Elementary
Statistics

Elementary Statistics

LOOKING AT THE BIG PICTURE

NANCY PFENNING

UNIVERSITY OF PITTSBURGH

BROOKS/COLE
CENGAGE Learning™

Australia • Brazil • Japan • Korea • Mexico • Singapore • Spain • United Kingdom • United States

Elementary Statistics:
Looking at the Big Picture
Nancy Pfenning

Publisher: Richard Stratton

Senior Sponsoring Editor: Molly Taylor

Associate Editor: Daniel Seibert

Editorial Assistant: Shaylin Walsh

Senior Marketing Manager: Greta Kleinert

Marketing Coordinator: Erica O'Connell

Marketing Communications Manager:
Mary Anne Payumo

Content Project Manager: Susan Miscio

Art Director: Linda Helcher

Senior Print Buyer: Diane Gibbons

Senior Rights Acquisition Account Manager,
Text: Katie Huha

Production Service: S4Carlisle Publishing
Services

Rights Acquisition Account Manager, Images:
Don Schlotman

Photo Researcher: Jennifer Lim

Interior and Cover Designer: KeDesign

Cover Image: © Veer Incorporated

Compositor: S4Carlisle Publishing Services

Library of Congress Control Number: 2009935400

ISBN-13: 978-0-495-83158-7

ISBN-10: 0-495-83158-1

Brooks/Cole
20 Channel Center Street
Boston, MA 02210
USA

Cengage Learning is a leading provider of customized learning solutions with office locations around the globe, including Singapore, the United Kingdom, Australia, Mexico, Brazil, and Japan. Locate your local office at: **international.cengage.com/region**

Cengage Learning products are represented in Canada by Nelson Education, Ltd.

For your course and learning solutions, visit
www.cengage.com

Purchase any of our products at your local college store or at our preferred online store **www.ichapters.com**

Printed in the United States of America
1 2 3 4 5 6 7 12 11 10 09

To Frank, Andreas & Mary, Marina, and Nils

Contents

PART II   Displaying and Summarizing Data   70

PART III Probability 224

PART IV ▶ **Statistical Inference**   386

> ## Teaching the Big Picture 747

Preface

Statistics: The Big Picture

Statistics, unlike any other discipline, provides a forum for us to tackle research questions about any topic imaginable. From the great pioneers of the discipline like Florence Nightingale and Carl Friedrich Gauss to modern-day pollsters or pharmaceutical researchers, statisticians have altered the way we view the world—changing the way we look at the big picture. By exposing students to this wonderfully wide variety of investigations and applications, I want to show them how to appreciate their statistics course as relevant to both their academic and everyday interests.

Because I learned statistics "the old way" more than thirty years ago, it took me several years of teaching the subject for me to really appreciate what lies at the heart of statistical thinking and practice. Over time I became convinced that, with the right textbook, students in a one-semester course could grasp the essence of statistics that goes beyond mastery of individual topics or procedures.

Students often learn statistics with too narrow a focus on specific formulas and not enough of a broad perspective of its power and problem-solving ability. Without a clear grasp of the big picture of statistics, they may pay the price when it comes time to take a final exam or, later on, apply what they have learned in future courses or on the job. Research has shown that even students who received an A in their introductory-statistics course are still poorly equipped to choose the right display, summary, or inference tool when confronted with a variety of problems, relying on trial-and-error instead of reason to decide what was appropriate.*

I was optimistic that students could grasp the big picture of statistics while also learning specific techniques, but I thought they needed a textbook designed to open them to a broader perspective of the material. I also discovered that certain devices could successfully be implemented to convey the big picture of statistics to students. In my teaching I adhered to a logical, natural structure based on the four interrelated processes of investigating a situation statistically. Within that structure, I stressed that a few basic situations—involving single categorical or quantitative variables or relationships between them—are possible. Relying on this simple structure, I wove in certain themes central to understanding how statistical thinking reflects the way we perceive and interpret the real world.

I field-tested these ideas over several semesters with a soft-cover draft manuscript of this textbook, used by hundreds of students in my introductory-statistics classes with encouraging results. Compared to their peers who were taught with

---

*Lovett, M. C. (2001). A collaborative convergence on studying reasoning processes: A case study in statistics. In S. Carver, & D. Klahr (Eds.) *Cognition and instruction: Twenty-five years of progress* (pp. 347–384). Mahwah, NJ: Erlbaum.

standard textbooks, these students showed better performance on exam questions requiring them to select the correct procedure in a variety of situations.

The Big Picture Approach: Rewarding for Instructors and Students

By using this book to teach introductory statistics, teachers can show students that the questions raised and discoveries made are truly intriguing. Students are guided to see the big picture of statistics as they gradually master specific techniques. Using the book's natural framework based on four processes and five variable situations, teachers can map out a course that flows logically from topic to topic and students can feel oriented throughout, keeping sight of the "forest" as they move through the "trees." Thanks to this innovative approach, statistics can be as exciting and as meaningful as it should be for teachers and students alike.

Framing the Big Picture: The Four Basic Processes of Statistics

Starting in the first chapter, I emphasize that all of the material aligns with four basic processes: producing data, displaying and summarizing the data, understanding probability, and using probability to perform statistical inference. An illustration, with accompanying explanations that convey to students the gist of the entire course, recurs throughout the textbook to orient students visually to which part of the big picture is being addressed. Further, each of the book's four parts—corresponding to the four basic processes—has its own designated color. Thus, the big-picture approach uses more than one tactic to strengthen visual information alerting students to the process in the foreground.

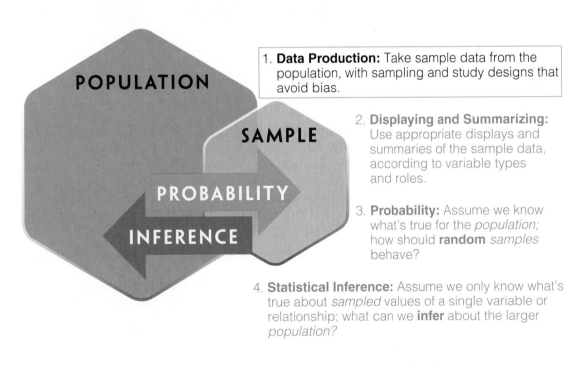

1. **Data Production:** Take sample data from the population, with sampling and study designs that avoid bias.

2. **Displaying and Summarizing:** Use appropriate displays and summaries of the sample data, according to variable types and roles.

3. **Probability:** Assume we know what's true for the *population;* how should **random** *samples* behave?

4. **Statistical Inference:** Assume we only know what's true about *sampled* values of a single variable or relationship; what can we **infer** about the larger *population?*

Typically, the second half of an introductory statistics course is devoted to the coverage of statistical inference. By demonstrating to students that inference is the last in a logical sequence of four processes, we reassure them that the material is inherently cumulative. We also impress on them that what we can accomplish with these four processes is a practical reason why researchers in so many fields in the natural sciences, social sciences, and the arts have come to rely on statistical methods.

To help students become familiar with these processes, earlier chapters feature fairly simple exercises that train students to identify which of the four processes is the focus of attention. Gradually, students are challenged to think about how all four processes fit together to provide insight into more advanced research questions.

Profiles of Data Types: The Five Variable Situations

If a statistician had to use just one word to tell what statistics is all about, he or she might well say "variability" or "variables." This book stresses to students that data consist of values of variables, either quantitative or categorical. In introductory statistics, we focus either on single variables or on relationships between two variables. For an introductory course, there are just five basic situations: one categorical variable, one quantitative, one each categorical and quantitative, two categorical, or two quantitative.

Whenever we choose a display, summary, or inference tool, knowing which of the five situations applies is key to making the correct selection. A simple icon showing C or Q, either singly or in pairs, reminds us of the situation we are studying. For relationships between two variables, we think carefully about which variable should be explanatory and which response, then sketch an arrow in the direction of the presumed causation.

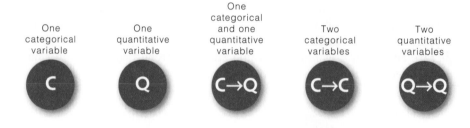

| One categorical variable | One quantitative variable | One categorical and one quantitative variable | Two categorical variables | Two quantitative variables |

Structuring of Chapters: Five Variable Situations within Four Processes

The clear, natural structure of *Elementary Statistics: Looking at the Big Picture* gives coherence to the broad range of topics in an introductory statistics course. Parts I through IV correspond to the four basic processes, with a systematic progression through the five variable situations. Specifically, the five situations are used in displaying and summarizing data in Part II and again in Part IV for the presentation of relevant inference procedures.

Recurrent Themes: The Essence of Statistical Thinking

This book highlights several recurrent themes that help develop a sense of what is most important in the science of statistics. These include the following issues:

- the distinction between the population and a sample
- the role played by sample size
- the possibilities and consequences of errors in a study's conclusions

Such issues are addressed repeatedly, both in the text and in the accompanying exercises. By revisiting these ideas within the context of particular procedures, students appreciate that they need not start from scratch each time they meet a new topic. Rather, they continually build on basic principles established early in the text. Along with the structure of five variable situations within four basic processes, these recurrent themes are the common threads woven into the tapestry of the book, making it possible to present statistics as one big picture.

Perspective: Looking Ahead, Looking Back, and A Closer Look

Another innovative device for conveying the big picture is the careful placement of marginal notes to integrate the topic at hand into the larger theme of the book. *Looking Ahead* notes foreshadow how a particular concept or skill fits into the book's general goals. *Looking Back* notes recall earlier material so students can draw on what they have already learned to incorporate new ideas. *A Closer Look* notes invite students to pause and consider important details, giving them the scrutiny they need.

These marginal notes show how each new topic fits into the bigger picture, relating it to material previously covered and anticipating what students will learn later on. Positioning these notes contextually in the margin lets students read the material without interruption, while providing connections to past and future material for them to digest at their own pace.

The Big Picture and Real Data

To keep students engaged throughout, the book features almost 400 examples and over a thousand exercises based on actual, current, fascinating statistical applications. For example:

- How do bees behave under the influence of alcohol?
- Is it a good strategy to go back and change one's answers before turning in a multiple choice test?
- What does children's selection of Halloween candy tell us about marketing strategies?

Data sets in this book are always given in context, so students can think about problems intuitively and see the relevance of the methods. One frequently used data set, available online on the companion website, consists of values of close to forty variables for over four hundred students. By exploring relationships among familiar variables for individuals like themselves, students can confirm some results that are to be expected—for instance, that males earn more than females—and others that may be counterintuitive.

Hundreds of other real data sets are featured in the book's examples and exercises. Also available on the companion website, these are mostly limited to one or two dozen values to make it easy to enter by hand into a computer or calculator.

Effective Teaching of Statistics through the Four-Step Structure of Examples

Well-chosen examples are my main vehicle for presenting ideas, with explanatory text in between to summarize the concept demonstrated and lead into the next topic. This succinct approach strengthens the book's highly efficient structure: a logical progression of ideas illustrated by a sequence of examples. Throughout the book, examples follow the same clear format:

- Background
- Question
- Response
- Practice Exercise

This structure lends itself to effective, coherent presentation in lectures. Example by example, instructors can elicit responses from the students once the background has been outlined and the question has been posed.

Comprehensive Section and Chapter Exercises for Practice and Assignments

One of my highest priorities was to fill the book with plenty of high-quality exercises to help teachers deliver an effective course that includes lectures, assignments, and exams. The more exercises available to an instructor, the more opportunity he or she has to enhance a course. Whatever applications an instructor prefers to focus on in class—such as medicine, or politics, or modern culture—the book provides more than enough exercises to discuss in lectures, assign for homework, or incorporate into quizzes or exams. The section and chapter exercises are designed to reveal the big picture of statistics to students in a gradual and manageable way, whether the exercises are assigned by hand or through Enhanced WebAssign, Cengage Learning's online learning and course-management system.

To ease access to relevant exercises for both instructors and students, problem sets are featured at the end of each major section. These section exercises deal more specifically with each new topic, ensuring that students have ample practice with concepts as they are introduced.

A more comprehensive set of exercises appears at the end of the chapter, encouraging students to integrate each topic into the Big Picture. The chapter exercises serve a broader purpose than the section exercises, and are grouped under headings orienting teachers and students to what kinds of skills are stressed.

- **Warming Up**
  These exercises set the stage by considering what types of variables are handled by the chapter's methods, any data production issues, and other important background information.

- **Exploring the Big Picture**
  These exercises get to the heart of what the chapter has covered, often incorporating ideas from more than one section into multipart problems.

- **Using Software**
  These exercises practice the use of technology to produce graphs, summaries, or inference output relevant to the chapter.

- **Discovering Research**
  These exercises ask students to seek out studies that rely on the methods presented in the chapter and comment on relevant details.

- **Reporting on Research**
  This type of exercise requires students to go beyond the results obtained in the chapter's exercises to highlight a particular topic, such as whether or not there is statistical evidence of the freshman year weight-gain phenomenon known as the "Freshman Fifteen." Combining what they have learned from those exercises and from outside sources like the Internet, students write a report according to their instructor's specifications.

Enhanced WebAssign: Online Learning and Practice

Enhanced WebAssign is an easy-to-use online teaching and learning system that provides assignable homework, automatic grading, and interactive assistance for students. Starting with the exercises with solutions at the back of the book, I have worked hand-in-hand with online homework experts at WebAssign to modify these solved exercises for effective online practice. As students progress through the examples, they can use a computer to practice applying new concepts and skills, receiving immediate feedback.

The unsolved exercises, numbering approximately 800, are also available via Enhanced WebAssign. Whereas the hardcopy textbook includes many exercises asking students to "explain" or "describe," I personally revised the exercises to keep such open questions to a minimum in online assignments, while still retaining the spirit of each question. The textbook's exercises tend to feature more questions concerning the active creation of a graph or computer output, while the Enhanced WebAssign exercises include more closed questions about graphs or output that have already been produced. Still, the length and the topic content of all exercises match up exactly from the text to Enhanced WebAssign.

Students Talk Stats: Realistic Student Conversations That Get at the Heart of Statistical Issues

Students appreciate a textbook that reflects an awareness of the challenges that they face in mastering both subtle and complex statistical concepts. This book features *Students Talk Stats* examples and exercises, discussions of statistics problems by four prototypical students whose experiences are based on those of real students in my own classes. These students who "talk stats" show levels of understanding that span a broad enough range so that actual students are sure to identify with their struggles and discoveries.

Adam gets the group started by plunging right into a problem—and typically getting in over his head. Brittany doesn't always know what is correct, but she's quick to pick up on obvious flaws in Adam's reasoning. Carlos often helps to steer the group in the right direction. Dominique tends to appreciate the sense of Carlos' explanations, and may offer further insights of her own.

Following each Students Talk Stats discussion is a brief assessment of who is on the right track and why. Besides these discussions within the text, some exercises present statements by each of the four students and ask whose claim makes the most sense.

Where to Begin? Considering Data Production Issues to Initiate a Semester-Long Discourse

A first step in an introductory statistics course that successfully engages students is having them consider and discuss the underlying study design used to produce data. Before presenting methods for displaying and summarizing data, this book sets the stage with a discussion of variables, then delves into aspects of study design that play a role in whether variables or relationships between variables will be summarized without bias. Also, sampling design is scrutinized to establish whether the summaries represent without bias what is true about the variables in the larger population. Raising questions like "How could a study be designed to test if sugar causes hyperactivity?" shows students from the start that the point of statistics is to answer important questions about ourselves and our world.

Curriculum Flexibility for More Advanced Topics

Many instructors do not have enough time to cover all the topics presented in this book, such as ANOVA, chi-square, or inference for regression. The presentation of each topic and its accompanying exercise set is self-contained to allow for any of these to be skipped, while still delivering a coherent course. Optional additional chapters on Non-parametric Methods, Two-Way ANOVA, and Multiple Regression are also provided on the text's Premium Website for courses that incorporate those topics. Even if particular topics are bypassed, the Big Picture approach gives students a much better sense of the types of situations that potentially arise.

Documentation of Adherence to Standards in the Discipline

It was important to me that my book support the standards approved by the most respected organizations, such as GAISE, AMATYC, and NCTM. After reviewing those standards thoroughly, I verified that the text's explanations, examples, and exercises work together to further the teaching of statistics in any context—in a high school, at a two-year college, as a course taught under the auspices of a mathematics department, or as a course offered by a separate statistics department. Interested instructors are encouraged to ask their Cengage Learning representative for a copy of the document.

Flexible Incorporation of Software

When instructors of introductory statistics were surveyed about the extent to which students used software in solving homework problems, responses varied from "not at all" to "practically always." This book includes a *Using Software* section near the end of chapter exercises to give instructors the flexibility to require anywhere from none to heavy use of software in their course. If an instructor chooses heavier reliance on software, he or she may also want to de-emphasize the use of tables. The book's exercise sets indicate where tables are needed so that teachers can assign as many or few as they want. Additionally, downloadable data sets and Online Technology Guides on the book's Premium Website offer support and instruction for using the book with a variety of popular statistical software packages.

For Instructors: Teaching the Big Picture

I created the instructor's supplement, placed in the back of the Annotated Instructor's Edition, to suit a wide range of individual needs and tastes in the teaching of introductory statistics. Called *Teaching the Big Picture,* it includes a variety of resources such as a guide to exercise topics in the book, additional worked examples and supplemental exercises, classroom activities for group or computer lab instruction, and teaching tips for more in-depth instruction of key topics.

Acknowledgments

The author is grateful for the thoughtful feedback of the reviewers whose ideas have helped to shape this text.

Robert F. Abbey, Jr.
Troy University

Anthony Aidoo
Eastern Connecticut State University

Olcay Akman
Illinois State University

Kathleen Almy
Rock Valley College

Hanan Amro
South Texas College

Polly Amstutz
University of Nebraska, Kearney

Alireza Arasteh
Western New Mexico University

Sonya Armstrong
West Virginia State University

Dean Barchers
Red Rocks Community College

David Bauer
Virginia Commonwealth University

Michael P. Bobic
Emmanuel College

R. B. Campbell
University of Northern Iowa

Guang-Hwa Chang
Youngstown State University

Jerry Chen
Suffolk County Community College

Jin Chen
Cuyahoga Community College

Shawn Chiappetta
University of Sioux Falls

Jessica Chisham
Iowa State University

Yvonne Chueh
Central Washington University

Dianna Cichocki
Erie Community College

Elizabeth Clarkson
Wichita State University

Michael Collyer
Iowa State University

John Curran
Eastern Michigan University

Larry G. Daniel
University of North Florida

John Daniels
Central Michigan University

Jimmy de la Torre
Rutgers University

Patricia Deamer
Skyline College

Beverly Eaton
Oakland Community College

Billy Edwards
University of Tennessee at Chattanooga

Benny Eichhorn
Rider University

Wade Ellis
West Valley College

Karen Estes
St. Petersburg College

Janet Evert
Erie Community College South

Maggie W. Flint
Northeast State Technical Community College

Sergio Fratarcangeli
College of New Rochelle

Larry Gache
Cincinnati State University

Jon Graham
University of Montana

Rachel Graham
Iowa State University

Ellen Gundlach
Purdue University

William V. Harper
Otterbein College

Kristin Hartford
Long Beach City College

Jolene Hartwick
Western Technical College

Emam Hoosain
Augusta State University

Bryan Ingham
Fingerlakes Community College

Mark Irwin
Harvard University

Pete Johnson
Eastern Connecticut State University

Martin Jones
College of Charleston

Joe Joyner
Tidewater Community College

Raj Jtla
Missouri State University

Grazyna Kamburowska
SUNY College at Oneonta

Phil Kavanagh
Mesa State College

Mohammed Kazemi
University of North Carolina, Charlotte

Raja Khoury
Collin County Community College

Richard Klein
Middlesex County College

Diane Koenig
Rock Valley College

Rita Kolb
CC of Baltimore City

Conrad Krueger
San Antonio College

Gerald J. LaPage
Bristol Community College

Louise Lawson
Kennesaw State University

Richard Leedy
Polk Community College

Susan Lenker
Central Michigan University

Kristin Lennox
Texas A&M University

Inwon Leu
Cuyamaca College

Jiawei Liu
Georgia State University

Adam Lynn
Clemson University

Syrous Marivani
Louisiana State University at Alexandria

Dave Matthews
Minnesota West Community and Technical College

Catherine Matos
Clayton State University

Nola McDaniel
McNeese State University

Vicki McMillian
Ocean County College

Jackie Miller
The Ohio State University

Jeff Mock
Diablo Valley College

Megan Mocko
University of Florida

Carla Monticelli
Camden County College

Jeff A. Morel
Jamestown College

Linda Myers
Harrisburg Area Community College

Charles Odion
Houston Community College

Roger G. Olson
Saint Joseph's College of Indiana

Ron Palcic
Johnson County Community College

Michael Pannucci
Rutgers University

What good is knowing *how* to use statistical techniques if students don't know *when* to use them?

If students learn statistics with too narrow a focus, they may pay the price later on when they have to apply what they have learned—often relying on trial-and-error instead of reason to determine the appropriate technique. In fact, research has shown that even students who receive an "A" in introductory statistics can be poorly equipped to choose the right display, summary, or inference tool when faced with a variety of problems.

Elementary Statistics: Looking at the Big Picture solves this dilemma. Successfully field-tested with an approach honed from the author's 15 years of teaching introductory statistics at the college level, this innovative text allows students to think about statistical material in its *entirety*. Students also learn problem-solving strategies applicable to *any* research situation. Guided by this framework, along with thoughtful pedagogy and visuals, students learn specific statistical techniques *and* see the common thread that ties them all together—the Big Picture.

IN THIS PREVIEW

- **Unique organization** around the four basic processes of statistics and five basic research situations
- **Structured examples** in a consistent Background–Question–Response–Practice Exercise sequence
- **Focus on connections** between concepts
- **Numerous real-data exercises** to practice concepts and integrate them into the Big Picture
- **Teaching and learning resources**, including **Enhanced WebAssign** for homework management, readymade lecture slides, videos, and a Multimedia eBook

"I like the easy pace of the text, the way in which the author makes sure the students understand the concepts before moving on. The Students Talk Stats will help them relate to the concepts being taught. Also, the step process is a good technique. . . . I would describe [this book] as a fresh and exciting look at what can be a boring subject."

— Richard Leedy, Polk Community College, Florida

A unique framework helps students think big (as in Big Picture)

Starting in the first chapter, Nancy Pfenning emphasizes that the introductory statistics course intuitively aligns around *four basic processes:* producing data, displaying and summarizing data, understanding probability, and using probability to perform statistical inference. She then organizes the presentation around these processes.

TABLE OF CONTENTS

Visual cues keep students on track

Throughout the book, this graphic—with the relevant process highlighted—visually orients students to the process in the forefront of the discussion. Pages in the book's four parts have color-coded tabs reflecting the same color scheme.

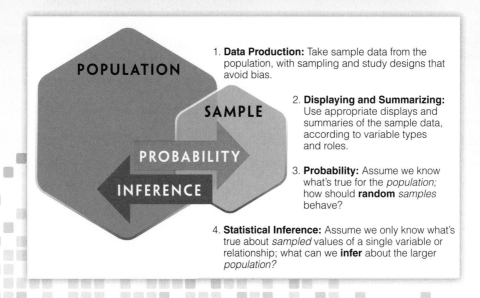

1. **Data Production:** Take sample data from the population, with sampling and study designs that avoid bias.

2. **Displaying and Summarizing:** Use appropriate displays and summaries of the sample data, according to variable types and roles.

3. **Probability:** Assume we know what's true for the *population;* how should **random** *samples* behave?

4. **Statistical Inference:** Assume we only know what's true about *sampled* values of a single variable or relationship; what can we **infer** about the larger *population?*

Within the process-based organization described to the left, Pfenning stresses *five basic research situations* involving types of variables (quantitative, categorical, or a blend). These situations are introduced and illustrated in Chapter 1, and designated with an icon wherever they are relevant in text examples. With this ongoing reinforcement, students learn to approach research problems by first identifying *which* situation applies. As a result, they are better able to choose the correct display, summary, or inference tool.

One categorical variable	One quantitative variable	One categorical and one quantitative variable	Two categorical variables	Two quantitative variables

Example 1.6 illustrates the five situations in a variety of contexts.

EXAMPLE 1.6 IDENTIFYING VARIABLE TYPES AND ROLES

Background: Consider these headlines:

- *Men are twice as likely as women to be hit by lightning*
- *35% of returning troops seek mental health aid*
- *Do Oscar winners live longer than less successful peers?*
- *Smaller, hungrier mice*
- *County's average weekly wages at $811, better than U.S. average*

Thanks for helping me live longer?

Questions: What type of variables are involved in each of these situations? If the relationship between two variables is of interest, which plays the role of explanatory variable and which is the response?

 Responses: *Men are twice as likely as women to be hit by lightning:* We consider two categorical variables-gender and whether or not a person is hit by lightning. Gender would be the explanatory variable and being hit by lightning or not is the response. The other way around wouldn't make sense because being hit by lightning could not have an impact on a person's gender.

 35% of returning troops seek mental health aid: Whether or not a returning soldier seeks mental health aid is a single categorical variable.

 Do Oscar winners live longer than less successful p[eers]? This involves a categorical explanatory variable—b[eing an] Oscar winner or not—and a quantitative response [which is] length of life.

 Smaller, hungrier mice: This brief headline suggests [a] relationship between two quantitative variables: the [size of a] mouse and its appetite. Size apparently plays the ro[le of the] explanatory variable, so that as size goes down, the [amount] of food desired goes up.

 County's average weekly wages at $811, better than U.S. average: This involves just one quantitative variable—weekly wages. If wages for one county had been compared to those of another county, then there would have been an additional categorical explanatory variable. Comparing this county's wages to those of the United States in general is a different kind of comparison, where the county residents may be thought of as a single sample, coming from the larger population of U.S. residents.

Practice: *Try Exercise 1.17 on page 13.*

Structured examples use real data

Well-chosen examples form the core of the text's presentation. The more than 300 examples and 1,000 exercises are based on a wide variety of actual statistical applications. *How do bees behave under the influence of alcohol? Is it a good strategy to go back and change one's answer on a multiple-choice test?* Along the way, the Big Picture approach reminds students that, no matter how diverse the applications, the same set of systematic methods can be applied.

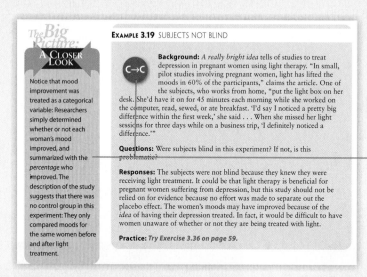

The Big Picture:
A CLOSER LOOK

Notice that mood improvement was treated as a categorical variable: Researchers simply determined whether or not each woman's mood improved, and summarized with the *percentage* who improved. The description of the study suggests that there was no control group in this experiment: They only compared moods for the same women before and after light treatment.

EXAMPLE 3.19 SUBJECTS NOT BLIND

Background: *A really bright idea* tells of studies to treat depression in pregnant women using light therapy. "In small, pilot studies involving pregnant women, light has lifted the moods in 60% of the participants," claims the article. One of the subjects, who works from home, "put the light box on her desk. She'd have it on for 45 minutes each morning while she worked on the computer, read, sewed, or ate breakfast. 'I'd say I noticed a pretty big difference within the first week,' she said . . . When she missed her light sessions for three days while on a business trip, 'I definitely noticed a difference.'"

Questions: Were subjects blind in this experiment? If not, is this problematic?

Responses: The subjects were not blind because they knew they were receiving light treatment. It could be that light therapy is beneficial for pregnant women suffering from depression, but this study should not be relied on for evidence because no effort was made to separate out the placebo effect. The women's moods may have improved because of the *idea* of having their depression treated. In fact, it would be difficult to have women unaware of whether or not they are being treated with light.

Practice: *Try Exercise 3.36 on page 59.*

Each example reflects a clear-cut structure—Background, Question, Response, and, finally, a Practice Exercise that students can try immediately, using the example as a model.

Note the icon and marginal note, which drive home the type of variables relevant to the situation.

Insightful peer discussions engage students in the learning process

Students Talk Stats examples and exercises—praised by the text's reviewers—are prototypical student discussions of very real statistics problems that illustrate their various levels of comprehension along with typical struggles and discoveries involved in learning statistics. Following each discussion is a brief assessment of who is on the right track and why.

Students Talk Stats

Interpreting a Confidence Interval

Suppose a group of students are discussing this report that appeared in 2007 on an Internet news site about the late Princess Diana: "A poll commissioned by Channel 4 television suggested that one in four Britons believe Diana was murdered. The telephone survey of 1,016 adults conducted this week had a margin of error of plus or minus 3 percentage points."

Adam: *"One in four is 25%. They always report a margin of error that goes with 95%, so the probability is 95% that the sample percentage who believe she was murdered falls between 22% and 28%."*

Brittany: *"The probability isn't 95%, it's 100% that the sample percentage falls in that interval, because they built the interval around the sample percentage! They're talking about the unknown population percentage: The probability is 95% that the population percentage falls between 22% and 28%."*

Carlos: *"You can't talk about the probability that the population percentage falls somewhere, because it's not a random variable, it's just one actual number. You can say they're 95% confident that the population percentage falls in that interval."*

Dominique: *"Carlos is right, but if Brittany really wants to talk about probability, she could say the probability is 95% that they produce an interval that captures the unknown population percentage."*

Both Carlos and Dominique are correct. Setting up confidence intervals is a form of statistical inference, where we make statements about population parameters. When a categorical variable is involved, it should be a statement about the population proportion or percentage. Because it is a fixed parameter, so it is not subject to the laws of random behavior. Therefore, it is incorrect to talk about the *probability* that population percentage falls in a certain interval. Either we can say we are 95% confident that the population percentage falls in the 95% confidence interval, or we can say that the probability is 95% that the 95% confidence interval (built around whatever sample percentage happened to be obtained) captures the unknown population percentage.

Practice: *Try Exercise 9.21 on page 000.*

Marginal notes connect concepts, placing topics in a broader context

Throughout the text, the strategic placement of marginal notes ensures that students never lose sight of how the topic at hand fits into the Big Picture.

Let's consider the use of randomization at two stages of selection in an experiment. First, a sample of subjects must be collected. Ideally, the sample would be perfectly representative of the entire population, but for practical purposes, researchers are almost always obliged to recruit volunteers. Thus, this stage rarely employs randomization. Second, individuals must be assigned to the treatment groups so that the only real difference between groups is what treatment was received, justifying claims of causation. At this stage, randomization is vital.

Double-Blind Experiments

Suppose the sugar/hyperactivity experiment had been carried out with randomized assignments to the two sugar treatments, and researchers determined that the percentage hyperactive for the high-sugar-intake group was higher than that for the low-sugar-intake group. In other words, suppose there is clear evidence of an *association* between sugar intake and hyperactivity. Could they then conclude that sugar *causes* hyperactivity?

Perhaps. Before such a conclusion is reached, it is important to think about how both subjects' and experimenters' awareness of treatment assignment can affect a study's results. First, we define some important terms.

The Big Picture: LOOKING AHEAD

Using volunteers helps to offset one of the drawbacks to experimentation that will be discussed later—namely, the problem of noncompliance.

Looking Ahead notes foreshadow how a particular concept or skill will fit into the course's general goals.

The Big Picture: LOOKING AHEAD

Using volunteers helps to offset one of the drawbacks to experimentation that will be discussed later—namely, the problem of noncompliance.

The Big Picture: LOOKING BACK

In Part I, we learned that samples need to be representative of the larger group (the population) of interest. In this example, we must be careful about who constitutes the larger population. A sample of shoppers in a downtown market district would not be representative of all shoppers in terms of foreign language ability.

EXAMPLE 9.5 A CONFIDENCE INTERVAL FOR THE POPULATION PROPORTION

Background: In recognition of 2005 being named the Year of Languages by the American Council on the Teaching of Foreign Languages, a group of students and teachers of foreign languages conducted a poll in a city's downtown market district. They asked 200 shoppers for the time in a foreign language, such as French ("Quelle heure est-il?"), Spanish ("Que hora es?") and German ("Wieviel Uhr ist es?"), and found that 66 were able to respond correctly in the given language. Thus, the sample proportion proficient enough to respond was $66/200 = 0.33$. It can be shown that the approximate standard deviation for the distribution of sample proportion is 0.03.

Question: What is a 95% confidence interval for the population proportion of shoppers who could respond correctly in the given language?

Response: The margin of error for a 95% confidence interval equals 2 standard deviations, or $2(0.03) = 0.06$. We can be 95% confident that the population proportion comes within 0.06 of 0.33. In other words, a 95% confidence interval for the population proportion is (0.27, 0.39).

Practice: *Try Exercise 9.8(a) on page 000.*

Other notes called **Looking Back** recall earlier material so that students can draw on what they have already learned to more effectively incorporate new ideas.

Errors in Studies' Conclusions: The Imperfect Nature of Statistical Studies

Statistics is, by nature, an inexact science. Studies are carried out to decide whether or not a claim is true concerning a single variable's values, or about a relationship between variables, but conclusions are rarely 100% certain. For instance, it is possible that a pharmaceutical study's results suggest a drug *is* effective when it actually is not. It is also possible that a study's results suggest that a drug does *not* produce side effects when it actually does. An important aspect of statistical research is to consider the consequences of drawing the wrong conclusions in one way or the other. Such mistakes, which are given the technical names *Type I Error* and *Type II Error*, will be discussed more formally in Part IV of this book. For now, we consider such errors less formally, as one more aspect of study design that warrants careful consideration.

EXAMPLE 3.4 TWO TYPES OF ERROR

Background: *Tests determine state police radar guns work*

The Big Picture: A CLOSER LOOK

The convention in statistical research is to designate the claim that "nothing is going on" as the default point of view. In general, the first type of error arises if we conclude something *is* going on when it actually isn't. The second type of error is to conclude something is *not* going on when it actually is.

A Closer Look notes invite students to stop and examine in more depth, giving important details the scrutiny they deserve without interrupting the flow of the primary narrative.

Categorized exercises (lots of them) build understanding and offer options for homework, quizzes, and exams

A set of problems after each major section assures that students master basic concepts as they are introduced. A more comprehensive set at the end of each chapter encourages them to integrate individual topics.

Warming Up

3.55 In 2003, The National Research Council estimated that obesity occurs in 25% of dogs and cats in Westernized societies. (Obesity can be determined by squeezing an animal in the lower chest area and seeing if the ribs can be felt.) Perhaps the 25% estimate was obtained by calling homeowners and, if they had a cat or dog, asking them to see if the animal's ribs could be felt by squeezing. Alternatively, the estimate could have been obtained by asking veterinarians to report what percentage of the animals they treat could be classified as obese, using the above method.

Keeping in mind that bias may arise either from a nonrepresentative sample or from inaccurately assessing a variable,

a. Which approach is more likely to lead to a nonrepresentative sample: calling homeowners or asking veterinarians?

b. Which approach is more likely to lead to inaccurate assessments: calling homeowners or asking veterinarians?

3.56 An article entitled *Family dinners benefit teens* claims that "eating dinner together as a family is one way of keeping teen-agers well adjusted and out of trouble."[36]

> **Warming Up** exercises help to orient students by getting them to think about types of variables involved, data production methods, or other background issues discussed in earlier chapters.

Exploring the Big Picture: CONFIDENCE INTERVALS AND HYPOTHESIS TESTS FOR PROPORTIONS

9.82 Forty employers in a variety of fields and cities were surveyed in 2004 on topics relating to company benefits, and the degree to which employees were supported in terms of flexible work hours and child-care assistance. One question asked if the employer had any experience or knowledge about attention-deficit hyperactive disorder (ADHD). Responses of either yes (y) or no (n) are shown below.

n	n	n	n	y	n	y	n	n	y	n	y	n	y	n	n	y	y	n	y
n	n	n	y	y	n	n	n	y	n	y	n	n	y	n	y	n	n	n	n

a. Find the sample proportion with a *yes* response.

b. Find the approximate standard deviation of sample proportion, rounding to the nearest thousandth.

> **Exploring the Big Picture** exercises get to the heart of what the chapter has accomplished, often incorporating ideas from more than one section into a multi-part problem.

Using Software: INFERENCE FOR PROPORTIONS [SEE TECHNOLOGY GUIDE]

9.93 *Why we don't come: Patient perceptions on no-shows*, published in the *Annals of Family Medicine* in December 2004, reports that 15 of 34 patients (44%) interviewed cited lack of respect by the health-care system as a reason for failing to keep doctor's appointments in the past. Specifically, being kept waiting for an appointment, in the waiting room, and in the exam room were taken as evidence of insufficient respect.

a. Explain why a formal test would not be necessary in order to decide if a majority of all patients miss appointments because of perceived lack of respect.

b. Use software to produce a 95% confidence interval for the proportion of all patients who miss appointments because of perceived lack of respect.

> **Using Software** provides practice with the use of technology to produce graphs, summaries, or inference output. Directions for using various software packages are available on the Premium Website for students.

Discovering Research: STUDY DESIGN

3.76 Find (and hand in) an article or Internet report about a sample survey. Tell if each variable of interest is quantitative or categorical. Tell what is the suggested population of interest. Then tell how the individuals were selected and whether or not you believe they adequately represent the population of interest. Discuss whether there are any clear sources of bias. Were the questions open or closed?

explanatory and response (if there are two variables). Are there any potential confounding variables that should have been controlled for?

3.78 Find (and hand in) an article or report about an experiment. Tell what the variables of interest are, whether they are quantitative or categorical, and which is explanatory and response. Describe the subjects, treatments, whether or not the subjects were blind,

> **Discovering Research** exercises ask students to seek out studies that rely on the methods presented in the chapter at hand, and comment on relevant details.

Reporting on Research: STUDY DESIGN

3.79 Use results of Exercises 3.18 and 3.21 and relevant findings from the Internet to make a report on gun control that relies on statistical information.

> **Reporting on Research** exercises require students to go beyond the results obtained in one or several of the chapter's exercises, combine what they have learned with outside sources, and write about it.

Automatically graded problems from the text—online!
More than 1,000 text problems, customized by Nancy Pfenning for online practice and assignment, are available online with **Enhanced WebAssign**.

Beyond the book, you and your students will have all the support you need

Teaching the Big Picture: An Instructor Supplement

Nancy Pfenning created this supplement, placed at the end of the Annotated Instructor's Edition, to suit a variety of individual tastes and needs in the teaching of introductory statistics. Resources include:

- Sample syllabus for a 15-week semester, easily adaptable to custom-design a course
- Additional details and examples
- Guide to exercise topics, useful for assigning end-of-section exercises that cover the basics and end-of-chapter exercises to help students grasp chapter material from a broader perspective
- Supplemental exercises with solutions
- Hands-on and computer-lab activities
- Solutions to the text's unsolved exercises

ENHANCED WebAssign

Enhanced WebAssign

Easy to Assign. Easy to Use. Easy to Manage.

Whether or not you've used online homework before, **Enhanced WebAssign** is an ideal time-saving solution. Its visual and interactive problems motivate students and get them involved. Every Practice Exercise referenced in the book's examples is available online. Students can also watch videos that walk them through many examples and exercises step-by-step.

For you, creating an assignment is as easy as choosing which questions you want your students to answer, when you want the assignment to be due, and how many attempts you want to grant. With the feature-rich gradebook, you can manage your class grades, set grade curves, extend deadlines, and export results to an offline spreadsheet-compatible format. For more information, visit **www.webassign.net/brookscole**.

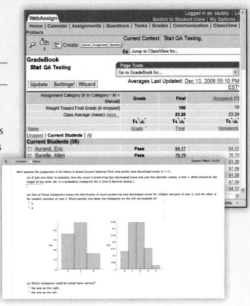

Solution Builder

www.cengage.com/solutionbuilder

This online instructors' database offers complete worked solutions to all exercises in the text, allowing you to create customized, secure printouts of solutions in PDF format, matched exactly to the problems you assign in class.

PowerLecture™

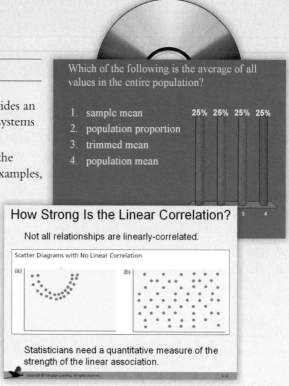

PowerLecture™ with ExamView® and JoinIn™

ISBN-13: 978-0-495-82997-3 • ISBN-10: 0-495-82997-8

The fastest, easiest way to build customized lectures, **PowerLecture™** provides an electronic test bank, book-specific lecture slides, and content for "clicker" systems to enhance your students' educational experience:

- A semester's worth of Microsoft® PowerPoint® lecture slides, based on the Background–Question–Response format of the book's well-received examples, have been customized to the text by Nancy Pfenning. Accompanying student handouts allow students to follow along in lectures with a manageable amount of note-taking.

- Featuring automatic grading and nearly 400 multi-part questions tailored to the text, the **ExamView®** electronic test bank allows you to quickly create, deliver, and customize tests and study guides in print and online. All test items are also provided in PDF and Microsoft® Word formats for instructors who opt not to use the software component.

- **JoinIn™** content (for use with most "clicker" systems) promotes active learning, allowing you to take polls and attendance, ask questions using readymade slides, and instantly assess students' responses.

Premium Website

This site offers flexible support for a variety of statistical software packages such as Microsoft® Excel, MINITAB®, SPSS®, and TI calculators. Online Technology Guides for each package provide specific instructions to students for applying software to problems in the text, and offer instructors flexibility to integrate as much technology as they need. Downloadable data sets are also provided for the text's examples and exercises in each software's native file formats. In addition, Video Lectures serve as a virtual teaching assistant by walking students through key statistical concepts. When you package access to the Premium Website with each new text, your students also gain access to an engaging Multimedia eBook (see description on this page).

Student Solutions Manual

ISBN-13: 978-0-495-82996-6 • ISBN-10: 0-495-82996-X

This manual offers full worked solutions to selected exercises from the text.

Multimedia eBook

Ideal for today's visual and technology-savvy students, this interactive version of the text motivates students and engages them in learning statistics. Students can easily navigate through the table of contents, index, and glossary, or use the search function to find specific areas and topics in an instant. They can also use highlighting and note-taking features, just as they would in a printed book. Access to the eBook is included for your students when you sign up for **Enhanced WebAssign** and/or request access to the **Premium Website** with each new text.

iChapters.com Downloadable eBook

Available at **www.iChapters.com**, this PDF version of the text looks just like the printed text but also provides a convenient menu of links to each chapter's main headings, allowing students to easily navigate from section to section. Using the Adobe® Acrobat® search feature, students can also search for key terms or other specific information.

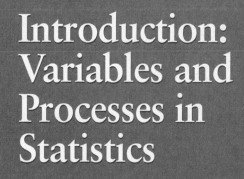

Introduction: Variables and Processes in Statistics

What can you accomplish with this book, and how?

What's the key to solving statistics problems?

Broker/BigstockPhoto.com

Before the semester starts, a statistics teacher wants to organize a box of hundreds of newspaper clippings and Internet reports collected in the past couple of years:

- ■ "Dark Chocolate Might Reduce Blood Pressure"
- ■ "Almost Half of U.S. Internet Users 'Google' Themselves"
- ■ "Vampire Bat Saliva Researched for Stroke"
- ■ "Environmental Mercury, Autism Linked by New Research"

There are several reports on smoking and on obesity, but for most of the topics—such as bat saliva—there is only one article. How can the teacher sort all of those articles in a way that will make them easy to access for future reference?

At the end of the semester, a group of statistics students are studying together, trying to solve practice final exam problems such as these:

- ■ Suppose systolic blood pressures for 7 patients who ate dark chocolate daily for two weeks dropped an average of 5 points, whereas those of a control group of 6 patients who ate white chocolate remained unchanged. If the standardized difference between blood pressure decreases was 2.1, do we have convincing evidence that dark chocolate is beneficial?

- ■ According to a 2007 report, 47% of 1,623 U.S. Internet users surveyed by the Pew Internet & American Life Project had searched for information about themselves online. Give a 95% confidence interval for the percentage of all U.S. Internet users who searched online for information about themselves.

■ Researchers found that 9 out of 15 stroke patients receiving vampire bat saliva had an excellent recovery, compared with 4 out of 17 who were untreated. Does this provide evidence that bat saliva is effective in treating stroke patients?

■ Research in a large sample of Texas school districts found that for every 1,000 pounds of environmentally released mercury, there was a 17% increase in autism rates. If one district has 300 additional pounds of environmental mercury compared to another, how much higher do we predict its autism rate to be?

The students may feel overwhelmed in trying to find the right approach to each of the problems, after having learned a whole semester's worth of various statistical procedures. How can the students figure out which procedure is the right one for each problem?

The answer for both teacher and students is a simple one, and it will also be the key for you to understand what this book is all about, from beginning to end. *The way we handle statistical problems depends on the number and types of variables involved.*

A *variable*, as the name suggests, is something that varies for different individuals: Blood pressure is a variable because it takes different values for different people; recovery from a stroke is a variable because some patients have an excellent recovery and others do not. The individuals with variable traits in many cases are people, but individuals can be anything that we are interested in—from penguins to school districts to planets.

Types of Variables: Categorical or Quantitative

Virtually all of the situations encountered in this book will involve either a *single variable* or the *relationship between two variables*. A variable's type is *categorical* if it takes qualitative values such as sex, race, or the response to a yes-or-no question. The type is *quantitative* if the variable takes number values for which arithmetic makes sense, such as age, number of siblings, or rating something on a scale of 1 to 10.

Categorical variables are sometimes referred to as "qualitative" and quantitative variables are sometimes called "numerical."

> *Definitions*   A **variable** is a characteristic that differs for different individuals. A **categorical variable** takes qualitative values that are not subject to the laws of arithmetic. A **quantitative variable** takes number values for which arithmetic makes sense. A **relationship** (also known as an **association**) exists between two variables if certain values of one tend to occur with certain values of the other.

Some number-valued variables, like ZIP codes, are categorical if the numbers are labels, not signifying an amount that can be quantified. For example, if half of a group of students have a ZIP code 15217 and the other half 15213, we can't say that the typical ZIP code is the average of these, 15215.

The statistics teacher can divide the clippings into just five piles:

1. One categorical variable
2. One quantitative variable
3. One categorical variable and one quantitative variable
4. Two categorical variables
5. Two quantitative variables

Likewise, the statistics students just need to identify the number and type of variables involved in each problem, and this will suggest what statistical procedure should be applied.

This book features "Students Talk Stats" examples and exercises that are discussions by four prototypical students, highlighting many of the most important ideas in statistics. As you gradually rise to higher levels of understanding of statistical concepts and procedures, you may find you can relate to their struggles and discoveries. Our first such discussion will help you begin to develop the skill of identifying what types of variables are involved when you are presented with any report containing statistical information.

Students Talk Stats

Identifying Types of Variables

*F*our students who have recently enrolled in a statistics class are browsing through news articles on the Internet, thinking about what kind of variables are involved.

Adam: *"I'm in the mood for chocolate, so I'm looking at this article that says 'Dark Chocolate Might Reduce Blood Pressure'. I'm pretty sure blood pressure is quantitative but couldn't chocolate go either way?"*

Brittany: *"Realistically, I think they'd just compare people who do and don't eat dark chocolate, which would make it categorical. Here's one that says 'Almost Half of U.S. Internet Users "Google" Themselves'. Half is a number so it's quantitative."*

Carlos: *"Half is talking about the overall fraction, but for each person, they just recorded whether or not they Googled themselves, so it's categorical. What about 'Vampire Bat Saliva Researched for Stroke'? I picture they handled bat saliva like Brittany said they'd handle chocolate—some people get it and others don't. I don't think it would be easy to put a number on recovery from a stroke, so that variable's probably categorical, too."*

Dominique: *"I'm confused about this one: 'Environmental Mercury, Autism Linked by New Research'. Mercury would be quantitative, and I think of autism as being categorical, but the report says they looked at autism rates in different school districts depending on how much mercury was in the area. Would that make autism quantitative?"*

Adam is correct that blood pressure is quantitative, and Brittany rightly guesses that chocolate consumption in this case would be categorical. Carlos has correctly identified Googling one's self as a categorical variable in the second article, and is on the right track that both bat saliva and stroke recovery would be categorical. Finally, although autism for individual people would be categorical, if a study considers autism *rates* for a sample of school districts, then the variable is quantitative. Dominique is right about both mercury and autism rate being quantitative variables in this study.

Practice: *Try Exercise 1.2 on page 11.*

Although variable type is usually fairly straightforward to identify, some "crossover" from one type to the other may take place, such as in the autism/mercury study discussed above by the four students, as well as in the following pair of examples.

EXAMPLE 1.1 WHEN A CATEGORICAL VARIABLE GIVES RISE TO A QUANTITATIVE VARIABLE

Background: Individual teenagers were surveyed as to whether they have used marijuana, and whether they have used harder drugs.

Teenager	Marijuana?	Harder Drugs?
#1	Yes	Yes
#2	No	No
#3	No	No
#4	Yes	No
…	…	…

Researchers then looked at the percentage of teenagers using marijuana and the percentage using harder drugs in various countries around the world to see if those two variables are related.

Country	% Marijuana	% Harder Drugs
#1	22	4
#2	37	16
#3	7	3
#4	23	14
…	…	…

Questions: What kinds of variables are involved in the first situation? What kinds of variables are involved in the second situation?

Responses: The first situation explores the relationship between two categorical variables. The second explores the relationship between two quantitative variables.

Practice: *Try Exercise 1.6(a,b) on page 12.*

EXAMPLE 1.2 WHEN A QUANTITATIVE VARIABLE GIVES RISE TO A CATEGORICAL VARIABLE

Researchers studied the effects of having dental X-rays during pregnancy. First they recorded birth weights of babies, along with information as to whether the mothers had been X-rayed while pregnant. When it came time to analyze the data, they simply classified the babies as being below 6 pounds (considered below normal) or not, along with information about whether the mothers had been X-rayed while pregnant.

Questions: What kind of variables were involved in the first situation? In the second situation?

Responses: The first situation involves one categorical variable (mother had dental X-rays or not) and a quantitative variable (baby's weight). The second situation involves two categorical variables because babies' weights are now categorized into two groups.

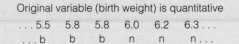

Original variable (birth weight) is quantitative

. . . 5.5   5.8   5.8   6.0   6.2   6.3 . . .
. . . b   b   b   n   n   n . . .

← Below normal | Normal →

Practice: *Try Exercise 1.8 on page 12.*

The **Big Picture:**
LOOKING AHEAD

Many real-life studies, including many discussed in this book, convert quantitative variables to categorical in order to simplify matters.

Handling Data for Two Types of Variables

We refer to recorded values of categorical or quantitative variables as *data*. The science of *statistics* is all about handling data.

> *Definitions*   **Data** are pieces of information about the values taken by variables for a set of individuals.
>
> The science of **statistics** concerns itself with gathering data about a group of individuals, displaying and summarizing the data, and using the information provided by the data to draw conclusions about a larger group of individuals.

Before we go into detail about the process of gathering data, it helps to have an idea of how we will handle the data when the time comes. Categorical variables are summarized by telling *count* or *proportion* or *percentage* in the category of interest. The most common way of summarizing quantitative variables is with their *mean* (same thing as *average*), although we will discuss other useful summaries a bit later in this book.

> *Definitions*   The **count** in a category of interest is simply the number of individuals in that category.
>
> The **proportion** in a category of interest is the number of individuals in that category, divided by the total number of individuals considered.
>
> The **percentage** in a category of interest is the proportion (as a decimal) multiplied by 100%.
>
> The **mean** of a set of values is their sum divided by the total number of values.

Students may be misled to think that the variable of interest in a situation is quantitative because they see a number attached to it. In fact, that number may be a count or a proportion or a percentage summarizing values of a categorical variable. It may help to think about how data values are being recorded *for each individual* in a sample in order to decide whether the variable of interest is categorical or quantitative, as Carlos did in the four students' discussion on page 3.

EXAMPLE **1.3** SUMMARIZING CATEGORICAL VARIABLES

Background: An article entitled "New Test-Taking Skill: Working the System" reports: "Indeed, although only a tiny fraction—1.9%—of students nationwide got special accommodations for the SAT, the percentage jumps fivefold for students at New England prep schools. At 20 prominent Northeastern private schools, nearly one in 10 students received special treatment."[1]

Question: What type of variable is featured here, and how is it summarized?

Response: For each student in the entire nation or in the private schools examined, it is recorded whether or not the student was granted special accommodations in taking the SAT test. This is a categorical variable, summarized by telling the percentage or proportion in the category of interest (receiving special accommodations).

Practice: *Try Exercise 1.10 on page 12.*

The **Big** *Picture:*
A Closer Look

In cases like this, where values of a quantitative variable are being compared for two or more categorical groups, a summary occasionally quantifies the differences by reporting what percent higher or lower another mean is from the original mean.

EXAMPLE **1.4** SUMMARIZING QUANTITATIVE VARIABLES

Background: An article entitled "Racial Gaps in Education Cause Income Tiers" reports: "On average, a white man with a college diploma earned about $65,000 in 2001. Similarly educated white women made about 40% less, while black and Hispanic men earned 30% less. . ."[2]

Question: How would earnings for each group (such as white women or Hispanic men) be summarized—with a mean or with a proportion?

Response: Earnings are a quantitative variable and could be summarized for each group with a mean, namely $65,000 for college-educated white men, and a mean that is less by 40% of $65,000 for college-educated white women—that is, $39,000.

Practice: *Try Exercise 1.11 on page 12.*

Most of the data that statisticians handle, and most of the data that we encounter in our everyday lives, come from some subgroup, called a *sample*, as opposed to the entire group of interest, called the *population*. Occasionally, we have access to information about the entire population, gathered via a *census*. This was the case in Example 1.4 about earnings of various demographic groups in the United States.

Definitions   A **sample** is a subset taken from a larger group, and the larger group of interest is the **population**.

A **census**, according to Webster's dictionary, is a "usually complete enumeration of the population," and we think of a census in general as a survey intended to include all citizens in a given area. When we talk about "*the* Census," we are referring to the U.S. Census, conducted regularly since 1790, and designed to gather more and more detailed information about America's population.

Once census results are summarized, as in Example 1.4, there are no further statistical procedures needed to draw conclusions about the "larger population."

EXAMPLE 1.5 WHEN INFORMATION IS PROVIDED FOR AN ENTIRE POPULATION

Background: "Are Feeding Tubes Over-Prescribed?" describes a Harvard Medical School study that "involved 1999 data from all 15,135 licensed U.S. nursing homes at the time."[3] The study found that "one-third of U.S. nursing home patients in the final stages of Alzheimer's and other forms of dementia are given feeding tubes, despite evidence that the practice serves no benefit and may even cause harm." The variable of interest here is whether or not nursing home patients in the final stages of Alzheimer's or other forms of dementia are given feeding tubes, a categorical variable that is summarized with the proportion 1/3.

Question: Why would it not be appropriate to generalize the study's results to a larger population?

Response: It is not possible to generalize this result to a larger group because it already refers to patients in *all* nursing homes at the time, rather than to a sample comprising a subset of those patients.

Practice: *Try Exercise 1.14 on page 13.*

In practice, some census variables are not necessarily assessed for all participants, but we tend to think of a census as a report that, unlike most other reports encountered in the world around us, tells us about *all* individuals, rather than just a *sample* of individuals.

Roles of Variables: Explanatory or Response

By far the most interesting and useful statistical studies involve *relationships* between variables. How we approach the data will depend on what roles the variables play in their relationship. There are occasionally situations where two variables have "equal footing" in the relationship, such as in a study of the relationship between football teams' rankings in offense and in defense. For the most part, however, one variable is thought to cause changes in, or at least to explain, values of the other: It is called the *explanatory variable*. The other variable is impacted by, or responds to, the first: It is called the *response variable*. A more complicated relationship can involve more than one explanatory or response variable.

> *Definitions*   **Causation** exists between two variables if changes in values of the first are actually responsible for changes in values of the second.
>
> The **explanatory variable** in a relationship between two variables is the one that is presumed to impact the other variable, called the **response variable.**

In the following diagram of the five possible situations introduced on page 2, the last three involve a relationship. The direction of the arrow goes from explanatory to response variable. Because relatively few actual situations of interest involve a quantitative explanatory and categorical response variable, and because the analysis is fairly advanced compared to the others, we will not analyze such situations in this book.

Methods of logistic regression can be used to handle situations in which the explanatory variable is quantitative and the response is categorical.

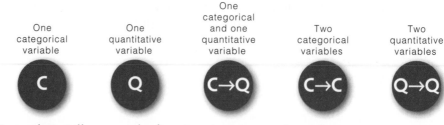

One categorical variable — **C**

One quantitative variable — **Q**

One categorical and one quantitative variable — **C→Q**

Two categorical variables — **C→C**

Two quantitative variables — **Q→Q**

Example 1.6 illustrates the five situations in a variety of contexts.

EXAMPLE 1.6 IDENTIFYING VARIABLE TYPES AND ROLES

Background: Consider these headlines:

- "Men Are Twice as Likely as Women to Be Hit by Lightning"
- "35% of Returning Troops Seek Mental Health Aid"
- "Do Oscar Winners Live longer Than Less Successful Peers?"
- "Smaller, Hungrier Mice"
- "County's Average Weekly Wages at $811, Better Than U.S. Average"

Questions: What type of variables are involved in each of these situations? If the relationship between two variables is of interest, which plays the role of explanatory variable and which is the response?

Thanks for helping me live longer?

 Responses: "Men Are Twice as Likely as Women to Be Hit by Lightning": We consider two categorical variables—gender and whether or not a person is hit by lightning. Gender would be the explanatory variable and being hit by lightning or not is the response. The other way around wouldn't make sense because being hit by lightning could not have an impact on a person's gender.

 "35% of Returning Troops Seek Mental Health Aid": Whether or not a returning soldier seeks mental health aid is a single categorical variable.

 "Do Oscar Winners Live Longer Than Less Successful Peers?": This involves a categorical explanatory variable— being an Oscar winner or not—and a quantitative response variable—length of life.

 "Smaller, Hungrier Mice": This brief headline suggests a relationship between two quantitative variables: the size of a mouse and its appetite. Size apparently plays the role of explanatory variable, so that as size goes down, the amount of food desired goes up.

"County's Average Weekly Wages at $811, Better Than U.S. Average": This involves just one quantitative variable—weekly wages. If wages for one county had been compared to those of another county, then there would have been an additional categorical explanatory variable. Comparing this county's wages to those of the United States in general is a different kind of comparison, where the county residents may be thought of as a single sample, coming from the larger population of U.S. residents.

Practice: *Try Exercise 1.17 on page 13.*

Statistics as a Four-Stage Process

Before we begin to learn about the first stage in the process of statistical analysis, we should consider how all the stages fit together to accomplish our overall goal. On page 5, we stated that, as a science, statistics is used to produce information from a sample, summarize it, and then draw conclusions about the larger population from which the sample came. Those conclusions, known as *statistical inference*, can be reached only if we have some knowledge of the workings of *random* behavior, which comes under the realm of the science of *probability*.

> *Definitions*   A **random** occurrence is one that happens by chance alone, and not according to a preference or an attempted influence.
>
> **Probability** is the formal study of the likelihood or chance of something occurring in a random situation. In the context of statistics, probability explores the behavior of random samples taken from a larger population.
>
> **Statistical inference** is the scientific process of drawing conclusions about a population based on information from a sample.

Thus, our goal can be reached in four stages, which will be addressed one at a time in the book's four parts.

1. **Data production:** How to select a representative sample, and how to properly assess values of variables for that sample.

2. **Displaying and summarizing data:** Depicting and describing single quantitative or categorical variables of interest, or relationships between variables if there are two variables involved.

3. **Probability:** The scientific process wherein we assume we actually know what is true for the entire population, and conclude what is likely to be true for a sample drawn at random from that population.

4. **Statistical inference:** Using what we have discovered about the variables of interest in a random sample to draw conclusions about those variables for the larger population.

It is easy for a student to lose sight of these long-term goals, as he or she concentrates on learning particular concepts and techniques. Throughout the book, the following diagram will help remind you of how each new topic fits into the "big picture." A reminder of variable types and roles is included because awareness of the variables involved is always an important part of the statistical picture.

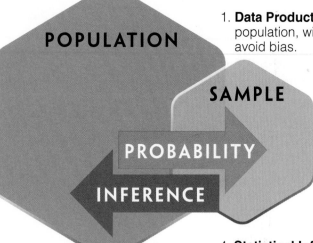

1. **Data Production:** Take sample data from the population, with sampling and study designs that avoid bias.

2. **Displaying and Summarizing:** Use appropriate displays and summaries of the sample data, according to variable types and roles.

3. **Probability:** Assume we know what's true for the *population;* how should **random** *samples* behave?

4. **Statistical Inference:** Assume we only know what's true about *sampled* values of a single variable or relationship; what can we **infer** about the larger *population?*

EXAMPLE 1.7 IDENTIFYING THE FOUR PROCESSES

Background: Consider the following situations:

■ A retail manager is asked to present some graphs and a brief report on her group's sales over the past several months, broken down into various types of merchandise.

■ Before a bookstore's owners make plans for extensive renovations, they want to find out what customers already like about the store and what aspects are in need of change.

■ A pharmaceutical company has carried out a study and determined proportions of patients experiencing nausea for those who take a certain medication and those who take a "dummy pill." The company wants to know what claims it can make about proportions of patients experiencing nausea in the general population for those who take the medication compared to those who don't.

■ The proportion of all Americans who are of Hispanic origin is 0.13. We'd like to know how unlikely it would be to take a random sample of 1,000 Americans and find only 0.06 to be Hispanic.

Question: Which of the four processes is involved in each situation?

Response:

■ The first is a task in displaying and summarizing data—namely, the information on sales of various types of merchandise.

■ The second requires data production—namely, the design and implementation of a survey of the bookstore's customers.

■ The third is a statistical inference problem, using information on tested patients to draw conclusions about side effects for any user of the medication.

■ The final one is a probability problem because we seek the likelihood of obtaining a certain proportion in our sample who are Hispanic.

Practice: *Try Exercise 1.23 on page 14.*

CHAPTER 1   SUMMARY

> Characteristics that can differ from one individual to another are called **variables.** Variables can be either categorical or quantitative. In statistics, we study single variables or relationships between variables. At times we merely focus on variables' values for a specific set of individuals, called a **sample.** More often, our goal is to generalize to a larger group, called the **population.**

Variables and Statistics

- **Data** are pieces of information about the values taken by variables for a set of individuals.

- The five variable situations to be covered in this book are:
  1. Single categorical variable
  2. Single quantitative variable
  3. Categorical explanatory and quantitative response variable
  4. Categorical explanatory and categorical response variable
  5. Quantitative explanatory and quantitative response variable

- **Categorical** variables can be summarized with **counts, proportions,** or **percentages.**

- **Quantitative** variables can be summarized with **means.**

- If individuals studied are entire groups, the percentage in a particular category for each group can be treated as a quantitative variable.

- A quantitative variable can be converted into a categorical variable by grouping into ranges of values.

- The science of statistics is concerned with gathering data, summarizing it, and using that information to draw conclusions about a larger population. The latter process is known as **statistical inference.**

- A **census** gathers information about an entire population rather than just a sample.

- When the relationship between two variables is of interest, it should be determined which (if any) plays the role of **explanatory variable** and which is the **response variable.**

- A **random** occurrence is one that happens by chance alone, and **probability** is the formal study of randomness.

- The four stages in the "big picture" of statistics are
  1. Data production
  2. Displaying and summarizing data
  3. Probability
  4. Statistical inference

CHAPTER 1   EXERCISES

Note: Asterisked numbers indicate exercises whose answers are provided in the Solutions to Selected Exercises section, on page 689.

*1.1 Students were asked to rate their instructor's preparation for class as being excellent, good, or needs improvement. Response to this question is what types of variable— quantitative or categorical?

*1.2 Suppose researchers want to investigate how weight can affect blood pressure. Tell what types of variables each of these situations involves.

a. Individuals' weights and blood pressures are recorded.

b. Individuals are classified as being normal or overweight, and their blood pressures are recorded.

More exercises for this chapter are featured in the **TBP** Supplement on pages 749. End-of-chapter activities are described on page 747.

c. Individuals are classified as having high or low blood pressure, and their weights are recorded in kilograms.

d. Individuals are assessed as having high or low blood pressure, and as being normal or overweight.

1.3 Prospective subjects for a study had their blood pressures recorded.

a. Is the variable of interest quantitative or categorical?

b. Would results best be summarized with a mean or with a proportion?

1.4 Before the 2004 presidential election in the United States, there was a great deal of interest concerning public opinion of the war in Iraq. For each of the following situations, tell what individuals are being studied, what variable is of interest, and whether the variable is categorical or quantitative.

a. People around the world were surveyed as to whether they approved or disapproved of the Iraq war.

b. People in various countries were surveyed as to whether they approved or disapproved of the Iraq war. For each country, it was determined what percentage of its people disapproved of the war.

c. The *Guardian*—a British newspaper—reported that 8 of 10 countries surveyed by leading newspapers (such as the *Guardian*, Canada's *La Presse*, and Japan's *Asahi Shimbun*) disapproved of the Iraq war.

1.5 Based on a survey of a few thousand people, a newspaper reporter wants to draw conclusions about how a country's citizens in general feel about the war in Iraq. At this point, is the reporter mainly concerned with data production, displaying and summarizing data, probability, or performing statistical inference?

*1.6 For parts (a) and (b), tell who or what individuals are being studied, identify the variable of interest, and tell whether it is categorical or quantitative; then answer the question in part (c).

a. Adults were surveyed as to whether they were married, single, or divorced.

b. The *New York Times* reported, state by state, the divorce rate per 1,000 married

adults in 2003. The lowest rate was in Massachusetts, with 5.7 divorces per 1,000 married people, and the highest was in Nevada, with 14.6 per 1,000.

c. Assume we have Census data on marital status of people in the United States. Are those people considered to be a sample or a population?

1.7 A *New York Times* reporter decides to convey information about American divorce rates by including a map of the United States. Each state is shaded from light to dark depending on how high its divorce rate is. At this point, is the reporter mainly concerned with data production, displaying and summarizing data, probability, or performing statistical inference?

*1.8 "Can Mom's Drinking Lower Kids' IQ?" examined the relationship between mothers' consumption of alcohol during pregnancy and their children's IQs. The mothers were classified as being abstainers (0 alcoholic drinks per day), light drinkers (up to 0.5 per day), moderate drinkers (0.5 to 1 per day), or heavy drinkers (more than 1 per day). Is alcohol consumption being treated as a categorical or a quantitative variable?

1.9 An article reported costs of ski-lift tickets in various resorts in a region as being less than $20, $20 to $40, $40 to $50, or more than $50. Is ticket price being treated as a categorical or a quantitative variable?

*1.10 A British survey reported in 2006 states: "Nearly 40 percent of 106 students who answered questionnaires about their attitudes said they couldn't cope without their cell phone."[4]

a. What type of variable is being considered?

b. How is the variable summarized?

*1.11 "In a study of 87 French and Swiss college students, researchers gave half of them sunscreen with a protection factor of 10 and the other half with a factor of 30. The students, who weren't told which lotion they received, went on summer vacations and recorded the amount of time they spent in the sun. Users of the stronger sunscreen spent 25% more time in the sun, mostly sunbathing, the study found . . . students in the study often waited until their skin turned red before rushing to the shade."[5]

a. Is time spent in the sun being treated as a quantitative or a categorical variable?

b. How would researchers summarize time spent in the sun for each group (those with the stronger and those with the weaker sunscreen)?

1.12 A newspaper article entitled "Teens Most Likely to Have Sex at Home" notes that of the sexually active teens surveyed in the year 2000, "56% said they first had sex at their family's home or at the home of their partner's family."[6]

a. What is the variable of interest?

b. Is the variable of interest quantitative or categorical?

c. How is the variable being summarized?

1.13 Based on results of a survey of sexually active teenagers, sociologists would like to be able to say whether or not a majority of all sexually active teenagers first had sex at their or their partner's home. At this point, are the sociologists mainly concerned with data production, displaying and summarizing data, probability, or performing statistical inference?

*1.14 The *New York Times* reports: "Three out of four workers drove to their jobs by themselves in 2006, according to another finding by the Census Bureau."[7] Should we consider the workers studied to be a sample or a population?

1.15 Mortality rates in the United States during the 1980s and 1990s were studied by county, race, gender, and income, with the following results: "Asian-Americans, average per-capita income of $21,566, have a life expectancy of 84.9 years . . . Western American Indians, $10,029, 72.7 years . . ."[8] Are these numbers referring to samples or populations?

1.16 The American Association of Retired People (AARP) conducted a survey in which it was discovered that 63% of adult Americans don't want to live to be at least 100. On average, those polled wanted to live to the age of 91.

a. Should we consider the Americans polled to be a sample or a population?

b. There is a categorical variable of interest in the survey; tell roughly how the survey question was phrased to obtain those responses.

c. There is a quantitative variable of interest in the survey; tell roughly how the survey question was phrased to obtain those responses.

*1.17 The *New York Times* reported on a study of gadgets and appliances in American homes. For each of the following results, tell which of the five variable situations is involved, choosing from the following:

- C: single categorical variable
- Q: single quantitative variable
- C → Q: categorical explanatory variable and quantitative response variable
- C → C: categorical explanatory variable and categorical response variable
- Q → Q: quantitative explanatory variable and quantitative response variable

a. For each of the 17 appliances studied, the *Times* reported the percentage of American homes in 2001 that had the appliance. For example, microwave ovens were in 96% of the homes and answering machines were in 78% of the homes. (1) C (2) Q (3) C → Q (4) C → C (5) Q → Q

b. The study made a comparison of percentage owning each appliance in 2001 to the percentage owning the appliance in 1987. For example, microwave ovens were in 66% of the homes in 1987 as opposed to 96% in 2001. Answering machines were in 10% of the homes in 1987 as opposed to 78% in 2001. (1) C (2) Q (3) C → Q (4) C → C (5) Q → Q

c. The study reported 2.5 television sets owned per household in 2001. (1) C (2) Q (3) C → Q (4) C → C (5) Q → Q

1.18 The *New York Times* reported on a study of gadgets and appliances in American homes. For each of the 17 appliances studied, it told the percentage of American homes in 2001 that had the appliance. For example, microwave ovens were in 96% of the homes and answering machines were in 78% of the homes.

a. Who or what are the individuals being studied?

b. What is the variable of interest?

c. Is the variable of interest quantitative or categorical?

1.19 The study that looked at prevalence of various appliances in homes in 2001, as described in Exercises 1.17 and 1.18, made a comparison to the percentages for each appliance in 1987. For example, microwave ovens were in 66% of the homes in 1987 as opposed to 96% in 2001. Answering machines were in 10% of the homes in 1987 as opposed to 78% in 2001.

    a. There are two variables involved; what is the explanatory variable?

    b. Tell whether the explanatory variable is quantitative or categorical.

    c. What is the response variable?

    d. Tell whether the response variable is quantitative or categorical.

    e. In which year would you expect percentages to be higher overall—1987 or 2001, or both the same?

1.20 The *New York Times* study of appliances reported 2.5 television sets per household in 2001.

    a. Is the variable of interest quantitative or categorical?

    b. Is the reported summary a mean or a proportion?

1.21 Suppose television advertisers want to know if age plays a role in people's response to a rather unconventional ad that might be aired during the next Super Bowl. The ad is shown to a variety of viewers. Keeping in mind that the explanatory variable is not necessarily the first one mentioned, classify each of the following possible approaches as involving one of these relationships:

    ■ $C \rightarrow C$: categorical explanatory variable and categorical response variable

    ■ $C \rightarrow Q$: categorical explanatory variable and quantitative response variable

    ■ $Q \rightarrow C$: quantitative explanatory variable and categorical response variable

    ■ $Q \rightarrow Q$: quantitative explanatory variable and quantitative response variable

    a. They ask whether or not a viewer likes the ad, and record his or her age.

    b. They classify a viewer as being youth, young adult, middle-aged, or senior citizen, and whether or not he or she likes the ad.

    c. Viewers' ages are recorded, along with their rating of the ad on a scale of 1 to 10 (most unfavorable) to 10 (most favorable).

    d. Viewers' ratings of the ad on a scale of 1 to 10 are recorded, along with the viewers' age group as being youth, young adult, middle-aged, or senior citizen.

1.22 Television advertisers are trying to decide which of the approaches outlined in Exercise 1.21 to use in an upcoming study of age and response to an advertisement. At this point, are they mainly concerned with data production, displaying and summarizing data, probability, or performing statistical inference?

*1.23 A department head wants to investigate the quality of teaching of a professor who is coming up for tenure. Tell which of the four processes (data production, displaying and summarizing, probability, or statistical inference) is involved in each of these stages:

    a. The department head considers whether to simply ask students to rate various aspects of the professor's performance on a 5-point scale, or whether to also ask them to write a paragraph describing their experience in that professor's class.

    b. A sample of students is surveyed, and scores on a 5-point scale are averaged for each aspect of the professor's performance.

    c. If all of the professor's students would give an average rating no higher than 4.0 on preparedness, it would be very unlikely to get a sample of 20 students' ratings averaging at least 4.3 on preparedness.

    d. Based on the responses of sampled students, the department head concludes that the mean preparedness rating for *all* of the professor's students is higher than 4.0.

1.24 *Men's Health* magazine used data on body mass index, back-surgery rates, usage of gyms, etc. to grade the quality of men's "abs" (abdominal muscles) in 60 cities across the country. If each city was given a rating between 0 and 4, such as 2.75 for Pittsburgh, then how is the variable of interest being treated—as quantitative or categorical?

1.25 Suppose *Men's Health* magazine wants to present the results of the survey described in Exercise 1.24 in a way that is both appealing and informative. Is the magazine mainly concerned with data production, displaying and summarizing data, probability, or performing statistical inference?

1.26 Anthropologists studied gender differences in public restroom graffiti, noting whether the graffiti occurred in a men's or women's room, and classifying writings as being competitive and derogatory or advisory and sympathetic.

    a. There are two variables mentioned here; what is the explanatory variable?

    b. Tell whether the explanatory variable is quantitative or categorical.

    c. What is the response variable?

    d. Tell whether the response variable is quantitative or categorical.

    e. Would type of writings for each gender be summarized with means or proportions?

Typical graffiti for women's room?

1.27 If researchers report that alcoholics are three times as likely to smoke compared to nonalcoholics, do they consider smoking to be the explanatory variable or the response?

1.28 If researchers report that smokers are 10 times as likely to be alcoholics compared to nonsmokers, do they consider smoking to be the explanatory variable or the response?

1.29 The Centers for Disease Control and Prevention noted that "the price of a pack of cigarettes went up 90% between 1997 and 2003."[9] Suppose students in an introductory statistics course have been asked to identify the two variables of interest here, then tell which is explanatory and which is response, and whether each is quantitative or categorical. Which student has the correct answer?

    Adam: The explanatory variable is price of cigarettes, and it's categorical because it was summarized with a percentage. The response is year, and it's quantitative because it takes number values.

    Brittany: The roles are reversed: Year is the quantitative explanatory variable and price is the categorical response.

    Carlos: Year is the explanatory variable, and because just two values are possible, it's categorical. Price is the response and it's quantitative—90% just tells how much the price has changed from the year 1997 to the year 2003.

    Dominique: Both variables are quantitative because they both take number values; year is explanatory because it affects the price.

1.30 One-third of all nursing home patients with Alzheimer's and other forms of dementia are given feeding tubes. Researchers want to know how unlikely it would be to find more than half in a random sample of 100 such patients to have been given feeding tubes. Are the researchers mainly concerned with data production, displaying and summarizing data, probability, or performing statistical inference?

Discovering Research: VARIABLE TYPES AND ROLES

1.31 Hand in an article or report about a statistical study; tell what variable or variables are involved and whether they are quantitative or categorical. If there are two variables, tell which is explanatory and which is response. If summaries are mentioned, tell whether they are reporting means or proportions or something else.

Reporting on Research: VARIABLE TYPES AND ROLES

1.32 Use the results of Exercise 1.6 and relevant findings from the Internet to make a report on divorce in the United States that relies on statistical information.

© Matthias Kulka/zefa/CORBIS

Part I

Data Production

The Big Picture:

LOOKING AHEAD

Obtaining an unbiased, representative sample is essential for performing statistical inference in Part IV. A study design that assesses sampled values without bias is a prerequisite for producing accurate summaries in Part II.

An Overview

In this part of the book, we focus on the two stages of data production:

1. Obtaining a sample
2. Designing a study to discover what we want to know about the variables of interest for the individuals in the sample

The principles of good data production play a vital role in what we aim to accomplish throughout the book. It is of the utmost importance at this stage to avoid any form of *bias*.

> *Definitions*   An **estimate** is an educated guess for a quantity; in statistics, the most common quantities to be estimated are means and proportions.
>
> **Bias** is the tendency of an estimate to deviate in one direction from a true value.
>
> A **biased sample** results in over- or underestimates because the sample is not representative of the population of interest.
>
> The **design** of a study is the plan for gathering information about the variables of interest. A **biased study design** results in over- or underestimates because of flaws in the way information about sampled individuals is gathered.

The Big Picture:

A CLOSER LOOK

Bias as a household word may suggest that the over- or underestimation is deliberate; in fact, bias is often unintentional.

Bias Due to Sampling

In an interview, Larry Flynt (controversial publisher of *Hustler* and similar magazines) was asked, "How would you like women to remember you—as someone who helped or hurt their position?"[1] His reply was ". . . of the thousands of girls who have posed for my magazines, I've never had one who felt she had been exploited. I think it's actually helped the women's movement. . . ." Obviously, the

16

sample of girls who posed for Flynt's magazines are not representative of women in general, so we cannot infer anything about the attitude of the larger population of women based on his sample of models.

Thus, it is extremely important that the very first step in data production—*sampling*—be carried out in such a way that the sample really does represent the population of interest. Also, we must remember that our summaries of variables and their relationships reflect the true nature of the variables and relationships in the sample only if the *design* for gathering the information is sound.

Bias Due to Study Design

According to an article entitle "Exercise Does Good Things for Teens' Moods," "Boys who reported less than an hour of vigorous physical activity a week were more likely to be depressed and withdrawn than those who exercised regularly." The design for assessing the boys' physical activity and mood was to simply observe the values for these variables as they naturally occurred. For this reason, we can't rule out a very different explanation for what the researchers observed in their sample of boys: Perhaps being in a good mood makes a teenager more likely to exercise.

Good data production is an essential part of the "big picture" of statistics. We must keep its principles in mind as we progress later on in the book to summarizing data, understanding probability, and performing statistical inference.

Throughout this part of the book, we will establish guidelines for ideal production of data. It is important for us to strive to achieve these standards. Realistically, however, it is rarely possible to carry out a study that is completely free of flaws. Therefore, we must frequently apply common sense to decide which imperfections we can "live with," and which ones could completely undermine a study's results.

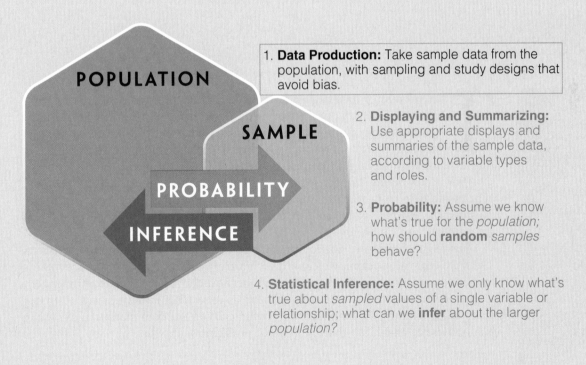

1. **Data Production:** Take sample data from the population, with sampling and study designs that avoid bias.

2. **Displaying and Summarizing:** Use appropriate displays and summaries of the sample data, according to variable types and roles.

3. **Probability:** Assume we know what's true for the *population;* how should **random** *samples* behave?

4. **Statistical Inference:** Assume we only know what's true about *sampled* values of a single variable or relationship; what can we **infer** about the larger *population?*

Sampling: *Which Individuals Are Studied*

How should we take a sample of individuals to gain information about the larger group?

© Tom Grill/CORBIS

How good is the food?
Who should be asked?

The *Big* Picture:

LOOKING BACK

We defined a *random* occurrence on page 9 to be one that happens by chance alone, and not according to a preference or an attempted influence. Our preferences, which may be subtle or subconscious, cannot be entirely suppressed at will.

The process of data production consists of two steps: (1) obtain the sample, and (2) carry out a properly designed study to assess the variables or relationships of interest. In this chapter we will concentrate on the first step, stressing that the sample must be taken in such a way as to ensure that it represents the larger population of interest without bias.

Pick a number at random from 1 to 20. This may sound easy, but unless you get outside help from something like a computer or a table of random digits or a 20-sided die, the task is impossible. Our brains are designed to recognize and create *patterns*, not randomness.

Just as our brains are not equipped to guide us in selecting a number between 1 and 20 truly at random, we cannot pick a truly random sample of participants for a study "off the top of our head" without the aid of some random number generator. *Random* as a household word often is used to describe a selection that a statistician would call "haphazard." Technically, a random sample must make planned use of chance so that the laws of probability apply.

Sources of Bias in Sampling: When Selected Individuals Are Not Representative

Bias, the tendency for an estimate to deviate in one direction from the true value, can enter into the selection process in a variety of ways. After we define some of the most common sources of bias in sampling, we will examine how they can arise in the context of an example.

Definitions   **Selection bias** occurs in general when the sample is nonrepresentative of the larger population of interest.

The **sampling frame** is the collection of all the individuals who have the potential to be selected. It should—but does not necessarily—match the population of interest.

A **self-selected sample** (also known as a **volunteer sample**) includes only individuals who have taken the initiative to participate, as opposed to having been recruited by researchers.

A **haphazard sample** is selected without a scientific plan, according to the whim of whoever is drawing the sample.

The main criterion for selection in a **convenience sample** is that the sampled individuals are found at a time or in a place that is handy for researchers.

Nonresponse occurs when individuals selected by researchers decline to be part of the sample. A sample is described as suffering from **nonresponse bias** when too many individuals decline, to the extent that there is a substantial impact on the composition of the sample.

Call-in or Internet polls are practically guaranteed to be biased, often quite heavily, because they result in volunteer samples.

EXAMPLE 2.1 HOW VARIOUS TYPES OF BIAS OCCUR IN SAMPLING

Background: A professor wants to survey a sample of six from 80 class members to get their opinion about the course textbook.

Questions: Are these sampling methods unbiased? If not, what type of bias enters in?

1. Ask for students to raise their hands if they would like to give their opinion of the textbook.

2. Sample the next six students who come in to office hours.

3. Look at a class roster and, without the aid of a random number generator, attempt to take a "random" sample of six names.

4. Assign each student in the classroom a number from 1 on up, then use software or a table of random digits to select six at random.

5. Take a random sample from the roster of students enrolled and mail them a questionnaire.

Responses:

1. Asking students to raise their hands yields a *volunteer sample*, which would be likely to favor people with strong positive or negative feelings about the book.

2. Asking students who come in to office hours would yield a *convenience sample*, and would result in bias because students who need help may tend to find the book difficult to understand.

Continued

Nonresponse bias is one of the hardest problems to combat in sample surveys, but researchers can successfully reduce it by providing incentives to respond or by following up with additional attempts to elicit a response.

3. If the professor picks names "off the top of his head," it results in a *haphazard sample* that may fail to be representative because of conscious or subconscious tendencies to pick certain types of students.

4. The problem with picking only from students in attendance is that the *sampling frame does not match the population*: Often, not all of the enrolled students attend class. Absent students might tend to feel negatively about the course in general, including the textbook; or, on the other hand, maybe they don't attend because they feel the book is good enough to teach them all they need to know!

5. Taking a random sample from the roster of students enrolled and mailing them a questionnaire may be one of the professor's best options. However, there is a good chance that not all six students would take the trouble to respond. Thus, *nonresponse bias* may result in a sample of students that are atypical.

Practice: *Try Exercise 2.6 on page 26.*

For a more technical definition of a *simple random sample* of size *n*, we can specify that every set of *n* individuals has an equal probability of being selected.

The last two sampling methods in Example 2.1 incorporated randomness in the selection process. This turns out to be a key feature of good sampling technique, to be discussed presently.

Probability Sampling Plans: Relying on Randomness

Remember that probability, defined on page 9, is the formal study of random behavior. Thus, a *probability sampling plan* is one that utilizes randomness. This turns out to be the best way to avoid selection bias in a survey. There are a variety of probability sampling plans that researchers can use.

A classic example of a simple random sample (sampling at random without replacement) is drawing names from a hat—once a name has been drawn, it is *not* put back into the hat.

> *Definitions*   A **probability sampling plan** incorporates chance in the selection process so that the rules of probability apply.
>
> - A **simple random sample** selects individuals at random and without replacement, so that the same individual cannot be selected twice.
> - A **stratified random sample** takes separate random samples from groups of similar individuals (strata) within the population.
> - A **cluster sample** selects small groups (clusters) at random from within the population; *all* units in each cluster are sampled.
> - A **multi-stage sample** stratifies in stages, randomly sampling from groups or areas that are successively more specific.

Page 750 of the *Teaching the Big Picture* **(TBP)** *Supplement* includes a discussion of modern-day challenges to effective sampling due to the shift from land-line to cell phones.

For the purpose of learning statistics, we often present methods that apply in the most straightforward setting, when we have a simple random sample. In real-life statistical practice, one of the more complicated sampling plans is generally used.

One type of sampling plan that does not rely on probability is a *systematic sample*.

> *Definition* A **systematic sampling plan** employs a methodical but nonrandom approach, such as selecting individuals at regularly spaced intervals on a list.

A systematic sampling plan, such as choosing every tenth name on an alphabetical roster of students, does not utilize randomness, but in some situations this would not prevent the sample from being representative of the population. Such a plan is at times a reasonable alternative to a probability sampling plan.

EXAMPLE 2.2 IDENTIFYING SAMPLING PLANS

Background: Suppose a representative sample of undergraduate students from a particular university is needed.

Question: What type of probability sampling plan is used in each of the following?

1. A random sample of classes is taken from all classes meeting at the university, and *all* students in each of the sampled classes are included in the sample.

2. First divide all the students into schools—such as arts, sciences, engineering, and so on. Within each school, a random sample of students is taken.

3. First all the students are divided into schools. Within each school, a random sample of majors is selected. Within each major, a random sample of classes is selected. At the last stage, either the entire cluster of students in each sampled class is included, or individual students are randomly sampled from each sampled class.

4. A random number generator is used to select a certain number of students from the list of all those who attend that university.

Response:

1. The first is a cluster sample.

2. The second is a stratified sample.

3. The third is a multi-stage sample.

4. The fourth is a simple random sample.

Practice: *Try Exercise 2.10 on page 27.*

The Role of Sample Size: Bigger Is Better If the Sample Is Representative

So far, we have made no mention of sample size. The first priority is to make sure the sample is representative of the population by using some form of probability sampling plan. Next, to get a more precise idea about the nature of the variables of interest or their relationship for the entire population, a larger sample does a better job than a smaller one.

EXAMPLE 2.3 SAMPLE SIZE AND SAMPLING PLAN

Background: Suppose a medical school's administrators would like to find out how its students would rate the quality of food in the cafeteria.

Question: Which one of the following four sampling plans would be best?

1. The person responsible for polling stands outside the cafeteria door and asks the next 5 students who exit the cafeteria to give the food a rating on a scale of 1 to 10.

2. The person responsible for polling stands outside the cafeteria door and asks the next 50 students who exit the cafeteria to give the food a rating on a scale of 1 to 10.

3. The person responsible for polling takes a random sample of 5 students from all those enrolled at the school and asks them to rate the cafeteria food on a scale of 1 to 10.

4. The person responsible for polling takes a random sample of 50 students from all those enrolled at the school and asks them to rate the cafeteria food on a scale of 1 to 10.

Response: The first two plans would be biased in favor of higher ratings because students with unfavorable opinions about the cafeteria food would be more likely to eat elsewhere. It does no good to poll 50 instead of 5 because this would just help us to pinpoint a biased typical rating more precisely. The third plan, because it is random, would be unbiased. However, with such a small sample, you run the risk of by chance including people who provide unusually low ratings, or those who provide unusually high ratings. In other words, the average rating could vary quite a bit depending on who happens to be included in that small sample. The fourth plan would be best: First of all, it has been chosen at random to avoid bias; secondly, the larger sample size gets us closer to the truth about the opinions of all the students.

Practice: *Try Exercise 2.13 on page 27.*

The Big Picture: LOOKING AHEAD

Sample size will turn out to play a crucial role in the statistical inference section of this book, when we use information from a sample to state specific conclusions about the population of interest. Larger samples are better because they provide more information about the population, but it should be noted that in statistics, as in real life, we are confronted with many trade-offs. A larger sample may be more informative, but it is also more costly in terms of time and money.

On pages 750–751 of the *TBP* Supplement we discuss how, for practical purposes, real-life sampling may deviate from what is ideal from a theoretical standpoint.

From Sample to Population: To What Extent Can We Generalize?

Knowing exactly what sort of group constitutes the sample does not automatically tell us which population the sample represents. To decide which group we can generalize to, we must take into account the variables of interest.

EXAMPLE 2.4 IDENTIFYING WHAT POPULATION IS REPRESENTED BY A GIVEN SAMPLE

Background: A study of the benefits of marijuana for pain management was conducted, with the sample consisting of 60 AIDS patients at the San Mateo County Health Center in California.

Question: What would be the largest population to which the researchers could draw conclusions, based on the study's results: people in general, any patients who seek medication for pain management, all AIDS patients, or all AIDS patients at that health center—or do the sampled patients really only represent themselves?

Response: It should be fairly safe to generalize to all AIDS patients. Before generalizing to *any* patients who seek medication for pain management, it is necessary to consider whether the chemical benefits would be the same, regardless of the pain's underlying cause. Interaction with other medications should also be considered—for example, the medications taken by AIDS patients would be quite different from those taken by cancer patients.

Practice: *Try Exercise 2.15 on page 27.*

The majority of real-world studies use a sample taken from some larger population, and an attempt is made to generalize from conclusions about the sample to conclusions about the population. Such a generalization *should* not be made if the sample is not a representative subset of the larger group of interest. It simply *cannot* be made if the sample is not a subset of any larger group.

EXAMPLE 2.5 SAMPLE NOT A SUBSET OF A LARGER POPULATION

Background: Astrophysicists looked at the diameters and orbits of the seven irregular moons of the planet Neptune.

Question: Can we use the data to draw more general conclusions?

Response: The data values, while of interest in their own right, would not be used to draw conclusions about any larger population because Neptune's seven irregular moons are not a subset of any larger group.

Practice: *Try Exercise 2.17 on page 28.*

Students Talk Stats

Seeking a Representative Sample

*E*ach year a large sample of potential jurors must be contacted for court trials in regions throughout the United States. In Pennsylvania's Allegheny County, over 100,000 potential jurors were to be contacted by May 1, 2004. Ordinarily, the best method would be to choose at random from all county residents. However, in early spring 2004, a lack of racial diversity in the daily jury pool delayed a homicide trial in Pittsburgh. Although 10.8% of the county's voting population is black, nonresponse led to jury pools that were typically only 5.5% black. The situation is described in an article entitled "Judge Moves to Boost Recruitment of Blacks for County Jury Pool." To rectify

Students Talk Stats continued ➔

Students Talk Stats continued

the county's chronic problem of too few African-Americans in its jury pools, the presiding judge, Joe James, ordered that in addition to the usual random selection, parts of the county with higher percentages of African-Americans would be targeted for 15,000 supplemental mailings. As a follow-up, jurors who were present in the daily jury pool would be asked to complete an anonymous questionnaire about their race, gender, age, and ZIP code, allowing the county to characterize the sampled individuals who *do* ultimately respond to the call for jury duty.

Suppose a group of statistics students is debating the merits of the judge's sampling method.

Adam: *"It works for me."*

Brittany: *"But the sample is supposed to be random. If the judge deliberately adds all those African-Americans to the sample, then it's not random anymore."*

Carlos: *"The main reason why you want the sample to be random is to make it representative of the population. That wasn't happening the way it was supposed to, so the judge made an improvement."*

Dominique: *"Carlos is right. They tried to make the sample random but it turned out that African-Americans were under-represented because of nonresponse. The bias from nonresponse could be worse than the bias from altering the sample."*

The students are on the right track here. Nonresponse was resulting in a biased sample and the judge helped to offset this flaw by modifying the sample to make it more representative. In the long run, the questionnaires' results could be used to try to offset the nonresponse and still mail the jury duty summons to a completely random sample. This would be accomplished by identifying what makes nonrespondents differ from respondents, and then trying more aggressively to reach nonrespondents successfully. According to a *Pittsburgh Post-Gazette* article published some time after the report of Judge James's attempts to draw a pool of jurors that was more representative of the county's racial distribution, the Allegheny Court of Common Pleas began to offer jurors discounts for shopping and parking, as a way of reducing the inconvenience of jury duty.

In the short run, mailing summons to a disproportionately high percentage of black residents would ideally result in a sample that was ultimately representative. In the long run, discovering reasons for why people fail to respond to the call for jury duty, and taking steps to make changes accordingly, could increase response to the truly random sample.

CHAPTER 2 | SUMMARY

The Big Picture:

Since our goal in statistics is to learn about single variables or relationships, the first step is to record values taken by the variables of interest. We accomplish this in two stages: First, obtain a sample of individuals to be studied; then assess the variables' values for those sampled indi-viduals, via some study design. At the sampling stage, we want to select individ-uals that are representative of the larger group of interest. Randomness, defined in Chapter 1 as a selection that depends on chance alone, is crucial for obtaining samples that are truly representative.

Sampling Methods

- Sampling should be carried out in a way that avoids bias, and produces a sample that truly represents the population of interest.

- The **sampling frame** (individuals with the potential to be sampled) should match the population (individuals about whom information is desired).

- **Self-selected/volunteer samples** are usually biased.

- **Convenience samples** may introduce bias because of which individuals are included and which are excluded.

- A **haphazard sample**, in which a person makes an informal attempt at randomness, can be biased in unforeseen ways. As household words, *random* and *haphazard* are often used interchangeably, but in statistics, there is an extremely important distinction between the two.

- **Nonresponse** can bias a sample because nonrespondents tend to differ from respondents in ways that could affect the variables of interest.

- **Systematic sampling**, such as choosing individuals at regular intervals, may or may not bias the results, depending on the circumstances. This is a technique that does *not* implement randomness.

- **Probability sampling plans** avoid bias by employing randomness to let chance govern the selection.

- The best-known probability sampling plan is a **simple random sample,** taken at random and without replacement.

- Other probability sampling plans are **stratified sampling** (where the population is first divided into groups of similar individuals), **cluster sampling** (where entire groups are sampled rather than single individuals), and **multi-stage sampling** (where groups are sampled at random, then groups from within the sampled groups, and so on).

- As long as the sample is unbiased, **larger samples are better.** However, larger samples are not always possible because of time or money constraints.

CHAPTER 2 | EXERCISES

Note: Asterisked numbers indicate exercises whose answers are provided in the Solutions to Selected Exercises section, on page 689.

Warming Up

2.1 A study was to be conducted at the San Mateo County Health Center in California, in which marijuana would be dispensed to 60 AIDS patients for pain management. Suppose patients were asked to report their level of pain on a scale of 0 to 10, and scores were compared for patients receiving marijuana and another group of patients receiving more conventional pain medication.

 a. Is the variable for pain quantitative or categorical, and which role is it playing (explanatory or response)?

More exercises for this chapter are featured in the **TBP** *Supplement* on pages 753 through 754. End-of-chapter activities are described on page 751.

b. Is the variable for treatment quantitative or categorical, and which role is it playing (explanatory or response)?

c. The goal of the study was to see if, in general, marijuana could be helpful in pain management for any AIDS patient. Is this focusing on data production, displaying and summarizing, probability, or statistical inference?

*2.2   Suppose a utility company polls customers to assess their satisfaction with its services.

a. Describe what stage of such a poll is concerned with sampling, and what stage is concerned with study design.

b. Describe a way to treat satisfaction as categorical and a way to treat it as quantitative.

2.3   Suppose people are being polled about their physical activity. The researchers who conduct the poll must decide how to assess people's physical activity; they must also decide which people should be polled.

a. Which of the above decisions focuses on sampling?

b. Which of the above decisions focuses on study design?

c. Describe a way to treat physical activity as a categorical variable.

d. Describe a way to treat physical activity as a quantitative variable.

*2.4   In October 2002, newsPolls.org posted results of a survey wherein people who said they would have a special meal at Thanksgiving were asked, "About how many people do you think you will have at the Thanksgiving meal?"[2]

a. Is the variable of interest quantitative or categorical?

b. Would the results be summarized with a mean or a proportion?

c. Which of these variables could have the greatest impact on the accuracy of individuals' responses to the question: gender, region of the United States, or political party?

Exploring the Big Picture

*2.5   A poll taken in October 2004, which was funded by the European Union and the Turkish government, found that 50.8% of the 8,075 married women surveyed in Turkey were married without their consent.

a. If the women had responded to a survey in a relatively progressive magazine, would this tend to result in bias due to a nonrepresentative sample or due to a poor design for assessing the sampled values?

b. If some of the women had doubts that their responses would be kept anonymous, would we have reason to believe the actual percentage married without consent to be higher or lower than 50.8%?

*2.6   Suppose a principal of a large high school wants to survey a sample of five teachers about conditions in the teachers' lounge. For each of the following sampling methods, tell which type of bias causes it to be flawed.

a. The principal randomly selects from a list that does not include the school's part-time teachers.

b. The principal puts a box outside the lounge, indicating that teachers can contribute anonymous comments about the condition of the lounge.

c. The principal thinks of several teachers to ask about conditions in the lounge.

d. A random sample taken from all the school's teachers receive an anonymous survey about the lounge in their mailboxes, with a request for them to complete and return it.

e. Whenever a teacher stops by the principal's office with other concerns, the principal can ask for his or her opinion about the condition of the lounge.

2.7   To determine who is the most famous athlete of all time, a student thinks up a sample of some acquaintances and calls to ask their opinion. Was this a systematic sample, a haphazard sample, or a random sample?

2.8   The Public Interest Research Group (PIRG) surveyed 197 credit reports and concluded that one in four contained serious errors. However, the survey's results were called into question because PIRG only surveyed its own members. Was this a convenience sample, a systematic sample, a cluster sample, or a stratified sample?

2.9 The Public Interest Research Group (PIRG) surveyed 197 credit reports and concluded that one in four contained serious errors. However, the survey's results were called into question: "Besides objecting to the way the survey was conducted, with PIRG surveying its own members, Norm Magnuson of the Consumer Data Industry Association protested that the group 'unilaterally decided what is a serious error' in presenting its findings."[3] Is Magnuson suggesting there is bias because the individuals are not representative of the larger population, or bias in the assessment of variables' values, or both, or neither?

*2.10 If a polling organization must be especially careful to represent all regions of the United States, which type of sampling plan is most useful: multi-stage sampling, cluster sampling, convenience sampling, or systematic sampling?

2.11 Four statistics students discuss the following design questions; who has the best answer about type of sample that should be taken? "Researchers want to survey teenagers to see if there is a link between how often they eat dinner with the family and how well-adjusted they are. If the researchers suspect that gender may play an important role in this relationship, should they take a convenience sample, a systematic sample, a cluster sample, or a stratified sample?"

Adam: Convenience sample sounds good. If they take it in a convenient way, they can use a larger sample size. That will include lots of both sexes.

Brittany: They should stratify the population into males and females, then take random samples, keeping track of gender along with the other variable.

Carlos: Isn't that a systematic sample? You systematically pick one male, then one female, then another male, and another female, and so on.

Dominique: If you want enough of both sexes, I think you should sample a cluster of males and a cluster of females, making the clusters as large as possible.

2.12 In August 2003, newsPolls.org posted results of a survey that included the question: "Do you use the Internet to get information about MAJOR LEAGUE BASEBALL often, sometimes, rarely, or never?"[4] Which of the following sampling methods would be most likely to obtain a sample that results in biased responses: telephone, e-mail, or ordinary mail?

*2.13 Suppose an e-mail survey asks respondents about how frequently they use the Internet to get information about Major League Baseball. If the survey takers want to use results to draw conclusions about how frequently all Americans use the Internet to get information about Major League Baseball, are the conclusions more accurate if there were 100 respondents or 1,000; or can't the design be improved with a different sample size?

2.14 Viewers of *American Idol* could vote for their favorite singer by using land-line telephones, cell phones, or text-messaging; the winner is presumably the favorite of all Americans.

a. Which of these best describes the potential source of bias: using a self-selected sample, sampling frame not matching population, using a convenience sample, or taking a haphazard sample?

b. In which case would we have a better idea of which singer is preferred by the American public in general—if 10,000 people or if 100,000 people call in their vote; or doesn't it make a difference?

*2.15 A survey is conducted that includes several hundred students at a large university, all taking an introductory statistics course. Proportions of students in the various year and gender categories are typical of those for college students in general.

a. Suppose that we are interested in the students' math SAT scores. Which of these is the *largest* population for which we can say the surveyed students probably constitute a representative sample: all humans, all college students, all students at that university, or all introductory statistics students at that university?

b. Suppose we are interested in the female students' heights. Which of these is the *largest* population for which we can say the surveyed female students probably constitute a representative sample: all females, all college-aged females, all female college students, all female students at that university, or all female introductory statistics students at that university?

2.16 A survey is conducted that includes several hundred students at a large university, all taking an introductory statistics course. Proportions of students in the various year and gender categories are typical of those for college students in general.

a. Suppose we are interested in whether or not individuals are left-handed. Which of these is the *largest* population for which we can say the surveyed students probably constitute a representative sample: all humans, all college students, or all students at that university?

b. Suppose we are interested in males' earnings for the past year. Which of these is the *largest* population for which we can say the surveyed male students probably constitute a representative sample: all males, all college-aged males, all male college students, or all male students at that university?

*2.17 A study looked at the percentages of low-income students with federally funded financial aid at the nation's top 20 universities. Why is it not appropriate to use the data to draw more general conclusions?

2.18 The Food and Agriculture Organization of the United Nations released a report in 2005 on the rate of deforestation around the world. It specified the percentage of forests depleted in each of South America's countries. Why should we not use the data to draw more general conclusions?

2.19 An advertisement for the online *Pricing Psychology Report* mentions the well-known phenomenon whereby people are much likelier to buy a product if it is priced at $9.99 rather than $10.00. It also recommends a way for online marketers to compare orders for merchandise advertised at two different prices, called "perfect A/B split price testing":[5]

a. The first visitor to your site sees price "A"

b. The second visitor sees price "B"

c. The third visitor sees price "A"

d. The fourth visitor sees price "B" etc.

Is this method characterized as cluster sampling, haphazard sampling, systematic sampling, stratified sampling, or random sampling?

2.20 In May 2003, newsPolls.org posted results of a survey that included the question: "Do you have a permanent tattoo somewhere on your body?"[6]

a. Is the variable of interest quantitative or categorical?

b. Would the results be summarized with a mean or a proportion?

c. If the survey was carried out on-line, and there is concern that the sampled individuals were not necessarily representative of the general population of the United States, do you think they would tend to be younger or older?

d. Considering your answer to the previous question, which is more likely to be the problem—results of an online survey causing us to overestimate or to underestimate the proportion of the entire population with permanent tattoos?

2.21 In the fall of 2004, after severe flooding in a town, a dog was found and brought to the Humane Society by a woman who expressed her willingness to adopt the dog if its owner could not be located. The dog initially failed their so-called "pinch test" by biting an evaluator who applied pressure to its toes, and so it was not released to the woman until 2 months later. After the incident was publicized in the local newspaper, the paper's *Pet tales* columnist reported: "I received more than 200 phone calls and e-mails from people who thought this was wrong. Only three defended the shelter."[7]

Was this a self-selected sample, a stratified sample, or a cluster sample?

2.22 An article from California's *Alameda Times-Star*, posted on a website called www.cannabisnews.com, described a study to be conducted at the San Mateo County Health Center, in which marijuana would be dispensed to 60 AIDS patients for pain management. Only those who had already used marijuana in the past would be eligible.

a. Would this be called a random sample, a systematic sample, or a convenience sample?

b. Why do you think the researchers used this type of sample?

2.23 An article entitled "Couch Potato Nation" describes a report by the federal Centers for Disease Control and Prevention that "analyzed responses from 119,000 people who were asked in 1996 about their physical activity during the month prior to the survey."[8] Suppose the survey was carried out by telephone, and the researchers had reason to suspect that whoever answers the phone might tend to be the least active household member. To offset this bias, they could ask about the physical activity of all household members. Would this be a convenience sample, a systematic sample, a cluster sample, or a stratified sample?

2.24 "Written Word Helps Wounds Heal" describes a British study: "In the study, which involved 36 people, half were asked to write about the most upsetting experience they had had, spelling out how they had felt. The rest of the study participants wrote about trival things, such as how they spent their free time. Both groups spent 20 minutes a day for three days writing. Following the writing exercise, researchers created a small skin puncture [under anesthesia] on the participants' upper arms. The wounds were examined two weeks later. It was found that the group who had written about their emotional experiences had smaller wounds, meaning they had healed more quickly. Those whose wounds were healing more slowly were found to have higher levels of stress and psychological distress."[9] The sample of study participants was clearly *not* which one of these: a convenience sample, a volunteer sample, or a random sample?

2.25 Suppose canvassers before a presidential election are going door-to-door and asking people which candidate they plan to vote for. One canvasser has just surveyed a cluster of four people from the same

household, and another has just surveyed four individuals each from a different household. Which canvasser will tend to get more variety in responses—the one who surveys a cluster of four or the one who surveys four individuals?

2.26 In the year 2000, there were just 9 single men for every 10 single women in urban United States (that is, in cities of 100,000 people or more). How can a survey conducted in major cities successfully reflect the opinions of all singles in the United States, who are equally divided between men and women—by taking cluster samples of men and women, by stratifying first according to gender, or by taking a volunteer sample?

2.27 A manual used by the Dallas County district attorney's office from 1968 to 1976 advised, "Do not take [. . .] a member of any minority race on a jury no matter how rich or well educated."

a. Was this an attempt to bias trial results at the sampling stage or at the stage where jurors must reach a conclusion of guilty/not guilty?[10]

b. In this example, which of these best describes the source of bias: using a volunteer sample, sampling frame not matching population, using a convenience sample, taking a haphazard sample?

2.28 An Internet report of a survey's results included a disclaimer that the sample was obtained in a purely "random, unscientific" way. Explain why this is a poor choice of words, and tell what they probably intended to say instead of *random*: stratified, clustered, systematic, or haphazard?

Discovering Research: SAMPLING DESIGN

2.29 Hand in an article or report about a study for which a sample has been taken. Tell what you know, or can reasonably guess, about what kind of sampling plan was used. Be sure to mention whether the sampling

plan included randomness and whether it seems susceptible to some kind of bias. Tell whether the sample size seems fairly large and, if not, whether it would be feasible to obtain a larger sample.

Reporting on Research: SAMPLING DESIGN

2.30 Use results of Exercises 2.8 and 2.9, and relevant findings from the Internet, to make a report on PIRG and credit reports that relies on statistical information.

CHAPTER **3**

Design: *How* Individuals Are Studied

How should we obtain information about variables or relationships for sampled individuals?

© moodboard/CORBIS

Does watching TV make us eat?

How can we find out?

After the first step in the data production process (actually obtaining a sample) is completed, we come to the second step—gaining information about the variables of interest.

In Chapter 2, we learned how to obtain an unbiased sample, so that when the time comes in Part IV to perform inference and draw conclusions about the larger population, we are justified in claiming our sample to be representative. In this chapter, we will learn how to design a study that assesses the variables of interest without bias for the sampled individuals. When the time comes to summarize those sampled values in Part II, we can safely claim our summaries to be accurate only if our study design is sound.

One of the examples we will consider in detail is the question of whether people tend to consume more snacks while they're watching TV. Even if we have a truly random sample of people to study, if we aren't careful about how to gather information about their television-watching and snacking habits, our summaries of how much snacking is done in the presence or absence of television will be incorrect.

3.1 Various Designs for Studying Variables

Depending on the information sought, values of the variables of interest can be assessed via one of several possible designs: an *observational study*, a *sample survey*, or an *experiment*. *Anecdotal evidence* is a way of gathering information that is nonscientific, and should be avoided.

30

Definitions   In an **observational study**, values of the variable or variables of interest are recorded as they occur naturally.

A **sample survey** is a particular type of observational study wherein individuals report variables' values themselves, frequently by giving their opinions.

In an **experiment**, researchers impose a treatment to manipulate values of the explanatory variable and note how the response variable is affected.

Anecdotal evidence focuses on personal accounts by one or just a few individuals selected haphazardly or by convenience.

When anecdotal evidence is cited, there is no reason to expect the individuals to be representative of anyone but themselves. Results should not be generalized to any larger group.

EXAMPLE 3.1 DISTINGUISHING A SCIENTIFIC STUDY FROM ANECDOTAL EVIDENCE

C→Q

Background: An article entitled "Study: Breast Milk is Better Brain Food" was published in the newspaper. It describes research that tracked the progress of more than 1,000 children in New Zealand from birth through the age of 18. Shortly thereafter, a mother wrote a letter to the editor, complaining that she had "a problem with the study that stated that breast-fed babies are smarter than bottle-fed . . . My 10-month-old son has always been bottle-fed and he is very smart. I have been told by his pediatrician that in some aspects he is ahead for his age. I feel that this study contains some inaccuracies. Obviously, the people who conducted this study have never met my son."[1]

Questions: What type of design did the New Zealand researchers use to assess the relationship between type of milk and intelligence? What type of design did the mother use?

Responses: The researchers apparently used an observational study, whereas the mother was using anecdotal evidence.

Is one of these mothers making her child smarter?

Practice: *Try Exercise 3.1 on page 36.*

The Big Picture: **LOOKING AHEAD**

The distinction between an ordinary observational study and a sample survey is not always clear-cut. Identifying the type of study should not be thought of as an end in itself, but rather as an aid in considering what types of pitfalls to be on the lookout for.

The Big Picture: **A CLOSER LOOK**

Anecdotal evidence may be persuasive to some people because of the "personal touch": The fact that a wealth of details are provided may make the individual results very vivid, so that the anecdote's claims seem more credible.

What makes the production of data "anecdotal" involves both sampling and study design issues. The sampling design is problematic because there are usually just a few individuals chosen by convenience. The study design tends to rely on the telling of a story, as opposed to an objective gathering of evidence.

Notice that Example 3.1 involves a categorical explanatory variable (breast-fed or bottle-fed) and a quantitative response (intelligence).

Unlike the chapters in Parts II and IV, each of which addresses a particular variable situation, this chapter features a variety of situations, mostly of the form C, Q, C —> Q, C —>C, and Q —> Q. By pointing out the types of variables in each example, we can train students to keep in mind the big picture of statistics.

The type of design used, and the details of the design, are crucial because we can obtain an accurate summary of variables' values—or of a relationship between variables—for the individuals studied only if the information about those variables is assessed properly.

Identifying Study Design

Because each type of study design has its own advantages and trouble spots, it is important to begin by determining what type of study we are dealing with. The next example helps illustrate how to distinguish among the three basic designs—sample surveys, observational studies, and experiments. It also demonstrates the distinction between *retrospective* and *prospective* observational studies.

Definitions A **retrospective observational study** seeks information about variables' values in the past, whereas a **prospective observational study** seeks information about variables' values to occur in the future.

EXAMPLE 3.2 IDENTIFYING STUDY DESIGNS

Background: Suppose researchers want to determine if people tend to snack more while they watch TV.

Question: Is each of the following designs a sample survey, a retrospective observational study, a prospective observational study, or an experiment?

- Recruit participants for the study. While they are presumably waiting to be interviewed, half of the individuals sit in a waiting room with snacks available and a TV on. The other half sit in a waiting room with snacks available and no TV. Researchers determine if people consume more snacks in the TV setting.

- Poll a sample of individuals with the following question: While watching TV, do you tend to snack (a) less than usual (b) more than usual or (c) the same as usual?

- Recruit participants for a study. Give them journals to record, hour-by-hour, their activities the following day, including TV watched and food consumed. Afterwards, assess if food consumption was higher during TV times.

- Recruit participants for a study. Ask them to recall, for each hour of the previous day, whether they were watching TV and what food they consumed each hour. Determine if food consumption was higher during the TV times.

Response:

- The first design is an *experiment* because the researchers take control of the explanatory variable (TV watched or not), and determine the effect on the response of interest (snack consumption).

- The second is a *sample survey* because the individuals self-assess the relationship between TV watching and snacking. Note that the situation has been simplified to involve a single categorical variable.
- The third is an *observational study* because the participants themselves determine whether or not to watch TV. Because the values of the variables of interest (TV and snacking habits) are recorded "forward in time," we would call the study *prospective*.
- The fourth is also an *observational study*. Again, it is the participants themselves who decide whether or not to watch TV. In this case, the values of the variables of interest are recorded "backward in time," making it a *retrospective* study.

Practice: *Try Exercise 3.7 on page 37.*

Notice that three of the four designs in Example 3.2 involve a categorical explanatory variable (watching TV or not) and a quantitative response (amount of food eaten).

Most sample surveys are designed to gather information about single variables. In contrast, most observational studies and experiments attempt to draw conclusions about the *relationship* between two variables.

When researching a relationship, almost always an attempt is made to establish causation, making a claim that the explanatory variable is actually *causing* changes in the response. Here are a few examples of media reports that suggest a causal relationship:

- "Moderate Walking Helps the Mind Stay Sharper," discussed in Exercise 3.30 on page 50
- "When Your Hair's a Real Mess, Your Self-Esteem Is Much Less," discussed in Exercise 3.48 on page 61
- "Family Dinners Benefit Teens," discussed in Exercise 3.56 on page 65

Such studies are especially useful and interesting, but they are also especially vulnerable to flaws that could invalidate the conclusion of causation. In many studies of relationships, whereas evidence of an *association* between two variables may be quite clear, the question of whether one variable is actually *causing* changes in the other may be too murky to ever be resolved entirely. One important factor in establishing causation is whether the explanatory variable's values occur naturally or have been assigned by researchers.

Observational Studies versus Experiments: Who Controls the Variables?

Before assessing the effectiveness of observational studies and experiments for producing evidence of a causal relationship between two variables, we illustrate the essential difference between these two designs. The context is a simple example that has gained quite a bit of attention for several decades now: Does sugar consumption cause hyperactivity in children?

Ever since the results of a study by Dr. Benjamin Feingold were published in the early 1970s, it has been a widely held belief that sugar intake can lead to hyperactive behavior. In fact, there was a serious potential flaw in Dr. Feingold's study design, which we will discuss later in this chapter. For now, let us consider how to design an observational study or experiment to test for a causal relationship.

In this situation, sugar intake is the explanatory variable. Typically, it would be treated as categorical, such as low or high. The response—activity—is also most likely categorical; namely, whether or not a child is diagnosed with a condition like Attention Deficit Hyperactive Disorder (ADHD).

EXAMPLE 3.3 DESIGNING AN OBSERVATIONAL STUDY OR EXPERIMENT

Background: Researchers seek to establish if sugar consumption can cause hyperactivity in children.

Questions: How could an observational study be designed to determine if there is a causal relationship? How could an experiment be designed?

Responses: In an **observational study**, researchers would obtain a sample of children and find out about their sugar intake as it occurs naturally. The information could be gathered via a retrospective study (asking parents about their children's past dietary habits) or a prospective study (having the parents record food intake in a journal). The response variable—activity—could be assessed by simply asking parents if their child has been diagnosed with something like ADHD. Alternatively, the researchers could use their own methods to assess the children's activity.

In an **experiment,** the researchers would dictate how much sugar the children are to consume. After a certain period of time, they would assess whether or not the children are hyperactive.

Practice: *Try Exercise 3.8 on page 37.*

These displays help to illustrate the key difference between our two studies: The explanatory variable, sugar intake, occurs naturally in the observational study, whereas it is assigned by researchers in the experiment.

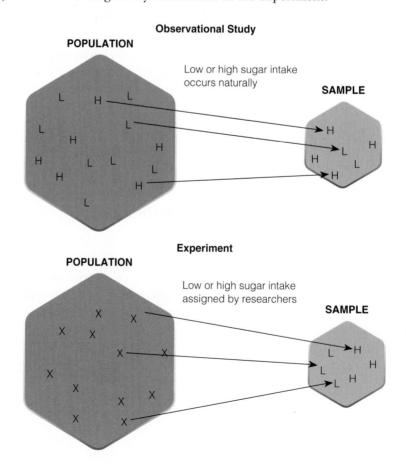

Errors in Studies' Conclusions: The Imperfect Nature of Statistical Studies

Statistics is, by nature, an inexact science. Studies are carried out to decide whether or not a claim is true concerning a single variable's values, or about a relationship between variables, but conclusions are rarely 100% certain. For instance, it is possible that a pharmaceutical study's results suggest a drug *is* effective when it actually is not. It is also possible that a study's results suggest that a drug does *not* produce side effects when it actually does. An important aspect of statistical research is to consider the consequences of drawing the wrong conclusions in one way or the other. Such mistakes, which are given the technical names *Type I Error* and *Type II Error*, will be discussed more formally in Part IV of this book. For now, we consider such errors less formally, as one more aspect of study design that warrants careful consideration.

EXAMPLE 3.4 TWO TYPES OF ERROR

Background: "Tests Determine State Police Radar Guns Work Properly" describes a study by a school of engineering that "contradicted claims the Decatur Genesis [handheld radar] guns were producing erroneous readings that could have led to unwarranted speeding tickets."[2] The $18,000 study most likely tested the guns on a sample of vehicles traveling at various speeds, checking whether a gun's reading of a vehicle's speed coincided correctly with the actual speed.

Questions: What are the two possible errors that can be made if a study must conclude whether or not radar guns work properly? What are the potential harmful consequences of each type of error?

Who stands to lose if a test of radar guns reaches the wrong conclusion?

Responses: In spite of the study's conclusion that the guns work properly, there is still a chance that the guns really are faulty under some circumstances. The consequence of this type of erroneous conclusion would be that speeding tickets are issued unfairly to some people who are *not* driving over the speed limit, as the article mentions. In addition, there may be speeders who continue to put lives at risk because the guns fail to catch them.

On the other hand, if the tests to assess the guns had been poorly designed, they could also have incorrectly determined the guns to be faulty, when in fact they function properly. The consequence of this type of erroneous conclusion would be that time and money would be spent on improving a speed detection system that actually needs no improvement.

Practice: *Try Exercise 3.9(a) on page 37.*

The **Big Picture:**

A CLOSER LOOK

The convention in statistical research is to designate the claim that "nothing is going on" as the default point of view. In general, the first type of error arises if we conclude something *is* going on when it actually isn't. The second type of error is to conclude something is *not* going on when it actually is.

The **Big Picture:**

A CLOSER LOOK

Notice that Example 3.4 involves a categorical explanatory variable (whether speed was actual or recorded by the radar gun) and a quantitative response (speed).

Sample size plays a role in the type of error to which a study is more susceptible. For instance, if a drug has harmful side effects when used by some patients but not others, then studying a very small sample of patients may not be enough to produce convincing evidence of the drug's risks.

EXAMPLE 3.5 SMALL SAMPLES LEADING TO SECOND TYPE OF ERROR

Background: A study tested whether or not police radar guns were working properly.

Question: Which type of erroneous conclusion is more likely to occur if only a very small sample of radar guns are tested: concluding that the guns do not function properly when they actually do, or concluding that the guns do function properly when they actually don't?

Response: If only a few handheld radar guns are tested, then there is a greater risk of concluding that the guns function properly when they actually don't. With a very small sample, there's a better chance that the sample doesn't happen to include any faulty guns.

Practice: *Try Exercise 3.9(b) on page 37.*

Example TBP 3.1 on page 755 of the *Teaching the Big Picture* **(TBP)** *Supplement* serves as a reminder that larger samples are generally better, but only if the study design is sound.

Designing a study to include a larger sample is one way to reduce the risk of concluding that "nothing is wrong" when, in fact, something *is* wrong.

Study designs are summarized in the Chapter Summary on page 64.

EXERCISES FOR SECTION 3.1

Various Designs for Studying Variables

Note: Asterisked numbers indicate exercises whose answers are provided in the Solutions to Selected Exercises section, on page 689.

*3.1 "Where You Will Live the Longest" is the title of a 2006 report on a study of mortality rates in the United States during the 1980s and 1990s. A resident of one of the top-ranked counties for longevity (Clear Creek, Colorado) followed up the report with her explanation of why people in that area tend to stay lively: "It's because it's too risky not to . . . Don't look closely at the droppings in the driveway and you might not realize they belong to a nearby ferocious animal. Fail to notice the morning ice along the creek and you won't order your propane or woodsplitter in time before winter . . ."[3]

a. What design (observational study, experiment, sample survey, or anecdotal evidence) was used to produce the original report?

b. What design did the Clear Creek resident use?

3.2 A 13-member panel was convened by the National Institutes of Health in 2004 to look for consensus on causes of youth violence and ways to prevent it. Its conclusion was that "boot camps and other get-tough programs for adolescents do not prevent criminal behavior, as intended, and may make the problem even worse."[4] Was their conclusion most likely based on one observational study, several observational studies, an experiment, a sample survey, or anecdotal evidence?

3.3 A newspaper article about a book entitled *Wilderness Within, Wilderness Without*, by Shannon Szwarc, tells how "living in a rugged outdoor environment with firm but nurturing counselors"[5] at a therapeutic wilderness camp transformed the author. Would a reader's conclusion that the wilderness program is effective be based on one observational study, several observational studies, an experiment, a sample survey, or anecdotal evidence?

3.4 The two preceding exercises describe, respectively, a study by the National Institutes of Health and a book by a former wilderness camp member. Both address the effectiveness of such camps.

   a. What aspects of the National Institutes of Health study would make its claims persuasive?

   b. What aspects of the book about a wilderness camp's benefits to the author would make its claims persuasive?

3.5 Suppose that get-tough programs as described in the previous exercises actually *are* beneficial, and a study erroneously concludes that they do nothing to prevent criminal behavior. Describe the potential harmful consequences of such a mistake.

3.6 Suppose that get-tough programs do *not* prevent criminal behavior, and a study erroneously concludes that they are beneficial. Describe the potential harmful consequences of such a mistake.

*3.7 A paper by Emily Oster of Harvard University, published in the Social Science Research Network's electronic library in 2004, explored the "possibility that the witchcraft trials [between 1520 and 1770] are a large-scale example of violence and scapegoating prompted by a deterioration in economic conditions. In this case, the downturn was brought on by a decrease in temperature and resulting food shortages. [. . .] Witches became target for blame because there was an existing cultural framework that both allowed their persecution and suggested that they could control the weather."[6] Would the relationship between witchcraft trials and weather be examined via a sample survey, an observational study, or an experiment?

*3.8 A drug for female sexual dysfunction called Intrinsa was tested in 2004, both for efficacy and for possible dangerous side effects before being considered for approval by the Food and Drug Administration. A report of clinical trials states: "Fifty-two percent of those [women] given the drug said they experienced a 'meaningful benefit' in their

sex-lives—but so did 31% of those who were given the placebo."[7] Who controlled the values of the explanatory variable in this study: the women or the researchers?

*3.9 "As Orders Soar, Concerns Over Stun Guns Grow" reported in 2004 that "Amnesty International says stun guns are being abused by police and wants more scientific study done to determine whether the devices are safe. Amnesty says at least 74 people have died in the United States and Canada in the past four years after being shocked with Tasers. The group also says officers have turned stun guns on the mentally disturbed, children, and the elderly."[8] On the other hand, Taser company chairman Phil Smith says, "We get e-mail from police every week . . . thanking us for developing a weapon so they didn't have to shoot somebody." According to the article, "Phoenix police officers credit Tasers with helping police shootings drop by more than half and fatal shootings by 31% last year."

   a. One issue involved here is whether or not Tasers can be lethal. Discuss the harmful consequences of incorrectly deeming them to be safe for use by police officers, if, in fact, they can cause fatal heart attacks. Discuss the consequences of deeming them to be unsafe if, in fact, the deaths mentioned in the article were not due to the Tasers.

   b. Suppose some Tasers are to be tested to see if the voltage delivered is dangerously high. If a very small sample of Tasers is tested, is there more risk of concluding Tasers in general are safe when, in fact, some are not, or more risk of concluding Tasers in general are not safe when, in fact, they are?

3.10 An article entitled "Stress Found in Returning Soldiers" includes the following information: "A desperate woman wearing a black robe and her young son walked up to Alan Lewis, a United States soldier who was working security. The boy had just picked up an unexploded piece of ordnance, which blew up, badly burning his face and hands . . . Weeks later, Lewis would lose parts of both his legs after a land mine exploded under the Humvee he was driving. But his most horrible experience, Lewis said, was the sight of the boy and his mother."[9] The article also found that of 6,200 members of four United States combat infantry units deployed in Iraq and Afghanistan, about 75% "reported encountering injured or ill women or children who they were unable to help." It was noted that "before the Sept. 11 terrorist attacks, an estimated 8% of Americans suffered from the [post traumatic stress] disorder."

This article includes information gathered via three designs: observational study, sample survey, and anecdotal evidence.

a. Which type of design accompanies the first quote above?

b. Which type of design accompanies the second quote above?

c. Which type of design accompanies the third quote above?

When soldiers return, how will we learn about possible stress disorders?

3.2 Sample Surveys: When Individuals Report Their Own Values

A *sample survey* is a particular type of observational study in which individuals report variables' values themselves, frequently by giving their opinions. Researchers have several options to choose from when deciding how to survey the individuals involved: in person, or via telephone, Internet, or mail.

Sample surveys are sometimes used to examine relationships, but usually they assess values of many separate variables, such as respondents' opinions on various matters.

Of course, the first step in carrying out a sample survey is to obtain the sample. We have discussed the fact that random samples are best at representing the larger population of interest, but other samples can be used if there is good reason to believe that they are not subject to any clear bias. Even if we have managed to select a representative sample for a survey, we are not yet "home free": We must still compose the survey question itself so that the information we gather from the sampled respondents correctly represents the unbiased truth about the variables of interest. The various issues that arise in the design of survey questions are best illustrated with a variety of concrete examples.

Sources of Bias in Sample Surveys

C All of the examples discussed in this section are typical of most sample surveys, in that they focus on just one categorical variable at a time. Even if multiple categorical variables are assessed in a survey, they are usually handled individually, rather than looking for a relationship among those variables.

An important feature of survey questions is whether they are open or closed.

The Big Picture:
A Closer Look

A yes-or-no question is considered to be closed, even if it does not explicitly state the words *yes* and *no* as response options. For example, "Do you like rap music?" is a closed question.

> *Definitions*   An **open question** (also called *open-ended*) is one without a fixed set of response options.
>
> A **closed question** either provides or implies a fixed set of possible responses.

EXAMPLE 3.6 OPEN OR CLOSED SURVEY QUESTIONS

Background: Suppose a music store owner wants to assess the music preferences of her customers via a survey. Here are two possible ways to query the customers:

- "What is your favorite kind of music?"
- "Which of these types of music do you prefer? (a) classical (b) rock (c) pop (d) rap"

Questions: Are the proposed survey questions open or closed? What are the advantages and disadvantages of each?

Responses: The first is an open question because it allows for more or less unlimited responses. It may be difficult for the store owner to make sense of all the possible categories and subcategories of music that survey respondents could come up with. Some may be more general than what she had in mind ("I like modern music the best") and others too specific ("I like Japanese alternative electronic rock by Cornelius"). On the other hand, it gives respondents the opportunity to choose categories of music that the owner did not anticipate.

The second is a closed question because response options are specified. This makes the responses much easier for the surveyor to handle. But what if a respondent is asked the closed question, as worded above, and he actually prefers jazz or folk music or gospel? He may pick a second-favorite from the options presented or try to "pencil in" the real preference, or maybe just not respond at all. Whatever the outcome, it is likely that overall the responses to the question posed in this way will not give the store owner very accurate information about all customers' music preferences.

Practice: *Try Exercise 3.14(a) on page 44.*

Example 3.6 reminds us that a surveyor should always think carefully about whether questions should be open or closed. For closed questions, great care should be taken to include all the reasonable options that are possible, including "not sure." Also, surveyors should consider including an option like "other: _____" for the sake of thoroughness, in case an option was overlooked. These issues are explored in our next example.

EXAMPLE 3.7 CLOSED QUESTIONS WITH OVERLY RESTRICTIVE OPTIONS

Background: According to an article entitled *Technicolor dreams*, a neuroscientist researched the phenomenon of dreaming in color as opposed to black and white by surveying people as to how often they dream in color. Response options were "always," "sometimes," and "never."

Question: What improvement could be made to this survey question?

Response: To obtain an accurate summary, an option of "don't know" or "not sure" or "can't remember" should have been included, because many people would fall into this category.

Practice: *Try Exercise 3.11 on page 44.*

The Big Picture: **A CLOSER LOOK**

Surveys taken in 1942 reported a much higher percentage of respondents (71%) claiming to dream in black and white compared to the percentage in 2003 (18%). Researchers are now inclined to attribute the difference to people's exposure to black-and-white movies, TV, and photos at the time, which influenced their mental image of what they had dreamed. The dreams themselves were probably no less colorful than dreams are today.

Many surveys ask respondents to assign a rating to a variable, such as in the following example.

EXAMPLE 3.8 UNBALANCED RESPONSE OPTIONS

Background: *USA Today* conducted a survey in 2002 asking respondents to rate their own health by choosing from these five options: excellent/very good/good/fair/poor. The survey found that 91% of Americans rated their own health as good to excellent.

Questions: Do the survey results seem consistent with reality? If not, what caused the results to be biased?

Responses: The number 91% seems unrealistically high. This is a result of the options provided being rather "top-heavy," with three favorable versus two not-so-favorable. If respondents feel their health is just mediocre, they may opt for the middle choice, "good." Thus, the summary of the survey's results distorts the respondents' true feelings about their health.

Practice: *Try Exercise 3.14(b) on page 44.*

Some survey questions are either deliberately or unintentionally biased toward certain responses.

Sometimes survey questions are ordered to deliberately bias the responses by planting an idea in an earlier question that will sway people's thoughts in a later question. Example TBP 3.2 on page 756 of the **TBP** *Supplement* features a series of survey questions that are clearly designed to bias responses in this way.

The Big Picture: A CLOSER LOOK

One way to test for bias in a survey question is to ask yourself, "Just from reading the question, would a respondent have a good idea of what response the surveyor is hoping to elicit?" If the answer is yes, then the question should have been worded more neutrally.

EXAMPLE 3.9 DELIBERATE BIAS VIA A LEADING QUESTION

Background: Hikers returning from a back-country camping trip in Glacier National Park were asked to complete a survey by University of Idaho researchers on interactions between back-country travelers and grizzly bears. One question read, "Because people and cattle live practically everywhere in the United States, and grizzly bears only in Wyoming, Montana, and Alaska, I think Montana should forego some grazing when there is a conflict with a bear: (circle one) strongly agree/agree/neither agree nor disagree/disagree/strongly disagree."[10]

Can the wording of a survey question lead to more rights for grizzlies?

Question: Do we know which response(s) the surveyors were hoping to elicit?

Response: Clearly, the surveyors wanted respondents to answer "strongly agree" or at least "agree." The question "puts words in people's mouths," urging them to report a particular opinion.

Practice: *Try Exercise 3.16 on page 44.*

Sometimes surveyors attempt to get feedback on more than one issue at a time.

EXAMPLE **3.10** COMPLICATED SURVEY QUESTION

Background: A Gallup surveyor conducting a telephone poll asked the following question, to which respondents were to assign a level at which they agreed: "I don't go out of my way to purchase low-fat foods unless they are also low in calories."

Question: If respondents don't go out of their way to purchase low-fat foods at all, regardless of whether or not they are low in calories, would they answer yes or no?

Response: Some may answer yes and others no: The logic of the question could easily escape the respondents, and they would be too confused to supply an answer that correctly conveys their grocery shopping habits.

Practice: *Try Exercise 3.21(d) on page 45.*

Clearly, simple questions are much better than complicated ones. Rather than try to gauge opinions on several issues at once, complex survey questions like the one in Example 3.10 should be broken down into shorter, more concise ones.

Another important issue for many surveys is the extent to which respondents are truthful. Depending on the topic, we cannot always assume that survey respondents will answer honestly.

EXAMPLE **3.11** SENSITIVE QUESTION

Background: Consider these two survey questions:

1. Have you eaten rutabagas in the past year?

2. Have you used illegal drugs in the past year?

Questions: If a respondent answers no to the first question, is it safe to conclude that he or she did not eat rutabagas? If a respondent answers no to the second question, is it safe to conclude that he or she did not use illegal drugs?

Responses: Respondents are unlikely to want to hide the fact that they ate rutabagas: If they answer no, we can assume this reflects the truth. In contrast, if respondents answer no to the second question, then it is still a good possibility that they did use illegal drugs, but don't want to admit it.

Practice: *Try Exercise 3.24 on page 45.*

Responses are more likely to reflect the truth if the survey provides respondents assurance that they are completely anonymous. Effective techniques for collecting accurate data on sensitive questions are an important area of inquiry in statistics. Careful wording of questions can be helpful in eliciting honest responses about behaviors that people are usually reluctant to admit. This approach is evident in the following survey.

Schools could refer to the survey results to improve their chances of acquiring grant money from the government to establish or bolster various drug and violence prevention programs. This means that schools stand to gain financially from larger percentages of children admitting to delinquent behavior.

As an exercise in careful wording of survey questions, students may try to think of a better way to phrase the question in Example 3.12 in such a way as to elicit honest answers but at the same time not suggest that such behaviors are being condoned.

EXAMPLE 3.12 WORDING QUESTIONS TO ELICIT HONEST RESPONSES

Background: This is an excerpt from a survey given to public school 6th through 12th graders every 2 years by a state's Commission on Crime and Delinquency:

How old were you when you first:

- Had more than a sip or two of beer, wine, or hard liquor?
- Began drinking alcoholic beverages regularly, that is, at least once or twice a month?
- Got suspended from school?
- Got arrested?
- Carried a handgun?
- Attacked someone with the idea of seriously hurting them?
- Belonged to a gang?

Options were "never have/10 or younger/11/12/13/14/15/16/17." Parents objected to the wording of this and similar survey questions, which seemed to suggest that such behaviors were inevitable.

Question: Why did the surveyors choose to word the questions this way?

Response: The surveyors wanted to make sure that students who had engaged in any of those behaviors felt comfortable in admitting to it.

Practice: *Try Exercise 3.25 on page 45.*

Giving people a feeling of anonymity by having them complete questionnaires via computer rather than paper and pencil is another commonly used technique for gathering responses to sensitive questions. It is a well-documented phenomenon that people are much less inhibited at the computer keyboard than they are otherwise.

EXAMPLE 3.13 KEYBOARDS FOR SENSE OF ANONYMITY

Background: An innovative statistics computer tutor was being piloted at a large university, and students who used the tutor identified themselves by name and social security number. Nevertheless, one student filled many of the textboxes for responses to open questions with strings of obscenities. The student's responses otherwise, for assignments and exams completed on paper, were perfectly appropriate.

Question: How can the student's inappropriate behavior be explained?

Response: Supplying answers on the keyboard gave the student a false sense of anonymity.

Practice: *Try Exercise 3.27 on page 46.*

Is one of these students less inhibited than the other?

The Big Picture: A Closer Look

People's lack of inhibition when using a keyboard can work to researchers' advantage when they seek candid responses that have the potential to be embarrassing or incriminating.

Notice that in the question on alcohol consumption in Example 3.12, the surveyors were careful to define what they meant by "regularly" (at least once or twice a month) so that all students would be addressing the same question in their minds. However, a survey's variable of interest is often so subjective that every respondent may be thinking of it in different terms.

EXAMPLE 3.14 HARD-TO-DEFINE CONCEPTS

Background: A survey found that 19% of adult Americans believe that money can buy happiness, but the concept of happiness was not defined for respondents. According to Robert Frost, "Happiness makes up in height for what it lacks in length."[11] On the other hand, Albert Camus has said, "But what is happiness except the simple harmony between a man and the life he leads?"

Questions: Does Frost's explanation suggest that money can buy happiness? How about Camus's definition?

Responses: Frost's claim suggests that temporary pleasures, such as a nice (expensive) weekend in the Caribbean, may bring about happiness. In contrast, Camus's definition suggests that happiness is something that money cannot buy in the long run.

Practice: *Try Exercise 3.28 on page 46.*

Sample surveys are summarized on page 64 of the Chapter Summary.

EXERCISES FOR SECTION 3.2

Sample Surveys: When Individuals Report Their Own Values

Note: Asterisked numbers indicate exercises whose answers are provided in the Solutions to Selected Exercises section, on page 689.

*3.11 For which of these is it more important to include a response option like "don't know" or "not sure": a question about whether the respondent owns a gun, or a question about whether the respondent feels the national firearms registry program should be abandoned?

3.12 A 2002 survey of 5,000 households found that 87% of the respondents said their employers prohibited smoking in the workplace. If the survey did not permit a response of "don't know," who would be more likely to give an incorrect response about whether smoking was permitted at their workplace—smokers or nonsmokers?

3.13 For which question is it more important to include an option of "don't know": asking if respondents have a permanent tattoo on their body, or asking how many people will be present at their upcoming Thanksgiving dinner?

*3.14 Many questionnaires use a scale of 1 to 5 for responses.

   a. Would such questions be considered open or closed?

   b. Explain why a scale of 1 to 5 is much more common than a scale of 1 to 4 or 1 to 6.

3.15 An article entitled "Survey Finds County Enjoys Good Health" reports that "the vast majority of [county] residents rate their health as good to excellent . . . 20% of nearly 5,000 adults surveyed described their health as excellent, 34% called it very good, and 30% called it good. Sixteen percent said they were in fair or poor health."[12]

   a. If the questionnaire included five response options, what were they?

   b. If the questionnaire included four response options, what were they?

   c. In which case would you say the options were unbalanced: if there were five options given, or four, or both of these, or neither?

*3.16 In the year 2000, Hamilton College sponsored a national survey to probe high school students' attitudes toward gun issues.

The survey included a question about whether or not the respondents were in favor of the following: "Require a 5-day waiting period between the purchase and delivery of a handgun, to keep the buyer from acting on impulse against himself or others."[13] Did the surveyors want respondents to be in favor or opposed; or is it impossible to tell from the wording of the question?

3.17 The following survey questions were posted on the website www.a-human-right.com:

   1. Is it morally correct for a police officer to shoot in order to save an innocent victim from an attack?

   2. If no police officer is present is it morally correct for the innocent victim to shoot to protect self or dependents from an attack?

   3. If my child or my spouse were assaulted, I would . . .
      ■ Run away and hope my kid or spouse can keep up with me
      ■ Be a good witness so I can tell the cops what happened later
      ■ Try to convince the attacker to stop through verbal persuasion
      ■ Fight to stop the attack

   4. Given a choice, I would prefer to defend myself with . . .
      ■ My bare hands
      ■ An ineffective weapon, such as pepper spray
      ■ An effective weapon, such as a firearm

   For which question(s) is it clear what answer the surveyors want respondents to give?

*3.18 "Data Found Lacking on Effects of Gun Control Efforts" explains that an analysis in 2004 of "efforts to control violence by restricting guns says there is not enough evidence to reach valid conclusions about their effectiveness. [. . .] A serious limit in such analyses is the lack of good data on who owns firearms and on individual encounters with violence, according to the study. Research scientists need appropriate access to federal and state data on gun use, manufacturing and sales, the study urged. [. . .] The report calls for the development of a National Violent Death Reporting System and a National Incident-Based Reporting System for collecting data."[14]

Are these scientists mainly concerned with data production, displaying and summarizing data, probability, or statistical inference?

*3.19 An exit poll surveyed 11,027 voters after the 2004 presidential election. Among the questions asked were, "Which one issue mattered most in deciding how you voted for president?"[15] and "How do you feel about the United States decision to go to war in Iraq?" As far as the ordering of questions is concerned, do you think there is less chance of bias if they are ordered as above, or in reverse order, or doesn't it matter?

3.20 An exit poll surveyed 11,027 voters after the 2004 presidential election. The survey asked voters, "Compared to four years ago, is your family's financial situation about the same, better today, or worse today?"[16] and also asked voters to tell their income bracket for the previous year, with choices ranging from under $15,000 to $200,000 or more. As far as the ordering of this pair of questions is concerned, do you think it is better to order them as above or in reverse order? Explain your reasons.

*3.21 Environics Research Group in Canada conducted a survey about firearms in which some respondents were asked to tell whether they agreed with the first or the second opinion described in the following: "The Auditor-General has found significant cost overruns in the national firearms registry program. Some people say that these cost overruns prove that the concept of the registry is unworkable and should be abandoned. Other people say that despite the cost overruns, the national firearms registry is still a good concept and should be completed."[17] Other respondents were presented with the same pair of opinions, but in the reverse order.

a. Why were two different forms of the question asked?

b. Describe how researchers could explore whether or not the ordering of the two opinions may affect people's responses.

c. Would the survey's results tell you more about how all Canadians feel regarding firearms registry if there were

10 respondents or 1,000 respondents; or doesn't it matter?

d. Which one of the following would most improve the above survey question: make it less complicated, give respondents more of a feeling of anonymity, or make it an open question?

3.22 Students were asked to rate their instructor's preparation for class as being excellent, good, or needs improvement.

a. If a student feels the instructor does an average job, what response will he or she probably select?

b. The options provided result in biased responses to the instructor's survey; will they tend to overestimate or underestimate the quality of the instructor's preparation?

c. Should the instructor summarize results with means or with proportions?

3.23 A survey of students found that only 10% of them liked brussels sprouts.

a. Was the survey question more likely to have been open or closed?

b. Which would do more to convince you that the percentage of all students who like brussels sprouts is close to 10%: if the survey included 200 students or 20 students?

*3.24 For which survey question is it more important to assure respondents of their anonymity: when asking how they rate their instructor's preparedness or when asking if they like brussels sprouts?

*3.25 A survey asked, "On how many occasions (if any) have you sniffed glue, breathed the contents of an aerosol spray can, or inhaled other gases or sprays, to get high during the past 30 days?" Response options were "0 occasions, 1–2 occasions, 3–5 occasions, 6–9 occasions, 10–19 occasions, 20–30 occasions, 40 or more occasions." An alternative wording would have been "Have you sniffed glue, breathed the contents of an aerosol can, or inhaled other gases or sprays, to get high during the past 30 days? If so, on how many occasions? _____" For which wording are students more likely to admit (or simply claim) to have engaged in the above-mentioned behaviors, the first or the second?

3.26 "Phantom Illness" poses the question, "Do you ever call in sick when you're not sick?" and reports results of a poll by CareerBuilder.com: "More than a third of workers, or 35%, said they had done so at least once in the past year."[18] Tell why there may be less bias in the responses to this e-mail survey than if it had been conducted by phone or in person.

*3.27 If students are asked by their statistics instructor in the course of the semester to complete a survey about quality of instruction, which method is more likely to elicit honest responses: asking them to complete the survey via computer lab facilities or via a pencil-and-paper survey?

*3.28 A survey asked, "How many close friends do you have?" Which of these is most worrisome: leading question, complicated question, sensitive question, or hard-to-define concept?

3.29 For each of these studies, a precise summary is used to assess an imprecise thing. Tell whether the imprecision involves the explanatory variable or the response variable.

a. A study in which people who were asked to think about bad hair scored 3 points lower on self-esteem than people who were asked to think about leaky packages.

b. A study that showed happy people lived 20 months longer than unhappy people.

3.3 Observational Studies: When Nature Takes Its Course

We discussed the distinction between observational studies and experiments on page 33. The fact that some individuals in an observational study have opted for certain values of the explanatory variable, whereas others have opted for other values, means those individuals may be different in additional ways that could also play a role in the response of interest. Those "additional ways," which we will define as *confounding variables*, are by far the most common flaw in observational studies.

Confounding Variables and Causation

> *Definition*   A **confounding variable** is one that clouds the issue of causation because its values are tied in with those of the so-called explanatory variable, and also play a role in the so-called response variable's values. Confounding variables are also known as *lurking variables*.

EXAMPLE 3.15 CONFOUNDING IN AN OBSERVATIONAL STUDY

Background: Suppose the observational study described in Example 3.3 on page 34 had been carried out, and researchers determined that the percentage who were hyperactive was lower for children with a low sugar intake, and higher for children with a high sugar intake. In other words, suppose there is clear evidence of an *association* between sugar intake and hyperactivity.

Question: How could gender enter in as a confounding variable, preventing the researchers from concluding that sugar *causes* hyperactivity?

Response: Perhaps one gender group—for instance, boys—is more likely to eat larger amounts of sugar, and suppose that boys also tend to be hyperactive more than girls. The data would make it appear that sugar itself was responsible for hyperactivity, whereas in truth it may just be that being male is the reason for hyperactive behavior. We can express this scenario in terms of the key variables involved: In addition to the explanatory variable (high or low sugar) and the response variable (normal or hyperactive), a third, *confounding variable* (gender) is tied in with the explanatory variable's values, and may itself cause the response to be normal or hyperactive. We can illustrate the situation with a diagram.

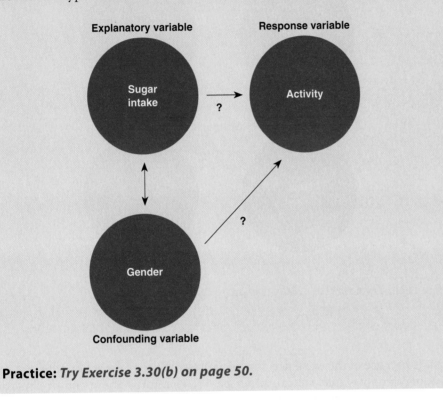

Practice: *Try Exercise 3.30(b) on page 50.*

The Big Picture:

A CLOSER LOOK

Notice that by considering the role of gender in the relationship, we are adding another possible categorical explanatory variable to our original design.

Fortunately, researchers do have a way of coping with confounding variables. In general, we *control* for the effects of a confounding variable by separately studying groups that are similar with respect to this variable.

EXAMPLE 3.16 CONTROLLING FOR CONFOUNDING VARIABLES

Background: It is thought that gender may be a confounding variable in the relationship between sugar intake and activity level.

Question: How can researchers take this possible confounding variable into account?

Response: The difficulty arises because of the confounding variable's values being "tied in with" those of the explanatory variable, so one way to attempt to unravel the true nature of the relationship between explanatory and response variables is to separate out the effects of the confounding variable.

Continued

We could control for the possible confounding variable of gender in our sugar/hyperactivity study by considering boys and girls separately. Then, if *both* boys and girls with high sugar intakes have higher rates of hyperactivity, we would be closer to producing evidence of causation. The following diagram demonstrates how straightforward it is to control for the confounding variable "gender."

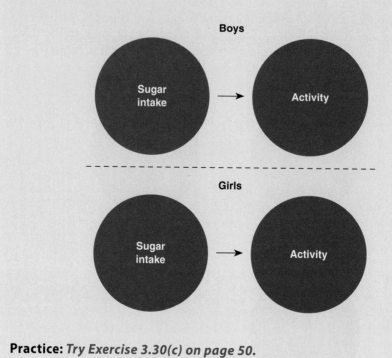

Practice: *Try Exercise 3.30(c) on page 50.*

Example TBP 3.3 on page 757 of the *TBP Supplement* discusses the possibility that several confounding variables may enter into a relationship.

We will define independent *events* in Part III: Whether or not one occurs does not impact the probability of the other occurring. When we describe two *groups* of individuals as being independent, we mean which individuals are sampled for one group has no effect on which individuals are sampled for the other. For example, a group of husbands and their wives would be *dependent*: Once a man is chosen, his wife must be included in the group of women studied.

It is because of the existence of a virtually unlimited number of potential confounding variables that we can never be 100% certain of a claim of causation based on an observational study. On the other hand, observational studies are an extremely common tool that researchers use to attempt to draw conclusions about causal connections. If great care is taken to control for the most likely confounding variables (and to avoid other pitfalls that we will discuss presently), and if common sense indicates that there is good reason for one variable to cause changes in the other, then researchers may assert that an observational study provides good evidence of causation.

Paired or Two-Sample Studies

A vast number of studies compare responses for two possible values of a categorical explanatory variable, with a design that is either *two-sample* or *paired*.

> *Definitions*   A **two-sample study design** compares responses for two independent groups. In a **paired study design**, there are two response values recorded for each unit. This design is sometimes called *matched pairs*.

EXAMPLE 3.17 TWO-SAMPLE VERSUS PAIRED STUDY DESIGN

Background: Suppose researchers seek evidence that sugar consumption causes hyperactivity in children.

Questions: How could evidence be gathered via a two-sample study design? Via a paired study design?

Responses: If the study compares activity for two groups of children, classified as being either low- or high-sugar-intake, then it would be a *two-sample design.*

Activity habits and levels vary greatly from family to family, depending on region, socio-economic status, and so on. One way to control for all of these influences would be to use a *paired design*: Study pairs of siblings, determining who has a higher intake of sugar and comparing activity levels within each pair. If age were thought to be a possible confounding variable, then twins could be used.

Practice: *Try Exercise 3.32 on page 50.*

The Big Picture: **LOOKING AHEAD**

Typical paired study designs that we will encounter include before-and-after studies and comparisons of responses for pairs of individuals, such as twins, siblings, or married couples.

In general, paired studies help to control for confounding variables by comparing responses for individuals occurring in pairs that are similar in important ways. Paired and two-sample studies will be revisited when we discuss the design of experiments.

Prospective or Retrospective Studies: Forward or Backward in Time

Observational studies are subject to other pitfalls besides confounding variables, arising from various aspects of the design for evaluating the explanatory and response values.

EXAMPLE 3.18 DRAWBACKS OF RETROSPECTIVE AND PROSPECTIVE STUDIES

Background: Suppose researchers want to determine if people tend to snack more while they watch TV. One possible design, considered in Example 3.2 on page 32, is to recruit participants for an observational study and give them journals to record, hour-by-hour, their activities the following day, including TV watched and food consumed. Then researchers could review the journals to determine if food consumption was higher during TV times. We identified this as being a *prospective* observational study, carried forward in time.

A second possible design is to recruit participants for a *retrospective* observational study, gathering data from the past. The participants are asked to recall, for each hour of the previous day, whether they were watching TV and what food they consumed each hour. Then researchers determine if food consumption was higher during the TV times.

Continued

Question: What are the disadvantages of the two designs described?

Response: Studying people in the more natural setting of their own homes makes it more realistic than assessing their behavior in a contrived, experimental setting. Still, when people in a prospective study are obliged to record their behavior as it occurs, they may be too self-conscious to act naturally. They may want to avoid embarrassment and so cut back on their TV viewing, or their snack consumption, or the combination of the two.

The retrospective design has the advantage of not disturbing people's natural behavior in terms of TV viewing or snacking. It has the disadvantage of relying on people's memories to record those variables' values from the day before. They may forget some of their TV viewing, or their snacking, or the combination of the two.

Practice: *Try Exercise 3.34(a,b) on page 51.*

Observational studies are summarized on page 64 of the Chapter Summary.

EXERCISES FOR SECTION 3.3

Observational Studies: When Nature Takes Its Course

Note: Asterisked numbers indicate exercises whose answers are provided in the Solutions to Selected Exercises section, on page 689.

*3.30 "Moderate Walking Helps the Mind Stay Sharper" is the title of an article that reports, "Women who walked 1 1/2 hours per week had a 20% lower risk of mental impairment than those who walked less than 40 minutes per week, according to a study of 18,766 elderly women conducted by researchers from the Harvard School of Public Health."[19]

a. Was this an observational study or an experiment?

b. Which one of these would be most worrisome here: confounding variables, people's behaviors affected by their awareness of participating in a prospective study, or anecdotal evidence?

c. Suppose age was thought to be a possible confounding variable in the relationship between walking and mental fitness. How could researchers handle this problem?

d. Report the explanatory variable using a single word from the article's title _____ and identify its variable type:
   1. Categorical
   2. Quantitative

e. Report the response variable using two words from the article's explanation in quotations _____ and identify its variable type:
   1. Categorical
   2. Quantitative

f. Do we compare means or proportions?

3.31 An article entitled "Men, Beer, and Lung Cancer" reported that men who regularly consumed red wine were less likely to contract lung cancer than were men who drank beer.

a. The fact that men were studied separately from women indicates that a certain variable is being controlled for as a potential confounding variable. What is it?

b. Another variable was *not* mentioned and could easily enter in as a confounding variable. What is it?

*3.32 A study compared percentages of men and of women who were illiterate in various countries around the world. For instance, in Zimbabwe, 7.2% of the men and 15.4% of the women were illiterate. Is this a paired or a two-sample study?

3.33 Pell grants provide federally funded financial aid to low-income students. A study looked at the percentage of students with Pell grants in 1992, compared to 2001, for the nation's top 20 universities. For instance, Harvard went from 4.6% of its students having Pell grants in 1992 to 6.8% in 2001, and Massachusetts Institute of Technology went from 16.3% to 12.4%.

    a. Was this a two-sample or paired study?

    b. Tell which of the following processes would *not* be relevant in this situation, and why: data production, displaying and summarizing data, or statistical inference.

*3.34 "TV Pro Wrestling Spurs Teen Violence" is the headline of an article that reports on a study that related the viewing of pro wrestling on television with violent behavior such as date fights (verbal or physical abuse taking place in social settings traditionally known as "dates").

    a. Describe how data could have been gathered via a retrospective observational study; what is a major drawback to such a study design?

    b. Describe how data could have been gathered via a prospective observational study; what is a major drawback to such a study design?

    c. Assuming there is, in fact, some relationship between watching pro wrestling and teen violence, give a brief alternative explanation that is different from the headline's claim that "TV pro wrestling spurs teen violence."

3.35 An article entitled *Couch potato nation* describes a report by the federal Centers for Disease Control and Prevention that "analyzed responses from 119,000 people who were asked in 1996 about their physical activity during the month prior to the survey."[20]

    a. This was an observational study. Was it retrospective or prospective?

    b. The article states that overall, nearly 30% of adults reported being inactive. Is physical activity treated here as a quantitative or a categorical variable?

    c. It was also reported that the rate of inactivity was 37% in small towns, compared with a rate of 27% in large urban areas. Now there are two variables of interest; describe the explanatory variable and tell whether it is quantitative or categorical.

3.4 Experiments: When Researchers Take Control

By now you should have an idea of how difficult—or perhaps impossible—it is to establish causation in an observational study, especially due to the problem of confounding variables. The key to establishing causation is to ensure that individuals differ *only* with respect to their values of the explanatory variable. In general, this is a goal that we have a much better chance of accomplishing by carrying out a well-designed experiment.

Recall that in an experiment, it is the researchers who assign values of the explanatory variable for the participants. The key to ensuring that individuals differ only with respect to explanatory values—which is also the key to establishing causation—lies in the way this assignment is carried out. We return to the sugar/hyperactivity study as a context to explore the essential ingredients of experimental design.

In Example 3.3 on page 34, we described the following experiment: Collect a sample of children and assign a low-sugar diet to some, and a high-sugar diet to others. After a certain period of time, assess whether each of the children is hyperactive or not. This is an experiment because the researchers themselves impose the values of the explanatory variable of interest for the individuals studied, rather than letting them occur naturally.

We will begin by using the context of this sugar/hyperactivity example to illustrate the specialized vocabulary of experiments, some of which are household

Many experiments test the impact of more than one explanatory variable via a *factorial design*. If we multiply the numbers of possible values (levels) of the various factors together, then we arrive at the number of possible combinations of levels that can be tested. For instance, a factorial design testing three types of sweetener in two amounts each would include six experimental conditions altogether.

words that do not require formal definitions. First of all, the explanatory variable, or *factor*, in this case is sugar intake. The different imposed values of the explanatory variable, or *treatments*, consist of low- or high-sugar intakes. The groups receiving different treatments are called *treatment groups*. A *control group* may be included for comparison; in this case, it could consist of children who consume as much sugar as they normally would, or perhaps children who are assigned to consume what researchers deem to be a normal amount of sugar, as opposed to unusually low or high. Ideally, the *subjects* (human participants in an experiment) in each treatment group differ from those in the other treatment groups only with respect to the treatment (sugar intake).

Definitions   A **factor** in an experiment is an explanatory variable. **Treatments** are values of the explanatory variable imposed by researchers.

As mentioned in our discussion of why confounding variables prevent us from establishing causation in observational studies, eliminating all other differences among treatment groups will be the key to asserting causation via an experiment. How can this be accomplished?

Randomized Controlled Experiments

The Big Picture:

LOOKING AHEAD

Almost all experiments that we will discuss are randomized controlled, even if not explicitly stated.

Your intuition may already tell you, correctly, that *random assignment* to treatments is the best way to prevent treatment groups of individuals from differing in additional ways besides the treatment assigned. Either computer software or random digits tables, or even something as simple as a coin flip, can be used to accomplish the random assignment. The resulting design is called a *randomized controlled experiment* because researchers *control* values of the explanatory variable with a randomization procedure. Under random assignment, the groups tend not to differ significantly with respect to any potential confounding variable. Then, if we see a relationship between the explanatory and response variables, we have evidence that it is a causal one.

Note that the word *control* is used in three different senses.

Definitions   In the context of observational studies, we **control** for a confounding variable by separating it out.

An experiment is called **controlled** because the values of its explanatory variables have been assigned by researchers, as opposed to having occurred naturally. In general, these assignments are made at random, and it is called a **randomized controlled experiment**.

The **control group** in an experiment consists of individuals who do not receive a treatment, but who otherwise are presumably handled the same as those who do receive the treatment.

Pages 757–758 of the **TBP** *Supplement* goes into more depth on the inclusion of control groups in experiments, with Example TBP 3.4, Example TBP 3.5, and Example TBP 3.6 exploring situations where there is no control group per se.

Let's consider the use of randomization at two stages of selection in an experiment. First, a sample of subjects must be collected. Ideally, the sample would be perfectly representative of the entire population, but for practical purposes, researchers are almost always obliged to recruit volunteers. Thus, this stage rarely employs randomization. Second, individuals must be assigned to the treatment groups so that the only real difference between groups is what treatment was received, justifying claims of causation. At this stage, randomization is vital.

Double-Blind Experiments

The **Big Picture:**
LOOKING AHEAD

Using volunteers helps to offset one of the drawbacks to experimentation that will be discussed later—namely, the problem of noncompliance.

Suppose the sugar/hyperactivity experiment had been carried out with randomized assignments to the two sugar treatments, and researchers determined that the percentage hyperactive for the high-sugar-intake group was higher than that for the low-sugar-intake group. In other words, suppose there is clear evidence of an *association* between sugar intake and hyperactivity. Could they then conclude that sugar *causes* hyperactivity?

Perhaps. Before such a conclusion is reached, it is important to think about how both subjects' and experimenters' awareness of treatment assignment can affect a study's results. First, we define some important terms.

Definitions   A **blind** subject in an experiment is unaware of which treatment he or she is receiving. A **placebo** is an inert treatment given to duplicate the psychological effects of the actual treatment. The **placebo effect** is the phenomenon whereby subjects respond to the idea of treatment rather than to the treatment itself.

A **blind experimenter** is one who, when assessing the response of interest, is not aware of which treatment a subject has received. The **experimenter effect** is the conscious or subconscious tendency of an experimenter to be influenced by knowledge of a subject's value of the explanatory variable when assessing the subject's response. In the extreme, the experimenter may attempt to bring about certain responses because of knowledge of which treatment has been assigned.

In a **double-blind experiment**, both subjects and researchers are blind.

"Blind" Subjects

Although randomized controlled experiments do give us a better chance of pinning down the effects of the explanatory variable of interest, they are not completely problem-free. For example, suppose that the children in our sugar/hyperactivity experiment, like many of us, had heard reports or jokes made about the "fact" that consuming high amounts of sugar can cause hyperactive behavior. Even with a randomized assignment to the two sugar treatments, there would be an important difference between the subjects: Those in the high-sugar-intake group might expect to become hyperactive, and there could be a psychological effect on their activity. Therefore, the ideal circumstance is for the subjects to be unaware themselves of which treatment is being administered to them. In other words, subjects in an experiment should be blind to which treatment they received.

When the treatment involved is a drug, researchers simply administer a placebo pill to the control group so that there are no psychological differences between those who receive the drug and those who do not. The word *placebo* means "I shall please," and is so named because of the natural tendency for human subjects to improve, thanks to the idea of being treated, regardless of the intended benefits of the treatment itself. This is the phenomenon known as the *placebo effect*.

EXAMPLE 3.19 SUBJECTS NOT BLIND

Background: "A Really Bright Idea" tells of studies to treat depression in pregnant women using light therapy. "In small, pilot studies involving pregnant women, light has lifted the moods in 60% of the participants," claims the article. One of the subjects, who works from home, "put the light box on her desk. She'd have it on for 45 minutes each morning while she worked on the computer, read, sewed, or ate breakfast. 'I'd say I noticed a pretty big difference within the first week,' she said . . . When she missed her light sessions for three days while on a business trip, 'I definitely noticed a difference.'"

Questions: Were subjects blind in this experiment? If not, is this problematic?

Responses: The subjects were not blind because they knew they were receiving light treatment. It could be that light therapy is beneficial for pregnant women suffering from depression, but this study should not be relied on for evidence because no effort was made to separate out the placebo effect. The women's moods may have improved because of the *idea* of having their depression treated. In fact, it would be difficult to have women unaware of whether or not they are being treated with light.

Practice: *Try Exercise 3.36 on page 59.*

How could researchers arrange for subjects to be blind when the treatment involved is sugar? The obvious answer is to give some subjects sugar in their food, and give others a "placebo" in the form of an artificial sweetener such as saccharin or aspartame. Even if researchers administer identical diets to the two groups, with the only difference being the type of sweetener (sugar or artificial), can we really be sure that no psychological difference enters in? People often are able to detect whether soft drinks are sweetened artificially; even ants have been known to seek out sugar-sweetened cola and not be tempted by the diet version! Thus, the optimal design may not be perfect. However, if researchers threw up their hands and refused to carry out any study with potential weaknesses, we would ultimately learn very little about the complicated world that we live in.

"Blind" Experimenters

When the response of interest is fairly cut-and-dried, then recording its values is a straightforward process in which researchers need not use their own judgment in making an assessment.

EXAMPLE 3.20 EXPERIMENTERS NEED NOT BE BLIND WHEN THE ASSESSMENT IS OBJECTIVE

Background: Recently, many experiments have been conducted to compare various antidepression drugs' role in teen suicides.

Question: In which case would it be important for researchers to be blind to what treatment the subjects have received: when the response of interest is committing suicide, or when the response of interest is having suicidal tendencies?

Response: If the response is actually committing suicide, then researchers need not be blind at the time of assessment. On the other hand, the assessment of suicidal *tendencies* can be rather subjective. In this case, it would be important for researchers to be blind.

Practice: *Try Exercise 3.37 on page 59.*

The Big Picture: A Closer Look

Notice that here the explanatory variable (drug taken or not) is categorical and the response (suicide in one case, having suicidal tendencies in the other) is also categorical.

In our sugar experiment, the response of interest (being hyperactive or not) is not so clear-cut. In cases like this, it is important for researchers who evaluate the response to be blind to which treatment the subject received, in order to prevent the experimenter effect from influencing their assessments. Now we come to the potential flaw in Dr. Feingold's experiment: He apparently knew which children had received higher amounts of sugar, and may have been swayed toward perceiving or reporting behavior as hyperactive when exhibited by a child in the high-sugar group.

In general, the most reliable way to determine whether the explanatory variable is actually causing changes in the response variable is to carry out a randomized controlled double-blind experiment. The closer researchers get to achieving this ideal design, the more convincing are their claims of causation (or lack thereof).

Depending on the variables of interest, a double-blind design may not be entirely feasible. Moreover, the benefits of researchers having total control over values of the explanatory variable are to some extent offset by the difficulties involved in creating a very controlled—and therefore unnatural—environment. This drawback of experimentation will be explored in Example 3.21.

Pitfalls in Experimentation

Some of the inherent difficulties that might be encountered in experimentation are the Hawthorne effect, lack of realism, noncompliance, and treatments that are unethical, impossible, or impractical to impose. Except for the first, these expressions are part of our everyday vocabulary.

> *Definition*   The **Hawthorne effect** is the phenomenon wherein people's performance is improved simply due to their awareness of being observed.

EXAMPLE 3.21 EXPERIMENT FLAWED BY HAWTHORNE EFFECT OR LACK OF REALISM

Background: In Example 3.2 on page 32, we introduced a hypothetical experiment to determine if people tend to snack more while they watch TV. While the subjects are presumably waiting to be interviewed, half of them

Continued

The Big Picture: A Closer Look

One of the greatest advantages of an experiment—that researchers themselves take control of the explanatory variable—can also be a disadvantage in that it may result in a rather unrealistic setting. Depending on the explanatory variable of interest, it may be quite easy or it may be virtually impossible to take control of the variable's values and still maintain a fairly natural setting.

The Big Picture: LOOKING BACK

On page 19, we saw that nonrespondents in a survey may differ from respondents in an important way. Similarly, noncompliant subjects in an experiment may be very different from compliant ones, so that excluding them may result in bias of some sort.

The Big Picture: A CLOSER LOOK

Families who volunteer for a study about hyperactivity may have children with a higher rate of hyperactivity than those in the general population. Still, if researchers are primarily concerned with the effect of sugar, then *relative rates* of hyperactivity for low versus high sugar groups should be roughly the same for the volunteer sample as they would be for the general population, as long as the sugar levels are assigned randomly.

sit in a waiting room with snacks available and a TV on. The other half sit in a waiting room with snacks available and no TV. Researchers determine if people consume more snacks in the TV setting.

Question: Suppose that, in fact, the subjects who sat in the waiting room with the TV consumed more snacks than those who sat in the room without TV. Could we conclude that in their everyday lives, and in their own homes, people eat more snacks when the TV is on?

Response: Not necessarily, because people's behavior in this very controlled setting may be quite different from their ordinary behavior. If they suspect their snacking behavior is being observed, they may alter their behavior either consciously or subconsciously, exhibiting the Hawthorne effect. Even if they don't suspect they are being observed in the waiting room, the relationship between TV and snacking there might not be representative of what it is in real life. Thus, we may not be justified in generalizing the experiment's results due to *lack of realism* (also called *lack of ecological validity*).

Practice: *Try Exercise 3.38 on page 59.*

In carrying out the observational study to explore the relationship between sugar consumption and hyperactivity, it shouldn't be too difficult to get most of the participants (or their parents) to cooperate with reporting their food intake. Cooperation tends to be more problematic in experiments.

EXAMPLE 3.22 NONCOMPLIANCE IN AN EXPERIMENT

Background: In an experiment designed to determine if sugar consumption causes hyperactivity in children, researchers intend to take total control over children's diets for a substantial length of time.

Question: Can the researchers count on most of the children adhering to the prescribed diet?

Response: It is quite possible that many of the children would be unwilling or feel unable to cooperate by eating exactly what they are told to eat. Thus, noncompliance (failure to submit to the assigned treatment) could enter in on such a large scale as to render the results useless.

Practice: *Try Exercise 3.39 on page 60.*

On one hand, a random sample is safer in terms of truly representing the larger population. On the other hand, using a sample of volunteers helps to reduce noncompliance in an experiment.

There are other, more serious drawbacks to experimentation, as illustrated in the following examples:

EXAMPLE 3.23 UNETHICAL EXPERIMENT

Background: A newspaper article entitled "Study Forced Orphans to Stutter" tells about a 1939 study carried out on 22 orphans in Iowa: One group of 11 was given positive speech therapy, and the other 11 were induced to stutter by constant badgering on the part of their speech therapist. Out of those 11, 8 became chronic stutterers. One of them, interviewed over 60 years later, said, "It's affected me right now. I don't like to read out loud because I'm afraid of making a mistake. I don't like talking to people because of saying the wrong word."[21] The therapist herself came to deeply regret her role in this experiment, in spite of the fact that it eventually led to a theory that helped in treating thousands of children for stuttering.

Question: Is it ethical to impose a treatment with the intention of causing orphans to become stutterers?

Response: Most people today would agree that the answer is a resounding "No!": The price of the knowledge gained was simply too high for the unwitting victims.

Practice: *Try Exercise 3.40(e) on page 60.*

A CLOSER LOOK

Notice that here the explanatory variable (positive speech therapy or badgering) and the response (being a chronic stutterer or not) are both categorical.

If time permits, this is an ideal opportunity for in-depth discussions of ethics in research. Notorious examples of unethical studies, such as the Tuskegee syphilis study conducted between 1932 and 1972 or the Milgram shock experiments of the 1960s, can be mentioned. Students can be assured that the Research Act of 1974 established requirements for Institutional Review Boards (IRBs) to screen research for any unethical treatment of humans or animals.

Because it is unethical to manipulate the explanatory variable in this and many other situations, researchers must often make do with a well-designed observational study rather than an experiment.

There are also many explanatory variables—such as salary, gender, or height—that are either impractical or downright impossible to manipulate. Observational studies are subject to flaws themselves, but often they are the only recourse.

Modifications to Randomization

In some cases, an experiment's design can be enhanced by relaxing the requirement of total randomization, and *blocking* the subjects first.

> *Definition*   **Blocking** in an experiment entails first dividing the subjects into groups of individuals who are similar with respect to an outside variable that may be important in the relationship being studied. Treatments are then assigned randomly within the blocks.

LOOKING BACK

Blocking subjects in an experiment is analogous to stratification in sampling, discussed on page 20.

Blocking can help ensure that the impacts of treatments are most effectively measured, without interference from background variables. For instance, if researchers suspect that gender is an important outside variable in the relationship between sugar intake and activity, they may not want to risk that a random assignment to treatments happens to result in a disproportionately high number of females being put on a low-sugar diet and males put on a high-sugar diet. To guard

Example TBP 3.7 on page 758 of the *TBP Supplement* demonstrates how blocking or pairing can improve an experiment's design.

against this, they can block by gender, splitting the sampled subjects into males and females, and then randomly allocating to treatments within each gender group.

In the extreme, researchers may carry out a *paired study* to examine a relationship for a sample of "blocks" of just *two* individuals who are similar in many important respects, or even the *same* individual whose responses are compared for two explanatory values. A paired design helps us to pinpoint the effects of the explanatory variable by comparing responses for the same individual under two explanatory values, or for two individuals who are as similar as possible except that the first gets one treatment and the second gets another (or serves as the control). Treatments should usually be assigned at random within each pair, or the order of treatments randomized for the same individual. Paired designs were discussed on page 48 in the context of observational studies.

In general, race is an explanatory variable whose values researchers cannot manipulate. Nevertheless, our next example describes an experiment in which researchers actually did randomly assign *perceived* race to pairs of resumes, allowing them to obtain fairly convincing evidence of discrimination.

EXAMPLE 3.24 ADVANTAGE OF PAIRED DESIGN

Background: "What's in a Name? Studies Find That Afrocentric Names Often Incur a Bias" tells about two economists who wanted to research racial discrimination in hiring practices. They created fictitious resumes, and for every pair of similar-quality resumes sent in response to a help-wanted ad, one was randomly assigned a white-sounding name (such as Emily Walsh or Greg Baker) and the other a black-sounding name (such as Lakisha Washington or Jamal Jones). The resumes with white-sounding names received call-backs 10% of the time, whereas those with black-sounding names received call-backs only 7.5% of the time.

Question: Why did the researchers work with *pairs* of similar-quality resumes instead of sending a variety of resumes, some with white-sounding names and others with black-sounding names?

Response: By sending pairs of similar resumes to the companies, the researchers were better able to pinpoint the discrimination due to perceived race. If they had used a two-sample design, one could argue that the group with white-sounding names just happened to include more high-quality resumes.

Practice: *Try Exercise 3.45(b–d) on page 60.*

Notice that in this paired study design, both the explanatory variable (white-sounding or black-sounding name) and the response (received call-back or not after sending in resume) are categorical.

Example TBP 3.8 on page 759 of the *TBP Supplement* features a simple before-and-after study.

Example TBP 3.9 on page 760 of the *TBP Supplement* illustrates the combination of two-sample and paired designs in a drug study.

"Before-and-after" studies are an extremely common type of paired design. For each individual, the response variable of interest is measured twice: before the treatment and after the treatment. The categorical explanatory variable is having the treatment applied or not.

A very common and effective study design for testing responses to a drug uses a combination of random assignment to one of two treatment groups (drug versus placebo) with pairs (before versus after). This lets researchers pin down the effect of the drug by comparing responses before and after for the same individual. At the same time, including a control group of subjects who do not receive the drug prevents the placebo effect or other possible confounding variables (such as

© Susan Steinkamp/CORBIS

Why is the Twins Day Festival a researcher's paradise?

natural changes due to time) from influencing their conclusions about the effect of the drug itself.

Note that we have explained data production as occurring in two stages: First obtain the sample, then evaluate the variables of interest via an appropriate design. Even though the steps are carried out in this order chronologically, it is generally best for researchers to decide on a study design before they actually obtain the sample. For the sugar/hyperactivity study, researchers would first decide if they want to conduct a paired or two-sample study, then recruit a sample of volunteers, and then carry out the study and assess the results.

Experiments are summarized on page 65 of the Chapter Summary.

EXERCISES FOR SECTION 3.4

Experiments: When Researchers Take Control

Note: Asterisked numbers indicate exercises whose answers are provided in the Solutions to Selected Exercises section, on page 689.

*3.36 A study was carried out to see whether acupuncture can relieve stress; another study looked at whether Rogaine results in significant hair restoration.

 a. Which of the two studies is more susceptible to the placebo effect? Explain.

 b. For which of the studies would it be easier to make the subjects blind to whether or not they are receiving the actual treatment?

*3.37 A news article reports on a study published in *Lancet* in 1996: "Researchers experimented on themselves, letting honeybees sting them repeatedly and then comparing whether scraping a stinger after two seconds resulted in a smaller weal than yanking it out as quickly."[22] Why did the

researchers compare weal sizes, instead of simply reporting how painful the sting was?

*3.38 In September of 2006, *Scientific American* reported that "Washing Hands Reduces Moral Taint."[23] To demonstrate that people are inclined to wash their hands as a response to a feeling of moral uncleanliness, researchers asked some students to recall an ethical action they had undertaken in their lives; others were asked to recall an unethical action. "After recalling an unethical memory, students were more likely to choose a free antiseptic wipe over a free pencil when offered the choice, as compared with untested subjects who showed little preference." Which of these would be most worrisome in this experiment: placebo effect, experimenter effect, lack of realism, or imposing a treatment that is unethical?

*3.39 In which study would noncompliance be more of a problem: a study where participants are to think about bad hair or leaky containers, or a study that asks participants to have tissue removed from their upper arm?

*3.40 "Written Word Helps Wounds Heal" describes a British study: "In the study, which involved 36 people, half were asked to write about the most upsetting experience they had had, spelling out how they had felt. The rest of the study participants wrote about trivial things, such as how they spent their free time. Both groups spent 20 minutes a day for three days writing. Following the writing exercise, researchers created a small skin puncture [under anesthesia] on the participants' upper arms. The wounds were examined two weeks later. It was found that the group who had written about their emotional experiences had smaller wounds, meaning they had healed more quickly. Those whose wounds were healing more slowly were found to have higher levels of stress and psychological distress."[24]

a. Explain why this experiment used volunteers, rather than a random sample.

b. Explain why some participants were asked to write about how they spent their free time.

c. Describe the response variable and explain whether it was likely to have been treated as quantitative or categorical.

d. Would the study's results be summarized with means or proportions?

e. Which of these is most problematic in attempting to use the study's results to conclude that writing about disturbing events can have healing benefits: placebo effect, experimenter effect, lack of realism, or imposing a treatment that is unethical?

f. What modification to the experiment's design would have been appropriate if researchers suspected that the benefits of releasing emotions by writing differs for men and women?

g. If researchers had recruited married couples and randomly assigned the man or woman to one or the other treatment, what would the design be called?

3.41 An article entitled "Study Offers Surprise on Working of Body's Clock" tells about a randomized controlled double-blind study in which subjects spent several days in a sleep lab. At night they "stayed awake in a dimly lighted room, reclining in a chair with a table over their laps. A thick black material was draped over their legs and fastened to their waists. Underneath this skirt, a knee pad with a fiber optic tube was attached to the back of their knees and a bright light was delivered through the tube for three hours."[25] Other subjects were kept under identical conditions except the light was not turned on. Those treated with light had significant changes in their body rhythms, while those untreated did not.

a. Which of these would be most worrisome in this experiment: placebo effect, experimenter effect, lack of realism, or imposing a treatment that is unethical?

b. Was the black skirt used to offset the placebo effect, the experimenter effect, lack of realism, or imposing a treatment that is unethical?

c. If body rhythms are assessed by measuring body temperature and level of melatonin in the blood, is it important for researchers to be unaware of which subjects were in the treatment group when it comes time to evaluate their responses?

3.42 Keeping in mind that volunteers in experiments must almost always be paid for their time, would you expect the study discussed in Exercise 3.41 about the effect of light on humans' body clocks to have been carried out on a fairly small or fairly large sample of subjects?

3.43 Which type of studies do you think tend to use larger sample sizes—experiments or observational studies—or do you think type of study plays no role in sample size used?

3.44 For which of these studies would it be easier to include a placebo so that subjects are blind to treatment: an experiment to test if piano lessons improve math scores, or an experiment to test if taking a blood pressure medication reduces the risk of heart attacks?

*3.45 An article entitled "Piano Lessons Boost Math Scores" states that "second-grade students who took piano lessons for four months scored significantly higher on math than children who did not."[26]

a. Tell why these results are more convincing if they are based on an experiment than they would be if they were based on an observational study.

b. One possible design is to take a sample of second graders and randomly assign some to be given piano lessons for 4 months, and others not. Is this a two-sample or a paired design?

c. Another possible design is to take a sample of second-grade twins and randomly assign one twin to be given piano lessons for 4 months, the other not. Is this a two-sample or a paired design?

d. Explain why the design described in part (c) could do a better job at pinpointing the effects of piano lessons on math skills, compared to the design described in part (b).

e. If an experiment is carried out to determine if piano lessons can increase math scores, is it important for the researchers who evaluate the response to be unaware of whether or not a student was in the treatment group?

*3.46 Which could be called a before-and-after design: a study to see if people can lower their cholesterol by eating oatmeal every day for a month, or a study to see if breast-fed infants have fewer infections than do bottle-fed infants?

*3.47 Describe how a study could test the effectiveness of the hair restoration drug Rogaine using a combination of paired and two-sample designs.

3.48 The article "When Your Hair's a Real Mess, Your Self-Esteem Is Much Less" describes a study wherein participants "were divided into three groups. One group was questioned about times in their lives when they had bad hair. The second group was told to think about bad product packaging, like leaky containers, to get them in a negative mindset. The third group was not asked to think about anything negative. All three groups then underwent basic psychological tests of self-esteem and self-judgment. The people who pondered their bad-hair days showed lower self-esteem than those who thought about something else."[27]

a. Was this an observational study, an experiment, or a sample survey?

b. Which group was included to see if thoughts about bad hair are worse for people's self-esteem than other negative thoughts—the second or third group?

c. Which is more important: obtaining a random sample of participants for the study, or randomly assigning participants to one of the three groups?

d. Which of these is most problematic in attempting to use the study's results to conclude that people having "bad hair days" suffer from low self-esteem: placebo effect, experimenter effect, lack of realism, non-compliance, or imposing a treatment that is unethical?

How's her self-esteem?

3.49 An article entitled "How Healthy Is Our State for Kids? Study Will Tell" describes a study that would recruit and enroll participants in 96 locations over the next 4 years and track them from conception through their children's twenty-first year. Participants would have at least 15 in-person visits by local research teams. For the $2.7 billion study, "workers will collect biological samples from the mother and child, as well as air, water, dirt and dust from the child's environment. The study also will examine many aspects of children's lives: genetics, neighborhoods, schools, chemical exposures linked to the atmosphere, food or water supplies, and social and behavioral environments."[28]

a. Will this be an observational study or an experiment?

b. Which of these would be most worrisome here: treatments that are unethical to impose, people's behaviors affected by their awareness of participating in a prospective study, or people's faulty memories in a retrospective study?

3.50 A 2004 article entitled "Study of Pesticides and Children Stirs Protest" describes a proposed Environmental Protection Agency (EPA) study to see how small children absorb pesticides and other household chemicals. The EPA would pay each family "$970, some children's clothing and a camcorder"[29] in exchange for their participation for two years, during which they would use various household chemicals and have their children tested for absorption rates. [Note: In 2005 it was decided not to carry out the study.]

a. Would this be an observational study or an experiment?

b. Which of these would be most worrisome here: treatments that are unethical to impose, people's behaviors affected by their awareness of participating in a prospective study, or people's faulty memories in a retrospective study?

3.51 Suppose a certain type of pesticide is actually *not* toxic to humans, but a study erroneously concludes that it *is* toxic, and the pesticide is banned.

a. Describe the potential harmful consequences of such a mistake.

b. Tell which group would be more in favor of avoiding this type of mistake: pesticide manufacturers or environmentalists.

3.52 Suppose a certain type of pesticide actually *is* toxic to humans, but a study erroneously concludes that it is *not* toxic, and the pesticide is kept in use.

a. Describe the potential harmful consequences of such a mistake.

b. Tell which group would be more in favor of avoiding this type of mistake: pesticide manufacturers or environmentalists.

3.53 Suppose that the effect of pesticides on children's absorption levels is thought to depend to some extent on two additional variables, namely the extent of previous exposure to those pesticides and the age of the child. For which of these two variables would it be easier to separate the data when examining the study's results?

3.54 One possible design to study the benefits to infants of breast milk would be a very large observational study. Another possibility would be a blind experiment wherein a very small group of women are provided daily with bottles of breast milk to feed their infants, while another small group is provided with bottles of formula. If differences between breast-fed and bottle-fed infants are, in fact, rather subtle, which study would be more likely to fail to find clear evidence of breast milk's benefits?

CHAPTER 3   SUMMARY

Before summarizing the various design issues discussed in this chapter, we picture a discussion by 4 students concerning television's effects on children's behavior.

Students Talk Stats

Does Watching TV Cause ADHD? Considering Study Design

"Study: Watching TV May Hurt Toddlers' Attention Spans" tells about a report in April 2004 in the journal *Pediatrics* that suggests that too much TV watching in one- and three-year-olds might overstimulate and permanently rewire the developing brain. "The study involved 1,345 children who participated in government-sponsored national health surveys. Their parents were questioned about the children's TV-viewing habits and rated their behavior at age 7 on a scale similar to measures used in diagnosing attention deficit disorders . . . About 36% of the 1-year-olds watched no TV, while 37% watched one to two hours daily and had a 10% to 20% increased risk of attention deficit problems. Fourteen percent watched three to four hours daily and had a 30% to 40% increased risk compared with children who watched no TV. The remainder watched at least 5 hours daily."[30]

Let's picture an in-class discussion of the study by four statistics students who have just learned about sampling and study design.

Adam: *"This experiment has a variable for watching TV, and it's quantitative because they count the hours."*

Brittany: *"You can't just call it quantitative every time you see numbers. They group the kids according to whether they watched no TV, or one to two hours, or three to four hours, or at least five, so really they made TV watching a categorical variable, and it's explanatory. The response is whether or not the kids are attention deficit, and that would be categorical, too. And by the way, it's not an experiment, it's an observational study, because nobody told the kids how much TV to watch."*

Carlos: *"That's a problem with their design. Kids who are likely to turn out to be attention deficit may be the ones who get hooked on TV early because it's more stimulating than shaking a rattle or whatever else they do when they're one year old."*

Dominique: *"The other problem is that parents whose kids turn out to have attention deficit disorder might have guilty consciences about how much TV they let them watch when they were little, and they might remember the TV watching time more clearly than parents whose kids turn out fine. It's one thing to have a retrospective study where people are asked how much TV was watched the day before, but this was like 5 or 6 years later."*

Brittany is correct that both explanatory and response variables would have been categorical, and Carlos is rightly concerned about confounding variables in this observational study. Specifically, the nature of children who would be seduced by the type of stimulation TV provides may predispose them to turn out to have attention deficit disorder. Dominique makes a good point about the dangers of relying on people's memories in a retrospective study.

The lead author of the TV/ADHD study supports his claim with a physiological explanation: "We know from studies of newborn rats that if you expose them to different levels of visual stimuli . . . the architecture of the brain looks very different . . ."[31] Overstimulation at a young age "can create habits of the mind that are ultimately deleterious."

The Big Picture: A CLOSER LOOK

Certainly the results of the TV/ADHD study would have been more convincing if the design had been an experiment. An observational study is much more practical for an explanatory variable like TV viewing, but there have, in fact, been experiments conducted in which researchers took some control over TV viewing. In one such study, researchers persuaded half of the school-age subjects to cut back on TV hours, then compared the subjects' weight gains who did and did not cut back on TV.

This discussion should help impress on statistics students that the answers the discipline provides are rarely black or white. Rather, claims made by statistical reports must be evaluated subjectively, and the reader must decide to what extent he or she is convinced. The expertise you have acquired by now puts you, like our 4 students, in a position to have intelligent discussions about the data production underlying any studies encountered in this book, in other college courses, and in your everyday life.

The Big Picture

Because our goal in statistics is to learn about single variables or relationships, the first step is to record values taken by the variables of interest. We accomplish this in two stages: First, obtain a sample of individuals to be studied; second, assess the variables' values for those sampled individuals via some study design. In Chapter 2, we discussed how to sample individuals that are representative of the larger group of interest. In this chapter, we turned our focus to designing a study that assesses the variables' values in such a way that they accurately reflect what is true for the sampled individuals.

There are several possible designs for gathering information about those individuals.

- **Sample survey:** This is a type of observational study in which individuals report variables' values (often opinions) themselves.

- **Observational study:** Variables' values are recorded as they occur naturally.

- **Experiment:** Researchers take control of the explanatory variables' values and see how changes in its values affect the response of interest.

- **Anecdotal evidence:** Personal accounts are given by just one or a few individuals, selected haphazardly.

When a sample is studied in order to generalize the results to a larger population, two types of error are possible:

- Erroneously conclude that something is "going on" when it isn't

- Erroneously conclude that something is not "going on" when it is

Consequences of both types of mistake should be kept in mind as conclusions are drawn.

Sample Surveys

- **Open questions** are less restrictive but responses are more difficult to summarize.

- **Closed questions** may be biased by options provided.

- Closed questions should permit options "other" or "not sure" if these may apply.

- Questions should be worded neutrally.

- Questions shouldn't be confusing or complicated.

- Survey methods and questions should be carefully designed to elicit honest responses if sensitive issues are involved.

- Beware of precise numbers summarizing hard-to-define concepts.

The type of design used—observational study or experiment—plays an important role in the extent to which we can believe claims that there is evidence of a causal relationship between two variables.

Observational Studies

- Because of confounding variables, it is difficult to establish causation.

- If possible, control for suspected confounding variables by studying groups of similar individuals separately.

- Some confounding variables are difficult to control for; others may not be identified.

- Other pitfalls of observational studies include people behaving differently for a **prospective study** (carried forward in time), and people's faulty memories for a **retrospective study** (carried backward in time).

- A two-sample or paired design is often used to make comparisons in an observational study.

Experiments

- Randomized assignment to treatments automatically controls for confounding variables.

- Making *subjects blind* avoids the **placebo effect** (people's tendency to improve because of the idea of treatment, not the treatment itself).

- Making *researchers blind* avoids conscious or subconscious influences on responses, or on their subjective assessment of responses (called the **experimenter effect**).

- A randomized controlled double-blind experiment is generally optimal for establishing causation.

- Lack of realism may prevent researchers from generalizing experimental results to real-life situations.

- Noncompliance may undermine an experiment.

- Some treatments are impossible, impractical, or unethical to impose.

- Many experiments employ a two-sample design if they compare responses for treatment and control groups. Before randomization, units in an experiment may be blocked (separated into groups of similar individuals) or paired.

CHAPTER 3   EXERCISES

Note: Asterisked numbers indicate exercises whose answers are provided in the Solutions to Selected Exercises section, on page 689.

Additional exercises appeared after each section: various study designs (Section 3.1) page 36, sample surveys (Section 3.2) page 44, observational studies (Section 3.3) page 50, and experiments (Section 3.4) page 59.

Warming Up

3.55 In 2003, The National Research Council estimated that obesity occurs in 25% of dogs and cats in Westernized societies. (Obesity can be determined by squeezing an animal in the lower chest area and seeing if the ribs can be felt.) Perhaps the 25% estimate was obtained by calling homeowners and, if they had a cat or dog, asking them to see if the animal's ribs could be felt by squeezing. Alternatively, the estimate could have been obtained by asking veterinarians to report what percentage of the animals they treat could be classified as obese, using the above method.

Keeping in mind that bias may arise either from a nonrepresentative sample or from inaccurately assessing a variable,

a. Which approach is more likely to lead to a nonrepresentative sample: calling homeowners or asking veterinarians?

b. Which approach is more likely to lead to inaccurate assessments: calling homeowners or asking veterinarians?

3.56 An article entitled "Family Dinners Benefit Teens" claims that "eating dinner together

as a family is one way of keeping teenagers well adjusted and out of trouble."[32]

a. The article's title suggests that which variable is explanatory and which is response?

b. Compose a brief title that would suggest the opposite assignment of explanatory and response roles.

c. The article goes on to say that "adjusted teens . . . ate with their families an average of five days a week; nonadjusted teens ate with their families only three days a week." This statement implies that eating dinner with the family is the response variable; is it being treated as quantitative or categorical?

3.57 Tell which process—data production, displaying and summarizing data, probability, or statistical inference—is the focus of each of these details concerning a survey about famous athletes:

a. The website includes a pie chart showing survey results, and reports that the highest percentage (38%) was for respondents who felt Michael Jordan was the most famous athlete.

b. The website suggests we can conclude that the percentage of all Americans who consider Michael Jordan to be the most

famous athlete is 38%, with a margin of error equal to about 3%.

c. The website tells who was included in the survey and how the question was phrased.

Exploring the Big Picture: SURVEYS

3.58 A survey of 122 families with epileptic children explored the behavior of the family dog in connection with epileptic seizures.

a. It was reported that "20% of families with epileptic children said their pets have the ability to anticipate a seizure. . ." Was this information most likely obtained with an open or a closed question? Is the variable of interest quantitative or categorical?

b. It was also reported that "anticipation time ranged from 10 seconds to five hours, with an average of 2.5 minutes." Was this information most likely obtained with an open or a closed question? Is the variable of interest quantitative or categorical?

c. Furthermore, "responses from the 122 families in the survey reveal protective behaviors by a variety of dogs. For example: A sheltie-spitz mixed breed sits on a child before a drop attack, a seizure that causes an epileptic to fall to the ground. An Akita keeps a young girl away from the stairs 15 minutes before a seizure. And a Great Pyrenees attaches itself to a 3-year-old, forgoing even food and water, hours before the girl has a convulsion." What is the name for this type of evidence?

3.59 "Don't Count Out Prostitutes" reports that "surveys for 15 years have shown that men have more sex partners than women, an

illogical conclusion that has puzzled experts. The General Social Surveys, conducted by the University of Chicago, and the National Health and Social Life Survey, found that men were claiming up to 74% more partners than women."[33]

a. One explanation for the discrepancy would be that there is bias resulting from which one of these difficulties: complicated questions, sensitive questions, or hard-to-define concepts?

b. Is the variable of interest quantitative or categorical?

*3.60 Tell whether the following questions are open or closed.

a. Patti LaBelle sang, "Voulez vous coucher avec moi ce soir?" (Do you want to sleep with me tonight?)

b. Beck sang, "Soy un perdedor. I'm a loser baby so why don't you kill me?"

3.61 Tell whether the following pairs of questions are open or closed.

a. Bill Withers sang, "Who is he (and what is he to you)?"

b. The Beatles sang, "Will you still need me? Will you still feed me when I'm sixty-four?"

3.62 Find song lyrics that pose a question, and tell whether it is open or closed.

Exploring the Big Picture: OBSERVATIONAL STUDIES AND EXPERIMENTS

3.63 Tall Tale? A Study Suggests That Spring Babies Have More Stature" reports that spring babies were found to be taller, by 0.23 of an inch, than those born in the fall. Tell why this had to be an observational study, not an experiment.

3.64 A Swedish researcher proposed a theory that links the production of shoes to the prevalence of schizophrenia: "Heeled footwear began to be used more than 1,000 years ago, and led to the occurrence of the first cases of schizophrenia . . .

Instructors might want to compile students' responses to Exercise 3.62 (including the artist's name, if provided.) A list can be handed out hard-copy or posted on the course website, as at www.pitt.edu/~nancyp/stat-0200/songquestions.html to give students an idea of what music their classmates are listening to.

Mechanization of the production started in Massachusetts, spread from there to England and Germany, and then to the rest of Western Europe. A remarkable increase in schizophrenia prevalence followed the same pattern."[34] Which one of these should make us hesitate before we agree that shoes must cause schizophrenia: confounding variables, people's behaviors affected by their awareness of participating in a prospective study, or people's faulty memories in a retrospective study?

3.65 An article entitled "Breast Milk Benefit" states: "In a review of 212 premature births from 1992 and 1993, the researchers found that 29% of the infants fed human milk acquired infections versus 47% of the babies fed formula."[35]

a. Was this an observational study or an experiment?

b. Which of these would be most worrisome here: confounding variables, people's behaviors affected by their awareness of participating in a prospective study, or people's faulty memories in a retrospective study?

3.66 An article entitled "Breast-Feeding Benefits Bolstered" explains that "hospitals were assigned at random to institute a breast-feeding program . . . in which doctors and midwives gave instruction and counseling. The other hospitals . . . provided the usual obstetric care."[36] Results showed that "about 9% of the infants who had been in the breast-feeding program had at least one intestinal infection in the first year, compared with about 13% in the control group."

a. Was this a paired or a two-sample study?

b. Was this an observational study or an experiment?

c. Are the results from this study more convincing than those from the study described in the previous exercise because of a larger sample size, because of a bigger difference in percentages acquiring infections for breast-fed versus bottle-fed children, or because of a better study design?

3.67 "Boozy Bees May Offer Clues About Pickled People" describes a study in which bees were given various amounts of alcohol, while some bees were given plain sugar water. Researchers noted that the alcohol killed some of the bees, and it also affected some of the bees' behavior in terms of sociability and industriousness.

a. Was this an experiment, an observational study, or a sample survey?

b. Was there a control group? If so, describe it.

c. The researchers actually were interested in learning more about how alcohol affects humans. Explain why they studied bees instead.

d. If a researcher must assess how sociable a bee is, is it important for the researcher to be unaware of how much alcohol (if any) the bee consumed?

e. If a researcher must assess whether or not a bee survived the study, is it important for the researcher to be unaware of how much alcohol (if any) the bee consumed?

f. It is reported that alcohol killed some of the bees. Would these results be summarized with a mean or with a proportion?

3.68 A Quaker Oatmeal box reported the following: "100 people in Lafayette, Colorado volunteered to eat a good-sized bowl of oatmeal for 30 days to see if simple lifestyle changes—like eating oatmeal—could help reduce cholesterol. After 30 days, 98 lowered their cholesterol. With these great results, the people in Lafayette proved to themselves that simple changes can make a real difference."[37]

a. Was this an observational study or an experiment?

b. There are two variables of interest. What was the explanatory variable?

c. Was the explanatory variable categorical or quantitative?

d. What was the response variable?

e. Was the response variable categorical or quantitative?

f. Describe the treatment group.

g. Was there a randomized assignment to treatment or control? Explain.

h. Describe other possible reasons, besides eating oatmeal, that could account for the participants' cholesterol being lowered.

i. Which one of these is more problematic here: experimenter effect or Hawthorne effect?

j. Would Quaker Oats' results have been more convincing if it had used 1,000 instead of 100 volunteers?

k. Describe details of a study design that might be more effective than this one in establishing whether or not oatmeal lowers cholesterol.

3.69 Suppose that the effect of consuming oatmeal on cholesterol level is thought to depend to some extent on two additional variables—gender and degree of fitness. For which of these two variables would it be easier to separate the data when exploring the relationship between oatmeal consumption and cholesterol level?

3.70 In which study would noncompliance be more of a problem: a study that asks participants to eat oatmeal for 30 days, or a study that asks participants to use pesticides for 2 years?

*3.71 In which study could the experimenter effect be more of a problem: a study in which the response of interest is cholesterol levels, or a study in which the response of interest is how sociable a bee's behavior is?

3.72 In which study could the experimenter effect be more of a problem: a study in which the response of interest is people's feelings of self-esteem, or a study in which the response of interest is the size of a wound, in square centimeters?

*3.73 Which of these studies would cost more money to carry out: the study that tests if eating oatmeal every day for a month lowers cholesterol levels, or the study that tests children's absorption of pesticides by paying their parents to use certain pesticides over the course of 2 years?

3.74 Which of these studies would cost more money to carry out: the study that tests whether writing has an effect on healing when tissue has been removed from the upper arm under anesthesia, or the study that tests whether people's self-esteem is lowered if they are asked to think about times when they had bad hair?

3.75 A study at Northwestern University "evaluated 67 normal, mentally healthy, suburban males initially in 1962, when the boys were 14, and in 1997, when the men were 48."[38] One interesting finding was that "44% of the men 'remembered' that when they were teenagers, they believed that it was OK to have sex during high school. However, only 15% of the participants felt this way when they were questioned as teenagers."

Four statistics students are asked to tell what this finding suggests, in terms of which of these study designs we should be skeptical of in general: retrospective observational studies, prospective observational studies, studies where the treatment is unethical, or experiments that are not double-blind. Which student gives the best response?

Adam: It shows you should be skeptical of experiments with a lack of realism. When you're in your forties, getting into the teenage mindset is too unrealistic.

Brittany: The difference in percentages is so big, I think the men must have been influenced by whoever was asking the questions. That's always a problem if a study isn't double-blind.

Carlos: This is a prospective observational study, carried forward in time from 1962 to 1997, so that's the type of study you should be skeptical of.

Dominique: The study itself is prospective, but the point is that people don't remember things from the past very accurately. So it teaches us to be skeptical of retrospective studies.

Discovering Research: STUDY DESIGN

3.76 Find (and hand in) an article or Internet report about a sample survey. Tell if each variable of interest is quantitative or categorical. Tell what is the suggested population of interest. Then tell how the individuals were selected and whether or not you believe they adequately represent the population of interest. Discuss whether there are any clear sources of bias. Were the questions open or closed?

3.77 Find (and hand in) an article or report about an observational study. Tell what the variables of interest are, whether they are quantitative or categorical, and which is explanatory and response (if there are two variables). Are there any potential confounding variables that should have been controlled for?

3.78 Find (and hand in) an article or report about an experiment. Tell what the variables of interest are, whether they are quantitative or categorical, and which is explanatory and response. Describe the subjects, treatments, whether or not the subjects were blind, whether or not the researchers were blind, and whether there are any obvious problems with the experiment's design.

Reporting on Research: STUDY DESIGN

3.79 Use results of Exercises 3.16, 3.17, 3.18 and 3.21 and relevant findings from the Internet to make a report on gun control that relies on statistical information.

Part II

Displaying and Summarizing Data

Displaying and Summarizing Data: An Overview

Before going into detail about the two steps in data production—sampling and design—we discussed the fact that the way we handle statistical problems depends on the number and type of variables involved. We either have a single categorical variable, a single quantitative variable, or a relationship between, respectively, a categorical and a quantitative variable, two categorical variables, or two quantitative variables. Categorical variables are summarized by telling counts, proportions, or percents in the category of interest, whereas quantitative variables are often summarized by reporting the mean. Whenever we are interested in the relationship between two variables, it is important to establish which (if any) plays the role of explanatory variable and which is the response. The roles played by the variables will determine which displays and summaries are appropriate.

Once we establish what is true about a variable or relationship in a random *sample,* we will be in a position to say something about what is true for the larger *population.* Throughout this book, we must take care to distinguish between samples and populations.

> *Definitions* A number that summarizes a sample is called a **statistic.** A number that summarizes the population is called a **parameter.**

The most common statistics of interest are the sample proportion $\hat{p}$ (called "p-hat") and the sample mean $\bar{x}$ (called "x-bar"), corresponding to the parameters population proportion p and population mean μ (called "mu"). These will be formally defined as we encounter them in Chapter 4.

Identifying Statistics and Parameters

Here are some situations featuring either statistics or parameters.

■ 19% of 2,366 surveyed Americans said they believed money can buy happiness.

In this situation, the sample proportion, 0.19, is a statistic $\hat{p}$. The unknown proportion of all Americans who believe money can buy happiness is a parameter p.

- A *New York Times* article entitled "The DNA 200" reports that the first 200 inmates to be cleared through DNA evidence, from January 1989 to April 2007, averaged 12 years in prison.[1]

  Here the number 12 is a parameter μ because it is talking about the mean years for the population of all 200 inmates exonerated thus far.

Keeping the Big Picture in Perspective

In Part I, we learned about good sampling technique, to ensure that the sample truly represents the larger population about which we want to draw conclusions. We also learned how to design good studies so that the information obtained about the variables or relationships accurately reflects the truth about the sampled individuals. Adhering to good principles of sampling and design is vital for the theory developed in Part III, when we assume a population parameter is known, and learn how the corresponding sample statistic behaves. The behavior is predictable only if the statistic summarizes data values that are unbiased. The same principles continue to be essential for the more practical techniques learned in Part IV, when we use sample statistics to draw conclusions about unknown population parameters. Again, those conclusions will be correct only if the statistic is unbiased.

Keeping in mind that the sampling technique and study design could have an impact on the data that are produced, we undertake in Part II to summarize data gathered about single variables and about relationships. In other words, we will now learn how to find relevant sample statistics for the data at hand. The following diagram shows how summarizing data fits into the "big picture" of statistics.

Some instructors prefer to obtain their own survey data. Their results can easily be substituted for those referenced in this book.

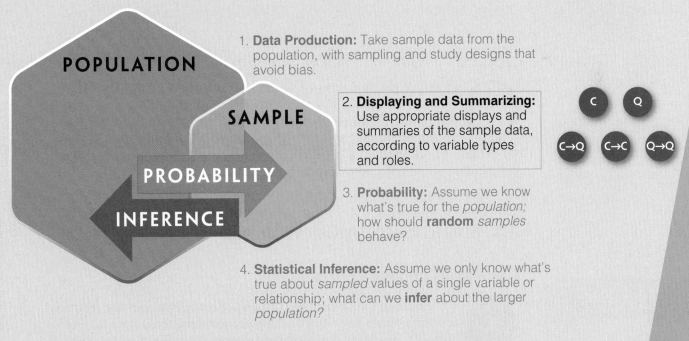

1. **Data Production:** Take sample data from the population, with sampling and study designs that avoid bias.

2. **Displaying and Summarizing:** Use appropriate displays and summaries of the sample data, according to variable types and roles.

3. **Probability:** Assume we know what's true for the *population;* how should **random** *samples* behave?

4. **Statistical Inference:** Assume we only know what's true about *sampled* values of a single variable or relationship; what can we **infer** about the larger *population?*

Results of a survey taken by several hundred students in introductory statistics classes at a particular university provide a good source of real-life examples corresponding to each of the 5 variable situations, from one categorical variable to two quantitative variables. These students reported their age, whether or not they'd eaten breakfast that day, how many minutes they spent on the computer the day before, and so on. To gain experience in working with real data, we will often produce displays and summaries, and later perform statistical inference, using this data set. Because our summaries of the survey data correspond to a sample, we will treat those summaries as statistics, not parameters.

Displaying and Summarizing Data for a Single Variable

For a sample of students, what percentage ate breakfast? What are the students' mean earnings?

Survey of breakfast habits: Which one of these surveyed students was typical?

O f the five possible types of situations for single variables or relationships discussed in this book, we start with situations involving a *single categorical variable*—typified by the question about breakfast posed above—and then those involving a *single quantitative variable*, as in the question about earnings. This chapter will deal more or less exclusively with such situations. We will cover relationships in Chapter 5.

4.1 Single Categorical Variable

Summaries and Pie Charts

C We begin with summaries and displays of categorical variables because they turn out to be quite a bit simpler than those for quantitative variables. Pie charts and bar graphs are the most common displays used for data about one categorical variable. To summarize the data, we report counts or percents or proportions.

We defined counts, proportions, and percentages on page 5 as ways of summarizing categorical variables: the number of individuals in a category of interest is called the *count* in this category. The count divided by the total number of individuals is called the *proportion* in the category of interest. The proportion can be multiplied by 100 to convert it to a *percentage*. These summaries are easily displayed with a pie chart.

The Big Picture:
A CLOSER LOOK

Other words such as *rate* or *risk* may be used to refer to percents or proportions; *risk* suggests an undesirable response such as injury, illness, or death.

> *Definition*   A **pie chart** displays categorical data by dividing a circular region into slices whose areas correspond to the proportions or percentages in each category. The total area of the pie is 1, or 100%.

EXAMPLE 4.1 ISSUES TO CONSIDER IN SUMMARIZING A CATEGORICAL VARIABLE

Background: In a survey of 446 students at a certain university, 246 had eaten breakfast that day.

Questions:

1. Do you think our sample—students in many introductory statistics classes at a certain university, offered at various times throughout the day—could be considered a fairly representative (unbiased) sample of all students at that university?

2. The data were gathered via an anonymous computer survey that asked, "Did you eat breakfast today? Answer *yes* or *no.*" Is there good reason to expect an unbiased response?

3. How can we display and summarize the information for our sample?

4. Note that more than half—55%—in our sample of 446 students ate breakfast. Assuming our sample is representative and responses are unbiased, can we be pretty sure that a majority of *all* college students eat breakfast on any given day? In other words, we know the *statistic* sample proportion is more than 0.5. Can we conclude that the *parameter,* unknown population proportion, is also more than 0.5?

Responses:

1. The students included in this sample do seem to comprise a good cross-section of the larger population of students at the university.

Pie Chart of Breakfast

No (200, 44.8%)

Yes (246, 55.2%)

2. There should be no reason to expect responses to be biased because eating breakfast is not at all controversial or sensitive.

3. The information can be displayed with a pie chart. The responses are summarized by hand or with software, reporting counts or percentages answering no or yes. These are included in the pie chart display. Thus, a majority of students (about 55%) in the sample ate breakfast.

4. The last question comes under the realm of statistical inference. At this point, it is not clear whether a sample proportion of 0.55 could convince us that the population proportion is greater than 0.50. However, we will eventually develop the skills to respond knowledgeably to this and similar questions.

Example TBP 4.1 on page 768 of the *Teaching the Big Picture* **(TBP)** *Supplement* shows how we produce and process

Because the distinction between statistics (which summarize samples) and parameters (which summarize populations) is so important, we take care to distinguish between these with correct notation. Sample proportion, a statistic, is denoted $\hat{p}$ (called "p-hat"), whereas population proportion, a parameter, is denoted p. In Example 4.1, we know $\hat{p} = 0.55$, and we are wondering if we can conclude that $p > 0.5$.

Definitions $\hat{p}$ is the **sample proportion** in a given category and p is the **population proportion**.

EXAMPLE 4.2 NOTATION FOR A PROPORTION FROM A SAMPLE OR A POPULATION

Background: A *New York Times* article from June 1, 2004 entitled "New York Fiction, by the Numbers" tells about an undergraduate engineering student at Princeton who performed a statistical analysis of stories published in *The New Yorker* under two different editors. She focused on many variables, such as writer's gender, characters' religion, and main story topics. She found that the proportion of all stories published between 1995 and 2001 that dealt with sex was 0.47.[2]

Questions: What notation do we use for the number 0.47? If the student had simply taken a sample of stories from that time period, how would we denote the sample proportion that dealt with sex?

Responses: Because 0.47 is a population proportion, we denote it p. A sample proportion would be denoted $\hat{p}$.

Practice: *Try Exercise 4.3(c) on page 78.*

Statistics is more than just a collection of tools like how to find proportions or draw pie charts. In order to interpret such summaries and displays, we need to consider other important aspects of the data, such as sample size and possible bias. We now address some of these issues, along with additional information about summaries and displays.

The Role of Sample Size: Why Some Proportions Tell Us More Than Others Do

Our intuition tells us that larger samples are more informative than smaller ones. The reason why this is in fact correct has to do with probability.

Students may be under the mistaken impression that probability is taught as a sort of side-dish to accompany statistics—a way of filling up a semester with material. We can assure them that probability is necessary in order to quantify the extent to which statisticians can use information from a sample to say what should be true for the larger population. Sample size plays an essential role in this quantification.

EXAMPLE 4.3 PROPORTIONS FROM DIFFERENT SAMPLE SIZES

Background: Suppose one sample includes 20 students, and 55% (that is, 11 out of 20) eat breakfast. A second sample includes 2,000 students, and 55% (that is, 1,100 out of 2,000) eat breakfast.

Question: Which of these would be more likely to convince you that a majority of all college students eat breakfast, or are they equally convincing?

Response: Even though the percentages are identical, there is a big difference between 55% of 20 and 55% of 2,000, and the difference has to do with *probabilities*. Your intuition should tell you that even if only half of all students eat breakfast, it is not so improbable that in a sample of just 20 students, as many as 11 would happen to eat breakfast. On the other hand, if only half of all students eat breakfast, it should seem rather improbable to you that as many as 1,100 in a sample of 2,000 eat breakfast.

Practice: *Try Exercise 4.3(i) on page 79.*

In our example about eating breakfast or not, the categorical variable of interest had just two possible values that could be expressed as a simple *yes* or *no*. There are plenty of situations allowing for more than two possibilities, such as in the following example.

EXAMPLE 4.4 PROPORTIONS IN THREE CATEGORIES

Background: A student wrote in to "Ask Marilyn" in *Parade* magazine about whether or not she should resist the urge to go back and change her answers in multiple-choice tests. Marilyn replied as follows:

"Nicholas Skinner, a psychologist at King's College in Ontario, says nearly every study on the matter shows the following surprise: About 50% of changes go from wrong to right; 25% go from right to wrong; and 25% go from wrong to wrong . . ."[3]

Question: Do we summarize or display differently when our categorical variable has more than 2 possibilities?

Response: In this case, where the nature of multiple-choice answer changes has three possibilities, we can still summarize with percentages and display with a pie chart.

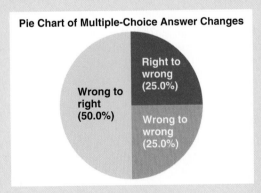

Pie Chart of Multiple-Choice Answer Changes

Practice: *Try Exercise 4.4(a–c) on page 79.*

Bar Graphs: Another Way to Visualize Categorical Data

Whereas a pie chart represents proportions or percentages in various categories using *areas* of the pie's slices, a bar graph represents proportions using *heights* of bars.

Although our main focus in this part of the book is to simply summarize variables and relationships, such as using sample proportion $\hat{p}$ to summarize values of a single categorical variable, it helps to keep in mind that eventually we will want to make some "educated guesses" about the unknown population proportion. Example 4.3 previews this formal inference process by exposing students to the natural, intuitive reasoning behind it.

When we develop a formal theory of categorical variables, we will concentrate on those that just have two possibilities, following the binomial model.

The Big Picture: A CLOSER LOOK

Students who seek the best test-taking strategy should remember that these percentages are referring to large numbers of test-takers who have been observed in studies. Certainly there are individual students who tend to change answers to their own advantage more often than what is typical, and other students who "shoot themselves in the foot" more often than 25% of the time.

Students may wonder if a bar graph is the same thing as a histogram. A bar graph is designed to summarize a categorical variable, whereas a histogram is designed to summarize a quantitative variable. An important difference is that because a bar graph has no numerical scale for the horizontal axis, the width of its bars is arbitrary. The width of bars in a histogram must correspond to the precise range of numerical values being accounted for. Histograms will be discussed in the next section.

> *Definition*   A **bar graph** shows proportions in various categories (marked on a horizontal axis) with bars of corresponding heights.

EXAMPLE 4.5 CONSTRUCTING A BAR GRAPH

Background: "Lab Still Most Popular Dog" reports American Kennel Club registrations for the year 2003[4]:

Breed	No. Registered
Labrador retrievers	144,934
Golden retrievers	52,530
Beagles	45,033
German shepherds	43,950
Dachshunds	39,473
Yorkshire terriers	38,256
Boxers	34,136
Poodles	32,176
Shih tzus	26,935
Chihuahuas	24,930
Other	433,318
Total	915,671

Question: How can we display this information?

Response: A pie chart might turn out to be a bit crowded because of all the different categories listed. Instead, we can construct a bar graph, identifying the values of our categorical variable (dog breed) along the horizontal axis. This graph uses the vertical axis to show *counts* of dogs in each breed category. Alternatively, we could have divided each count by 915,671 to show *proportions* or *percentages*.

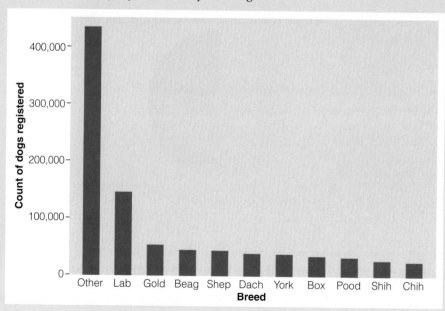

Either way, the graph makes it obvious to what extent Labrador retrievers were the most popular breed in 2003, numbering almost three times as much as the next most popular breed.

Practice: *Try Exercise 4.6(a) on page 80.*

Examples TBP 4.2 and TBP 4.3 on page 769 of the *TBP Supplement* discuss the relative merits of pie charts and bar graphs, and the ordering of bars.

Mode and Majority: The Value That Dominates

Besides summarizing a categorical variable by reporting percentages in the various possible categories, we may also point out—as we did in Example 4.5 on dog breeds—which category has the highest percentage. This value is referred to as the *mode*. The theory that we will develop for categorical variables will be restricted for the most part to situations where the variable has just two possible values. In this case, the mode is just the value for which the percentage is more than 50%. Therefore, rather than referring to the "mode" in many examples, we will point out which value is in the majority or which is in the minority.

> *Definitions*   The **mode** is the most common value taken by a variable. If a categorical variable has just two possible values, the one with a higher percentage shows the **majority** and the one with a lower percentage shows the **minority**.

EXAMPLE 4.6 MODE, MAJORITY, AND MINORITY

Background: In Example 4.1, 55% of sampled students ate breakfast. In Example 4.4, it was reported that 25% of students' exam response changes go from right to wrong.

Question: What is the mode for each of the variables mentioned, and what can we say in terms of a majority or minority of values?

Response: Eating breakfast is the mode, because it is more common than not eating breakfast, and a *majority* of sampled students ate breakfast because 55% is more than 50%. Changing to a right answer is the mode for the second variable, whereas a *minority* of answer changes go from right to wrong.

Practice: *Try Exercise 4.7(b) on page 80.*

Revisiting Two Types of Bias

Next we consider a survey for which we encounter bias due to the sampling method, as well as bias due to how the categorical variable's values are recorded.

For the various statistical skills developed in this book, students need to become accustomed to thinking about categorical data in terms of both counts and proportions. The theory to be developed in Part III on probability is based on the behavior of binomial counts, such as *122* workers. However, in order to perform inference in Part IV, we will gradually shift our focus to proportions, such as *0.71* of the workers revealing their passwords.

Students Talk Stats

Biased Sample, Biased Assessment

Suppose a group of statistics students are discussing a report they've encountered on a news website, entitled "Office Workers Give Away Passwords for a Chocolate Bar!" The report, from Infosecurity Europe in April 2004, goes on to describe how 71% of 172 office workers—that is, 122—willingly revealed their computer password to a surveyor posted outside a London subway station at rush hour.[5]

Adam: *"I can't believe that 71% of the people in England are willing to sell their passwords for a candy bar. Those Cadbury bars aren't even that good."*

Brittany: *"Don't believe it. The report is only about those 172 workers, and they weren't a random sample or anything."*

Carlos: *"It was an easy way to get a free candy bar. How's that surveyor going to check if the passwords were real?"*

Dominique: *"I guess if you really want to find out anything useful, you'd have to try to get a random sample, and then have some way of checking if the passwords were authentic. But I still believe a lot of people aren't very security-conscious, in this country too."*

In a situation like this, we must be careful about drawing conclusions like, "71% of *all* London office workers are willing to reveal their computer password." Those 172 workers were a convenience sample, as we discussed on page 19 of Part I, not a random sample. There was no follow-up to verify that the "passwords" exchanged for a candy bar were authentic. Therefore, bias may enter in on two fronts: through a sample that is nonrepresentative of the larger population, and through incorrect assessment of the variable's values. Nevertheless, the poll's results do suggest that many workers are not as security-conscious as they should be.

EXERCISES FOR SECTION 4.1

Single Categorical Variables

Note: Asterisked numbers indicate exercises whose answers are provided in the Solutions to Selected Exercises section, on page 689.

4.1   According to the Centers for Disease Control, the risk of dying by suicide in the year 2000 was 1 in 12,091, whereas the risk of dying by homicide was 1 in 15,440. Which type of death was more likely?

4.2   National Football League coaches are supposed to classify injured players as being "doubtful" if their chance of playing in the next game is 25%, "questionable" if the chance is 50%, and "probable" if the chance is 75%. On a Friday in November 2004, 20 football players were listed as doubtful, 76 as questionable, and 88 as probable.

   a. Draw a pie chart to display the information from that Friday, using three "slices."

   b. Draw a bar graph to display the information from that Friday, using the vertical axis for counts.

   c. Draw a bar graph to display the information from that Friday, using the vertical axis for percents.

   d. Your displays were only for injured players. What additional information would you need in order to display percentages for all the NFL players that day?

*4.3   An article entitled "Study Indicates Racial Disparity in Traffic Stops" reports on a study of more than 2,000 traffic stops by police in a certain city. "Overall, the study showed 25% of all stops during a 6-month period involved black motorists, even though blacks account for 12% of the driving-age population. Whites were involved in 67% of the stops, but are 83% of the city's driving-age population."[6]

a. Was this an experiment, an observational study, or a sample survey?

b. Consider the traffic stops over that 6-month period to constitute a sample taken from all traffic stops over a period of years. Which of the above percentages are statistics? Which of the above percentages are parameters?

c. Would we denote the proportion 0.25 as p or $\hat{p}$?

d. Which of these pie charts represents the percentages of traffic stops that involved each race (not the overall percentages of the driving-age population)—the one on the left or the one on the right?

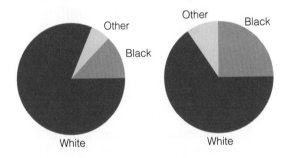

e. As far as the "Other" minorities were concerned, did the police stop a higher or a lower percentage than what occurs in the driving-age population?

f. Let's assume that if there is any chance of discrimination on the part of the traffic police, we want to be sure it is identified and rectified. Which type of mistake should experts try harder to avoid when drawing general conclusions from the study: making a claim that racial profiling exists when, in fact, it does not, or making a claim that racial profiling does not exist when, in fact, it does?

g. The information provided may cause us to wonder: "If only 12% of the city's drivers are black, and if police really weren't discriminating against black drivers, then what is the chance that in over 2,000 stops they just happened to get at least 25% who were black?" Which statistical process applies here—displaying and summarizing data, probability, or statistical inference?

h. One could argue that the difference between 12% and 25% seems significant because the larger percentage is more than _____ times the size of the smaller percentage.

i. Does the fact that the sample size (2,000) is very large make it more convincing or less convincing that there is systematic bias on the part of the traffic police?

*4.4 A survey of college students asked them to report their height, age, favorite color, living situation (on or off campus), whether they smoked or not, how many cigarettes were smoked the previous day for those who identified themselves as smokers, and if they'd eaten breakfast that day.

a. Identify all the categorical variables in this data set.

b. Which of these categorical variables has more than two possible values?

c. Use the fact that there are 20 cigarettes in a pack to describe a way to treat the number of cigarettes smoked as a categorical variable with two possible values.

d. Taking the survey respondents to be a sample from a larger population of students, if we report percentages of surveyed students in the various category responses, would these be statistics (summarizing a sample) or parameters (summarizing a population)?

e. In a face-to-face interview with a health center nurse, if 15% of the students claim to be smokers, can we conclude that about 15% of the larger population of students smoke?

4.5 A survey of college students asked them to report their math SAT score, verbal SAT score, whether or not they were vegetarian, their weight, how many credits they were taking, whether or not they had pierced ears, how much money they'd earned the previous year, how much cash they were carrying, and year at school as 1st, 2nd, 3rd, 4th, or "other."

a. Identify all the categorical variables in this data set.

b. Which of these categorical variables has more than two possible values?

c. Use the fact that students with 12 credits or more are considered "full-time" to describe a way to treat credits taken as a categorical variable with just two possible values.

d. Taking the survey respondents to be a sample from a larger population of students, if we report percentages of surveyed students in the various category responses, would these be statistics or parameters?

*4.6 Exercise 4.3 considered a study of more than 2,000 traffic stops by police in a certain city.

  a. The pie charts convey the extent of racial profiling by allowing us to compare the size of the pie slice for blacks in the population with the size of the slice for blacks who were stopped by traffic police. How would bar graphs convey this information?

  b. Which type of display is better to show evidence of racial profiling: two pie charts, two bar graphs, or both about the same?

  c. If bar graphs are used, is there one "best" way to order the bars according to race?

*4.7 A study was to be conducted to explore the effects of sugar intake on activity level of children. Researchers recruited 48 children for the study, and began by classifying the children as being of preschool age (P) or in elementary school (E).

```
E  P  P  P  P  E  E  P  P  P  E  P
E  E  E  P  E  P  E  P  E  P  E  E
E  P  P  E  P  P  P  P  P  E  E  E
E  E  P  E  P  E  E  E  P  P  P  P
```

  a. What percentage of children were in preschool and what percentage were in elementary school?

  b. Which type of school is in the majority?

  c. What other word can be used in general to describe a value that is in the majority?

  d. If a researcher wants to report the proportion of participants in elementary school, should this be denoted as p or $\hat{p}$?

  e. If the researchers suspect that age may play an important role in the extent to which sugar intake affects activity, tell how this should be incorporated into the study's design.

4.8 In an informal anonymous survey in a statistics class in October 2004, students were asked:

"Will you vote in the presidential election this November?" Their responses are listed in this table.

Yes	Unsure	Yes	No	Yes	Yes	Yes	Yes
Yes	Yes	Yes	Yes	Yes	Yes	No	Yes
No	No	Unsure	Yes	No	Yes	Yes	Yes
Yes	Yes	No	Unsure	Yes	Yes	Yes	Yes
Yes	Yes	Yes	No	Yes	Yes	Yes	Yes
Yes	Yes	Yes	Yes	Yes	Yes	Yes	Yes
Yes	Yes	Yes	Yes				

  a. What percentage answered *Yes*?

  b. What percentage answered *No*?

  c. What percentage answered *Unsure*?

  d. Display the results in a pie chart.

  e. A telephone survey of a random sample of 1,202 college undergraduates by Harvard University's Institute of Politics in October 2004 reported that a record high, 84%, would "definitely" be voting in the upcoming presidential election. Does the percentage for the informal survey above come within 10% of Harvard's percentage?

  f. Suppose the option "*Unsure*" had not been provided in the survey, and the students who were unsure all answered "*Yes.*" Draw the pie chart for this scenario and tell how it differs from the original one.

4.9 A *New York Times* article called "A Big Professional Headache" reports that "neurologists suffer many more migraines than the general population, [. . .] and for those neurologists who specialize in treating headaches, the incidence is even higher [. . .] Eighteen percent of women and 6% of men in the general population say they have at least one migraine in a given year. Among women practicing neurology, the figure was 58%, and among the men, 34%. The difference was even more pronounced for headache specialists. Seventy-four percent of the women reported having migraines, as did 59% of the men."[7]

  a. Was this an experiment or an observational study?

  b. If we are only interested in whether or not a person suffers from migraines, then we are considering a single categorical variable. The study described above actually features two additional variables. Tell what they are and if they are quantitative or categorical.

c. Does this pair of pie charts depict percentages for men and women in the general population, among neurologists, or among headache specialists?

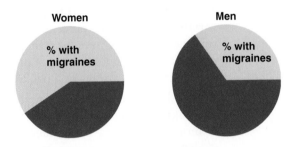

Women   **Men**

% with migraines   % with migraines

d. Report results for female and male neurologists, using the word "risk."

e. Report results for female and male neurologists, using the words "majority" and "minority."

f. The researchers who reported these results wrote that, "perhaps the prevalence of migraine in the general population is greater than studies would suggest, and neurologists are either better able to self-diagnose or better able to remember headaches with specific features." Is this suggesting bias in the assessment of the variable's values, or is it providing an explanation for why neurologists may actually be different from the rest of the population with respect to suffering from migraines?

g. An alternative explanation, according to the article, is that "doctors with histories of migraines are drawn to study them, or that the kind of people who become neurologists are the kind of people who get migraines." Is this suggesting bias in the assessment of the variable's values, or is it providing an explanation for why neurologists may actually be different from the rest of the population with respect to migraines?

4.10 A newspaper article entitled "Study: TV Shows Tend to Be Bi-coastal" reports in November 2004 that of all that year's 1,696 cable and network series, "a whopping 601 called California home and 412 were set in New York state."[8]

a. What percentage of series were located in other settings besides California and New York?

b. Would this percentage be considered a statistic or a parameter?

c. Draw a pie chart to display the information, using three "slices."

d. Draw a bar graph to display the information, using the vertical axis for counts.

e. Draw a bar graph to display the information, using the vertical axis for percents.

f. Describe at least two possible ways to order the bars in your graph.

g. Explain why the process of statistical inference would not be appropriate for the data presented.

4.11 For which situation is it most appropriate to talk about a proportion as a "risk": when considering locations of TV shows, when considering destinations of tourists, or when considering whether a child suffers from strep throat?

4.12 Psychology researchers from the University of California, San Diego, set about finding an answer to the question, "Do dogs resemble their owners?" In their study, "28 student judges were asked to match photos of dogs with their owners. Each student was presented with a photo of a dog owner and photos of two dogs; one dog was the actual pet, the other was an imposter. If more than half of the judges correctly paired a given dog with his or her owner, this was considered a "match." Forty-five dogs took part in the study—25 purebreds and 20 mutts. [. . .] Overall, there were just 23 matches (as defined above). However, the judges had an easier time with the purebred dogs: 16 matches, versus 7 for the mixed breeds."[9]

a. Overall, what proportion of the 45 dogs were correctly matched with their owners?

b. Of the 25 purebreds, what proportion were correctly matched with the dogs' owners?

c. Suppose only 3 dogs were included in the study. Would it be common, or would it be unusual, for at least two-thirds to be matched correctly, purely by chance?

d. Your answer to part (b) indicates that a clear majority in the sample were able to match correctly for the purebred dogs. If this proportion were being used as evidence that, in general, people can match purebred dogs to their owners, would it be more convincing, less convincing, or equally convincing if it arose from a sample of 250 dogs instead of 25?

Were this dog and owner made for each other?

© Morgan David de Lossy/CORBIS

Using Software [see Technology Guide]

4.13 Access the student survey data, completed by 446 students in introductory statistics courses at a large university in the fall of 2003.

a. Use software to report the percentage who *did* carry a cell phone at the time.

b. Use software to report the percentage who did *not* carry a cell phone at the time.

c. Do you think that by now the percentage who do carry a cell phone is higher, lower, or about the same?

*4.14 Access the student survey data, completed by 446 students in introductory statistics courses at a large university in the fall of 2003.

a. Use software to sort the numbers of cigarettes smoked by the students who are smokers, then convert to a categorical variable by telling the percentage who smoked less than a pack, and the percentage who smoked a pack or more. (There are 20 cigarettes in a pack.)

b. Which should be higher—the percentage of smoking students who smoke a pack or more a day, or the percentage of all students who smoke a pack or more a day?

4.15 Access the student survey data, completed by 446 students in introductory statistics courses at a large university in the fall of 2003. Use software to sort the numbers of credits taken by the surveyed students, then convert to a categorical variable by telling the percentage who were part-time (took less than 12 credits) and the percentage who were full-time.

4.16 Access the student survey data, completed by 446 students in introductory statistics courses at a large university in the fall of 2003. Use software to report the percentages in the various years (1st, 2nd, 3rd, 4th, and other). Are the percentages fairly evenly divided? Explain.

4.2 Single Quantitative Variables and the Shape of a Distribution

Q Displays and summaries for single categorical variables, presented in the preceding section, were relatively simple: display with a pie chart or bar graph, and summarize with a proportion. In contrast, there is a lot more going on when we consider a number-valued data set. Whenever we are interested in the overall pattern of behavior of a quantitative variable, we consider the *distribution* of its values.

Definition A **distribution** consists of all the possible values of a variable and how frequently they occur.

Thinking about Quantitative Data

To begin thinking about number-valued variables, we look at a simple example.

EXAMPLE 4.7 ISSUES TO CONSIDER IN SUMMARIZING
A QUANTITATIVE VARIABLE

Background: Suppose a large sample of students in introductory statistics classes at a particular university were asked via an anonymous computer survey, "How much money did you earn last year, to the nearest thousand dollars?"

Questions:

1. Would the data be fairly representative of earnings of the population of all students at that particular university? Would they be representative of earnings of students at *any* university?

2. Is there good reason to expect an unbiased response to the question about earnings?

3. How should we summarize the information for this sample?

4. If earnings for the sample of students averaged $3,776, can we be pretty sure that *all* students at that university averaged less than $5,000?

Responses:

1. The earnings of introductory statistics students at a particular university should be fairly representative of earnings of all students at that university, as long as students in a wide variety of majors and years have reason to take statistics. But we should not generalize to students attending *all* universities, because socio-economic levels of students may vary quite a bit from school to school, depending on tuition and other factors.

2. If students are asked to report their earnings out loud to the rest of the class, they may not do so honestly if they have no earnings at all, or if their earnings are unusually high. In contrast, the anonymous responses to a computer survey described above should be fairly accurate.

3. To summarize the information, we would like to report a few key words or numbers, instead of reporting a long list of earnings values. This will be the main task of this section and the next.

4. Once again we must recognize the distinction between summarizing sample data and performing inference about the larger population. It's one thing to observe that our *sampled* students averaged less than $5,000. At this point, however, we cannot claim that the same would necessarily be true for earnings of the larger *population* of students.

The Big Picture: LOOKING BACK

In Chapter 2 (on sampling) we stated that in *theory*, the best way to guarantee that the sample truly represents the population is for the sample to be random. In *practice*, samples are chosen in a wide variety of ways. Common sense is often the best guideline in deciding whether or not a sample truly represents the population.

Clearly, we will not be in a position to draw conclusions about the larger population unless we have good reason to believe that our sample summary is unbiased.

EXAMPLE **4.8** BIAS FROM A NONREPRESENTATIVE SAMPLE

Background: While most courses at a university are worth 3 credits, the introductory statistics course is worth 4 credits.

Question: Can we use the number of credits taken by introductory statistics students to draw conclusions about the number of credits taken by all students at that university?

Response: No: These students would tend to have an extra credit that semester, leading to a biased sample.

Practice: *Try Exercise 4.17 on page 92.*

EXAMPLE **4.9** A BIASED ASSESSMENT OF SAMPLED VALUES

Background: After the fatal crash of a small plane in North Carolina in January 2002, the FAA became concerned about excess weight on planes. An article entitled "F.A.A. Reviews Rules on Passenger Weight After Crash" reports that thousands of passengers flying on small planes in the following month would "have to tell ticket agents how much they weigh, or step on a scale, to check whether existing estimates of average passenger weight are accurate [. . .]. The airlines will be adding 10 pounds to whatever passengers tell them they weigh. Peggy Gilligan, director of flight standards at the FAA, said people 'usually lie in the single digits.'"[10]

Question: How does the possible source of bias here differ from the bias discussed in Example 4.8?

Response: Gilligan's comment makes it clear that the FAA realizes its sample of weights would be biased toward underestimates if the design used to collect the data were to ask passengers themselves to report their weights, instead of to actually weigh them. The concern here is not about the sample failing to be representative of the larger population. Rather, the FAA must guard against a biased assessment of the sampled values *after* a representative sample has been obtained.

Practice: *Try Exercise 4.18 on page 92.*

Once we have screened our sampling and study designs for possible bias, we are ready to display and summarize our quantitative data set. To describe the distribution of values of a quantitative variable, we report its *shape, center,* and *spread.*

Definitions The **shape** of a distribution indicates which values tend to be more or less common. The **center** is a measure of what is typical. The **spread** is a way of measuring how much the distribution's values vary.

In most distributions, certain values tend to be more common than others. Knowing the shape gives us an idea of which values are more common or less common.

One aspect of shape is how balanced or lopsided the distribution is.

Definitions   A **symmetric** distribution has a balanced shape, showing that it is just as likely for the variable to take lower as higher values. A **skewed** distribution is lopsided. If it is **skewed left,** there are a few values that are relatively low compared to the bulk of the data values. If it is **skewed right,** there are a few values that are relatively high compared to the bulk of the data values.

In the extreme, values that are noticeably low or high compared to most of those in the distribution are called **outliers.** Often a display shows a gap separating outliers from the bulk of values.

Another important aspect of shape is if the distribution has one or more "clumps" of values that are common, seen as peaks in the display.

Definitions   A **unimodal** distribution has one peak. Otherwise, a distribution can be **bimodal** if there are two peaks. It is **uniform** if there are no peaks, showing that all possible values are equally common.

All sorts of shapes are possible for real-life quantitative distributions. However, one shape in particular warrants our attention.

Definition   One particular symmetric, unimodal, "mound-shaped" or "bell-shaped" pattern is called **normal.**

By far the easiest way to get a feel for the shape of a quantitative distribution is to look at a display of its values. The most common display tools for single quantitative variables are stemplots, histograms, and boxplots. Each of these has its own advantages and disadvantages.

Stemplots: A Detailed Picture of Number Values

Stemplots are a relatively straightforward display because they preserve information about individual values of the quantitative variable more than is seen in histograms or boxplots. Because they are more practical for smaller samples, we will keep our example data sets small and manageable.

We can easily identify the mode for categorical data by referring to the percentages in each category. For quantitative variables, we are obliged to make a visual assessment of what constitute peaks in our display.

The *Big Picture:*

LOOKING AHEAD

Example 4.12 on page 88 shows how to distinguish between left and right skewness. Normally shaped distributions will play a crucial role in much of the theory that is developed and utilized in this book. This shape arises naturally in many contexts, including physical characteristics of living things.

The normal curve applies to the distributions of both sample proportion and sample mean, and thus has relevance in Part III to both categorical and quantitative variables. When we perform inference in Part IV, we refer to the standard normal (z) curve for both single proportions and single means. Even when we perform inference for relationships, students can best understand the behavior of t, F, and χ^2 distributions by using the familiar z curve as a starting point.

Definition   A **stemplot** (also known as a stem-and-leaf plot) consists of a vertical list of stems, after each of which follows a horizontal list of one-digit leaves.

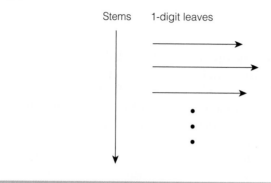

Although stemplots are not as commonly used in practice as histograms and boxplots, they function especially well as a teaching tool, because they provide enough information to specify all the relevant summaries.

EXAMPLE 4.10 CONSTRUCTING A STEMPLOT

Background: Weights were recorded for a sample of 19 female college students:

110 135 133 145 120 134 120 132 148 159 112 125 135 130 125 130 135 110 120

Question: How can we construct a stemplot for the data and use it to describe the shape of the distribution of weights?

Response: Sorting the data helps if we must construct the stemplot by hand:

110 110 112 120 120 120 125 125 130 130 132 133 134 135 135 135 145 148 159

Then we construct the plot, using ones digits as leaves, and hundreds and tens as stems:

```
11 | 0  0  2
12 | 0  0  0  5  5
13 | 0  0  2  3  4  5  5  5
14 | 5  8
15 | 9
```

The shape is just a bit lopsided, but we can call it fairly symmetric and unimodal. This makes sense because many females would be expected to have a weight about halfway between the extremes. Relatively low or high weights should be less common. The bell shape suggests the distribution is fairly normal, which might be expected because weight is a physical characteristic.

Practice: *Try Exercise 4.19 on page 92.*

If the simplest stemplot construction doesn't provide a good picture, various modifications are possible.

EXAMPLE 4.11 SPLITTING STEMS

Background: Students reported the number of credits they were taking, and if their year was first, second, third, fourth, or other. Here are the credits taken by "other" students:

4 7 11 11 11 13 13 14 14 15 17 17 17 18

Questions: Could you make a good guess at the shape of the distribution of credits taken by students who reported their year as "other," rather than first, second, third, or fourth? How can a stemplot be constructed to make clear the shape of this distribution?

Responses: Most students take about five courses of about 3 credits each, but this group of students could include several part-timers. Therefore, we have reason to expect the bulk of values to be around 15, with a few unusually low numbers for students taking only one or two courses. These would not be balanced out at the other end by students taking seven or eight courses because the upper limit is generally six.

Our first attempt at a stemplot could look like this:

```
0 | 4 7
1 | 1 1 1 3 3 4 4 5 7 7 7 8
```

As displayed, it is difficult to say anything about the shape, because there are *too few stems* for the number of leaves. In such cases, we can *split stems* for more detail, either two, five, or ten ways. One possibility would be to split stems in two: the first stem gets leaves 0–4 and the second stem gets leaves 5–9. The software used below (MINITAB) opted to split five ways: the first stem gets leaves 0–1, the second stem gets leaves 2–3, and so on.

```
Stem-and-leaf of Credits  N = 14
Leaf Unit = 1.0
   1     0 4
   2     0 7
   2     0
   5     1 111
   7     1 33
   7     1 445
   4     1 777
   1     1 8
```

Even though the third 0 stem has no leaves, we did not exclude it from the display because this would have prevented us from grasping that 4 and 7 are unusually low values. Stems must be consistent with a regular numerical scale.

Practice: *Try Exercise 4.20 on page 92.*

The Big Picture: A CLOSER LOOK

The information "Leaf Unit = 1.0" lets us know how to read the stemplot entries—for example, "0   4" in the first row represents a value of 4 credits. The digits in the left-most column just count number of observations from the bottom and top ends toward the middle, and may be ignored for most purposes.

A well-constructed stemplot clearly shows if a distribution is skewed. Left-skewed data sets have a few unusually low values, and right-skewed data sets have a few unusually high values.

EXAMPLE 4.12 SEEING LEFT OR RIGHT SKEWNESS

Background: The stemplot in Example 4.11 makes it clear that the distribution is somewhat lopsided, or skewed.

Question: Is the distribution of credits skewed left or right?

Response: First, we must adjust for the fact that our display was vertical rather than horizontal: Picture the stemplot rotated so that smaller numbers are to the left and larger to the right, as is conventional along any horizontal axis. Then, imagine the profile of the stemplot as the silhouette of some creature, and decide if the long "tail" is to the left or right.

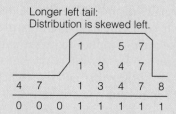

Longer left tail:
Distribution is skewed left.

For our credits data, the tail is to the left, and so the distribution is skewed left. This is consistent with the fact that most students' numbers of credits correspond to a full-time load, but a few students take just 1 or 2 courses.

Practice: *Try Exercise 4.21 on page 92.*

Example 4.11 showed how to handle cases in which a stemplot would have too *few* stems. The next example shows what to do to avoid having too *many* stems.

EXAMPLE 4.13 TRUNCATING DIGITS FOR A STEMPLOT

Background: A sample of 20 students were asked to report how much time (in minutes) they had spent on the computer the day before.

    0 10 20 30 30 30 30 45 45 60 60 60 67 90 100 120 200 240 300 420

Question: How can a stemplot be constructed to make clear the shape of this distribution?

Response: If the leaves are to be one digit, then the stems will consist of hundreds and tens digits, from 0 all the way to 42. Such a stemplot would be too strung out to give us any idea of the shape. If there are too many stems for the number of leaves, then we can reduce the number of stems by *truncating* or *rounding* the last digit (or even several digits) and working with the remaining, more important digits. Because a stemplot constructed by hand is meant as a quick, easy display tool, we prefer to simplify matters by truncating, rather than rounding, the ones digit. Here is the modified data set

    0 1 2 3 3 3 3 4 4 6 6 6 6 9 10 12 20 24 30 42

and our stemplot looks like this:

```
0 | 0  1  2  3  3  3  3  4  4  6  6  6  6  9
1 | 0  2
2 | 0  4
3 | 0
4 | 2
```

If we rotate the shape to a horizontal position, with small stems to the left and large stems to the right, we see a conspicuous right tail: The shape is very right-skewed. In other words, there are a few values that are unusually high compared to most of the values. From the appearance of our stemplot, we conclude that most students spent less than 100 minutes on the computer, but a few students reported unusually high numbers of minutes.

Practice: *Try Exercise 4.25(b) on page 92.*

Histograms: A More General Picture of Number Values

Stemplots have the advantage of giving us a detailed look at all the data values, but the disadvantage that they become unwieldy for a large number of observations. In such cases, a histogram would be preferable.

> *Definition*   A **histogram** shows possible values of a quantitative variable along the horizontal axis, with vertical bars showing the count or percentage or proportion of values in certain interval ranges.

To construct a histogram, we

1. Divide the range of data into intervals of equal width.
2. Find the count or percentage or proportion of observations in each interval.
3. Draw the histogram, using the horizontal axis for the range of data values and the vertical axis for counts or percents or proportions.

EXAMPLE 4.14 CONSTRUCTING A HISTOGRAM BY HAND

Background: A local newspaper article in February 2007 entitled "Colleges Still Unsure How to Use New SAT" reported average SAT Writing Test scores for 70 county schools[11]:

244	325	347	365	367	378	383	401	401	405	414	423	433	433
438	445	447	450	451	451	464	465	467	468	468	472	473	475
478	479	479	480	484	484	485	489	490	490	496	496	497	500
502	503	506	509	512	515	516	518	519	522	523	528	529	532
542	543	546	550	555	557	558	560	573	575	585	600	620	668

Question: How do we construct a histogram for this data set?

The Big Picture:
LOOKING BACK

It is important to note that a histogram and a bar graph, although their appearances are similar, are two very different things. A bar graph represents the distribution of one or more *categorical* variables, whereas a histogram represents the distribution of a single *quantitative* variable.

The horizontal axis in a bar graph is for identifying the various possible categories, in whatever order seems preferable. The horizontal axis in a histogram must follow a consistent numerical scale. Typically, the histogram bars are of equal width, but they need not be, and bar width is important. The bars in bar graphs are generally spaced apart, but those in a histogram tend to touch unless there are significant gaps in the variable's values, such as those due to outliers.

LOOKING BACK

Just as we want to avoid too few or too many stems in stemplots, we should opt for intervals of a reasonable length in histograms so that the number of rectangles isn't too few or too many. Five to 10 intervals are usually about right.

It is also possible to adjust the scale in Example 4.14 to represent "percent per 50 points," and have rectangles of heights $\frac{1}{50}$, $\frac{0}{50}$, $\frac{3}{50}$, $\frac{6}{50}$, $\frac{14}{50}$, $\frac{34}{50}$, $\frac{26}{50}$, $\frac{11}{50}$, $\frac{3}{50}$, and $\frac{1}{50}$, resulting in a total *area* of 100%. We can mention this to students at some point because we will gradually focus more on the area of the rectangles in a histogram whose total area is 100%.

Response: We follow the three steps outlined previously:

1. The schools' average scores range from 244 to 668, so we could work with a range of 200 to 700 and divide into 10 intervals of width 50.

2. A table helps to record the count of schools with average scores in each interval, and we can convert these to percents.

Interval	Count	Percent
200 to 250	1	1/70 = 1%
250 to 300	0	0/70 = 0%
300 to 350	2	2/70 = 3%
350 to 400	4	4/70 = 6%
400 to 450	10	10/70 = 14%
450 to 500	24	24/70 = 34%
500 to 550	18	18/70 = 26%
550 to 600	8	8/70 = 11%
600 to 650	2	2/70 = 3%
650 to 700	1	1/70 = 1%

3. Our horizontal axis identifies the writing averages. When we come to the value 450, we must make a choice: Should we include it as the right endpoint of the interval from 400 to 450, or as the left endpoint of the interval from 450 to 500? Arbitrarily, we've included it in the latter. Then we must be consistent and continue to include the left endpoint and not the right in all the intervals. The vertical axis is identified as "frequency" (same as "count"), and we draw rectangles of heights 1, 0, 2, 4, 10, 24, 18, 8, 2, and 1.

The appearance of the histogram would not be affected by switching from counts to percents or proportions—all that would change would be the labeling on the vertical axis.

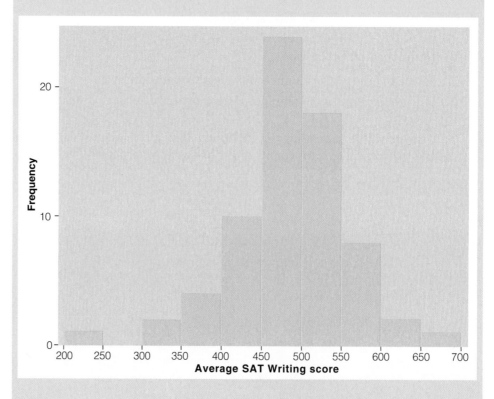

The shape is unimodal, with the peak between 450 and 500. It is fairly bell-shaped, with a low outlier between 200 and 250. Our histogram shows that almost all the schools' average writing test scores were between 300 and 700, but students in the outlier school averaged substantially less than the rest.

Histograms are the display of choice when we use software to handle data for a single quantitative variable. Software packages are designed to make judicious "choices" in terms of interval width, the marking of axes, and so on. These defaults can be overridden if a user has particular preferences. Our next example involves a huge data set that would not lend itself to producing a display by hand.

EXAMPLE 4.15 A HISTOGRAM CONSTRUCTED WITH SOFTWARE

Background: Researchers Robert W. Fogel and Stanley L. Engerman investigated a sample of 5,000 slave sales in New Orleans between the years 1804 and 1862.[12] Software was used to create a histogram displaying the amounts on the notarized bills of sale stored in the New Orleans Notarial Archival Office.

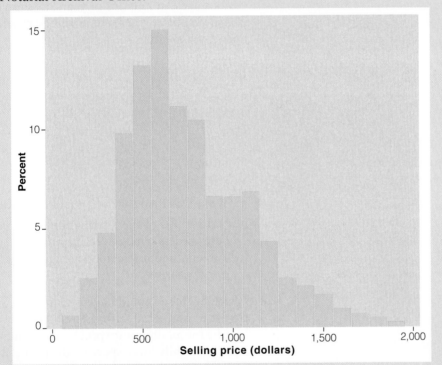

Question: How does this histogram differ from the one constructed in Example 4.14?

Response: The horizontal axis is constructed to identify the histogram's bars with midpoints instead of endpoints. The vertical axis records percents instead of frequencies. Still, the basic appearance of this histogram is similar to that of the histogram in Example 4.14, except that the shape happens to be right-skewed: There were relatively few unusually high selling prices reaching almost $2,000. This would be roughly $40,000 by today's standards.

Practice: *Try Exercise 4.25(c,d) on page 92.*

The Big Picture:
LOOKING AHEAD

On page 96 we will present an objective way of identifying outliers; for now, we identify them subjectively as remote values often separated from others in the display by gaps.

EXERCISES FOR SECTION 4.2

Single Quantitative Variables and the Shape of a Distribution

Note: Asterisked numbers indicate exercises whose answers are provided in the Solutions to Selected Exercises section, on page 689.

*4.17 Can we use information about the vertical drop of 23 ski slopes in the Middle Atlantic States to draw conclusions about the average vertical drop of all the nation's ski slopes?

*4.18 The Inter-university Consortium for Political and Social Research (ICPSR) published results of a survey of thousands of 12th graders conducted in 2004. One question asked, "Compared with others your age throughout the country, how do you rate yourself on school ability?"[13] If we were to estimate the mean *actual* ability of all 12th graders based on these self-ratings, our estimate would be biased. Does this bias come about because our sample is nonrepresentative, or because of the way the variable's values are assessed?

*4.19 Here are estimated weights, in thousands of kilograms, for 20 dinosaur specimens:

0.0   0.0   0.1   0.2   0.4   0.6   0.7   0.7   1.0   1.1   1.1   1.2   1.5   1.7   1.7   1.8   2.9   3.2   5.0   5.6

Construct a stemplot for the data, using thousands as stems and tenths of thousands as leaves.

*4.20 What is wrong with this stemplot?

```
0   012333344
0   66669
1   02
1
2   04
3   0
3
4   2
```

*4.21 Comment on the shape of the stemplot of dinosaur weights in Exercise 4.19.

4.22 What is wrong with this histogram?

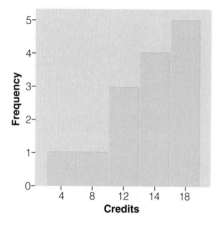

4.23 Oceanographers obtained fish fossils of various ages, in millions of years, as shown in this stemplot, where stems represent tens and leaves are ones.

```
3   3
3   8
4   1
4   555889
5   03
5   67888
6   1124
6   88999
```

a. What was the range of ages of the fossils?

b. Is the shape of the distribution best described as left-skewed, having low outliers, symmetric, having high outliers, or right-skewed?

4.24 Which of these should have a shape that is closest to normal: distribution of femur bone lengths for all dinosaur specimens (including a few especially large species), distribution of femur bone lengths for all *Tyrannosaurus rex* specimens (including a few that died in childhood), or distribution of femur bone lengths for all *Tyrannosaurus rex* specimens that died in adulthood?

*4.25 Here are data for prices of 12 used upright pianos in the classified section of a newspaper.

100   450   500   650   695   1,100   1,200   1,200   1,600   2,100   2,200   2,300

a. Who or what are the individuals of interest?

b. Display the data with a stemplot, first truncating the tens and ones digits. Use thousands for stems, splitting in two, and hundreds for leaves.

c. Construct a histogram for the data, using intervals of width 500 starting at 0 and including left endpoints, so the price 500 would be included in the second interval, not the first.

d. Modify your histogram from part (c) to identify *midpoints* along the horizontal axis.

e. How would the appearance of the histogram change if the vertical axis recorded percents instead of frequencies?

4.3 Center and Spread: What's Typical for Quantitative Values, and How They Vary

There are two approaches to summarizing center and spread. We will discuss the *five-number summary* first because it is easier to calculate. It also gives rise to our third display tool, the *boxplot*. The five-number summary is especially useful for summarizing distributions with pronounced skewness or outliers. In subsequent sections of the book we will almost always summarize quantitative variables with the *mean* and *standard deviation*.

Five-Number Summary: Landmark Values for Center and Spread

Reporting each and every value, especially for large data sets, would result in so much of an information overload that it would not accomplish much. Instead, we need a way of reporting just a few key "landmark" values that help put the whole distribution in perspective. These include the *median* as a measure of center and *quartiles* as a measure of spread.

> *Definition* The **median** tells the center of a distribution by reporting the single middle value for an odd number of observations, or the average of the two middle values for an even number of observations. The median has half of the data values below it and the other half above it.

EXAMPLE 4.16 THE MEDIAN FOR AN EVEN NUMBER OF VALUES

Background: Full-time students typically take about five classes, worth about 3 credits each, so the median number of credits taken by students in general is about 15. Here is the stemplot for credits taken by a group of 14 "nontraditional" students (those who reported their year as "other"), as constructed in Example 4.11:

```
0  4
0  7
0
1  111
1  33
1  445
1  777
1  8
```

Continued

Question: What is the median number of credits taken by these nontraditional students?

Response: The median of 14 values is between the 7th and 8th values. We average these values to find that the median is $\frac{13 + 14}{2} = 13.5$.

Practice: *Try Exercise 4.28(a) on page 103.*

Once we have reported what value is typical for a data set, it is also useful to summarize the extent to which values vary.

Definitions

The **quartiles** help measure the spread of a distribution:

- The **first quartile** (Q_1) has one-fourth of the data at or below it; it is the middle of the values below the median. One-fourth is 25%, so Q_1 is also the 25th percentile.

- The **third quartile** (Q_3) has three-fourths of the data at or below it; it is the middle of the values above the median, and is the 75th percentile.

In general, a **percentile** tells what value has the given percentage of a distribution's values falling at or below it.

LOOKING BACK

We already have a name for the second quartile: It is the median.

The five-number summary includes information about both center and spread.

Definitions   The **five-number summary** of a distribution consists of its minimum value, first quartile (Q_1), median, third quartile (Q_3), and maximum value.

The difference between the minimum and maximum values is called the **range**, telling the spread of all the data values. The difference $Q_3 - Q_1$ is called the **interquartile range**, abbreviated **IQR**, telling the spread of the middle half of the data values.

LOOKING BACK

In Example 4.14, we used the word *range* informally, and reported that the range of schools' average SAT writing scores was from 244 to 668. According to the more technical definition, the range would be a single number, 424.

For an odd number of values, we will exclude the median when finding the quartiles, which fall in the middle of the values below and above the median. Software, or even other textbooks, may use a different algorithm and produce slightly different quartiles.

EXAMPLE 4.17 FINDING THE FIVE-NUMBER SUMMARY, THE RANGE, AND THE IQR

Background: Weights were recorded for a sample of 19 female students, as in Example 4.10, and sorted from lowest to highest.

110 110 112 120 120 120 125 125 130 130 132 133 134 135 135 135 145 148 159

Question: What are the five-number summary, range, and interquartile range for this data set?

Response:

■ The minimum and maximum weights, in pounds, are 110 and 159. The median of 19 weights is the 10th value, or 130 pounds. As for quartiles, since we can't divide 19 values evenly in half, we leave out the median and find Q_1 to be the middle of the smaller nine values, or the 5th, which is 120. Q_3 is the middle of the larger nine values—that is, 135. The *five-number summary* is 110, 120, 130, 135, 159.

■ The *range* of all weights is $159 - 110 = 49$ pounds.

■ The *IQR*, or range of the middle half of weights, is $135 - 120 = 15$ pounds.

Practice: *Try Exercise 4.28(b) on page 103.*

The Big Picture:
A CLOSER LOOK

A useful skill in assessing output is extracting what is needed and ignoring the rest, at least temporarily. For now, we focus on the five-number summary (and sample size). Later on we'll pay attention to the mean and standard deviation.

Here is computer output for a general summary of the variable *Female Weights*.

```
Descriptive Statistics: Female Weights
Variable                     N        Mean      Median      TrMean      StDev     SE Mean
Female Weights              19      129.37      130.00      128.76      12.82        2.94
Variable              Minimum     Maximum          Q1          Q3
Female Weights         110.00      159.00      120.00      135.00
```

The previous output, like most of the output in this textbook, happens to have been produced with MINITAB. The following summaries of the same data set (female weights) have been produced by SPSS, Excel, and a TI84 calculator.

SPSS Weight Summaries

	Descriptive Statistics													
	N	Range	Minimum	Maximum	Sum	Mean		Std. Deviation	Variance	Skewness		Kurtosis	
	Statistic	Statistic	Statistic	Statistic	Statistic	Statistic	Std. Error	Statistic	Statistic	Statistic	Std. Error	Statistic	Std. Error
Female_weight	19	49.00	110.00	159.00	2458.00	129.3684	2.94214	12.82450	164.468	.430	.524	.303	1.014
Valid N (listwise)	19												

Excel Weight Summaries

Female Weights	
Mean	129.3684
Standard Error	2.942142
Median	130
Mode	120
Standard Deviation	12.8245
Sample Variance	164.4678
Kurtosis	0.303326
Skewness	0.429856
Range	49
Minimum	110
Maximum	159
Sum	2458
Count	19

TI84 Weight Summaries

```
1-Var Stats
x̄ = 129.3684211
Σx = 2458
Σx² = 320948
Sx = 12.8245014
σx = 12.48245306
↓n = 19
```

```
1-Var Stats
↑n = 19
minX = 110
Q1 = 120
Med = 130
Q3 = 135
maxX = 159
```

If students wonder about values in the output, they can be told that for most purposes we disregard the trimmed mean (TrMean), calculated after omitting the most extreme observations. SE Mean will not be relevant until Part IV, and is at any rate somewhat redundant because it could be calculated as the standard deviation divided by the square root of the sample size.

Boxplots: Depicting the Key Number Values

We began learning to display data for one quantitative variable with stemplots and histograms. The five-number summary gives rise to a third commonly used display tool: the *boxplot*, which lets us take in the information from the five-number

Students may ask which of our displays is "best." Stemplots and histograms give us a much better idea of the shapes of distributions, but boxplots are still a popular display tool for quantitative data, especially when the presence of an additional categorical variable of interest warrants a visual comparison of distributions for two or more groups at once. These situations will be encountered in Chapter 5 on relationships, and again in Chapter 11, which covers two-sample *t* and *F* procedures.

summary visually, and also makes outliers conspicuous. The "box" part of it shows where the middle half of data values occur, and the "whiskers" represent the lower and upper fourths of values. The height of the box is the interquartile range $IQR = Q_3 - Q_1$, which tells the range of the middle half of the data. The width of the box has no role except to stress that the box is where the middle half of values occur.

Definition   A **boxplot** (also known as a *box-and-whiskers plot*) is a display of a distribution's median, quartiles, and extreme values, with special treatment for outliers.

1. The bottom whisker extends to the minimum non-outlier.
2. The bottom of the box is at Q_1.
3. There is a line through the box at the median.
4. The top of the box is at Q_3.
5. The top whisker extends to the maximum non-outlier.

Outliers are denoted with an asterisk (*).

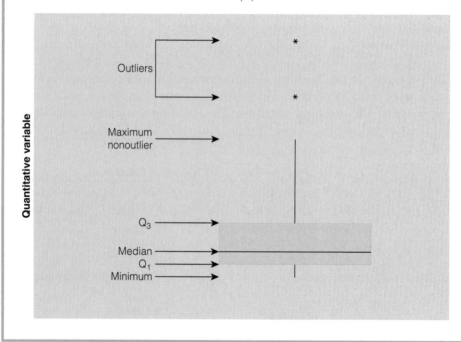

The Big Picture:
A CLOSER LOOK

Histograms are left-skewed if the left tail is longer, and right-skewed if the right tail is longer. Similarly, a boxplot exhibits left skewness if it is "bottom heavy," with the lower whisker longer than the upper whisker, or more of the box below than above the median line. It exhibits right skewness if it is "top heavy," with the upper whisker longer than the lower whisker, or more of the box above than below the median line.

A simple criterion to identify outliers is based on the interquartile range *IQR*, and is called the *1.5 × IQR Rule*.

Definition   The **1.5 × IQR Rule** identifies outliers as follows: Any value below $Q_1 - (1.5 \times IQR)$ is considered a low outlier, and any value above $Q_3 + (1.5 \times IQR)$ is considered a high outlier.

1.5 × *IQR* Rule to identify outliers

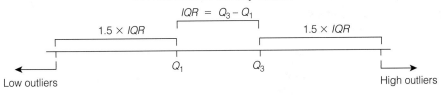

Example **4.18** Identifying Outliers by Hand or with Software

Background: Recall our data from Example 4.13 for time (in minutes) spent on the computer by 20 students, and the accompanying stemplot.

0 10 20 30 30 30 30 45 45 60 60 60 67 90 100 120 200 240 300 420

```
Stem-and-leaf of computer  N = 20  Leaf Unit = 10
  0 012333344
  0 66669
  1 02
  1
  2 04
  2
  3 0
  3
  4 2
```

Questions: Which values strike us visually as being outliers? Are the same values classified as outliers, whether we carry out the rule by hand or look at a boxplot produced by the computer?

Responses: Certainly the last value (420) and, most likely, the next to last (300) appear to be outliers; perhaps the 200 and 240 as well.

We can find the five-number summary values by hand, noting that the median of 20 values is between the 10th and 11th. Q_1 is in the middle of the smaller 10 (between the 5th and 6th), and Q_3 in the middle of the larger 10 (between the 15th and 16th).

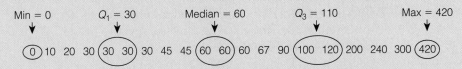

Thus, the values are 0, 30, 60, 110, 420. The *IQR* is $110 - 30 = 80$. There are no low outliers. High outliers would be above $110 + 1.5(80) = 230$. Officially, we would designate 240, 300, and 420 as outliers because those are the values above 230.

Alternatively, we can locate the five values in computer output:

Descriptive Statistics: computertime					
Variable	N	Mean	Median	TrMean	StDev	SE Mean
computer	20	97.9	60.0	85.4	109.7	24.5
Variable	Minimum	Maximum	Q1	Q3	
computer	0.0	420.0	30.0	115.0	

The software's (MINITAB's) use of a different algorithm to find quartiles results in a slightly different value for Q_3 (115 instead of 110), which means the *IQR* would be $115 - 30 = 85$. High outliers would be above $115 + 1.5(85) = 242.5$. The output only designates 300 and 420 as outliers because those are the values above 242.5.

Continued

Here is the boxplot produced by the computer:

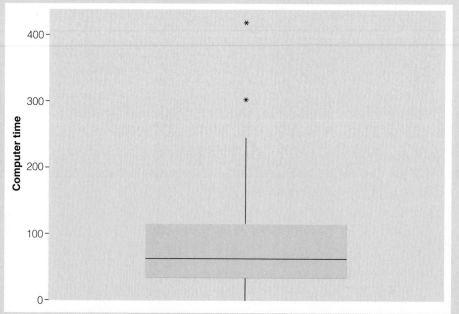

Although there is a minor discrepancy between the results we obtained by hand and those produced by software, in the end both methods show the distribution to have some high outliers.

Practice: *Try Exercise 4.28(c–e) on page 103.*

To decide whether to omit or include outliers, we should consider how they arose. If they are the result of an error in measurement or recording, they should be omitted. If they truly represent individuals that happen to be unusual, they should be included.

EXAMPLE 4.19 HANDLING OUTLIERS

Background: Example 4.18 featured outlier times spent on the computer by students the day before they were surveyed, with a maximum of 420 minutes, or 7 hours. The same survey also produced a low outlier height value of 51 inches.

Question: Should the outlier values be retained in the data sets or removed?

Response: It is plausible that a student spent as much as 7 hours on the computer, due to either work- or school-related tasks, and so these outliers should be retained. In contrast, the outlier height value (unless the survey's coordinator is aware of a student who is not much taller than 4 feet) can best be attributed to a mistake made by a student in reporting her height of 5-foot-1 to be 51 instead of 61 inches. This outlier should probably be removed, or converted to 61 instead.

Practice: *Try Exercise 4.28(f) on page 104.*

The Big Picture:
A CLOSER LOOK

In statistics, "how many there are" is a vital piece of information, telling us the sample size. The convention is to denote this sample size as "*n*." In our computer output, it is denoted "*N*."

Mean and Standard Deviation: Center and Spread in a Nutshell

The most commonly used measure of the center of a data set is the *mean*, or arithmetic average, introduced on page 5: Just add up all the numbers and divide by how many there are.

> *Definition*   The **mean** of n observations $x_1, x_2, \ldots, x_n$ is
>
> $$\overline{x} = \frac{x_1 + \ldots + x_n}{n}$$
>
> and is called "x-bar."

Example TBP 4.4 on page 770 of the **TBP** *Supplement* illustrates how the mean can be misleading when the data include outliers. Example TBP 4.5 on page 771 of the **TBP** *Supplement* walks students through the steps of calculating a standard deviation by hand.

With the next two examples we explore how shape affects the relationship between the mean and the median.

EXAMPLE **4.20** MEAN VERSUS MEDIAN FOR A SYMMETRIC DISTRIBUTION

Background: Weights were recorded for a sample of 19 female students in Example 4.10, and sorted from lowest to highest.

110 110 112 120 120 120 125 125 130 130 132 133 134 135 135 135 145 148 159

Question: Find the mean weight and compare it to the median, using a histogram to show the role played by the shape of the distribution.

Response: The mean weight of 19 females is

$$\overline{x} = \frac{110 + \ldots + 159}{19} = 129.37$$

which can be found by hand or, even easier, with software:

Variable	N	Mean	Median	TrMean	StDev	SE Mean
Female Weights	19	129.37	130.00	128.76	12.82	2.94

The mean ($\overline{x} = 129.37$) and the median (130) are approximately the same because the distribution is fairly symmetric.

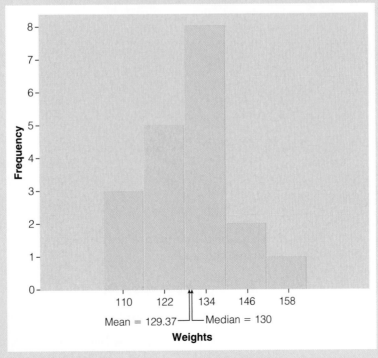

Practice: *Try Exercise 4.29(a) on page 104.*

EXAMPLE **4.21** MEAN VERSUS MEDIAN FOR LEFT-SKEWED AND RIGHT-SKEWED DISTRIBUTIONS

Background: Credit loads, as recorded for a sample of 14 nontraditional students in Example 4.11, can be found to have a mean of 13 and a median of 13.5. We identified the shape as left-skewed.

4 7 11 11 11 13 13 14 14 15 17 17 17 18

Times spent on the computer in a day by a sample of 20 students, discussed in Example 4.13, have a mean of 97.9 and a median of 60. The shape is very right-skewed.

0 10 20 30 30 30 30 45 45 60 60 60 67 90 100 120 200 240 300 420

Question: How does the shape of each distribution affect the relationship between the mean and the median?

Response: The left-skewness in the distribution of credits pulls the mean down below the median. The difference between the mean ($\bar{x} = 13$) and the median (13.5) is fairly minor because the skewness is not extreme.

The right-skewness and high outliers in the distribution of computer times pull the value of the mean above the median. The difference between the mean (97.9) and the median (60) is more pronounced than it was for credits because here the right-skewness is so extreme.

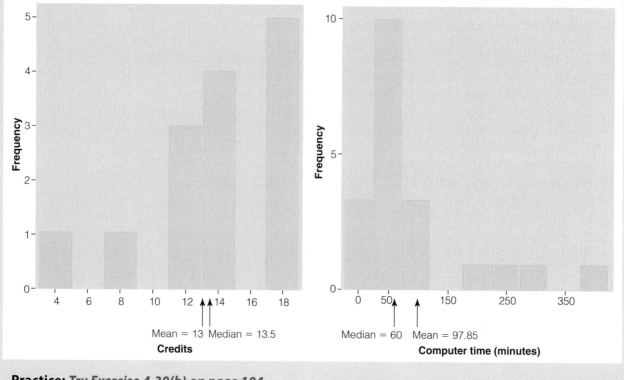

Mean = 13 Median = 13.5
Credits

Median = 60 Mean = 97.85
Computer time (minutes)

Practice: *Try Exercise 4.30(b) on page 104.*

Example TBP 4.6 on page 772 of the ***TBP Supplement*** guides students in intuiting how the shape, the mean, and the standard deviation would compare for distributions of ages of three groups.

Thus, the shape of a quantitative distribution plays a role in the comparative size of the mean and the median:

Shape	Mean versus Median	Example
Symmetric	mean = median	Female weights
Skewed left/low outliers	mean < median	Credits for nontraditional students
Skewed right/high outliers	mean > median	Time spent on computer

In general, we prefer the mean as a measure of center because it includes information from all the observations. However, if a distribution has pronounced skewness or outliers, the median may be better because it is less affected by those few extreme values. For this reason, we call the median a *resistant* measure of center.

The measure of spread to accompany the mean is the *standard deviation*, *s*, which tells us how far the observations tend to be from their mean, $\bar{x}$. The units of the standard deviation are the same as those of the variable itself, and of its mean. Occasionally, we are more interested in the squared standard deviation, or *variance*.

LOOKING AHEAD

It is natural for students to wonder why our "average" divides by $n - 1$ instead of n. Ultimately, the variance s^2 from a sample is used to estimate the variance of the entire population. It does a better job of estimating when we divide by $n - 1$ instead of n.

> **Definitions**   The **standard deviation**, written *s*, is the square root of the "average" squared deviation from the mean. The standard deviation of *n* observations $x_1, x_2, \ldots, x_n$ is calculated as
>
> $$s = \sqrt{\frac{(x_1 - \bar{x})^2 + \ldots + (x_n - \bar{x})^2}{n - 1}}$$
>
> where $\bar{x}$ is the mean of those observations. The **variance**, written s^2, is
>
> $$s^2 = \frac{(x_1 - \bar{x})^2 + \ldots + (x_n - \bar{x})^2}{n - 1}$$

Example TBP 4.7 on page 773 of the **TBP** *Supplement* includes graphs with incorrect standard deviations (0.14 and 14.0) for household size to illustrate how the distributions could not conform to reality if they had too little or too much spread.

Standard deviations play a vital role in statistics. After all, it could be said that statistics is all about the behavior of variables, and it is the *variability*, or spread, of variables that we seek to understand. The standard deviation is *the* single number most commonly used to measure variability of distributions. Software can easily be used to calculate a standard deviation, but it is up to you to understand what this number means.

EXAMPLE 4.22 INTERPRETING THE MEAN AND STANDARD DEVIATION

Background: The number of credits taken by 14 nontraditional students, introduced in Example 4.11, has a mean of 13.00 and a standard deviation of 4.00.

```
              4  7  11  11  11  13  13  14  14  15  17  17  17  18

Variable    N      Mean    Median    TrMean    StDev    SE Mean
credits     14     13.00    13.50     13.33     4.00      1.07
```

Question: How do we interpret these numbers?

Response: These students were taking 13 credits on average. Some took close to 13 credits and for others the number of credits was farther from 13; typically, their number of credits differed from 13 by about 4 points.

Practice: *Try Exercise 4.30(c) on page 104.*

As long as we're familiar with the variable in question, most of us find it fairly easy to make an educated guess at its mean value. Standard deviation is less intuitive, but we can try to estimate it by keeping in mind that it measures the typical distance of values from their mean.

The Big Picture:

LOOKING AHEAD

Although the mean and standard deviation are of limited usefulness for describing data sets with skewness or outliers, we will see in Part IV that the role they play in statistical inference makes skewness and outliers less problematic.

EXAMPLE 4.23 ESTIMATING THE STANDARD DEVIATION

Background: Household size in the United States has a mean of approximately 2.5 people.

Question: Which one of these numbers—0.014, 0.14, 1.4, and 14.0— would be a good guess for the standard deviation, and why?

Response: 1.4 would be a good guess for the standard deviation. Many households have 2 or 3 people, which are just 0.5 away from the mean of 2.5. A few households have as many as 7 people, which is 4.5 away from the mean. Typically, the household sizes could differ from the mean by about 1.4. The values 0.014 and 0.14 would be too small (not enough spread) and 14.0 would be too large (too much spread).

Practice: *Try Exercise 4.36(d) on page 106.*

It is important to consider the shape of a distribution before we decide which summaries to report.

EXAMPLE 4.24 WHEN THE STANDARD DEVIATION IS AFFECTED BY SKEWNESS OR OUTLIERS

Background: Consider this output summarizing a sample of students' earnings (where the units are thousands of dollars), along with a histogram displaying the data.

Variable	N	Mean	Median	TrMean	StDev	SE Mean
Earned	446	3.776	2.000	2.823	6.503	0.308

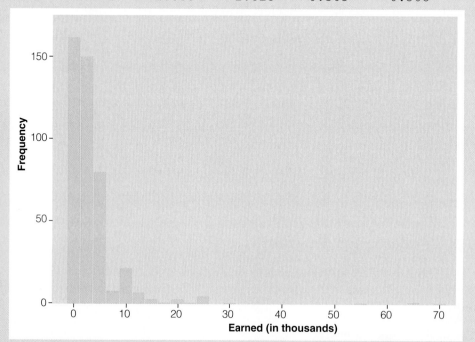

Question: Should we say that typically the students earned about $3,776, and earnings differed from this amount by about $6,503?

Response: The histogram shows the earnings to be extremely skewed to the right. Most of the earnings are between zero and $2,000, so $3,776 seems high for what is "typical." And most of the earnings are within only about $1,000 of the median, $2,000, so $6,503 seems too high as a measure of the typical distance of values from their center. The right skewness inflates the mean and—to an even greater extent—the standard deviation, so they would be misleading if used as reported summaries.

Practice: _Try Exercise 4.38 on page 107._

EXERCISES FOR SECTION 4.3

Center and Spread: What's Typical for Quantitative Values, and How They Vary

Note: Asterisked numbers indicate exercises whose answers are provided in the Solutions to Selected Exercises section, on page 689.

*4.26 Oceanographers obtained fish fossils at various depths, in meters below sea floor (mbsf), as shown in this stemplot, where stems represent hundreds and leaves are tens.

```
1  1
1  3
1  4445
1  6677
1  8
2  01111
2  2233
2
2  66667
```

a. Who or what are the individuals studied?

b. What was the range of depths at which the fossils were obtained?

c. What is the median of the 25 depths?

d. Is the shape of the distribution best described as left-skewed, having low outliers, symmetric, having high outliers, or right-skewed?

e. Would you expect the mean to be less than, greater than, or about the same size as the median?

f. Are the fossil depths likely to have been a random sample? Explain.

4.27 This stemplot shows the number of medals won at the 2008 Olympics by 87 countries, including the 110 medals won by the United States.

```
0   111111111111111111112222222222223333334444445555556666666777889
1   00013456889
2   4578
3   1
4   0167
5
6
7   2
8
9
10  0
11  0
```

a. Construct a histogram for the data, with the rectangles covering intervals of width 10.

b. Find the five-number summary.

c. The top 25% of countries won at least how many medals?

*4.28 Data for prices of 12 used, upright pianos in the classified section of a newspaper were discussed in Exercise 4.25 on page 92.

        100   450   500   650   695   1,100   1,200   1,200   1,600   2,100   2,200   2,300

a. What is the median price?

b. Report the five-number summary values and the IQR.

c. Use the $1.5 \times IQR$ Rule to determine which values, if any, should be considered outliers.

d. Sketch a boxplot of the data.

e. Would the distribution best be described as left-skewed, having low outliers, fairly symmetric, right-skewed, or having high outliers?

f. Suppose a typed list of 14 piano prices included additional values of −600 and 3,100. How should these outliers be handled?

*4.29 Data for prices of 12 used, upright pianos in the classified section of a newspaper were discussed in Exercise 4.28.

a. Explain why the mean is approximately the same as the median.

b. The mean of these 12 values is 1,175. Find what the mean would be if we included a 13th value—the price for a used, baby grand piano being offered for $8,000.

c. Suppose a buyer wants to use the mean price of those 12 pianos, $1,175, to estimate the mean price of all used pianos. Is she mainly concerned with data production, displaying and summarizing data, probability, or statistical inference?

d. Based on the information from this sample of 12 pianos, which of these would be the most plausible value for the mean price of all used pianos: $700, $1,100, or $1,700?

e. The standard deviation for piano prices is 739 dollars, and the variance is 546,121 squared dollars. Which one of these tells the typical distance of prices from the mean price?

f. The mean price is $1,175 and the standard deviation is $739. How much does one of the pianos cost (to the nearest dollar) if it is 0.65 standard deviations below the mean?

g. To estimate the mean and standard deviation of all used piano prices, would you recommend obtaining a sample of 12 pianos or 24 pianos, or doesn't it make a difference?

*4.30 Data for vertical drop (difference in feet between top and bottom of a continuous slope or trail) of 23 ski slopes in the Middle Atlantic states are displayed both with a histogram and with a boxplot.

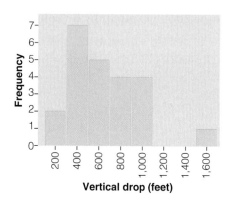
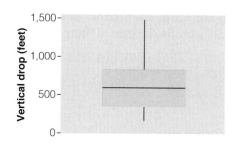

a. The boxplot fails to show one important feature of the data that the histogram makes obvious. What is that feature?

b. Explain why we can expect the mean to be greater than the median.

c. Based on the output shown, we can say the drops average _____ feet, and differ from this average by about _____ feet.

Variable	N	Mean	Median	TrMean	StDev	SE Mean
Vertical	23	627.0	610.0	606.7	317.4	66.2
Variable	Minimum	Maximum	Q1	Q3		
Vertical	180.0	1500.0	360.0	850.0		

4.31 The number of reported hate crimes committed against persons, as well as the number of reported hate crimes involving destruction of property (such as vandalism), were recorded by the federal government for each of the 50 states in the year 2002, with results displayed in these histograms.

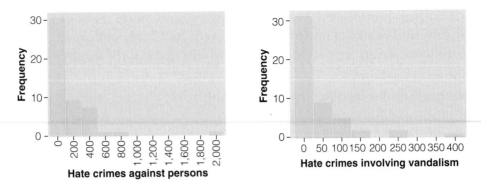

a. One of the distributions has a mean of 47 and the other has a mean of 177. Which is the mean for crimes against persons?

b. One of the distributions has a standard deviation of 78 and the other has a standard deviation of 307. Which is the standard deviation for crimes involving vandalism?

c. The histogram for hate crimes against persons shows that 31 of the 50 states had fewer than how many such crimes?

d. The histogram for hate crimes involving vandalism shows that 31 of the 50 states had fewer than how many such crimes?

e. Redraw the histogram for hate crimes against persons, using percents of states instead of frequencies (counts) of states.

f. Can we assume the numbers mentioned above are actual measurements of hate crimes reported for the entire population, or are they most likely just estimates based on samples?

4.32 Running times (in minutes) of 29 movies currently showing in early December 2004 are listed here, from a 73-minute European film called "The Big Animal," about a couple who unwittingly adopt a camel into their home when the circus leaves town, to the 173-minute Oliver Stone film about Alexander the Great.

> 73 90 90 93 94 97 98 99 100 100 102 105 105 106 106
> 107 108 113 115 115 115 120 123 130 130 140 150 152 173

a. Display the data with a stemplot.

b. Report the five-number summary values.

c. Use the $1.5 \times IQR$ Rule to determine which values, if any, should be considered outliers.

d. Sketch a boxplot of the data.

e. Which is a better summary of the "typical" movie length—the mean or the median? Explain.

f. If these movies are taken to be a sample of all the movies showing in 2004, is their mean length a statistic or a parameter? Do we call it $\bar{x}$ or μ?

g. In which case would you expect $\bar{x}$ to be closer to μ: when our sample consists of 29 movies or 59 movies?

4.33 A survey of 122 families with epileptic children explored the behavior of the family dog in connection with epileptic seizures. Many families claimed that their dog was able to anticipate an upcoming seizure, and demonstrated its concern in a variety of ways. It was reported that "anticipation time ranged from 10 seconds to 5 hours, with an average of 2.5 minutes."[14] Based on this information, we can make a good guess with regard to the shape of the distribution of anticipation times—Is it skewed left, skewed right, or symmetric?

*4.34 Between 2001 and 2002, astrophysicists discovered new irregular moons of Neptune, with diameters (in kilometers) of 31, 33, 36, 37, 43, and 54. [Subsequently, five of the six discoveries were made official.]

a. Find the mean diameter of these six moons.

b. Does it make sense to use this mean as an estimate for a population mean? Explain.

c. Explain why the median would do a better job of reporting what diameter is typical for Neptune's six new irregular moons.

4.35   The ages of the male beach volleyball players for the United States in the 2004 Olympics were 33, 32, 32, and 32. The ages of the female players were 26, 27, 34, and 35.

   a. Which group of players' ages is more spread out—the males or the females?

   b. Find the mean age for males.

   c. Find the mean age for females.

   d. Which gender group is older, on average?

   e. The standard deviation of the females' ages is

$$\sqrt{((26 - 30.5)^2 + (27 - 30.5)^2 + (34 - 30.5)^2 + (35 - 30.5)^2)/(4 - 1)} = 4.65.$$

      Calculate the standard deviation of the male players' ages by hand.

   f. Are the units of the standard deviation years or squared years?

*4.36   The Inter-University Consortium for Political and Social Research (ICPSR) published results of a survey of thousands of 12th graders conducted in 2004. One question asked, "Compared with others your age throughout the country, how do you rate yourself on school ability?"[15] Response options were:

1 = Far below average, 2 = Below average, 3 = Slightly below average, 4 = Average, 5 = Slightly above average, 6 = Above average, 7 = Far above average

Results are shown in this histogram, with rounded percentages shown above each response from 1 to 7.

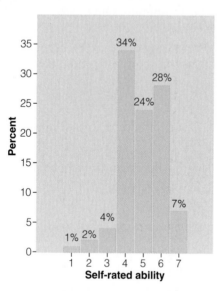

   a. The median rating is the one for which we can say, "50% of the students rated themselves at this level or below." What is the median?

   b. The distribution bulges at the middle and tapers at the ends, but is clearly non-normal; how can we best describe the shape?

   c. Which one of these is your best guess for the mean rating: 2.9, 4.9, 5.9, or 6.9?

   d. Which one of these is your best guess for the standard deviation of the ratings (which tells the typical distance of ratings from their mean): 0.012, 0.12, 1.2, or 12.0?

   e. If *actual* (not self-rated) abilities were approximately normally distributed, what should their mean and median be?

   f. If we were to estimate the mean actual ability of all 12th graders based on their self-ratings, our estimate would be biased. Does this bias come about because our sample is nonrepresentative, or because of the way the variable's values are assessed?

4.37   The same ICPSR survey discussed in Exercise 4.36 also asked students, "During a typical week, on how many evenings do you go out for fun and recreation?" Results are displayed in a histogram.

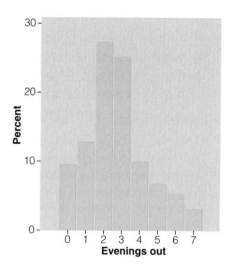

   a. Almost exactly 50% responded 2 or fewer, and almost exactly 50% responded 3 or more, so the median number of evenings out in a typical week is 2.5. Keeping in mind the shape of the distribution, which of these would be your best guess for the mean: 2.0, 2.7, 4.0, or 4.7?

b. Which of these would be your best guess for the standard deviation (which tells typical distance of values from their mean): 0.017, 0.17, 1.7, or 17.0?

*4.38 Graduate students in a statistics department recorded hours spent consulting on 21 different projects in a particular semester:

```
     1  1  2  2  3  5 ·5  8  10  15  15  18  20  20  24  30  30  30  48  50  148
```

Variable	N	Mean	Median	TrMean	StDev	SE Mean
Hours	21	23.10	15.00	17.68	32.09	7.00

a. Just by looking at the data values, describe the general appearance of a display (such as histogram or stemplot) of the data.

b. How many values are more than one standard deviation away from the mean?

c. Is 32 a good summary for the typical distance of values from their mean? Explain.

4.39 The *New York Times* published an article called "In Michigan, a Milestone for a Mouse Methuselah" about a dwarf mouse that surprised scientists by living to the age of 4 years, much older than the average life span of 2 years.[16] Based on this information, which one of these would be the best guess for standard deviation of dwarf mouse ages: one week, a couple of weeks, a few months, one year, or a few years?

4.40 In 2004, a 42-year-old man underwent surgery to reduce his weight of 1,072 pounds.

a. If all male weights have mean 190 pounds and standard deviation 30 pounds, how many standard deviations above average was his weight?

b. Tell whether in this context 190 is a statistic or a parameter, and whether we should call it $\bar{x}$ or μ.

Using Software [see Technology Guide]

4.41 A *New York Times* article in July 2004 was subtitled, "Symphony Orchestras Are Going Begging. So Why Are Top Conductors Getting Rich?" To make his point, the journalist reported compensations for various music directors "derived from the latest IRS forms publicly available," which were from around the year 2002.[17]

Symphony	Director	Salary
New York Philharmonic	Lorin Maazel	$2,280,000
San Francisco Symphony	Michael Tilson Thomas	$1,470,000
Dallas Symphony	Litton	$551,719
Chicago Symphony	Daniel Barenboim	$2,140,000
Los Angeles Philharmonic	Esa-Pekka Salonen	$1,240,000
Atlanta Symphony	Robert Spano	$505,615

a. The article mentions that "among the 18 American orchestras with 52-week contracts, at least 7 pay their music directors more than $1 million . . ." If 7 of the 18 directors receive more than $1 million, what percentage is this?

b. What percentage of the six directors listed in the table receive more than $1 million?

c. Use software to calculate the mean of the six directors' salaries reported.

d. Use software to calculate the standard deviation of the six directors' salaries reported.

e. Explain why the mean you calculated is not necessarily a good estimate for the mean salary of all 18 American orchestras' directors.

*4.42   Oceanographers obtained fish fossils at various depths, in meters below sea floor (mbsf):

115   134   142   147   147   153   164   167   172   178   186   205   210
213   214   215   224   227   230   236   264   266   269   269   270

Use software to fill in the blanks: On average, the fossils were obtained from about _____ meters below sea floor, and they differed from this average by about _____ meters.

4.43   Oceanographers obtained fish fossils of various ages, in millions of years:

34   38   41   45   45   46   48   49   49   50   53   57   58   59   59   59   61   62   63   65   69   69   69   69   70

Use software to fill in the blanks:

a. On average, the fossils were about _____ million years old.

b. They differed from this average by about _____ million years.

*4.44   Some physical characteristics, like height, naturally follow a normal shape for specific age and gender groups. Heights of college-aged females are normal and centered at about 65 inches, whereas heights of college-aged males are normal and centered at about 70 inches. Use software to access the student survey data and complete the following tasks.

a. Produce a histogram of heights of all students. Describe its shape.

b. Are there roughly equal numbers of males and females in the data set? If not, which group is larger?

c. Separate the data by gender and produce a histogram of heights of female students. Describe its shape.

d. Produce a histogram of heights of male students. Describe its shape.

e. To better understand the behavior of the variable height, is it better to study males and females separately, or to combine them?

4.45   Use software to access the student survey data and complete the following tasks.

a. Report the five-number summary values for the weights of all the students.

b. Use the 1.5 × IQR Rule to tell whether the weights of all the students have low outliers, high outliers, or neither.

c. Report the five-number summary values for the weights of the female students.

d. Use the 1.5 × IQR Rule to tell whether the weights of the female students have low outliers, high outliers, or neither.

e. Report the five-number summary values for the weights of the male students.

f. Use the 1.5 × IQR Rule to tell whether the weights of the male students have low outliers, high outliers, or neither.

g. These boxplots are for weights of females, males, and combined students, but not necessarily in that order.

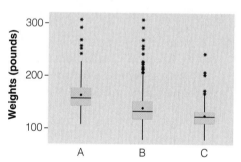

Which of the three groups is represented by boxplot A?

h. Which of the three groups is represented by boxplot B?

i. Which of the three groups is represented by boxplot C?

4.4   Normal Distributions: The Shape of Things to Come

We continue our study of sample values for a single quantitative variable, such as weight, number of credits taken, SAT score, or age. By now we have seen left-skewed distributions—such as number of credits taken by a group of students that includes part-time students. We've also seen right-skewed distributions—such as earnings of students, where most earned just a few thousand dollars but a few had substantial salaries. We focus now on distributions that are *not* skewed, but symmetric, and also bell-shaped. Such a shape occurs in all sorts of contexts, such as physical characteristics of living things (as in our example of female weights). Exam scores also frequently follow this pattern (as in the "bell curve" of people's IQ scores).

Following is a typical histogram for a fairly normal-shaped data set. First, the vertical scale has been adjusted so that the total area within the histogram is 100%, or 1. By this construction, the area above any interval corresponds to the percentage or proportion of values in that interval. What makes us characterize the histogram as "normal" is the particular bell shape exhibited. It is symmetric about the mean, indicating that it is just as likely for the quantitative variable to take a value a certain distance below its mean as above. It bulges in the middle, indicating that values closest to the mean are most common. And it tapers at the ends, indicating that it becomes less and less common to take values increasingly farther from the mean.

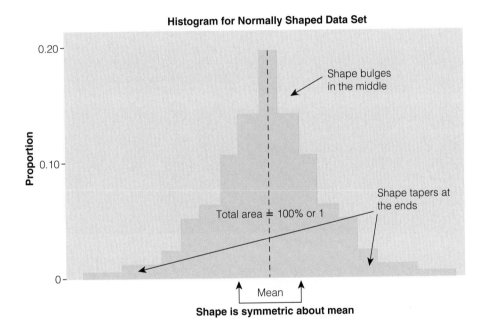

From now on, we will focus almost exclusively on a histogram's area, rather than the heights of its bars. Therefore, many of the histograms presented—such as that in the next example—will not specify the vertical scale. We can assume that the scale has been adjusted so that the total area enclosed is 100%.

EXAMPLE 4.25 HOW A HISTOGRAM SHOWS PERCENTAGES

Background: IQ scores for a large representative sample have a mean of 100. The distribution is normal because of the way human intelligence naturally varies.

Continued

Questions: What would be the center and shape of a histogram of IQ scores? How can a histogram of IQ scores be used to find the percentage of scores between 90 and 120?

Responses: Because the mean of all scores is 100, the histogram will be centered at 100. Its shape will be symmetric on either side of 100. IQ scores close to 100 are most common (the histogram's area is concentrated around 100). It is less common to see scores far from 100 in either direction (the histogram flattens down toward a height of zero for scores far from 100).

Just as for any histogram that is constructed to have a total area of 100%, we can find the percentage of IQ scores in any interval by taking the area inside the histogram over that interval. Thus, the percentage of IQ scores between 90 and 120 would be the area inside the histogram from 90 to 120.

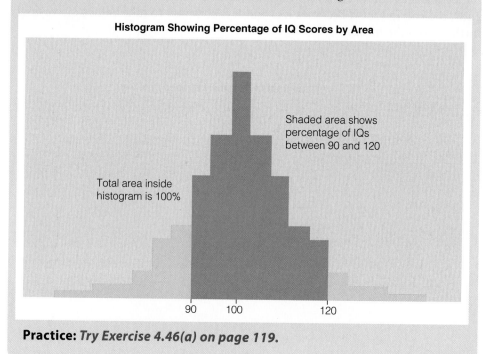

Histogram Showing Percentage of IQ Scores by Area

Shaded area shows percentage of IQs between 90 and 120

Total area inside histogram is 100%

Practice: *Try Exercise 4.46(a) on page 119.*

In fact, the histogram sketched in Example 4.25 is not the only one possible for a normal distribution centered at 100. In order to uniquely determine a normal distribution, we must also identify its spread. Once we know both the mean and the standard deviation, there is an easy way to get a feel for the behavior of a normal distribution via a simple rule that specifies a few key "guidepost" values.

The 68-95-99.7 Rule for Samples: What's "Normal" for a Data Set

In actual statistical practice we rely on *all* the information provided by the knowledge that a distribution with a certain mean and standard deviation has a normal shape. For now, however, we present a small but useful piece of information that will help us begin to get a grasp of the behavior of these distributions.

68-95-99.7 Rule for Normally Distributed Data

Suppose a sample set of values for a quantitative variable has mean $\overline{x}$ and standard deviation s, and the distribution has the particular symmetric, bell-shape known as normal. Then approximately

- 68% of the data values fall within 1 standard deviation of the mean: in the interval $(\overline{x} - s, \overline{x} + s)$
- 95% of the data values fall within 2 standard deviations of the mean: in the interval $(\overline{x} - 2s, \overline{x} + 2s)$
- 99.7% of the data values fall within 3 standard deviations of the mean: in the interval $(\overline{x} - 3s, \overline{x} + 3s)$

The Big Picture: **A Closer Look**

The 68-95-99.7 Rule is also called the *Empirical Rule* because it reports what we observe in actuality: what our *experience* shows us to occur.

Based on this rule, we can sketch a histogram for a normally shaped data set.

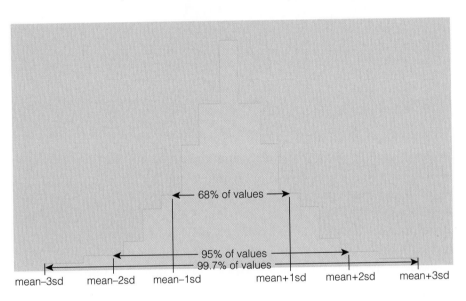

The normal shape fits so many data sets well because it is common for quantitative variables to fall naturally into a pattern where values tend to cluster around their average, and taper away at the extremes. The symmetry arises because in so many contexts it is just as common for a quantitative variable to take a value a certain distance below its mean as above.

In previous examples, we started with a data set and determined its shape, center (mean), and spread (standard deviation) by looking at a display and by calculating the summaries, either by hand or with the aid of software. Another kind of problem is to start with the information that a distribution's shape is normal with a given mean and standard deviation, and then give a rough sketch of what it must look like.

Example TBP 4.11 on page 775 of the **TBP** *Supplement* demonstrates how well a normally shaped data set can conform to the 68-95-99.7 rule. In contrast, Exercise TBP 4.22 shows that a skewed data set does not conform well at all.

EXAMPLE **4.26** USING THE 68-95-99.7 RULE TO SKETCH A HISTOGRAM

Background: Shoe sizes for a sample of 163 adult males are approximately normal with a mean of 11 and a standard deviation of 1.5.

Questions: How would a histogram for the data look? What does the 68-95-99.7 Rule tell us about these adult male shoe sizes?

Continued

Responses: First, we sketch a bell-shaped histogram centered at the mean, 11. We mark off 3 standard deviations to the left and to the right of the mean, making a standard deviation worth 1.5.

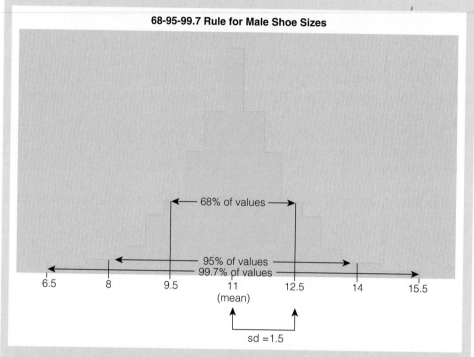

68-95-99.7 Rule for Male Shoe Sizes

According to the 68-95-99.7 Rule, approximately

- 68% of the shoe sizes should fall within 1 standard deviation of the mean: in the interval $(11 - 1.5, 11 + 1.5) = (9.5, 12.5)$;
- 95% of the shoe sizes should fall within 2 standard deviations of the mean: in the interval $(11 - 2(1.5), 11 + 2(1.5)) = (8.0, 14.0)$;
- 99.7% of the shoe sizes should fall within 3 standard deviations of the mean: in the interval $(11 - 3(1.5), 11 + 3(1.5)) = (6.5, 15.5)$.

Practice: *Try Exercise 4.54(a) on page 121.*

Although the 68-95-99.7 Rule is formulated in terms of falling *within* a certain distance of the mean, it is easy enough to use it to find percentages *beyond* a certain distance. We simply use the fact that altogether 100% of the values must be accounted for, and use subtraction to focus on the percentage of values in the "tails" of the distribution.

EXAMPLE 4.27 USING THE 68-95-99.7 RULE TO IDENTIFY PERCENTAGES IN A HISTOGRAM'S TAILS

Background: Shoe sizes for a sample of 163 adult males are approximately normal with a mean of 11 and a standard deviation of 1.5.

Questions:

1. What percentage of shoe sizes are greater than 15.5?
2. What male shoe size corresponds to the bottom 2.5%?

Responses:

1. Because 99.7% of the shoe sizes fall between 6.5 and 15.5, almost nobody has a shoe size over 15.5. We can say this is close to 0%, or we can be more precise and take $(100\% - 99.7\%)/2 = 0.15\%$.

2. Because 95% of the shoe sizes fall between 8 and 14, the remaining 5% is shared below 8 and above 14. Thus, the bottom 2.5% are below size 8.

The graph on the left illustrates our answer to the first question, whereas the one on the right illustrates the solution to the second question.

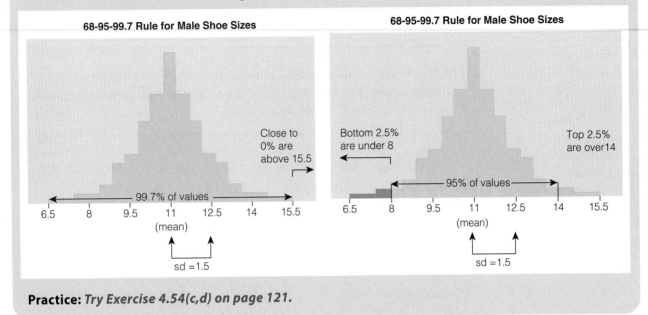

Practice: *Try Exercise 4.54(c,d) on page 121.*

Notice that the first question in Example 4.27 asked for a percentage, given a value. The second question asked for a value, given a percentage. It is useful to be able to solve problems about normally distributed variables "in both directions."

From a Histogram to a Smooth Curve

The 68-95-99.7 Rule works fairly well for data sets with histograms that exhibit a symmetric bell shape, along the lines of what we call "normal." Technically, for a distribution to be truly normal, it must allow for any possible value over a *continuous* range, unlike shoe sizes, which cannot fall in between half sizes. The normal curve actually represents an *infinite* number of values, not just a set of, say, 163 males. Often in statistics we consider rather abstract distributions representing populations of infinite size (all adult males in the United States is close enough), and a variable (such as foot length) that is not limited to distinct, incremental values. The result is a smooth curve like the one shown below for foot lengths of all adult males in the United States.

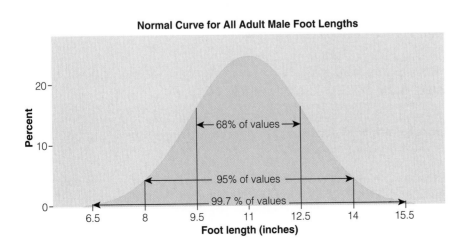

Normal Curve for All Adult Male Foot Lengths

The distinction between a *sample* of values for a variable, displayed with a histogram, and the variable's values for the entire *population*, displayed with a smooth curve if the variable is continuous, is extremely important for students to grasp. Our ultimate goal in introductory statistics is to use information from a sample—such as sample mean—to draw conclusions about the larger population from which the sample was taken—such as inferring a range of plausible values for unknown population mean. Throughout this process, then, students must distinguish between the sample mean and the population mean with proper notation.

Whereas the mean for a sample is denoted $\bar{x}$, the mean for a population is denoted μ (the Greek letter "mu"). Whereas the standard deviation for a sample is denoted s, the standard deviation for a population is denoted σ (the Greek letter "sigma"). Because $\bar{x}$ and s summarize the sample, they are statistics. In contrast, μ and σ—because they summarize the population—are parameters. A convention in statistics is to use Greek letters to denote parameters.

> *Definitions*   The **population mean**—the average of all values—is μ. The **population standard deviation**—the square root of the average of all squared deviations from the mean—is σ.

EXAMPLE 4.28 DISPLAYING AND SUMMARIZING SAMPLES OR POPULATIONS

Background: We are interested in displaying and summarizing adult male or female brain weights, which are normally distributed.

Questions: How do we denote the mean and standard deviation, and display the distribution, for a *sample* of adult males? What if the information comes from a *population* of adult females?

Responses: We write $\bar{x}$ and s for the mean and standard deviation of a *sample* of male brain weights. We would display the distribution with a histogram that is normally shaped. In contrast, we write μ and σ for the mean and standard deviation of the *population* of female brain weights. We would display this distribution with a normal curve.

Practice: *Try Exercise 4.55(a) on page 121.*

Examples TBP 4.8 and TBP 4.9 on page 774 of the *TBP* Supplement provide students with a preview to inference by having them consider whether a given sample mean suggests that a proposed value for the unknown population mean is plausible. Example TBP 4.10 on page 775 foreshadows inference by pointing out that, in general, the mean from a larger sample provides a better estimate for the unknown population mean.

Standardizing Values of Normal Variables: Storing Information in the Letter z

In general, about two-thirds (68%) of the values in a normal distribution are within 1 standard deviation σ of the mean μ. Most values (95%) are within 2 standard deviations of the mean. Practically all (99.7%) are within 3 standard deviations of the mean. We measure distance from the mean, in standard deviations, through a process called *standardizing*.

EXAMPLE 4.29 FINDING STANDARDIZED VALUES

Background: Male foot lengths (in inches) have a mean of 11 and a standard deviation of 1.5.

Questions: How many standard deviations below or above the mean foot length is 13 inches? What about a foot length of 7 inches?

Responses: The mean is 11 inches, so 13 inches is 2 *inches* above the mean. Because a standard deviation is worth 1.5 inches, this would be 2/1.5 = 1.33 *standard deviations* above the mean. Combining these two steps, we could write

$$\frac{13 \text{ inches} - 11 \text{ inches}}{1.5 \text{ inches per standard deviation}}$$

$$= \frac{13 - 11}{1.5} \text{ standard deviations} = +1.33 \text{ standard deviations}$$

Similarly, we take $\frac{7 - 11}{1.5} = \frac{-4}{1.5} = -2.67$ and report that 7 inches is 2.67 standard deviations below the mean.

Practice: *Try Exercise 4.55(d) on page 121.*

In the language of statistics, we have just found the *z-score* for a male foot length of 13 inches to be $z = +1.33$ and the *z*-score for 7 inches to be -2.67. Or, to put it another way, we have *standardized* the values 13 inches and 7 inches. We will see how standardizing helps put the size of a value in perspective.

Definitions   The **z-score** of a value tells how many standard deviations below or above the mean the original value is:

$$z = \frac{\text{value} - \text{mean}}{\text{standard deviation}}$$

We also call z the **standardized value.**

The convention is to denote a value from our data set with the letter x. If we only know the mean $\overline{x}$ and standard deviation s of *sample* values, then the standardized value would be

$$z = \frac{x - \overline{x}}{s}$$

If we standardize with the *population* mean and standard deviation, μ and σ, we write

$$z = \frac{x - \mu}{\sigma}$$

Either way, standardizing "wipes out" the original units of measurement. Because standard deviation is always positive, z will be positive for values of x above the mean and negative for values of x below the mean. If x exactly equals the mean, then z equals zero. Because a distribution of values x of a normal variable is symmetric about the mean, it follows that the standardized normal scores z are symmetric about zero. Because z counts the number of standard deviations below or above the mean a value is, our 68-95-99.7 Rule "translates" as follows.

> Although we may standardize a value x from any sample or population, in some contexts using the letter z suggests we have standardized a value from a normally distributed sample or population.

68-95-99.7 Rule for Standard Normal Distributions

For standardized scores z of a normally distributed data set or population,

- ■ 68% of z-scores are between -1 and $+1$
- ■ 95% of z-scores are between -2 and $+2$
- ■ 99.7% of z-scores are between -3 and $+3$

Continued

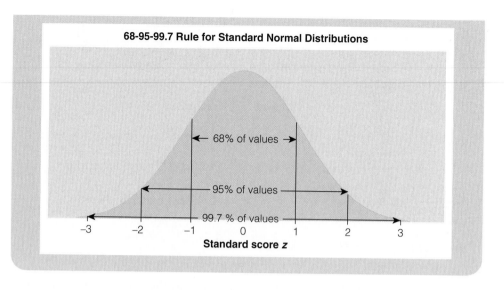

68-95-99.7 Rule for Standard Normal Distributions

Because 95% of z-scores are less than 2 in absolute value, we start to think of values as "unusual" when they get close to 2 or more standard deviations away from the mean. A foot length of 13 inches is only 1.33 standard deviations above the mean, so it is not unusual. On the other hand, 7 inches is 2.67 standard deviations below the mean, which is quite unusual.

EXAMPLE 4.30 WHAT Z-SCORES TELL US

Background: Two students ask their statistics professor how they did on a recent exam. They are told that the distribution of scores was normal, and one of them had a z-score of -0.4; the other had a z-score of $+1.5$.

Question: How should the students interpret these results?

Response: Since the middle 68% of z-scores are between -1 and $+1$, a score of -0.4 is somewhat below average but not alarmingly so. A z-score of $+1.5$ is somewhere between the top 16% and the top 2.5%, so it's a good score but not among the very best.

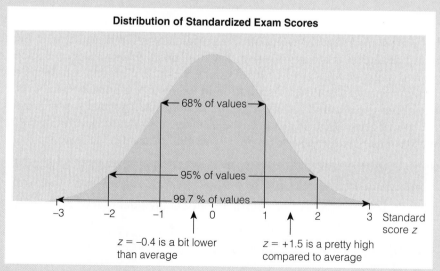

Distribution of Standardized Exam Scores

Practice: *Try Exercise 4.55(e) on page 121.*

Most people realize that 13 inches is a fairly common foot length for an adult male, and 7 inches would be unusually small. On the other hand, we often work with variables that we know less about. Nevertheless, as long as we are told that the distribution's shape is normal, and what the values of the mean and standard deviation are, we can get a pretty good idea of what to expect. This table classifies various ranges of z-scores informally, according to how someone might reasonably react in terms of how usual or unusual they feel such z-scores to be:

Size of z	Unusual?
$|z|$ greater than 3	Extremely unusual
$|z|$ between 2 and 3	Very unusual
$|z|$ between 1.75 and 2	Unusual
$|z|$ between 1.5 and 1.75	Maybe unusual (depends on circumstances)
$|z|$ between 1 and 1.5	Somewhat low/high, but not unusual
$|z|$ less than 1	Quite common

EXAMPLE 4.31 USING Z-SCORES TO IDENTIFY UNUSUAL VALUES

Background: Systolic blood pressure readings for a large group of students are fairly normal with a mean of 120 and a standard deviation of 16.

Questions: One of the individuals had a systolic blood pressure of 102; is this unusually low? Another had a reading of 171; is this unusually high?

Responses: The z-score for 102 is $(102 - 120)/16 = -1.125$, which means 102 is not especially far below the mean. The z-score for 171 is $(171 - 120)/16 = +3.19$, which means this blood pressure is extremely high. This student should have his or her blood pressure rechecked to make sure the reading wasn't in error, and then be seen by a doctor if the value really is as high as 171.

Practice: *Try Exercise 4.55(f) on page 121.*

Students *Talk Stats*

When the 68-95-99.7 Rule Does Not Apply

*A*ges of all undergraduate students at a certain university have mean 20.5 and standard deviation 2.9. Is $16\frac{1}{2}$ unusually young for one of these students?
  Suppose a group of statistics students encounters this problem on a practice exam and wants to reach a consensus on the answer.

Adam: *"The z-score for 16.5 is 16.5 minus 20.5, divided by 2.9, which is negative 1.38. It's not unusual to be 1.38 standard deviations below the mean, right?"*

Students Talk Stats continued ➔

The Big Picture:

LOOKING AHEAD

The ability to classify a summary as "unusual" or not plays a key role in the statistical inference part of the book, Part IV. There we will either construct an interval of plausible values for an unknown parameter, or decide whether a particular proposed value for the parameter is plausible.

Later on, when we perform inference about a population proportion or population mean, sample size is incorporated into the standardized sample proportion or sample mean. For now, we can alert students that when we consider values of a variable for a very large group of individuals, we may expect to encounter a few whose z-scores are quite extreme.

If a distribution is not normal, we can't apply the 68-95-99.7 Rule, but we can apply a result called *Chebyshev's Theorem*. This asserts that the probability is at least $1 - \frac{1}{k^2}$ that a variable takes a value within k standard deviations of its mean. It provides no useful information for $k = 1$. For $k = 2$, it tells us that the probability is at least $1 - \frac{1}{2^2} = 0.75$ that a variable falls within 2 standard deviations of the mean. If we know the variable is normal, then we know the probability to be 0.95, which tells us much more than Chebyshev's Theorem does.

Students Talk Stats continued

Brittany: *"Look around. How many $16\frac{1}{2}$-year-olds do you see on campus? Do you know anybody in college who's that young?"*

Carlos: *"Overall the standard deviation might be 2.9 years, but most of the spread is coming from students who are a lot older than the average."*

Dominique: *"This is a trick question. It doesn't say the distribution is normal, so Adam shouldn't be talking about the z-score as if it's from a normal distribution. We have to use our common sense and say it is an unusually young age, even though its standardized value isn't so extreme. That's because some of the students are really old, like Carlos said, so the distribution isn't normal, it's skewed right."*

This example was designed to remind students of the importance of the requirement that *the shape of the distribution must be normal if we want to apply the guidelines of the 68-95-99.7 Rule.* The shape of ages of college students is quite skewed to the right. The rule does not apply because being a certain distance below the mean could be next to impossible, whereas being that same distance above the mean is not so unusual.

"Unstandardizing" z-Scores: Back to Original Units

If we know the mean and standard deviation of a variable's values, and are told the z-score for a particular value, it is quite easy to "unstandardize," keeping in mind that the z-score tells us how many standard deviations below or above the mean a value is.

EXAMPLE 4.32 FROM Z-SCORE TO ORIGINAL VALUE

Background: An IQ test has a mean of 100. The standard deviation is 15.

Question: If a student's z-score is +1.2, what is the student's IQ?

Response: The z-score tells us that the student scored 1.2 standard deviations above the mean, where a standard deviation is 15 and the mean is 100. We calculate $100 + 1.2(15) = 118$.

Practice: *Try Exercise 4.55(g) on page 121.*

In general, $z = \dfrac{\text{value} - \text{mean}}{\text{standard deviation}}$, so we can express a value in the original units by finding

$$\text{value} = \text{mean} + z(\text{standard deviation})$$

being careful to get the correct sign for z. If the mean and standard deviation are given for the population, we can express a value x as

$$x = \mu + z\sigma$$

Because σ is always positive, a positive z results in a value that is greater than the mean, whereas a negative z results in a value that is less than the mean.

The Normal Table: A Precursor to Software

Before software was widely available, tables were essential for finding proportions or percentages involving normal variables. This book does not require the use of tables, but they are included at the end of the book, and a section of "Using the Normal Table" exercises is featured in some of the chapters that involve normal variables.

Most statistical applications involving normal distributions are carried out with software that automatically provides the needed proportions. Still, using normal tables is one way for beginners to become familiar with how these distributions behave.

Pages 775 through 778 of the *TBP* Supplement explain the structure of normal tables and illustrate their use with Examples TBP 4.12, TBP 4.13, and TBP 4.14.

EXERCISES FOR SECTION 4.4

Normal Distributions: The Shape of Things to Come

Note: Asterisked numbers indicate exercises whose answers are provided in the Solutions to Selected Exercises section, on page 689.

*4.46 The histogram in Exercise 4.36 on page 106 shows the distribution of self-rated school ability scores, on a scale of 1 to 7.

a. What percentage of 12th graders rated themselves less than 4?

b. What percentage of 12th graders rated themselves 4 or less?

c. What percentage of 12th graders rated themselves at least 4?

d. What percentage of 12th graders rated themselves more than 4?

4.47 The histogram in Exercise 4.37 on page 106 shows the distribution of evenings out per week for a large group of students. Was the percentage of students who went out fewer than 2 nights per week about 10% to 15%, 15% to 20%, 20% to 25%, or 25% to 30%?

*4.48 Data for vertical drop (difference in feet between top and bottom of a continuous slope or trail) of 23 ski slopes in the Middle Atlantic states are summarized below.

Variable	N	Mean	Median	TrMean	StDev	SE Mean
Vertical	23	627.0	610.0	606.7	317.4	66.2

Variable	Minimum	Maximum	Q1	Q3		
Vertical	180.0	1500.0	360.0	850.0		

a. Use the output to tell how many standard deviations above the mean the maximum value is.

b. Did all of the 23 values fall within 2 standard deviations of the mean (between $627 - 2(317.4) = -7.8$ and $627 + 2(317.4) = 1261.8$)?

c. The minimum drop is 180 feet. Would its z-score be positive or negative?

d. One of the ski slopes has a z-score of $+0.86$. What is its vertical drop, to the nearest foot?

e. The mean drop is 627 feet. If this is taken as a summary of all the region's ski slopes, is it a statistic or a parameter? Do we refer to it as $\bar{x}$ or μ?

f. The mean drop is 627 feet. If this is taken as a summary of a sample of some of the nation's ski slopes, is it a statistic or a parameter? Do we refer to it as $\bar{x}$ or μ?

g. How would a histogram of the data appear if the standard deviation were only 3 instead of 317.4?

4.49 Here is a stemplot for ages at death (in years) of 20 dinosaur specimens, ranging from 2 years up to 28 years.

```
0  22
0  57
1  0444
1  5567888
2  1224
2  8
```

a. The mean age at death is 15 years and the standard deviation is 7 years. What percentage of the dinosaurs' ages were within 1 standard deviation of the mean?

b. What percentage of the dinosaurs' ages were within 2 standard deviations of the mean?

c. The units of standard deviation s are years. What would be the units of variance s^2?

d. The shape of the stemplot is fairly normal, with only a bit of left-skewness. Tell how the shape of the distribution for age at death of humans would differ.

e. If paleontologists want to use the mean age, 15 years, to estimate the mean age at death of all dinosaurs, are they mainly concerned with data production, displaying and summarizing data, probability, or statistical inference?

f. Based on the information from this sample, which of these would be the most plausible value for mean age at death of all dinosaurs: 10 years, 14 years, or 18 years?

4.50 Here are data for per capita beer consumption (in liters per person per year) in 18 countries during 2002.[18]

Country	Beer Consumption
Ireland	155
Germany	119
Austria	106
Belgium	98
Denmark	98
United Kingdom	97
Australia	89
United States	85
Netherlands	80

Country	Beer Consumption
Finland	79
New Zealand	78
Canada	70
Switzerland	57
Norway	56
Sweden	56
Japan	55
France	41
Italy	29

a. Display the data with a histogram, using rectangles with intervals of width 20 liters.

b. Explain why the shape of the data suggests that the 68-95-99.7 Rule should work reasonably well.

c. The mean per capita consumption is approximately 80, and the standard deviation is approximately 30. What are the endpoints of the interval that extends within 1 standard deviation of the mean?

d. The 68-95-99.7 Rule estimates about 68% of values should fall in the interval you reported in part (c); what percentage of those 18 values actually fall within the interval?

e. What are the endpoints of the interval that extends within 2 standard deviations of the mean?

f. What percentage of those 18 values actually fall within the interval you reported in part (e)?

g. What are the endpoints of the interval that extends within 3 standard deviations of the mean?

h. What percentage of those 18 values actually fall within the interval you reported in part (g)?

i. Find the z-score for Ireland and report how many standard deviations below or above the mean its value is.

j. Which country has a z-score of $+0.3$?

k. Countries with consumption values even less than Italy's were not included. Would their z-scores be positive or negative?

4.51 Total viewerships, in millions, for all the presidential debates held every 4 years from 1976 to 2004 are summarized in this output. (Note that there were typically two or three debates held in each of those eight election years.)

```
Variable              N     Mean    Median    TrMean    StDev    SE Mean
Debate Viewership     19    57.66    62.70     57.58    13.58       3.12
```

a. How many presidential debates were there altogether from 1976 to 2004?

b. The viewership for the first Bush-Kerry debate in 2004 was 62.5 million. What is the z-score for this value?

c. Based on the z-score, how does the viewership for the Bush-Kerry debate compare to the data set as a whole—pretty low, pretty high, or fairly typical?

d. There was only one Carter-Reagan debate in 1980, and the viewership was 80.6 million. What is the z-score for this value?

e. Based on the z-score, how does the viewership for the Carter-Reagan debate compare to the data set as a whole—pretty low, pretty high, or fairly typical?

f. Explain why the z-score for the number of viewers watching the very first televised debate (between Kennedy and Nixon in 1960) might be misleading as a measure of public interest.

*4.52 Weights of male Gadwall ducks at the "gawky downy" age follow a distribution like the one shown. What are the mean and standard deviation?

Weight of Male Gawky-Downy Gadwall Ducks

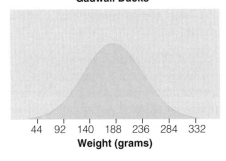

44   92   140   188   236   284   332
Weight (grams)

4.53 Weights of 1-year-old boys (in kilograms) follow a distribution like the one shown. What are the mean and standard deviation?

6   18
Weight of 1-year-old boys (kilograms)

*4.54 Waist circumference of women in their twenties follows a somewhat normal distribution with mean 32 inches, standard deviation 5 inches.

a. Use the 68-95-99.7 Rule to sketch a histogram for a large data set of women's waist circumferences, marking off the circumferences that are within 1, 2, and 3 standard deviations of the mean.

b. Sketch a normal curve for the waist circumferences of all women.

c. Approximately what is the percentage of waists that are larger than 42 inches?

d. The smallest 16% of waists are less than how many inches?

e. More precisely, the mean for women in their twenties is 32.2, and their median is 30.6. The mean for women in their eighties is 36.7, and their median is 36.4. Which age group has more skewness in the distribution of waist circumferences?

f. Is the skewness observed in part (e) left or right?

*4.55 Waist circumference of women in their twenties follows a somewhat normal distribution with mean 32 inches, standard deviation 5 inches.

a. How do we denote the number 32?

b. How would we denote the mean waist circumference for a sample of women in their twenties?

c. The mean, 32 inches, is actually just an estimate made by researchers. Is it closer to the truth if it was based on information from a well-designed study of 1,000 women, or of 10,000 women, or doesn't it matter?

d. How many standard deviations away from the mean is a waist circumference of 32?

e. If the z-score for a woman's waist circumference is $+2.4$, should we report it to be somewhere in the top 50%, the top 16%, the top 2.5%, or the top 0.15%?

f. If the z-score for a woman's waist circumference is $+2.4$, would we consider it to be fairly common, unusually small, or unusually large?

g. Find the waist circumference for a woman whose z-score is $+2.4$.

h. Find the waist circumference for a woman whose z-score is -1.2.

4.56 Weights of 1-year-old male children are fairly normally distributed with mean 26 pounds, standard deviation 3 pounds.

   a. Use the 68-95-99.7 Rule to sketch a curve for this distribution, marking off the weights that are within 1, 2, and 3 standard deviations of the mean.

   b. Find the z-score for a male 1-year-old who weighs 20 pounds.

   c. Find the weight (to the nearest pound) of a 1-year-old male whose z-score is -1.67.

   d. What percentage of male 1-year-olds weigh less than 20 pounds?

   e. Would a 19-pound, 1-year-old male be considered pretty light, pretty heavy, or fairly typical?

   f. Would a 28-pound, 1-year-old male be considered pretty light, pretty heavy, or fairly typical?

4.57 Suppose you are told the mean and standard deviation for amounts that a sample of students have in their bank accounts. Why is this not enough to sketch the distribution of amounts?

4.58 Students' scores on a final exam had a mean of 79%. If a student had a z-score of -0.3, which one of these could be her exam score: 75%, 85%, or 95%?

*4.59 On an exam with scores that followed a normal distribution, a student's z-score was $+1$. What percentage of students scored better than he did?

4.60 On an exam with scores that followed a normal distribution, a student's z-score was $+2$. What percentage of students scored worse than he did?

4.61 In a certain population of smokers, the number of cigarettes smoked per day followed a fairly normal curve with a mean of 15 and a standard deviation of 6.

   a. Use the 68-95-99.7 Rule to sketch a curve for this distribution, marking off the numbers of cigarettes smoked daily that are within 1, 2, and 3 standard deviations of the mean.

   b. Explain why the lower end of the curve is not perfectly consistent with reality.

   c. Find the z-score for a person who smokes one pack (20 cigarettes) a day.

   d. Characterize one pack a day as being unusually low, unusually high, or not unusual.

   e. Find the z-score for a person who smokes two packs a day.

   f. Characterize two packs a day as being unusually low, unusually high, or not unusual.

*4.62 Keep in mind that certain distributions, such as exam scores or some physical characteristics for specific age and gender groups, naturally follow a normal shape. Other distributions are naturally skewed left or have low outliers if there tend to be relatively few values that are unusually low compared to the rest. Yet other distributions are naturally skewed right or have high outliers if there tend to be relatively few values that are unusually high compared to the rest.

Decide if each of the following variables is most likely to have a shape that is approximately normal, or skewed left/low outliers, or skewed right/high outliers:

   a. Math SAT scores

   b. Number of credits taken by a large group of students, including part-time and full-time

   c. Number of minutes that students spend exercising on a given day

   d. Number of minutes that students spend watching TV on a given day

   e. Ages of students' fathers

   f. Heights of students' mothers

   g. Number of siblings that students have

   h. How much money students earned the previous year

4.63 Keep in mind that certain distributions, such as exam scores or some physical characteristics for specific age and gender groups, naturally follow a normal shape. Other distributions are naturally skewed left or have low outliers if there tend to be relatively few values that are unusually low compared to the rest. Yet other distributions are naturally skewed right or have high outliers if there tend to be relatively few values that are unusually high compared to the rest.

Decide if each of the following variables is most likely to have a shape that is approximately normal, or skewed left/low outliers, or skewed right/high outliers:

a. Number of minutes that students spend on the computer on a given day

b. Number of minutes that students spend on the phone on a given day

c. Verbal SAT scores

d. Number of cigarettes smoked in a day by a large group of students who smoke

e. Amount of cash carried by students

f. Heights of students' fathers

g. Ages of students' mothers

h. Number of hours that students slept on a given night in a large group of students that includes a few who got little or no sleep

4.64 "Remains Found of Downsized Human Species" reports that "once upon a time, on a tropical island midway between Asia and Australia, there lived a race of little people, whose adults stood just 3.5 feet high."[19] The article goes on to tell about the excavation in 2003 of an adult female skeleton, the first of several whose size was small enough to warrant identification as a new human species, called *Homo floresiensis* after the island of Flores where they were discovered.

a. If heights of adult females today have mean 64.5 inches and standard deviation 2.5 inches, what would be the z-score of a 3.5-foot-tall woman?

b. The article explains that "because the downsizing is so extreme, smaller than that in modern human pygmies, they [scientists] assigned it to a new species." The smallest race of pygmies is said to have an average height of 54 inches. If their standard deviation is about 2 inches, find how many standard deviations below average the Floresian would be compared to pygmies.

c. Do we refer to the standard deviation of all pygmy heights as $\bar{x}$, μ, s, or σ?

Using Software [see Technology Guide]

*4.65 Here are estimated weights (in thousands of kilograms) of 20 dinosaur specimens:

> 5,654   5,040   3,230   2,984   1,807   1,761   30   1,105   747   607
> 229   127   1,142   1,282   1,013   762   50   1,791   1,518   496

a. Use software to calculate the mean and standard deviation.

b. If a distribution is normal, about 16% of values are less than the value that is one standard deviation below the mean. What percentage of these 20 weights are less than the value that is one standard deviation below the mean?

c. If a distribution is normal, only about 2.5% of values are more than two standard deviations above the mean. What percentage of these 20 weights are more than two standard deviations above the mean?

d. Comment on how well or how badly this data set conforms to the 68-95-99.7 Rule.

4.66 This data set reports the number of McDonald's restaurants in various European countries as of 2004:

> 1115   1091   857   290   276   227   205   181   148   133
> 119   99   93   91   76   64   62   60   55   48   10   6   3

a. Use software to find the mean and standard deviation for number of restaurants in those countries.

b. For what percentage of countries is the number of restaurants at or below the mean?

c. If a distribution is normal, about 16% of values are less than the value that is 1 standard deviation below the mean. What percentage of these 23 values are less than the value that is 1 standard deviation below the mean?

d. If a distribution is normal, only about 2.5% of values are more than 2 standard deviations above the mean. What percentage of these 23 values are more than 2 standard deviations above the mean?

e. Comment on how well or how badly this data set conforms to the 68-95-99.7 Rule.

4.67 Running times (in minutes) of 29 movies currently showing in early December 2004 are listed here, from a 73-minute European film called "The Big Animal", about a couple that unwittingly adopts a camel into their home when the circus leaves town, to the 173-minute Oliver Stone film about Alexander the Great.

> 73 90 90 93 94 97 98 99 100 100 102 105 105 106 106
> 107 108 113 115 115 115 120 123 130 130 140 150 152 173

a. Use software to find the mean and standard deviation.

b. Report the z-score for the shortest film, about the camel.

c. Report the z-score for the longest film, about Alexander the Great.

Using the Normal Table [see end of book] or Software

4.68 Part (j) of Exercise 4.50 on page 120 refers to the country whose z-score for per capita beer consumption is $+0.3$. Find the probability of z being greater than $+0.3$, if the distribution were perfectly normal.

*4.69 According to Exercise 4.52 on page 121, weights of male Gadwall ducks at the "gawky downy" age follow a normal distribution with mean 188 grams, standard deviation 48 grams.

a. The lightest 1% weigh less than how many grams?

b. The lightest 10% weigh less than how many grams?

c. The heaviest 20% weigh more than how many grams?

d. The heaviest 2% weigh more than how many grams?

4.70 According to Exercise 4.53 on page 121, weights of 1-year-old boys follow a normal distribution with mean 12 kilograms, standard deviation 2 kilograms.

a. The lightest 5% weigh less than how many kilograms?

b. The lightest 25% weigh less than how many kilograms?

c. The heaviest 50% weigh more than how many kilograms?

d. The heaviest 3% weigh more than how many kilograms?

*4.71 Part (h) of Exercise 4.55 on page 121 refers to the waist circumference of a woman whose z-score is -1.2, where the mean is 32 inches and standard deviation is 5 inches.

a. Find the proportion of z values less than -1.2.

b. What proportion of z values are greater than -1.2?

4.72 According to Exercise 4.56 on page 122, weights of 1-year-old boys are normal with mean 26 pounds, standard deviation 3 pounds.

a. Part (c) refers to the weight of a 1-year-old boy whose z-score is -1.67. Find the proportion of 1-year-old boys who weigh less than this amount.

b. Part (e) refers to a 1-year-old boy whose weight is 19 pounds. Find the proportion of 1-year-old boys who weigh less than this.

c. What proportion of 1-year-old boys weigh *more* than 19 pounds?

d. Part (f) refers to a 1-year-old boy whose weight is 28 pounds. Find the proportion of 1-year-old boys who weigh *less* than this.

4.73 Exercise 4.58 on page 122 refers to a student whose exam score had $z = -0.3$. If the distribution of scores is normal, what proportion of z-scores are less than -0.3?

*4.74 Exercise 4.59 on page 122 refers to a student whose exam score had $z = +1$. According to the normal table or a computer, exactly what proportion of z-scores are greater than $+1$?

4.75 Exercise 4.60 on page 122 refers to a student whose exam score had $z = +2$. According to the normal table or a computer, exactly what proportion of z-scores are greater than $+2$?

4.76 Exercise 4.61 on page 122 states that in a certain population of smokers, daily number of cigarettes smoked is approximately normal with mean 15, standard deviation 6.

a. Find the proportion smoking at least one pack a day (20 cigarettes).

b. Find the proportion smoking at least two packs a day (40 cigarettes).

CHAPTER 4 SUMMARY

Often we are interested in sampled values of a single variable. The variable may be categorical (such as whether or not a student eats breakfast), or quantitative (such as how much money the student earned). Which displays and summaries are appropriate depends on whether the variable is categorical or quantitative. In this chapter, we concentrated on displaying and summarizing *sampled* values of a variable. We did, however, make an exception in the case of a normal curve, which shows a bell-shaped distribution of number values for an entire *population*.

Single Categorical Variable

- Summarize results for all individuals in a categorical data set with **counts, percents,** or **proportions** in the various categories.

- Display categorical values with a **pie chart** or **bar graph.**

- Categorical variables may have any number of possible values, but much of the theory developed later in this book will be restricted to situations where just two values are possible.

- A proportion that summarizes categorical values for a *sample* is a **statistic,** written $\hat{p}$. If it summarizes values for a *population*, it is a **parameter,** written p.

- The **mode** is the most common category value. If there are only two possibilities, then the mode is the same as the value taken by the *majority*.

- The percentage that summarizes a categorical variable may be **biased** because the sample was not representative, or because of flaws in the design for assessing the variable's values, or both.

Single Quantitative Variable

When we are interested in values of a single quantitative variable, we can summarize the general pattern of those values by reporting shape, center, and spread.

Shape

- Shape is best assessed by producing a display of the data. A **stemplot** is one display for a quantitative data set. Each stem in a vertical list is followed by a horizontal list of one-digit leaves, representing all observations with that stem.

- Stems may be **split** if there are too few stems for the number of leaves.

- Leaves may be **truncated** or rounded if there are too many stems for the number of leaves.

- The list of stems must form a consistent numerical scale, and stems that happen not to have any leaves must still be included.

- A **histogram** is a display consisting of rectangles with heights that correspond to the count or percentage or proportion of values occurring in the given horizontal interval.

- The shape of a distribution is called **symmetric** if it is fairly balanced.

- If a distribution has one major peak it is called **unimodal.**

- A particular shape that frequently occurs is called **normal.** It is symmetric and unimodal, often called bell-shaped because of the way it bulges at the center and tapers at the ends.

- The shape is called **skewed** if it is lopsided. It is **skewed left** if there is a longer left tail, indicating there are a few values that are relatively low compared to the rest of the values. It is **skewed right** if there is a longer right tail, indicating there are a few values that are relatively high compared to the rest of the values.

- **Outliers** are values that are far from the bulk of displayed values.

Center and Spread

- The **median** of a quantitative data set is the single middle value for an odd sample size. It is the average of the two middle values for an even sample size.

- The **first quartile** (Q_1) has one-fourth of the data values at or below it. It is the middle of the values below the median.

■ The **third quartile** (Q_3) has three-fourths of the data values at or below it. It is the middle of the values above the median.

■ The **interquartile range** is $IQR = Q_3 - Q_1$. We designate as outliers any values below $Q_1 - 1.5(IQR)$ or above $Q_3 + 1.5(IQR)$.

■ The **five-number summary** lists the minimum, first quartile, median, third quartile, and maximum.

■ A **boxplot** displays the five-number summary, with special treatment for outliers. The box spans the quartiles, with a line through the box at the median. The whiskers extend to the minimum and maximum non-outliers. Outliers are marked "*". Boxplots are skewed left if "bottom heavy," skewed right if "top heavy."

■ The **sample mean** is the arithmetic average

$$\overline{x} = \frac{x_1 + \ldots + x_n}{n}$$

■ The **sample standard deviation** is the square root of the "average" squared deviation from the mean

$$s = \sqrt{\frac{(x_1 - \overline{x})^2 + \cdots + (x_n - \overline{x})^2}{n - 1}}$$

It tells the typical distance of values from their mean.

Normal Distributions

■ If a data set has a normal shape, the **68-95-99.7 Rule** tells us that approximately 68% of the values fall within 1 standard deviation of the mean, 95% within 2 standard deviations of the mean, and 99.7% within 3 standard deviations of the mean.

■ Since 100% of a variable's values must be accounted for, the 68-95-99.7 Rule can be used to tell percentages on the **tails** of a normal distribution, beyond a certain distance from the mean.

■ The distribution of values of a normal variable may be represented with a smooth bell-shaped curve instead of a histogram. The **normal curve** is generally meant to display values for an entire population, modeled as having an infinite number of individuals, where the variable's values constitute a continuum of possibilities.

■ The standardized value of any data value x, or **z-score**, tells how many standard deviations below or above the mean x is: $z = \frac{x - \overline{x}}{s}$.

■ The mean of a population is denoted μ and the standard deviation is denoted σ. A standardized value is $z = \frac{x - \mu}{\sigma}$.

■ A z-score can be "unstandardized" to the actual value by finding value = mean + z(standard deviation), or $x = \mu + z(\sigma)$.

■ For a normal data set, the 68-95-99.7 Rule applied to standardized scores tells us that 68% of z-scores are between -1 and $+1$; 95% are between -2 and $+2$; 99.7% are between -3 and $+3$.

■ If a sample data set or population is normal, then the z-score gives us a good idea of how usual or unusual a value is. The cut-off for what would be considered unusual is around $z = -2$ or $z = +2$.

■ Besides estimating normal percentages with the 68-95-99.7 Rule or finding them with software, a normal table (provided at the end of the book) can be used.

CHAPTER 4   EXERCISES

Note: Asterisked numbers indicate exercises whose answers are provided in the Solutions to Selected Exercises section, on page 689.

Additional exercises appeared after each section: categorical variables (Section 4.1) page 78, quantitative variables (shape, Section 4.2) page 92, quantitative variables (center and spread, Section 4.3) page 103, and quantitative variables (normal, Section 4.4) page 119.

Warming Up: SINGLE CATEGORICAL VARIABLE

4.77 Use the definition of *experiment* to explain why we would not expect an experiment to involve just a single categorical variable.

4.78 Explain why a random sample of college students has a higher percentage of females, whereas a random sample of high school students is almost evenly divided between males and females.

4.79 Four statistics students are answering a homework problem that asks them to explain why a very large sample of college students shows a significantly higher percentage of students with pierced ears than does a sample of high school students. Which *two* answers are best?

Adam: Probably because of people like me—I didn't get my ear pierced until I started college. Once you have them pierced, you don't get them unpierced, so the number with pierced ears accumulates as students get older.

Brittany: I think it's because high school students are pretty much evenly divided

between males and females, but there are more females in college and they tend to be the ones with pierced ears.

Carlos: Maybe it's because the college students feel less inhibited, so they're the ones who are willing to admit that they have pierced ears.

Dominique: Inhibitions have nothing to do with it unless you're talking about something more personal like a hidden tattoo. I think the difference in proportions with ears pierced just came about by chance. Anything's possible with random samples.

4.80 For which one of the following variables would you expect high school and college students may have very different percentages in the various categories: whether they ate breakfast or not; whether they are right-handed, left-handed, or ambidextrous; what number they picked between 1 and 20 when asked to pick a number at random?

Exploring the Big Picture: SINGLE CATEGORICAL VARIABLE

4.81 In "Compliance with the Item Limit of the Food Supermarket Express Checkout Lane: An Informal Look," researcher J. Trinkaus reported, "75 15-min observations of customers' behavior at a food supermarket showed that only about 15% of shoppers observed the item limit of the express lane."[20]

a. Is 15% a statistic or a parameter? Should it be denoted p or $\hat{p}$?

b. Can we tell the approximate count of shoppers who observed the item limit? If so, what is it? If not, explain why not.

c. Which type of sample is suggested by the word *informal*: volunteer, random, convenience, or stratified?

d. If these results are used to estimate that about 15% of all shoppers observe the item limit of the express lane, are we performing data production, displaying and summarizing data, probability, or inference?

4.82 In November 2004, a newspaper article announced, "Caesarean Deliveries Hit U.S. Record" and stated that "roughly 1.13 million, or 27.6% [of births], were caesarean deliveries" in the United States in 2003.[21]

a. Approximately how many births were there altogether in the United States that year?

More exercises for this chapter are featured in the *TBP* Supplement on pages 779 through 786. End-of-chapter activities are described on page 778.

b. If the proportion 0.276 refers to the entire proportion of births, should it be written as p or $\hat{p}$?

4.83 An Internet survey first asked a sample of 2,065 men and women how many sexual partners they'd had altogether. When subsequently asked about their truthfulness in responding to the question, 5% said they had lied.

a. If the original survey had been used to estimate the mean number of sexual partners for men and women in general, would it result in bias due to a nonrepresentative sample or bias due to inaccurately assessing a variable's values?

b. What notation do we use for the number 0.05?

c. How do we denote the unknown proportion of all people who would lie when answering such a question?

4.84 "Antarctic Birds Use Scent to Find Their Mates" reports that "Antarctic birds returning to a nesting colony after feeding at sea sniff out their mates, literally . . .

Scientists studying the birds [Antarctic prions] found that they have a noticeable odor, which remained behind on the bags used to hold them. So the researchers set up a Y-shaped maze. On the end of each arm, they placed a bag that had previously held a bird. In 17 out of 20 cases, the returning bird selected the bag that smelled like its mate . . ."[22]

a. Which statistical process concerned the researchers when they decided on a Y-shaped maze to test their theory—data production, displaying and summarizing, probability, or statistical inference?

b. If the birds could *not* identify the smell of their mates, approximately what percentage of all returning birds would select the correct bag?

c. Is your answer to part (b) a statistic or a parameter?

d. Use percentages to explain why the results seem convincing.

e. What is the largest population for which the researchers may be justified in generalizing their results?

Using Software [see Technology Guide]: SINGLE CATEGORICAL VARIABLE

4.85 Access the student survey data completed by 446 students in introductory statistics courses at a large university in the fall of 2003.

a. Use software to report the percentages of males and females.

b. Keeping in mind that introductory statistics is required for most majors, do the data suggest that a majority of all students at the university are female?

4.86 Access the student survey data completed by 446 students in introductory statistics courses at a large university in the fall of 2003.

a. What was the students' favorite color?

b. What percent preferred the favorite color?

c. What was the students' least favorite color?

d. What percent preferred the least favorite color?

e. During that same school year, 267 high school students taking a college statistics course for credit were surveyed. Their favorite color was blue, with a percentage of 42%, and their least favorite was yellow, with a percentage of 3%. Is taste in colors apparently similar for high school and college students?

Discovering Research: SINGLE CATEGORICAL VARIABLE

4.87 Find (and hand in) a newspaper article or Internet report about a study that involves just a single categorical variable. Besides providing a copy of the article or report, tell how the data were produced (experiment, observational study, or sample survey). Tell if the variable is summarized with counts, percents, or both. Tell if results are being reported for a sample or for an entire population, and report the number of individuals studied, if known. Tell if there is reason to suspect bias that arises if the sample is not representative, or bias in the design for assessing the variable's values.

Reporting on Research: SINGLE CATEGORICAL VARIABLE

4.88 Use the results of Exercise 4.3 on page 78 and relevant findings from the Internet to make a report on racial profiling that relies on statistical information.

Warming Up: SINGLE QUANTITATIVE VARIABLE

4.89 The United Nations and the World Health Organization expressed alarm regarding the extent to which AIDS has reduced life expectancy in Southern Africa. In Swaziland, children born between 2000 and 2005 could expect to live an average of only 34.4 years, compared to a worldwide life expectancy that is about twice that long.[23]

   a. Consider age at death for people in a developed country like the United States. Would the distribution's shape be left-skewed, symmetric, or right-skewed?

   b. Consider age at death for people in Swaziland. Would the distribution's shape be more symmetric or less symmetric than that for the United States?

4.90 In an e-mail interview in December 2004, a *New York Times* reporter asked the renowned physicist Stephen Hawking, "What is your IQ?" to which he replied, "I have no idea. People who boast about their IQ are losers," and went on to say that "there really is a continuous range of abilities with no clear dividing line."[24] Given this comment, would Hawking seem to advocate treating intelligence as a categorical variable, classifying an individual as "moron" for an IQ under 70, "genius" for an IQ over 140, and so on?

Exploring the Big Picture: SINGLE QUANTITATIVE VARIABLE

4.91 A newspaper article on salaries of college presidents reported compensations for a sample of 11 college presidents in area schools during the year 2002–2003, as well as compensations for the 10 highest-paid leaders of public universities in the entire United States. (Leaders of private universities, not included in the latter data set, have been known to receive more than $1 million in yearly pay.) The data, recorded in thousands of dollars, have been summarized with software.

Variable	N	Mean	Median	TrMean	StDev	SE Mean
AreaCollegePres	11	288.4	270.0	277.5	129.4	39.0
TopUSCollegePres	10	643.8	644.7	641.4	82.9	26.2

   a. Find the salary of a college president whose z-score for that area was approximately +2.

   b. The same college president was also included in the list of the top 10 salaries for the entire United States; find his z-score in reference to this group.

   c. Discuss the drawbacks in using the mean for college presidents in a particular area as an estimate for the mean salary of all college presidents.

   d. Explain why the mean salary of top college presidents is useless as an estimate for any larger group.

4.92 A *New York Times* review of the book *The State Boys Rebellion* by Michael D'Antonio cites this chilling quote: "to make sure every last moron was captured, many states, including Massachusetts, would establish traveling 'clinics' to administer IQ tests at public schools." The review mentions that by 1949, approximately 150,000 Americans were institutionalized.[25]

   a. The U.S. population in 1949 was about 150,000,000. What proportion of all Americans were institutionalized at that time?

   b. Scores for the Wechsler IQ test are normal with mean 100 and standard deviation 15. Use the 68-95-99.7 Rule to sketch a curve for this distribution, marking off the scores that are within 1, 2, and 3 standard deviations of the mean.

c. Apparently, people were being institutionalized in the 1940s if their IQ was approximately how many standard deviations below the mean?

d. The reviewer cites that of the 150,000 institutionalized Americans at that time, an estimated 12,000 were in fact "of relatively normal intelligence." Discuss the harmful consequences of using the results of an IQ test to institutionalize people who, in fact, are capable of functioning normally in society.

e. Discuss the harmful consequences of failing to institutionalize people who are unable to function in society.

4.93 Typical age, in days, at which various species of ducks begin to fly range from 39.5 (for blue-winged teals) to 62.5 (for canvasbacks).

39.5 47.0 47.0 50.0 50.5 51.0 51.5 56.0 60.5 61.5 62.5

a. Display the data with a stemplot.

b. Report the "typical" flying age of the various species by finding the median age and converting to weeks.

*4.94 In 1954, researchers Gollop and Marshall defined age classes of ducks based on their plumage, from the earliest stages "bright ball of fluff," and "fading ball of fluff," to the next-to-last stage "feathered-flightless," and, finally, "flying."[26]

a. Suppose female mallards at the "bright ball of fluff" stage have weights (in grams) with mean 32.4 and standard deviation 2.4. Find the z-score of a female mallard at this stage that weighs 40 grams.

b. Suppose female mallards at the "fading ball of fluff" stage have weights (in grams) with mean 115.3 and standard deviation 37.6. Find the z-score of a female mallard at this stage that weighs 40 grams.

c. If a female mallard weighs 40 grams, is she more likely to be at the "bright ball of fluff" stage or the "fading ball of fluff" stage? (Base your answer on the z-scores.)

4.95 In 1954, researchers Gollop and Marshall defined age classes of ducks based on their plumage, from the earliest stages "bright ball of fluff," and "fading ball of fluff," to the next-to-last stage "feathered-flightless," and, finally, "flying."

a. Suppose male mallards at the "feathered-flightless" stage have weights (in grams) with mean 864 and standard deviation 100. Find the z-score of a male mallard at this stage that weighs 840 grams.

b. Suppose male mallards at the "flying" stage have weights (in grams) with mean 818 and standard deviation 91. Find the z-score of a male mallard at this stage that weighs 840 grams.

c. If a male mallard weighs 840 grams, is he more likely to be at the "feathered-flightless" stage or the "flying" stage? Explain.

4.96 In 2004, a 59-year-old woman, about to give birth in December, set the record for age when pregnant.

a. If age of all mothers at the time of delivery has a mean of 27 and a standard deviation of 6, tell how many standard deviations above average this woman's age is.

b. Explain why the distribution of ages at time of delivery cannot be normal.

c. If we incorrectly applied the 68-95-99.7 Rule, it would tell us that half of 100% minus 99.7%, or 0.15%, of mothers are less than 9 years old at the time of delivery. Is the actual percentage higher or lower than this?

4.97 Four statistics students discuss the question, "Which of these variables could take a value that is so low as to be surprising: age of a mother at the time of delivery, or age of a mouse at time of death, or both, or neither?" Whose answer is best?

Adam: Any data set can have low outliers, so I'd say both.

Brittany: You shouldn't be surprised by low outliers, they happen all the time. So I'd say neither.

Carlos: We saw an example of a mouse that died at an unusually old age. There must also be mice that die at an unusually young age, so I'd say age of a mouse at time of death could have a surprisingly low value.

Dominique: Mice die at birth all the time, so the lowest possible value is zero but it wouldn't surprise us at all. On the other hand, mothers are usually at least in their teens when they deliver, but I read that there are a few girls who develop early and give birth when they're still children themselves.

Using Software [see Technology Guide]:
SINGLE QUANTITATIVE VARIABLE

4.98 This stemplot shows the number of medals won at the 2008 Olympics by 87 countries, including the 110 medals won by the United States and 100 won by China.

```
 0  11111111111111111111222222222222233333344444445555556666666777889
 1  00013456889
 2  4578
 3  1
 4  0167
 5
 6
 7  2
 8
 9
10  0
11  0
```

a. Use software to find the mean and standard deviation for number of medals won by the various countries.

b. Find the mean and standard deviation, if the two highest outliers—for China and the United States—are omitted.

c. Which is apparently more affected by outliers: the mean or the standard deviation?

4.99 Rents of one-bedroom apartments near a university were recorded in 2005

475   550   450   350   485   430   650   350   495   425   475   350

Use software to fill in the blanks, to the nearest dollar: the rents average to $_____, and they tend to differ from this average by about $_____.

Using the Normal Table [see end of book] or Software:
SINGLE QUANTITATIVE VARIABLE

*4.100 Exercise 4.94 discusses weights of female mallards at various stages of development.

a. The "bright ball of fluff" stage has mean weight 32.4 grams and standard deviation 2.4 grams. Find the proportion of female mallards at this stage that weigh more than 40 grams.

b. The "fading ball of fluff" stage has mean weight 115.3 grams and standard deviation 37.6 grams. Find the proportion of female mallards at this stage that weigh less than 40 grams.

4.101 Exercise 4.95 discusses weights of male mallards at various stages of development.

a. The "feathered-flightless" stage has mean weight 864 grams and standard deviation 100 grams. Find the proportion of male mallards at this stage that weigh less than 840 grams.

b. The "flying" stage has mean weight 818 grams and standard deviation 91 grams. Find the proportion of male mallards at this stage that weigh more than 840 grams.

Discovering Research: SINGLE QUANTITATIVE VARIABLE

4.102 Find (and hand in) a newspaper article or Internet report about a study that involves just a single quantitative variable. Besides providing a copy of the article or report, tell how the data were produced—was it an experiment or an observational study? Tell if the variable is summarized with mean, median, or neither. Tell if results are being reported for a sample or for an entire population, and the number of individuals studied, if known. Tell if there is reason to suspect bias that arises if the sample is not representative, or bias in the design for assessing the variable's values.

Reporting on Research: SINGLE QUANTITATIVE VARIABLE

4.103 Use results of Exercises 4.90 and 4.92 (page 129) and relevant findings from the Internet to make a report on IQ that relies on statistical information.

Displaying and Summarizing Relationships

For sampled students, are Math SAT scores related to their year of study?
Is the wearing of corrective lenses related to gender for sampled students?
Are ages of sampled students' mothers and fathers related?

Did surveyed males wear glasses more than the females did?

These questions typify situations where we are interested in data showing the relationship between two variables. In the first question, the explanatory variable—year of study—is categorical, and the response—Math SAT score—is quantitative. The second question deals with two categorical variables—gender as the explanatory variable and lenswear as the response. The third question features two quantitative variables—ages of mothers and ages of fathers. We will address these three types of situations one at a time, because for different types of variables we use very different displays and summaries. The first type of relationship is the easiest place to start, because the displays and summaries for exploring the relationship between a categorical explanatory variable and a quantitative response variable are natural extensions of those used for single quantitative variables, covered in Chapter 4.

5.1 Relationships between One Categorical and One Quantitative Variable

Different Approaches for Different Study Designs

In this book, we will concentrate on the most common version of this situation, where the categorical variable is explanatory and the response is quantitative. This type of situation includes various possible designs: two-sample, several-sample, or paired. Displays, summaries, and notation differ depending on which study design was used.

A CLOSER LOOK

When the explanatory variable is quantitative and the response is categorical, a more advanced method called *logistic regression* (not covered in this book) is required.

133

Other displays for relationships between categorical and quantitative variables are mentioned on page 789 of the *Teaching the Big Picture (**TBP**) Supplement.*

Displays

- **Two-Sample or Several-Sample Design:** Use side-by-side boxplots to visually compare centers, spreads, and shapes.
- **Paired Design:** Use a single histogram to display the differences between pairs of values, focusing on whether or not they are centered roughly at zero.

Summaries

To make comparative summaries, there are also several options, which are again extensions of what is used for single samples.

- **Two-Sample or Several-Sample Design:** Begin by referencing the side-by-side boxplot to note how centers and spreads compare by looking at the medians, quartiles, box heights, and whiskers. As long as the distributions do not exhibit flagrant skewness and outliers, we will ultimately compare their means and standard deviations.
- **Paired Design:** Report the mean and standard deviation of the differences between pairs of values.

Notation

This table shows how we denote the above-mentioned summaries, depending on whether they refer to a sample or to the population. Subscripts 1, 2, . . . are to identify which one of two or more groups is being referenced. The subscript d indicates we are referring to differences in a paired design.

	Two- or Several-Sample Design		Paired Design	
	Means	**Standard Deviations**	**Mean**	**Standard Deviation**
Sample	$\bar{x}_1, \bar{x}_2, \ldots$	$s_1, s_2, \ldots$	$\bar{x}_d$	s_d
Population	$\mu_1, \mu_2, \ldots$	$\sigma_1, \sigma_2, \ldots$	μ_d	σ_d

LOOKING AHEAD

The appropriate inference tools for drawing conclusions about the relationship between one categorical and one quantitative variable (to be presented in Chapter 11) will differ, depending on whether the categorical variable takes two or more than two possible values.

Our opening question about Math SAT scores for students of various years involves a categorical variable (year) that takes more than two possible values. This question will be addressed a little later, after we consider an example where the categorical variable of interest takes only two possible values. In fact, the same display tool—side-by-side boxplots—will be used in both situations. Summaries are also compared in the same way.

Data from a Two-Sample Design

First, we consider possible formats for data arising from a two-sample study.

EXAMPLE 5.1 TWO DIFFERENT FORMATS FOR TWO-SAMPLE DATA

Background: Our original earnings data, analyzed in Example 4.7 on page 83, consisted of values for the single quantitative variable

"earnings." In fact, since there is also information on the (categorical) gender of those students, we can explore the difference between earnings of males and females. If there is a noticeable difference between earnings of males and females, this suggests that gender and earnings are related in some way.

The way that we get software to produce side-by-side boxplots and descriptive statistics for this type of situation depends on how the data have been formatted. If we were keeping track of the data by hand, one possibility is to set up a column for males and one for females, and in each column list all the earnings for sampled students of that gender.

Male Earnings	Female Earnings
12	3
1	7
10	2
…	…

Question: What is another possible way to record the data values?

Response: An alternative is to set up one column for earnings and another for gender:

Earnings	Gender
12	Male
3	Female
7	Female
…	…

Practice: *Try Exercise 5.2 on page 144.*

The second formatting method presented in this example is more consistent with the correct perspective that the two variables involved are gender (categorical explanatory variable) and earnings (quantitative response variable). A common mistake would be to think there are two quantitative variables involved—male earnings and female earnings. This is *not* the case because for each individual sampled, we record a categorical value and a quantitative value, not two quantitative values.

Next, we consider the most common display and summaries for data from a two-sample design.

EXAMPLE 5.2 DISPLAYING AND SUMMARIZING TWO-SAMPLE DATA

Background: Data have been obtained for earnings of male and female students in a class, as discussed in Example 5.1. Here are side-by-side boxplots for the data, produced by the computer, along with separate

Continued

summaries of earnings (in thousands of dollars) for females and for males:

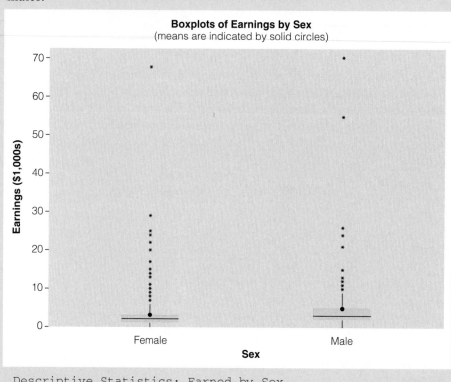

Boxplots of Earnings by Sex
(means are indicated by solid circles)

```
Descriptive Statistics: Earned by Sex
Variable   Sex       N         Mean     Median    TrMean    StDev
Earned     female    282       3.145    2.000     2.260     5.646
           male      164       4.860    3.000     3.797     7.657
Variable   Sex       SE Mean   Minimum  Maximum   Q1        Q3
Earned     female    0.336     0.000    65.000    1.000     3.000
           male      0.598     0.000    69.000    2.000     5.000
```

Question: What do the boxplots and descriptive statistics tell us?

Response: The side-by-side boxplots, along with the reported summaries, make the differences in earnings between the sexes clear.

- **Center:** Typical earnings for males are seen to be higher than those for females, regardless of whether means ($3,145 for females versus $4,860 for males) or medians ($2,000 for females versus $3,000 for males) are used to summarize center.

- **Spread:** Whereas both females and males have minimum values of 0, the middle half of female earnings are concentrated between $1,000 and $3,000, whereas the middle half of male earnings range from $2,000 to $5,000. Thus, the male earnings exhibit more spread.

- **Shape:** Both groups have high outliers (marked "*"), with a maximum somewhere between $60,000 and $70,000. The fact that both boxes are "top-heavy" indicates right-skewness in the distributions.

Because the distributions have such pronounced skewness and outliers, it is probably better to refrain from summarizing them with means and standard deviations, all of which are rather distorted. Looking at the boxplots, it makes much more sense to report the "typical" earnings with medians: $2,000 for females and $3,000 for males.

Practice: *Try Exercise 5.7(a–f) on page 145.*

Some software packages produce "side-by-side" boxplots that are actually stacked vertically instead of alongside one other. Because the convention in other displays of relationships—in bar graphs for two categorical variables and scatterplots for two quantitative variables—is to plot the explanatory variable horizontally, we favor the side-by-side arrangement of boxplots. This stresses the point of view that the categorical variable is explanatory.

Data from a Several-Sample Design

Now we return to the chapter's first opening question, about Math SAT scores and year of study for a sample of students.

EXAMPLE 5.3 DISPLAYING AND SUMMARIZING SEVERAL-SAMPLE DATA

Background: Our survey data set consists of responses from several hundred students taking introductory statistics classes at a particular university. Side-by-side boxplots were produced for Math SAT scores of students of various years (first, second, third, fourth, and "other").

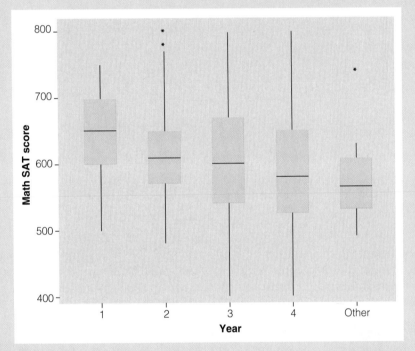

Questions: Would you expect Math SAT scores to be comparable for students of various years? Do the boxplots show that to be the case?

Responses: We would expect the scores to be roughly comparable because SAT scores tend to be quite stable over time. However, looking at the median lines through the boxes in the side-by-side plots, we see a noticeable downward trend: Math SAT scores tend to be highest for freshmen and decline with each successive year. They tend to be lowest for the "other" students. One possible explanation could be that the university's standards for admission have become increasingly rigorous, so that the most recent students would have the highest SAT scores.

Practice: *Try Exercise 5.8 on page 146.*

The Big Picture:
A CLOSER LOOK

Note that besides the obviously quantitative variable *Math SAT* score, we have the variable *Year*, which may have gone either way (quantitative or categorical) except for inclusion of the group *Other*, obliging us to handle *Year* as categorical.

The preceding example suggested a relationship between year of study and Math SAT score for sampled students. Our next example expands on the investigation of this apparent relationship.

EXAMPLE 5.4 CONFOUNDING VARIABLE IN RELATIONSHIP BETWEEN CATEGORICAL AND QUANTITATIVE VARIABLES

Background: Consider side-by-side boxplots of Math SAT scores by year presented in Example 5.3, and of Verbal SAT scores by year for the same sample of students, shown here:

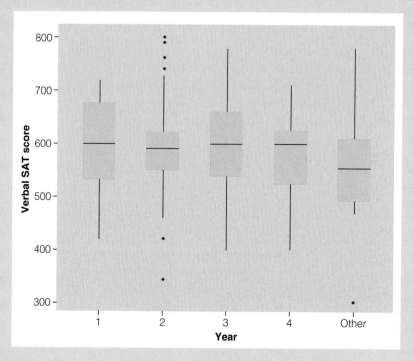

Questions: Do the Verbal SAT scores reinforce the theory that increasingly rigorous standards account for the fact that math scores were highest for first-year students and decreased for students in each successive year? If not, what would be an alternative explanation?

Responses: The Verbal SAT scores, unlike those for math, are quite comparable for all the groups except the "other" students, for whom they appear lower. The theory of tougher admission standards doesn't seem to hold up, so we should consider alternatives. It is possible that students with the best math scores are willing—perhaps even eager—to take care of their statistics or quantitative reasoning requirement right away. Students whose math skills are weaker may be the ones to postpone enrolling in statistics, resulting in survey respondents in higher years having lower Math SATs. We can say that willingness to study statistics early is a confounding variable that is tied in with what year a student is in when he or she signs up to take the course, and also is related to the student's Math SAT score.

Practice: *Try Exercise 5.10 on page 146.*

> To avoid stigmatizing older students, we can observe here that some students are inclined to "save the best for last," making their intro stats course the "dessert" of their undergraduate career.

Data from a Paired Design

In the Data Production part of the book, we learned of two common designs for making comparisons: a *two-sample design* comparing independent samples, and a *paired design* comparing two responses for each individual (or pair of similar individuals). We display and summarize data about a quantitative variable produced via a two-sample design as discussed in Example 5.2 on page 135—with side-by-side boxplots and a comparison of centers and spreads. In contrast, we display and summarize data about a quantitative variable produced via a paired design by reducing to a situation involving the *differences in responses* for the individuals studied. This single sample of differences can be displayed with a histogram and summarized in the usual way for a *single quantitative variable*.

A hypothetical discussion among students helps to contrast paired and two-sample designs.

Students Talk Stats

Displaying and Summarizing Paired Data

What displays and summaries would be appropriate if we wanted to compare the ages of students' fathers and mothers, for the purpose of determining whether fathers or mothers tend to be older?

Suppose a group of statistics students are discussing this question, which appeared on an exam that they just took.

Outlier age differences in the media

Adam: *"Ages of fathers is quantitative and ages of mothers is quantitative. I know we didn't cover scatterplots yet, but that's how you display two quantitative variables. I learned about them when I failed this course last semester. So I said display with a scatterplot and summarize with a correlation."*

Brittany: *"Those don't count as two quantitative variables, if you're making a comparison between father and mother. There's just one quantitative variable—age—and one categorical variable, for which parent it is. So I said display with side-by-side boxplots and summarize with five-number summaries, because that's what goes with boxplots."*

Carlos: *"You're thinking of how to display data from a two-sample design, but fathers and mothers are pairs, even if they're divorced like mine. So you subtract their ages and display the differences with a histogram. I said summarize with mean and standard deviation, because it should be pretty symmetric, right?"*

Students Talk Stats continued →

Whereas the relationship between *parents'* genders and ages arises from a paired design, the relationship between *students'* genders and ages arises from a two-sample design because there is nothing to link individual males and females together.

Example TBP 5.1 on page 789 of the *TBP Supplement* shows how we would display and summarize the relationship between *students'* genders and ages.

Students Talk Stats continued

Dominique: *"I said histogram too. But I was thinking it would be skewed, because of older men marrying younger women, like Michael Douglas and Catherine Zeta-Jones, so I put five-number summary. Do you think we'll both get credit, Carlos?"*

Carlos is right: Because each student in the survey reported the age of both father and mother, the data occur in pairs, not in two independent samples. We could compute the difference in ages for each pair, then display those differences with a histogram and summarize them with mean and standard deviation, as long as the histogram is reasonably symmetric. Otherwise, as Dominique suggests, report the five-number summary. Let's take a look at the histogram to see if it's symmetric or skewed, after a brief assessment of the center and spread.

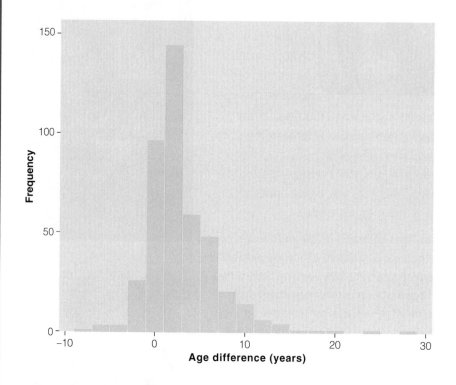

■ **Center:** Our histogram of "father's age minus mother's age" is clearly centered to the right of zero: The fact that the differences tend to be positive tells us that fathers tend to be older than mothers. The histogram's peak is at about 2, suggesting that it is common for the fathers to be approximately 2 years older than their wives.

■ **Spread:** Most age differences are clumped within about 5 years of the center; the standard deviation should certainly be less than 5 years.

■ **Shape:** Right-skewness/high outliers represent fathers who are much older than their wives. The reverse phenomenon is not evident; apparently it is rare for women to be more than a few years older than their husbands. This wouldn't necessarily be obvious without looking at the histogram, so we'll hope that both Dominique and Carlos would get credit for their answers.

Practice: *Try Exercise 5.13 on page 147.*

Generalizing from Samples to Populations: The Role of Spreads

In this section, we have focused on comparing sampled values of a quantitative variable for two or more groups. Even if two groups of sampled values were picked at random from the exact same population, their sample means are almost guaranteed to differ somewhat, just by chance variation. Therefore, we must be careful not to jump to broader conclusions about a difference in general. For example, if sample mean ages are 20.5 years for male students and 20.3 years for female students, this does not necessarily mean that males are older in the larger population from which the students were sampled. Conclusions about the larger population, based on information from the sample, can't be drawn until we have developed the necessary theory to perform statistical inference in Part IV. This theory requires us to pay attention not only to how different the *means* are in the various groups to be compared, but also to how large or small the groups' *standard deviations* are. The next example should help you understand how the interplay between centers and spreads gives us a clue about the extent to which a categorical explanatory variable accounts for differences in quantitative responses.

EXAMPLE 5.5 HOW SPREADS AFFECT THE IMPACT OF A DIFFERENCE BETWEEN CENTERS

Background: Wrigley gum manufacturers funded a study in an attempt to demonstrate that students can learn better when they are chewing gum. A way to establish whether or not chewing gum and learning are related is to compare mean learning (assessed as a quantitative variable) for gum-chewers versus non-gum-chewers. All students in the Wrigley study were taught standard dental anatomy during a 3-day period, but about half of the students were assigned to chew gum while being taught. Afterwards, performance on an objective exam was compared for students in the gum-chewing and non-gum-chewing groups. The mean score for the 29 gum-chewing students was 83.6, whereas the mean score for the 27 non-gum-chewing students was 78.8.[1]

Taken at face value, the means tell us that scores tended to be higher for students who chewed gum. However, we should keep in mind that if 56 students were all taught the exact same way, and we randomly divided them into two groups, the mean scores would almost surely differ somewhat. What Wrigley would like to do is convince people that the difference between $\bar{x}_1 = 83.6$ and $\bar{x}_2 = 78.8$ is too substantial to have come about just by chance.

Both of these side-by-side boxplots represent scores wherein the mean for gum-chewing students is 83.6 and the mean for non-gum-chewing students is 78.8. Thus, the differences between *centers* are the same for both of these scenarios. As far as the *spreads* are concerned, however, the boxplot on the left is quite different from the one on the right.

Continued

The Big Picture:
A CLOSER LOOK

These boxplots show the location of each distribution's mean with a dot.

The Big Picture:
LOOKING AHEAD

Consideration of not just the difference between centers but also of data sets' spreads as well as sample sizes, will form the basis of formal inference procedures, to be presented in Part IV. These methods provide researchers—like those from the Wrigley Company—with evidence to convince people that a treatment—like gum-chewing—has an effect. Or, they may fail to provide them with evidence, as was in fact the case with this study: The data turned out roughly as in Scenario A (on the left), not like Scenario B (on the right).

Example TBP 5.2 on page 790 of the *TBP Supplement* compares spreads in more detail by looking at standard deviations in computer output for the gum-chewing experiment discussed in Example 5.5.

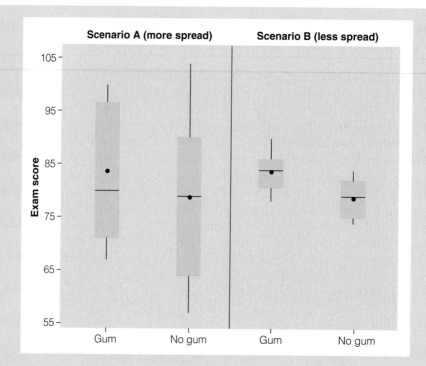

Questions: Assuming sample sizes in Scenario A are the same as those in Scenario B, for which Scenario (A or B) would it be easier to believe that the difference between means for chewers versus non-chewers came about by chance? For which scenario does the difference seem to suggest that gum chewing really can have an effect?

Responses: Scores for the gum-chewing and non-gum-chewing students in Scenario A (on the left) are so spread out—all the way from around 60 to around 100—that we hardly notice the difference between their centers. Considering how much these two boxes overlap, it is easy to imagine that gum makes no difference, and the scores for gum-chewing students were higher just by chance. In contrast, scores for the two groups of students in Scenario B (on the right) have considerably less spread. They are concentrated in the upper 70s to upper 80s, and this makes the difference between 83.6 and 78.8 seem more pronounced. Considering how much less these two boxes overlap, we would have more reason to believe that chewing gum really can have an effect.

Is chewing gum the key to getting higher exam scores?

© Tim Pannell/CORBIS

Practice: *Try Exercise 5.15(a–g) on page 148.*

As always, we should keep in mind that good data production must also be in place, especially if we want to demonstrate that different values of the categorical explanatory variable actually *cause* a difference in responses. For example, if Wrigley had asked people to volunteer to chew gum or not, instead of randomly assigning them, then even a dramatic difference between mean scores of gum-chewers and non-gum-chewers could not be taken as evidence that chewing gum provides a benefit. Also, the possibility of a placebo effect cannot be ruled out: If students suspected that the gum was supposed to help them learn better, there may have been a "self-fulfilling prophecy" phenomenon occurring.

The Role of Sample Size: When Differences Have More Impact

Besides taking spreads into account, it is important to note that sample size will play a role in how convinced we are that a difference in sample means extends to the larger population from which the samples originated. For example, the side-by-side boxplot for gum-chewers versus non-gum-chewers on the right in Example 5.5 would be less convincing if there were only 10 students in each group, and more convincing if there were 100 students in each group. The formal inference procedures to be presented in Part IV will always take sample size into account. For now, we should keep in mind that sample size can have an impact on what conclusions we draw from sample data.

EXAMPLE 5.6 HOW SAMPLE SIZE AFFECTS THE IMPACT OF A DIFFERENCE BETWEEN CENTERS

Background: A sample of workers in France averaged about 1,600 hours of work a year, compared to 1,900 hours of work a year for a sample of Americans.[2]

Questions: If 2 people of each nationality had been sampled, would this convince you that French workers in general average fewer hours than American workers? Would it be enough to convince you if 200 people of each nationality had been sampled?

Responses: Clearly, even if mean hours worked per year were equal for all French and American workers, a sample of just 2 French people could easily happen to include someone who worked relatively few hours, whereas the sample of 2 Americans could happen to include someone who worked relatively many hours. This could result in sample means as different as 1,600 and 1,900, even if the population means were equal. On the other hand, if mean hours worked per year were equal for all French and American workers, it would be very difficult to imagine that a sample of 200 each happened to include French people working so few hours on average, and Americans working so many hours on average, resulting in sample means 1,600 and 1,900. If these means arose from samples of 200 people of each nationality, it would do more to convince us that French workers in general average fewer hours than American workers.

Practice: *Try Exercise 5.15(h) on page 149.*

Relationships between categorical and quantitative variables are summarized on page 204 of the Chapter Summary.

Relationships between One Categorical and One Quantitative Variable

Note: Asterisked numbers indicate exercises whose answers are provided in the Solutions to Selected Exercises section, on page 689.

5.1 According to "Films and Hormones," "researchers at the University of Michigan report that the male hormone [testosterone] rose as much as 30% in men while they watched *The Godfather, Part II.* Love stories and other 'chick flicks' had a different effect: They made the 'female hormone' progesterone rise 10% in *both* sexes. But not all films will make you more aggressive or romantic. Neither sex got a hormone reaction from a documentary about the Amazon rain forest."[3] This study involved four variables: testosterone, progesterone, type of film, and gender.

   a. Classify the variable for testosterone as being quantitative or categorical, and as explanatory or response. If it is categorical, tell how many possible values it can take.

   b. Classify the variable for type of film as being quantitative or categorical, and as explanatory or response. If it is categorical, tell how many possible values it can take.

   c. Classify the variable for gender as being quantitative or categorical, and as explanatory or response. If it is categorical, tell how many possible values it can take.

*5.2 This table provides information on the eight U.S. Olympic beach volleyball players in 2004.

Male Age	Female Age
32	26
32	35
33	27
32	34

   a. Is the data set formatted with a column for values of quantitative responses and a column for values of a categorical explanatory variable, or is it formatted with two columns of quantitative responses—one for each of two categorical groups?

   b. Create a table formatting the data the opposite way from that described in part (a). List ages in increasing order.

5.3 The federal government created the Pell Grant in 1972 to assist low-income college students. This table provides information on Pell Grant recipients for the academic year 2001–2002 at schools of various types in a certain state.

Number of Recipients	School Type
434	Private
365	Private
2,195	State
353	Private
893	Private
2,050	State
2,566	State
4,627	State
273	Private
604	State-related
7,047	State-related
761	Private
329	Private
2,338	State
5,369	State-related
409	Private
4,296	State-related
340	Private
380	Private

   a. Is the data set formatted with a column for values of quantitative responses and a column for values of a categorical explanatory variable, or is it formatted with columns of quantitative responses for various categorical groups?

b. Create a table formatting the data the opposite way from that in part (a). List data values in increasing order.

c. To better put the data in perspective, which one of these additional variables' values would be most helpful to know: school's location, number enrolled, or percentage of women attending?

5.4   The Pell Grant was created in 1972 to assist low-income college students. This table provides information on percentages of students who were Pell Grant recipients for the academic year 2001–2002 at schools of various types in a certain state.

Private	State	State-Related
21	38	66
12	33	19
41	36	35
11	36	22
24	30	
40		
22		
41		
22		
20		

a. Use a calculator or computer to find the mean and standard deviation of percentages of students with Pell Grants at private schools.

b. Use a calculator or computer to find the mean and standard deviation of percentages of students with Pell Grants at state schools.

c. Use a calculator or computer to find the mean and standard deviation of percentages of students with Pell Grants at state-related schools.

d. The highest mean is for state-related schools. Explain why it might be misleading to report that the percentage of students receiving Pell Grants is highest at state-related schools.

e. For which type of school are the Pell Grants most evenly allocated, in the sense that percentages for all schools of that type are most similar to each other?

f. Explain why side-by-side stemplots may be a better choice of display than side-by-side boxplots for this data set.

g. When deciding whether to use side-by-side stemplots or boxplots, are we mainly concerned with data production, displaying and summarizing data, probability, or statistical inference?

*5.5   One type of school in Exercise 5.4 has a high outlier value. Would it be better to summarize its values with a mean or a median?

5.6   Construct side-by-side stemplots for the Pell Grant percentages data from Exercise 5.4, all using stems 1 through 6.

*5.7   These side-by-side boxplots show mean assessment test scores for various schools in a certain state, grouped according to whether they are lower-level elementary schools, or schools that combine elementary and middle school students in kindergarten through eighth grade.

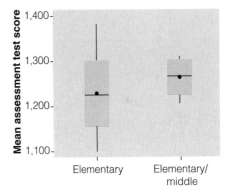

a. Was the study design paired, two-sample, or several-sample?

b. Do the boxplots have comparable centers, or does it appear that one type of school has mean scores that are noticeably higher or lower than the other type?

c. Given your answer to part (b), is there reason to suspect that scores are related to the type of school (ordinary elementary or combination elementary and middle school)?

d. Do the boxplots have comparable spreads, or does it appear that one type of school has mean scores that are noticeably more or less variable than the other type?

e. The standard deviation of scores for one type of school is 40, for the other is 82. Which one of these is the standard deviation for the combination schools (boxplot on the right)?

f. Does either of the boxplots exhibit pronounced skewness or outliers?

g. There were in fact only 6 combination schools in the data set. Would you be more convinced or less convinced that type of school plays a role in scores if the boxplot were for 60 schools instead of 6—or wouldn't it matter?

*5.8   These side-by-side boxplots show mean assessment test scores for various schools in a state, grouped according to whether they are elementary, middle, or high schools.

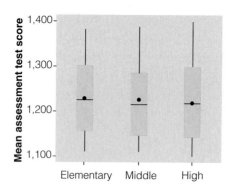

a. Was the study design paired, two-sample, or several-sample?

b. Do the boxplots have comparable centers, or does it appear that one type of school

has mean scores that are noticeably higher or lower than the other types?

c. Given your answer to part (b), is there reason to suspect that scores are related to the type of school (elementary, middle, or high school)?

d. Do the boxplots have comparable spreads, or does it appear that one type of school has mean scores that are noticeably more or less variable than the other types?

e. Do any of the boxplots exhibit pronounced skewness or outliers?

5.9   Scores on a state assessment test were averaged for all the schools in a particular district, which were classified according to level (such as elementary, middle, or high school).

a. Mean scores for elementary schools had a mean of 1,228, and a standard deviation of 82. What would be the z-score for an elementary school whose mean score was 1,300?

b. Mean scores for middle schools had a mean of 1,219, and a standard deviation of 91. What would be the z-score for a middle school whose mean score was 1,300?

c. Mean scores for high schools had a mean of 1,223, and a standard deviation of 105. What would be the z-score for a high school whose mean score was 1,300?

d. Explain why the z-scores in parts (a), (b), and (c) are quite similar.

*5.10   A large group of students were asked to report their earnings in thousands of dollars for the year before, and were also asked to tell their favorite color. Apparently, students who preferred the color black tended to earn more than students who liked pink or purple. What is the most obvious confounding variable that could be causing us to see this relationship between favorite color and earnings?

Variable	N	Mean	Median	TrMean	StDev	SE Mean
Earned_black	35	5.260	3.000	4.350	6.070	1.030
Earned_pink	37	3.135	2.000	2.545	3.845	0.632
Earned_purple	53	3.415	2.000	2.298	5.783	0.794

5.11   Researchers monitored the food and drink intake of 159 healthy black and white adolescents aged 15 to 19. "They found that those who drank the most caffeine—more than 100 milligrams a day, or the equivalent of about four 12-ounce cans, had the highest pressure readings."[4] Weight was acknowledged as a possible confounding variable—one whose values are tied in with those of the explanatory variable, and also has an impact on the response.

a. Based on your experience, do people who consume a lot of soft drinks tend to weigh more or less than those who do not?

b. Based on your experience, do people who weigh a lot tend to have higher or lower blood pressures?

c. Explain how consumption of soft drinks could be a confounding variable in the relationship between caffeine and blood pressure.

d. If weight is a possible confounding variable, should adolescents of all weights be studied together, or should they be separated out according to weight?

e. Was this an observational study or an experiment?

5.12 These side-by-side boxplots show percentages participating in assessment tests for various schools in a certain state, grouped according to whether they are elementary, middle, or high schools.

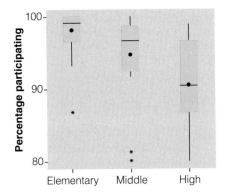

a. Because the boxplots have noticeably different centers, it appears that participation percentages are substantially different, depending on the level (elementary, middle, or high school). Can you think of any explanation for why participation would be higher at one level of school and lower at another?

b. Do the boxplots have comparable spreads? If not, which type of school has the least amount of variability in percentages taking the test?

c. Mean percentage participating was 91% for one type of school, 95% for another type, and 98% for the other type. Which of these is the mean for high schools?

d. The standard deviation for percent participating was 3% for one type of school, and 6% for the other two types. Which type of school had the standard deviation of 3%?

e. Which type of school would have a histogram of percentages participating

that is closest to normal: elementary, middle, or high school?

f. Can you tell by looking at the boxplots how many schools of each type were included?

*5.13 "OH, DEER!" reports on the number of people killed in highway crashes involving animals (in many cases, deer) in 1993 and 2003 for 49 states.[5] Typically, each state had about 2 such deaths in 1993 and about 4 in 2003. Results are displayed with a histogram and summarized with descriptive statistics.

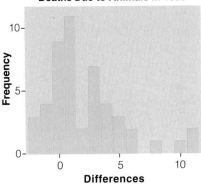

Deaths Due to Animals in 2003 Minus Deaths Due to Animals in 1993

	N	Mean	StDev
Deaths2003	49	4.286	4.072
Deaths1993	49	2.061	2.035
Difference	49	2.224	3.138

a. When we examine the data to decide to what extent highway deaths involving animals have increased or decreased, should we think in terms of a two-sample design or a paired design?

b. Typically, how did the number of deaths in a state change—down by about 4, down by about 2, up by about 2, or up by about 4?

c. Change in the number of deaths varied from state to state; typically, about how far was each change from the mean— 2, 3, or 4?

d. Based on the shape of the histogram, can we say that in a few states, there was an unusually large *decrease* in deaths due to animals, or an unusually large *increase* in deaths due to animals, or both, or neither?

5.14 A newspaper reported that prices were comparable at two area grocery stores. Here are the lowest prices found in each of two grocery stores for six items in the fall of

2004, along with a histogram of the price differences.

Item	Wal-Mart	Giant Eagle	Difference
Frozen peas	$0.87	$0.79	+$0.08
Dozen eggs	$0.78	$1.20	−$0.42
Wheat bread	$1.07	$1.59	−$0.52
Cocoa cereal	$1.66	$3.99	−$2.33
Decaf coffee	$1.87	$3.59	−$1.72
Sandwich bags	$1.94	$0.70	+$1.24

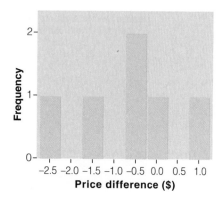

a. Did the data arise from an experiment or an observational study?

b. Find the mean of the differences.

c. For those six items, the sign of the mean suggests that which of the two grocery stores is cheaper?

d. If the same mean of differences had come about from a sample of 60 items instead of just 6, would it be more convincing that one store's prices are cheaper, less convincing, or would it not make a difference?

e. If we want to use relative prices for a sample of items to demonstrate that mean price of all items is less at one of the grocery stores, are we mainly concerned with data production, displaying and summarizing data, probability, or statistical inference?

f. Suppose one store's prices really are cheaper overall, but a sample of prices taken by a shopper failed to produce evidence of a significant difference. Who stands to gain from this erroneous conclusion: the shopper, the store with cheaper prices, or the store with more expensive prices?

g. Is the type of mistake described in part (f) more likely to occur with a smaller or a larger sample?

*5.15 The boxplots on the left show weights (in grams) of samples of female and male mallard ducks at age 35 weeks (not quite fully grown), whereas the boxplots on the right show weights of samples of female and male mallard ducks of all ages (newborn to adult).

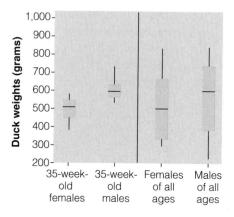

a. As far as the centers of the distributions are concerned, whether the ducks are 35 weeks old or of all ages, females weighed about 100 grams less than males. To the nearest 100 grams, about how much did the females tend to weigh?

b. To the nearest 100 grams, about how much did the males tend to weigh?

c. If a 35-week-old female weighed 550 grams, would her z-score be positive or negative?

d. If a 35-week-old male weighed 550 grams, would his z-score be positive or negative?

e. Which ducks had weights that were more spread out around the center—the 35-week-old ducks or the ducks of all ages?

f. In which case does the difference of 100 grams in weight between females and males do more to convince us that males tend to be heavier: when looking at 35-week-old ducks only or when looking at ducks of all ages?

g. In general, when does a given difference between means seem more pronounced: when the distributions' values are concentrated close to the means or when the distributions' values are very spread out around the means?

h. If a sample of male ducks weighs 100 grams more on average than a sample of female ducks, in which case would we be more convinced that males in general weigh more: if the samples were of 4 ducks each or if the samples were of 40 ducks each?

i. The standard deviation for one group of females was about 30 and the other was about 90. Which was the standard deviation for weights of females of all ages?

5.16 "Dream Drug Too Good to Be True?" reported in 2004 on a weight-loss drug called *rimonabant*: "It will make a person uninterested in fattening foods, they have heard from news reports and word of mouth. Weight will just melt away, and fat accumulating around the waist and abdomen will be the first to go. And by the way, those who take it will end up with higher levels of HDL, the good cholesterol. If they smoke, they will find it easier to quit. If they are heavy drinkers, they will no longer crave alcohol. 'Holy cow, does it also grow hair?' asked Dr. Catherine D. DeAngelis, editor of the *Journal of the American Medical Association*. [. . .] With an analysis limited to those who completed the study, rimonabant resulted in an average weight loss of about 19 pounds. In comparison, patients who received a placebo and who, like the rimonabant patients, were given a diet and consultations with a dietician, lost about 5 pounds per year."[6]

a. These boxplots show two possible configurations of data where drug-takers lose an average of 19 pounds and placebo-takers lose an average of 5 pounds.

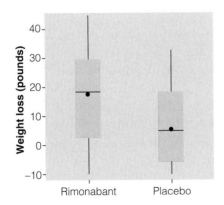

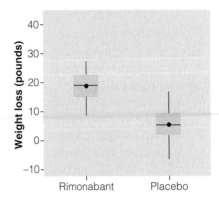

Which one of these would convince you the *most* that rimonabant is effective for weight loss?

1. 35 people were studied, and the data resulted in the first side-by-side boxplots.
2. 35 people were studied, and the data resulted in the second side-by-side boxplots.
3. 3,500 people were studied, and the data resulted in the first side-by-side boxplots.
4. 3,500 people were studied, and the data resulted in the second side-by-side boxplots.

b. Which one of the four situations described in part (a) would convince you the *least* that rimonabant is effective for weight loss?

c. In fact, the study involved 3,500 people. However, the results may not be so convincing, for this reason: "In presenting its findings, Sanofi-Aventis [the manufacturer] discarded thousands of participants who dropped out. Some say that is reasonable because it shows what can happen if people stay with a treatment. But statisticians often criticize it, saying it can make results look better than they are." Suppose weight losses were averaged not just for participants who remained a full year in the study, but also including participants who dropped out. Which of these would more likely be true about mean weight losses?

1. Mean loss (for both drug-takers and for placebo-takers) would be *less* if participants who dropped out were included.
2. Mean loss (for both drug-takers and for placebo-takers) would be *more* if

participants who dropped out were included.

d. When weight losses or gains of participants who dropped out before the end of the study are excluded, are researchers more likely to make the mistake of concluding the drug *is* effective when it actually is not, or the mistake of concluding the drug is *not* effective when it actually is?

e. When the researchers decided that placebo-takers should be given a diet and consultations with a dietician, just like the drug-takers, were they mainly

concerned with data production, displaying and summarizing data, probability, or statistical inference?

f. When the researchers decided to report mean rather than median weight loss, were they mainly concerned with data production, displaying and summarizing data, probability, or statistical inference?

g. If the researchers want to estimate that all people taking rimonabant would lose an average of 19 pounds, are they mainly concerned with data production, displaying and summarizing data, probability, or statistical inference?

5.2 Relationships between Two Categorical Variables

In our discussion of types of variables in Example 1.2 on page 4, we demonstrated that even if the original variable of interest is quantitative—such as an infant's birth weight—researchers often simplify matters by turning it into a categorical variable—such as whether or not an infant is below normal birth weight. Later, in our discussion of study design on page 33, we stressed that the goal of many studies is to establish causation in the relationship between two variables. Merging these two points, we note now that an extremely common situation of interest, which applies in a vast number of real-life problems, is the relationship between two categorical variables. The data values may have been produced via an observational study or survey, or they may be obtained via an experiment. We will consider results of both types of design in the examples to follow.

EXAMPLE 5.7 SUMMARIZING TWO SINGLE CATEGORICAL VARIABLES

Background: We can summarize the categorical variable "gender" for a sample of 446 students as follows.

■ **Counts:** 164 males and 282 females; or

■ **Percentages:** 164/446 = 37% males and 282/446 = 63% females; or

■ **Proportions:** 0.37 males and 0.63 females

We can also summarize the categorical variable "lenswear" for the same sample of 446 students.

■ **Counts:** 163 wearing contacts, 69 wearing glasses, and 214 with no corrective lenses; or

■ **Percentages:** 163/446 = 37% wearing contacts, 69/446 = 15% wearing glasses, and 214/446 = 48% with no corrective lenses; or

■ **Proportions:** 0.37 wearing contacts, 0.15 wearing glasses, and 0.48 with no corrective lenses

Question: Does the information provided tell us something about the relationship between gender and lenswear?

Response: The information provided about those two categorical variables—gender and lenswear—treats the variables one at a time. It tells us nothing about the relationship, only about the individual variables.

Practice: *Try Exercise 5.17 on page 160.*

Summaries and Displays: Two-Way Tables, Conditional Percentages, and Bar Graphs

Our gender/lenswear example provides a good context to explore the essentials of displaying and summarizing relationships between two categorical variables. A new dimension is added when we are concerned not just with the individual variables, but with their relationship.

> *Definition*   A **two-way table** presents information about two categorical variables. The table shows counts in each possible category-combination, as well as totals for each category.

A common convention is to record the explanatory variable's categories in the various rows of a two-way table, and the response variable's categories in the columns. However, sometimes tables are constructed the other way around.

Some students might be familiar with two-way tables being called "contingency tables," so named because frequencies are shown *contingent* on being in a particular category or combination of categories.

EXAMPLE 5.8 PRESENTING INFORMATION ABOUT INDIVIDUAL CATEGORICAL VARIABLES IN A TWO-WAY TABLE

Background: Raw data show each individual's gender and whether he or she wears contacts (c), glasses (g), or neither (n).

Sex	f	m	f	f	f	f	f	f	f	f	f	m	m	m	...
Lenswear	c	c	n	n	g	c	c	g	n	c	g	g	c	n	...

Question: If we construct a two-way table for gender and lenswear, what parts of the table convey information about the individual variables?

Response: First, we should decide what roles are played by the two variables to decide which should be along rows and which along columns. It would be absurd to suspect that the wearing of corrective lenses or not could affect someone's gender. On the other hand, it is possible that being male or female could play a role in students' need for corrective lenses, or in their choice of contacts versus glasses. Therefore, we take gender to be the explanatory variable and present its values in rows. Lenswear will be the response variable, presented in columns.

If we are interested in just the individual variables, we count up the number of females and the number of males and show those counts in the "Total" column along the right margin. Likewise, we count up the number of students in each of the three lenswear categories and show those along

Continued

the bottom margin. Total counts are shown here for the complete data set of over 400 students. The "inside" of the table, which would tell us about how the two variables are related, has not yet been filled in.

Information about Relationship Would Appear in Shaded Region				
	Contacts	Glasses	None	Total
Female				282
Male				164
Total	163	69	214	446

Practice: *Try Exercise 5.20(a,b) on page 160.*

The information about gender and lenswear as conveyed in Examples 5.7 and 5.8 is fine as a summary of the individual variables, but it tells us nothing about their relationship. Of the 163 with contacts, are almost all of them male? (This would suggest that being male causes a tendency to wear contacts.) Or is it the other way around, suggesting that being female causes a tendency to wear contacts? Or are the contact-wearers evenly split between males and females? Or are they split *in proportion* to the numbers of males and females surveyed?

We must take the roles of explanatory and response variables into account when we decide which comparison to make in our summary of the relationship. Because of unequal group sizes, we need to summarize with percentages (or proportions) rather than counts. When we focus on one explanatory group at a time, we find a percentage or proportion in the response of interest, given the *condition* of being in that group. Thus, we refer to a *conditional* percentage or proportion.

> *Definition*   A **conditional percentage** or **proportion** tells the percentage or proportion in the response of interest, given that an individual falls in a particular explanatory group.

In the following examples, we delve into the relationship between gender and lenswear by recording counts in various category combinations, then reporting relevant conditional percentages.

EXAMPLE 5.9 ADDING INFORMATION ABOUT THE RELATIONSHIP BETWEEN TWO CATEGORICAL VARIABLES IN A TWO-WAY TABLE

Background: We refer again to raw data showing each individual's gender and whether he or she wears contacts (c), glasses (g), or neither (n).

Sex	f	m	f	f	f	f	f	f	f	f	m	m	m	...
Lenswear	c	c	n	n	g	c	c	g	n	c	g	g	c	n	...

Question: How can we record information about the *relationship* between gender and lenswear?

Response: We need to find counts in the various gender/lenswear combinations, and include them in the table. This has been done for all 446 students surveyed.

	Contacts	Glasses	None	Total
Female	121	32	129	282
Male	42	37	85	164
Total	163	69	214	446

Practice: *Try Exercise 5.21(a) on page 161.*

Our next example stresses the importance of comparing relevant *proportions* as opposed to counts.

EXAMPLE 5.10 SUMMARIZING THE RELATIONSHIP BETWEEN TWO CATEGORICAL VARIABLES IN A TWO-WAY TABLE

Background: It turns out that 85 males wore no corrective lenses, as opposed to 129 females who wore no corrective lenses.

Questions: Should we report that fewer males went without corrective lenses? If not, how can we do a better job of summarizing the situation?

Responses: Because there were fewer males surveyed, it would be misleading to report that fewer males went without corrective lenses. We need to report the *relative* percentages (or proportions) in the various lens categories, taking into account that there are only 164 males altogether, compared to 282 females.

Since gender is our explanatory variable, we want to compare percentages in the various response groups (contacts, glasses, or none) for the two sexes males versus females. These are the conditional percentages wearing contacts, glasses, or none, given that a student was male or female. Computer software can be used to produce a table of counts and conditional percentages.

```
Rows:  Gender      Columns:  Lenswear
          contacts     glasses      none       All
 female       121          32        129        282
            42.91       11.35      45.74     100.00
 male         42          37         85        164
            25.61       22.56      51.83     100.00
 All         163          69        214        446
```

The conditional percentages reveal that although the *count* with no corrective lenses was higher for females (129 versus 85), the *percentage* is somewhat higher for males (51.83% versus 45.74%). Noticeably more pronounced are the differences between females and males with respect to type of lenses worn: about 43% of the females wore contacts, versus only about 26% of the males, and about 23% of the males wore glasses compared to just 11% of the females.

Practice: *Try Exercise 5.21(b,c) on page 161.*

Before presenting a bar graph to display these results, it is important to note that bar graphs can be constructed in many different ways, especially when several categorical variables are involved. If care is not taken to identify the roles of variables correctly, you may end up with a graph that displays the conditional percentages in each gender category, given that a person wears contacts versus glasses versus neither. These percentages are completely different from the ones that are relevant for our purposes, having decided that gender is the explanatory variable. Here is a useful tip for the correct construction, either by hand or with software, of bar graphs to display the relationship between two categorical variables: *The explanatory variable is identified along the horizontal axis, and percentages (or proportions or counts) in the responses of interest are graphed according to the vertical axis.*

EXAMPLE 5.11 DISPLAYING THE RELATIONSHIP BETWEEN TWO CATEGORICAL VARIABLES

Background: Conditional percentages in the various lenswear categories for males and for females were found in Example 5.10.

Question: How can we display information about the relationship between gender and lenswear?

Response: An appropriate graph under the circumstances—comparing lenswear for males and females—is shown here. Note that the explanatory variable (gender) is identified horizontally, and percentages in the various lenswear responses are graphed vertically. We see that the contact lens bar is higher for females than males, whereas the glasses bar is higher for the males. The bars for no lenses are almost the same height for both sexes. Depending on personal preferences, one may also opt to arrange the same six bars in three groups of two instead of two groups of three; this still treats gender as the explanatory variable.

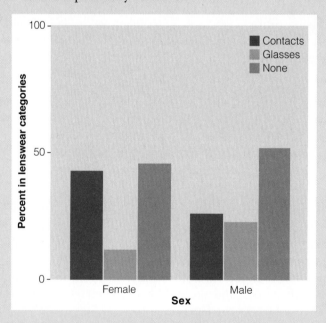

Practice: *Try Exercise 5.21(d) on page 161.*

Now that we have summarized and displayed the relationship between gender and lenswear, here are some questions to consider.

- Can you think of any reasons why females, in general, may tend to wear contacts more than males do? If the difference in sample percentages wearing contacts is 43% for females versus 26% for males, do you think this difference could have come about by chance in the sampling process? Or do you think it could provide evidence that the percentage wearing contacts is higher for females in the larger population of college students?

- Can you think of any reasons why students of one gender would consistently have less of a need for corrective lenses? If not, do you think the difference in sample percentages needing no lenses (roughly 52% for males versus 46% for females) could have come about by chance in the sampling process?

These questions are in the realm of probability and statistical inference. We may already have some intuition about which differences seem "significant," but we will learn formal methods to draw such conclusions more scientifically in Part IV. Our answers will rely heavily on the theory of probability, so that we can state what would be the *chance* of a sample difference as extreme as the one observed, if there were actually no difference in population percentages. For now, we can safely say that a higher percentage of sampled females wore contacts, and higher percentages of sampled males wore glasses or no corrective lenses. The differences between percentages of males and females seem more pronounced in the contacts and glasses responses, and less pronounced in the case of not needing any corrective lenses.

Whereas our example of the relationship between gender and lenswear arose from a survey, the next example presents results of an experiment. Another difference is that we constructed our gender/lenswear table from raw data; this next example will start with summaries that have already been calculated for us.

> In general, we are interested in conditional percentages in the response of interest, given a particular explanatory category. For Example 5.12, the article compares conditional percentage with decreased sweating, given that a subject received Botox (75%) versus the conditional percentage with decreased sweating, given that a subject received the placebo injection (one-quarter, which is 25%).

EXAMPLE 5.12 CONSTRUCTING A TWO-WAY TABLE FROM SUMMARIES

Background: "Wrinkle Fighter Could Help Reduce Excessive Sweating" tells of a study where "researchers gave 322 patients underarm injections of either Botox or salt water . . . A month later, 75% of the Botox users reported a significant decrease in sweating, compared with a quarter of the placebo patients. . . ." (The explanation provided is that Botox "seems to temporarily paralyze a nerve that stimulates sweat glands.")[7] Assume that the 322 patients were evenly divided between Botox and placebo (161 in each group).

Question: How can the summary information be shown in a two-way table?

Response: We can construct a complete two-way table, based on the information provided, because 75% of 161 is 121 (and the remaining 40 report no decrease) and a quarter of 161 is 40 (and the remaining 121 report no decrease).

	Sweating Decreased	Sweating Not Decreased	Total	Percent Decreased
Botox	121	40	161	75%
Placebo	40	121	161	25%
Total	161	161	322	

Treatment with Botox or placebo is the explanatory variable, so we place those categories in the rows of our table. Sweating responses go in the columns.

Practice: *Try Exercise 5.23(a–d) on page 161.*

The Big Picture:

LOOKING BACK

Remember that a study is an experiment if researchers impose values of the explanatory variable. Example 5.12 is an experiment because researchers assigned subjects to be injected with Botox or a placebo. Notice that the response—sweating— was treated as a categorical variable, as subjects either did or did not report a significant decrease in sweating.

The Role of Sample Size: Larger Samples Let Us Rule Out Chance

In order to provide statistical evidence of a difference in responses for *populations* in certain explanatory groups, and convince skeptics that the difference cannot be attributed to chance variation in the sample of individuals, we will need to do more than just eyeball the percentages. Another detail that must be taken into account at some point is the sample size. As our intuition suggests, the larger the sample size, the more convincing the difference.

EXAMPLE 5.13 SMALLER SAMPLES LESS CONVINCING

Background: In Example 5.12, there seemed to be a substantial difference in conditional percentages reporting a decrease in sweating—75% for Botox versus 25% for placebo.

Question: Would you be as convinced of the sweat-reducing properties of Botox if the same percentages arose from an experiment involving only eight subjects, as summarized in this hypothetical table?

	Sweating Decreased	Sweating Not Decreased	Total	Percent Decreased
Botox	3	1	4	75%
Placebo	1	3	4	25%
Total	4	4	8	

Response: The difference between 3 out of 4 and 1 out of 4 is not nearly as impressive as the difference between 121 out of 161 and 40 out of 161. If there were only 4 people in each group, it's easy to believe that even if Botox had no effect on sweating, by chance a couple more in the Botox group showed improvement.

Practice: *Try Exercise 5.25 on page 162.*

Example 5.13 suggests that a difference between proportions in a *sample* does not necessarily convince us of a difference in the larger *population*. Appropriate notation is important so that we can distinguish between conditional proportions in samples versus populations.

Sample proportions with decreased sweating for Botox versus placebo can be written as $\hat{p}_1$ and $\hat{p}_2$. The proportion of *all* people who would experience reduced sweating through the use of Botox is denoted p_1, and the proportion of all people who would experience (or claim to experience) reduced sweating just by taking a placebo is written p_2. As usual, the population proportions p_1 and p_2 are unknown.

LOOKING AHEAD

Statistical inference for two-way tables, presented in Part IV of this book, is typically based on a comparison of observed and expected counts, rather than on a comparison of observed proportions.

Comparing Observed and Expected Counts

One way to summarize the impact of a categorical explanatory variable on the categorical response is to compare conditional proportions, as was done in Example 5.10 on page 153 and Example 5.12 on page 155. A different approach would be to compare *counts:* How different are the observed counts from those that would be *expected* if the two variables were not related?

A *table of expected counts* shows us what would be the case on average in the long run if the two categorical variables were not related.

> *Definitions*　　The **expected value** of a variable is its mean. An **expected count** in a two-way table is the average value the count would take if there were no relationship between the two categorical variables featured in the table.

EXAMPLE 5.14 TABLE OF EXPECTED COUNTS

Background: Counts of respondents from the United States and Canada agreeing or not with the statement "It is necessary to believe in God to be moral," are shown in the table on the left. This table shows an overall percentage $\frac{1,020}{2,000} = 51\%$ answering *yes*, but percentages are quite different for U.S. ($\frac{870}{1,500} = 58\%$) and Canadian ($\frac{150}{500} = 30\%$) respondents.[8] The table on the right has the same total counts in the margins, but counts inside the table reflect what would be *expected* if the same percentage (51%) of the 1,500 Americans and the 500 Canadians had answered *yes*.

It is necessary to believe in God to be moral...(observed counts)

	Yes	No (or no answer)	Total
U.S.	870	630	1,500
Canada	150	350	500
Total	1,020	980	2,000

It is necessary to believe in God to be moral...(Counts of responses expected if percentages were equal for the U.S. and Canada)

	Yes	No (or no answer)	Total
U.S.	765	735	1,500
Canada	255	245	500
Total	1,020	980	2,000

Question: How different are the four actual observed counts from the four expected counts?

Response: Over 100 more Americans answered *yes* (870) than what we'd expect to see (765) if nationality had no impact on response. Conversely, fewer Canadians answered *yes* (150) than what we'd expect (255) if there were no relationship. The other two pairs of table entries likewise differ by 105. Taking these four differences at face value, without being able to justify anything formally, we can say that they do seem quite pronounced.

Practice: *Try Exercise 5.29 on page 163.*

The Big Picture:

LOOKING AHEAD

In Part IV, we will learn how to calculate a number called "chi-square" that rolls all the differences between observed and expected counts into one value. This number tells, in a relative way, how different our observed table is from what would be expected if response to the question about God and morality were not related to a person's nationality.

Example TBP 5.3 on page 790 of the ***TBP Supplement*** goes into detail in terms of summarizing the relationship in the observed table (on the left) in Example 5.14.

Confounding Variables and Simpson's Paradox: Is the Relationship Really There?

Whenever the relationship between two variables is being explored, there is almost always a question of whether one variable actually *causes* changes in the other. Does being female cause a choice of contact lenses over glasses? Does Botox cause less sweating? In Part I, which covered data production, we stressed the difficulty in establishing causation in observational studies due to the possible influence of confounding variables. The following example demonstrates how confounding variables, if they are permitted to lurk in the background without being taken into account, can result in conclusions of causation that are misleading.

Example 5.15 CONSIDERING CONFOUNDING VARIABLES

Background: Data for 430 full-time students yielded the following two-way table and bar graph for the variables *Major* (decided or not) and *Living situation* (on or off campus). Relevant conditional percentages are included in the right-most column.

	On Campus	Off Campus	Total	Rate On Campus
Undecided	124	81	205	124/205 = 60%
Decided	96	129	225	96/225 = 43%

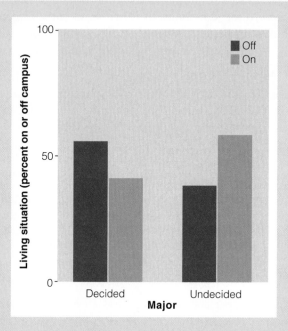

Question: Is there a relationship between whether or not a student's major is decided and whether the student lives on or off campus?

Response: The table and the bar graph (which take major decided or not as the explanatory variable and living situation as the response) show a fairly dramatic difference in percentages: A minority (43%) live on campus for the decided majors, whereas a clear majority (60%) live on campus for the undecided majors.

Does having an undecided major *cause* a student to live on campus? If this doesn't sound right, we could reverse roles of explanatory and response variables, and wonder if living on campus *causes* a student's major to be undecided. This wouldn't make much sense, either. Therefore, we should ask ourselves if there is some other variable lurking in the background that could play a role in whether or not a student's major is decided, and could also play a role in whether a student lives on or off campus. As you may have already suspected, a student's age or year at school is the missing variable that should have been taken into account.

Practice: *Try Exercise 5.32(b) on page 164.*

As we have discussed in Part I of this book, on data production, the way to handle a potential confounding variable is to separate it out.

EXAMPLE 5.16 HANDLING CONFOUNDING VARIABLES

Background: Year at school is suspected to be a confounding variable in the relationship between major decided or not and living situation on or off campus. The data from the table in Example 5.15, with the help of additional information about students' year at school, actually decomposes into the following two tables, with accompanying bar graphs, when students are separated into underclassmen (first or second year) and upperclassmen (third or fourth year).

Underclassmen	On Campus	Off Campus	Total	Rate On Campus
Undecided	117	55	172	117/172 = 68%
Decided	82	37	119	82/119 = 69%

Upperclassmen	On Campus	Off Campus	Total	Rate On Campus
Undecided	7	26	33	7/33 = 21%
Decided	14	92	106	14/106 = 13%

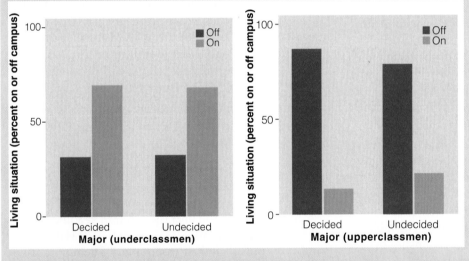

Question: Do the tables and bar graphs suggest a relationship between major decided or not and living situation?

Response: Now we see that for the underclassmen, a majority live on campus, whether major is decided or not, and the percentages are almost identical (68% and 69%). Likewise for the upperclassmen, a small minority live on campus, whether major is decided or not. The percentages differ somewhat (21% and 13%), but it seems plausible enough that a difference this small could have come about by chance, if there were no relationship between major decided or not and living situation. In other words, looking at the underclassmen and upperclassmen separately, there is no apparent relationship between major being decided or not, and the student living on or off campus. In contrast, when underclassmen and upperclassmen were lumped together, as in Example 5.15, the undecided majors seemed much more likely to live on campus, and the decided majors much more likely to live off campus.

Practice: *Try Exercise 5.32(d) on page 164.*

The Big Picture:

LOOKING AHEAD

Methods to be developed in Part IV will show that the difference between 21% and 13%, taking sample sizes into account, is not "statistically significant."

The above phenomenon, wherein the nature of a relationship changes when data for two groups are combined and those groups differ in an important way besides the explanatory and response variables of interest, is called **Simpson's Paradox**. It is a manifestation of the impact of a confounding variable on a relationship, and serves as a reminder that possible confounding variables must be controlled for in a study. When we recognize that being an under- or upperclassman plays a role, we actually begin to consider the relationship among *three* categorical variables. Being an under- or upperclassman would be the explanatory variable; major decided or not and living on or off campus would be the responses. Each of these two does respond to the explanatory variable, but they have no real impact on each other.

Relationships between two categorical variables are summarized on page 204 of the Chapter Summary.

EXERCISES FOR SECTION 5.2

Relationships between Two Categorical Variables

Note: Asterisked numbers indicate exercises whose answers are provided in the Solutions to Selected Exercises section, on page 689.

*5.17 High school students were surveyed about a variety of activities.

   a. 44.3% of the males had engaged in a physical fight during the past year, compared to 27.2% of the females. Is this information dealing with two single categorical variables individually, or the relationship between two categorical variables?

   b. 73.5% of the students met standards for engaging in adequate exercise; 14.7% had consumed the recommended servings of fruits and vegetables the day before. Is this information dealing with two single categorical variables individually, or the relationship between two categorical variables?

5.18 A newspaper article entitled "You Do What?!?" reports that "in a study of more than 160,000 resumes, ResumeDoctor.com found that . . . nearly 13% of the resumes told a company the applicant had 'communication skills,' while more than 7% said the person was a 'team player.'"[9] Is this information dealing with two single categorical variables individually, or the relationship between two categorical variables?

5.19 Workers were surveyed about neatness, as well as other background information. Of the people making more than $75,000 annually, 11% described themselves as "neat freaks," but 66% of those earning less than $35,000 claimed that description.[10]

   a. Is this information dealing with two single categorical variables individually, or the relationship between two categorical variables? Tell what the variables are, and if there is a relationship, tell which is explanatory and which is response.

   b. Do the results suggest that neater workers are the ones who earn more or earn less?

*5.20 The *New York Times* reported on "The Other Troops in Iraq": "In addition to the United States, 36 countries have committed troops to support the operation in Iraq at some point. Eight countries [. . . (as of fall 2004)] have pulled all their troops out." The report also indicated when the various countries sent their troops—some were earlier (spring of 2003) and others were later (summer/fall of 2003).[11] This table classifies those 36 countries as sending troops early or late, and as having pulled troops out early or not.

	Pulled Troops Early	Troops Remained by Fall 2004	Total
Sent Troops Early	3	12	15
Sent Troops Late	5	16	21
Total	8	28	36

   a. Which particular row or column reports the counts that are relevant if we are interested only in whether troops were sent early or late?

b. Which particular row or column reports the counts that are relevant if we are interested only in whether troops were pulled early or late?

c. Overall, what proportion of countries pulled their troops early?

d. Of the countries that sent troops early, what proportion also pulled their troops early?

e. Of the countries that sent troops late, what proportion pulled their troops early?

f. Which variable are we taking to be the explanatory variable: whether troops were sent early or late, or whether troops were pulled early or not?

g. Which of the following best summarizes the situation?

1. The countries that sent troops early were much more likely to pull their troops early.

2. The countries that sent troops early were a bit more likely to pull their troops early.

3. The countries that sent troops late were much more likely to pull their troops early.

4. The countries that sent troops late were a bit more likely to pull their troops early.

*5.21 Responses are shown for 18 students who were asked to report their gender as male or female, and answer *yes* or *no* to whether they'd eaten breakfast that day.

Sex	f	m	f	f	f	f	f	f	f	f	f	m	m	m	f	m	f	f
Breakfast?	n	n	y	n	n	y	y	n	y	y	y	n	n	n	y	y	n	y

a. Tabulate the results in a two-way table, taking gender as the explanatory variable and breakfast as the response; include totals for both variables.

b. What percentage of the males ate breakfast?

c. What percentage of the females ate breakfast?

d. Sketch a bar graph of the data.

e. Explain why this sample should not convince us that those are necessarily the percentages of *all* male and female college students who eat breakfast.

5.22 Responses are shown for 20 high school juniors and seniors who were asked to report their year, and whether their means of transportation was to drive themselves to school (d) or not (n).

Year	s	j	s	j	s	s	s	s	s	s	j	j	j	j	s	s	j	j	j	j
Trans	d	n	d	d	d	n	d	d	n	n	d	n	n	n	d	d	n	d	n	n

a. Which students should you expect to have a higher percentage driving themselves to school: juniors or seniors?

b. Tabulate the results in a two-way table, taking year as the explanatory variable and transportation as the response; include totals for both variables.

c. What percentage of the juniors drove to school?

d. What percentage of the seniors drove to school?

e. Sketch a bar graph of the data.

f. Overall, what percentage of the students drove to school?

g. Construct a table of what the counts would be if there were still 10 juniors and 10 seniors, and still 10 each driving to school and not driving to school, but equal percentages driving to school for juniors and for seniors (same as the overall percentage that you found in part [f]).

*5.23 The BBC News website reported in 2003 that "Tight Ties Could Damage Eyesight," citing that "researchers from the New York Eye and Ear Infirmary in New York tested 40 men, half of whom were healthy, and half of whom had already been diagnosed with glaucoma. Their 'intraocular pressure' was measured, then they were asked to put on a 'slightly uncomfortable' tie for 3 minutes.

They were tested again, and 60% of the glaucoma patients and 70% of the healthy men were found to have significant rises in pressure. As soon as the ties were removed, the pressure fell again." The researchers warned that long-term pressure rises have been linked to the condition glaucoma, which is the most common cause of irreversible blindness in the world.[12]

a. The study was an experiment; what was the treatment?

b. How many subjects were in a control group receiving no treatment?

c. The reported results involve two categorical variables. Tell what they are and which is explanatory and which is response.

d. Use the information to construct a two-way table of counts, with the explanatory variable in rows and the response in columns.

e. The researchers apparently suspected that a potential confounding variable could play a role in whether a tight necktie increases intraocular pressure. What is that variable?

© Barry Lewis/CORBIS

Can a necktie hurt your eyes?

5.24 An Internet report from January 2005 is titled, "Study: Anti-seizure Drug Reduces Drinking in Bipolar Alcoholics." This table is consistent with results mentioned in the report, which explains that drug- and placebo-takers were questioned after 6 months to see if they had engaged in heavy drinking (five or more drinks daily for men, four or more daily for women).[13]

	Heavy Drinking	No Heavy Drinking	Total
Valproate	14	18	32
Placebo	15	7	22
Total	29	25	54

a. What percentage of the valproate-takers had engaged in heavy drinking?

b. What percentage of the placebo-takers had engaged in heavy drinking?

c. The report also states that the valproate group had about half as many drinks on heavy-drinking days as those in the placebo group. In this case, is the response being treated as quantitative or categorical?

d. When sample size is small, there is a greater risk of failing to provide evidence that a drug is effective when, in fact, it is. Discuss the harmful consequences of drawing this type of incorrect conclusion in this particular situation.

*5.25 The results obtained in Exercise 5.24 would have been more convincing if they had come from a larger sample. Discuss the difficulties in carrying out this type of study on a large number of people.

*5.26 The U.S. government collects hate crime data each year, and classifies such criminal offenses according to motivation (race, religion, sexual orientation, etc.) and also according to race of the offender. Of the 3,712 offenses committed by whites, 679 were about the victim's sexual orientation; of the 1,082 offenses committed by blacks, 210 were about the victim's sexual orientation. [In both cases, most of the incidents were anti-male homosexual.] Clearly, the *count* of offenses that were about sexual orientation was higher for whites than for blacks. Find the *proportions* of hate crimes motivated by the victim's sexual orientation for white and for black offenders and tell which is higher.

5.27 In Exercise 5.26, proportions of hate crimes motivated by the victim's sexual orientation are compared for white and for black offenders.

a. Would the proportions be called statistics or parameters? Should they be denoted p_1 and p_2 or $\hat{p}_1$ and $\hat{p}_2$?

b. Of the 3,712 offenses committed by whites, 327 were about the victim's religion; of the 1,082 offenses committed by blacks, 46 were about the victim's religion. [In both cases, most of the incidents were anti-Jewish.] Find the proportions of hate crimes motivated by victim's religion for white and for black offenders.

c. In one of the two situations described in Exercise 5.26 and in part (b) of this exercise, the difference between proportions for whites and for blacks is small enough to have come about by chance. For which type of hate crime does race of the offender seem to make little difference: those motivated by victim's sexual orientation or those motivated by victim's religion?

d. In another of the two situations described above, the difference between proportions for whites and for blacks is too dramatic to be attributed to chance. For this type of hate crime, is the proportion higher for whites or for blacks?

e. Based on the information provided, complete this two-way table. [Almost all of the "Other" crimes were motivated by race and ethnicity.]

	Sexual Orientation	Religion	Other	Total
White Offender				
Black Offender				
Total				

5.28 The *New York Times* reported in 2004 on the "Values Gap" in the United States by comparing a variety of percentages. For example, the number of divorces per 1,000 married people was 15 in Nevada and 6 in Massachusetts, whereas the number of abortions per 1,000 births was 30 in New York and 20 in Washington.[14] Four statistics students are asked to tell which difference, if any, is larger: the one for divorces or the one for abortions. Whose answer is best?

Adam: So, 15 minus 6 is 9, and 30 minus 20 is 10. The difference is larger for abortions.

Brittany: But 9 and 10 are close enough that we can say the difference between them is negligible. Really the situations are comparable for divorces and for abortions.

Carlos: They're talking about divorces per thousand, out of millions of married people, or abortions per thousand, out of millions of

births. So 10 is actually much larger than 9—the difference is definitely larger for abortions.

Dominique: To put things in perspective you have to look at proportions: 0.0015 is more than twice as big as 0.0006, and 0.0030 is only half again as large as 0.0020. The difference in divorce rates is actually larger than the difference in abortion rates.

*5.29 Refer to Exercise 5.23 on page 161 about the possibility that wearing tight neckties causes glaucoma. The study found that 60% of 20 glaucoma patients and 70% of healthy men had significant rises in intraocular pressure after wearing a tight necktie for 3 minutes.

a. Create a table where the same overall percentage (65%) of subjects show an increase in intraocular pressure, and where the percentage is the same for the 20 subjects with glaucoma and the 20 subjects without glaucoma.

b. Each of the counts in the table showing equal percentages is different from the counts in the original table by how many?

c. Does it appear that whether or not someone already has glaucoma plays a significant role in whether or not a tightened necktie increases intraocular pressure?

d. If the same results had been obtained based on 10 subjects in each group instead of 20, would it then appear that whether or not someone already has glaucoma plays a significant role in whether or not a tightened necktie increases intraocular pressure?

5.30 An article in *Nature* reports on a study of the relationship between kinship and aggression in wasps. In a controlled experiment, the proportion of 31 *brother* embryos attacked by soldier wasp larvae was 0.52, whereas the proportion of 31 *unrelated* male embryos attacked was 0.77.[15]

a. What are the explanatory and response variables?

b. Construct a table of whole-number counts in the four possible category combinations, using rows for the explanatory variable and columns for the response.

c. Altogether, there were 40 attacks. If attacks had not been at all related to kinship, how many of these would be against brothers and how many would be against unrelated males?

d. Discuss the role of sample size in comparing a difference such as the difference between 0.52 and 0.77.

5.31 CBS reported on its website in September 2004: "Should Parents Talk to Their Dying Children About Death? A Swedish study found that parents whose children died of cancer had no regrets about talking to them about death, while some who didn't do so were sorry later. [. . .] Using Sweden's comprehensive cancer and death records, the researchers found 368 children under 17 who had been diagnosed with cancer between 1992 and 1997 and who later died. They contacted the children's parents, and 80% of them filled out a long, anonymous questionnaire. Among the questions: 'Did you talk about death with your child at any time?' Of the 429 parents who answered that, about one-third said they had done so, while two-thirds had not. None of the 147 who did so regretted talking about death. Among those who had not talked about death, 69 said they wished they had."[16]

a. The researchers focused on two categorical variables: Tell what they are and which is explanatory and which is response.

b. Construct a two-way table to classify the 429 parents in the survey, with the explanatory variable in rows and response variable in columns.

c. Altogether, 16% of the 429 respondents experienced regrets. If 16% of the 147 who had talked about death with their children had experienced regrets (instead of 0%), how many would that have been?

d. If only 16% of the 282 parents who had not talked about death had experienced regrets (instead of 69/282 = 24%), how many would that have been?

e. If we want to compare the results to what they would have been if equal percentages experienced regrets for parents who did and did not talk about death with their children, which of these is a better summary?
   1. Results are a bit different from what they would have been if equal percentages experienced regrets among parents who did and did not talk about death with their children.
   2. Results are very different from what they would have been if equal percentages experienced regrets

among parents who did and did not talk about death with their children.

f. When the researchers decided to make the questions anonymous, were they mainly concerned with data production, displaying and summarizing data, probability, or statistical inference?

g. If researchers want to use the results of their survey to conclude that all parents of dying children should consider talking about death with their children, are they mainly concerned with data production, displaying and summarizing data, probability, or statistical inference?

*5.32 Students were surveyed as to whether or not they had their ears pierced, and were also asked their favorite color. This table shows the approximate results for students who preferred pink or black.

	Pink	Black	Total
Not Pierced	17	19	36
Pierced	28	11	39

a. Compare the proportions preferring pink (as opposed to black) for those with and without pierced ears to demonstrate that students with pierced ears tend to prefer pink.

b. What is the most obvious confounding variable in the relationship between ear piercings and color preference?

c. These tables show results separately for males and females surveyed. Now compare the proportions preferring pink (as opposed to black) for those with and without pierced ears, one gender group at a time. Do female students or male students with pierced ears tend to prefer pink?

Females	Pink	Black	Total
Not Pierced	9	3	12
Pierced	27	9	36

Males	Pink	Black	Total
Not Pierced	8	16	24
Pierced	1	2	3

d. Which is the better approach to exploring the relationship between ear piercings and color preference: the one in part (a) or the one in part (c)?

5.3 Relationships between Two Quantitative Variables

Q→Q

So far, we have considered data for a single categorical variable or a single quantitative variable. We have also explored data for the relationship between a categorical and a quantitative variable, and for the relationship between two categorical variables. The last type of relationship to be examined is for data about two quantitative variables—that is, for each individual in the sample, values for two number-valued variables are recorded. In many situations, values taken by one quantitative variable play a role in the values taken by a second quantitative variable. Some examples to follow are male students' heights and weights, ages of students' mothers and fathers, and used cars' ages and prices. We will begin with an example involving students' heights and weights, since most of us have a pretty good feel for how these variables should be related. If and how ages of mothers and fathers are related (the issue raised at the beginning of the chapter) will be considered later on.

EXAMPLE 5.17 DISPLAYING AND SUMMARIZING TWO SINGLE QUANTITATIVE VARIABLES

Background: The following data, histograms, and descriptive statistics are for heights and weights of a sample of 17 male college students:

Ht	72	73	68	70	71	70	69	71	69	71	74	69	68	68	65	69	69
Wt	195	175	130	168	175	180	180	214	172	145	235	125	181	150	140	185	150

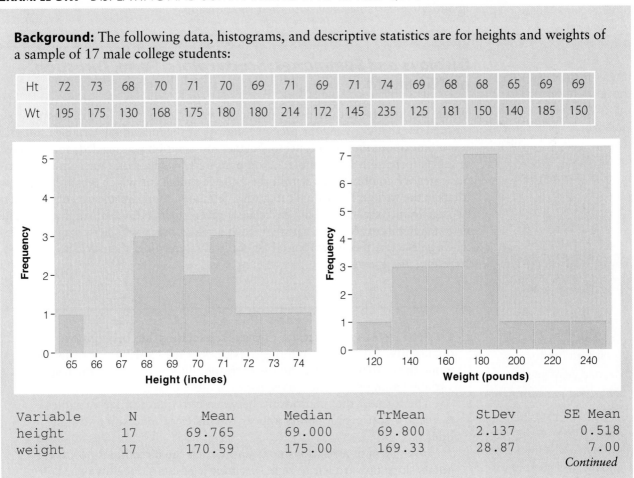

Variable	N	Mean	Median	TrMean	StDev	SE Mean
height	17	69.765	69.000	69.800	2.137	0.518
weight	17	170.59	175.00	169.33	28.87	7.00

Continued

- We can display and summarize the quantitative variable "height" for the sample. A histogram shows the distribution's shape to be reasonably symmetric (fairly normal, in fact), and so we could summarize by reporting the mean to be 69.765 inches and standard deviation 2.137 inches: These male students were about 70 inches tall, and their heights tended to differ from 70 inches by about 2 inches.

- Similarly, we can display and summarize the quantitative variable "weight" for the sample. A histogram shows the distribution's shape to be reasonably symmetric (also roughly normal), and so we could summarize by reporting the mean to be 170.59 pounds and standard deviation 28.87 pounds: These male students weighed about 171 pounds, and their weights tended to differ from 171 pounds by about 29 pounds.

Question: What do these displays and summaries tell us about the relationship between height and weight for the sampled males?

Response: In fact, these displays and summaries tell us nothing about how the two variables are related; they only tell us about the individual variables.

Practice: *Try Exercise 5.33 on page 192.*

For the relationship between two categorical variables, we first produce summaries (conditional percentages), and from these we create the display (a bar graph). For the relationship between two quantitative variables, it makes sense to begin with the display (a scatterplot) before producing summaries.

A CLOSER LOOK

If the form of a relationship is *curved,* then methods that go beyond elementary statistics can be used to transform the variables in such a way as to result in a linear form, and then proceed. In this book, if the form is curved, we will take the analysis no further.

Example 5.17 discusses two quantitative variables—height and weight—but the variables are treated one at a time, and so the example deals with two *single* quantitative variables, not with their relationship.

Displays and Summaries: Scatterplots, Form, Direction, and Strength

When we first looked at two categorical variables earlier in this chapter, we pointed out that knowing the precise behavior of the individual variables still told us nothing about their relationship. Further information was needed, and we filled in that information in Example 5.9 on page 152 by specifying the counts in various category combinations within the two-way table for which we already knew totals in the various individual categories. Similarly, there are all sorts of ways that two quantitative variables can be related, given their individual summaries. The first step in discovering the nature of such a relationship will be to display the interplay between those two variables with a *scatterplot,* then discuss its *form, direction,* and *strength.*

Definitions   A **scatterplot** displays the relationship between two quantitative variables by plotting x_i (values of the explanatory variable) along the horizontal axis, and the corresponding y_i (values of the response variable) along the vertical axis, for each individual i.

The **form** of the relationship between two quantitative variables is *linear* if scatterplot points appear to cluster around some straight line.

If the form of a relationship is linear, then the **direction** is *positive* if points slope upward left to right, *negative* if points slope downward.

The **strength** of a linear relationship between two quantitative variables is *strong* if the points are tightly clustered around a straight line, and *weak* if they are loosely scattered about a line.

The histograms and summaries for height and weight as described in Example 5.17 were fine for giving insight into the individual data sets, but they told us nothing about the interplay between the height and weight values. Thus, we need a scatterplot to give us a look at how the two variables are related. We also need additional summaries. These are introduced in the following example.

Example TBP 5.4 on page 792 of the *TBP Supplement* discusses a curved relationship between two quantitative variables.

EXAMPLE 5.18 RELATIONSHIP BETWEEN TWO QUANTITATIVE VARIABLES: FORM AND DIRECTION

Background: As in Example 5.17, we have data on heights and weights of 17 male students.

Ht	72	73	68	70	71	70	69	71	69	71	74	69	68	68	65	69	69
Wt	195	175	130	168	175	180	180	214	172	145	235	125	181	150	140	185	150

Question: How can we display and summarize the *relationship* between heights and weights to convey the information provided by the fact that the first height (72 inches) accompanies the first weight (195 pounds), and so on, for all 17 height/weight pairs?

Response: Whenever we explore a relationship, we should begin by thinking about the roles played by the variables involved. Whereas heights are almost completely predetermined, people do have some control over their weights, and we can think of a student's weight as responding to his height, at least to some extent. Therefore, we will assign *height* the role of explanatory variable and *weight* the response.

To display the relationship between heights and weights, we draw a scatterplot. Because height is the explanatory variable, we plot each height value horizontally and plot the corresponding weight vertically. For example, for the first sampled male, we would mark a point with a horizontal value of 72 and a vertical value of 195. Altogether, there will be 17 points in our scatterplot, for the 17 male students studied.

Once we have plotted all the points, we sketch a "cloud" around them to help give us a feel for how the points behave as a group. They do seem to cluster around a straight line, rather than a curve, so we can say the *form* is linear. As far as the *direction* is concerned, the scatterplot confirms what common sense would already tell us: If a male is naturally short, he tends to weigh less; if he is tall, he tends to weigh more. This circumstance results in scatterplot points that tend to fall in the lower left quadrant (lower weights accompanying shorter heights) and in the upper right quadrant (higher weights accompanying taller heights). Taken together, concentrations of points in the lower-left and upper-right quadrants lead to a cloud of points (and the line they cluster around) rising from left to right: The direction of the relationship is positive.

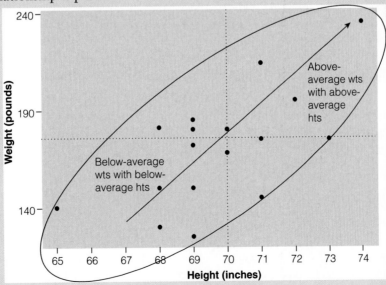

Practice: *Try Exercise 5.36(a–c) on page 193.*

If a relationship is negative, then below-average *x*-values tend to occur with above-average *y*-values, and vice-versa, and the scatterplot points tend to slope downwards, from the upper-left to the lower-right quadrant. Note that for some forms that are curved, it is impossible to assess the direction as being either positive or negative, if scatterplot points rise and then fall, or vice versa, as in a horseshoe shape.

Besides form and direction, an extremely important aspect of the relationship between two quantitative variables is its strength. If a relationship is very strong, then knowing a value of the explanatory variable gives us a very good idea of what the corresponding response should be. If a relationship is weak, then the explanatory variable only plays a minor role in what values the response takes.

EXAMPLE 5.19 RELATIONSHIP BETWEEN TWO QUANTITATIVE VARIABLES: STRENGTH

Background: These scatterplots display the relationships between the heights of students' mothers and fathers (on the top), weights and heights of male students (in the middle), and ages of students' mothers and fathers (on the bottom).

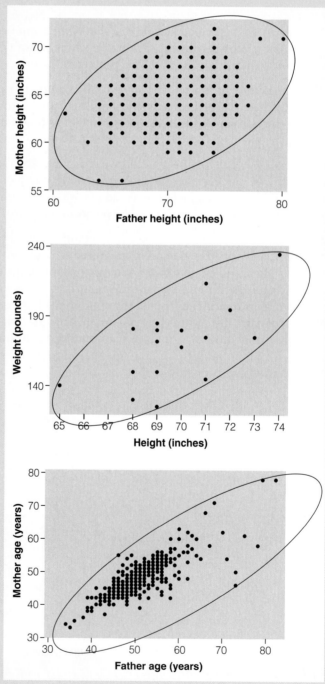

Notice that we arbitrarily took father's age to be the explanatory variable, mother's age the response. These two variables are on such equal footing that we could just as well have made the reverse assignment. Similarly, we could just as easily have taken mother's height to be the explanatory variable and father's height the response.

Question: Compare the three scatterplots' clouds of points to rank the scatterplots from weakest to strongest.

Response: First, we note that all three relationships are positive and appear linear, not curved.

Although there may be a slight tendency for shorter men to marry shorter women, and taller men to marry taller women, knowing a father's height gives us very little information about the mother's height. The scatterplot points for *Mother height* versus *Father height* are very loosely scattered in an oval cloud that is almost circular, and the relationship is very weak.

Knowing a father's age gives us a great deal of information about a mother's age because there is a tendency for people of similar ages to marry. If we know a father's age, we have a pretty good idea of the mother's age, give or take a couple of years. The scatterplot points for *Mother age* versus *Father age* are rather tightly clustered in a cigar-shaped cloud, and the relationship is fairly strong.

The relationship between male students' heights and weights is stronger than the one for heights of mothers and fathers, and weaker than the one for ages of mothers and fathers. The scatterplots are shown with weakest on the top (loosest scattering) and strongest on the bottom (tightest clustering).

Practice: *Try Exercise 5.37 on page 193.*

The **Big Picture:**

LOOKING AHEAD

To assess strength, we should concentrate on how "fat" or "skinny" the cloud of points is, not on how many data points happen to be included. Sample size will be taken into account when we study statistical inference for regression in Part IV.

It is worth noting that direction and strength are two separate considerations: a strong relationship may be positive or negative, likewise for a weak relationship. The next example gives us a look at a negative relationship that happens to be quite strong.

EXAMPLE 5.20 A NEGATIVE RELATIONSHIP

Background: Below is a scatterplot for price versus age of 14 used Pontiac Grand Ams.

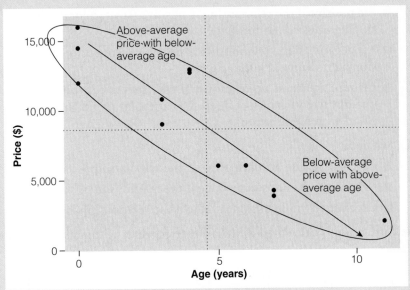

Continued

Recall our displays and summaries of the distribution of a single quantitative variable. Depending on our choice of stems in a stemplot, or interval widths in a histogram, the appearance of *spread* can be arbitrarily small or large. Fortunately, we can rely on the standard deviation to give us a succinct measurement of the spread of a distribution. Instead of saying "the weights are pretty spread out," we can make a very precise statement like, "the standard deviation of the weights is 31 pounds." Analogously, correlation lets us be precise about the *strength* of a relationship.

Notice that we use subscripts *x* and *y* to identify whether we are referring to the mean and standard deviation of the explanatory values *x* or the response values *y*.

Questions: In general, would you expect the direction of the relationship between used cars' ages and prices to be positive or negative? Does the scatterplot confirm your expectations? Does the relationship appear weak or strong?

Responses: It makes sense that newer cars should be worth more; as their age increases, their price should decrease. We would expect a scatterplot of price (response variable) versus age (explanatory variable) to show points in the upper-left quadrant (high prices for newer cars) and in the lower-right quadrant (low prices for older cars). Taken together, the cloud of points would slope down from left to right: We expect a negative relationship.

As for what the scatterplot shows, first we note that the form appears to be linear. The direction is clearly negative, as expected.

Finally, the relationship appears quite strong because the points are clustered fairly tightly around some imaginary line.

Practice: *Try Exercise 5.38(c,d) on page 194.*

Correlation: One Number for Direction and Strength

Choice of scale in a scatterplot can impact the appearance of strength of a relationship between two quantitative variables. Fortunately, there is a precise summary of strength (and direction) of a linear relationship, called the *correlation*, written *r*. Instead of saying "the relationship between the male students' heights and weights is moderately strong," we will be able to make a very precise statement like, "the correlation between the male students' heights and weights is 0.646." There is actually a great deal of information packed into this one number.

Definition   The **correlation, *r*,** is a number between −1 and +1 that tells the direction and strength of the linear relationship between two quantitative variables.

1. Direction:
   - *r* is positive if the relationship is positive (scatterplot points sloping upward left to right).
   - *r* is negative if the relationship is negative (scatterplot points sloping downward left to right).
   - *r* is zero if there is no relationship whatsoever between the two quantitative variables of interest (scatterplot points in a horizontal cloud with no direction).

2. Strength:
   - *r* is close to 1 in absolute value if the relationship is strong.
   - *r* is close to 0 in absolute value if the relationship is weak.
   - *r* is close to 0.5 in absolute value if the relationship is moderate.

The correlation is calculated as the average product of standardized *x* and *y* values:

$$r = \frac{1}{n-1}\left[\left(\frac{x_1 - \bar{x}}{s_x}\right)\left(\frac{y_1 - \bar{y}}{s_y}\right) + \cdots + \left(\frac{x_n - \bar{x}}{s_x}\right)\left(\frac{y_n - \bar{y}}{s_y}\right)\right]$$

On pages 792–793 of the *TBP Supplement*, we show how to calculate the correlation by hand.

When the Correlation Is 0, +1, or −1

In almost all real-life examples, there is some relationship between the two quantitative variables involved, but it is not perfect. The next three examples, to serve as a contrast, explore the three extremes that we rarely encounter.

The correlation equals zero when knowing which value the explanatory variable takes tells us absolutely nothing about the value of the response. In this case, the scatterplot points are scattered randomly about a horizontal line at the mean response value.

EXAMPLE 5.21 NO RELATIONSHIP

Background: As students handed in their final exams at the end of a statistics course, their professor recorded the chronological number for each (first was 1, last was 71) and then plotted each student's exam score versus this number.

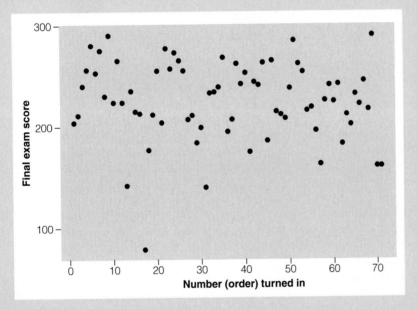

Questions: What does the plot reveal about the strength of the relationship between order turned in and score on the exam? What value (approximately) would we expect for the correlation *r*?

Responses: The plot shows completely random scatter, suggesting a relationship so weak as to be nonexistent. Apparently, time order for when each exam was handed in would tell the professor nothing about what the score was going to be. The two variables don't appear to be related at all. Therefore, we would expect the correlation to be just about zero.

Practice: *Try Exercise 5.39 on page 194.*

The correlation equals +1 when knowing which value the explanatory variable takes tells us everything about the value of the response, and the relationship is positive: Below-average explanatory values go with below-average responses, and above-average values also go together.

EXAMPLE 5.22 A PERFECT POSITIVE RELATIONSHIP

Background: In April 2001, Britain's "metric martyr" Steven Thoburn was convicted for selling bananas by the pound (25 pence per pound), instead of by the kilogram (55 pence per kilogram).[17] This scatterplot shows food prices per kilogram versus prices per pound for a variety of groceries.

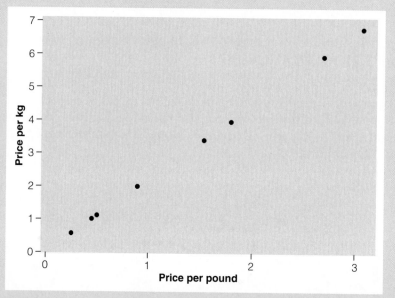

Questions: Why are the scatterplot points arranged exactly along a line with positive slope? What value would we expect for the correlation r?

Responses: Knowing price per pound gives us complete information about price per kilogram, and obviously, the more something costs per pound the more it will cost per kilogram. Thus, the scatterplot should show a perfect positive relationship, with points falling exactly on a line that slopes up from left to right. We expect r to equal $+1$.

Practice: *Try Exercise 5.40(a) on page 194.*

The correlation equals -1 when knowing which value the explanatory variable takes tells us everything about the value of the response, and the relationship is negative: Below-average explanatory values go with above-average responses, and vice-versa. Now the points fall exactly on a straight line with a negative slope.

EXAMPLE 5.23 PERFECT NEGATIVE RELATIONSHIP

Background: A commuter looking at used cars could record the age of the car in years; she could also record what year the car was made. This scatterplot shows age plotted versus year.

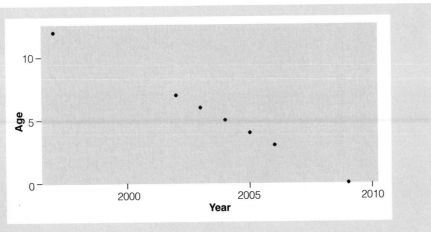

Questions: Why are the scatterplot points arranged exactly along a line with negative slope? What value would we expect for the correlation r?

Responses: The points fall exactly on a line because year completely determines age. The relationship is negative because as the year gets higher, the age gets lower. The correlation must be $r = -1$.

Practice: *Try Exercise 5.40(b) on page 194.*

Correlation as a Measure of Direction and Strength

The relationship between year and age of a car may be perfect, but it is not very interesting. Imperfect relationships are the ones that warrant our attention, as we attempt to determine to what extent one variable causes or explains changes in another, in situations that are much more complex than a simple conversion from year to age.

EXAMPLE 5.24 CORRELATIONS FOR RELATIONSHIPS OF VARIOUS STRENGTHS

Background: Recall the scatterplots in Example 5.19, all of which were for positive relationships.

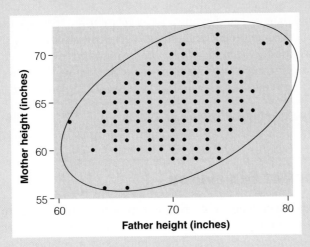

Continued

The Big Picture:
A CLOSER LOOK

What the software identifies as the "Pearson correlation" is the conventionally used measure of the relationship between two quantitative variables that we call *r*.

The Big Picture:
LOOKING AHEAD

Note that in addition to the value of the correlation, the output also reports the "*P*-value." This value will play a vital role later on, when we use statistical inference procedures to decide to what extent we can generalize what we see for the sample data to the larger population from which the data came. In fact, we will learn to interpret a *P*-value of 0 as strong evidence that heights of mothers and fathers are related in the larger population, not just in the sample that we happened to obtain from that population.

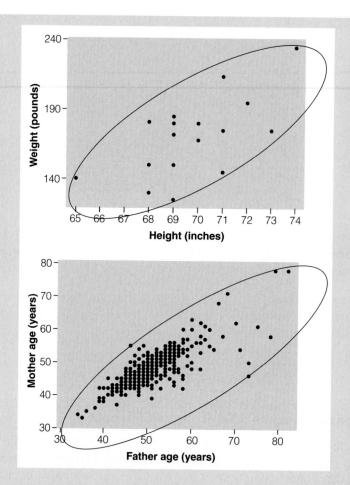

Question: Which scatterplot should have *r* closest to +1 and which should have *r* closest to 0?

Response: Because the relationship for mothers' versus fathers' heights appears weakest, we expect its correlation to be closest to 0. With software we can find the correlation *r* to be +0.225:

```
Pearson correlation of MotherHT and FatherHT = 0.225
P-Value = 0.000
```

The correlation is, in fact, positive (the scatterplot points do slope upward a bit) and closer to 0 than to 1, indicating a weak relationship. Because the relationship between mothers' and fathers' ages is the strongest, it should have a correlation closest to 1. In fact, this *r* can be found to equal +0.781, evidence of a fairly strong positive relationship. The medium-strength relationship in the middle has *r* = +0.646, which is in fact between 0.225 and 0.781.

Practice: *Try Exercise 5.42 on page 194.*

A Closer Look at Correlation

In order to keep the concept of correlation in perspective, it is helpful to remember that correlation tells the direction and strength of the *linear relationship between two quantitative variables*. There may exist a relationship between two categorical variables, but the word "correlation" should not be used to describe such a relationship. Correlation is for quantitative variables only, and there is no way to compute an average product of standardized explanatory and response values unless the values themselves are quantitative. Also, before using r as a summary, you must first have evidence that the relationship between those quantitative variables is linear.

In the remainder of this section, we discuss various properties of r that you should keep in mind when you refer to it as a summary of the direction and strength of a linear relationship between two quantitative variables.

Correlation Is Unaffected by the Roles of Explanatory and Response Variables

In fact, the correlation remains the same regardless of assignment of roles to the two variables. This makes sense if you think of r as the average product of standardized x and y values, according to its formula. It also makes sense if you consider r as a measure of the direction and tightness or looseness of the clustering of scatterplot points, seen in an example to follow.

As far as the formula for r (introduced on page 170) is concerned, multiplying standardized x_i times standardized y_i in our expression

$$ r = \frac{1}{n-1}\left[\left(\frac{x_1-\bar{x}}{s_x}\right)\left(\frac{y_1-\bar{y}}{s_y}\right) + \cdots + \left(\frac{x_n-\bar{x}}{s_x}\right)\left(\frac{y_n-\bar{y}}{s_y}\right)\right] $$

would give the same result as multiplying standardized y_i times standardized x_i. Known as the *commutative law* in arithmetic, the fact that $ab = ba$ confirms that the correlation is unchanged if the roles of x and y are reversed.

As far as the scatterplot is concerned, our next example uses it in taking a more visual approach to the fact that switching roles affects neither the direction nor the strength.

EXAMPLE 5.25 SCATTERPLOT AND CORRELATION WHEN ROLES ARE SWITCHED

Background: First, consider the relationship for male heights (explanatory variable) and weights (response variable), as illustrated in the scatterplot on the left. Next, consider what happens to the direction and strength of the relationship if we reverse roles, so that the axes are flipped as in the scatterplot on the right.

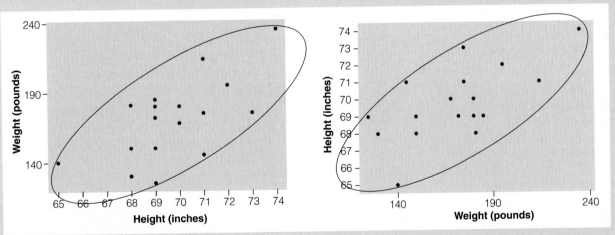

Questions: How are the direction and strength affected by switching roles? What should happen to the value of r?

Responses: The tightness or looseness of the clustering would not be affected by flipping the axes so that x becomes y and y becomes x. Also, if the axes are flipped, a relationship that slopes up will still slope up; a relationship that slopes down will still slope down. Thus, the value of r should be unchanged.

Practice: *Try Exercise 5.45 on page 195.*

Correlation Is Unaffected by Units of Measurement

The fact that the correlation remains the same if we change units of measurement also can be verified by looking at the formula for r or at the scatterplot.

Whatever units are used for x and for y, those units are cancelled out in the process of standardizing in the formula for r. For example, male students' heights had a mean of 69.765 inches and a standard deviation of 2.137 inches. If we standardize a height of 65 inches, we get

$$(65 \text{ inches} - 69.765 \text{ inches})/2.137 \text{ inches} = -2.22976$$

This standardized value is unitless, and so are all the others. We would get the same value if heights had been recorded in centimeters, where there are 2.5 centimeters per inch:

$$(162.5 \text{ cm} - 174.4125 \text{ cm})/5.3425 \text{ cm} = -2.22976$$

Likewise, changing the scale on the horizontal or vertical axis in the scatterplot does not affect the direction of the clustering, nor the strength.

EXAMPLE 5.26 SCATTERPLOT AND CORRELATION WHEN UNITS ARE CHANGED

Background: Instead of male heights in inches and weights in pounds (shown on the left), we could work with heights in centimeters and weights in kilograms (shown on the right).

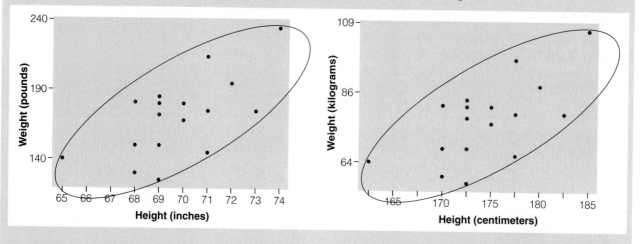

Questions: How are the direction and strength affected by changing units? What should happen to the value of r?

Responses: As long as both scales extend from minimum to maximum data values without any "dead space," all that changes in the scatterplot when we change units would be the numbers along the axes. The value of r should be unchanged.

Practice: *Try Exercise 5.47 on page 196.*

Example TBP 5.5 on page 794 of the ***TBP*** *Supplement* illustrates how a correlation based on averages tends to be stronger than one calculated from individual responses.

It is often the case that there are quite a few responses for each explanatory value. Sometimes, researchers decide to explore the relationship between explanatory values and *average* response values. Although this is a perfectly legitimate approach, you should be aware that a correlation based on averages tends to overstate the strength of a relationship: Averaging tends to eliminate much of the scatter arising from individual responses.

Least Squares Regression Line: What We See in a Linear Plot

As soon as a scatterplot has been produced to display the relationship between two quantitative variables, the form of the relationship should be assessed as appearing linear or not. If it appears curved, then the correlation should not be used as a measure of direction and strength—correlation is for linear relationships only. If it appears linear, then besides reporting direction and strength with r, it makes sense to pin down the nature of the linear relationship by summarizing with the equation of a straight line. In our next example, we begin to think about this line, while still keeping an eye on the behavior of the two individual variables involved.

EXAMPLE 5.27 SCATTERPLOT SUGGESTING INDIVIDUAL SUMMARIES AND A LINE

Background: A commuter would like to buy a used Pontiac Grand Am, and hears about an 8-year-old Grand Am going for $4,000. To get a feel for whether or not this is a reasonable price, the would-be buyer (who has recently taken an introductory statistics course) checks the ages and prices of 14 Grand Ams listed in the used car section of the classified ads. She creates a scatterplot for the data, sketching in a cloud around the points and a line about which they seem to be clustering, as well as lines at the approximate mean age and price values. Also, she uses software to produce the correlation r.

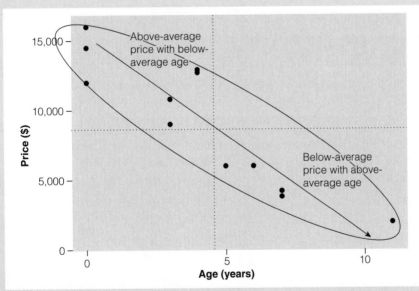

```
Pearson correlation of age and price = −0.886
P-Value = 0.000
```

Questions: What does the plot suggest about the individual distributions of age values and of price values? What does it suggest about the form and direction of the relationship? What does the correlation tell us?

Responses: Average age seems to be a bit less than 5 years, and the typical distance from this average (standard deviation of ages) seems to be about 2 or 3 years. Average price looks to be about $8,000 or $9,000, and the typical distance from this average (standard deviation of prices) could be

Continued

about \$4,000. There do not appear to be outliers in either direction for either distribution, except maybe the car whose age was about 11 years.

The relationship appears linear and is clearly negative: Below-average ages (to the left of the vertical dotted line) accompany above-average prices (above the horizontal dotted line) and above-average ages accompany below-average prices.

The fact that r is pretty close to -1 tells us that the prices of used Grand Ams correspond pretty closely to their ages. Even without a scatterplot, the commuter would know that the relationship should be negative: For example, an 8-year-old Grand Am shouldn't cost as much as one that's just a few months old.

Practice: *Try Exercise 5.50(a–d) on page 196.*

Now that we are focusing our attention on the apparent line in a linear relationship, we must also pay attention to the *residuals*, which are the distances of our scatterplot points from the line.

> *Definition*   The **residual** is the difference between an observed response and the response indicated by the line intended to summarize the relationship between two quantitative variables.

Residuals turn out to be the key to summarizing a linear relationship with the appropriate line.

EXAMPLE 5.28 THE LEAST SQUARES REGRESSION LINE

Background: A commuter has gathered information about ages and prices of used Grand Ams and would like to determine if \$4,000 is a fair price for an 8-year-old Grand Am. To see if the price is "in line," she refers to the line that the scatterplot points presumably cluster around.

Questions:

1. Is there only one "best" line?

2. If so, how can it be found?

3. If found, how could she make use of it?

Responses: We'll answer these questions in reverse order:

3. If she finds the line, she can use it to predict the price (response) for an 8-year-old car (explanatory value 8) and see how \$4,000 compares to the prediction.

2. Since she wants to use the line to make a prediction, the desired line should be one that makes the best price predictions. Or, to put it another way, she would like a line for which the prediction errors (residuals) are as small as possible.

The line sketched below, for example, would *not* be what she is looking for because the actual prices are too far from what the line would predict: It underpredicts for the newer cars (large positive prediction errors) and overpredicts for the older cars (large negative prediction errors).

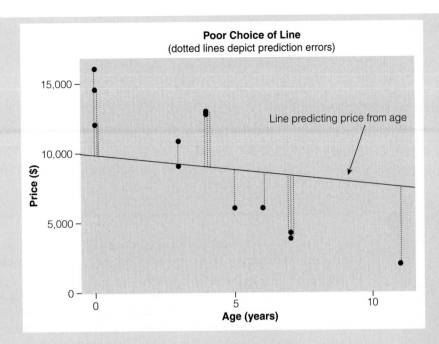

Poor Choice of Line
(dotted lines depict prediction errors)

These prediction errors, displayed as distances from each scatterplot point to the line, are residuals: They are the differences between observed responses and responses indicated by the line. The best line would be the one that minimizes these residuals for all the sampled points as a group.

1. Methods of calculus can be employed to prove that there is a *unique* line, called the "least squares line," which minimizes the sum of squared residuals and thereby makes the best overall predictions. Thus, there is, in fact, just one "best" line, written

$$\hat{y} = b_0 + b_1 x$$

The formula for calculating the least squares line will be presented in detail. For now, rather than carrying out the needed calculations by hand, the equation of the least squares line—fitted onto a scatterplot of the data—has been produced with computer software.

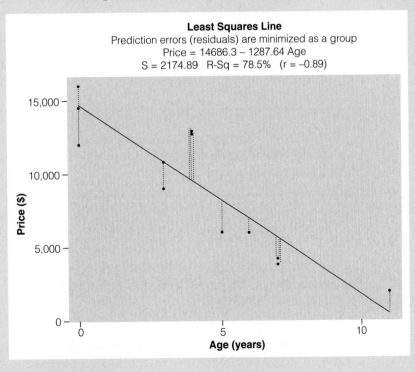

Least Squares Line
Prediction errors (residuals) are minimized as a group
Price = 14686.3 – 1287.64 Age
S = 2174.89   R-Sq = 78.5%   (r = –0.89)

Continued

According to the output, the "best" line predicts price to be 14,686.3 minus 1,287.64 times age, where the price units are dollars. For an age of 8 years, the predicted price is $14,686.3 - 1,287.64(8) = 4,385.18$. Apparently a price of \$4,000 is a bit of a bargain, at least as far as the age of the car is concerned.

Practice: *Try Exercise 5.50(e,f) on page 196.*

The Big Picture:
LOOKING AHEAD

Besides the regression equation and fitted line plot, the output reports a value S = 2,174.89. This measures the typical residual size, to be discussed later in this chapter.

Students may be familiar with the equation for a straight line, $y = mx + b$ as taught in algebra class. In statistics, instead of using one letter for the slope and another for the intercept, it is more convenient to work with the same letter (*b*), labeled with subscripts. This way, we can easily handle any number of explanatory variables in the multiple regression setting. For example, $\hat{y} = b_0 + b_1x_1 + b_2x_2$ would represent a prediction of price based on age x_1 and mileage x_2.

Example TBP 5.6 on page 795 of the *TBP Supplement* goes into detail about how to interpret the slope and intercept of the regression line.

Before presenting more details, we formally define the least squares regression line, its slope, and its intercept.

> *Definitions*   The **least squares regression line** is the unique line that fits the observed explanatory and response values in such a way as to minimize the sum of squared residuals.
>
> The **slope** b_1 of the regression line $\hat{y} = b_0 + b_1x$ relating sampled values of two quantitative variables tells how much we predict the response y to change for every unit increase in the explanatory variable x, where predicted response is denoted $\hat{y}$. The slope satisfies
>
> $$b_1 = r\frac{s_y}{s_x}$$
>
> The **intercept** b_0 tells where the line crosses the y-axis. It can be calculated as
>
> $$b_0 = \bar{y} - b_1\bar{x}$$
>
> and it follows that the regression line must pass through the point of averages $(\bar{x}, \bar{y})$.

Combining the above results for slope and intercept, we can say that the least squares line is the line that passes through the point of averages $(\bar{x}, \bar{y})$ and has slope $r\frac{s_y}{s_x}$.

When interpreting the intercept, we should keep in mind that in many situations, the explanatory variable cannot equal zero. In general, we must avoid making predictions for inappropriate explanatory values, a pitfall known as *extrapolation*.

> *Definition*   **Extrapolation** in the regression context is using the regression line to make predictions for explanatory values that are outside the range of values used to fit the line.

The next example shows how extrapolation can lead to nonsensical results.

EXAMPLE 5.29 EXTRAPOLATION AND THE CORRECT INTERPRETATION OF SLOPE AND INTERCEPT

Background: In Example 5.18 on page 167 we considered the relationship between weight and height for a sample of 17 male students. The correlation turned out to be $r = +0.646$, indicating a moderately strong positive relationship. The slope of the least squares regression line tells us that for every additional inch in height, we predict a male student to weigh an additional 8.72 pounds.

```
The regression equation is
weight = -438 + 8.72 height
```

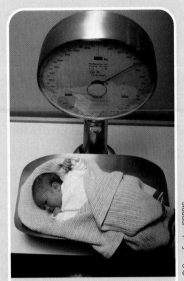

Questions: What happens if we use this regression equation to predict the weight of a newborn baby boy whose height is 20 inches? How can we correctly interpret the slope and intercept?

Responses: The predicted weight for a height of 20 inches is $-438 + 8.72(20) = -263.6$. Obviously, something went wrong, even though the arithmetic was done correctly, because a baby cannot weigh -263.6 pounds. Our regression line may do a decent job of predicting weights

Should we predict his weight to be −264 pounds?

for male heights in the approximate range of our explanatory data values, from 65 to 74 inches, but the linear relationship apparent in our scatterplot does not necessarily continue indefinitely in either direction. Our error was to *extrapolate* beyond height values for which the line was constructed.

To correctly interpret the regression line's slope and intercept, we can say that we predict a male student who is 1 inch taller than another to weigh 8.72 pounds more. The line that best fits the sampled students' heights and weights crosses the y-axis at $y = -438$.

Practice: *Try Exercise 5.54(c) on page 197.*

In some contexts, emphasis is put on r^2, which tells us the fraction of variation in the response that can be explained by least squares regression on the explanatory variable.

EXAMPLE 5.30 THE SQUARE OF THE CORRELATION

Background: The output for regression of Grand Am price on age in Example 5.28 on page 179 also reports "R-Sq = 78.5%," the square of the correlation r. When we specifically requested the correlation between age and price, it was reported to be -0.886.

Questions: How are R-Sq and r related? How can we interpret R-Sq?

Responses: We can convert R-sq to a decimal—R-sq = 78.5% = 0.785— then take the *negative* square root, because the slope of the regression line is negative. The result is the correlation $r = -\sqrt{r^2} = -\sqrt{0.785} = -0.886$.

We can say that 78.5% of the variation in a Grand Am's price can be explained by regressing on age.

Practice: *Try Exercise 5.55 on page 197.*

A Closer Look at Least Squares Regression

As long as a relationship between two quantitative variables is not perfect, it is in some sense a "stretch" to summarize everything with a simple equation of a straight line. We will now discuss some of the most important aspects of this process, so we can better understand the limitations of least squares regression.

Residuals: Prediction Errors in a Regression

We introduced the concept of residuals on page 178 when we discussed the construction of the least squares regression line. There is a residual for each pair of explanatory and response values, calculated as the observed response y_i minus the predicted response $\hat{y}_i$. Residuals are positive for scatterplot points above the least squares line (the line has underpredicted) and negative for scatterplot points below the line (it has overpredicted). Residuals play an important role in the relationship between two quantitative variables. If the relationship appears linear, we summarize it with the equation of the line that minimizes the sum of squared residuals. Constructing the line in such a way as to minimize the squared prediction errors yields a line that overall makes the best predictions for the sampled explanatory/response pairs. This gives us the best chance of making good response predictions for new explanatory values.

As part of the regression output, a number S (which we will write with a lowercase *s*) is reported, telling us the typical size of the residuals.

The calculation of s in regression is best left to software. Its interpretation is worthwhile for students as a reminder of how imperfect our regression predictions tend to be. It plays an important role in regression inference, to be covered in Chapter 13.

> *Definition*   The typical **residual** size in a regression is calculated as
>
> $$s = \sqrt{\frac{(y_1 - \hat{y}_1)^2 + \cdots + (y_n - \hat{y}_n)^2}{n - 2}}$$
>
> where the y_i are observed responses (in the scatterplot) and $\hat{y}_i$ are predicted responses (on the line).

Because residuals measure differences between observed responses and predicted responses, their units are the same as those of the response variable. In relative terms, *s* is larger for weak relationships with very loose scatter, and *s* is smaller for strong relationships with very tight clustering.

EXAMPLE 5.31 INTERPRETING S, THE TYPICAL RESIDUAL SIZE

Background: A local magazine published information in 1999 on average SAT scores of various public high schools in a particular city. Regression of average Math on average Verbal scores showed a very strong positive relationship, with a very high correlation ($r = 0.97$, since R-sq = 93.9%). The typical size of prediction errors was $s = 7.1$.

In addition, the magazine reported the percentage of faculty at those schools with advanced degrees. Regression of average Math SAT on percentage with advanced degrees showed a fairly weak positive relationship, with correlation $r = 0.41$ (since R-sq = 16.9%). The typical size of prediction errors was $s = 26.2$.

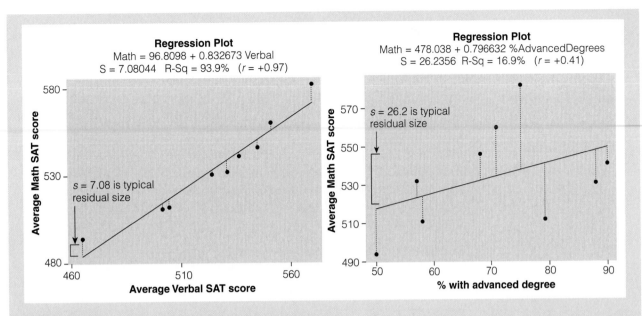

Question: What do the respective values of *s* tell us?

Response: The fact that *s* = 7.1 for regression of average Math on average Verbal SAT score means that if we use the regression on the left to predict average Math SAT from average Verbal SAT score for a school, we would tend to be off by only about 7 points in our prediction.

The fact that *s* = 26.2 for regression of average Math on percentage of faculty with advanced degrees tells us that if we use the regression line on the right to predict average Math SAT, we would tend to be off by about 26 points in our prediction.

Practice: *Try Exercise 5.56(a) on page 197.*

Taken together, the two regressions in Example 5.31 show us that the typical residual size *s* in predicting average Math SAT score was very small (about 7) when predicting from a school's average Verbal SAT score, because average Math and Verbal SAT scores have a strong relationship. In contrast, *s* is much larger (about 26) when predicting from percentage of teachers with advanced degrees, because this relationship is much weaker. The standard deviation of Math SAT scores itself is $s_y = 27$, indicating that a "blind" guess equal to the mean Math SAT score (typical error size 27) is only slightly worse than a prediction based on regression on percent with advanced degrees (typical error size 26). The relative sizes of *s* and s_y will now be discussed in more detail.

Because our approach to regression emphasizes the correlation, as opposed to its square, most of the book's fitted line plots have been modified from the original software output, noting the value of r by taking the positive or negative square root of R-sq.

Spread *s* about the Line versus Spread s_y about the Mean Response

Information about the explanatory variable helps us predict a response whenever the two variables are related, and our prediction error *s* will be less than s_y, which is how far off our prediction would tend to be if we didn't make use of information about the explanatory variable, and simply guessed *y* to equal its mean. If the two variables are *not* related, then *s* will be about the same as s_y, because the regression line doesn't really help us predict responses.

Page 796 of the ***TBP*** *Supplement* includes further discussion of the distinction between *s* and s_y.

EXAMPLE 5.32 TYPICAL RESIDUAL SIZE *S* VERSUS RESPONSE STANDARD DEVIATION S_Y

Background: The standard deviation of mothers' ages is 5.5 years. The typical residual size *s* in the regression of mother's age on father's age is 3.3 years.

Continued

Question: What do these two values tell us?

Response: Without information about the father's age, we'd predict a student's mother's age to be the average, and our prediction would tend to be off by about 5.5 years, the standard deviation.

If we predict the mother's age from the father's age, with the help of the least squares regression line, our prediction would tend to be off by the value of s, which is only 3.3 years. Thus, our error is reduced considerably, from 5.5 to 3.3 years. We saw a moderately strong relationship between ages of students' fathers and ages of their mothers in Example 5.19 on page 168, so knowing the age of a student's father is quite helpful in predicting the age of his or her mother.

Practice: *Try Exercise 5.58 on page 198.*

The Effect of Explanatory and Response Roles on the Regression Line

An important property of the correlation r is that it is unaffected by our assignment of roles—which variable is explanatory and which is response. If we request the correlation with a calculator or computer software, it makes no difference which variable we enter first. The scatterplot points are just as tightly clustered or as loosely scattered whether we plot y versus x or x versus y.

In contrast, the equation of the regression line *is* impacted by the assignment of roles for explanatory and response variables.

EXAMPLE 5.33 THE REGRESSION LINE IS AFFECTED BY EXPLANATORY/RESPONSE ROLES

Background: Consider a scatterplot consisting of the four points (0,2), (1,1), (4,3), and (5,0). If we want to predict y values, given x values, we must produce the line that minimizes the sum of squared *vertical* distances of the points to the line, as shown in the scatterplot on the left. If, on the other hand, we want to predict x values, given y values, we must produce the line that minimizes the sum of squared *horizontal* distances, as shown in the scatterplot on the right.

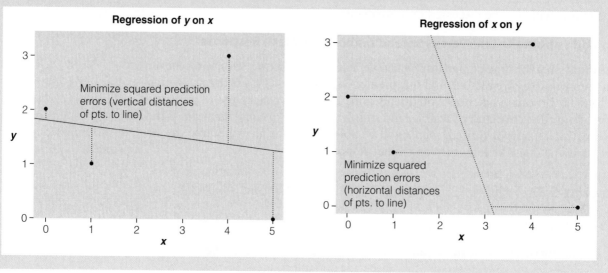

Question: Do we get the same line regressing *y* on *x* as we do regressing *x* on *y*?

Response: Clearly, the resulting lines are quite different: The line in the scatterplot on the left has only a slight negative slope, whereas the line on the right has a very steep slope. The lines are certainly not interchangeable: We must have a clear idea from the beginning as to which variable is explanatory and which is response, so that we use the correct line for the situation at hand. Presenting sample values as above, with no context or identification of variables, deprives us of information that is essential to the construction of the "best" regression line.

Practice: *Try Exercise 5.60(b) on page 198.*

Influential Observations and Outliers

When we looked at distributions of a *single* quantitative variable, we were careful to take note of outliers. Sometimes they signal a typographical or measurement error, sometimes they correspond to individuals who are different in a meaningful way from the rest of the sampled individuals (such as part-time students with noticeably fewer credits than full-time students), and sometimes they are present because individuals naturally may vary a great deal (such as a student who is a very poor test-taker getting an unusually low exam score).

When we look at *relationships* between two quantitative variables, there is an added dimension to the potential for outliers. Besides those individuals that would be considered outliers with respect to the single *x* and *y* variables, it is possible for an individual to be an outlier because of an unusual *combination* of *x* and *y* values. For instance, it is fairly common for a female to be 69 inches tall, and it is also common enough to wear a size 6 shoe. But the combination of being a few inches taller than average but wearing shoes a couple of sizes smaller than average is unusual. We define an *outlier* in regression to be a point that is unusually far from the regression line; thus, its residual is unusually large.

Because of the mechanics of the construction of the least squares line, which minimizes the sum of squared *vertical* distances of sampled points from the line, individuals that are on the fringe with respect to the horizontal explanatory variable *x* may be very *influential*. That is, an influential observation "pulls" the line away from the slope it would otherwise have, to avoid creating a huge residual.

Unlike other data sets that you encounter in this book, the points in Example 5.33 were presented simply as number pairs without any context. In actual statistical practice, it is essential to know what the numbers represent. Otherwise, as this example demonstrates, it is possible to reach two very different conclusions, based on a decision that is made arbitrarily due to lack of background information.

Definitions   An **outlier** in regression is a point with an unusually large residual. An **influential observation** is a point that has a high degree of influence on the position of the regression line or the value of the correlation or both.

A point can be an outlier without being influential, or influential without being an outlier. A point can also be both an outlier and an influential observation.

Even if an observation does not influence the position of the line imposed by the other scatterplot points, and has a small residual, it might cause the cloud of points to appear more elongated than it would otherwise, and inflate the value of the correlation. This is one of many reasons why it is important to examine the scatterplot carefully before taking either the correlation or the regression equation at face value.

Students Talk Stats

How Outliers and Influential Observations Affect a Relationship

*I*n 2004, several low-cost airlines were experiencing a growth spurt. This scatterplot displays fleet sizes for a sample of airlines at the time, and their orders for new planes. Four students are discussing what the data suggest in terms of a relationship between fleet size and orders for new planes.

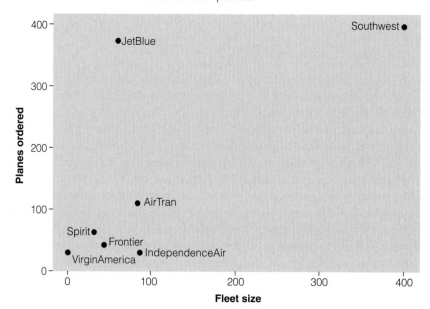

Adam: *"I found that the correlation for the relationship is 0.69, so there's a moderately strong relationship."*

Brittany: *"I omitted Southwest, because it's so far over to the right that it would be very influential. Without Southwest, the correlation is only 0.22, so there's hardly any relationship between the two variables."*

Carlos: *"Instead of leaving out Southwest, I deleted JetBlue, because it's an obvious outlier with a large residual. Then the correlation is 0.97, suggesting an extremely strong relationship."*

Dominique: *"We can't just pick and choose to eliminate one or the other airline and come up with all different answers. Part of the problem is that the sample is so small, each individual airline can have a major impact. But I don't know exactly where sample size comes in for relationships like this."*

This example illustrates how an outlier (like JetBlue) can reduce the apparent strength of a relationship, and how an influential observation (like Southwest) can have a major impact on the regression.

Practice: *Try Exercise 5.36(d,e) on page 193.*

The Big Picture: LOOKING AHEAD

Although the first three students have calculated correlations correctly, Dominique raises a valid point. The role of sample size will be discussed briefly a bit later in this section. Eventually, in Part IV, we will see how sample size helps us to quantify the extent to which we can use sample data to draw conclusions about a relationship in the larger population.

As the discussion among students demonstrates, there is no simple answer to the question about how to handle outliers and influential observations. The safest policy would be to report results both with and without the unusual observations, and discuss what makes them unusual. In some cases, they can be excluded because they represent individuals that don't really "belong" for some concrete reason. On the other hand, we should not indiscriminately remove all individuals that do not conform nicely to a uniform cloud of scatterplot points, because this may result in successively chopping away at the data until the remaining values no longer constitute a representative sample.

Sample versus Population: Thinking Beyond the Data at Hand

Throughout this section, we have dealt with relationships between *sampled* values of two quantitative variables. The correlation *r* tells the direction and strength of the relationship for the sample. The least squares regression line is the one that best fits the sample, in the sense that it minimizes the prediction errors for the sampled points as seen in the scatterplot.

For a *single* variable like age of father, mean age from a sample of college students may give us a clue about the mean age of all college students' fathers. Similarly, *r* and the equation of the least squares regression line calculated from ages of fathers and mothers for a sample of college students may give us a clue about the *relationship* between fathers' and mothers' ages for the larger population of college students. However, it is important to remember that the correlation and line that summarize the *sample* relationship, and the correlation and line that summarize the *population* relationship, are not the same thing. When we perform statistical inference for regression in Part IV, we will rely on notation that distinguishes between the sample regression line and the population regression line.

We have used the Roman letters $\bar{x}$ and s to denote the mean and standard deviation of a sample, contrasted by the Greek letters μ and σ, which denote the mean and standard deviation for the population. Similarly, whereas b_0 and b_1 are used to denote the intercept and slope of the line that summarizes the sample relationship, β_0 and β_1 are used to denote the intercept and slope of the line that summarizes the population relationship.

> *Definitions*   The **slope** β_1 of the regression line relating values of two quantitative variables for an entire population tells how much the response y changes in general for every unit increase in the explanatory variable x. The **intercept** β_0 tells where the line crosses the y-axis.

EXAMPLE 5.34 NOTATION FOR SLOPE AND INTERCEPT, SAMPLE VERSUS POPULATION

Background: In Example 5.19 on page 168, we considered the relationship between the ages of sampled students' fathers (the explanatory variable) and those of their mothers (the response). The least squares regression line is reported as follows:

```
The regression equation is
MotherAge = 14.5 + 0.666 FatherAge
```

Continued

The Big Picture: LOOKING AHEAD

In general, the values β_0 and β_1 are almost always unknown, but we will learn in Part IV the extent to which b_0 and b_1 can serve as estimates for them.

Question: What are b_0, b_1, β_0, and β_1 in this context, and which of these are known?

Response: The intercept and slope reported are $b_0 = 14.5$ and $b_1 = 0.666$ because they correspond to the line that best fits the sampled points. The intercept β_0 and slope β_1 for the equation that relates ages of *all* students' fathers and mothers are not known.

Practice: *Try Exercise 5.63 on page 200.*

The Role of Sample Size: Larger Samples Get Us Closer to the Truth

When sample values of a single quantitative variable are summarized, there is generally no explicit mention of sample size. Whether we have a sample of 4 fathers or 400 fathers, we could simply report that the ages of sampled students' fathers have a mean of 51 years. Information about sample size becomes most essential when we want to use a sample mean as an estimate for the unknown population mean. If our mean was produced from a sample of only 4 students' fathers, we wouldn't expect it to be as accurate an estimate as it would be if it came from a sample of size 400.

Similarly, our summaries of the relationship between two quantitative variables (the correlation r and the equation of the least squares regression line $\hat{y} = b_0 + b_1x$), as reported, do not tell us how many sampled x and y values have been used to produce them. A relationship may be strong or weak, with a steep or shallow slope, regardless of sample size. However, if we want to use sampled explanatory and response values to produce evidence of a relationship between the variables in the larger population, then sample size plays an important role. As your common sense may already suggest, evidence of a relationship obtained from a large sample is more convincing than evidence of a relationship obtained from a small sample. Furthermore, if we use b_0 and b_1 produced from sample data to estimate the intercept β_0 and slope β_1 relating x and y in the entire population, they tend to be more accurate if the sample was large.

EXAMPLE 5.35 WHAT SAMPLE SIZE TELLS US ABOUT A RELATIONSHIP

Background: Our original sample of over 400 ages of students' fathers and mothers (shown on the left) had correlation $r = +0.78$. A sample of just five age pairs (shown on the right) also happens to have $r = +0.78$.

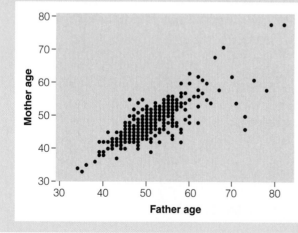 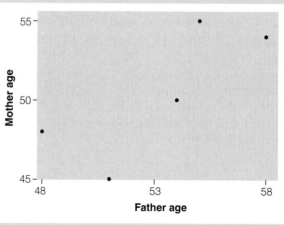

Question: Does one of the scatterplots provide more evidence of a strong positive relationship between mother's age and father's age for all students?

Response: The scatterplot on the left provides much more compelling evidence of a strong positive relationship because it is inconceivable that over 400 points would cluster this closely around a line of positive slope just by coincidence. In contrast, it is plausible that the five points shown in the scatterplot on the right could have fallen into their somewhat linear position by chance, even if the two variables were unrelated.

Practice: *Try Exercise 5.64 on page 200.*

Time Series: When Time Explains a Response

A very common situation involving two quantitative variables is when the explanatory variable is a time measurement. Often there is just one response recorded at regular time intervals, and rather than display the data with a scatterplot, we use a *time series plot* to highlight the progression made by the response variable over time.

Definitions   A **time series plot** records responses vertically for each explanatory value (time) graphed along the horizontal axis. The points are connected with line segments.

    The **trend** is the general progression of the response variable over time, either negative or positive or no clear tendency in either direction.

    A **peak** occurs when the response variable takes a relatively high value, and a **trough** occurs when the response is unusually low.

    There are all sorts of units possible in a time series, from nano-seconds to millennia; the units in the following example are months.

EXAMPLE 5.36 ELEMENTS OF A TIME SERIES

Background: A newspaper article from July 2002 entitled "Perspiration, Not Procreation" reports that "Births are seasonal, but 'too hot for sex' theory has problems." It goes on to explain that, "for decades in the United States, there has been a seasonal pattern in which more babies are born in August and September than any other months, and relatively few are born in April . . . Count backwards and that means more conceptions occur around the Christmas holidays and fewer during the dog days of summer."[18]

The time series plot of U.S. births by month during 2000 "shows the average daily births during each month in 2000 by dividing total births in a month by total days. This adjustment eliminates the variability in month length.

"Birth statistics from 2000 demonstrated the 'American pattern' of birth seasonality because the daily average in April was lower than during any other month. While April was the low month in 2000, the high months

Continued

came in late summer. Demographers divide the world into countries such as the United States that see a decline in births during April and countries such as those in Europe that experience a birth peak during April."

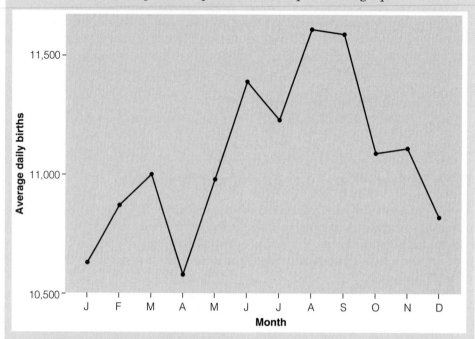

Question: Why would there be fewer conceptions in the United States in July, and more in December?

Response: The first explanation that may occur to you, as it did to researchers, would be a biological one: Perhaps fertility is diminished in hot weather. The problem with this theory is that there are many countries (quite a few of which are in Europe) for which the conception rate actually hits a peak during the hot months instead of a trough as in the United States. Attempts have been made to attribute the conception patterns to economic trends in various countries, or to social/psychological effects on couples' family-planning strategies. So far none of the theories seem to be completely consistent with conception trends overall throughout the world. You may have your own theory or opinion about what is the predominant influence on conception patterns in the various months of a year."

Practice: *Try Exercise 5.66 on page 201.*

'Tis the season to conceive—in some countries.

© Richard T. Nowitz/CORBIS

This example demonstrates the limitations of statistics—and science—in attempting to explain all aspects of our world with a tidy theory. On the other hand, a simple graphic tool like time series plots does go a long way toward helping us see *what* is going on in the world around us, even if we can't always explain *why*.

Additional Variables: Confounding Variables, Multiple Regression

Recall that in relationships between two categorical variables, we witnessed the phenomenon of Simpson's Paradox in Example 5.15 on page 158 when the analysis neglected to take into account possible confounding variables. The same phenomenon can occur in relationships between two quantitative variables.

Students Talk Stats

Confounding in a Relationship between Two Quantitative Variables

*A*s an extra-credit assignment, statistics students are to choose two quantitative variables from survey data gathered by their instructor, and analyze the relationship between them. A group of students, working together, have chosen the variables "weight" and "time spent on the phone."

Adam: *"R-squared is 0.013. You take the square root and get r equal to 0.11. There's a slight tendency for people who weigh more to talk on the phone more. I guess they're not as active."*

Brittany: *"The regression line has a negative slope, so you have to take the negative square root and get r equal to minus 0.11. So the more you weigh, the less you talk on the phone."*

Carlos: *"Why should weighing more make you talk on the phone less? There must be something else going on. Like maybe it's because guys usually weigh more, and they talk on the phone less."*

Dominique: *"How can we prove that? Or maybe we should just pick two other variables?"*

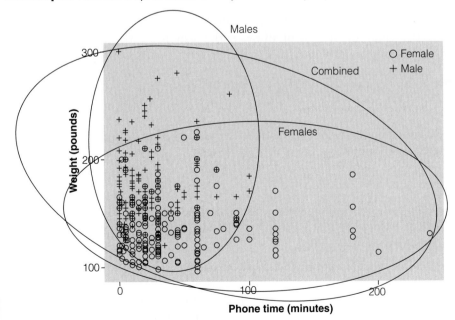

Since there doesn't seem to be any other reasonable theory to explain a negative relationship between weights and phone times, Carlos is right to consider the

Students Talk Stats continued →

Students Talk Stats continued

possibility of confounding variables, starting with gender, which should almost always be taken into account when exploring relationships in human beings. A helpful device for displaying relationships between two quantitative variables, with an added categorical variable, is a labeled scatterplot. In this case, a labeled plot would show one randomly scattered cloud for females, who tend to weigh less and talk on the phone more, and another randomly scattered cloud for males, who tend to weigh more and talk on the phone less. Putting these two non-relationships together results in a cluster of points with a slight downward slope.

As stressed in discussions of study design in Chapter 3, potential confounding variables are controlled for by studying groups of similar individuals separately. Software could be used to separate out the weight and phone values for males and females, then perform a regression for each gender group. Individually, the correlations would suggest no relationship between weight and phone time.

Practice: *Try Exercise 5.69(a) on page 201.*

Sometimes there is an additional quantitative explanatory variable whose values should be taken into account. In this case, a *multiple regression* would be performed, using methods that go beyond the scope of this textbook.

EXAMPLE 5.37 THE MULTIPLE REGRESSION SETTING

Background: A used-car buyer might want to base price predictions not only on the age of a car, but also on how many miles it has been driven.

Question: What would be the explanatory and response variables if a multiple regression were to be used?

Response: Instead of a simple regression of price on age, the buyer could perform a multiple regression of price (the response variable) on age and miles (the explanatory variables).

Practice: *Try Exercise 5.69(b) on page 201.*

Relationships between two quantitative variables are summarized on page 205 of the Chapter Summary.

EXERCISES FOR SECTION 5.3

Relationships between Two Quantitative Variables

Note: Asterisked numbers indicate exercises whose answers are provided in the Solutions to Selected Exercises section, on page 689.

*5.33 A newspaper report on results of the American Time Use Survey of 2003 states that "Americans like to keep it short on their cell phones: Last year, the average call lasted 2.87 minutes, while the average monthly bill was $49.91."[19]

Is this information about two single quantitative variables or about the relationship between two quantitative variables?

5.34 "Americans Like to Drive a Lot and Eat Cheese" reports results of the American

Time Use Survey of 2003, to be found in the U.S. Statistical Abstract 2004–2005.[20] Specifically, drivers in a typical household log 21,200 miles in a year, and the average American consumes 31 pounds of cheese in a year.

Is this information about two single quantitative variables or about the relationship between two quantitative variables?

5.35 A newspaper report on results of the American Time Use Survey of 2003 speculates that Americans' love of cheese may play a role in the fact that they're getting heavier.

If we consider whether people tend to weigh more if they eat more cheese, are we considering two single quantitative variables or the relationship between two quantitative variables?

*5.36 State assessment tests were administered to public school students in 89 schools in a certain school district in the year 2002. The percentage who passed in each school was regressed on the mean score for each school. The regression on the top includes data for a special education center that was clearly an outlier, and the regression on the bottom has omitted this data point.

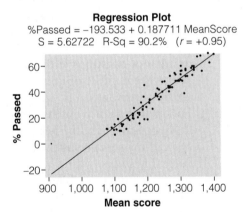

Regression Plot
%Passed = −193.533 + 0.187711 MeanScore
S = 5.62722   R-Sq = 90.2%   (r = +0.95)

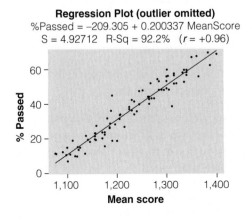

Regression Plot (outlier omitted)
%Passed = −209.305 + 0.200337 MeanScore
S = 4.92712   R-Sq = 92.2%   (r = +0.96)

a. Does the form of the relationship appear to be linear or curved?

b. Explain why a strong positive relationship should exist between the two variables (mean score and percent passing).

c. Do the scatterplots show a positive direction?

d. To the nearest 5%, estimate what percentage of students the regression line on the top predicts should pass in the outlier school (mean score was about 900).

e. Use your answer to part (d) to justify omitting the outlier from the regression.

f. When deciding whether to report correlation for the regression with or without the outlier, are we mainly concerned with data production, displaying and summarizing data, probability, or statistical inference?

*5.37 These plots show the percentages voting Republican versus Democratic for each of the 50 states, in the 1996 presidential election on the top, and in the 2000 presidential election on the bottom.

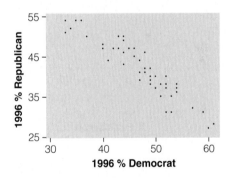

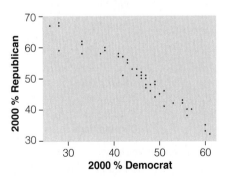

a. Which relationship is stronger: the one for 1996 or the one for 2000?

b. In which election were there apparently more votes for a third-party candidate? Explain.

*5.38   An annual state assessment test (PSSA) is a standards-based, criterion-referenced assessment used to measure a student's attainment of the academic standards while also determining the degree to which school programs enable students to attain proficiency of the standards. For a sample of schools, three relationships are considered: percentage passing versus school mean score, percentage passing versus percentage who participated (took the test) in each school, and percentage passing versus percentage of disadvantaged students in the school.

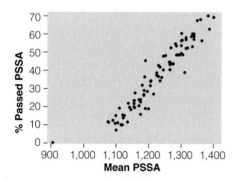

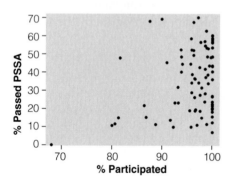

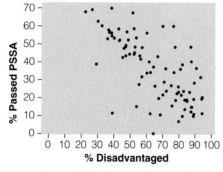

a. Which of the three relationships (on the top, in the middle, or on the bottom) is the strongest?

b. Which of the three relationships is the weakest?

c. Which of the three relationships (on the top, in the middle, or on the bottom) is most clearly negative?

d. Explain why we could expect the particular relationship that you identified in part (c) to be negative.

*5.39   The relationship between two columns of 40 random digits each was displayed in a scatterplot.

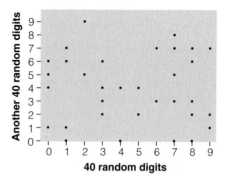

a. What correlation should we expect to see for the relationship between two random sets of numbers?

b. Does the scatterplot appear to have that approximate correlation?

*5.40   Consider the following relationships:
    1. For each student who is about to take a 20-question exam, the number of questions that will be answered correctly versus the number of hours the student has studied.
    2. For each student in a classroom taking a 20-question exam, the number of questions left to answer versus the number of questions already answered.
    3. For each student who has taken a 20-question exam, the percentage of correct answers versus the number of correct answers.
    4. For each student who has taken a 20-question exam, the number of correct answers versus the number of correct answers that the student was hoping to get.

a. Which one of the three relationships is perfectly positive?

b. Which one of the three relationships is perfectly negative?

5.41   For which of the four relationships described in Exercise 5.40 should we expect the typical residual size to equal zero? (There may be more than one.)

*5.42   Exercise 5.38 shows scatterplots for three relationships: percentage passing state assessment tests versus, respectively, mean score, percentage participating, and percentage of disadvantaged students. The individuals are schools in a particular district.

a. Correlations of the three relationships, in scrambled order, are -0.70, $+0.30$, $+0.95$. Which one is the correlation for the relationship in the middle (percentage passing versus percentage participating)?

b. Correlations of the three relationships, in scrambled order, are -0.70, $+0.30$, $+0.95$. Which one is the correlation for the relationship on the top (percentage passing versus school mean score)?

5.43 "Exercise Beats Calcium at Boosting Girl's Bones" reports on a study published in the *Journal of Pediatrics* in 2004 that found that "girls with better muscle development also had stronger bones." Muscle development was measured in terms of the girls' lean body mass, and the study's author explained: "A 1 kilogram increase in lean mass was associated with a $2\frac{1}{2}\%$ increase in their bone strength."[21]

a. Can we assume this was an experiment or an observational study?

b. Did the individuals studied constitute a sample or an entire population?

c. Did the study find a positive or a negative correlation?

d. Is the number $2\frac{1}{2}$ referring to the correlation r, the intercept b_0, or the slope b_1?

e. Is the number $2\frac{1}{2}$ a statistic or a parameter?

f. If researchers want to conclude that there is a relationship between muscle development and bone strength for all girls, are they mainly concerned with data production, displaying and summarizing data, probability, or statistical inference?

5.44 An article entitled "Too Few Z's May Result in Too Many Pounds" tells about two studies published in 2004 in the *Annals of Internal Medicine*, which show that "loss of sleep boosts levels of a hormone that tells us we're hungry, while dropping levels of a hormone that signals the body that we're full. Researchers have noticed that increased obesity among Americans has coincided with less time spent asleep. In 1960, U.S. adults slept an average of more than 8 hours a night; by 2002, the average had fallen to less than

7 hours. At the same time, in 1960, one in four adults was considered overweight and one in nine was considered obese; now two in three are overweight and nearly one in three is obese."[22]

a. Apparently there is a relationship between amount of sleep and levels of a hormone that tells us we're hungry. Is this relationship positive or negative?

b. There is also an apparent relationship between amount of sleep and levels of a hormone that tells us we're full. Is this relationship positive or negative?

c. The last two sentences of the previous quote have to do with the relationship between sleep and weight. Tell whether the variable for sleep is being treated as quantitative or categorical.

d. Tell whether the variable for weight is being treated as quantitative or categorical.

*5.45 Exercise 5.44 suggests that sleep loss is responsible for people eating more. On the other hand, one could argue that eating more may cause people to sleep less. If this is the case, how would it affect the correlation between hours of sleep and levels of the hunger hormone?

5.46 A survey was taken of students at a large university in the fall of 2003; among other things, students were asked to report their weight and how many minutes of television they had watched the day before.

a. Use software to access the student survey data and produce a scatterplot of weights versus television times.

b. Report the correlation r.

c. Tell whether the relationship is strong and negative, weak and negative, weak and positive, or strong and positive.

d. It is possible that the relationship seen between weight and TV time is really due to gender. Separate the weights and TV times for males and females, and produce correlations separately for males and females.

e. It is commonly believed that because of the sedentary nature of TV viewing, heavier people tend to watch more TV. Is this claim supported by the survey data set?

f. The regression equation for males is $Weight = 167 + 0.06(TV)$. Report the y-intercept and tell what it means in this context.

g. The regression equation predicts an additional 0.06 pound for every additional *minute* of TV watched for the males. How many additional pounds does it predict for every *hour* of TV watched?

*5.47 If weights were recorded in kilograms instead of pounds in Exercise 5.46, would r increase, decrease, or stay the same?

5.48 A survey was taken of students at a large university in the fall of 2003; among other things, students were asked to report their age and how much money they had earned the year before.

a. Use software to access the student survey data. Decide which variable should be explanatory, and produce a scatterplot.

b. Tell if either of the variables appears to have outliers, and if so, whether the outliers are high or low.

c. Find the correlation r.

d. Explain why it makes sense for there to be a moderately strong positive relationship between age and earnings.

5.49 Exercise 5.48 considered the relationship between students' ages and earnings. If instead we considered how *mean* earnings were related to each age value, would the correlation be closer to 0, closer to 1, or the same?

*5.50 The scatterplot on the bottom in Exercise 5.36 on page 193 shows the relationship between percentage of students who passed state assessment tests and the mean score for all the schools in a district, with one outlier school omitted.

a. Which of these is the most reasonable guess for mean of the school means (outlier omitted): 1,050, 1,150, 1,250, or 1,350?

b. Which of these is the most reasonable guess for standard deviation of the school means (outlier omitted): 20, 80, 200, or 800?

c. Which of these is the most reasonable guess for mean of the percentages passing (outlier omitted): 0%, 20%, 40%, or 80%?

d. Which of these is the most reasonable guess for standard deviation of the percentages passing (outlier omitted): 0%, 20%, 40%, or 80%?

e. A line is shown around which the scatterplot points are clustered. Would the line appear to fit equally well if it were shifted up, so that the intercept would be closer to 20 than to 0?

f. Would the line appear to fit equally well if it still passed through the mean x and y values, but had a slope close to zero, so that it would appear roughly horizontal?

5.51 The regression on the bottom in Exercise 5.36 on page 193 is for the relationship between percentage of students who passed state assessment tests and the mean score for all the schools in a district, with one outlier school omitted. If one school has a mean score that is 1 point higher than another school, about how much higher should the percent passing be?

5.52 A sample of 88 Puget Sound butter clams' widths had mean 4.4 and standard deviation 1.8. Their lengths had mean 5.7 and standard deviation 2.2 (units are centimeters). The correlation between widths and lengths was found to be 0.99.[23] How could we use this information to sketch the line that regresses length on width?

5.53 What sort of relationship is there between a football team's performance on offense and on defense? Rankings of the 32 NFL teams in the middle of the 2004 season, based on total yards gained on offense and total yards given up on defense, are graphed in this scatterplot.

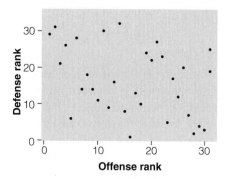

a. Does the relationship appear to be strong and negative, weak and negative, weak and positive, or strong and positive?

b. One of these is the correct value for the correlation r; which is it: -0.86, -0.36, $+0.36$, or $+0.86$?

c. Suppose Sports Fan #1 claims that teams tend to be better or worse all around in both offense and defense, whereas Sports Fan #2 claims that there is a tradeoff, in that good offense tends to come at the expense of defense and vice versa. Sports Fan #3 claims the two are not related at all. Which sports fan's claim is supported by the data?

d. Explain why the regression line must pass through the point (16.5, 16.5).

e. Keeping in mind that the numbers 1 to 32 constitute both the set of explanatory (x) values and the set of response (y) values, and that the slope of the regression line always satisfies $b_1 = r\frac{s_y}{s_x}$, explain why in this case the slope b_1 is equal to the correlation r.

f. The scatterplot takes offense to be the explanatory variable and defense the response. Would it have been better, worse, or equally good to take defense as the explanatory variable?

g. Which of these would change if we took defense as the explanatory variable: the equation of the regression line, the value of the correlation r, both of these, or neither of these?

*5.54 A survey was taken of students at a large university in the fall of 2003; among other things, students were asked to report their age and how much money they had earned the year before.

  a. Use software to access the student survey data. Report the regression equation.

  b. To the nearest thousand dollars, how much additional earnings does the line predict for every additional year in age?

  c. Explain why the y-intercept has no practical significance in this context.

*5.55 The scatterplot on the top in Exercise 5.37 on page 193 shows percentage voting Republican versus Democrat in the 50 states in the 1996 presidential election.

  a. The regression on the top, for the year 1996, shows "R-Sq = 85.8%." What was the correlation r?

  b. How much of the variation in percentage voting Republican in 1996 can be explained by the regression on percentage voting Democratic?

*5.56 The regression on the bottom in Exercise 5.36 on page 193 is for the relationship between percentage of students who passed state assessment tests and the mean score for all the schools in a district, except for an outlier that has been omitted.

  a. What is the typical size of the residuals (prediction errors)?

b. Considering that all the schools in the district were studied, would the slope of the regression line be considered a statistic b_1 or a parameter β_1?

5.57 This scatterplot shows the relationship between vertical drop of slope (in feet) and adult weekend lift ticket price for various ski resorts in the Middle Atlantic states, as of November 2004.[24]

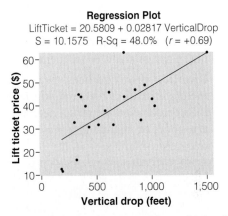

Regression Plot
LiftTicket = 20.5809 + 0.02817 VerticalDrop
S = 10.1575   R-Sq = 48.0%   (r = +0.69)

  a. Looking at the scatterplot, which of these is your best guess for the mean vertical drop of the slopes: 600, 1,000, 1,400, or 1,800?

  b. Looking at the scatterplot, which of these is your best guess for the standard deviation of vertical drop of the slopes: 3, 30, 300, or 3,000?

  c. Looking at the scatterplot, which of these is your best guess for the mean lift ticket price: $10, $20, $30, or $40?

  d. Looking at the scatterplot, which of these is your best guess for the standard deviation of lift ticket price: $0.15, $1.50, $15, or $150?

  e. Which one of these best describes the situation?
    1. There is no relationship between vertical drop and lift ticket price at these resorts.
    2. There is a slight tendency for ski resorts with more of a vertical drop to charge more for a lift ticket.
    3. There is a moderately strong relationship between vertical drop and price of a lift ticket at these resorts.
    4. Knowing the vertical drop, we can predict lift ticket price almost exactly for these resorts.

  f. Blue Knob's slope has a vertical drop of 1,025 feet. Use the regression equation to predict the lift ticket price there.

g. In fact, the lift ticket price at Blue Knob was $40. Is this relatively expensive or inexpensive for the size of the drop there?

h. What is the size of the residual in your prediction in part (f), if the actual price was $40?

i. Is this residual size quite a bit smaller than usual, fairly typical, or quite a bit larger than usual for this regression?

j. The y-intercept is about 20, predicting a lift ticket price of $20 for a downhill ski resort whose slopes have a vertical drop of zero. How often would this actually be the case: never, occasionally, or frequently?

k. If vertical drop had been measured in meters instead of feet, would the value of the correlation r increase, decrease, stay the same, or change in a way that is unforeseeable?

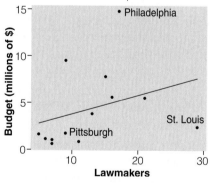

Regression at ski resorts: What's the slope?

*5.58   Exercise 5.39 on page 194 shows a scatterplot for the relationship between two columns of random digits. If we performed a regression, how would the typical residual size s compare to the value of the standard deviation s_y of y-values?

5.59   This scatterplot is for the number of gates in Southwest's top 10 airports, and the year they were established in that airport.

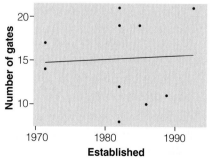

Regression Plot
Gates = –68.4375 + 0.0421922 Established
S = 5.08458   R-Sq = 0.4%   ($r = +0.06$)

a. In airports where Southwest was more recently established, does it tend to have considerably more gates, considerably fewer gates, or neither?

b. The typical residual size for predicting number of gates, based on the year established, is $s = 5$. How would this compare to the standard deviation s_y of number of gates: much more, much less, or about the same size?

*5.60   A survey was taken of students at a large university in the fall of 2003; among other things, students were asked to report their weight and how many minutes of television they had watched the day before.

a. If we take TV times as the explanatory variable, are we implying that watching a lot of TV could make you heavier, or that people who are heavier tend to watch more TV?

b. If weights were taken as the explanatory variable instead of TV times, which of these would change: the equation of the regression line, the value of the correlation, or both, or neither?

5.61   This scatterplot, with fitted regression line, is for number of lawmakers and the city council budget (in millions of dollars) in a recent sample of similarly sized cities in the United States. Some of the cities are identified by name.

Regression Plot
Budget = 1.76 + 0.20 Lawmakers
S = 4.20   R-Sq = 10.7%

a. Which of these is the approximate value of the correlation r: -0.83, -0.33, -0.03, $+0.33$, or $+0.83$?

b. Only one of the cities was identified as an outlier, with an unusually large residual—was it Philadelphia, Pittsburgh, or St. Louis?

c. If we removed St. Louis from the regression, would the slope of the regression line increase quite a bit, decrease quite a bit, or stay about the same?

d. What budget would the regression line predict for Pittsburgh, which had 9 lawmakers?

e. In fact, Pittsburgh's budget was $1.7 million. What is the residual (prediction error) for your prediction in part (d)?

f. According to the regression output, what is the typical size of prediction errors?

5.62 "EPA Cuts Pollution Levels with Refinery Settlements" reported in the *New York Times* in 2004 that "enforcement efforts begun in the Clinton Administration have led to negotiated settlements with a dozen companies in the last four years, resulting in [. . .] promises by the companies to spend $2.2 billion for equipment upgrades that reduce toxic emissions. The improvements are projected to eliminate nearly 170,000 tons of sulfur dioxide and nitrogen oxide, substances that cause problems for human health and the ozone."[25] The data for those 12 companies are organized in a table, and pollution reduction has been regressed on cost of upgrades. Two regression lines will be considered—one including and one omitting an influential observation.

Company	Upgrades Cost (in millions)	Pollutant Reduction (in tons)
Motiva Enterprises	550	57,550
BP Exploration	457	30,900
Marathon Ashland	360	20,800
Citgo	320	30,434
Chevron Texaco	275	9,558
Conoco	110	7,210
Koch	80	5,200
Holly	19	2,595
Lion	17	1,180
Cenex	10	2,430
Coastal Eagle Point	7	600
Ergon Refining	5	888
Total	$2,210	169,345

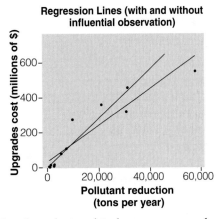

Regression Lines (with and without influential observation)

a. Explain why it makes sense for the relationship between upgrades cost and pollutant reduction to be positive.

b. The original regression was carried out with pollutant reduction as the explanatory variable, and cost as the response. However, one could argue that amount of money spent can explain the extent to which a refinery can reduce its pollutants, so that the roles of explanatory and response are reversed. How would this affect the correlation r: increase it, decrease it, no effect, or effect unpredictable?

c. If roles of explanatory and response variables are reversed, would the regression line be different or the same?

d. When deciding which regression to use—the one with pollutant reduction as the explanatory variable or the one with cost as the explanatory variable—are we mainly concerned with data production, displaying and summarizing data, probability, or statistical inference?

e. One company turned out to be an influential observation in the regression, exerting a great amount of influence on the equation of the regression line—which company was it?

f. Was that company unusual because the cost was surprisingly high or surprisingly low, given the amount of pollutants reduced?

g. One of the two regression lines shown was produced for the data with the influential observation omitted—is it the line with the steeper slope or the one with the shallower slope?

*5.63 Exercise 5.44 on page 195 discusses the relationship between amount of sleep and levels of a hormone that tells us we're hungry.

a. Would the slope of the regression line that summarizes this relationship in the *sample* of individuals studied be denoted b_1 or β_1?

b. How would we denote the slope for the relationship in the general population?

*5.64 Exercise 5.39 on page 194 shows a scatterplot for the relationship between two columns of 40 random digits each. The correlation was close to zero. Another regression was performed on two columns of just 5 random digits each, and there was a substantial negative correlation $(r = -0.48)$. What is the best explanation for this?

5.65 "Law to Increase Adoptions Results in More Orphans," a newspaper article published in December 2004, reports: "A 1997 federal law intended to increase adoptions of foster

children has accomplished that goal, but it also produced an unintended consequence: an increase in the number of children who were legally made orphans but not adopted." A psychologist explained the rationale for the law, which accelerated the process of terminating ties between foster children and their birth parents: "For some youngsters, the ties to birth parents must be broken so the children can feel emotionally freed to bond with new parents. And sometimes, the relationship between the parent and child is emotionally destructive and should be ended, whether adoptive parents are lined up or not." A critic of the law stated: "It is a birthright to have a parent, and shame on anybody who gratuitously denies a child a parent." These scatterplots show the numbers of terminated ties with birth parents, adoptions, and children left unadopted, respectively, for the years between 1997 and 2003.[26]

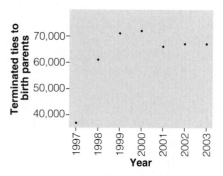

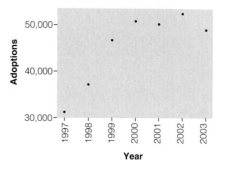

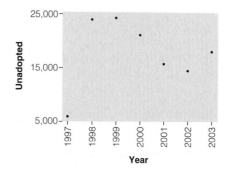

Tell which of the relationships, if any, conforms well to a straight-line pattern: terminated ties versus year, adoptions versus year, or unadopted versus year.

*5.66 Exercise 5.65 shows scatterplots for number of terminated ties, adoptions, and unadopted children, respectively, versus year.

    a. All three variables (terminated ties, adoptions, and unadopted) showed a dramatic rise after the Adoption and Safe Families Act was passed in 1997. Which variable rose most rapidly?

    b. Which variable rose most gradually?

    c. Which variable showed a noticeable increase again from 2002 to 2003?

    d. Discuss the relative merits and feasibility of each of these remedies for too many orphans: decreasing the number of terminated ties between foster children and birth parents, or increasing the number of adoptions.

5.67 "Cars Becoming Weapon of Choice" reported on the situation in Iraq as of January 2005: "There were two car bombs on the last days of June, 11 in July and 12 in August. The numbers then surged, with 26 in September, 43 in October, and 48 in November. December saw 27, and January is averaging about one a day—a dozen in the first 11 days." The article mentions that "those bombs killed about 1,000 people, both Iraqis and Americans, and wounded twice as many."[27]

    a. Sketch a time series plot of the data for June through December 2004.

    b. Explain how a prediction for January 2005 would differ, depending on whether it was based on the most recent trend in the time series plot or based on a regression line for the data.

    c. What was the average number of people killed in each of those 181 car bombings?

5.68 A paper by Emily Oster of Harvard University, published in the Social Science Research Network's electronic library in 2004, explored the "possibility that the witchcraft trials [between 1520 and 1770] are a large-scale example of violence and scapegoating prompted by a deterioration

in economic conditions. In this case, the downturn was brought on by a decrease in temperature and resulting food shortages. [. . .] Witches became target for blame because there was an existing cultural framework that both allowed their persecution and suggested that they could control the weather."[28] Time series plots of standardized temperatures and standardized trials, both of which incorporated trends over all of Europe, show a rather convincing pattern: Many decades for which there was a relative trough in temperature showed an accompanying spike in trials; most notably, when temperatures reached an extreme low-point around 1740, trials hit an all-time high.

    a. If we consider the relationship between witchcraft trials and weather, which should play the role of explanatory variable and which response?

    b. Suppose that instead of looking at time series plots for both variables, we looked at a scatterplot for trials and temperature. Would the correlation be positive or negative?

*5.69 The relationship between students' weights and earnings was explored. Because gender would play a role in both variables' values, regression was performed separately for males and females. Still, a positive correlation was found.

    a. What additional confounding variable is the best explanation for the positive correlation?

    b. If the interplay among weight, earnings, and age were explored, what role would weight play—explanatory or response?

    c. If the interplay among weight, earnings, and age were explored, what role would earnings play—explanatory or response?

    d. If the interplay among weight, earnings, and age were explored, what role would age play—explanatory or response?

5.70 This table shows the gross earnings in millions of dollars for the top 25 tours of 2004, along with average ticket prices and number of shows, as reported by PollstarOnline. The website mentions that all figures are for North American dates only.

Artist	Gross	Average Ticket Price	Shows
Prince	87.40	61.04	96
Celine Dion	80.40	136.33	154
Madonna	79.50	143.59	39
Metallica	60.50	57.39	83
Bette Midler	59.40	99.12	66
Van Halen	54.30	76.44	79
Kenny Chesney	50.80	44.40	77
Sting	50.10	66.84	83
Toby Keith	43.70	47.83	75
Elton John	43.30	158.22	60
Rod Stewart	42.50	74.78	81
Dave Matthews	41.20	43.32	47
Tim McGraw	40.10	52.48	64
Jimmy Buffett	34.60	59.57	30
Shania Twain	34.50	65.55	42
A.Jackson/M.McBride	34.00	51.50	58
Cher	29.10	65.17	54
Usher	29.10	58.45	42
Eric Clapton	29.00	69.25	33
Josh Groban	28.00	53.96	80
Aerosmith	25.60	57.54	41
George Strait	24.80	63.40	29
Phil Collins	23.80	76.52	26
Kid Rock	23.70	32.72	92
John Mayer	23.60	34.18	78

a. Two of the histograms for the individual distributions are clearly right-skewed, whereas one is actually quite symmetric except for a single high outlier. Which artist is responsible for that outlier?

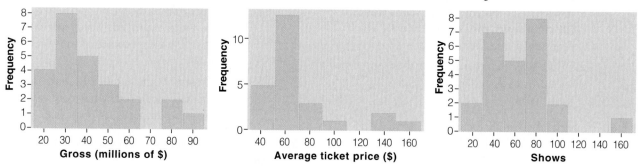

b. The regression on the left on page 203, for gross earnings versus average ticket price, has an obvious outlier in the upper-left-hand portion of the graph. Does this represent a concert tour that made a lot of money in spite of high ticket prices, a concert tour that made a lot of money in spite of low ticket prices, a concert tour that made little money in spite of high ticket prices, or a concert tour that made little money in spite of low ticket prices? (The regression on the right will be introduced in part [g].)

Regression Plot
Gross = 22.0288 + 0.298516 AvgTkPrice
S = 16.2966   R-Sq = 26.5%   (r = +0.51)

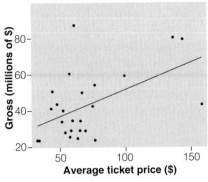

Regression Plot
Gross = 20.1852 + 0.353244 Shows
S = 16.0316   R-Sq = 28.9%   (r = +0.54)

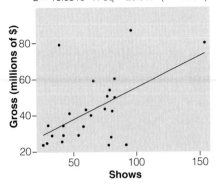

c. Identify the artist responsible for the outlier in part (b).

d. If the outlier discussed in part (b) were removed from the regression, would the value of the correlation r decrease, increase, or stay about the same? [Hint: Sketch two clouds around the scatterplot points, one including and one removing the outlier. Then decide which cloud, if any, seems to be more oval-shaped, as opposed to circular-shaped. Thinner, more oval-shaped clouds suggest tighter clustering and a larger value of correlation.]

e. For which performer was the average ticket price unusually high, considering the amount that the concerts grossed?

f. For every additional dollar in average ticket price, did a tour tend to gross an additional $22 million, $300,000, $16 million, or $26.5 million?

g. In the regression shown above on the right, for gross earnings versus number of shows, we see the point for Celine Dion's concert in the upper-right-hand corner (154 shows and a gross of $80.4 million). Would this point be considered an outlier (with an unusually large residual), an influential observation (which greatly impacts r and the equation of the regression line), or both, or neither?

h. For every additional show, did a tour tend to gross an additional $20 million, $350,000, $16 million, or $28.9 million?

i. If we use average ticket price to predict gross earnings, what is the approximate size of our prediction error, to the nearest million dollars?

j. If we use number of shows to predict gross earnings, what is the approximate size of our prediction error, to the nearest million dollars?

k. Which is more useful for predicting gross earnings: average ticket price, number of shows, or both about the same?

l. If a multiple regression were to be performed, tell which two of the variables (gross, average ticket price, and shows) would be explanatory and which one would be response.

Who is the artist responsible for the outlier?

CHAPTER 5   SUMMARY

The most important research done by statisticians involves relationships between variables. In this chapter we focus on relationships between a categorical explanatory variable and a quantitative response, between two categorical variables, and between two quantitative variables. Our summaries and displays for a quantitative response, compared for two or more categorical groups, are extensions of those used for single quantitative variables. Similarly, summaries and displays for two categorical variables expand on those used for single categorical variables. For the relationship between two quantitative variables, we introduced new summary and display tools. Whatever relationship we study, we must be careful to use sampling and study designs that help us avoid bias and confounding variables. This is especially important if our goal is to draw conclusions about the relationship in a larger population, based on our sample.

Relationships between a Categorical and a Quantitative Variable

- To display and compare quantitative responses for two or more independent groups, use **side-by-side boxplots**.

- Summarize and compare quantitative responses for two or more independent groups with **mean** and **standard deviation**, or with **five-number summary** if distributions show skewness and outliers.

- **Sample means** for groups in a two-sample or several-sample study can be denoted $\bar{x}_1$, $\bar{x}_2$, and so on. **Sample standard deviations** are denoted s_1, s_2, and so on. **Population means** are written μ_1, μ_2, etc., and **population standard deviations** are written σ_1, σ_2, etc.

- Display and summarize data from a paired study by handling the differences as values of a single quantitative variable.

- In a paired study design, **sampled differences** have mean $\bar{x}_d$ and standard deviation s_d, whereas **population differences** have mean μ_d and standard deviation σ_d.

- The difference in means for two or more categorical groups tends to be less pronounced if the distributions have a lot of spread (large standard deviations) and more pronounced if the distributions have little spread (small standard deviations).

- The difference in sample means for two or more categorical groups should be taken more seriously if it is based on large samples, and less seriously if it is based on small samples.

Relationships between Two Categorical Variables

- First establish if there is a natural assignment of roles—**explanatory** and **response**.

- Report data in a **two-way table**, preferably with the explanatory variable in rows.

- Summarize with **conditional percentages** or **conditional proportions** in the response categories of interest, given each explanatory category. Compare proportions to determine if they differ; if so, consider the extent to which they differ.

- Display with a **bar graph**, where the horizontal axis is for explanatory categories and the vertical axis shows conditional percentages or proportions in various response categories.

- **Sample proportions** in the response of interest for two explanatory groups are written $\hat{p}_1$ and $\hat{p}_2$. The corresponding **population proportions** are written simply p_1 and p_2.

- Instead of comparing observed proportions, we can compare the table of observed counts to the table of **expected counts**—the values that would occur if there were no relationship at all between the two variables.

- **Simpson's Paradox** is the phenomenon whereby the nature of the relationship between two variables changes, depending on whether results for different groups are summarized separately or combined.

- If an additional **confounding variable** may be influencing the relationship, study separately groups of individuals that are similar with respect to the confounding variable.

Relationships between Two Quantitative Variables

- Relationships between two quantitative variables are displayed with a **scatterplot**. To summarize, there should be mention of **form** (linear or not), **direction** (positive or negative), and **strength**.

- **Correlation r** tells the direction and strength of a linear relationship between two quantitative variables. It reports the direction of a relationship with its sign. Correlation r is closer to 0 for weaker relationships, and closer to -1 or $+1$ for stronger relationships.

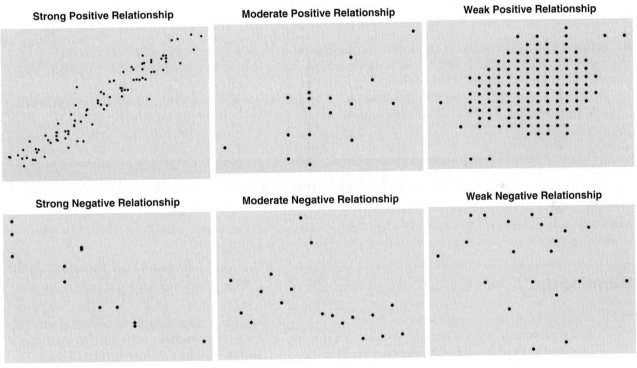

- In general, **software** should be used to calculate r. By hand you would need to find the "average" product of standardized x and y values.

- r is the same regardless of which variable is termed explanatory and which response, and regardless of measurement units. If one or both of the variables report **averages** as opposed to individual values, then the correlation may be overstated.

- If the relationship between two quantitative variables is deemed linear, it is summarized with an equation of a straight line, called the **least squares regression line**.

  - In general, software should be used for regression calculations. By hand you would find the line with **slope** $b_1 = r\frac{s_y}{s_x}$ and **intercept** $b_0 = \bar{y} - b_1\bar{x}$.

  - The slope b_1 of the regression line tells how much we predict the response to increase or decrease for every unit increase in the explanatory variable. The intercept b_0, technically, is the response predicted for an explanatory value of zero, a prediction that has practical value only if zero is a plausible explanatory value. **Extrapolation** is using the regression line to predict a response for an explanatory value that is outside the range of values used to construct the line; this may result in poor or even nonsensical predictions.

■ Residuals are **prediction errors**—the differences between each observed response and the response predicted for the given explanatory value. They are represented as vertical distances of scatterplot points from the least squares regression line. The number s in the regression output tells the **typical residual size**.

■ Although assignment of roles to the two quantitative variables, explanatory or response, does not affect r, it does impact the regression line, depending on whether it is constructed to minimize vertical or horizontal distances of scatterplot points from the line.

■ The scatterplot and output should be scrutinized for outliers and influential observations, and a decision should be made carefully as to whether or not they should be included in the regression analysis. In general, an **outlier** is a point with an unusually large residual. An **influential observation** is a point that has a great deal of impact on the position of the regression line, usually by virtue of being far from the other points in a horizontal direction.

■ Corresponding to the intercept b_0 and slope b_1 of the line that summarizes the sample data are the (generally unknown) intercept β_0 and slope β_1 of the line that summarizes the relationship for the larger population.

■ **Time series plots** display the relationship between two quantitative variables when the explanatory variable is time. Trends, peaks, and troughs provide information about how time affects the response.

■ Before drawing a conclusion about the relationship between two quantitative variables based on regression analysis, the possibility of **confounding variables** should be considered, and controlled for if warranted (and if values of the confounding variables are available) by performing the regression separately for groups of similar individuals. If an additional quantitative explanatory variable is taken into account, then methods of **multiple regression** (not covered in this book) would be used.

CHAPTER 5   EXERCISES

Note: Asterisked numbers indicate exercises whose answers are provided in the Solutions to Selected Exercises section, on page 689.

Additional exercises appeared after each section: relationships between a categorical and a quantitative variable (Section 5.1) on page 144, two categorical variables (Section 5.2) on page 160, and two quantitative variables (Section 5.3) on page 192.

Warming Up: CATEGORICAL AND QUANTITATIVE VARIABLES

*5.71   Suppose a sample of college students shows that students who live off campus tend to weigh more than students who live on campus.

  a. Which of the following, if any, is a possible confounding variable: gender (males tend to live off campus, and they tend to weigh more), or age (older students tend to live off campus, and they tend to weigh more), or both of these, or neither of these?

  b. Are mean weights of sampled students who live on and off campus denoted $\bar{x}_1$ and $\bar{x}_2$ or μ_1 and μ_2?

5.72   Suppose a large sample of college students shows that students who have pierced ears tend to earn less money. Which of the following, if any, is a possible confounding variable: gender (females tend to have pierced ears, and they tend to earn less money), or handedness (left-handed students tend to have pierced ears, and they tend to earn less money), or both of these, or neither of these?

5.73   Environmentalists concerned about global warming can take a variety of approaches to

More exercises for this chapter are featured in the *TBP* Supplement on pages 799 through 807. End-of-chapter activities are described on page 796.

produce evidence that temperatures are on the rise. Which one of these designs involves a categorical explanatory variable and a quantitative response?

a. Record the mean global temperature for each year over the past century.

b. Record the mean global temperature over the past 25 years and compare it to the mean global temperature for the previous 75 years.

5.74 The *New York Times* article "Modern German Duty: The Obligation to Play" reports that "Germans work fewer hours per year than anybody else in the advanced industrial world—1,557 hours a year in the former West Germany, compared with 1,605 for France, 1,683 for Britain and more than 1,900 for the United States . . ."[29]

a. Find the difference in mean hours worked per year, Americans minus Germans, and divide by 40 to find approximately how many fewer work-weeks there are for Germans.

b. Tell whether the variable for hours worked is explanatory or response, and whether it is quantitative or categorical.

c. Tell whether the variable for country is explanatory or response, and whether it is quantitative or categorical.

5.75 According to a newspaper article, "the change years ago from manual typewriters to computers has caused the average full-time secretary to gain 5 to 10 pounds."[30]

a. Describe an experiment that could be carried out to support this claim. What are the experiment's weaknesses?

b. Describe an observational study that could be carried out to support this claim. What are the observational study's weaknesses?

5.76 According to the *New York Times*, "Studies Find That for Men, It Pays to Be Married." Economists "drew on a unique data set, the Minnesota Twins Registry, which tracked most twins born in Minnesota between 1936 and 1955 . . . They found that the married men in their sample earned about 19% more than the unmarried men . . . They

found that married twins had 26% higher wages than their unmarried siblings."[31]

a. Did the first result (19% more) come about from a paired or a two-sample design?

b. Did the second result (26% higher) come about from a paired or a two-sample design?

c. Explain how it is possible that causation may occur in the opposite direction from what the title suggests.

5.77 Why are these boxplots not very useful for making a side-by-side comparison of heights of mothers and heights of fathers?

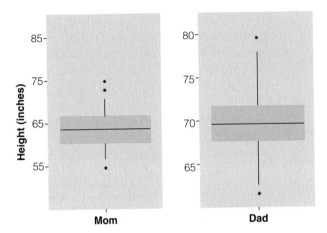

5.78 A newspaper article compares median net worth for black, Hispanic, and white households, as reported by the Pew Hispanic Center: The medians in 2002 were approximately $6,000 for black households, $8,000 for Hispanic households, and $89,000 for white households.[32] Four statistics students are asked in a homework exercise to explain why researchers would report medians instead of means. Who gives the best answer?

Adam: Probably because medians are easier to compute.

Brittany: I think they reported medians to make the results seem more dramatic, and make people aware of how discrimination against minorities can result in lower pay.

Carlos: If they'd wanted results to seem more dramatic, they would have used means. The reason they used medians was so they wouldn't be inflated by high outliers.

Dominique: In case they don't have the exact values for the households that they used, as long as the middle one is correct, the median will be accurate. Reporting the median is the best way to handle these data values.

5.79 "Busting the Nursery Rhymes" reports that "Research from a team at Bristol Royal Hospital for Children [in England] found that there's more violence in traditional nursery rhymes than in early-evening television." The study reported "that there were more than 52 violent scenes per each hour spent listening to 25 of the most popular nursery rhymes—or more than 10 times the five violent scenes witnessed per each hour of TV viewing. [. . .] Authors of the study admitted their research was done slightly tongue-in-cheek. But they also said they hoped to make the important assertion that parents worried about bad behavior shouldn't only point fingers at television. After all, there's Jack and Jill's hill-climbing tragedies and Rock-a-Bye-Baby's tale of a newborn tumbling out of a tree to consider. Other disturbing examples included Humpty

Dumpty's fall off the wall and Simple Simon's pricking of his finger."[33]

a. Certainly a mean of 52 is dramatically higher than a mean of 5. However, is the response of interest—number of violent scenes—really measuring the same thing for the two groups being compared (nursery rhymes and TV)? Discuss.

b. Suppose nursery rhymes are not harmful to children, but parents read about this study and substitute TV for bedtime reading of nursery rhymes. What are the potential harmful consequences of this mistake?

c. Suppose nursery rhymes are harmful to children, but parents conclude they are fine and expose their children to violent rhymes on a regular basis. What are the potential harmful consequences of this mistake?

d. Which mistake would you personally prefer to avoid: the one described in part (b) or the one described in part (c)?

Exploring the Big Picture: CATEGORICAL AND QUANTITATIVE VARIABLES

5.80 The *New York Times* reported that "from 2001 to 2003, World Health Organization surveys measured the prevalence of serious mental disorders in the populations of various countries." A comparison was made between eight developed and seven less-developed countries.[34]

Developed Countries	%	Less-Developed Countries	%
United States	7.7	Colombia	5.2
France	2.7	Ukraine	4.8
Belgium	2.4	Lebanon	4.6
Netherlands	2.3	Mexico	3.7
Japan	1.5	China (Shanghai)	1.1
Germany	1.2	China (Beijing)	0.9
Italy	1.0	Nigeria	0.4
Spain	1.0		

a. Find the mean rate of mental illness for the eight developed countries.

b. Is the mean for the developed countries higher or lower than the mean for the seven less-developed countries, which is 3.0%?

c. To compare rates of mental illness for developed and less-developed countries, is it better to report means or medians? Explain.

d. Explain why the rate of mental illness for all people in the seven less-developed countries *combined* is not necessarily 3.0%.

e. Find the standard deviation for rate of mental illness in the eight developed countries.

f. Is the standard deviation for the eight developed countries higher or lower than that for the seven less-developed countries, which is 2.1%?

g. The article mentions that "embarrassment about disclosing mental illness varies" from country to country; in some places, like Nigeria, women are reluctant to admit being depressed. Does this result in bias due to a nonrepresentative sample, or bias in the assessment of a variable's values?

5.81 Archaeologists investigated starch grains recovered from a grinding stone used by inhabitants of a region on the shore of the Sea of Galilee some 23,000 years ago. Grain size played a role in its attractiveness to seed-gatherers, and archaeologists can often distinguish one grain species from another by virtue of their sizes. This side-by-side boxplot has been reconstructed from summaries reported on lengths of two archaeological starch grains, in micrometers, by researchers Piperno, Weiss, Hoist, and Nadel.[35]

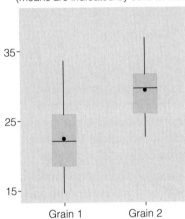

Boxplots of Grain Lengths (micrometers)
(means are indicated by solid circles)

a. If a grain was found with length 20 micrometers, is it probably the first type, or the second type, or could it easily be either?

b. If a grain was found with length 25 micrometers, is it probably the first type, or the second type, or could it easily be either?

c. If a grain was found with length 30 micrometers, is it probably the first type, or the second type, or could it easily be either?

d. One of the two types of grain had lengths that were somewhat more spread out; was it the first or the second type?

e. Do the boxplots suggest that overall grain length follows a distribution with a shape that is symmetric, or skewed left, or skewed right?

f. Keeping in mind that the data arose from a sample of grains, how should the mean length for the first grain type be denoted?

g. Keeping in mind that the data arose from a sample of grains, how should the standard deviation of lengths for the second grain type be denoted?

h. The researchers in this study took "two probes, each at five different locations on the [grinding] stone." At this stage, were they mainly concerned with data production, displaying and summarizing data, probability, or statistical inference?

5.82 Percentages of economically disadvantaged students are listed for 17 middle schools and 12 high schools in a certain school district around the year 2000.

Middle Schools	High Schools
30	22
38	27
39	37
43	39
52	40
56	46
56	49
57	53
62	55
68	57
71	62
72	70
80	
82	
84	
88	
89	

a. Are the data values formatted with a column for values of quantitative responses and a column for values of a categorical explanatory variable, or are they formatted with two columns of quantitative responses (one for each of two categorical groups)?

b. Find the five-number summary values for middle schools.

c. Find the five-number summary values for high schools.

d. Neither type of school has outlier values. Construct a side-by-side boxplot to display percentages of disadvantaged students in the two types of schools.

e. Are the centers comparable? If not, which type of school tends to have higher percentages of economically disadvantaged students?

f. Suppose students are classified as being economically disadvantaged based on a form that must be completed by parents regarding household income, and sent in to make students eligible for free or reduced school lunches. Explain how this could bring about a difference in reported percentages for the two types of schools.

g. Disadvantaged students might tend to drop out before they have completed high school. Explain how this could bring about a difference in reported percentages for the two types of schools.

h. Are the spreads comparable? If not, which type of school tends to have more variable percentages of economically disadvantaged students?

i. The shapes of the two distributions are similar: Are they markedly left-skewed, fairly symmetric, or markedly right-skewed?

j. Considering the shapes of the distributions, do mean and standard deviation do a good job of summarizing centers and spreads?

5.83 The so-called "freshman 15" refers to the purported tendency for students to gain about 15 pounds during their first year living in a college dormitory.[36] To see whether or not data support this theory, we display boxplots for weights of samples of freshman and sophomore females, as well as weights of freshman and sophomore males, from students surveyed at a large university in 2003. We also use software to produce means and standard deviations of weights for those groups.

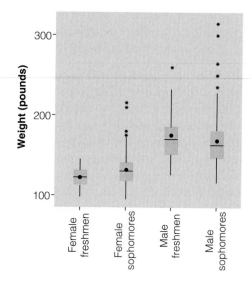

Level	N	Mean	StDev
WtFemaleFreshmen	24	122.04	12.16
WtFemaleSophomores	172	131.98	20.74
WtMaleFreshmen	11	175.00	39.83
WtMaleSophomores	84	168.11	34.89

a. Do sampled sophomore females appear to be heavier on average than sampled freshman females? If so, are they heavier by about 5 pounds, 10 pounds, or 15 pounds?

b. Do sampled sophomore males appear to be heavier on average than sampled freshman males? If so, are they heavier by about 5 pounds, 10 pounds, or 15 pounds?

c. Do the data support the notion of the "freshman 15"? Explain.

d. Which of the gender groups has a greater amount of spread in their weights—females or males?

e. Which group has less spread in their weights—female freshmen or female sophomores?

f. Do the distributions of weights tend to be normal, or skewed left/low outliers, or skewed right/high outliers?

g. Describe a paired design for gathering evidence for or against the notion of the "freshman 15."

Using Software [see Technology Guide]: CATEGORICAL AND QUANTITATIVE VARIABLES

*5.84 Lengths (in minutes) of movies showing during a week in 2004 were recorded to see if there was a difference in lengths for movies rated PG, PG-13, or R.

PG	PG-13	R
100	130	134
99	143	173
106	102	113
115	169	108
90	103	98
140	120	118
90	105	102
	120	123
	106	

a. Use software to produce side-by-side boxplots of the data.

b. Which one of these do the boxplots suggest: Movies with one of the ratings tend to be longer but lengths are comparable for movies with the other two ratings; or, movies with one of the ratings tend to be shorter but lengths are comparable for movies with the other two ratings.

c. Use software to produce sample sizes, means, and standard deviations of lengths of movies with the three different ratings.

d. Would we be more convinced of a difference in lengths of all movies with the various ratings if the samples sizes were larger, or doesn't it matter?

e. Fill in the blank with the number 10, 20, 30, 40, or 50: "Movies rated PG-13 tended to be about 2 hours long; some were shorter and others longer, but they tended to differ from the mean by about _____ minutes."

f. Are the standard deviations of the sampled movies denoted $\bar{x}_1, \bar{x}_2, \bar{x}_3$, or μ_1, μ_2, μ_3, or s_1, s_2, s_3, or $\sigma_1, \sigma_2, \sigma_3$?

5.85 Off-campus students at a certain university usually opt for housing in one of three areas:

Oakland (a somewhat run-down area in the direct neighborhood of the campus), Shadyside (an upscale area a couple of miles northeast), and Squirrel Hill (a residential area a couple of miles southeast). Here are rents charged for one-bedroom apartments advertised for these areas in the classified section of the local newspaper:

Oakland	Shadyside		Squirrel Hill
475	790	600	625
550	597	550	545
450	702	720	595
350	739	650	550
485	750	625	650
430	865	665	550
650	750	675	425
350	750	550	400
495	525	550	779
425	675	780	690
475	795	765	
350	675	725	
	575	425	
	750		

a. Use software to produce side-by-side boxplots of the data.

b. Use software to produce sample sizes, means, and standard deviations of rents in the three areas.

c. Use the results from part (b) to fill in the blanks in this summary, using words or whole numbers: "The cheapest area is _____; to live in the moderately priced area you have to pay about _____ hundred more dollars a month, and to live in the most expensive area you have to pay about _____ hundred more dollars a month."

d. Use the results from part (b) to fill in the blank in this summary, using a whole number: "Whichever area you choose, rents tend to differ from the mean by about _____ hundred dollars."

e. Use the appearance of the boxplots to fill in the blank in this comment: "If you're wondering whether any unusually high rents are inflating the value of the mean, that's actually the case in _____." (Choose from Oakland, Shadyside, Squirrel Hill, or none of the three areas.)

5.86 A car buyer wanted to compare prices of 3-year-old BMW and Mercedes Benz automobiles, and found these prices (in thousands of dollars) listed in the classified ads:

BMW	32	35	29	33	35	42	34	35	47	53
	27	54	27	27	34	32	28	51	28	
Mercedes	26	47	32	39						

a. Use software to find the mean and standard deviation of prices for BMWs, to the nearest thousand dollars.

b. Use software to find the mean and standard deviation of prices for Mercedes, to the nearest thousand dollars.

c. The means and standard deviations are almost identical. For which type of car would you feel the sample mean is a more accurate guess for the mean price of all such cars—BMW, Mercedes, or both the same?

d. If we use $\bar{x}_1$ to denote the mean price of the 19 BMWs, and s_1 to denote the standard deviation of their prices, what should we use to denote the mean price of the four Mercedes?

e. How should we denote the standard deviation of Mercedes Benz prices?

f. How should we denote the mean price of all 3-year-old BMWs?

g. How should we denote the standard deviation of prices of all 3-year-old BMWs?

5.87 Suppose someone claims that students in higher years at school tend to earn more money, because they are older and have more work experience.

a. Use software to access the student survey data, and find the sample sizes, medians, means, and standard deviations for earnings of 1st, 2nd, 3rd, 4th, and other year students.

b. Do the means seem to support the claim that students in higher years earn more?

c. Do the medians seem to support the claim?

d. Use software to produce side-by-side boxplots of the data.

e. Considering the appearances of the distributions, which would be better to report the centers: means or medians?

f. The three highest outliers occur in which two of the groups? Do earnings in these two years also have the highest standard deviations?

*5.88 Students were surveyed as to how many minutes they had exercised the day before. They were also asked whether or not they smoked.

a. If one group exercised more, would you expect it to be the smokers or the nonsmokers?

b. Use software to access the student survey data, and report the mean minutes exercised for smokers and for nonsmokers.

c. Which sample mean is higher?

d. Does the difference appear to be major or minor?

e. Can we conclude that smoking causes someone to exercise less? Explain.

5.89 On-campus students may get more sleep than off-campus students because they don't have to get up earlier to commute; or perhaps they get less sleep because of late-night noise in the dormitories; or perhaps they get about the same amount of sleep as off-campus students.

a. Use software to access the student survey data, and report the mean hours of sleep for on-campus and for off-campus students.

b. Which sample mean is higher?

c. Does the difference appear to be major or minor?

d. If we want to use mean hours slept by samples of on- and off-campus students to decide if there is evidence that all on-campus students sleep longer than all off-campus students, are we mainly concerned with data production, displaying and summarizing data, probability, or statistical inference?

5.90 Commuting students get to school by various means of transportation, such as taking a bus, driving a car, or walking. We may suspect that students who walk would tend to be youngest (because they are fittest or have the least money) whereas students who drive a car would tend to be oldest (because they are least fit or have the most amount of money).

a. Use software to access the student survey data. Report the mean ages of students who commute by bus, car, or walking.

b. Which group is youngest on average?

c. Which group is oldest?

d. Report the median ages.

e. Which group has the lowest median?

f. Which group has the highest median?

g. There were three students who commuted by bike. Which estimate should be better: using their sample mean age to estimate the mean age of all students who commute by bike, or using the sample mean age of 110 walkers to estimate the mean age of all students who commute by walking; or should the estimates be equally good?

Discovering Research: CATEGORICAL AND QUANTITATIVE VARIABLES

5.91 Find (and hand in) a newspaper article or Internet report about a study that involves values of a quantitative variable being compared for two or more categorical groups. Besides providing a copy of the article or report, tell how the data were produced—was it an experiment or an observational study? Report, if known, which group apparently has the highest values for the quantitative variable and which has the lowest. Tell if results are being reported for a sample or for an entire population, and the number of individuals studied, if known. Tell if there is reason to suspect bias that arises if the sample is not representative, or bias in the design for assessing the variable's values.

Reporting on Research: CATEGORICAL AND QUANTITATIVE VARIABLES

5.92 Use results of Exercise 5.83 and relevant findings from the Internet to make a report on the "freshman 15" that relies on statistical information.

Warming Up: TWO CATEGORICAL VARIABLES

5.93 "Coral Reefs Less Healthy Now Than 2 Years Ago" warns that "Only about 30% of the world's coral reefs are healthy, down from 41% 2 years ago, according to a study released yesterday [in 2004] that lists global warming as the top threat."[37] Tell what the two categorical variables of interest are, what possible values they can take, and which is explanatory and which is response.

5.94 A study by the European School Survey Project on Alcohol and Other Drugs

(ESPAD) found that 277 in a sample of 543 15-to-16-year-olds in the Faroe Islands had consumed five or more alcoholic beverages in a row at least once in the past month, compared to 1,207 in a sample of 8,940 15-to-16-year-olds in Poland.[38]

a. Which one of these is a better summary of the results, or are they both equally good?

1. Because 1,207 is more than four times as much as 277, we can say that the

Polish youths were more than four times as likely to have engaged in excessive drinking in the past month.

2. Because 277/543 = 0.51 is almost four times as much as 1,207/8,940 = 0.135, we can say that the Faroe Island youths were almost four times as likely to have engaged in excessive drinking in the past month.

b. Alcohol consumption is treated here as a categorical variable. Would it have been just as easy to find out how many liters of alcohol the youths had consumed in the past month, and compared means for the two countries? Explain.

c. If researchers are deciding whether to ask the youths, "How much alcohol did you drink in the past month?" or "Did you consume five or more alcoholic beverages in a row at least once in the past month?" are they mainly concerned with data production, displaying and summarizing data, probability, or statistical inference?

Exploring the Big Picture: TWO CATEGORICAL VARIABLES

5.95 In "An Informal Look at Use of Bakery Department Tongs and Tissues," a researcher named Trinkaus reported: "Of 108 people observed extracting for purchase rolls or pastries from displayed bulk stock in food supermarket bakery departments, about 90% used their hands for item selection and withdrawal rather than the store provided tongs. In stores where tissues were provided instead of tongs, approximately 60% of the 133 people who were observed used their hands."[39]

a. Was this an experiment or an observational study?

b. Are the relevant proportions (0.90 and 0.60) statistics or parameters?

c. Should the proportions be denoted p_1 and p_2 or $\hat{p}_1$ and $\hat{p}_2$?

d. Does the difference between 90% and 60% seem large enough to suggest that, in general, people opt for hands instead of tongs more than they opt for hands instead of tissues?

e. What if the difference (0.90 versus 0.60) had come about from observing just 10 people each in stores with tongs and with tissues; would this be more convincing or less convincing that, in general, people opt for hands instead of tongs more than they opt for hands instead of tissues?

5.96 A study, conducted for Planned Parenthood by Rand whose results were published in 2004, claims to be the first to find a "direct cause-and-effect link" between watching suggestive TV shows and early teen sex. The study "resulted from phone interviews of adolescents ages 12 to 17, first in 2001 and again a year later in 2002. It found that children who watched the most sex-saturated television [. . .] were twice as likely to engage in sexual activity within the next year than those who reported a low level of television watching."[40]

a. From the researchers' standpoint, what are the explanatory and response variables involved here?

b. Was this an experiment or an observational study?

c. Describe what would be the case if the roles of explanatory and response variables were reversed; is this a plausible scenario?

d. Discuss the researchers' claim to have found a "direct cause-and-effect link."

e. Researchers must decide whether to report the percentages engaging in sexual activity for those who did versus those who did not watch suggestive TV shows, or the percentages watching suggestive TV shows for those who did versus those who did not engage in sexual activity. At this stage, are they mainly concerned with data production, displaying and summarizing data, probability, or statistical inference?

5.97 *Parade* magazine reported the following story from *The Commercial Appeal* publication: "In an unusual taste test, a bear chose Rainier beer over Busch. The black bear was found passed out on the lawn of Baker Lake Resort near Concrete,

Washington, surrounded by 36 empty beer cans. It had gotten into the coolers of some nearby campers, who had stocked up on both brands of beer for their trip. Fish and Wildlife Enforcement Sgt. Bill Heinck said the bear did try one can of Busch, but ignored the rest. The beast then consumed all the campers' Rainier."[41]

a. Was this an experiment or an observational study?

b. What are the two categorical variables involved here?

c. The following table is one possibility, given the reported information. What are the percentages of Busch beers consumed and Rainier beers consumed by the bear in this case?

	Consumed	Not Consumed
Busch	1	1
Rainier	35	0

d. The following table is another possibility, given the reported information. What are the percentages of Busch beers consumed and Rainier beers consumed by the bear in this case?

	Consumed	Not Consumed
Busch	1	34
Rainier	35	0

e. Which of the tables would do more to convince you that the bear preferred Rainier beer—the one shown in part (c) or in part (d)—or are they equally convincing?

f. Considering the information that the campers "had stocked up on both brands of beer for their trip," which table is probably closer to the actual situation—the one shown in part (c) or part (d)?

Bears as beer experts?

5.98 A study published in April 2000 in the *British Medical Journal* reported on a Scotland survey regarding the numbers of surveyed high school students carrying weapons and engaging in illegal drug use.[42]

	Weapon	No Weapon	Total
Drugs	389	496	885
No Drugs	248	1,978	2,226
Total	637	2,474	3,111

a. To demonstrate that drug users were more likely than non-users to carry weapons, what two percentages should be compared? (Report them.)

b. The table shows that drug users were how many times as likely to carry weapons as non-users?

c. To demonstrate that students who carried weapons were more likely to use illegal drugs than those who didn't carry weapons, what two percentages should be compared? (Report them.)

d. The table shows that those who carried weapons were how many times as likely to use illegal drugs as those who didn't carry weapons?

Using Software [see Technology Guide]: TWO CATEGORICAL VARIABLES

*5.99 A survey was taken of students at a large university in the fall of 2003 who were enrolled in one of three introductory statistics courses: Stat 200, commonly taken by students in the social sciences; Stat 1000, taken by students in the natural sciences; and Stat 1100, taken by business majors. We would like to explore whether the courses differ in terms of the percentages of males and females enrolled, and so we will treat "Course" as the explanatory variable, and "Gender" as the response.

a. Explain why "Course" should be treated as a categorical variable, in spite of the fact that it takes number values.

b. Use software to access the student survey data. Report the percentage of females in Stat 200, Stat 1000, and Stat 1100.

c. Which course has the highest percentage of females and which has the lowest?

d. Should we assume that the difference in percentages is due to chance, or is there a good possibility that males and females would have a tendency to major in different subject areas?

5.100 A survey was taken of students at a large university in the fall of 2003; among other things, students were asked to report their gender, and which of these colors they preferred: black, blue, green, orange, pink, purple, red, yellow.

a. Which one of these colors could be expected to be preferred more by males than by females: black, pink, purple, or yellow?

b. Of all the colors, which two could be expected to be preferred more by females than by males: black, pink, purple, or yellow?

c. Use software to access the student survey data. Report the percentage preferring each color for males and for females.

d. For four of the colors, the difference in percentages between males and females is close enough that it could conceivably have come about by chance; in other words, it is plausible that the percentage preferring these colors is the same for the general populations of male and female students. Which colors are they?

5.101 A survey was taken of students at a large university in the fall of 2003 who were enrolled in one of three introductory statistics courses: Stat 200, commonly taken by students in the social sciences; Stat 1000, taken by students in the natural sciences; and Stat 1100, taken by business majors. Among other things, students were asked if they had pierced ears.

a. Use software to access the student survey data. Report the percentage with pierced ears for students in the social science-oriented course, students in the natural science-oriented course, and students in the business-oriented course.

b. The percentage with pierced ears is substantially higher among social science students, and substantially lower among business students. What is a possible confounding variable that is the real reason for a relationship between course taken and having pierced ears or not?

c. To determine the true nature of the relationship between course taken and having ears pierced or not, what would be the next step to take: Construct separate tables for each of the values of the possible confounding variable, or take larger samples in all groups?

Discovering Research: TWO CATEGORICAL VARIABLES

5.102 Find a newspaper article or Internet report about a study that involves two categorical variables. Besides providing a copy of the article or report, tell how the data were produced—was it an experiment or an observational study? Which variable is explanatory and which is response? Report, if known, which group apparently has the highest percentage in the response of interest and which has the lowest. Tell if results are being reported for a sample or for an entire population, and the number of individuals studied, if known. Tell if there is reason to suspect bias that arises if the sample is not representative, or bias in the design for assessing the variable's values. If there is enough information provided, construct a two-way table of counts.

Reporting on Research: TWO CATEGORICAL VARIABLES

5.103 Use results of Exercise 5.26 and relevant findings from the Internet to make a report on hate crimes in the United States that relies on statistical information.

Warming Up: TWO QUANTITATIVE VARIABLES

*5.104 "Drinking water rich in minerals, or hard water, may play a role in reducing heart disease, Finnish researchers say."[43] For one of these study designs, it would be appropriate to summarize results with a correlation; which is it? For the other designs, tell why correlation would not be appropriate.

    a. Take a sample of individuals from around the country; record the hardness (parts per million of calcium carbonate) of water where they live, and whether they die of a heart attack.

    b. Take a sample of communities from around the country; record the hardness (parts per million of calcium carbonate) of water in each community, and the rate of death by heart attack.

    c. Take a sample of communities from around the country; record whether the water in each community is hard or soft, and record the rate of death by heart attack in each community.

    d. Take a sample of individuals from around the country; record whether the water where they live is hard or soft, and whether they die of a heart attack.

5.105 According to a newspaper article, "the stronger an onion tastes, the more likely it is to help fight cancer and other diseases, scientists at Cornell have found."[44] For one of these study designs, it would be appropriate to summarize results with a correlation; which is it? For the other designs, tell why correlation would not be appropriate.

    a. For various types of onions, record whether or not they have a strong taste, and record whether or not they contain cancer-fighting compounds called phenolics and flavonoids.

    b. For various types of onions, record whether or not they have a strong taste, and measure amounts of cancer-fighting compounds called phenolics and flavonoids.

    c. For various types of onions, rank them according to how strong they taste, and record whether or not they contain cancer-fighting compounds called phenolics and flavonoids.

    d. For various types of onions, rank them according to how strong they taste, and measure amounts of cancer-fighting compounds called phenolics and flavonoids.

Exploring the Big Picture: TWO QUANTITATIVE VARIABLES

5.106 A newspaper report on results of the American Time Use Survey of 2003 mentions the "decades-long trend of people moving farther away from their jobs to find larger or more affordable homes."[45]

    If we look at a time series plot of Americans' distance from their jobs over the past two decades, are we considering two single quantitative variables, or the relationship between two quantitative variables?

5.107 Before the presidential election of 2004, there was much discussion of the relative intelligence of the two candidates, George W. Bush and John Kerry. After critics of Bush suggested that his IQ was on the low side, his defenders used a regression on his SAT score (1206) to estimate his IQ to be 124. Kerry's IQ was presumably about 122, based on his purported SAT score of 1190.

    a. Correlation between SAT score and IQ is somewhere between 0.5 and 0.6. Is the relationship weak, moderate, or strong?

    b. Standard deviation for IQ is about 15, and s (typical error size) for the prediction of IQ based on SAT score would be about 10. What is the range of IQ scores that are within about one s of the prediction for Bush's IQ, 124?

    c. What is the range of IQ scores that are within about one s of the prediction for Kerry's IQ, 122?

    d. Comment on the validity of a claim that Bush's IQ was about 2 points higher than Kerry's, based on their SAT scores.

e. Which should we be able to predict more accurately: IQ of one individual whose SAT score was 1206, mean IQ of all those whose SAT score was 1206, or both the same?

f. Based on samples, we can get a rough idea of the equation for the regression line that relates IQ to SAT for everyone who took the SAT test, but the actual intercept and slope for the entire population are unknown. Are these denoted b_0 and b_1 or β_0 and β_1?

5.108   "African AIDS Patients More Diligent in Taking Medicine Than in U.S." was reported in 2003. On average, "American patients tell their doctors that they are doing 20 percentage points better than they really are—that is, a patient who says he takes 90% of his pills will, when tested with unannounced home pill counts or electronic pill-bottle caps, turn out to be taking 70%."[46]

a. If we regressed claimed percentage on actual percentage of pills taken, would the number 20 correspond to intercept, slope, or correlation?

b. The article mentions that "a study of 29 Ugandan patients found that, on average, they estimated that they were taking 93% of pills and proved to be taking 91%." If two regression lines for pills claimed versus pills taken were drawn on the same graph, one for Uganda and one for the United States, would the line for Uganda be higher than or lower than the one for the United States?

5.109   "Warming Reducing Rice Yields" reported in 2004 that, according to the latest *Proceedings of the National Academy of Sciences*, "an average daily temperature increase of 1 degree Celsius resulted in a 10% reduction in the rice crop." In the United States, corn and soybean yields were found to reduce in a manner similar to that of rice in the Philippines.[47]

a. Which of the variables, rice yield and temperature, is the explanatory variable?

b. Was the relationship found to be positive or negative?

c. Which one of these is referred to in the above report: intercept, slope, or correlation?

d. The article reports that "most earlier studies of the effects of global warming on crops have involved computer simulations. This is one of the first to try to measure the effects directly." When the researchers opted to measure effects directly instead of using a computer simulation, were they mainly concerned with data production, displaying and summarizing data, probability, or statistical inference?

5.110   "Drop in Temperatures Could Lower Ticket Prices, Too," was a sports page article that pointed out that "cold weather might reduce the cost of tickets for [Steelers] fans who are trying to scalp their way into Heinz Field for the AFC playoff game against the New York Jets Saturday [January 15, 2005]." Some ticket brokers, however, believed that "the cold weather in the forecast isn't diminishing demand."[48]

How could data be gathered to determine if prices tend to go down as the weather gets colder?

5.111   Professor Adams of California State University posts Roman Census data on his website, based on research by Arnold Toynbee and Frank Tenney. The data production methods should be questioned, but examination of the scatterplot, with particular attention to outliers, can give us an idea of how the population of the Roman Republic changed over time.

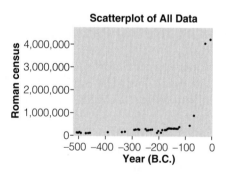

Scatterplot of All Data

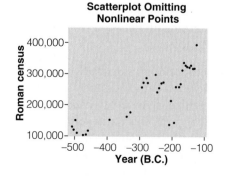

Scatterplot Omitting Nonlinear Points

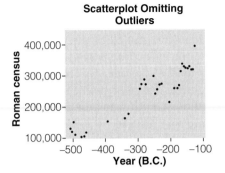

Scatterplot Omitting Outliers

a. The first scatterplot on page 218, with Census figures from 508 B.C. to 8 B.C., shows a rapid rise in the population after what year (to the nearest century)?

b. The second scatterplot on page 218 has eliminated data points that were most responsible for the original nonlinear appearance. Now there are two outliers apparent, which might represent serious errors in the measuring process. In roughly what century did they occur?

c. The scatterplot on this page has eliminated the two outliers that are the most obvious suspected errors in the measuring process. According to this plot, each year during those centuries the population of the Roman Republic increased by about how much: 60, 600, 6,000, or 60,000?

d. If regression were performed using the data between 500 and 100 B.C., would the prediction for the year 1 A.D. turn out to be an underestimate, an overestimate, or just about right?

5.112 A survey was taken of students at a large university in the fall of 2003; among other things, students were asked to report their Math SAT scores and their weight. The standard deviation for weights was $s_y = 32$ pounds. When weight was regressed on Math SAT, the correlation was found to be 0, indicating no relationship between the two variables. Four statistics students attempt to answer a homework question that asks for the typical size s of the prediction error if we try to predict weight from Math SAT score. Whose answer is correct?

Adam: If they're not related then you make the same size mistakes predicting weight whether you know SAT or not. So s should also be around 32.

Brittany: Doesn't the correlation tell how good your predictions are? So in this case the prediction error equals correlation, which is zero.

Carlos: If prediction error size equaled zero, then your predictions would be perfect. That's not the case, so s must be somewhere between zero and 32.

Dominique: If the correlation is zero, then that means your predictions will be really bad. So s will be much greater than 32.

5.113 A survey was taken of students at a large university in the fall of 2003; among other things, students were asked to report their weight and how much money they had earned in the previous year. When earnings were regressed on weights, the correlation was found to be $+0.19$, suggesting that heavier students tended to earn more. However, there may be confounding variables entering in.

a. Which of these may be tied in with a student's weight and also have an impact on earnings: gender, age, both of these, or neither of these?

b. If gender is a suspected confounding variable, how should the regression be handled?

5.114 A survey was taken of students at a large university in the fall of 2003; among other things, students were asked to report how many credits they were taking and their SAT scores. There is a positive correlation between number of credits taken and Math SAT score. When outliers whose number of credits is below 12 are omitted, there is no longer a substantial correlation between number of credits taken and Math SAT score. If we want to see if Math SAT scores are lower for part-time students compared to full-time students, what display could be used?

Using Software [see Technology Guide]: TWO QUANTITATIVE VARIABLES

5.115 "On July 10, 2004 Andre Tolme Became the First Person to Golf Across Mongolia" is the headline of the www.golfmongolia.com website. A *New York Times* article by James Brooke described the feat: "Andre Tolme sized up the day's golfing terrain, thousands of yards of treeless steppe rolling toward a distant horizon. Without a golfer to be seen for 100 miles around, he loosened up at his own pace, taking practice swings with a 3-iron. Then, with a powerful clockwise whirl and a satisfying swak! he sent the little white ball soaring far into the clear blue Mongolian sky. 'I feel good about that shot,' Mr. Tolme said, intently tracking the ball until it disappeared from view. 'You could just hit the ball forever here.' In a sense, he is. This summer, Mr. Tolme, a civil engineer from New Hampshire, is golfing across Mongolia. Treating this enormous Central Asian nation as his private course, he has divided Mongolia into 18 holes. The total fairway distance is 2,322,000 yards. Par is 11,880 strokes. 'You hit the ball,' he said, explaining his technique in a land without fences, a nation that is twice the size of Texas. 'Then you go and find it. Then you hit it again. And again. And again.'" Tolme's website includes data on the 18 holes that stretch across Mongolia.[49]

Hole	Miles	Par	Shots	Balls Lost
1	82	711	833	40
2	47	403	430	23
3	35	694	344	18
4	67	493	631	34
5	73	901	771	43
6	41	683	436	28
7	64	711	609	35
8	86	638	893	72
9	87	839	907	59
10	84	699	891	22
11	41	414	387	21
12	80	565	748	17
13	112	845	1,096	20
14	56	772	527	9
15	69	621	778	21
16	75	677	627	10
17	78	706	756	26
18	57	508	506	11
Total	1,234	11,880	12,170	509

a. Use software to produce a scatterplot and regression of *par on miles*. The relationship is positive because longer stretches should require more shots. Is it weak, moderate, or strong?

b. If regression is used to predict the par for a hole, based on how many miles it covers, what is the approximate size of the prediction error for those 18 holes?

c. Use software to produce a scatterplot and regression of actual *shots on miles*. The relationship is positive, because longer stretches really did require more shots. Is it weak, moderate, or strong?

d. If regression is used to predict the number of shots Tolme needed for a hole, based on how many miles it covers, what is the approximate size of the prediction error for those 18 holes?

e. Which relationship is stronger: the one between *par and miles*, or the one between *shots and miles*?

f. Which prediction error is smaller, and by how much: the one for predicting *par from miles*, or the one for predicting *shots from miles*?

g. Produce a scatterplot of *balls lost versus hole*, and pick one of the following to summarize the situation:

1. There was no apparent relationship between number of balls lost and which hole was played.

2. There was a weak positive relationship between number of balls lost and which hole was played, suggesting that Tolme may have become somewhat less careful as he advanced across the country.

3. There was a weak negative relationship between number of balls lost and which hole was played, suggesting that Tolme may have become somewhat better at keeping track of balls as he advanced across the country.

h. Which of the following best summarizes the amount of scatter for balls lost on holes 1 through 18?

1. The scatter was fairly uniform throughout, from beginning to end.

2. The number of balls lost varied more for the first nine holes and less for the last nine.

3. The number of balls lost varied less for the first nine holes and more for the last nine.

i. Produce a scatterplot of *balls lost versus miles*, and pick one of the following to summarize the situation:

1. There was no apparent relationship between number of balls lost and how many miles long a hole was.

2. There was a weak positive relationship between number of balls lost and how many miles long a hole was, suggesting that it was somewhat more likely to lose balls on the longer stretches.

3. There was a weak negative relationship between number of balls lost and how many miles long a hole was, suggesting that the shorter stretches may have had more obstructions where a ball could be hidden from view.

j. Which of the following best summarizes the amount of scatter for balls lost on holes of various lengths?

1. The scatter was fairly uniform throughout, from beginning to end.

2. The number of balls lost varied more for shorter holes and less for longer ones.

3. The number of balls lost varied less for shorter holes and more for longer ones.

k. On average, how many shots did Tolme use per ball before losing it? [Hint: Use information from the Totals row.]

l. On average, how many yards did Tolme hit each shot?

Golfing across Mongolia: Use a scatterplot to track lost balls?

5.116 A hunting incident is defined as an occurrence when a person is injured as the result of a discharge of a firearm or bow and arrow while hunting or trapping. After a 12-year-old girl accidentally shot herself and died during deer season in 2004, a newspaper reported that "Experts say sport safer now than it's ever been," and listed numbers of hunting incidents in the state for the years 1994 to 2003.[50]

Year	Incidents
1994	104
1995	97
1996	85
1997	92
1998	91
1999	83
2000	69
2001	62
2002	68
2003	57

a. For that particular state and the time period specified, do the data represent a sample or the entire population?

b. Use software to produce a scatterplot of the data.

c. Use software to perform a regression of incidents on year, and state the regression equation.

d. Report the correlation.

e. Characterize the relationship as being strong and negative, weak and negative, weak and positive, or strong and positive.

f. Each year, the number of incidents goes down by about how many?

g. Use the regression equation to predict the number of incidents for 2004.

h. Your prediction from part (g) is probably not entirely correct. What is the approximate size of your prediction error?

i. To decide if hunting really has gotten safer, what additional information would be most helpful: time of day that the incidents occurred, the number of active hunters for each year, or whether the hunters each year included children?

5.117 A newspaper published box-office data on summer movies showing from the first weekend in May through Labor Day for several years running.

Year	Average Ticket Price	Gross (millions)	Attendance (millions)
1998	4.69	2,683	572
1999	5.08	3,201	630
2000	5.40	3,151	584
2001	5.65	3,450	611
2002	5.80	3,799	655
2003	6.03	3,875	643

a. Use software to regress each of the variables—average ticket price, gross, and attendance—on year. Which of the three variables is least accurately predicted from year?

b. Use the regression equations to predict average ticket price, gross, and attendance for 2004.

c. The industry's prediction for average ticket price in 2004 was $6.25. Tell whether your regression line prediction was higher than, lower than, or equal to the industry prediction.

d. The industry's prediction for gross in 2004 was $3,950 million. Tell whether your regression line prediction was higher than, lower than, or equal to the industry prediction.

e. The industry's prediction for attendance in 2004 was 632 million. Tell whether your regression line prediction was higher than, lower than, or equal to the industry prediction.

f. In fact, one of the three response variables is the product of the other two; which one is it?

g. Suppose we had a large sample of movie ticket prices for each year, and we regressed all the individual prices on year, instead of the average. Would the value of the correlation r increase, decrease, or stay the same?

5.118 A survey was taken of students at a large university in the fall of 2003; among other things, students were asked to report their weight and their age.

a. Use software to access the student survey data and produce a scatterplot of weights versus ages.

b. Report the correlation r and tell whether the relationship is strong and negative, weak and negative, weak and positive, or strong and positive.

c. It is possible that the relationship seen between weight and age is really due to gender. If male students tended to be older than female students, would the correlation between weight and age be positive or negative?

d. Separate the weights and ages for males and females, and produce correlations separately for males and females.

e. The relationship seems to be a bit stronger for one group—is it males or females?

f. The regression equation for females is approximately $Weight = 112 + 1(Age)$. This suggests that for every additional year, a female student will weigh how many more pounds?

g. The regression equation for males is approximately $Weight = 92 + 3.9(Age)$. Predict the weight of a 20-year-old male.

h. The standard deviation of male weights is 33 pounds. If we use the regression equation to predict a male's weight, given his age, is the typical prediction error less than 33, equal to 33, or greater than 33?

5.119 A survey was taken of students at a large university in the fall of 2003; among other things, students were asked to report how many credits they were taking and how many hours they had slept the night before.

a. Use software to access the student survey data. Find the correlation between credits and hours slept, and describe the relationship as strong and negative, weak and negative, nonexistent, weak and positive, or strong and positive.

b. Students completed this survey during their first week of classes. Explain how this might have an impact on the relationship between credits taken and hours slept.

Discovering Research: TWO QUANTITATIVE VARIABLES

5.120 Find a newspaper article or Internet report about a study that involves two quantitative variables. Besides providing a copy of the article or report, tell how the data were produced—was it an experiment or an observational study? Which variable is explanatory and which is response? Is there a positive or negative relationship between the two variables? Does the report suggest that the relationship is strong or weak? Tell if results are being reported for a sample or for an entire population, and the number of individuals studied, if known. Tell if there is reason to suspect bias that arises if the sample is not representative, or bias in the design for assessing the variables' values.

Reporting on Research: TWO QUANTITATIVE VARIABLES

5.121 Use results of Exercise 5.107 and relevant findings from the Internet to make a report on presidential IQs that relies on statistical information.

© Fred Prouser/CORBIS

Part III

Probability

Introduction to Probability

O ur ultimate goal in this book is to perform *statistical inference*: Use a sample statistic (such as sample mean or sample proportion) to draw conclusions about an unknown population parameter (like population mean or population proportion).

Political polls provide a straightforward example of the kind of reasoning involved in performing statistical inference. First, keeping in mind principles established in Part I, researchers would design and implement a survey to poll people about their views before a presidential election. Methods of Part II would indicate that the results (categorical) could be summarized with a percentage. Suppose that 54% in the *sample* of 1,000 voters intend to vote for a particular candidate, and we would like to decide whether or not the majority—more than 50%—of *all* voters intend to vote for that candidate.

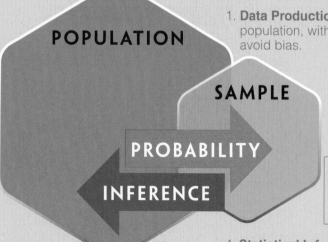

1. **Data Production:** Take sample data from the population, with sampling and study designs that avoid bias.

2. **Displaying and Summarizing:** Use appropriate displays and summaries of the sample data, according to variable types and roles.

3. **Probability:** Assume we know what's true for the *population*; how should **random** *samples* behave?

4. **Statistical Inference:** Assume we only know what's true about *sampled* values of a single variable or relationship; what can we **infer** about the larger *population*?

A way to tackle this problem would be to assume, at least temporarily, that 50% (no more) of all voters favor that candidate. Then we would determine how probable or improbable it would be to find as many as 54%, in a random sample of 1,000 voters, intending to vote for that candidate. If it turns out to be extremely unlikely to get a sample percentage as high as 54% when the population percentage is only 50%, then we'd conclude that the population percentage is *not* so low as 50%. It is almost certainly more.

The key to making a decision in our election example is finding the likelihood (or unlikelihood) of obtaining a certain sample percentage, given a claimed population percentage. Thus, it is a **probability** that brings about our final decision. Referring to our sketch of the "big picture," we are ready now to tackle the third major step in the four-step process of learning to perform statistical inference.

By the end of Part III, we will have established the necessary theory to evaluate probabilities like the one needed to solve the election example above. This theory is by no means simple, and must be developed gradually. We will begin by learning basic and more general rules of **probability** (the science), which is the formal study of *random* behavior. Next, we learn about the behavior of **random variables**, which are a particular kind of quantitative variable whose values are a result of some random process (such as random sampling). This leads to the chapter on **sampling distributions**, which tell the behavior of two random variables of particular interest—sample proportion and sample mean. By this time we will be able to determine, for a given population parameter, how the corresponding statistic behaves in the long run for random samples. This sets the stage for inference in Part IV, when we turn this knowledge around, and for a given statistic (such as sample proportion), determine what should be true about the corresponding parameter (such as unknown population proportion).

Now that we are about to begin our formal study of random behavior—the science of probability—it is a good time to remind ourselves of the importance of techniques learned in Part I, on data production. Randomization was the key to producing unbiased samples for observational studies, and the key to establishing causation in experiments. Now we should take note of the fact that the entire theory of probability developed in Part III, on which the applications in Part IV depend, requires that selections or assignments have been made at *random*.

In Part II, when we learned various display and summary techniques, we compartmentalized the topics according to number and type of variables involved. There were five basic situations, as illustrated in the diagram below: one categorical variable, one quantitative variable, one each categorical and quantitative, two categorical variables, and two quantitative variables.

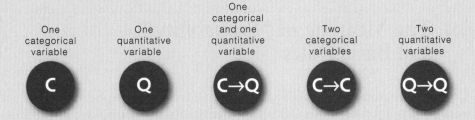

One categorical variable	One quantitative variable	One categorical and one quantitative variable	Two categorical variables	Two quantitative variables
C	Q	C→Q	C→C	Q→Q

In Part IV, when we learn to draw conclusions about the larger population, based on sample data, we will again handle one situation at a time, depending on number and type of variables. Now, in Part III, there will occasionally be subtle shifts from one to two categorical variables, or from quantitative to categorical variables and vice versa. Instead of focusing on number and type of variables, we concentrate, especially in Chapter 6, on the general rules that govern random behavior in *any* of these five situations.

CHAPTER 6

Finding Probabilities

How can we find probabilities of certain values or combinations of values for variables?

Can we determine probabilities in situations besides the usual dice rolls and card selections?

The Big Picture: LOOKING BACK

On page 9 we defined a *random occurrence* as one that happens by chance alone, and not according to a preference or an attempted influence. The science of probability is the formal study of the likelihood or chance of something occurring in a random situation.

In a more mathematical, rather than statistical, approach to probability, we define the **sample space** as the set of all possible outcomes in a random process.

The word **statistics** has two meanings: First, it refers to the science of producing, summarizing, and drawing conclusions from data. Secondly, *statistics* are summaries about sample data (as opposed to parameters, which refer to the entire population). Similarly, the word **probability** has two meanings: First, it is the scientific study of random behavior, an essential process on the way to performing statistical inference. Secondly, the *probability* of something is its chance of happening. For the purpose of our formal treatment of probabilities to come, we must scrutinize what we mean by the "probability" of an occurrence.

6.1 The Meaning of "Probability" and Basic Rules

Most people naturally have a sound, intuitive understanding of the meaning of the word *probability* if we say something like, "the probability of picking a heart from a deck of cards is 0.25" or "the probability of getting an A in this class is 0.25" or "the probability of this candidate being re-elected is 0.25." What most people do *not* realize is that these represent three very different ways of arriving at a probability. To discuss the formal meaning of a probability, we now present a few specialized vocabulary terms.

When a random process, such as picking a card, is being carried out, there exists a set of all the possible individual *outcomes*. If the random process is picking a card from a deck of 52, then there are 52 possible outcomes, corresponding to each card that may be selected. Often we are interested in some *event* made up of

226

several of these outcomes together. For example, we mentioned the event that a randomly chosen card was a heart: This event is made up of 13 of the 52 outcomes.

> *Definitions*   The **outcomes** in a random process are all the individual possible ways for it to turn out. An **event** is a set of one or more outcomes taken together.

Our intuition tells us that when there is a set of *equally likely outcomes*, then the probability of some event is the number of outcomes in that event, divided by the total number of outcomes. We know that a die has 6 faces, 3 of which show even numbers. The probability of getting an even number when a balanced die is tossed must be $3/6 = 0.5$. The principle of equally likely outcomes often applies when a *physical* selection is being made from a set of possibilities.

Our intuition also tells us that if we made a *long-run set of observed outcomes*, then the probability of an event is the number of those observed outcomes that make up the event, divided by the total number of observed outcomes. For example, the Centers for Disease Control and Prevention may obtain data on weights of a large number of Americans, then report that the probability of being overweight in America is 60%.

It is also possible to make a *subjective* assessment of a probability, measuring the extent to which a person believes an event will or will not happen. This method of assigning a probability may seem too arbitrary to form the basis of a legitimate scientific theory. In fact, our theory will still apply to subjective probabilities, as long as we insist that they conform to the basic rules that will be established in the next section. For example, if a student says that his chance of being chosen for a varsity sports team is 0.3, he cannot say that his chance of not being chosen is 0.8.

> *Definition*   The **probability** of an event is its chance of occurring, determined in one of the following ways:
>
> ■ the proportion of equally likely outcomes that comprise the event; or
>
> ■ the proportion of outcomes observed in the long run that comprised the event; or
>
> ■ the likelihood of occurring assessed subjectively.

EXAMPLE 6.1   THREE WAYS TO DETERMINE A PROBABILITY

Background: We consider three probability statements.

1. The probability of a randomly chosen card being a heart is 0.25.

2. A statistics professor reports that the probability of a randomly chosen student from her classes getting an A is 0.25.

3. A participant in a political discussion says he feels the probability of the incumbent candidate being re-elected is 0.25.

Question: Which way is each probability being determined: by the principle of equally likely outcomes, by observing a long-run set of outcomes, or by a subjective probability?

Continued

The **Big Picture:**

LOOKING AHEAD

In discussions to come, probabilities will be expressed in various forms: in decimal form (such as 0.25), in percents (such as 25%), and in the form of a fraction (such as 1/4). The words *chance* and *likelihood* are sometimes substituted for the word *probability*.

If students are curious about the word *odds*, this would be a good time to mention that odds are a ratio of occurrence to non-occurrence: The odds of getting a heart when picking a card from an ordinary deck are 1 to 3.

Response:

1. In the case of the randomly chosen card, the probability 0.25 is dictated by the principle of *equally likely outcomes*: We are physically selecting from 52 cards, of which 13 are known to be hearts, and so the probability of choosing a heart is 13/52 = 0.25.

2. In the case of the randomly chosen student, the professor does not assign a grade by picking randomly from a set of options, 25% of which are A's. Rather, the professor must be reporting her *long-run set of observed outcomes* (grade assignments), 25% of which were A's.

3. If the chance of a candidate being re-elected is claimed to be 0.25, it is not as if a card is randomly drawn from a set where 25% are labeled with that candidate's name. Nor is it the case that anyone has observed that in the long run, 25% of the time when that candidate runs for re-election, he is successful. Rather, the probability of 0.25 was based on a *subjective* assessment.

Practice: *Try Exercise 6.1 on page 236.*

It is worth noting at this point that the line between statistics and parameters is often blurred. Experts may look at weights of a large number of Americans and state that the probability of an American being overweight is 60%. Technically, 60% would be a statistic, because we don't really know the weights of all Americans. Nevertheless, this number may be treated as a parameter, assuming enough weights have been observed that 60% (approximately) really does hold for the entire population. This is suggesting that we have moved from the realm of the "short run" to that of the "long run," in the sense of interpreting a probability based on a long-run set of observed outcomes.

Recall the distinction made between a *statistic* that summarizes a sample and a *parameter* that summarizes the population. To avoid blurring the lines between statistics in the "short run" and parameters in the "long run," we will make use of many examples like card selections, dice rolls, and coin flips, where the physical circumstances and the principle of equally likely outcomes reassure us that a stated parameter really does correctly summarize the entire population of possible outcomes.

Much about probability can be understood using common sense—for example, the basic rules that we are about to develop are very intuitive. However, there are many situations for which intuition is inadequate or even downright misleading. Systematic application of the rules of probability can often accomplish what our intuition cannot. Clear definitions and notation are essential to this systematic approach.

The convention is to denote events with capital letters. For instance, we could write "H" for the event of getting a heart in a card selection. The probability of an event is denoted with a capital P, with the event following in parentheses. Thus, instead of writing "the probability that the card selected is a heart," we can simply write "$P(H)$." More explicit notation is sometimes helpful, and so we may also write "$P(Heart)$" instead. The "$P(\ \ )$" notation helps to streamline computations and focus on general laws that hold no matter what specific events we happen to be dealing with.

Students often have a misconception about probability as being difficult or mysterious. In fact, the basic rules about to be stated are quite intuitive. To stress their intuitive nature, we will precede each rule with an example that requires thinking about what should be true in a specific situation. Then we will state the rule as a generalization of this concept. Finally, another simple example will be worked through as an application to reinforce the rule just established. Also, we name the rules as straightforwardly as possible, so that in future references they will be more easily remembered.

Permissible Probabilities

EXAMPLE 6.2 INTUITING THE PERMISSIBLE PROBABILITIES RULE

Background: A six-sided die is rolled once.

Questions: What is the probability of rolling a nine? What is the probability of rolling a number that is less than nine?

Responses: Because it is impossible to roll a nine with one die, the probability must be zero: $P(N) = 0$. It is certain that the number rolled will be less than nine, so the probability must be 1: $P(L) = 1$. An event can't be any less probable than impossible, and it can't be any more probable than certain.

Permissible Probabilities Rule

The probability of an impossible event is 0, the probability of a certain event is 1, and all probabilities must be between 0 and 1.

EXAMPLE 6.3 APPLYING THE PERMISSIBLE PROBABILITIES RULE

Background: We consider the values -1, -0.1, 0.1, and 10.

Question: Which of these values is/are legitimate probabilities?

Response: The only legitimate probability is 0.1 because it is the only one that is between 0 and 1.

Practice: *Try Exercise 6.3(a) on page 237.*

Probabilities Summing to One

EXAMPLE 6.4 INTUITING THE SUM-TO-ONE RULE

Background: Consider the roll of an ordinary die.

Question: What do we get if we sum the probabilities of rolling a 1, a 2, a 3, a 4, a 5, and a 6?

Response: These represent all the possible outcomes, so their probabilities should sum to 1.

Sum-to-One Rule

The sum of probabilities of all possible outcomes in a random process must be 1.

EXAMPLE 6.5 APPLYING THE SUM-TO-ONE RULE

Background: A survey allows for three possible responses: *yes*, *no*, or *unsure*. We let $P(Y)$ denote the probability that a randomly chosen respondent answers *yes*, $P(N)$ the probability of answering *no*, and $P(U)$ the probability of answering *unsure*.

Question: What must be true about the probabilities $P(Y)$, $P(N)$, and $P(U)$?

Response: It must be true that $P(Y) + P(N) + P(U) = 1$.

Practice: *Try Exercise 6.5 on page 237.*

A pie chart helps depict the logic of this rule: If the possible outcomes are the possible values of the categorical variable represented, then the slices of various sizes, representing probabilities of those possible values, must amount altogether to the one entire pie. For this particular pie chart, 100% is the sum of the probabilities 42%, 49%, and 9%.

“Would you favor an amendment to the
U.S. Constitution saying that no state
can allow two men to marry each other
or two women to marry each other?”[1]

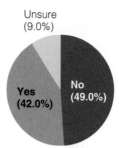

Notice that in the dice example, we were interested in a quantitative variable—the number rolled. In the survey example, we were interested in a categorical variable—whether the response was *yes* or *no* or *unsure*. Probability rules can be applied in situations involving either type of variable.

C   In a vast number of situations, we are simply interested in the probability that an event *does* occur, or that it *does not* occur: That is, we consider a categorical variable with just two possible values. In fact, the most commonly used theory for categorical variables (based on a “binomial” model, to be presented in Chapter 7) applies only in such situations: Either the variable’s value is in the category of interest or it is not. There are several different notations used for the negation of an event E, such as $\sim E$, E^C, $\overline{E}$, $\neg E$. In this book, we will simply write “not E” for the event that E does not occur.

Probability of "Not" Happening

In many useful applications, we need to know the probability that an event does *not* occur.

EXAMPLE 6.6 INTUITING THE "NOT" RULE

Background: A statistics professor reports that the probability of a randomly chosen student getting an A in her course is 0.25.

Question: What is the probability of not getting an A?

Response: Common sense tells us that if $P(A) = 0.25$, then $P(\text{not } A) = 1 - 0.25 = 0.75$. Alternatively, we could apply the Sum-to-One Rule: Getting an A or not getting an A constitute the only possible outcomes, and so their probabilities must sum to 1.

"Not" Rule (Law of Complements)

For any event A, $P(\text{not } A) = 1 - P(A)$. This is algebraically the same as $P(A) = 1 - P(\text{not } A)$.

This rule is commonly referred to as the "Law of Complements" because the "complement" of an event A is what we write as "not A."

EXAMPLE 6.7 APPLYING THE "NOT" RULE

Background: The probability of a randomly chosen American owning at least one TV set is 0.98.

Question: What is the probability of not owning any TV set?

Response: $P(\text{not } TV) = 1 - P(TV) = 1 - 0.98 = 0.02$. Notice that the event TV for owning *at least* one TV set lumps together people who own one, two, three, etc.

Practice: *Try Exercise 6.6 on page 237.*

Probability of One "Or" the Other for Non-overlapping Events

In some contexts, we need to find the probability of one event *or* another occurring.

EXAMPLE 6.8 INTUITING THE "OR" RULE FOR NON-OVERLAPPING EVENTS

Background: A statistics professor reports that the probability of a randomly chosen student in her class getting an A is 0.25, and the probability of getting a B is 0.30.

Continued

Question: What is the probability of getting an A or a B?

Response: Your instinct probably tells you to add the probabilities: $P(A \text{ or } B) = P(A) + P(B) = 0.25 + 0.30 = 0.55$.

To avoid being too hasty in stating a rule for the probability of one event *or* another happening, let us consider yet another example.

EXAMPLE 6.9 WHEN EVENTS OVERLAP

Background: A statistics professor reports that the probability of a randomly chosen student in her class getting an A is $P(A) = 0.25$, and the probability of being a female is $P(F) = 0.60$.

Question: What is the probability of getting an A or being a female?

Response: In this case, it would not be correct to simply add probabilities because the two events—getting an A and being a female—overlap, and we'd be counting the females who get A's twice.

The first in the pair of examples, about getting an A or a B, was simpler because these two events do not overlap: If one occurs, the other cannot, and vice versa. Such events are often referred to as *disjoint* or *mutually exclusive*. For now, we will state a rule that applies only in such special cases. It is sometimes called the "Addition Rule" for disjoint events because the word *or* entails adding probabilities.

> ### Non-overlapping "Or" Rule
> ### (Addition Rule for Disjoint Events)
>
> For any two *non-overlapping* events A and B, $P(A \text{ or } B) = P(A) + P(B)$.

Example TBP 6.1 on page 814 of the *Teaching the Big Picture* **(TBP)** *Supplement* illustrates an application of the Non-overlapping "Or" Rule that will be useful in finding *P*-values for two-sided hypothesis tests in Part IV.

EXAMPLE 6.10 APPLYING THE "OR" RULE FOR NON-OVERLAPPING EVENTS

Background: The probability of a purebred dog registered with the American Kennel Club being a Labrador Retriever is 0.158; the probability of being a Golden Retriever is 0.057.

Question: What is the probability of being either of the two types of retriever?

Purebred dogs as non-overlapping events

© Roger Tidman/CORBIS

Response: Because the dogs are purebred, we do not allow for the possibility that the breeds overlap, and we can simply add their probabilities: $P(L \text{ or } G) = P(L) + P(G) = 0.158 + 0.057 = 0.215$.

Practice: *Try Exercise 6.10(a) on page 237.*

Probability of One "And" the Other for Two Independent Events

Besides the probability of one event *or* another happening, we are often interested in the probability of one event *and* another happening. A series of examples will help us establish a rule for such probabilities. First, we need to define the concepts of *independence* and *dependence*.

Definitions Two events are **independent** if whether or not one occurs does *not* have an impact on the probability of the other occurring. They are **dependent** if whether or not one occurs *does* have an impact on the probability of the other occurring.

We will see that one circumstance that gives rise to some degree of dependence is when individuals or outcomes are removed from the set of possibilities when they are observed, called *sampling without replacement*. A less straightforward, but no less important, explanation for dependence is when the events of interest are naturally related to one another. A fairly intuitive example to be considered later on in this chapter has to do with the events "being male" and "having one's ears pierced." Because males are less likely than females to have their ears pierced, these two events are dependent. Much of statistics involves the exploration of relationships, and the concepts of independence and dependence are essential to our understanding of the relationship—or lack thereof—between two variables.

EXAMPLE 6.11 INTUITING THE "AND" RULE FOR INDEPENDENT EVENTS

Background: A balanced die is rolled twice.

Question: What is the probability of getting a one both times?

Response: One way to solve this is to note that the event of getting two ones is 1 out of the set of 36 equally likely outcomes that could be written $(1, 1), (1, 2), \cdots, (6, 6)$, so it has probability 1/36. Another way would be to note that on the first roll, the probability of getting a one is 1/6; on the second roll, the probability of getting a one is also 1/6. Therefore, 1/6 of 1/6 of the time, two rolls result in two ones, so the probability of two ones is $1/6 \times 1/6 = 1/36$.

Dice rolls are independent because we do not physically remove the spots on whatever face turned up, and we start over with the same set of possibilities on each roll. In contrast, selections of objects like coins from a pocket or people from a population are dependent if the objects are not replaced. They would be independent if we would replace the coin or person after each selection has taken place, called *sampling with replacement*.

EXAMPLE 6.12 INTUITING THE "AND" RULE: SAMPLING WITH REPLACEMENT

Background: In a child's pocket are two quarters and two nickels. He randomly extracts one of the coins and, after looking at it, replaces it before picking a second coin.

Question: What is the probability of getting a quarter both times?

Response: One way to solve this is to note that the event of getting two quarters is 1 out of the set of 4 equally likely outcomes that could be written QQ, QN, NQ, NN, and so it has probability 1/4. Another way would be to note that at the first selection, the probability of getting a quarter is 2/4 = 1/2; at the second selection, the probability of a quarter is also 2/4 = 1/2.

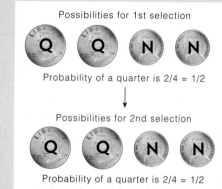

Possibilities for 1st selection

Probability of a quarter is 2/4 = 1/2

Possibilities for 2nd selection

Probability of a quarter is 2/4 = 1/2

So 1/2 of 1/2 of the time, there will be a quarter on both picks: The probability of getting a quarter both times is 1/2 × 1/2 = 1/4.

Before we express what we have learned in the form of a rule, let's consider another, slightly different, example that involves *sampling without replacement*.

EXAMPLE 6.13 WHEN SAMPLING IS DONE WITHOUT REPLACEMENT

Background: In a child's pocket are two quarters and two nickels. He randomly extracts one of the coins and, *without replacing it*, picks a second coin.

Question: What is the probability of getting a quarter both times?

Response: In this case, we can't simply multiply 2/4 by 2/4 to get 1/4 because of the fact that the successive selections were carried out *without replacement*: The probability of getting a quarter on the first selection is still 2/4, but once that quarter has been removed, the possibilities for the second selection consist of only one quarter and two nickels. If the quarter had not been removed, the possibilities for the second selection would have been two quarters and one nickel.

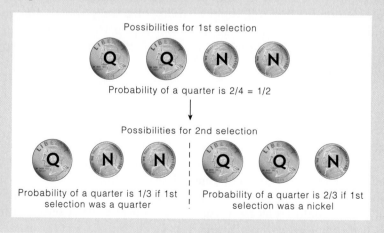

Possibilities for 1st selection

Probability of a quarter is 2/4 = 1/2

Possibilities for 2nd selection

Probability of a quarter is 1/3 if 1st   Probability of a quarter is 2/3 if 1st
selection was a quarter   selection was a nickel

In the first coin-selection example, where the child samples with replacement, the events "first coin a quarter" and "second coin a quarter" are *independent* because whether or not the first coin is a quarter has no impact on the probability of the second coin being a quarter. In the second example, where the child samples without replacement, the events "first coin a quarter" and "second coin a quarter" are *dependent* because whether or not the first coin was a quarter *does* affect the probability of the second coin being a quarter (less likely to get a quarter if one of the quarters has already been removed, more likely to get a quarter if a nickel was removed). For now, we will state a rule for the special case of *independent* events (whether or not one occurs has no effect on the probability of the other occurring). It is sometimes called the "Multiplication Rule" for independent events because the word *and* entails multiplying probabilities.

> ## Independent "And" Rule
> ## (Multiplication Rule for Independent Events)
>
> For any two *independent* events A and B, $P(A \text{ and } B) = P(A) \times P(B)$.

Our next example guides us to judge under what circumstances this rule applies.

EXAMPLE 6.14 APPLYING THE INDEPENDENT "AND" RULE

Background: Consider various situations where, at the outset, the probability of being female is 0.6 and the probability of being male is 0.4.

Questions:

1. Three out of the five people in a certain household—that is, 0.6—are female. If one of their names is selected at random, then replaced, and a second name is selected, what is the probability that the first is female and the second is male?

2. Three out of the five people in a certain household—that is, 0.6—are female. If one of their names is selected at random, and a second name is selected *without* replacing the first, what is the probability that the first is female and the second is male?

3. Three out of every five students—that is, 0.6—are female in a university with thousands of students. If one of the students is selected at random, and a second is selected without replacing the first, what is the probability that the first is female and the second is male?

Responses:

1. If two people are selected *with replacement* from five, where the proportion of females is 0.6, the probability of the first being female is, of course, 0.6. The second selection is independent because the first was replaced, and the probability of being male is $1 - 0.6 = 0.4$. Because of independence, the Independent "And" Rule applies: The probability of the first being female *and* the second being male is $0.6 \times 0.4 = 0.24$.

Continued

A CLOSER LOOK

As a household word, "and" suggests combining things together in a way that might be associated with addition. As far as probabilities are concerned, "and" requires multiplication, not addition. Stipulating the occurrence of yet another event reduces the overall chances of happening. Multiplying by a number that is generally less than 1 (and cannot be greater than 1) reduces the probability accordingly.

2. If two people are selected *without replacement* from five, where the original proportion of females is 0.6, the selections are not independent, and so the above rule does not apply. We will need to establish another, more general, rule to solve this kind of problem.

3. If two people are selected *without replacement* from thousands, where the proportion of females is 0.6, the selections are not completely independent. However, picking one student from thousands will have practically no effect on the probability of getting a male or female when a second student is selected. The Independent "And" Rule will give us a probability that is *approximately* correct, namely $0.6 \times 0.4 = 0.24$.

Practice: *Try Exercise 6.10(b,c) on page 237.*

We often would like to assume approximate independence when sampling without replacement, as we did in the third part of Example 6.14. The most commonly accepted rule of thumb is to require that the population be at least 10 times the sample size. This was *not* the case when sampling two from five people in a household, but it *was* the case when sampling two from thousands of students at a large university. In most real-life statistical applications, samples have been taken without replacement, whereas the needed theory—to be established in Chapter 7—requires independence. Thus, it is important to keep this rule of thumb in mind as we progress through the rest of the book.

> ## Rule of Thumb for Approximate Independence
>
> When sampling without replacement, random selections are approximately independent as long as the population is at least 10 times the sample size.

Examples TBP 6.2 and TBP 6.3 beginning on page 814 of the **TBP** *Supplement* utilize several of our basic rules, and demonstrate the power of the "Not" Rule.

See page 256 at the end of this chapter for a summary that includes the basic probability rules established in this section.

EXERCISES FOR SECTION 6.1

The Meaning of "Probability" and Basic Rules

Note: Asterisked numbers indicate exercises whose answers are provided in the Solutions to Selected Exercises section, on page 689.

*6.1 Probabilities are based on equally likely outcomes, a long-run set of observed outcomes, or subjective assessment. Tell which of these three applies in each of the following situations.

a. A football coach assesses an injured player as being "doubtful," meaning the probability is 0.25 that he will play in the upcoming game.

b. A coin is flipped to determine which football team will get the ball first; the probability is 0.50 that a given team will win the coin flip.

c. A particular football team has won four out of its five home games so far, so the coach states that the probability of winning a home game is 0.80.

6.2 Probabilities are based on equally likely outcomes, a long-run set of observed outcomes, or subjective assessment. Tell which of these three applies in each of the following situations.

a. A participant in a weekly poker game keeps track of how often he wins, and reports that his probability of winning is 0.2.

b. A poker player feels lucky, and states that his probability of winning the next game is 0.6.

c. The probability is 0.002 that a hand of five cards will produce a flush (all the same suit).

*6.3 A newspaper reports the probability that a certain airline's flights arrive on time.

a. Which of these is it: -6.86, -0.686, 0.686, or 6.86?

b. Was the probability based on equally likely outcomes, a long-run set of observed outcomes, or subjective assessment?

6.4 Investigators in a clinical trial use a random number generator to determine which treatment group each subject will be assigned to; in particular, there is a certain probability of being placed in the placebo group.

a. Which of these is it: 0.25, 2.5, or 25?

b. Was the probability based on equally likely outcomes, a long-run set of observed outcomes, or subjective assessment?

*6.5 In the American Nurses Association online Health and Safety Survey of 2001, several thousand nurses reported the usual length of the shift they worked at their main job.[2] What is the probability that one of these nurses worked a 12-hour shift?

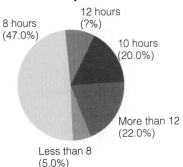

*6.6 In a large group of high school students, the probability of having siblings is 0.95. What is the probability of being an only child?

6.7 An estimated 1,690,000 children were runaways in 1999.[2]

a. For the runaway children in 1999, the probability of running away was 0.2 in the winter, 0.2 in the spring, and 0.2 in the fall. What was the probability of running away in the summer?

b. Altogether, about 1,676,200 of those children returned to their homes. What was the probability of returning?

*6.8 For each of these situations, tell whether selections are dependent, independent, or approximately independent.

a. Four of a company's 10 clients are selected at random and contacted to fill out a survey.

b. Four of a company's 50 clients are selected at random and contacted to fill out a survey.

6.9 For each of these situations, tell whether selections are dependent, independent, or approximately independent.

a. Each weekday evening a television viewer randomly selects one from five 6 o'clock news shows to watch.

b. A television viewer randomly selects one from five 6 o'clock news shows to watch Monday night; Tuesday night he randomly selects one from the remaining four shows to watch, and so on through Friday night.

*6.10 In a large group of Americans in 2001–2002, the probability of visiting the emergency room once in the past 12 months was 0.14, and the probability of visiting twice was 0.04.

a. What was the probability of visiting the emergency room one or two times?

b. For two randomly chosen Americans in 2001–2002, what is the probability that both visited the emergency room exactly once?

c. Explain why we cannot solve for the probability that two people chosen from the same household both visited the emergency room exactly once.

*6.11 In a large group of Americans in 2001–2002, the probability of visiting a doctor's office in the past 12 months was 0.8.

a. For two randomly chosen Americans in 2001–2002, what is the probability of at least one of them (either the first and not the second, or the second and not the first, or both) visiting a doctor that year?

b. Show how to get the answer to part (a) by subtracting from 1 the probability that neither of them visits a doctor.

6.12 The probability of an American adult flying a kite at least once in the year 2003 was

0.023. The probability of dancing at least once that year was 0.077. Why is it not correct to conclude that the probability of flying a kite or dancing was 0.100?

6.13 The health department in a certain county surveyed nearly 5,000 households in 2002 about health and sexual behavior. Of the respondents aged 18 to 29, the probability of being abstinent that year was 0.06; the probability of having one sex partner was 0.53, and the probability of having three or more sex partners was 0.23.[3]

   a. Tell whether the number 0.06 is a statistic or a parameter and whether it should be denoted $\hat{p}$ or p.

   b. Which was more common—having two sex partners or having three or more sex partners? Explain how you got your answer.

   c. Suppose two people living in the same household are picked from all those surveyed who were aged 18 to 29. Either find the probability that both of them had one sex partner, or tell why the probability cannot be found with the given information.

   d. Suppose two people are picked at random from all those surveyed who were aged 18 to 29. Either find the probability that both of them had one sex partner, or tell why the probability cannot be found with the given information.

6.2 More General Probability Rules and Conditional Probability

The most basic probability rules, established in the preceding section, are quite straightforward and intuitive. Most of the situations we considered involved just a single categorical variable, such as whether a selected individual was male or female, or what grade was received by a student. As we progress to the more general rules, we will add another dimension to our problems as we introduce a second variable to the situation, such as the *relationship* between a student's gender and what grade he or she received (both categorical variables).

Because most of the situations of interest now will involve two categorical variables, we will make use of two-way tables (as studied in Section 5.2) to keep track of the relevant information. To get a feel for the interplay between the two variables involved, we concentrate on certain aspects of the two-way table.

On page 816 of the **TBP Supplement**, we show how to illustrate the "and" and "or" probabilities by shading our two-way table with vertical and/or horizontal lines.

EXAMPLE 6.15 PARTS OF A TWO-WAY TABLE SHOWING "OR" AND "AND"

Background: A professor takes note of whether a student is male or female, and whether the student gets an A in her class or not. Gender would be the natural choice for explanatory variable, so she sets up a two-way table showing gender in the rows and grade in the columns.

Questions: What part of the table shows students who are female *or* get an A? What part shows students who are female *and* get an A?

Responses: The first two-way table below highlights the circumstance of being female *or* getting an A. The second highlights the circumstance of being female *and* getting an A.

	A	not A	Total
Female	Female or A		
Male			
Total			

	A	not A	Total
Female	Female and A		
Male			
Total			

Practice: *Try Exercise 6.14(a,c) on page 252.*

In the preceding section, we established a rule for the probability of one event *or* another occurring when those events could not both occur together, called the Non-overlapping "Or" Rule. We also established a rule for the probability of one event *and* another occurring when those events had no effect on each other, called the Independent "And" Rule. Our first goal in this section is to establish a general "Or" rule, for the probability of one event *or* another happening, where the events may overlap. Next, we'll establish a general "And" rule, for the probability of one event *and* another happening, where the events may be dependent. As before, the word "or" will entail addition and the word "and" will entail multiplication.

Some of the two-way tables presented in this chapter will be in terms of counts, like the tables encountered in Section 5.2. Others will be in terms of probabilities. Under the "equally likely outcomes" principle, the *probability* of a randomly sampled individual falling in the category of interest is just the count of individuals in the category of interest, divided by the total number of individuals.

EXAMPLE 6.16 A TWO-WAY TABLE FOR PROBABILITIES INSTEAD OF COUNTS

Background: A statistics professor sets up a two-way table of counts for all 2,000 students in her history of teaching, keeping track of gender and whether or not a student received an A. The table shows that 1,200 were female. Also, 500 of the students received A's. Altogether, 300 students were females who got A's.

Questions: What was the probability of being female? What was the probability of receiving an A? What was the probability of being female and receiving an A? How could these be shown in a table?

Responses: Based on the long-run set of observed outcomes, the probability of being female was 1,200/2,000 = 0.60; the probability of getting an A was 500/2,000 = 0.25; the probability of being female *and* getting an A was 300/2,000 = 0.15. In a table, we'd substitute probabilities for counts, with all four probabilities inside the table summing to 1.00. Note that the remaining probabilities could be filled in by subtraction.

	A	not A	Total
Female	0.15		0.60
Male			
Total	0.25		1.00

Practice: *Try Exercise 6.14(b,d) on page 252.*

Probability of One "Or" the Other for Any Two Events

In Example 6.8 on page 231, we concluded that to find the probability of getting an A or a B, the individual probabilities can simply be added. There were no complications because the two events were non-overlapping. On the other hand, to find the probability of getting an A or being a female in Example 6.9 on page 232, we could not simply add probabilities because those events do overlap, and we don't want to count the females with A's twice. In the next example, we will refer to the two-way table representation of the information provided in order to solve for the required probability.

EXAMPLE 6.17 INTUITING THE GENERAL "OR" RULE

Background: A statistics professor reports that the probability of one of her students getting an A is 0.25; the probability of being female is 0.60. If we want to find the probability of being a female *or* getting an A, we actually don't yet have enough information. In addition, we need to know the probability of being female *and* getting an A, which tells us something about how the two individual variables, gender and getting an A, are related. Suppose the probability of being female *and* getting an A is 0.15.

Question: What is the probability of being a female or getting an A?

Response: A two-way table displays the information provided. Note that we also include the information that the overall probability for all individuals together must be 1, according to the Sum-to-One Rule. Alongside is sketched a table for the probability sought, that of being a female *or* getting an A.

	A	not A	Total
Female	0.15		0.60
Male			
Total	0.25		1.00

	A	not A	Total
Female	P (Female or A)		
Male	= ?		
Total			

To find $P(Female$ or $A)$, we add $P(Female)$ and $P(A)$, then subtract the overlap $P(Female$ and $A)$. Thus, $P(Female$ or $A) = 0.60 + 0.25 - 0.15 = 0.70$.

	A	not A	Total
Female	0.60		
Male			
Total			

+

	A	not A	Total
Female	0.25		
Male			
Total			

—

	A	not A	Total
Female	0.15		
Male			
Total			

=

	A	not A	Total
Female	P (Female or A) = 0.60 + 0.25 – 0.15 = 0.70		
Male			
Total			

On page 816 of the **TBP** *Supplement*, we show how to establish the General "Or" Rule by solving for the probabilities of the individual cells, then summing probabilities for the relevant cells.

This example suggests a general rule for finding the probability of one event or another happening: Just add their individual probabilities and subtract the overlap so as not to count it twice. Traditionally, it is known as the **General Addition Rule**: It applies in general, whether or not the events are disjoint, and the word "or" entails the addition of probabilities.

The Big Picture:
LOOKING BACK

If A and B happen not to overlap, then P(A and B) will be zero and the General "Or" Rule reduces to the Non-overlapping "Or" Rule presented on page 232: P(A or B) = P(A) + P(B).

General "Or" Rule (General Addition Rule)

For *any* two events A and B, $P(A$ or $B) = P(A) + P(B) - P(A$ and $B)$.

EXAMPLE 6.18 APPLYING THE GENERAL "OR" RULE

Background: For a large group of high school students surveyed in Scotland and reported on in the *British Medical Journal* in 2000, the probability of engaging in illegal drug use was 0.28. The probability of carrying weapons was 0.20. The probability of engaging in illegal drug use *and* carrying weapons was 0.13.[4]

Question: According to the General "Or" Rule, what is the probability of engaging in illegal drug use or carrying weapons?

Response: Denoting the events as D for drug use and W for weapons, we have

$$P(D \text{ or } W) = P(D) + P(W) - P(D \text{ and } W) = 0.28 + 0.20 - 0.13 = 0.35$$

Practice: *Try Exercise 6.14(h) on page 252.*

Probability of Both One "And" the Other Event Occurring

By now we have realized our goal of establishing a general rule for the probability of one event *or* another happening. To realize our goal of establishing a general rule for the probability of one event *and* another happening, we must first explore probabilities of *dependent* events (as opposed to *independent* events, for which our Independent "And" Rule applied). To demonstrate the difference between independent and dependent events, we already considered a simple problem of picking two coins at random from two quarters and two nickels. If the sampling was done *with* replacement, then whether or not the second coin was a quarter was *independent* of whether or not the first coin was a quarter. If the sampling was done *without* replacement, then the events were *dependent*. In order to take into account the occurrence of the first event, on which the probability of the second event depends, we need the concept of a *conditional probability*.

Definition   The **conditional probability** of a second event, given a first event, is the probability of the second event occurring, assuming that the first event has occurred. We write $P(B \text{ given } A)$ to denote the conditional probability of event B, given that event A occurs.

EXAMPLE 6.19 INTUITING CONDITIONAL PROBABILITIES

Background: In a child's pocket are two quarters and two nickels. He randomly extracts one of the coins, and *without replacing it* picks a second coin.

Question: What is the probability of getting a quarter both times?

Response: The following sketch shows how to get the answer by multiplying relevant probabilities: We take the probability of the first coin being a quarter (6/12), times the conditional probability that the second coin is a quarter given that the first coin was a quarter (2/6). The probability of getting a quarter both times is

$$\frac{6}{12} \times \frac{2}{6} = \frac{2}{12} = \frac{1}{6}$$

Continued

On page 816 of the **TBP** *Supplement* we show how to find the probability in Example 6.19 by applying the principle of equally likely outcomes.

Pages 839 to 849 in the supplement material on binomial distributions present techniques for counting combinations, yet another approach to solving sampling-without-replacement problems: The probability of both coins being quarters is the number of ways to choose 2 from 2 quarters and 0 from 2 nickels, divided by the number of ways to choose 2 from 4 coins:

$$\frac{\binom{2}{2}\binom{2}{0}}{\binom{4}{2}} = \frac{1}{6}$$

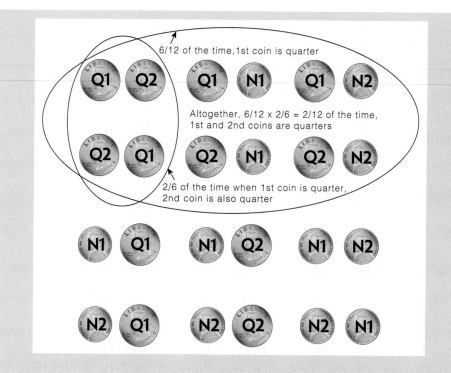

Notice that the second factor is not simply the probability of the second coin being a quarter. It is the probability of the second coin being a quarter, *given* that the first was a quarter. This is a conditional probability because it depends on the *condition* of the first selection being a quarter.

Before stating a formal rule, we look at another example involving a pair of events that our intuition will tell us must be dependent, not independent. The counts in the following table are representative of those for the students featured in our survey data file, but have been rounded for the purpose of working with "nicer" numbers.

EXAMPLE 6.20 INTUITING THE GENERAL "AND" RULE

Background: Surveyed students are classified according to the variable gender (female F or male M) and the variable whether or not they have ears pierced (E or *not* E).

	Ears Pierced	Ears Not Pierced	Total
Female	270	30	300
Male	20	180	200
Total	290	210	500

Questions: What are the following probabilities?

1. Probability of being male, written $P(M)$

2. Conditional probability of having ears pierced, given that a student is male, written $P(E$ given $M)$

3. Probability of being male and having ears pierced, written $P(M$ and $E)$

Responses:

1. The probability of being male is $P(M) = 200/500 = 0.40$.

2. The conditional probability of having ears pierced, given that a student is male, is $P(E \text{ given } M) = 20/200 = 0.10$. The sketch below stresses that once the condition is given that the student is male, the total number of possible outcomes is just 200. Of those 200, 20 have pierced ears.

$$P (E \text{ given } M) = 20/200 = 0.10$$

	Ears Pierced	Ears Not Pierced	Total
Female	270	30	300
Male	20	180	200
Total	290	210	500

3. Because 20 out of the 500 students are in both the "Male" row and the "Ears pierced" column, the probability of being male and having ears pierced is $P(M \text{ and } E) = 20/500 = 0.04$.

The last of these probabilities is perfectly correct, but for the purpose of stating a general rule, we now explore how to produce an expression for $P(M \text{ and } E)$ in terms of other probabilities. Recall our solution to Example 6.19, where coins were sampled without replacement: To find the probability of both coins being quarters, we took the probability of the first coin being a quarter, times the probability that the second coin is a quarter *given* that the first coin was a quarter. Similarly, we can find the probability of being male and having ears pierced by multiplying the probability of being male, times the conditional probability of having ears pierced, *given* that a student is male:

$$P(M \text{ and } E) = P(M) \times P(E \text{ given } M) = 0.40 \times 0.10 = 0.04$$

We can remind students that, according to the principle of equally likely outcomes, the probability of any event equals the number of outcomes in that event, divided by the total number of possible outcomes. For ordinary probabilities about students represented in the table, the total number of possible outcomes is 500. For conditional probabilities, the total number of possible outcomes is reduced to the number of outcomes possible under the given condition. In particular, when solving for a conditional probability *given that a student is male*, the total number of possible outcomes is only 200, not 500.

Now that we have reasoned through a couple of specific examples, we are ready to state a general rule that the probability of two events occurring is the probability of the first, times the probability of the second, given that the first has occurred. Traditionally, it is known as the General Multiplication Rule: It applies in general, whether or not the events are independent, and the word "and" entails the multiplication of probabilities.

General "And" Rule (General Multiplication Rule)

For *any* two events A and B, $P(A \text{ and } B) = P(A) \times P(B \text{ given } A)$.

EXAMPLE 6.21 APPLYING THE GENERAL "AND" RULE

Background: Polygraph (lie-detector) tests are often routinely administered to government employees or prospective employees in sensitive positions. The article "How Not to Catch a Spy: Use a Lie Detector" describes a National Research Council study in 2002, headed by

Continued

The Big Picture: A Closer Look

One of the most challenging aspects of a problem like our lie detector example is "translating" the *background* information—as well as the *desired* information—into the more standard language of probability, so that the rules can be applied properly. Conditional probabilities are described not only with the word "given," but also with such words as "if," "when," "for those who," or "out of those who."

Lie detector tests: high probabilities of two types of error

Stephen Fienberg from Carnegie Mellon University. The study found that lie detector results are "better than chance, but well below perfection." Typically, the test will conclude someone is a spy 80% of the time when he or she actually is a spy; but 16% of the time, the test will conclude someone is a spy when he or she is not. We'll assume that 10 of every 10,000 employees are actual spies.[5]

Questions: What are the following probabilities?

1. The probability that an employee is a spy and is "detected" to be one

2. The probability that an employee is not a spy and is nevertheless "detected" to be one

3. The overall probability that the polygraph "detects" an employee as being a spy

Responses: We will label the basic events as S (the employee is a spy), not S, D (the polygraph "detects" the employee as being a spy), and not D.

- Reporting that "the test will conclude someone is a spy 80% of the time when he or she actually is a spy" is telling us the *conditional* probability of the test concluding someone is a spy, *given* that he or she actually is a spy: $P(D \text{ given } S) = 0.80$.

- Similarly, "16% of the time, the test will conclude someone is a spy when he or she is not" tells us $P(D \text{ given not } S) = 0.16$.

- Assuming that "10 of every 10,000 employees are actual spies" can be written simply as $P(S) = 0.001$.

To find the first two probabilities, we just apply the General "And" Rule.

1. The probability that an employee is a spy and is detected to be one is $P(S \text{ and } D) = P(S) \times P(D \text{ given } S) = 0.001 \times 0.80 = 0.0008$

When we calculated the probability of a positive polygraph test to be 0.16064, most of the proportion (0.15984) comes from people who actually are not spies. Due to the relatively high probabilities of "detecting" non-spies and failing to detect actual spies, Fienberg and the National Research Council urged the government to "place high priority on the development of a new, significantly scaled-back program that focuses on the use of the polygraph as an interrogation tool and not for employee screening." The study panel also urged increased funding for the development of new techniques to replace the polygraph.

2. The probability that an employee is *not* a spy and is detected to be one is

$$P(\text{not } S \text{ and } D) = P(\text{not } S) \times P(D \text{ given not } S) = 0.999 \times 0.16 = 0.15984$$

Here we have also applied the "Not" Rule: If $P(S) = 0.001$, then $P(\text{not } S) = 0.999$.

3. Looking at a sketch of the two-way table helps us figure out the overall probability of being "detected" by the polygraph, $P(D)$, which may occur whether someone actually is *or* is not a spy.

	D	not D	Total
S	S and D		
not S	not S and D		
Total			

$D = (S \text{ and } D) \text{ or } (\text{not } S \text{ and } D)$, where those two events are non-overlapping

To find $P(D)$, the overall probability of being "detected" by the polygraph, we add the individual probabilities of being a spy and being detected, and of *not* being a spy and being detected. The Non-overlapping "Or" Rule can be applied because those two events do not overlap. $P(D) = P(S \text{ and } D) + P(\text{not } S \text{ and } D) = 0.0008 + 0.15984 = 0.16064$.

Thus, overall a bit more than 16% of the time, the test "detects" a spy.

Practice: *Try Exercise 6.16(a,b,d) on page 253.*

Before mechanically applying one rule after another to solve relatively complicated probability problems like the preceding lie-detector example, it is helpful to first get a feel for what kind of answer we should expect. In particular, when a final outcome is conditional on whether one or the other event occurred at an interim stage, we can think of the probability of the final outcome as a *weighted average* of the probabilities of occurring, given one or the other event occurred at the interim stage.

LOOKING AHEAD

Notice that Example 6.21 featured the possibility of two types of error being made: concluding that someone is a spy when in fact he or she is not, and failing to conclude that someone is a spy when in fact he or she is a spy. The probability of the first type of error in this example was 16%, and the probability of the second type of error was 20%. The example helps to remind us that probability problems by nature involve uncertainty. We have touched on these two types of error already in Part I, and will return to them again in Part IV.

Students Talk Stats

Probability as a Weighted Average of Conditional Probabilities

*F*our students are trying to make sense of the results in Example 6.21 on page 243: The probability $P(S)$ of a government employee being a spy is 0.001. The probability $P(D \text{ given } S)$ of a lie detector correctly detecting a spy is 0.80; the probability $P(D \text{ given not } S)$ of incorrectly identifying a non-spy as being one is 0.16. The overall probability of being identified as a spy by the lie detector is $P(D) = 0.16064$.

Adam: *"So I guess P(D given not S) and P(D) are the same but for some reason the first one was rounded."*

Brittany: *"Shouldn't P(D) be halfway between P(D given S) and P(D given not S)? Why isn't it the average of 0.80 and 0.16, which would be 0.48?"*

Students Talk Stats continued →

Students Talk Stats continued

Carlos: *"Since the vast majority aren't spies, we'd expect P(D) to be much closer to P(D given not S), which is 0.16."*

Dominique: *"So it's like a weighted average, and a lot less weight is given to the probability that comes from being a spy. The answer combines 0.001 of 0.80 with 0.999 of 0.16."*

Dominique has explained the outcome very well: 0.16064 is a weighted average of 0.80 and 0.16, much closer to 0.16 because the associated outcome is much more probable.

Practice: *Try Exercise 6.16(c) on page 253.*

On page 817 of the *TBP Supplement*, we show how the Rule of Conditional Probability makes intuitive sense when we look at a two-way table. On pages 817 to 818 we discuss the pros and cons of various display techniques, such as Venn diagrams and tree diagrams.

Conditional Probability in Terms of Ordinary Probabilities

The General "And" Rule, established on page 243 and applied in Example 6.21, can be re-arranged algebraically to yield a useful rule for how a conditional probability relates to ordinary probabilities. We simply take the rule $P(A \text{ and } B) = P(A) \times P(B \text{ given } A)$ and divide both sides by $P(A)$. Some go so far as to define conditional probabilities with this expression.

Rule of Conditional Probability

For any two events A and B,

$$P(B \text{ given } A) = \frac{P(A \text{ and } B)}{P(A)}$$

EXAMPLE 6.22 APPLYING THE RULE OF CONDITIONAL PROBABILITY

Background: Once again, we consider the lie-detector example, where the probability $P(S)$ of a government employee being a spy is 0.001. The probability $P(D \text{ given } S)$ of a lie detector correctly detecting a spy is 0.80; the probability $P(D \text{ given not } S)$ of incorrectly identifying a non-spy as being a spy is 0.16. We now know that the probability of being a spy and being detected is $P(S \text{ and } D) = 0.001(0.8) = 0.0008$. Also, the overall probability of a positive lie-detector test is $P(D) = 0.16064$.

Question: If the lie-detector indicates that an employee is a spy, what is the probability that he or she actually is one?

Response: Although we originally established the rule for the probability of a second event occurring, given that a first event has occurred, the rule also works for finding the probability that a first event *had* occurred, given that in the end a second event occurred:

$$P(S \text{ given } D) = \frac{P(D \text{ and } S)}{P(D)} = \frac{0.0008}{0.16064} = 0.00498$$

The Big Picture: A CLOSER LOOK

When the rule for conditional probability is applied to find the probability that a first event *had* occurred, given that a later event is known to have ultimately occurred (as in Example 6.22), the rule is known as *Bayes' Theorem*.

If the lie detector has identified an employee as being a spy, the probability is less than half of 1% that the employee actually is a spy! This surprising result comes about because the chance of being a spy (0.001) is so small compared to the chance of not being a spy. Also, because the polygraph is not perfect, of all the non-spies who are tested, an unfortunately high proportion (0.16) are erroneously "detected" as being spies.

Practice: *Try Exercise 6.16(e) on page 253.*

The Big Picture:
A CLOSER LOOK

Note the dramatic difference between $P(D$ given $S) = 0.80$ and $P(S$ given $D) = 0.00498$ in Example 6.22. A similar contrast arises in a medical context. Typically, the probability of testing positive, given that someone has a certain disease, is quite high, whereas the probability of having the disease, given that someone has tested positive, is quite low. There is a tendency for laymen and even physicians to confuse these two conditional probabilities, which are actually quite different.

Checking for Independence

One of the primary goals in statistics is to discover whether or not two variables are related. The concept of conditional probability, when combined with our Independent "And" Rule, will provide us with a test for independence.

First, we return to our gender/ears pierced example and think about how dependence results in conditional probabilities that are different from ordinary probabilities.

EXAMPLE 6.23 INTUITING CONDITIONAL PROBABILITIES WHEN EVENTS ARE DEPENDENT

Background: Surveyed students are classified according to the variable gender (female or male) and the variable whether or not they have ears pierced.

Questions:

1. Do you think having ears pierced or not depends to some extent on gender? Consider the overall probability of having ears pierced, compared to the probability of having ears pierced, given that a student is male. Do you think they should be approximately the same? If not, which should be lower?

2. What are the following probabilities?
   a. The probability of having ears pierced, written $P(E)$
   b. The conditional probability of having ears pierced, given that a student is male, written $P(E$ given $M)$

3. Does being male affect the probability of having ears pierced? If so, to what extent?

	Ears Pierced	Ears Not Pierced	Total
Female	270	30	300
Male	20	180	200
Total	290	210	500

Responses:

1. Because males are much less likely than students in general (and females in particular) to have their ears pierced, the probability of having ears pierced should be much lower if we are given the information that a student is male.

Continued

The Big Picture:
LOOKING BACK

It is important to be aware that a conclusion of dependence is not the same as a conclusion of causation. Statistical tests do provide us with a way of determining whether or not two variables are related, but issues of causation must be addressed by careful consideration of study design, as in Chapter 3.

Note that we sometimes refer to two specific *events* as being independent, and other times refer to two *variables* as being independent. When each variable allows for just two possibilities, then independent events and independent variables amount to the same thing, because as soon as one of four possible category combinations is determined, the remaining three follow by subtraction from the totals.

2. **a.** The probability of having ears pierced is $P(E) = 290/500 = 0.58$.
   b. In Example 6.20, we found the conditional probability of having ears pierced, given that a student is male, to be $P(E$ given $M) = 20/200 = 0.10$.

3. As expected, the probability of having ears pierced is much lower for males (0.10) than it is for students in general (0.58). Apparently, being male greatly reduces the probability of having one's ears pierced.

Next, we consider how ordinary and conditional probabilities compare when events are independent.

Notice that the table about gender and ear piercing was in terms of counts, whereas our table about gender and grade is in terms of probabilities. The rules are applied in the same way, but we no longer need to divide by the total count of students.

EXAMPLE 6.24 INTUITING CONDITIONAL PROBABILITIES WHEN EVENTS ARE INDEPENDENT

Background: Surveyed students are classified according to the variable gender (female or male) and the variable whether or not they received an A in their statistics course. Results are summarized in this table, which can be obtained from the information provided in Example 6.17 on page 240.

	A	not A	Total
Female	0.15	0.45	0.60
Male	0.10	0.30	0.40
Total	0.25	0.75	1.00

Questions:

1. Consider the overall probability of getting an A, compared to the probability of getting an A, given that a student is female. Do you think they should be approximately the same? If not, which should be higher?

2. What are the following probabilities?
   a. The probability of getting an A, written $P(A)$
   b. The conditional probability of getting an A, given that a student is female, written $P(A$ given $F)$

3. Does being female affect the probability of getting an A? If so, to what extent?

Responses:

1. Without any additional information, there is no obvious reason why the probability of getting an A should be affected by gender. $P(A)$ and $P(A$ given $F)$ should be about the same.

2. **a.** The probability of getting an A is $P(A) = 0.25$.
   b. The conditional probability of getting an A, given that a student is female, is $P(A$ given $F) = 0.15/0.60 = 0.25$.

3. For this group of students, the probability of getting an A is the same for students in general (0.25) as it is for females in particular (0.25). The probability of getting an A is apparently independent of gender.

The probability of getting an A turned out to be the same, whether or not we were given the information that a student was female. This confirmed our suspicion that the events were *independent*. In contrast, the probability of having pierced ears changed, if we were given the additional information that a student was male. This confirmed our suspicion that the events were *dependent*.

Now we are ready to formulate a rule, based on what was learned in these intuitive examples: If two events are independent, then the probability of one is the same, whether or not we are given the information that the other has occurred.

Simple algebra can show that $P(\text{not } B)$ and $P(\text{not } B$ given not $A)$ are the same when A and B are independent, different if they are dependent.

Rule of Independent Events

If two events A and B are independent, then $P(B) = P(B$ given $A)$.

In fact, implication also works in the opposite direction: If $P(B) = P(B$ given $A)$, then the events A and B must be independent.

Checking for Independence

If $P(B) = P(B$ given $A)$, then A and B are independent.

In addition, we can formulate results about *dependent* events: If two events are dependent, then the ordinary and conditional probabilities *differ*, and vice versa.

Notice that the above rule and check for independence can be used to solve two types of problems. First of all, if we know two events are independent, then we can use the rule to state that the ordinary and conditional probabilities must be the same. Alternatively, and more practically, we can compare the ordinary and conditional probabilities from a two-way table to determine whether two events are independent.

EXAMPLE 6.25 APPLYING THE CHECK FOR INDEPENDENT EVENTS

Background: Researchers have reason to suspect that Botox injections could decrease sweating.[6] We'll label the events B for getting Botox, D for decreased sweating.

Questions:

1. Do the researchers suspect that Botox and decreased sweating are independent or dependent?

2. If their hunch is right, which will be higher, $P(D)$ or $P(D$ given $B)$; or would these be the same?

3. Find $P(D)$ and $P(D$ given $B)$; are Botox and decreased sweating independent?

	Sweating Decreased	Sweating Not Decreased	Total
Botox	121	40	161
Placebo	40	121	161
Total	161	161	322

Continued

The Big Picture:
LOOKING AHEAD

For now, our claims of dependence must be limited to the sampled individuals. In Part IV, methods of statistical inference will let us decide if the degree of dependence in the sample is high enough to conclude that the variables in question are related in the larger population as well.

A table of expected counts was constructed for Example 5.14 on page 157 by making *proportions* equal; now we think of the same process in terms of *probabilities* being equal.

Responses:

1. The researchers suspect the two events to be *dependent*: They suspect a decrease in sweating may depend on Botox being injected or not.

2. If their hunch is right, there will be a higher probability of decreased sweating for subjects who receive Botox: $P(D$ given $B)$ will be higher than $P(D)$.

3. According to the table, $P(D$ given $B) = 121/161 = 0.75$, whereas $P(D) = 161/322 = 0.50$. The fact that the two are different tells us that, for these 322 subjects, decreased sweating does indeed depend on whether or not a subject received Botox injections.

Practice: *Try Exercise 6.16(f) on page 253.*

Counts Expected If Two Variables Are Independent

One of our main goals in Part IV will be to establish whether or not two variables are related. When the two variables are categorical, our method will be to consider the two-way table of counts that would be *expected* if the events involved were independent, and then compare to what was actually *observed* in reality. If the difference is too extreme, then we conclude that the variables are related (dependent). In fact, the table of counts expected if the explanatory and response variables were independent is identical to the table of counts expected if proportions in the responses of interest were the same for the various explanatory groups.

Recall our Independent "And" Rule, which stated that for independent events A and B, $P(A$ and $B) = P(A) \times P(B)$. This rule enables us to set up a table of what counts we expect would be in the various category combinations if two variables were independent.

EXAMPLE 6.26 FINDING COUNTS EXPECTED IF VARIABLES ARE INDEPENDENT

Background: A sample of 500 students consists of 300 females and 200 males. Altogether, 290 students have pierced ears and 210 do not.

Questions: What counts would we expect to see in the various gender/ear pierced categories, if gender and pierced ears were independent? How do these counts compare to the actual observed counts, shown in the table on the left?

Responses: To make our table conform better to the formulation of the rule, we will list students as M for male, not M for female, E for having ears pierced, and not E for not having ears pierced.

Counts Actually Observed

	E	not E	Total
not M	270	30	300
M	20	180	200
Total	290	210	500

Counts Expected If Gender and Pierced Ears Were Independent

	E	not E	Total
not M	?	?	300
M	?	?	200
Total	290	210	500

We can fill in the blanks by systematically applying the above rule to each combination of events: If gender and ears pierced are independent, then so are pairwise not M and E, not M and not E, and we would have

- $P(\text{not } M \text{ and } E) = P(\text{not } M) \times P(E) = \frac{300}{500} \times \frac{290}{500} = \frac{300 \times 290}{500}/500$, so the *count* in the first cell in the first column would be $\frac{300 \times 290}{500} = 174$.

- $P(M \text{ and } E) = P(M) \times P(E) = \frac{200}{500} \times \frac{290}{500} = \frac{200 \times 290}{500}/500$, so the *count* in the second cell in the first column would be $\frac{200 \times 290}{500} = 116$.

- $P(\text{not } M \text{ and not } E) = P(\text{not } M) \times P(\text{not } E) = \frac{300}{500} \times \frac{210}{500} = \frac{300 \times 210}{500}/500$, so the *count* in the first cell in the second column would be $\frac{300 \times 210}{500} = 126$.

- $P(M \text{ and not } E) = P(M) \times P(\text{not } E) = \frac{200}{500} \times \frac{210}{500} = \frac{200 \times 210}{500}/500$, so the *count* in the second cell in the second column would be $\frac{200 \times 210}{500} = 84$.

Counts Actually Observed

	E	not E	Total
not M	270	30	300
M	20	180	200

Counts Expected If Gender and Pierced Ears Were Independent

	E	not E	Total
not M	174	126	300
M	116	84	200
Total	290	210	500

Pairwise, the expected and observed counts are quite different: 174 versus 270, 116 versus 20, 126 versus 30, and 84 versus 180.

Practice: *Try Exercise 6.18(e–h) on page 253.*

Although the concepts of events being non-overlapping or being independent are completely different, students sometimes confuse the two. Examples TBP 6.4 and TBP 6.5 on page 819 of the ***TBP*** *Supplement* help to illustrate the distinction. Example TBP 6.6 on page 820 illustrates the difference between $P(B \text{ given } A)$ and $P(A \text{ given } B)$.

Example 6.26 suggests quite a difference between the observed and expected counts. This difference comes about because, in reality, the choice to have one's ears pierced has quite a lot to do with gender; the two variables are far from being independent. In Part IV, we will learn to summarize these differences with a single number, and use it to decide if we have evidence of a relationship between gender and ear piercings in the larger population of students. Because the expected counts will play such an important role in drawing general conclusions based on information in a two-way table, it is useful to note the pattern in the above calculations: Each expected count equals the row total, multiplied by the column total, divided by the table total.

$$\text{expected count} = \frac{\text{row total} \times \text{column total}}{\text{table total}}$$

See page 256 at the end of this chapter for a summary that includes the general probability rules established in this section.

EXERCISES FOR SECTION 6.2

More General Probability Rules and Conditional Probability

Note: Asterisked numbers indicate exercises whose answers are provided in the Solutions to Selected Exercises section, on page 689.

*6.14 Leon James and Diane Nahl posted results of a survey conducted in August 2000, where respondents were asked about various driving habits. This table classifies the 1,030 participants as being young (aged 15 to 24) or middle-aged/older, and whether or not they were in the habit of swearing at other drivers.

	Swear	Don't Swear	Total
Young	335	170	505
Middle-Aged/Old	306	219	525
Total	641	389	1,030

a. How many of the respondents were young *and* in the habit of swearing?

b. What was the probability (to three decimal places) of being young and in the habit of swearing?

c. How many of the respondents were young *or* in the habit of swearing?

d. What was the probability (to three decimal places) of a respondent being young *or* in the habit of swearing?

e. Find the probability (to three decimal places) that a randomly chosen respondent was "young" (aged 15 to 24).

f. Does your answer to part (e) suggest that the surveyed drivers were fairly representative of the general population of drivers in terms of age?

g. Find the probability (to three decimal places) that a randomly chosen respondent was in the habit of swearing at other drivers.

h. If we label the events as Y for being young and S for swearing, show that your answer to part (d) is $P(Y \text{ or } S) = P(Y) + P(S) - P(Y \text{ and } S)$.

i. Find the probability that a randomly chosen respondent was in the habit of swearing at other drivers, *given* that the respondent was young.

j. Were young drivers more likely or less likely to swear than drivers in general? Is the difference quite substantial or just a few percentage points?

k. The survey also gathered information about whether or not drivers were in the habit of making insulting gestures at others while driving. Tell whether the events "swears at other drivers" and "makes insulting gestures at other drivers" are likely to be independent, and whether they are likely to overlap.

6.15 Leon James and Diane Nahl posted results of a survey conducted in August 2000, where respondents were asked about various driving habits. This table classifies 1,086 participants according to type of car driven, and whether or not they were in the habit of making insulting gestures at other drivers. Notice that, unlike most tables encountered in this book, the explanatory variable (type of car) is indicated in columns and the response (gestures or not) is in rows.

	Economy	Family	Luxury	Sports	Truck	Utility	Van	Total
Gestures	79	65	16	58	42	32	8	300
No Gestures	281	170	45	95	77	79	39	786
Total	360	235	61	153	119	111	47	1,086

a. Before calculating any conditional probabilities, identify the types of cars whose owners you would suspect to have a tendency to make insulting gestures at other drivers.

b. For each type of car, find the (conditional) probability that surveyed drivers of that type of car make insulting gestures.

c. Comment on whether or not your suspicions in part (a) were correct.

d. To three decimal places each, find the probability of driving a van ($P(V)$), the probability of making insulting gestures ($P(G)$), and the probability of driving a van *and* making insulting gestures ($P(V$ and $G)$).

e. Check if $P(V$ and $G) = P(V) \times P(G)$ to see if the events V and G are independent, and explain the outcome.

f. You found $P(G$ given $V)$ in part (b). Check if $P(V$ and $G) = P(V) \times P(G$ given $V)$ and explain the outcome. (It may help you to work with the original fractions instead of converting to decimals.)

g. Which would you suspect to be higher: the probability of making insulting gestures ($P(G)$), or the probability of making insulting gestures *given* that someone drives a sports car ($P(G$ given $S)$)? Report the two probabilities to three decimal places.

h. Find the overall probability of driving an economy car, a family car, a luxury car, or a van.

i. Find the probability of making insulting gestures, given that someone drives an economy car, a family car, a luxury car, or a van.

j. Are drivers of economy cars, family cars, luxury cars, and vans less likely in general to make insulting gestures?

k. Did the surveyors allow for overlapping of categories, in cases where someone drives more than one type of car?

*6.16 According to exit polls from the 2000 presidential election, the probability of a voter supporting stricter gun control laws was $P(C) = 0.60$. The probability of voting for Bush, given that a voter supported stricter gun control laws, was $P(B$ given $C) = 0.34$, and the probability of voting for Bush, given that a voter did *not* support stricter gun control laws, was $P(B$ given not $C) = 0.74$.

a. Find $P(C$ and $B)$, the probability of supporting stricter gun control laws and voting for Bush.

b. Find $P($not C and $B)$, the probability of not supporting stricter gun control laws and voting for Bush.

c. Note that a majority of voters supported stricter gun control laws. Would we expect $P(B)$ to be closer to $P(B$ given $C) = 0.34$ or to $P(B$ given not $C) = 0.74$?

d. Find $P(B)$, the overall probability of voting for Bush, keeping in mind that a voter either supported gun control and voted for Bush *or* did not support gun control and voted for Bush.

e. Use the definition of conditional probability and your answers to parts (a) and (d) to find $P(C$ given $B)$, the probability of supporting stricter gun control laws, given that a voter voted for Bush.

f. Compare $P(C)$ and $P(C$ given $B)$, and discuss why they are quite different.

6.17 According to exit polls from the 2000 presidential election, the probability of a

voter self-identifying as gay (including lesbians) was $P(G) = 0.04$. The probability of voting for Bush, given that a voter was gay, was $P(B$ given $G) = 0.25$, and the probability of voting for Bush, given that a voter was not gay, was $P(B$ given not $G) = 0.50$.

a. Find $P(G$ and $B)$, the probability of being gay and voting for Bush.

b. Find $P($not G and $B)$, the probability of not being gay and voting for Bush.

c. Note that a minority of voters were gay. Would we expect $P(B)$ to be closer to $P(B$ given $G) = 0.25$ or to $P($given not $G) = 0.50$?

d. Find $P(B)$, the overall probability of voting for Bush, keeping in mind that a voter was either gay and voted for Bush *or* not gay and voted for Bush.

e. Use the definition of conditional probability and your answers to parts (a) and (d) to find $P(G$ given $B)$, the probability of being gay given that a voter voted for Bush.

*6.18 "Ultrasound Improves Stroke Blood Clot Clearance," reported on the FuturePundit website, reports: "Using ultrasound in combination with the drug t-PA can improve response to an ischemic stroke, according to a study involving 126 patients. This first-of-its-kind human trial compared the safety and efficacy of ultrasound and t-PA versus use of t-PA alone."[7]

This table is consistent with the study's reported results:

Observed	Clots Removed	Not Removed	Total
Just TPA	7	53	60
TPA & Ultrasound	25	41	66
Total	32	94	126

a. One way to assess the extent to which ultrasound enhances the standard clot-removal effectiveness of TPA is to compare $P(R$ given $T)$ (probability of clot removal with just TPA) and $P(R$ given $TU)$ (probability of clot removal with both TPA and ultrasound). First find $P(R$ given $T)$.

b. Next find $P(R$ given $TU)$.

c. Comment on whether the two probabilities you found in parts (a) and (b) are very different, slightly different, or identical.

d. Which of these is correct notation to use for the probabilities you found in parts (a) and (b): p_1 and p_2 or $\hat{p}_1$ and $\hat{p}_2$?

e. Another way to assess the extent to which ultrasound enhances the standard clot-removal effectiveness of TPA is to compare the numbers of cases with clots removed and not removed with each treatment method (7, 25, 53, and 41) with what the numbers would have been if the rate of clot removal were identical for the two treatment groups. The overall rate of clot removal was 32/126 = 0.25 and so the rate of not being removed was 0.75. To the nearest whole number, how many of the 60 subjects in the "Just TPA" group would have their clots removed, if their removal rate had been 0.25?

f. How many of the 66 subjects in the "TPA & Ultrasound" group would have their clots removed, if the rate had been 0.25? [Note that the total with clots removed should sum to 32.]

g. How many of the 60 "Just TPA" subjects would *not* have their clots removed, at a rate of 0.75?

h. How many of the 66 "TPA & Ultrasound" group would *not* have their clots removed, at the rate of 0.75? Make a table showing these four counts of what would be expected if the probability of cure were identical for both treatment groups.

Expected	Clots Removed	Not Removed
Just TPA		
TPA & Ultrasound		

i. Comment on whether the counts in your table are very different from, slightly different from, or identical to the counts that were actually observed.

j. Do the researchers seem justified in their claim that ultrasound enhances the standard clot-removal effectiveness of TPA?

k. Suppose ultrasound truly is helpful in attempting to remove clots with TPA. Discuss the potential harmful consequences of erroneously concluding that ultrasound is not helpful.

6.19 *Pediatrics* published an electronic article in September 2004, reporting that a "dry-on, suffocation-based, pediculicide lotion treats head lice without neurotoxins, nit removal, or extensive house cleaning." One group of subjects had lice treated with the new lotion only, while another group was treated with both the lotion and nit removal (a rather tedious process), and the following counts were observed.[8]

Observed	Cured	Not Cured	Total
Just Lotion	38	2	40
Lotion & Nit Removal	90	3	93
Total	128	5	133

a. One way to assess the extent to which nit removal improves the effectiveness of the lotion treatment is to compare $P(C$ given $L)$ (probability of cure with just lotion) and $P(C$ given $LN)$ (probability of cure with both lotion and nit removal). Find these two probabilities.

b. Comment on whether the probabilities you found in part (a) are very different, slightly different, or identical.

c. Which of these is correct notation to use for the probabilities you found in part (a): p_1 and p_2 or $\hat{p}_1$ and $\hat{p}_2$?

d. Another way to assess the extent to which nit removal improves the effectiveness of the lotion treatment is to compare the numbers not cured and cured with each treatment method (38, 90, 2, and 3) with what the numbers would have been if the rate of cure were identical for the two treatment groups. Use the formula

$$\text{expected count} = \frac{\text{row total} \times \text{column total}}{\text{table total}}$$

to calculate these expected counts, which represent the situation if type of treatment method had no impact whatsoever on whether or not the subject is cured of lice. (Report your answers to the nearest tenth—that is, to one decimal place.)

Expected	Cured	Not Cured
Just Lotion		
Lotion & Nit Removal		

e. Comment on whether the counts in your table are very different from, slightly different from, or identical to the counts that were actually observed.

f. Do the researchers seem justified in their claim that the lotion by itself is effective enough?

g. Suppose that lotion alone is actually effective, but a consumer with head lice erroneously believes that it is not. What would be the most obvious consequence of this mistake?

CHAPTER 6 SUMMARY

Probability tells us what to expect in the long run, assuming a context of randomness. In this chapter, we established rules to determine the probability of specific events. These rules are essential in order to expand our view in future chapters, and understand the more global behavior of variables like sample proportion and sample mean, which are subject to the laws of probability.

Probability Definitions and Rules

The **probability** of an event is its chance of happening. If there is a set of **equally likely outcomes**, then the probability of some event is the number of outcomes in that event, divided by the total number of outcomes. If we make a **long-run set of observed outcomes**, then the probability of an event is the number of those observed outcomes that make up the event, divided by the total number of observed outcomes. Probability may also be evaluated as a **subjective assessment**. In any case, probabilities must adhere to the following rules.

- **Permissible Probabilities Rule**
  The probability of an impossible event is 0, the probability of a certain event is 1, and all probabilities must be between 0 and 1.

- **Sum-to-One Rule**
  The sum of probabilities of all possible outcomes in a random process must be 1.

- **"Not" Rule (Law of Complements)**
  For any event A,

  $$P(\text{not } A) = 1 - P(A) \quad P(A) = 1 - P(\text{not } A)$$

  That is, the probability of not happening is one minus the probability of happening; the probability of happening is one minus the probability of not happening.

- **Non-overlapping "Or" Rule (Addition Rule for Disjoint Events)**
  For any two *non-overlapping* events A and B, the probability of one or the other is the sum of their probabilities:

  $$P(A \text{ or } B) = P(A) + P(B)$$

- **Independent "And" Rule (Multiplication Rule for Independent Events)**
  Two events are independent if whether or not one occurs has no impact on the probability of the other occurring. For any two *independent* events A and B, the probability of both happening is the product of their probabilities:

  $$P(A \text{ and } B) = P(A) \times P(B)$$

- **Rule of Thumb for Approximate Independence**
  When sampling without replacement, random selections are approximately independent as long as the population is at least 10 times the sample size.

- **General "Or" Rule (General Addition Rule)**
  For *any* two events A and B, the probability of one or the other is the sum of their probabilities, minus the probability that both happen:

  $$P(A \text{ or } B) = P(A) + P(B) - P(A \text{ and } B)$$

- **General "And" Rule (General Multiplication Rule)**
  For *any* two events A and B, the probability of both happening is the probability of the first, times the probability of the second, given that the first has occurred:

  $$P(A \text{ and } B) = P(A) \times P(B \text{ given } A)$$

- **Rule of Conditional Probability**
  For any two events A and B, the conditional probability of the second given the first is the probability of both, divided by the probability of the first (given) event:

  $$P(B \text{ given } A) = \frac{P(A \text{ and } B)}{P(A)}$$

- **Rule of Independent Events**
  If two events A and B are independent, then the probability of one is the same, whether or not the other event is given (has occurred):

  $$P(B) = P(B \text{ given } A)$$

- **Checking for Independence**
  If $P(B) = P(B \text{ given } A)$—that is, if the ordinary probability of one equals its conditional probability, given that the other has occurred—then the events A and B are independent.

CHAPTER 6 EXERCISES

Note: Asterisked numbers indicate exercises whose answers are provided in the Solutions to Selected Exercises section, on page 689.

Additional exercises appeared after each section: basic probability rules (Section 6.1) on page 236 and more general rules (Section 6.2) on page 252.

Warming Up: PROBABILITY

6.20 Of the 2,346 U.S. prisoners under sentence of death in 1990, 23 were executed. Of the 3,556 under sentence of death in 2002, 71 were executed.

 a. To the nearest hundredth, find the probability of being executed in each of those two years.

 b. Summarize the change in execution rates from 1990 to 2002.

 c. Are your probabilities in part (a) statistics $\hat{p}_1$ and $\hat{p}_2$ or parameters p_1 and p_2?

6.21 Based on information in the *U.S. Statistical Abstract*, this table shows populations of the various continents in the year 2000, and the projected proportion of world population for each continent in 2050.

	Africa	North America	South America	Asia	Europe	Oceania	Total
Millions in 2000	803	487	348	3,686	730	31	6,085
Projected Proportion in 2050	0.197	0.082	0.054	0.590	0.072	0.005	1.00

 a. The probability of being from one continent in particular is projected to increase substantially by 2050; which is it?

 b. The probability of being from one continent in particular is projected to decrease substantially by 2050; which is it?

*6.22 For each of the following variables, tell whether the various possible values may or may not overlap.

 a. The variable is medication taken for blood pressure, and the possibilities include beta blockers, calcium channel blockers, diuretics, and ACE inhibitors. [Hint: Physicians often prescribe combinations of these medications.]

 b. The variable is gender.

 c. The variable is instruments played by children in a gifted class, and the possibilities are piano, violin, flute, guitar, saxophone, other.

 d. The variable is which candidate a voter plans to cast his or her ballot for, in a presidential election.

6.23 For each of the following variables, tell whether the various possible values may or may not overlap.

 a. The variable is which parent a child lives with.

 b. The variable is which street drugs a teenager has tried.

 c. The variable is the subject of a student's first class Monday morning.

 d. The variable is highest degree attained: high school diploma, bachelor's, master's, or doctorate.

 e. The variable is degree attained: high school diploma, bachelor's, master's, or doctorate.

6.24 In the American Nurses Association (ANA) online Health and Safety Survey of 2001, nurses were first asked if they had been injured on the job in the past year. In a later question, they were asked if they had been physically assaulted at work in the past year.[9] If the questions had been asked in reverse order, would the percentage saying they'd been injured most likely be the same as, or less than, or greater than the original percentage?

More exercises for this chapter are featured in the *TBP Supplement* on pages 825 through 828. End-of-chapter activities are described on page 821.

6.25 Some nurses erroneously answered the question, "Of these injuries, how many did you report?" when in fact they had not been injured. The American Nurses Association had to make a choice whether or not to include such responses. At this point, were they mainly concerned with data production, displaying and summarizing, probability, or statistical inference?

6.26 When deciding on the ordering of questions in its survey, was the American Nurses Association mainly concerned with data production, displaying and summarizing, probability, or statistical inference?

6.27 The American Nurses Association can calculate the probability that a *surveyed* nurse had over 25 years of experience to be $1,189/4,507 = 0.26$.

a. If the ANA wants to draw conclusions about the probability that *any* nurse has over 25 years experience, is it mainly concerned with data production, displaying and summarizing, probability, or statistical inference?

b. If older nurses are less likely to complete an online survey than younger nurses, would 0.26 tend to be an overestimate or an underestimate for the probability that any nurse has over 25 years' experience?

Exploring the Big Picture: PROBABILITY

6.28 In the American Nurses Association online Health and Safety Survey of 2001, participants were asked, "In the past year, have you been physically assaulted at work?"; 3,915 of 4,722 nurses answered *no*. What is the probability that one of the surveyed nurses *had* been physically assaulted at work in the past year?

6.29 Of the estimated 105,397,000 popular votes cast in the 2000 presidential election, 50,992,000 were Democratic and 50,455,000 were Republican.

a. Does this problem involve a single variable or a relationship?

b. What was the probability of a vote being neither Democratic nor Republican?

*6.30 Assuming IQ scores have mean 100 and standard deviation 15, if we randomly sample 225 people's scores, the probability of their sample mean IQ being less than 99 is 0.16, and the probability of being greater than 101 is also 0.16. What is the probability of the sample mean being more than 1 point away from 100?

6.31 Weights of 1-year-old male children are fairly normal with mean 26 pounds, standard deviation 3 pounds. If we randomly sample nine 1-year-old boys, the probability of their sample mean weight being less than 23 pounds is 0.0015, and the probability of being greater than 29 pounds is also 0.0015. What is the probability of the sample mean weight being more than 3 pounds away from 26?

6.32 A newspaper reported on an AARP Singles Survey of men and women ages 40 to 69 conducted in June 2003, in which 3,501 singles were asked, "What for you is the desirable or preferred age of a dating partner?"[10] Results for men and women are shown in separate bar charts. We'll assume that the remaining proportions in each gender group had no preference.

a. Find the probability that a man picked at random from those surveyed would prefer a younger woman.

b. Find the probability that a woman picked at random from those surveyed would prefer an older man.

c. Suppose a man and a woman are picked at random from those surveyed. What is the probability that the man prefers a younger woman and the woman prefers an older man?

d. Suppose a man and a woman are picked at random from those surveyed. What is the probability that both of them prefer a partner of the same age?

e. Suppose a man and a woman are picked at random from those surveyed. What is the probability that the man prefers an older woman and the woman prefers a younger man?

f. Assuming the ages of the surveyed men and women are equally represented, does it seem likely that a randomly chosen man and woman will be compatible in terms of age preferences? Explain.

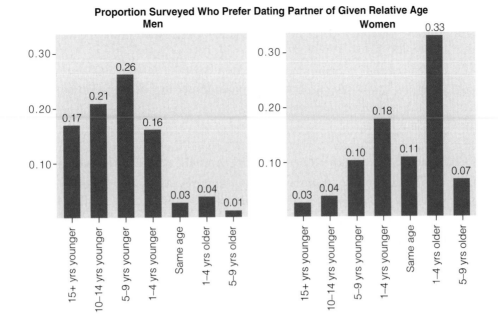

Proportion Surveyed Who Prefer Dating Partner of Given Relative Age

6.33 This table shows proportions of college freshmen in 1970 and in 2003 with various average grades in high school.

	Year 1970	Year 2003
A	0.196	0.466
B	0.625	0.483
C	0.177	0.005
D	0.003	0.001

a. Is the explanatory variable identified along the rows or the columns?

b. Discuss how the data provide evidence of "grade inflation."

c. In which one of the two years (1970 or 2003) were there students who were not accounted for in the four grade categories?

*6.34 "Taunts Cut Girls More Than Sticks or Stones" tells about a survey conducted in 2003 by the Girl Scouts Research Institute. "The institute surveyed 2,279 girls, only some of them Girl Scout members, in April, using a self-administered online questionnaire." The article includes a table entitled "What scares girls most?" that reports percentages in various categories for all the girls surveyed (aged 8 to 17).[11]

Being teased or made fun of	32%
Being attacked with a weapon (such as gun or knife)	28%
Being kidnapped	26%
Being forced to do something sexual	24%
Being gossiped about	24%
Getting into a car accident	21%
Getting a disease such as AIDS or cancer	21%
Being called names	18%
Natural disasters such as earthquakes or tornadoes	18%
Terrorist attacks	16%
War	15%

a. Explain how you know that some topics must overlap.

b. What could be the *minimum* percentage of girls who responded both "being gossiped about" and "being called names"?

c. If a girl is picked at random from those who completed the survey, what is the maximum possible probability that she feared either "being gossiped about" or "being called names" (or both)?

d. What could be the *maximum* percentage of girls who responded both "being gossiped about" and "being called names"?

e. If a girl is picked at random from those who completed the survey, what is the minimum possible probability that she feared either "being gossiped about" or "being called names" (or both)?

f. Do we have good reason to expect the various responses to be independent—for instance, is a girl just as likely to fear "being called names" whether she does or does not fear "being gossiped about"?

6.35 A *New York Times* article from June 1, 2004, entitled "New York Fiction, by the Numbers" tells about an undergraduate engineering student at Princeton who performed a statistical analysis of stories published in *The New Yorker* under two different editors. She focused on many variables, such as writer's gender, characters' religion, and main story topics.[12] The percentages of topics for all stories published between 1995 and 2001 were listed as follows:

Sex	47%
Children	26%
Travel	25%
Drugs	5%
Money	10%
Religion	9%
Illness	12%

a. Explain how you know that some topics must overlap.

b. What could be the *minimum* percentage of stories that were about both sex and drugs?

c. If a story is picked at random, what is the maximum possible probability that the story is about sex or drugs (or both)?

d. What could be the *maximum* percentage of stories that were about both sex and drugs?

e. If a story is picked at random, what is the minimum possible probability that the story is about sex or drugs (or both)?

f. If the student must decide in what order to arrange the topics in a bar graph, is she mainly concerned with data production, displaying and summarizing, probability, or statistical inference?

g. If the student wants to conclude that approximately 47% of all fiction stories are about sex, is she mainly concerned with data production, displaying and summarizing, probability, or statistical inference?

h. When the student decided what years to examine, was she mainly concerned with data production, displaying and summarizing, probability, or statistical inference?

6.36 A journal article reported in September 2003 that a Swiss dermatologist established a link between smoking and gray hair in women under 40, with results as shown in this table.[13]

	Gray	Not Gray	Total
Smoker	13	10	23
Nonsmoker	0	32	32
Total	13	42	55

a. Was this an observational study or an experiment?

b. For the women in this study, find the probability of having gray hair ($P(G)$), the probability of not smoking ($P(\text{not } S)$), and the probability of having gray hair or not smoking ($P(G \text{ or not } S)$).

c. Use your answers from part (b) to determine whether or not $P(G \text{ or not } S) = P(G) + P(\text{not } S)$.

d. For the women in this study, find the probability of having gray hair ($P(G)$), the probability of smoking ($P(S)$), and the probability of having gray hair or smoking ($P(G \text{ or } S)$).

e. Use your answers from part (d) to determine whether or not $P(G \text{ or } S) = P(G) + P(S)$.

f. Explain why the probability of one event *or* the other did equal the sum of probabilities in one case, but not in the other.

6.37 A study reported in February 2008 that an Australian dermatologist established a link between alcoholism/drug addiction and gray hair in people in their early thirties, with results as shown in this table.[14]

	Gray	Not Gray	Total
Drugs/Alcohol	104	92	196
Not Addicted	13	66	79
Total	117	158	275

a. Was this an observational study or an experiment?

b. For the people in this study, find the probability of having gray hair, $P(G)$, and the probability of being addicted to drugs or alcohol, $P(A)$.

c. How many people had gray hair *and* were addicted to drugs or alcohol?

d. What was the probability of having gray hair and being addicted to drugs or alcohol?

e. Show that the product $P(G)P(A)$ does not equal $P(G \text{ and } A)$.

f. Does suffering from alcoholism/drug addiction have an impact on the probability of having gray hair?

*6.38 A student is chosen at random from a large university. We consider the events N (the student's last name starts with the letter "N"), D (the student lives in the dormitories), and C (the student commutes by car).

a. Should the events N and D be non-overlapping, independent, both, or neither?

b. Should the events D and C be non-overlapping, independent, both, or neither?

*6.39 Let W be the event that someone in the United States is a woman of child-bearing age, and A be the event that someone in the United States has an abortion this year.

Which of the numbers 0.02 and 1.00 is $P(A \text{ given } W)$ and which is $P(W \text{ given } A)$?

6.40 This table reports the number of abortions, in thousands, for unmarried and married women in the United States in 1990 and in 2000.

	Unmarried	Married	Total
1990	1,268	341	1,609
2000	1,067	246	1,313

a. Is the variable "Year" considered to be quantitative or categorical?

b. For the abortions in 1990, find the probability of the woman being married.

c. For the abortions in 2000, find the probability of the woman being married.

d. From 1990 to 2000, did the probability of being married for women who had abortions decrease substantially, decrease slightly, increase slightly, or increase substantially?

6.41 In 2003, the probability of a worker in the United States being employed only part-time was 0.27. Some of the workers were part-time for economic reasons, such as slack work conditions, or inability to find full-time work. Others were part-time for noneconomic reasons, such as child-care problems, health problems, or being in school. Given that a worker was part-time, the probability of this being for noneconomic reasons was 0.85. What was the overall probability of a worker in the United States being employed part-time for noneconomic reasons?

6.42 The probability of a high school student in 2001 acknowledging having carried a weapon in the past month was 0.174. For those students who carried a weapon, the probability that it was on school property was 0.368. What was the overall probability of carrying a weapon on school property?

6.43 Suicides are most common between the ages of 5 and 54. This table shows the number of suicides and the number of total deaths in the United States in 2001 for various age groups.

	Suicides	Total Deaths
Age 5–14	189	7,094
Age 15–24	3,971	32,252
Age 25–34	5,070	41,683
Age 35–44	6,635	91,674
Age 45–54	5,942	168,065

a. Which variable was originally quantitative and transformed into categorical by grouping values?

b. For which two of these age groups is the probability of death by suicide the highest?

c. For which two of these age groups is the probability of death by suicide the lowest?

d. The five probabilities in this situation can be written as proportions; are they statistics or parameters?

e. Should the five proportions be denoted p_1 to p_5 or $\hat{p}_1$ to $\hat{p}_5$?

6.44 This table shows the numbers of college-aged and other Americans, in millions, who did or did not have health insurance in 2002.

	Age 18–24	Other	Total
Insured	19.3	223.0	242.3
Uninsured	8.1	35.5	43.6
Total	27.4	258.5	285.9

a. Is the explanatory variable shown in the rows or in the columns of this table?

b. Suppose a claim is made that college-aged Americans are twice as likely to be uninsured (for health) as others. State the relevant probabilities.

c. Tell whether or not the claim mentioned in part (b) is justified.

6.45 The U.S. Statistical Abstract published data on Advanced Placement (AP) exams taken in 2003, classified by gender and by subject. Some of the data are shown in this table.

a. To the nearest hundredth, what is the probability that an AP test in 2003 was taken by a male?

	Males	Females	Total
Calculus	115,587	97,207	212,794
English	149,331	255,896	405,227
Environmental Science	12,954	16,952	29,906
Statistics	29,078	29,152	58,230
…	…	…	…
Total	791,597	954,634	1,746,231

b. Is your answer to part (a) a statistic or a parameter?

c. If gender and subject were independent, then your answer to part (a) should also be the probability that a student taking the Statistics AP exam was male. What was the actual probability that a student taking the Statistics AP exam was male?

d. Was a student taking the Statistics AP exam more likely than a test-taker in general to be male, or less likely?

e. For which one of the subjects listed was the probability of being male much lower than it would have been if gender and subject were independent?

6.46 According to the *U.S. Statistical Abstract*, the probability of a high school student playing on a sports team was 0.65 for white males, 0.56 for white females, 0.68 for black males, and 0.40 for black females. Assume that the composition of high school students was 0.43 white males, 0.43 white females, 0.07 black males, and 0.07 black females.

a. Was playing on a sports team independent of race and gender group?

b. What was the overall probability of a high school student playing on a sports team?

c. Given that a high school student played on a sports team, what was the probability of being a white male?

*6.47 In 2001, the probability of a college student being male was 0.44. For males, the probability of being a part-time student was 0.38. For females, the probability of being a part-time student was 0.43.

a. To the nearest hundredth, find the probability of a college student in 2001 being part-time.

b. Which is taken to be the explanatory variable here—gender or type of student?

6.48 In 1988, the probability of a college student being part-time was 0.43. For part-time students, the probability of being male was 0.39. For full-time students, the probability of being male was 0.49.

a. To the nearest hundredth, find the probability of a college student in 1988 being male.

b. Which is taken to be the explanatory variable here—gender or type of student?

*6.49 An Internet review of home pregnancy tests reports: "Home pregnancy testing kits usually claim accuracy of over 95% (whatever that may mean). The reality is that the literature contains information on only four kits evaluated as they are intended to be used—by women testing their own urine. The results we have suggest that for every four women who use such a test and are pregnant, one will get a negative test result. It also suggests that for every four women who are not pregnant, one will have a positive test result."[15] For the purpose of this exercise, assume that the website's claims are correct (one in four pregnant women tests negative, one in four non-pregnant women tests positive).

a. Assume that 50% of all women who use these kits are actually pregnant. Use probability notation to denote and identify the probability of being pregnant, the probability of not being pregnant, the probability of testing positive if a woman is pregnant, and the probability of testing positive if a woman is not pregnant. Then find the overall probability of testing positive, and the probability of actually being pregnant, given that a woman has tested positive.

b. Assume that 80% of all women who use the kits are pregnant. Find the probability of being pregnant, given that a woman has tested positive.

c. Now assume that only 20% of all women who use the kits are actually pregnant. Find the probability of being pregnant, given that a woman has tested positive.

d. Discuss how the above results suggest that, if a person tests positive for a disease that is quite rare, there tends to be just a small probability of actually having the disease.

6.50 Gonorrhea is a common infectious disease. In 1999, the rate of reported gonorrhea infections was 132.2 per 100,000 persons. A polymerase chain reaction (PCR) test for gonorrhea is known to have sensitivity 97% and specificity 98%. A sensitivity of 97% means that if someone has the disease, the probability of correctly testing positive is 97%, so the probability of testing negative (when someone has the disease) is 3%. A specificity of 98% means that if someone does not have the disease, the probability of correctly testing negative is 98%, so the probability of testing positive (when someone does not have the disease) is 2%.

a. Based on the information provided, complete a two-way table where the total count is 100,000; counts having gonorrhea or not are shown along the rows, and counts testing positive or negative are shown along the columns.

b. If a randomly chosen person in the United States is routinely screened for gonorrhea, and the test comes up positive, what is the probability of actually having the disease?

c. The probability you found in part (b) applies to a *randomly* chosen person being screened. If someone is screened because of exhibiting symptoms, would the probability of having the disease be higher or lower than your answer to part (b)?

6.51 For the various organ transplants performed in the United States in 2003, the probability of surviving for at least a year was 0.98 for kidney transplants, and 0.88 for other transplants.

a. If exactly half of the transplants had been kidneys, what would be the overall probability of surviving for at least a year?

b. In fact, the probability of being a kidney transplant was 0.59. What was the actual overall probability of surviving any transplant for at least a year?

c. If there were approximately 26,000 organ transplants in 2003, about how many patients did not survive for one year?

d. Are 0.98 and 0.88 describing the population or a sample?

e. Should 0.98 and 0.88 be denoted p_1 and p_2 or $\hat{p}_1$ and $\hat{p}_2$?

6.52 This table shows probabilities of college freshmen in 1970 and in 2003 calling themselves liberal, being in favor of legalizing marijuana, and agreeing that capital punishment should be abolished, as reported in the U.S. *Statistical Abstract*.

	Liberal?	Legalize Marijuana?	Abolish Capital Punishment?
Year 1970	0.36	0.41	0.59
Year 2003	0.24	0.39	0.33

For which topic did the trend in probability of being liberal from 1970 to 2003 play a stronger role—attitude toward marijuana or attitude toward capital punishment?

*6.53 Let's suppose 100 students surveyed in 1970 and another 100 in 2003 said whether or not they were liberal, with counts corresponding to the probabilities reported in the preceding exercise.

Counts Observed

	Liberal	Not Liberal	Total
1970	36	64	100
2003	24	76	100
Total	60	140	200

Counts Expected If Year and Liberal or Not Were Independent

	Liberal	Not Liberal	Total
1970			100
2003			100
Total	60	140	200

a. Use the formula

$$\text{expected count} = \frac{\text{row total} \times \text{column total}}{\text{table total}}$$

to fill in the table of counts that would be expected if year and being liberal or not were independent.

b. By how many does each of the counts in your table differ from the corresponding observed count?

c. The actual surveys included hundreds of thousands of incoming freshmen at colleges across the country. If 100,000 freshmen had been surveyed each year instead of 100, then each of the

expected counts would differ from the corresponding observed count by how many?

6.54 Let's suppose 100 students surveyed in 1970 and another 100 in 2003 said whether or not they were against the death penalty, with counts corresponding to the probabilities reported in Exercise 6.52.

Counts Observed

	For Death	Against Death	Total
1970	59	41	100
2003	33	67	100
Total	92	108	200

Counts Expected If Year and Opinion about Death Penalty Were Independent

	For Death	Against Death	Total
1970			100
2003			100
Total	92	108	200

a. Use the formula

$$\text{expected count} = \frac{\text{row total} \times \text{column total}}{\text{table total}}$$

to fill in the table of counts that would be expected if year and opinion about the death penalty were independent.

b. By how many does each of the counts in your table differ from the observed counts?

c. If attitudes about the death penalty really didn't change from 1970 to 2003, would it be surprising to see counts as reported in the observed table, instead of as in the expected table (where probability of being against the death penalty is exactly the same in 1970 as in 2003)?

*6.55 This table provides information on probabilities of American households in 2001 owning a cat or not, and owning a dog or not.

	Cat	No Cat	Total
Dog			0.361
No Dog			0.639
Total	0.316	0.684	1.000

a. If dog and cat ownership were independent, what would be the probability of a household owning both a cat and a dog?

b. If dog-owning households were more likely than households in general to own cats, would the actual probability of owning both a cat and a dog be higher or lower than your answer to part (a)?

6.56 This table shows the number of homicide victims in the United States in 2001 for four gender/race groups, as well as the total numbers (in thousands) of the U.S. population in those groups.

	Homicide Victims	Total (in thousands)
White Male	8,254	113,796
White Female	3,074	116,705
Black Male	6,780	17,245
Black Female	1,446	19,002

In a statistics assignment, students are asked to report which race/gender combination had the highest probability of being a homicide victim, and which had the lowest. Which one of the four students' answers is correct?

Adam: The total number of victims is 116,705 for white females—that's the highest, and 17,245 for black males—that's the lowest.

Brittany: Those are total populations in the four groups. You have to look at the numbers of victims: highest for white males at 8,254 and lowest for black females at 1,446.

Carlos: You have to look at conditional probability of being a homicide victim, given that you're in a certain race/gender group. I calculate it to be highest for black males and lowest for white females.

Dominique: Are you supposed to divide or multiply to get conditional probabilities? Because I multiplied and the answer was highest for white males and lowest for black females.

6.57 This table classifies wartime veterans as of the year 2003 by their age and the war in which they served. The data are in thousands.

	Gulf War	Vietnam Era	Korean War	World War II	Total
Under 45	3,119	0	0	0	3,119
45–49	307	705	0	0	1,012
50–54	223	2,111	0	0	2,334
55–59	101	3,301	0	0	3,402
60–64	28	1,390	0	0	1,418
65 or over	6	703	3,580	4,370	8,659

a. Which of the variables could allow for overlapping categories: age, war served in, both, or neither?

b. If G represents the event of having served in the Gulf War, and U represents the event of being under 45, find $P(G$ given $U)$ and $P(U$ given $G)$.

c. What was the most probable age group for a Vietnam War veteran in 2003?

d. If a veteran was 65 or over, what was the most probable war in which to have fought?

e. Suppose a similar table is constructed in 2008. How would the probability of a veteran having fought in World War II compare to the probability in 2003: would it have increased, decreased, or stayed the same?

6.58 According to the *U.S. Statistical Abstract*, for the millions of illegal immigrants coming to the United States in 2000, the probability of coming *from* Mexico was 0.69. The probability of coming *to* Texas was 0.15.

a. If the event of coming to Texas and the event of coming from Mexico were independent, what would be the probability of an illegal immigrant coming from Mexico and to Texas?

b. Explain why those two events should be dependent, not independent.

c. The actual probability of coming from Mexico and to Texas is almost surely different from the one you calculated in part (a); is it higher or lower?

6.59 This table provides information on estimated probabilities of unauthorized immigrants in the year 2000 coming *from* China or elsewhere, and coming *to* California or elsewhere.

	Destination California	Destination Other	Total
Origin China			0.02
Origin Other			0.98
Total	0.32	0.68	1.000

a. If country of origin and state of destination were independent, what would be the probability of an unauthorized immigrant coming from China and to California?

b. If unauthorized immigrants from China were more likely than others to come to California, would the actual probability be higher or lower than your answer to part (a)?

6.60 Which is easier for the government to keep track of: origin and destination of illegal immigrants, or race and marital status of citizens?

Discovering Research: PROBABILITY

6.61 Find an article or report on a news website that uses the word "probability." Tell whether the probability is calculated as one of a set of equally likely outcomes, or based on a long-run set of observed outcomes, or made as a subjective assessment.

Reporting on Research: PROBABILITY

6.62 Use results of Exercises 6.14 and 6.15 and relevant findings from the Internet to make a report on driving in the United States that relies on statistical information.

Random Variables

What patterns are exhibited by variables in the long run, when their values are subject to the laws of probability?

Counting heads in coin flips: One of the simplest possible random variables

From the beginning, we have stressed the fact that statistics is all about variables, which are categorical or quantitative characteristics of individual people or things. In Part I (Data Production), we learned how to properly produce sample data about the variables of interest, with *random sampling* a top priority. In Part II, we learned how to summarize categorical or quantitative sample data with a proportion or a mean. Our ultimate goal in Part IV will be to perform statistical inference—such as draw conclusions about the unknown population proportion or mean, based on a sample proportion or sample mean that has actually been observed. As long as the sample has been taken at random, sample proportion and sample mean are what we call *random variables*.

> *Definition*   A **random variable** is a quantitative variable whose values are results of a random process.

Assuming the underlying sampling process is random, the theory of the behavior of sample proportions and sample means comes under the realm of probability—the formal study of random behavior. Thus, an important task in Part III is to apply the rules of probability, established in Chapter 6, to random variables, and learn what we need to know about their behavior. As for any quantitative variables, the key features that tell about their behavior are shape, center, and spread.

Sample proportion and sample mean are rather abstract random variables, because the individuals they represent are entire samples that are taken only theoretically, not in actuality. For example, we could think about all the different

The Big Picture:
LOOKING AHEAD

Although random variables such as sample proportion and sample mean are themselves quantitative, these variables tell the long-run behavior of both categorical and quantitative variables. The theory developed in this chapter will apply to any of the five possible situations for single variables and relationships discussed in this book.

values taken by the sample mean IQ of 100 people, if we were to randomly select 100 people over and over again from the general population. We would denote this random variable as $\overline{X} = \frac{1}{100}(X_1 + \cdots + X_{100})$, where each X_i itself is a random variable.

Such random variables are also rather complicated, because of all the possibilities that can arise when we take a random sample and find the proportion of values that happen to fall in a given category, or calculate the mean of the values that happen to be selected. Imagine all the possible sample mean IQs we could obtain in repeated random samples of 100 people, and their varying probabilities, depending on how usual or unusual each sample mean is.

Instead of trying to tackle these complicated random variables right away, we will begin by considering some very simple random variables, such as the number of tails that occur if a coin is flipped once. These simple random variables will serve as building blocks for the more complicated ones that we ultimately need to understand.

The Big *Picture:*

LOOKING AHEAD

The letter *Z* is specially designated for standardized *normal* random variables, to be discussed later in this chapter.

7.1 Discrete Random Variables

One of the simplest, most straightforward random processes is to toss a coin a certain number of times. The random variable we usually consider for this experiment is the number of heads or the number of tails appearing. In this and in many examples to follow, we use conventional notation for random variables, namely, capital letters such as X, Y, or Z.

EXAMPLE 7.1 A SIMPLE RANDOM VARIABLE

Background: Toss a balanced coin twice, and let the random variable X be the number of tails appearing.

Question: What are the possible values of X?

Response: X can take the values 0, 1, and 2.

Practice: *Try Exercise 7.1(a) on page 285.*

The random variable for number of tails, like many random variables of interest, has distinct possible values like the counting numbers. Such random variables are called *discrete*. In contrast, a random variable whose possible values cover an entire interval of possibilities, such as the height of a randomly chosen person, is called *continuous*. Ultimately, we will need the theory of continuous random variables to handle sample proportion and sample mean. For now, we begin with discrete random variables, which are much easier to grasp.

Definitions   A **discrete random variable** is one whose possible values are finite or countably infinite (like the numbers 1, 2, 3, . . .). A **continuous random variable** is one whose values constitute an entire (infinite) range of possibilities over an interval.

Probability Distributions of Discrete Random Variables

When we learned how to find probabilities by applying the rules in Chapter 6, we generally focused on just one particular outcome or event, like the probability of getting at least one tail when a coin is tossed twice, or the probability of getting an even number when a die is rolled. Now that we have mastered the solution of individual probability problems, we proceed to take a more global view of probabilities, by considering *all* the possible values of a discrete random variable, along with their associated probabilities. This list of possible values and their probabilities is called the *probability distribution* of the random variable.

> *Definition*   The **probability distribution** of a random variable tells all of its possible values, along with their associated probabilities.

A probability distribution tells us about the entire population of values of a random variable. For this reason, our examples tend to arise from situations like coin flips or census results, where we can know *everything* about the variable of interest.

We begin our exploration of probability distributions with some examples that demonstrate how the probability rules established in Chapter 6 apply to random variables.

EXAMPLE 7.2 THE PROBABILITY DISTRIBUTION OF A RANDOM VARIABLE

Background: The random variable X is the number of tails appearing in two tosses of a coin.

Question: What is the probability distribution of X?

Response: We first note that each of the four possible outcomes HH, HT, TH, TT shown below is equally likely, so each has probability 1/4. Alternatively, the Independent "And" Rule can be applied to find the probability of each outcome to be $1/2 \times 1/2 = 1/4$.

X takes the value 0 only for the outcome HH, so the probability that $X = 0$ is 1/4. X takes the value 1 for the outcomes HT or TH; by the Non-overlapping "Or" Rule, the probability that $X = 1$ is $1/4 + 1/4 = 1/2$. Finally, X takes the value 2 only for the outcome TT, so the probability that $X = 2$ is 1/4. The probability distribution is easily specified in a table that shows the possible values of X in the first row and their probabilities in the second row.

X = Number of tails	0	1	2
Probability	1/4	1/2	1/4

Practice: *Try Exercise 7.1(b) on page 285.*

We can alert students
that much of what is
done in this section
parallels what was done
for quantitative data sets
in Chapter 4. For
example, we displayed
the distribution of *sample*
values in a quantitative
data set with a histogram,
and summarized them by
reporting their mean and
standard deviation,
$\bar{x}$ and *s*. In this section, we
will display the
population of values of a
random variable with a
probability histogram,
and summarize with
population mean and
standard deviation,
μ and σ.

Producing a probability distribution table for the population of all possible values of a random variable is analogous to producing a data set of values for the sample. Once we have this information, the first thing to do is display it with a graph, namely a *probability histogram*.

> **Definition**   A **probability histogram** shows the possible values of a random variable along the horizontal axis. The vertical axis specifies the probability of the random variable taking a particular value (if the variable is discrete) or a value in a sub-interval (if the variable is continuous).

For a discrete random variable, technically only single point values are possible, but the histogram still has bars over intervals, often of width 1.

EXAMPLE 7.3 CONSTRUCTING A PROBABILITY HISTOGRAM

Background: The probability distribution of the number of tails in two coin flips was established in Example 7.2.

Question: What does the probability histogram for this random variable look like, and what does it suggest about shape, center, and spread?

Response: The horizontal axis shows the possible values 0, 1, and 2. Bars are sketched over these points with heights equal to the corresponding probabilities $\frac{1}{4}$, $\frac{1}{2}$, and $\frac{1}{4}$.

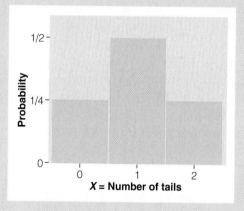

The shape is symmetric and single-peaked (unimodal). The histogram is centered over the value 1, and the typical distance (spread) from 1 would be less than 1 because half of the values don't differ from the mean at all, and the other half are 1 away from the mean.

Practice: *Try Exercise 7.3(b–d) on page 285.*

A random variable, *X*, is a quantitative variable whose values are subject to the laws of probability. The random occurrence that *X* takes a particular value *x* can be treated as an *event* that has a certain probability. Thus, we can write "$P(X = x)$" to denote "the probability that the random variable *X* takes the value *x*." The laws of probability established in Chapter 6 apply to such events, and they will provide us with a way of systematically exploring the behavior of random variables. In particular, our Permissible Probabilities Rule and Sum-to-One Rule, in the context of random variables, are stated as follows.

The convention is to use capital letters to denote random variables, and lowercase letters to denote their values. Because the distinction between the two is subtle, we will avoid confusing students with the use of notation like "$P(Z \leq z)$" when we do inference in Part IV.

Permissible Probabilities Rule and Sum-to-One Rule for Discrete Random Variables

Any probability distribution of a discrete random variable X must satisfy:

- $0 \leq P(X = x) \leq 1$ where x is any value of X
- $P(X = x_1) + P(X = x_2) + \cdots + P(X = x_k) = 1$, where $x_1, x_2, \cdots, x_k$ are all the possible values of X

The implications of the above requirements in terms of our probability histogram will play an important role in our understanding of continuous distributions, such as the normal distribution. Rather than focus on *heights* of histogram bars, as is usual for histograms representing sample data, we now focus on *areas* of the bars. If the horizontal intervals have width 1, then the Sum-to-One Rule states that the total area of all bars in a probability histogram must be 1.

EXAMPLE 7.4 THE SUM-TO-ONE RULE FOR A PROBABILITY DISTRIBUTION

Background: In Example 7.3, we sketched a probability histogram for the number of tails in two coin flips.

Question: What is the total area of the bars in the probability histogram?

Response: The total area is $1/4 + 1/2 + 1/4 = 1$.

Practice: *Try Exercise 7.3(a) on page 285.*

Recall that the *median* of a distribution is the middle, with half of the values below it and half above. The probability histogram represents probabilities by area, so the value of the random variable with half of the area to the left of it (and the other half to the right) must be the median.

EXAMPLE 7.5 THE MEDIAN OF A PROBABILITY DISTRIBUTION

Background: The random variable X for the number of tails in two coin flips is depicted in the probability histogram in Example 7.3 on page 270.

Question: What is the median value of X?

Response: The median is 1 because 1 is the value of X that divides the area of the histogram in half.

Practice: *Try Exercise 7.4(a) on page 286.*

Recall our discussions comparing mean to median in Part II: For a symmetric distribution, the two are equal. Whereas the median is seen as the equal-area point on a histogram, the mean can be interpreted as the balance point. In fact, statisticians' formula for the mean is equivalent to physicists' formula for the center of gravity. For symmetric distributions, the balance point on a histogram is the same as the equal-area point, so the mean and median are equal.

EXAMPLE 7.6 MEAN AND MEDIAN OF A SYMMETRIC PROBABILITY DISTRIBUTION

Background: The random variable X for the number of tails in two coin flips, depicted in the probability histogram in Example 7.3 on page 270, has a median of 1.

Question: How does the mean of X compare to the median?

Response: Because the probability histogram is symmetric, the mean must also be 1.

Practice: *Try Exercise 7.4(b) on page 286.*

The probability distribution for two coin tosses was simple enough to construct at once. For more complicated random processes, it is common to first construct an interim table of all the possible outcomes and their probabilities, then use the Non-overlapping "Or" Rule to condense that information into the actual probability distribution table.

EXAMPLE 7.7 AN INTERIM TABLE AND THE PROBABILITY DISTRIBUTION

Background: A coin is tossed three times. Let the random variable X be the number of tails tossed.

Questions: How can we use our knowledge of the possible outcomes in three coin flips to find the probability distribution of X? What are the shape and center of the distribution? What can we say about the spread?

Responses: First, we can specify all the possible outcomes (there are 8 of them), the number of tails X in each case, and the probability of each outcome. Because they are all equally likely, each has probability 1/8. Alternatively, by the Independent "And" Rule, each particular sequence of three coin faces has probability $1/2 \times 1/2 \times 1/2 = 1/8$.

Outcome	X = Number of tails	Probability
HHH	0	1/8
HHT	1	1/8
HTH	1	1/8
THH	1	1/8
HTT	2	1/8
THT	2	1/8
TTH	2	1/8
TTT	3	1/8

Next, we use the Non-overlapping "Or" Rule to assert that

$$P(X = 1) = P(HHT \text{ or } HTH \text{ or } THH) = P(HHT) + P(HTH) + P(THH)$$
$$= 1/8 + 1/8 + 1/8 = 3/8$$

Similarly,

$$P(X = 2) = P(HTT \text{ or } THT \text{ or } TTH) = P(HTT) + P(THT) + P(TTH)$$
$$= 1/8 + 1/8 + 1/8 = 3/8$$

The resulting probability distribution and accompanying histogram are shown here.

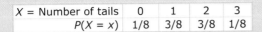

X = Number of tails	0	1	2	3
P(X = x)	1/8	3/8	3/8	1/8

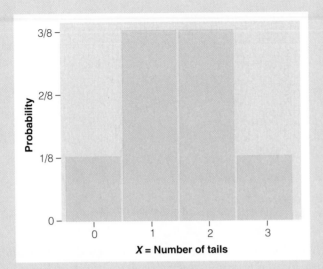

The shape, like that of the histogram for just two coin flips, is symmetric and single-peaked. The median, or equal-area point, is halfway between 1 and 2, or 1.5. This must also be the mean, because of symmetry. The typical distance of values from the mean value of 1.5 may be a bit less than 1 because 1 and 2 (which are more common) are only 0.5 away from 1.5, and 0 and 3 (which are less common) are 1.5 away from 1.5.

Practice: *Try Exercise 7.5 on page 286.*

The Big *Picture:*

LOOKING AHEAD

Later on in this section we will define the standard deviation as a way to measure the spread of a probability distribution by calculating the typical distance of its values from their mean.

   In Examples 7.2 and 7.7, we were able to specify the probability distributions ourselves, based on the physical circumstance of a coin toss. In most situations, the probability distribution is simply provided for us, as in the next example. We can assume that the probabilities have been established according to the principle of long-run observed outcomes.

EXAMPLE 7.8 A PROBABILITY DISTRIBUTION BASED ON LONG-RUN OBSERVED OUTCOMES

Background: The Census Bureau reports the following probability distribution of household size X in the United States for the year 2000. Values beyond 7 are not included because the probability of any more than 7 people, rounded to two decimal places, is zero. The distribution has been displayed with a probability histogram.

Continued

X	1	2	3	4	5	6	7
P(X = x)	0.26	0.34	0.16	0.14	0.07	0.02	0.01

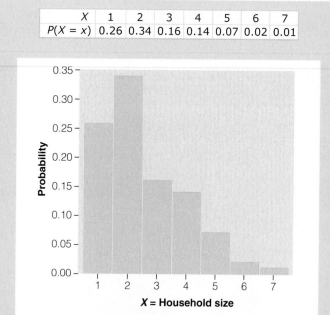

Question: What is the difference between the way these probabilities have been assessed and the way we assessed probabilities for situations involving coin flips?

Response: Coin flip probabilities are based on the known physical properties of a coin (there are two possible faces—heads and tails—and both are equally likely) whereas the household size probabilities have been based on sizes observed in the "long run" (over the entire United States in 2000).

Practice: *Try Exercise 7.7(b) on page 287.*

The following example serves to review the probability rules established in Chapter 6 and to confirm that the rules naturally apply to events about random variables.

EXAMPLE 7.9 RANDOM VARIABLES MUST OBEY PROBABILITY RULES

Background: Household sizes in the United States in the year 2000 have a probability distribution as shown in Example 7.8.

Questions:

1. How do the probabilities in the distribution of household size conform to the Permissible Probabilities Rule?

2. Without actually adding the probabilities, can you say what their sum is?

3. What is the probability of a household *not* consisting of just 1 person?

4. What is the probability that a household has fewer than 3 people?

5. Suppose a polling organization has sampled two households at random. What is the probability that the first has 3 people and the second has 4 people?

6. Again suppose two households have been sampled at random. What is the probability that one or the other has 3 people?

7. Suppose a marketing poll samples only from households with fewer than 3 people. What is the probability that a household with fewer than 3 people has only 1 person?

8. Suppose a polling organization has sampled two households at random. What is the probability that the second has 7 people, given that the first has 6 people?

Responses:

1. All the probabilities in the distribution of household size are between 0 and 1, and therefore conform to the Permissible Probabilities Rule.

2. According to the Sum-to-One Rule, the sum of all the probabilities must be 1.

3. By the "Not" Rule, the probability of not consisting of just one person is

$$P(X \neq 1) = 1 - P(X = 1) = 1 - 0.26 = 0.74.$$

4. Having fewer than 3 people is the same as having 1 or 2 people, and those two events are non-overlapping. Applying the Non-overlapping "Or" Rule, we have

$$P(X < 3) = P(X = 1 \text{ or } X = 2) = P(X = 1) + P(X = 2)$$
$$= 0.26 + 0.34 = 0.60$$

5. The Independent "And" Rule can be applied because there is virtually no dependence when sampling two households without replacement from millions. If we want to express our answer using probability notation, we must expand on our notation in order to represent two random variables, one (X_1) for the size of the first household selected, and the other (X_2) for the size of the second household selected.

$$P(X_1 = 3 \text{ and } X_2 = 4) = P(X_1 = 3) \times P(X_2 = 4) = 0.16 \times 0.14 = 0.0224$$

6. To find the probability that one or the other household has 3 people, we must apply our General "Or" Rule because the two events are overlapping: It is possible that *both* sampled households have 3 people, and the probability of that event should not be counted twice.

$$P(X_1 = 3 \text{ or } X_2 = 3) = P(X_1 = 3) + P(X_2 = 3) - P(X_1 = 3 \text{ and } X_2 = 3)$$
$$= 0.16 + 0.16 - (0.16 \times 0.16) = 0.2944$$

7. To find the probability that a household with fewer than 3 people has only 1 person, we can apply our Rule of Conditional Probability:

$$P(X = 1 \text{ given } X < 3) = \frac{P(X = 1 \text{ and } X < 3)}{P(X < 3)} = \frac{0.26}{0.26 + 0.34} = 0.43$$

8. We have already established that household sizes in a sample of two taken from the whole United States are independent, so the information that the first household has 6 people is superfluous when we want to know the probability that the second household has 7 people. According to the Rule of Independent Events,

$$P(X_2 = 7 \text{ given } X_1 = 6) = P(X_2 = 7) = 0.01$$

Practice: *Try Exercise 7.8 on page 287.*

The Big Picture: A Closer Look

If #5 had asked instead for the probability of one household having 3 people and the other 4 people, *in either order,* the answer would be 0.0224 + 0.0224 = 0.0448, by the Non-overlapping "Or" Rule.

The Mean of a Random Variable

In Section 4.3, we used the mean of a sample of quantitative values—their arithmetic average—to tell the center of their distribution. Summing all the values in a data set, and then dividing by how many there are, naturally gives more weight to values that occur more often. Similarly, we now tell the center of a probability distribution for a random variable by reporting its mean, which will be a *weighted average* of its values: The more probable a value is, the more weight it gets. For perfectly symmetric distributions, the mean is identical to the median, which is the point for which the probability is 50% of being below, and 50% above, that value. For left-skewed distributions, the mean is less than the median, and for right-skewed distributions, the mean is more than the median.

As always, it is important to distinguish between a concrete sample of observed values for a variable as opposed to an abstract population of all values taken by a random variable in the long run. Whereas we denoted the mean of a *sample* as $\bar{x}$, we now denote the mean of a *random variable X* as μ, because it summarizes the entire *population* of values of the random variable. If we are considering more than one random variable at a time, we can use a subscript to be more specific: μ_X is the mean of X and μ_Y is the mean of Y.

EXAMPLE 7.10 THE WEIGHTED AVERAGE OF A RANDOM VARIABLE'S VALUES

Background: Consider the probability distribution and histogram for year at school, where the population consists of undergraduate students enrolled in introductory statistics courses at a certain university.

X = Year	1	2	3	4
P(X = x)	0.08	0.60	0.24	0.08

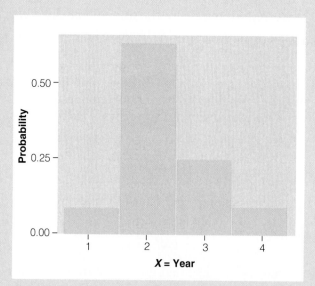

The median value is 2 because the 50% mark would occur somewhere within the group of 2nd-year students.

Questions: What is the weighted average of the four possible values, giving each value the weight of its probability? How does it compare to the middle (2.5) of the four numbers 1, 2, 3, 4, and to their median (2)?

Responses: If we weight each possible value with its probability, so that less probable values get less weight and more probable values get more weight, they average out to

$$1(0.08) + 2(0.60) + 3(0.24) + 4(0.08) = 2.32$$

This average is less than the middle of the four numbers (1, 2, 3, 4) because although 1 and 4 are equally likely, 2 is more likely than 3. It is more than the median (2) because of the right skewness.

Practice: *Try Exercise 7.9 on page 287.*

Motivated by Example 7.10, we define the mean of a random variable as a weighted average of its values: Each value is weighted with its probability of occurring.

> *Definition*   The **mean of a discrete random variable X**, whose possible values are $x_1, x_2, ..., x_k$, is
>
> $$\mu = x_1 P(X = x_1) + \cdots + x_k P(X = x_k)$$

EXAMPLE 7.11 CALCULATING THE MEAN OF A RANDOM VARIABLE

Background: Recall the probability distribution and histogram constructed for the random variable X = number of tails in two coin flips.

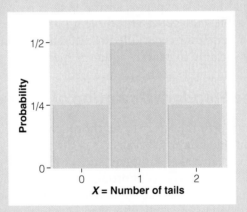

X = Number of tails	0	1	2
Probability	1/4	1/2	1/4

By "eyeballing" the distribution in Example 7.6 on page 272, we said that both the median and the mean must be 1.

Question: Does the formula given above confirm that the mean is 1?

Response: Yes: We simply calculate

$$\mu = (0 \times 1/4) + (1 \times 1/2) + (2 \times 1/4) = 0 + 1/2 + 2/4 = 1$$

Practice: *Try Exercise 7.10(g,h) on page 288.*

Besides intuiting the mean as a weighted average of possible values of a random variable, we can also picture the mean as the average of values in a "data" set that actually represents the entire population.

Technically, the equal-area point in Example 7.10 would fall somewhere between 2 and 2.5 on the horizontal axis, but we should keep in mind that the random variable is discrete, with only whole number values possible. For simplicity's sake, let's picture a population size of 100. Then the median would be found as the middle of 8 1's, 60 2's, 24 3's, and 8 4's: The middle number is a 2.

EXAMPLE 7.12 THE MEAN OF A RANDOM VARIABLE ANALOGOUS TO THE MEAN OF A DATA SET

Background: Consider again the probability distribution for year at school from Example 7.10 on page 276 where the population consists of undergraduate students enrolled in introductory statistics courses at a certain university. The mean of the random variable was found to be 2.32.

X = Year	1	2	3	4
$P(X = x)$	0.08	0.60	0.24	0.08

Question: According to the probability distribution, if there were exactly 1,000 students in the population, there would be 80 1st-year students, 600 2nd-year students, 240 3rd-year students, and 80 4th-year students. What is the average of 80 1's, 600 2's, 240 3's, and 80 4's?

Response: The average is [80(1) + 600(2) + 240(3) + 80(4)]/1,000 = 2.32, which is the same as the mean of the random variable.

Practice: *Try Exercise 7.10(i) on page 288.*

Example TBP 7.1 on page 830 of the *Teaching the Big Picture* **(TBP)** *Supplement* demonstrates that the "expected" value isn't necessarily a possible value for the random variable to take.

Especially in more mathematical contexts, the mean μ_X of a random variable X is also known as its "expected value" $E(X)$, in which case the standard deviation is denoted $SD(X)$. We do not "expect" a random variable to always—or even often—take its mean value. Rather, this is the average value of the random variable expected in the long run. When we take a weighted average of possible values that are whole numbers, the resulting mean is often *not* a whole number. Thus, especially for discrete random variables, it may be impossible for the variable to exactly equal its mean.

The Standard Deviation of a Random Variable

It is worth the effort to be thorough in discussing the spread of distributions of random variables, because it is the relatively small spread of sampling distributions that makes sampling such a powerful tool for performing statistical inference. For the sake of thoroughness, we will begin with two examples in which we actually calculate the standard deviation. Then we will focus on the more important skill of correctly interpreting the value of a standard deviation.

In Part II, we learned that the standard deviation of a data set measures the typical distance of sample values from their mean, by computing the square root of the average squared distance from the mean. Analogously, the standard deviation of a random variable is the square root of the average squared distance from the mean, where a weighted average is taken—heavier weights for more probable values, lighter weights for less probable values.

Just as for the mean, we must distinguish between a concrete sample of observed values for a variable as opposed to an abstract population of all values that a random variable can take in the long run. Whereas we denoted the standard deviation of a *sample* as s, we now denote the standard deviation of a *random variable X* as σ. Our notation reflects the fact that this standard deviation summarizes the behavior of the entire *population* of values for the random variable. Just as for means, notation for standard deviations can be more specific if appropriate, so that the standard deviation of X is sometimes written σ_X.

LOOKING BACK

As was pointed out in Section 4.4, the letter σ (pronounced "sigma") is the Greek lowercase *s*. Once again, we use a Roman letter for a statistic summarizing a sample, and a Greek letter for a parameter summarizing a population.

EXAMPLE **7.13** THE STANDARD DEVIATION AS THE TYPICAL DISTANCE FROM THE MEAN

Background: For the random variable X = number of tails in two coin flips, we found in Example 7.11 that the mean is 1.

Question: What is the standard deviation, or square root of average squared distance from the mean?

Response: Because the three possible values are 0, 1, and 2, their distances from the mean are $0 - 1$, $1 - 1$, and $2 - 1$. Instead of simply averaging the squared distances (whereby each would have weight $\frac{1}{3}$), we weight them with their respective probabilities $\frac{1}{4}$, $\frac{1}{2}$, and $\frac{1}{4}$, then take the square root:

$$\sigma = \sqrt{(0 - 1)^2\left(\frac{1}{4}\right) + (1 - 1)^2\left(\frac{1}{2}\right) + (2 - 1)^2\left(\frac{1}{4}\right)}$$

$$= \sqrt{\frac{1}{4} + 0 + \frac{1}{4}} = \sqrt{\frac{1}{2}} = 0.71$$

Practice: *Try Exercise 7.12(b) on page 288.*

The calculations in Example 7.13 are formalized in the following definition.

> *Definition* The **standard deviation of a discrete random variable X**, whose possible values are $x_1, x_2, ..., x_k$, is
> $$\sigma = \sqrt{(x_1 - \mu)^2 P(X = x_1) + \cdots + (x_k - \mu)^2 P(X = x_k)}.$$
> σ tells the typical distance of the random variable's values from their mean μ.

The Big Picture: A Closer Look

Just as many discrete random variables can never take their mean value, it may also be the case that there are no single values that fall exactly the "typical" distance away from the mean. In Example 7.13, none of the values falls exactly 1 standard deviation from the mean. We can think of the standard deviation, 0.71, as a way of "averaging" the distances $0 - 1$, $1 - 1$, and $2 - 1$, taking into account the probabilities of these distances.

EXAMPLE **7.14** USING THE FORMULA FOR STANDARD DEVIATION

Background: Example 7.8 on page 273 reported the distribution of household size in the United States.

X	1	2	3	4	5	6	7
$P(X = x)$	0.26	0.34	0.16	0.14	0.07	0.02	0.01

The mean household size can be calculated as $1(0.26) + 2(0.34) + 3(0.16) + 4(0.14) + 5(0.07) + 6(0.02) + 7(0.01) = 2.5$, rounded to the nearest tenth.

Question: How far do the values of X tend to be from their mean?

Response: We find the square root of the average squared deviation from the mean by calculating

$$\sigma = \sqrt{(1 - 2.5)^2(0.26) + (2 - 2.5)^2(0.34) + \cdots + (7 - 2.5)^2(0.01)}$$

$$= \sqrt{0.5850 + 0.0850 + 0.0400 + 0.3150 + 0.4375 + 0.2450 + 0.2025} = \sqrt{1.91} = 1.38$$

Practice: *Try Exercise 7.13(a) on page 288.*

We can point out to students that in Example 7.14, because of the skewness, there are *no* households with number of persons farther than 2 standard deviations below the mean, but there *are* households (those with seven people) with number of persons farther than 3 standard deviations above the mean. In contrast, we will see in a future section that random variables with a normal shape conform to the 68-95-99.7 Rule established for data sets in Part II.

More important than being able to calculate the standard deviation by hand is understanding what it is telling us.

EXAMPLE 7.15 INTERPRETING THE STANDARD DEVIATION OF A RANDOM VARIABLE

Background: The random variable X = household size has a mean of 2.5 and a standard deviation of approximately 1.4.

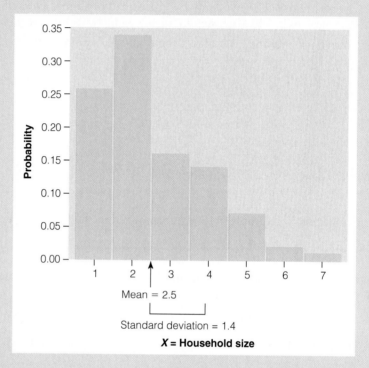

Question: How can the mean and standard deviation be interpreted in the context of the probability histogram for X?

Response: The mean household size, or "typical" value, is 2.5. Some household sizes, like 2 and 3, are quite close to this mean. Others, like 6 and 7, are farther away. The typical distance of household sizes from the mean 2.5 is the standard deviation, 1.4.

Practice: *Try Exercise 7.15(c) on page 288.*

Rules for the Mean and Standard Deviation of a Random Variable

Remember that our long-term goal is to make inferences about population parameters, based on sample statistics. For example, we may want to use the sample proportion of voters in favor of a presidential candidate to estimate the proportion of all voters in the population who are in favor of that candidate. Or we may want to use the mean weight of a sample of airline passengers to estimate the mean weight of all passengers. Such tasks can be accomplished if we know enough about how sample proportions or sample means tend to behave for a random sample taken from a population with a known proportion or mean. In this context, sample proportion and sample mean are random variables. The answer to the question, "How do they behave?" must be expressed in terms of the usual features that highlight the behavior of a quantitative distribution: shape, center (mean), and spread (standard deviation).

As we mentioned at the beginning of this chapter, sample proportion and sample mean are rather abstract random variables, because they represent theoretical behavior, if repeated random samples were taken. They are also rather complicated, because they are constructed as *combinations* of simpler random variables—namely, the proportions or means in individual samples. For example, sample mean IQ for repeated random samples of 100 people can be written as $\overline{X} = \frac{1}{100}(X_1 + \cdots + X_{100})$, where each X_i itself is a random variable. Therefore, we learn about the mean and standard deviation of sample proportion or sample mean by establishing rules for the behavior of means and standard deviations of random variables that are formed as *combinations* of simpler random variables.

Our first example shows what happens to the mean and standard deviation when a random variable is transformed by adding a constant, or multiplying by a constant.

Examples TBP 7.2 through TBP 7.5 starting on page 831 of the ***TBP Supplement*** explore rules for combinations of random variables where the underlying situation is the roll of a die.

EXAMPLE 7.16 INTUITING THE MEAN AND STANDARD DEVIATION OF A TRANSFORMED RANDOM VARIABLE

Background: Suppose a worker averages 36 hours a week, with a standard deviation of 4 hours.

Questions: If the worker is paid $10 an hour, what should be the mean and standard deviation of his weekly earnings? What should be the mean and standard deviation of his weekly earnings if he must subtract $30 a week for parking?

Responses: His weekly earnings should average $10(36) = $360, with a standard deviation of $10(4) = $40. If he must subtract $30 for parking each week, then he'd average $360 − $30 = $330 a week, still with standard deviation $40: The fixed payment for parking has no effect on the variability of his earnings.

If we let H denote his weekly hours worked, then his weekly earnings (minus parking) are written $-30 + 10H$ and the mean and standard deviation of his weekly earnings are

$$\mu_{-30+10H} = -30 + 10\mu_H = -30 + 10(36) = 330$$

$$\sigma_{-30+10H} = 10\sigma_H = 10(4) = 40$$

We can confirm that $\mu_D = 2\mu_X$ and $\sigma_D = 2\sigma_X$ in Example 7.17 on the following page by working "from scratch" with the distribution of D, which has values 2, 4, 6, 8, 10, 12, each with probability $\frac{1}{6}$.

Now we are ready to generalize our results with a rule.

We multiply by $|b|$ instead of b because standard deviation always measures the typical distance from the mean with a positive number.

Rule for Mean and Standard Deviation of a Transformed Random Variable

If X is a random variable with mean μ_X and standard deviation σ_X, then the new random variable $a + bX$ has mean and standard deviation
$$\mu_{a + bX} = a + b\mu_X$$
$$\sigma_{a + bX} = |b|\sigma_X$$

We confirm the sense of this rule by considering the mean and standard deviation for the roll X of a die, and for double the roll, $D = 2X$.

EXAMPLE 7.17 APPLYING THE RULE TO FIND THE MEAN AND STANDARD DEVIATION OF 2X

Background: X, the random variable for the number rolled on a single die, is known to have a mean of 3.5 and a standard deviation of 1.7.

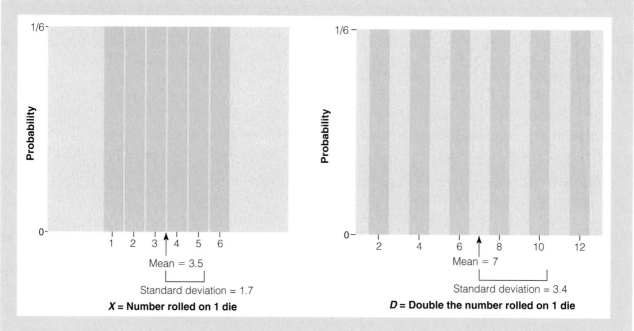

Question: What are the mean and standard deviation of double the roll on a die, $D = 2X$?

Response: We apply the rule, with $a = 0$ and $b = 2$:
$$\mu_{0 + 2X} = 0 + 2\mu_X = 2(3.5) = 7$$
$$\sigma_{0 + 2X} = |2|\sigma_X = 2(1.7) = 3.4$$

The distribution of X, the single roll, is shown on the left, and the distribution of $2X$, double the roll, is shown on the right. The histograms reinforce the fact that if the value of X is doubled, so are its center and spread.

Practice: *Try Exercise 7.18 on page 290.*

Another way that we can form new random variables is by taking the sum of other random variables. This will be an important step in constructing the random variable sample proportion or sample mean, based on counts or means occurring in individual samples.

EXAMPLE 7.18 INTUITING THE MEAN AND STANDARD DEVIATION OF A SUM OF RANDOM VARIABLES

Background: A coin is tossed once and X_1 is the random variable for the number of tails appearing. X_1 takes the values 0 and 1 each with probability 0.5. Its mean is 0.5 and its standard deviation is 0.5. The coin is tossed again and X_2 is the random variable for number of tails appearing on the second toss. X_2 also takes the values 0 and 1 each with probability 0.5. It also has mean 0.5 and standard deviation 0.5. Note that X_2 is *independent* of X_1 because what appears on one toss does not affect subsequent tosses.

The random variable $X_1 + X_2$ represents the number of tails appearing in two tosses of a coin. In Example 7.11 on page 277, we found the random variable $X_1 + X_2$ to have a mean of 1. In Example 7.13 on page 279, we found its standard deviation to be 0.7, to the nearest tenth.

Question: How do the mean and standard deviation of $X_1 + X_2$ (the number of tails in two flips) relate to the mean and standard deviation of X_i (the number of tails in one flip)?

Response: The mean of $X_1 + X_2$ is the sum of the means of X_1 and X_2, namely $0.5 + 0.5 = 1.0$. However, the standard deviation is *not* the sum of the standard deviations of X_1 and X_2. It is not $0.5 + 0.5 = 1.0$, but only 0.7. The distribution of X, the number of tails in a single coin flip, is shown on the left. The distribution of $X_1 + X_2$, the number of tails in two coin flips, is shown on the right. The new random variable obtained by summing the two individual random variables has a spread that is less than the sum of the individual spreads.

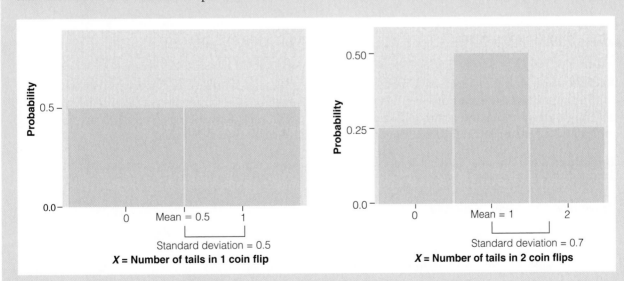

Practice: *Try Exercise 7.20 on page 290.*

Example 7.18 illustrated that the standard deviation of the sum of random variables was less than the sum of the standard deviations. This comes about because it is actually the *squared* standard deviations that are additive. For our coin-flip example, we have $\sigma^2_{X_1 + X_2} = 0.5^2 + 0.5^2 = 0.25 + 0.25 = 0.5$, so $\sigma_{X_1 + X_2} = \sqrt{0.5} = 0.7$.

We now generalize, stating a rule for the mean and standard deviation of the sum of any two random variables. It is important to note that our results for standard deviation hold only if the random variables are independent.

Rule for Mean and Standard Deviation of the Sum of Two Random Variables

If X_1 and X_2 are random variables, then the mean of their sum is the sum of their means:

$$\mu_{X_1+X_2} = \mu_{X_1} + \mu_{X_2}$$

If X_1 and X_2 are independent, then the variance (*squared* standard deviation) of their sum is the sum of their variances (*squared* standard deviations):

$$\sigma^2_{X_1+X_2} = \sigma^2_{X_1} + \sigma^2_{X_2}$$

To find the standard deviation of their sum, we must apply this formula, then take the square root:

$$\sigma_{X_1+X_2} = \sqrt{\sigma^2_{X_1} + \sigma^2_{X_2}}$$

We can confirm that $\mu_T = \mu_{X1} + \mu_{X2}$ and $\sigma^2_T = \sigma^2_{X_1} + \sigma^2_{X_2}$ in Example 7.19 by working "from scratch" with the distribution of T, which has values 2, 3, 4, 5, 6, 7, 8, 9, 10, 11, 12 with accompanying probabilities $\frac{1}{36}, \frac{2}{36}, \frac{3}{36}, \cdots, \frac{1}{36}$.

We confirm the sense of this rule by considering the mean and standard deviation for the roll X_i of a die, and for the total of two rolls, $T = X_1 + X_2$.

EXAMPLE 7.19 APPLYING THE RULE FOR THE SUM OF RANDOM VARIABLES

Background: X_1, the random variable for the number rolled on a single die, is known to have a mean of 3.5 and a standard deviation of 1.7. X_2, the random variable for the number rolled on a second die, also has a mean of 3.5 and a standard deviation of 1.7. The random variables X_1 and X_2 are independent because the roll of one die does not impact the roll of another die.

Question: What does the rule tell us about the mean and standard deviation of the total of two dice, $T = X_1 + X_2$?

Response: The mean of the sum is the sum of the means:

$$\mu_T = \mu_{X_1 + X_2} = \mu_{X_1} + \mu_{X_2} = 3.5 + 3.5 = 7$$

The variance of the sum is the sum of the variances:

$$\sigma^2_T = \sigma^2_{X_1 + X_2} = \sigma^2_{X_1} + \sigma^2_{X_2} = 1.7^2 + 1.7^2$$

and the standard deviation of the sum is the square root of the sum of the squared standard deviations:

$$\sigma_T = \sigma_{X_1 + X_2} = \sqrt{1.7^2 + 1.7^2} = \sqrt{2.9 + 2.9} = \sqrt{5.8} = 2.4$$

The distribution of X, a single roll, is shown on the left, and the distribution of $X_1 + X_2$, the total of two rolls, is shown on the right.

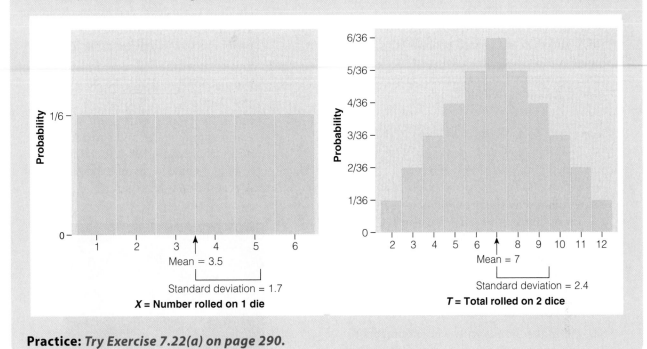

Practice: *Try Exercise 7.22(a) on page 290.*

Notice that the standard deviation for the total rolled on two dice (2.4) is less than just summing their individual standard deviations (1.7 + 1.7 = 3.4).

Discrete random variables are summarized on page 335 of the Chapter Summary.

EXERCISES FOR SECTION 7.1

Discrete Random Variables

Note: Asterisked numbers indicate exercises whose answers are provided in the Solutions to Selected Exercises section, on page 689.

*7.1 If an American woman is chosen at random, the number of days X that she typically works in a week is a random variable.

a. What are the possible values of X?

b. Suppose 50% of women work 5 days a week, 20% don't work at all, and the remaining 30% are evenly divided among the other possibilities. What would be the probability distribution of X?

7.2 If a high school student is chosen at random, the student's year of study X is a random variable.

a. What are the possible values of X?

b. Suppose the school has equal numbers of freshmen, sophomores, juniors, and

seniors. What would be the probability distribution of X?

c. If the school has fewer juniors and seniors, due to dropouts, would the mean of X be more than 2.5 or less than 2.5?

d. If we constructed a probability histogram for X, what would be the total area of its bars?

*7.3 Exercise 4.36 in Chapter 4 examined center, spread, and shape of the distribution of 12th-graders' answers to the question, "Compared with others your age throughout the country, how do you rate yourself on school ability?" Response options range from 1 (far below average) to 7 (far above average). We can approach the same information more formally by setting up a random variable X for the self-rating of a randomly chosen surveyed student. This table shows the possible values of X and their associated probabilities, consistent with results published by the Inter-university Consortium for Political and Social Research (ICPSR).[1]

X	1	2	3	4	5	6	7
Probability	?	0.02	0.04	0.34	0.24	0.28	0.07

a. Explain why the probability of a student rating himself/herself 1 must be 0.01. That is, show why $P(X = 1) = 0.01$.

b. Display the distribution with a probability histogram.

c. Tell whether the shape is symmetric, left-skewed, or right-skewed.

d. Fill in the blanks with whole numbers to report on center and spread: The mean of the distribution appears to be about _____ and the typical distance from this mean is about _____.

*7.4   In part (b) of Exercise 7.1 on page 285, we set up a probability distribution for the number of days per week worked by a randomly chosen American woman.

a. The median value of a random variable is the value for which at least 50% of the time, the random variable falls at or below it. If the distribution was as described on page 285, what would be the median number of days worked?

b. Explain why the mean would not equal the median for this random variable.

*7.5   Sickle-cell disease is a condition common in persons of African ancestry, where red blood cells contain an abnormal type of hemoglobin. Individuals whose cells produce both normal and abnormal hemoglobin are said to have "sickle-cell trait" and they are generally healthy. If both parents have sickle-cell trait, then each of their children has probability 0.25 of having the actual disease. Suppose two parents with sickle-cell trait have three children.

a. Using "D" to indicate having the disease and "N" for not having it, construct an

interim table of all possible outcomes, the accompanying values of the random variable X that equals the number of children with sickle-cell disease, and the associated probabilities. Then construct a probability distribution table for X.

b. Tell whether the shape of a histogram of the distribution would be skewed left, skewed right, or symmetric.

c. Fill in the blanks with whole numbers to comment on center and spread: The mean of X is somewhat less than _____ and the standard deviation of X is somewhat less than _____.

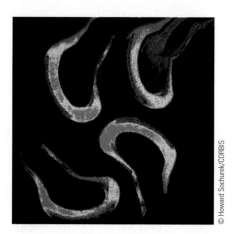

Sickle-cell disease: Laws of probability tell us what to expect.

7.6   Exercise 7.5 describes circumstances for children being born with sickle-cell disease if both of their parents have sickle-cell trait, when the couple has *three* children. Now, we let X be the number of children with sickle-cell trait when the couple has *two* children.

a. Construct an interim table for X, the number of children with sickle-cell disease.

b. Construct the probability distribution for X.

c. Find the mean of X by taking the appropriately weighted average of the numbers 0, 1, and 2.

d. Find the distances of the values 0, 1, and 2 from their mean, square them, and weight each with its respective probability. Then take the square root to find the standard deviation.

e. Fill in the blanks: When the parents both have sickle-cell trait and they have two children, on average the number of children with sickle-cell disease will be _____, and the numbers typically differ from this average by about

_____.

*7.7 A survey of households in a farming village in Nepal asked, "Do women from your household collect firewood?" and "How many women from your household collect firewood?"[2]

a. For which of these questions could researchers calculate a mean—the first, the second, both, or neither?

b. If we set up a probability distribution for the number of women in a household in that village collecting firewood, would it be based on the principle of equally likely outcomes, the principle of long-run observed outcomes, or a subjective assessment?

*7.8 Exercise 7.3 dealt with self-rated school ability X, on a scale of 1 to 7, for a large group of 12th graders. Based on the results, published by ICPSR, we present this probability distribution table:

X	1	2	3	4	5	6	7
Probability	0.01	0.02	0.04	0.34	0.24	0.28	0.07

a. What is the probability of a student rating himself or herself below average? That is, find $P(X < 4)$.

b. To find the probability in part (a), which rule was being applied—the Non-overlapping "Or" Rule or the Independent "And" Rule?

c. The probability of a student rating himself or herself above average is $P(X > 4) = 0.59$. Obviously it would be incorrect to state that the probability of *any* 12th grader being above average in school ability is 0.59. Does the problem arise because of working with a non-representative sample, or because of the way the values of X are assessed (by self-rating)?

d. If X_1 is the self-rating of a randomly chosen student, and X_2 is the self-rating of the student's best friend, explain why

we cannot use the Independent "And" Rule to find $P(X_1 = 1 \text{ and } X_2 = 1)$—that is, the probability that both of them rate themselves 1 (far below average).

e. If X_1 is the self-rating of a randomly chosen student, and X_2 is the self-rating of another randomly chosen student, find $P(X_1 = 1 \text{ and } X_2 = 1)$—namely, the probability that both of them rate themselves 1.

f. If two students are chosen at random, find the probability that at least one of them has a self-rating of 4—in other words, find $P(X_1 = 4 \text{ or } X_2 = 4)$, keeping in mind that the events $X_1 = 4$ and $X_2 = 4$ may overlap.

g. Given that a student rates herself above average, what is the probability that her self-rating is 7? In other words, find $P(X = 7 \text{ given } X > 4)$.

*7.9 If two brown-eyed parents, each with a recessive gene for blue eyes, have two children, the probability of having 0 children with blue eyes is $\frac{9}{16}$, the probability of having 1 child with blue eyes is $\frac{6}{16}$, and the probability of having 2 children with blue eyes is $\frac{1}{16}$. Use the fact that the mean is the weighted average of possible values to find the mean number of children with blue eyes.

*7.10 A survey taken in a farming village in Nepal asked, "How many bullocks does your household have?" and "How many cows does your household have?" The probability distributions of number of bullocks B and number of cows C shown here are consistent with the data published by the Inter-university Consortium for Political and Social Research (ICPSR).[3]

B	0	1	2	3
Probability	0.66	0.04	0.28	0.02

C	0	1	2	3	4
Probability	0.78	0.11	0.06	0.03	0.02

a. Draw a probability histogram for B.

b. Draw a probability histogram for C; discuss similarities and differences between the shapes of B and C.

c. Which are more likely to be kept in pairs—bullocks or cows?

d. Find the probability of no more than two bullocks, $P(B \leq 2)$.

e. Find the probability of no more than two cows, $P(C \leq 2)$.

f. If a household is chosen at random, can we say that the probability of owning no bullocks and no cows is $0.66 \times 0.78 = 0.51$? Explain.

g. Use the formula
$$\mu = x_1 P(X = x_1) + \ldots + x_k P(X = x_k)$$
to find the mean number of bullocks, μ_B, owned by a randomly chosen household.

h. Use the formula
$$\mu = x_1 P(X = x_1) + \ldots + x_k P(X = x_k)$$
to find the mean number of cows, μ_C, owned by a randomly chosen household.

i. Suppose the village had exactly 100 households. According to the probability distribution, 66 would have 0 bullocks, 4 would have 1, 28 would have 2, and 2 would have 3. Find the average of 66 0's, 4 1's, 28 2's, and 2 3's, and confirm that this average equals the mean.

j. What is the probability that the random variable for number of cows owned exactly equals its mean value?

7.11 The mean number of cows in a household in a particular Nepal village was calculated in part (h) of Exercise 7.10. According to the probability distribution, if the village had exactly 100 households, 78 would have 0 cows, 11 would have 1 cow, 6 would have 2 cows, 3 would have 3 cows, and 2 would have 4 cows. Find the average of 78 0's, 11 1's, 6 2's, 3 3's, and 2 4's, and confirm that this average equals the mean.

*7.12 The random variable X for number of heads in a single coin toss has possible values 0 and 1, each with probability 0.5.

a. Explain why 0.5 is the mean of X.

b. Each of the two values of X has a distance of 0.5 away from the mean. Find the weighted average of the two squared distances from the mean, weighting each with probability 0.5, and take the square root to find the standard deviation of X.

c. Explain why your answer to part (b) makes sense as a measure of the typical distance of values from their mean.

*7.13 Exercise 7.10 presented the probability distributions for number of bullocks and number of cows owned by randomly chosen households in a Nepal farming village.

a. Use the formula
$$\sigma = \sqrt{(x_1 - \mu)^2 P(X = x_1) + \cdots + (x_k - \mu)^2 P(X = x_k)}$$
to find the standard deviation σ_B of the number of bullocks owned.

b. If $B + C$ is the total number of bullocks and cows owned by a household, use the formula $\mu_{X_1 + X_2} = \mu_{X_1} + \mu_{X_2}$, along with your answers to parts (g) and (h) of Exercise 7.10, to find the mean total, $\mu_{B + C}$.

c. Explain why the formula $\sigma_{X_1 + X_2} = \sqrt{\sigma_{X_1}^2 + \sigma_{X_2}^2}$ cannot be used to find the standard deviation of the total number of bullocks and cows owned by a household.

7.14 Exercise 7.10 presented the probability distributions for number of bullocks and number of cows owned by randomly chosen households in a Nepal farming village. Use the formula
$$\sigma = \sqrt{(x_1 - \mu)^2 P(X = x_1) + \cdots + (x_k - \mu)^2 P(X = x_k)}$$
to find the standard deviation σ_C of the number of cows owned.

*7.15 Exercise 7.3 dealt with self-rated school ability X, on a scale of 1 to 7, for a large group of 12th graders. Based on the results, published by ICPSR, we present this probability distribution table:

X	1	2	3	4	5	6	7
Probability	0.01	0.02	0.04	0.34	0.24	0.28	0.07

a. Explain why we cannot use the 68-95-99.7 Rule to find the probability that X takes values over certain intervals.

b. Use the formula
$$\mu = x_1 P(X = x_1) + \ldots + x_k P(X = x_k)$$
to prove that μ, the mean value of X, equals 4.9.

c. Keeping in mind that standard deviation σ measures the typical distance of values of X from their mean μ, tell why 1.2 is the only reasonable guess for σ from the options 0.012, 0.12, 1.2, and 12.0.

d. Find the value of X that is 2 standard deviations σ above the mean μ.

e. Report the probability that X takes a value more than 2 standard deviations σ above its mean μ.

f. Based on your response to part (e), comment on how well or poorly this distribution conforms to the 68-95-99.7 Rule for normal distributions.

g. Suppose an administrator transforms the random variable X to a new random variable $Y = -\frac{50}{3} + \frac{50}{3}X$, so that the self-ratings range from 0 to 100. Show that $Y = 0$ when $X = 1$ and $Y = 100$ when $X = 7$.

h. The mean value of X is $\mu_X = 4.9$. What is the mean value of $Y = -\frac{50}{3} + \frac{50}{3}X$?

i. The standard deviation of X is 1.2. What is the standard deviation of $Y = -\frac{50}{3} + \frac{50}{3}X$?

7.16 An exercise in Chapter 4 examined center, spread, and shape of the distribution of 12th graders' answers to the question, "During a typical week, on how many evenings do you go out for fun and recreation?" We can approach the same information more formally by setting up a random variable X for the response of a randomly chosen surveyed student. This table shows the possible values of X and their associated probabilities, consistent with results published by the Inter-university Consortium for Political and Social Research (ICPSR).[4]

X	0	1	2	3	4	5	6	7
Probability	?	0.13	0.27	0.25	0.10	0.07	0.05	0.03

a. According to what principle was the probability distribution determined: equally likely outcomes, long-run observed outcomes, or a subjective assessment?

b. Explain why the probability of a student reporting zero evenings must

be 0.10. That is, show why $P(X = 0) = 0.10$.

c. Find the probability of a student going out at least three evenings in the week; that is, find $P(X \geq 3)$.

d. To find the probability in part (c), which rule was being applied—the Non-overlapping "Or" Rule or the Independent "And" Rule?

e. If students had reason to believe that their peers would discover their responses to this question, would there be a tendency of bias toward higher numbers or lower numbers?

f. If students had reason to fear that their teachers would discover their responses to this question and make adjustments to homework load accordingly, would there be a tendency of bias toward higher numbers or lower numbers?

g. If X_1 is the number of evenings out for a randomly chosen student, and X_2 is the number of evenings out for the student's best friend, explain why we cannot use the Independent "And" Rule to find $P(X_1 = 7$ and $X_2 = 7)$—that is, the probability that both of them go out every evening of the week.

h. If X_1 is the number of evenings out for a randomly chosen student, and X_2 is the number of evenings out for another randomly chosen student, find $P(X_1 = 7$ and $X_2 = 7)$—namely, the probability that both of them go out every evening of the week.

i. If two students are chosen at random, find the probability that at least one of them goes out exactly three evenings a week: In other words, find $P(X_1 = 3$ or $X_2 = 3)$, keeping in mind that the events $X_1 = 3$ and $X_2 = 3$ may overlap.

j. Given that a student goes out fewer than three evenings a week, what is the probability of going out two evenings? In other words, find $P(X = 2$ given $X < 3)$.

7.17 Exercise 7.16 dealt with 12th graders' responses to the question, "During a typical week, on how many evenings do you go out for fun and recreation?" Based on the results, published by ICPSR, we present this probability distribution table:

X	0	1	2	3	4	5	6	7
Probability	0.10	0.13	0.27	0.25	0.10	0.07	0.05	0.03

a. Display the distribution with a probability histogram.

b. The median value of a random variable is the value for which at least 50% of the time, the random variable falls at or below it; it is seen as the equal area point on a probability histogram. Report the median of X.

c. Explain why we cannot use the 68-95-99.7 Rule to find the probability that X takes values over certain intervals.

d. Considering the shape of the histogram in part (a), should the mean be less than, greater than, or equal to the median?

e. Use the formula
$$\mu = x_1 P(X = x_1) + \ldots + x_k P(X = x_k)$$
to prove that μ, the mean value of X, equals approximately 2.7.

f. Keeping in mind that standard deviation σ measures the typical distance of values from their mean μ, tell why 1.7 is the only reasonable guess for σ from the options 0.017, 0.17, 1.7, and 17.0.

g. Find the value of X that is 2 standard deviations σ below the mean μ.

h. Report the probability that X takes a value smaller than 2 standard deviations σ below its mean μ.

i. Use your answer to part (h) to comment on how well or how poorly that probability conforms to the 68-95-99.7 Rule for normal distributions.

j. Suppose we transform the random variable X_i (number of evenings out in a week) to a new random variable $Y = X_1 + X_2 + \ldots + X_{52}$, for number of evenings out per year. The mean value of X_i is $\mu_{X_i} = 2.7$. What is the mean of Y?

k. Explain why surveyors would probably get less accurate responses if they asked the students, "During a typical year, on how many evenings do you go out for fun and recreation?"

l. The standard deviation of X_i is 1.7. Refer to Example 7.18 on page 283 and tell whether the standard deviation of Y would be less than 52(1.7), equal to 52(1.7), or more than 52(1.7).

*7.18 Mid-summer temperatures at noon in a certain city have a mean of 30 degrees Celsius with a standard deviation of 5 degrees Celsius. Converting Celsius to Fahrenheit with the equation $F = \frac{9}{5}C + 32$, what are the mean and standard deviation of the temperatures in degrees Fahrenheit?

7.19 Suppose a waitress's tips average $40 a day, with a standard deviation of $10. A busboy earns $50 a day, plus 20% of the waitress's tips, so his earnings B satisfy $B = 0.20W + 50$. What are the mean and standard deviation of the busboy's daily earnings?

*7.20 According to Exercises 7.10 and 7.13, the number of bullocks in a randomly chosen household in a farming village in Nepal has a mean of 0.66 and a standard deviation of 0.95.

a. What is the mean of the combined number of bullocks $B_1 + B_2$ in two randomly chosen households?

b. Can we say that the standard deviation of the combined number of bullocks is $0.95 + 0.95 = 1.90$?

7.21 According to Exercises 7.10 and 7.14, the number of cows in a randomly chosen household in a farming village in Nepal has a mean of 0.40 and a standard deviation of 0.88.

a. What is the mean of the combined number of cows $C_1 + C_2$ in two randomly chosen households?

b. What is the standard deviation of the combined number of cows?

*7.22 The average number of days worked per week for married women in the early 1990s had mean 4.7 and standard deviation 1.0.

a. If two married women are chosen at random, what should be the mean and standard deviation of the total days worked by the two of them in a week?

b. If two married women are co-workers, each of whose days worked per week has mean 4.7 and standard deviation 1.0, which of these can we compute: mean of the total days worked by both of them in a week, or standard deviation of the total days worked by both of them in a week, or both of these, or neither of these? Explain.

7.23 The average number of hours worked per week for married men in the early 1990s had a mean of 42.6 and a standard deviation of 12.9.

a. If two married men are chosen at random, what should be the mean and standard deviation of the total hours worked by the two of them in a week?

b. If two married men are co-workers, each of whose hours worked per week has a mean of 42.6 and a standard deviation of 12.9, which of these can we compute: mean of the total hours worked by both of them in a week, or standard deviation of the total hours worked by both of them in a week, or both of these, or neither of these? Explain.

7.2 Binomial Random Variables

A long-term goal for readers of this book is to understand the behavior of sample proportions when random samples are taken from a population of values for a categorical variable. Because the sample *proportion* $\hat{p}$ in a given category is actually the sample *count* X divided by the sample size n, a first step to understanding the behavior of proportions is understanding the behavior of counts. Counts falling into a specified category, under the right conditions, conform to a particular type of distribution known as *binomial*. The behavior of a binomial random variable is very predictable by virtue of the laws of probability. We begin by defining a binomial random variable.

What Makes a Random Variable "Binomial"?

Definition   The random variable that counts sampled individuals falling into a particular category is **binomial** if the following conditions are met:

1. There must be a fixed sample size n.
2. Each selection must be independent of the others.
3. Each sampled individual may take just two possible values.
4. The probability of each individual falling in the category of interest is always p.

The Big Picture:
LOOKING BACK

We defined independence on page 233 in Chapter 6. Selections are independent if the probability of being in the category of interest on any given selection is not impacted by whether or not other selected individuals were in the category of interest.

If these four conditions hold, then the random variable X that counts how many of those sampled individuals fall in the category of interest is called "binomial with parameters n and p." We are already familiar with the parameters n (sample size) and p (population proportion in the category of interest). Notice that because a binomial random variable X takes distinct values like the counting numbers, it is discrete.

EXAMPLE 7.20 A SIMPLE BINOMIAL RANDOM VARIABLE

Background: A coin is flipped twice, and we consider the random variable X for the number of tails.

Question: Explain why X is binomial, and report n and p.

Response: The number of flips is fixed, so there is a fixed sample size $n = 2$. The coin flips are independent of each other, and on each flip there are just two possibilities: tails or heads. There is the same probability of tails each time, $p = 0.5$. Thus, X is binomial with parameters $n = 2$ and $p = 0.5$. We introduced this random variable in Example 7.2 and constructed its probability histogram in Example 7.3.

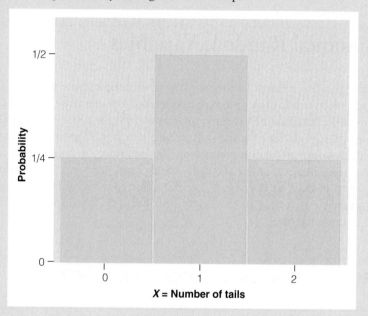

Practice: *Try Exercise 7.24 on page 307.*

Our next example illustrates how a random variable may fail to meet the various conditions for being called "binomial."

EXAMPLE 7.21 DETERMINING WHETHER A RANDOM VARIABLE IS BINOMIAL

Background: We consider various random variables based on card selections:

1. Pick a card from a deck of 52, replace it, pick another, and so on. Let X be the number of cards picked until you get an ace.

2. Pick 16 cards without replacement from a deck of 52. Let X be the number of red cards picked.

3. Pick a card from a deck of 52, replace it, pick another, etc. Do this 16 times. Let the random variables W, X, Y, and Z denote the numbers of selected cards that are clubs, hearts, diamonds, and spades, respectively. [Our goal is to find the probability that certain numbers of each suit are picked.]

4. Most card games in Germany are played with a deck of only 32 cards (the numbers 2 through 6 are not included). Pick a card from an American deck of 52, replace it, pick a card from a German deck of 32, replace it, back to 52, etc. After 16 selections, let X be the number of aces picked.

Card selections in Germany: Aren't they playing with a full deck?

5. Pick a card from a deck of 52, replace it, pick another, etc. Do this 16 times. Let X be the random variable for the number of hearts picked.

Question: Are these random variables binomial?

Response:

1. In the first situation, X is not binomial because the sample size n is not fixed. It might take any number of selections until you get an ace, from 1 on up to infinity (because the cards are replaced).

2. In the second situation, X is not binomial because sampling *without* replacement makes the selections *dependent*, as we discussed in Chapter 6 on probability. Especially after quite a few cards have been picked, the probability of a card being red is diminished if many red cards have already been removed, increased if few red cards have been removed. Note that the probability p of the first card being red is 0.5, but then p keeps changing, and the fourth condition is also violated.

3. In the third situation, W, X, Y, and Z are not binomial because the sampled individuals may take four possible values instead of just two.

4. In the fourth situation, X is not binomial because the probability p of getting an ace is not fixed; it alternates between 1/13 and 1/8.

5. In the fifth situation, X *is* binomial, with parameters $n = 16$ and $p = 0.25$.

Practice: *Try Exercise 7.25 on page 307.*

The theory of binomial random variables is essential in order to get all the results we need for handling categorical variables throughout the remainder of this book. Therefore, the four conditions on page 291 need to be met whenever we take a random sample from a categorical population for the purpose of drawing conclusions about the unknown population proportion falling in the category of interest. This may sound reasonable, until you think back to our discussions of sampling in Part I of the book: For practical purposes, samples are almost always taken *without replacement*, as in the definition of a simple random sample. When we got to probability theory in Part III, we learned that sampling without replacement results in *dependence*. How can we reconcile the reality of dependence in our samples with the theory that requires independence?

Fortunately, we may overlook the requirement of independence whenever the degree of dependence is slight, so the theory remains more or less intact. The next example demonstrates that under certain circumstances, the condition of independence may be "fudged," without having much impact on probabilities.

EXAMPLE 7.22 HOW SAMPLE SIZE RELATIVE TO POPULATION SIZE AFFECTS DEPENDENCE

Background: We consider two situations. In the first, two people are picked at random without replacement from a class where 25 out of 75 (proportion one-third) are male, and we let X be the number of males picked. In the second situation, two people are picked from a group of only three where one is male (proportion one-third), and again we let X be the number of males picked. In both situations, the probability of being male for the first selection is one-third, or 0.333.

Questions: For each of the two situations, what is the probability of the second person being male if the first is male? What is the probability of the second person being male if the first is not male? In either situation, can we assert that X is approximately binomial?

Responses: When we pick two from 75 where one-third are male, the probability of being male for the second person is $\frac{24}{74} = 0.324$ if the first was male, $\frac{25}{74} = 0.338$ if the first was female—pretty close to one-third, or 0.333. Because the population size (75) is much larger than the sample size (2), X is approximately binomial with $n = 2$, $p = \frac{1}{3}$.

When we pick two from only three where one-third are male, the probability of the second being male is either 0 or 0.5—very different from each other, and from 0.333! In this case, X is not close to being binomial because there is a high degree of dependence, and the probability p is far from remaining constant.

Practice: *Try Exercise 7.27(a) on page 308.*

This example suggests that it is not simply the size of the sample or the size of the population that matters. Rather, the sample must not be too large *relative* to the population size. As long as our sample doesn't dip too deeply into the population, selections are reasonably independent. We state a rule that reasserts our rule of thumb for approximate independence when sampling without replacement from page 236 in Chapter 6, now in the context of binomial distributions.

Rule of Thumb for an Approximate Binomial Distribution

If the population is at least 10 times the sample size n, non-replacement has little effect. In such cases, when taking a simple random sample (without replacement) of size n from a population with proportion p in a certain category, the sample count X in the category of interest is approximately binomial.

Most problems for binomial random variables take the form of a question like this: "If X is binomial with a certain n and p given, what is the probability that X

equals some value, or lies within some range of values?" There are several options available for answering such questions, but the most efficient approach for our purposes will be to reformulate the question in terms of proportions instead of counts. For large enough samples, we can use a normal approximation to find probabilities about the sample *proportion* $\hat{p}$ in the category of interest, such as $P(\hat{p} \leq ?)$. Here, sample proportion is simply sample count divided by sample size: $\hat{p} = X/n$.

Because our normal approximation will be based on a variable having the same mean and standard deviation as the sample proportion $\hat{p} = X/n$, we must establish what those are. In fact, they are constructed by careful application of the definitions and rules for means and standard deviations of discrete random variables, applied to the underlying binomial variable of interest X. This random variable can be thought of as a combination of simpler random variables, each corresponding to one sampled individual.

Other approaches to solving binomial problems are outlined on page 834 of the **TBP** *Supplement*. Solving for probabilities with the binomial formula is discussed, along with a thorough introduction to permutations and combinations, on pages 839 to 849. Solution of a small-sample binomial problem with software is also presented.

The Mean and Standard Deviation of Sample Proportions

We will begin with the mean of binomial counts X, then shift to the mean of proportions $\hat{p} = \frac{X}{n}$. Similarly, standard deviations are discussed first for counts and then for proportions.

The mean of a binomial random variable is easy to grasp intuitively.

EXAMPLE 7.23 INTUITING THE MEAN OF A BINOMIAL RANDOM VARIABLE

Background: Based on the principle of long-run observed outcomes, the probability of being left-handed is said to be approximately 0.1. Suppose we sample 100 people at random.

Question: On average, what should be the count of left-handed people in our sample?

Response: On average, we should get about $100(0.1) = 10$ left-handed people in our sample.

Practice: *Try Exercise 7.27(b) on page 308.*

Our intuition suggests that the mean count in the category of interest should be the number sampled, times the probability of being in that category. The mean of proportions is also easy to intuit.

EXAMPLE 7.24 INTUITING THE MEAN OF SAMPLE PROPORTIONS

Background: The probability of being left-handed is said to be approximately 0.1. Suppose we sample 100 people at random.

Question: What proportion of left-handed people should we expect to get in our sample?

Response: The proportion of left-handed people in our sample should be about 0.1, since that proportion holds for the larger population. For some samples our proportion might be less than 0.1 and for others more, but overall they should average out to 0.1.

Practice: *Try Exercise 7.27(c) on page 308.*

Examples 7.23 and 7.24 taken together suggest the following rule.

Rule for the Mean of Counts and Proportions

If count X is a binomial random variable with parameters n and p, then the mean of X is

$$\mu_X = np$$

and the mean of the proportion $\hat{p} = \frac{X}{n}$ is

$$\mu_{\hat{p}} = p$$

Notice that because $\hat{p}$ is X divided by n, the mean of $\hat{p}$ is the mean of X divided by n.

We explain on page 837 of the *TBP* Supplement how to derive the formula for the mean of proportions from the formula for the mean of counts.

The fact that the mean of the distribution of sample proportion $\hat{p}$ equals the population proportion p is one of the three key pieces in the theory that will enable us to draw conclusions about an unknown population proportion, based on the sample proportion. Its consequences are far-reaching, because it reassures us that if the sample proportion $\hat{p}$ from a random sample is used to estimate the unknown population proportion p, it may sometimes underestimate and sometimes overestimate, but in the long run, it tends to be "right on target." Statisticians say that sample proportion $\hat{p}$ is an *unbiased estimator* of the population proportion p. Remember that the rules apply to *random* variables, and that random selection of the sample is vital.

EXAMPLE 7.25 THE MEAN OF PROPORTIONS FOR BIASED SAMPLES

Background: The overall probability of being left-handed is 0.1. Suppose we take a sample of major league baseball pitchers.

Question: On average, will the proportion who are left-handed in our sample equal 0.1?

Response: We cannot say on average what proportion will be left-handed, because major league baseball pitchers do not constitute a random sample from the general population in terms of handedness: There are disproportionately many "lefties" among baseball pitchers. The formula $\mu_{\hat{p}} = p$ does not hold for biased samples.

Practice: *Try Exercise 7.28 on page 308.*

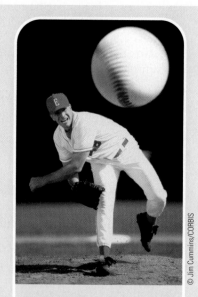

Baseball pitchers: a biased proportion of lefties

Some sources report the proportion of left-handers among baseball pitchers to be approximately 0.33.

We intuited in Examples 7.23 and 7.24 that when a random sample of size n is taken from a population with proportion p in the category of interest, then the count of sampled individuals falling in that category has a mean of np and the proportion has a mean of p. Formulas for the standard deviation of counts and proportions are less intuitive. When we apply them, we should keep in mind that the standard deviation of counts tells us the typical distance of counts from their mean np, and the standard deviation of proportions tells us the typical distance of proportions from their mean p.

> ## Rule for the Standard Deviation of Counts and Proportions
>
> If sample count X is a binomial random variable with parameters n and p, then X has standard deviation
>
> $$\sigma_X = \sqrt{np(1-p)}$$
>
> and sample proportion $\hat{p} = \frac{X}{n}$ has standard deviation
>
> $$\sigma_{\hat{p}} = \sqrt{\frac{p(1-p)}{n}}$$

A CLOSER LOOK

Notice that because $\hat{p}$ is X divided by n, the standard deviation of $\hat{p}$ is the standard deviation of X divided by n.

To better understand the formulas, it helps to think about what the mean and standard deviation of sample count or proportion are measuring in a given setting. A discussion by the four students can remind you about how to use the above formulas to measure the typical distance of a binomial count from its mean np, or of a proportion from its mean p.

Starting on page 835 of the *TBP* Supplement, we derive formulas for the mean and standard deviation of counts and proportions. We explain on page 837 how to derive the formulas for the standard deviation of proportions from the formula for the standard deviation of counts.

Students Talk Stats

Calculating and Interpreting the Mean and Standard Deviation of Count or Proportion

*A*n assignment asks students to report the mean and standard deviation of sample count and sample proportion when a random sample of size 100 is taken from a population where the proportion who are left-handed is 0.1.

Adam: *"If you sample 100 people, on average the number who are left-handed will be one-tenth, because the mean of $\hat{p}$ is p."*

Brittany: *"You're getting your formulas confused. If we're talking about the **number** who are left-handed, we use the fact that the mean of counts X is np, which would be 100 times one-tenth, or 10. The standard deviation is the square root of p times 1 minus p divided by n, so that's the square root of one-tenth times nine-tenths over 100, or 0.03."*

Carlos: *"You shouldn't report a mean for counts with a standard deviation for proportions. The formulas for means have n in the numerator, and the formulas for proportions divide by n. The **number** left-handed uses the formulas for counts: The mean is np = 100(0.1) = 10 and the standard deviation is $\sqrt{100(0.1)(1-0.1)} = \sqrt{9} = 3$. The **proportion** left-handed has a mean of p = 0.1 and a standard deviation of $\sqrt{\frac{0.1(1-0.1)}{100}} = 0.03."*

Dominique: *"So if you pick 100 people at random, on average you should get 10 left-handed people. Sometimes you get a number close to 10, and sometimes it's farther away. Typically, the count who are left-handed should differ from 10 by about 3. And the proportion who are left-handed should be about 0.1. Sometimes the sample proportion will be close to 0.1, and sometimes it's farther away. Typically, the sample proportion of left-handed people should differ from 0.1 by about 0.03. That seems right."*

Practice: *Try Exercise 7.29(d,h) on page 308.*

Page 837 of the **_TBP Supplement_** includes a reminder that information about the mean and standard deviation of counts and proportions can be combined with information about normal probabilities only if the sample size is large enough.

   The fact that the standard deviation of the distribution of sample proportion equals $\sqrt{\frac{p(1-p)}{n}}$ is another key piece in the theory that will enable us to draw conclusions about the unknown population proportion, based on a sample proportion. It may be considered one of the most vital results in all of introductory statistics, mainly because of the appearance of sample size n *in the denominator* of our expression for the standard deviation of the random variable sample proportion. This means that *as sample size increases, the spread of the distribution of sample proportion decreases*. In Part IV, we will see how to take advantage of this phenomenon when using a sample proportion to estimate the unknown population proportion: The larger the sample, the less spread there is in the distribution of sample proportion, and the closer $\hat{p}$ comes to its mean p. In other words, there is theoretical justification for what our intuition may already suggest: Larger samples provide better estimates.

EXAMPLE 7.26 HOW SAMPLE SIZE AFFECTS THE STANDARD DEVIATION OF SAMPLE PROPORTION

Background: If the overall probability of being left-handed is 0.1 and we sample 10,000 people at random instead of 100, then on average the proportion of left-handed people in our sample will still be 0.1.

Question: What will the standard deviation of sample proportion be if we sample 10,000 people instead of 100?

Response: Now the standard deviation is only $\sqrt{\frac{0.1(1-0.1)}{10,000}} = 0.003$. With such a large sample size, sample proportions tend to be much closer to the population proportion, 0.1.

Practice: _Try Exercise 7.29(i) on page 308._

Sampling without replacement from a relatively small population results in a standard deviation of sample proportions that is smaller than the claimed value $\sqrt{\frac{p(1-p)}{n}}$. In the extreme, if we take repeated samples of size 100 from a population of size 100, the mean of the sample proportions will be p but the standard deviation will be 0, because the sample proportions will all be the same! Real-life population sizes N are typically much larger than sample sizes n, so it is probably enough to give students a warning, rather than teach them about the correction factor $\sqrt{\frac{N-n}{N-1}}$ to adjust the formula for standard deviation $\sqrt{\frac{p(1-p)}{n}}$ that assumes independence.

   Remember that each selection had to be independent from the others (or at least approximately so) in order to apply the rule for the standard deviation of a sum of random variables.

EXAMPLE 7.27 FORMULA FOR STANDARD DEVIATION REQUIRES INDEPENDENCE

Background: Suppose 20 people in a group of 200 are left-handed, and we sample 100 people at random *without replacement* from those 200.

Question: What are the mean and standard deviation of sample proportion who are left-handed?

Response: The mean of sample proportions is 20/200 = 0.10. However, the standard deviation is not $\sqrt{\frac{0.10(1-0.10)}{100}} = 0.03$. Because of the dependence that arises when we sample too many people from a small population, the standard deviation would actually be less than 0.03.

Practice: _Try Exercise 7.30 on page 308._

   Notice that our results for proportions are perfectly compatible with the results for counts. If the overall probability of being left-handed is 0.10, and 100 people are sampled, then the *count* of left-handed people in our sample will be about 10, and sampled counts will differ from 10 by about 3. The *proportion* of left-handed people will be about 0.10, and sampled proportions will differ from 0.10 by about 0.03. In the next section, we will begin to concentrate more on proportions as our preferred summary of the behavior of categorical variables.

LOOKING AHEAD

The mean and standard deviation are reported for each distribution in Example 7.28. These will be discussed in Example 7.29, which will consider center and spread in addition to shape.

The Shape of the Distribution of Counts or Proportions: The Central Limit Theorem

We have already made a great deal of progress in this chapter: We now know how to find the center (mean) and spread (standard deviation) of the distribution of sample counts or proportions taking a certain categorical value when the binomial conditions hold. Specifically, there must be a fixed sample size n, independent selections, just two possible categories, and a constant probability p of falling in the category of interest.

Besides center and spread, we also need to know about the shape of the distribution. It will turn out to depend both on the *sample size n* and on the shape of the underlying distribution for the selection of a single individual, which itself depends directly on the *value of p*.

In the following example, we begin by focusing on the role of sample size.

EXAMPLE 7.28 SHAPE OF THE DISTRIBUTION OF COUNTS OR PROPORTIONS AS SAMPLE SIZE INCREASES

Background: Flip a coin a certain number of times n. The probability of getting a tail each time is $p = 0.5$. The *count* of tails obtained in each sample of n flips is a binomial random variable, whose mean and standard deviation can be calculated with the formulas recently presented. Alternatively, we may consider the *proportion* of tails obtained in each sample. The following are probability histograms for count and proportion, for various sample sizes n.

1. $n = 1$: Sample count has mean 0.50, standard deviation 0.50. Sample proportion also has mean 0.50, standard deviation 0.50. (Count X and proportion $\hat{p} = X/n$ are identical when the sample size n is 1.)

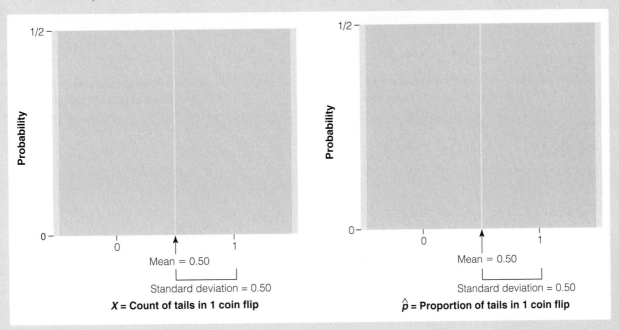

Continued

2. $n = 2$: Sample count has mean 1.00, standard deviation 0.71. Sample proportion has mean 0.50, standard deviation 0.35.

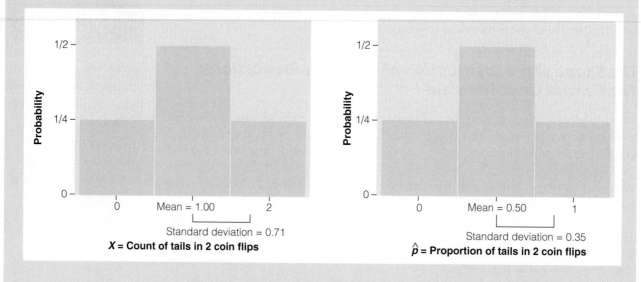

3. $n = 3$: Sample count has mean 1.50, standard deviation 0.87. Sample proportion has mean 0.50, standard deviation 0.29.

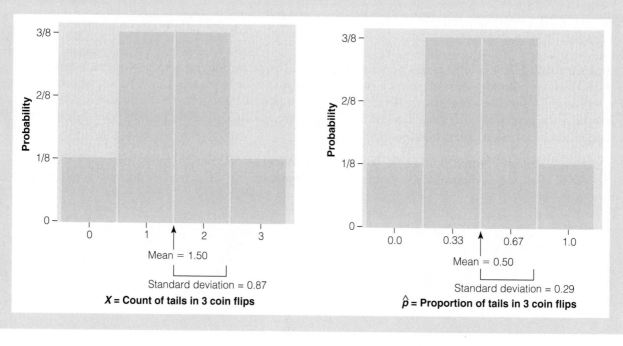

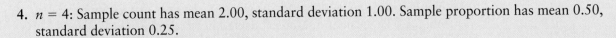

4. $n = 4$: Sample count has mean 2.00, standard deviation 1.00. Sample proportion has mean 0.50, standard deviation 0.25.

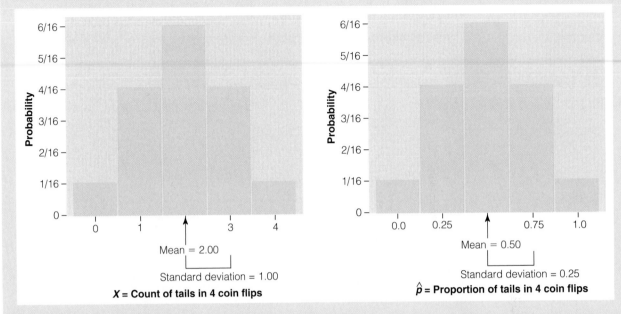

Questions: How do the shapes compare for counts and proportions? How do the shapes compare for various sample sizes n?

Responses: For any given sample size, the shape of the distribution of sample count is identical to that of sample proportion. Shapes do differ, however, for various sample sizes:

1. $n = 1$: Shape is flat.
2. $n = 2$: Shape is unimodal and very rough (not at all like a smooth curve).
3. $n = 3$: Shape is less rough.
4. $n = 4$: Shape is more normal.

Thus, as the sample size increases, the shape of the distribution of counts or proportions becomes more normal.

Practice: *Try Exercise 7.32(b,c) on page 308.*

The probability histograms in Example 7.28 were presented side-by-side for counts and proportions in order to impress upon you the fact that the two distributions are directly related. All that changes as we shift from counts to proportions is that the horizontal scale is divided by the sample size n. Now that this fact has been established, we shift our emphasis for the remainder of the book to the behavior of sample proportions, not counts. After all, when we learn to perform inference about categorical variables, we will want to make statements about the unknown population *proportion*, not count, based on the sample proportion that we have observed.

The Big Picture:
LOOKING BACK

The normal shape, as it applied to distributions of data, was discussed throughout Section 4.4.

EXAMPLE 7.29 CENTER, SPREAD, AND SHAPE OF SAMPLE PROPORTION AS SAMPLE SIZE INCREASES

Background: Flip a coin a certain number of times n. The probability of getting a tail each time is $p = 0.5$. Example 7.28 showed probability

Continued

histograms (on the right) for proportions of tails, for various sample sizes *n*. The mean and standard deviation were reported for each distribution. We present here one more histogram, for the distribution of sample proportions for *n* = 16, where a smooth curve has been sketched over the histogram's bars.

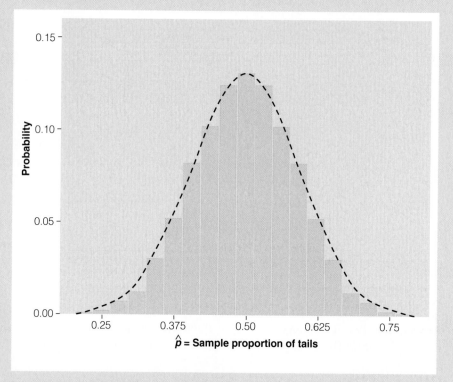

Question: How are the mean, standard deviation, and shape of the distribution of sample proportion affected as *n* increases?

Response:

1. The *mean* of the distribution of sample proportion is always *p*. In the case of coin flips, the mean proportion of tails is always 0.5. As long as the coin is balanced, we can rely on a sample proportion of tails that in the long run reflects the population proportion 0.5 without bias.

2. The *standard deviation* of the distribution of sample proportion is $\sqrt{\frac{p(1 - p)}{n}}$. No matter what *p* is, the standard deviation decreases as *n* increases because *n* appears in the denominator. For our coin flips example, the standard deviation of the proportion of tails goes from 0.50 to 0.35 to 0.29 to 0.25 as *n* increases from 1 to 2 to 3 to 4. For *n* = 16, the standard deviation is only $\sqrt{\frac{0.5(1 - 0.5)}{16}} = 0.125$.

3. The *shape* of the underlying distribution (*n* = 1) is balanced, with a flat-topped histogram reflecting the fact that both possible outcomes (tails or not tails) are equally likely. As the sample size *n* increases, the shape remains symmetric, but develops more and more of a bulge in the middle, with a tapering of the ends. From our discussions of distributions of quantitative data sets in Part II, we should already suspect that the *shape is becoming more normal* as sample size *n* increases. By the time the sample size is up to 16, a normal curve fits the histogram quite closely.

Practice: *Try Exercise 7.34 on page 309.*

Before we jump to conclusions about the shape of the distribution of sample proportion, we consider an example where the underlying proportions are *not* balanced. Our example looks at distributions of sample proportion when the population proportion is 0.1 and 0.9, respectively, to stress that we need to look out for population proportions that are far from 0.5 *in either direction*.

EXAMPLE 7.30 THE DISTRIBUTION OF SAMPLE PROPORTIONS FOR AN UNBALANCED POPULATION

Background: Assume the proportion of left-handed people in the population is 0.1 and we sample n people at random. We consider the behavior of sample proportion $\hat{p}$ of left-handed people as the sample size n increases. Simultaneously, we consider the behavior of sample proportion $\hat{q}$ of right-handed people. For each distribution, we report the mean and standard deviation of sample proportions.

1. $n = 1$: Sample proportion left-handed has mean 0.1; sample proportion right-handed has mean 0.9. Standard deviations are 0.30.

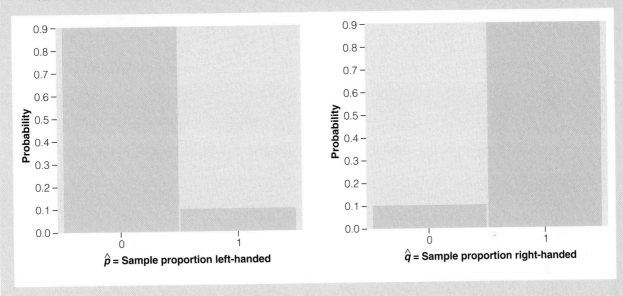

2. $n = 4$: Sample proportion left-handed has mean 0.1; sample proportion right-handed has mean 0.9. Standard deviations are 0.15.

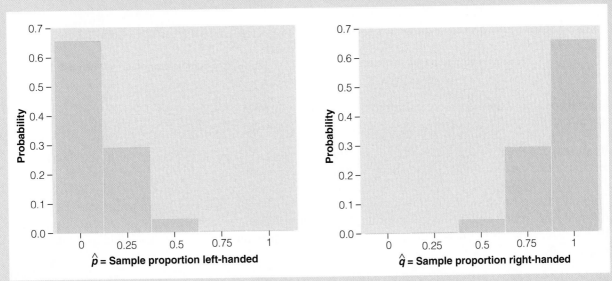

Continued

3. $n = 16$: Sample proportion left-handed has mean 0.1; sample proportion right-handed has mean 0.9. Standard deviations are 0.075.

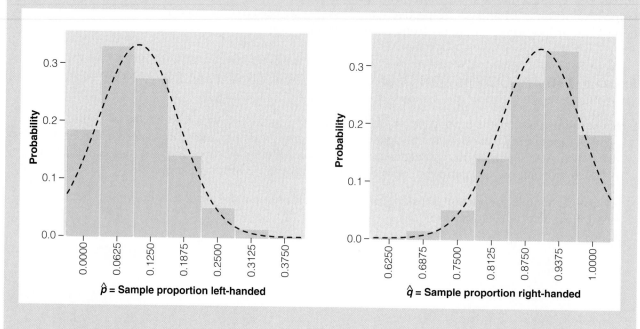

4. $n = 100$: Sample proportion left-handed has mean 0.1; sample proportion right-handed has mean 0.9. Standard deviations are 0.03.

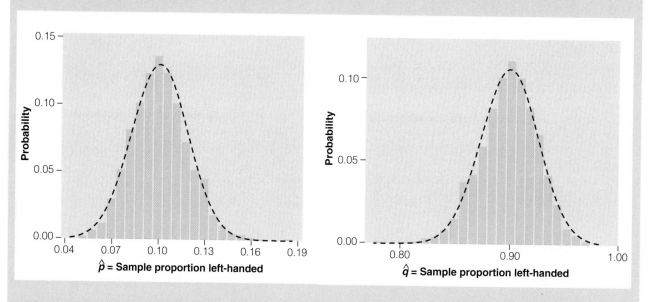

Questions: How do the shapes compare for underlying proportions 0.1 and 0.9? What can we say about the shapes of the distributions as sample size increases?

Responses: When $p = 0.1$, the distribution is always skewed right, and when $p = 0.9$, the distribution is always skewed left. For any given sample size, the degrees of right- and left-skewness are the same. For samples of size 1, the skewness is very pronounced. As the sample size increases, the skewness gradually diminishes. By the time sample size reaches 16, the shapes are showing some normality, but a normal curve would still provide a poor approximation. When the sample size is increased all the way to $n = 100$, we arrive at distributions that exhibit only a tiny bit of skewness (still right and left, respectively).

Practice: *Try Exercise 7.35(a) on page 309.*

In the case of coin flips, where the underlying distribution was nicely balanced on either side of 0.5, the shape of sample proportion could already be called symmetric and single-peaked for samples of just 2. In contrast, the distributions of sample proportion left-handed or right-handed started out very unbalanced (right-skewed and left-skewed, respectively) and the skewness persists as sample size increases from 1 to 4 to 16 to 100, although it does become gradually less pronounced.

Examples 7.28, 7.29, and 7.30 are rather lengthy, but taken together they give us a glimpse at the single most powerful law that comes into play in introductory statistics, namely the **Central Limit Theorem**. Although our examples were about categorical variables, the theorem will also apply to the behavior of means when the variables of interest are quantitative.

Implications of the Central Limit Theorem

The distribution of sample proportion has a shape that becomes closer and closer to normal as the sample size increases. The same is true for the distribution of sample mean.

Thus, for large enough sample sizes, we can use the normal distribution to find the probability that sample proportion takes a value over any given interval.

A natural question to ask at this point is, "How large a sample is 'large enough'?" It would certainly simplify matters if we could specify a particular sample size n that guarantees the sample proportion to be approximately normally distributed. However, as we saw in our recent examples, the shape of the distribution of sample proportion depends on the *combination* of sample size n and underlying shape, as determined by p.

If the underlying shape is nice and balanced, as for coin flips where probabilities of 0 tails and 1 tail are each 0.5 on a single flip (shown next on the left), then the shape becomes normal fairly quickly. It already followed a normal curve closely for $n = 16$, but just to be safe, we could set $n = 20$ as our minimum sample size.

If the shape is skewed right or left, as for proportions of left-handed or right-handed people (underlying distributions have blocks of height 0.9 versus 0.1, shown in the middle, or 0.1 versus 0.9, shown on the right), then larger samples are needed if we want sample proportion to exhibit the symmetric single-peaked shape characteristic of the normal distribution. A sample size of $n = 16$ was not nearly large enough, but $n = 100$ should do the trick.

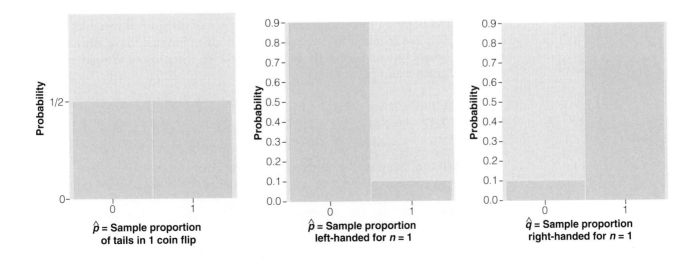

Thus, the answer to "How large a sample is 'large enough'?" depends on how balanced or skewed the distribution is. The requirement of larger samples for more skewed underlying distributions can be formulated neatly with the following pair of conditions.

> ### Rule of Thumb for Approximate Normality of Sample Proportion
>
> If independent samples of size n are taken from a population with probability p of being in the category of interest, then the distribution of sample proportion $\hat{p}$ has a shape that is approximately normal if
>
> $$np \geq 10 \text{ and } n(1 - p) \geq 10$$

Requiring both of the inequalities to hold is how we take care of unbalanced underlying distributions that may be skewed right *or* left. To check the rule of thumb in practice, it is enough to get a rough estimate for the sizes of np and $n(1 - p)$.

Example TBP 7.6 on page 838 of the **TBP** *Supplement* verifies that our Rule of Thumb's requirements conform to what we saw in our probability histograms of coin flips or left-handed/right-handed people, for a variety of sample sizes.

EXAMPLE 7.31 APPLYING THE RULE OF THUMB FOR APPROXIMATE NORMALITY

Background: The president of a city's Downtown Council hosted a meeting with 800 participants on January 27, 2005, and was curious about the probability that a certain proportion of participants would have a birthday that day. We know that for a randomly chosen individual, the probability of having been born on January 27 is 1/365.

Question: Is the rule of thumb for approximate normality of the distribution of sample proportion satisfied?

Response: The rule is not satisfied because 800(1/365) is a bit less than 3, which is certainly less than 10. The probability of interest would need to be computed as an exact binomial probability, not approximated with a normal curve.

Practice: *Try Exercise 7.35(b) on page 309.*

The laws of probability, applied to the behavior of categorical variables under the circumstances required to call a random variable binomial, have gotten us to the point where we can succinctly summarize the distribution of sample proportion for a given n and p.

EXAMPLE 7.32 SUMMARIZING THE DISTRIBUTION OF SAMPLE PROPORTION

Background: Suppose the proportion of voters in a certain population favoring a particular candidate is 0.5, and a sample of 1,000 voters is taken.

Question: What can we say about the distribution of sample proportion $\hat{p}$ of voters favoring that candidate?

Response: The distribution of $\hat{p}$ has a mean of $p = 0.5$, a standard deviation of $\sqrt{\frac{p(1-p)}{n}} = \sqrt{\frac{0.5(1-0.5)}{1,000}} = 0.0158$, and a shape that is approximately normal because $np = 1,000(0.5) = 500$ and $n(1-p) = 1,000(1-0.5) = 500$ are both at least 10.

Practice: *Try Exercise 7.36 on page 309.*

We can summarize the general behavior of sample proportions in just two short sentences. Nevertheless, the theory behind this brief summary has a great deal of depth, and there are far-reaching consequences for performing statistical inference in Part IV.

Summary: Center, Spread, and Shape of Sample Proportion

If X, the count of sampled individuals in the category of interest, is binomial with parameters n and p, then sample proportion $\hat{p} = X/n$ has mean p and standard deviation $\sqrt{\frac{p(1-p)}{n}}$.
The shape of the distribution of sample proportion $\hat{p}$ is approximately normal if $np \geq 10$ and $n(1-p) \geq 10$.

Binomial random variables are summarized on page 336 of the Chapter Summary.

EXERCISES FOR SECTION 7.2

Binomial Random Variables

Note: Asterisked numbers indicate exercises whose answers are provided in the Solutions to Selected Exercises section, on page 689.

*7.24 Exercise 7.5 on page 286 stated that if both parents have sickle-cell trait, then each of their children has probability 0.25 of having the actual disease. Suppose two parents with sickle-cell trait have three children.

   a. Explain why the number of children X with sickle-cell disease is a binomial random variable.

   b. Report the values of n and p.

*7.25 Tell whether each of these random variables is binomial; if not, tell which condition is not met (fixed sample size n, independence of selections, just two possible values, and constant probability p of being in the category of interest).

   a. X is the number of times each high school senior in a sample of size 100 has been married.

   b. Overall, approximately 2% of high school seniors are married. The random

variable X is set up for the number of high school seniors that are sampled by a school district until it finds five who are married.

   c. Two percent of all high school seniors are married. 500 seniors are randomly surveyed across the country, and the random variable X is the number of surveyed seniors who are married.

   d. Two percent of a high school's 100 seniors are married. A school survey randomly selects 40 seniors; the random variable X is the number of surveyed seniors who are married.

7.26 Tell whether each of these random variables is binomial; if not, tell which condition is not met (fixed sample size n, independence of selections, just two possible values, and constant probability p of being in the category of interest).

a. Approximately 5% of a school district's 1,000 seniors have no siblings. A random sample of 300 seniors is taken from that district, and X counts the number with no siblings.

b. Approximately 5% of high school seniors have no siblings. A random sample of 300 high school seniors is taken, and X counts the number with no siblings.

c. Approximately 5% of high school seniors have no siblings, 29% have one, 27% have two, and the remaining 39% have three or more. A random sample of 100 high school seniors is taken, and the random variable X counts the number of siblings for each of the sampled seniors.

d. Approximately 5% of high school seniors have no siblings. A survey is taken and X counts the number needed until 20 high school seniors with no siblings have been selected.

*7.27 We assume the probability of being born in the winter (as opposed to spring, summer, or fall) is 0.25, and the random variable X counts the number of people born in the winter when we take a sample of a given size.

a. In which case is X approximately binomial: when we sample 5 from 10 people, when we sample 5 from 100 people, or both, or neither?

b. If we sample 100 people, on average how many do we expect to have been born in the winter?

c. For any sample size, on average what proportion of people do we expect to have been born in the winter?

*7.28 Assume that, overall, the proportion of high school seniors with no siblings is 0.05. If we take a sample of seniors from a particular private high school, can we say that sample proportion with no siblings has mean 0.05?

*7.29 The binomial random variable X counts the *number* of married students in a random sample of high school seniors, where $p = 0.02$ of all high school seniors are married. The random variable $\hat{p} = X/n$ is for the *proportion* of married students in the sample.

a. If $X = 3$ in a random sample of 100 students, find $\hat{p}$.

b. If $\hat{p} = 0.01$ in a random sample of 200 students, find X.

c. Find the mean and standard deviation of X if the sample consists of $n = 50$ students. (Round to the nearest tenth.)

d. Interpret the mean and standard deviation found in part (c).

e. Find the mean and standard deviation of $\hat{p}$ if the sample consists of $n = 50$ students. (Round to the nearest hundredth.)

f. Find the mean and standard deviation of X if the sample consists of $n = 500$ students. (Round to the nearest tenth.)

g. Find the mean and standard deviation of $\hat{p}$ if the sample consists of $n = 500$ students. (Round to the nearest hundredth.)

h. Interpret the mean and standard deviation found in part (g).

i. In which case does our sample proportion tend to come closer to the population proportion 0.02: for samples of 50 or 500 or both the same?

*7.30 Two percent of a high school's 100 seniors are married. A school survey randomly selects 40 seniors; can you report the mean and standard deviation of sample proportion who are married? Explain.

7.31 The probability of a live birth resulting in a child with Down syndrome is approximately 0.001.

a. Report the mean and standard deviation of sample proportion with Down syndrome in a sample of 5,000 births.

b. Tell whether the shape of the distribution of sample proportion is approximately normal.

*7.32 The proportion of all hikers in Grand Canyon National Park who preferred less-developed areas was 0.30.[5]

a. If just one hiker is sampled, then the count X preferring less-developed areas has just two possible values, 0 and 1. Sketch a probability histogram for X.

b. One of these histograms shows the distribution of count preferring less-developed areas for random samples of size 2, and the other is for random samples of size 4. Is the histogram on the top for samples of 2 or 4?

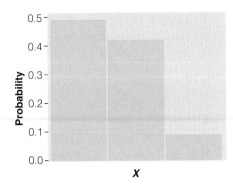

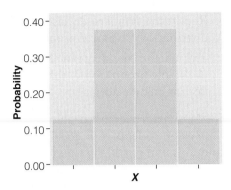

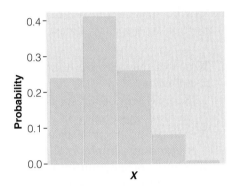

c. Which histogram could be called more normal—the one on the top or the one on the bottom?

7.33 Researchers at Harvard Medical School reported in 2005 that 50% of all U.S. bankruptcies were due to medical bills.[6]

   a. If just one bankruptcy is sampled, then the proportion $\hat{p}$ due to medical bills has just two possible values, 0 and 1. Sketch a probability histogram for $\hat{p}$.

   b. One of these histograms shows the distribution of proportion due to medical bills for a random sample of 3 bankruptcies, and the other is for proportion in random samples of 5 bankruptcies. Is the first histogram for samples of 3 or 5?

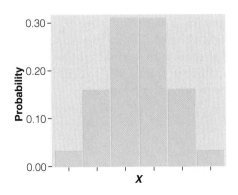

c. Which histogram could be called more normal—the first one or the second?

*7.34 We assume the probability of being born in the winter is 0.25, and consider the sample proportion born in the winter for random samples of various sizes.

   a. Tell how the centers of the distribution of sample proportion compare for samples of 4 people versus samples of 40 people.

   b. Tell how the spreads of the distribution of sample proportion compare for samples of 4 people versus samples of 40 people.

   c. Tell how the shapes of the distribution of sample proportion compare for samples of 4 people versus samples of 40 people.

*7.35 The binomial random variable X counts the *number* of married students in a random sample of high school seniors, where $p = 0.02$ of all high school seniors are married. The random variable $\hat{p} = X/n$ is for the *proportion* of married students in the sample.

   a. In which case is the distribution of X closer to normal—for samples of 50 or samples of 500?

   b. In which case is the rule of thumb for approximate normality satisfied—for samples of 50, 500, both, or neither?

   c. For samples of 10 students, the distribution of X is very right-skewed. What can we say about the shape of the distribution of $\hat{p}$?

*7.36 We assume the probability of being born in the winter is 0.25, and consider the sample proportion born in the winter for random samples of size 40.

   a. Report the mean of the distribution of sample proportion.

b. Report the standard deviation of the distribution of sample proportion.

c. Tell whether the shape of the distribution of sample proportion in this case is approximately normal.

7.37 The binomial random variable X counts the *number* of students with no siblings in a random sample of high school seniors, where $p = 0.05$ of all high school seniors have no siblings. The random variable $\hat{p} = X/n$ is for the *proportion* of students with no siblings in the sample.

a. For each student in the sample, are we treating information about siblings as a quantitative or categorical variable?

b. If $\hat{p} = 0.06$ in a random sample of 150 students, find X.

c. If $X = 8$ in a random sample of 200 students, find $\hat{p}$.

d. Find the mean and standard deviation of X if the sample consists of $n = 50$ students. (Round to the nearest tenth.)

e. Find the mean and standard deviation of $\hat{p}$ if the sample consists of $n = 50$ students. (Round to the nearest hundredth.)

f. Find the mean and standard deviation of X if the sample consists of $n = 400$ students. (Round to the nearest tenth.)

g. Find the mean and standard deviation of $\hat{p}$ if the sample consists of $n = 400$ students. (Round to the nearest hundredth.)

h. In which case is the distribution of X approximately normal—for samples of 50, 400, both, or neither?

i. For samples of 20 students, the distribution of $\hat{p}$ is very right-skewed. What can we say about the distribution of X?

*7.38 In the state of Connecticut, the proportion of blacks is about 0.10 and the proportion of females is about 0.50.

a. Which of these has the most normal distribution, and which has the least normal distribution?

1. Sample proportion of females in random samples of 10.
2. Sample proportion of females in random samples of 100.
3. Sample proportion of blacks in random samples of 10.
4. Sample proportion of blacks in random samples of 100.

b. Which of the four distributions in part (a) has the least spread, and which has the most spread?

7.39 The proportion of people in the United States who speak Spanish is about 0.11; the proportion who speak Chinese is about 0.01.

a. Which of these has the least normal distribution?

1. Sample proportion speaking Chinese in random samples of 20.
2. Sample proportion speaking Chinese in random samples of 200.
3. Sample proportion speaking Spanish in random samples of 20.
4. Sample proportion speaking Spanish in random samples of 200.

b. Which of the distributions in part (a) has the most normal distribution?

c. Which of the four distributions in part (a) has the least spread?

d. Which of the four distributions in part (a) has the most spread?

*7.40 The proportion of whites in Connecticut is 0.90. The distribution of sample *proportion* of whites in samples of size 20 is somewhat left-skewed. Would the shape of the distribution of sample *count* of whites in samples of size 20 be less normal, more normal, or the same?

7.41 The proportion of people in the United States who speak Spanish is about 0.11. The distribution of sample *count* speaking Spanish in samples of size 50 is somewhat right-skewed. Would the shape of the distribution of sample *proportion* speaking Spanish in samples of size 50 be less normal, more normal, or the same?

7.3 Continuous Random Variables and the Normal Distribution

Remember that we summarize distributions of quantitative variables by reporting the shape, center, and spread. In Part II, we explained that having reason to believe a distribution's shape to be normal, and knowing its mean and standard deviation, provided enough information to draw very precise conclusions about where the distribution's values tended to occur. We learned to make use of the 68-95-99.7 Rule to estimate proportions of data values in a given interval. In this section, we will go into more depth with regard to the normal distribution, in contexts where it refers to an entire population of values, not just a sample data set. Future results will rely heavily on the fact that if a random variable is known to have a normal distribution, and we know its mean and standard deviation, then we know absolutely everything about how that random variable behaves.

The standardized normal distribution (often identified by the letter z) will apply when we perform inference for a single categorical variable of interest, and in certain circumstances when there is a single quantitative variable. By the end of the book, we will have introduced several other useful continuous standardized distributions, known as t, F, and chi-square. These will allow us to draw conclusions in situations with one or two quantitative variables, or with values of a quantitative variable compared for two or more categorical groups, or with two categorical variables.

In this chapter, only the z distribution will be discussed in detail. Sketches of the other distributions, which are to be introduced gradually throughout Part IV, are shown here in order to impress upon you that not all distributions of interest are symmetric and bell-shaped like the standard normal distribution z.

The Big Picture:

LOOKING AHEAD

Combining detailed knowledge of the normal distribution with the Central Limit Theorem (which states that sample proportions and sample means are approximately normal for large enough samples) will put us in a position to draw conclusions about unknown population proportion or mean, based on what we see in the sample. This is statistical inference—the final goal of the book.

The normal curve is not to be "abandoned" once we shift our focus to other distributions like t, F, and χ^2. In fact, normal distributions serve as building blocks for these other, more complicated, distributions.

One categorical variable

C

z

One quantitative variable

Q

z or t

One categorical and one quantitative variable

C→Q

t or F

Two categorical variables

C→C

chi-square

Two quantitative variables

Q→Q

t

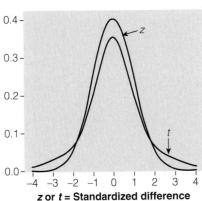

z or t = Standardized difference between sample mean and proposed population mean

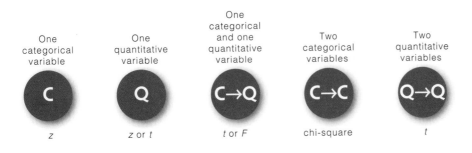

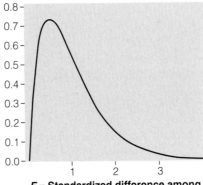

F = Standardized difference among observed sample means

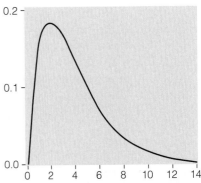

chi-square = Standardized difference between counts observed and counts expected if proportions in various responses were equal for various explanatory groups (in 3 by 3 table)

Even if our variable of interest is categorical, or if a quantitative variable is discrete, our summaries—sample proportion and sample mean—behave as continuous random variables when we consider their behavior in the long run for repeated random samples of a given size, as long as the sample size is large enough.

Discrete versus Continuous Distributions

When we introduced discrete random variables, we explained that their possible values are distinct, like the counting numbers. Note that discrete random variables may still have an infinite number of possible values: There is no limit to the size of counting numbers.

EXAMPLE 7.33 A DISCRETE RANDOM VARIABLE WITH INFINITE POSSIBILITIES

Background: Suppose we roll a die repeatedly and let X be the number of rolls until a 6 appears.

Question: Is X discrete or continuous?

Response: Even though the possible values of X are infinite, X is discrete because those values are distinct and correspond to the counting numbers 1, 2, 3, and so on.

Practice: *Try Exercise 7.42 on page 330.*

In contrast, a continuous random variable not only has an infinite number of possible values, but these comprise an entire interval, such as all real numbers between 0 and 1. Whereas discrete variables are limited to particular values, often at evenly spaced intervals, continuous variables can take any value in between.

For practical purposes, we often either consciously or unconsciously restrict our recording of a quantitative variable's values to certain distinct possibilities. For instance, students may have been asked to record their height to the nearest inch, or they may have done so naturally. But in reality, if a large number of students were lined up in height order, their heights would not conform to distinct steps like a staircase—they could take any of an infinite number of possible heights between the whole-inch values. Thus, although the data may appear to have only whole-inch values, the variable height is still continuous.

The next example should help us get a feel for distinguishing among categorical, discrete quantitative, and continuous quantitative variables.

EXAMPLE 7.34 VARIABLES CATEGORICAL OR DISCRETE QUANTITATIVE OR CONTINUOUS QUANTITATIVE

Background: Our survey data file contains information about the values of many variables for several hundred students:

Age	Breakfast?	Comp	Credits	Earnings	Ht	Math SAT	Random #	Sex	...
19.67	No	120	15	1,000	59	620	13	F	
20.08	No	120	16	6,000	76	420	13	M	
19.08	Yes	40	14	0	65	650	13	F	
...	...	...	...	...	...	...	...	...	

Question: What type of variable is each of those that appears in the table excerpt?

Response:

1. Age: continuous quantitative

2. Breakfast: categorical

3. Comp (time spent on the computer the day before): continuous quantitative

4. Credits: discrete quantitative

5. Earnings: discrete or continuous quantitative, depending on whether you want to disallow "in-between" earnings, like one-third of $1,000

6. Ht: continuous quantitative

7. Math SAT: discrete quantitative

8. Random # (number picked from 1 to 20): discrete quantitative

9. Sex: categorical

Practice: *Try Exercise 7.43 on page 330.*

A display for values of a continuous random variable must allow for the fact that the population may have infinitely many individuals, and that the values taken by the variable have infinitely many possibilities. This brings us to the notion of *density curves*, which we will think of as idealized probability histograms.

> *Definition*   A **density curve** is a smooth curve that represents the probability distribution of a continuous random variable. The total area under the curve is one, and the area under the curve between any two points shows the probability that the random variable takes a value between those points.

The data sets used in this book are real, and the author resisted the temptation to make the data appear more real by modifying values like the first three students' selection of a "random" number, all of which happened to be 13.

To shift our focus from discrete to continuous random variables, let's first consider the probability histogram below for shoe size X of adult males. X is a discrete random variable, because shoe sizes can take only whole and half number values—nothing in between.

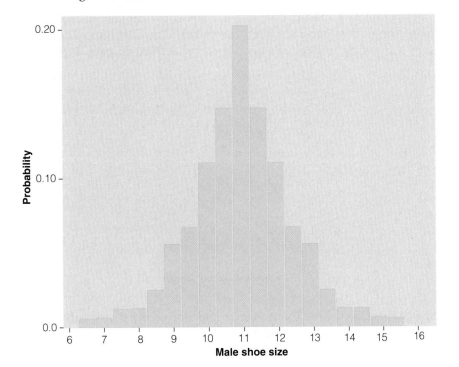

Due to the Sum-to-One Rule, which states that the sum of probabilities of all possible outcomes must be one, the heights of all the rectangles in the histogram must sum to one. It is always possible to adjust the histogram so that it represents probabilities by area instead of height. As is, the total area of the rectangles in our male shoe-size histogram is 0.50, since each rectangle has width 0.50 and the total of heights is one. If we change the vertical scale so that all vertical axis values are doubled, then the total area will be exactly one. The shape and the horizontal scale remain unchanged. Now we can tell the probability of shoe size taking a value in any interval, just by finding the area of the rectangles over that interval. For instance, the area of the rectangles up to and including 9 shows the probability of having a shoe size less than or equal to 9, shown below on the left.

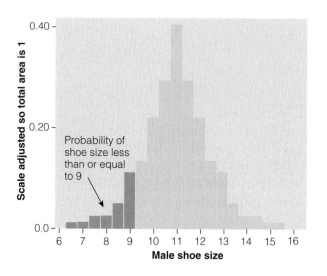
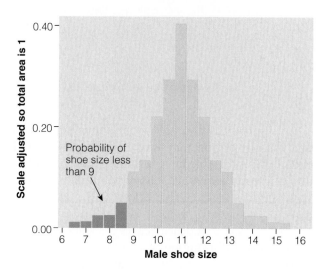

Notice that for a discrete random variable like shoe size, the probability is affected by whether we want strict inequality or not. For example, the area—and corresponding probability—is reduced if we consider only shoe sizes *strictly* less than 9, shown above on the right.

Now consider another random variable X = foot length of adult males. Unlike shoe size, this variable is not limited to distinct, separate values, because foot lengths can take any value over a continuous range of possibilities. If we have in mind a population of infinite size, and are somehow capable of measuring foot lengths to the utmost accuracy, then the probability distribution can be represented by a smooth curve called a *density curve*, defined on page 313.

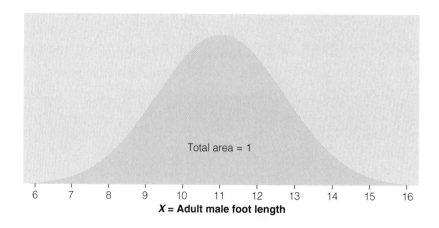

Like the modified probability histograms above, a density curve represents probabilities by area: The area under the curve between any two points shows the probability that the random variable takes a value between those points. Just as the Sum-to-One Rule requires the total of the histogram areas to equal one (when we are representing probability by area, not height), the total area under any density curve likewise must equal one. The vertical scale here would be similar to that of the modified probability histograms for shoe size, but it has been omitted because we are concentrating on area, not height, to find probabilities.

For example, the probability of a foot length less than 9 is represented by the shaded area below.

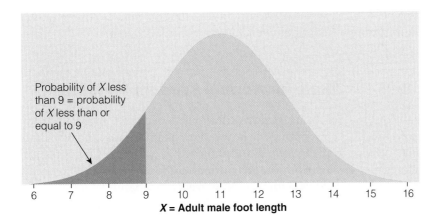

Probability of *X* less than 9 = probability of *X* less than or equal to 9

X = Adult male foot length

© Roy McMahon/CORBIS

What's the difference between a foot length and a shoe size?

We have seen that for a discrete random variable like shoe size, strict inequality or not matters when solving for probabilities. In contrast, for a continuous random variable like foot length, the probability of a foot length less than or equal to 9 will be the same as the probability of a foot length strictly less than 9. Because a continuous random variable has infinitely many possible values, technically, the probability of any single value occurring is zero! In terms of our density curve, the area under the curve up to and including a certain point is the same as the area up to and excluding the point, because there is no area over a single point.

Density curves, like probability histograms, can have any shape imaginable as long as the total area underneath the curve is 1. As anyone who has studied calculus can attest, finding the area under a curve can be difficult. In this book, our approach to normal probabilities will be to refer to the 68-95-99.7 Rule or other key points of the distribution that are often singled out for the purpose of performing statistical inference. Eventually, we will rely on software to report relevant probabilities.

Example TBP 7.18 on page 850 of the ***TBP Supplement*** illustrates when ordinary and strict inequalities result in the same probability. There follows a more technical discussion of how we solve for areas under continuous curves.

When a Random Variable Is Normal

Q In Part II on displaying and summarizing data, we encountered quantitative data sets—such as weights of female college students—whose distributions naturally followed a symmetric bell shape, bulging in the middle and tapering at the ends. Many variables, like IQ scores or shoe sizes or foot lengths, exhibit these properties. Symmetry indicates that the variable is just as likely to take a value a certain distance below its mean as it is to take a value that same distance above its mean. The bell shape indicates that values closer to the mean are more likely, and it becomes increasingly unlikely to take values far from the mean in either direction. The particular shape exhibited by these variables has been studied since the early part of the 19th century, when they were first called "normal" as a way of suggesting their depiction of a common, natural pattern.

Even more important than the fact that many quantitative variables themselves follow the normal curve is the role played by the normal curve in the theory of the behavior of repeated samples. Under the right conditions, the normal curve will describe the behavior of the random variable sample mean or sample proportion when repeated random samples of a given size are taken from a quantitative or categorical population, even though the population distribution itself may not be normal. Understanding the normal distribution is therefore an important step in the direction of our overall goal, which is to relate sample means or proportions to population means or proportions.

It should be noted that a true normal population is an idealized model representing an infinite number of individuals with a precise pattern of values that is not necessarily encountered in reality. Thus, if we suppose a variable like foot lengths to be normal, we have in mind a distribution that is close enough to normal that a normal model fits it well.

The 68-95-99.7 Rule for Normal Random Variables

We began to get a feel for normal distributions in Section 4.4 of Part II, when we introduced the 68-95-99.7 Rule for how values in a normally shaped sample data set behave relative to their mean $\bar{x}$ and standard deviation s. This is the same rule that dictates how the distribution of a normal random variable behaves relative to its mean μ and standard deviation σ. Now we use probability language and notation to tell about the random variable's behavior. For example, in Part II, we would have said "If the weights in our data set have a normal shape and they have mean $\bar{x}$ and standard deviation s, then about 68% of those weights should fall within s of $\bar{x}$." The analogous statement now would be "If X, the weight of a randomly chosen female college student, follows a normal distribution with mean μ and standard deviation σ, then the probability is 0.68 that a randomly chosen weight falls within σ of μ."

68-95-99.7 Rule for Normal X

If X is a normal random variable, then the probability is

- 0.68 that X takes a value within 1σ of μ—that is, in the interval $\mu \pm 1\sigma$
- 0.95 that X takes a value within 2σ of μ—that is, in the interval $\mu \pm 2\sigma$
- 0.997 that X takes a value within 3σ of μ—that is, in the interval $\mu \pm 3\sigma$

If students are comfortable with probability notation, we can write

- $0.68 = P(\mu - \sigma \leq X \leq \mu + \sigma)$
- $0.95 = P(\mu - 2\sigma \leq X \leq \mu + 2\sigma)$
- $0.997 = P(\mu - 3\sigma \leq X \leq \mu + 3\sigma)$

Notice that the information from the rule can be interpreted from the perspective of the outside "tails" of the normal curve: Since 0.68 is the probability of being within 1 standard deviation of the mean, the "Not" Rule tells us that $(1 - 0.68) = 0.32$ is the probability of being farther than 1 standard deviation away. By the symmetry of the normal density curve, we can state that for a normal random variable X, the probability is

- $(1 - 0.68)/2 = 0.16$ that X takes a value below $\mu - 1\sigma$ (also 0.16 that X takes a value above $\mu + 1\sigma$)
- $(1 - 0.95)/2 = 0.025$ that X takes a value below $\mu - 2\sigma$ (also 0.025 that X takes a value above $\mu + 2\sigma$)
- $(1 - 0.997)/2 = 0.0015$ that X takes a value below $\mu - 3\sigma$ (also 0.0015 that X takes a value above $\mu + 3\sigma$)

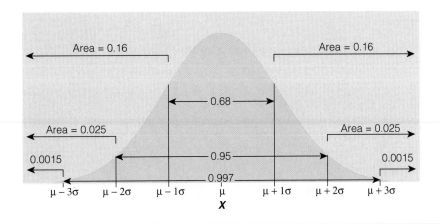

EXAMPLE 7.35 THE 68-95-99.7 RULE FOR A NORMAL RANDOM VARIABLE

Background: IQ for a randomly chosen adult, as measured by the Wechsler Adult Intelligence Scale, is a normal random variable X with a mean of $\mu = 100$ and a standard deviation of $\sigma = 15$.

Question: What does the 68-95-99.7 Rule tell us about the probability distribution of X?

Response: We can sketch a normal curve centered at 100, along with probabilities 68%, 95%, and 99.7%, respectively, of falling within 1, 2, or 3 standard deviations of 100, where a standard deviation equals 15. Tail probabilities are shown as well.

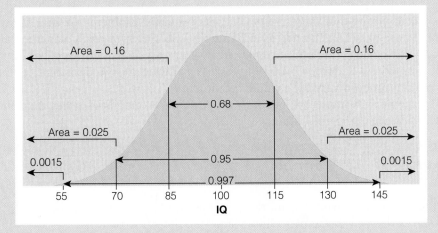

Practice: *Try Exercise 7.47 on page 331.*

A probability distribution sketch based on the 68-95-99.7 Rule helps us answer questions about the probability that our random variable takes values over certain intervals.

EXAMPLE 7.36 FINDING PROBABILITIES WITH A SKETCH BASED ON THE 68-95-99.7 RULE

Background: We begin with a sketch of the probability distribution of IQ, as constructed in Example 7.35 with the help of the 68-95-99.7 Rule.

Continued

Questions:

1. What is the probability that a randomly chosen person will have an IQ between 70 and 130?

2. What is the probability that a randomly chosen person will have an IQ less than 70?

3. What is the probability that a randomly chosen IQ is less than 100?

4. An IQ is almost guaranteed (probability 0.997) to fall between what two values?

5. The probability is only 0.025 that an IQ will be greater than what score?

Responses:

1. 0.95 or 95%, because $P(70 \leq X \leq 130) = 0.95$ [same as $P(70 < X < 130)$]

2. 0.025 or 2.5%, because $P(X < 70) = 0.025$ [same as $P(X \leq 70)$]

3. 0.50 or 50%, because $P(X < 100) = 0.50$ [Since 100 is the mean, by the symmetry of the normal density curve, it is also the median. Half of *any* normal random variable's values fall below its mean and the other half above.]

4. 55 and 145, because $0.997 = P(55 \leq X \leq 145)$.

5. 130, because $0.025 = P(X > 130)$.

Practice: *Try Exercise 7.48 on page 331.*

It is worth noting that there are two types of normal problems we may want to solve. Those like (1), (2), and (3) in Example 7.36 specify a particular interval of values of a normal random variable, and we are asked to find a probability. In problems like (4) and (5), a probability is given and we are asked to identify where the normal random variable's values would be.

In the next example, we begin to think about probabilities other than those featured in the 68-95-99.7 Rule.

EXAMPLE 7.37 USING THE 68-95-99.7 RULE TO ESTIMATE PROBABILITIES

Background: Consider again the distribution of male foot lengths, which is normal with a mean of 11 and a standard deviation of 1.5:

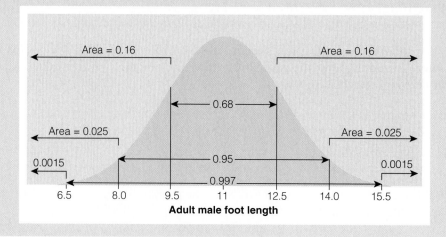

There are various ways to determine normal probabilities, such as the one sought in Example 7.37, more precisely. Before software became readily available, tables were used. In this book, we will concentrate on the use of computers to solve such problems, as is done in almost all current applications. We will also stress the usefulness of estimation skills for getting a "ballpark range" for a probability, as we did when we concluded that the probability of interest in Example 7.37 must lie between 0.16 and 0.025.

Question: What is the approximate probability of a foot length larger than 13 inches?

Response: Since 13 inches is somewhere between 1 and 2 standard deviations above the mean, we can use the 68-95-99.7 Rule to give a rough estimate for the probability of being greater than 13: It is somewhere between 0.16 and 0.025.

Practice: *Try Exercise 7.49(c,d) on page 331.*

There is a different normal distribution for every different combination of values for μ and σ. The easiest way to put any value of a normal variable in perspective is to *standardize*—that is, determine exactly how many standard deviations below or above the mean that value is.

Standardizing and Unstandardizing: From Original Values to z or Vice Versa

The first step in assessing a probability associated with a value of a normal variable is to determine the relative value with respect to all the other values taken by that normal variable. This is accomplished by determining how many standard deviations below or above the mean that value is.

The process of standardizing the value of a normal random variable exactly parallels the process of standardizing a value in a normal data set. In Section 4.4 of Part II, we found the z-score of a value x in a normal *data* set to be that value minus the mean of all the *data* values, divided by the standard deviation of the *data* values: $z = \frac{x - \bar{x}}{s}$. Now, in the context of a normal *random variable* X, the standardized normal value z tells how many standard deviations σ below or above the mean μ a certain value x of X is. The standardized value z is now written as

$$z = \frac{x - \mu}{\sigma}$$

Notice that, since σ is always positive, for values of x above the mean μ, z will be positive. For values of x below μ, z will be negative.

Sometimes, a standardized value is reported, and we would like to know what the original value was. We can isolate x in the above formula for z, and write

$$x = \mu + z\sigma$$

You can think of this process as "unstandardizing" from z to x.

It is common for students to learn to evaluate normal probabilities with the use of a table that fills in a large amount of detail between the sparse information provided by the 68-95-99.7 Rule. On one hand, it is useful to have the skill to assess the probability that a normal variable takes a value in *any* given interval, assuming you know the mean and standard deviation. On the other hand, there is often considerable time and effort expended in order to acquire this skill, which is not really essential, now that software is so readily available. Therefore, we will stress getting a feel for how usual or unusual a value of a normal variable is—a skill that will be useful in Part IV when we want to make decisions about the unknown value of a population parameter.

Estimating z Probabilities with a Sketch of the 68-95-99.7 Rule

The fact that the standard normal curve is symmetric about 0 and encompasses a total area of 1 tells us that the areas on either side of $z = 0$ are both 0.5. The

---

The process of standardizing occurs not just in the context of normal distributions, but also for the other distributions mentioned, such as t, F, and χ^2. Thus, getting a feel for how standardized values relate to probabilities is a very important skill throughout much of Part IV.

Examples TBP 7.19 and TBP 7.20 starting on page 850 of the *TBP Supplement* review the process of standardizing and unstandardizing that we saw for normally distributed data values in Chapter 5.

The other disadvantage of using a table, as opposed to a curve showing the 68-95-99.7 Rule or the 90-95-98-99 Rule to be presented later in this section, is that there is a greater risk of a disconnect between the hundreds of numbers in the table—both z values and probabilities—and their meanings. In other words, too often students using tables "can't see the forest for the trees."

68-95-99.7 Rule, expressed for the standard normal random variable Z whose mean is 0 and standard deviation is 1, is stated as follows.

68-95-99.7 Rule for Standard Normal Z

If Z is a standard normal random variable, then the probability is

- 0.68 that Z takes a value in the interval $(-1, +1)$
- 0.95 that Z takes a value in the interval $(-2, +2)$
- 0.997 that Z takes a value in the interval $(-3, +3)$

If we want to focus on "outside" regions instead of "inside," the rule tells us that the probability is

- 0.16 that Z takes a value below -1
  (also 0.16 that Z takes a value above $+1$)
- 0.025 that Z takes a value below -2
  (also 0.025 that Z takes a value above $+2$)
- 0.0015 that Z takes a value below -3
  (also 0.0015 that Z takes a value above $+3$)

The above information from the 68-95-99.7 Rule, displayed in the sketch below, provides us with a quick tool for estimating probabilities associated with z values, or estimating z values for a given probability.

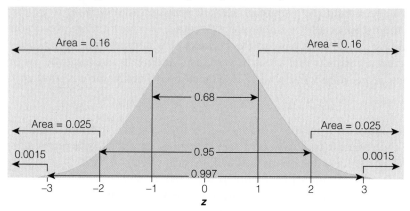

Once we have found the z-score for the value of a normal random variable, we can use the rule or the sketch to characterize how usual or unusual that value is. This is especially helpful in situations where we have little instinct for what should be typical.

The same criteria can be used as those that applied to standardized values from a normally distributed data set in Section 4.4, with these guidelines that were presented on page 117.

Size of z	Unusual?
$|z|$ greater than 3	Extremely unusual
$|z|$ between 2 and 3	Very unusual
$|z|$ between 1.75 and 2	Unusual
$|z|$ between 1.5 and 1.75	May be unusual (depends on circumstances)
$|z|$ between 1 and 1.5	Somewhat low/high, but not unusual
$|z|$ less than 1	Quite common

EXAMPLE 7.38 CHARACTERIZING NORMAL VALUES BASED ON Z-SCORES

Background: An experiment explored the neural activity in rats that were injected with a substance to increase their blood pressure. Blood pressure rises (where the units were mmHg) for the dosage given are approximately normal with a mean of $\mu = 52$ and a standard deviation of $\sigma = 23$.[7]

Question: How would we characterize a blood pressure rise of 102?

Response: The z-score for 102 is $(102 - 52)/23 = 2.17$. Based on what we know about the z curve, this value can be characterized as being "very unusual" on the high side (toward the outer fringe of the right side of the curve), but not "extremely high" (not completely beyond the extreme right edge in our sketch).

Practice: *Try Exercise 7.51 on page 332.*

We can use the sketch of the 68-95-99.7 Rule to estimate probabilities for values of z that are not exactly 1, 2, or 3.

EXAMPLE 7.39 ESTIMATING PROBABILITIES WITH THE 68-95-99.7 RULE

Background: The 68-95-99.7 Rule tells us the probabilities of being within 1, 2, or 3 standard deviations of the mean. Combined with the fact that the total area under the normal curve is 1, the rule also tells us the probabilities of being farther than 1, 2, or 3 standard deviations from the mean in either direction.

Questions: Referring to the sketch of the 68-95-99.7 Rule, what is the approximate probability that a normal random variable takes a value

1. Less than the value that is 2.8 standard deviations above the mean?

2. Less than the value that is 1.47 standard deviations below the mean?

3. More than the value that is 0.75 standard deviations above the mean?

Responses:

1. Since $+2.8$ is toward the right-most extreme of the z curve, $P(Z < +2.8)$ will be close to the area under the entire curve, which is 1. [Tables or software give a precise answer of 0.9974.]

2. Since -1.47 is between -2 and -1, $P(Z < -1.47)$ will be somewhere between 0.025 and 0.16. [Tables or software give a precise answer of 0.0708.]

3. Since $+0.75$ is between 0 and $+1$, $P(Z > +0.75)$ is more than 0.16 but less than 0.50. [See the illustration on the next page; tables or software give a precise answer of 0.2266.]

Continued

Page 851 of the *TBP Supplement* features sketches of the probabilities estimated in parts 1 and 2 of Example 7.39.

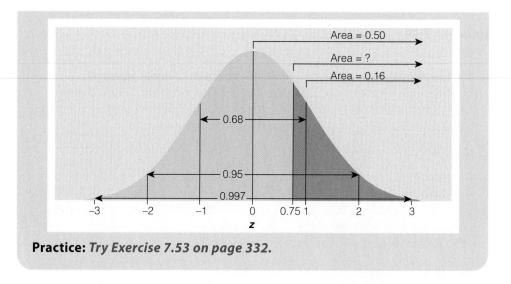

Practice: *Try Exercise 7.53 on page 332.*

When normal probability problems involve z values that go beyond -3 or $+3$, we can either refer to the sketch or simply use common sense.

We can alert students that z-scores as extreme as those seen in Example 7.40 may never occur for certain normal variables: There has never been an adult male whose height was 34.4 standard deviations above the mean. However, it is not so uncommon to encounter such extreme z-scores when we perform inference. In this context, z will measure how far what we observe is from what would be the case if there was "nothing going on." Thus, if a drug is very effective for treating an illness, experiments may produce a z as extreme as 34.4.

EXAMPLE 7.40 PROBABILITIES FOR EXTREME Z-SCORES

Background: According to the 68-95-99.7 Rule, the probability is 0.997 that z is between -3 and $+3$.

Questions: What is the approximate probability of a normal random variable being

1. Less than 11.62 standard deviations below the mean?

2. Greater than 25.1 standard deviations below the mean?

3. Less than 6.009 standard deviations above the mean?

4. Greater than 34.4 standard deviations above the mean?

Responses:

1. There is practically no area under the z curve below -11.62, so we say the probability is approximately 0.

2. Virtually all the z curve area occurs to the right of -25.1, so we say the probability is approximately 1.

3. Almost all the area is to the left of $+6.009$: the probability is approximately 1.

4. The probability of being greater than 34.4 standard deviations above the mean is approximately 0.

Practice: *Try Exercise 7.54 on page 332.*

The problems in the following example present information given and information sought in reverse order from those in Examples 7.39 and 7.40. Now a probability is given and we are asked to find a z value. Again, our answers using the 68-95-99.7 Rule will just be rough estimates.

EXAMPLE 7.41 ESTIMATING Z-SCORE GIVEN A PROBABILITY

Background: Again, we have the information provided by the 68-95-99.7 Rule.

Questions: Based on a sketch of the 68-95-99.7 Rule, what are the approximate values of the following z-scores?

1. The probability is 0.01 that a standardized normal variable takes a value below what value of z?

2. The probability is 0.15 that a standardized normal variable takes a value above what value of z?

Responses:

1. According to a sketch, since 0.01 is between 0.0015 and 0.025, z must be somewhere between -3 and -2. [Tables or software give a precise answer of $z = -2.33$.]

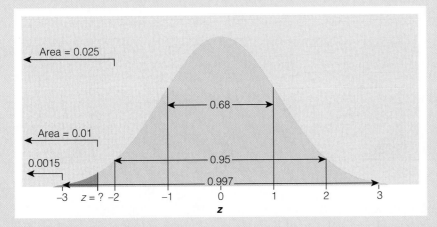

2. Again we can look at a sketch of the 68-95-99.7 Rule for z. Since 0.15 is just under 0.16, z must be just over 1. [Tables or software give a precise answer of $z = +1.04$.]

Practice: *Try Exercise 7.57 on page 332.*

Page 852 of the **TBP** *Supplement* shows a sketch for the response to the second part of Example 7.41.

Page 852 of the **TBP** *Supplement* shows a sketch of the quartiles of the normal curve, encountered in Response 2 of Example 7.42.

The Big *Picture:*

LOOKING BACK

The fact that the middle 50% of students' sleep times fall between 6 and 8 hours tells us that 6 and 8 are the *quartiles* of the distribution to be discussed in Example 7.42. Quartiles were intoduced in Chapter 4. In general, z-scores of -0.67 and $+0.67$ correspond to the quartiles of any normal distribution.

Nonstandard Normal Probabilities

In Example 7.35 on page 317, we used the 68-95-99.7 Rule to sketch the distribution of IQ scores. In Example 7.37 on page 318, we used the rule to sketch the distribution of foot lengths. Instead of drawing a new sketch for every different normal variable encountered, a more efficient approach is to work with standardized values, for which the same sketch of z values and associated probabilities always applies.

EXAMPLE 7.42 ESTIMATING PROBABILITIES BY STANDARDIZING AND USING THE 68-95-99.7 RULE

Background: Typical nightly hours slept by college students are normal with a mean of 7 and a standard deviation of 1.5.

Questions: What is the approximate probability of a randomly chosen student sleeping

1. More than 9 hours?

2. Between 6 and 8 hours?

3. Exactly 6.14 hours?

Responses:

1. To find the probability of sleeping more than 9 hours, we first standardize: $z = (9 - 7)/1.5 = +1.33$. The probability that we seek, $P(X > 9)$, is the same as the probability $P(Z > +1.33)$ that a normal random variable takes a value greater than 1.33 standard deviations above its mean. According to the sketches below, this probability is somewhere between 0.025 and 0.16. Sleeping more than 9 hours is on the long side, but not too unusual. [Tables or software would give a precise answer of 0.0918.]

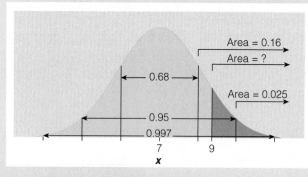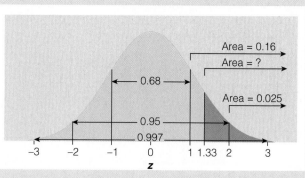

2. The standardized values of 6 and 8 are, respectively, $z = (6 - 7)/1.5 = -0.67$ and $(8 - 7)/1.5 = +0.67$. According to the sketch, the probability of being between these values is substantial, but clearly less than the area between -1 and $+1$, which is 0.68. [Tables or software give a precise answer of 0.4972.]

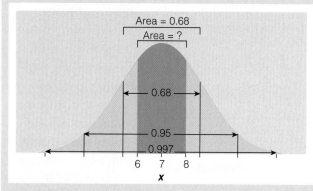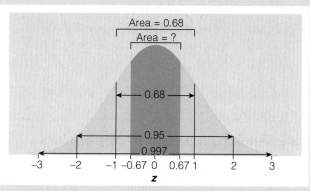

3. Time is a continuous random variable, with an infinite number of possible values. The probability of exactly taking any one particular value (such as 6.14) is zero. This is consistent with the fact that the area under the normal curve over any single *point* is zero: There is a nonzero area only when we work with probabilities over *intervals*.

Practice: *Try Exercise 7.59 on page 333.*

In Example 7.42, we were given values of a normal random variable, and asked to find an associated probability. The two basic steps in the solution process are to (1) standardize to z; and (2) estimate probabilities by looking at a sketch. The next example will be a different type of problem: Given a certain probability, you will be asked to estimate the associated value x of the normal random variable X. The solution process will go more or less in reverse order from what it was for the preceding example.

EXAMPLE 7.43 ESTIMATING NORMAL VALUES BY USING THE 68-95-99.7 RULE AND UNSTANDARDIZING

Background: Again, typical nightly hours slept by college students are normal with a mean of 7 and a standard deviation of 1.5.

Questions: What are the following sleep times, approximately?

1. The probability is 0.04 that a randomly chosen student will sleep less than how many hours?

2. The probability is 0.20 that a randomly chosen student will sleep more than how many hours?

Responses:

1. According to the sketch on the left, a probability of 0.04 below is associated with z somewhere between -2 and -1 (closer to -2). So the time we seek is somewhere between 2 and 1 standard deviations below the mean time: between $7 - 2(1.5)$ and $7 - 1(1.5)$—that is, between 4 and 5.5 hours. The sketch on the right shows the unstandardized value sought, in terms of x instead of z. [Tables or software give a precise answer of $z = -1.75$, which unstandardizes to $x = 7 - 1.75(1.5) = 4.375$ hours.]

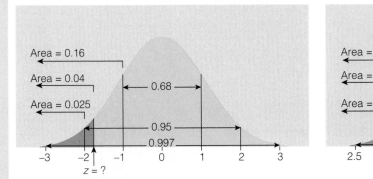
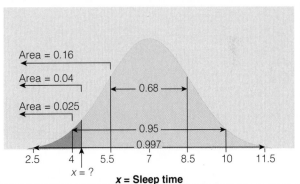

2. Since 0.20 is somewhat more than 0.16, the associated z value is somewhat less than 1 (but greater than 0, because the value sought is above average). The unstandardized value must be between the average and 1 standard deviation above average: between 7 and 8.5. [Tables or software give a precise answer of $z = +0.84$, which unstandardizes to $x = 7 + 0.84(1.5) = 8.26$ hours.]

Practice: *Try Exercise 7.61(a) on page 333.*

Note that part 1 of Example 7.43, which asked, "The probability is 0.04 that a randomly chosen student will sleep less than how many hours?" could have been rephrased as: "0.04 is the proportion of all students' sleep times that are below what value?" The latter phrasing takes the perspective of thinking about the probability as a *proportion of occurrences in the long run*, as discussed at the beginning of Chapter 6. The original question, in terms of probability, focuses on the

Example TBP 7.21 on page 853 of the **TBP** *Supplement* is formulated in terms of percentiles.

chance of a randomly chosen individual from a normal population having a value in a given interval. We also could have phrased it as follows: "What sleep time is in the 4th percentile?"

By now we have had practice in getting approximate answers to normal probability problems "in both directions": those where a value of a normal variable is given and we are asked to estimate a probability, and those where a probability is given and we are asked to estimate the value. Strategies for solving such problems are summarized on page 337 of the Chapter Summary.

Tails of the Normal Curve: The 90-95-98-99 Rule

In Part IV, we will learn to perform two types of statistical inference, known as "confidence intervals" and "hypothesis tests." When we set up a confidence interval, we state our conclusions in terms of an interval that has a fairly high probability—such as 90%, 95%, or 99%—of containing the parameter of interest. When we carry out a hypothesis test, we state our conclusions in terms of whether or not the probability of obtaining a sample statistic as extreme as the one observed is very low—such as lower than 5% or 1%. Thus, both types of inference require us to focus on probabilities for values that are on the tails of the normal curve, in the vicinity of $z = -2$ or $z = +2$. With that goal in mind, we now provide information about normal probabilities to supplement what we already know from the 68-95-99.7 Rule. If you like, you can think of it as the "90-95-98-99 Rule."

The following sketch illustrates detailed z-scores and probabilities for *inside* areas in the vicinity of $z = \pm 2$.

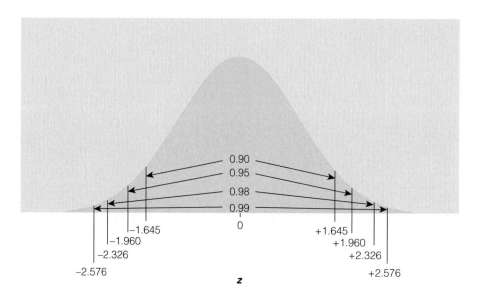

We can put this information into words as follows.

90-95-98-99 Rule for the Tails of a Standard Normal Curve

If Z is a standardized normal random variable, then the probability is

- 0.90 that Z takes a value in the interval $(-1.645, +1.645)$
- 0.95 that Z takes a value in the interval $(-1.960, +1.960)$
- 0.98 that Z takes a value in the interval $(-2.326, +2.326)$
- 0.99 that Z takes a value in the interval $(-2.576, +2.576)$

The following sketch illustrates the same *z*-scores and corresponding probabilities on the *outside* tails of the standard normal curve. Notice that the same information from the preceding sketch is being presented in a different way.

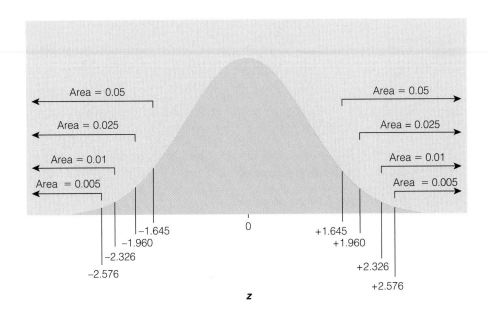

Again, we can express this information with words as follows:

If *Z* is a standardized normal random variable, then the probability is

- 0.05 that *Z* takes a value less than −1.645 and
  0.05 that *Z* takes a value greater than +1.645

- 0.025 that *Z* takes a value less than −1.960 and
  0.025 that *Z* takes a value greater than +1.960

- 0.01 that *Z* takes a value less than −2.326 and
  0.01 that *Z* takes a value greater than +2.326

- 0.005 that *Z* takes a value less than −2.576 and
  0.005 that *Z* takes a value greater than +2.576

Notice that these "landmarks" of the tails of the standard normal curve include the "95" part of the 68-95-99.7 Rule, with the *z*-score reported more precisely as 1.96 instead of 2. All of the *z*-scores are stated with a high degree of precision because researchers use them to report very accurate results.

Once we know what is true for *z*-scores, we can deduce what is true about values of any normal random variable, as long as we know its mean and standard deviation.

Page 853 of the **TBP Supplement** previews solving for *P*-values by using these tail probabilities and the "Or" Rule.

EXAMPLE 7.44 ESTIMATING PROBABILITIES BASED ON INFORMATION ABOUT THE TAILS OF THE NORMAL CURVE

Background: According to one source, waist circumference in inches for women in their twenties is a normal random variable with a mean of 32 and a standard deviation of 5.

Questions: What does the sketch of the tails of the normal curve tell us about the probability of a waist circumference being

Continued

1. More than 43 inches?

2. Less than 23 inches?

3. More than 39 inches?

Responses:

1. $z = (43 - 32)/5 = +2.2$ is between $+1.96$ and $+2.326$, so the probability of being more than this is between 0.025 and 0.01.

2. $z = (23 - 32)/5 = -1.8$ is between -1.96 and -1.645, so the probability of being less than this is between 0.025 and 0.05.

3. $z = (39 - 32)/5 = +1.4$ is less than $+1.645$, so the probability of being more than this is greater than 0.05.

Practice: *Try Exercise 7.63 on page 333.*

A useful skill for performing inference in the future will involve standardizing a value of a normal random variable and deciding if the probability of being this extreme is more or less than a given cut-off value, like 0.01 or 0.05.

EXAMPLE 7.45 COMPARING A PROBABILITY TO A CUT-OFF VALUE

Background: Heights in centimeters of girls at the start of 1st grade are approximately normal with a mean of 122 and a standard deviation of 5.

Question: Is the probability of being taller than 130 centimeters greater or less than 0.05?

Response: The standardized height is $z = \frac{130 - 122}{5} = +1.6$. Since this is not as extreme as $+1.645$, the probability of being taller than 130 centimeters must be greater than 0.05.

Practice: *Try Exercise 7.67 on page 334.*

In Example 7.44, we were given values of a normal random variable in the vicinity of $+2$ or -2, and asked to find an associated probability. The two basic steps in the solution process are to (1) standardize to z; and (2) estimate probabilities by looking at a sketch of the tails of the normal curve. The next example will be a different type of problem: Given a certain probability, you will be asked to find the associated value x of the normal random variable X. Again, we are working with probabilities that take us to the outer fringes of the normal curve. The solution process will go more or less in reverse order from what it was for Example 7.44.

EXAMPLE 7.46 FINDING VALUES BASED ON TAIL PROBABILITIES OF THE NORMAL CURVE

Background: Math SAT scores for a certain population of college students may be considered to be a normal random variable with a mean of 610 and a standard deviation of 72.

Questions: What does the sketch of the tails of the normal curve tell us about the following SAT scores?

1. If a student is chosen at random, the probability is 0.98 that his or her Math SAT score is between what two values (that are equally distant from the mean)?

2. If a student is chosen at random, the probability is 0.05 that his or her Math SAT score is below what value?

3. The top half of a percent scored how high?

Responses:

1. According to the sketch on page 326, the probability is 0.98 that a normal random variable takes a value within 2.326 standard deviations of its mean. In this case, that would be in the interval from 610 − 2.326(72) to 610 + 2.326(72). The interval is (443, 777).

2. According to the sketch, the probability is 0.05 that a normal random variable takes a value less than 1.645 standard deviations below its mean. In this case, that would be below 610 − 1.645(72) = 492. In other words, 492 is the cut-off for the lowest 5% of scores for this population of students.

3. The probability is 0.005 that a normal random variable takes a value more than 2.576 standard deviations above its mean. Therefore, half a percent would be above 610 + 2.576(72) = 795.

Practice: *Try Exercise 7.69 on page 334.*

A government ruling about the use of growth hormones provides the context for a thought-provoking discussion of the tails of the normal curve.

Students Talk Stats

Means, Standard Deviations, and Below-Average Heights

*A*n article entitled, "Tall Enough?" is being discussed by students in a statistics course:

"In July of 2003, the Food and Drug Administration decided doctors could prescribe a growth hormone preparation called Humatrope, made by Eli Lilly Co., for children who aren't lacking the hormone but were still more than 2.25 standard deviations below the average height for their age and sex . . ."[8]

The students are supposed to find how short a male or female adult would be, at 2.25 standard deviations below average, and comment on ethical issues involved in the use of such a drug. They are to work under the assumption that female heights have a mean of 64.5 inches and a standard deviation of 2.5 inches; male heights have a mean of 70.0 inches and a standard deviation of 3.0 inches. Both distributions are normal.

Students Talk Stats continued →

Students Talk Stats continued

Adam: *"2.25 standard deviations below average for the men is 70 minus 2.25 times 3, that's 63 and a quarter inches. You couldn't do anything at that height except maybe get the midget part in some movies. I'd say go for the hormone."*

Brittany: *"63 and a quarter inches is only half a standard deviation below what's average for women. Almost a third of all women get by at that height, so why should it be so hard for men? But if women are 2.25 standard deviations below average, that's 64.5 minus 2.25 times 2.5, which is about 59 inches. You can't even see a movie in the theater at that height unless you sit way in the front!"*

Carlos: *"If you look up the area under the standard normal curve to the left of minus 2.25, it's a little more than 0.01. One in 100 would turn out to be an awful lot of people. To me it sounds like the drug manufacturers are trying to create a superior race, by eliminating the shortest 1%. Why not just let the kids stay short, as long as their health isn't affected?"*

Dominique: *"The problem is that everybody wants to be average or above average. As long as the standard deviation isn't zero, there's got to be some spread, and that means some people are below average and others are above. People may only want variability in one direction, but it doesn't work that way."*

Normal random variables are summarized on page 336 of the Chapter Summary.

EXERCISES FOR SECTION 7.3

Continuous Random Variables and the Normal Distribution

Note: Asterisked numbers indicate exercises whose answers are provided in the Solutions to Selected Exercises section, on page 689.

*7.42 Suppose a student is asked to choose any odd (positive) number at random, and X is the value chosen. Tell whether X is a discrete or continuous random variable; if it is discrete, report its possible values.

*7.43 Tell whether each of the following involves a categorical variable, a discrete quantitative variable, or a continuous quantitative variable.

   a. Depth of fish fossils found below the sea floor

   b. Whether a country's government pays for at least half of higher education costs

   c. How many evenings a student went out in the week preceding a survey

   d. The proportion of higher education costs paid by the government in each of many countries around the world

   e. Vertical drop of various ski slopes

   f. Body mass of dinosaur specimens

   g. Number of 2004 Olympic medals won by various countries

7.44 Tell whether each of the following involves a categorical variable, a discrete quantitative variable, or a continuous quantitative variable.

   a. Number of McDonald's restaurants in various countries around the world

   b. Time before a child's epileptic seizure that the family dog shows signs of anticipation

   c. Whether or not a pedometer reports mileage accurately

   d. Students' self-rating of intelligence, on a scale of 1 to 7

   e. Femur bone lengths of dinosaur specimens

   f. What language is spoken in various American households

g. The proportion of households with Spanish as the first language in each of the 50 states

*7.45 For each of the following situations, tell whether the two probabilities should be equal:

a. The probability of a student going out at least two evenings in a week, and the probability of going out more than two evenings in a week

b. The probability that the mean number of evenings out for all 12th-graders is at least 2, and the probability that the mean number of evenings out for all 12th-graders is more than 2

c. The probability that a mallard duck weighs less than 500 grams, and the probability that a mallard duck weighs no more than 500 grams

d. The probability that more than one-third of all high school seniors cut classes at least once in a month, and the probability that at least one-third of all high school seniors cut classes at least once in a month

7.46 For each of the following situations, tell whether the two probabilities should be equal:

a. The probability that the mean Verbal SAT score of all students in a state is below 500, and the probability that the mean Verbal SAT score of all students in a state is 500 or less

b. The probability of a household having fewer than three cats, and the probability of a household having no more than three cats

c. The probability of a particular baseball player pitching more than one no-hitter in a season, and the probability of the baseball player pitching one or more no-hitters in a season

*7.47 A young woman is chosen at random from the population of women in their twenties, whose waist circumference is a normal random variable with mean 32 inches, standard deviation 5 inches. Use the 68-95-99.7 Rule to sketch the probability distribution of the woman's waist circumference X.

*7.48 Heights in centimeters of girls at the start of 1st grade are approximately normal with

mean 122, standard deviation 5. Use the 68-95-99.7 Rule to answer the following.

a. Find $P(107 \leq X \leq 137)$, the probability that a randomly chosen girl at the start of 1st grade is between 107 and 137 centimeters tall.

b. Find $P(X > 127)$, the probability that a randomly chosen girl at the start of 1st grade is more than 127 centimeters tall.

c. The probability is 0.95 that a randomly chosen girl at the start of 1st grade has a height between what values, in centimeters?

d. The probability is 2.5% that a randomly chosen girl at the start of 1st grade has a height below what value, in centimeters?

*7.49 A young woman is chosen at random from the population of women in their twenties, for whom waist circumference is a normal random variable with mean 32 inches, standard deviation 5 inches. Exercise 7.47 asked for a sketch of this distribution, based on the 68-95-99.7 Rule.

a. Find the probability of a waist more than 42 inches.

b. Tell whether or not 42 inches can be considered unusually large.

c. Estimate the probability of a waist less than 20 inches.

d. Tell whether 20 inches can be considered unusually small.

e. If a woman's waist circumference is 20 inches, how many standard deviations below or above the mean is it?

f. What is the z-score for a waist circumference of 20 inches?

g. Find the waist circumference of a woman whose z-score is $+0.8$.

7.50 Weights in kilograms of boys at the start of 1st grade are approximately normal with mean 25, standard deviation 5. Use the 68-95-99.7 Rule to answer the following.

a. Find $P(15 \leq X \leq 35)$, the probability that a randomly chosen boy at the start of 1st grade weighs between 15 and 35 kilograms.

b. Find $P(X < 20)$, the probability that a randomly chosen boy at the start of 1st grade weighs under 20 kilograms.

c. The probability is 99.7% that a randomly chosen boy at the start of 1st grade has a weight between what values, in kilograms?

d. The probability is 0.16 that a randomly chosen boy at the start of 1st grade weighs more than how many kilograms?

*7.51 Children's gross motor development is assessed with an overall motor quotient, MQ, which follows an approximate normal distribution, with mean 100 and standard deviation 15. The following MQs are all above average; find their z-scores and characterize each as being exceptional, borderline, or unexceptional, if we decide to call the MQ "exceptional" if it is considerably more than 2 standard deviations above the mean, "borderline" if it is close to 2 standard deviations above the mean, and "unexceptional" otherwise.

   a. MQ = 117

   b. MQ = 144

   c. MQ = 132

   d. MQ = 129

7.52 Children's fitness is assessed by finding the distance, in meters, that they can run in 6 minutes. Overall, this distance varies fairly normally, with mean 835 and standard deviation 111. The following distances are all below average; find their z-scores and characterize each as showing fitness to be exceptionally poor, borderline, or unexceptional, if we decide to call fitness "exceptionally poor" when distance run is considerably less than 2 standard deviations below the mean, "borderline" if it is close to 2 standard deviations below the mean, and "unexceptional" otherwise.

   a. 600 meters

   b. 354 meters

   c. 742 meters

   d. 623 meters

*7.53 The 68-95-99.7 Rule for normal distributions asserts that the probability is 0.95 that a standardized score z falls between −2 and +2. Tell whether each of the following probabilities is more than 0.025 or less than 0.025:

   a. The probability of a z-score for weight being less than −4.5

   b. The probability of a z-score for weight being less than −1.5

c. The probability of a z-score for weight being less than +1.5

d. The probability of a z-score for weight being greater than +2.1

e. The probability of a z-score for weight being greater than +1.7

f. The probability of a z-score for weight being greater than −0.7

*7.54 Report the approximate probability of z taking a value in the given range:

   a. z greater than +6.2

   b. z greater than −5

   c. z less than −21.83

   d. z less than 4.06

7.55 Report the approximate probability of z taking a value in the given range:

   a. z greater than −10

   b. z less than −4.85

   c. z greater than +9.14

   d. z less than +6.1

7.56 The 68-95-99.7 Rule for normal distributions asserts that the probability is 0.95 that a standardized score z falls between −2 and +2. Tell whether each of the following probabilities is more than 0.025 or less than 0.025:

   a. The probability of a z-score for height being less than −1.5

   b. The probability of a z-score for height being less than −2.5

   c. The probability of a z-score for height being less than +3.9

   d. The probability of a z-score for height being greater than +3.4

   e. The probability of a z-score for height being greater than +0.3

   f. The probability of a z-score for height being greater than −1.3

*7.57 Use the 68-95-99.7 Rule to estimate the z-score corresponding to the given probabilities:

   a. The probability is 0.10 that a z-score is below what value?

   b. The probability is 0.001 that a z-score is above what value?

7.58 Use the 68-95-99.7 Rule to estimate the z-score corresponding to the given probabilities:

a. The probability is 0.4 that a z-score is below what value?

b. The probability is 0.02 that a z-score is above what value?

*7.59 Heights in centimeters of girls at the start of 1st grade are approximately normal with mean 122, standard deviation 5. Based on the z-score for each of the following heights, use the 68-95-99.7 Rule to estimate the probability of being this short or shorter (if below average), or the probability of being this tall or taller (if above average).

a. 106 centimeters

b. 125 centimeters

c. 116 centimeters

7.60 Weights in kilograms of boys at the start of 1st grade are approximately normal with mean 25, standard deviation 5. Based on the z-score for each of the following weights, use the 68-95-99.7 Rule to estimate the probability of being this light or lighter (if below average), or the probability of being this heavy or heavier (if above average).

a. 31.7 kilograms

b. 47 kilograms

c. 24 kilograms

*7.61 Heights in centimeters of girls at the start of 1st grade are approximately normal with mean 122, standard deviation 5. Use the 68-95-99.7 Rule to estimate the following heights:

a. The probability is 0.02 that a girl at the start of 1st grade is taller than what height?

b. A girl's height is in the 20th percentile.

7.62 Weights in kilograms of boys at the start of 1st grade are approximately normal with mean 25, standard deviation 5. Use the 68-95-99.7 Rule to estimate the following weights:

a. The probability is 0.002 that a boy at the start of 1st grade is less than what weight?

b. The probability is 0.12 that a boy at the start of 1st grade is more than what weight?

*7.63 Chest sizes are approximately normal, with mean and standard deviation (in inches) 37.35 and 2.64 for males, 35.15 and 2.64 for females. Find the z-score for each of these chest sizes; if it is negative, give a range for the probability of a chest size that low or

lower; if positive, give a range for the probability of being that high or higher. At the extremes, one limit may be zero. [Make use of normal curve tail probabilities shown in this sketch.]

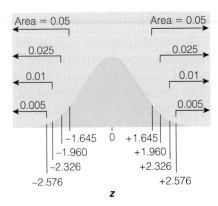

a. Male chest size 32.60 inches: z = _____, probability between _____ and _____

b. Male chest size 45.00 inches: z = _____, probability between _____ and _____

c. Female chest size 41.00 inches: z = _____, probability between _____ and _____

d. Female chest size 28.80 inches: z = _____, probability between _____ and _____

7.64 Waist sizes are approximately normal, with mean and standard deviation (in inches) 32.35 and 3.31 for males, 28.15 and 2.89 for females. Find the z-score for each of these waist sizes; if it is negative, give a range for the probability of a waist size that low or lower; if positive, give a range for the probability of being that high or higher. At the extremes, one limit may be zero. [Make use of normal curve tail probabilities shown in the preceding exercise.]

a. Male waist size 38.30 inches: z = _____, probability between _____ and _____

b. Male waist size 25.00 inches: z = _____, probability between _____ and _____

c. Female waist size 20.00 inches: z = _____, probability between _____ and _____

d. Female waist size 37.70 inches: z = _____, probability between _____ and _____

*7.65 Heights in centimeters of girls at the start of 1st grade are approximately normal with mean 122, standard deviation 5. Find the z-score for each of the following heights, and characterize it as "very short," "somewhat short," "somewhat tall," or "very tall."

a. 106 centimeters

b. 125 centimeters

c. 116 centimeters

7.66 Weights in kilograms of boys at the start of 1st grade are approximately normal with mean 25, standard deviation 5. Find the z-score for each of the following weights, and characterize it as "very light," "somewhat light," "somewhat heavy," or "very heavy."

a. 31.7 kilograms

b. 47 kilograms

c. 24 kilograms

*7.67 Information about the tails of the normal curve asserts that the probability is 0.01 that a standardized score z falls below -2.326, and 0.01 that z falls above $+2.326$. Tell whether each of the following probabilities is more than 0.01 or less than 0.01:

a. The probability of a z-score for MQ being greater than $+2.4$

b. The probability of a z-score for MQ being greater than $+1.9$

c. The probability of a z-score for MQ being less than -3.7

d. The probability of a z-score for MQ being less than -0.4

7.68 Information about the tails of the normal curve asserts that the probability is 0.05 that a standardized score z falls below -1.645, and 0.05 that z falls above $+1.645$. Tell whether each of the following probabilities about fitness (measured as distance run in 6 minutes) is more than 0.05 or less than 0.05:

a. The probability of a z-score for fitness being less than -1.9

b. The probability of a z-score for fitness being less than -1.4

c. The probability of a z-score for fitness being greater than $+1.7$

d. The probability of a z-score for fitness being greater than $+1.6$

*7.69 Ear lengths are approximately normal, with mean and standard deviation (in inches) 2.45 and 0.17 for males, 2.06 and 0.17 for females. Find the following ear lengths, making use of the z values for normal curve tail probabilities shown in Exercise 7.63.

a. The length for which the probability of a male's ear being shorter is 0.005

b. The length for which the probability of a male's ear being longer is 0.05

c. The length for which the probability of a female's ear being shorter is 0.025

d. The length for which the probability of a female's ear being longer is 0.01

7.70 Upper thigh circumferences are approximately normal, with mean and standard deviation (in inches) 22.00 and 1.88 for males, 22.30 and 1.88 for females. Find the following upper thigh circumferences, making use of the z values for normal curve tail probabilities shown in Exercise 7.63.

a. The circumference for which the probability of a male's upper thigh being smaller is 0.025

b. The circumference for which the probability of a male's upper thigh being larger is 0.005

c. The circumference for which the probability of a female's upper thigh being larger is 0.01

d. The circumference for which the probability of a female's upper thigh being smaller is 0.05

CHAPTER 7   SUMMARY

Random variables are quantitative variables whose values are subject to the laws of probability. **Discrete random variables,** whose possible values are distinct like the counting numbers, are relatively simple to understand because we usually spell out those values and their probabilities precisely in a probability distribution table or histogram. A particular type of discrete random variable, called **binomial,** is relevant when we are interested in single categorical variables. **Continuous random variables** may take any (quantitative) value over a continuous range of possibilities. These include **normal random variables,** which exhibit a particular symmetric, bell-shaped pattern. We study the normal curve in depth because of its relevance in performing statistical inference for single variables, either categorical or quantitative, and also for relationships.

Summary of Discrete Random Variables

- The **probability distribution** of a discrete random variable X is a list of its possible values x_i and their accompanying probabilities $P(X = x_i)$. The same information can be displayed in a **probability histogram**.

- Probabilities of all possible values of the random variable must sum to one, and if the probability histogram's bars are of width one, its total area must be one.

- When considering the event that a random variable X takes certain values, the probabilities of such events must obey the laws of probability established in Chapter 6.

- The **median** of a discrete random variable is the value such that the probability is 0.50 of being above or below that value. The median equals the mean for symmetric probability distributions.

- The **mean μ** of a discrete random variable X is the average of its possible values, where each value is weighted with its probability:

$$\mu = x_1 P(X = x_1) + \cdots + x_k P(X = x_k)$$

- The **standard deviation σ** of a discrete random variable X is the square root of the average squared deviation from the mean, where each squared deviation is weighted with the probability of the particular value x_i of the random variable:

$$\sigma = \sqrt{(x_1 - \mu)^2 P(X = x_1) + \cdots + (x_k - \mu)^2 P(X = x_k)}$$

- The standard deviation σ tells the typical distance of the random variable's values from its mean μ.

- The shape of the distribution of a discrete random variable can be assessed by looking at the probability histogram. Shape may be roughly normal, but other shapes are possible, such as uniform, skewed left, or skewed right.

- If a random variable X is transformed to a new random variable $aX + b$, then its mean undergoes the same transformation. Its standard deviation is simply multiplied by $|b|$:

$$\mu_{a + bX} = a + b\mu_X$$

$$\sigma_{a + bX} = |b|\sigma_X$$

- The mean of the sum $X_1 + X_2$ of two random variables X_1 and X_2 is the sum of their means:

$$\mu_{X_1 + X_2} = \mu_{X_1} + \mu_{X_2}$$

If they are independent, then their squared standard deviations are also additive:

$$\sigma^2_{X_1 + X_2} = \sigma^2_{X_1} + \sigma^2_{X_2}$$

To find the standard deviation, we must take the square root of the above expression:

$$\sigma_{X_1 + X_2} = \sqrt{\sigma^2_{X_1} + \sigma^2_{X_2}}$$

Summary of Binomial Random Variables

- A **binomial random variable** arises in a particular set of circumstances that involve counting the number of values falling in a certain category when sampling from a variable that allows for just two possible categories.

- The random variable X that counts how many of n sampled individuals fall in the category of interest (whose probability is p) is called **binomial with parameters n and p** if the following conditions are met:
  - There must be a fixed sample size n.
  - Each selection must be independent of the others.
  - X may take just two possible values for each individual sampled.
  - The probability is always p that each individual falls in the category of interest.

- The requirement of independence may be relaxed when we sample without replacement from a population that is at least 10 times the sample size n; under such circumstances, we can say the count in the category of interest is approximately binomial.

- A binomial random variable for **sample count X** has mean np and standard deviation $\sqrt{np(1 - p)}$.

- **Sample proportion** $\hat{p} = X/n$ in the category of interest has mean p and standard deviation $\sqrt{\frac{p(1 - p)}{n}}$. The fact that the mean of sample proportion equals population proportion tells us that sample proportion is unbiased as an estimator for population proportion. Because sample size n appears in the denominator of the expression for standard deviation, sample proportion has less spread for larger sample sizes.

- For any given binomial random variable, the shape of the distribution of sample proportion $\hat{p} = X/n$ is the same as the shape of sample count X.

- For large enough samples, the distribution of a binomial random variable X—and therefore also the sample proportion $\hat{p} = \frac{X}{n}$—has a shape that is approximately normal. This is generally the case if $np \geq 10$ and $n(1 - p) \geq 10$.

Although binomial counts or proportions technically are discrete random variables because their possible values are countable, we begin to think of them as continuous when large samples are taken.

Summary of Normal Random Variables

- In general, **continuous random variables** have an infinite number of possible values over an entire interval. A variety of other continuous random variables are mentioned on page 311, but for the time being we focus on those that are normal.

- A continuous random variable has a probability distribution that can be represented by a smooth curve called a **density curve**. The probability of taking a value over any given interval equals the area under the curve over that interval. The total area under any density curve must be 1. One particular density curve that arises naturally in many contexts is the **normal curve**, which is bell-shaped and symmetric about its mean. The **68-95-99.7 Rule** outlines the roles played by mean μ and standard deviation σ for a normal random variable X: The probability is
  - 68% that X falls within 1 standard deviation σ of its mean μ
  - 95% that X falls within 2 standard deviations σ of its mean μ
  - 99.7% that X falls within 3 standard deviations σ of its mean μ

- Traditionally, normal tables were used for more detailed information about normal probabilities, but current practice relies almost exclusively on software.

- The 68-95-99.7 Rule tells us that for a standard normal random variable Z, the probability is
  - 68% that Z takes a value in the interval $(-1, +1)$
  - 95% that Z takes a value in the interval $(-2, +2)$
  - 99.7% that Z takes a value in the interval $(-3, +3)$

- Standardized values z considerably greater than 2 in absolute value are generally considered unusual; values close to 2 in absolute value may be called borderline; otherwise, a value may be considered not unusual.

- The two basic types of normal problems for which we seek solutions are:
  - Given a value of a normal variable, find the associated probability.
  - Given a probability (or proportion or percentile), find the associated value of the normal variable.

Each type of problem can be solved in two steps:

- If we are given a value, and need to find the associated probability,
  1. Standardize the given value x to $z = \frac{x - \mu}{\sigma}$.
  2. Using a sketch of the 68-95-99.7 Rule, get a range for the relevant area under the curve.
- If we are given a probability, and need to find the associated value,
  1. Shade in the desired area under the curve, and use a sketch of the 68-95-99.7 Rule to get a range for the associated value z.

2. Unstandardize to $x = \mu + z(\sigma)$, either as a precise answer or to get a range for x.

- Besides the information provided by the 68-95-99.7 Rule, it is helpful to know more about probabilities for the tails of the normal distribution: If Z is a standard normal random variable, then the probability is
  - 0.90 that Z takes a value in the interval $(-1.645, +1.645)$
  - 0.95 that Z takes a value in the interval $(-1.960, +1.960)$
  - 0.98 that Z takes a value in the interval $(-2.326, +2.326)$
  - 0.99 that Z takes a value in the interval $(-2.576, +2.576)$

This information can be reformulated by reporting that the probability is 0.05, 0.025, 0.01, 0.005 (respectively) that a normal random variable takes a value *less* than 1.645, 1.960, 2.326, 2.576 (respectively) standard deviations *below* its mean. The same probabilities hold for taking a value *more* than those same numbers of standard deviations *above* the mean.

CHAPTER 7   EXERCISES

Note: Asterisked numbers indicate exercises whose answers are provided in the Solutions to Selected Exercises section, on page 689.

Additional exercises appeared after each section: discrete random variables (Section 7.1) on page 285, binomial random variables (Section 7.2) on page 307, and continuous random variables—including normal distributions (Section 7.3)—on page 330.

Warming Up: RANDOM VARIABLES

7.71 A survey of high school students inquires about siblings.
  a. If a question asks how many siblings each student has, would the best display be a pie chart, a histogram, side-by-side boxplots, or a scatterplot?
  b. Would results be summarized with a mean or a proportion?
  c. If a question asks whether or not the students have siblings, would the results be displayed with a pie chart, a histogram, side-by-side boxplots, or a scatterplot?
  d. Would the proportion of sampled students with no siblings be denoted p or $\hat{p}$?

*7.72 Twenty percent of all assaults on law enforcement officers are with firearms, knives, or other dangerous weapons (the rest are with hands, feet, fists, etc.).

  a. Which one of these would provide an appropriate display of the information: pie chart, histogram, side-by-side boxplots, or scatterplot?
  b. Should the proportion 0.20 be written as p or $\hat{p}$? Explain.
  c. If we look at a sample of 87 assaults on law enforcement officers, will 20% of these assaults be with dangerous weapons? Explain.
  d. If we looked at a larger sample, would we expect proportion of assaults with dangerous weapons to be closer to 0.20 or farther from 0.20? Explain.
  e. One of these represents the count X of assaults on a sample of 87 law enforcement officers that employed weapons; which is it—23 or 0.23?

More exercises for this chapter are featured in the *TBP Supplement* on pages 858 through 862. End-of-chapter activities are described on page 854.

f. One of these represents the proportion $\hat{p}$ of assaults on a sample of 87 law enforcement officers that employed weapons; which is it—15 or 0.15?

g. Was the information in this exercise obtained from an experiment or an observational study?

7.73   Ninety percent of all drug seizures are of cannabis (marijuana or hashish); the remaining 10% involve a variety of other drugs.

a. Which one of these would provide an appropriate display of the information: bar graph, single boxplot, back-to-back stemplots, or scatterplot?

b. Should the proportion 0.90 be written as p or $\hat{p}$? Explain.

c. If we looked at a sample of 180 drug seizures, will 90% of these be of cannabis? Explain.

d. If we look at a smaller sample, would we expect proportion of cannabis seizures to be closer to 0.90 or farther from 0.90? Explain.

e. One of these represents the proportion $\hat{p}$ in a sample of 180 drug seizures that were of cannabis; which is it—0.087, 0.87, 8.7, or 87?

f. One of these represents the count X in a sample of 180 seizures that were of cannabis; which is it—0.17, 1.7, 17, or 170?

g. Was the information in this exercise obtained from an experiment or an observational study?

7.74   Assuming the proportion of all potential jury members who are women is 0.50, we would like to see how unlikely it is that of the last 80 jury members selected, only 31 were women. Is this mainly dealing with the process of data production, displaying and summarizing, probability, or statistical inference?

7.75   Suppose the proportion of blacks selected for a jury in Connecticut is considered in order to decide if it is plausible that, in general, 10% of chosen jury members in the state are black. Is this mainly dealing with the process of data production, displaying and summarizing, probability, or statistical inference?

7.76   What weight is to be considered "average" in a population may change over time. If researchers must be sure to keep such summaries up to date, which one of these is

the issue: data production, displaying and summarizing, probability, or inference?

*7.77   For each of the following variables, tell whether using self-reported values (instead of values assessed by researchers) would tend to result in overestimates of the true value, or underestimates, or if the potential for bias is not obvious.

a. Heights of college-aged males

b. Weights of college-aged females

c. Distance that middle school boys can run in 6 minutes

d. Knee heights of college-aged females

7.78   For each of the following variables, tell whether using self-reported values (instead of values assessed by researchers) would tend to result in overestimates of the true value, or underestimates, or if the potential for bias is not obvious.

a. Female hip sizes

b. Male ear lengths

c. Relative intelligence of high school seniors, in answer to the question, "Compared with others your age throughout the country, how do you rate yourself on intelligence"

d. Number of siblings of high school seniors

7.79   For each of the following situations, choose one of these as an appropriate display: single pie chart, bar graph, histogram, side-by-side boxplots, or scatterplot.

a. 1st-grade boys' heights and weights

b. Heights of 1st-grade girls

c. Whether a 1st-grade student is a boy or a girl, and whether he/she is light, medium, or heavy

d. Heights of 1st-grade girls compared to heights of first grade boys

7.80   For each of the following situations, choose one of these as the appropriate display: single pie chart, histogram, side-by-side boxplots, or scatterplot.

a. Distance run in 6 minutes by middle school and by high school students

b. Gross motor quotient (MQ) scores for a large group of students

c. Children's MQ scores and the distance they can run in 6 minutes

d. Fitness levels of students, classified as being exceptionally poor, unexceptional, or exceptionally good

Exploring the Big Picture: DISCRETE RANDOM VARIABLES

7.81 A survey taken in a farming village in Nepal asked, "How many male buffaloes does your household have?" and "How many female buffaloes does your household have?" The probability distributions of number of male buffaloes M and number of female buffaloes F shown here are consistent with the data published by the Inter-university Consortium for Political and Social Research (ICPSR).[9]

M	0	1	2
Probability	0.88	0.07	0.05

F	0	1	2	3	4	5	6
Probability	0.26	0.29	0.24	0.14	0.05	0.01	0.01

a. The median value of a random variable is the value for which at least 50% of the time, the random variable falls at or below it. Report the median of M and the median of F.

b. Draw separate probability histograms for M and F; discuss similarities and differences between their shapes.

c. Find the probability of at least one male buffalo, $P(M \geq 1)$.

d. Find the probability of at least one female buffalo, $P(F \geq 1)$.

e. If a household is chosen at random, can we say that the probability of owning at least one male and at least one female buffalo is $0.12 \times 0.74 = 0.09$? Explain.

f. Suppose that a family with at least one male buffalo is guaranteed to have at least one female buffalo; in other words, suppose $P(F \geq 1$ given $M \geq 1) = 1$. Find $P(M \geq 1$ and $F \geq 1)$, the probability of owning at least one male and at least one female buffalo.

g. Use the formula $\mu = x_1 P(X = x_1) + \ldots + x_k P(X = x_k)$ to find the mean number of male buffaloes, μ_M, owned by a randomly chosen household.

h. Use the formula $\mu = x_1 P(X = x_1) + \ldots + x_k P(X = x_k)$ to find the mean number of female buffaloes, μ_F, owned by a randomly chosen household.

i. If $M + F$ is the total number of buffaloes owned by a household, use the formula $\mu_{X_1 + X_2} = \mu_{X_1} + \mu_{X_2}$, along with your answers to parts (g) and (h), to find the mean total, $\mu_{M + F}$.

j. Judging from the looks of your probability histograms, which distribution has a larger standard deviation (typical distance of values from their mean)—M or F?

k. Explain why the formula $\sigma_{X_1 + X_2} = \sqrt{\sigma_{X_1}^2 + \sigma_{X_2}^2}$ cannot be used to find the standard deviation of the total number of buffaloes owned by a household, $\sigma_{M + F}$.

7.82 A survey of households in a farming village in Nepal asked, "How many women from your household collect firewood?" and "How many men from your household collect firewood?" The probability distributions of number of women W and men M collecting firewood shown here are consistent with the data published by the Inter-university Consortium for Political and Social Research (ICPSR).

W	0	1	2	3
Probability	0.15	0.61	0.21	0.03

M	0	1	2	3	4
Probability	0.30	0.54	0.13	0.02	0.01

a. Report the mean number collecting firewood for the women and for the men.

b. On average, was the number of women collecting firewood much less, a bit less, a bit more, or much more than the number of men collecting? Justify your answer.

c. On average, what was the total number of adults in each household collecting firewood? Justify your answer.

d. Is it reasonable to assume that for a given household, W and M are independent? Explain.

e. Is it reasonable to suppose that if no women in a household collected firewood, then at least one of the men would have to collect it? If this is indeed the case, find the probability of zero men collecting, given that zero women collect; in other words, find $P(M = 0 \text{ given } W = 0)$.

f. In part (e), we assume numbers of men and women collecting firewood are known for all households in the population, and we want to draw conclusions about an individual randomly sampled household. Is this the process of data production, displaying and summarizing, probability, or statistical inference?

7.83 Preceding exercises dealt with ownership of cattle and the collection of firewood by households in a particular Nepal village. Statistics students are asked if the same probability distributions should apply to other Nepal villages; who gives the best answer?

Adam: As long as they're all in the same country, the villages should be about the same, so the probability distributions should be the same, too.

Brittany: I don't know anything about Nepal, but I can picture that some villages could be a lot different from others, depending on how much they need cattle to farm and what kind of traditions they have for who collects firewood. The probability distributions don't necessarily apply to other Nepal villages.

Carlos: They didn't say if the village was sampled at random. If it was sampled at random, then it should be the same as other villages in terms of firewood collection and cattle, right?

Dominique: If it's sampled at random, then the probability distributions for other villages should be close, but they wouldn't be exactly the same.

*7.84 Picture bread that is sliced with thickness X_i that is uniform in a given slice i, but varies from slice to slice.

a. The usual way to construct a sandwich is with two slices of bread, but it can also be constructed by folding over a single slice of bread. Which of the random variables $2X_1$ and $X_1 + X_2$ represents the thickness of bread for a sandwich constructed from two individual slices, and which represents the thickness of bread for a sandwich constructed by folding a single slice?

b. If *two* slices are randomly selected for constructing a sandwich, and one of the slices is on the thin side, the other slice may be thick, so that the sandwich itself is not unusually thin. If *one* slice is randomly selected, and it is on the thin side, then the folded-over part must also be thin. In which case is there more of a tendency for extremely thin or thick sandwiches—when a sandwich is constructed from two independent slices, or when it is constructed by folding over a single slice?

c. Suppose thickness X_i of any randomly chosen slice has mean 0.5 inches. Find the mean of $2X_1$ and find the mean of $X_1 + X_2$. Are they equal? If not, tell which is larger and why.

d. Suppose thickness X_i of any randomly chosen slice has standard deviation 0.01 inches. Find the standard deviation of $2X_1$ and find the standard deviation of $X_1 + X_2$. Are they equal? If not, tell which is larger and why.

7.85 Suppose a statistics professor offers two midterm exams, each worth 100 points. A student plans to do a lot of traveling during the semester for job interviews, and asks if she can miss one of the midterms. The professor gives her the option of taking both midterms as scheduled, or taking just one midterm and doubling the score.

a. Which of the random variables $2X_1$ and $X_1 + X_2$ represents the student's score if she takes both midterms? Which represents her score if she takes just one midterm and doubles the score?

b. If the student takes both midterms, and does somewhat worse than usual on one, she may do somewhat better than usual on the other, so that her combined midterm score isn't too bad. If she takes just one midterm, and does somewhat worse than usual, then the doubled score is also worse than usual; if she does somewhat better, then the doubled score is also better than usual. In which case is there more of a tendency for unusually low or high scores—if she takes both midterms, or if she takes just one midterm and doubles the score?

c. This is a fairly average student, and her exam performance X_i is a random variable with mean 80. Find the mean of $2X_1$ and find the mean of $X_1 + X_2$.

d. Are the means you found in part (c) equal? If not, tell which is larger and why.

e. Suppose a student's exam performance X_i has standard deviation 5. Find the standard deviation of $2X_1$ and find the standard deviation of $X_1 + X_2$, according to formulas on page 282 and 284.

f. Are the standard deviations you found in part (e) equal? If not, tell which is larger and why.

g. To find the standard deviation of $X_1 + X_2$ in part (e), one must assume that a student's scores X_1 and X_2 on the first and second midterm exams are independent. Is this a reasonable assumption?

Exploring the Big Picture: BINOMIAL RANDOM VARIABLES

7.86 The president of a city's Downtown Council hosted a meeting with 800 participants on January 27, 2005, and was curious about how many participants would have a birthday that day.

a. If the probability of having a birthday on that day for each individual is 1/365, what is the mean number of January 27 birthdays that we expect to see in a group of 800 people?

b. What is the standard deviation of the number of birthdays on January 27?

c. The council president discovered that 1 of the 800 participants was born on January 27. Find the z-score for this value.

d. Based on the z-score, is 1 a surprisingly low number of January 27 birthdays?

e. Explain why the sample size is not large enough to guarantee an approximate normal distribution.

f. According to the 68-95-99.7 Rule, the probability would be 0.95 that the number of birthdays on January 27 falls between what two values?

g. The actual binomial probability of more than 5 birthdays on January 27 in a group of 800 people can be shown to be 0.02. Explain why this is fairly consistent with the 68-95-99.7 Rule.

h. The actual probability of fewer than 0 birthdays on January 27 is, of course, zero. Explain why this is not consistent with the 68-95-99.7 Rule.

*7.87 A study of organized hiking groups to Grand Canyon National Park in the 1980s concluded that 15% of all group leaders were college-aged (under 23 years old). Suppose a random sample of 80 group leaders is taken.

a. Did the study treat age as a quantitative or a categorical variable?

b. The number X of group leaders in the sample who are college-aged has mean 12 and standard deviation 3.2, and the distribution is approximately normal because $np = 80(0.15) = 12$ and $n(1 - p) = 80(0.85) = 68$ are both at least 10. Use the 68-95-99.7 Rule to sketch the distribution of X.

c. Is it likely that fewer than 20 of the 80 group leaders are college-aged?

d. The proportion $\hat{p}$ of group leaders in the sample who are college-aged has mean 0.15 and standard deviation 0.04, and the distribution is approximately normal because $np = 80(0.15) = 12$ and $n(1 - p) = 80(0.85) = 68$ are both at least 10. Use the 68-95-99.7 Rule to sketch the distribution of $\hat{p}$.

e. Is it likely that the sample proportion of group leaders who are college-aged is less than 0.05?

7.88 A study of hikers in Grand Canyon National Park in the 1980s concluded that 30% of all hikers express a preference for less-developed areas. Suppose a random sample of 84 hikers is taken.

a. The number X of hikers in the sample who prefer less-developed areas has mean 25.2 and standard deviation 4.6, and the distribution is approximately normal because $np = 84(0.3) = 25.2$ and $n(1 - p) = 84(0.7) = 58.8$ are both at least 10. Use the 68-95-99.7 Rule to sketch the distribution of X.

b. Is it likely that at least 40 of the 84 hikers prefer less-developed areas? Explain.

c. The proportion $\hat{p}$ of hikers in the sample who prefer less-developed areas has mean

0.3 and standard deviation 0.05, and the distribution is approximately normal because $np = 84(0.3) = 25.2$ and $n(1 - p) = 84(0.7) = 58.8$ are both at least 10. Use the 68-95-99.7 Rule to sketch the distribution of $\hat{p}$.

d. Is it likely that the sample proportion of hikers preferring less-developed areas is at least 0.2? Explain.

*7.89 Researchers at Harvard Medical School reported in 2005 that 50% of all U.S. bankruptcies were due to medical bills. Suppose a random sample of 25 bankruptcies is taken.

a. Find the mean and standard deviation for the count X of bankruptcies in the sample that are due to medical bills.

b. Recall that we standardize a value by calculating

$$z = \frac{\text{value} - \text{mean}}{\text{standard deviation}}$$

Find the standardized value if the count X of bankruptcies due to medical bills is found to be 11.

c. If 11 in a sample of 25 bankruptcies are found to be due to medical bills, would we characterize this number as surprisingly low, a bit low, a bit high, or surprisingly high?

d. Find the mean and standard deviation for the proportion $\hat{p}$ of bankruptcies in the sample of 25 that are due to medical bills.

e. Find the standardized value if the proportion $\hat{p}$ of bankruptcies due to medical bills is found to be $11/25 = 0.44$.

f. In general, if the sample count is 0.6 standard deviations below the mean count, how many standard deviations below the mean proportion will the sample proportion be?

7.90 A study of high school seniors in 2002 found that 0.32 had cut classes for a day at least once in a month. Suppose a sample of 36 high school seniors is taken.

a. Assuming the sample is random, find the mean and standard deviation for the count X of seniors in the sample who cut at least one day of classes in a month, rounding each to the nearest tenth (one decimal place).

b. Recall that we standardize a value by calculating

$$z = \frac{\text{value} - \text{mean}}{\text{standard deviation}}$$

Find the standardized value if the count X of sampled seniors cutting classes at least one day in a month is found to be 20.

c. If 20 in a sample of 36 high school seniors cut at least one day of classes in a month, would we characterize this number as surprisingly low, a bit low, a bit high, or surprisingly high?

d. If 20 in a sample of 36 high school seniors cut at least one day of classes in a month, would we have reason to suspect that those 20 were not representative of a population where the proportion cutting class was 0.32? Explain.

e. Find the mean and standard deviation for the proportion $\hat{p}$ of seniors in the sample who cut at least one day of classes in a month, rounding each to the nearest hundredth (two decimal places).

f. Find the standardized value if the proportion $\hat{p}$ of sampled seniors cutting classes at least one day in a month is found to be $20/36 = 0.56$.

g. In general, if the sample count is 3 standard deviations above the mean, how many standard deviations above the mean is the sample proportion?

h. The fact that the study was conducted by surveying high school seniors *during class time* may have resulted in bias; in this case, should we suspect that 0.32 is an overestimate or an underestimate of the actual proportion p who cut at least one day of classes in a month?

i. If bias results because of surveying students during class time, is it arising because of a non-representative sample or because of the way the variable's values were assessed?

j. If the surveyed seniors feared that their responses were not anonymous, this may have resulted in bias; keeping this in mind, should we suspect that 0.32 is an overestimate or an underestimate of the actual proportion p who cut at least one day of classes in a month?

k. If bias results because students fear their responses are not anonymous, is it arising because of a non-representative sample or because of the way the variable's values were assessed?

l. Cutting classes was treated here as a categorical variable. Describe how a survey question could be phrased if it were to be treated as a quantitative variable.

Exploring the Big Picture: CONTINUOUS RANDOM VARIABLES AND THE NORMAL DISTRIBUTION

*7.91 Children's gross motor development is assessed with an overall motor quotient, MQ, which follows an approximate normal distribution, with mean 100 and standard deviation 15, as shown with details based on the 68-95-99.7 Rule.

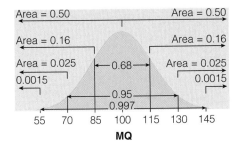

Tell whether the probability of an MQ being *less* than each of these values is between 0 and 0.0015, between 0.0015 and 0.025, between 0.025 and 0.16, between 0.16 and 0.50, between 0.50 and 0.84, between 0.84 and 0.975, between 0.975 and 0.9985, or between 0.9985 and 1.

a. MQ = 117
b. MQ = 132
c. MQ = 89
d. MQ = 144
e. MQ = 129
f. MQ = 51

7.92 Children's fitness is assessed by finding the distance, in meters, that they can run in 6 minutes. Overall, this distance varies fairly normally, with mean 835 and standard deviation 111, as shown with details based on the 68-95-99.7 Rule.

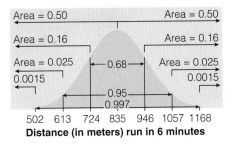

Distance (in meters) run in 6 minutes

Tell whether the probability of a distance being *greater* than each of these values is between 0 and 0.0015, between 0.0015 and 0.025, between 0.025 and 0.16, between 0.16 and 0.50, between 0.50 and 0.84, between 0.84 and 0.975, between 0.975 and 0.9985, or between 0.9985 and 1.

a. 600 meters
b. 1,092 meters
c. 354 meters
d. 742 meters
e. 960 meters
f. 623 meters

Discovering Research: RANDOM VARIABLES

7.93 Find an article or report that involves a quantitative variable. Tell whether that variable is clearly discrete or continuous, and whether or not we can assume that it follows a fairly normal distribution. If it is unlikely to be normal, tell whether it is likely to have left skewness or low outliers, right skewness or high outliers, or some other shape.

Reporting on Research: RANDOM VARIABLES

7.94 Use results of Exercises 7.3 to 7.17 and relevant findings from the Internet to make a report on the typical American 12th grader that relies on statistical information.

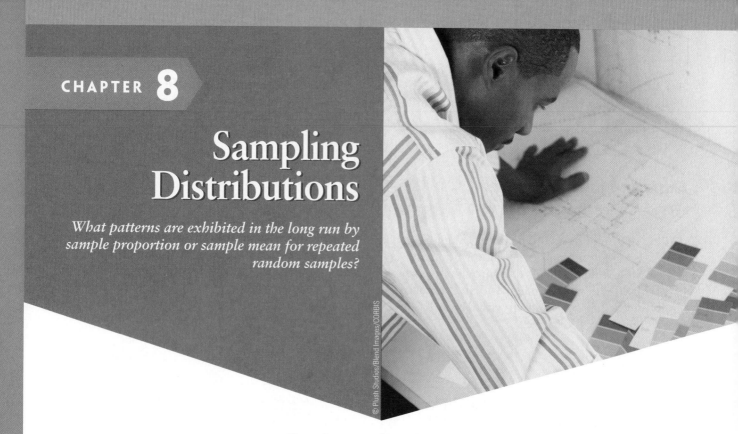

Sampling Distributions

What patterns are exhibited in the long run by sample proportion or sample mean for repeated random samples?

© Plush Studios/Blend Images/CORBIS

Choosing samples: What kind of behavior do we expect in the long run?

For simplicity's sake, we will concentrate on results that can be obtained from the 68-95-99.7 Rule, or from the details recently presented with regard to probabilities around the tails of the normal curve. However, students should remember that precise information regarding *any* normal values and probabilities can be obtained via tables or software.

Categorical Variables: The Behavior of Sample Proportions

C In this chapter, we combine results from Chapter 7 on the mean, standard deviation, and shape of the distribution of sample proportion (in Section 7.2 on binomial random variables) with techniques for assessing normal probabilities (in Section 7.3 on normal random variables).

Taken together, these will allow us to make definitive statements about the probability that the sample proportion in a random sample of a given size takes a value in a certain interval. For example, we will learn to draw conclusions like, "If a random sample of 100 people is taken from a population where the proportion who are left-handed is 0.10, then the probability is approximately 16% that the sample proportion of left-handed people is more than 0.13."

The relevance of such conclusions will be seen in Part IV, when we formulate problems typical of what researchers face in real-life applications. For instance, they might wonder if it really is true that the proportion of all students who are left-handed is only 0.10. They could discover that the sample proportion left-handed in a sample of 100 students is, say, 0.13. Then they would use this result to decide if 0.10 is still a plausible population proportion. Their decision is based on the *probability* of a sample proportion being as high as 0.13, when sampling from a population whose proportion of left-handers is supposedly 0.10.

When the variable of interest in a problem is categorical, then the center, spread, and shape of the distribution of sample proportion are entirely determined by the sample size n and the population proportion p in the category of interest. As long as the sample size n is large enough relative to the underlying shape (determined by p), then the shape of the distribution of sample proportion is approximately normal. We identified this result as being an expression of the *Central Limit Theorem*.

Quantitative Variables: The Behavior of Sample Means

Q When the variable of interest in a problem is quantitative, then the center and spread of the distribution of sample mean are determined by the population mean and standard deviation. The Central Limit Theorem still applies, in that the shape of the distribution is approximately normal for large enough sample sizes. However, there is no neat rule of thumb based on population parameters as we had in the case of sample proportions, when we required that $np \geq 10$ and $n(1 - p) \geq 10$. For a given mean and standard deviation, a quantitative population may exhibit *any* shape, from perfectly normal to extremely skewed. Therefore, some guesswork will be required in order to make a claim that the distribution of sample mean is approximately normal.

Again, we will take advantage of easily referenced normal probabilities (those expressed in the 68-95-99.7 Rule or the rule about the tails of the normal curve) when we solve probability problems about sample mean. For instance, we will learn to draw conclusions like, "If nightly hours slept by college students are normally distributed with a mean of 7.0 and a standard deviation of 1.5, then the probability is 5% that the mean hours slept by a random sample of 25 students is less than 6.51."

Just as for categorical variables, the relevance of such conclusions for quantitative variables will be seen in Part IV, when more realistic problems are addressed. For instance, researchers might wonder if it really is true that the mean nightly hours slept by all college students is as high as 7.0. They could discover that the sample mean hours slept by 25 students is, say, 6.51. Then they would use this result to decide if 7.0 is still a plausible population mean. Their decision is based on the *probability* of a sample mean being as low as 6.51, when sampling from a population whose mean is supposedly 7.0.

Whether we are tackling a problem involving categorical or quantitative variables, the key to drawing conclusions about unknown population parameters is to know how sample statistics behave in repeated random samples. That is, we need to understand the *sampling distribution* of the variable sample proportion or sample mean.

> *Definition* The **sampling distribution** of a sample statistic tells the probability distribution of values taken by the statistic in repeated random samples of a given size.

As long as the sample is random, sample proportion—or sample mean—is, in fact, a *random variable*. The behavior of such random variables can be neatly summarized thanks to the laws established in our chapters on probability and random variables. Specifically, we can report the mean and standard deviation of the sampling distribution, and state whether or not circumstances allow us to claim its shape to be approximately normal. If such a claim is justified, then we can find out the probability of taking a value in a given interval. Being able to solve for such probabilities will let us answer questions about categorical and quantitative variables that are typically asked in real-life research problems.

THE BIG PICTURE: LOOKING AHEAD

When we perform inference, we will make educated guesses about the population's shape, just as statisticians do in real-life applications, by looking at the shape of our sample data. Then we will consider the sample size, to decide if sample means taken from that population would follow an approximately normal distribution.

8.1 The Behavior of Sample Proportion in Repeated Random Samples

Thinking about Proportions from Samples or Populations

The goal of this section—which focuses on categorical variables—is to draw formal conclusions about the behavior of sample proportion $\hat{p}$ (called "p-hat") based on the known value of population proportion p. The difference in notation is slight (one p has a "hat" and the other doesn't), but the difference between $\hat{p}$ and p as entities is enormous. Sample proportion $\hat{p}$ is a *statistic* that summarizes a sample, and can be measured from data about a categorical variable. It may also be thought of as a *random variable*, if we are considering its behavior in the long run for repeated random samples. Still, it refers to a sample.

In contrast, population proportion p is a *parameter* that summarizes the population. In reality, p cannot be known unless we happen to have access to data about the entire population (such as in a census), or if the situation involves a random experiment such as a coin flip, where physical circumstances, and the principle of equally likely outcomes, dictate the overall proportion in the category of interest. Establishing a link between statistics like $\hat{p}$ and parameters like p lies at the heart of the science of statistics. To understand the most essential results, students must think carefully about the distinction between the two.

Example TBP 8.1 on page 867 of the *Teaching the Big Picture (TBP) Supplement* features a parameter that is *not* based on the principle of equally likely outcomes.

The Big Picture:

LOOKING BACK

In Part I, we mentioned use of tables or software to pick random samples, or to randomly assign individuals to treatment groups in an experiment. Without the aid of such tools, human beings are not well-equipped to generate random selections off the top of their heads—a phenomenon that you can verify by observing various types of bias that arise when people are asked to pick a number "at random." Results of such selections are scrutinized in several examples presented in this chapter.

EXAMPLE 8.1 DISTINGUISHING BETWEEN SAMPLE PROPORTION AND POPULATION PROPORTION

Background: When 400 students in a survey were asked to pick a number at random from one to twenty, 30 of them (proportion 0.075) picked the number seven. If students picked numbers completely at random from the numbers one to twenty, the proportion of times that the number seven would be picked in the long run is 0.05.

Question: What are the parameter and accompanying statistic in this situation?

Response: The parameter is the population proportion of random selections resulting in the number seven, which is $p = 0.05$. The accompanying statistic is the sample proportion of selections resulting in the number seven, which is $\hat{p} = 0.075$.

Practice: *Try Exercise 8.1 on page 353.*

Before stating formal results, we consider an example in which we use our intuition to anticipate how sample proportions $\hat{p}$ should behave relative to the population proportion p. Our example looks at the behavior of $\hat{p}$ for two different sample sizes because of the crucial role played by sample size in both the spread and the shape of the distribution of $\hat{p}$. Because we are thinking about the behavior of $\hat{p}$ in the long run for repeated random samples, it is playing the role of a random variable rather than a statistic.

EXAMPLE 8.2 INTUITING THE DISTRIBUTION OF SAMPLE PROPORTION FOR TWO DIFFERENT SAMPLE SIZES

Background: According to the U.S. Census, the proportion of part-time college students in this country who are female is 0.60.

Questions: What kind of values would the sample proportion $\hat{p}$ of females take for repeated random samples of

1. $n = 10$ part-time students?

2. $n = 100$ part-time students?

Responses: The sample proportion $\hat{p}$ of females takes various values subject to the laws of chance—it is a random variable. We can summarize its sampling distribution—just as we summarized distributions of data values in Part II—by telling about its **center, spread,** and **shape.**

1. First we consider the behavior of sample proportion for samples of **size 10** taken from a population whose proportion in the category of interest (female) is 0.60.

■ **Center:** Some sample proportions will be less than 0.60, and some more. Overall, they'll tend to go below 0.60 just as much as they go above: The *mean* of sample proportions $\hat{p}$ should equal the population proportion $p = 0.60$.

■ **Spread:** For samples of size 10, the sample count of females could easily vary all the way from about 3 to about 9, so the sample proportion could easily vary from about $\frac{3}{10} = 0.30$ to about $\frac{9}{10} = 0.90$.

■ **Shape:** The most common sample proportion in the long run will be about 0.60, with proportions below and above 0.60 becoming less and less likely: We'd expect a single-peaked, symmetric, bell shape with tapering ends. In other words, the distribution of sample proportion should appear sort of normal.

2. Next we consider the behavior of sample proportion for samples of **size 100** taken from a population whose proportion in the category of interest (female) is 0.60.

■ **Center:** This distribution should also be *centered* at 0.60.

■ **Spread:** Whereas sample proportions from 0.3 to 0.9 would be plausible for samples of size 10, common sense tells us that a random sample of 100 part-time students will virtually never produce as few as 30 females or as many as 90 females, if the population proportion of females is 0.60. Clearly, how much the sample proportions vary depends on the size of the sample. There should be less *spread* for samples of 100 compared to that for samples of size 10.

■ **Shape:** The *shape* should be fairly normal, more so than for samples of size 10 because a histogram's profile would conform more closely to a smooth bell curve.

Practice: *Try Exercise 8.5 on page 354.*

The activity on randomly sampling teaspoons or tablespoons of M&M's on page 872 of the **TBP** *Supplement* can be discussed and carried out as a substitute for Example 8.2.

Students' intuition about spread is more easily framed in terms of a range. Eventually, we must summarize the spread with a standard deviation.

Page 866 of the **TBP** *Supplement* depicts a variety of sample proportions of females when sampling from a population with proportion 0.60.

Our conclusions about the center, spread, and shape of the random variable sample proportion were reached by applying the rules of probability established in Chapter 6.

We can teach students about the correction factor for a relatively small population, described in a marginal note on page 298. Still, we should also impress on students that other circumstances— such as asking for a show of hands among sampled individuals—can result in dependence, which undermines our formula for the standard deviation.

The conclusions we reach by thinking about what should constitute reasonable behavior of sample proportion are actually confirmed by the laws of probability. Under the right circumstances, probability theory dictates the occurrence of precisely the same phenomena that our intuition tells us we'd expect to observe in practice. To draw formal conclusions about the behavior of sample proportion, we refer back to relevant results about center, spread, and shape that were presented in Chapter 7.

Center, Spread, and Shape of the Distribution of Sample Proportion

In Section 7.2 on binomial random variables, we stated that a random variable X for the count of sampled individuals in the category of interest is *binomial with parameters n and p* if each of the following holds:

1. There is a fixed sample size n.
2. Each selection is independent of the others.
3. Each sampled individual takes just two possible values.
4. The probability of each individual falling in the category of interest is always p.

The second condition isn't really met when we sample without replacement (which is usually the case), but there is approximate independence as long as the sample is not too large relative to the population size. For this reason, the results in this section, which rely on a binomial model, should be applied only if the population size is at least $10n$ (that is, 10 times the sample size).

Key results in Section 7.2 on binomial random variables were our formulas for the mean and standard deviation of sample proportion $\hat{p} = X/n$ in the category of interest when a random sample of size n is taken from a population having proportion p in the category of interest. We also discussed the Central Limit Theorem, which tells us about the shape of the distribution of $\hat{p}$.

Rule for the Distribution of Sample Proportion

If random samples of size n are drawn from a population that has proportion p in the category of interest, then sample proportion $\hat{p}$ has mean p, standard deviation $\sqrt{\frac{p(1-p)}{n}}$, and a shape that is approximately normal for a large enough sample size n.

To specify how large a sample is "large enough," we have a rule with a built-in requirement for n to be larger if p is far from 0.5 in either direction, a circumstance that causes the underlying distribution to be asymmetric.

Guidelines for Approximate Normality of Sample Proportion

To ensure that the distribution of sample proportion $\hat{p}$ is approximately normal, a rule of thumb is to require that np and $n(1-p)$ both be at least 10.

Now that we have organized the relevant results established in Chapter 7, we present some examples. First, we explore circumstances under which we can or cannot determine the center, spread, or shape of the distribution of sample proportion.

EXAMPLE 8.3 WHEN THE RULE FOR THE DISTRIBUTION OF SAMPLE PROPORTION APPLIES

Background: The proportion of part-time college students in this country who are female is 0.60. We consider the distribution of sample proportion $\hat{p}$ of females when taking repeated random samples of n part-time college students.

Question: Can we claim that the results about the mean, standard deviation, and shape in the Rule for the Distribution of Sample Proportion apply in each of the following situations?

1. $n = 100$ taken from all part-time students at a particular college

2. $n = 100$ taken from a college that enrolls just 200 part-time students, of whom the proportion of females is 0.60

3. $n = 5$ taken from all part-time college students

4. $n = 100$ taken from all part-time college students

Response:

1. For $n = 100$ part-time students at a particular college, we cannot say what the *mean* of the distribution of $\hat{p}$ is, due to the fact that the sample is biased: The proportion of part-time students who are female at a particular college might be higher or lower than the proportion 0.60 that applies to all colleges and universities in the United States.

2. If $n = 100$ are randomly sampled without replacement from only 200 students, the *standard deviation* cannot be calculated with our usual formula because there is too much dependence when the population is only twice the sample size, instead of 10 times.

3. For $n = 5$ part-time students, the *shape* of the distribution of $\hat{p}$ is not normal because the sample size is too small: $np = 5(0.60) = 3$, which is less than 10.

4. For a representative sample from a much larger population, the results about mean and standard deviation *do* apply. The shape is approximately normal because a sample size of $n = 100$ is large enough: $np = 100(0.60) = 60$ and $n(1 - p) = 100(0.40) = 40$, both of which are more than 10.

Practice: *Try Exercise 8.6 on page 354.*

Next, we solve for probabilities about sample proportion in the situation for which the rule about center, spread, and shape does apply.

Example TBP 8.2 on page 867 of the *TBP Supplement* uses the 68-95-99.7 Rule to identify a sample proportion that is clearly unusual.

Example TBP 8.3 on page 869 of the *TBP Supplement* serves as a reminder that probabilities based on the normal curve cannot be used if the sample is too small and our rule of thumb (np and $n(1 - p)$ both at least 10) is not satisfied.

EXAMPLE 8.4 APPLYING THE RULE FOR THE DISTRIBUTION OF SAMPLE PROPORTION

Background: The proportion of part-time students in this country who are female is 0.60.

Question: 95% of the time, the proportion of females in a random sample of 100 part-time students will fall in what interval?

Response: The mean of the distribution of $\hat{p}$ is the population proportion $p = 0.60$ and the standard deviation is $\sqrt{\frac{0.60(1 - 0.60)}{100}} = 0.05$. The shape is approximately normal. According to the 68-95-99.7 Rule, the probability is 0.95 that the sample proportion falls within 2 standard deviations of the mean: in the interval (0.50, 0.70).

Practice: *Try Exercise 8.7 on page 354.*

Whereas Example 8.4 referred to the 68-95-99.7 Rule, our next example utilizes the picture with details about the tails of the normal curve, in the vicinity of 2 standard deviations away from the mean. These details will turn out to be especially useful for the purpose of performing statistical inference.

Because the numbers of standard deviations in the 90-95-98-99 Rule are no longer "nice" numbers (1.645, 1.960, 2.326, and 2.576 instead of 1, 2, and 3), it's much easier in this case to first standardize our sample proportion, then refer to a sketch of the standard normal (z) curve.

When the rule for sample proportions on page 348 applies, it can tell us what values of sample proportion could be considered unusual, for a given population proportion and sample size.

The Big Picture:
LOOKING BACK

The result found in Example 8.5, which suggests that students were incapable of a truly random number selection "off the top of their heads," provides a valuable lesson relating to data production. Selections for a sample or assignments to experimental treatments that rely on people's judgments, as opposed to a true random number generator, are chronically vulnerable to bias.

EXAMPLE 8.5 USING THE TAILS OF THE NORMAL CURVE TO DECIDE IF A SAMPLE PROPORTION IS UNUSUAL

Background: If each student picks a whole number at random from one to twenty, the overall proportion picking each of the numbers should be $1/20 = 0.05$. Suppose 400 students in a survey are asked to pick a number at random from one to twenty. For truly random selections, the distribution of sample proportion picking the number seven has a mean of 0.05, a standard deviation of $\sqrt{\frac{0.05(1 - 0.05)}{400}} = 0.01$, and a shape that is approximately normal.

Questions:

1. According to a sketch of the tails, what is the approximate probability that the sample proportion who pick the number seven is 0.075 or more?

2. If the sample proportion of 400 students picking the number seven was in fact 0.075, would this cause you to doubt the claim that students' selections were truly random, with probability only 0.05 that the number seven is picked?

Responses:

1. The standardized value of 0.075 is $z = (0.075 - 0.05)/0.01 = +2.5$. The probability that the sample proportion picking seven is at least 0.075 is the same as the probability that z takes a value greater than or equal to $+2.5$. According to the sketch, since $+2.5$ is a little to the left of $+2.576$, the probability we seek is a bit more than 0.005. It is certainly less than 0.01, since $+2.5$ is more than $+2.326$.

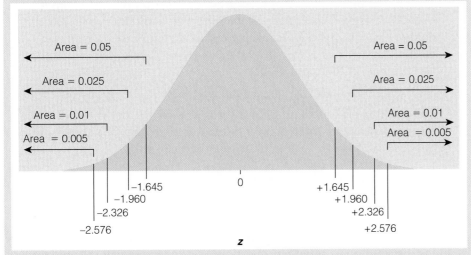

2. It is extremely unlikely (probability approximately 0.005) for the sample proportion picking the number seven to be 0.075 or more, if the population proportion were only 0.05. This does cast doubt on the claim that selections were truly random. It seems that students are biased in favor of the number seven when asked to make a random selection.

Practice: *Try Exercise 8.11(a–d) on page 354.*

The following example illustrates the importance of the role played by sample size in the distribution of sample proportion.

EXAMPLE 8.6 SAMPLE PROPORTION MORE VARIABLE FOR SMALLER SAMPLES

Background: Suppose only 200 (not 400) students are asked to pick a number at random from one to twenty. Now 15 of them select the number seven, so the sample proportion is again 0.075.

Questions:

1. What are the center, spread, and shape of the distribution of sample proportion picking the number seven for samples of size 200?

2. What is the approximate probability that the sample proportion who pick the number seven is 0.075 or more?

3. Suppose the sample proportion of 200 students picking the number seven was in fact 0.075. Would this cause you to doubt the claim that students' selections were truly random, with probability only 0.05 that the number seven is picked?

Continued

The Big Picture:
LOOKING AHEAD

The issue of how small a probability would have to be for us to characterize an event as "unlikely" is a thought-provoking one, which we will discuss at length in Part IV.

The Big Picture:
LOOKING AHEAD

The second response in Example 8.5 gives you a foretaste of the type of conclusions we will seek to draw in Part IV, when we perform inference in the form of "hypothesis tests."

To contrast Example 8.7, Example TBP 8.4 on page 869 of the *TBP Supplement* reminds us that often, a study *fails* to produce evidence that something—like bias—is going on. Due to the "file-drawer" effect (bias toward publication of more newsworthy or interesting conclusions that "rock the boat"), we are less likely to be made aware of studies that fail to find something exceptional.

A watchdog group by the name of Children Now observed prime-time characters for six broadcast networks at the start of the season in 2002–2003, and found that only 6% were Hispanic. As we will see in Example 8.7, this proportion is too low to be considered representative. The group cited these results as it campaigned for better representation of minorities on television.

Responses:

1. The mean is still $p = 0.05$, but now the standard deviation is
$\sqrt{\frac{p(1 - p)}{n}} = \sqrt{\frac{0.05(1 - 0.05)}{200}} = 0.0154$ instead of 0.01. Our conditions for approximate normality are just barely met: $np = 200(0.05) = 10 \geq 10$ and $n(1 - p) = 200(0.95) = 190 \geq 10$.

2. Now the standardized value of 0.075 is $z = (0.075 - 0.05)/0.0154 = +1.62$. The probability that the sample proportion picking seven is at least 0.075 is the same as the probability that z takes a value greater than or equal to $+1.62$. According to our sketch of the tails of the normal curve, since $+1.62$ is a little less than $+1.645$, the probability we seek is a bit more than 0.05.

3. Obtaining a sample proportion as high as 0.075 in a sample of 200 students isn't as improbable as it is in a sample of 400 students (probability approximately 0.05 instead of approximately 0.005). In this case, we may be willing to believe that $p = 0.05$.

Practice: *Try Exercise 8.11(f) on page 355.*

Examples 8.5 and 8.6 taken together demonstrate the role played by sample size in the distribution of sample proportion: For larger samples, sample proportions tend not to stray as far from the population proportion. In this case, with a population proportion of 0.05, sample proportion in samples of size 400 would almost never stray as high as 0.075, whereas sample proportion in samples of size 200 would occasionally stray that high.

Our examples involving "random" number selection provided a valuable lesson in the dangers of bias when taking samples for statistical purposes. The next example shows how statistical methods can be used to provide evidence of bias as a manifestation of discrimination.

EXAMPLE 8.7 SAMPLE PROPORTION AS EVIDENCE OF BIAS

Background: According to the U.S. Census, the proportion of Americans who were of Hispanic origin in the year 2002 was 0.13.

Questions: If 125 characters in prime-time TV shows for all six broadcast networks constituted a *random* sample in terms of race/ethnicity, what would be the probability of a sample proportion of Hispanics less than or equal to 0.06? What can we conclude if only 6% of all prime-time TV characters at that time were found to be Hispanic?

Responses: We use the fact that sample proportions should be centered at the population proportion, 0.13, and the standard deviation for sample proportions in this case is
$\sqrt{\frac{0.13(1 - 0.13)}{125}} = 0.03$. The shape is approximately normal because $125(0.13) = 16.25$ and $125(1 - 0.13) = 108.75$ are both at least 10. A sketch of the distribution of sample proportion based on the 68-95-99.7 Rule (shown on the left) indicates that the probability of being below 0.06 is certainly less than 0.025.

Hispanics—even more of a minority on TV

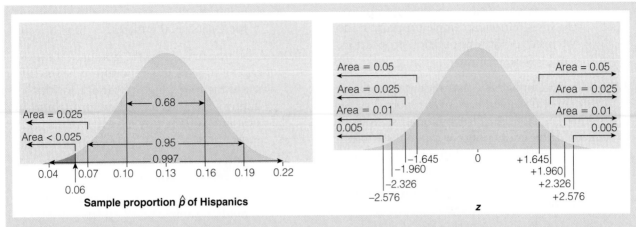

Alternatively, we can standardize 0.06 to $z = (0.06 - 0.13)/0.03 = -2.33$ and refer to a sketch of the tails of the standard normal curve (shown on the right). Since $z = -2.33$ is basically equivalent to $z = -2.326$, the probability of a sample proportion this low or lower is only 0.01. Our results suggest that Hispanics were systematically underrepresented in prime-time TV shows.

Practice: *Try Exercise 8.11(e) on page 355.*

EXERCISES FOR SECTION 8.1

The Behavior of Sample Proportion in Repeated Random Samples

Note: Asterisked numbers indicate exercises whose answers are provided in the Solutions to Selected Exercises section, on page 689.

*8.1 According to a 2005 newspaper report about financial aid for college students, about three-fourths of all full-time students seeking degrees or certificates receive some form of financial aid; on average, undergraduates borrow about $20,000 during college. Identify each of the numbers mentioned as being sample proportion $\hat{p}$, population proportion p, sample mean $\bar{x}$, or population mean μ, and tell whether it is a statistic or a parameter:

  a. three-fourths (0.75)

  b. 20,000

8.2 A survey of several hundred college students found that they averaged 20.4 years of age. According to a 2005 newspaper report about college students, 39% of all students in degree-granting institutions in the year 2000 were 25 and older. Identify each of the numbers mentioned as being sample proportion $\hat{p}$, population proportion p, sample mean $\bar{x}$, or population mean μ, and tell whether it is a statistic or a parameter:

  a. 20.4

  b. 0.39

*8.3 Suppose we are interested in the behavior of sample proportion of college students who

are receiving financial aid, for random samples of a certain size.

  a. To draw conclusions about the *center* of the distribution of sample proportion, do we need to know population proportion, sample size, or both?

  b. To draw conclusions about the *spread* of the distribution of sample proportion, do we need to know population proportion, sample size, or both?

  c. To draw conclusions about the *shape* of the distribution of sample proportion, do we need to know population proportion, sample size, or both?

8.4 Suppose we are interested in the behavior of sample proportion of all college students who are over the age of 25, for random samples of a certain size.

  a. To draw conclusions about the *center* of the distribution of sample proportion, do we need to know population proportion, sample size, or both?

  b. To draw conclusions about the *spread* of the distribution of sample proportion, do we need to know population proportion, sample size, or both?

c. To draw conclusions about the *shape* of the distribution of sample proportion, do we need to know population proportion, sample size, or both?

*8.5   At a large university, the graduation rate for the general student body was reported to be 0.66. Consider the distribution of sample proportion graduating for random samples of 5 students, compared to the distribution for random samples of 50 students.

a. Compare the centers of the distributions for 5 versus 50 students.

b. Compare the spreads of the distributions for 5 versus 50 students.

c. Compare the shapes of the distributions for 5 versus 50 students.

*8.6   At a large university, the graduation rate for the general student body was reported to be 0.66. For two of the following, we cannot use this chapter's methods to find the probability in question; explain why in each case.

a. The probability that at least 2 in a random sample of 4 from the general student body graduate.

b. The probability that at least 64 in a sample of 90 pre-med students graduate.

c. The probability that at least 64 in a random sample of 90 from the general student body graduate.

*8.7   For one of the situations in the preceding exercise, we *can* use this chapter's methods to find the probability in question. In this case, calculate the standard deviation of sample proportion, the sample proportion to two decimal places, the standardized sample proportion z, and use the 68-95-99.7 Rule to report the probability.

8.8   At a large university, the graduation rate for student athletes was reported to be 0.61. Consider the distribution of sample proportion graduating for random samples of 4 athletes, compared to the distribution for random samples of 20 athletes.

a. Compare the centers of the distributions for 4 versus 20 athletes.

b. Compare the spreads of the distributions for 4 versus 20 athletes.

c. Compare the shapes of the distributions for 4 versus 20 athletes.

8.9   At a large university, the graduation rate for student athletes was reported to be 0.61. For two of the following, we cannot use this chapter's methods to find the probability in question; explain why in each case.

a. The probability that fewer than 3 in a random sample of 6 athletes at the university graduate.

b. The probability that fewer than 10 in a random sample of 29 athletes at the university graduate.

c. The probability that fewer than 10 in a random sample of 29 football players at the university graduate.

8.10   For one of the situations in the preceding exercise, we *can* use this chapter's methods to find the probability in question. In this case, calculate the following:

a. standard deviation of sample proportion

b. the sample proportion to two decimal places

c. the standardized sample proportion z

d. the probability (using the 68-95-99.7 Rule)

*8.11 In a comprehensive study of 12th graders across the country in 2002, the proportion who claimed never to have tried marijuana was 0.88. The distribution of sample proportion claiming never to have tried marijuana for samples of size 250 has mean 0.88, standard deviation 0.02, and a shape that is approximately normal, due to the large sample size.

a. Suppose that in a sample of 250 12th graders, the proportion claiming never to have tried marijuana was 0.93. Standardize to find the z-score for this sample proportion.

b. Use your z-score and the sketch of the 68-95-99.7 Rule (shown on the top) to estimate the probability that a random sample of size 250 from this population would produce a sample proportion of 0.93 or more (choose one of the following): greater than 0.16, between 0.16 and 0.025, between 0.025 and 0.0015, or less than 0.0015.

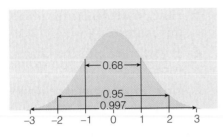

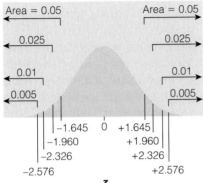

c. Use your z-score and the sketch of the tails of the normal curve (shown on the bottom) to estimate the probability that a random sample of size 250 from this population would produce a sample proportion of 0.93 or more (choose one of the following): greater than 0.05, between 0.05 and 0.025, between 0.025 and 0.01, between 0.01 and 0.005, or less than 0.005.

d. Based on your estimate for the probability of a sample proportion equal to 0.93 or higher when random samples of 250 are taken from a population with proportion 0.88 in the category of interest, characterize such a sample proportion as being not improbable, very unlikely, or virtually impossible.

e. Which of these scenarios is supported by the sample data?
   1. Some of those 250 12th-graders had reason to believe their peers would be aware of their responses, and they adjusted their responses to seem less conservative than they actually were.
   2. Some of those 250 12th-graders had reason to believe their teachers would be aware of their responses, and they adjusted their responses to seem more conservative than they actually were.
   3. Both (1) and (2).
   4. Neither (1) nor (2).

f. Now suppose that the sample proportion 0.93 arose from a sample of only 86 12th

graders. In this case, the standard deviation would be 0.035 and the z-score would be +1.43. Characterize the probability of a z-score this high as being not improbable, very unlikely, or virtually impossible.

8.12 In a comprehensive survey of teenagers across the country in 2002, the proportion who did not attend religious services was 0.16.[1] The distribution of sample proportion who do not attend religious services for samples of size 3,000 has mean 0.16, standard deviation 0.007, and a shape that is approximately normal, due to the large sample size.

a. Suppose that in a sample of 3,000 teenagers, the proportion who did not attend religious services was 0.18. Standardize to find the z-score for this sample proportion.

b. Use your z-score and the sketch of the 68-95-99.7 Rule (shown on the top in Exercise 8.11) to estimate the probability that a random sample of size 3,000 from this population would produce a sample proportion of 0.18 or more (choose one of the following): greater than 0.16, between 0.16 and 0.025, between 0.025 and 0.0015, or less than 0.0015.

c. Use your z-score and the sketch of the tails of the normal curve (shown on the bottom in Exercise 8.11) to estimate the probability that a random sample of size 3,000 from this population would produce a sample proportion of 0.18 or more (choose one of the following): greater than 0.05, between 0.05 and 0.025, between 0.025 and 0.01, between 0.01 and 0.005, or less than 0.005.

d. Based on your estimate for the probability of a sample proportion equal to 0.18 or higher when random samples of 3,000 are taken from a population with proportion 0.16 in the category of interest, characterize such a sample proportion as being not improbable, rather unlikely, or extremely unlikely.

e. In fact, a study of 3,000 teenagers in 2005 claimed that 0.18 did not attend religious services, but one of the study's critics felt this number was biased because, "Kids who are going to church are more likely to stay for the entire survey." Is this critic suggesting that the true population proportion not attending religious services is less than 0.18 or greater than 0.18?

*8.13 "U.S. Teens Share Parents' Religion, Survey Finds" reported in 2005 that religious values were more important than they had been for teenagers in the 1960s. "God functions for most teenagers as a combination cosmic therapist and a divine butler . . . He is distant until you need him to solve a problem or make you feel better,"[2] explained a University of North Carolina sociologist. In any case, the study found that 80% of teenagers reported they believed in God.

a. Find the mean and standard deviation of sample proportion believing in God for random samples of 64 teenagers.

b. Tell why the distribution's shape will be approximately normal.

c. Use the 68-95-99.7 Rule to sketch the distribution of sample proportion for samples of size 64 taken from a population where the proportion believing in God is 0.80.

d. If 48 in a sample of 64 teenagers report that they believe in God, is there reason to suspect that they are not a representative sample of all teenagers in terms of belief in God? Explain.

e. This exercise features two proportions: 0.80 and $\frac{48}{64} = 0.75$. Tell whether 0.80 plays the role of statistic or parameter.

f. How do we denote the number 0.80 in this context?

g. Tell whether 0.75 is a statistic or a parameter.

h. How do we denote the number 0.75 in this context?

8.14 A survey of 3,000 teenagers in 2005 found that 0.80 believed in God, and 0.18 did not attend religious services. Is this evidence that some sampled teenagers attended religious services in spite of not believing in God, or that some sampled teenagers did not attend religious services in spite of believing in God, or neither? Tell which of these four statistics students provides the best answer.

Adam: There's not enough information to answer the question.

Brittany: The problem is that we know what's true for the sample but we can't say what's true for the population.

Carlos: We're only asked to say what's true for the sample. 18% didn't attend services, so that means 82% did. And only 80% believed in God, so 2% attended services even though they didn't believe in God.

Dominique: I agree that the evidence shows some sampled teenagers attended services in spite of not believing in God, but it may be even more than 2%, if there were also some teenagers who didn't attend services, even though they did believe in God.

8.2 The Behavior of Sample Mean in Repeated Random Samples

Thinking about Means from Samples or Populations

In this section—whose focus is on situations involving a quantitative variable—we establish a theory for the behavior of sample mean $\overline{X}$ relative to the population mean μ. Just as for proportions, it is very important to distinguish between a statistic (a number that summarizes a sample) and a parameter (a number that summarizes a population).

EXAMPLE 8.8 DISTINGUISHING BETWEEN SAMPLE MEAN AND POPULATION MEAN

Background: IQ in the United States has a mean of 100. Suppose a random sample of 9 individuals has a mean IQ of 90.

Question: What are the parameter and accompanying statistic in this situation?

Response: The parameter is the population mean IQ, $\mu = 100$. The accompanying statistic is the sample mean IQ, $\bar{x} = 90$.

Practice: *Try Exercise 8.15(a) on page 366.*

Before stating formal results, we consider an example in which we use our intuition to anticipate how the sample mean $\bar{X}$ as a random variable should behave relative to the population mean μ. Because of the importance of sample size, our example considers results for two possible values of n.

EXAMPLE 8.9 INTUITING THE DISTRIBUTION OF SAMPLE MEAN FOR TWO DIFFERENT SAMPLE SIZES

Background: The population of possible rolls X for a single die consists of equally likely values {1, 2, 3, 4, 5, 6}. It has a mean of $\mu = 3.5$ and a standard deviation of $\sigma = 1.7$.

Questions: What kind of values would sample mean roll $\bar{X}$ take for repeated rolls of

1. $n = 2$ dice?

2. $n = 8$ dice?

Responses: The sample mean roll $\bar{X}$ takes various number values subject to the laws of chance—it is a random variable. We can summarize its sampling distribution—just as we summarized distributions of data values in Part II—by telling about its *center, spread,* and *shape.*

1. First we consider the center, spread, and shape of the distribution of sample mean roll of **2 dice.**

■ *Center:* Sometimes the mean roll of 2 dice will be less than 3.5, sometimes greater than 3.5. It should be just as likely to get a lower-than-average mean as a higher-than-average mean: The sampling distribution of sample mean roll $\bar{X}$ should be *centered* at 3.5.

■ *Spread:* For 2 dice, the sample mean roll $\bar{X}$ will have a fair amount of *spread:* sample means all the way from 1.0 (if two 1's are rolled) to 6.0 (if two 6's are rolled) are not uncommon.

■ *Shape:* The most likely mean roll is 3.5 (resulting from rolls (1, 6), (2, 5), (3, 4), (4, 3), (5, 2), or (6, 1)). Lower or higher mean rolls are progressively less likely, with 1.0 (two 1's are rolled) and 6.0 (two 6's are rolled) being least likely. Thus, the *shape* should be somewhat triangular: highest in the middle at 3.5, descending on either side.

2. Next we consider the center, spread, and shape of the distribution of sample mean roll of **8 dice.**

■ *Center:* The distribution of $\bar{X}$ should again be *centered* at $\mu = 3.5$.

■ *Spread:* For the roll of 8 dice, the distribution of sample mean roll $\bar{X}$ should have less *spread* than for 2 dice. All eight 1's or 6's will almost

Continued

The Big Picture:

A CLOSER LOOK

When we think about the behavior of $\bar{X}$ in the long run for repeated random samples, it is playing the role of a random variable rather than a statistic, and we use a capital X instead of a lowercase x.

Example TBP 8.5 on page 871 of the *TBP Supplement* considers a parameter and accompanying statistic when students choose a number "at random" from 1 to 20. Now, instead of being concerned with a categorical variable (whether or not the number seven was picked), we are concerned with the size of the number as a quantitative variable.

Page 870 of the *TBP Supplement* depicts a variety of sample means when rolling two dice, where the population mean is 3.5. An activity that parallels this example is described on page 874.

Here we employ conventional notation, which is to write $\bar{x}$ with a lowercase x when referring to the *statistic* sample mean, measured on a one-time basis. We write $\bar{X}$ with an uppercase X when referring to the *random variable* sample mean, which takes values that vary from one sample to the next in repeated random samples. Curiously, there is no analogous distinction between notations for the statistic $\hat{p}$ and the random variable $\hat{p}$.

never happen: If you roll this many dice at once, there tend to be some low numbers that balance out the high numbers.

■ *Shape:* The most likely mean roll is still 3.5, with lower or higher mean rolls progressively less likely. But now there is a much better chance of the mean being close to 3.5, and a much worse chance of being as low as 1.0 or as high as 6.0: The *shape* of the sampling distribution should bulge at the mean 3.5 and taper away at either end. In other words, it should appear normal.

Practice: *Try Exercise 8.19 on page 367.*

Just as we saw for sample proportions, the laws of probability will confirm that the behavior we expect to see in practice for sample means also holds in theory.

The Mean of the Distribution of Sample Mean

When we sample at random from a population whose mean is μ, the quantitative random variable of interest, X_i, has the same mean μ for each sampled individual i. In Section 7.1, we established that the mean of the sum equals the sum of the means. We also showed that the mean transforms along with a random variable if that variable is multiplied by some constant. Therefore, for the entire sample, the mean of the random variable sample mean $\bar{X} = \frac{1}{n}(X_1 + \cdots + X_n)$ is

$$\frac{1}{n}(\mu + \cdots + \mu) = \frac{1}{n}(n\mu) = \mu$$

LOOKING AHEAD

The fact that the mean of $\bar{X}$ is μ, the underlying population mean, may not appear to be especially interesting, but it actually has far-reaching importance in what we want to accomplish in Part IV. It tells us that if we take a random sample and use the statistic sample mean $\bar{x}$ to estimate the unknown population mean μ, although any single time it may under- or overestimate, in the long run, $\bar{x}$ estimates μ *without bias*. Statisticians say that the random variable $\bar{X}$ is an "unbiased estimator" of μ.

EXAMPLE 8.10 APPLYING THE RULE FOR THE MEAN OF SAMPLE MEANS

Background: IQ scores for the general population have a mean of 100 and a standard deviation of 15. Suppose many samples of a given size were taken repeatedly, and each time the sample mean IQ was recorded.

Questions: What should be the mean of all the sample means for random samples of size 9? What about for random samples of size 36? What about for samples of 36 inmates from U.S. prisons?

Responses: As long as the sample is unbiased, the mean of all sample means should be the same as the population mean, 100. This will be the case regardless of sample size. However, if we take a non-representative sample, such as prison inmates, then we cannot say where the sample means will be centered.

Practice: *Try Exercise 8.21 on page 367.*

The above example demonstrates that sample size has no effect on the center of the distribution of sample mean. In contrast, sample size *does* impact the spread of the distribution, a fact that directly entails advantages in gathering information from larger groups, rather than from just a few individuals.

The Standard Deviation of the Distribution of Sample Mean

As far as the standard deviation of $\bar{X}$ is concerned, we must apply the rules for standard deviations of constant multiples and of sums of random variables. Since the sample mean $\bar{X} = \frac{1}{n}(X_1 + \cdots + X_n)$ multiplies the sum of the X_i by $\frac{1}{n}$, the standard deviation of $\overline{X}$ also multiplies the sum by $\frac{1}{n}$. Remember that each individual random variable X_i has standard deviation σ, the same as the standard deviation of the underlying quantitative population. Keeping in mind that the standard deviation of a sum of independent random variables is the square root of the sum of their squared standard deviations, we can show that the standard deviation of $\overline{X} = \frac{1}{n}(X_1 + \cdots + X_n)$ is

$$\frac{1}{n}\sqrt{\sigma^2 + \cdots + \sigma^2} = \frac{1}{n}\sqrt{n\sigma^2} = \frac{\sigma}{\sqrt{n}}$$

> Again, we may remind students that if sampling is done without replacement, then the sample size should not be more than one-tenth the population size. Otherwise, our expression for the standard deviation, which relied on independence of the individual X values, will be incorrect.

EXAMPLE 8.11 APPLYING THE RULE FOR THE STANDARD DEVIATION OF SAMPLE MEANS

Background: IQ scores for the general population have a mean of 100 and a standard deviation of 15. Suppose many samples of a given size were taken repeatedly, and each time the sample mean IQ was recorded.

Questions:

1. What is the standard deviation of all the sample means for random samples of size 9?

2. What about for random samples of size 36?

3. What about for random samples of 36 people taken from a population of 60 people whose IQ scores have a mean of 100 and a standard deviation of 15?

Responses:

1. As long as the sampled IQ scores are independent of one another, the standard deviation of sample means for samples of size 9 would be the population standard deviation, 15, *divided by the square root of the sample size 9:* $\frac{15}{\sqrt{9}} = \frac{15}{3} = 5$.

2. The standard deviation of sample means for samples of size 36 would be the population deviation, 15, *divided by the square root of the sample size 36:* $\frac{15}{\sqrt{36}} = \frac{15}{6} = 2.5$.

3. If the 36 people are sampled *without replacement* from a group of only 60, then the selections are *dependent* and our formula for standard deviation is incorrect.

Practice: *Try Exercise 8.23 on page 367.*

> Our result about the standard deviation of sample mean will be exploited in Part IV, when we use sample mean as an estimate for unknown population mean. For now, we want students to concentrate on understanding how sample mean as a random variable behaves, relative to *known* population mean μ (and standard deviation σ). Example 8.11 demonstrates how the appearance of $\sqrt{n}$ in the denominator impacts the standard deviation: If sample size is multiplied by 4, standard deviation of sample mean is divided by the square root of 4, or 2. Specifically, increasing n from 9 to 36 decreased the standard deviation of our sample mean from 5 to 2.5.

When we established formulas for the mean and standard deviation of sample proportion $\hat{p}$, for situations with a categorical variable of interest, we stressed on page 352 the importance of the fact that n appears in the denominator of the standard deviation of $\hat{p}$, $\sqrt{\frac{p(1-p)}{n}}$. This told us that as the sample size n increases, the spread of the distribution of sample proportion decreases. Analogously, because the standard deviation of sample mean $\overline{X}$ is $\frac{\sigma}{\sqrt{n}}$, the spread of the distribution of sample mean also decreases as the sample size increases. Thus, there is theoretical justification for what our intuition may already suggest: Larger samples provide better estimates.

The Shape of the Distribution of Sample Mean: The Central Limit Theorem

Now that we know the center (mean) and spread (standard deviation) of the distribution of sample mean, the last issue to be resolved is that of shape. When we examined behaviors of counts and proportions in Chapter 7, we looked at variables like "proportion of tails in n coin flips" or "proportion of left-handed people in a sample of size n" for sample sizes n increasing from 1. The population distribution of tails was perfectly balanced (probability of tails and heads both 0.5), and we saw that sample proportion exhibited a fairly symmetric, single-peaked shape even for relatively small sample sizes ($n = 16$). In contrast, the population distribution of left-handed people was very unbalanced (probability of left-handed 0.1, probability of right-handed 0.9), and the distribution of sample proportion was still quite skewed for samples of size $n = 16$. Because the shape of the population distribution is completely determined by the population proportion p, statisticians could easily establish a rule of thumb for use of a normal approximation, based on the interplay between n and p: smaller n acceptable for p close to 0.5, larger n needed for p farther from 0.5 in either direction.

The behavior of sample means is similar to that of sample proportions, in that smaller samples are adequate for normal approximations if the population distribution itself is close to normal, and larger samples are required if the population distribution is very non-normal (for instance, if it is very skewed). The Central Limit Theorem guarantees the shape of the distribution of sample mean to become increasingly normal as the sample size increases. It provides us with the third key element in our quest to characterize the behavior of the random variable sample mean.

Center, Spread, and Shape of the Distribution of Sample Mean

Now we consolidate our results about the center, spread, and shape of the random variable sample mean.

> ### Rule for the Distribution of Sample Mean
>
> If random samples of size n are taken from a relatively large population with a mean of μ and a standard deviation of σ, then the distribution of sample mean $\overline{X}$ has
>
> - mean μ
> - standard deviation $\frac{\sigma}{\sqrt{n}}$
> - shape approximately normal if sample size n is large enough

Unlike p for categorical variables, the mean μ and standard deviation σ of a quantitative variable do not supply us with any information about the shape of the population distribution. Therefore, our guidelines for use of a normal approximation are unfortunately less clear-cut than the rule of thumb for sample proportions (normal approximation acceptable if $np \geq 10$ and $n(1 - p) \geq 10$). There is no analogous rule of thumb for sample means that is universally implemented; in this book we will utilize the following guidelines for what values of n would be considered "large enough."

One of the most common questions asked by students in statistics is, "How large is large enough?" This question, unfortunately, has no simple answer. If we say that $n = 30$ should be large enough to offset skewness, this does not mean that the distribution of $\overline{X}$ is terribly skewed for $n = 29$ and perfectly normal for $n = 30$. Progress toward normality as n increases is a gradual thing, and for this reason different textbook authors offer different guidelines. Breaking up the range of sample sizes into small (less than 15), medium (between 15 and 30), and large (greater than 30) may help to guide students toward understanding that there is no magic sample size n that makes the Central Limit Theorem's claims of normality come true.

Guidelines for Approximate Normality of Sample Mean

The shape of the distribution of sample mean $\overline{X}$ for random samples of size *n* is approximately normal if

- the population itself is approximately normal; or
- the population is fairly symmetric (not necessarily single-peaked) and *n* is at least 15; or
- the population is moderately skewed and *n* is at least 30.

At the one extreme, if the population distribution is exactly normal, then sample mean is also normal for any sample size *n*. At the other extreme, if the population distribution is severely skewed, caution should be exercised in deciding whether or not the sample size is large enough to render a normal shape for the distribution of sample mean.

EXAMPLE 8.12 THE SHAPE OF THE DISTRIBUTION OF SAMPLE MEAN

Background: Exercise 7.81 on page 339 in Chapter 7 looked at probability distributions for numbers of male or female buffaloes owned by farming villagers in Nepal.

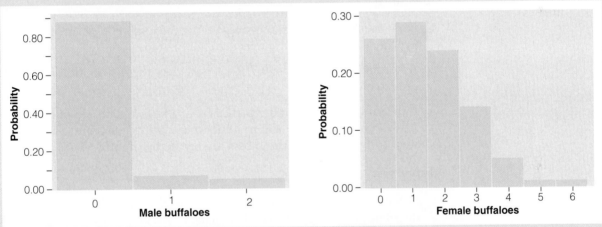

Both histograms are skewed right but the one for males has much more extreme right-skewness than that for females, because such a high proportion of villagers have zero male buffaloes. As is, the histograms can be thought of as representing the distribution of sample mean number of buffaloes for samples of size 1.

Questions: What can we say about the shape of the distribution of sample mean number of *male* buffaloes for random samples of 30 households? What about the shape of the distribution of sample mean number of *female* buffaloes for random samples of 30 households?

Responses: Because the histogram for *male* buffaloes is very right-skewed, the distribution of sample mean may still be somewhat right-skewed for samples of size 30. In contrast, because the underlying distribution for *females* is closer to normal, the distribution of sample mean number of female buffaloes may achieve a fairly normal shape for samples of size 30.

Distribution of sample mean number of buffaloes: Gender affects shape.

Practice: *Try Exercise 8.25 on page 368.*

Normal Probabilities for Sample Means

By now we know the mean and standard deviation of the distribution of sample mean, and can assert its shape to be normal under the right conditions. This puts us in a position to be able to answer questions about the behavior of sample mean by solving probability problems.

In Example 8.1 on page 346, we introduced random number selection as a categorical random variable, focusing on whether or not the number selected was a seven. In the following example, we treat it as a quantitative random variable, focusing on the *size* of the number selected.

EXAMPLE 8.13 USING THE 68-95-99.7 RULE TO DECIDE IF A SAMPLE MEAN IS UNUSUAL

Background: If students each pick a whole number completely at random from 1 to 20, then the mean of all numbers selected should be the mean of the numbers from 1 to 20, which is 10.5. The standard deviation of the numbers from 1 to 20 is 5.77. Suppose 400 students are asked to think of a number at random from 1 to 20.

Questions:

1. How does the probability histogram for the underlying distribution appear, assuming the numbers are chosen at random?

2. According to the 68-95-99.7 Rule, how does the distribution of sample mean appear?

3. If the sample mean number picked by 400 students turned out to be 11.6, would this cause you to doubt the claim that students' selections were truly random, with no bias toward higher numbers?

Responses:

1. Because each number 1 to 20 is equally likely, the underlying distribution has a symmetric flat shape called *uniform*.

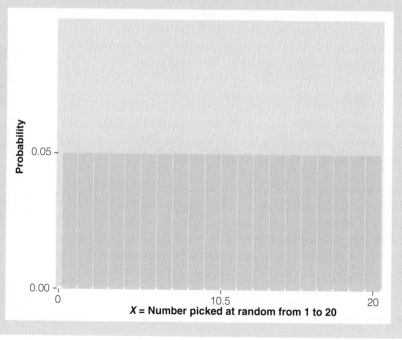

2. The distribution of sample mean has a mean of $\mu = 10.5$ and a standard deviation of $\frac{\sigma}{\sqrt{n}} = \frac{5.77}{\sqrt{400}} = 0.2885$, or 0.3 if we round to the nearest tenth for simplicity's sake. The shape is approximately normal because $n = 400$ is very large. The 68-95-99.7 Rule yields the following sketch for the distribution of sample mean number picked:

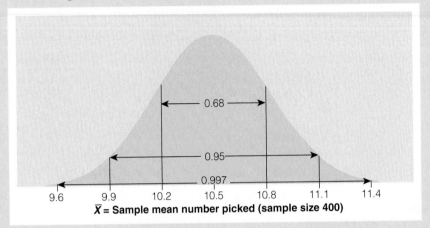

$\overline{X}$ = Sample mean number picked (sample size 400)

3. Since 11.6 is even larger than 11.4, it is virtually impossible (probability less than $(1 - 0.997)/2 = 0.0015$) for the sample mean number picked to be as high as 11.6, if the students are truly picking numbers at random. It seems that students are biased in favor of higher numbers when asked to make a random selection.

Practice: *Try Exercise 8.27 on page 368.*

Once again, we concluded our example with the type of thought question that will be addressed more thoroughly in Part IV when we perform the form of inference known as *hypothesis testing*. Just as Example 8.5 on page 350 suggested bias in favor of certain particular numbers (like seven) when we treated number selection as a categorical variable, this example indicates danger of another type of bias, in terms of the quantitative size of the number selected. Thus, making selections without the benefit of true randomness can easily result in sample summaries that fail to reflect the true nature of the underlying population.

The Central Limit Theorem allowed us to invoke normal probabilities in Example 8.13, because the population distribution was symmetric and the sample size was very large. In the next example, the Central Limit Theorem is not needed because the population distribution itself is normal. Whereas Example 8.13 made use of the 68-95-99.7 Rule, Example 8.14 will reach its conclusions based on probabilities for the tails of the normal curve. The former is simpler and the latter is more detailed in the region around $z = \pm 2$. It is helpful to have both techniques at our disposal.

EXAMPLE 8.14 USING THE TAILS OF THE NORMAL CURVE TO DECIDE IF A SAMPLE MEAN IS UNUSUAL

Background: IQ scores are known to be normal with a mean of 100 and a standard deviation of 15.

Question: Based on a sketch of the tails of the normal curve, can we say 88 is an unusually low value under the following circumstances?

1. A randomly chosen individual has an IQ of 88.

2. A random sample of 4 individuals has a sample mean IQ of 88.

3. A random sample of 9 individuals has a sample mean IQ of 88.

Continued

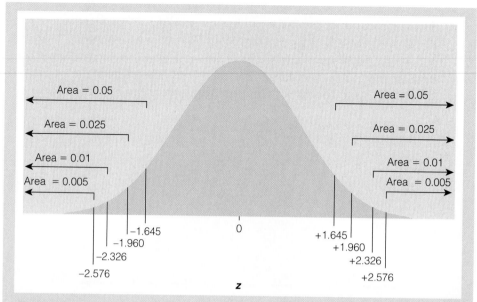

Response:

1. The z-score for an individual IQ of 88 is $z = (88 - 100)/15 = -0.8$. The sketch shows that this is not unusual at all. We also know from the 68-95-99.7 Rule that a score this low occurs for more than 16% of the population.

2. Sample mean IQ for a random sample of 4 individuals has a mean of 100 and a standard deviation of $15/\sqrt{4} = 7.5$. The z-score for a sample mean IQ of 88 is $z = (88 - 100)/7.5 = -1.6$. Since -1.6 is just to the right of -1.645 in the sketch, the probability of being this low is a bit more than 0.05. We could consider a sample mean IQ this low to be slightly unusual.

3. Sample mean IQ for a random sample of 9 individuals has a mean of 100 and a standard deviation of $15/\sqrt{9} = 5$. The z-score for a sample mean IQ of 88 is $z = (88 - 100)/5 = -2.4$. Since -2.4 is between -2.576 and -2.326 in the sketch, the probability of being this low is between 0.005 and 0.01. We could consider a sample mean this low to be very unusual.

Practice: *Try Exercise 8.28 on page 368.*

In our IQ example, the shape of the distribution of sample mean was guaranteed to be normal, regardless of sample size, because the shape of the underlying population itself is normal. The following discussion by four students should impress on you the need to be vigilant, and report normal probabilities only when the Central Limit Theorem allows us to do so. It refers to a sketch of the distribution of household size, introduced on page 274 in Example 7.8.

When Normal Approximations Are Appropriate

Suppose a group of four students have been given permission to work together on their statistics homework problems. They decided to divide up the first four problems, stated as follows:

Household size *X* for a randomly chosen household in the United States for the year 2000 follows a probability distribution as shown in the histogram, with a mean of 2.5, a standard deviation of 1.4, and a shape that is quite skewed to the right.

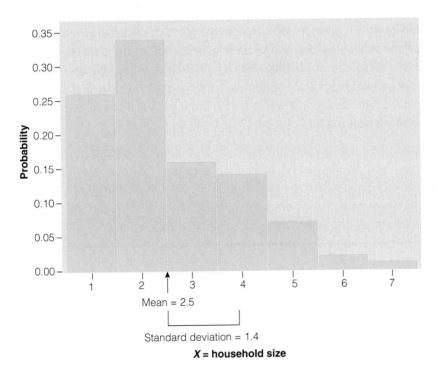

1. Suppose an individual household is selected. What is the probability that its size is less than −0.3 people?

2. Suppose an individual household is selected. What is the probability that its size is at least 3 people?

3. Suppose a random sample of 10 households is taken. What is the probability that the sample mean household size is at least 3?

4. Suppose a random sample of 100 households is taken. What is the probability that the sample mean household size is at least 3?

Adam: *"I got mine done. I took negative 0.3, minus 2.5, divided by 1.4, and got z equals negative 2. The 68-95-99.7 Rule says the probability of being less than 2 standard deviations below the mean is 0.025. So the answer is 2.5%."*

Students Talk Stats continued ➔

Students Talk Stats continued

Brittany: *"What were you thinking? There's no households that have a negative number of people. You shouldn't standardize to z and find the probability because that only works for normal distributions. Look how skewed the histogram is. Anyway the histogram confirms the answer is zero without doing any work.*

"To solve my problem, I just looked at the histogram. The probability of at least three people is the total area of the rectangles from 3 on up, which is about 0.40. The probability of at least three people is about 40 percent."

Carlos: *"I started to do mine by standardizing, like Adam did, and then I realized that because the distribution is skewed, the sample mean isn't going to be normal for a small sample like 10. This is like a trick question, because there's no way we can answer it with what's given."*

Dominique: *"So I guess I'm the only one who got to do an actual normal problem. Sample mean has mean 2.5, and for samples of size 100, its standard deviation is 1.4 divided by the square root of 100, which is 0.14. Because the sample size is so large, the shape of sample mean should be approximately normal. The standardized value of 3 is 3 minus 2.5, divided by 0.14, which is 3.57. This is really extreme so we could say the probability is close to zero."*

Standardizing values and finding normal probabilities can become so routine to students that they may get the mistaken impression—as Adam did—that this solution technique is always appropriate. Remember that normal approximations are valid for sample proportions and sample means only if the sample size is large enough to offset non-normality in the underlying population.

EXERCISES FOR SECTION 8.2

The Behavior of Sample Mean in Repeated Random Samples

Note: Asterisked numbers indicate exercises whose answers are provided in the Solutions to Selected Exercises section, on page 689.

*8.15 The mean price paid for an ounce of gold in 2003 was $350.

a. Tell whether 350 is a sample mean or a population mean, and identify it with the proper notation.

b. For which sample size will the distribution of sample mean price have more spread: 20 or 30?

c. For which sample size will the shape of the distribution of sample mean be less normal: 20 or 30?

8.16 The mean price paid for an ounce of silver in 2003 was $5.

a. Tell whether 5 is a sample mean or a population mean, and identify it with the proper notation.

b. For which sample size will the distribution of sample mean price have less spread: 10 or 100?

c. For which sample size will the shape of the distribution of sample mean be more normal: 10 or 100?

*8.17 Suppose we are interested in the behavior of sample mean amount borrowed by undergraduates for college tuition, for random samples of a certain size.

a. To draw conclusions about the *center* of the distribution of sample mean, which of these do we need to know (there may be more than one needed): population mean, population standard deviation, population shape, sample size?

b. To draw conclusions about the *spread* of the distribution of sample mean, which of these do we need to know (there may be more than one needed): population mean, population standard deviation, population shape, sample size?

c. To draw conclusions about the *shape* of the distribution of sample mean, which of these do we need to know (there may be more than one needed): population mean, population standard deviation, population shape, sample size?

8.18 Suppose we are interested in the behavior of sample mean age of college undergraduates, for random samples of a certain size.

a. To draw conclusions about the *center* of the distribution of sample mean, which of these do we need to know (there may be more than one needed): population mean, population standard deviation, population shape, sample size?

b. To draw conclusions about the *spread* of the distribution of sample mean, which of these do we need to know (there may be more than one needed): population mean, population standard deviation, population shape, sample size?

c. To draw conclusions about the *shape* of the distribution of sample mean, which of these do we need to know (there may be more than one needed): population mean, population standard deviation, population shape, sample size?

*8.19 The numbers 1 through 20 have a mean of 10.5 and a standard deviation of 5.8. The shape of the distribution is uniformly flat because all numbers are equally likely. Consider the distribution of sample mean number when 9 students pick a number at random from 1 to 20, compared to the distribution when 16 students pick a number at random from 1 to 20.

a. Compare the centers of the distributions for 9 versus 16 selections.

b. Compare the spreads of the distributions for 9 versus 16 selections.

c. Compare the shapes of the distributions for 9 versus 16 selections.

8.20 The numbers 1 through 10 have a mean of 5.5 and a standard deviation of 2.9. The shape of the distribution is uniformly flat

because all numbers are equally likely. Consider the distribution of sample mean number when 4 students pick a number at random from 1 to 10, compared to the distribution when 25 students pick a number at random from 1 to 10.

a. Compare the centers of the distributions for 4 versus 25 selections.

b. Compare the spreads of the distributions for 4 versus 25 selections.

c. Compare the shapes of the distributions for 4 versus 25 selections.

*8.21 Assume heights of adult males have a mean of 69 inches. Tell whether each of the following distributions would be centered to the left of 69, at 69, or to the right of 69.

a. Sample mean height for samples of 16 college basketball players

b. Sample mean height for random samples of 6 adult males

c. Sample mean height for random samples of 16 adult males

d. Sample mean height for random samples of 16 students from a school that includes grades 7 through 12

8.22 Assume weights of women in their thirties to have a mean of 144 pounds. Tell whether each of the following distributions would be centered to the left of 144, at 144, or to the right of 144.

a. Sample mean weight for random samples of 9 women in their thirties

b. Sample mean self-reported weight for random samples of 9 women in their thirties

c. Sample mean weight for random samples of 9 women in their thirties, with coats and shoes on

*8.23 Assume heights of adult males have a standard deviation of 2.8 inches. Tell the standard deviation of each of the following distributions.

a. Sample mean height for random samples of 16 adult males

b. Sample mean height for random samples of 49 adult males

8.24 Assume weights of women in their thirties to have a standard deviation of 33 pounds. Tell the standard deviation of each of the following distributions.

a. Sample mean weight for random samples of 9 women in their thirties

b. Sample mean weight for random samples of 121 women in their thirties

*8.25 Keeping in mind that practically all houses in a city would be just one to three stories tall, whereas a small minority of buildings would have many stories, tell whether each of these distributions would have a shape that is extremely left-skewed, somewhat left-skewed, close to normal, somewhat right-skewed, or extremely right-skewed:

a. Heights of all buildings in a city

b. Sample mean heights for random samples of 30 buildings in a city

c. Sample mean heights for random samples of 300 buildings in a city

Are a few tall buildings represented by tall bars on a histogram?

8.26 Tell whether each of these distributions would have a histogram that is extremely left-skewed, somewhat left-skewed, close to normal, somewhat right-skewed, or extremely right-skewed:

a. Lengths of trunks of all adult African elephants

b. Sample mean trunk lengths for random samples of 5 adult African elephants

c. Sample mean trunk lengths for random samples of 50 adult African elephants

*8.27 The distribution of hours worked per week by husbands in the United States in the early 1990s had a mean of 42.6 and a standard deviation of 12.9. The distribution itself was fairly symmetric and single-peaked but not normal because of the relatively high probability of working very close to 40 hours, and because the distribution has a small spike at 0, instead of tapering off

gradually. For samples of size 18, the shape of sample mean hours would be very close to normal, with a mean of 42.6 and a standard deviation of $12.9/\sqrt{18} = 3.0$, as shown in this sketch based on the 68-95-99.7 Rule. Identify the correct range for each of the following probabilities, referring to random samples of size 18.

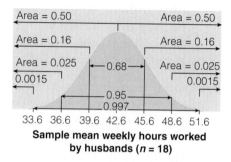

Sample mean weekly hours worked by husbands ($n = 18$)

a. The probability that sample mean hours worked exceeds 40: less than 0.5 or more than 0.5

b. The probability that sample mean hours worked falls below 38: less than 0.16 or more than 0.16

c. The probability that sample mean hours worked falls below 37: less than 0.025 or more than 0.025

*8.28 The distribution of hours worked per week by husbands in the United States in the early 1990s had a mean of 42.6 and a standard deviation of 12.9. For samples of size 18, the shape of sample mean hours would be very close to normal, with a mean of 42.6 and a standard deviation of $12.9/\sqrt{18} = 3.0$. Estimate the probability that sample mean hours worked exceeds 50 by standardizing to z and using information from the tails of the normal curve, shown below.

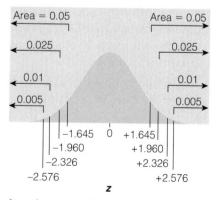

8.29 The distribution of hours worked per week by wives in the United States in the early 1990s had a mean of 26.0 and a standard deviation of 17.2.

a. Tell whether 26.0 is a sample or population mean, and identify it with proper notation.

b. Without actually calculating values of z, tell whether each of these sample means will have a positive or negative standardized score: 40, 30, 25, 20.

c. Without actually calculating values of z, tell which one of these sample means will have the most extreme standardized score: 40, 30, 25, 20.

d. Tell which of these samples means will have the least extreme standardized score: 40, 30, 25, 20.

8.30 The distribution of hours worked per week by wives in the United States in the early 1990s had a mean of 26.0 and a standard deviation of 17.2. The distribution itself was fairly symmetric and double-peaked because of the relatively high probability of working either 0 hours or very close to 40 hours. For samples of size 74, the shape of sample mean hours would be close to normal, with a mean of 26.0 and a standard deviation of $17.2/\sqrt{74} = 2.0$, as shown in this sketch based on the 68-95-99.7 Rule. Identify the correct range for each of the following probabilities, referring to random samples of size 74.

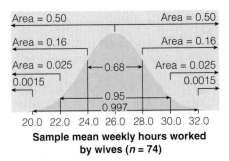

Sample mean weekly hours worked by wives (n = 74)

a. The probability that sample mean hours worked exceeds 40: less than 0.0015 or more than 0.0015

b. The probability that sample mean hours worked falls below 25: less than 0.5 or more than 0.5

c. The probability that sample mean hours worked falls below 20: less than 0.025 or more than 0.025

8.31 The distribution of hours worked per week by wives in the United States in the early 1990s had a mean of 26.0 and a standard deviation of 17.2. For samples of size 74, the shape of sample mean hours would be close

to normal, with a mean of 26.0 and a standard deviation of $17.2/\sqrt{74} = 2.0$.

a. To estimate the probability that sample mean hours worked exceeds 30, first find the standardized value z.

b. Next, use the sketch of the tails of the normal curve (the second curve in Exercise 8.32[b]) to identify the approximate probability that sample mean hours exceeds 30.

*8.32 The National Center for Education Statistics reported 4th-grade *reading* scores in 2003 to have a mean of 217 and a standard deviation of 126 (where possible scores range from 0 to 500).

a. Suppose that in a sample of 3,115 4th graders, the mean reading score was 212. Standardize to find the z-score for this sample mean.

b. Use your z-score and the sketch of the 68-95-99.7 Rule (shown on the top) to estimate the probability that a random sample of size 3,115 from this population would produce a sample mean of 212 or lower (choose one of the following): greater than 0.16, between 0.16 and 0.025, between 0.025 and 0.0015, or less than 0.0015.

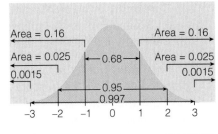

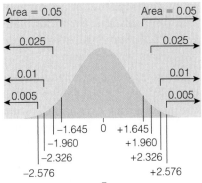

c. Use your z-score and the sketch of the tails of the normal curve (shown on the bottom) to estimate the probability that a random sample of size 3,115 from this population would produce a sample mean of 212 or lower (choose one of the following): greater than 0.05, between 0.05 and 0.025, between 0.025 and 0.01, between 0.01 and 0.005, or less than 0.005.

d. Based on your estimate for the probability of a sample mean equal to 212 or lower when random samples of 3,115 are taken from a population whose mean is 217 and standard deviation is 126, characterize such a sample mean as being not improbable, very unlikely, or extremely unlikely.

e. In fact, the sample of 3,115 4th graders were all charter school students. Which of the following is supported by the sample data?
1. The mean reading score for charter school 4th graders is fairly close to the mean score for all 4th graders.
2. The mean reading score for charter school 4th graders is unusually low compared to the mean score for all 4th graders.
3. The mean reading score for charter school 4th graders is unusually high compared to the mean score for all 4th graders.

f. Suppose a sample of just 9 charter schools had a mean score of 212. Find the z-score in this case, and characterize the sample mean as being fairly close to 217, unusually low compared to 217, or unusually high compared to 217.

8.33 The National Center for Education Statistics reported 4th-grade *math* scores in 2003 to have mean 234 and standard deviation 85 (where possible scores range from 0 to 500).

a. Suppose that in a sample of 3,154 4th graders, the mean math score was 228. Standardize to find the z-score for this sample mean.

b. Use your z-score and the sketch of the 68-95-99.7 Rule (shown on the top in the preceding exercise) to estimate the probability that a random sample of size 3,154 from this population would produce a sample mean of 228 or lower (choose one of the following): greater than 0.16, between 0.16 and 0.025, between 0.025 and 0.0015, or less than 0.0015.

c. Use your z-score and the sketch of the tails of the normal curve (shown on the bottom in the preceding exercise) to estimate the probability that a random sample of size 3,154 from this population

would produce a sample mean of 228 or lower (choose one of the following): greater than 0.05, between 0.05 and 0.025, between 0.025 and 0.01, between 0.01 and 0.005, or less than 0.005.

d. Based on your estimate for the probability of a sample mean equal to 228 or lower when a random sample of size 3,154 is taken from a population whose mean is 234 and standard deviation is 85, characterize such a sample mean as being not improbable, very unlikely, or extremely unlikely.

e. In fact, the sample of 3,154 4th graders were all charter school students. Which of the following is supported by the sample data?
1. The mean math score for charter school 4th graders is fairly close to the mean score for all 4th graders.
2. The mean math score for charter school 4th graders is unusually low compared to the mean score for all 4th graders.
3. The mean math score for charter school 4th graders is unusually high compared to the mean score for all 4th graders.

f. Suppose a sample of just 25 charter schools had a mean score of 228. Find the z-score in this case.

g. Based on the z-score you found in part (f), characterize a sample mean of 228 from a sample of size 25 as being fairly close to 234, unusually low compared to 234, or unusually high compared to 234.

8.34 The National Center for Education Statistics reported 4th-grade *reading* scores in 2003 to have mean 217 and standard deviation 126, while *math* scores had mean 234 and standard deviation 85. The z-score for a mean reading score of 212 for a sample of size 3,115 is $z = (212 - 217)/(126/\sqrt{3{,}115}) = -2.21$ and the z-score for a mean math score of 228 for a sample of size 3,154 is $z = (228 - 234)/(85/\sqrt{3{,}154}) = -3.96$. Tell whether or not each of the following contributes to the result that z is more extreme for the mean math score than it is for the mean reading score.

a. 228 is farther from 234 than 212 is from 217.

b. The standard deviation for math is smaller than that for reading.

c. The sample size is larger for math than it is for reading.

CHAPTER 8   SUMMARY

Results about the center, spread, and shape of the distribution of sample proportion and sample mean can be summarized in just a few lines (shown later in this summary). Their impact is nevertheless far-reaching, and vital to virtually all subsequent results to be presented in this book. To demonstrate how to apply these results, we revisit a question (posed on pae 224 at the beginning of Part III) whose purpose was to motivate our pursuit of the study of probability:

"Suppose that 54% in a sample of 1,000 voters intend to vote for a particular candidate. Can we conclude that the majority—more than 50%—of *all* voters intend to vote for that candidate?" By now we have developed the necessary skills to solve for the probability that is the key to making a decision in this voting problem.

If we assume that the population proportion favoring that candidate is just $p = 0.50$, then the sample proportion for a sample of size $n = 1,000$ follows an approximately normal distribution with a mean of $p = 0.50$ and a standard deviation of $\sqrt{\frac{0.50(1 - 0.50)}{1,000}} = 0.016$. Because the standardized value of 0.54 is $(0.54 - 0.50)/0.016 = 2.5$, our sketch of the tails of the normal curve, shown in Example 8.5 on page 351, tells us the probability of a sample proportion this high is somewhere between 0.01 and 0.005. Most people instinctively feel that something with a probability less than 1% is very unlikely to happen. Thus, we are inclined not to believe that the population proportion is only 0.50: There *is* evidence that a majority of the population are in favor of that candidate.

Now we summarize what has been established in this chapter about the behavior of sample proportion and sample mean as random variables. For these results to hold, the samples must be taken at random from relatively large populations, and the sample size must be large enough to ensure that the Central Limit Theorem applies.

The Behavior of Sample Proportion

Sample proportion is an appropriate summary of *categorical* data values. Sample proportion $\hat{p}$ is a random variable if we consider its behavior in the long run for repeated random samples of a given size n. If the population proportion in the category of interest is p, then the distribution of sample proportion $\hat{p}$ satisfies:

■ The *mean* of $\hat{p}$ is p, as long as the sampling and study design are unbiased.

■ The *standard deviation* of $\hat{p}$ is $\sqrt{\frac{p(1 - p)}{n}}$, assuming population is at least 10 times sample size so that samples taken without replacement are roughly independent.

■ The *shape* of $\hat{p}$ is approximately normal for a large enough sample size n, relative to underlying shape as determined by p: We need to have np and $n(1 - p)$ both at least 10.

As long as the above condition for approximate normality is met, probabilities about sample proportion may be estimated using the 68-95-99.7 Rule or the information provided about the tails of the normal curve. For more precise probabilities, tables or software may be used.

The Behavior of Sample Mean

Sample mean is an appropriate summary of *quantitative* data values. Sample mean $\overline{X}$ is a random variable if we consider its behavior in the long run for repeated random samples of a given size n. If the population mean is μ and the population standard deviation is σ, then

- The *mean* of sample mean $\overline{X}$ is the population mean μ, as long as the sampling and study design are unbiased.

- The *standard deviation* of $\overline{X}$ is $\frac{\sigma}{\sqrt{n}}$, assuming the population is at least 10 times sample size so that samples taken without replacement are roughly independent.

- The *shape* of $\overline{X}$ is approximately normal for a large enough sample size n, relative to the underlying shape (a smaller sample is adequate if the population distribution is close to normal, and a larger sample is needed if the population distribution is far from normal).

As long as the guidelines for approximate normality on page 361 are met, probabilities about sample mean may be estimated using the 68-95-99.7 Rule or the information provided about the tails of the normal curve. For more precise probabilities, tables or software may be utilized.

CHAPTER 8   EXERCISES

Note: Asterisked numbers indicate exercises whose answers are provided in the Solutions to Selected Exercises section, on page 689.

Additional exercises appeared after each section: the distribution of sample proportions (Section 8.1) on page 353 and the distribution of sample means (Section 8.2) on page 366.

Warming Up: SAMPLING DISTRIBUTIONS

*8.35 Researchers might explore the question of the effect of work habits on marriage in a variety of ways. Tell whether each of these possible designs features one categorical, one quantitative, one each quantitative and categorical, two categorical, or two quantitative variables:

   a. For a large sample of couples, determine whether the husband averages more than 50 hours of work a week and whether they get divorced.

   b. Compare hours worked in a week for a sample of husbands who stay married to hours worked in a week for a sample of husbands who get divorced.

   c. Find the average hours worked per week for a sample of husbands who get divorced, and compare it to the known national average for all husbands.

   d. For a sample of husbands who work more than 50 hours a week, find the proportion who get divorced, and compare it to the known national divorce rate for all husbands.

*8.36 One of the designs in the preceding exercise would focus on a single sample mean. Which is it?

8.37. Tell whether each of the following uses a paired, a two-sample, or a several-sample design:

   a. Work hours for a sample of husbands are compared to work hours for a sample of wives.

   b. For a sample of couples, the difference between husband's and wife's work hours is examined.

   c. Work hours are compared for samples of husbands who are single, married, and divorced.

8.38 Researchers might explore public attitude toward wolves in Croatia in a variety of ways.[3] Tell whether each of these possible designs features one categorical, one quantitative, one each categorical and quantitative, two categorical, or two quantitative variables:

   a. Survey people as to whether they approve of setting poisons for wolves.

   b. Survey a random sample of people and another random sample several years later, asking whether they approve of setting poisons for wolves, to determine if they are becoming more tolerant of wolves.

   c. Ask people how many times in the past year they have heard a wolf howling, and ask them to rank wolves in terms of their undesirability as pests compared to other animals such as bears, wild boars, insects, rodents, and foxes, to see if people tend to disapprove of wolves

More exercises for this chapter are featured in the *TBP* Supplement on pages 876 through 881. End-of-chapter activities are described on page 871.

more if they are more aware of their presence.

   d. Survey people, asking them to rank wolves' undesirability on a scale of 1 to 10.

8.39 One of the designs in the preceding exercise would focus on a single sample proportion. Which is it?

*__8.40__ Entering students at the University of Washington were asked to complete a survey in the fall of 1999. Out of about 4,000 entering students, roughly 2,000 completed the survey. The sample of 2,000 students who completed the survey were found to differ in a variety of ways (age, ethnicity, SAT scores) from the population of 4,000 entering students. Explain why our formulas for standard deviation of sample proportion or sample mean, which require independent selections, do not apply in this situation.

8.41 In a newspaper article entitled "Criminal Pasts Cited for Many City School Bus Drivers," it is reported that "state auditors checking the records of a random sample of 100 city bus drivers have found that more than a quarter of them had criminal histories . . . A series of problems last year with school bus drivers . . . prompted [state Auditor General] Casey to take a closer look at the city's staff of 750 drivers . . ."[4] Show that our rule of thumb for approximate independence for sampling without replacement is not quite satisfied.

8.42 A newspaper report on recycling unwanted gifts states that "about 31% of shoppers have regifted one or more times, with three times being the average,"[5] according to a 2003 American Express Retail Index survey of 803 adults. Identify each of the numbers mentioned with the correct variable name, $\hat{p}$, p, $\bar{x}$, μ, or n:

   a. 31%

   b. 3

   c. 803

8.43 Marketers are interested in the phenomenon of "regifting"—that is, recycling unwanted gifts. For each of the following situations, tell which of these is the focus: data production, displaying and summarizing data, probability, or statistical inference.

   a. We'll assume that a certain percentage of Americans recycle gifts. If we consider the likelihood of sample percentage being below a certain value for a sample of a given size, then the focus is on which of the four processes?

   b. If we want to use information from a sample survey to draw conclusions about gift recycling habits of all Americans, then the focus is on which of the four processes?

   c. Based on results from a survey about regifting, a reporter considers whether to use two pie charts or a single bar graph to compare habits of men and women. Which of the four processes is the focus at this stage?

   d. To discover how common gift recycling is, a survey question must be worded carefully to elicit honest and accurate responses. Which of the four processes is the focus at this stage?

8.44 Researchers are interested in the amount of time it takes Americans to get to work. For each of the situations below, tell which of these is the focus: data production, displaying and summarizing data, probability, or statistical inference.

   a. Based on results from a survey, a researcher considers whether to report the median or the mean travel time. What is the focus at this stage?

   b. Researchers consider asking people not to include any additional time spent stopping for breakfast, dropping children off at school, etc., when they report their typical travel-to-work time. What is the focus at this stage?

   c. If we want to use information from a sample survey to draw conclusions about time it takes all Americans to get to work, then the focus is on which of the four processes?

   d. We'll assume Americans take a certain time on average to get to work. If we consider the likelihood of sample mean being above a certain value for a sample of a given size, then the focus is on which of the four processes?

*__8.45__ Tell whether the shape of each of these population distributions would be left-skewed/low outliers, right-skewed/high outliers, fairly symmetric but non-normal, or approximately normal:

a. Length at birth of all full-term babies born in a particular year

b. Age at death of Americans who died in a particular year

c. Income of all full-time workers in the United States

d. Household size in the United States

8.46 Tell whether the shape of each of these population distributions would be left-skewed/low outliers, right-skewed/high outliers, fairly symmetric but non-normal, or approximately normal:

a. Age of people who made their first visit to a dentist in a particular year

b. Number of fillings for U.S. college students

c. Length of adults' incisor teeth

d. Number of teeth (their own) retained by Americans in their sixties

*8.47 For large random samples, the z-score representing standardized sample proportion may be called extremely improbable if it is greater than _____, very improbable if it is in the vicinity of _____, somewhat improbable if it is in the vicinity of _____, and not at all improbable if it is less than _____. (To fill in the blanks, choose from the numbers 1, 2, 3, 4, using each of the numbers exactly once.)

8.48 For large random samples, if the z-score representing standardized sample mean is less than 1 we may call it _____; if its value is in the vicinity of 2 we may call it _____; if in the vicinity of 3 it may be called _____, and greater than 4 may be called _____. (To fill in the blanks, choose from extremely unlikely, very unlikely, fairly unlikely, not unlikely, using each of the four options exactly once.)

Exploring the Big Picture: DISTRIBUTION OF SAMPLE PROPORTIONS

*8.49 Roughly one in 4,000 babies is born with both male and female traits, a condition known as "intersex." What is the smallest sample size for which probability calculations regarding this condition can rely on normal approximations?

8.50 The probability of being born on a particular day of the year is 1/365. What is the smallest sample size for which probability calculations regarding a particular birthday can rely on normal approximations?

*8.51 According to a 2005 newspaper report about college students, the proportion who seek help at counseling centers is 0.40 at expensive private institutions and 0.10 at larger, public institutions.

a. Regardless of sample size, what is the mean of the distribution of sample proportion when the population proportion is 0.40?

b. For samples of size 100, find the standard deviation of the distribution of sample proportion when the population proportion is 0.40 (rounding to the nearest hundredth).

c. In general, if the sample proportion seeking help at counseling centers at

private institutions is greater than 0.40, will the standardized sampled proportion (z) be positive or negative?

d. Regardless of sample size, what is the mean of the distribution of sample proportion when the population proportion is 0.10?

e. For samples of size 100, find the standard deviation of the distribution of sample proportion when the population proportion is 0.10 (rounding to the nearest hundredth).

f. In general, if the sample proportion seeking help at counseling centers at public institutions is less than 0.10, will the standardized sampled proportion (z) be positive or negative?

g. Find the standardized score $z = \frac{\text{value} - \text{mean}}{\text{standard deviation}}$ for each of the following sample results, and use it to characterize each count as being unusually high, unusually low, or not unusual, given the type of institution:

1. 25 in a sample of 100 students from expensive private institutions seek counseling

2. 25 in a sample of 100 students from larger, public institutions seek counseling

3. 46 in a sample of 100 students from expensive private institutions seek counseling

4. 16 in a sample of 100 students from larger, public institutions seek counseling

8.52 A 2005 newspaper report compared smoking habits in Europe and the United States.

a. The proportion of adults in *Europe* who smoke is 0.34. For samples of size 45, find the standard deviation of the distribution of sample proportion for Europe (rounding to the nearest hundredth).

b. Find the standardized score $z = \frac{\text{value} - \text{mean}}{\text{standard deviation}}$ if in a sample of 45 adult Europeans, the proportion smoking is 0.29.

c. Based on your z-score, characterize the proportion 0.29 as being unusually low, somewhat low but not unusual, somewhat high but not unusual, or unusually high (for Europeans).

d. The proportion of adults in the *United States* who smoke is 0.23. For samples of size 45, find the standard deviation of the distribution of sample proportion for the United States (rounding to the nearest hundredth).

e. Find the z-score if in a sample of 45 adult Americans, the proportion smoking is 0.29.

f. Based on your z-score, characterize the proportion 0.29 as being unusually low, somewhat low but not unusual, somewhat high but not unusual, or unusually high (for Americans).

g. Note that if sample size is multiplied by 100, z-score is multiplied by 10; should we be surprised if a random sample of 4,500 adults from either Europe or the United States resulted in a sample proportion of smokers equal to 0.29? Explain.

h. To display information about smoking in Europe and the United States, would we use a bar graph, side-by-side boxplots, or a scatterplot?

*8.53 According to the U.S. *Statistical Abstract*, the proportion of new single-family houses completed in 2003 that had exactly three bedrooms was 0.51.

a. Is the variable for number of bedrooms being treated here as quantitative or categorical? Describe a way to treat it as the other type of variable.

b. The underlying distribution has just two possible values, 0 and 1. Sketch its probability histogram, and describe it as left-skewed, right-skewed, or close to symmetric.

c. If we took repeated random samples of 6 new single-family houses in 2003 and recorded the proportion of houses with exactly three bedrooms in each sample, what should be the mean of all these sample proportions?

d. What should be the standard deviation (to the nearest hundredth) of all sample proportions for samples of size 6?

e. Tell whether the shape of the distribution of sample proportions for samples of size 6 would be left-skewed, right-skewed, symmetric but not normal, or approximately normal. (Justify your answer.)

f. If we took repeated random samples of 24 new single-family houses in 2003 and recorded the proportion of houses with exactly three bedrooms in each sample, what should be the mean of all these sample proportions?

g. What should be the standard deviation (to the nearest hundredth) of all sample proportions for samples of size 24?

h. Tell whether the shape of the distribution of sample proportions for samples of size 24 would be left-skewed, right-skewed, fairly symmetric but not normal, or approximately normal. (Justify your answer.)

*8.54 According to the U.S. *Statistical Abstract*, the proportion of new single-family houses completed in 2003 that had exactly three bedrooms was 0.51. Without actually calculating values of z, tell whether each of these sample proportions will have a positive or negative standardized score: 0.40, 0.53, 0.90.

*8.55 According to the U.S. *Statistical Abstract*, the proportion of new single-family houses completed in 2003 that had exactly three bedrooms was 0.51. Without actually calculating values of z, tell which one of these sample proportions will have the most extreme and which will have the least extreme standardized score: 0.40, 0.53, 0.90.

*8.56 According to the *U.S. Statistical Abstract,* the proportion of new single-family houses completed in 2003 that had exactly three bedrooms was 0.51. For samples of 30 new single-family houses completed in 2003, the distribution of sample proportion with exactly three bedrooms has mean 0.51, standard deviation 0.09, and a shape that is approximately normal. Find the sample proportion and the z-score for each of these sample counts, and characterize each as having unusually few three-bedroom houses, unusually many three-bedroom houses, or a proportion of three-bedroom houses that is not unusual:

   a. 12 of 30 houses have three bedrooms

   b. 16 of 30 houses have three bedrooms

   c. 27 of 30 houses have three bedrooms

*8.57 According to the *U.S. Statistical Abstract,* the proportion of new single-family houses completed in 2003 that had exactly three bedrooms was 0.51. For samples of 30 new single-family houses completed in 2003, the distribution of sample proportion with exactly three bedrooms has mean 0.51, standard deviation 0.09, and a shape that is approximately normal.

   a. The probability is 0.95 that sample proportion falls between what two values?

   b. If a sample of 30 single-family houses completed in 2003 in a particular town has 0.70 with exactly three bedrooms, could we say that this sample represents what was typical for the United States?

   c. What is the probability that sample proportion is less than 0.42 *or* greater than 0.60?

8.58 According to the *U.S. Statistical Abstract,* the proportion of new single-family houses completed in 2003 that had two or more stories was 0.53.

   a. Is the variable for number of stories being treated here as quantitative or categorical?

   b. The underlying distribution has just two possible values, 0 and 1. Sketch its probability histogram, and describe it as left-skewed, right-skewed, fairly symmetric but not normal, or normal.

   c. If we took repeated random samples of 4 new single-family houses in 2003 and recorded the proportion of houses with two or more stories in each sample, what should be the mean of all these sample proportions?

   d. What should be the standard deviation (to the nearest hundredth) of all sample proportions for samples of size 4?

   e. Tell whether the shape of the distribution of sample proportions for samples of size 4 would be left-skewed, right-skewed, symmetric but not normal, or approximately normal. (Justify your answer.)

   f. If we took repeated random samples of 50 new single-family houses in 2003 and recorded the proportion of houses with two or more stories in each sample, what should be the mean of all these sample proportions?

   g. What should be the standard deviation (to the nearest hundredth) of all sample proportions for samples of size 50?

   h. Tell whether the shape of the distribution of sample proportions for samples of size 50 would be left-skewed, right-skewed, fairly symmetric but not normal, or approximately normal. (Justify your answer.)

8.59 According to the *U.S. Statistical Abstract,* the proportion of new single-family houses completed in 2003 that had two or more stories was 0.53. Without actually calculating values of z, tell whether each of these sample proportions will have a positive or negative standardized score:

   a. 0.20

   b. 0.70

   c. 0.50

8.60 According to the *U.S. Statistical Abstract,* the proportion of new single-family houses completed in 2003 that had two or more stories was 0.53.

   a. Without actually calculating values of z, tell which one of these sample proportions will have the most extreme standardized score: 0.20, 0.70, 0.50.

   b. Tell which one of these sample proportions will have the least extreme standardized score: 0.20, 0.70, 0.50.

8.61 According to the *U.S. Statistical Abstract,* the proportion of new single-family houses completed in 2003 that had two or more stories was 0.53. For samples of 70 new single-family houses completed in 2003, the distribution of sample proportion with two or more stories has mean 0.53, standard deviation 0.06, and a shape that is approximately normal. Find the sample proportion and the *z*-score for each of these sample counts, and characterize each as having unusually few multi-story houses, unusually many multi-story houses, or a proportion of multi-story houses that is not unusual:

a. 14 of 70 houses have two or more stories

b. 49 of 70 houses have two or more stories

c. 35 of 70 houses have two or more stories

8.62 According to the *U.S. Statistical Abstract,* the proportion of new single-family houses completed in 2003 that had two or more stories was 0.53. For samples of 70 new single-family houses completed in 2003, the distribution of sample proportion with two or more stories has mean 0.53, standard deviation 0.06, and a shape that is approximately normal.

a. The probability is 0.68 that sample proportion falls between what two values?

b. If a sample of 70 single-family houses completed in 2003 in a particular town has 0.49 with two or more stories, could we say that this sample represents what was typical for the United States?

c. What is the probability that sample proportion is less than 0.41 *or* greater than 0.65?

8.63 According to a 2004 report from the Centers for Disease Control, 5% of teenagers are gay or lesbian.

a. Find the mean and standard deviation of sample proportion who are gay or lesbian for random samples of 400 teenagers.

b. Tell why the distribution of sample proportion for random samples of 400 teenagers will have a shape that is approximately normal.

c. Use the 68-95-99.7 Rule to sketch the distribution of sample proportion for samples of size 400 taken from a population where the proportion who are gay or lesbian is 0.05.

d. If 160 in a sample of 400 homeless teenagers are found to be gay or lesbian, does this suggest that homeless teenagers are not representative of teenagers in general with respect to sexual orientation? Use the value of standardized sample proportion (*z*) to justify your answer.

e. If 160 in a sample of 400 homeless teenagers are found to be gay or lesbian, does this lend support to claims that many teenagers who tell their parents they are gay are thrown out of their homes? Explain.

*8.64 Each year over 1,000 college students die in alcohol-related deaths, often in cases that involve binge drinking. Harvard School of Public Health reported in 2004 that 44% of college students are binge drinkers. In an informal anonymous survey conducted in a statistics class shortly after the Harvard report was released, students were asked: "In the past two weeks, have you had (males) more than five alcoholic drinks on one occasion? (females) more than four alcoholic drinks on one occasion?" [This is how experts classify a student as being a binge drinker or not.] The proportion answering *yes* was 28/66 = 0.42.

a. Report the center, spread, and shape of the distribution of sample proportion, when population proportion is 0.44 and sample size is 66.

b. How usual or unusual is a sample proportion as low as 0.42 in this situation?

Using Software [see Technology Guide]: PROPORTIONS

This chapter's software exercises are based on survey data, which for this purpose are considered to represent an entire population of over 400 individuals. Whereas our theory about the behavior of sampling distributions requires an infinite number of repetitions, for the purpose of these exercises only 20 random samples of a given size are taken. Distributions of sample proportion (pages 377–379) and sample mean (pages 382–384) are considered for small (*n* = 10), and for larger (*n* = 40) samples, for populations that are symmetric or close to normal, and for populations that are far from normal.

*8.65 This exercise explores the distribution of sample proportion for *small* random samples taken from a *balanced* population (population proportion close to 0.5): a population of several hundred students where half live on campus and the other half do not.

a. First, verify that the population of categorical values for the variable *Live* is very symmetric by accessing the survey data and finding the proportion who live on campus. Then sketch a histogram for the population proportion who live on campus.

b. If the population proportion is 0.5, the mean of all sample proportions for samples of any size should be _____; the standard deviation for samples of size 10 should be $\sqrt{\frac{0.5(1 - 0.5)}{10}}$ = _____. Explain why the shape of the distribution of sample proportion for random samples of size 10 should be symmetric and somewhat normal.

c. Twenty random samples of size $n = 10$ have been taken from several hundred values of the variable *Live* (on or off campus), and the sample proportion living on campus has been calculated each time:

| 0.6 | 0.4 | 0.5 | 0.5 | 0.5 | 0.5 | 0.4 | 0.6 | 0.2 | 0.5 | 0.5 | 0.4 | 0.4 | 0.4 | 0.6 | 0.6 | 0.5 | 0.7 | 0.2 | 0.3 |

Use software to find the mean and standard deviation of the sample proportions (report them to the nearest hundredth) and to produce a histogram.

d. Tell briefly how center, spread, and shape of the distribution of sample proportion for the twenty random samples of size 10 compare to the theoretical mean, standard deviation, and shape, as discussed in part (b).

8.66 This exercise explores the distribution of sample proportion for *larger* random samples taken from a *balanced* population (population proportion close to 0.5): a population of several hundred students where half live on campus and the other half do not.

a. First, verify that the population of categorical values for the variable *Live* is very symmetric by accessing the survey data and finding the proportion who live on campus.

b. If the population proportion is 0.5, the mean of all sample proportions for samples of any size should be _____; the standard deviation for samples of size 40 should be _____.

c. Explain why the shape of the distribution of sample proportion for random samples of size 40 should be approximately normal.

d. Twenty random samples of size $n = 40$ have been taken from several hundred values of the variable *Live* (on or off campus), and the sample proportion living on campus has been calculated each time:

| 0.500 | 0.575 | 0.425 | 0.650 | 0.400 | 0.450 | 0.475 | 0.525 | 0.550 | 0.475 |
| 0.400 | 0.500 | 0.5128 | 0.625 | 0.475 | 0.500 | 0.550 | 0.475 | 0.550 | 0.600 |

Use software to find the mean and standard deviation of the sample proportions (report them to the nearest hundredth) and to produce a histogram.

e. Tell briefly how center, spread, and shape of the distribution of sample proportion for the 20 random samples of size 40 compare to the theoretical mean, standard deviation, and shape, as discussed in parts (b) and (c).

8.67 This exercise explores the distribution of sample proportion for *small* random samples taken from an *unbalanced* population (population proportion close to 0.03).

a. First, verify that the population of categorical values for the variable *Handed* is very unbalanced by accessing the survey data and finding the proportion who are ambidextrous.

b. Sketch a histogram for the population proportion who are ambidextrous (as opposed to not ambidextrous).

c. If the population proportion is 0.03, the mean of all sample proportions for samples of any size should be _____; the standard deviation for samples of size 10 should be _____.

d. Explain why the shape of the distribution of sample proportion should be skewed right for repeated random samples of size 10.

e. Twenty random samples of size $n = 10$ have been taken from several hundred values of the variable *Handed* (ambidextrous or not, for our purposes), and the sample proportion who are ambidextrous has been calculated each time:

0	0	0	0	0	0	0	0.1	0.1	0	0.1	0	0	0	0	0	0.1	0	0	0

Use software to find the mean and standard deviation of the sample proportions (report them to the nearest hundredth) and to produce a histogram.

f. Tell briefly how the center, spread, and shape of the distribution of sample proportion for the 20 random samples of size 10 compare to the theoretical mean, standard deviation, and shape, as discussed in parts (c) and (d).

8.68 This exercise explores the distribution of sample proportion for *larger* random samples taken from an *unbalanced* population (population proportion close to 0.03).

a. First, verify that the population of categorical values for the variable *Handed* is very unbalanced by accessing the survey data and finding the proportion who are ambidextrous.

b. If the population proportion is 0.03, the mean of all sample proportions for samples of any size should be _____; the standard deviation for samples of size 40 should be _____.

c. Explain why the shape of the distribution of sample proportion should be somewhat skewed right for repeated random samples of size 40, but not as skewed as for samples of size 10.

d. Twenty random samples of size $n = 40$ have been taken from several hundred values of the variable *Handed* (ambidextrous or not, for our purposes), and the sample proportion who are ambidextrous has been calculated each time:

0.025	0.05	0	0.05	0.025	0.025	0.05	0.05	0	0.025
0.025	0.025	0	0.025	0.025	0.10	0.025	0.025	0	0.05

Use software to find the mean and standard deviation of the sample proportions (report them to the nearest hundredth) and to produce a histogram.

e. Tell briefly how the center, spread, and shape of the distribution of sample proportion for the 20 random samples of size 40 compare to the theoretical mean, standard deviation, and shape, as discussed in parts (b) and (c).

Discovering Research: SAMPLE PROPORTION

8.69 Find an article or report on a survey featuring a categorical variable of interest, which mentions sample size and the proportion in the category of interest. Is the sample large enough to produce at least 10 individuals in and out of that category?

Exploring the Big Picture: DISTRIBUTION OF SAMPLE MEANS

8.70 Tell whether each of these distributions would have a histogram that is extremely left-skewed, somewhat left-skewed, close to normal, somewhat right-skewed, or extremely right-skewed:

a. Heights of all male students in a large school that includes grades 6 to 12

b. Sample mean heights for random samples of 5 male students in a large school that includes grades 6 to 12

c. Sample mean heights for random samples of 50 male students in a large school that includes grades 6 to 12

*8.71 The distribution of hours worked per week by husbands in the United States in the early 1990s had mean 42.6 and standard deviation 12.9.

a. Tell whether 42.6 is a sample or population mean, and identify it with proper notation.

b. Without actually calculating values of z, tell whether each of these sample means (for a sample of any size) will have a positive or negative standardized score: 40, 50, 38, 37.

c. Without actually calculating values of z, tell which one of these sample means (for a sample of any size) will have the most extreme and which will have the least extreme standardized score: 40, 50, 38, 37.

*8.72 The number of days per week worked by husbands in the United States in the early 1990s had mean 5.2 and standard deviation 0.7.

a. Assuming each husband reported a whole number in answer to the question, "Typically, how many days do you work each week?" the random variable X for number of days worked has eight possible values; what are they?

b. The distribution of days worked in a week by husbands in the United States would have a peak at what value of X?

c. Would the shape of the distribution of X be left-skewed, fairly symmetric, or right-skewed?

d. One of these curves represents the distribution of sample mean days worked per week for random samples of 50 husbands, and the other is for random samples of 200 husbands. What is the sample size for the curve on the top?

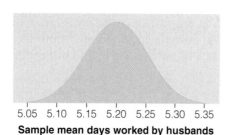

5.05 5.10 5.15 5.20 5.25 5.30 5.35
Sample mean days worked by husbands

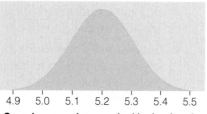

4.9   5.0   5.1   5.2   5.3   5.4   5.5
Sample mean days worked by husbands

e. Characterize each of these as being not improbable, somewhat improbable, very improbable, or extremely improbable.

1. Sample mean days worked by a random sample of 200 husbands is less than 5.0.

2. Sample mean days worked by a random sample of 50 husbands is less than 5.0.

3. Days worked by a randomly chosen husband is less than 5.0.

f. To compare days worked per week for husbands and wives, would we compare percentages, compare means, or look at the correlation?

8.73 The number of days per week worked by wives in the United States in the early 1990s had mean 4.7 and standard deviation 1.0.

a. Assuming each wife reported a whole number in answer to the question, "Typically, how many days do you work each week?" the random variable X for number of days worked has eight possible values; what are they?

b. The distribution of days worked in a week by wives in the United States would have peaks at what two values of X?

c. Would the shape of the distribution of X be fairly symmetric? Explain.

d. One of these curves represents the distribution of sample mean days worked per week for random samples of 100 wives, and the other is for random samples of 400 wives. What is the sample size for the curve on the top?

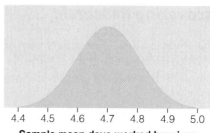

4.4   4.5   4.6   4.7   4.8   4.9   5.0
Sample mean days worked by wives

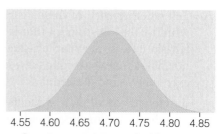

4.55 4.60 4.65 4.70 4.75 4.80 4.85
Sample mean days worked by wives

e. Characterize this event as being not improbable, somewhat improbable, very improbable, or extremely improbable: Sample mean days worked by a random sample of 400 wives is at least 5.0.

f. Characterize this event as being not improbable, somewhat improbable, very improbable, or extremely improbable: Sample mean days worked by a random sample of 100 wives is at least 5.0.

g. Characterize this event as being not improbable, somewhat improbable, very improbable, or extremely improbable: Days worked by a randomly chosen wife is at least 5.0.

h. To display a comparison of days worked per week for husbands and wives, if the data are comprised of pairs, would we use a bar graph, a histogram, or side-by-side boxplots?

i. To display a comparison of days worked per week for men and women, if the data are comprised of two independent samples, would we use a bar graph, a histogram, or side-by-side boxplots?

8.74 Birth weights of babies in Guatemala were found to have mean 2,860 grams and standard deviation 440 grams.[6]

a. The distribution of birth weights would be somewhat left-skewed, but sample mean birth weight for samples of several hundred babies would be close to normal, according to what theorem?

b. The mean weight of 572 babies of mothers who cooked on open wood fires (as opposed to cleaner fuels like gas or electricity) was 2,820 grams. Find the z-score for this sample mean.

c. Characterize a sample mean weight of 2,820 for samples of size 572 taken from the population of Guatemalan birth weights as unusually low, a bit low, or quite typical.

d. If those 572 babies differed from the general population of babies only with respect to type of cooking fuel used by the mother, would the sample suggest that cooking with open wood fires while pregnant may lead to smaller babies?

e. What are some other variables whose values may differ for mothers who cook with various types of fuel, and which

may also impact the babies' birth weights? (In other words, what are some possible confounding variables?)

Does cooking over a wood fire lead to smaller babies?

*8.75 Children's gross motor development is assessed with an overall motor quotient, MQ, which was found to follow an approximate normal distribution for a large group of school children, with mean 93 and standard deviation 15.

a. What are the mean and standard deviation of sample mean MQ for a random sample of 144 children?

b. What are the mean and standard deviation of sample mean MQ for a random sample of 36 children?

c. In general, what values of sample mean MQ will result in a standardized sample mean (z) that is positive?

d. A sample of 144 children *who participated in both club sports and regular sports* had a mean MQ of 96.5. Report the z-score for this sample mean and use it to explain whether or not these children appear to be representative of the larger group in terms of MQ.

e. A sample of 36 *obese* children had a mean MQ of 85.7. Report the z-score for this sample mean and use it to explain whether or not these children appear to be representative of the larger group in terms of MQ.

*8.76 Children's gross motor development is assessed with an overall motor quotient, MQ, which was found to follow an approximate normal distribution for a large group of school children, with mean 93 and standard deviation 15.

a. What is the standard deviation of sample mean for samples of size 25?

b. Report the interval centered at the mean that has a 95% probability of containing the sample mean for random samples of size 25.

c. What is the probability that sample mean is less than 90 or greater than 96?

8.77 Children's fitness is assessed by finding the distance, in meters, that they can run in 6 minutes. Overall, this distance varies fairly normally, with mean 835 and standard deviation 111.

a. What are the mean and standard deviation (to one decimal place) of sample mean distance run for a random sample of 289 children?

b. What are the mean and standard deviation (to one decimal place) of sample mean distance run for a random sample of 38 children?

c. In general, what values of sample mean fitness will result in a standardized sample mean (z) that is negative?

d. A sample of 289 children who *watched TV daily* ran a mean distance of

834.1 meters. Find the z-score for this sample mean.

e. Use the z-score from part (d) to explain whether or not these children appear to be representative of the larger group in terms of distance run.

f. A sample of 38 *underweight* children ran a mean distance of 838 meters. Find the z-score for this sample mean.

g. Based on your z-score, do these underweight children appear to be representative of the larger group in terms of distance run?

8.78 Children's fitness is assessed by finding the distance, in meters, that they can run in 6 minutes. Overall, this distance varies fairly normally, with mean 835 and standard deviation 111.

a. What is the standard deviation of sample mean for samples of size 9?

b. Report the interval centered at the mean that has a 95% probability of containing sample mean for random samples of size 9.

c. What is the probability that sample mean is less than 761 or greater than 909?

8.79 A large number of people responded to a Community Tracking Study survey question that asked them to rate their satisfaction with their health plan, on a scale of 0 to 10.

X	0	1	2	3	4	5	6	7	8	9	10
Probability	0.01	0.00	0.01	0.02	0.02	0.09	0.07	0.17	0.29	0.14	0.18

a. Tell whether the distribution is left-skewed, right-skewed, or fairly symmetric.

b. What is the probability of a rating greater than 9?

c. It can be shown that the ratings have mean 7.6 and standard deviation 1.9. What would be the mean and standard deviation of the distribution of sample mean rating, for random samples of size 100?

d. What is the z-score for a mean rating of 9 in a sample of size 100?

e. Characterize a mean rating greater than 9 in a random sample of size 100 taken from this distribution as being not improbable, somewhat improbable, very improbable, or virtually impossible.

f. Explain why the methods of this chapter cannot be used to find the probability of a mean rating greater than 9 in a sample of size 10, instead of 100.

Using Software [see Technology Guide]: MEANS

8.80 This exercise explores the distribution of sample mean for *small* random samples taken from a population with a shape that is *close to normal* (Math SAT scores).

a. First verify that the population of values for the variable *Math* is close to normal by accessing the survey data and producing a histogram of the values.

b. Because our population mean is 610 and standard deviation is 72, the mean of all sample means for samples of any size should be _____; the standard deviation for samples of size 10 should be _____.

c. Explain why the shape of the distribution of sample mean for random samples of size 10 should be close to normal.

d. Twenty random samples of size $n = 10$ have been taken from several hundred values of the variable *Math SAT*, and the sample mean has been calculated each time:

603.8	607.5	607.1	583.3	660.0	612.2	628.8	613.8	583.8	572.5
619.0	600.0	598.8	612.5	645.6	620.0	584.0	620.0	611.4	555.6

Use software to find the mean and standard deviation of the sample means (report them to the nearest tenth) and to produce a histogram.

e. Tell briefly how center, spread, and shape of the distribution of sample mean for the 20 random samples of size 10 compare to the theoretical mean, standard deviation, and shape, as discussed in parts (b) and (c).

*8.81 This exercise explores the distribution of sample mean for *larger* random samples taken from a population with a shape that is *close to normal* (Math SAT scores).

a. Because our population mean is 610 and standard deviation is 72, the mean of all sample means for samples of any size should be _____; the standard deviation for samples of size 40 should be _____. Explain why the shape of the distribution of sample mean for random samples of size 40 should be very close to normal.

b. Twenty random samples of size $n = 40$ have been taken from several hundred values of the variable *Math SAT*, and the sample mean has been calculated each time:

615.4	595.1	605.9	606.7	613.4	602.7	625.3	624.2	596.3	608.7
622.8	608.1	614.4	614.1	582.5	597.7	627.6	616.5	619.7	613.3

Use software to find the mean and standard deviation of the sample means (report them to the nearest tenth) and to produce a histogram.

c. Tell briefly how center, spread, and shape of the distribution of sample mean for the 20 random samples of size 40 compare to the theoretical mean, standard deviation, and shape, as discussed in part (a).

d. The set of 20 sample means has a low outlier, resulting in an asymmetric histogram. Explain why the histogram should be symmetric if we would continue to take repeated random samples and record sample mean, instead of stopping after just 20 samples.

8.82 This exercise explores the distribution of sample mean for *small* random samples taken from a population with a shape that is quite *skewed* (students' earnings).

a. First verify that the population of values for the variable *Earned* is very right-skewed by accessing the survey data and producing a histogram of the values.

b. Because our population mean is 3.776 and standard deviation is 6.503, the mean of all sample means for samples of any size should be _____; the standard deviation for samples of size 10 should be _____. (The units are thousands of dollars.)

c. Explain why the shape of the distribution of sample mean for random samples of size 10 should be right-skewed.

d. Twenty random samples of size $n = 10$ have been taken from several hundred values of the variable *Earned*, and the sample mean has been calculated each time:

3.6	2.6	4.6	2.5	4.3	1.6	2.5	3.2	4.3	2.9
1.9	3.2	2.4	5.2	3.1	3.4	3.0	3.0	2.7	5.7

Use software to find the mean and standard deviation of the sample means (report them to the nearest tenth) and to produce a histogram.

e. Tell briefly how center, spread, and shape of the distribution of sample mean for the 20 random samples of size 10 compare to the theoretical mean, standard deviation, and shape, as discussed in parts (b) and (c).

8.83 This exercise explores the distribution of sample mean for *larger* random samples taken from a population with a shape that is quite *skewed* (students' earnings).

a. Because our population mean is 3.776 and standard deviation is 6.503, the mean of all sample means for samples of any size should be _____; the standard deviation for samples of size 40 should be _____. (The units are thousands of dollars.)

b. Explain why the shape of the distribution of sample mean for random samples of size 40 should be somewhat right-skewed but less so than for samples of size 10.

c. Twenty random samples of size $n = 40$ have been taken from several hundred values of the variable *Earned*, and the sample mean has been calculated each time:

2.775	3.275	3.400	4.200	4.350	3.650	4.500	4.830	3.050	2.875
4.575	2.925	3.225	2.400	4.075	3.875	3.025	2.675	3.100	2.75

Use software to find the mean and standard deviation of the sample means (report them to the nearest tenth) and to produce a histogram.

d. Tell briefly how center, spread, and shape of the distribution of sample mean for the 20 random samples of size 40 discussed in part (c) compare to the theoretical mean, standard deviation, and shape, as discussed in parts (a) and (b).

Reporting on Research: SAMPLE PROPORTIONS AND MEANS

8.84 Use results of Exercises 8.75 to 8.78 and relevant findings from the Internet to make a report on children's fitness, weight, and TV-watching habits that relies on statistical information.

© Ariel Skelley/CORBIS

Part IV

Statistical Inference

Statistical Inference: An Overview

Whether or not we state it explicitly, whenever information is gathered about a group of individuals, we almost always want to generalize to a larger group. A poll finds what proportion of surveyed voters favor a particular candidate, to get an idea of what proportion of *all* voters favor that candidate. An experimenter determines how much more weight is lost by some dieters who exercise, compared to some dieters who don't, to draw conclusions about weight loss by *all* dieters who do or don't exercise.

Most people, even if they have never taken a statistics course, are not so naive as to believe that what is true for a sample must also be exactly true for the larger population. But unless they have a knowledge of statistical principles, people are unable to judge to what degree information about a sample can be extended to the general population. This book teaches you to be an educated consumer of statistical information, so that by the time you have finished this final (and most important) part, you will have the skills to make such generalizations carefully and correctly. These skills will enable you to decide, given poll results, whether or not a majority of *all* voters favor a candidate. They will let you estimate, given results of an experiment, how many more pounds *any* dieter stands to lose if he or she exercises regularly.

Inference in the Big Picture

Our diagram of the four processes should help remind you of how this fourth and final process fits into the "big picture" of statistics.

By now we have considered how to produce an unbiased sample, and how to display and summarize the sample data, depending on what types of variables are involved. We have established important principles of probability theory, and are ready to make practical use of these results: Now that we know how samples tend to behave relative to populations, we turn this knowledge around and discover what is likely to be true about a population, given what we have observed in a sample. Our knowledge about the population, based on the sample, will not be perfect, but methods about to be presented will enable us to quantify the uncer-

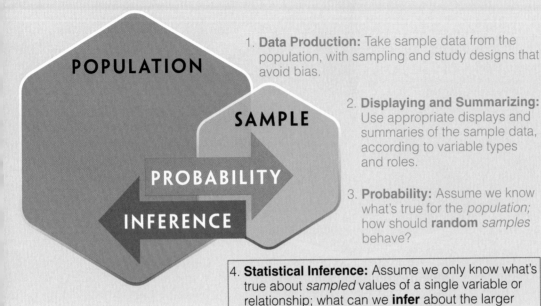

1. **Data Production:** Take sample data from the population, with sampling and study designs that avoid bias.

2. **Displaying and Summarizing:** Use appropriate displays and summaries of the sample data, according to variable types and roles.

3. **Probability:** Assume we know what's true for the *population*; how should **random** *samples* behave?

4. **Statistical Inference:** Assume we only know what's true about *sampled* values of a single variable or relationship; what can we **infer** about the larger *population*?

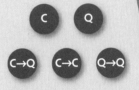

tainty of our conclusions. This final step, inference, is highlighted in our diagram because it is the task at hand. The five variable situations are also shown because each situation calls for a different approach to inference.

The various inference procedures encountered will require us to work with a variety of statistics besides z, such as t, F, and χ^2. Notation for these statistics and for the corresponding random variables is discussed on page 887 of the *Teaching the Big Picture* **(TBP)** *Supplement.*

Two Major Forms of Inference

No matter which of the five situations applies, our inference about the larger population, based on the sample, may take one of two forms: confidence intervals or hypothesis tests.

■ Setting up a **confidence interval** is a way of presenting a **range of plausible values** for the unknown population parameter. The interval tells us what values are, in a sense, believable.

■ Carrying out a **hypothesis test** is a way of deciding whether or not a particular proposed value for the unknown parameter is plausible. In the case of relationships between two variables, a hypothesis test is especially important because it helps us decide whether or not there is convincing evidence that those variables are related in the larger population, not just in the sample.

Graphic illustrations of the workings of confidence intervals and hypothesis tests in the five situations are provided on pages 887 to 888 of the **TBP** *Supplement.*

In the next five chapters we will systematically consider both forms of inference—confidence intervals and hypothesis tests—for each of the five variable situations. As you advance through these chapters, you may want to refer back to this overview occasionally, to help keep the "big picture" in perspective throughout.

CHAPTER 9

Inference for a Single Categorical Variable

Do more than 50% of all college students eat breakfast?

© Peter Yates/CORBIS

Thinking about the population of breakfast-eaters: An inference problem

In this chapter, we consider only situations involving a single categorical variable, such as whether or not a student eats breakfast. The parameter we want to draw conclusions about is the population proportion p in the category of interest (such as the proportion of *all* students who eat breakfast) and the corresponding statistic is the sample proportion $\hat{p}$ (such as the proportion of *surveyed* students who ate breakfast).

We introduced Section 4.1, on displays and summaries for a single categorical variable, by considering the question, "What percentage of sampled students ate breakfast?" This question referred to survey results for 446 students at a particular university, which found that 246 of them had eaten breakfast that day. We displayed the results with a pie chart, shown on the left, and summarized by reporting that the sample proportion was 246/446 = 0.55, or 55%. Alternatively, the results could be displayed using a bar graph (shown in the middle) with one bar each for students answering no or yes. If we assume that only two responses are possible, then the information can also be conveyed using a single bar (shown on the right) for the proportion answering yes.

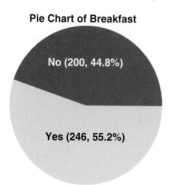

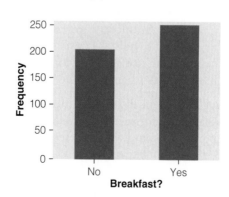

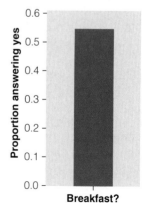

Now we want to use the sample results to draw conclusions about the percentage of *all* college students who eat breakfast on a given day. Before attempting to make any connections between the sample (some students taking introductory statistics courses at a particular university) and the population (all college students), we should think about whether or not the sample is fairly representative of the population in terms of the variable of interest—eating breakfast or not. There are perhaps somewhat differing trends for students who live on or off campus, which would result in differences among various colleges and universities, depending on their percentages of students living on campus. In fact, our data set shows almost identical proportions eating breakfast for on and off campus students, which is reassuring. If all of the surveyed students were enrolled in a class meeting at a particular time of day (such as 8:00 in the morning), then the tendency to eat breakfast could be affected. In fact, the students were enrolled in statistics classes meeting at various times of the day, so this possible source of bias should not be a problem. It is probably safe to assert that these students represent all students at that university in terms of their breakfast habits. Arguably, they could represent all college students reasonably well.

We begin by considering three different ways we might want to do inference about the unknown proportion p of all college students who eat breakfast.

The Big Picture: LOOKING AHEAD

In future chapters we will perform inference about a single quantitative variable, or about relationships between two variables. Although the specifics will differ, depending on what types of variables are involved, many of the general principles developed in this chapter will apply in the other inference chapters as well.

EXAMPLE 9.1 THINKING ABOUT AN UNKNOWN POPULATION PROPORTION

Background: In a representative sample of 446 college students, 246 ate breakfast the day of the survey.

Questions:

■ What is our *best guess* for the proportion of all college students who eat breakfast?

■ What *interval* should contain the proportion of all college students who eat breakfast on a given day?

■ Is there evidence that *more than half* (proportion greater than 0.50) of all college students eat breakfast?

Responses: Intuitively, our best guess for the population proportion would be the sample proportion, 246/446 = 0.55. Our intuition provides no obvious answers to the second and third questions. What we need is a way to establish a range of plausible values for an unknown population proportion, or to decide if a proposed value for the population proportion is plausible.

Statistics is a science, but handling data is also an art that relies to some extent on matters of taste. Students' (and teachers') opinions may be discussed here, with regard to whether or not the breakfast-eating habits of students at one large university are fairly representative of those of all college students.

The three questions posed in Example 9.1 represent three basic forms of statistical inference that we may want to perform when drawing conclusions about population parameters based on sample statistics: *point estimates, confidence interval estimates,* and *hypothesis tests.* Point estimates are the least informative, but they are a good place to start because they are the simplest.

Definition   A **point estimate** is a single number used to estimate an unknown quantity.

9.1 Point Estimate and Confidence Interval: A Best Guess and a Range of Plausible Values for Population Proportion

When we used the rules of probability in Chapter 8 to summarize the behavior of the sample proportion $\hat{p}$ for random samples of a certain size taken from a population with proportion p in the category of interest, we arrived at results concerning the center, spread, and shape of the distribution of sample proportion. As far as center is concerned, we stated that the distribution of sample proportion $\hat{p}$ has a mean equal to the population proportion p. This result provides theoretical justification for the most intuitive answer to the first question in Example 9.1, namely to estimate the unknown population proportion with an observed sample proportion (in this case, $246/446 = 0.55$). While there is no guarantee that the population proportion will exactly equal our guessed value, the theory established in Part III (summarized on page 307) tells us that, in the long run, our guess is on target. At some times we might underestimate and other times we might overestimate, but in the long run, sample proportion $\hat{p}$ is an *unbiased estimator* for population proportion p.

The ***Big Picture:***
LOOKING BACK

Because all of our inference procedures will require us to begin with an unbiased estimator, the principles of good data production from Part I, which ensure unbiased samples and summaries, are crucial.

> *Definition* An **unbiased estimator** is a random variable with a mean that equals the quantity to be estimated.

EXAMPLE 9.2 SAMPLE PROPORTION AS THE BEST GUESS FOR THE POPULATION PROPORTION

Background: In a random sample of 1,001 adult Americans, the proportion intending to celebrate Thanksgiving with a special meal was 0.90.

Question: What would be a good estimate for the proportion of all Americans intending to celebrate Thanksgiving with a special meal?

Response: The best guess for the unknown population proportion is the sample proportion, 0.90.

Practice: *Try Exercise 9.5(b) on page 406.*

The word *random* in the above example is important. Contrast that example with the following one.

EXAMPLE 9.3 WHEN A SAMPLE PROPORTION IS A POOR ESTIMATE FOR THE POPULATION PROPORTION

Background: A large sample of high school seniors were surveyed during class time. Responses to one of the survey questions showed that the proportion who had cut classes for at least a day in the past month was 0.32.

Question: Based on this sample, what would be a good estimate for the proportion of all seniors cutting class at least once a month?

Response: In this situation, the sample proportion is *not* a good estimate for the population proportion. The fact that the survey was conducted during class time resulted in a sample of students who were not representative of all students in terms of cutting class: Obviously, the survey failed to include information from students who were not in class the day it was administered, many of whom could have been cutting class. Moreover, the students may not have answered honestly if they feared their teachers would find out they'd been cutting class. Sample proportion is an unbiased estimator for the population proportion only when it arises from an unbiased sample.

Practice: *Try Exercise 9.6 on page 407.*

Are these students busy causing biased samples?

Point estimates are a good place to start, but they do not provide enough information for most purposes. Although it is reassuring to know that in the long run, the sample proportion from a random sample is an unbiased estimate for the unknown population proportion, the fact is that this estimate is almost always "off" by some amount. If the sample proportion intending to vote for a particular candidate is 0.54, then it's not at all certain that the population proportion is also 0.54. However, we may estimate it to be somewhere in the vicinity of 0.54. Is it somewhere between 0.53 and 0.55? Or somewhere between 0.44 and 0.64? The difference between these intervals is clearly important, because in the former case we could assert that the majority of all voters favor that candidate, whereas in the latter case we could not.

Knowing the mean of the distribution of sample proportion to be the population proportion lets us take the first step, forming an estimate that is unbiased. The next step, that of "closing in" on the value of the unknown population proportion, utilizes what we have established in terms of the spread (standard deviation) of the distribution of sample proportion. Two different ways to get a handle on the value of unknown population proportion will be presented: first confidence intervals, and then hypothesis tests. Confidence intervals provide us with a range of plausible values for the unknown population proportion, whereas hypothesis tests let us decide whether or not a particular proposed value of the population proportion is plausible.

The groundwork for performing inference in the form of confidence intervals has already been laid in Part III. All that remains now is to reverse the reasoning process: Instead of using probability to conclude how samples behave in the long run, based on information that is known about the population, we must learn to draw conclusions about an unknown population value, based on information measured from a sample. We now make this transition as we shift from probability intervals to confidence intervals.

Probability versus Confidence: Talking about Random Variables or Parameters

To better understand the long-run behavior of sample proportions in Chapter 8, we considered the following in Example 8.5:

"If students each pick a whole number at random from one to twenty, then the overall proportion picking each of the numbers should be $1/20 = 0.05$. Suppose 400 students are asked to pick a number at random from one to twenty . . ."

Notice that the population proportion p was known, as we assumed it to be 0.05, and we had $n = 400$. Probability theory told us the following:

- The distribution of sample proportion $\hat{p}$ picking the number seven has *mean* 0.05. In other words, if repeated random selections of 400 numbers were made, in the long run the proportions of sevens in all those selections would vary, but they would average out to 0.05.
- The *standard deviation* of $\hat{p}$ is $\sqrt{0.05(0.95)/400} = 0.01$: In the long run, this is how far those sample proportions tend to be from 0.05.
- The *shape* of the distribution of $\hat{p}$ is approximately normal, thanks to the large sample size. Thus, we can use normal probabilities to be specific about the tendency for sample proportions to fall a certain distance from the population proportion 0.05.

If the population proportion is known, we learned in Part III how to make a *probability* statement about sample proportions in a random sample. But in real-life problems, we want to do the opposite: If a sample proportion has been found, we want to make an *inference* statement about the unknown population proportion. On one level, such a transition is trivial, as demonstrated by the following example.

The Big Picture: A CLOSER LOOK

In literature, we discuss the "turning point" of a novel or play, when a dramatic shift takes place in the story. We can think of the transition from probability to inference as the turning point of introductory statistics. This is the critical point where we go from a statement about the sample based on the population to a statement about the population based on the sample.

EXAMPLE 9.4 HOW FAR IS ONE FROM THE OTHER, AND VICE VERSA?

Background: Suppose an old friend is passing through the vicinity of your neighborhood, and calls to say, "I'm within half a mile of your house."

Question: What can be said about where your house is in relation to the friend?

Response: Of course, the house is within half a mile of your friend.

Guided by this reasoning, we make a very useful observation: *Whenever the sample proportion falls within a certain distance of the population proportion, then the population proportion is within that same distance of the sample proportion.* Therefore, since 95% of the time the sample proportion picking the number seven falls within 0.02 of the population proportion, it is also true that 95% of the time the population proportion picking the number seven is within 0.02 of the sample proportion.

On another level, however, there is a subtle but important distinction that must be made between statements about the long-run behavior of sample proportions and statements about the population proportion. Because the *sample proportion* for repeated random samples is a random variable, its values are subject to the laws of probability. For one sample of 400 students, the proportion of students who pick the number seven may be 0.06. For another sample it may be 0.04, for another it may be 0.05, and so on.

In contrast, the *population proportion* is fixed. Whether or not we know its value, it does not "jump around" according to the laws of random behavior. Thus, it is incorrect to make statements like, "The probability is 95% that the population proportion . . ." because probability is for *random variables*, not fixed parameters. The correct language to use is to say, "We are 95% *confident* that the population proportion picking the number seven comes within 0.02 of the sample proportion."

The graph on the left illustrates long-run behavior of sample proportions, which under the right conditions vary with a predictable normal pattern. Because sample proportion is a random variable, we produce a *probability interval* for its values, based on the population mean and standard deviation. On the right, we see how to obtain a range of plausible values for the unknown population proportion, based on a single sample proportion that has been observed. Population proportion is a parameter, so we produce a *confidence interval* for what values are plausible, where spread is incorporated via *margin of error*. Margin of error is calculated using the standard deviation of the sample statistic; details will be discussed presently.

> The **TBP** *Supplement* presents another approach to this issue on page 889 with a discussion of whether sample proportion or population proportion is the *subject* of our statement.
>
> Another way to stress the distinction between probability and confidence is to say that sample proportions, because they can vary, have a *distribution*. Under the right circumstances, we can model this distribution with a normal curve. Population proportion does not have a distribution because it does not vary.

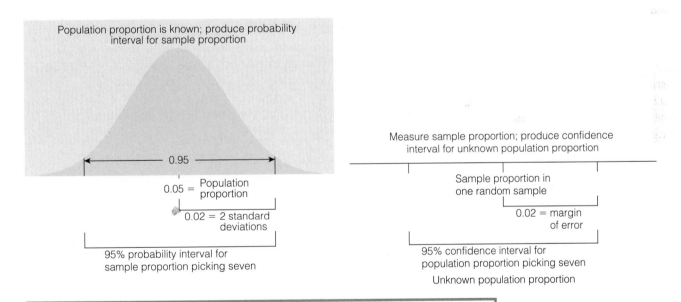

Population proportion is known; produce probability interval for sample proportion

0.95

0.05 = Population proportion

0.02 = 2 standard deviations

95% probability interval for sample proportion picking seven

Measure sample proportion; produce confidence interval for unknown population proportion

Sample proportion in one random sample

0.02 = margin of error

95% confidence interval for population proportion picking seven

Unknown population proportion

Definitions   The **margin of error** is the *distance* around a sample statistic, within which we have reason to believe the corresponding parameter falls.

A **confidence interval** for a parameter is an *interval* within which we have reason to believe the parameter falls.

Now that the correct language for statements about population parameters has been established, we can present a general method for constructing a confidence interval for an unknown population proportion, given the sample proportion and the sample size.

95% Confidence Intervals: Building around Our Point Estimate

Whereas our point estimate stood alone, the estimate in our confidence interval is accompanied by a margin of error. The margin of error tells within what distance of the estimate (sample proportion, in this case) we can fairly safely claim the unknown parameter (population proportion) to be. Clearly it is better to present a range of plausible values for the population proportion, rather than to present a single guess that is almost surely incorrect. We continue to make use of the specific part of the 68-95-99.7 Rule telling us that 95% of the time normal variables take a value within 2 standard deviations of their mean. Later on, we will develop intervals at other levels of confidence besides 95%.

Given a sample proportion and its standard deviation, we can easily construct a confidence interval for the unknown population proportion, as seen in the next example.

The Big Picture: LOOKING BACK

In Part I, we learned that samples need to be representative of the larger group (the population) of interest. In this example, we must be careful about who constitutes the larger population. A sample of shoppers in a downtown market district would not be representative of all shoppers in terms of foreign language ability.

EXAMPLE 9.5 A CONFIDENCE INTERVAL FOR THE POPULATION PROPORTION

Background: In recognition of 2005 being named the Year of Languages by the American Council on the Teaching of Foreign Languages, a group of students and teachers of foreign languages conducted a poll in a city's downtown market district. They asked 200 shoppers for the time in a foreign language, such as French ("Quelle heure est-il?"), Spanish ("Que hora es?") and German ("Wieviel Uhr ist es?"), and found that 66 were able to respond correctly in the given language.[1] Thus, the sample proportion proficient enough to respond was 66/200 = 0.33. It can be shown that the approximate standard deviation for the distribution of sample proportion in this situation is 0.03.

Question: What is a 95% confidence interval for the population proportion of shoppers who could respond correctly in the given language?

Response: The margin of error for a 95% confidence interval equals 2 standard deviations, or 2(0.03) = 0.06. We can be 95% confident that the population proportion comes within 0.06 of 0.33. In other words, a 95% confidence interval for the population proportion is (0.27, 0.39).

Practice: *Try Exercise 9.8(a) on page 407.*

Where did the standard deviation 0.03 in Example 9.5 come from? Remember that the standard deviation of the sample proportion $\hat{p}$ is calculated from the population proportion p and the sample size n. Applying various probability rules in Chapter 7 enabled us to express the standard deviation of sample proportion on page 297 as $\sqrt{\dfrac{p(1-p)}{n}}$. We now want to set up a confidence interval to estimate the population proportion p because it is unknown. Therefore, the standard deviation $\sqrt{\dfrac{p(1-p)}{n}}$ of sample proportion $\hat{p}$ is also unknown. However, it can be estimated by substituting $\hat{p}$ for p in the formula. Throughout this section on confidence intervals, we will work with approximate standard deviation $\sqrt{\dfrac{\hat{p}(1-\hat{p})}{n}}$, called the *standard error*.

> *Definition*   The **standard error** is the estimated standard deviation of a sampling distribution.

EXAMPLE 9.6 CALCULATING THE STANDARD ERROR

Background: The population proportion of people who can respond to a question about the time in a foreign language is unknown. The sample proportion in a sample of 200 shoppers is found to be 0.33.

Question: What is the standard error (approximate standard deviation of the distribution of sample proportion)?

Response: The standard error is $\sqrt{\dfrac{0.33(1-0.33)}{200}} = 0.033$, which we may round to 0.03.

Practice: *Try Exercise 9.9(a) on page 407.*

Confidence intervals are used to estimate all sorts of parameters—such as population proportion, population mean, difference between population means, difference between population proportions, or population slope—depending on which of the five variable situations is involved. They always take the form

confidence interval = estimate ± margin of error

The estimate is the statistic that accompanies the parameter of interest, and the margin of error is a certain multiple of the standard deviation of the sampling distribution of that statistic. When the situation involves one categorical variable, the estimate is the sample proportion $\hat{p}$. The standard deviation is approximated with the standard error $\sqrt{\dfrac{\hat{p}(1-\hat{p})}{n}}$. The multiplier for 95% confidence and a normal sampling distribution is 2, but we will introduce other multipliers for other levels of confidence later in this section. For now, we state the formula for calculating a 95% confidence interval to estimate the unknown population proportion.

Remember that the multiplier 2 is appropriate because *in a normal distribution*, the probability of being within 2 standard deviations of the mean is 95%. If the sample size isn't large enough, then the normal approximation is invalid. Our rule of thumb presented on page 306 in Part III was for np and $n(1-p)$ both to be at least 10. Now that we are performing statistical inference because the population proportion p is unknown, we must modify the rule of thumb, substituting the sample proportion $\hat{p}$ for the population proportion p. It is useful to note that

There are many situations in statistics where we substitute information about the sample for needed (but unknown) information about the population. Some other such situations to be encountered in this chapter include our test on page 396 for large enough sample size n, and a method described in a marginal note on page 400 for determining what sample size n will produce a desired margin of error.

The question of whether to use 1.96 or the rounded value 2 as the multiplier for our confidence interval presents a trade-off. The former gives us a slightly higher level of accuracy, whereas the latter gives students a better chance of making estimates in their heads. In keeping with this book's philosophy of facilitating an intuitive feel for data, we begin with the multiplier 2. Later on, we offer 1.96 as an alternative after students have developed a general sense for the size of the margin of error.

> ## 95% Confidence Interval for Population Proportion
>
> An approximate **95% confidence interval for the unknown population proportion** p based on the sample proportion $\hat{p}$ from a large random sample of size n is
>
> $$\text{estimate} \pm \text{margin of error}$$
> $$= \text{sample proportion} \pm 2 \text{ standard deviations}$$
> $$\approx \text{sample proportion} \pm 2 \text{ standard errors}$$
> $$= \hat{p} \pm 2\sqrt{\frac{\hat{p}(1 - \hat{p})}{n}}$$

since $\hat{p} = X/n$, where X is the count in the category of interest, the rule of thumb requires

$$n\hat{p} = nX/n = X \geq 10$$

$$n(1 - \hat{p}) = n - nX/n = n - X \geq 10$$

In other words, the sample count (X) *in* the category of interest and sample count ($n - X$) *out* of the category of interest must both be at least 10. This requirement is easy to check.

EXAMPLE 9.7 CHECKING THE SAMPLE SIZE FOR A NORMAL APPROXIMATION

Example TBP 9.1 on page 889 of the *TBP Supplement* shows a situation where the condition for a normal approximation is *not* met because there are too few sampled individuals in the category of interest.

> **Background:** Suppose we want to set up a confidence interval for the population proportion, based on the sample proportion eating breakfast, where 246 out of 446 students had eaten breakfast.
>
> **Question:** Is the sample size large enough?
>
> **Response:** The count in the category of interest (breakfast) is 246 and the count outside the category of interest is $446 - 246 = 200$. Both are greater than 10, so the sample is large enough.
>
> **Practice: *Try Exercise 9.9(b) on page 407.***

We must check that sample size is large enough to justify using the multiplier 2 (from a normal distribution) in our confidence interval. Our next concern is whether or not our formula for standard deviation is accurate. This formula assumes sampling *with replacement*. If the sample is taken *without replacement*, then the formula is accurate only if the sample size is not too large relative to the population size. Our rule of thumb, presented on page 236 in Part III, is to check that the population is at least 10 times the sample size.

EXAMPLE **9.8** A SAMPLE THAT IS TOO LARGE RELATIVE TO THE POPULATION SIZE

Background: In a newspaper article entitled *Criminal pasts cited for many city school bus drivers*, it is reported that "state auditors checking the records of a random sample of 100 city bus drivers have found that more than a quarter of them had criminal histories . . . A series of problems last year with school bus drivers . . . prompted [state Auditor General] Casey to take a closer look at the city's staff of 750 drivers. . . ."[2]

Question: Should we set up a 95% confidence interval for the proportion of all city school bus drivers with criminal records, based on a sample of size 100 and sample proportion approximately 0.25 (one quarter)?

Response: Certainly the sample is large enough: The sample counts with and without criminal histories are 25 and 75, respectively. However, because the population size (750) is not more than 10 times the sample size (100), the approximated standard deviation $\sqrt{\dfrac{0.25(1 - 0.25)}{100}} = 0.043$ is not quite accurate: Sampling 100 drivers without replacement from only 750 results in too much dependence among the selections.

Practice: *Try Exercise 9.9(f) on page 407.*

An interval to show our lack of confidence in school bus drivers?

© Envision/CORBIS

The Big Picture: A CLOSER LOOK

If the population is less than 10 times the sample size, the formula for standard deviation can be adjusted for more accuracy. We do not present the modified formula here because the need for it rarely arises.

Before progressing to intervals with other levels of confidence, we return to the questions in our opening example.

EXAMPLE **9.9** REVISITING OUR ORIGINAL QUESTION ABOUT THE PROPORTION WHO EAT BREAKFAST

Background: In a representative sample of 446 college students, 246 (proportion 0.55) ate breakfast the day of the survey.

Questions: What interval should contain the proportion of all college students who eat breakfast on a given day? Is there evidence that more than half of all college students eat breakfast?

Responses: The approximate standard deviation of the distribution of sample proportion is $\sqrt{0.55(1 - 0.55)/446} = 0.02$. We are approximately 95% confident that the unknown population proportion eating breakfast is within 2 standard deviations of the sample proportion—that is, within $2(0.02) = 0.04$ of 0.55. A 95% confidence interval for the population proportion eating breakfast is (0.51, 0.59). Because the entire interval is greater than 0.5, this suggests that more than half (a majority) of all college students eat breakfast.

Practice: *Try Exercises 9.11 on page 408 and 9.17(a) on page 409.*

Page 890 of the *TBP Supplement* outlines how the steps in constructing a confidence interval correspond to the four basic processes of statistics.

Our next task is to explore the effect of sample size on the width of our confidence interval.

The Role of Sample Size: Closing In on the Truth

We stressed on page 391 that a simple guess for the unknown population proportion in the form of a point estimate is of limited usefulness. In reality, the guess is likely to be wrong, and we need to have an idea of how much "give-or-take" there is surrounding our guess. This is the role played by the margin of error in our confidence interval. The size of the margin of error conveys a great deal of information, because it tells how good or bad our guess is likely to be. The size of the margin of error for a 95% confidence interval is 2 standard deviations, where the standard deviation is approximated with $\sqrt{\dfrac{\hat{p}(1 - \hat{p})}{n}}$. Whoever takes the random sample has no control over the value of the sample proportion $\hat{p}$, but sometimes it is possible to have a say in what size sample is taken. The following example demonstrates how the sample size n impacts the margin of error in a confidence interval.

EXAMPLE **9.10** HOW LARGER SAMPLES PRODUCE NARROWER CONFIDENCE INTERVALS

Background: Suppose a sample of voters is taken before an election, and it is found that 0.54 of them favor a particular candidate. We are interested in finding a 95% confidence interval for the population proportion favoring that candidate.

Questions:

1. What would the confidence interval be if the proportion 0.54 arose from a sample of size 50?

2. What would the confidence interval be if the proportion 0.54 arose from a sample of size 200?

3. What would the confidence interval be if the proportion 0.54 arose from a sample of size 1,000?

Responses: This table shows how to produce the three intervals, all of which are centered at the sample proportion, 0.54. The number lines that follow illustrate how the intervals become narrower as the sample size gets larger.

Sample Size n	Standard Error of $\hat{p}$	Margin of Error	95% Confidence Interval
50	$\sqrt{\dfrac{0.54(1-0.54)}{50}} = 0.070$	$2(0.070) = 0.14$	$(0.40, 0.68)$
200	$\sqrt{\dfrac{0.54(1-0.54)}{200}} = 0.035$	$2(0.035) = 0.07$	$(0.47, 0.61)$
1,000	$\sqrt{\dfrac{0.54(1-0.54)}{1,000}} = 0.016$	$2(0.016) = 0.03$	$(0.51, 0.57)$

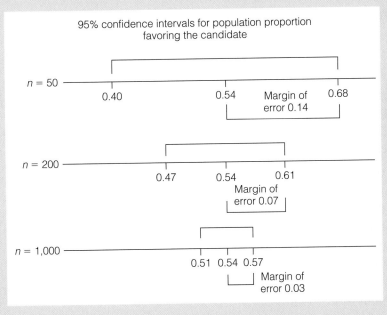

95% confidence intervals for population proportion favoring the candidate

Practice: *Try Exercise 9.17(b) on page 409.*

The first interval, based on the smallest sample, is not especially useful because it is so wide. The second interval, based on a sample that is four times the size of the first sample, is half as wide. The third interval does the best job of pinpointing the unknown population proportion favoring that candidate. In particular, it lets us claim with confidence that a majority of all voters favor the candidate, because the interval contains only values greater than 0.5.

Samples of size roughly 1,000 are extremely common in polling. Just as we saw in Example 9.10, a sample of size 1,000 yields a margin of error approximately equal to 0.03. When newspapers, magazines, or Internet reports provide details of a poll, there is often mention of a margin of error equal to plus or minus 3 percentage points.

Our intuition suggests that larger samples provide more information, so larger samples should increase our ability to pinpoint what is true about the population. This is confirmed by the mechanics of the construction of confidence intervals, whereby larger sample sizes produce smaller margins of error and therefore narrower intervals.

We can use the fact that $\sqrt{\dfrac{p(1-p)}{n}}$ is largest for $p = 0.5$ to make a conservative estimate as to what sample size is needed to obtain a desired margin of error m. Because the margin of error for a 95% confidence interval is $m = 2\sqrt{\dfrac{p(1-p)}{n}}$,

If a report goes into detail and provides separate figures for two demographic groups, such as men and women, or Democrats and Republicans, then the margin of error must be revised. A sample of size 500 yields a margin of error between 4% and 5%.

Taking the proportion to be $p = 0.5$ is the "worst case scenario"; the margin of error decreases if proportion is closer to 0 or 1. A geometric argument may help students see why $\sqrt{\frac{p(1-p)}{n}}$ is largest for $p = 0.5$. Picture a rectangle for which the sum of width plus length equals 1. If we call the width p, then the length is $1 - p$. The area $p(1 - p)$ is largest when the rectangle is a square with $p = 1 - p = 0.5$. The area shrinks as the width gets farther from 0.5, and the shape of the rectangle gets skinnier and skinnier.

Another approach to estimating the sample size needed to produce a desired margin of error is to substitute sample proportion $\hat{p}$ into the formula for n: approximate $n = \frac{4\hat{p}(1 - \hat{p})}{m^2}$. This assumes that a trial sample has been taken in order to obtain an initial guess $\hat{p}$.

it follows that $n = \dfrac{4p(1-p)}{m^2}$. Taking $p = 0.5$, we can say that the margin of error will be *at most m* when

$$n = \frac{1}{m^2}$$

EXAMPLE 9.11 DETERMINING APPROXIMATE SAMPLE SIZE FOR A DESIRED MARGIN OF ERROR

Background: Suppose a polling agency desires a margin of error no more than $m = 0.01$ for a 95% confidence interval.

Question: What sample size should be used?

Response: The sample size should be $n = \dfrac{1}{0.01^2} = 10{,}000$.

Practice: *Try Exercise 9.17(c) on page 409.*

Confidence at Other Levels

Although 95% confidence intervals are by far the ones most commonly encountered, under certain circumstances researchers may prefer to work with other levels of confidence. Detailed information about the tails of the normal curve (90-95-98-99 Rule) will help us establish formulas for confidence intervals at other levels besides 95%.

Recall what we learned about the tails of the normal curve on page 326 of Chapter 7. The probability is:

- 0.90 that a normal random variable takes a value within 1.645 standard deviation of its mean
- 0.95 that the random variable takes a value within 1.960 standard deviations of its mean
- 0.98 that the random variable takes a value within 2.326 standard deviations of its mean
- 0.99 that the random variable takes a value within 2.576 standard deviations of its mean

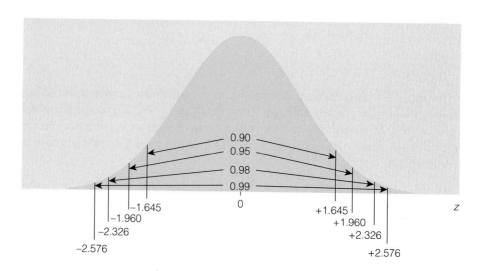

When we set up 95% confidence intervals for the unknown population proportion, based on a sample proportion, we would have achieved a bit more accuracy by producing the interval of values within 1.96 standard deviations of the mean, instead of 2. Moreover, we could have set up a 90% confidence interval if we produced the interval within 1.645 standard deviations of the mean, or a 99% confidence interval if we produced the interval within 2.576 standard deviations of the mean. Although 95% is the most widely used confidence level (and by default the level used in media reports of survey results), it is instructive to explore other confidence intervals that are sometimes employed by researchers.

EXAMPLE 9.12 HOW HIGHER LEVELS OF CONFIDENCE LEAD TO WIDER INTERVALS

Background: Students in committed relationships were asked by psychologists if they at times took comfort by sniffing their partner's clothing, when the partner was out of town.[3] In a sample of 108 students, the proportion who answered yes was 0.70, and the approximate standard deviation of the distribution of sample proportion is $\sqrt{0.70(1 - 0.70)/108} = 0.04$.

Question: Construct 90%, 95%, 98%, and 99% confidence intervals for the unknown population proportion p. How do the intervals compare?

Response: This table shows how to produce the four intervals.

Confidence Level	Margin of Error	Confidence Interval
90%	1.645(0.04) = 0.07	(0.63, 0.77)
95%	1.960(0.04) = 0.08	(0.62, 0.78)
98%	2.326(0.04) = 0.09	(0.61, 0.79)
99%	2.576(0.04) = 0.10	(0.60, 0.80)

All the intervals are centered at the sample proportion 0.70, but the spread is more for intervals at higher levels of confidence.

Practice: *Try Exercise 9.18(a) on page 409.*

The **Big Picture:** **A CLOSER LOOK**

If we used 2 instead of 1.960 in our 95% confidence interval, the margin of error would still be 0.08 to two decimal places. The difference resulting from using 2 or 1.960 is usually so minor that we may consider it to be inconsequential. Nevertheless, 1.960 is the multiplier to use for maximum accuracy.

We may philosophize that in statistics, as in life, you "can't have your cake and eat it too." In terms of producing a nice, precise interval to close in on the unknown value of the population proportion, the first interval in Example 9.12 is optimal because it is the narrowest. In terms of producing an interval for which we have maximum confidence, the fourth interval is optimal because our level of confidence (99%) is highest.

On page 891 of the *TBP Supplement,* we discuss higher probabilities of success for wider intervals in the context of long-run repetitions.

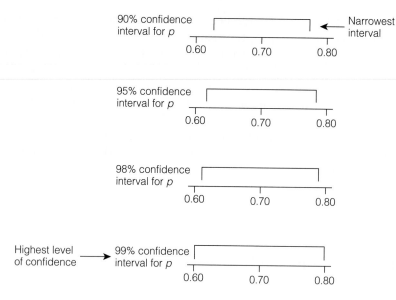

The trade-off is that we may state more precise intervals with less confidence, or less precise intervals with more confidence. The commonly used 95% level is a moderate choice in terms of precision of the interval and degree of confidence. This is also the default level in producing confidence intervals with software.

EXAMPLE 9.13 HOW CONFIDENCE INTERVALS MAY APPEAR IN COMPUTER OUTPUT

Background: A 95% confidence interval for the proportion of all students eating breakfast is to be calculated with software.

Question: How do these outputs produced with two types of software compare?

MINITAB:

```
Variable     X    N   Sample p        95.0% CI        Z-Value   P-Value
Bkfst?     246  445   0.552809   (0.506613, 0.599005)    2.23     0.026
```

SPSS:

Case Processing Summary						
	Cases					
	Valid		Missing		Total	
	N	Percent	N	Percent	N	Percent
Bkfst	445	99.8%	1	0.2%	446	100.0%

Descriptives			Statistic	Std. Error
Bkfst	Mean		.55	.024
	95% Confidence Interval for Mean	Lower Bound	.51	
		Upper Bound	.60	
	…		…	

Response: Both packages omit the one student out of 446 who did not respond. Besides showing sample count in the category of interest (eating breakfast), sample size, sample proportion, and the confidence interval, MINITAB also reports a "Z-Value" and "P-Value." (These will be discussed in detail in Section 9.2 on hypothesis tests.) SPSS requires a conversion from *no's* and *yes's* to 0's and 1's, and the reported "Mean" of 0.55 is the average of 199 0's and 246 1's, which is actually the sample proportion. The lower and upper bounds of the confidence interval, 0.51 and 0.60, are reported to just two decimal places, and there is no mention of a "Z-Value" or "P-Value."

A Closer Look

In Example 9.9, we constructed by hand the confidence interval (0.51, 0.59) for the population proportion eating breakfast. Due to rounding the standard error to 2 decimal places, our interval turned out to be less accurate than the one produced with software in Example 9.13.

When we see a confidence interval for population proportion, we can easily deduce what the sample proportion must have been, because it is, by construction, exactly in the middle.

EXAMPLE 9.14 SAMPLE PROPORTION AS THE MIDPOINT OF A CONFIDENCE INTERVAL

Background: Commuting students at a university were surveyed about their usual means of transportation to school—car, bus, bike, or walking. Software was used to construct a 95% confidence interval for the proportion of all commuters at the university who usually walked to school.

```
Sample   X   N   Sample p        95.0% CI          Z-Value  P-Value
1       111 230  0.482609  (0.418030, 0.547188)     −0.53    0.598
```

Question: What is the midpoint of the confidence interval?

Response: The midpoint is $(0.418030 + 0.547188)/2 = 0.482609$. This is the same as the reported sample proportion because the confidence interval is constructed symmetrically on either side of the sample proportion.

Practice: *Try Exercise 9.18(b) on page 409.*

Deciding If a Particular Value Is Plausible: An Informal Approach

In Example 9.9, we used a 95% confidence interval for the proportion of all students eating breakfast to make an informal decision about whether or not a majority of all students eat breakfast. Our next example contrasts the interval in Example 9.9 with the one in Example 9.14 about the proportion of all commuters who walk to school.

EXAMPLE 9.15 USING A CONFIDENCE INTERVAL TO DECIDE IF A PROPOSED POPULATION PROPORTION IS PLAUSIBLE

Background:

- In Example 9.9, we found an approximate 95% confidence interval for the unknown population proportion of students eating breakfast to be (0.51, 0.59).
- In Example 9.14, we found an approximate 95% confidence interval for the unknown population proportion of commuters who walk to be (0.42, 0.55).

Questions:

- Is it plausible that only 0.50, no more, of all students eat breakfast?
- Is it plausible that 0.50, no less, of all commuters walk to school?

Responses:

- The confidence interval (0.51, 0.59) suggests that 0.50 is too low a guess for the unknown population proportion, because 0.50 is less than all the values in the interval.
- The confidence interval (0.42, 0.55) suggests that 0.50 is a plausible guess for the unknown population proportion walking, because 0.50 is contained in the 95% confidence interval.

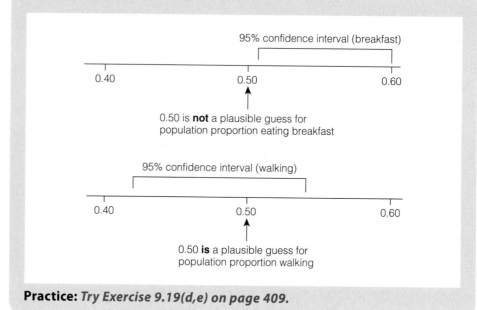

Practice: *Try Exercise 9.19(d,e) on page 409.*

Before moving on to the other type of inference, hypothesis testing, we should clarify exactly what it means to be "confident."

The Meaning of a Confidence Interval: What Exactly Have We Found?

The calculation of a confidence interval is quite simple, even by hand. What takes more thought is correctly interpreting the interval once it is produced.

Students Talk Stats

Interpreting a Confidence Interval

Suppose a group of students are discussing this report that appeared in 2007 on an Internet news site about the late Princess Diana: "A poll commissioned by Channel 4 television suggested that one in four Britons believe Diana was murdered. The telephone survey of 1,016 adults conducted this week had a margin of error of plus or minus 3 percentage points."[4]

Adam: *"One in four is 25%. They always report a margin of error that goes with 95%, so the probability is 95% that the sample percentage who believe she was murdered falls between 22% and 28%."*

Brittany: *"The probability isn't 95%, it's 100% that the sample percentage falls in that interval, because they built the interval around the sample percentage! They're talking about the unknown population percentage: The probability is 95% that the population percentage falls between 22% and 28%."*

Carlos: *"You can't talk about the probability that the population percentage falls somewhere, because it's not a random variable, it's just one actual number. You can say they're 95% confident that the population percentage falls in that interval."*

Dominique: *"Carlos is right, but if Brittany really wants to talk about probability, she could say the probability is 95% that they produce an interval that captures the unknown population percentage."*

Both Carlos and Dominique are correct. Setting up confidence intervals is a form of statistical inference, where we make statements about population parameters. When a categorical variable is involved, it should be a statement about the population proportion or percentage. Because it is a fixed parameter, it is not subject to the laws of random behavior. Therefore, it is incorrect to talk about the *probability* that population percentage falls in a certain interval. Either we can say we are 95% confident that the population percentage falls in the 95% confidence interval, or we can say that the probability is 95% that the 95% confidence interval (built around whatever sample percentage happened to be obtained) captures the unknown population percentage.

Practice: *Try Exercise 9.21 on page 410.*

The Big Picture: LOOKING AHEAD

Example 9.15 demonstrated a way to rather informally decide whether or not we are willing to believe that an unknown population proportion takes a proposed value. In Section 9.2 on hypothesis tests, we will present a more formal method of making such decisions.

Example TBP 9.2 on page 890 of the **TBP** *Supplement* explores confidence interval results in the long run. Wilson's estimate (page 892) can be discussed as an improvement over the basic formula, providing more justification for the claim that in the long run, 95% of our 95% confidence intervals contain *p*.

In practice, only one sample is taken, and a single confidence interval is produced. That confidence interval either succeeds in capturing the unknown population parameter or it doesn't. The level of confidence is referring to what should occur in the long run. If repeated random samples were taken, and we constructed a 95% confidence interval for each sample, then in the long run 95% of those 95% confidence intervals would contain the population parameter.

EXERCISES FOR SECTION 9.1

Point Estimate and Confidence Interval: A Best Guess and a Range of Plausible Values for Population Proportion

Note: Asterisked exercise numbers indicate exercises whose answers are provided in the Solutions to Selected Exercises section, on page 689.

9.1   There is evidence that eating breakfast can benefit academic performance, not just for younger students but also at the college level.[5] Besides recording whether or not a student eats breakfast, what additional variable could be examined for a sample of students in order to obtain evidence about this relationship?

9.2   "Sleep Face Down for Lower Blood Pressure" reported online in October 2004 about a study involving "271 healthy men not taking blood pressure medication. They ranged in age from 19 to 64, with an average age of 50. The researchers put automatic blood-pressure cuffs on the men and asked them to lie face up. Then they had them turn over and lie face down while they again measured the men's blood pressure. The men's overall blood pressure went down slightly—but significantly—when the men rested face down. Twenty-five of the men had a dramatic decrease in blood pressure— more than 15 points—when they flipped from face up to face down."[6]

   a. Was this a paired, two-sample, or several-sample study design?

   b. Which of the results mentioned above could be analyzed using the methods of this chapter: that the men's overall blood pressure went down slightly when they rested face down, or that 25 of the men had a dramatic decrease in blood pressure?

   c. Would the number 25 be denoted n, X, $\hat{p}$, or p?

   d. Would the number 25/271 be denoted n, X, $\hat{p}$, or p?

   e. Explain why the study design would have been better if some of the men (randomly assigned) flipped from face up to face down and the rest flipped from face down to face up.

9.3   "Seizure-Alerting and -Response Behaviors in Dogs Living with Epileptic Children" reported in the journal *Neurology* in June 2004 that 9 out of 60 dogs in families with epileptic children were able to anticipate a seizure, as evidenced by licking, whimpering, or standing next to the child. According to the families, these dogs predicted 80% of the children's seizures, with no "false positives."[7]

   a. Does "false positive" mean predicting a seizure and it does not occur, or not predicting a seizure and it does occur?

   b. Keep in mind that the data were reported by the families themselves, via surveys and telephone interviews. Should we suspect 0.80 to be an overestimate, an underestimate, or an accurate estimate of the proportion of the children's seizures that the dogs were able to anticipate?

   c. Could an experiment be designed as a future study to gather data on this phenomenon? If so, describe it. If not, explain why not.

*9.4   In Topeka, Kansas, in 2005, Reverend Fred Phelps "failed in his effort to repeal an anti-discrimination ordinance in an election."[8] Final results showed 14,285 of all voters (53%) opposing the repeal.

   a. If repeated random samples of a certain size were taken from all the Topeka voters, what would be the mean of all the sample proportions of voters opposing the repeal?

   b. Keep in mind that statistical inference uses information from a sample to draw a conclusion about the larger population. Explain why it would be inappropriate to use the data to set up a 95% confidence interval for the proportion of all Topeka voters in that election who opposed the repeal.

   c. Should 0.53 be denoted p or $\hat{p}$?

*9.5   A survey conducted in the United Kingdom in 1999 showed that "66% of people said they chose books on the basis of their jackets, and nearly 75% said they were influenced by book reviews."[9] A survey conducted in 2004 showed that "one in four of those polled said the last book they read was on the basis of what a colleague or family member had told them [. . .] Only loyalty to a favoured author counted as much, with 26% of readers saying their last choice of a book for pleasure was because they had read others by the same author. In a disappointing result for the promotional teams who spend up to 100 million pounds on book advertising every year, only 6% said they chose a book because they saw it advertised, with 7% citing the cover design as the deciding factor."[10]

a. Which survey apparently allowed for overlapping categories: the one from 1999 or the one from 2004, or both, or neither?

b. Based on the first survey, what is your best guess for the proportion of all people who choose books on the basis of their jackets?

c. The percentage of people who "judge a book by its cover" seems to be 66% according to the first survey, and only 7% according to the second one. What is the best explanation for these percentages being so different?

d. Suppose about 1,000 people had been sampled for the second survey, and a 95% confidence interval for population proportion who judge a book by its cover was found to be (0.05, 0.09). Which one of these is the best interpretation of this interval?

1. We have produced an interval with a 95% probability of containing the proportion of all people for whom a book's cover was *the* deciding factor in choosing the last book they read.

2. We have produced an interval with a 95% probability of containing the proportion of all people for whom a book's cover was among the deciding factors in choosing the last book they read.

3. We have produced an interval with a 95% probability of containing the sample proportion of people for whom a book's cover was *the* deciding factor in choosing the last book they read.

4. We have produced an interval with a 95% probability of containing the sample proportion of people for whom a book's cover was among the deciding factors in choosing the last book they read.

*9.6 The U.S. Conference of Catholic Bishops' second annual report on the sexual abuse crisis in the church stated that about 80% of the 1,083 victims who came forward in 2004 were male.[11] Explain why we cannot use their data to set up a confidence interval for the proportion of all church abuse victims who were male.

*9.7 A 2007 survey by The Marlin Company of 752 U.S. workers asked if their company had used e-mail to fire or lay off employees.[12] Fill in the first blank with words and the second with a number: Because the sample proportion who answered *yes* is 0.10, and the margin of error is 0.02, we are 95% confident that the _____ is within 0.02 of _____.

*9.8 Experience Inc., a career website for college students and alumni, surveyed more than 200 recent college graduates and found that 60% had accepted a job in a new city, state, or country. The approximate standard deviation for the distribution of sample proportion in this case is 0.035.

a. What is an approximate 95% confidence interval for the population proportion who accepted a job in a new city, state, or country?

b. What should be checked before we use the interval to estimate the proportion of all recent U.S. college graduates who accept a job in a new city, state, or country?

*9.9 "Antibiotic Resistance Puzzle" reports that children in a certain city "are resistant to common antibiotics at a rate that is double the national average [. . .] To look at local resistance rates, the Children's Hospital researchers tested 708 cultures of Group A strep that were obtained from pediatric patients between September 2001 and May 2002. Overall, 68 (or 9.6%) of the strep samples were resistant to macrolides. [. . .] Studies conducted elsewhere indicate a national macrolide resistance rate of about 5%."[13]

a. Based on a sample size of 708 and a sample proportion of 0.10 (0.096 rounded to the nearest hundredth), use the formula for approximate standard deviation, $\sqrt{\hat{p}(1-\hat{p})/n}$, to show that the error (standard deviation of sample proportion) is roughly 0.01.

b. To justify use of a normal approximation, the observed numbers in and out of the category of interest must be at least 10. What are those two numbers in this case?

c. Report an approximate 95% confidence interval for the proportion of all Group A strep cultures from the area that would be resistant to macrolides.

d. Does your confidence interval contain the national resistance rate, 0.05, or does it contain only values less than 0.05, or contain only values greater than 0.05?

e. Does your interval suggest that all Group A strep cultures from that city are more resistant to macrolides than all Group A strep cultures in the United States? Explain.

f. Is a representative sample of size 708 small enough relative to the population size to ensure that the formula for standard deviation of sample proportion in part (a) is approximately correct?

9.10 Suppose strep resistance rates in all cities across the country are actually 0.05.

a. If samples are taken in a particular city to produce a 90% confidence interval for the proportion of all strep cultures in the city that are resistant to antibiotics, what is the probability that the 90% confidence interval succeeds in capturing the true population proportion for that city?

b. If samples are taken in 100 cities across the country, to produce 100 90% confidence intervals for the proportion of all strep cultures in each city that are resistant to antibiotics, about how many of the intervals should succeed in capturing the city's true population proportion?

c. About how many of the 100 90% confidence intervals would fail to capture the true population proportion?

*9.11 A survey conducted in 2004 revealed that 20% of 504 respondents said they had in the past sold unwanted gifts over the Internet.[14] Use this information to construct a 95% confidence interval for the population proportion who sold unwanted gifts over the Internet, rounding your margin of error to the nearest hundredth.

9.12 In a sample of 16 students, 15 were right-handed. Is $\hat{p} \pm 2\sqrt{\hat{p}(1-\hat{p})/n}$ a 95% confidence interval for the proportion of all students who are right-handed?

9.13 A study conducted in the fall of 2003 found that 5 of 58, or 9%, of St. Louis Rams football players had methicillin-resistant *Staphylococcus aureus* (MRSA), a highly contagious infection of turf-abrasion wounds.[15] Give two reasons why we should not use the data and a normal approximation to set up a confidence interval for the proportion of all football players with such infections.

*9.14 A study by speech therapists looked at whether or not a certain type of therapy was successful in eliminating lisps in the speech of 19 patients with frontal open bites. Each patient was categorized as either success (s) or no success (n):

s n s s s s n s s s s s s s s s s s s

Which would be preferable for performing inference about the proportion of all such patients who could eliminate their lisps with the therapy: using actual binomial probabilities as discussed in Section 7.2, or using a normal approximation, or are they both equally good? Explain.

9.15 A study by speech therapists looked at whether or not a certain type of therapy was successful in eliminating upper respiratory allergies in 11 patients with frontal open bites. Each patient was categorized as either success (s) or no success (n):

s s s s n s s s s n s

Which would be preferable for performing inference about the proportion of all such patients who could eliminate upper respiratory allergies with the therapy: using actual binomial probabilities as discussed in Section 7.2, or using a normal approximation, or are they both equally good? Explain.

9.16 Researchers from Harvard Medical School noted that Rembrandt's self-portraits show him to be "exotropic," with eyes pointing outward more than what is normal: "Rembrandt depicted himself as significantly exotropic, by an average of 10 degrees and in some cases by up to 30 degrees."[16] By reporting the data in this way, are researchers treating Rembrandt's vision as a categorical or a quantitative variable? Explain.

*9.17 Exercise 9.5 describes two surveys conducted in the United Kingdom: one in 1999 and one in 2004.

    a. A 95% confidence interval for the population proportion who judge a book by its cover would be (0.63, 0.69) based on a sample of 1,000 people in the first survey, and (0.05, 0.09) based on a sample of 1,000 people in the second survey. Which survey suggests that a majority of people judge a book by its cover: the first, the second, both, or neither?

    b. If the surveys had each used 2,000 people instead of 1,000, would the confidence intervals be narrower or wider?

    c. Suppose the surveyors decided in advance that they wanted a margin of error no more than $m = 0.04$. What sample size should be used?

*9.18 "Hospital Chiefs Wary of Mandate on Error Reports" states that "many hospital administrators are leery of the push toward mandatory reporting of medical errors."[17] Specifically, in a survey conducted between 2002 and 2003, a certain proportion of chief executives and operating officers in various states said that a state-run, mandatory, nonconfidential reporting system would encourage lawsuits, despite evidence that patients are less likely to sue if doctors admit their mistakes and apologize. Based on the observed sample proportion, a 95% confidence interval for the proportion of all hospital administrators who believe such a system would encourage lawsuits is (0.67, 0.91).

    a. Would a 90% confidence interval be wider or narrower?

    b. The point estimate for population proportion must be at the center of the reported interval. What is it?

    c. What is the margin of error in this estimate?

    d. What is the approximate standard deviation of the sample proportion?

    e. Tell which one of these is the correct interpretation of the interval (0.67, 0.91):

       1. The probability is 0.95 that the population proportion falls in this interval.

       2. The probability is 0.95 that the sample proportion falls in this interval.

       3. We are 95% sure that the population proportion falls in this interval.

       4. We are 95% sure that the sample proportion falls in this interval.

    f. Suppose 75 executives and officers were surveyed. Is our formula for approximate standard deviation accurate if we want to draw conclusions about a population of several thousand executives and officers?

*9.19 According to a CNN online article, a 1997 nationwide Centers for Disease Control survey of about 16,000 students showed the lowest proportion of students having sex since the bi-yearly survey was started by the CDC in 1991: about 52% of surveyed students had never had sexual intercourse, compared with 46% in 1991. If we assume the population proportion to be roughly 0.5, the margin of error will be $2\sqrt{0.5(1 - 0.5)/n} = 1/\sqrt{n}$, where n is the sample size.

    a. To the nearest thousandth, find the approximate error margin for students in general ($n = 16,000$).

    b. Based on the sample proportion 0.52 and margin of error from part (a), is the article's title *Majority of U.S. "Teens Are Not Sexually Active"* justified? Explain.

    c. Find the approximate error margin for boys, assuming that half of the 16,000 students (or 8,000) were boys.

    d. Find the approximate error margin for Hispanics, assuming that 13% of the 16,000 students were Hispanic.

    e. The article reports that proportions who were sexually active dropped substantially for whites and African-Americans from 1991 to 1997, but for Hispanics, the proportion only dropped from 0.53 to 0.52. Should we be convinced that the Hispanics' rate dropped at all? Based on sample proportion 0.52 and margin of error from part (d), tell whether or not 0.53 is still a plausible value for Hispanics' population proportion.

f. In general, are we better able to pinpoint a change with larger samples or with smaller samples?

9.20 In 2005, CNN.com reported on a survey of 1,000 young adults, including those with college degrees, college students, college dropouts, and full-time workers. The report mentions that "only 32% of young adults without a degree said parents strongly expected them to go to college—a huge gap from the 67% with degrees who got such encouragement. The survey's margin of sampling error was plus or minus 3 percentage points."[18]

a. In fact, the margin of sampling error is plus or minus 3 percentage points only when reporting on the entire sample of 1,000 individuals. Is it more or less than 3% when reporting on subgroups such as those with and those without college degrees?

b. Keep in mind that fewer than 30% of all Americans older than their late twenties have a college degree. Which subgroup has a smaller margin of error: those with or those without a college degree?

*9.21 A survey in 2007 of 447 parents nationwide by the nonprofit organization College Saving Foundation found that 27% had saved nothing for their children's future college expenses. Based on the data, a 95% confidence interval is (0.23, 0.31). How should we interpret this interval?

a. The probability is 0.95 that the sample proportion falls in this interval.

b. The probability is 0.95 that the population proportion falls in this interval.

c. We are 95% confident that the sample proportion falls in this interval.

d. We are 95% confident that the population proportion falls in this interval.

9.22 The *Journal of Genetic Counseling* compiled statistics on thousands of births over a long period of time, and reported that otherwise healthy first cousins are at no great risk of passing chance birth defects onto their children: "normal" parents have a 3 to 4% chance of bearing a child with a serious birth defect, compared to a 5 to 7% chance for first cousins.

a. Sample percentages were presumably at the center of each reported range. Report the sample percentage of birth defects for "normal" parents and for first cousins.

b. For which group did they apparently have a larger sample size—"normal" parents or first cousins? Explain.

9.23 A survey of 1,200 college students in mid-November 2004 asked, "Outside of class, how often do you discuss politics and current events?" Based on their responses, a 95% confidence interval for the proportion of all students who would answer "almost every day" is (0.30, 0.36).

a. What is the point estimate for population proportion?

b. What is the margin of error in this estimate?

c. What is the approximate standard deviation of the sample proportion?

d. Would a 99% confidence interval be wider or narrower?

e. Tell which one of these is the correct interpretation of the interval (0.30, 0.36):
  1. The probability is 0.95 that the sample proportion falls in this interval.
  2. The probability is 0.95 that the population proportion falls in this interval.
  3. We are 95% confident that the sample proportion falls in this interval.
  4. We are 95% confident that the population proportion falls in this interval.

f. Is the interval approximately accurate for any year, or just for 2004 (a presidential election year)? Explain.

g. Is the interval approximately accurate for any month that year, or just for November? Explain.

9.24 An Internet article reports on results of a study completed in 2004 by psychologists at universities in Washington and Oregon: "65 Percent of Children Have Had an Imaginary Companion." "The researchers originally recruited 152 preschoolers, ages 3 and 4, and their parents several years ago. Each child and parents were interviewed separately about imaginary companions. [. . .]

Three years later, 100 of those children (50 girls and 50 boys) and their parents volunteered for the newly published study. The children and their parents again were interviewed separately about imaginary companions. [. . .] Children were considered to have imaginary companions if they said they had one and provided a description of it."[19] Some examples cited in a newspaper report of the study included Rose (an invisible 9-year-old squirrel), Skateboard Guy (an invisible 11-year-old who lived in a boy's pocket and popped up at boring moments to do tricks on his skateboard), and Elephant (a 7-inch-tall pachyderm that wore a tank top and shorts and sometimes was mean).

How many millions of imaginary friends are out there?

a. Is there reason to believe that the 100 children (with parents) who volunteered to continue in the study 3 years after the initial interview were no different from the 52 children who abstained? If not, would you expect those 100 children to be more likely or less likely to have imaginary companions?

b. The researchers focused on children up to the age of 7. Use the reported proportion (0.65) and the sample size (100) to construct a 95% confidence interval for the proportion of all such children who have an imaginary companion, rounding your margin of error to the nearest hundredth.

c. There are roughly 20,000,000 children aged three to seven in the United States. Use your confidence interval in part (b) to give a range for the *number* of imaginary friends they have altogether. (Note that some children may have more than one imaginary friend, and others may share the same imaginary friend, but we will disregard those here.)

9.25 In Exercise 9.11, we used the fact that 20% of 504 respondents said they had in the past sold unwanted gifts over the Internet to construct a 95% confidence interval for the unknown population proportion.

a. Now use the information to construct a 90% confidence interval for the population proportion who sold unwanted gifts over the Internet, rounding your margin of error to the nearest hundredth.

b. Use the information to construct a 98% confidence interval for the population proportion who sold unwanted gifts over the Internet, rounding your margin of error to the nearest hundredth.

c. Which interval has a higher probability of containing the true population proportion— the 90% or the 98% confidence interval?

d. Which interval is narrower—the 90% or the 98% confidence interval?

9.26 A survey conducted in 2004 by researchers at the University of Connecticut was intended to gauge understanding of our First Amendment rights by asking questions such as whether respondents thought flag burning was illegal, or whether the government can restrict indecent material on the Internet.[20] If we assume sample proportion to be roughly 0.5, the margin of error will be $2\sqrt{0.5(1-0.5)/n} = 1/\sqrt{n}$, where n is the sample size. The survey included approximately 100,000 students, 8,000 teachers, and 500 administrators. Tell whether each of these margins of error is for students, for teachers, or for administrators: (a) 0.045 (b) 0.011 (c) 0.003.

9.27 If population proportion of people who can respond to a question about the time in a foreign language is unknown, but the sample proportion in a sample of 200 shoppers is found to be 0.33, then the standard deviation of the distribution of sample proportion is approximately

$$\sqrt{\frac{0.33(1-0.33)}{200}} = 0.033, \text{ which we may}$$

round to 0.03. A 95% confidence interval for proportion of *all* shoppers who can respond to a question about the time in a foreign language is (0.27, 0.39).

a. Explain why the above interval is incorrect if surveyors glanced at the shoppers' wrist while posing the question.

b. Explain why the above interval is incorrect if the survey was carried out in an international market district.

9.28 British researchers reported that four young men suffered from collapsed lungs as a result of listening to loud music.[21] Explain why we cannot use this information to estimate the proportion of all listeners of loud music who would suffer from collapsed lungs.

*9.29 University researchers were able to produce cloned embryos of rhesus macaque monkeys and transferred them to 25 surrogate mothers. The number of viable pregnancies that resulted was 0. Which would be preferable for performing inference about the proportion of all transferred embryos that would result in a viable pregnancy: using actual binomial probabilities as discussed in Section 7.2, or using a normal approximation, or are they both equally good? Explain.

9.30 "Contraception Shots Work in Male Monkeys" tells about an injection that results in levels of certain antibodies that are high enough to prevent conception. "In the experiments, designed in the United States and carried out in India, seven of the nine males tested developed high antibody levels. Five of the seven recovered fertility once the immunization stopped."[22] Can a normal approximation be used to set up a confidence interval for the proportion of all monkeys that would develop high antibody levels, or for the proportion that would recover fertility, or both of these, or neither of these? Explain.

9.31 Researchers at the University of North Carolina calculated body mass index (BMI) for 2,168 NFL players, "nearly all those playing in the 2003–04 season," and found that 56% qualify as being obese.[23] Statistics students are asked to tell whether or not it is appropriate to use the data to set up a

confidence interval for the proportion of all the NFL players that season who were obese. Whose answer is correct?

Adam: It's not appropriate because we already know what's true for almost all the players.

Brittany: A confidence interval is appropriate because the rule of thumb holds: If we take np and $n(1-p)$ they're both about 1,000, which is way more than 10.

Carlos: If BMI is a quantitative variable, shouldn't we be setting up an interval for a mean? I think it's inappropriate to set up an interval for a proportion in this case.

Dominique: It's inappropriate to set up the confidence interval because the information only comes from "nearly all" of the players. We'd need to know about *all* of the players in order for the interval to be accurate.

Using Software [see Technology Guide]

9.32 "Kids Overdo Headache Meds" reports on a study by Dr. David Rothner, a pediatric neurologist at the Cleveland Clinic: "In a study of 680 headache patients ages 6 to 18, Rothner found that 22% were overusing nonprescription pain relievers. Overuse is defined as taking at least three doses each week for longer than 6 weeks."[24]

a. Use software to produce a 95% confidence interval for the proportion of all headache patients in that age group who overuse nonprescription pain relievers.

b. Suppose we had sampled from all children ages 6 to 18 (not just headache patients) to set up a confidence interval for the proportion of all children in that age group who overuse nonprescription pain relievers. Would the interval be centered the same as the one you produced in part (a), or centered to the left of it, or centered to the right of it?

c. Suppose overuse was defined as taking at least three doses each week for longer than 6 *months*, instead of 6 *weeks*. Would a confidence interval for the proportion of all headache patients ages 6 to 18 who overuse nonprescription pain relievers be centered the same as the one you produced in part (a), or centered to the left of it, or centered to the right of it?

9.33 In a survey, 446 students were asked to pick their favorite color from black, blue, green, orange, pink, purple, red, yellow.

   a. If colors were equally popular, what proportion (to three decimal places) of students would choose each color?

   b. Pick a color that you suspect will be *less* popular than others. Using software to access the survey data, report the sample proportion who preferred the color you chose.

   c. Tell whether or not the sample proportion is, in fact, lower than the proportion you calculated in part (a).

   d. Use software to produce a 95% confidence interval for the proportion of all students who would choose that color.

   e. Does your confidence interval contain the proportion you calculated in part (a), or is it strictly above, or strictly below?

9.34 In a survey, 446 students were asked to pick a whole number at random, anywhere from 1 to 20.

   a. If all 20 numbers were equally likely to be chosen, what proportion of students would choose each number?

   b. Pick a number that you suspect would be chosen *more* often than others. Using software to access the survey data, report the sample proportion who picked the number you suspected would be chosen more often.

   c. Tell whether or not the sample proportion you found in part (b) is in fact higher than the proportion you calculated in part (a).

   d. Use software to produce a 95% confidence interval for the proportion of all students who would choose that number. (Report the interval to three decimal places.)

   e. Does your confidence interval contain the proportion you calculated in part (a), or is it strictly above, or strictly below?

   f. Tell whether a 99% confidence interval would be wider or narrower than the interval you produced in part (d).

*9.35 Suppose we had a population of cancer deaths within a week of a special day, where exactly half died in the week before. If we took 100 repeated random samples of a certain size and for each sample used the sample proportion who died in the week before the special day to set up a 95% confidence interval for population proportion, about how many of those confidence intervals would contain 0.5 (the true population proportion)?

9.2 Hypothesis Test: Is a Proposed Population Proportion Plausible?

Throughout this book, we have occasionally encountered examples in which sample data were summarized, and based on that sample statistic, we speculated whether or not we believed the corresponding population parameter could equal a proposed value. Such speculations are a common aspect of real-life statistical applications. We call this form of inference a **hypothesis test**. In this section, we take a systematic approach to problems in which we test a hypothesis to decide whether or not to believe that the population proportion takes a certain value, given the value of a sample proportion that has been observed. In the end, our decision hinges on a probability called the *P-value*.

> *Definition*   The **P-value** of a test is the probability, assuming the population parameter takes the proposed value, of obtaining sample data at least as extreme as what has been observed.

As a prototype, we return to our opening example on page 389, and solve it in four steps, after the preliminary step of formulating a formal problem statement.

EXAMPLE 9.16 USING A FOUR-STEP PROCESS TO TEST A HYPOTHESIS

Background: In a representative sample of 446 students, 246 ate breakfast.

Question: Do more than 50% of all students eat breakfast?

Response:

0. We can pose the question as a choice between two opposing statements about the population proportion eating breakfast: Is it just 0.50 or is it more?

1. The first step in the solution process is to consider issues concerning **data production**, as presented in Part I. In particular, we must make sure that our claims about the center, spread, and shape of sample proportion are justified.

    ■ If the survey question had been poorly formulated, or if the sampled students were not representative of all students with respect to eating breakfast, then our sample proportion would not be an unbiased estimator of the population proportion. Our assumptions about the *center* of the distribution would be incorrect. [Fortunately, in this situation the sample proportion should in fact be a fairly unbiased estimator of the population proportion.]

    ■ If the population were not at least 10 times the sample size, then our formula for standard deviation (*spread*) of sample proportion would be incorrect. [This is not a problem because the population of interest is certainly larger than 10(446) = 4,460.]

    ■ If the sample size were too small, then the *shape* of the distribution of sample proportion would not be normal. We could not draw any conclusions based on a normal curve. [If about half of all students eat breakfast, we should expect to see about 223 who do and 223 who don't eat breakfast in our sample (both greater than 10). Thus, our sample size is large enough that we can assume sample proportion to have an approximately normal shape.]

2. Next, we **summarize** the sample data, as we learned to do in Part II, both as the original sample proportion $\hat{p}$ and as the standardized sample proportion z. If the population proportion is indeed 0.50, then the sample proportion has a mean of 0.50 and a standard deviation of $\sqrt{0.50(1 - 0.50)/446}$. Once we calculate the sample proportion $\hat{p}$ itself, we use its mean and standard deviation to calculate its standardized value z:

$$\hat{p} = 246/446 = 0.55 \qquad z = \frac{0.55 - 0.50}{\sqrt{0.50(1 - 0.50)/446}} = +2.11$$

It is helpful to note that our sample proportion, 0.55, is indeed more than 0.50. The value of z, $+2.11$, gives us a feel for how much larger 0.55 is than 0.50: It is more than 2 standard deviations higher.

3. The third step corresponds to Part III, the process of **probability**. How unlikely would it be, if the population proportion were 0.50, to get a sample proportion $\hat{p}$ as high as 0.55 (first graph shown below)? In terms of the standardized sample proportion z, how unlikely is it for z to take a value as high as $+2.11$ (second graph shown below)? We can refer to the 68-95-99.7 Rule and assess this probability—our "P-value"—as being between 0.025 and 0.0015, since z is between 2 and 3. A probability of this size could be called "fairly unlikely."

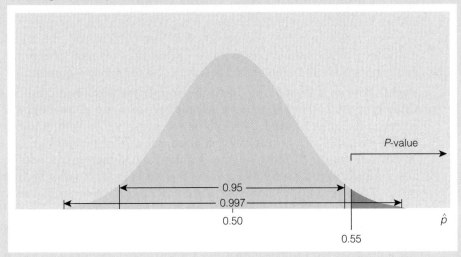

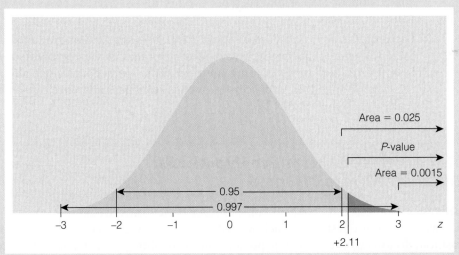

4. The fourth step embodies the process of **statistical inference**, which is the crux of Part IV, because it requires us to take our sample summary, and the accompanying probability, and use these to infer something about the population from which our sample was obtained. Because our P-value is less than 0.025, we can say our sample proportion, 0.55, is improbably high compared to the proposed value of population proportion, 0.50.

We conclude that the population proportion is *not* 0.50—it is apparently more than this. Thus, we conclude that a majority of all students—at least at that particular university—eat breakfast.

Practice: *Try Exercise 9.36 on page 439.*

A CLOSER LOOK

The standardized statistic, z in this case, is often referred to as the "test statistic" because of its importance in carrying out the hypothesis test.

LOOKING AHEAD

After establishing some details with technical vocabulary and notation, we will present these steps again on page 453 in a more useful form for practical applications.

LOOKING BACK

We have noted that the transition from probability to confidence can be considered the "turning point" of introductory statistics. We could also say that the "turning point" occurs when we progress from Step 3 of our test (finding a P-value) to Step 4 (performing inference based on the P-value).

Taking our solution of Example 9.16 to be a model, we can outline the solution of any hypothesis test question about an unknown population proportion in four steps, besides a preliminary step of posing the question in a structured way. Those four steps correspond to the four basic processes of statistics.

0. Express the question as a choice between two opposing statements about the population proportion.

1. Consider the **data production** as discussed in Part I. Check if there is reason to believe that the sample proportion is unbiased. Check that the population of interest is at least 10 times the sample size, and that the sample size is large enough to assume $\hat{p}$, and therefore z, is approximately normal.

2. **Summarize** the sample data both as original sample proportion $\hat{p} = X/n$ and as standardized sample proportion z, taking the value of the population proportion to be the one proposed in Step 0. "Eyeball" the sample proportion to see how it compares to proposed population proportion, and get a feel for the value of z. These reflect skills developed in Part II.

3. Decide how unlikely it would be, if the population proportion took the value proposed in Step 0, to get a sample proportion $\hat{p}$ as low/high/different as the one observed. This can be accomplished with software, or the 68-95-99.7 Rule, or information about the tails of the normal curve or normal tables. In terms of the standardized sample proportion z, how unlikely is it for z to take a value this far below/above/away from zero? [Our choice of "low/high/different" and "below/above/away from" is dictated by the particular problem statement. This issue will be discussed shortly.] This step reflects skills developed in Part III on **probability**. The "unlikelihood" is the probability on which our final conclusion in Step 4 hinges. This probability is referred to as the P-value of the test.

4. Based on the probability—that is, the P-value—estimated or evaluated in Step 3, decide between the two opposing points of view expressed in Step 0. This step involves using sample data to draw conclusions about the larger population, a process known as **statistical inference**, which is really the essence of Part IV.

Three Forms of Alternative Hypothesis: Different Ways to Disagree

Because hypothesis test problems come in three basic forms, we present an example with a trio of questions, which we will subsequently answer in a methodical fashion, following the four-step process outlined above. The main difference among the three types of questions has to do with the formulation of two opposing points of view in Step 0, but there are repercussions for the remaining steps as well. First, we establish some useful vocabulary and notation.

In general, a hypothesis test problem is expressed in terms of two opposing points of view. The *null hypothesis* claims that the population proportion equals some "traditional" value, in the sense that this is the status quo or situation if nothing special is going on. In an experiment, the null hypothesis would say that the treatment has no effect on the response of interest. Conventional shorthand notation for the null hypothesis is to write it as H_0, called "aitch naught" (*naught* means nothing). The proposed value of the population proportion is written as p_0, called "pee naught."

The point of view that disagrees with the null hypothesis is called the *alternative hypothesis*, written H_a. In contrast to the null hypothesis, the alternative hypothesis claims there *is* something going on, or things are not what they used to be, or a treatment in an experiment does have an effect on the response.

Definitions   The **null hypothesis** in a test, written H_0, claims the population parameter equals a proposed value. The **alternative hypothesis**, written H_a, claims the parameter differs in some way from the proposed value.

When there is a single categorical variable of interest, the null and alternative hypotheses can be written $H_0 : p = p_0$ versus $H_a : \begin{Bmatrix} p > p_0 \\ p < p_0 \\ p \neq p_0 \end{Bmatrix}$ where p_0 is the disputed value of the population proportion.

Because correct formulation of the problem statement is so important, we will discuss the three basic forms in detail before actually solving any of our example problems.

EXAMPLE 9.17 THREE POSSIBLE FORMS OF THE ALTERNATIVE HYPOTHESIS

Background: Consider these three hypothesis test questions:

A. To test whether humans can successfully mimic random behavior, 400 students are asked to pick a number at random from one to twenty. Of those 400, 30 pick the number seven. Is the population proportion picking the number seven just 0.05, or is there evidence of bias in that *more* than one-twentieth, or 0.05, of all students would pick the number seven?

B. Do fewer than half of all commuters walk to school? In a sample of 230 commuting students, 111 reported that they generally walk to school (sample proportion $111/230 = 0.48$). Can we conclude that the population proportion walking to school is *less* than 0.50?

C. In the fall of 2006, the proportion of Florida's Community College Associates of Arts (AA) program students who were economically or academically disadvantaged was 0.43. Is the rate significantly *different* at Florida Keys Community College? In order to decide, we'll use the fact that 169 of its 356 AA students in the fall of 2006 were classified as disadvantaged (sample proportion $169/356 = 0.475$).

Continued

In the *TBP Supplement* on page 892, we explain that when the alternative is one-sided, the null hypothesis could also be written as a (not strict) inequality.

The Big *Picture:*
LOOKING BACK

Each of the three questions posed in this example supplies information in the form of a sample size and observed sample proportion. Using this information, we could go the route of inferring something about the unknown population proportion by setting up a confidence interval, as done in Section 9.1. Instead, our inference will take the form of a yes-or-no decision in answer to a question about whether the population proportion equals a proposed value.

Question: How would we express the null and alternative hypotheses in each case?

Response:

A. In the random number selection example, it may be that the overall proportion selecting seven is 0.05. Or, if our suspicions of bias in favor of the number seven are correct, then the overall proportion selecting seven is *greater than* 0.05. We write $H_0 : p = 0.05$ versus $H_a : p > 0.05$.

B. In the commuters example, it could be that the proportion of walkers among all commuting students at the university is 0.50. Or perhaps the population proportion is *less than* 0.50. We write $H_0 : p = 0.50$ versus $H_a : p < 0.50$.

C. In the example concerning disadvantaged students, perhaps the proportion at Florida Keys Community College just happens to be a bit different from 0.43. Or it may *differ (in either direction)* significantly from 0.43. We write $H_0 : p = 0.43$ versus $H_a : p \neq 0.43$.

The three situations vary in terms of the "direction" in which the claim of equality is disputed.

Practice: *Try Exercise 9.37 on page 439.*

Some students might profit from a discussion of key words or phrases—such as 'lower,' 'less,' 'no more than,' 'minority,' 'different,' 'the same,' 'equal,' 'higher,' 'more,' 'no less than,' or 'majority'—that suggest which alternative hypothesis is appropriate in a given problem.

In this book, we avoid the expressions "one-tailed test" and "two-tailed test" because of the confusion that can arise once we are dealing with *F* and chi-square distributions: The test is two-sided but the relevant area is under a single tail.

The first two examples, [A] and [B], each feature a *one-sided alternative*, with an explicit suspicion of the direction in which population proportion differs from the proposed value p_0, expressed with a ">" or "<" sign. The third example, [C], features a *two-sided alternative*, which disagrees more generally with the claim that $p = p_0$, expressed with a "≠" sign.

Definitions   A **one-sided alternative hypothesis** refutes equality with a greater- or less-than sign. A **two-sided alternative hypothesis** features a not-equal sign.

The form of our alternative hypothesis directly affects the *P*-value, which assesses how improbable it would be for a random sample to produce a sample proportion *at least as extreme* as the one observed. "At least as extreme" means "as high as" if the alternative hypothesis expresses a suspicion that the population proportion is higher than the one claimed in the null hypothesis. It means "as low as" if the alternative hypothesis has a less-than sign, and "as different in either direction as" if the alternative has a not-equal sign. Thus, the *P*-value corresponds to a *right-tail area* in the case of a greater-than alternative (first graph shown below), a *left-tail area* in the case of a less-than alternative (second graph shown below), and a *two-tailed area* in the case of a not-equal alternative (third graph shown below).

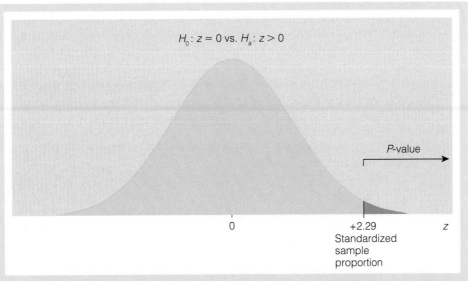

Because z is between $+2$ and $+3$, the P-value is between 0.025 and 0.0015, according to our sketch of the 68-95-99.7 Rule for the standard normal curve (first graph shown below). Alternatively, because z is between $+1.96$ and $+2.326$, the P-value is between 0.025 and 0.01, referring to the tails of the normal curve (90-95-98-99 Rule in the second graph shown below).

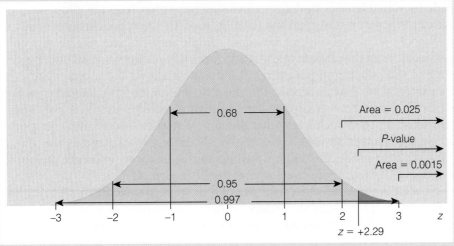

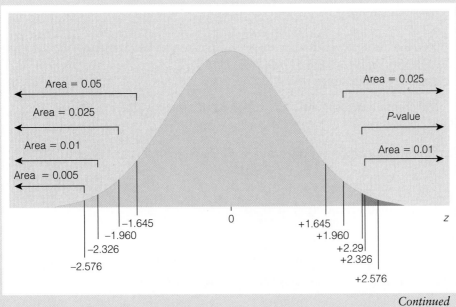

Continued

4. Most people would agree that an occurrence whose probability is less than 0.025 could be characterized as very unlikely. This casts doubt on our initial assumption that the population proportion is only 0.05. A sample proportion as high as 0.075, in samples of size 400, suggests a population proportion that is higher than 0.05. In other words, there *is* evidence of bias in favor of the number seven, in that the proportion of students picking that number was disproportionately high.

If the test had been carried out with the aid of software, the output would look something like this:

```
Test and CI for One Proportion
Test of p = 0.05 vs p > 0.05
Sample   X    N   Sample p  95.0% Lower Bound  Z-Value  P-Value
1       30   400  0.075000         0.053338       2.29    0.011
```

Because z is just below $+2.326$, the P-value is slightly greater than 0.01.

Practice: *Try Exercise 9.38(a,b) on page 439.*

Many instructors have their own students attempt to choose a number "at random" (haphazardly) from 1 to 20, and obtain similar evidence of bias. The implications of this subtle bias can be impressed on students by discussing what would happen if a researcher used a comparable method to divide a group of 20 subjects in two groups— treatment and control— for an experiment. In other words, what if the researcher considered those 20 subjects and off the top of his head, picked one, then another, and so on up to 10, to receive the actual drug being tested as opposed to the placebo?

The final conclusion that there was bias in those attempted random selections (made by actual college students), carries an important message about data production. Whenever statistical inference is used to draw conclusions about unknown population parameters, based on sample statistics, we rely heavily on the theoretical result that the sample statistic *for random samples* is an unbiased estimator of the population parameter. Randomness allows us to center our confidence interval for p at $\hat{p}$, or state that the distribution of $\hat{p}$ is centered at p_0 if the null hypothesis is true. It is often the case that a real-life sample is not random, and was obtained in such a way that the sample statistic—like sample proportion picking the number seven—is *biased*. We should always scrutinize the way the data have been produced before drawing conclusions with inference methods. If the design is flawed, those conclusions may be incorrect.

Now let's follow the same sequence of four steps to solve Example 9.19, keeping in mind that the alternative takes a different form from that in Example 9.18. Instead of calculating $\hat{p}$ and z by hand, we refer this time to computer output.

EXAMPLE 9.19 TESTING A HYPOTHESIS WITH A LESS-THAN ALTERNATIVE

Background: In a sample of 230 commuting students, 111 reported that they walked to school (sample proportion about 0.48).

Question: Can we conclude that the population proportion p walking to school is less than 0.50?

Response:

0. Using symbols, we write $H_0 : p = 0.50$ versus $H_a : p < 0.50$.

1. There are no obvious problems with how the data were produced.

2. The relevant statistic is sample proportion 0.482609, which is indeed less than 0.50, but not by much. The standardized test statistic is $z = -0.53$, which tells us that our sample proportion is 0.53 standard deviations below the mean.

```
Test and CI for One Proportion
Test of p = 0.5 vs p < 0.5
Sample    X    N   Sample p  95.0% Upper Bound   Z-Value   P-Value
1       111  230   0.482609        0.536805        -0.53     0.299
```

3. Certainly there is nothing unusually low about a value that is roughly half a standard deviation below its mean. The output confirms this by reporting the P-value to be 0.299, not a small probability at all.

   The first sketch shown below illustrates the desired P-value as a probability about the sample proportion itself, while the second sketch shows the P-value in terms of the standardized sample proportion z.

4. The assumption that the proportion of commuters who walk is 0.50 is not an unreasonable one, given that our sample proportion is 0.48. We know this because our P-value (0.299) is not at all small.

Practice: Try Exercise 9.40 on page 440.

Are walkers in a minority among commuting college students?

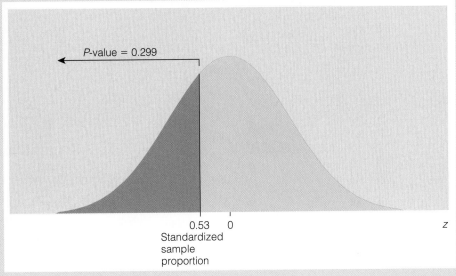

Now we consider our third example, featuring a two-sided alternative.

EXAMPLE 9.20 TESTING A HYPOTHESIS WITH A TWO-SIDED ALTERNATIVE

Background: In the fall of 2006, the proportion of Florida's Community College Associates of Arts (AA) program students who were economically or academically disadvantaged was 0.43.

Question: Is the rate significantly *different* at Florida Keys Community College? In order to decide, we'll use the fact that 169 of its 356 AA students in the fall of 2006 were classified as disadvantaged.

Response:

0. The null and alternative hypotheses are $H_0 : p = 0.43$ and $H_a : p \neq 0.43$.

1. There are no obvious problems with the data production.

2. The sample proportion is $169/356 = 0.475$. The standardized distance between 0.475 and 0.43 is $z = +1.70$, as shown in the output below.

```
Test and CI for One Proportion
Test of p = 0.43 vs p not = 0.43
Sample    X    N  Sample p          95.0% CI         Z-Value  P-Value
1        169  356  0.474719  (0.422847, 0.526592)     1.70    0.088
```

3. Now the desired *P*-value is the two-tailed area under the normal curve (which is centered at hypothesized population proportion 0.43). It represents the probability of being at least as far from 0.43 *in either direction* as 0.475 is. This is the same as the combined area to the right of the standardized test statistic $+1.70$ and to the left of -1.70 under the *z* curve.

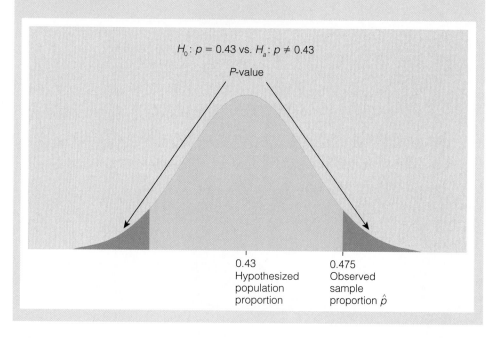

$H_0 : p = 0.43$ vs. $H_a : p \neq 0.43$

P-value

0.43
Hypothesized
population
proportion

0.475
Observed
sample
proportion $\hat{p}$

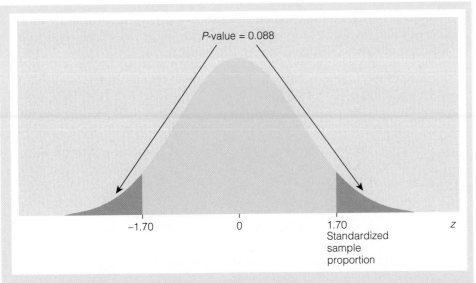

A value that is 1.70 standard deviations away from its mean *in either direction* is a bit far, but not necessarily what we would call "unusually far" because its probability—according to the output—is 0.088.

4. We conclude that the students at Florida Keys are not significantly different in terms of being disadvantaged or not—apparently they are reasonably representative of the larger student population with respect to this particular variable.

Practice: *Try Exercise 9.41 on page 441.*

If software were not available, we could refer to the tails of the normal curve, which show 1.70 to be just over 1.645, and so the two-tailed probability is just under 2(0.05) = 0.10.

Examples 9.18, 9.19, and 9.20 provide models for solving any test of hypotheses about a population proportion. A formal outline of the steps to be followed is presented on page 453 in our chapter summary.

One-Sided or Two-Sided Alternative Hypothesis

The form of the alternative hypothesis can "make or break" the test decision. We explore this phenomenon by looking at what happens if we make one minor change to our third example: Instead of wondering if the proportion disadvantaged at Florida Keys is significantly *different* from 0.43, we wonder if the proportion is significantly *higher* than 0.43.

In Example 9.20 (and for two-sided tests in general) we apply the "Or" Rule for Non-Overlapping Events, (same as the Special Addition Rule) in combination with the fact that the *z* curve is symmetric about 0. The probability of *z* being at least $+1.70$ *or* at most -1.70 is twice the probability of being at least $+1.70$.

EXAMPLE 9.21 HOW THE FORM OF THE ALTERNATIVE HYPOTHESIS AFFECTS THE TEST

Background: In the fall of 2006, the proportion of Florida's Community College Associates of Arts (AA) program students who were economically or academically disadvantaged was 0.43.

Question: If we want to decide if the proportion disadvantaged at Florida Keys is significantly *higher* than 0.43, how would our response change from that in Example 9.20, in which we sought evidence that the proportion *differs* significantly from 0.43?

Continued

Response: We reformulate the null and alternative hypotheses, and proceed again through the four basic steps, making a note of which aspects of the test are unchanged and which are changed.

0. The null hypothesis is still $H_0 : p = 0.43$ but now the alternative is $H_a : p > 0.43$.

1. The background information remains the same.

2. The sample proportion is still $169/356 = 0.475$, and now we note that it is indeed greater than 0.43. The standardized sample proportion is still $z = +1.70$.

3. Now the *P*-value is the probability of being at least 1.70 standard deviations *above* the mean, a right-tail area only. The *P*-value for the two-sided alternative was 0.088, but now the *P*-value is just half that, 0.044. An occurrence whose probability is less than 0.05 could be considered to be rather improbable.

```
Test of p = 0.43 vs p > 0.43
Sample    X    N  Sample p  95.0% Lower Bound  Z-Value  P-Value
1       169  356  0.474719       .  0.431186      1.70    0.044
```

4. When the test was carried out with the two-sided alternative, the *P*-value didn't seem small enough to reject $H_0 : p = 0.43$, so we concluded that the proportion disadvantaged does not differ significantly from 0.43. Now, formulated with the one-sided alternative, we can conclude that the proportion disadvantaged at Florida Keys is significantly higher than 0.43. In a way, the initial suspicion that the proportion disadvantaged at this school was higher helped provide us with enough evidence to push things over the edge in terms of evidence of a difference.

The graphs below illustrate the difference in *P*-values from the two-sided to the one-sided alternative. Quite simply, the *P*-value for the two-sided test is twice that for the one-sided test; the *P*-value for the one-sided test is half that for the two-sided test.

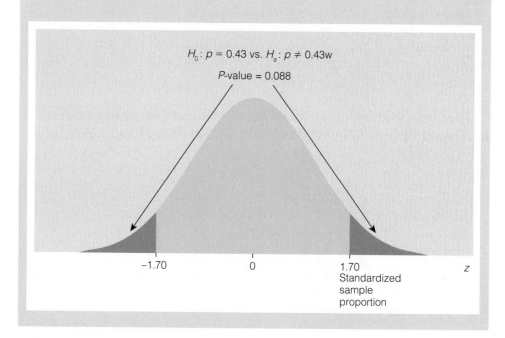

$H_0 : p = 0.43$ vs. $H_a : p \neq 0.43$w

P-value = 0.088

−1.70   0   1.70   z
                         Standardized
                         sample
                         proportion

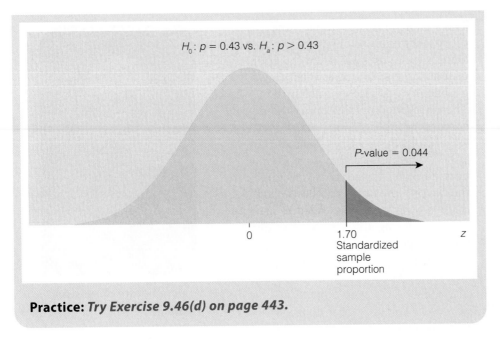

$H_0: p = 0.43$ vs. $H_a: p > 0.43$

P-value = 0.044

0   1.70   *z*
Standardized
sample
proportion

Practice: *Try Exercise 9.46(d) on page 443.*

The Big Picture:
A CLOSER LOOK

The switch from a two-sided alternative in Example 9.20 to a one-sided alternative in Example 9.21 was done to make a point about how the form of the alternative affects the *P*-value. In practice, the form of the alternative should *not* be revised merely for the purpose of obtaining a smaller *P*-value.

Clearly, the form of the alternative hypothesis plays an important role in the hypothesis test process, and impacts our final decision. Let's consider another example before discussing guidelines for choosing the appropriate alternative hypothesis.

EXAMPLE 9.22 SAMPLE DATA OBVIOUSLY FAILING TO SUPPORT THE ALTERNATIVE HYPOTHESIS

Background: The moon has four phases: new moon, first quarter, full moon, and last quarter. Each of these is in effect for 25% of the time, so if the phase of the moon has no impact on the occurrence of epileptic seizures, it should be the case that the proportion of all epileptic seizures occurring during a full moon is 0.25. A neurologist whose patients claimed that their seizures tended to be triggered or worsened when the moon was full gathered data for a large number of seizures. He found that 94 of 470 seizures occurred during a full moon.[25]

```
Test of p = 0.25 vs p > 0.25
Sample   X    N  Sample p  95.0% Lower Bound  Z-Value  P-Value
1       94  470  0.200000             0.169651    -2.50    0.994
```

The hypotheses shown in the output are consistent with the problem statement: The null hypothesis claims the population proportion of seizures during a full moon to be 0.25, while the alternative claims it to be greater than 0.25.

Question: Why is it unnecessary to carry out all four steps in the hypothesis test?

Response: The data cannot provide convincing evidence that more than one-fourth of seizures occur during a full moon. On the contrary, it turns out that the proportion in the sample (0.20) is considerably *less* than 0.25! No further steps are needed after establishing that the sample proportion is less than 0.25.

Continued

The *P*-value in this example is the probability of a sample proportion greater than or equal to 0.20, when the population proportion is 0.25, the same as the probability of a *z*-score greater than −2.50. The corresponding area under the normal curve is most of its total area, 1. Specifically, the *P*-value is found to be 0.994. Obviously, such a huge *P*-value provides no evidence whatsoever against the claim in the null hypothesis. That is, there is no evidence that seizures are more common during a full moon than during the other phases.

More seizures during full moon?

Taylor S. Kennedy/Getty Images

The Big Picture:
A Closer Look

Example 9.22 demonstrates that the alternative hypothesis does not necessarily "match" the observed sample proportion. Ideally, the null and alternative hypotheses are formulated before the sample is taken, or at least before the sample is evaluated. There is no guarantee that the sample proportion will tend in the direction claimed by the alternative.

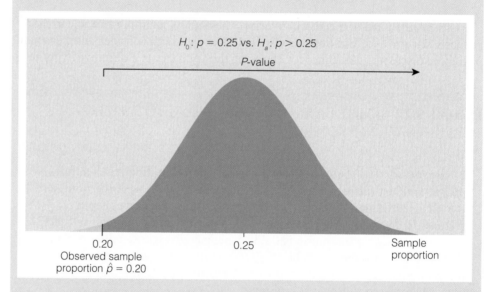

$H_0 : p = 0.25$ vs. $H_a : p > 0.25$

P-value

0.20
Observed sample proportion $\hat{p} = 0.20$

0.25

Sample proportion

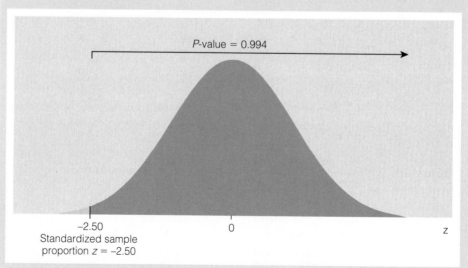

P-value = 0.994

−2.50
Standardized sample proportion $z = -2.50$

0

z

Practice: *Try Exercise 9.47(a,b) on page 444.*

So far, the hypothesis test examples encountered in this section were worded in such a way that the correct form of the alternative was quite obvious. In some real-life problems, things may be a bit murkier. In keeping with the spirit of the test—whose approach is conservative in that a null hypothesis, expressing the status quo, is not rejected unless there is very convincing evidence to the contrary— we will adopt a conservative policy and opt for a two-sided alternative when in doubt. The two-sided alternative makes it more difficult to reject the null hypothesis because the *P*-value is twice its value for the one-sided alternative. This was the case in our two versions of question about disadvantaged students at community colleges: We did *not* reject the null hypothesis about proportion disadvantaged, $p = 0.43$, against the two-sided alternative $p \neq 0.43$ in Example 9.20, but we *did* reject the null hypothesis against the one-sided alternative $p > 0.43$ in Example 9.21.

You may wonder, quite rightly, why a *P*-value of 0.088 was not considered small enough to reject the null hypothesis, while a *P*-value of 0.044 was considered to be small enough. We will now discuss this rather complex issue.

How Small Is a "Small" P-Value?

First, let's recall the *P*-values produced in the examples we've looked at so far, and our accompanying decisions about the null hypothesis.

EXAMPLE 9.23 REVIEWING EXAMPLE P-VALUES AND CONCLUSIONS

Background: So far, we have solved three prototypical examples: about random number selections in Example 9.18, commuters walking to school in Example 9.19, and disadvantaged students in Examples 9.20 and 9.21.

Question: What were the *P*-values for each of those examples, and what conclusions did we draw based on those *P*-values?

Response:

A. In our random number selection problem, the *P*-value was 0.011 and we considered this to be a small enough probability to reject the null hypothesis.

B. In our commuters walking to school problem, the *P*-value was 0.299, which we considered not small at all, so we did not reject the null hypothesis.

C. In our problem about disadvantaged students, the *P*-value was 0.088 for the two-sided alternative and we did not reject the null hypothesis. It was 0.044 for the one-sided alternative and we did reject the null hypothesis.

These decisions were, in fact, consistent with what is generally taken to be the cutoff probability between small and not-small *P*-values—namely, 0.05. However, users of hypothesis tests should be careful not to latch on to any one cutoff level too tightly. There are various additional considerations that we should make when we are faced with a decision based on a *P*-value that is on the small side, but perhaps not convincingly so. In general, the particular circumstances of a problem should always be considered before automatically using 0.05 as the cutoff level. In some contexts, other levels like 0.01 or 0.10 might be more appropriate.

Students should be reminded that statistical inference is the process of making statements about unknown population parameters. Thus, our null and alternative hypotheses need to be statements about population proportion p, not about sample proportion $\hat{p}$. Sample proportion enters into the solution process, not into the conjecture process. The null hypothesis should be formulated according to what the traditional or status quo situation was; the alternative hypothesis should express what a researcher hopes or fears or suspects is true, based on the context of circumstances. It is improper to "snoop" at the data first and then formulate the alternative hypothesis. If this method were employed, there would be no such thing as a two-sided alternative!

Examples TBP 9.3, TBP 9.4, TBP 9.5, and TBP 9.6 (starting on page 892) go into detail about when past or future considerations may warrant setting high or low values for α.

Because predetermined cutoff levels are often employed, there is special notation that is conventionally used.

Definition   The cutoff level that signifies a *P*-value being small enough to reject the null hypothesis is **alpha**, denoted α, the lowercase Greek letter *a*.

Whenever a level α is prescribed, we reject the null hypothesis for a *P*-value less than α. If the *P*-value is not less than α, then we do not reject. The most commonly used level is $\alpha = 0.05$.

The Role of Sample Size in Conclusions for Hypothesis Tests

Obviously, larger samples provide us with more information than smaller samples do. It follows that larger samples tend to provide us with more evidence to reject a null hypothesis. This idea is explored in the next pair of examples.

EXAMPLE 9.24 A LARGE SAMPLE SIZE LEADING TO A SMALL P-VALUE

Background: Suppose one demographer claims that there are equal proportions of male and female births in a certain state, whereas another claims there are more males. They use hospital records from all over the state to sample 10,000 recent births, and find 5,120 to be males, or $\hat{p} = 0.512$. They test $H_0 : p = 0.5$ versus $H_a : p > 0.5$ and calculate

$$z = \frac{0.512 - 0.5}{\sqrt{\dfrac{0.5(1 - 0.5)}{10,000}}} = 2.4,$$ so the *P*-value is 0.0082, quite small. The null hypothesis is emphatically rejected.

Question: Which of these is the correct interpretation of the very small *P*-value?

a. There is evidence that the population proportion of male births is much higher than 0.5.

b. There is very strong evidence that the population proportion of male births is higher than 0.5.

Response: The difference between these two interpretations is subtle but important; only the second interpretation, (b), is correct.

Practice: *Try Exercise 9.49 on page 444.*

Especially when the sample size is large, we may produce very strong evidence of a relatively minor difference from the claimed p_0. Thus, it is important to distinguish between "statistical significance" (due to a small *P*-value) and *practical significance* (a difference is substantial enough to impress us). Statistical significance can be quantified, whereas practical significance is a matter of opinion.

> *Definition*   Data are said to be **statistically significant** if they produce a *P*-value that is small enough to reject the null hypothesis.

The ***TBP*** *Supplement* discusses statistical significance in a bit more detail on page 894, and includes Example TBP 9.7, which helps students think about hypothesis test conclusions in the long run.

In contrast to what we saw in Example 9.24, the next example demonstrates that for rather small samples, we may fail to gather evidence about a difference that seems quite substantial.

EXAMPLE 9.25 A SMALL SAMPLE SIZE LEADING TO A LARGE P-VALUE

Background: A statistics lab instructor suspects there to be a higher proportion of females overall in statistics classes. She observes 12 females in a group of 20 students, so $\hat{p} = 0.6$. To confirm her suspicions, she would test $H_0 : p = 0.5$ versus $H_a : p > 0.5$. She calculates

$$z = \frac{0.6 - 0.5}{\sqrt{\dfrac{0.5(1 - 0.5)}{20}}} = 0.89.$$ The *P*-value is 0.1867, providing her with no

statistical evidence to support her suspicion.

Question: Because the *P*-value is not small at all, can we conclude that the overall proportion of females is only 0.5 and no more?

Response: Technically, the test results oblige us to continue to believe the null hypothesis: $p = 0.5$. Nevertheless, it is quite possible that the population proportion of females really is greater than 0.5, but the sample size was just too small to be convincing. In contrast, a lecture class of 80 students with $\hat{p} = 0.6$ would produce a *z* statistic of 1.79 and a *P*-value of 0.0367: The larger sample *would* let us conclude that $p > 0.5$.

Practice: *Try Exercise 9.50 on page 444.*

When to Reject the Null Hypothesis: Three Contributing Factors

To get a better feel for what circumstances would lead us to reject a null hypothesis, we can examine the specific quantities that enter into our calculation of *z*. For this purpose, we rewrite *z* as

$$z = \frac{\hat{p} - p_0}{\sqrt{\dfrac{p_0(1 - p_0)}{n}}} = \frac{(\hat{p} - p_0)\sqrt{n}}{\sqrt{p_0(1 - p_0)}}$$

We reject H_0 for a small *P*-value, which in turn has arisen from a *z* that is large in absolute value, on the fringes of the normal curve. There are three components that may result in a *z* that is large in absolute value, which in turn cause us to reject H_0:

- **Difference** $\hat{p} - p_0$: What we tend to focus on as the cause of rejecting H_0 is a large difference $\hat{p} - p_0$ between the observed proportion and the proportion proposed in the null hypothesis. Clearly, if the sample proportion $\hat{p}$

shows itself to be very different from the claimed population proportion p_0, this should lead us to reject the claim that $p = p_0$. Because $\hat{p} - p_0$ is multiplied in the numerator, a large difference naturally makes z large and the P-value small.

- **Sample size n:** A large sample size, because $\sqrt{n}$ is actually multiplied in the numerator of the test statistic z, brings about a large z and a small P-value. Conversely, a small sample size n may lead to a smaller z and failure to reject H_0, even if it is false.

- **Standard deviation $\sqrt{p_0(1 - p_0)}$:** If p_0 is close to 0 or 1, then $\sqrt{p_0(1 - p_0)}$ is considerably smaller than it is for p_0 close to 0.5.

For example, $\sqrt{p_0(1 - p_0)}$ is 0.1 for $p_0 = 0.01$ or $p_0 = 0.99$, but it is 0.5 for $p_0 = 0.5$.

A smaller standard deviation results in a larger z statistic, which in turn results in a smaller P-value. In general, we stand a better chance of rejecting a null hypothesis when the distribution has little spread, because this allows us to detect even subtle differences between what is hypothesized and what is observed.

Thus, the difference between the sample statistic and what the null hypothesis claims, the sample size, and the standard deviation of the sample statistic all play a role in whether or not the data are statistically significant.

Remember that a *small* P-value suggests that the difference $\hat{p} - p_0$ is relatively *large*, and thus statistically significant. This terminology is sometimes a source of confusion for students.

Students Talk Stats

Interpreting a *P*-Value

Computer output for the test about the population proportion of male births in a state is shown below.

```
Test and CI for One Proportion
Test of p = 0.5 vs p > 0.5

Sample      X      N   Sample p   95.0% Lower Bound   Z-Value   P-Value
1        5120   10000   0.512000            0.503778      2.40     0.008
```

Suppose a group of statistics students are preparing for their next exam, and each one proposes his or her interpretation of the P-value and test results.

Adam: *"The P-value is 0.008, which is very small, so we say the P-value is insignificant."*

Brittany: *"If the P-value is small, then for some reason we have to say the opposite. The P-value is significant."*

Carlos: *"It's not really the P-value that we should call significant, it's the difference between what the data show and what the null hypothesis claimed. That's what's significant."*

Dominique: *"Carlos is right. And even though the difference between 0.512 and 0.5 may not seem like much, the fact that we had such a big sample made the difference statistically significant."*

Carlos and Dominique are correct: Based on the output showing a P-value of 0.008, we can say that the difference between 0.512 and 0.5 is statistically significant. In other words, the small P-value is telling us that statistically, a difference this large is extremely unlikely to come about by chance.

It is noteworthy that in Example 9.25 about the proportion of females in statistics classes, the lab teacher risked erroneously failing to reject a false null hypothesis because her sample size was too small. Failing to reject a false null hypothesis is one type of mistake that is possible when we make a decision based on a test of hypotheses. The other type of mistake is that of incorrectly rejecting a null hypothesis when, in fact, it is true. The circumstances and implications of these two types of error are interesting and important, and they are worthy of exploration.

Type I or II Error: What Kind of Mistakes Can We Make?

On page 35 in Part I on data production, we discussed the imperfect nature of statistical studies. Now that we have presented the methods of statistical inference, we can be more specific about the incorrect conclusions that may be drawn when carrying out a test of hypotheses. Our hope is that when we reject a null hypothesis, it was in fact false, and when we fail to reject a null hypothesis, it was true. In contrast to correct conclusions such as these, there is always a possibility that an error has been made.

> *Definitions*   The mistake of rejecting a null hypothesis, even though it is true, is called a **Type I Error**. Failing to reject a null hypothesis, even though it is false, is called a **Type II Error**.

	Do Not Reject H_0	Reject H_0
H_0 true	Correct	Type I Error
H_0 false	Type II Error	Correct

To get a feel for the two types of error that can be committed in a hypothesis test about a proportion, we consider results of a recent survey.

EXAMPLE 9.26 CONSIDERING TWO POSSIBLE TYPES OF ERROR

Background: In a survey of teenagers, the proportion reported to be virgins was 0.62. For those reported to be virgins, the proportion of mothers who said their teenage child was a virgin was 0.97. For those who had had sex, the proportion of mothers who said their teenage child was a virgin was 0.50.[26]

Question: How would we formulate null and alternative hypotheses about a child's virginity status, and what are the errors mothers could make in drawing their conclusions?

Response: The assumption of "nothing going on" would, of course, be that the teenager is a virgin, so this is the claim of the null hypothesis. The alternative claims that the child is not a virgin. Plenty of mothers (97%) correctly identified their teenagers as being virgins when they were actually virgins, but there were a few mothers (3%) who believed their children to have had sex when they hadn't. This would be a Type I Error because they incorrectly rejected a true null hypothesis.

Continued

A CLOSER LOOK

Another way to remember the error types—I and II—is to recognize that the null hypothesis is the one that we assume to be true by default. Thus, the first type of error considered is the one encountered when the null hypothesis is, in fact, true.

Thinking about Type I and II Errors is a good way to remind students that statistics is by no means an exact science. We gather evidence to convince someone that an experiment is effective, but there is always the possibility that a Type I Error has been committed and the data turned out to be unusual just by chance, not because the treatment made a difference. Or we might fail to produce evidence that one population is essentially different from another, but there is always the possibility that a Type II Error has been committed and the data did not reveal a difference, even though one actually exists.

The other type of error was made by mothers who mistakenly believed their children to be virgins, when, in fact, they had had sex. This was a very common mistake in our example, made by 50% of the mothers. It is a Type II Error because they incorrectly failed to reject the null hypothesis, even though it was false.

Practice: *Try Exercise 9.52(a,b) on page 445.*

This rhyme may help you remember which error is which:

Type One: Reject null, even though true;
If false, but you don't reject, this Type is Two.

Errors are a fact of life when we make decisions based on hypothesis tests. Being aware of the risks and implications of these errors is an important aspect of the test process. Whenever we set a cutoff probability α in advance, with the intention of rejecting the null hypothesis if the P-value is less than α, then we are in effect setting the probability of a Type I Error. Remember that P-values are probabilities. They convey to us the long-run relative frequency of occurrences: In the long run, how often would it happen that the distribution of sample proportion, if its mean really equals the hypothesized population proportion, takes a value as high/low/different as the one observed?

Because inference draws conclusions about a population based on a relatively small subset of values (fewer than 10%), both types of error are inevitable in the long run. Therefore, we should think carefully about the implications of making Type I or II Errors in a variety of settings.

EXAMPLE 9.27 CONSIDERING CONSEQUENCES OF TWO TYPES OF ERROR

Background: Type I and Type II Errors are both possible in medical testing.

Question: Why does the medical community often set the criterion for a positive diagnosis in such a way that Type II Errors are less common than Type I Errors?

Response: If a healthy person initially tests positive (Type I Error), then the consequence—besides considerable anxiety—is a subsequent, more discerning test, with a better chance of making the correct diagnosis the second time around. If an infected person tests negative (Type II Error), then the consequences are more dire because treatment will be withheld, or at best delayed, and there is the risk of further infecting other individuals. Thus, in this case it makes sense to tolerate a higher probability of Type I Error in order to diminish the probability of Type II Error.

Practice: *Try Exercise 9.52(c) on page 445.*

EXAMPLE 9.28 TWO TYPES OF ERROR IN A LEGAL CONTEXT

Background: If a defendant is on trial for a crime, the null hypothesis is that he or she is innocent. The alternative claims the defendant is guilty. The trial weighs evidence as in a hypothesis test to decide whether or not to reject the null hypothesis of innocence.

Question: What would Type I and II Errors signify in this context, and which type of error would have more disturbing consequences?

Response: A Type I Error means rejecting a null hypothesis that is true—in other words, finding an innocent person guilty. A Type II Error would be failing to convict a guilty person. Most people would agree that the former is worse than the latter.

© Gaetano/CORBIS

Guilty or not guilty: What if the verdict is wrong?

Many situations encountered in everyday life may be thought of in terms of Type I and Type II Error.

Students Talk Stats

What Type of Error Was Made?

Students in a statistics class are to complete a group assignment where they must find a report about an error that has been made which can be classified as Type I or Type II. One of the students has discovered an article entitled *New rules for safer surgery*, about "new protections against one of the most devastating and preventable medical errors—surgery on the wrong body part . . . Cases included the removal of the wrong breast and a noncancerous kidney, a biopsy on the wrong side of the brain . . ."[27] The students wonder what kind of error it is to operate on the wrong body part.

Adam: *"Two breasts so it's two errors."*

Brittany: *"The null hypothesis is that a body part is healthy. If you operate by mistake on a healthy body part, then you're rejecting the null hypothesis even though it's true, so it's a Type I Error."*

Carlos: *"The mistake is failing to operate on the body part that needs fixing, so it's a Type II Error."*

Dominique: *"I think Adam must be right. They're making two errors at once, so it involves both Type I and Type II."*

In fact, Adam and Dominique are correct that these mistakes in the operating room entail both types of error.

The *TBP Supplement* presents a table on page 896 that includes the α and β probabilities. Examples TBP 9.8 and TBP 9.9 deal with sensitivity and specificity of medical tests, and an accompanying graph illustrates how physicians make the trade-off between committing one or the other type of error.

Example TBP 9.10 on page 898 of the *TBP Supplement* discusses the consequences of mothers making errors when drawing conclusions about their children's virginity status.

Relating Results of Test with Confidence Interval: Two Sides of the Same Coin

Statistical inference can be carried out in the form of confidence intervals or hypothesis tests. The former let us set up a range of plausible values for the unknown population parameter, whereas the latter let us decide whether a proposed value for that parameter is plausible. In fact, these two forms of inference go hand in hand.

EXAMPLE 9.29 HOW CONFIDENCE INTERVALS RELATE TO HYPOTHESIS TESTS

Background: In Example 9.9, we found an approximate 95% confidence interval for the unknown population proportion of all students eating breakfast to be (0.51, 0.59). Later on, in Example 9.16, we obtained a small P-value (less than 0.025) and rejected the null hypothesis in favor of the alternative that the population proportion is greater than 0.5.

Question: How are the confidence interval and hypothesis test results consistent with one another?

Response: Because the interval did not contain 0.50, it suggested that we would reject the hypothesis that just half of all students eat breakfast.

Practice: *Try Exercise 9.65(a) on page 448.*

The link between confidence intervals and tests becomes more complicated in the case of a one-sided alternative. Fortunately, because software easily provides us with results either in the form of confidence intervals or hypothesis tests, it is not necessary for us to precisely convert results of one form of inference to another by hand.

There is in fact a direct relationship between the information provided in a confidence interval and that provided by a hypothesis test. This relationship is fairly straightforward in the case of a two-sided alternative. If the proposed population proportion p_0 is contained in the 95% confidence interval, then the P-value for the two-sided test will not be less than 0.05 and we will not reject $H_0 : p = p_0$, using 0.05 as our cutoff probability. On the other hand, if p_0 is not contained in the 95% interval, then the P-value will be less than 0.05 and we will reject H_0.

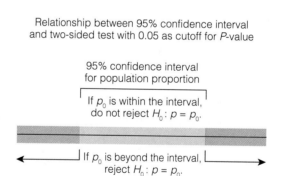

Similarly, if p_0 is in the 99% confidence interval, the P-value for the two-sided test will not be less than 0.01. If p_0 is not in the 99% confidence interval, then the P-value will be less than 0.01.

The Language of Hypothesis Tests: What Exactly Do We Conclude?

Having explored the possibility of Type I and II Errors as a "necessary evil" in the use of hypothesis tests, we should keep in mind the imperfect nature of such tests when stating our conclusions.

Caution must also be exercised in interpreting results when the null hypothesis is *not* rejected.

For a one-sided alternative, we sometimes reject H_0 even though p_0 *is* contained in our confidence interval. For example, if p_0 is contained in the 95% confidence interval, then the P-value for the *one-sided* test will not be less than 0.025. If it happens to be, say, 0.03, then we *would* reject H_0 using 0.05 as our cutoff probability.

Students Talk Stats

The Correct Interpretation of a Small *P*-Value

Suppose students in a statistics computer lab class use software to test if a majority of the population of students eat breakfast, based on the sample data analyzed in this chapter. Besides producing the relevant computer output, the students are required to interpret the test results.

```
Test and CI for One Proportion
Test of p = 0.5 vs p > 0.5
Sample    X    N  Sample p  95.0% Lower Bound  Z-Value  P-Value
1        246  445  0.553              0.514040     2.23    0.013
```

Adam: *"The P-value is 0.013, so the probability is 0.013 that the population proportion equals 0.5. The test proves that the alternative hypothesis is true, and the proportion of all students eating breakfast is greater than 0.5."*

Brittany: *"The P-value isn't a probability about the population proportion, it's a probability about the sample proportion. It says that if the population proportion were equal to 0.5, the probability that the sample proportion equals 0.553 would be 0.013."*

Carlos: *"Brittany is right, the P-value is about the sample proportion. But we're not talking about the probability of the sample proportion exactly equaling any particular value—it's the probability that the sample proportion is at least as high as 0.553. And since that probability is so small, we have proven that the population proportion can't be 0.5."*

Dominique: *"Carlos is right about what the P-value is measuring, but his conclusion isn't exactly right. We can't prove anything 100%, but we can say that we have very convincing evidence that the population proportion is not 0.5. It's something higher."*

Dominique is correct: Based on the computer output that shows a *P*-value of 0.013, we can say that if the proportion of all students eating breakfast were only 0.5, the probability of observing a sample proportion as high as 0.553 (or higher) is 0.013. This provides fairly strong evidence against the null hypothesis $p = 0.5$, in favor of the alternative $p > 0.5$.

Practice: *Try Exercise 9.66 on page 448.*

Students Talk Stats

The Correct Interpretation When a *P*-Value Is Not Small

The students' next task requires them to test if a minority of all commuting students walk to school. Again, they produce output and propose various interpretations of the *P*-value and test results.

```
Test and CI for One Proportion
Test of p = 0.5 vs p < 0.5
Sample    X    N  Sample p  95.0% Upper Bound  Z-Value  P-Value
1        111  230  0.482609           0.536805    -0.53    0.299
```

Students Talk Stats continued →

Sometimes the opposite of rejecting the null hypothesis is referred to as "accepting" it, but this word may give the false impression that we have produced evidence that the null hypothesis is true, which is not really the case. Rather, the opposite of rejecting the null hypothesis should be referred to as "failing to reject it," which is a more accurate expression.

Example TBP 9.11 on page 899 of the **TBP** *Supplement* demonstrates that sample data can support more than one null hypothesis, reminding us to avoid using the word "prove" when stating conclusions. Also, it may be helpful for students to think in terms of a court trial, as in Example 9.28 on page 892. Further explanation is given on page 899 of the **TBP** *Supplement*.

In this chapter, our tests were always about a categorical variable that allowed for only two possibilities, conforming to the binomial model. On page 900 of the **TBP** *Supplement*, we discuss situations where there are more than two possible values for the variable.

Students Talk Stats continued

Adam: *"The P-value is 0.299, so that's the probability that the proportion of all students who walk is 0.5."*

Brittany: *"No, you have to explain the P-value the same way we did for the last problem: If the proportion of all commuters who walk is 0.5, then the probability that our sample proportion would be 0.482609 or lower is 0.299. Since the P-value isn't small, we accept the null hypothesis and so we've proven that the proportion of all commuters who walk is 0.5."*

Carlos: *"How can we use a sample proportion of 0.48 to prove that the population proportion is 0.5? That doesn't make sense to me."*

Dominique: *"Carlos is right—as usual. When the P-value isn't small, then we just can't reject the null hypothesis. That's not the same thing as proving the null hypothesis is true."*

Carlos and Dominique are correct: Based on the output, which shows a *P*-value of 0.299, we can say that if the proportion of all commuters who walk were equal to 0.5, the probability of observing a sample proportion as low as 0.482609 is 0.299. The fact that the *P*-value is not small tells us that we cannot reject the null hypothesis. We haven't proven that $p = 0.5$, but we should continue to believe that it is plausible, since we have no compelling evidence to the contrary.

Practice: *Try Exercise 9.67 on page 448.*

The "Critical Value" Approach: Focusing on the Standard Score

Instead of focusing on the size of the *P*-value in a hypothesis test, a different approach (more in use before calculators and computers became common) is to focus on the size of the standardized statistic. Using this approach, we would reject the null hypothesis if the test statistic exceeds a certain value, called the *critical value*.

Definition   The **critical value** in the formulation of a hypothesis test is the value such that the null hypothesis will be rejected if the standardized test statistic exceeds this value.

For instance, it may be decided in advance to reject H_0 in a *z*-test if |*z*| exceeds 2.576. Note that this is equivalent to setting our cutoff probability α equal to 0.01 in a two-sided test. Similarly, the critical *z*-value of 1.96 accompanies a two-sided *P*-value of 0.05. Here the emphasis is on looking for large test statistics, rather than looking for small *P*-values.

The advantage to scrutinizing the *P*-value is that it tells us exactly how improbable such an extreme test statistic would be, if the claim in H_0 were true. For one test the *P*-value may be 0.049 and for another it may be 0.002. These provide much more information than simply noting that in both cases, |*z*| exceeds the critical value of 1.96.

Hypothesis Test: Is a Proposed Population Proportion Plausible?

Note: Asterisked numbers indicate exercises whose answers are provided in the Solutions to Selected Exercises section, on page 689.

*9.36 "Antibiotic Resistance Puzzle," discussed in Exercise 9.9, reports that children in a certain city "are resistant to common antibiotics at a rate that is double the national average."[28] The national average was 0.05, but researchers found that 68 of 708 Group A strep cultures taken from children in the area were resistant to the antibiotics.

a. Formulate two opposing points of view to test whether or not the resistance rate of all Group A strep cultures in that city is higher than the national rate.

b. Is there reason to suspect bias in the sample of cultures?

c. Is the sample too large relative to the population?

d. Is the sample too small to justify use of a normal approximation?

e. Find the sample proportion $\hat{p}$ that were resistant, to the nearest hundredth, and find the value of standardized sample proportion z, using the fact that standard deviation of sample proportion under the null hypothesis is
$$\sqrt{0.05(1 - 0.05)/708} = 0.01 \text{ (to the nearest hundredth)}.$$

f. Use your z-score and a sketch of the 68-95-99.7 Rule to tell whether the probability of a sample proportion equal to 0.10 or higher, from a population with proportion resistant equal to 0.05, is greater than 0.16, between 0.16 and 0.025, between 0.025 and 0.0015, or less than 0.0015.

g. Tell which one of the following background scenarios would convince you more that resistance rates are higher in a particular city, and explain why:
  1. Researchers suspected that resistance rates were going to be higher in that city because antibiotics are overprescribed there, and patients often don't take the full course of medication, thereby helping the bacteria to develop resistance.
  2. Researchers just tested for resistance at many cities across the country to see what would turn up.

*9.37 Exercise 9.18 discussed the fact that some hospital administrators fear that mandatory reporting of medical errors would encourage lawsuits, in spite of evidence that suggests patients are less likely to sue if doctors admit their mistakes and apologize.

a. If we want to show that a majority of administrators believe mandatory reporting of errors would encourage lawsuits, would we be disputing a claim of equality with a greater-than, less-than, or not-equal sign?

b. Write the appropriate null and alternative hypotheses using mathematical notation.

*9.38 In a survey of 446 students, the sample proportion wearing corrective lenses is $\hat{p} = 0.52$, and standardized sample proportion (comparing to $p_0 = 0.50$) is $z = +0.85$.

a. Shade the area of the normal curve for distribution of sample proportion (first graph shown below) to indicate the area represented by the P-value if we test against the alternative that the population proportion is greater than 0.5. [Please see the three graphs on p. 000 for examples of P-value as a shaded area.]

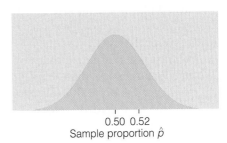

0.50 0.52
Sample proportion $\hat{p}$

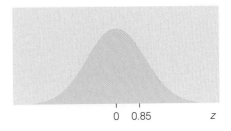

0   0.85 z

b. Shade the area of the normal curve for distribution of standardized sample proportion z (graph shown above) to indicate the area represented by the P-value if we test against the alternative that the population proportion is greater than 0.5.

c. Shade the area of the normal curve for distribution of sample proportion to indicate the area represented by the P-value if we test against the (two-sided) alternative that population proportion does not equal 0.5.

d. Shade the area of the normal curve for distribution of standardized sample proportion z to indicate the area represented by the P-value if we test against the (two-sided) alternative that the population proportion does not equal 0.5.

e. Will the null hypothesis be rejected against either the one-sided or two-sided alternative? Explain.

f. Should we expect a confidence interval for population proportion, based on our sample proportion, to contain 0.5? Explain.

9.39 In a survey completed by students in introductory statistics courses at a large university in the fall of 2003, the sample proportion of off-campus students who walk to school is $\hat{p} = 0.48$, and standardized sample proportion (comparing to $p_0 = 0.50$) is $z = -0.53$.

a. Shade the area of the normal curve for distribution of sample proportion (first graph shown below) to indicate the area represented by the P-value if we test against the alternative that population proportion is less than 0.5. [Please see the three graphs on p. 000 for examples of P-value as a shaded area.]

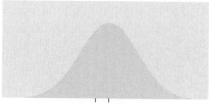

0.48 0.50
Sample proportion $\hat{p}$

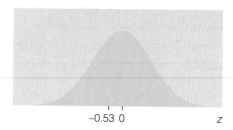

−0.53 0 z

b. Shade the area of the normal curve for distribution of standardized sample proportion z (graph shown above) to indicate the area represented by the P-value if we test against the alternative that population proportion is less than 0.5.

c. Shade the area of the normal curve for distribution of sample proportion to indicate the area represented by the P-value if we test against the (two-sided) alternative that population proportion does not equal 0.5.

d. Shade the area of the normal curve for distribution of standardized sample proportion z to indicate the area represented by the P-value if we test against the (two-sided) alternative that population proportion does not equal 0.5.

e. Will the null hypothesis be rejected against either the one-sided or two-sided alternative? Explain.

f. Should we expect a confidence interval for population proportion, based on our sample proportion, to contain 0.5? Explain.

*9.40 A journal article entitled "Holidays, Birthdays, and Postponement of Cancer Death" begins: "Health-care workers and others involved with patients dying of cancer commonly recall those who apparently held on to life and defied the odds by surviving a major holiday or significant event, only to die immediately thereafter."[29] The authors gathered data from thousands of cancer deaths and focused on the 2-week periods surrounding Christmas, Thanksgiving, and each patient's birthday. They looked at various sex, race, and age groups separately, as well as all results combined. They also took into account that Jewish patients would not be expected to consider Christmas to be a special day. The null hypothesis states that the overall proportion of cancer patients who die in the week before a special day is 0.5 (the same as the proportion who die in the week following). Of 5,776 women who died within a week of Christmas, 2,858 died in the week before, as opposed to after.

a. Calculate the sample proportion of women who died in the week before Christmas, to three decimal places.

b. Is your answer to part (a) denoted p, $\hat{p}$, or p_0?

c. If the alternative hypothesis $H_a : p < 0.5$ claims that, in general, people hold on to life in order to survive a holiday, does the sample proportion tend in the right direction to support this claim?

d. The standardized sample proportion is -0.79. Based on the 68-95-99.7 Rule, which of these intervals reports the correct range for the P-value: less than 0.0015, between 0.0015 and 0.025, between 0.025 and 0.16, or greater than 0.16?

e. Do we denote -0.79 as $\hat{p}$ or z?

*9.41 In a survey of 446 students, it was found that 50% of the sampled students lived on campus and 50% lived off campus.

a. Tell the value of standardized sample proportion z, if we want to test whether the proportion of all students living on campus could be 0.50.

b. If we sketch a normal curve for the distribution of sample proportion (centered at 0.50), what portion should be shaded to indicate the area represented by the P-value for testing against the alternative that population proportion is greater than 0.5? [Please see the three graphs on p. 000 for examples of P-value as a shaded area.] What does the P-value equal in this case?

c. What portion of the standard normal (z) curve should be shaded to indicate the area represented by the P-value for testing against the alternative that the population proportion is greater than 0.5?

d. What portion of the normal curve for the distribution of sample proportion should be shaded to indicate the area represented by the P-value for testing against the (two-sided) alternative that population proportion does not equal 0.5?

e. What portion of the normal curve for the distribution of standardized sample proportion z should be shaded to indicate the area represented by the P-value for testing against the (two-sided) alternative that population proportion does not equal 0.5? What does the P-value equal in this case?

f. Will the null hypothesis be rejected against either the one-sided or two-sided alternative? Explain.

9.42 In the same survey used in 9.41, 88% of the sampled students were right-handed.

a. The proportion of all people who are right-handed is said to be 0.88. Tell the value of standardized sample proportion z, if we want to test whether the proportion of all students who are right-handed could be 0.88.

b. If we sketch a normal curve for the distribution of sample proportion (centered at 0.88), what portion should be shaded to indicate the area represented by the P-value for testing against the alternative that population proportion is less than 0.88? [Please see the three graphs on p. 000 for examples of P-value as a shaded area.]

c. What portion of the standard normal (z) curve should be shaded to indicate the area represented by the P-value for testing against the alternative that the population proportion is less than 0.88? What does the P-value equal in this case?

d. What portion of the normal curve for the distribution of sample proportion (again, centered at 0.88) should be shaded to indicate the area represented by the P-value for testing against the (two-sided) alternative that population proportion does not equal 0.88? What does the P-value equal in this case?

e. What portion of the normal curve for the distribution of standardized sample proportion z should be shaded to indicate the area represented by the P-value for testing against the (two-sided) alternative that population proportion does not equal 0.88?

f. Will the null hypothesis be rejected against either the one-sided or two-sided alternative? Explain.

9.43   Exercise 9.40 explains that to test whether there is a tendency for cancer patients to hold on to life long enough to survive for a holiday or birthday, researchers gathered data from thousands of cancer deaths and focused on the 2-week periods surrounding Christmas, Thanksgiving, and each patient's birthday. The null hypothesis states that the overall proportion of cancer patients who die in the week before a special day is 0.5 (the same as the proportion who die in the week following). They looked at various sex, race, and age groups separately, as well as all results combined. Of 1,309 blacks who died within a week of Thanksgiving, 700 died in the week before, as opposed to after.

    a. Calculate the sample proportion of blacks who died in the week before Thanksgiving.

    b. Is this sample proportion denoted $\hat{p}$, p, or p_0?

    c. If we use a *one-sided* alternative hypothesis $H_a : p < 0.5$ to claim that, in general, people hold on to life in order to survive a holiday, does the sample proportion tend in the right direction to support this claim?

    d. The standardized sample proportion is $z = +2.52$. If we test H_0 against the *two-sided* alternative $H_a : p \neq 0.5$, use the tails of the normal curve to tell which of these intervals reports the correct range for the P-value: less than 2(0.005), between 2(0.005) and 2(0.01), between 2(0.01) and 2(0.025), between 2(0.025) and 2(0.05), greater than 2(0.05).

    e. Use $\alpha = 0.05$ as the cutoff for what we would consider to be a "small" P-value. Which one of these is the correct conclusion to draw from the results of testing against the two-sided alternative:
       1. There is no convincing evidence that the proportion of all black cancer patients dying before Thanksgiving differs from 0.5.
       2. There is convincing evidence that the proportion of all black cancer patients dying before Thanksgiving differs from 0.5.
       3. Black cancer patients tend to hold on to life until after Thanksgiving.

9.44   To test whether there is a tendency for cancer patients to hold on to life long

enough to survive for a holiday or birthday, researchers gathered data from thousands of cancer deaths and focused on the 2-week periods surrounding Christmas, Thanksgiving, and each patient's birthday. The null hypothesis states that the overall proportion of cancer patients who die in the week before a special day is 0.5 (the same as the proportion who die in the week following). They looked at various sex, race, and age groups separately, as well as all results combined. Of 6,968 elderly (at least 70 years old) cancer patients who died within a week of their birthday, 3,547 died in the week before, as opposed to after.

    a. Calculate the sample proportion $\hat{p}$ of elderly patients who died in the week before their birthday.

    b. If we use a *one-sided* alternative hypothesis $H_a : p < 0.5$ to claim that, in general, people hold on to life in order to survive a holiday, does the sample proportion tend in the right direction to support this claim?

    c. The standardized sample proportion is $z = +1.51$. If we test H_0 against the *two-sided* alternative $H_a : p \neq 0.5$, use the 68-95-99.7 Rule to tell which of these intervals reports the correct range for the P-value: less than 2(0.0015), between 2(0.0015) and 2(0.025), between 2(0.025) and 2(0.16), greater than 2(0.16).

    d. Use $\alpha = 0.05$ as the cutoff for what we would consider to be a "small" P-value. Which one of these is the correct conclusion to draw from the results of testing against the two-sided alternative:
       1. There is no convincing evidence that proportion of all elderly cancer patients dying before their birthday differs from 0.5.
       2. There is convincing evidence that proportion of all elderly cancer patients dying before their birthday differs from 0.5.
       3. Elderly cancer patients tend to hold on to life until after their birthday.

    e. In this problem, should we denote 0.5 as $\hat{p}$, p, or p_0?

9.45   To test whether there is a tendency for cancer patients to hold on to life long enough to survive for a holiday or birthday, researchers gathered data from thousands of cancer deaths and focused on the 2-week periods surrounding Christmas, Thanksgiving, and each patient's birthday. The null hypothesis states that the overall proportion of cancer patients who die in the week before a special day is 0.5 (the same as the proportion who die in the week following) and the (two-sided) alternative hypothesis says the proportion dying in the week before differs from 0.5. They looked at various sex, race, and age groups separately for each of the three special days, and calculated P-values for 18 tests. (These are precise binomial probabilities, which tend to differ slightly from normal approximations.)

Event/Group	P-Value	Event/Group	P-Value	Event/Group	P-Value
Xmas/Men	0.10	Tgiving/Men	0.93	Bday/Men	0.49
Xmas/Women	0.44	Tgiving/Women	0.09	Bday/Women	0.05
Xmas/White	0.24	Tgiving/White	0.71	Bday/White	0.11
Xmas/Black	0.19	Tgiving/Black	0.01	Bday/Black	0.23
Xmas/< 70	0.16	Tgiving/< 70	0.23	Bday/< 70	0.26
Xmas/≥ 70	0.75	Tgiving/≥ 70	0.66	Bday/≥ 70	0.13

a. In general, if a null hypothesis is true, what is the probability that, by chance, sample data produce evidence to reject it at the 0.05 level?

b. If we tested a true null hypothesis 100 times, about how many times would it be rejected, just by chance?

c. If we test a true null hypothesis about 20 times, about how many times would it be rejected, just by chance?

d. How many of the P-values in the table above are small enough (*less than* 0.05) to reject the null hypothesis that the proportion of cancer patients dying the week before a special day (as opposed to the week after) equals 0.5?

e. Which is the best conclusion to draw from the study's results?
   1. There is no convincing evidence that cancer patients die any more or less often before a special day as opposed to after.
   2. Special days have no effect on cancer patients' time of death, except that blacks in general tend to die in the week before Thanksgiving, instead of the week after.

*9.46 A 2005 report on the 109th Congress included information on race and religion of the 434 members of the House and 100 members of the Senate.

a. Whereas 7% of the U.S. adult population is Methodist, 12% of the House and 12% of the Senate members are Methodist. Explain why standardized proportion (z) of Methodists would be larger for the House than for the Senate.

b. If we tested for a significant difference between sample proportion of Methodists and proportion in the general population, which P-value would be smaller: for the House, for the Senate, or both the same? Explain.

c. Out of 434 House members, 42 were black. A test was carried out against the two-sided alternative hypothesis, but because we would have reason to suspect in advance that blacks are underrepresented, a one-sided test would have been more appropriate. Use the output below to report what the P-value would be for a one-sided test.

```
Test of p = 0.13 vs p not = 0.13
Sample   X    N   Sample p        95.0% CI        Z-Value   P-Value
1       42   434  0.096774  (0.068959, 0.124589)   -2.06     0.040
```

d. Suppose we used 0.025 as our cutoff for a small *P*-value. Referring to the output produced for a two-sided alternative in part (c), in which case would we reject the claim that $p = 0.13$: against the one-sided alternative, or the two-sided alternative, or both, or neither?

e. According to the test carried out in part (c), what is the assumed proportion of all adult Americans who are black?

*9.47 A specialist in mood disorders has stated that there is a 15% risk of suicide for children with untreated depression.

a. If we test $H_0 : p = 0.15$ versus $H_a : p < 0.15$, tell which of these sample proportions would provide the *most* evidence against the null hypothesis, in favor of the alternative: 0.11, 0.14, 0.20

b. If we test $H_0 : p = 0.15$ versus $H_a : p < 0.15$, tell which of these sample proportions would provide the *least* evidence against the null hypothesis: 0.11, 0.14, 0.20

c. If we test $H_0 : p = 0.15$ versus $H_a : p \neq 0.15$, tell which of these sample proportions would provide the *most* evidence against the null hypothesis, in favor of the alternative: 0.11, 0.14, 0.20

d. If we test $H_0 : p = 0.15$ versus $H_a : p \neq 0.15$, tell which of these sample proportions would provide the *least* evidence against the null hypothesis: 0.11, 0.14, 0.20

9.48 It is reported that the proportion of college students at large public institutions who seek help at counseling centers is 0.10.

a. If we test $H_0 : p = 0.10$ versus $H_a : p \neq 0.10$, tell which of these sample proportions would provide the *most* evidence against the null hypothesis, in favor of the alternative: 0.05, 0.11, 0.13

b. If we test $H_0 : p = 0.10$ versus $H_a : p \neq 0.10$, tell which of these sample proportions would provide the *least* evidence against the null hypothesis: 0.05, 0.11, 0.13

c. If we test $H_0 : p = 0.10$ versus $H_a : p > 0.10$, tell which of these sample proportions would provide the *most* evidence against the null hypothesis, in favor of the alternative: 0.05, 0.11, 0.13

d. If we test $H_0 : p = 0.10$ versus $H_a : p > 0.10$, tell which of these sample proportions would provide the *least* evidence against the null hypothesis: 0.05, 0.11, 0.13

*9.49 The proportion of all births in the United States that were Caesarian deliveries in 2002 was 0.26. One particular county found that 35,600 of its 143,000 births were Caesarian that year, and so $\hat{p} = 0.249$. A test of $H_0 : p = 0.26$ against $H_a : p \neq 0.26$ produces $z = -9.48$ and so the *P*-value is 0.000, which is very small. Does this mean proportion of Caesarians in that county is very different from 0.26, or that we have very strong evidence that this county's proportion of Caesarians does not conform to the national rate of 0.26?

*9.50 Suppose contraception shots have a slight effect overall on antibody levels in monkeys. If the shots are tested on a sample of just nine monkeys, would you expect a *P*-value that is extremely small or not very small?

9.51 "Study Proves Number Bias in UK Lottery" reported on the Internet about a document completed in 2002, "The Randomness of the National Lottery," which was meant to offer irrefutable proof that it was random. But the authors hit a snag when they found that one numbered ball, 38, was drawn so often that they believed there was bias in the selections, perhaps due to a physical difference in the ball: "Haigh and Goldie found that over 637 draws you would expect each number to be drawn between 70 and 86 times. But they found that 38 came up 107 times, 14 times more than the next most drawn ball. 'That some number has been drawn 107 times is very unusual—the chance is under 1%.'"[30]

a. If each number is expected to be drawn between 70 and 86 times, on average how many times is it expected to be drawn?

b. Based on your answer to part (a), what *proportion* of times is each number expected in 637 draws? (Round to the nearest thousandth.)

c. Show that standard deviation of sample proportion in this situation would be 0.013.

d. What *proportion* of the 637 draws did the number 38 come up? (Round to the nearest thousandth.)

e. Find z, the standardized difference between sample proportion (your answer to part [d]) and ideal proportion (your answer to part [b]).

f. Were the authors correct that the chance is under 1%?

g. A spokesperson defending the lottery's randomness criticized the authors' conclusions: "If you trawl through an awful lot of data you are always going to uncover patterns somewhere." Is her statement consistent with the decision-making process of hypothesis testing? Explain.

*9.52 Critics of the U.K. lottery described in Exercise 9.51 claimed that the draws were not random. A supporter claimed that the draws were random.

a. If the critics were wrong, did they commit a Type I or Type II Error?

b. If the supporter was wrong, did she commit a Type I or Type II Error?

c. Which type of error would cause more inconvenience to the lottery's organizers, Type I or Type II? Explain.

9.53 In 2004, controversy arose regarding the issue of whether or not eating dairy products could help people lose weight.[31] The null hypothesis would state that dairy products have no effect.

a. Michael Zemel, director of The Nutrition Institute at the University of Tennessee, carried out a study from which he concluded that eating dairy products *does* help people lose weight. If his conclusion is erroneous, would it be a Type I or a Type II Error?

b. Jean Harvey-Berino, chair of the Department of Nutrition and Food Sciences at the University of Vermont, carried out a study from which she concluded that eating dairy products does *not* help people lose weight. If her conclusion is erroneous, would it be a Type I or a Type II Error?

c. Which type of error would the dairy industry most want to avoid committing?

d. Describe the impact each type of error would have on dieters.

9.54 In Example 6.21, we looked at probabilities associated with the administration of lie-detector tests. A National Research Council

study in 2002, headed by Stephen Fienberg from Carnegie Mellon University, found that lie-detector results are "better than chance, but well below perfection."[32] Typically, the test will conclude someone is a spy 80% of the time when he or she actually is a spy. However, 16% of the time, the test will conclude someone is a spy when he or she is not.

a. What is the probability of committing a Type I Error?

b. What would be the consequences of committing a Type I Error?

c. What is the probability of committing a Type II Error?

d. What would be the consequences of committing a Type II Error?

9.55 According to the alwaystestclean.com website, a report by the *Los Angeles Times* News Service stated that in a study of 161 prescription and over-the-counter medications, 65 of them produced false positive drug test results in the most widely administered urine test. Some examples cited were ibuprofen leading to false positive tests for THC, poppy seeds on bagels leading to false positive tests for opiates, amoxicillin leading to false positive tests for cocaine, and black skin leading to false positive tests for marijuana.

a. Do false positive tests mean that the medications, poppy seeds, etc. make it look like people use illegal drugs when they actually don't, or do they mean that it looks like people don't use illegal drugs when they actually do?

b. Is the report referring to Type I or Type II errors?

*9.56 Urine tests are commonly used to test for drugs. The null hypothesis would say there were no illegal drugs used. Pick the most appropriate cutoff level for the P-value, 0.10 or 0.05 or 0.01, under each of the following circumstances.

a. No other information is provided.

b. If illegal drugs are detected, an athlete is immediately barred from participation in his sport.

c. If illegal drugs are detected, a more accurate follow-up test is carried out.

9.57 Legislation was proposed in Indiana in 2001 to require HIV testing of all pregnant women in the state. The null hypothesis in a test would say that HIV is not present. Pick the most appropriate cutoff level for the P-value, 0.10 or 0.01, under each of the following circumstances.

a. If the test is positive, a woman who cannot afford the time or money for a follow-up test will avoid further prenatal care for fear of being discovered.

b. If the test is positive, for any woman, a confidential, no-cost follow-up test is immediately carried out.

9.58 A news article reported in 2005 that "Amgen Inc. said it would stop giving an experimental drug for Parkinson's disease to 48 people who received it as part of a trial because tests found it worked no better than a placebo. [. . .] There is no cure for Parkinson's, and the drug had been seen as promising when a preliminary trial found all five patients showed measurable improvement."[33] If the null hypothesis is that the drug does not help patients with Parkinson's then the preliminary trial apparently committed which type of error: Type I or Type II?

*9.59 A New York Times report from March 2005 provided information on the U.S. military personnel who had been killed in Iraq as of March 9. The proportion of those killed who had graduated from high school was $\hat{p} = 0.955$, versus 0.942 of all military personnel and 0.855 of all Americans aged 18 to 44. We could test if the proportion of those killed who had graduated from high school is significantly higher than the proportion of all military personnel who had graduated from high school by comparing $\hat{p} = 0.955$ to $p_0 = 0.942$. Or, we could test if the proportion of those killed who had graduated from high school is significantly higher than the proportion of all Americans aged 18 to 44 who had graduated from high school by comparing $\hat{p} = 0.955$ to $p_0 = 0.855$.

a. The z statistic in one case is 2.16 and in one case is 11.04. Which of these z statistics is for the test making a comparison to all Americans aged 18 to 44?

b. Is there convincing evidence that among those killed, the proportion who had graduated from high school is significantly higher than for all Americans aged 18 to 44?

9.60 A New York Times report from March 2005 provided information on the U.S. military personnel who had been killed in Iraq as of March 9. Software has been used to carry out various tests about the gender, race, and rank of those killed.

a. Test of p = 0.16 vs p < 0.16

Sample	X	N	Sample p	95.0% Upper Bound	Z-Value	P-Value
1	38	1512	0.025132	0.031754	−14.30	0.000

The output above is for a test about whether the proportion of women among those killed is less than 0.16, the proportion of all military personnel who are women. Is it significantly less than 0.16? Tell what part of the output you referred to.

b. Test of p = 0.855 vs p > 0.855

Sample	X	N	Sample p	95.0% Lower Bound	Z-Value	P-Value
1	1349	1512	0.892196	0.879077	4.11	0.000

The output above is for a test about whether the proportion who were enlisted (as opposed to officers) was representative of the proportion of all military personnel who were enlisted (0.855). Was it apparently suspected that the number of killed who were enlisted would be disproportionately high, or disproportionately low, or simply different from the overall proportion?

c. Test of p = 0.087 vs p not = 0.087

Sample	X	N	Sample p	95.0% CI	Z-Value	P-Value
1	174	1512	0.115079	(0.098994, 0.131164)	3.87	0.000

The output above is for a test about whether the proportion of those killed who were Hispanic was representative of the proportion of all military personnel who were Hispanic (0.087). Was it apparently suspected that the number of killed who were Hispanic would be disproportionately high, or disproportionately low, or simply different from the overall proportion?

d. Test of p = 0.67 vs p < 0.67

Sample	X	N	Sample p	95.0% Upper Bound	Z-Value	P-Value
1	1096	1512	0.724868	0.743759	4.54	1.000

The output above is for a test about whether the proportion of those killed who were white was less than the proportion of all military personnel who were white (0.67). Explain why the *P*-value is so large.

9.61 A *New York Times* report from March 2005 provided information on race of U.S. military personnel who had been killed in Iraq as of March 9. The proportion of blacks was 0.109.

   a. Which would produce a larger standardized difference (*z*): testing for a difference from proportion of all military personnel who were black (0.186) or testing for a difference from proportion of all Americans who are black (0.130)?

   b. Which would produce a smaller *P*-value: testing for a difference from proportion of all military personnel who were black (0.186) or testing for a difference from proportion of all Americans who are black (0.130)?

9.62 Psychology researchers from the University of California, San Diego, set about finding an answer to the question, "Do dogs resemble their owners?" In their study, "28 student judges were asked to match photos of dogs with their owners. Each student was presented with a photo of a dog owner and photos of two dogs. One dog was the actual pet, the other was an imposter. If more than half of the judges correctly paired a given dog with his or her owner, this was considered a "match." Forty-five dogs took part in the study—25 purebreds and 20 mutts. [. . .] Overall, there were just 23 matches (as defined above). However, the judges had an easier time with the purebred dogs: 16 matches, versus 7 for the mixed breeds."[34] Output is shown here for three tests: both types together, purebreds, and mixed breeds ("mutts"), in that order.

Sample	X	N	Sample p	95.0% Lower Bound	Z-Value	P-Value
1	23	45	0.511111	0.388541	0.15	0.441

Sample	X	N	Sample p	95.0% Lower Bound	Z-Value	P-Value
1	16	25	0.640000	0.482094	1.40	0.081

Sample	X	N	Sample p	95.0% Lower Bound	Z-Value	P-Value
1	7	20	0.350000	0.174570	−1.34	0.910

   a. State the null and alternative hypotheses to test if the proportion of all dogs that can be successfully matched by judges is more than half, using words and then symbols.

   b. For which types of dogs, if any, do the tests indicate that dogs really do resemble their owners: both types together, purebreds, mixed breeds, or none of these?

   c. For which types of dogs is use of a normal approximation most appropriate for the given data: both types together, purebreds, or mixed breeds?

   d. For which types of dogs is use of a normal approximation least appropriate for the given data: both types together, purebreds, or mixed breeds?

   e. Explain why, for mixed breeds, our rules of thumb indicate that a normal approximation should not be used to construct a confidence interval but it may be used to carry out the test.

9.63 In March 2005, the husband of Terry Schiavo, the woman who had been in a persistent vegetative state for 15 years, succeeded in having her feeding tube removed, as he stated she would have wished. When Congress moved to intervene and order the tube to be replaced, ABC News polled a random sample of 501 adults, and found that 0.63 agreed that the tube should have been removed.[35] If the standardized sample proportion is $z = +5.85$, is it clear that a majority of all American adults were in favor of the tube's removal?

9.64 Four students are discussing the meaning of a *P*-value.

   Adam: My last stats prof said when you explain a *P*-value you want to make it so clear that even your mom could understand what you mean.

Brittany: That's so sexist. Why not make it so clear, even your *dad* could understand it?

Carlos: It is kind of insulting. Like "your mom is so bad at statistics, she doesn't know a *P*-value from a *z*-statistic."

Dominique: And *your* mom is so bad at statistics, she rejects the null hypothesis when her *P*-value is *greater* than 0.05.

Carlos: Ouch!

Create a new insult of your own: "Your mother/father is so bad at statistics . . ."

*9.65 Exercise 9.46 discussed a 2005 report on the 109th Congress that included information on race and religion of the 434 members of the House and 100 members of the Senate. Out of 434 House members, 42 were black. A test was carried out against the two-sided alternative hypothesis $p \neq 0.13$, because 13% of the general population of the U.S. were black.

```
Test of p = 0.13 vs p not = 0.13
Sample   X    N   Sample p         95.0% CI         Z-Value  P-Value
1        42  434  0.096774  (0.068959, 0.124589)    -2.06    0.040
```

a. The *P*-value for the two-sided test is a bit less than 0.05, and the confidence interval doesn't quite contain 0.13. What would you be able to say about the confidence interval if the *P*-value was much less than 0.05?

b. Based on the confidence interval in the output, which of these would be rejected: $H_0 : p = 0.06$, $H_0 : p = 0.08$, $H_0 : p = 0.10$, $H_0 : p = 0.12$, $H_0 : p = 0.14$? (Your answer can include anywhere from none to all five of these hypotheses.)

c. What notation should be used for the assumed proportion of all adult Americans who are black: p, p_0, or $\hat{p}$?

d. Of 100 Senate members, 24 were Roman Catholic. What is the value of standardized proportion (z), if 24% of all adult Americans are Roman Catholic?

e. If a two-sided test is carried out to see if the proportion of Catholics in the Senate is significantly different from the proportion in the general population, would the *P*-value be 0, 0.5, or 1? Explain.

*9.66 "Antibiotic Resistance Puzzle," discussed in Exercise 9.9, reports that children in a certain city "are resistant to common antibiotics at a rate that is double the national average."[36] The national average was 0.05, but researchers found that 68 of 708 Group A strep cultures taken from children in the area were resistant to the antibiotics. The *P*-value to test for a significantly higher rate in that city was less than 0.0005. Which one of these is the correct conclusion to draw, based on the size of the *P*-value?

a. The data prove that Group A strep in that city is more resistant to macrolides than it is in the United States in general.

b. The data fail to provide evidence that Group A strep in that city is more resistant to macrolides than it is in the United States in general.

c. The data prove that Group A strep in that city is no more resistant to macrolides than it is in the United States in general.

d. The data provide evidence that Group A strep in that city is more resistant to macrolides than it is in the United States in general.

*9.67 Exercise 9.40 discussed a one-sided test of the null hypothesis that the overall proportion of cancer patients who die in the week before a special day is 0.5 (the same as the proportion who die in the week following). Because the test statistic was less than 1 in absolute value, the *P*-value was greater than 0.16. Tell which one of these is the correct conclusion to draw, based on the size of the *P*-value:

a. The data prove that women are more likely to die in the week after Christmas than in the week before.

b. The data fail to provide evidence that women are more likely to die in the week after Christmas than in the week before.

c. The data prove that women are no more likely to die in the week after Christmas than they are to die in the week before.

d. The data provide evidence that women are more likely to die in the week after Christmas than in the week before.

Using Software [see Technology Guide]

9.68 In a national poll of 1,706 Americans aged 45 and older conducted in 2004 for the AARP, 1,228 of respondents agreed with the statement, "Adults should be allowed to legally use marijuana for medical purposes if a physician recommends it."[37] We want to use software to test if a majority (more than 0.5) of all Americans aged 45 and older support legalization of marijuana for medical purposes.

a. First state H_0 and H_a mathematically.

b. Next, report the sample proportion $\hat{p}$ from the test output.

c. Report the standardized sample proportion z.

d. Report the P-value.

e. Does the poll provide convincing evidence that a majority of all Americans aged 45 and older support legalization of marijuana for medical purposes? Explain.

9.69 "2004 a Bad Year for the Grizzly Bear" reported that "31 bears were killed illegally or had to be destroyed in a mountain habitat of 6 million acres that has Glacier National Park and federal wilderness areas at its core. That is the largest number of deaths caused by humans in the region since 1974, when the grizzly was listed as threatened under the Endangered Species Act. More worrisome is that 18 of the dead bears were females, which are more important than males to the reproductive health of the entire population."[38] This exercise requires you to use software to test if a disproportionate number of killed bears were female, assuming that half of all grizzlies are female.

a. In choosing whether to formulate a one-sided or two-sided alternative hypothesis, keep in mind that most of us are not familiar enough with grizzly bear behavior to have any expectations as to whether females would be more or less likely to be killed. State H_0 and H_a mathematically.

b. Report the sample proportion $\hat{p}$.

c. Report the standardized sample proportion z.

d. Report the P-value.

e. Was a disproportionate number of killed bears female, or could the sample proportion have come about by chance?

f. Would your answer to part (e) be the same if you had formulated the alternative hypothesis as $H_a : p > 0.5$? Explain.

g. Report a 95% confidence interval for population proportion of bears that are female, based on sample proportion of females in the killed bears.

h. Does your 95% confidence interval contain 0.5?

9.70 A survey was completed by 446 students at a large university in the fall of 2003. Students were asked to pick their favorite color from black, blue, green, orange, pink, purple, red, yellow.

a. If colors were equally popular, what proportion (to three decimal places) of students would choose each color?

b. Pick a color that you suspect will be *more* popular than others. Using software to access the survey data, report the sample proportion who preferred the color you chose.

c. Tell whether or not your sample proportion is in fact higher than the proportion you calculated in part (a).

d. Use software to produce a 95% confidence interval for the proportion of all students who would choose that color.

e. Does your confidence interval contain the proportion you calculated in part (a), or is it strictly above, or strictly below?

f. Tell whether a 90% confidence interval would be wider or narrower than the interval you produced in part (d).

g. Software should be used to carry out a hypothesis test to see if the sample proportion choosing your color was high enough to assert that, overall, students picked that color more than if they were choosing at random from eight colors. Report the standardized sample proportion z.

h. Report the P-value.

i. State your conclusions, using 0.05 as the cutoff for small P-values.

9.71 In a survey of 446 students, respondents were asked to pick a whole number at random, anywhere from 1 to 20.

a. If all 20 numbers were equally likely to be chosen, what proportion of students would choose each number?

b. Pick a number that you suspect could be chosen *less* often than others. Using software to access the survey data, report the sample proportion who picked the number you suspected would be chosen less often.

c. Is the sample proportion in fact lower than the proportion you calculated in part (a)?

d. Use software to produce a 95% confidence interval for the proportion of all students who would choose that number. (Report your interval to three decimal places.)

e. Does your confidence interval contain the proportion you calculated in part (a), or is it strictly above, or strictly below?

f. Use software to carry out a hypothesis test to see if the sample proportion choosing your number was low enough to assert that, overall, students picked that number less than if they were choosing at random from twenty numbers: Report the standardized sample proportion z.

g. Report the P-value for your test.

h. State your conclusions, using 0.05 as the cutoff for small P-values.

Using the Normal Table [see end of book] or Software

9.72 Exercise 9.86 will carry out a test of the hypothesis that the proportion of misaligned eyes in a sample of artists' self-portraits (0.09) is significantly higher than 0.05, which is the proportion in the general population. Output shows z to be $+7.78$. Explain why a normal table would not be helpful in finding the P-value, given the value of z.

*9.73 Exercise 9.40 asked for the standardized sample proportion z when testing if, in general, a minority of female terminal cancer patients die the week before (as opposed to after) Christmas, given the sample proportion was 2,858 out of 5,776. Find the exact P-value, if z was found to be -0.79 in a test against the alternative $H_a : p < 0.5$.

9.74 Exercise 9.43 asked for the standardized sample proportion z when testing if, in general, a minority of black terminal cancer patients die the week before (as opposed to after) Thanksgiving, given the sample proportion was 700 out of 1,309. Find the exact P-value, if z was found to be $+2.52$ in a test against the alternative $H_a : p < 0.5$, keeping in mind that the P-value for this alternative is the probability of z being *less* than or equal to $+2.52$.

9.75 Exercise 9.44 asked for the standardized sample proportion z when testing if, in general, a minority of elderly terminal cancer patients died the week before (as opposed to after) Christmas, given sample proportion was 3,547 out of 6,968. Find the exact P-value, if z was found to be $+1.51$ in a test against the two-sided alternative $H_a : p \neq 0.5$, keeping in mind that the P-value for this alternative is twice the probability of z being this far from zero in either direction.

*9.76 Exercise 9.59 mentioned a z statistic of 2.16 in testing to see if the sample proportion of soldiers killed in Iraq was significantly higher than a proposed population proportion. What would the P-value be in this case?

*9.77 Exercise 9.38 looked for evidence that the population proportion of students wearing corrective lenses is greater than 0.5, given a standardized sample proportion of $z = +0.85$. Report the P-value for this test.

9.78 Exercise 9.39 looked for evidence that the population proportion of off-campus students walking to school is less than 0.5, given a standardized sample proportion of $z = -0.53$. Report the P-value for this test.

CHAPTER 9   SUMMARY

Results for inference about a population proportion in the form of confidence intervals and hypothesis tests are summarized separately below. First, we discuss in more general terms the contexts in which such inferences are performed.

The examples presented in this chapter all involved just a **single categorical variable**. Whether the specific variable was about eating breakfast or about the moon being full during an epileptic seizure, the binomial model introduced in Section 7.2 of Chapter 7 was in place, in that each individual either did or did not belong in the category of interest. Whenever inference is to be performed for a single categorical variable, we have in mind a larger population of individuals, and in each case, the individual either does or does not have the quality of interest. With respect to that variable, the population consists of a large num-

ber of *yes's* and *no's*. The proportion in the *yes* category in the population is unknown, and to gain information about it, a random sample is taken. By looking at the sample proportion in the *yes* category, we can draw conclusions about the unknown population proportion.

The simplest way to do this is with a **point estimate**: Use the sample proportion as a guess for the population proportion. Much more informative is the **confidence interval**, which supplements the point estimate with a margin of error. The confidence interval reports a range of plausible values for the population proportion, and the level of confidence with which this report is made. The other form of inference is a **hypothesis test**, which uses the sample proportion to decide whether or not a particular proposed value of the population proportion is plausible.

Most of the principles established in this chapter will also apply to situations where the single variable of interest is quantitative instead of categorical. Inference methods for single quantitative variables are presented in the next chapter.

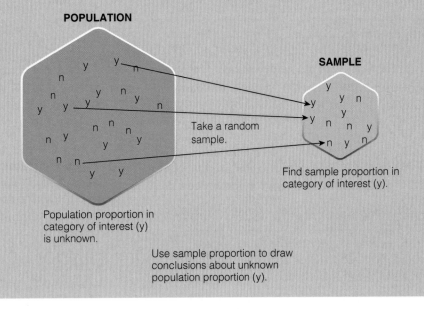

POPULATION

SAMPLE

Take a random sample.

Population proportion in category of interest (y) is unknown.

Find sample proportion in category of interest (y).

Use sample proportion to draw conclusions about unknown population proportion (y).

Confidence Intervals for Proportions

A confidence interval lets us report a **range of plausible values** for the unknown population proportion, based on the sample proportion and sample size.

When performing inference about a single categorical variable, a confidence interval supplements our point estimate with a *margin of error* that tells within what distance of the sample proportion we can fairly safely claim the unknown population pro-

portion to be. The methods presented here yield approximately correct results as long as the sample is random and large enough so that a normal approximation applies:

■ Our general rule of thumb is that $n\hat{p} \geq 10$ and $n(1 - \hat{p}) \geq 10$, which is the same as requiring that the observed counts in (X) and out $(n - X)$ of the category of interest be at least 10.

- The population should be at least 10 times the sample size to guarantee approximate independence of selections when sampling without replacement, so that our formula for standard deviation is correct.

- Larger samples yield narrower confidence intervals. It is common for opinion polls to survey about 1,000 people, in which case the margin of error is about 0.03.

- We can obtain narrower, more precise intervals at lower levels of confidence and wider, less precise intervals at higher levels of confidence.

- Informally, we can judge whether a particular proposed value of the parameter is plausible by checking whether or not it is contained in the confidence interval.

- One correct interpretation of a 95% confidence interval is to say we are 95% confident that the population proportion is in the interval. Another correct interpretation is to say the probability is 95% that an interval produced by this method succeeds in capturing the population proportion.

Confidence Interval for Population Proportion

An approximate 95% confidence interval for the unknown population proportion p based on a sample proportion $\hat{p}$ from a random sample of size n is

$$\hat{p} \pm 2\sqrt{\frac{\hat{p}(1 - \hat{p})}{n}}$$

Intervals at other levels of confidence can be found by replacing 2 with appropriate multipliers based on normal probabilities, or with 1.96 for a more accurate 95% confidence interval.

- 1.645 for 90% confidence
- 2.326 for 98% confidence
- 2.576 for 99% confidence

Hypothesis Tests about Proportions

A hypothesis test helps us decide whether a proposed value for the population proportion is plausible. The mechanics of the test require us to calculate a number that measures how different the sample proportion is from that proposed value, taking sample size and spread of the distribution of sample proportion into account. This standardized difference follows a standard normal (z) distribution if certain conditions are met.

- Once the question has been framed in terms of two opposing points of view, there are four basic steps in a test of hypotheses about population proportion, corresponding to the four basic statistical processes (see page 67).

  Conclusions of the hypothesis test should always be stated in context, in terms of the specific categorical variable of interest.

- Whether to use a one-sided or two-sided alternative must be decided from the problem statement, not from the value of observed sample proportion. When in doubt, a two-sided alternative should be used, because it is more conservative in that it makes it more difficult to reject the null hypothesis. In general, the P-value for a two-sided alternative is twice that for a one-sided alternative.

- The most common cutoff probability α for what P-values should be considered "small" is 0.05. In some contexts, other cutoff probabilities such as 0.10 or 0.01 are more appropriate.

- Larger samples tend to make it easier to reject a null hypothesis. A very small P-value means there is very strong evidence against the null hypothesis. It does not necessarily mean that there is a huge difference between the observed sample proportion $\hat{p}$ and p_0. Conversely, a very small sample may result in a P-value that is not small, failing to produce statistical evidence of a difference, even if the difference actually exists.

- A **Type I Error** is made when the null hypothesis is rejected, even though it is actually true. Setting a cutoff probability α is tantamount to dictating the probability of committing a Type I Error. A **Type II Error** is made when the null hypothesis is not rejected, even though it is actually false. Tests with very small sample sizes are especially susceptible to Type II Errors. Users of hypothesis tests should think carefully about the consequences of committing either type of error.

Testing Hypotheses about a Population Proportion

If a problem about a single categorical variable is expressed as a question of whether or not the population proportion equals a certain proposed value, a test of hypotheses can be carried out as follows.

0. **Problem Statement:** State null and alternative hypotheses about unknown population proportion p. These are expressed mathematically as

$$H_0 : p = p_0 \text{ vs. } H_a : \begin{cases} p > p_0 \\ p < p_0 \\ p \neq p_0 \end{cases}$$

where p_0 is the hypothesized value of the population proportion.

1. **Data Production:** Check if the sample is unbiased and that the population is at least 10 times the sample size. Verify that the sample size is large enough to permit a normal approximation: Check if np_0 and $n(1 - p_0)$ are both at least 10.

2. **Summarizing:** Find the observed sample proportion $\hat{p}$, and if the alternative is one-sided, check if this sample proportion tends in the direction claimed by the alternative.

Find the standardized sample proportion $z = \dfrac{\hat{p} - p_0}{\sqrt{\dfrac{p_0(1 - p_0)}{n}}}$.

3. **Probability:** Identify the P-value as the probability, assuming the null hypothesis $H_0 : p = p_0$ is true, of a sample proportion $\hat{p}$ at least as extreme as the one observed. Specifically, in terms of standardized sample proportion z, the P-value is the probability of a standard normal variable

   - *greater than or equal to z,* if we have $H_a : p > p_0$.
   - *less than or equal to z,* if we have $H_a : p < p_0$.
   - at least as far from zero *in either direction* as z, if we have $H_a : p \neq p_0$.

4. **Inference:** If the P-value is "small," then the observed sample proportion is improbable under the assumption that the null hypothesis $H_0 : p = p_0$ is true. We deem the assumption unreasonable and *reject* the null hypothesis in favor of the alternative. In this case, we conclude the population proportion is greater/less/different than the proposed value.

   If, on the other hand, the P-value is not small, we have not produced compelling statistical evidence against the null hypothesis. Because it was the "status quo" or default situation, we continue to believe the proportion proposed in H_0 to be plausible.

■ Results of hypothesis tests are never completely conclusive. If we reject the null hypothesis, then we have evidence that the alternative hypothesis is true. This evidence does not mean that we have proven the null hypothesis to be false. If we do not reject the null hypothesis, then we have failed to produce evidence to refute it. Our lack of evidence does not mean that we have proven the null hypothesis to be true.

Confidence Intervals and Hypothesis Tests

Confidence intervals and hypothesis tests are directly related. We can invoke this relationship informally by saying that if a proposed value of population proportion is contained in our confidence interval, we expect not to reject the null hypothesis that population proportion equals that value. If the value falls outside the confidence interval, we anticipate that the null hypothesis will be rejected. To relate confidence intervals and hypothesis tests more formally, it would be necessary to take into account the confidence level and cutoff probability α, as well as whether the test alternative is one-sided or two-sided.

CHAPTER 9   EXERCISES

Note: Asterisked numbers indicate exercises whose answers are provided in the Solutions to Selected Exercises section, on page 689.

Additional exercises appeared after each section: confidence intervals (Section 9.1) on page 406, and hypothesis tests (Section 9.2) on page 439.

Warming Up: INFERENCE FOR SINGLE CATEGORICAL VARIABLES

9.79 An article entitled "Courtship in the Monogamous Convict Cichlid; What Are Individuals Saying to Rejected and Selected Mates?" considered courtship behavior of male and female convict cichlids (damselfish). "The courtship of both male and female convict cichlids is characterized by movements (i.e., events) such as tail beating, quivering and brushing . . ."[39]

a. For each couple (female fish and her selected mate), the researchers looked at average daily courtship rate for the female and for the male, to see if the two were related. Were the researchers focusing here on one categorical, one quantitative, one each categorical and quantitative, two categorical, or two quantitative variables?

b. To display the relationship between female courtship rate and male courtship rate for 11 fish couples, would researchers use a histogram, side-by-side boxplots, bar graph, or scatterplot?

c. Researchers wanted to see if females' courtship rates toward selected males turned out to be higher than their courtship rates toward rejected males. Were they focusing here on one categorical, one quantitative, one each categorical and quantitative, two categorical, or two quantitative variables?

d. To display the difference between courtship rates toward selected versus rejected males, if a paired design was used, would researchers use a histogram, side-by-side boxplots, bar graph, or scatterplot?

e. To diplay the difference between courtship rates toward selected versus rejected males, if a two-sample design was used, would researchers use a histogram, side-by-side boxplots, bar graph, or scatterplot?

9.80 An article entitled "Courtship in the Monogamous Convict Cichlid; What Are Individuals Saying to Rejected and Selected Mates?" considered courtship behavior of male and female damselfish. The author writes, "I randomly selected 12 videotaped trials for analysis of courtship behaviour. When I collected data from the videotapes, I had no knowledge of which male was ultimately selected for the particular tank I was watching."[40] Was this done to avoid the placebo effect, the experimenter effect, the problem of faulty memory in retrospective studies, or the problem of participants' behavior being influenced in prospective studies?

9.81 A report on amyotrophic lateral sclerosis (ALS) found that the proportion having the disease was higher for Italian soccer players compared with the general population. The researchers suggested several explanations, none of them with certainty. For example, they speculated that therapeutic drugs may

More exercises for this chapter are featured in the **TBP** Supplement on pages 902 through 909. End-of-chapter activities are described on page 900.

be involved, in which case it would make sense to compare rates of ALS for soccer players who do and do not use therapeutic drugs.[41] Describe two groups whose data could be compared, in order to test each of the following additional possible explanations offered by the researchers:

a. Perhaps ALS is related to heavy physical exercise, and therefore not related particularly to soccer.

b. Environmental toxins like fertilizers or herbicides used on soccer fields might play a role.

Exploring the Big Picture: CONFIDENCE INTERVALS AND HYPOTHESIS TESTS FOR PROPORTIONS

9.82 Forty employers in a variety of fields and cities were surveyed in 2004 on topics relating to company benefits, and the degree to which employees were supported in terms of flexible work hours and child-care assistance. One question asked if the employer had any experience or knowledge about attention-deficit hyperactive disorder (ADHD). Responses of either yes (y) or no (n) are shown below.

n	n	n	n	y	n	y	n	n	y	n	y	y	n	n	y	y	n	y	n
n	n	n	y	y	n	n	n	y	y	n	n	y	n	y	n	n	n	n	n

a. Find the sample proportion with a *yes* response.

b. Find the approximate standard deviation of sample proportion, rounding to the nearest thousandth.

c. Are there at least 10 each in the two categories of interest (yes and no)?

d. Set up a 95% confidence interval for the proportion of all employers who have experience or knowledge of ADHD.

e. Does the correctness of your interval depend on those 40 employers being a representative sample of all employers, or on the survey question eliciting accurate responses, or on both of these, or on neither of these?

f. Based on your interval, which one of the following conclusions is most appropriate?

1. The data show without a doubt that the proportion of all employers with experience or knowledge about ADHD is less than 0.5.

2. The data provide no evidence at all that the proportion of all employers with experience or knowledge about ADHD is less than 0.5.

3. The data may barely indicate that the proportion of all employers with experience or knowledge about ADHD is less than 0.5.

9.83 A study of wolf spiders by Persons and Uetz, published in the online journal *Animal Behavior* in November 2004, reports that, "of the 120 virgin females paired with males, 87 attempted cannibalism by lunging repeatedly at the male. Ten of these attempts at premating cannibalism were successful."[42] For the following, round your answers to the nearest thousandth (three decimal places).

a. Find the sample proportion $\hat{p}$ that attempted cannibalism.

b. What is the approximate standard deviation of sample proportion that attempted cannibalism?

c. Report a 95% confidence interval for population proportion, if we are interested in the proportion of all virgin female wolf spiders that would attempt cannibalism.

d. Of the 120 females observed, find the sample proportion $\hat{p}$ that succeeded at cannibalism.

e. What is the approximate standard deviation of sample proportion in part (d)?

f. Report a 95% confidence interval for population proportion, if we are interested in the proportion of all virgin female wolf spiders that would attempt cannibalism *and* succeed.

g. In general, is a confidence interval for a given sample size wider or narrower for sample proportions that are farther from 0.5?

h. Of the 87 females that attempted cannibalism, find the sample proportion that succeeded.

i. What is the approximate standard deviation of the sample proportion in part (h)?

j. Report a 95% confidence interval for the population proportion, if we are interested in the proportion that succeed, *given* that a virgin female wolf spider has attempted cannibalism.

9.84 A poll conducted by the Siena College Research Institute in 2005 found that "81%

of people surveyed would vote for a woman for president."[43]

a. Is this enough information to report a point estimate for the proportion of all people who would vote for a woman for president?

b. What other information would be needed to set up a 95% confidence interval for the proportion of all people who would vote for a woman for president?

c. If the pollsters desired a margin of error no bigger than 0.02, how many people should be sampled?

d. Besides sample size, what other detail must be provided if conclusions are to be drawn in the form of a hypothesis test at the 0.05 level of significance?

9.85 "New Transplant Protocol Improves Survival Rate" reported in 2004 about a new drug treatment whereby intestine transplant recipients were given an injection beforehand that killed the immune system cells that typically attack a donor organ. It states that "96% of the [123] patients survived after one year. The normal one-year survival rate for intestine transplant recipients is around 80%."[44] This output shows results of a test carried out with software.

```
Test of p = 0.8 vs p > 0.8
Sample    X    N   Sample p   95.0% Lower Bound   P-Value
1        118  123  0.959350        0.916432        0.000
```

a. Explain why the alternative hypothesis uses ">" instead of "<" or "≠."

b. Explain why the *P*-value was found using binomial probabilities, instead of with a normal approximation.

c. Is there significant improvement with the new protocol? Tell what part of the output you used to get your answer.

d. Given the results of the test, would you expect a confidence interval for overall proportion surviving with the new protocol to contain 0.80? Explain.

9.86 Researchers at Harvard Medical School proposed that Rembrandt may have been stereoblind, judging by the misalignment of his eyes in some self-portraits. Furthermore, the researchers state that "we have been examining frontal photographs of famous artists in the collection of the National Portrait Gallery in Washington, D.C. So far, a larger proportion of the artists (28% [15 of 53]) than of members of the general population (5%) show misaligned eyes by the light reflex test—a finding consistent with our hypothesis that stereoblindness is not a handicap to an artist and that it may even be an asset."[45] Based on the data provided, a formal hypothesis test may be carried out.

a. State the null and alternative hypotheses about the proportion of all artists with misaligned eyes, first with words and then mathematically, if we seek to provide evidence that misaligned eyes are more common in artists than in the general population.

b. Does the sample proportion tend in the direction of your alternative hypothesis?

c. Do we verify that the general population size is much larger than 530 in order to assert that sample count is approximately binomial, or in order to assert that sample count and proportion are approximately normal?

d. If we expect 5% to have misaligned eyes, can we expect to get at least 10 each with eyes that are misaligned and aligned in our sample of 53 faces?

e. Software was used to carry out a test, first requesting the *P*-value to be calculated as an actual binomial probability, then requesting a normal approximation. Tell which one of the two results should be reported, and why.

```
Test of p = 0.05 vs p > 0.05

Sample    X    N    Sample p    95.0% Lower Bound    Exact P-Value
1         15   53   0.283019          0.183252              0.000

Sample    X    N    Sample p    95.0% Lower Bound    Z-Value    P-Value
1         15   53   0.283019          0.181242        7.78       0.000
```

f. Tell which one of these is the correct conclusion to draw, based on the size of the *P*-value:

1. The data prove that misaligned eyes are more common in artists.

2. The data fail to provide evidence that misaligned eyes are more common in artists.

3. The data prove that misaligned eyes are no more common in artists than they are in others.

4. The data provide evidence that misaligned eyes are more common in artists.

g. The researchers propose that "stereoblindness is not a handicap to an artist." The null hypothesis would be that 5% of all artists are stereoblind (with misaligned eyes), and if the alternative claims that stereoblindness is a handicap for artists, it would state that *fewer* than 5% of all artists are stereoblind. Explain why this alternative hypothesis could be discounted just by looking at sample proportion, without carrying out a formal test.

Was Rembrandt stereoblind?

9.87 In June 1999, Microsoft was found guilty of anti-competitive behavior and ordered to be split in two. In January 2001, Microsoft argued in a filing to the U.S. Court of Appeals that the trial court had made a mistake. Would this have been a Type I or a Type II Error? Explain.

9.88 "Radiation Risk Overstated" reported in 2005 that women receiving radiation for breast cancer may no longer face an increased risk of potentially deadly heart damage from the treatment.[46] In earlier decades, radiation doses were high enough, and inaccurate enough, to put the heart in jeopardy, but radiation therapy became much safer over the years.

a. If the null hypothesis states that radiation for breast cancer does not damage the heart, the report suggests that as of 2005, people may be committing which type of error: Type I or Type II?

b. What is the potential harm of thinking radiation for breast cancer damages the heart, when in fact it does not: avoiding beneficial treatment for breast cancer, or putting the heart in jeopardy?

9.89 Teen athletes often wear ankle and knee braces to protect themselves from sports injuries.

a. Suppose the proportion of all teen athletes who suffer ankle and knee injuries is p_0. The null hypothesis would state that the proportion p of teen athletes with ankle and knee braces who suffer such injuries is the same—$H_0 : p = p_0$. State the alternative hypothesis, first in words and then mathematically, if we suspect that ankle and knee braces help protect against injuries.

b. A study of student athletes in 100 North Carolina high schools in the late 1990s found that "North Carolina teens who wore ankle and knee braces were 1.6 to 1.7 times more likely to become injured than their fellow athletes." Explain why there is no need to find a standardized sample proportion and a *P*-value to decide between the null and alternative hypotheses (from part [a]) in this case.

c. Before concluding that ankle and knee braces actually increase the likelihood of injury, possible confounding variables should be taken into account. Give at least one reason why someone wearing such a brace might be more susceptible to injury, besides the brace itself causing the injury.

9.90 An annual Gallup poll survey asked about 1,000 American adults, "If you could have only one child, would you want a boy or a girl?"[47] Assuming those surveyed were evenly divided between men and women, and based on the information that 64% of the men and 68% of the women had a preference, there were about 320 men and 340 women with a preference.

a. Of the 320 men who expressed a preference, 225 wanted a boy. Based on the output below, can we conclude that a majority of all men with a preference would want a boy? Explain.

```
Sample    X    N   Sample p         95.0% CI
1        225  320  0.703125   (0.653067, 0.753183)
```

b. Of the 340 women who expressed a preference, 180 wanted a girl. Based on the output below, can we conclude that a majority of all women with a preference would want a girl? Explain.

```
Sample    X    N   Sample p         95.0%  CI
1        180  340  0.529412   (0.476357, 0.582467)
```

c. For which of the two data sets would standardized sample proportion (z) be larger: that for men or for women?

d. For which of the two data sets would the P-value be smaller: that for men or for women?

9.91 In a population of several hundred students, the proportion who are ambidextrous (neither left- nor right-handed) is 0.03. Repeated random samples of size 40 were taken, and for each sample a 95% confidence interval was constructed for population proportion ambidextrous. This was done 20 times, for a total of 20 confidence intervals.

```
X   N   Sample p          95.0% CI            Exact P-Value
1   40  0.025000   (0.000633, 0.131586)         1.000
2   40  0.050000   (0.006114, 0.169197)         0.634
0   40  0.000000   (0.000000, 0.072158)         0.327
2   40  0.050000   (0.006114, 0.169197)         0.634
1   40  0.025000   (0.000633, 0.131586)         1.000
1   40  0.025000   (0.000633, 0.131586)         1.000
2   40  0.050000   (0.006114, 0.169197)         0.634
2   40  0.050000   (0.006114, 0.169197)         0.634
0   40  0.000000   (0.000000, 0.072158)         0.327
1   40  0.025000   (0.000633, 0.131586)         1.000
1   40  0.025000   (0.000633, 0.131586)         1.000
1   40  0.025000   (0.000633, 0.131586)         1.000
0   40  0.000000   (0.000000, 0.072158)         0.327
1   40  0.025000   (0.000633, 0.131586)         1.000
1   40  0.025000   (0.000633, 0.131586)         1.000
4   40  0.100000   (0.027925, 0.236637)         0.031
1   40  0.025000   (0.000633, 0.131586)         1.000
1   40  0.025000   (0.000633, 0.131586)         1.000
0   40  0.000000   (0.000000, 0.072158)         0.327
2   40  0.050000   (0.006114, 0.169197)         0.634
```

a. Explain why exact binomial confidence intervals were requested, instead of confidence intervals based on a normal approximation.

b. In general, what is the probability that a 95% confidence interval does *not* contain the true value of the parameter?

c. If 20 intervals are produced, each with 95% confidence, in the long run about how many will fail to capture the true value of the parameter?

d. How many of the 20 intervals above fail to contain the population proportion, 0.03?

e. Will your answer to part (d) be exactly the case in every set of 20 confidence intervals? Explain.

9.92 In a population of several hundred students, the proportion who are ambidextrous (neither left- nor right-handed) is 0.03. Repeated random samples of size 40 were taken, and for each sample a hypothesis test was carried out, testing if population proportion ambidextrous equals 0.03. This was done twenty times, for a total of 20 tests. The preceding exercise shows sample proportion $\hat{p}$ and the accompanying P-value for each test.

  a. Because the rule of thumb $np \geq 10$ and $n(1 - p) \geq 10$ is not satisfied (40(0.03) is only 1.2), binomial P-values were produced. Explain why there are no z statistics.

  b. In general, what is the probability that a test of a null hypothesis that is actually true rejects it, using 0.05 as the cutoff level α for what is considered to be a small P-value?

  c. If 20 tests of a true null hypothesis are carried out at the 0.05 level, in the long run about how many will (correctly) fail to reject it? How many will (incorrectly) reject it?

  d. How many of the 20 P-values above are small enough to reject $H_0 : p = 0.03$ at the $\alpha = 0.05$ level? (If any are small enough, tell what they are.)

  e. Will your answer to part (d) be exactly the case in every set of 20 tests? Explain.

  f. How many of the 20 P-values above are small enough to reject $H_0 : p = 0.3$ at the $\alpha = 0.10$ level?

Using Software [see Technology Guide]: INFERENCE FOR PROPORTIONS

9.93 *Why we don't come: Patient perceptions on no-shows*, published in the *Annals of Family Medicine* in December 2004, reports that 15 of 34 patients (44%) interviewed cited lack of respect by the health-care system as a reason for failing to keep doctor's appointments in the past. Specifically, being kept waiting for an appointment, in the waiting room, and in the exam room were taken as evidence of insufficient respect.[48]

  a. Explain why a formal test would not be necessary in order to decide if a majority of all patients miss appointments because of perceived lack of respect.

  b. Use software to produce a 95% confidence interval for the proportion of all patients who miss appointments because of perceived lack of respect.[48]

  c. If a higher level of confidence were desired, would the interval be wider or narrower?

9.94 A survey was completed by 446 students in introductory statistics courses at a large university in the fall of 2003. We will consider students to never eat meat if they answered "yes" (as opposed to "no" or "sometimes") to a question that asked if they were vegetarian.

  a. Use software to access the survey data and produce a 95% confidence interval for the proportion of all students who never eat meat, assuming the surveyed students were a representative sample.

  b. The proportion of adult Americans who never eat meat is reported to be 0.03. Does your interval contain 0.03?

  c. Test whether the proportion who never eat meat in the larger population from which surveyed students were sampled could equal 0.03. Draw your conclusions, using 0.05 as the cutoff for a small P-value.

  d. Explain how your answers to parts (b) and (c) are consistent with one another.

  e. Report the P-value if you had tested against the one-sided alternative that proportion of all such students who never eat meat was *greater than* 0.03.

9.95 A survey was completed by 446 students in introductory statistics courses at a large university in the fall of 2003. Students reported whether or not they had pierced ear(s).

  a. Use software to access the survey data and produce a 95% confidence interval for the proportion of all students with pierced ear(s), assuming the surveyed students were a representative sample.

  b. Does your interval contain 0.50?

c. Test whether the proportion with pierced ear(s) in the larger population from which surveyed students were sampled could equal 0.50; report the z statistic.

d. Draw your conclusions, using 0.05 as the cutoff for a small P-value.

e. Explain how your answers to parts (b) and (d) are consistent with one another.

f. Would sample proportion be higher or lower if only females were surveyed?

g. Would standardized sample proportion z be higher or lower if only female students were surveyed?

h. Would the P-value be larger or smaller if only female students were surveyed?

Using the Normal Table [see end of book] or Software: INFERENCE FOR PROPORTIONS

*9.96 Exercise 9.36 asked for the z-score when a sample of 708 strep cultures had a sample proportion of 0.10 resistant to antibiotics, if in general 0.05 are resistant (noting that the standard deviation of sample proportion is 0.01). It also asked for an estimate of the probability that the sample proportion would be this high. Would a normal table be helpful in order to report this P-value more precisely? Explain.

9.97 Exercise 9.62 produced z statistics for various tests about how well subjects could match photos of dogs and their owners. Use the normal table or software to report the P-value if each of these z-statistics is used to test against the one-sided alternative $H_a : p > 0.5$.

a. $z = 0.15$

b. $z = 1.40$

c. $z = -1.34$

*9.98 Exercise 9.46 produced a z statistic of -2.06 when testing if the proportion of blacks in the

House of Representatives was significantly lower than the proportion in the U.S. population. Use the normal table or software to find the P-value for this (one-sided) test.

9.99 Exercise 9.90 on page 000 explored whether a majority of all men would prefer a boy, based on a sample of 320 men with a preference in which 225 would rather have a boy. It also explored whether a majority of all women would prefer a girl, based on 180 out of 340 with that preference.

a. Calculate the z statistic for testing against the alternative $H_a : p > 0.5$, based on the data for the men.

b. Use the normal table or software to find the P-value for the test in part (a).

c. Calculate the z statistic for testing against the alternative $H_a : p > 0.5$, based on the data for the women.

d. Use the normal table or software to find the P-value for the test in part (c).

Discovering Research: INFERENCE FOR PROPORTIONS

9.100 Find an article or report that includes mention of sample size and summarizes values of a categorical variable with a count, proportion, or percentage. Based on that information, set up a 95% confidence interval for population proportion in the category of interest. If the article reports a margin of error, tell whether or not it is consistent with the one you calculated.

9.101 Find an Internet report or newspaper article about a mistake that has been made in a yes-or-no decision.

a. State the null hypothesis in words.

b. Tell whether the mistake was a Type I or Type II Error.

Reporting on Research: INFERENCE FOR PROPORTIONS

9.102 Use results of Exercises 9.40, 9.43, 9.44, and 9.45 and relevant findings from the Internet to make a report on postponement of cancer

death until after holidays that relies on statistical information.

Inference for a Single Quantitative Variable

Are mean yearly earnings of all students at a university less than $5,000?

Juan Silva/Getty Images

Thinking about the population of students' earnings— an inference problem

Q In Chapter 9, we established methods for drawing conclusions about the unknown population proportion, based on a sample proportion, for situations where the variable of interest was categorical. Now we turn to situations where the single variable of interest is quantitative, as in the above question about earnings. In this case, we focus on the mean as the main summary of interest, and we want to infer something about the unknown population mean, based on an observed sample mean. Much of what we established for categorical variables still applies.

The underlying concepts in performing inference for single categorical variables continue to apply when we perform inference for single quantitative variables. The mechanics of the inference procedures, on the other hand, require us to summarize and standardize a different type of variable—quantitative instead of categorical. The main summaries for quantitative samples and populations were first introduced in Chapter 4.

Pages 911 to 913 of The *Teaching the Big Picture (TBP) Supplement* outline in detail the similarities and differences between inference procedures for means and proportions.

- **Population mean** is μ (called "mu"), a parameter.
- **Sample mean** is $\bar{x}$ (called "x-bar"), a statistic.
- **Population standard deviation** is σ (called "sigma"), a parameter.
- **Sample standard deviation** is s, a statistic.

When we perform inference about means, a different distribution often applies instead of the standard normal (z) distribution with which we are so familiar by now. The sample mean $\bar{x}$ standardizes in some situations to z but in others to a new type of random variable, t. We will begin to address the distinction between inference with z and with t in Example 10.4 on page 464, after establishing $\bar{x}$ to be our point estimate for μ.

Instead of using capital letters to distinguish random variables from statistics or distributions, we will write them in boldface in Part IV; for example, *z*, $\bar{x}$, or *t*. The distinction is subtle, and students can generally overlook it without confusion.

First, let's return to our opening question about students' earnings, and phrase it in three different ways to parallel the three forms of inference that will be presented.

EXAMPLE 10.1 POINT ESTIMATE, CONFIDENCE INTERVAL, AND HYPOTHESIS TEST QUESTIONS

Background: In a representative sample of 446 students at a university, mean earnings for the previous year were $3,776.

Questions:

1. What is our best guess for the mean earnings of all students at this university the previous year?

2. What interval should contain the mean earnings of all students at this university for the previous year?

3. Is there evidence that the mean of earnings of all students at this university was less than $5,000?

Response: We will answer these questions as we develop a theory for performing the three types of inference about an unknown population mean.

10.1 Inference for a Mean When Population Standard Deviation Is Known or Sample Size Is Large

When we used the rules of probability in Chapter 8 to summarize the behavior of sample mean for random samples of a certain size taken from a population with mean μ, we arrived at results concerning center, spread, and shape of the distribution of sample mean. As far as the center is concerned, we stated that the distribution of sample mean $\bar{x}$ has a mean equal to the population mean μ.

EXAMPLE 10.2 SAMPLE MEAN AS A POINT ESTIMATE FOR THE POPULATION MEAN

Background: The unknown mean of earnings of all students at a university is denoted μ.

Questions: If we take repeated random samples of a given size from the population of all students, where should their sample mean earnings be centered? If we take a single sample, what is our best guess for μ?

Responses: Some random samples would have a sample mean less than μ and others greater than μ, but overall the sample means should average out to μ. Therefore, sample mean earnings is our best guess for unknown population mean earnings μ.

Practice: *Try Exercise 10.1(a) on page 477.*

This example justifies answering the first question of Example 10.1 in the most natural way: Our best guess for the mean earnings of *all* students at that university would be the mean earnings of the *sampled* students—$3,776. Probability theory assures us that sample mean $\bar{x}$ is an unbiased estimator for population mean μ as long as our sample is random and earnings are reported accurately.

Just as we saw for proportions, we must exercise caution whenever we make generalizations from a sample mean to the mean of the larger population.

EXAMPLE 10.3 WHEN A SAMPLE MEAN IS A POOR ESTIMATE FOR THE POPULATION MEAN

Background: When students come for help in office hours during a given week, a professor asks them how much time they took to complete the previous week's assignment. Their mean completion time was 3.5 hours.

Question: What is the professor's best guess for the mean time all of her students took to complete the assignment?

Response: In this situation, sample mean is *not* an unbiased estimator for the population mean because the sampled students were not a representative sample of the larger population of students. If the professor were to guess 3.5, it would almost surely be an overestimate, because students coming for help in office hours would tend to take longer to get their homework done. There is no "best guess" in this case.

Practice: *Try Exercise 10.1(b) on page 477.*

Students in office hours—a biased sample?

Just as we saw in the case of sample proportion as a point estimate in Chapter 9, use of sample mean as a point estimate for population mean is of limited usefulness. Because the distribution of sample mean is continuous, there are infinitely many sample means possible, and our point estimate is practically guaranteed to be *incorrect*. Instead of making a single incorrect guess at the unknown population mean, we should either produce an interval that is likely to contain it, or conclude whether or not a proposed value of the population mean is plausible. In

Our point estimate, sample mean $\bar{x}$, does not include information from the distribution's spread, so it is the same whether we know the population standard deviation σ or not.

Admittedly, the assumption of known population standard deviation in most situations is a stretch: If the population mean is unknown, how could we somehow know the value of the population standard deviation? Once we have developed a theory that works for this simpler case, we can show students how to handle the more realistic case—when the population standard deviation is unknown.

other words, our goal is to perform inference in the form of confidence intervals or hypothesis tests. The key to how well we can close in on the value of population mean lies in the spread of the distribution of sample mean.

Once we begin to set up confidence intervals or carry out hypothesis tests to close in on the value of μ, standard deviation enters in and the process will differ, depending on whether or not the population standard deviation is known. To keep things as simple as possible at the beginning, we will assume at first that σ is known, in which case the standardized value of sample mean follows a standard normal (z) distribution.

If σ is not known, we must resort to standardizing with sample standard deviation s instead of population standard deviation σ, and the standardized value no longer follows a z distribution, but rather what is called a t distribution.

To clarify the contrast between situations where the standardized sample mean follows a z or t distribution, we consider two situations that are identical except that the population standard deviation is known in the first case and unknown in the second.

EXAMPLE 10.4 INFERENCE ABOUT A MEAN WHEN THE POPULATION STANDARD DEVIATION IS KNOWN VERSUS UNKNOWN

Background: In a sample of 12 students attending a particular community college, the mean travel time to school was found to be 18 minutes.

Question: For which of these two scenarios would inference be based on z and for which would it be based on t?

1. We want to draw conclusions about the mean travel time of all students at that college; travel time for *all* students at that college is assumed to have a standard deviation of $\sigma = 20$ minutes.

2. We want to draw conclusions about the mean travel time of all students at that college; travel time for the *sample* was found to have a standard deviation of $s = 20$ minutes.

Response: The first problem would be answered using inference based on z because the population standard deviation is known. The second problem would be answered using inference based on t because the population standard deviation is unknown.

Practice: *Try Exercise 10.3 on page 477.*

A Confidence Interval for the Population Mean Based on z

We begin with situations where the population standard deviation is known, as in the first problem in Example 10.4. We will also include situations where the sample is so large that the population standard deviation σ can be very closely approximated with the sample standard deviation s. First, we see how to set up a range of plausible values for an unknown population mean μ, based on the sample mean $\bar{x}$. After that, we will see how to test a hypothesis to decide whether or not to believe that the population mean μ equals some proposed value.

Because knowledge about an unknown population mean comes from understanding the distribution of sample mean, we should recall the most important results about sample mean obtained in Chapter 8.

Reviewing Results for the Distribution of Sample Mean

If random samples of size n are taken from a population with mean μ and standard deviation σ, then the distribution of sample mean $\bar{x}$ has

- mean μ
- standard deviation $\frac{\sigma}{\sqrt{n}}$
- shape approximately normal if sample size n is large enough

The claim about the mean of $\bar{x}$ requires that the sample be representative. The claim about the standard deviation requires the population to be at least 10 times the sample size so that samples taken without replacement are roughly independent. The claim about the shape holds if n is large enough to offset non-normality in the shape of the underlying population.

95% Confidence Intervals with *z*

Calculations are simplified if we seek a 95% confidence interval for the mean. In this case, the multiplier is approximately 2, as long as the population standard deviation is known and a z distribution applies.

Let's begin with a situation where both the population mean and standard deviation are known, and we use them to construct a *probability* interval for the sample mean when random samples of a given size are taken from that population.

EXAMPLE 10.5 A PROBABILITY INTERVAL FOR THE SAMPLE MEAN BASED ON A KNOWN POPULATION MEAN

Background: Assume the distribution of IQ to be normal with a mean of 100 and a standard deviation of 15, illustrated in the graph on the left. Suppose a random sample of 9 IQs is observed. Then the mean IQ for that sample has a mean of 100, a standard deviation of $15/\sqrt{9} = 15/3 = 5$, and a shape that is normal because IQs themselves are normally distributed. This distribution is shown in the graph on the right.

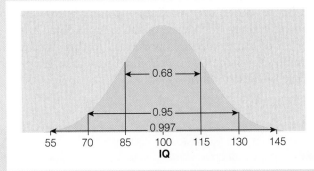
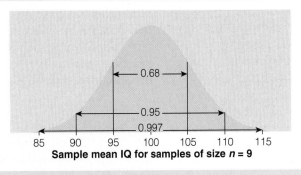

Question: What does the 95% part of the 68-95-99.7 Rule tell us about sample mean IQ in this situation?

Response: The rule tells us the probability is 95% that sample mean IQ in a sample of size 9 comes within 2 standard deviations of population mean IQ, where a standard deviation is 5 points: that is, in the interval (90, 110).

Practice: *Try Exercise 10.4(b) on page 477.*

A probability interval, such as the one we saw in Example 10.5, paves the way for our construction of a confidence interval. In order to make this transition for proportions when the variable of interest was categorical, we observed in Example 9.4 on page 392 that if a friend is within half a mile of your house, then your house is within half a mile of the friend. Similarly, if the sample mean falls within a certain distance of the population mean, then the population mean falls within the same distance of the sample mean.

However, sample mean is a random variable that obeys the laws of probability—the formal study of random behavior. The population mean is a fixed parameter (even if its value is unknown) and it does not behave randomly. The correct way to shift from probability statements about the sample mean to inference statements about the population mean is to use the word "confidence," as demonstrated in the next example.

On page 913 of the *TBP Supplement* is a graphical depiction of how the margin of error arises from a probability interval.

The guidelines for normality presented in Chapter 8 were established in the context of probability theory, when we were assuming the population distribution to be known. Now that we are in the "real world" and want to perform inference about unknown values of a population, we cannot know exactly what the population is shaped like. As usual, if there's something we would like to know about the population, we look to the sample. Thus, our criteria for setting up a confidence interval for an unknown population mean, which are based on a normal approximation, will be the same as those in Chapter 8 except we look at the shape of the *sample* instead of that of the population. Normal probability plots, described on page 914 of the *TBP Supplement*, are a good way to assess the normality of sample data.

EXAMPLE 10.6 THE MARGIN OF ERROR IN A CONFIDENCE INTERVAL FOR THE MEAN

Background: The distribution of IQ scores is normal with a standard deviation of 15.

Question: If we take a random sample of 9 IQs and use the sample mean IQ to set up a 95% confidence interval for the unknown population mean IQ, what would be the margin of error?

Response: The standard deviation of sample mean is population standard deviation divided by square root of sample size, or $15/\sqrt{9} = 5$. The margin of error is 2 standard deviations (of sample mean), or $2(5) = 10$.

Practice: Try Exercise 10.6 on page 478.

Now we are almost ready to present an extremely useful formula for constructing a 95% confidence interval for population mean. Because the formula requires the sample mean to be normal, you need to refer back to the guidelines established on page 361 of Chapter 8. These guidelines—which are now modified because in reality we can only assess the shape of the sample data, not the population—must be met for *all* of the procedures presented in this chapter. In practice—especially if the sample size is small—you should always check a graph of the sample data to justify use of these methods.

Guidelines for Approximate Normality of Sample Mean

We can assume the shape of the distribution of sample mean for random samples of size n to be approximately normal if

- a graph of the sample data appears approximately normal; or
- a graph of the sample data appears fairly symmetric (not necessarily single-peaked) and n is at least 15; or
- a graph of the sample data appears moderately skewed and n is at least 30.

If these guidelines are followed, then we may construct the confidence interval.

The Big Picture:
LOOKING BACK

95% Confidence Interval for Population Mean When Population Standard Deviation Is Known

An approximate 95% confidence interval for unknown population mean μ based on sample mean $\bar{x}$ from a random sample of size n is

$$\text{estimate} \pm \text{margin of error}$$
$$= \text{sample mean} \pm 2 \text{ standard deviations of sample mean}$$
$$= \bar{x} \pm 2\frac{\sigma}{\sqrt{n}}$$

where σ is the population standard deviation.

Notice the similarity between this confidence interval and the one for an unknown population proportion presented on page 396: sample proportion $\pm$ 2 standard deviations of sample proportion

$$\approx \hat{p} \pm 2\sqrt{\frac{\hat{p}(1-\hat{p})}{n}}$$

Here is an illustration of the sample mean, its standard deviation, the margin of error, and the confidence interval:

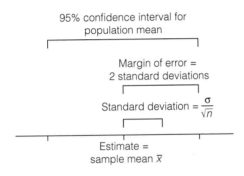

95% confidence interval for population mean

Margin of error = 2 standard deviations

Standard deviation = $\frac{\sigma}{\sqrt{n}}$

Estimate = sample mean $\bar{x}$

The above formula can be applied if a confidence interval is to be produced by hand. Otherwise, the interval can be requested using software by entering the data values and specifying the population standard deviation.

EXAMPLE 10.7 CONFIDENCE INTERVALS FOR A MEAN BY HAND OR WITH SOFTWARE

Background: A random sample of weights of female college students has been obtained:

| 110 | 110 | 112 | 120 | 120 | 120 | 125 | 125 | 130 | 130 | 132 | 133 | 134 | 135 | 135 | 135 | 145 | 148 | 159 |

Assume the standard deviation for weights of all female college students is 20 pounds.

Questions: How would we check background conditions and use the data to construct a 95% confidence interval for mean weight of all female college students by hand? How would we proceed if we were using software?

Responses: First we need to consider the sample size and the shape of the distribution, to make sure that n is large enough to offset any non-normality, so that sample mean would be approximately normal. A stemplot can easily be constructed by hand, and we see that the distribution is reasonably normal. At any rate, the sample size (19) is large enough to offset the small amount of right skewness that we should expect to see in a distribution of weight values.

Continued

```
11  002
12  00055
13  00234555
14  58
15  9
```

To set up the interval, we calculate the sample mean weight, 129.37. Since the population standard deviation is assumed to be 20 and the sample size is 19, our 95% confidence interval is $129.37 \pm 2\frac{20}{\sqrt{19}} = 129.37 \pm 9.18 = (120.19, 138.55)$.

If we had software at our disposal, we could start by producing a histogram of the weight values. Again, we would conclude that, although the shape is somewhat non-normal, 19 should be a large enough sample size to allow us to proceed.

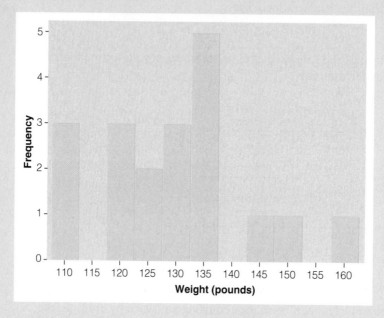

We can request a 95% confidence interval for the population mean, after entering the sample of 19 female weights listed above and specifying the population standard deviation σ to be 20.

```
One-Sample Z: Weight
The assumed sigma = 20
Variable          N      Mean     StDev    SE Mean        95.0% CI
Weight           19    129.37     12.82       4.59    ( 120.37, 138.37)
```

The 95% confidence interval for mean weight of all female college students is (120.37, 138.37). It is slightly different from the interval produced by hand because we used the multiplier 2 and the computer uses 1.96.

Practice: *Try Exercise 10.8(c) on page 478.*

Many teachers of statistics will agree that **variability** is the most important concept for students to understand. Individuals vary, and samples vary too, but sample mean does not vary as much as individual values do. This is the reason why statistics is so useful: We can close in on an unknown population parameter by using the corresponding statistic from a random sample. Probability theory taught us the exact nature of the variability of sample mean: Its standard deviation is population standard deviation *divided by square root of sample size*. Thus, in a very straightforward way, larger samples lead to statistics that tend to be closer to the unknown parameters that they estimate.

The following discussion by four students reminds us that this variability can be assessed as the entire width of the confidence interval, or as the margin of error around the sample mean, or as the standard deviation of sample mean. The last of these is estimated as $\frac{s}{\sqrt{n}}$ if σ is unknown.

Students Talk Stats

Confidence Interval for a Mean: Width, Margin of Error, Standard Deviation, and Standard Error

Suppose the four students have been asked to find the margin of error in the confidence interval for mean female weight, with output as shown in Example 10.7:

```
The assumed sigma = 20
Variable   N    Mean   StDev  SE Mean        95.0% CI
Weight    19  129.37   12.82     4.59  ( 120.37, 138.37)
```

Adam: *"It's standard deviation, right? So that would be 12.82."*

Brittany: *"For a 95% confidence interval, the margin of error is twice the standard deviation, which is twice 12.82, or 25.64."*

Carlos: *"The whole interval from 120 to 138 isn't even that wide. You forgot to divide by the square root of the sample size. The standard deviation of sample mean is 12.82 divided by the square root of 19. That's what you multiply by 2."*

Dominique: *"That's still not right. Remember we're supposed to work with population standard deviation sigma, which is 20. The standard deviation of sample mean is 20 divided by square root of 19, which is 4.59. That's the SE Mean in the output. The margin of error is 2 times that, or 9.18. The confidence interval is 129.37 plus or minus 9.18. That comes out to the interval from 120.19 to 138.55, which is just a little different from the output because the exact multiplier is 1.96, not 2."*

When you are deciding between the use of 2 or 1.96 as a multiplier in our confidence interval, it may be helpful to keep in mind that the *z* confidence interval is best used as a teaching tool. Students have a better chance of internalizing the process if the numbers are "nice." Furthermore, σ is rarely known in practice, and software produces an interval based on the appropriate *t* multiplier. This *t* multiplier is often closer to 2 than it is to 1.96. This book takes the approach of starting with 2 to make the formulas more streamlined for students. Eventually there is the option of replacing 2 with 1.96 for more accuracy.

On page 914 of the **TBP** *Supplement* is a graphical depiction of the margin of error for female weights, as discussed by the four students.

So far, we have required the population standard deviation σ to be known if we wanted to set up a 95% confidence interval for the unknown population mean using the multiplier 2 that comes from the z distribution. In fact, if the sample size is reasonably large—say, at least 30—then we can assume that the sample standard deviation s is close enough to σ that $\frac{s}{\sqrt{n}}$ is approximately the same as the standard deviation $\frac{\sigma}{\sqrt{n}}$ of $\overline{x}$. Thus, the z multiplier can be used if σ is known *or* if n is large.

95% Confidence Interval for μ When σ Is Unknown But n Is Large

If sample size n is fairly large (at least 30), an approximate 95% confidence interval for unknown population mean μ based on sample mean $\overline{x}$ and sample standard deviation s is

$$\overline{x} \pm 2\frac{s}{\sqrt{n}}$$

Additional details about *z* confidence intervals are included in the ***TBP Supplement.*** In Example TBP 10.1 on page 914, we refrain from using a *z* procedure because the sample is small and non-normal. Examples TBP 10.2 and TBP 10.3 starting on page 915 show how we can use the confidence interval to decide if a proposed value for μ is plausible or not.

Use of *z* probabilities simplifies matters when we hand-calculate a confidence interval for the mean based on a sample mean and sample standard deviation from a fairly large sample size. However, when we use software, we cannot request a *z* confidence interval or hypothesis test procedure unless we can specify the population standard deviation.

EXAMPLE 10.8 USING A Z MULTIPLIER IF THE POPULATION STANDARD DEVIATION IS UNKNOWN BUT THE SAMPLE SIZE IS LARGE

Background: In a representative sample of 446 students at a university, mean earnings for the previous year was \$3,776. The standard deviation for earnings of all students is unknown, but the sample standard deviation is found to be \$6,500.

Question: Can we use this information to construct a 95% confidence interval for mean earnings of all students at this university for the previous year?

Response: First, we note that although the distribution of earnings is extremely skewed, a sample of size 446 is so large that the Central Limit Theorem ensures the distribution of sample mean earnings to have a normal shape.

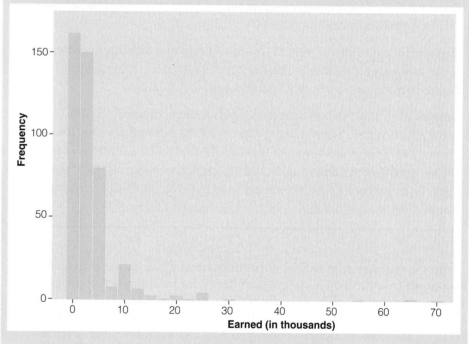

Because *n* is so large, we can substitute sample standard deviation $s = 6,500$ for the unknown population standard deviation σ and still use the multiplier 2 from the *z* distribution. Our 95% confidence interval for μ is

$$3,776 \pm 2\frac{6,500}{\sqrt{446}} = 3,776 \pm 616 = (3,160, 4,392)$$

Practice: *Try Exercise 10.9(b) on page 478.*

Now we have two different reasons for checking the sample size *n*.

1. If σ is unknown and we want to set up a confidence interval by hand, we make sure *n* is large enough so that *s* is close enough to σ to allow for use of probabilities based on the *z* distribution instead of *t*.

2. Even if σ is known, n must be large enough to offset non-normality in the population distribution's shape. Otherwise the Central Limit Theorem does not guarantee $\bar{x}$ to be normal, so it does not standardize to z.

Besides playing a role in ensuring that a confidence interval based on normal probabilities is legitimate, sample size is important for its impact on the width of our confidence interval.

Role of Sample Size: Larger Samples, Narrower Intervals

Recall that an approximate 95% confidence interval for the unknown population mean μ is

$$\bar{x} \pm 2\frac{\sigma}{\sqrt{n}}$$

where σ is the population standard deviation. The fact that n appears in the denominator in our expression for margin of error means that larger samples will produce narrower intervals.

EXAMPLE 10.9 HOW THE SAMPLE SIZE AFFECTS THE WIDTH OF A CONFIDENCE INTERVAL

Background: Based on a sample of 100 California condor eggs with sample mean length 105.7 centimeters, a 95% confidence interval was found, assuming the standard deviation of all lengths to be 2.5 centimeters.

```
One-Sample Z: Length
The assumed sigma = 2.5
Variable          N      Mean     StDev    SE Mean        95.0% CI
Length          100     105.7      2.5        .25     ( 105.21, 106.19)
```

The interval is constructed as

$$105.7 \pm 1.96 \left(\frac{2.5}{\sqrt{100}}\right) = 105.7 \pm 1.96(0.25) = 105.7 \pm 0.49 = (105.21, 106.19)$$

Question: How would the interval change if the data had come from a sample that was one-fourth as large (25 instead of 100)?

Response: Dividing n by 4 results in a standard deviation of sample mean that is multiplied by the square root of 4, or 2. The 95% confidence interval would change to

$$105.7 \pm 1.96 \left(\frac{2.5}{\sqrt{25}}\right) = 105.7 \pm 1.96(0.5) = 105.7 \pm 0.98 = (104.72, 106.68)$$

Thus, dividing sample size by 4 produces an interval with twice the original width, about 2 cm instead of about 1 cm. With a smaller sample size, we have less information about the population. The result is a wider, less precise confidence interval.

Practice: *Try Exercise 10.9(e) on page 478.*

Environmentalists and statisticians agree: Larger samples of animals would be better.

Roy Toft/Getty Images

The Big
Picture:
LOOKING
BACK

When the variable of interest was categorical, we worked with a standard deviation of sample proportion that was approximately

$$\sqrt{\frac{\hat{p}(1 - \hat{p})}{n}}.$$ The fact

that the square root of sample size enters into the denominator impacts the width of our confidence interval in a precise way. The same relationship between sample size and interval width also holds for confidence intervals to estimate population mean. For example, dividing *n* by 4 in Example 10.9 resulted in an interval width that was multiplied by 2.

Intervals at Other Levels of Confidence with *z*

Intervals at other levels of confidence besides 95% are easily obtained by hand (using other multipliers instead of 2) or with software (requesting another level besides the default 95%). As illustrated in our sketch of the tails of the normal curve, different levels of confidence require different multipliers to replace 2 (or, more precisely, 1.96).

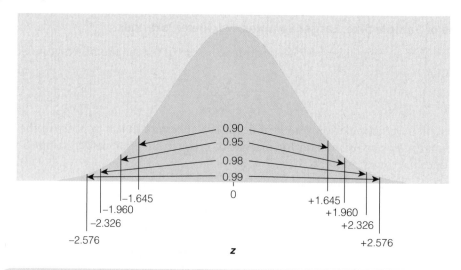

EXAMPLE 10.10 INTERVALS AT VARIOUS LEVELS OF CONFIDENCE

Background: Our sample of 19 female weights has a mean of 129.37. The standard deviation of all female weights is assumed to be 20.

Question: How do 90%, 95%, 98%, and 99% confidence intervals for population mean weight compare?

Response: By hand, we would calculate

$$129.37 \pm \text{multiplier } \frac{20}{\sqrt{19}}$$

substituting 1.645, 1.96, 2.326, or 2.576 for the multiplier, depending on what level of confidence is desired. Alternatively, we can produce the intervals with software. As the sketch below illustrates, the interval is narrowest at the lowest level of confidence and widest at the highest level of confidence.

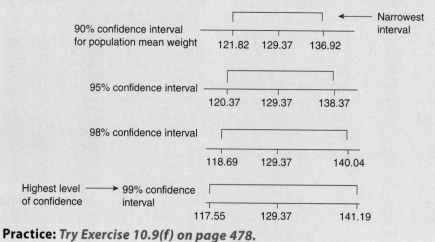

Practice: *Try Exercise 10.9(f) on page 478.*

Thus, we confront the usual trade-off: We would like a narrow, precise interval estimate, but we would also like to be very confident that it contains the unknown population mean weight. We can gain precision at the expense of level of confidence, or vice versa.

Interpreting a Confidence Interval for the Mean

Calculation of a confidence interval, by hand or with software, is a very straightforward process that is easily mastered. Interpreting the interval correctly requires more thought. Students should appreciate the fact that reporting an interval to someone who wants information about an unknown population mean is of little value unless we can also explain what the interval actually is.

Students Talk Stats

Correctly Interpreting a Confidence Interval for the Mean

*F*our students, in preparation for a test, discuss the 95% confidence interval for mean household size produced on the computer, based on a random sample of 100 households in a certain city, where the population standard deviation for household size is assumed to be 1.4.

```
One-Sample Z: Householdsize
The assumed sigma = 1.4
Variable         N    Mean   StDev   SE Mean      95.0% CI
Householdsize  100   2.440   1.336     0.140   ( 2.166, 2.714)
```

Adam: *"95% of all households in the city have between 2.166 and 2.714 people."*

Brittany: *"Adam, there's not a single household in the whole world that has between 2.166 and 2.714 people. Do you know any households that have like two-and-a-half people in them? That's definitely wrong."*

Carlos: *"The interval tells us that* mean *household size should be between 2.166 and 2.714 people."*

Dominique: *"Are you talking about population mean or sample mean? I guess it has to be population mean, because that's what's unknown. So we're 95% confident that the mean household size for the entire city is somewhere between 2.166 and 2.714 people. That makes sense."*

The fact that various confidence levels are produced, depending on what level of confidence is requested, should remind us that statistics is full of answers that are not as hard-and-fast as we sometimes would like them to be. Example TBP 10.4 on page 917 of the ***TBP Supplement*** shows how the plausibility of a proposed value can depend on which confidence level is used.

Remember that we are continuing to perform inference, whereby we use sample statistics to make statements about unknown population parameters. When the single variable of interest is quantitative, our confidence interval makes a statement about the unknown *population* mean, as Dominique correctly points out. The word "confidence" is used instead of "probability" because the level (95% in this case) refers to how sure we are that the population mean is contained in our interval. Alternatively, we can say that the probability is 95% that our method produces an interval that succeeds in capturing the unknown population mean.

Now that we have completed our discussion of *z* confidence intervals for means, summarized on page 503 of the Chapter Summary, we consider the other major form of inference for means—hypothesis tests.

A z Hypothesis Test about the Population Mean

Just as we saw for tests about a proportion, the process of carrying out a hypothesis test about the unknown population mean varies, depending on which of three forms the alternative hypothesis takes. What sort of values of sample mean provide evidence against the null hypothesis in favor of the alternative depends on the sign of the alternative hypothesis. Our decision of whether or not to reject the null hypothesis in favor of the alternative hinges on the P-value, which reports the probability of sample mean being greater than, less than, or as extreme in either direction as the one observed, under the assumption that the population mean μ equals the value μ_0 proposed in the null hypothesis.

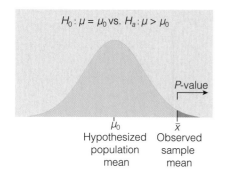

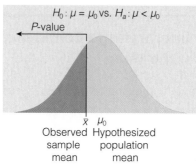

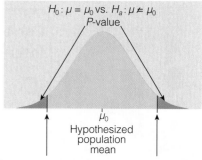

Any formal hypothesis test—including that for a population mean, which we are about to present—can be outlined as a series of four steps, once we've formulated our question about the unknown population parameter as two opposing points of view from which we must ultimately choose one.

1. The first step in the solution process is to carry out a "background check" of the study design, using principles established in Part I to look for possible sources of bias in the sampling process, or in the way variables were evaluated. The population should be at least 10 times the sample size, and we must follow the same guidelines as those for confidence intervals, detailed on page 466. These require us to check if the sample size is large enough to offset possible non-normality in the underlying distribution.

2. The second step corresponds to skills acquired in Part II: We summarize the quantitative variable with its mean and standard deviation, then standardize.

3. The third step is to find a probability, as we learned to do in Part III. Specifically, we seek the probability of a sample mean as low/high/different as the one observed, if population mean equaled the value μ_0 proposed in the null hypothesis. This is the P-value of the test.

4. The fourth step requires us to make a statistical inference decision, the crux of Part IV. If the observed sample mean $\bar{x}$ is improbably far from the claimed population mean μ_0, we reject that claim and conclude that the alternative is true. Otherwise, we continue to believe that the population mean may equal μ_0.

The Chapter Summary features a more technical outline of hypothesis tests for means on page 504.

If we use software, it is a good idea to start by graphing the data set and considering if the sample size is large enough to offset whatever skewness (if any) we suspect in the population. To carry out the test it is necessary to input the proposed mean μ_0, the sign of the alternative hypothesis, the known value of σ, and, of course, the quantitative data set from which the sample mean is obtained. Output will include the sample mean $\bar{x}$, the standardized sample mean z, and the P-value.

Our first hypothesis test example for means addresses the question of whether or not our sample of students' earnings provides compelling evidence that the population mean of earnings is less than $5,000. The word "less" indicates the alternative should be one-sided.

EXAMPLE 10.11 TESTING ABOUT A MEAN AGAINST A ONE-SIDED ALTERNATIVE

Background: In a representative sample of 446 students, mean earnings for the previous year were $3,776. As we saw when we set up a confidence interval for population mean earnings in Example 10.8 on page 470, the sample size is large enough that we can assume σ to approximately equal s, $6,500.

Question: Is there evidence that mean earnings of all students at that university were less than $5,000?

Response: Just as we did when carrying out hypothesis tests for proportions, we pose the problem formally and then follow a four-step solution process.

0. The null hypothesis claims the population mean equals $5,000, and the alternative claims it is less. We write $H_0 : \mu = 5$ versus $H_a : \mu < 5$, where the units are thousands of dollars. If software is used, we must enter the proposed mean 5 thousand and the sign "<" for the alternative.

1. We are given to understand that the sample is unbiased. The population size is presumably larger than $10(446) = 4,460$. Even though earnings are sure to be skewed right, the sample size (446) is large enough to guarantee sample mean to be approximately normal.

2. The relevant statistic is sample mean earnings $3,776, which is indeed less than $5,000. The standardized test statistic is $z = -3.98$. Software would produce these automatically from the quantitative data set entered. Alternatively, z could have been calculated by hand as $z = \frac{\bar{x} - \mu_0}{\sigma/\sqrt{n}} = \frac{3.776 - 5}{6.5/\sqrt{446}}$.

3. The P-value is the probability of a sample mean as low as (or lower than) 3.776, if the population mean is 5. This is the same thing as z being less than or equal to -3.98, which is virtually zero, because a standard normal random variable almost never takes a value this extreme. Computer output would show the P-value to be 0.000.

4. Because the P-value is very small, we have very strong evidence to reject the null hypothesis in favor of the alternative. We conclude that we are quite convinced the alternative is true: The mean of earnings of all students at that university was less than $5,000.

```
One-Sample Z: Earned
Test of mu = 5 vs mu < 5
The assumed sigma = 6.5
Variable            N        Mean      StDev      SE Mean
Earned            446       3.776      6.503        0.308
Variable      95.0% Upper Bound          Z           P
Earned                      4.282      -3.98       0.000
```

Practice: *Try Exercise 10.11 on page 479.*

The Big Picture: A CLOSER LOOK

The sign of z in Example 10.11 is negative because the observed sample mean was less than the hypothesized population mean. The fact that z is very large in absolute value—considerably larger than 2—indicates that the sample mean $\bar{x} = 3.776$ is very far from the hypothesized population mean $\mu_0 = 5$.

Just as we saw with proportions, if we carry out a two-sided test about the population mean, our *P*-value will be a two-tailed probability.

EXAMPLE 10.12 TESTING ABOUT A MEAN AGAINST A TWO-SIDED ALTERNATIVE

Background: Assume the standard deviation for shoe sizes of all male college students is 1.5. Shoe sizes of 9 sampled male college students have a mean of 11.222.

Question: Is 11.0 a plausible value for the mean shoe size of all male college students?

Response: Before following the usual four-step solution strategy, it's a good idea to "eyeball" the data to see what our intuition suggests. The sample mean (11.222) seems very close to the proposed population mean (11.0). Furthermore, the sample size is quite small, which makes it more difficult to reject a proposed value as implausible. Therefore, we can anticipate that our test will *not* reject the claim that $\mu = 11.0$. Now we proceed formally.

0. We formulate the hypotheses $H_0 : \mu = 11.0$ versus $H_a : \mu \neq 11.0$.

1. There is no reason to suspect a biased sample. Certainly, the size of the population of interest is greater than 10(9) = 90. Although the sample size is small, sample mean should be normally distributed because shoe sizes themselves would be normal.

2. The relevant statistic is sample mean shoe size 11.222, and the standardized test statistic is $z = +0.44$. This information would be provided in computer output. Alternatively, z could have been calculated by hand as $z = \frac{11.222 - 11.0}{1.5/\sqrt{9}}$.

3. The *P*-value is the probability of sample mean as different (in either direction) from 11.0 as 11.222 is. This is the same thing as z being greater than 0.44 in absolute value, or twice the probability of z being greater than +0.44. Since 0.44 is a lot less than 1, the "68" part of the 68-95-99.7 Rule tells us that the *P*-value is much larger than 2(0.16) = 0.32. Computer output confirms the *P*-value to be quite large, 0.657.

```
One-Sample Z: Shoe
Test of mu = 11 vs mu not = 11
The assumed sigma = 1.5
Variable      N       Mean      StDev     SE Mean
Shoe          9      11.222     1.698       0.500
Variable        95.0% CI              Z         P
Shoe       ( 10.242, 12.202)       0.44     0.657
```

4. The *P*-value isn't small at all: We have no evidence whatsoever to reject the null hypothesis in favor of the alternative. We acknowledge 11.0 to be a plausible value for the population mean shoe size, based on the data provided.

Practice: *Try Exercise 10.13(c) on page 480.*

The ***TBP*** *Supplement* includes graphical depictions of the *P*-value for Example 10.12, in terms of both shoe size *x* and standardized shoe size *z*.

The Big Picture: A Closer Look

The sign of *z* in Example 10.12 is positive because the observed sample mean was greater than the hypothesized population mean. The fact that *z* is fairly small in absolute value—less than 1— suggests that the sample mean $\bar{x} = 11.222$ is relatively close to the hypothesized population mean $\mu_0 = 11.0$.

We will discuss other important hypothesis test issues, such as Type I and II Errors and the correct interpretation of test results, once we have made the transition to more realistic situations in which the population standard deviation σ is *not* known.

Inference for a Mean When Population Standard Deviation Is Known or Sample Size Is Large

Note: Asterisked numbers indicate exercises whose answers are provided in the Solutions to Selected Exercises section, on page 689.

*10.1 "Sources of Individual Shy-Bold Variations in Antipredator Behaviour of Male Iberian Rock Lizards," published online in *Animal Behavior* in 2005, considered a variety of traits and measurements for lizards noosed in the mountains of central Spain. "Many male lizards also have a conspicuous row of small but distinctive blue spots that runs along the side of the body on the outer margin of belly."[1] The number of blue spots was measured for each of two sides for 34 lizards, and was found to have mean 6.5.

   a. Assuming the lizards were a representative sample, what is our best guess for the mean number of side spots on all Iberian rock lizards?

   b. If the 34 lizards had all been obtained from a particular pet shop instead of from their natural habitat, could we say that 6.5 is our best guess for mean number of side spots on all Iberian rock lizards?

10.2 A 2002 survey by the American Pet Product Manufacturers Association estimated that the average number of ferrets in ferret-owning households nationwide was 1.9.

   a. What was apparently the sample mean number of ferrets found by the survey?

   b. What additional information would be needed in order to set up a confidence interval for the average number of ferrets in all ferret-owning households?

   c. If the probability of a household owning any ferrets at all is 0.005, what do we estimate to be the average number of ferrets for *all* households nationwide?

*10.3 When Pope John Paul II died in April 2005 after serving 27 years as pontiff, newspapers reported years of tenure of popes through the ages, starting with St. Peter, who reigned for 35 years (from 32 to 67 A.D.). Tenures of all 165 popes averaged 7.151 years, with standard deviation 6.414 years. A test was carried out to see if tenures of the eight 20th-century popes were significantly longer than those throughout the ages. Explain why a z test is carried out instead of t.

*10.4 The 676,947 females who took Verbal SAT tests in the year 2000 scored an average of 504, with standard deviation 110.

   a. Should the numbers 504 and 110 be denoted $\hat{p}$ and p, $\bar{x}$ and s, or μ and σ?

   b. The probability is 0.95 that sample mean Verbal SAT score for a random sample of 121 females falls within what interval?

   c. Explain why it would not be appropriate to use this information to set up a confidence interval for population mean female Verbal SAT score in the year 2000.

   d. Suppose that instead of information on all scores, we only know about a random sample of females' Verbal SAT scores. Tell which of these intervals would be the *narrowest*.
      1. 95% confidence interval for population mean score, based on a sample of size 60
      2. 90% confidence interval for population mean score, based on a sample of size 60
      3. 95% confidence interval for population mean score, based on a sample of size 600
      4. 90% confidence interval for population mean score, based on a sample of size 600

   e. Which of the intervals would be the *widest*?

10.5 The American Academy of Physician Assistants website reported on results of its 1999 census survey of all practicing PAs in the United States. Mean income was $68,000 and standard deviation was $17,000.

   a. Should the numbers 68,000 and 17,000 be denoted $\bar{x}$ and s or μ and σ?

   b. Can we use this information to find the interval for which the probability is 95% that mean income in a random sample of 100 practicing PAs falls within that range?

   c. Can we use this information to find a 95% confidence interval for mean income of all practicing PAs?

d. One of the intervals described in parts (b) and (c) is in fact appropriate; report it.

e. Suppose that instead of a census, only a random sample had been taken. Tell which of these intervals would be the *narrowest*.
   1. 90% confidence interval for population mean income, based on a sample of size 100
   2. 99% confidence interval for population mean income, based on a sample of size 100
   3. 90% confidence interval for population mean income, based on a sample of size 10
   4. 99% confidence interval for population mean income, based on a sample of size 10

f. Which of the four intervals would be the *widest*?

*10.6 According to the 1990 U.S. Census, travel time to work had a standard deviation of 20 minutes. If we were to take a random sample of 16 commuters to set up a 95% confidence interval for population mean travel time, what would be the margin of error?

10.7 Length in centimeters of newborn babies has standard deviation 5. If we were to take a random sample of 25 newborns to set up a 95% confidence interval for population mean length, what would be the margin of error?

*10.8 Several hundred students enrolled in introductory statistics courses at a large university were surveyed and asked to pick a whole number at random from 1 to 20. Because the mean of the numbers from 1 to 20 is 10.5, for truly random selections they should average 10.5 in the long run.

a. Tell whether we would opt for a z or t procedure if the population standard deviation was unknown.

b. Tell whether we would opt for a z or t procedure if we take into account that the standard deviation of the numbers 1 through 20 is 5.766.

c. Use software to access the data and, with 5.766 as population standard deviation, construct a 95% confidence interval for mean selection by all students.

d. Use software to access the data and, with 5.766 as population standard deviation, carry out a test to see if the students'

random number selections were consistent with random selections from a population whose mean is 10.5. Report the sample mean and *P*-value.

e. Do the data suggest that the selections could have been truly random?

f. Would the null hypothesis have been rejected against the one-sided alternative $H_a: \mu > 10.5$? Explain.

g. Would the null hypothesis have been rejected against the one-sided alternative $H_a: \mu < 10.5$? Explain.

h. Do people apparently perceive larger or smaller numbers to be more random? Explain.

i. Note that the sample standard deviation $s = 5.283$ is smaller than the assumed population standard deviation $\sigma = 5.766$. [This is partly due to the phenomenon that students tend to avoid the extremes 1 and 20 when making a "random" selection.] If $t = \frac{\bar{x} - \mu_0}{5.283/\sqrt{n}}$ had been used instead of $z = \frac{\bar{x} - \mu_0}{5.766/\sqrt{n}}$, would t have been larger or smaller than z?

j. If $t = \frac{\bar{x} - \mu_0}{5.283/\sqrt{n}}$ had been used instead of $z = \frac{\bar{x} - \mu_0}{5.766/\sqrt{n}}$, would the *P*-value have been larger or smaller than the one obtained using z?

*10.9 "eBay's Buy-It-Now Function: Who, When, and How," published online in *Topics in Economic Analysis & Policy* in 2004, describes an experiment involving the sale of 2001 American Eagle silver dollars on eBay. In a controlled auction, 82 of the dollars sold for a mean of $9.04, with standard deviation $1.28.[2]

a. What is our best guess for the overall mean selling price of 2001 American Eagle silver dollars?

b. Explain why we can assume the unknown population standard deviation to be fairly close to the sample standard deviation, $1.28.

c. Give a 95% confidence interval for the overall mean selling price.

d. Would you be willing to believe a claim that overall online auction sale prices of these dollars average $9.00?

e. If the same results had been obtained with a larger sample size, would the interval be wider, narrower, or the same?

f. If the interval had been constructed at the 90% level instead of 95%, would it be wider, narrower, or the same?

g. To test the claim in part (d), how would the alternative hypothesis be written: $H_a : \bar{x} \neq 9.04$, $H_a : \mu \neq 9.04$, $H_a : \bar{x} \neq 9.00$, or $H_a : \mu \neq 9.00$?

10.10 According to a paper by Sokal and Hunter published in the *Annals of the Entomological Society of America* in 1955, wing lengths were measured for a sample of 100 houseflies. The data were used to produce a 95% confidence interval; lengths were recorded in millimeters.

```
Variable    N      Mean     StDev    SE Mean         95.0% CI
length     100    4.5500    0.3920    0.0392    ( 4.4722, 4.6278)
```

a. Report the sample mean wing length.

b. Find the center point of the 95% confidence interval.

c. Explain why your answers to parts (a) and (b) are equal.

d. Show that the interval is approximately equal to sample mean plus or minus 2 standard errors, where a standard error is the standard deviation divided by the square root of the sample size.

e. Which one of these is the correct interpretation of the interval?
   1. There is a 95% probability that we produce an interval that contains population mean wing length.
   2. There is a 95% probability that we produce an interval that contains sample mean wing length.
   3. The probability is 95% that population mean wing length falls in this interval.
   4. The probability is 95% that sample mean wing length falls in this interval.

f. Standardize the sample mean, if population mean equals 4.50.

g. Use the result of part (f) to argue that 4.50 is a plausible value for the population mean wing length.

*10.11 "An Analysis of the Study Time-Grade Association," published in *Radical Pedagogy* in 2002, reported that scores on a standardized test for cognitive ability for a group of over 100 students in an Introductory Psychology course had mean 22.6 and standard deviation 5.0. For the 6 students who reported studying zero hours per week for the course, the mean was 25.3 and standard deviation was 7.7.

a. State the null and alternative hypotheses if we want to test for evidence that mean cognitive ability score for those 6 students was significantly higher than for the population of students in the course.

b. Explain why the standardized sample mean can be called z if we use 5 as the standard deviation.

c. Calculate z.

d. Recall that values of z between 0 and 1 are quite common; values closer to 1 than to 2 may be considered not unusual; values close to 2 are borderline, values close to 3 are unusually large, and values considerably greater than 3 are extremely large. Based on the relative size of your z

statistic, would the P-value for the test be small, not small, or borderline?

e. Is there evidence that mean cognitive ability score for those 6 students was significantly higher than for the population of students in the course?

f. Note that since $z = \frac{\bar{x} - \mu_0}{\sigma / \sqrt{n}}$, the size of z is doubled if the sample size is multiplied by 4. Report the value of z if a sample of 24 students (instead of 6) had a mean score of 25.3, and tell whether this would be significantly higher than the population mean.

10.12 "An Analysis of the Study Time-Grade Association," published in *Radical Pedagogy* in 2002, reported that scores on a standardized test for cognitive ability for a group of over 100 students in an Introductory Psychology course had mean 22.6 and standard deviation 5.0. For the 7 students who reported studying the most for the course (9 hours or more per week), the mean was 17.6 and standard deviation was 2.8.

a. Calculate the standardized sample mean, using 5 as the standard deviation.

b. Recall that values of z between 0 and 1 are quite common; values closer to 1 than to 2 may be considered not unusual; values close to 2 are borderline, values close to 3 are unusually large, and values considerably greater than 3 are extremely large. Based on the relative size of your z statistic, explain why there is evidence that mean cognitive ability score for those 7 students was significantly lower than for the population of students in the course.

c. Can we conclude that studying diminishes a student's cognitive ability? Explain.

*10.13 When Pope John Paul II died in April 2005 after serving 27 years as pontiff, newspapers reported years of tenure of popes through the ages, starting with St. Peter, who reigned for 35 years (from 32 to 67 A.D.). Tenures of all 165 popes averaged 7.151 years, with standard deviation 6.414 years. Output is shown for a test that was carried out to see if tenures of the eight 20th-century popes were significantly longer than those throughout the ages.

```
Test of mu = 7.151 vs mu > 7.151
The assumed sigma = 6.414
Variable            N    Mean    StDev   SE Mean   95.0% Lower Bound   Z      P
PopeTenures1900s 8    12.75    8.56    2.27          9.02            2.47   0.007
```

a. Explain why we can assert that average tenure was significantly longer in the 20th century.

b. Keeping in mind that, as a rule, popes remain in office until death, what is one possible explanation for the test's results?

c. What would the P-value have been if a two-sided alternative had been used?

10.2 Inference for a Mean When the Population Standard Deviation Is Unknown and the Sample Size Is Small

In Chapter 8, we established that if the underlying population variable x is normal with mean μ and standard deviation σ, then for a random sample of size n, the random variable $\bar{x}$ is normal with mean μ and standard deviation $\frac{\sigma}{\sqrt{n}}$. We used this fact to transform an observed sample mean $\bar{x}$ to a standard normal value $z = \frac{\bar{x} - \mu}{\sigma/\sqrt{n}}$, which tells how many standard deviations below or above the population mean μ our sample mean $\bar{x}$ is. Note that the standardized random variable z always has standard deviation 1, regardless of sample size n.

In situations involving a large sample size n, the sample standard deviation s is approximately equal to σ, and probabilities for $\frac{\bar{x} - \mu}{s/\sqrt{n}}$ are approximately the same as for a standard normal z.

In contrast, if the sample size n is small, s may be quite different from σ, and the standardized statistic that we call $t = \frac{\bar{x} - \mu}{s/\sqrt{n}}$ does *not* follow a standard normal distribution.

■ Because of subtracting the mean of $\bar{x}$ (that is, μ) from $\bar{x}$ in the numerator, the distribution of $t = \frac{\bar{x} - \mu}{s/\sqrt{n}}$ is (like z) centered at zero.

■ As long as n is large enough to make $\bar{x}$ approximately normal, the standardized random variable t can be called "bell-shaped."

■ Because of dividing by the standard error $s/\sqrt{n}$ (which is *not* the exact standard deviation of $\bar{x}$), the standard deviation of t is *not* fixed at 1 as it is for z. Sample standard deviation s contains less information than σ, so the spread of t is greater than that of z, especially for small sample sizes n. Because s approaches σ as sample size n increases, the t distribution approaches the standard normal z distribution as n increases. Thus, the spread of sample mean standardized using s instead of σ depends on the sample size n. We say the distribution has $n - 1$ "degrees of freedom," abbreviated "df."

> *Definition*   The **degrees of freedom** in a mathematical sense tell us how many values are unknown in a problem. For the purpose of performing statistical inference, the degrees of freedom tell which particular distribution applies.

Since there are many different t distributions—one for each df—it would take too much space to provide rules for each of them corresponding to the 68-95-99.7 Rule for normal distributions, or detailed probabilities on the tails of every t curve. Instead, we will cite and compare key values with tail probabilities for a few t distributions, to give you an idea of how t relates to z. In particular, you will see that t has somewhat more spread for smaller sample sizes and is virtually identical to z for larger sample sizes.

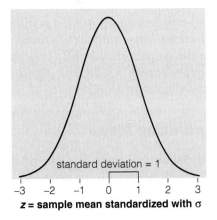

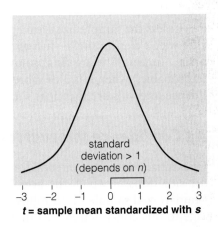

The Big Picture:

LOOKING AHEAD

There is only one z distribution, and its standard deviation is always 1. As we learn about inference for different types of variables, we encounter other distributions—such as t, F, and chi-square—that are actually families of distributions with varying spreads, depending on how many degrees of freedom apply.

EXAMPLE 10.13 CONTRASTING SPREADS OF Z AND T DISTRIBUTIONS

Background: When sample mean for a sample of size 7 is standardized with $s/\sqrt{n}$ instead of $\sigma/\sqrt{n}$, the resulting random variable t has $7 - 1 = 6$ degrees of freedom. Its distribution is shown below along with the z distribution for comparison.

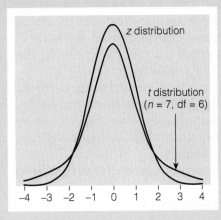

Continued

Question: How do the two distributions compare?

Response: Both are centered at 0, symmetric, and bell-shaped. The z distribution bulges more at 0, showing that it has less spread. The t distribution is "heavier" at the tails, showing that it has more spread.

Practice: *Try Exercise 10.14 on page 489.*

A heavy tail: Is that why they call it t-rex instead of z-rex?

© DK Limited/CORBIS

Unless the sample size is exceptionally small (say, less than 5 or 6), it is still the case with t distributions—just as with z distributions—that we start to consider a value "unusual" when its absolute value is in the neighborhood of 2, and "very improbable" when it is 3 or more. The t multipliers for 90, 95, 98, and 99% confidence intervals are therefore somewhere in the vicinity of 2 or 3.

A t Confidence Interval for the Population Mean

Our initial confidence interval for an unknown population mean was constructed for situations in which the population standard deviation σ is known, and the standardized sample mean follows a standard normal z distribution. The advantage to this construction was that it allowed us to remain on familiar ground as far as the multiplier in the confidence interval was concerned: 2 (or, more precisely, 1.96) for a confidence level of 95%, because 95% of the time a *normal variable* falls within 2 standard deviations of its mean. The drawback is that it is, in most cases, unrealistic to assume the population standard deviation to be known.

Now we develop a method to find a confidence interval for an unknown population mean when the population standard deviation σ is unknown, and the sample mean standardized with $s/\sqrt{n}$ instead of $\sigma/\sqrt{n}$ follows a t distribution. The advantage of this construction is that it has the most practical value: We rarely know the value of population standard deviation, and the t procedure lets us set up a confidence interval when all we have is a set of quantitative data values. The drawback is that we must keep in mind that the multiplier varies, depending on sample size, which dictates degrees of freedom for the t distribution. Carrying out the procedure with software is actually a bit simpler than the z procedure because we do not need to report a value for σ.

In order for the t confidence interval formula to produce accurate intervals, either the population distribution must be normal or the sample size must be large enough for sample mean to follow an approximately normal distribution. The usual guidelines for the relationship between sample size and shape, presented on page 466, should be consulted.

We begin with the most common level of confidence, 95%.

95% Confidence Intervals with t

Notice that our t confidence interval formula, unlike z, cannot be stated with one specific multiplier.

> ## Confidence Interval for Population Mean When σ Is Unknown and n Is Small
>
> A 95% confidence interval for unknown population mean μ based on sample mean $\bar{x}$ from a random sample of size n is
>
> estimate ± margin of error
>
> = sample mean ± multiplier × standard deviation of sample mean
>
> $$\approx \bar{x} \pm \text{multiplier}\left(\frac{s}{\sqrt{n}}\right)$$
>
> where s is the sample standard deviation. The multiplier (from the t distribution) depends on sample size n, which dictates degrees of freedom df $= n - 1$. The multiplier is at least 2, with values close to 3 for very small samples.

The confidence intervals based on z or t in Example 10.14 are quite different because the sample size (9) is so small. Example TBP 10.5 on page 918 in the *TBP Supplement* shows that for a sample of size 19 the difference is minor. Example TBP 10.6 on page 919 stresses that regardless of sample size, a t procedure must be used with software when σ is unknown.

In order to contrast confidence intervals based on t as opposed to z, we revisit an earlier example in which we originally made an assumption about the population standard deviation σ.

EXAMPLE 10.14 COMPARING CONFIDENCE INTERVALS FOR A POPULATION MEAN WITH T VERSUS Z

Background: We have a random sample of 9 shoe sizes of college males:

11.5	12.0	11.0	15.0	11.5	10.0	9.0	10.0	11.0

This data set has a mean of 11.222 and a standard deviation of 1.698.

Below are side-by-side sketches of the tails of the z distribution and the tails of the t distribution with 8 degrees of freedom, which corresponds to a sample of size 9.

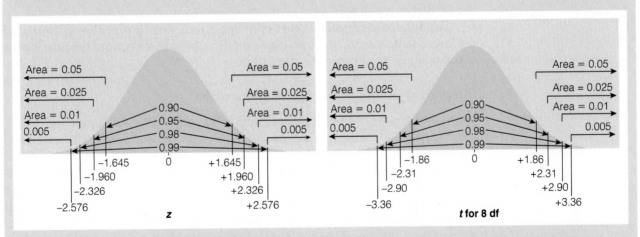

Questions: What is an approximate 95% confidence interval for the mean shoe size of all college males? What would the interval have been if 1.698 were known to be the population standard deviation σ instead of the sample standard deviation s? How do the intervals compare?

Continued

Responses: A 95% confidence interval for the population mean μ, based on the sample mean 11.222, sample standard deviation 1.698, and sample size 9, uses the multiplier 2.31 from the t distribution (shown on the right) for $9 - 1 = 8$ degrees of freedom and 95% confidence level:

$$\bar{x} \pm \text{multiplier} \left(\frac{s}{\sqrt{n}} \right)$$

$$= 11.222 \pm 2.31 \left(\frac{1.698}{\sqrt{9}} \right) = 11.222 \pm 1.307 = (9.92, 12.53)$$

We can also produce the confidence interval with software, simply entering the nine data values and requesting a one-sample t procedure.

```
One-Sample T: Shoe
Variable         N      Mean     StDev    SE Mean        95.0% CI
Shoe             9    11.222     1.698      0.566   ( 9.917, 12.527)
```

If 1.698 had been the known population standard deviation, the multiplier would have come from the z distribution and the interval would have been

$$11.222 \pm 1.96 \left(\frac{1.698}{\sqrt{9}} \right) = 11.222 \pm 1.109 = (10.11, 12.33)$$

To produce the interval with software, we would request a one-sample z procedure and we would need to enter the assumed population standard deviation. In any case, both intervals are centered at the sample mean 11.222 but the z interval is narrower: Its width is $12.33 - 10.11 = 2.22$, whereas the width of the t interval is $12.53 - 9.92 = 2.61$.

Practice: *Try Exercise 10.16(a,b) on page 489.*

The Big Picture: A Closer Look

When we construct a t confidence interval for the mean, we need not check that sample size is large enough so that s approximately equals σ. We do still need to check that sample size is large enough to guarantee the shape of sample mean $\bar{x}$ to be approximately normal. In the case of shoe sizes, the distribution itself should be roughly normal, so even a very small sample is acceptable.

To make a point about how the width of a confidence interval is impacted by whether the standard deviation is a known value σ or is estimated with s, Example 10.14 produced a z confidence interval with software, entering sample standard deviation as the presumed population standard deviation. This would *not* be done in practice. When σ is unknown and confidence intervals or hypothesis tests are carried out with software, a t procedure is required, not z.

The difference between z and t confidence intervals becomes less pronounced for larger sample sizes, in which case s tends to be closer to σ and the t multiplier is only slightly larger than the z multiplier.

Intervals at Other Levels of Confidence with t

With software, we can easily obtain t intervals at other levels of confidence. Again, the multipliers are greater than those used to construct z confidence intervals when the population standard deviation σ was known. They are considerably larger for very small samples, and they become closer to the z multipliers as sample size n increases. The following table gives you an idea of how different—or similar—the t multipliers are. Notice that except for the extremely small sample size ($n = 4$), all the multipliers are around 2 or 3. As long as single sample inference is being performed (as is the case throughout this chapter), the degrees of freedom are simply sample size n minus 1.

	Confidence Level			
	90%	95%	98%	99%
z (infinite n)	1.645	1.960 or 2	2.326	2.576
t: df = 19 (n = 20)	1.73	2.09	2.54	2.86
t: df = 11 (n = 12)	1.80	2.20	2.72	3.11
t: df = 3 (n = 4)	2.35	3.18	4.54	5.84

Using the appropriate multiplier, we construct our confidence interval as

$$\bar{x} \pm \text{multiplier} \frac{s}{\sqrt{n}}$$

As usual, higher levels of confidence are associated with larger multipliers, farther out on the tails of the curve, and thus produce wider intervals.

EXAMPLE 10.15 WIDER INTERVALS AT HIGHER LEVELS OF CONFIDENCE

Background: A sample of 12 one-bedroom apartments near a university had monthly rents (in dollars) with a mean of 457 and a standard deviation of 88. According to the table on page 484, the multiplier for a sample of size 12 (with df = 12 − 1 = 11) and 95% confidence is 2.20; for 99% confidence it is 3.11.

Question: What is a 99% confidence interval for the mean monthly rent of all one-bedroom apartments in the area, and how does it compare to a 95% confidence interval?

Response: Our 99% confidence interval by hand is

$$\bar{x} \pm \text{multiplier} \left(\frac{s}{\sqrt{n}} \right)$$

$$= 457 \pm 3.11 \left(\frac{88}{\sqrt{12}} \right) = 457 \pm 79 = (378, 536)$$

and with software it looks like this:

```
Variable    N    Mean   StDev   SE Mean        99.0% CI
Rent        12   457.1   87.9     25.4   ( 378.2, 535.9)
```

The interval is wider than a 95% interval would be because we are multiplying by 3.11 for 99% confidence, as opposed to 2.20 for 95% confidence.

```
Variable    N    Mean   StDev   SE Mean        95.0% CI
Rent        12   457.1   87.9     25.4   ( 401.3, 512.9)
```

We have the usual trade-off: Higher levels of confidence produce less-precise intervals. In this case, the interval width is about $158 for 99% confidence and $112 for 95% confidence.

Practice: *Try Exercise 10.16(e) on page 489.*

In contrast to Example 10.15, Example TBP 10.7 on page 919 in the **TBP** *Supplement* demonstrates that *t* intervals at a lower level of confidence are narrower.

Page 920 in the **TBP** *Supplement* compares and contrasts the *z* and *t* confidence intervals in a bit more depth.

The information provided by the table on page 484, telling us which multipliers to use to obtain confidence intervals for specific *t* distributions, focused on "inside areas" of those *t* distributions. If we want to perform hypothesis tests, we simply convert the information so that it tells us probabilities on the outside tails of the *t* curves.

Now that we have completed our discussion of *t* confidence intervals, summarized on page 503 of the Chapter Summary, we consider hypothesis tests for means when the population standard deviation is unknown and the sample size is small.

A t Hypothesis Test about the Population Mean

To facilitate the transition from z to t hypothesis tests about a population mean, we recall this pair of sketches for the standard normal z distribution. The first sketch was used to produce confidence intervals; it shows what z values correspond to inside probabilities 0.90, 0.95, 0.98, and 0.99. These z values were our multipliers for the various levels of confidence. The second sketch was used to perform hypothesis tests; it shows that those same z values correspond to tail probabilities 0.05, 0.025, 0.01, and 0.005. By comparing our standardized test statistic to those values, we were able to report a range for the P-value, which was represented by a left-tail, right-tail, or two-tailed probability.

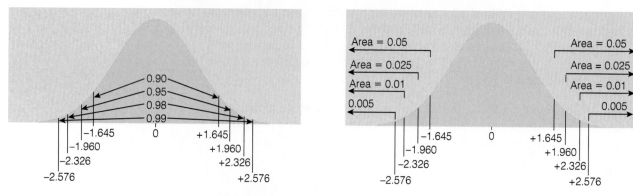

Now we can look at analogous sketches for a particular t distribution, with specific degrees of freedom df $= n - 1$, to see that the t multipliers for confidence intervals are also cutoff values for corresponding tail probabilities. These tail probabilities enable us to report a range for the P-value when performing a test of hypotheses about a proposed value of the unknown population mean, when the population standard deviation is also unknown.

EXAMPLE 10.16 TEST ABOUT A MEAN WHEN THE POPULATION STANDARD DEVIATION IS UNKNOWN

Background: A random sample of 19 female students at a university reported their weights as follows:

| 110 | 110 | 112 | 120 | 120 | 120 | 125 | 125 | 130 | 130 | 132 | 133 | 134 | 135 | 135 | 135 | 145 | 148 | 159 |

Because the sample size is 19, we need to refer to a t distribution for 18 degrees of freedom.

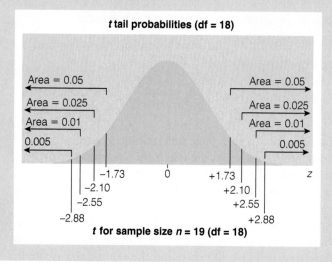

t tail probabilities (df = 18)

t for sample size *n* = 19 (df = 18)

Question: The population mean weight for young women is reported by the National Center for Health Statistics (NCHS) to be 141.7. Is this plausible, or do we have evidence that the mean weight—or at least the mean reported weight—of all female college students is less than this?

Response: We make a formal problem statement and then carry out the test in four steps.

0. The null and alternative hypotheses may be written mathematically as $H_0: \mu = 141.7$ versus $H_a: \mu < 141.7$.

1. These students may well be a representative sample of all female students at that university, but their reported weights may be biased toward lower values, as H_a suggests. Population size is not a problem, nor is sample size, since the distribution of weights would have a fairly normal shape.

2. By hand, we would find sample weights to have a mean of 129.36 and a standard deviation of 12.82. The mean, 129.36, is indeed less than 141.7. The standardized mean weight is

$$t = \frac{129.36 - 141.7}{12.82/\sqrt{19}} = -4.19$$

Because of standardizing with $s/\sqrt{n}$ instead of $\sigma/\sqrt{n}$, our standardized statistic is called t, not z. Because t values, even for small sample sizes, rarely exceed 3 in absolute value, the value -4.19 is clearly extreme, indicating the sample mean weight (129.36) to be much less than the claimed population mean (141.7).

3. Because the alternative hypothesis claimed $\mu < 141.7$, the P-value is the probability, assuming $\mu = 141.7$, of obtaining a standardized sample mean at least as *low* as -4.19. Thus, the P-value is the area under the t curve for $19 - 1 = 18$ degrees of freedom to the *left* of -4.19. Because we know that -4.19 is far from 0 on any t curve, we know the P-value must be very small. This is confirmed by the sketch provided: The probability of t with 18 df being less than -2.88 is only 0.005. It follows that the P-value is even smaller than 0.005.

4. The P-value is certainly small enough to reject the null hypothesis. We conclude that the alternative hypothesis is true. There is evidence that the mean weight of all college females, based on our sample, is less than the population mean reported by NCHS. Either our sample represents a different population from theirs, or the students were under-reporting their weights.

Practice: *Try Exercise 10.18 on page 490.*

If it is not obvious that the t statistic is "large" (considerably greater than 3) or "not large" (considerably less than 2), then a t test about a mean carried out by hand requires information about the t distribution with relevant degrees of freedom, $n - 1$. For practical purposes, such tests are almost always carried out with software.

The next example serves as a reminder that use of a t procedure does *not* mean that normality is no longer an issue. In fact, sample mean $\overline{x}$ standardized with $s/\sqrt{n}$ follows the t distribution only if $\overline{x}$ is normal.

Example TBP 10.8 on page 920 in the **TBP** *Supplement* contrasts z and t hypothesis test results.

The Big Picture: LOOKING BACK

Remember that t, like z, is symmetric and bell-shaped. It just has a different spread from z.

EXAMPLE 10.17 THE T TEST REQUIRES A NORMALLY DISTRIBUTED SAMPLE MEAN

Background: Below is a sample of credits taken by 14 nontraditional students:

4	7	11	11	12	13	13	14	14	17	17	17	17	18

Continued

The **Big** *Picture:*
LOOKING BACK

The results of Example 10.16 suggest that our surveyed females may have been under-reporting weights, a phenomenon that has been documented in other settings. In Example 4.9 on page 84, we learned that the airlines add 10 pounds to weights reported by passengers in order to obtain a more accurate estimate of actual weights. It seems doubtful that these female students would shave that much off their actual weights. Perhaps a better explanation is that these students were not a representative sample of the population considered by the NCHS. Women who attend college may tend to weigh less than those who don't. This explanation is supported by research that shows obesity to be more common in women with a low socio-economic status.

Example TBP 10.9 on page 921 in the **TBP** *Supplement* demonstrates that a *t* test *is* appropriate for a small sample that comes from a normal distribution.

Question: Do these students represent a population whose mean number of credits is less than 15?

Response: First, we should examine a histogram of the data.

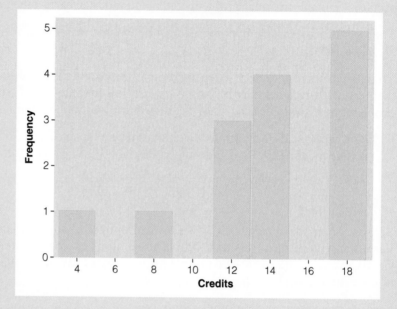

Because the shape is fairly skewed to the left, and the sample size 14 is on the small side, we conclude that the Central Limit Theorem cannot guarantee an approximately normal distribution of the sample mean. If $\bar{x}$ is not normal, then the standardized test statistic $\frac{\bar{x} - \mu}{s/\sqrt{n}}$ does not follow a t distribution, so we should not carry out a t test.

Practice: *Try Exercise 10.20 on page 490.*

As long as the data values are easily accessed, carrying out a t test with software is a very simple and practical skill, as evidenced in the following scenario.

Students Talk Stats

Practical Application of a *t* Test

Adam: *"So me and my roommates are buying a used pool table for $1,500. It's a really good deal—the guy who's selling it said they generally average at least $1,700 second-hand."*

Brittany: *"And you believed him? Not me. Here, I'll check on eBay . . . there's one for $600, one for $1,500, one for $1,800, and one for $675. Offhand it looks like they probably average less than $1,700."*

Carlos: *"Do a t test. Null hypothesis is mean equals 1,700, alternative is mean less than 1,700, to see if we can show that guy is wrong. The P-value is 0.08. Should we reject the null hypothesis?"*

Dominique: *"If it was like your minister or priest telling you they average $1,700, then you'd make the cutoff smaller, since you'd start out trusting him. But if it's just some guy*

Students Talk Stats continued ➜

Students Talk Stats continued

who's trying to make a profit, then the cutoff for a small P-value could be 0.10. I think we can reject the null hypothesis, in which case they average less than $1,700 overall and he's lying. I think you should look around for a cheaper pool table, Adam."

```
One-Sample T: PoolTablePrice
Test of mu = 1700 vs mu < 1700
Variable            N       Mean      StDev       SE Mean
PoolTablePri        4       1144      598             299
Variable      95.0%  Upper Bound       T           P
PoolTablePri                 1847     -1.86       0.080
```

The steps in carrying out a hypothesis test about μ are summarized in the Chapter Summary on page 504.

EXERCISES FOR SECTION 10.2

Inference for a Mean When the Population Standard Deviation Is Unknown and the Sample Size Is Small

Note: Asterisked numbers indicate exercises whose answers are provided in the Solutions to Selected Exercises section, on page 689.

*10.14 Two columns of data have been summarized; one consisted of a random sample of 100 values from the z distribution and the other consisted of a random sample of 100 values from the t distribution with 4 degrees of freedom. Explain how we know that the second column, C2, represents a t distribution.

Variable	N	Mean	Median	TrMean	StDev	SE Mean
C1	100	0.0928	0.2137	0.0828	0.9929	0.0993
C2	100	0.004	-0.058	-0.045	1.362	0.136

10.15 Two columns of data are displayed with side-by-side boxplots. One column consisted of a random sample of 100 values from the z distribution and the other consisted of a random sample of 100 values from the t distribution with 4 degrees of freedom. Which boxplot represents the t distribution: the one on the left or the one on the right?

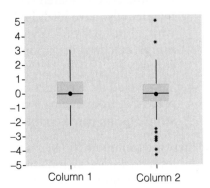

*10.16 "Adults Who Stutter: Responses to Cognitive Stress," published in the *Journal of Speech*

and *Hearing Research* in 1994, reported that speech rate, in words per minute, for 9 stutterers had mean 90.4 and standard deviation 9.7.

a. Use the fact that the t multiplier for 8 degrees of freedom at 90% confidence is 1.86 to construct a 90% confidence interval for mean speech rate of all stutterers.

b. If 9.7 were known population standard deviation, instead of sample standard deviation, what would the multiplier be instead of 1.86?

c. If standard deviation had been smaller than 9.7, would the interval be wider or narrower?

d. If the sample size had been larger than 9, would the interval be wider or narrower?

e. If a higher level of confidence were desired, would the interval be wider or narrower?

10.17 "Adults Who Stutter: Responses to Cognitive Stress," published in the *Journal of Speech and Hearing Research* in 1994, reported that speech rate, in words per minute, for 9 stutterers under conditions of stress had mean 52.6 and standard deviation 3.2.

a. Use the fact that the t multiplier for 8 degrees of freedom at 99% confidence is 3.36 to construct a 99% confidence interval for mean speech rate of all stutterers under conditions of stress.

b. If a lower level of confidence were desired, would the interval be wider or narrower?

c. If standard deviation had been larger than 3.2, would the interval be wider or narrower?

d. If the sample size had been smaller than 9, would the interval be wider or narrower?

e. If 3.2 were known population standard deviation, instead of sample standard deviation, would the interval be wider or narrower?

*10.18 In "Reproduction, Growth and Development in Captive Beluga," published in the journal *Zoo Biology* in 2005, researchers observed captive male beluga whales in various aquariums. Number of calves sired was recorded for all 10 males included in the study.

a. Formulate the appropriate null and alternative hypotheses (using mathematical symbols) if we want to test whether the mean number of calves sired by all captive male belugas exceeds 1.0.

b. The mean number of calves sired by sampled males was found to be 1.4 (thus, greater than 1) and the standard deviation was 1.35. Find the standardized sample mean.

c. Explain why the standardized sample mean should be identified as t and not z.

d. Based on your alternative hypothesis, would the P-value be a left-tailed, right-tailed, or two-tailed probability?

e. For most t distributions (including that for samples of size 10), values between 0 and 1 are quite common; values close to 2 may be considered borderline, values close to 3 are unusually large, and values considerably greater than 3 are extremely large. Characterize the P-value as being not small at all, somewhat small, quite small, or extremely small (close to zero).

f. Tell whether or not the data provide evidence that mean number of calves sired by all male beluga whales in captivity exceeds 1.0.

10.19 In "Husbandry, Overwinter Care, and Reproduction of Captive Striped Skunks," published in the journal *Zoo Biology* in 2005, researchers recorded litter size of 16 captured female striped skunks.

a. Formulate the appropriate null and alternative hypotheses (using mathematical symbols) if we want to test whether the mean litter size for all captive female striped skunks is less than 6.

b. The mean litter size for sampled females was found to be 5.813 (thus, less than 6), and the standard deviation was 1.109. Find the standardized sample mean, under the assumption that the null hypothesis is true.

c. Explain why the standardized sample mean should be identified as t and not z.

d. Based on your alternative hypothesis, would the P-value be a left-tailed, right-tailed, or two-tailed probability?

e. For most t distributions (including that for samples of size 16), values between 0 and ± 1 are quite common; values close to ± 2 may be considered borderline, values close to ± 3 are unusually large, and values considerably greater than 3 in absolute value are extremely large. Characterize the P-value as being not small at all, somewhat small, quite small, or extremely small (close to zero).

f. Tell whether or not the data provide evidence that mean litter size for all captive female striped skunks is less than 6.

g. Researchers considered separately three females who gave birth in 2002, each with a litter size of 7. Explain why the sample standard deviation in this case is zero.

h. Why would the mechanics of the t test prevent us from finding a standardized sample mean, based on the data in part (g)?

*10.20 Here are stemplots for ages at death (with leaves representing years) and weights (with leaves representing hundreds of kilograms) of 20 dinosaur specimens.

```
Ages              Weights
0  22             0  00124677
0  57             1  01125778
1  0444           2  9
1  5567888        3  2
2  1224           4
2  8              5  06
```

For which data set is the shape close enough to normal, given the sample size (20), so that sample mean $\bar{x}$ would be approximately normal and a t procedure would be appropriate to perform inference about the larger population of dinosaurs: ages, weights, both, or neither? Explain.

10.21 Here are histograms showing number of days skipped in a typical month, and number of evenings out in a typical week, for a sample of thousands of 12th graders who participated in the Inter-university Consortium of Political and Social Research survey in 2004.

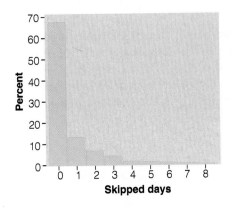
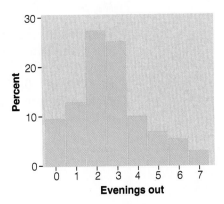

a. For which data set is the shape close enough to normal, given the sample size, so that sample mean $\bar{x}$ would be approximately normal and a z procedure would be appropriate to perform inference about the larger population of students: skipped days, evenings out, both, or neither? Explain.

b. Suppose that only 30 students had been sampled. For which data set would a z or t procedure be appropriate: skipped days, evenings out, both, or neither? Explain.

10.3 A Closer Look at Inference for Means

Pages 923 to 924 in the ***TBP*** *Supplement*, which include Examples TBP 10.10 and TBP 10.11, discuss the use of t tables for both confidence intervals and hypothesis tests.

Now that the basic steps in a test of hypotheses about a population mean have been presented, we consider several important aspects of such tests, including how they relate to confidence intervals:

- Impact of the form of the alternative hypothesis in borderline cases
- Role of sample size and spread
- Type I and II Errors
- Relationship between tests and confidence intervals
- Correct language for stating conclusions
- Robustness of procedures

A One-Sided or Two-Sided Alternative Hypothesis about a Mean

If the size of our test statistic is "borderline," then testing against a one-sided or two-sided alternative can have a major impact on our test's conclusions.

EXAMPLE 10.18 A T TEST WITH A ONE-SIDED OR TWO-SIDED ALTERNATIVE

Background: A sample of 4 Math SAT scores is taken: 570, 580, 640, 760. Their mean is 637.5 and the standard deviation is 87.3, so if we want to test if the population mean is 500, the standardized sample mean is $t = \frac{637.5 - 500}{87.3/\sqrt{4}} = 3.15$.

Questions: How does our t statistic compare to relevant values in our sketch of the t distribution for 3 degrees of freedom? What do we conclude if we test at the $\alpha = 0.05$ level against $H_a : \mu > 500$ or if we test against $H_a : \mu \neq 500$?

Responses: The t statistic, 3.15, is just below 3.18, which is the value associated with a right-tail probability of 0.025. For the one-sided alternative, the P-value is slightly more than 0.025, small enough to reject H_0 at the $\alpha = 0.05$ level. For the two-sided alternative, the P-value is slightly more than 2(0.025) = 0.05, which is *not* small enough to reject H_0.

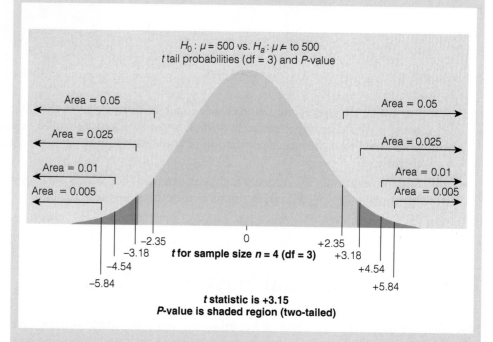

If the test is carried out using software, the P-value is 0.026 for the one-sided test and 0.051 for the two-sided test.

Practice: *Try Exercise 10.22(f) on page 498.*

Concluding that 500 is a plausible population mean, when the sample values are 570, 580, 640, and 760, might seem inconsistent with common sense. There are several weaknesses in our testing process in Example 10.18 that bear thinking about:

1. Under the circumstances, a two-sided alternative would be a poor choice. There are good reasons for suspecting our population of college students in a statistics course to average *higher* on their Math SAT than the population of high school students, which includes all those who don't go on to college.

2. The sample size was extremely small. Because of the mechanics of the test, which we will review shortly, small samples make it difficult to reject the

null hypothesis, and make us vulnerable to Type II Errors (failing to reject H_0, even though it's false).

3. Blind adherence to a cutoff probability of 0.05 is not a good tactic. A P-value of 0.051 coming from a sample of size 4 could easily be considered "small."

4. A t test makes it more difficult to reject a null hypothesis than a z test, because the t distribution is more spread out than z, especially for a small sample size like 4. The fact that it has more spread means that values must be farther from 0 to be considered "unusual." A little bit of research into SAT scores could be used to find the population standard deviation so that a z test could have been carried out. If σ turned out to be close to our sample standard deviation, 87.3, we would have z approximately 3.15, which would yield a very small P-value and allow us to reject the null hypothesis that population mean equals 500.

The Role of Sample Size and Spread: What Leads to Small P-Values?

Observe that

$$t = \frac{\bar{x} - \mu_0}{s/\sqrt{n}} = \frac{(\bar{x} - \mu_0)\sqrt{n}}{s}$$

We reject H_0 for a small P-value, which in turn has arisen from a t that is large in absolute value, on the fringes of the t curve. There are three components that can result in a t that is large in absolute value, which in turn causes us to reject H_0.

1. What we tend to focus on as the cause of rejecting H_0 is a *large difference* $\bar{x} - \mu_0$ between the observed sample mean $\bar{x}$ and the mean μ_0 proposed in the null hypothesis. Because $\bar{x} - \mu_0$ is multiplied in the numerator of t, a large difference naturally makes t large and the P-value small.

2. Because $\sqrt{n}$ is actually multiplied in the numerator of the test statistic t, a *large sample size n* (shown on the right) tends to produce a larger t and a smaller P-value, making it more likely that H_0 will be rejected. If a very large sample size leads to a conclusion of a statistically significant difference between the observed $\bar{x}$ and the claimed μ_0, we should consider whether this difference also has practical significance. Conversely, as the graph on the left shows, a small value of n tends to result in a t that is not large and a P-value that is not small.

The **Big Picture: A CLOSER LOOK**

If we happen to know σ and our standardized test statistic is z, then the same three components affect the size of our z statistic, with σ substituted for s in #3.

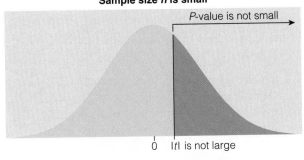

Sample size n is small

P-value is not small

0 |t| is not large

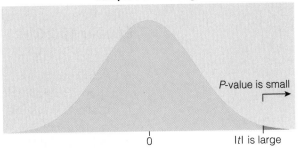

Sample size n is large

P-value is small

0 |t| is large

3. Because the standard deviation s is in the denominator, *smaller s* results in a larger t statistic, which, in turn, results in a smaller P-value. In general, we stand a better chance of rejecting a null hypothesis when the distribution has little spread. When values are concentrated very close to their mean, we are in a better position to detect even subtle differences between what is hypothesized and what is observed. This phenomenon will be explored in the next example.

EXAMPLE 10.19 THE ROLE OF SPREAD IN TESTING ABOUT A MEAN

Background: A sample of weights of female mallard ducks could be used to test against the alternative hypothesis $\mu < 600$ to see if there is evidence that, in general, female mallards weigh less than the known average for males (600 grams).

Female mallards at a *particular* age—say, 35 weeks—have weights that are concentrated around what is typical for that age. A sample of 4 female mallards at 35 weeks of age is found to have a mean weight of 500 grams, with a standard deviation of 30 grams. The P-value in a test against $H_a : \mu < 600$ is 0.0034.

In contrast, female mallard ducks of *all* ages have weights with a great deal of spread because they include sizes all the way from hatchlings to full-grown. If a sample of 4 female mallards of various ages also has a mean weight of 500 grams, but a much larger standard deviation of 90 grams, then the P-value is 0.0564.

Question: Why is there such a dramatic difference in the P-values, depending on whether the standard deviation is 30 grams or 90 grams?

Response: For $s = 30$, our test statistic is $t = \frac{500 - 600}{30/\sqrt{4}} = -6.67$, which is clearly large, even for a small sample size. If $s = 90$ (three times as large), then the t statistic is one-third the original size: $t = \frac{500 - 600}{90/\sqrt{4}} = -2.22$, which could be considered borderline. Samples with a great deal of spread make it more difficult for us to pinpoint what is true for the population, or to reject a proposed value as being implausible.

Practice: *Try Exercise 10.23(b) on page 499.*

Type I and II Errors: Mistakes in Conclusions about Means

If we keep testing a true null hypothesis, in the long run, the laws of probability indicate that we will reject it occasionally. Therefore, we should be cautious about performing **multiple tests** and then singling out the cases where the P-value is small.

EXAMPLE 10.20 HOW MULTIPLE TESTS CAN LEAD TO TYPE I ERROR

Background: Assume all ACT test scores in a state have a mean of 21. Suppose an education expert randomly samples ACT scores of 20 students each in 100 schools across the state, and finds that in 4 of those schools, the sample mean ACT score is significantly lower than 21, using a cutoff level of $\alpha = 0.05$.

Question: Are these 4 schools necessarily inferior in that their students do significantly worse than 21 on the ACTs?

Response: No. We should first note that 20 indicates the sample size here, and 100 is the number of tests—in other words, we test $H_0 : \mu = 21$ versus $H_a : \mu < 21$ again and again, 100 times. If $\alpha = 0.05$ is used as a cutoff, then 5% of the time in the long run we will reject H_0 even when it is true. Roughly, 5 schools in 100 will produce samples of students with ACT scores low enough to reject H_0, just by chance in the selection process, even if the mean for all students at those schools is in fact 21.

Practice: *Try Exercise 10.26 on page 500.*

Multiple testing makes us vulnerable to committing a Type I Error—rejecting a null hypothesis even when it is true. Running many tests at once with 0.05 as a cutoff for small P-values is also prescribing 0.05 to be the probability of a Type I Error. If only one test is carried out, then the chance of rejecting a true null hypothesis is small. If 100 tests are run, we're almost sure to commit several Type I Errors.

We were vulnerable to a Type II Error (failing to reject a false null hypothesis) in Example 10.18 on page 492, when we concluded that $\mu \neq 500$ based on a sample of 4 Math SAT scores whose mean was 637.5. A common circumstance for committing this type of error is when the sample size is too small.

Relating Tests and Confidence Intervals for Means

After learning how to perform inference about a population proportion using confidence intervals and then hypothesis tests, we discussed the relationship between results of these two forms of inference. The same sort of relationship holds for confidence intervals and tests about a population mean, and just as we saw with inference about proportions, this relationship can be invoked either formally or informally. We will again stress the latter approach, keeping in mind that our ad hoc conclusion should be confirmed using more precise methods, if a definitive answer is required.

> ### Informal Guidelines Relating Confidence Interval to Test Results
>
> If a proposed value of population mean is *inside* a confidence interval for population mean, we expect *not* to reject the null hypothesis that population mean equals that value. If the value falls *outside* the confidence interval, we anticipate that the null hypothesis *will* be rejected. To relate confidence intervals and hypothesis tests more formally, it would be necessary to take into account the confidence level and cutoff probability α, as well as whether the test alternative is one-sided or two-sided.

We explore the relationship between confidence intervals and tests by considering situations where the proposed mean is well outside the interval, where it is well-contained in the interval, and where it is on the border.

EXAMPLE 10.21 RELATING TEST AND CONFIDENCE INTERVAL RESULTS

Background: We have produced confidence intervals for the following unknown population means:

Continued

The Big Picture: A Closer Look

Example 10.20 reminds us to think about the cutoff level for a small P-value in a hypothesis test about μ as the long-run probability that our test will incorrectly reject a true null hypothesis. Similarly, level of confidence in a confidence interval about μ tells us the long-run probability of producing an interval that succeeds in capturing μ.

1. Earnings:

```
Variable         95.0% CI           T         P
Earned        ( 3.171, 4.381)     -3.98     0.000
```

2. Male shoe size:

```
Variable         95.0% CI           T         P
Shoe          ( 9.917, 12.527)     0.39     0.705
```

3. Math SAT score:

```
Variable         95.0% CI           T         P
MathSAT       ( 498.6,  776.4)     3.15     0.051
```

Question: What do the confidence intervals suggest we would conclude about the following claims?

1. Population mean earnings equals $5,000.

2. Population mean male shoe size equals 11.0.

3. Population mean Math SAT score equals 500.

Response: In each case, we check to see if the proposed population mean is contained in the confidence interval.

1. Because $5,000 is far above the upper bound of the first interval, we anticipate that a formal hypothesis test would reject the claim that $\mu = 5,000$. The P-value 0.000 is consistent with this, because it is so small.

2. Because 11.0 is well inside the second interval, we anticipate that a formal hypothesis test would not reject the claim that $\mu = 11.0$. The P-value 0.705 is consistent with this, because it is not small at all.

3. Because 500 is extremely close to the lower bound of our third confidence interval, 498.6, we expect a test might be a close call. In fact, the P-value 0.051 is what we generally consider to be borderline.

Practice: *Try Exercise 10.27(c,i) on page 500.*

For simplicity's sake, Example 10.21 did not specify alternative hypotheses. Of course, if our proposed sample mean falls outside the interval in the opposite direction from what the alternative claims, we could not reject the null hypothesis. For instance, if a 95% confidence interval for population mean earnings is (3.171, 4.381), and we test against the alternative hypothesis $H_a : \mu > 5.000$, then we would have no evidence at all to reject the null hypothesis in favor of the alternative because the entire interval falls *below* 5.000.

Correct Language in Hypothesis Test Conclusions about a Mean

When we discussed hypothesis tests about population proportion, we stressed that results of a test are not 100% conclusive. The only way to know for sure what is true about the entire population is to gather data about every individual, as the U.S. Census attempts to do. The goal of statistical inference is to use information from a sample to draw conclusions about the larger population, and our theory even *requires* the population to be at least 10 times the sample size. This means that at least 90% of the population values (usually a much larger percentage) remain unknown. We should keep this built-in uncertainty in mind when we are stating results of a test about an unknown population mean.

EXAMPLE 10.22 CORRECT INTERPRETATION OF TEST RESULTS WHEN THE P-VALUE IS SMALL

Background: Based on a sample of 445 students, we test a claim that the mean number of credits taken by all introductory statistics students at a certain university equals 15, against the alternative that the mean exceeds 15. The *P*-value is quite small, just 0.005.

```
Test of mu = 15 vs mu > 15
Variable            N      Mean     StDev      SE Mean
Credits           445   15.2517    2.0290       0.0962
Variable      90.0% Lower Bound          T         P
Credits                   15.1282       2.62     0.005
```

Questions: Because the *P*-value is so small, can we conclude that the population mean for credits is much larger than 15? Have we proven that the population mean exceeds 15?

Responses: We can say we have very strong evidence that the population mean exceeds 15. In fact, the true population mean might be quite close to 15—after all, the sample mean is 15.25. Apparently, the small *P*-value is due to the very large sample size.

Even though the evidence against the null hypothesis is very strong, we still can't say we've proven it to be false. In the long run, even large samples sometimes happen to consist of values that, as a group, turn out to be nonrepresentative.

Practice: *Try Exercise 10.30(a) on page 501.*

EXAMPLE 10.23 CORRECT INTERPRETATION OF TEST RESULTS WHEN THE P-VALUE IS NOT SMALL

Background: A test was carried out on the claim that the mean number of cigarettes smoked in a day by all smoking students at a certain university equals 6, against the two-sided alternative. The *P*-value is 0.841, not small at all, so there is no evidence at all to reject the null hypothesis.

Question: Have we proven that the population mean equals 6?

Response: We can say we have no evidence at all that the population mean differs from 6. This is *not* the same as proving that the mean equals 6.

Practice: *Try Exercise 10.33(d) on page 502.*

In general, if we reject the null hypothesis, then we can say we have convincing evidence that the alternative is true (not the same thing as proving the alternative to be true, or proving the null hypothesis to be false). If we do not reject the null hypothesis, then we say we can continue to believe it to be true (not the same thing as proving it to be true, or proving the alternative to be false).

Robustness of Procedures

On page 466, we presented guidelines that require us to use larger samples if the underlying distribution is apparently non-normal. In practice, users of statistics are often faced with the question of what to do if the data set is small and somewhat skewed. In other words, how *robust* are our procedures against violations of normality?

> *Definition* A statistical procedure is **robust** against violations of a needed condition if the procedure still gives fairly accurate results when the condition is not satisfied.

The most important condition of concern is for the underlying population to be normal. When we report a confidence interval or a P-value for a z or t procedure, it is technically accurate only if we have sampled from a normal population. Fortunately, the confidence interval and the P-value are usually pretty accurate if the population is not normal, unless there is pronounced non-normality and the samples are quite small.

Many aspects of the t test that we have discussed in this section apply just as well to the z test. These include the importance of formulating a proper alternative hypothesis, the roles of sample size and spread, the implications of Type I and II Errors, the relationship between test results and confidence intervals, the correct interpretation of the test results, and robustness.

EXERCISES FOR SECTION 10.3

A Closer Look at Inference for Means

Note: Asterisked numbers indicate exercises whose answers are provided in the Solutions to Selected Exercises section, on page 689.

*10.22 The mean price per bottle of all wines sold by a New York company is $44. A test on the 10 types of Merlot on the company's price list is carried out to see if Merlot is, on average, cheaper than all the wines in general.

```
Test of mu = 44 vs mu < 44
Variable           N      Mean      StDev     SE Mean
Merlot             10     XXXXX     13.73       4.34
Variable      90.0% Upper Bound       T          P
Merlot                     33.30    -3.85      0.002
```

a. State the null and alternative hypotheses using mathematical notation.

b. A histogram of the prices appears fairly normal. Why is this important?

c. The value of the sample mean has been crossed out. Was it greater than or less than 44?

d. Report the P-value and characterize it as being small, not small, or borderline.

e. What do we conclude about the average price of Merlot wines, compared to the company's wine prices in general?

f. What would the P-value have been if we had tested against the alternative $H_a: \mu \neq 44$?

*10.23 *USA Today* reported on a study in which researchers called medical specialists' offices posing as new patients and requesting appointments for non-urgent problems. The mean waiting time (in days) was reported, based on a sample of such requests. Boxplots are shown to accompany the questions in (a), (b), and (c), respectively.

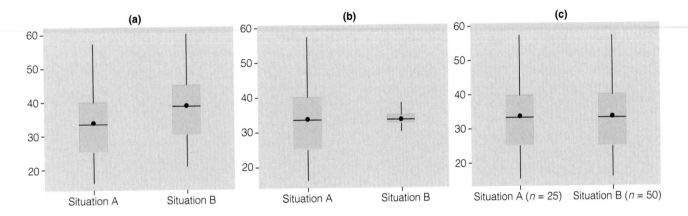

a. In which of the two situations depicted by the boxplots on the left would you be more convinced that the population mean is greater than 30 days: A or B?

b. In which of the two situations depicted by the boxplots in the middle would you be more convinced that the population mean is greater than 30 days: A or B?

c. In which of the two situations depicted by the boxplots on the right would you be more convinced that the population mean is greater than 30 days: A or B?

10.24 A study by the Kaiser Family Foundation looked at how 8- to 18-year-olds spend their leisure time, including how many minutes per day they spend reading books. Boxplots are shown to accompany the questions in (a), (b), and (c), respectively.

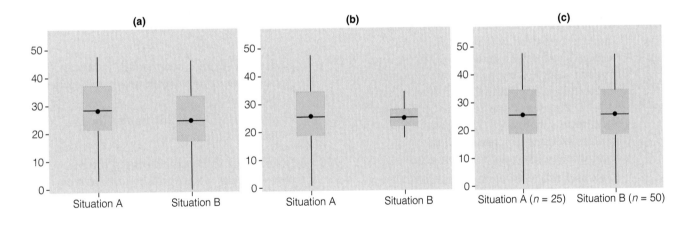

a. In which of the two situations depicted by the boxplots on the left would you be more convinced that the population mean is less than 30 minutes: A or B?

b. In which of the two situations depicted by the boxplots in the middle would you be more convinced that the population mean is less than 30 minutes: A or B?

c. In which of the two situations depicted by the boxplots on the right would you be more convinced that the population mean is less than 30 minutes: A or B?

10.25 In a population of several hundred students, the mean Math SAT score was 610.44, and standard deviation was 72.14. Repeated random samples of size 40 were taken, and for each sample a 95% confidence interval was constructed for population mean score. This was done 20 times, for a total of 20 confidence intervals.

Variable	N	Mean	StDev	SE Mean	95.0% CI	Z	P
Mathlargen	39	615.4	58.4	11.6	(592.7, 638.0)	0.43	0.669
Mathlargen	35	595.1	67.4	12.2	(571.2, 619.0)	-1.25	0.210
Mathlargen	34	605.9	62.0	12.4	(581.6, 630.1)	-0.37	0.713
Mathlargen	36	606.7	86.6	12.0	(583.1, 630.2)	-0.31	0.754
Mathlargen	35	613.4	76.5	12.2	(589.5, 637.3)	0.25	0.806
Mathlargen	33	602.7	76.9	12.6	(578.1, 627.3)	-0.61	0.539
Mathlargen	34	625.3	73.1	12.4	(601.0, 649.5)	1.20	0.230
Mathlargen	33	624.2	76.1	12.6	(599.6, 648.9)	1.10	0.272
Mathlargen	35	596.3	66.3	12.2	(572.4, 620.2)	-1.16	0.246
Mathlargen	38	608.7	73.7	11.7	(585.7, 631.6)	-0.15	0.881
Mathlargen	36	622.8	61.1	12.0	(599.2, 646.3)	1.03	0.305
Mathlargen	36	608.1	75.2	12.0	(584.5, 631.6)	-0.20	0.843
Mathlargen	34	614.4	76.1	12.4	(590.2, 638.7)	0.32	0.748
Mathlargen	34	614.1	78.7	12.4	(589.9, 638.4)	0.30	0.766
Mathlargen	36	582.5	78.1	12.0	(558.9, 606.1)	-2.32	0.020
Mathlargen	39	597.7	66.5	11.6	(575.1, 620.3)	-1.10	0.270
Mathlargen	34	627.6	87.2	12.4	(603.4, 651.9)	1.39	0.164
Mathlargen	34	616.5	84.8	12.4	(592.2, 640.7)	0.49	0.626
Mathlargen	37	619.7	58.4	11.9	(596.5, 643.0)	0.78	0.433
Mathlargen	36	613.3	60.4	12.0	(589.8, 636.9)	0.24	0.810

a. In general, what is the probability that a 95% confidence interval contains the true value of the parameter?

b. If 20 intervals are produced, each with 95% confidence, in the long run about how many will succeed in capturing the true value of the parameter?

c. How many of the 20 intervals above contain the population mean 610.44?

d. Will the same number of intervals contain the population mean in every set of twenty 95% confidence intervals? Explain.

*10.26 In a population of several hundred students, the mean Math SAT score was 610.44, and standard deviation was 72.14. Repeated random samples of size 40 were taken, and for each sample a hypothesis test was carried out, testing if population mean score equals 610.44. This was done 20 times, for a total of 20 tests. Exercise 10.25 showed standardized mean score z and the accompanying P-value for each test.

a. In general, what is the probability that a test of a null hypothesis that is actually true rejects it, using 0.05 as the cutoff level α for what is considered to be a small P-value?

b. If 20 tests of a true null hypothesis are carried out at the 0.05 level, on average, about how many will (correctly) fail to reject it? How many will (incorrectly) reject it?

c. How many of the 20 P-values above are small enough to reject $H_0 : \mu = 610.44$ at the $\alpha = 0.05$ level? (If any are small enough, tell what they are.)

d. Will the same number of P-values be small enough to reject H_0 in every set of 20 tests? Explain.

e. If the P-value is very small, what can you say about the corresponding confidence interval?

f. Explain why roughly half of the z statistics are negative.

*10.27 A survey of 192 medical school interns, whose results were published in the *New England Journal of Medicine* in January 2005, found them to average 57 hours of work a week, with standard deviation 16 hours.

a. Explain why the distribution of sample mean, $\bar{x}$, will have an approximately normal shape even if the distribution of hours worked is not normal.

b. Explain why standardized sample mean will follow an approximate z distribution, even if we standardize with sample standard deviation s instead of population standard deviation σ.

c. Report an approximate 95% confidence interval for mean hours worked per week by the population of interns, rounding to the nearest tenth (one decimal place).

d. If the interval were to be constructed with software, would we use a z or a t procedure?

e. Explain why 40 is not a plausible value for population mean hours worked per week, based on your confidence interval.

f. Find the value of standardized sample mean, if population mean were 40.

g. Explain why 40 is not a plausible value for population mean hours worked per week if sample mean is 57, based on the standardized value of 57.

h. If we were to carry out a formal test to see if the population mean could be 40, based on a sample mean of 57, how should the alternative hypothesis be written: $H_a : \bar{x} \neq 40$, or $H_a : \mu \neq 40$, or $H_a : \bar{x} > 40$, or $H_a : \mu > 40$, or $H_a : \bar{x} \neq 57$, or $H_a : \mu \neq 57$, or $H_a : \bar{x} > 57$, or $H_a : \mu > 57$?

i. Based on your confidence interval in part (c), would you reject the null hypothesis $H_0 : \mu = 40$?

10.28 A survey of 2,737 medical school interns found their average age to be 28.0 years, with standard deviation 3.9 years.

a. Explain why the distribution of sample mean, $\bar{x}$, will have an approximately normal shape even if the distribution of ages is not normal.

b. Explain why standardized sample mean will follow an approximate z distribution, even if we standardize with sample standard deviation s instead of population standard deviation σ.

c. Report an approximate 95% confidence interval for population mean age of interns, rounding to the nearest hundredth (two decimal places).

d. Use your confidence interval to report whether or not each of these is a plausible value for population mean age: 27.9, 28.0, 28.1, 28.2, 30.0.

e. Find the value of standardized sample mean, if population mean is 30.

f. Explain why 30 is not a plausible value for population mean age if sample mean is 28, based on the standardized value of 28.

g. If we were to carry out a formal test, how should the alternative hypothesis be written: $H_a : \bar{x} \neq 28$, or $H_a : \mu \neq 28$, or $H_a : \bar{x} < 28$, or $H_a : \mu < 28$, or $H_a : \bar{x} \neq 30$, or $H_a : \mu \neq 30$, or $H_a : \bar{x} < 30$, or $H_a : \mu < 30$?

h. Based on your confidence interval in part (c), would you reject the null hypothesis $H_0 : \mu = 30$?

10.29 Results for a 1997 survey of about 25,000 male nonfarm wage and salary workers were published in the *Monthly Labor Review* in 1998. Hours worked in the week prior to the survey were found to have mean 42.66 and standard deviation 12.46.

a. Find the standardized sample mean weekly hours worked, if population mean was equal to 40.

b. Based on your answer to part (a), what can we assert about the population mean hours worked by male nonfarm wage and salary workers?

*10.30 The *P*-value for testing if male workers average significantly more than 40 hours in a week is extremely small, close to zero.

a. Does this mean we have evidence that all male workers average much more than 40 hours a week, or does it mean we have strong evidence that all male workers average more than 40 hours a week?

b. Would 40 be contained in a 99% confidence interval for population mean hours worked by all male workers?

10.31 Results for a 1997 survey of about 25,000 female nonfarm wage and salary workers were published in the *Monthly Labor Review* in 1998. Hours worked in the week prior to the survey were found to have mean 36.90 and standard deviation 11.93.

a. Find the standardized sample mean weekly hours worked, if population mean was equal to 40.

b. Based on your answer to part (a), what do we conclude about the population mean hours worked by female nonfarm wage and salary workers?

10.32 The *P*-value for testing if female workers average significantly less than 40 hours in a week is extremely small, close to zero.

a. Does this mean we have evidence that all female workers average much less than 40 hours a week, or does it mean we have strong evidence that all female workers average less than 40 hours a week?

b. Would 40 be contained in a 99% confidence interval for population mean hours worked by all female workers?

*10.33 "Domestic Goats Follow Gaze Direction and Use Social Cues in an Object Choice Task," published online in *Animal Behavior* in January 2005, included information on 23 goats' performance in a bucket-selection task under control conditions.[3] Here are their scores (each on a test of 18 trials), which can be shown to have mean 8.8 and standard deviation 1.8:

4	6	7	7	8	8	8	8	8	8	9	9	9	9	9	10	10	10	10	11	11	11	12

a. Construct a histogram to verify that the shape of the distribution of scores is roughly normal.

b. If we want to see if this sample provides evidence that all goats would average better than chance, how would the null and alternative hypotheses be formulated: $H_0: \mu = 9$ versus $H_a: \mu > 9$, or $H_0: \bar{x} = 9$ versus $H_a: \bar{x} > 9$, or $H_0: \mu = 8.8$ versus $H_a: \mu > 8.8$, or $H_0: \bar{x} = 8.8$ versus $H_a: \bar{x} > 8.8$?

c. If a goat performed at chance level, its score would be 9. Explain why a formal test is not necessary to establish that the goats failed to perform significantly better than chance.

d. The *P*-value for the test to see if the goats did significantly better than chance is 0.715, which is not small at all. Can we say we have proven that goats in general do not perform better than chance with the given social cues?

e. Use the fact that the *t* distribution multiplier for 22 degrees of freedom at 95% confidence is roughly 2 to construct an approximate 95% confidence interval for mean score of all goats under these conditions (round to the nearest hundredth).

The fact that sample size is being checked for two reasons (see the summary on page 503) is a common source of confusion for students. The standardized statistic

$$\frac{\bar{x} - \mu}{s/\sqrt{n}}$$

may be written *t* only if $\bar{x}$ follows an approximately normal distribution. We look at a graph of the data, and must rule out the use of a *t* procedure if the sample size is not large enough to take care of non-normality in the underlying distribution of *x* values. At this stage, we presented in this book guidelines according to whether *n* is small (less than 15), medium (between 15 and 30), or large (greater than 30). Even if σ is known, we cannot refer to $\frac{\bar{x} - \mu}{\sigma/\sqrt{n}}$ as *z* unless $\bar{x}$ is approximately normal. The second reason for checking sample size is when σ is unknown and we want to decide if $t = \frac{\bar{x} - \mu}{s/\sqrt{n}}$ can be treated as *z*. For this decision, we offer the Rule of Thumb that *n* be at least 30.

CHAPTER 10 SUMMARY

The Big Picture: The examples presented in this chapter all involved just a single quantitative variable, such as earnings, shoe sizes, weights, or lengths of condor eggs. Whatever the variable, we were interested in drawing conclusions about its mean value for the larger population from which a sample was obtained, performing inference in the usual ways (confidence intervals or hypothesis tests).

■ **σ known or unknown:** The details of both intervals and tests differ depending on whether or not population standard deviation σ is known. In real-life applications, the population standard deviation is rarely known.

■ **Checking sample size:** Regardless of whether or not σ is known, we must always check that we have n large enough to offset non-normality as evidenced in displays of the data; otherwise, neither z nor t is appropriate. As far as approximating σ with s is concerned, what size n can be considered "large" is a matter of personal taste, but 30 may be a reasonable choice. This table outlines proper procedures to be used under various conditions.

	σ **Known**	σ **Unknown**
Small sample ($n < 30$)	$\dfrac{\bar{x} - \mu}{\sigma/\sqrt{n}} = z$	$\dfrac{\bar{x} - \mu}{s/\sqrt{n}} = t$
Large sample ($n \geq 30$)	$\dfrac{\bar{x} - \mu}{\sigma/\sqrt{n}} = z$	$\dfrac{\bar{x} - \mu}{s/\sqrt{n}} \approx z$ by hand; t procedure with software

With software, we must use a t procedure unless σ happens to be known (which is rare). By hand or "in our heads" for estimation purposes, the table guides us to think in terms of a z distribution when σ is known or if the sample is large.

■ **Three forms of inference:** To draw conclusions about unknown population mean for a single quantitative variable, we begin by using sample mean $\bar{x}$ as a **point estimate** for unknown population mean μ. We elaborate on this estimate with a **confidence interval** to set up a range of plausible values for μ, or with a **hypothesis test** to decide whether or not population mean equals a proposed value.

Confidence Intervals

■ **σ known:** A confidence interval for unknown population mean μ is

$$\bar{x} \pm \text{multiplier} \, \frac{\sigma}{\sqrt{n}}$$

where the multiplier is based on the standard normal (z) distribution:

Confidence Level	z Multiplier
90%	1.645
95%	$1.960 \approx 2$
98%	2.326
99%	2.576

The level tells how confident we are that μ is contained in the interval, or it tells the probability that we produce an interval that succeeds in capturing μ.

■ **σ unknown:** A confidence interval for unknown population mean μ is

$$\bar{x} \pm \text{multiplier} \, \frac{s}{\sqrt{n}}$$

where the multiplier is based on the t distribution with $n - 1$ degrees of freedom.

For a given level of confidence, the t multiplier is always larger than the z multiplier. When the sample size n is fairly large (at least 20 or 30), the t multiplier is just slightly larger than 2. When the sample size n is small, the t multiplier is closer to 3.

In general, we obtain a narrower confidence interval with larger n and with lower levels of confidence.

Hypothesis Tests

The **Big** *Picture:*

A CLOSER LOOK

Remember that z or t tell us, relative to sample size and spread, how different the sample mean $\bar{x}$ is from the proposed population mean μ_0.

Note that focusing on the size of z, as in the table below, is reminiscent of the traditional way of deciding between the null and alternative hypotheses that used "critical values": Reject the null hypothesis if the test statistic exceeds a certain value. Here the emphasis is on looking for large test statistics, rather than looking for small P-values. In the end, knowing the exact P-value helps us assess the strength of evidence (or lack thereof) against H_0.

Summary of Hypothesis Test about Population Mean

0. State null and alternative hypotheses about unknown population mean μ:

$$H_0 : \mu = \mu_0 \text{ versus } H_a : \begin{cases} \mu > \mu_0 \\ \mu < \mu_0 \\ \mu \neq \mu_0 \end{cases}$$

   where μ_0 is the hypothesized value of population mean.

1. The sample must be unbiased, the population must be relatively large, and the sample size must be large enough to guarantee the shape of sample mean $\bar{x}$ to be approximately normal.

2. Find the observed sample mean $\bar{x}$. If the alternative is one-sided, check if $\bar{x}$ tends in the direction claimed by the alternative. If $\bar{x}$ tends in the right direction, standardize it to z or t, depending on whether or not σ is known:

$$z = \frac{\bar{x} - \mu_0}{\sigma/\sqrt{n}} \text{ or } t = \frac{\bar{x} - \mu_0}{s/\sqrt{n}}$$

3. Identify the P-value as the probability, assuming the null hypothesis $H_0 : \mu = \mu_0$ is true, of a sample mean $\bar{x}$ at least as extreme as the one observed. Specifically, the P-value is the probability of a sample mean

   ■ greater than or equal to $\bar{x}$, if we have $H_a : \mu > \mu_0$.

   ■ less than or equal to $\bar{x}$, if we have $H_a : \mu < \mu_0$.

   ■ at least as far from μ_0 in either direction as $\bar{x}$, if we have $H_a : \mu \neq \mu_0$.

4. If the P-value is small, reject the null hypothesis $H_0 : \mu = \mu_0$ in favor of the alternative: Conclude that the population mean is greater/less/different than the proposed value. If the P-value is not small, do not reject the null hypothesis: Conclude that the population mean may well equal the proposed value.

This table provides some rough guidelines for estimating the relative size of a z statistic if software or tables are unavailable. In fact, a careful look at the t table at the end of the book shows that t is quite similar to z unless the degrees of freedom are very small—that is, unless sample size n is very small.

Whether the P-value is found based on z for known σ or t for unknown σ, $H_0 : \mu = \mu_0$ is rejected if the P-value is deemed "small." Often $\alpha = 0.05$ is used as a cutoff probability for what P-values are considered small, but other levels such as 0.10 or 0.01 may be more appropriate, depending on the circumstances.

	Common	Not Unusual	Borderline	Quite Unusual	Extremely Improbable
$|z|$	less than 1	closer to 1 than to 2	around 2	considerably greater than 2	greater than 3

CHAPTER 10 EXERCISES

Note: Asterisked numbers indicate exercises whose answers are provided in the Solutions to Selected Exercises section, on page 689.

Additional exercises appeared after each section: inference for means with *z* (Section 10.1) on page 477, inference for means with *t* (Section 10.2) on page 489, and a closer look at inference for means (Section 10.3) on page 498.

Warming Up: INFERENCE FOR SINGLE QUANTITATIVE VARIABLES

10.34 "Domestic Goats Follow Gaze Direction and Use Social Cues in An Object Choice Task," published online in *Animal Behavior* in January 2005, included information on goats' performance in a bucket-selection task, when cued by a handler who gazed at the correct bucket. If a goat performed at chance level, its score would be 9; each of the goats' performances was tested to see if it performed significantly better than chance on the 18 trials. Tell whether the standardized score *z* for each of these goats would be positive or negative:

   a. Trudi: score 7

   b. Weissohr: score 14

   c. Stumpfhorn: score 10

   d. Weisshuf: score 8

10.35 "Domestic Goats Follow Gaze Direction and Use Social Cues in An Object Choice Task," published online in *Animal Behavior* in January 2005, included information on 23 goats' performance in a bucket-selection task, when cued in one of two ways. The mean score when cued by a handler *touching* the correct bucket was 14.3; the mean score when cued by *pointing* was 11.4. Both standard deviations are the same.

   a. If the goats perform at chance level, they would average 9 overall. Which standardized sample mean would be higher: the one for touching or the one for pointing?

   b. Explain why your answer to part (a) would not necessarily be correct if the standard deviations differed.

   c. Explain why your answer to part (a) would not necessarily be correct if the sample sizes differed.

   d. Which *P*-value would be smaller: the one for touching or the one for pointing?

   e. The standardized test statistic for pointing, which follows an approximate

z distribution, is 5.4. Did the goats perform significantly better than chance when cued by touching, pointing, both, or neither?

10.36 "Domestic Goats Follow Gaze Direction and Use Social Cues in An Object Choice Task," published online in *Animal Behavior* in January 2005, reports how researchers "tested goats' ability to use gaze and other communicative cues given by a human in a so-called object choice situation." Tell whether each of the following focuses on data production, displaying and summarizing data, probability, or statistical inference.

   a. "Across trials, food location was counterbalanced and randomly varied, with the stipulation that it was never placed in the same bucket/location for more than two consecutive trials."

   b. The goat known as "Weissohr" (White Ear) successfully chose 14 out of 18 food buckets. The chance of performing this differently from the expected 9 out of 18 correct choices, if gaze direction actually does not help a goat in making its choice, is 0.031.

   c. On average, when cued with gazing, the goats scored 9.6 correct bucket choices out of 18.

   d. "In both conditions [Touch and Point, as opposed to Gaze] the subjects chose the correct bucket significantly more often in the experimental than in the control condition."

*10.37 "A Survey Method for Characterizing Daily Life Experience: The Day Reconstruction Method," published in *Science* magazine in December 2004, asked a large sample of women to report what they did throughout the day, and how they felt at the time. They were to rate each activity in terms of

More exercises for this chapter are featured in the *TBP Supplement* on pages 927 through 931. End-of-chapter activities are described on page 924.

"positive affect" (among other things), reporting their feeling of happiness/ enjoyment on a scale of 0 to 6. The overall mean positive affect was 3.89.[4] Tell whether the standardized score for each of these specific activities' means (for all the women) would be positive or negative.

a. Commuting: 3.45

b. Eating: 4.34

c. Exercising: 4.31

d. Housework: 3.73

e. Interacting with Boss: 3.52

f. Interacting with Co-workers: 3.76

g. Shopping: 3.95

10.38 "Time in Purgatory: Examining the Grant Lag for U.S. Patent Applications," published online by the Berkeley Electronic Press in 2003, examined grant lag (period of time between an initial patent application and its final granting, in months) for patents on record between 1976 and 1996. There were well over 1 million patents during this period, and their grant lag time had mean 28.4 months, standard deviation 19.7 months.[5] Mean grant lag was found for various smaller subgroups taken from the larger population, depending on who held property rights to the patent. Tell whether each of these would have a positive or negative standardized score z:

a. Government: mean 31.1

b. Independent: mean 28.7

c. Unassigned: mean 26.4

10.39 In "Behavioral Biases Meet the Market: The Case of Magazine Subscription Prices," published in *Advances in Economic Analysis & Policy* in 2005, the authors looked at the ratio of subscription price to newsstand price for all the major magazines in the United States. Values ranged from 0.163 to 1.24, indicating that the best subscription price was just about one-sixth of the newsstand price, whereas the worst was 24% higher than the newsstand price. The mean was found to be 0.553 and the

standard deviation 0.200.[6] If we wanted to verify that, on average, subscription prices are lower than newsstand prices, how should the alternative hypothesis about population mean ratio μ be written (mathematically)?

10.40 In "Predicting Reproduction in Captive Sea Otters," published in the journal *Zoo Biology* in 2005, gestation lengths for an otter named Mali who became pregnant four times from 1998 to 2001 are listed: 220 days, 255 days, 249 days, and 188 days.[7] Explain why these lengths should not be used to estimate the mean gestation length of all captive sea otters.

10.41 When Pope John Paul II died in April 2005, there was some discussion of ages of cardinals throughout the world, in terms of who would be a good candidate for successor, and who could vote for the successor, because only those under 80 years of age were eligible to vote.

a. How would we report the data values if age is treated as a quantitative variable?

b. How would we report the data values if age is treated as a categorical variable?

10.42 An experiment looked at amount of weight lost in a year by subjects assigned to the Atkins diet. Tell whether each of the following focuses on data production, displaying and summarizing, probability, or statistical inference:

a. Researchers randomly assigned some patients to follow the Atkins diet.

b. Mean weight loss at one year was 2.1 kg.

c. If the subjects were a random sample taken from a population whose mean weight loss equaled zero, the probability of a sample mean weight loss as high as 2.1 kg is found to be 0.009.

d. Because the sample mean weight loss is significantly higher than zero, researchers concluded that the Atkins diet is effective.

Exploring the Big Picture: INFERENCE FOR MEANS WITH Z

10.43 "Can Economic Theory Explain Piracy Behavior?," published online in 2003 by Berkeley Electronic Press, reports results for

the survey question, "Assume that your friend has a computer program that is priced in retail stores at _____ and that you are very anxious to get. Assume also that you are offered to copy your friend's program for free. What is the maximum amount you would be willing to pay for the program in a retail store under these circumstances? I would be willing to pay _____."[8] Resulting values of the variable NWTPO (net willingness to pay for the original) were recorded as follows: If retail price was $100 and an individual would be willing to pay $15, then his value of NWTPO would be 0.15. Values of NWTPO for 264 respondents had a mean of 0.1822 and a standard deviation of 0.1899.

a. Suppose a program had been priced at $100. On average, how much would the respondents have been willing to pay for the original?

b. Notice that the standard deviation is more than the mean. Explain why this suggests that the shape of the distribution is skewed, and tell whether it is skewed left or right.

c. Explain why we cannot use the given information and a normal approximation to estimate what proportion of *individual* responses were 0.5 or more.

d. Explain why we *can* use the normal multiplier 2 to set up a 95% confidence interval for the population mean value of NWTPO; report the interval.

e. Is it plausible that, overall, people are willing to pay more than half price for the original instead of pirating it for free?

f. Is it plausible that, overall, people are willing to pay more than one-fourth price for the original instead of pirating it for free?

10.44 "Can Economic Theory Explain Piracy Behavior?," published online in 2003 by Berkeley Electronic Press, reports results for the survey question, "Assume that your friend has a computer program that is priced in retail stores at _____ and that you are very anxious to get. Assume also that you are offered to copy your friend's program for free. What is the maximum amount you would be willing to pay for the program in a retail store under these circumstances? I would be willing to pay _____."[9]

a. Explain why the values of the variable of interest (NWTPO = net willingness to pay for the original) were measured via a survey rather than an observational study or an experiment.

b. Can we assume that the reported values of NWTPO are fairly close to what they are "in real life"? Explain.

c. Another survey question asked, "How large a share of your collection of music is illegally copied?" with response options 0–25%, 26–50%, 51–75%, or 76–100%. What are the advantages to permitting four specific ranges of percentages, instead of phrasing it as an open question?

d. Should results for the question described in part (c) be summarized with a mean or with proportions? Explain.

10.45 In "Egg Size, Fertility, Hatchability, and Chick Survivability in Captive California Condors," published in the journal *Zoo Biology* in 2005, researchers considered the lengths in millimeters of 100 eggs that were in the second laying of the season. They reported results *Mean* ± *SE* to be 105.70 ± 0.48.[10]

a. Explain why the multiplier in a confidence interval for population mean may be identified as z instead of t.

b. Keeping in mind that an approximate 95% confidence interval is sample mean plus or minus 2 standard errors, report an approximate 95% confidence interval for the mean length of all captive condor eggs in the second laying of the season.

c. Keeping in mind that standard error is calculated as sample standard deviation divided by square root of sample size ($s/\sqrt{n}$), report the sample standard deviation s for those 100 eggs.

10.46 Results for a 1997 survey of about 25,000 each male and female nonfarm wage and salary workers were published in the *Monthly Labor Review* in 1998. Hours worked in the week prior to the survey were found to have mean and standard deviation 42.66 and 12.46 for the men, 36.90 and 11.93 for the women.

a. The test statistic $\frac{\bar{x} - 40}{s/\sqrt{25,000}}$ turns out to be larger in absolute value for the women than it is for the men. Is this because the women's sample mean 36.90 is further from 40 than 42.66 is, or because the women's standard deviation 11.93 is smaller than the men's, or both of these, or neither of these?

b. If we tested against the alternative hypothesis $H_a: \mu \neq 40$, which P-value would be smaller—that for the women or that for the men?

c. Explain why we would not need to carry out all the steps of a formal test if we formulated the alternative hypothesis $H_a: \mu < 40$ for the men.

d. Explain why we would not need to carry out all the steps of a formal test if we formulated the alternative hypothesis $H_a: \mu > 40$ for the women.

10.47 "Time In Purgatory: Examining the Grant Lag for U.S. Patent Applications," published online by the Berkeley Electronic Press in 2003, examined grant lag (period of time between an initial patent application and its final granting, in months) for *all* patents on record between 1976 and 1996. There were well over 1 million patents during this period, and their grant lag time had mean 28.4 months, standard deviation 19.7 months.

a. For the 1,278 patents whose assignees (those who hold the property rights bestowed by the invention) were *nonprofit* organizations, the mean grant lag was 30.3 months. State the null and alternative hypotheses to see if the mean for nonprofit organizations differs significantly from the overall mean lag, 28.4 months. Report your z statistic.

b. What can you say about the size of the P-value for the test in part (a)?

c. What do you conclude about the mean grant lag time for nonprofit organizations?

d. For the 17,209 patents whose assignees were listed as "*independent*," the mean grant lag was 28.6 months. State the null and alternative hypotheses to see if the mean for independent organizations differs significantly from the overall mean lag, 28.4 months. Report your z statistic.

e. What can you say about the size of the P-value for the test in part (d)?

f. What do you conclude about the mean grant lag time for independent organizations?

g. Sample mean grant lag for patents whose assignees were from the *government* was *further* from the population mean than sample mean lag for *nonprofit* organizations. If the sample size was the same, would the P-value for the government be larger or smaller than the one for nonprofits?

h. The sample size for patents whose assignees were from the *government* was *larger* than the sample size for *nonprofit* organizations. If the sample mean was the same, would the P-value for the government be larger or smaller than the one for nonprofits?

i. Patents whose assignees were *private* firms made up 78% of all the patents recorded. Explain why we should not use a z procedure to test if their mean grant lag time (28.6 months) differs significantly from the overall mean lag, 28.4 months.

j. The authors present a histogram of grant lags, with the following caution: "The actual tail of the distribution continues beyond what is shown in the graph, as our data set includes patents with lags up to 1143 months long."[11] Is the distribution left-skewed or right-skewed?

k. Would median grant lag be greater than or less than 28.4? Explain.

10.48 "An Analysis of the Study Time-Grade Association," published in *Radical Pedagogy* in 2002, reported scores on a standardized test for cognitive ability for subgroups of students in an Introductory Psychology course, classified according to how much they studied for the course per week. Standard deviation was 7.74 for scores of students who studied zero hours per week, and 2.82 for scores of students who studied nine or more hours per week.[12] What does this suggest about performances of students? Choose one of these:

a. Students who don't study have a higher cognitive ability.

b. Students who don't study have a lower cognitive ability.

c. Students who don't study are more predictable in terms of their cognitive ability.

d. Students who don't study are less predictable in terms of their cognitive ability.

10.49 "An Analysis of the Study Time-Grade Association," published in *Radical Pedagogy* in 2002, looked at self-reported study time for the course, in hours per week, by 140 students enrolled in an Introductory Psychology course. Times had mean 3 hours and standard deviation 2.6 hours.

   a. The article reports that according to the National Survey of Student Engagement, the Carnegie Foundation benchmark is 6 hours of study per week for a course that meets three hours a week. Standardize the sample mean time and explain why we can consider it to follow the z distribution.

   b. Could the difference between sample mean study time (3 hours) and recommended study time (6 hours) have come about by chance in the process of sampling? Explain.

Exploring the Big Picture: INFERENCE FOR MEANS WITH T

10.50 A newspaper article on growing tomatoes reported days needed to germinate for a sample of varieties, including "Bloody Butcher," "Sweet Baby Girl," and others:

55	48	50	65	52	60	49	60	56	50	63
58	57	52	50	60	57	52	65	60	45	50

   a. Construct a stemplot of the data, splitting stems in two, and tell whether it is roughly normal, roughly symmetric but non-normal, fairly skewed, or extremely skewed.

   b. A 95% confidence interval for population mean days needed to germinate is (52.63, 57.73). Use this to tell what the sample mean must be.

   c. Given that the width of the confidence interval is $57.73 - 52.63 = 5.10$ days, what is the margin of error?

   d. Given that the t multiplier is roughly 2, what is the approximate standard error?

   e. Is two months a plausible guess for mean days needed to germinate for all tomato varieties from which the sample originated, or is it too long, or is it too short? Explain.

10.51 When Pope John Paul II died in April 2005, it was reported that only cardinals younger than 80 would be eligible to vote for a new pontiff. Out of all cardinals worldwide, 64% were eligible to vote. Software can be used to test if the proportion of U.S. cardinals who were eligible (12 out of 14) was unusually high. The *P*-value in the first half of the output is calculated as an exact binomial probability, and in the second half it is calculated as a normal approximation. Notice that because the variable of interest is categorical and summarized with a proportion, this problem is a review of material covered in Chapter 9.

```
Test of p = 0.64 vs p > 0.64
Sample       X       N  Sample p  95.0% Lower Bound  Exact P-Value
1           12      14  0.857143           0.614610           0.073
Test of p = 0.64 vs p > 0.64
Sample       X       N  Sample p  95.0% Lower Bound  Z-Value  P-Value
1           12      14  0.857143           0.703313     1.69    0.045
*Note * The normal approximation may be inaccurate for small samples.
```

   a. Explain why it is not a good idea to use a normal approximation in this situation.

   b. If 0.05 is used as a cutoff probability, does the binomial *P*-value suggest that disproportionately many U.S. cardinals were eligible?

   c. If 0.05 is used as a cutoff probability, does the normal approximation *P*-value suggest that disproportionately many U.S. cardinals were eligible?

   d. If 0.05 is used as a cutoff probability, and a two-sided alternative had been formulated, would the normal approximation *P*-value suggest that a disproportionate number of U.S. cardinals were eligible?

10.52 When Pope John Paul II died in April 2005, newspapers reported ages of all 183 cardinals; their mean was 76.0 and standard deviation 8.236. Software can be used to test if U.S. cardinals were significantly younger on average than cardinals worldwide. The z test below standardizes sample mean using 8.236 as known population standard deviation; the t test uses sample standard deviation of ages of the 14 U.S. cardinals.

```
One-Sample Z: CardinalAgesUS
Test of mu = 76 vs mu < 76
The assumed sigma = 8.236
Variable        N     Mean   StDev   SE Mean   95.0% Upper Bound    Z      P
CardinalAgesUS 14    74.29   4.94      2.20                77.91   -0.78  0.218

One-Sample T: CardinalAgesUS
Test of mu = 76 vs mu < 76
Variable        N     Mean   StDev   SE Mean   95.0% Upper Bound    T      P
CardinalAgesUS 14    74.29   4.94      1.32                76.62   -1.30  0.108
```

a. Explain why in this situation the z test is appropriate.

b. Which is larger for this sample, population standard deviation σ or sample standard deviation s?

c. Which is larger in absolute value, the z or t statistic?

d. Which is smaller, the P-value based on a z procedure or the one based on a t procedure?

10.53 A test to see if U.S. cardinals are significantly younger than cardinals worldwide produces a P-value that is considerably greater than 0.05. Based on this result, statistics students are asked to reach a conclusion about the mean age of U.S. cardinals compared to that of cardinals worldwide. Whose answer is best?

Adam: If the P-value is not small then there must be a large difference. We've proven that U.S. cardinals are younger.

Brittany: You can't say we've proven them to be younger, but you can say we have evidence that they're younger.

Carlos: If the P-value is not small, then the difference we observed is not so improbable if U.S. cardinals were the same age as cardinals worldwide. So we've proven that U.S. cardinals are the same age as cardinals worldwide.

Dominique: The P-value is not small, so we failed to produce evidence that U.S. cardinals are significantly younger. That's not the same thing as proving them to be the same age.

10.54 "Domestic Goats Follow Gaze Direction and Use Social Cues in An Object Choice Task," published online in *Animal Behavior* in January 2005, included information on 13 adult goats' performance in a bucket-selection task, when cued by a handler who gazed at the correct bucket. Here are their scores (each on a test of 18 trials), along with descriptive statistics:

| 6 | 7 | 8 | 8 | 8 | 8 | 8 | 9 | 9 | 10 | 10 | 12 | 14 |

Variable	N	Mean	Median	TrMean	StDev	SE Mean
AdultGoatsGaze	13	9.000	8.000	8.818	2.121	0.588

Variable	Minimum	Maximum	Q1	Q3
AdultGoatsGaze	6.000	14.000	8.000	10.000

a. If a goat performed at chance level, its score would be 9. Explain why a formal test is not necessary to establish that the goats, as a group, did not perform significantly better than chance.

b. Explain why the value of standardized sample mean would be zero.

c. Explain why a 95% confidence interval for the population mean score is guaranteed to contain 9.

d. Recall that the $1.5 \times IQR$ Rule identifies an observation as being a high outlier if it is more than $1.5(Q_3 - Q_1)$ above Q_3. Under this criterion, is 14 a high outlier?

e. Each of the 13 goats' performances was tested to see if it performed significantly better than chance on the 18 trials. Using binomial probabilities, the goat with a score of 14 was shown to have scored significantly better than chance. However, the study's authors concluded that certain other cues (such as touching or pointing) could be effective, but not gaze by itself. Explain why there is not necessarily anything special about one individual out of 13 doing "unusually well" on such a task.

10.55 Hourly wages for bus drivers in a sample of urban areas across the country were reported in the newspaper in 2005; here they are rounded to the nearest dollar:

26	22	21	21	21	21	21	21	21	21	21

Produce a stemplot of the data and explain why standardized sample mean would not follow a z or t distribution.

10.56 Hourly wages for bus drivers, in the 20 U.S. urban areas where earnings for drivers were highest, had mean $22.61 and standard deviation $1.45. Explain why we should not use this information to estimate mean hourly wages of all bus drivers in the United States.

10.57 Top swimming times for male members of a college team were found for various events. For these problems, use the fact that the t multiplier for 95% confidence and 4 degrees of freedom is 2.78.

a. Times for the top five swimmers of the 50 freestyle had a mean of 20.7 and a standard deviation of 0.4. Produce a 95% confidence interval (rounding to the nearest tenth).

b. Times for the top five swimmers of the 100 freestyle had a mean of 46.0 and a standard deviation of 0.9. Produce a 95% confidence interval (rounding to the nearest tenth).

c. Should we consider the population to be times for *all* male college swim team members in the given event?

d. Use your confidence intervals from parts (a) and (b) to argue whether or not top swimmers on average can swim the 100 freestyle in twice the time it takes to swim the 50 freestyle.

10.58 A master's thesis by M. Purser at the University of Washington in 1988 looked at soil density in a conifer forest. Bulk densities (in grams per cubic cm) for 33 samples were reported in the Quantitative Environmental Learning Project (QELP) posted on www.seattlecentral.org. Their mean was 0.37 and standard deviation was 0.27.

a. Use the fact that the t multiplier for 32 degrees of freedom and 99% confidence is 2.74 to report a 99% confidence interval for the mean density of all soil samples in the forest, rounding to the nearest hundredth.

b. Report a 99% confidence interval for the mean density of all soil samples in the forest, rounding to the nearest hundredth, if the z multiplier is used instead of t.

c. Characterize your intervals in parts (a) and (b) as being very different, slightly different, or identical.

d. Tell whether use of z instead of t multipliers for samples of size 33 makes a big difference, a slight difference, or no difference when constructing confidence intervals.

10.59 "Weighty Matter Pits Passengers Against Airlines" reported in 2005 about a controversy arising over airline seat size. The situation was sparked when a 300-pound dentist was told by Southwest Airlines that he would have to pay for a second seat on the return flight, claiming his large frame would not fit entirely in the 17-inch-wide space. The article provided information on seat widths for a sample of airlines. Here are the data values for coach seats (as opposed to first class), along with computer output for the data:

16	19	17	17	17	18	17	17.7	17.05	19	18	18

Variable	N	Mean	StDev	SE Mean	95.0% CI
PlaneSeatWidth	12	17.563	0.889	0.257	(16.998, 18.127)

a. Based on the confidence interval, how would you characterize a proposed population mean seat width of 16—as plausible, implausible, or borderline?

b. How would you characterize a proposed population mean seat width of 17?

c. How would you characterize a proposed population mean seat width of 18?

d. How would you characterize a proposed population mean seat width of 19?

e. The passenger argued that Southwest seats, at 17 inches, were way too narrow compared to those of other airlines. In order to see if his claim has merit, should you look at the data values themselves or at the confidence interval? Explain.

*10.60 "Self-Report of Cochlear Implant Use and Satisfaction by Prelingually Deafened Adults," published in *Ear & Hearing* in June 1996, evaluated noise and voice recognition, with use of a hearing aid, by 12 adults who had been deaf all their lives.[13]

| 52 | 40 | 97 | 62 | 75 | 57 | 45 | 55 | 70 | 65 | 62 | 77 |

a. Construct a stemplot of the data to verify that the shape is roughly normal.

b. One of these is a 90% and the other a 95% confidence interval for population mean recognition score: (53.27, 72.90) and (55.07, 71.09). Which one is the 90% interval?

c. The scores have mean 63 and standard deviation 15. If a patient just guessed at answers on the hearing test, he or she would be expected to score only 50. To get an idea of how much higher 63 is than 50 in this situation, standardize to $t = \frac{\bar{x} - \mu_0}{s/\sqrt{n}}$.

d. For t distributions with 11 degrees of freedom, the probability of being greater than 2.72 is 0.01. Is a score of 63 significantly higher than 50?

e. The null hypothesis states that $\mu = 50$. What does the alternative state?

f. One year after these 12 patients received cochlear implants, they were tested again on noise and voice recognition. Is this a paired, two-sample, or several-sample design?

10.61 "Self-Report of Cochlear Implant Use and Satisfaction by Prelingually Deafened Adults," published in *Ear & Hearing* in June 1996, evaluated performance on a multiple-choice hearing test, with use of a hearing aid, by 11 adults who had been deaf all their lives.

| 35 | 50 | 30 | 45 | 15 | 20 | 10 | 25 | 35 | 70 | 30 |

a. Construct a stemplot of the data to verify that the shape is roughly normal.

b. One of these is a 95% and the other a 99% confidence interval for population mean hearing test score: (16.86, 49.50) and (21.71, 44.65). Which one is the 99% interval?

c. The scores have a mean of 33 and a standard deviation of 17. If a patient just guessed at answers on the hearing test, he or she would be expected to score 25. To get an idea of how much higher 33 is than 25 in this situation, standardize to $t = \frac{\bar{x} - \mu_0}{s/\sqrt{n}}$.

d. For t distributions with 10 degrees of freedom, the probability of being greater than 1.81 is 0.05. Is a score of 33 significantly higher than 25?

e. Besides this multiple-choice hearing test, the patients were also tested on noise and voice recognition. If researchers want to look for a relationship between patients' scores on the multiple-choice test and on the noise and voice recognition test, are they considering the relationship between one categorical and one quantitative variable, or two categorical variables, or two quantitative variables?

10.62 A *New York Times* article entitled "How Long is Too Long for the Court's Justices?" reported in 2005 that the average Supreme Court justice between 1789 and 1970 served for 15.2 years. More recently, tenures tended to be longer, with the following times for the 9 justices serving in the first half of 2005:

Justice	Appointed	Tenure as of 2005
Rehnquist	1971	34
Stevens	1975	30
O'Connor	1981	24
Scalia	1986	19
Kennedy	1988	17
Souter	1990	15
Thomas	1991	14
Ginsburg	1993	12
Breyer	1994	11

a. The mean tenure (in years) was 19.6 and the standard deviation was 8.1. Find the standardized tenure score, if these 9 were a random sample of tenures taken from a population with mean 15.2.

b. Explain why the standardized score should be written t and not z.

c. What information would be needed if we want to report a z statistic for the standardized score?

d. For 8 degrees of freedom, the probability of a t score being greater than 1.86 is

0.05. Explain why we cannot reject the hypothesis that these 9 tenures constitute a random sample from a population with mean 15.2.

e. By the second half of 2005, Rehnquist died and was replaced by Roberts; O'Connor retired, and was replaced in early 2006 by Alito. Explain why the new sample mean tenure, 14.0, could not be used as convincing evidence that tenure times averaged significantly longer than 15.2 years.

Exploring the Big Picture: MORE INFERENCE FOR MEANS WITH Z AND T

10.63 In this chapter, we learned to use the mean, standard deviation, and size of a sample to test whether population mean was actually different from a claimed value. For each of the following, tell which circumstance makes it easier to convince someone that population mean differs from the mean (μ_0) proposed in the null hypothesis:

a. Sample mean is close to μ_0 or sample mean is far from μ_0.

b. Values are concentrated around a sample mean that is different from μ_0 or values are very spread out around a sample mean that is different from μ_0.

c. Sample size is small or sample size is large.

10.64 When a particular diet is tested for effectiveness there is always the possibility, due to such factors as flaws in the study design or inadequate sample size, of drawing the wrong conclusion about the null hypothesis (which states that the diet has no benefit). Discuss the potential harmful consequences of committing a Type I Error in this situation, and the potential harmful consequences of committing a Type II Error.

10.65 "Comparison of the Atkins, Ornish, Weight Watchers, and Zone Diets for Weight Loss and Heart Disease Risk Reduction," published in the *Journal of the American Medical Association* in January 2005, describes an experiment in which 160 participants were randomly assigned to one of four diets. Forty-two percent had dropped out by the end of a year, and it was assumed that those 67 subjects neither lost nor gained weight.[14]

a. For the 40 subjects assigned to the Atkins diet, weight loss at one year had mean 2.1 kg, standard deviation 4.8 kg. The standardized difference of sample mean from zero is $t = \frac{2.1 - 0}{4.8/\sqrt{40}} = 2.77$, and the P-value is quite small, 0.009. Is this evidence of average weight after one year being very much less than what it was originally, or is it very compelling evidence that average weight after one year is less than what it was originally?

b. Mean weight loss with the Zone diet was 3.2 kg, and with the Weight Watchers diet was 3.0 kg. Since the sample sizes were the same (40), if standard deviations were equal, which diet would have a smaller P-value?

c. The P-value was 0.002 for Zone, 0.001 for Weight Watchers. Keeping in mind that a small P-value arises from a large test statistic, which is calculated with standard deviation in the denominator, which diet must have had a smaller standard deviation?

d. Explain why dieters might prefer to adopt a diet for which the amount of weight lost has a smaller standard deviation.

10.66 Suppose researchers want to test if a particular diet is successful.

a. If μ is the mean amount of weight lost by all users of the diet, should the alternative hypothesis state $\mu < 0$, $\mu \neq 0$, or $\mu > 0$?

b. If μ is the mean change in all dieters' weights from beginning to end, with negative numbers representing a decrease in weight and positive numbers representing an increase, should the alternative hypothesis state $\mu < 0$, $\mu \neq 0$, or $\mu > 0$?

c. If critics of a diet aren't sure whether it helps somewhat or even actually leads to some weight gain, should the alternative hypothesis about population mean weight loss state $\mu < 0$, $\mu \neq 0$, or $\mu > 0$?

d. Suppose H_a states $\mu < 0$ and the P-value is found to be 0.002. What would the P-value have been if H_a had stated $\mu \neq 0$?

10.67 Forty subjects were assigned to a particular weight loss diet. By the end of a year, 20 of the subjects had dropped out of the study.

The mean weight loss for those who remained was 2.1 kilograms.

a. Is 2.1 kilograms an unbiased estimate for the mean weight loss by all subjects who would be assigned that diet?

b. What would the mean weight loss for the original 40 subjects be if the 20 who dropped out actually *gained* an average of 2.1 kilograms?

10.68 An experiment found that subjects on the Atkins diet lost a significant amount of weight in a year, with P-value equal to 0.009. Would zero be contained in a 95% confidence interval for population mean weight loss on the Atkins diet? Explain.

10.69 In a population of several hundred students, the mean amount earned in the previous year was $3.776 thousand. Repeated random samples of size 40 were taken, and for each sample a 95% confidence interval was constructed for population mean amount. This was done 20 times, for a total of 20 confidence intervals.

Variable	N	Mean	StDev	SE Mean	95.0% CI	T	P
Earnedlargen	40	2.775	4.041	0.639	(1.483, 4.067)	−1.57	0.125
Earnedlargen	40	3.275	3.130	0.495	(2.274, 4.276)	−1.01	0.318
Earnedlargen	40	3.400	3.425	0.542	(2.305, 4.495)	−0.69	0.492
Earnedlargen	40	4.200	8.810	1.390	(1.380, 7.020)	0.30	0.763
Earnedlargen	40	4.350	5.021	0.794	(2.744, 5.956)	0.72	0.474
Earnedlargen	40	3.650	4.753	0.752	(2.130, 5.170)	−0.17	0.868
Earnedlargen	40	4.500	10.850	1.720	(1.030, 7.970)	0.42	0.675
Earnedlargen	40	4.830	10.910	1.730	(1.330, 8.320)	0.61	0.547
Earnedlargen	40	3.050	3.896	0.616	(1.804, 4.296)	−1.18	0.246
Earnedlargen	40	2.875	3.098	0.490	(1.884, 3.866)	−1.84	0.074
Earnedlargen	40	4.575	5.153	0.815	(2.927, 6.223)	0.98	0.333
Earnedlargen	40	2.925	3.238	0.512	(1.890, 3.960)	−1.66	0.104
Earnedlargen	40	3.225	3.324	0.526	(2.162, 4.288)	−1.05	0.301
Earnedlargen	40	2.400	2.827	0.447	(1.496, 3.304)	−3.08	0.004
Earnedlargen	40	4.075	5.731	0.906	(2.242, 5.908)	0.33	0.743
Earnedlargen	40	3.875	5.630	0.890	(2.074, 5.676)	0.11	0.912
Earnedlargen	40	3.025	4.780	0.756	(1.496, 4.554)	−0.99	0.326
Earnedlargen	40	2.675	2.258	0.357	(1.953, 3.397)	−3.08	0.004
Earnedlargen	40	3.100	3.671	0.580	(1.926, 4.274)	−1.16	0.251
Earnedlargen	40	2.750	3.256	0.515	(1.709, 3.791)	−1.99	0.053

a. Explain why the test statistic is t and not z.

b. In general, what is the probability that a 95% confidence interval contains the true value of the parameter?

c. If 20 intervals are produced, each with 95% confidence, in the long run about how many will succeed in capturing the true value of the parameter?

d. How many of the 20 intervals above contain the population mean 3.776?

e. Will your answer to part (d) be exactly the case in every set of 20 confidence intervals? Explain.

10.70 In a population of several hundred students, the mean amount earned the previous year was $3.776 thousand. Repeated random samples of size 40 were taken, and for each

sample a hypothesis test was carried out, testing if population mean earnings equals 3.776. This was done 20 times, for a total of 20 tests. The preceding exercise shows standardized mean earnings t and the accompanying P-value for each test.

a. In general, what is the probability that a test of a null hypothesis that is actually true rejects it, using 0.05 as the cutoff level α for what is considered to be a small P-value?

b. If 20 tests of a true null hypothesis are carried out at the 0.05 level, in the long run about how many will (correctly) fail to reject it?

c. How many of the true null hypotheses will (incorrectly) be rejected?

d. How many of the 20 P-values in Exercise 10.69 are small enough to reject $H_0 : \mu = 3.776$ at the $\alpha = 0.05$ level? (If there are any, tell what they are.)

e. Will your answer to part (d) be exactly the case in every set of 20 tests? Explain.

f. If a P-value in the situation described in this exercise is very small, what can you say about the corresponding confidence interval?

*10.71 "Adults Who Stutter: Responses to Cognitive Stress," published in the *Journal of Speech and Hearing Research* in 1994, reported that speech rate, in words per minute, for nine stutterers had mean 90.4 and standard deviation 9.7.[15]

a. A test was carried out against the two-sided alternative $H_a : \mu \neq 100$ and the P-value was found to be 0.0178. What would the P-value be if we wanted to test if mean speech rate for all stutters is *less* than 100 words per minute?

b. If a test were carried out against the alternative $H_a : \mu \neq 90$, the P-value

would be 0.9044. What is the correct conclusion to draw?

1. We have proven that the mean rate for all stutterers is 90 words per minute.

2. We have strong evidence that the mean rate for all stutterers is 90 words per minute.

3. We have failed to produce evidence that the mean rate for all stutterers differs from 90 minutes.

10.72 "Adults Who Stutter: Responses to Cognitive Stress," published in the *Journal of Speech and Hearing Research* in 1994, reported that speech rate, in words per minute, for nine stutterers under conditions of stress had mean 52.6 and standard deviation 3.2.[16]

a. A test was carried out against the one-sided alternative $H_a : \mu > 50$ and the P-value was found to be 0.0204. What would the P-value be if we wanted to test if mean speech rate under conditions of stress for all stutterers *differs* from 50 words per minute?

b. Based on the P-value 0.0204 for the one-sided test $H_a : \mu > 50$, what is the correct conclusion to draw?

1. We have proven that the mean rate for all stutterers under stress conditions is more than 50 words per minute.

2. We have evidence that the mean rate for all stutterers under stress conditions is more than 50 words per minute.

Using Software [see Technology Guide]: INFERENCE FOR MEANS

*10.73 In "Reproduction, Growth and Development in Captive Beluga," published in the journal *Zoo Biology* in 2005, researchers observed captive male beluga whales in various aquariums. Age (in years) at first conception was recorded for the seven whales who sired calves during the period from 1969 to 1987:[17]

| 12 | 16 | 9 | 13 | 17 | 12 | 12 |

a. The shape of the data set is roughly normal but somewhat right-skewed.

Explain why age at first conception would also be right-skewed for human males.

b. Use software to produce a 95% confidence interval for the mean age at first conception of all captive beluga males.

c. The sample mean age was 13 years. For which one of these alternative hypotheses could we automatically conclude that the null hypothesis cannot be rejected, without needing to standardize and carry out a formal test: $H_a : \mu < 12$, $H_a : \mu > 12$, $H_a : \mu < 14$, or $H_a : \mu \neq 14$?

10.74 In "Energy and Mineral Nutrition and Water Intake in the Captive Indian Rhinoceros," published in the journal *Zoo Biology* in 2005, total daily dry-matter intake (in kg) was recorded for 11 rhinoceri in various zoos before placing them on a roughage-only diet.[18]

| 23.4 | 16.3 | 28.8 | 20.3 | 22.6 | 20.4 | 15.7 | 20.8 | 22.2 | 24.1 | 13.7 |

a. Use software to produce a histogram of the intakes.

b. Characterize the shape of the histogram as being roughly normal, roughly symmetric but non-normal, fairly skewed with possible outliers, or extremely skewed.

c. Is it appropriate to use t procedures to perform inference on population mean dry-matter intake, based on this sample? Explain.

d. Use software to produce a 95% confidence interval for the mean dry-matter intake of all captive Indian rhinoceri.

e. The sample mean intake was 20.75 kilograms. For which one of these alternative hypotheses could we automatically conclude that the null hypothesis cannot be rejected, without needing to standardize and carry out a formal test: $H_a : \mu < 21$, $H_a : \mu > 20$, $H_a : \mu < 20$, or $H_a : \mu \neq 21$?

10.75 Graduate students in a statistics department recorded hours spent consulting on 21 different projects in a particular semester:

| 1 | 1 | 2 | 2 | 3 | 5 | 5 | 10 | 15 | 15 |
| 18 | 20 | 20 | 24 | 30 | 30 | 30 | 48 | 50 | 148 |

a. Just by looking at the data values, describe the general appearance of a display (such as histogram or stemplot) of the data.

b. Use software to produce a 95% confidence interval for mean hours spent on a consulting project for all semesters, assuming this semester was typical.

c. Report the center of your confidence interval (sample mean) and width of the interval.

d. Delete the value "148" from the data set and produce a 95% confidence interval.

e. Report the center and width of the new confidence interval.

f. Discuss the effect that an outlier can have on a confidence interval; is there an equally dramatic effect on its center and its width?

10.76 Researchers Madsen and Lof carried out a study involving reforestation in southern Scandinavia where oaks were seeded with acorns under a variety of circumstances. Germination rates (as percents) in 25 sites were recorded:

| 70 | 61 | 86 | 43 | 43 | 90 | 43 | 90 | 90 | 61 | 61 | 86 | 86 |
| 61 | 86 | 43 | 90 | 43 | 90 | 61 | 43 | 90 | 61 | 43 | 90 |

a. Produce a histogram of the data and characterize it as roughly normal, roughly symmetric but not close to normal, or showing pronounced skewness and/or outliers.

b. Considering that the sample size (25) is moderately large, can we count on the distribution of sample mean to be fairly normal?

c. Use software to produce a 95% confidence interval for the mean germination rate of all sites in similar circumstances.

10.77 "By the Numbers: Border Communities" reported on county taxes for a sample of counties in the same state as Allegheny County, a populous county in which we may assume the taxes to be relatively high. Taking into account what percentage of a property's market value was taxed in the various counties, the mills for the four counties mentioned were 4.51, 5.35, 2.86, and 0.41. These were compared with Allegheny County's tax rate of 4.69 mills.

a. Use software to test if the mean for all this state's counties is significantly lower than 4.69, based on the sample of four counties; report the *P*-value.

b. State your conclusion.

10.78 Verbal SAT scores of incoming students at a large university were reported to have a mean of 580. At about the same time (2003), several hundred students in a variety of introductory statistics courses there were surveyed, and asked to report their Math and Verbal SAT scores.

a. Use software to access the survey data, and test whether or not the sampled students' mean Verbal SAT score is consistent with a population mean of 580: Test $H_0 : \mu = 580$ versus $H_a : \mu \neq 580$ and report the *P*-value.

b. Using $\alpha = 0.05$ as your cut-off for a small *P*-value, was the sampled students' mean significantly different from 580?

c. Now carry out the same test, but assume population standard deviation to be 115, which is considerably larger than the sample standard deviation (73.24). Report the test statistic and the *P*-value.

d. With a larger standard deviation, is the test statistic $\frac{\bar{x} - \mu_0}{s/\sqrt{n}}$ larger or smaller?

e. With a larger standard deviation, is the *P*-value larger or smaller?

f. Assuming population standard deviation to be 115, report a 95% confidence interval for population mean Verbal SAT score.

10.79 Several hundred students in a variety of introductory statistics courses at a large university were surveyed and asked to report their Math and Verbal SAT scores.

a. Math SAT scores of these students were significantly higher than the reported mean for the university. Can this be attributed to possible bias in the sampling process (these students were not representative in terms of their math skills), or bias in assessing the variable's values (some students "remembered" their scores to be higher than they actually were), or both?

b. Use software to report a 95% confidence interval for mean Math SAT score of the larger population of students from which the sample originated.

10.80 Several hundred male and female college students were surveyed and asked to report their height and weight. An informal website reports that men's heights have mean 69 inches and women's heights have mean 64 inches. College-aged men are reported to have mean weight 168 pounds, and college-aged women have mean 132 pounds. Use software to access the survey data and test each of those claims against a two-sided alternative:

a. Are you willing to believe that college-aged men have mean height 69 inches? (Report the *P*-value and answer yes or no.)

b. Are you willing to believe that college-aged women have mean height 64 inches? (Report the *P*-value and answer yes or no.)

c. Are you willing to believe that college-aged men have mean weight 168 pounds? (Report the *P*-value and answer yes or no.)

d. Are you willing to believe that college-aged women have mean weight 132 pounds? (Report the *P*-value and answer yes or no.)

10.81 Several hundred students enrolled in introductory statistics courses at a large university were surveyed and asked to report the number of credits they were taking that semester. Use software to access the survey data and test whether or not the students constitute a sample from a population where the mean number of credits is more than 15:

a. Report the sample mean number of credits.

b. Report the *P*-value.

c. Choose one of the following as the best way to state conclusions:

1. There is strong evidence that the population mean number of credits is much higher than 15.

2. There is strong evidence that the population mean number of credits is higher than 15, but apparently not by much.

3. There is weak evidence that the population mean number of credits is much higher than 15.

4. There is weak evidence that the population mean number of credits is

higher than 15, but apparently not by much.

5. There is no evidence that the population mean number of credits is higher than 15.

*10.82 Several hundred students enrolled in introductory statistics courses at a large university were surveyed on various days of the week and asked to report the number of minutes they'd spent watching television the day before.

a. Use software to access the survey data and construct a 95% confidence interval for the mean number of minutes of daily television watched by the population of students.

b. According to the American Time Use Survey published by the Bureau of Labor Statistics, the mean daily hours of television watched by Americans aged 15 to 24 at that time (2003) was 2.23 hours (about 134 minutes). Use your confidence interval to decide whether or not this is a plausible value for mean daily amount of television watched by the population of students. If it is not plausible, tell whether the population of students watch more or less television than Americans aged 15 to 24 in general.

c. Use mathematical notation to write null and alternative hypotheses to test if the population mean time for students could be 134 minutes.

10.83 Several hundred students enrolled in introductory statistics courses at a large university were surveyed on various days of the week and asked to report the number of minutes they'd spent exercising the day before.

a. Use software to access the survey data and construct a 95% confidence interval for the mean number of minutes of daily exercise for the population of students.

b. According to the American Time Use Survey published by the Bureau of Labor Statistics, the mean daily hours of exercise for Americans aged 15 to 24 at that time (2003) was about 31 minutes. Use your confidence interval to decide whether or not this is a plausible value for mean daily amount of exercise for the population of students. If it is not plausible, tell whether the population of

students exercise more or less than Americans aged 15 to 24 in general.

c. Use mathematical notation to write null and alternative hypotheses to test if the population mean time for students could be 31 minutes.

10.84 Several hundred students enrolled in introductory statistics courses at a large university were surveyed on various days of the week and asked to report the number of minutes they'd spent talking on the phone the day before.

a. Use software to access the survey data and construct a 95% confidence interval for the mean number of minutes on the phone for the population of students.

b. According to the American Time Use Survey published by the Bureau of Labor Statistics, the mean daily time on the phone for Americans aged 15 to 24 at that time (2003) was 14.4 minutes. Use your confidence interval to decide whether or not this is a plausible value for mean daily amount of phone time for the population of students. If it is not plausible, tell whether the population of students talk on the phone more or less than Americans aged 15 to 24 in general.

c. Use mathematical notation to write null and alternative hypotheses to test if the population mean time for students could be 14.4 minutes.

10.85 Several hundred students enrolled in introductory statistics courses at a large university were surveyed and asked if they smoked. Smokers were to report how many cigarettes they had smoked the day before.

a. Use software to access the survey data and construct a 95% confidence interval for the number of cigarettes smoked in a day by the smoking students.

b. Based on cigarette sales and percentage of people who smoked, the Centers for Disease Control estimates the number of cigarettes smoked per day by smokers in 1990 to be 30.3. Explain why your confidence interval provides evidence that the mean for the population of students is much less than this.

c. Based on the National Health Interview Survey of thousands of smokers, the Centers for Disease Control states that the self-reported number of cigarettes smoked per day by smokers in 1990 was 19.1. Explain why your confidence interval provides evidence that the mean for the population of students is much less than this.

d. Give a possible explanation for why the self-reported number of cigarettes smoked (19.1) is considerably smaller than what the actual number apparently was (30.3).

e. Give a possible explanation for why the mean number of cigarettes smoked in 2003 would be less than what it was in 1990.

f. Give a possible explanation for why the mean number of cigarettes smoked by college student smokers would be less than what it is for smokers in general.

Discovering Research: INFERENCE FOR MEANS

10.86 Find a newspaper article or Internet report about a study that involves just a single quantitative variable, where value of a population mean is inferred, based on an observed sample mean. Explain whether there is reason to suspect bias because the sample is not representative of the larger population of interest.

Reporting on Research: INFERENCE FOR MEANS

10.87 Use results of Exercises 10.43 and 10.44 and relevant findings from the Internet to make a report on piracy of music and other software that relies on statistical information.

Inference for Relationships between Categorical and Quantitative Variables

For all students at a university, are Math SAT scores related to what year of study they are in?

© Genevieve Naylor/CORBIS

Relating other variables to SAT scores:

A source of research since the 1940s

The *Big* Picture: A CLOSER LOOK

The original SAT test was created in 1942 by Carl Brigham, a Princeton psychologist. Brigham is known for his claims in the 1920s that standardized tests provided evidence of the superiority of the Nordic race. By the time he created the SAT, he refuted such claims, acknowledging that the "evidence" was actually a result of culturally biased questions in the tests he had developed for the army that were predecessors to the SAT.

C→Q   In this chapter, we are interested in the relationship (if any) between a categorical explanatory variable and a quantitative response variable, not simply for a sample but for an entire population.

In Chapters 9 and 10, when we did inference about a *single* categorical or quantitative variable, we first learned to set up a confidence interval for the unknown population proportion or mean, then learned to carry out a hypothesis test. When the *relationship* between two variables is of interest, the most natural place to start is with a hypothesis test, to determine whether or not there is statistical evidence of a relationship in the larger population.

EXAMPLE 11.1 INFERENCE ABOUT A RELATIONSHIP: HYPOTHESIS TESTS BEFORE CONFIDENCE INTERVALS

Background: Researchers gathered data on the amount of time per day spent watching television for 1-year-olds and 3-year-olds.

Question: Which form of inference should be carried out first: setting up a confidence interval for the difference between mean television times, 3-year-olds minus 1-year-olds, or testing to see if age (1 or 3 years old) plays a role in how much television is watched?

Do kids watch more TV at age 1 or 3?

Response: It makes sense to perform the hypothesis test first. Then, if age does apparently play a role, we would use a confidence interval to estimate the difference between mean times for 3-year-olds and 1-year-olds.

Practice: *Try Exercise 11.1 on page 525.*

Whenever a relationship is being explored, the null hypothesis states that the variables are *not* related and the alternative hypothesis states that they *are* related. These hypotheses apply no matter what types of variables are involved—categorical or quantitative. Besides the general formulation of null and alternative hypotheses in terms of whether or not the *variables* are related, the hypotheses are also typically formulated in terms of the relevant *parameters*. Here is where we see a big difference, depending on what types of variables are involved. For a categorical explanatory variable and a quantitative response variable, the parameters of interest would be population means μ_i for independent samples, or a population mean of differences μ_d if the design is paired.

EXAMPLE 11.2 HYPOTHESES STATED IN TERMS OF VARIABLES OR PARAMETERS

Background: Researchers gathered data on the amount of time per day spent watching television for 1-year-olds and 3-year-olds.

Questions:

1. How would we formulate a null hypothesis in terms of variables?

2. How would we formulate a null hypothesis in terms of parameters?

Responses:

1. **Variables:** The null hypothesis would state that age (1 or 3 years old) and television watching time are not related.

2. **Parameters:** The null hypothesis would state that the population mean television watching time for all 1-year-olds, μ_1, is the same as the mean for all 3-year-olds, μ_2.

Practice: *Try Exercise 11.2(b) on page 525.*

In the case of our opening example, instead of phrasing it as a question of whether or not year and Math SAT are related for populations of students in various

The Big Picture:

LOOKING BACK

Paired, two-sample, and several-sample designs were introduced in Chapter 3 on designing studies, and discussed further in Section 5.1 on displaying and summarizing data from those types of design.

If the sample sizes are large enough or the population standard deviation is known, then a *z* or two-sample *z* distribution may replace the *t* or two-sample *t*. Allowing for a *t* procedure is most general, and it will be correct in any case. In practice it is rare to carry out a *z* procedure with software, because it requires us to state population standard deviations, which are typically not known.

Example TBP 11.1 on page 933 in the *Teaching the Big Picture* (**TBP**) *Supplement* reviews proper notation for the various designs. Page 933 presents supplemental material on the distinction between paired and two-sample inference.

Page 935 of the **TBP** *Supplement* includes illustrations to stress the difference between handling the parents' ages as paired data or as two samples.

years, we may alternatively express it as a question of whether or not mean Math SAT could be the same for populations of students in the various years.

Depending on whether the underlying design is paired, two-sample, or several-sample, the specific parameters of interest vary. It follows that the formulation of hypotheses and the construction of a confidence interval also vary, depending on what design was used to produce the data. Also, three different distributions apply: *t*, two-sample *t*, or *F*.

- **Paired samples:** Test if the mean of population differences, μ_d, is zero. Set up an interval estimate for how far μ_d is from zero. Because we focus on the *single* sample of differences, we can use the *t* distribution, discussed in Chapter 10.

- **Two independent samples:** Test if the difference between population means $\mu_1 - \mu_2$ is zero. Set up an interval estimate for that difference. This situation involves a new distribution, called the two-sample *t*, which is the distribution of the standardized *difference* between two sample means.

- **Several samples:** Test if all the population means μ_i are equal. In a more advanced setting, we could scrutinize confidence intervals and make multiple comparisons. (In this book, we focus on the hypothesis test results.) This situation also involves a new distribution, called *F*, which is a standardized measure for how different several means are from one another.

Of the three situations covered in this chapter, the solution method for comparing more than two groups, such as in our opening question about Math SAT scores for students in various years, is the most complex and will be covered last. The method for a paired design is by far the simplest, because it reduces to a method used in Chapter 10 for situations involving a single quantitative variable. We will therefore begin with the paired situation.

11.1 Inference for a Paired Design with *t*

As usual, conclusions about the population can be drawn in the form of confidence intervals or hypothesis tests. Because our primary concern is to establish whether or not a relationship exists between a categorical explanatory variable and a quantitative response variable in the larger population, we begin with hypothesis test methods.

Hypothesis Test in a Paired Design

Good inference procedures involve more than just assessing the size of a *P*-value. Before drawing conclusions about the larger population, we should pay attention to summaries and displays of the sample data. A discussion by the four students on page 140 in Chapter 5 explored the summaries and displays for comparing ages of students' mothers and fathers. Because the design is paired, it is appropriate to focus on the single sample of age differences. It was established that the sampled fathers were older by 2.448 years, with a standard deviation of 3.877 years. A histogram of the age differences exhibited right-skewness, suggesting that a few of the fathers were considerably older than their wives.

Once we've considered displays and summaries of the data, we are ready to extend our knowledge of the sample to draw conclusions about the larger population. In practice, a paired *t* procedure would be requested using software, and we would test the null hypothesis that the population mean of age differences is zero.

We usually rely on computer output when performing inference on any single variables or relationships. However, the same results can be obtained by hand if

necessary. To perform a hypothesis test in a paired setting, we have to calculate the standardized sample mean of differences.

> ## Standardized Test Statistic and P-Value in Paired Design
>
> To test the null hypothesis $H_0: \mu_d = 0$ in a paired study, we calculate
>
> $$t = \frac{\bar{x}_d - 0}{s_d/\sqrt{n}}$$
>
> and find the P-value as a right-tailed, left-tailed, or two-tailed probability of a value this extreme in a t distribution with $n - 1$ degrees of freedom. The particular form of the P-value depends on the alternative hypothesis.

One-sided and two-sided alternatives were defined on page 418 in Chapter 9, and scrutinized in subsequent examples.

Now we are ready to perform the actual inference procedure.

EXAMPLE 11.3 HYPOTHESIS TEST FOR A PAIRED STUDY

Background: We have data on the ages of students' mothers and fathers and want to determine if there is a relationship between the variables "age of a parent" and "sex of a parent" (that is, if fathers or mothers tend to be older). A request for a paired inference procedure results in the following output:

```
Paired T for DadAge - MomAge
                N       Mean      StDev     SE Mean
DadAge         431     50.831     6.167      0.297
MomAge         431     48.383     5.258      0.253
Difference     431      2.448     3.877      0.187
95% CI for mean difference: (2.081, 2.815)
T-Test of mean difference = 0 (vs not = 0): T-Value = 13.11 P-Value = 0.000
```

Question: What does the output tell us about each of the steps in a formal test of hypotheses?

Response:

0. No suggestion has been made in advance that fathers or mothers are suspected to be older, so the default two-sided alternative makes sense. The last line of the output confirms that these are the null and alternative hypotheses tested: $H_0: \mu_d = 0$ versus $H_a: \mu_d \neq 0$.

1. The sample of ages of parents of students taking introductory statistics should be fairly representative of the ages of the parents of all college students. The population is much larger than the sample, and although the histogram for the distribution of differences is skewed, the sample size is large enough that sample mean difference should be normal.

2. The sample differences have a mean of $\bar{x}_d = +2.448$ years and a standard deviation of $s_d = 3.877$ years. The standardized difference of $+2.448$ from zero is

$$t = \frac{\bar{x}_d - 0}{s_d/\sqrt{n}} = \frac{2.448 - 0}{3.877/\sqrt{431}} = +13.11$$

as seen in the output. For a large sample size, t is virtually indistinguishable from a standard normal z distribution, so a t statistic of 13.11 is obviously huge.

Continued

3. The *P*-value for our two-sided test is the probability of a *t* statistic this far from zero in either direction. Given that it behaves virtually the same as a *z* statistic, a *t* statistic as large in absolute value as 13.11 is almost impossible. The output confirms this by reporting the *P*-value to be 0.000.

4. Because the *P*-value is so small, we emphatically reject the claim of the null hypothesis—that the population mean of differences equals zero. We conclude that the mean is non-zero. Or, we can say the sex of a parent *does* play a role in age for the general population of students' parents.

Practice: *Try Exercise 11.6(e–f) on page 526.*

Because sampled fathers were significantly older than sampled mothers, we have good reason to believe that fathers are older in the larger population as well. However, we should keep our formal conclusions more general because our original alternative hypothesis was two-sided.

Example TBP 11.3 on page 935 of the ***TBP Supplement*** demonstrates that we may reach an incorrect conclusion if we erroneously handle paired data with a two-sample *t* procedure. Example TBP 11.4 on page 936 looks at a paired design with a very small *n*, checking the guidelines to see if a paired *t* is appropriate. There is also further discussion of paired confidence intervals and tests.

Now that we are convinced there is a significant difference in ages for the population of parents, a confidence interval helps to quantify that difference.

Confidence Interval in a Paired Design

To fine-tune our conclusion in Example 11.3—that age *is* related to sex of the parent—we look to a confidence interval for μ_d.

If a confidence interval for the mean μ_d of all differences is to be constructed by hand, we simply modify the single-sample formula for μ,

$$\bar{x} \pm \text{multiplier } \frac{s}{\sqrt{n}}$$

by substituting the sample mean of differences $\bar{x}_d$ for $\bar{x}$ and the standard deviation of differences s_d for s.

Confidence Interval for Population Mean Difference

A confidence interval for the population mean of differences in a paired study is

$$\bar{x}_d \pm \text{multiplier } \frac{s_d}{\sqrt{n}}$$

The multiplier comes from the *t* distribution with $n - 1$ degrees of freedom, when the data consist of *n* pairs, and varies a bit depending on what level of confidence is desired. A graph of the differences should be checked for non-normality if the sample isn't large.

EXAMPLE 11.4 CONFIDENCE INTERVAL FOR A PAIRED STUDY

Background: A sample of 431 age differences, *DadAge* minus *MomAge*, have a mean of 2.45 and a standard deviation of 3.88.

Question: What is a 95% confidence interval for the mean of age differences for the population of parents?

Response: For such a large sample, the *t* multiplier is approximately the same as the *z* multiplier for 95% confidence, 2. Our interval is

$$2.45 \pm 2(3.88/\sqrt{431}) = 2.45 \pm 0.37 = (2.08, 2.82)$$

Based on this interval, which was automatically provided in the output for our two-sided hypothesis test in Example 11.3, we can say we are 95% confident that the mean of age differences is somewhere between 2.08 and 2.82 years. On average, fathers are apparently older by at least 2 years, but not as many as 3 years.

Practice: *Try Exercise 11.6(g) on page 526.*

We should remind students that software is especially helpful in the middle stages of our inference procedure. Before "crunching the numbers," a human being must perform the necessary background checks to ensure that the data have been produced in such a way that the paired *t* procedure is valid. Also, it must be decided in advance which alternative hypothesis is appropriate. Afterwards, the output does not state conclusions for us: It is our job to decide between the null and alternative hypotheses, based on the size of the reported *P*-value. Then we must state our conclusions in the context of the variables discussed.

Recall that assuming our standardized test statistic to follow a *t* distribution implicitly assumes that the original statistic (in this case, sample mean of differences) follows a normal distribution. Thanks to the Central Limit Theorem, such an assumption can be made safely when the sample size is very large, as was the case for our 431 age pairs. On the other hand, when the sample of pairs is small, a histogram of the sample mean of differences should be examined, keeping in mind the following guidelines for use of a paired *t* procedure.

Guidelines for Use of a Paired t Procedure

We can assume the shape of the distribution of sample mean difference for random samples of *n* pairs to be approximately normal, and the standardized statistic $\frac{\bar{x}_d - 0}{s_d/\sqrt{n}}$ to follow a *t* distribution, if

- the sample of differences looks approximately normal; or
- the sample of differences looks fairly symmetric (not necessarily bell-shaped) and *n* is at least 15; or
- the sample of differences is moderately skewed and *n* is at least 30.

The context for the paired *t* test is that two observations are made on the *same* individual or paired unit in our sample. Next we will learn to perform inference in situations where values of a quantitative variable are being compared for two *independent* groups of individuals. This will require us to become familiar with a new distribution that is similar, but not identical, to the one-sample *t* distribution.

EXERCISES FOR SECTION 11.1

Inference for a Paired Design with t

Note: Asterisked numbers indicate exercises whose answers are provided in the Solutions to Selected Exercises section, on page 689.

*11.1 "Adults Who Stutter: Responses to Cognitive Stress," published in the *Journal of Speech and Hearing Research* in 1994, reported speech rate, in words per minute, for nine stutterers under conditions of stress.[1] Which form of inference should be performed first: a confidence interval for population mean difference in speech rates (stress versus normal conditions), or a hypothesis test to determine if conditions of stress affect speech rates of stutterers in general?

*11.2 "Domestic Goats Follow Gaze Direction and Use Social Cues in An Object Choice Task," published online in *Animal Behavior* in January 2005, included information on 23 goats' performance in a bucket-selection task.[2]

a. If a comparison is to be made between performances of adults and juveniles, would this be a paired, two-sample, or several-sample design?

b. State the appropriate null hypothesis, first in terms of variables and then in terms of parameters.

11.3 "Domestic Goats Follow Gaze Direction and Use Social Cues in An Object Choice Task," published online in *Animal Behavior* in January 2005, included information on 23 goats' performance in a bucket-selection task.

a. If a comparison is to be made for each goat's performance when cued by touching versus pointing, would this be a paired, two-sample, or several-sample design?

b. State the appropriate null hypothesis, first in terms of variables and then in terms of parameters.

*11.4 "Adults Who Stutter: Responses to Cognitive Stress," published in the *Journal of Speech and Hearing Research* in 1994, reported speech rate, in words per minute, for nine stutterers under conditions of stress.

a. If a comparison is to be made between these and their speech rates under normal conditions, would this be a paired, two-sample, or several-sample design?

b. Would the spread of the data best be summarized by reporting standard deviations of speech rates under normal and stressed conditions, respectively, or by reporting the standard deviation of the differences between normal and stressed speech rates?

c. Would the data best be displayed with a histogram or side-by-side boxplots?

d. In order to draw conclusions about speech rates for all stutterers under conditions of stress as opposed to normal conditions, should we perform inference about μ_d based on $\bar{x}_d$ or about $\mu_1 - \mu_2$ based on $\bar{x}_1 - \bar{x}_2$?

11.5 "Adults Who Stutter: Responses to Cognitive Stress," published in the *Journal of Speech and Hearing Research* in 1994, reported speech rate, in words per minute, for nine stutterers under conditions of stress.

a. If a comparison is to be made between these and speech rates under conditions of stress for nine non-stutterers, would this be a paired, two-sample, or several-sample design?

b. Would the data best be summarized by reporting means and standard deviations of speech rates under stress of stutterers and non-stutterers, respectively, or by reporting the mean and standard deviation of the differences between speech rates, pairing up each stutterer with a non-stutterer?

c. Would the data best be displayed with a histogram or side-by-side boxplots?

d. In order to draw conclusions about speech rates for all stutterers under stress conditions compared to non-stutterers under stress conditions, should we perform inference about μ_d based on $\bar{x}_d$ or about $\mu_1 - \mu_2$ based on $\bar{x}_1 - \bar{x}_2$?

e. Which form of inference should be performed first: a confidence interval for population difference in mean speech rates (stutterers versus non-stutterers), or a hypothesis test to determine if stutterers in general are different from non-stutterers in terms of their speech rates?

*11.6 The effectiveness of an intervention program for teaching children about child abuse was examined by administering a 16-question test to children before and after participating in the program. As an example, the first question asked what would be the best thing to do if you saw someone shaking a baby. (The correct response was to tell the person to stop and tell another adult.) The change in percentage correct, posttest minus pretest, was recorded for each question, and a test was carried out to see if the results provide convincing evidence that the program was effective.

```
              N        Mean      StDev    SE Mean
Post         16        76.75     20.96      5.24
Pre          16        60.06     23.66      5.92
Diff         16        16.69     14.81      3.70
95% CI for mean difference: (8.79, 24.58)
T-Test of mean difference = 0 (vs not = 0): T-Value = XXXX P-Value = 0.000
```

a. Was this a paired or two-sample test?

b. Which of these is a better summary of spread?
1. The standard deviations were 23.66 on the pretest and 20.96 on the posttest.
2. The standard deviation of the difference, posttest minus pretest, was 14.81.

c. Would side-by-side boxplots provide the best display of the data?

d. Does the null hypothesis state $\mu_1 - \mu_2 = 0$ or $\mu_d = 0$?

e. The *t* statistic has been crossed out. Standardize the sample mean difference to find its value.

f. Does the test suggest that the program significantly improved percentages correct on the various questions?

g. The *t* multiplier for 95% confidence and 15 degrees of freedom is 2.131. Show how the interval for the population mean difference was calculated to be (8.79, 24.58).

h. Are there any other possible explanations for why students would do better on the posttest, besides having learned something from the intervention program?

i. What would be a better design for producing evidence of the program's effectiveness, instead of just comparing pretest and posttest scores for students who participated in the program?

j. A histogram of the 16 score differences has been produced. Explain why it reassures us that inference with a *t* procedure is appropriate.

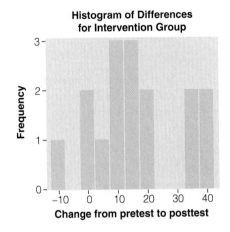

Histogram of Differences for Intervention Group

11.7 The Quantitative Environmental Learning Project (QELP) cited a study by the King County Division of Water and Land Resources on bacteria in various public beaches near Seattle, Washington. For each water sample, bacterial concentrations in colony forming units per 100 milliliters were recorded for two types of bacteria: coliform and *E. coli*.[3]

Sample	#1	#2	#3	#4	#5	#6	#7	#8	#9	#10	#11	#12	#13	#14	#15	#16	#17
Coliform	350	73	180	150	200	130	2,200	6,300	360	1,200	560	1,700	19	430	320	87	380
E. coli	350	90	120	330	200	120	1,600	5,800	300	980	630	1,800	16	270	270	160	210

a. Was this a paired or two-sample design?

b. Explain why the best summary of spread would *not* be to report the individual standard deviations.

c. As far as the sample was concerned, which type of bacteria was more common?

d. Produce a histogram of the differences and verify that it is mildly skewed. Does it suggest that there are a few unusually small differences, or a few unusually large differences?

e. The differences in concentrations have mean 81.9 and standard deviation 203.3. To test whether there is evidence that one type of bacteria is more common than the other, first report the standardized sample mean.

f. Tell whether the *P*-value would be less than 0.05.

g. State your conclusions about whether or not one type of bacteria is more common overall.

h. Use the fact that the *t* multiplier for 16 degrees of freedom and 95% confidence is 2.12 to produce a confidence interval for the population mean difference.

i. What aspect of your confidence interval in part (h) shows it to be consistent with your conclusion in part (g)?

j. Suppose researchers want to determine whether one type of bacteria tends to increase as the other increases. In this case, does the situation involve one quantitative and one categorical variable, two categorical variables, or two quantitative variables?

11.8   Samples of rainbow trout taken from the Spokane River were tested for lead and for zinc content, in milligrams per kilogram.[4]

Lead	Zinc
0.73	45.3
1.14	50.8
0.60	40.2
1.59	64.0

a. Suppose we consider performing a paired t test on the differences, lead minus zinc. Just by looking at the numbers, predict whether the t statistic will be very large in absolute value and negative, very close to zero, or very large in absolute value and positive; explain.

b. Based on your response to part (a), predict whether the P-value will be very small, not small at all, or borderline.

c. By hand or with software, carry out the paired test; first report the t statistic.

d. Report the P-value of the test.

e. Comment on whether or not your predictions in parts (a) and (b) were correct.

11.2 Inference for a Two-Sample Design with t

The Big Picture:
LOOKING BACK

In Section 5.1, we learned that side-by-side boxplots are a useful tool for displaying quantitative data obtained for two or more independent categorical groups. As far as summaries are concerned, we can compare means and standard deviations as long as the data sets appeared reasonably symmetric. Otherwise, we compare five-number summaries (or medians and *IQRs*).

In this section, we go beyond displays and summaries for data from a two-sample design. We will learn to draw conclusions about such relationships in the larger populations from which the data originated. Unlike the paired data from the preceding section, this section will involve data that have been obtained from two separate populations.

The key difference between paired and two-sample inference is that in a paired design we focus on the *mean of differences*. In a two-sample design, we focus on the *difference between means*.

The Two-Sample t Distribution and Test Statistic

Before we carry out a specific example in detail, it will be helpful to first discuss in more general terms how we will go about deciding whether or not to believe that means may be equal for two independent populations. Our test statistic should somehow measure the difference between the two sample means ($\bar{x}_1$ and $\bar{x}_2$), taking into account how spread out the data sets are (sample standard deviations s_1 and s_2), and also the respective sample sizes (n_1 and n_2). All of this is in fact accomplished via the **two-sample t statistic**, which can be thought of as the standardized difference between sample means, and is calculated as

$$t = \frac{(\bar{x}_1 - \bar{x}_2) - (\mu_1 - \mu_2)}{\sqrt{\dfrac{s_1^2}{n_1} + \dfrac{s_2^2}{n_2}}} = \frac{(\bar{x}_1 - \bar{x}_2) - 0}{\sqrt{\dfrac{s_1^2}{n_1} + \dfrac{s_2^2}{n_2}}}$$

The standard deviation of $\bar{x}_1 - \bar{x}_2$ is found to be $\sqrt{\dfrac{\sigma_1^2}{n_1} + \dfrac{\sigma_2^2}{n_2}}$ by applying the rule from Part III which asserts $\sigma_{\bar{X}_1-\bar{X}_2}^2 = \sigma_{\bar{X}_1}^2 + (-1)^2\sigma_{\bar{X}_2}^2 = \sigma_{\bar{X}_1}^2 + \sigma_{\bar{X}_2}^2$ as long as X_1 and X_2 are independent. This would *not* be the case if the data actually arose from a paired study.

where we have set the difference between population means $\mu_1 - \mu_2$ equal to zero, because that will be the assumption of the null hypothesis.

As a random variable, the two-sample t can be assumed to follow the symmetric bell-shaped distribution known as "two-sample t" only if the two samples are normally shaped or if the sample sizes are large enough. Guidelines for how large is "large enough" are analogous to those that apply in the case of single samples: Smaller samples will do if those samples appear fairly normal, whereas larger samples are needed if the shapes exhibit outliers or skewness.

As long as these guidelines are met, the behavior of the test statistic that we refer to as the "two-sample t" is quite predictable. Under the null hypothesis of equal population means, the two-sample t is bell-shaped and symmetric about zero, with a standard deviation somewhat larger than 1. The particular spread depends on the two-sample t degrees of freedom, which are based on sample sizes.

Degrees of Freedom for the Two-Sample t *Procedure*

The appropriate two-sample *t* degrees of freedom can be estimated using a very complicated formula, best left to software. They fall somewhere between the smaller sample size minus one and the combined sample size minus two.

If n_1 and n_2 are both at least 10 or so, we can get rough estimates with the familiar *z* distribution when performing inference by hand.

EXAMPLE 11.5 SIMILARITY BETWEEN TWO-SAMPLE OR ORDINARY T AND Z DISTRIBUTIONS

Background: If the standard deviations σ_1 and σ_2 are equal and the sample sizes n_1 and n_2 are equal, then the two-sample *t* distribution is the same as the ordinary *t* distribution with $n_1 + n_2 - 2$ degrees of freedom. For instance, if the standard deviations are equal and the sample sizes are both 4, the two-sample *t* distribution is the same as the *t* distribution with $4 + 4 - 2 = 6$ degrees of freedom. This graph shows the *t* distribution for 6 degrees of freedom (heavier tails) and the *z* distribution (a higher bulge at the center).

Once students have learned to carry out two-sample hypothesis testing, they might confuse the expressions "two-sample" and "two-sided." Exercise 11.47 on page 572 highlights the distinction between the two via a discussion by the four students.

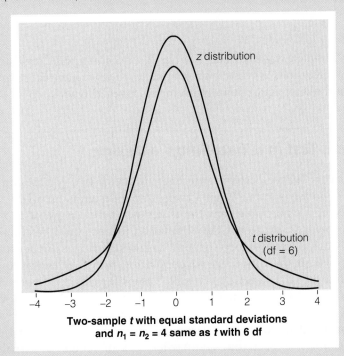

Two-sample *t* with equal standard deviations and $n_1 = n_2 = 4$ same as *t* with 6 df

Details about the two-sample *t* distribution are provided on page 938 of the ***TBP*** *Supplement*.

Question: How do the two distributions compare?

Response: The two distributions are quite similar: Both are symmetric about zero and "bell-shaped." The *t* distribution shows a bit more spread: Its tails are heavier, whereas the *z* distribution has more area concentrated around the mean, zero.

Practice: *Try Exercise 11.9 on page 538.*

Even if the population standard deviations and sample sizes are not equal, the two-sample t distribution is similar to "the" single-sample t distribution. We write "the" in quotes because there are many t distributions, depending on the degrees of freedom.

Now that we have an idea of the behavior of the *distribution* known as two-sample t, we consider the two-sample t *statistic*, which calculates the standardized difference between sample means for the purpose of performing inference.

The Big Picture:
A CLOSER LOOK

The quantity $\sqrt{\dfrac{s_1^2}{n_1} + \dfrac{s_2^2}{n_2}}$ is just an approximation of the true standard deviation of $\overline{x}_1 - \overline{x}_2$, $\sqrt{\dfrac{\sigma_1^2}{n_1} + \dfrac{\sigma_2^2}{n_2}}$. If we knew population standard deviations, we would be able to standardize using the latter, and the result would simply be a standard normal z statistic.

Standardized Test Statistic and P-Value in Two-Sample Design

To test the null hypothesis $H_0: \mu_1 - \mu_2 = 0$ in a two-sample study, we calculate

$$t = \frac{(\overline{x}_1 - \overline{x}_2) - 0}{\sqrt{\dfrac{s_1^2}{n_1} + \dfrac{s_2^2}{n_2}}}$$

and find the P-value as a right-tailed, left-tailed, or two-tailed probability of a value this extreme in a two-sample t distribution with appropriate degrees of freedom. The df fall somewhere between the smaller $n_i - 1$ and $n_1 + n_2 - 2$, with the former providing a more conservative estimate. The particular form of the P-value depends on the alternative hypothesis.

The Big Picture:
LOOKING AHEAD

Two-sample data, like several-sample data, can appear in stacked or unstacked formats. Data for our next example, 11.6, could consist of one column of age values and another column of gender values. Alternatively, it could consist of a column of female ages and a column of male ages. Example 11.12 on page 544 gives a detailed illustration of stacked and unstacked formats for a several-sample design.

If a two-sample t statistic takes a value that is known to be highly unusual for the particular two-sample t distribution at hand, then we have cause to doubt that the null hypothesis of equal population means is really true.

Hypothesis Test in a Two-Sample Design

Throughout Part IV, we perform inference in one of two forms: confidence intervals and hypothesis tests. When a two-sample design is involved, we'd probably test first if it's plausible that the difference between population means is zero. In other words, we test if the population means could be equal, in which case the categorical explanatory variable has no significant impact on the quantitative response. If the difference in population means does not appear to be zero, we could set up a range of plausible values for this difference. This confidence interval would help to quantify the impact of the explanatory variable on the response.

Our first detailed example will concern ages of female and male students. Initially, one might expect that comparing ages of female and male students would involve the same procedures as those used to compare ages of students' mothers and fathers. In fact, the data arise from two different types of design: Ages of mothers and fathers consisted of *pairs* of values (one age pair for each student) whereas ages of female and male students consist of two *independent* data sets.

To draw conclusions about populations of ages of male and female students, we'll test if it's plausible that both populations share the same mean. If the population means apparently differ, we'll construct a range of plausible values for this difference, female minus male.

EXAMPLE 11.6 A TWO-SAMPLE HYPOTHESIS TEST

Background: We have data on students' age and sex, and want to determine if there is a relationship between the variables "age of a student" and "sex of a student" (that is, if males or females tend to be older). A request for a two-sample inference procedure results in the following side-by-side boxplots and output.

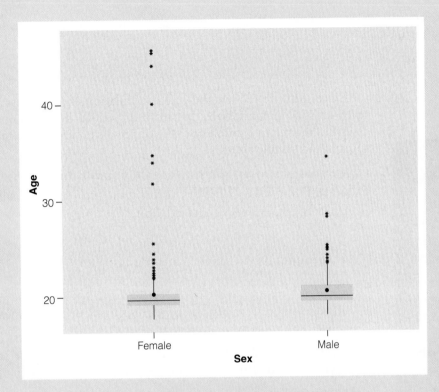

```
Two-sample T for Age
Sex          N     Mean     StDev   SE Mean
female      281    20.28     3.34     0.20
male        163    20.53     1.96     0.15
Difference = mu (female) - mu (male )
Estimate for difference: -0.250
95% CI for difference: (-0.745, 0.245)
T-Test of difference = 0 (vs not =): T-Value = -0.99 P-Value = 0.321 DF = 441
```

Question: What do the boxplots and output tell us about the relationship between sex and age for the larger group of students?

Response: The box for males appears to be slightly higher than that for females. On the other hand, the outliers tend to be higher for the females. Due to many high outliers for both groups, both boxplots display so much spread that whatever differences we see between the two groups seem relatively inconsequential. Nevertheless, both sample sizes are large enough (281 females and 163 males) that our test might be sensitive to a subtle but statistically significant difference in mean ages.

The relative difference in sample mean ages (20.28 for females and 20.53 for males), taking sample spreads and sizes into account, is measured via the two-sample *t* statistic, shown to be −0.99. The P-value, or probability of a sample mean this extreme, is 0.321, which is *not* small.

Continued

Therefore, we do not reject the null hypothesis, and we conclude that the mean age of all female students may be the same as the mean age of all male students. The data provide no evidence of a relationship between sex and age for the larger population of students.

Practice: *Try Exercise 11.13(a–d) on page 539.*

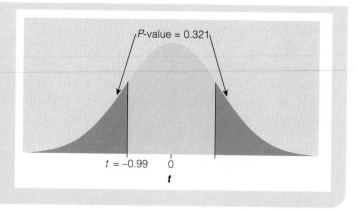

The Big Picture: **A CLOSER LOOK**

It is worth noting that the sketch above, which shows the *P*-value for two-sample $t = -0.99$, demonstrates how close this curve is to that of a standard normal *z*, due to the large sample sizes. According to the 68-95-99.7 Rule, the combined tail area when *z* is 1 away from 0 is $1 - 0.68 = 0.32$. Our two-sample *t* is just about 1 below zero, and the combined tail area (*P*-value) is 0.321.

An illustration of sampling for the two-sample design in Example TBP 11.6 is shown on page 942 of the ***TBP** Supplement.*

Since software renders the actual calculation of *t* unnecessary, we should not dwell on such computations, but instead consider how this quantity succeeds in assessing the relative difference between two sample means, taking into account spreads and sample sizes.

EXAMPLE 11.7 HOW THE DIFFERENCE BETWEEN SAMPLE MEANS AFFECTS THE TWO-SAMPLE TEST RESULTS

Background: A two-sample *t* statistic, $t = \dfrac{(\bar{x}_1 - \bar{x}_2) - 0}{\sqrt{\dfrac{s_1^2}{n_1} + \dfrac{s_2^2}{n_2}}}$, has been computed in order to test the hypothesis that population means are equal, against the two-sided alternative.

Question: How does the size of the difference between the sample means affect the size of our *P*-value for the test?

Response: First and foremost, the two-sample *t* statistic measures how different the observed sample means are, due to the presence of $\bar{x}_1 - \bar{x}_2$ in the numerator. If this difference is large in absolute value, suggesting that sample means are very different from one another, then the two-sample *t* statistic will tend to be large in absolute value, putting us far on the fringe of the *t* distribution curve, resulting in a small *P*-value and a conclusion that the population means differ. If $\bar{x}_1 - \bar{x}_2$ is not especially large, then the two-sample *t* will be closer to zero and the *P*-value will not be small enough to conclude that the population means differ.

Practice: *Try Exercise 11.14(a) on page 540.*

The role of standard deviations is more subtle than that of the difference between sample means, but they do have the potential to impact our conclusions.

EXAMPLE 11.8 HOW THE SAMPLE STANDARD DEVIATIONS AFFECT THE TWO-SAMPLE TEST RESULTS

Background: A two-sample *t* statistic, $t = \dfrac{(\bar{x}_1 - \bar{x}_2) - 0}{\sqrt{\dfrac{s_1^2}{n_1} + \dfrac{s_2^2}{n_2}}}$, has been computed in order to test the hypothesis that population means are equal, against the two-sided alternative.

Question: How do the sizes of the sample standard deviations affect the size of our *P*-value for the test?

Response: Because of their appearance in the denominator of our two-sample *t* statistic, large values of s_1 or s_2 tend to result in values of *t* closer to zero. If *t* is close to zero, then the *P*-value, which equals a tail probability, will not be especially small, and we will not have enough evidence to conclude that population means differ. Whenever the individual distributions have a great deal of spread about their means, the observed difference between those means is less prominent.

If, on the other hand, the sample standard deviations are quite small, then their appearance in the denominator of *t* makes its value large, which in turn results in a small *P*-value. Whenever the individual distributions have little spread about their means, the difference between those means is magnified.

Practice: *Try Exercise 11.14(b) on page 540.*

An illustration of how the size of the difference between sample means affects the size of the two-sample *t* statistic and the size of the *P*-value, as discussed in Example 11.7, is shown on page 939 of the **TBP** *Supplement.*

An illustration of the role played by standard deviations in the size of the two-sample *t* statistic and the size of the *P*-value, as discussed in Example 11.8, is shown on page 939 of the **TBP** *Supplement.*

The following side-by-side boxplots illustrate how large sample standard deviations contribute to a conclusion of equal population means, and small sample standard deviations contribute to a conclusion of different population means. To put the data in context, you could imagine that the boxplot on the left in each scenario represents monthly salary (in thousands of dollars) for a sample of female workers, whereas the boxplot on the right in each scenario represents monthly salary for a sample of male workers. Our visual intuition should suggest that population means may be equal in Scenario A—for instance, 3.5 would be a plausible value for population mean monthly earnings of both females and males. In Scenario B, because of the small degree of spread in each of the two samples, the amount of overlap is reduced, and any population mean that would be plausible for the females (on the left) would be too low to be plausible for the males (on the right).

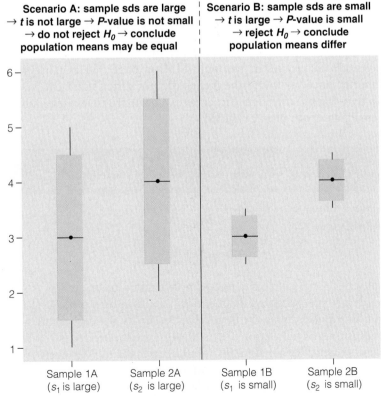

Sample means, indicated by solid circles, are 3 and 4 in both scenarios

TheBig Picture:

LOOKING BACK

In Example 5.5 on page 141 in Chapter 5, we discussed the role of distributions' spreads when we considered how impressed we should be by a difference in mean test scores for gum-chewers versus non-chewers. At the time, we could only speculate because we had not yet developed any tools for performing inference.

An illustration of the role played by sample sizes in the size of the two-sample *t* statistic and the size of the *P*-value, as discussed in Example 11.9, is shown on page 940 of the **TBP** *Supplement.*

As always, sample size plays an important role in our inference conclusions.

EXAMPLE 11.9 HOW SAMPLE SIZES AFFECT THE TWO-SAMPLE TEST RESULTS

Background: A two-sample *t* statistic, $t = \dfrac{(\bar{x}_1 - \bar{x}_2) - 0}{\sqrt{\dfrac{s_1^2}{n_1} + \dfrac{s_2^2}{n_2}}}$, has been computed in order to test the hypothesis that population means are equal, against the two-sided alternative.

Question: How do the sample sizes affect the size of our *P*-value for the test?

Response: The sample sizes n_1 and n_2 appear in the denominator of the denominator of our two-sample *t* statistic. Therefore, large sample sizes will ultimately make *t* large (and the *P*-value small) and small sample sizes make *t* small (and the *P*-value large). Large sample sizes in general give us more information about the population, and lend more impact to differences observed in the samples, thus giving us a better chance of rejecting the null hypothesis of equal population means. Small sample sizes tend to oblige us to take such differences less seriously, because they could more easily have come about by chance.

Practice: *Try Exercise 11.14(e) on page 540.*

Of course, the situation has been over-simplified in Examples 11.7, 11.8, and 11.9, for the purpose of stressing individually the roles of the difference between sample means, the sizes of the sample standard deviations, and the sample sizes. In reality, the combination of all three circumstances can be a rather complex matter to consider. This combination of circumstances is what makes the formula for our two-sample *t* statistic so "messy."

Confidence Interval in a Two-Sample Design

We did not pursue the issue of a confidence interval for the difference between male and female mean ages in Example 11.6 on page 531 because we opted to close the matter once we found the means did not differ significantly. In general, however, a two-sample confidence interval can be instructive, especially if hypothesis test results have not been provided.

Confidence Interval for Difference between Population Means

A confidence interval for the difference between population means in a two-sample study is

$$(\bar{x}_1 - \bar{x}_2) \pm \text{multiplier} \sqrt{\frac{s_1^2}{n_1} + \frac{s_2^2}{n_2}}$$

The multiplier comes from the two-sample *t* distribution, which is similar to the ordinary one-sample *t* distribution, which in turn is close to the *z* distribution if the samples are large. If the samples are very small, then the multiplier is closer to 3 than to 2. As always, the multiplier is smaller for lower levels of confidence (like 90%) and larger for higher levels (like 99%). Graphs of each of the two sample data sets should be checked for non-normality if the samples are not large.

Calculations for a two-sample confidence interval are more involved than those for a single mean. It helps to keep in mind that the formula simply builds a margin of error around the difference between sample means. Like all confidence intervals, it takes the form estimate ± margin of error, where the margin of error is a multiple of the standard deviation of the estimate. Here, as is often the case, we can only approximate the true standard deviation.

The above formula is cumbersome enough to discourage students from constructing confidence intervals for differences between population means by hand—certainly, software is much preferred. However, in case software is not available, the following example shows how to produce the interval.

EXAMPLE 11.10 CONSTRUCTING A TWO-SAMPLE CONFIDENCE INTERVAL BY HAND

Background: Ages of a sample of 281 female students have a mean of 20.28 and a standard deviation of 3.34 (in years). Ages of 163 males have a mean of 20.53 and a standard deviation of 1.96.

Question: What is a 95% confidence interval for the difference $\mu_1 - \mu_2$ in population mean ages, female minus male?

Response: We note that

$$\bar{x}_1 - \bar{x}_2 = 20.28 - 20.53 = -0.25$$

and the standard error of the difference between sample means is

$$\sqrt{\frac{s_1^2}{n_1} + \frac{s_2^2}{n_2}} = \sqrt{\frac{3.34^2}{281} + \frac{1.96^2}{163}} = 0.25$$

Although the distributions of ages are both skewed right with high outliers, the sample sizes are large enough that we can assume $\bar{x}_1$ and $\bar{x}_2$ to follow approximate normal distributions, so that their standardized difference follows a two-sample t distribution. The two-sample t, in turn, is close to the z distribution because the sample sizes are large enough that s_1 and s_2 should be quite close to σ_1 and σ_2. Therefore, the multiplier is approximately 2, and the interval is

$$\bar{x}_1 - \bar{x}_2 \pm \text{multiplier} \sqrt{\frac{s_1^2}{n_1} + \frac{s_2^2}{n_2}} = -0.25 \pm 2(0.25) = (-0.75, +0.25)$$

In the population of students, the average age of females is anywhere from 0.75 year (9 months) less to 0.25 year (3 months) more than that for males. Note that this is consistent with the interval $(-0.745, 0.245)$ obtained via software as part of the output for the two-sample test carried out in Example 11.6 on page 531.

Practice: *Try Exercise 11.18 on page 541.*

When inference in the form of a confidence interval is performed in the two-sample setting, our foremost concern is usually to check if the interval of plausible values for the difference between population means contains zero. If it does, this suggests the population means may be equal. If it does not, it suggests that they differ. In case the interval does not contain zero, we first check if it contains only positive values (providing evidence that the first population mean is greater than the second) or only negative values (providing evidence that the first population mean is less than the second). Then we examine it to get an idea of how much larger one population mean is than the other.

EXAMPLE 11.11 EXAMINING TWO-SAMPLE CONFIDENCE INTERVALS

Background: We consider some 95% confidence intervals:

1. The confidence interval for the difference between population mean ages of male and female students is $(-0.745, +0.245)$.

2. The confidence interval for the difference between population mean heights, *female minus male* (in inches), based on the same samples of males and females, is $(-6.392, -5.294)$.

3. The confidence interval for the difference between population mean heights, *male minus female*, is $(5.294, 6.392)$.

Question: What does each of these intervals tell us about the difference between population means?

Response:

1. The first interval contains 0, so it is plausible that there is no difference between population mean ages.

2. The second interval does not contain 0, so we have evidence that the population mean heights differ for males and females. The fact that the interval contains only negative values supports what our intuition would have told us already—namely, that females are shorter than males. The interval gives us a good estimate for how much shorter females are on average: about 5 or 6 inches.

3. The third interval is the "opposite" of the second one, so to speak. We can think of our conclusion in terms of males being taller than females, instead of females being shorter than males. Because most people find positive differences easier to grasp, it is usually better to subtract a smaller mean from a larger one, if we have control over how the data are processed.

Practice: *Try Exercise 11.19(e) on page 541.*

The Pooled Two-Sample t Procedure

When carrying out a two-sample t procedure with software, you may notice an option provided where you can request a "pooled" procedure, or specify "Assume equal variances" as part of the test. These options are referring to the unknown population variances σ_1^2 and σ_2^2. Assuming them to be equal is the same as assuming population standard deviations σ_1 and σ_2 to be equal. If this is the case, then there is only one unknown population variance, and it can be estimated by *pooling* together a weighted average of the two sample variances. Under these circumstances, the standardized test statistic has a bona fide t distribution (not just approximate, as is the case with unequal population variances) and the degrees of freedom are calculated to be higher than for the ordinary two-sample t. In general, higher degrees of freedom, just like larger sample sizes, tend to make it easier to reject the null hypothesis, and they result in narrower confidence intervals.

Users of statistical software might be tempted to first run an ordinary two-sample procedure, and if that doesn't quite succeed in producing significant results, then try the pooled procedure. This is not a good approach because the decision of whether or not to use a pooled *t* should be based on background circumstances, not on desired results.

Is there some way to decide whether or not it is reasonable to assume that population variances are equal? One common method is to eyeball the sample standard deviations. If the larger is no more than twice the smaller, we may decide that they are close enough to suggest they are coming from populations with equal standard deviations—and, therefore, equal variances. This rule of thumb has not been proven to work especially well. However, it is worth mentioning as a way to start comparing sample standard deviations, and we will rely on a generalization of this rule when carrying out several-sample procedures. There are formal tests for equal variances that may be carried out using software, but these also have their drawbacks: They tend to perform quite poorly when the distributions are not normal.

By the mechanics of the complicated computations involved, the interplay between the relative sizes of samples and relative sizes of sample standard deviations affects how a pooled test's results compare to that of an ordinary test. Often, but not always, conclusions are the same whether or not the pooled procedure is used.

Students Talk Stats

Ordinary versus Pooled Two-Sample *t*

*F*our students are working together on a two-sample homework problem. They are given samples of monthly rents for one-bedroom apartments either downtown (a couple of miles from their university) or in the vicinity of their campus. They are to use software to determine if the mean rent of all downtown one-bedroom apartments could equal that of all one-bedroom apartments near campus.

The students are considering the boxplot and summary statistics for the data, and trying to decide what procedure would be appropriate.

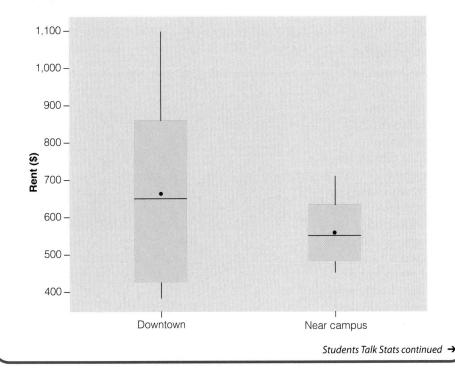

Students Talk Stats continued →

The data set of rents, downtown and near campus, is provided on page 940 of the ***TBP Supplement***.

Students Talk Stats continued

Variable	N	Mean	Median	TrMean	StDev	SE Mean
Downtown	7	662.1	650.0	662.1	257.8	97.4
NearCamp	8	557.5	550.0	557.5	88.8	31.4

Variable	Minimum	Maximum	Q1	Q3
Downtown	380.0	1100.0	425.0	860.0
NearCamp	450.0	710.0	481.3	631.3

Adam: *"Let's give the pooled t a whirl."*

Brittany: *"Bad idea. I read that you shouldn't use a pooled procedure if the larger standard deviation is more than twice the smaller. 257.8 is more than two times 88.8, so we have to use the ordinary two-sample t."*

Carlos: *"I didn't think we were supposed to use that rule, but anyway, think about it. Downtown there are some really classy expensive apartments, and some inner-city places that are falling apart. The rents for all of those are going to be more spread out than the rents of the apartments around here, which are pretty much all priced for students."*

Dominique: *"Just out of curiosity I tried it both ways and no matter what, the P-value is around 0.3, which isn't small at all so we can't reject the null anyway. But officially we better use the ordinary procedure, because of what Carlos just said. And write down the conclusion that mean rents for downtown and near campus could be equal."*

The students are wise to be wary of using the pooled two-sample procedure. Carlos's approach is commendable, because he thinks about the specific variables involved in order to decide that an assumption of equal population standard deviations is not justified.

Practice: *Try Exercise 11.20 on page 542.*

EXERCISES FOR SECTION 11.2

Inference for a Two-Sample Design with t

Note: Asterisked numbers indicate exercises whose answers are provided in the Solutions to Selected Exercises section, on page 689.

*11.9   "Psychiatric Symptoms of Adolescents with Physical Complaints Admitted to An Adolescent Unit" reported in *Clinical Pediatrics* in March 2005: "The aim of this study was to evaluate the psychiatric symptoms among adolescents who were seen in the outpatient clinic for their physical complaints." The study, which excluded any patients with known psychiatric disorders, included 290 outpatients between 13 and 17 years of age. It compared psychometric scores of a large number of male and female adolescents, using a two-sample *t* procedure.[5] For large samples, the two-sample *t* behaves roughly the same as a *z* distribution, shown here with details about tail probabilities.

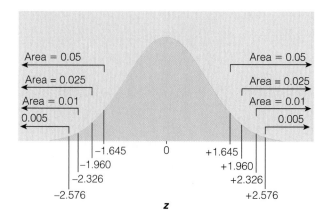

Tell whether or not each of the following t statistics provides evidence of a significant difference between the males and females studied.

  a. Anxiety: $t = 2.89$

  b. Depression: $t = 3.83$

  c. Negative Self: $t = 0.70$

  d. Somatization (physical complaints caused by psychological problems) $t = 3.50$

  e. Hostility $t = 1.11$

11.10 The study described in Exercise 11.9 also compared psychometric scores of early versus mid-adolescents, using a two-sample t procedure. For large samples, the two-sample t behaves roughly the same as a z distribution. Tell whether or not each of the following two-sample t statistics provides evidence of a significant difference between the two age groups.

  a. Anxiety: $t = 3.36$

  b. Depression: $t = 3.56$

  c. Hostility: $t = 1.25$

  d. Negative Self: $t = 2.85$

  e. Somatization $t = 1.35$

11.11 In Exercise 11.9, based on the following t statistics, either the null hypothesis of no difference between males and females is rejected or it is not rejected. When the test conclusion is reached, there is always a possibility that it is incorrect. Tell whether the potential error in each case is Type I or Type II, depending on whether or not the null hypothesis is rejected.

  a. Anxiety: $t = 2.89$

  b. Depression: $t = 3.83$

  c. Negative Self: $t = 0.70$

  d. Somatization $t = 3.50$

  e. Hostility $t = 1.11$

11.12 In the study described in Exercise 11.9, tests were run to compare mean scores on quite a few symptoms, including anxiety, depression, negative self, somatization, and hostility.

  a. Suppose 20 symptoms were studied altogether, and 20 hypothesis tests were carried out. If one or two of those tests produced a relatively small P-value, we should not necessarily conclude that males and females really differ with respect to those symptoms. Explain why not. [Note: In fact, fewer than 20 tests were carried out, and more than just one or two produced small P-values.]

  b. What type of error do we run the risk of committing, if we carry out a large number of tests to compare males and females?

*11.13 "An Analysis of the Study Time-Grade Association," published in *Radical Pedagogy* in 2002, reported that scores on a standardized test for cognitive ability for a group of 6 students who reported studying zero hours per week for the course had mean 25.30 and standard deviation 7.72. Scores for a group of 7 students who studied nine or more hours per week had mean 17.57 and standard deviation 2.82.[6]

  a. Find the difference between sample mean scores.

  b. As far as the samples were concerned, who did better: those who didn't study or those who studied a lot?

  c. Use the fact that the standard error for the difference between sample means is

$$\sqrt{\frac{7.72^2}{6} + \frac{2.82^2}{7}} = 3.33$$ to find the standardized difference between sample mean scores.

  d. The conservative approach would be to assess the P-value based on $6 - 1 = 5$ degrees of freedom. For this distribution, the two-tailed area beyond $|t| = 2.57$ is 0.05. Would we have evidence at the $\alpha = 0.05$ level of a population difference in mean scores in this case?

  e. A less conservative approach would be to assess the P-value based on $6 + 7 - 2 = 11$ degrees of freedom. For this distribution, the two-tailed area beyond $|t| = 2.20$ is 0.05. Would we have evidence at the $\alpha = 0.05$ level of a population difference in mean scores in this case?

  f. To get more conclusive results, would it help if larger or smaller sample sizes were used?

  g. Discuss the possibility of certain types of students under-reporting hours studied, and other types of students over-reporting. Discuss various ways of recording number of hours studied per week for samples of students.

*11.14 A study published in *Physiological Genomics* in 2002 investigated the genetic basis of limb bone lengths (measured in millimeters) in over 400 mice. We'll assume the sample to be comprised of 200 each males and females. Suppose a *t* statistic is to be computed to test for a significant difference between lengths of various bones for males versus females. If the standard deviation *s* for a given bone length is common for both sexes, the two-sample *t* statistic would be

$$t = \frac{(\bar{x}_1 - \bar{x}_2) - 0}{\sqrt{\dfrac{s^2}{200} + \dfrac{s^2}{200}}} = \frac{10(\bar{x}_1 - \bar{x}_2)}{s}$$

a. For males versus females, femur lengths averaged 17.0 and 16.7, whereas ulna lengths averaged 15.4 and 15.0. If standard deviations were the same for both types of bone, which *t* statistic would be larger: the one for the difference between femur lengths or the one for the difference between ulna lengths?

b. The standard deviation was 0.75 for femurs, 0.55 for ulnas. If differences between sample means were the same for both types of bone, which *t* statistic would be larger: the one for the difference between femur lengths or the one for the difference between ulna lengths?

c. One of the two-sample *t* statistics is 4.0 and the other is 7.3. Which of these is the test statistic for femurs and which is for ulnas?

d. Keeping in mind that a two-sample *t* for large samples is approximately the same as *z*, is there evidence of a difference between males' and females' bone lengths for femurs, ulnas, both, or neither?

e. If the sample sizes had been larger, would the *t* statistics in part (c) tend to be larger or smaller?

11.15 A study published in *Physiological Genomics* in 2002 investigated the genetic basis of organ weights in over 400 mice. We'll assume the sample to be comprised of 200 each males and females. Suppose a *t* statistic is to be computed to test for a

significant difference between weights of various organs for males versus females. If standard deviation *s* for a given organ weight is assumed to be the same for both sexes, the two-sample *t* statistic would be

$$t = \frac{(\bar{x}_1 - \bar{x}_2) - 0}{\sqrt{\dfrac{s^2}{200} + \dfrac{s^2}{200}}} = \frac{10(\bar{x}_1 - \bar{x}_2)}{s}$$

a. For males versus females, *liver* weights averaged 3.5 and 2.7 grams; the common standard deviation was 0.4 gram. Calculate the two-sample *t* statistic to test for a difference between population mean liver weights of males versus females.

b. For males versus females, *spleen* weights averaged 0.214 and 0.211 gram; the common standard deviation was 0.053 gram. Calculate the two-sample *t* statistic to test for a difference between population mean spleen weights of males versus females.

c. One of the *P*-values is 0.57 and the other is 0.0000. Which is the *P*-value for testing for equal mean *spleen* weights between males and females?

11.16 This boxplot displays heights, in inches, of female Olympic beach volleyball players and gymnasts.

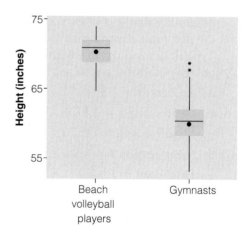

a. Assuming the samples were fairly large, do the boxplots suggest that it is plausible for populations of Olympic beach volleyball players and gymnasts to have the same mean height?

b. For which group is it plausible that the population mean height is 65, as it is for adult females in general: beach volleyball players, or gymnasts, or both, or neither?

11.17 Software was used to produce side-by-side boxplots of duration of stuttering for patients who had already been classified as having mild, moderate, or severe speech disabilities.

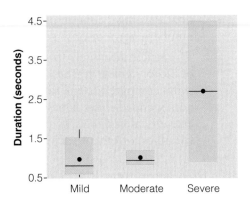

a. Clearly, the mean duration is noticeably higher for the patients whose disability had been classified as severe. Based on the appearance of the boxplots, tell whether the standard deviation for this group is much larger, much smaller, or about the same as for the other two.

b. With a calculator or by hand, find the mean duration of stuttering for patients in the mild group (values 0.75, 0.84, 0.52, and 1.73) and in the moderate group (values 1.18, 0.93, 0.83).

c. The sample standard deviations are 0.53 for the mild group and 0.18 for the moderate group; the standard error for the difference between sample means is

$$\sqrt{\frac{0.53^2}{4} + \frac{0.18^2}{3}} = 0.29.$$ Find the

standardized difference between sample means, which is a two-sample t statistic.

d. Which alternative is appropriate in this situation: one-sided or two-sided? Explain.

e. Keeping in mind that t statistics less than 1 in absolute value are common; closer to 1 than 2 are not unusual; around 2 or 3 are borderline; greater than 4 or 5 are extremely improbable, tell whether the P-value would be not small at all, small, or borderline.

f. Tell whether the data provide convincing evidence that, on average, duration of stuttering differs for patients classified with a mild disability compared to those classified with a moderate disability.

g. If the sample standard deviations had been much larger than 0.53 and 0.18, would the standard error have been larger or smaller than 0.29?

h. If the sample standard deviations had been much larger than 0.53 and 0.18, would the t statistic have been larger or smaller than the one you calculated in part (c)?

i. If the sample standard deviations had been much larger than 0.53 and 0.18, would the P-value have been larger or smaller?

j. Which type of error is committed if you conclude that overall mean duration of stuttering is no greater for those classified with a moderate disability than for those classified with a mild disability, when in fact the mean *is* greater?

*11.18 Samples of fish taken from the Spokane River were tested for lead content in milligrams per kilogram. Because most of the lead is thought to be concentrated in bones and fat, tests were carried out on filets, which are more representative of the fish that people actually consume. A sample of 22 rainbow trout filets had mean lead content 0.16 and standard deviation 0.11; a sample of 20 largescale suckers had mean 0.09 and standard deviation 0.06.[7] Use the formula

$$\bar{x}_1 - \bar{x}_2 \pm \text{multiplier} \sqrt{\frac{s_1^2}{n_1} + \frac{s_2^2}{n_2}}$$

and the fact that the two-sample t multiplier for a fairly large combined sample size is approximately 2 to produce a 95% confidence interval for the difference between mean lead contents, trout minus suckers.

*11.19 "Extended Work Shifts and the Risk of Motor Vehicle Crashes Among Interns," published in the *New England Journal of Medicine* in January 2005, looked at the consequences of sleep deprivation on a sample of thousands of medical school interns. Some programs offered night-float coverage, "the assignment of another physician to take calls for the on-call participant during an overnight shift for a period of time so that the participant could rest." "The average number of sleep hours per extended shift for those with night-float coverage was significantly greater than the number for those without night-float coverage (3.2 ± 1.6 hours vs. 2.6 ± 1.7 hours; $t = 21.3$; $P < 0.001$)."[8]

a. What was the difference in sample mean hours of sleep for the two groups?

b. Convert the difference in sample means to minutes.

c. Which of these is more responsible for the fact that the t statistic (21.3) is extremely large: that the sample sizes are very large, or that the difference between sample means is very large?

d. How do we interpret a P-value that is extremely small: Does it provide evidence that population means are very different, or does it provide very strong evidence that population means are different?

e. Would a confidence interval for the difference between population means, sleep hours with minus without night-float coverage, contain only negative numbers, zero, or only positive numbers?

f. The article ultimately looked at the rate of motor vehicle crashes after extended shifts compared to the rate after nonextended shifts. Does this involve two categorical variables, two quantitative variables, or one of each?

*11.20 Exercise 11.18 described how samples of fish were taken from the Spokane River and tested for lead content in milligrams per kilogram. The mean and standard deviation were 0.16 and 0.11 for trout, 0.09 and 0.06 for largescale suckers.

a. Software was used to carry out first an ordinary two-sample test, then a *pooled* two-sample t test (assuming population standard deviations to be equal).

```
T-Test of difference = 0 (vs not =): T-Value = 2.41 P-Value = 0.021 DF = 34
T-Test of difference = 0 (vs not =): T-Value = 2.35 P-Value = 0.024 DF = 40
```

For which test is there evidence of a difference in mean lead concentration for all filets of rainbow trout and largescale suckers: ordinary, pooled, both, or neither?

b. Are the sample standard deviations close enough to justify use of the pooled procedure?

c. Suppose that researchers had suspected before the samples were taken that concentrations of lead are higher in trout filets than sucker filets. Do the sample means tend in the direction of that suspicion?

d. What would the P-value have been if a one-sided pooled test had been carried out?

11.21 Duration of stuttering (in seconds) was compared for patients who had already been classified as having mild or moderate speech disabilities. The standard deviations were 0.53 and 0.18. Are these close enough to justify use of a pooled t procedure?

11.22 "Early Television Exposure and Subsequent Attentional Problems in Children," published in *Pediatrics* in April 2004, included information on television watching habits of 1,278 children aged 1 and 1,345 children aged 3. "Children watched an average of 2.2 hours (SD: 2.91) of television per day at age 1 and 3.6 hours (SD: 2.94) per day at age 3."[9]

a. Find the difference between sample mean watching times, aged 1 minus aged 3.

b. Is this difference denoted $\bar{x}_1 - \bar{x}_2$ or $\bar{x}_d$?

c. Use the fact that the standard error for the difference between sample means is

$$\sqrt{\frac{2.91^2}{1,278} + \frac{2.94^2}{1,345}} = 0.1,$$ and the fact that

the two-sample t distribution for large samples is approximately the same as the z distribution, to produce a 95% confidence interval for the difference between population mean watching times.

d. Does the interval convince you that 3-year-olds average more TV than 1-year-olds? If so, do they average at least one hour more? Explain.

e. If the sample sizes had been only 13 instead of about 1,300, then the standard error would have been about 1.0 instead of 0.1. The t multiplier would be about 2.1. What would the approximate 95% confidence interval for difference between population means have been in this case?

f. If the sample sizes had been only 13, would the confidence interval contain zero, or only negative numbers, or only positive numbers?

g. What would your answer to part (f) suggest with respect to whether or not, on average, 3-year-olds watch more television than 1-year-olds?

11.23 "Science Lifts 'Mummy's Curse'" reported on the BBC news website in December 2002 that "the infamous mummy's curse of Tutankhamen's tomb has little basis in hard science, research has found. The curse was allegedly placed upon all those present at the opening of the tomb in the Valley of the Kings near Luxor, Egypt, in February 1923. The legend is thought to have originated with the death of the expedition financier Lord Carnarvon, who died in 1923 after being bitten by a mosquito. [. . .] It was said that Lord Carnarvon's three-legged dog howled at the very time his master died, and promptly gave up the ghost. According to the writings of archaeologist Howard Carter, 25 westerners were present at the breach of sacred seals in a previously undisturbed area of the pharaoh's tomb and were therefore potentially exposed to the curse. A further 11 were in Egypt at the time but were not recorded by him to have been present at the site at the relevant time. Mark Nelson, of Monash University in Australia, followed up the personal history of all those present to see if they had indeed died young."[10] The mean and standard deviation of age at death were 70.0 and 12.4 for those present, 75.0 and 13.0 for those not present.

a. If $\bar{x}_1$ is the mean age at death for those present and $\bar{x}_2$ the mean for those not present, choose one of these as the correct alternative hypothesis: $\mu_1 - \mu_2 = 0$, $\mu_1 - \mu_2 < 0$, $\mu_1 - \mu_2 > 0$, $\mu_1 - \mu_2 \neq 0$.

b. Use the formula $t = \dfrac{(\bar{x}_1 - \bar{x}_2) - 0}{\sqrt{\dfrac{s_1^2}{n_1} + \dfrac{s_2^2}{n_2}}}$ to calculate the two-sample *t* statistic.

c. Note that two-sample *t* statistics, like those for single samples, are common if less than 1; not unusual if closer to 1 than to 2; borderline if in the neighborhood of 2 or 3 (depending on sample size); quite unusual if considerably greater than 3; extremely unusual if greater than 4. Could the *P*-value of your test be considered not small at all, borderline, or very small?

d. Based on the size of your *P*-value, do you agree with Nelson's conclusion that the data provide no evidence of a curse? Explain.

e. Without constructing a confidence interval for the difference between population mean ages at death, tell whether or not it will contain zero; explain.

Statistics refutes mummy's curse!

11.3 Inference for a Several-Sample Design with *F*: Analysis of Variance

So far in this chapter we have learned how to perform statistical inference in situations that involved comparing values of a quantitative variable for paired and for two-sample designs. Now we will learn how to compare values of a quantitative variable across several independent groups. Thus, the situation is a generalization of the two-sample situation, both conceptually and in terms of some of the details of how the test statistic is calculated. However, the distribution that applies, called an *F distribution*, looks quite different from the two-sample *t* distribution because it is based on *squared* differences. Once a method has been established for solving such problems, we will be able to answer our opening question, which involved comparing mean Math SAT scores for students of various years.

First, we consider two possibilities for formatting data in a several-sample design. One possibility is for the data to occur in a "stacked" column of quantitative values, along with another column containing values for the categorical explanatory variable. Another common way for the data to be presented is in "unstacked" columns—that is, several columns of quantitative data that are already grouped according to category.

EXAMPLE 11.12 SEVERAL-SAMPLE DATA IN STACKED OR UNSTACKED FORM

Background: Data for this chapter's opening question on Math SAT score and year of study, shown on the left, originated from a student survey. For another example, data have been gathered on mileages (miles per gallon driven in the city) for samples of three types of cars. These are shown on the right.

Math	Year
550	3
580	2
550	other
620	2
. . .	. . .

Sedan	Minivan	SUV
21	20	22
21	19	22
20	19	21
20	18	19
20	18	17
19	17	16
18	16	16
18	16	16
		15
		10
		13
		13

Question: Do the columns in both of our examples each represent a different variable?

Response: The answer in the first case is yes: Math SAT score is the response variable, comprising a column of its own, and year of study is the explanatory variable, also in a column of its own. We call this data set "stacked" because all the scores are combined into one column.

In contrast, the mileage data presents a column of quantitative responses for each of three categorical groups. These are *not* three quantitative variables. In fact, we are considering two variables: type of car (categorical) and mileage (quantitative). This data set would be called "unstacked."

Although the formats are different, both data sets arose from several-sample designs.

Practice: *Try Exercise 11.24(a) on page 559.*

As a preliminary step to performing inference in a several-sample design, we consider the test statistic that will measure, in a standardized way, how different several sample means are.

The F *Statistic*

In Section 11.2, we introduced and examined the two-sample *t* statistic. In particular, we explored how the difference between sample means, the sizes of sample standard deviations, and the sample sizes affected the size of the two-sample *t* statistic and, thus, the outcome of a hypothesis test for equal population means. The spread of the individual distributions played an important role in our final decision: When the sample standard deviations were relatively large, side-by-side boxplots tended to have plenty of overlap, and we were willing to believe that the population means were equal. In contrast, when the sample standard deviations were relatively small, side-by-side boxplots tended to have less overlap, and we rejected the hypothesis of equal population means. The role of sample size was also important: Minor differences between means could still turn out to be significant for very large samples.

When several populations, not just two, are being compared, we still base our final decision on how different the sample means are, taking into account how spread out the sample data are, as well as the sample sizes. The technicalities of the test lead us to focus on the *squared* differences among means in the numerator, and squared standard deviations (variances) in the denominator. The procedure itself is referred to as **Analysis of Variance**, abbreviated **ANOVA**.

When comparing the differences among several means, we use the letter *I* to denote how many groups are being compared. The letter *N* denotes the total sample size obtained when the individual group sample sizes $n_1, n_2, \ldots, n_I$ are combined. Also, $\bar{x}$ denotes the overall sample mean, a weighted average of the individual (group) sample means $\bar{x}_1, \bar{x}_2, \ldots, \bar{x}_I$. The individual sample standard deviations are denoted $s_1, s_2, \ldots, s_I$.

	Sizes	Means	Standard Deviations
Sample	I = no. of groups compared $n_1, n_2, \ldots, n_I$ sum to N	$\bar{x}_1, \bar{x}_2, \ldots, \bar{x}_I$ (overall $\bar{x}$)	$s_1, s_2, \ldots, s_I$
Population		$\mu_1, \mu_2, \ldots, \mu_I$	$\sigma_1, \sigma_2, \ldots, \sigma_I$

> *The* **Big** *Picture:*
> **A Closer Look**
>
> Note that if *I* equaled 2, as in the two-sample case, *N* would equal $n_1 + n_2$, and our data would simply consist of the two sample means, $\bar{x}_1$ and $\bar{x}_2$, and the two sample standard deviations, s_1 and s_2.

EXAMPLE 11.13 NOTATION FOR THE F TEST (ANOVA) IN A SEVERAL-SAMPLE DESIGN

Background: We want to compare Math SAT scores of 32 first-year, 233 second-year, 87 third-year, 28 fourth-year, and 10 "other" students.

Question: What are the number of groups *I* and the total sample size *N*?

Response: Since five groups are being compared, *I* = 5. We total the individual sample sizes to get *N* = 390.

Practice: *Try Exercise 11.24(b) on page 559.*

The *F* statistic calculates the standardized sum of squared differences between sample means $\bar{x}_i$ and the overall mean $\bar{x}$. In other words, *F* measures, in a relative way, how different the various sample means are from one another.

Standardized Test Statistic and P-Value in Several-Sample Design

To test the null hypothesis $H_0: \mu_1 = \mu_2 = \ldots = \mu_I$ in a several-sample study, we calculate

$$F = \frac{[n_1(\overline{x}_1 - \overline{x})^2 + n_2(\overline{x}_2 - \overline{x})^2 + \cdots + n_I(\overline{x}_I - \overline{x})^2]/(I - 1)}{[(n_1 - 1)s_1^2 + (n_2 - 1)s_2^2 + \cdots + (n_I - 1)s_I^2]/(N - I)}$$

and find the P-value as the probability of a value this extreme in an F distribution with appropriate degrees of freedom.

The rather daunting formula for our test statistic F is easier to grasp if we consider its similarities to the two-sample t statistic

$$t = \frac{(\overline{x}_1 - \overline{x}_2) - 0}{\sqrt{\dfrac{s_1^2}{n_1} + \dfrac{s_2^2}{n_2}}}$$

The Big Picture: LOOKING AHEAD

The degrees of freedom for the F distribution will be discussed on page 551.

Notice that both expressions feature the following:

- differences of sample means ($\overline{x}_i$) in the numerator
- sample standard deviations (s_i) in the denominator
- sample sizes (n_1 and n_2 for two-sample t, and N for F) divided in the denominator

Now let us discuss the specifics of the roles of means, standard deviations, and sample sizes in the F statistic. The F statistic is similar to the two-sample t statistic in that it assesses the relative difference among sample means, taking into account spreads and sample sizes. Obviously, the formula for F is a lot "messier" because it combines information for any number of groups, not just two. However, if there are just two groups being compared, with equal sample sizes and standard deviations, then F is exactly the square of the two-sample t statistic!

EXAMPLE 11.14 SQUARING THE TWO-SAMPLE T STATISTIC

Background: The histogram on the left is for a random sample of 100 values from a t distribution. The degrees of freedom are large, so that a two-sample t distribution is quite similar to a standard normal z. Thus, the distribution looks to be centered at zero, with a standard deviation close to one and a symmetric bell shape. The histogram on the right is for the *squares* of those 100 t values.

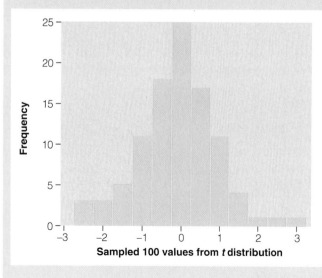

Sampled 100 values from t distribution

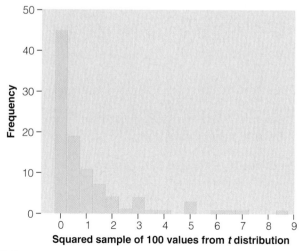

Squared sample of 100 values from t distribution

Question: How does the distribution of squared two-sample t values, on the right, compare to the distribution of original values on the left?

Response: The squared values are strictly non-negative and centered roughly at one, with a shape that is clearly right-skewed.

Practice: *Try Exercise 11.26 on page 560.*

Squaring values taken from a two-sample t distribution with large degrees of freedom would be just like taking values from an F distribution with the appropriate degrees of freedom. Like the distribution of squared two-sample t values on the right in Example 11.4, F distributions are non-negative, right-skewed, and centered roughly at 1.

Instead of dwelling on the lengthy computation of F by hand, we consider how this quantity succeeds in assessing the relative difference among several sample means, taking into account spreads and sample sizes.

EXAMPLE 11.15 HOW THE DIFFERENCE AMONG SAMPLE MEANS AFFECTS THE F TEST RESULTS

Background: An F statistic has been computed to test the hypothesis that several population means are equal.

Question: How does the size of the difference among the sample means affect the size of our P-value for the test?

Response: Most importantly, the F statistic measures overall how much variation there is *among* the observed sample means $\overline{x}_i$ from the overall mean $\overline{x}$, due to the presence of all the squared differences $(\overline{x}_i - \overline{x})^2$ in the numerator. If the sample means are very different from one another, then the F statistic will tend to be large, resulting in a small P-value and a conclusion that not all population means are the same.

Practice: *Try Exercise 11.27(a) on page 560.*

In the numerator of F, each squared difference $(\overline{x}_i - \overline{x})^2$ is weighted with the accompanying group size n_i, so that larger groups are given more weight than smaller groups. This quantity

$$[n_1(\overline{x}_1 - \overline{x})^2 + n_2(\overline{x}_2 - \overline{x})^2 + \cdots + n_I(\overline{x}_I - \overline{x})^2]$$

is known as the **Sum of Squares for Groups**, or **SSG**.

The fact that spreads play an important role in our conclusions about several population means is evident in the name "ANOVA," which stands for "Analysis of Variance." Not only do differences among sample means enter in, but also the squared sample standard deviations, or variances.

EXAMPLE 11.16 HOW SAMPLE STANDARD DEVIATIONS AFFECT THE F TEST RESULTS

Background: An F statistic has been computed to test the hypothesis that several population means are equal.

Question: How do the sizes of the sample standard deviations affect the size of our P-value for the test?

Response: As was the case for the two-sample t statistic, because the squared sample standard deviations appear in the denominator of our F statistic, large values of s_i tend to result in values of F that are not large. If F is not large, then the P-value will not be small, and we will not have enough evidence to conclude that population means differ. Whenever the individual distributions have a great deal of spread about their means, the observed difference among those means is less prominent.

If, on the other hand, the sample standard deviations are quite small, then their appearance in the denominator of F makes its value large, which, in turn, results in a small P-value. Whenever the individual distributions have little spread about their means, the difference among those means is magnified.

Practice: *Try Exercise 11.27(b) on page 560.*

The expression

$$[(n_1 - 1)s_1^2 + (n_2 - 1)s_2^2 + \cdots + (n_I - 1)s_I^2]$$

in the denominator of our F statistic measures overall how much spread there is *within* all the various groups, and is known as the **Sum of Squared Error** within groups, or **SSE**. Just as with group mean differences, group standard deviations (squared) for larger groups are given more weight, via multiplication by $n_i - 1$.

The following figure illustrates how large sample standard deviations contribute to a conclusion of possibly equal population means, and small sample standard deviations contribute to a conclusion of different population means. To put the data in context, you could imagine that the boxplots on the left, in the middle, and on the right in each scenario represent monthly salary (in thousands of dollars) for samples of black, Hispanic, and white workers, respectively. Our visual intuition suggests that the population means may be equal in Scenario A—for instance, 4 thousand dollars might be a plausible value for population mean monthly earnings of all three racial/ethnic groups. In Scenario B, because of the small degree of spread in each of the three samples, the three boxplots do not even overlap, and any population mean that would be plausible for the Hispanics (in the middle) would be too high to be plausible for the blacks (on the left) and too low to be plausible for the whites (on the right).

An illustration of the several-sample design for producing the salary data is shown on page 940 of the **TBP** Supplement.

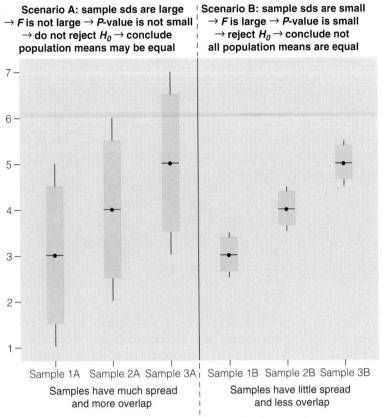

Scenario A: sample sds are large
→ *F* is not large → *P*-value is not small
→ do not reject H_0 → conclude
population means may be equal

Scenario B: sample sds are small
→ *F* is large → *P*-value is small
→ reject H_0 → conclude not
all population means are equal

Sample 1A Sample 2A Sample 3A   Sample 1B Sample 2B Sample 3B

Samples have much spread
and more overlap

Samples have little spread
and less overlap

Sample means are 3, 4, and 5 in both scenarios

The role of sample sizes is more complicated in the case of more than two groups because of the combined effect of total sample size *N* and number of groups *I*.

EXAMPLE 11.17 HOW THE SAMPLE SIZES AFFECT THE F TEST RESULTS

Background: An *F* test about population means is carried out based on three small samples ($n_i = 5$), then based on three larger samples ($n_i = 12$). The data are such that sample means (3, 4, and 5) are identical for the small versus large samples, and all the groups have the same standard deviation ($s_i = 1.58$). Thus, both side-by-side boxplots would look exactly the same—in fact, they appear just like those in Scenario A above.

Small samples ($n_i = 5$):

```
One-way ANOVA: smallsample1, smallsample2, smallsample3
Analysis of Variance
Source      DF          SS          MS          F           P
Factor       2       10.00        5.00        2.00       0.178
Error       12       30.00        2.50
Total       14       40.00
```

Large samples ($n_i = 12$):

```
One-way ANOVA: largesample1, largesample2, largesample3
Analysis of Variance
Source      DF          SS          MS          F           P
Factor       2       24.00       12.00        4.80       0.015
Error       33       82.47        2.50
Total       35      106.47
```

Continued

Question: How do the sample sizes affect the size of our *P*-value for the test?

Response: $N - I$ appears in the denominator of the denominator of F, so that a large overall sample size N tends to make F large, which makes the *P*-value small, and gives us a better chance of rejecting the null hypothesis.

In the first case, the observed differences among the means 3, 4, and 5 are *not* significant (*P*-value = 0.178) because the sample sizes are too small (each $n_i = 5$). We conclude in this case that the samples may be coming from populations that share the same overall mean.

In the second case, the differences among sample means *are* significant (*P*-value 0.015), due to the larger sample sizes (each $n_i = 12$). Now we would conclude that not all the population means are equal.

Practice: *Try Exercise 11.27(c) on page 560.*

To put the conclusions of Example 11.17 in context, we can say that differences among mean earnings for *small* samples of blacks, Hispanics, and whites might not be sufficient to convince us of a general inequity for larger populations. On the other hand, if such differences are observed for *larger* samples of workers, then we would have statistical evidence of inequity.

Although the data sets in Example 11.17 are hypothetical, they are roughly consistent with Census data, which show that, on average, whites are paid more than Hispanics, who are paid more than blacks.

The F Distribution

By now we are familiar with three standardized distributions—*z*, single-sample *t*, and two-sample *t*.

- **z distribution:** When we take a normally distributed sample mean $\bar{x}$, subtract its mean μ, and divide by its standard deviation $\sigma/\sqrt{n}$, the result is a standard normal random variable *z*, which by definition has a mean of 0, a standard deviation of 1, and a normal shape.

- **t distribution:** If instead we divide $\bar{x} - \mu$ by the estimated standard deviation $s/\sqrt{n}$, the result is a *t* random variable. Its mean is 0, its standard deviation is greater than 1 to an extent dictated by sample size, and it is symmetric and bell-shaped, although not quite normal.

- **Two-sample t distribution:** If we take the difference between two normally distributed sample means $\bar{x}_1 - \bar{x}_2$, subtract the mean $\mu_1 - \mu_2$, and divide by the estimated standard deviation of the difference $\sqrt{\dfrac{s_1^2}{n_1} + \dfrac{s_2^2}{n_2}}$, the result is a two-sample *t* random variable. It has a mean of 0, a standard deviation greater than 1 (as for single-sample *t*) and dependent on degrees of freedom, and is symmetric and bell-shaped but not normal.

Graphs of these three distributions look very much alike, and are distinguished from one another by their different spreads, which turn out to be roughly the same if the sample sizes are reasonably large.

In contrast, the random variable *F* that results when we take the ratio of mean Sum of *Squares* for Groups and mean Sum of Squared Errors within groups, based as usual on normally distributed sample means, has a very different appearance from the *z*, *t*, or two-sample *t* distributions.

- **Center:** The values of this random variable *F* are strictly non-negative, so *F* certainly cannot be centered at 0. In fact, its mean is close to 1.
- **Shape:** *F* is not symmetric but right-skewed, because of squaring differences in the numerator.
- **Spread:** The spread of the distribution of *F* depends not only on the total sample size *N* but also on the number of groups compared *I*. Together, *N* and *I* dictate the degrees of freedom in the numerator and in the denominator of *F*.

Page 947 features a computer activity that gives students a first-hand look at how the spreads of both the *F* statistic and the *F* distribution are impacted by the total sample size *N* and the number of groups *I*.

Degrees of Freedom for F

The *F* distribution has $I - 1$ degrees of freedom in the numerator and $N - I$ degrees of freedom in the denominator.

For the *F* distribution on the left, with $I - 1 = 5 - 1 = 4$ degrees of freedom in the numerator and $N - I = 390 - 5 = 385$ degrees of freedom in the denominator, there is a relatively small amount of spread, so that 3 turns out to be a relatively large value for *F*. (The tail probability to the right of 3 is 0.0185.) In contrast, for the *F* distribution on the right, with $I - 1 = 3 - 1 = 2$ degrees of freedom in the numerator and only $N - I = 15 - 3 = 12$ degrees of freedom in the denominator, there is enough spread so that 3 is not an unusually large value of *F*. (The tail probability to the right of 3 is 0.0878.)

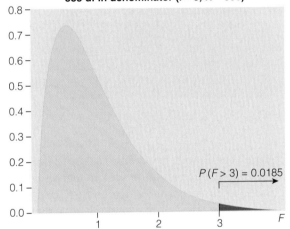

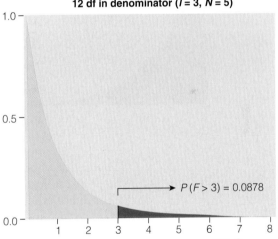

Because it is the degrees of freedom that tell us which particular *F* distribution we are dealing with, they constitute an important part of the several-sample data.

EXAMPLE 11.18 DEGREES OF FREEDOM IN THE NUMERATOR AND DENOMINATOR OF F

Background: We want to compare Math SAT scores of 32 first-year, 233 second-year, 87 third-year, 28 fourth-year, and 10 "other" students with an *F* test.

Question: What are the degrees of freedom in the numerator and the denominator of *F*?

Continued

The *Big Picture*:

A CLOSER LOOK

The shorthand notation often employed by researchers would refer to the distribution on the left as "*F*(4, 385)" and the one on the right as "*F*(2, 12)." Alternatively, the degrees of freedom may be shown as subscripts.

Students should be alerted to avoid misreading the denominator df as $N - 1$ instead of $N - I$.

Response: We have already established in Example 11.13 on page 545 that $I = 5$ and $N = 390$. The degrees of freedom in the numerator are $I - 1 = 4$ and in the denominator are $N - I = 390 - 5 = 385$.

Practice: *Try Exercises 11.29(e) on page 561.*

The shape of F is very different from that of the other distributions with which we are familiar. However, as far as the most important aspect of our test statistics is concerned, F operates in the same way as the z, t, and two-sample t statistics. Namely, F is a number that measures how extreme the sample data are, assuming the null hypothesis is true. Values of F that are not large suggest that the observed differences among sample means are not so extreme: The P-value will not be small, and the null hypothesis of equal population means is plausible. Conversely, large values of F suggest that the observed differences are extreme enough to reject the hypothesis of equal population means. In this case the P-value will be small.

The graphs below illustrate the relationship between the size of the statistic F and the size of the P-value.

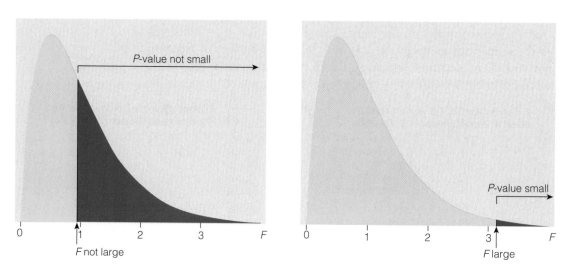

The question of how large is "large" cannot be answered so easily for an F distribution because spreads vary considerably, depending on which degrees of freedom F has in both the numerator and the denominator (which, in turn, depend on the number of groups I and the total sample size N). For example, 3 would be a large value for the F distribution depicted on the left on page 551, for 4 and 385 degrees of freedom. On the other hand, 3 is not especially large for the F distribution on the right, for 2 and 12 degrees of freedom.

Solving Several-Sample Problems

Whenever we perform statistical inference, drawing conclusions about larger populations based on samples, the first step should always be an examination of the sample data via displays and summaries. If an analysis of variance were to be carried out by hand as in the "old days," we would begin by finding means and standard deviations, and five-number summaries (assuming side-by-side boxplots are to be used for display). Then the calculation process (which is long and tedious even for comparing very small samples) would be followed to produce the F statistic, after which a range for the P-value would be found using tables.

In current practice, use of software makes much more sense, both for producing the initial displays and summaries, and for finding the F statistic and the P-value. It is common for software packages to offer side-by-side boxplots as an option when ANOVA is requested. Sample means and standard deviations, included in the ANOVA output, should be scrutinized to get a feel for the centers and spreads of the individual distributions.

EXAMPLE 11.19 SOLVING SEVERAL-SAMPLE PROBLEMS WITH SOFTWARE

Background: Data have been gathered on students in introductory statistics courses at a particular university, including their year of study and their Math SAT scores. Software was used to carry out an analysis of variance, and then to produce side-by-side boxplots of sample scores for each of the five year possibilities (1st, 2nd, 3rd, 4th, and Other).

```
One-way ANOVA: Math versus Year
Analysis of Variance for Math
Source      DF         SS        MS        F         P
Year         4      78254     19563      3.87     0.004
Error      385    1946372      5056
Total      389    2024626

                                   Individual 95% CIs For Mean
                                   Based on Pooled StDev
Level        N       Mean      StDev -------+---------+---------+---------
1           32     643.75      63.69                     (-----*-----)
2          233     613.91      61.00                 (-*--)
3           87     601.84      89.79                (--*---)
4           28     581.79      89.73          (-----*------)
other       10     578.00      72.08 (-----------*------------)
                                          -------+---------+---------+---------
Pooled StDev =     71.10                        560       600       640
```

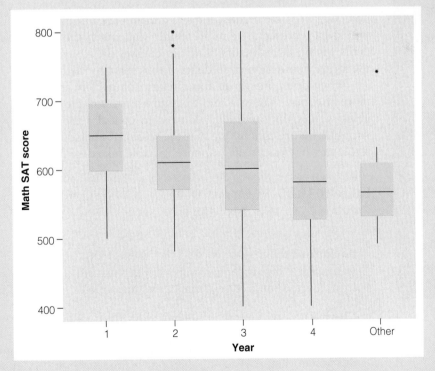

Question: For all students at the university, are Math SAT scores related to what year of study the students are in? In other words, is there evidence that mean Math SAT scores are not all the same for populations of students in various years?

Continued

Response: Although it is tempting to go directly to the so-called "bottom line"—which in any test is the *P*-value—a more thorough approach would begin with an examination of the side-by-side boxplots, along with the sample means and standard deviations. As we already discussed when we displayed the data on page 137 in Part II, the boxplots show that Math SAT scores tend to decrease as year increases from 1 to 4, and are the lowest for the "Other" students. The sample means, provided with the output, show means steadily decreasing from 643.75 for first-year students to 578.00 for "Other" students. The sample standard deviations, which take values between 60 and 90, are fairly large in that the five boxplots show considerable overlap.

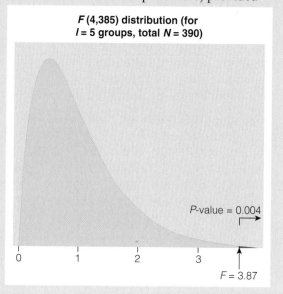

F (4,385) distribution (for *I* = 5 groups, total *N* = 390)

P-value = 0.004

F = 3.87

Ultimately, the sample sizes are large enough to render the observed differences among sample means statistically significant. This can be asserted because the *P*-value is quite small, just 0.004.

Apparently, 3.87 is "large" for an *F* statistic calculated for 5 groups of the given sizes. In any case, we reject the null hypothesis of equal population means, and conclude that not all the mean Math SATs are the same for populations of students in the various years.

Practice: *Try Exercise 11.29(h) on page 561.*

The Big Picture:

A CLOSER LOOK

The confidence intervals in Example 11.19, which are automatically provided in the ANOVA output, do not overlap enough so that any one mean population Math SAT score would be plausible for all five groups. Thus, they are consistent with our decision to reject the null hypothesis of equal population means.

In Example 11.19, we concluded that mean Math SAT scores differed among populations of first, second, third, fourth, and other students. But what "populations" are we talking about? Perhaps if we saw a significant difference among *weights* of female students of various years, we could conclude that mean weights differ for all female students of various years at this university. As far as the variable *Weight* is concerned, female students taking introductory statistics courses would be representative of all female students at the university. In contrast, students taking introductory statistics courses are *not* necessarily representative of the larger population of students with respect to their Math SAT scores.

When doing inference about relationships between variables, we should pay more attention than ever to the design used to sample the data and assess the variables' values. In particular, we need to consider the possibility of confounding variables before concluding that the so-called explanatory variable actually plays a role in what values the response variable takes.

EXAMPLE 11.20 HOW BIAS DUE TO NONREPRESENTATIVE SAMPLES CAN AFFECT THE F TEST RESULTS

Background: Suppose we find that mean Math SAT scores differ significantly for students in various years of study, based on sample data from several hundred students taking introductory statistics courses.

Question: Can we really conclude that Math SAT scores differ for all students in various years of study at that university?

Response: Before reaching this conclusion, we should think about possible bias in the sampling process, due to confounding variables. As far as Math SAT scores are concerned, students in introductory statistics courses in each year of study are *not* a representative sample of all students in that year of study. Students who are proficient in math would be inclined to take statistics in their freshman year, whereas students who have difficulty with math might postpone fulfilling a stats requirement. We could say that confidence (or lack thereof) in ability to do well in statistics is a confounding variable in the relationship between Math SAT score and year of study for students enrolled in introductory statistics courses.

Practice: *Try Exercise 11.31 on page 562.*

We can contrast the results in Example 11.20 with Example TBP 11.5 on page 941 of the ***TBP Supplement***, which suggests there are *no* additional variables confounding the relationship between *Verbal* SAT scores and year. Example TBP 11.6 shows that bias may also enter in at the stage where the sampled values are assessed.

The ANOVA Table: Organizing What We Know about F

Whether ANOVA calculations need to be performed by hand (as in the "old days"), or whether software takes care of those calculations (which is now almost always the case), a table helps to keep track of the various components of the *F* statistic and to report the *P*-value. An ANOVA table is typically provided as part of the computer output. It would be easy enough to complete by hand if it weren't for the tedious calculations of sums of squares that appear in both the numerator and the denominator of the *F* statistic.

$$F = \frac{[n_1(\bar{x}_1 - \bar{x})^2 + n_2(\bar{x}_2 - \bar{x})^2 + \cdots + n_I(\bar{x}_I - \bar{x})^2]/(I - 1)}{[(n_1 - 1)s_1^2 + (n_2 - 1)s_2^2 + \cdots + (n_I - 1)s_I^2]/(N - I)}$$

The numerator and denominator of *F* each measure variation from a different source.

- The **numerator** measures variation arising from differences among sample means for the various groups. This variation represents the impact of the categorical explanatory variable (or *Factor* in the table shown on page 556) on the quantitative response of interest.

- The **denominator** measures the usual variation that arises due to the fact that individuals naturally vary. This source is called *Error* in the table, not in the sense of a measurement error or decision error, but as in a standard error, which is an estimated standard deviation and, thus, a measure of the data's spread.

As noted earlier, if the numerator of this ratio dominates, then *F* will turn out to be large (and the *P*-value small), providing evidence that the categorical explanatory variable plays a significant role in the response. If instead the denominator is relatively large, then *F* will turn out not to be large (and the *P*-value not small), and whatever differences we see among sample means are insignificant, given how spread out the data are overall.

We fill out the five columns of an ANOVA table from left to right, ending with the *P*-value, which is the "bottom line" in any hypothesis test.

1. **Degrees of freedom.** Recall that we use *I* to denote the number of groups being compared, and *N* to denote the combined sample size. The group degrees of freedom, which tell us how to average out the variation in the numerator, are **DFG** $= I - 1$. The error degrees of freedom, which tell us how to average out the variation in the denominator, are **DFE** $= N - I$.

2. **Sums of Squares.** The number that measures how different the *I* group means are from one another is the Sum of Squared Variation among Groups, **SSG**. The number that measures how spread out the *N* observations are around their *I* group means is the Sum of Squared Error within groups, **SSE**. Both of these sums of squares are quite tedious to calculate by hand.

3. **Mean Squares.** The numerator of *F* is the Mean Sum of Squared variation among Groups, **MSG**, which is the **SSG** divided by its corresponding

degrees of freedom, $\mathbf{DFG} = I - 1$. The denominator of F is the Mean Sum of Squared Error within groups, $\mathbf{MSE}$, which is $\mathbf{SSE}$ divided by its corresponding degrees of freedom, $\mathbf{DFE} = N - I$.

4. **Test statistic.** F is the ratio of average variation *among* group means, MSG, to average error variation *within* groups, MSE. If this ratio is *not* especially large, then we will continue to believe that the population means may all be equal. If F *is* large, we have evidence that the means differ and we will reject the null hypothesis' claim of equal population means.

5. **P-value.** Shown in the right-most column of the ANOVA table, the P-value tells us how probable or improbable our observed F statistic is, under the assumption that the null hypothesis is true (the population means are equal). As always, a small P-value constitutes evidence against the null hypothesis, in favor of the alternative.

Source	Degrees of Freedom	Sum of Squares	Mean Sum of Squares	F	P
Factor	$DFG = I - 1$	SSG	$MSG = SSG/DFG$	$F = \dfrac{MSG}{MSE}$	P-value
Error	$DFE = N - I$	SSE	$MSE = SSE/DFE$		
Total	$N - 1$	SST			

EXAMPLE 11.21 COMPLETING AN ANOVA TABLE

Background: City mileages are being compared for 8 sedans, 8 minivans, and 12 SUVs in an ANOVA test for a difference among population mean mileages for the three types of vehicle. The sums of squares have been calculated as 42.01 for Groups and 181.42 for Error.

Question: What are the values belonging in the five columns of the ANOVA table?

Response:

1. The degrees of freedom are $I - 1 = 3 - 1 = 2$ for Groups and $N - I = (8 + 8 + 12) - 3 = 25$ for Error.

2. SSG = 42.01 and SSE = 181.42 have been provided.

3. The mean squares are SSG/DFG = 42.01/2 = 21.01 for Groups and SSE/DFE = 181.42/25 = 7.26 for Error.

4. The test statistic is $F = $ MSG/MSE = 21.01/7.26 = 2.89.

5. The only remaining information in the ANOVA table is the P-value, which must be obtained with software or estimated using F tables. Software shows the P-value to be 0.074, which can be considered borderline.

Source	Degrees of Freedom	Sum of Squares	Mean Sum of Squares	F	P
Factor	$DFG = 3 - 1 = 2$	42.01 (Given)	$MSG = \frac{42.01}{2} = 21.01$	$\frac{MSG}{MSE} = \frac{21.01}{7.26} = 2.89$	?
Error	$DFE = 28 - 3 = 25$	181.42 (Given)	$MSE = \frac{181.42}{25} = 7.26$		

Practice: *Try Exercise 11.32 on page 562.*

The ANOVA Alternative Hypothesis

Stating the null hypothesis for a several-sample design is a very straightforward matter: We write $H_0 : \mu_1 = \mu_2 = \ldots = \mu_I$ and say that all the population means are equal. Another way to express the null hypothesis is to say that the categorical explanatory and quantitative response variable are not related: Which explanatory group an individual belongs to does not play a role in the individual's response.

Keeping in mind that the alternative hypothesis should refute what is claimed in the null hypothesis, how can H_a be written and stated correctly?

The next example demonstrates a common mistake that students should strive to avoid.

EXAMPLE 11.22 INCORRECT WORDING IN REFUTING A CLAIM

Background: In a medical advice column called *DearDoctor*, written by various doctors for a county medical society and published in the newspaper, readers receive responses to their questions about medical issues. One reader inquired, "Does everyone with Parkinson's disease shake?" to which an M.D. in neurology replied, "All patients with Parkinson's disease do not shake." He went on to explain that while most Parkinson's patients do have tremors, there are some who exhibit only a shuffling gait.

A doctor misspeaks: "All patients with Parkinson's do not shake."

Question: Is the doctor's reply what he truly meant to say?

Response: The statement "All patients with Parkinson's disease do not shake," suggests that *no* patients with Parkinson's disease shake, which is surely not what the doctor intended to say. In fact, a correct reply should have been, "Not all patients with Parkinson's disease shake."

Practice: *Try Exercise 11.36(d) on page 564.*

To refute the claim that all population means are equal, we should say that *not all the population means are equal*. It would be incorrect to express the alternative hypothesis by saying that all the population means are not equal. Perhaps some of them are the same.

EXAMPLE 11.23 CORRECT WORDING IN THE ANOVA
ALTERNATIVE HYPOTHESIS

Background: In Example 11.19 on page 553 we rejected the null hypothesis that population mean Math SAT scores were equal for students of all years (1, 2, 3, 4, and Other), and we concluded the alternative to be true.

Continued

Page 943 of the *TBP Supplement* elaborates on Example 11.23 by discussing how the ANOVA alternative hypothesis could be expressed correctly using mathematical notation.

Question: How is the alternative hypothesis correctly worded?

Response: The alternative should state that not all population means are equal. It does *not* say that all of the means must differ.

Correct H_a: not all the population means are equal

Incorrect H_a: $\mu_1 \neq \mu_2 \neq \mu_3 \neq \mu_4 \neq \mu_5$

Looking at the side-by-side boxplots in Example 11.19 on page 553, the mean for 1st-year students is noticeably high, but the rest appear to be fairly close to one another. For instance, the sample means for 2nd- and 3rd-year students are 613.9 and 601.8, and in fact, a two-sample *t* test concludes that there is *no* significant difference between these two.

Practice: *Try Exercise 11.37 on page 564.*

In general, the ANOVA null and alternative hypotheses can either be written

$$H_0: \mu_1 = \mu_2 = \cdots = \mu_I \text{ versus } H_a: \text{not all the } \mu_i \text{ are equal}$$

or

$$H_0: \text{the two variables are } \textit{not} \text{ related } \text{ versus } H_a: \text{the two variables } \textit{are} \text{ related}$$

The fact that the word "not" appears in the null hypothesis in one formulation, and in the alternative in the other, can be a source of confusion to students. A statement that population means are equal and a statement that variables are not related both take the point of view that "nothing is going on." This is always the essence of the claim made by the null hypothesis.

Assumptions of ANOVA

We are really only justified in claiming the ratio $\frac{\text{MSG}}{\text{MSE}}$ to follow what is known as an *F* distribution if the sample means in MSG are normally distributed and if we have sampled from populations with equal standard deviations. The following guidelines should be kept in mind.

Guidelines for Use of ANOVA (F) Procedures

What we call an *F* statistic can be assumed to follow the *F* distribution only if all the samples are normally shaped, or if the sample sizes are large enough. Guidelines for how large is "large enough" are analogous to those that apply in the case of single samples: Smaller samples will do if those samples appear fairly normal, whereas larger samples are needed if the shapes exhibit outliers or skewness. In general, the *F* procedure is fairly robust: It tends to produce fairly accurate results unless there is a rather extreme violation of these guidelines.

The *F* procedure is based on an assumption of equal population standard deviations. If sample standard deviations appear quite different—for instance, if the largest is more than twice the smallest—then we should look for an especially small *P*-value as sufficient evidence to reject the null hypothesis of equal population means.

Page 943 of the *TBP Supplement* discusses the assumptions of ANOVA in more detail.

EXAMPLE 11.24 CHECKING GUIDELINES FOR ANOVA

Background: Two recent examples involved Math SAT scores compared for students in five different year levels, and mileages compared for three types of car. Sample standard deviations were included as part of the ANOVA output.

s_i (Math)	s_i (Mileage)
63.69	1.188
61.00	1.458
89.79	3.774
89.73	
72.08	

Question: For which ANOVA procedure do we have more reassurance from the sample standard deviations that the standardized statistic actually follows an F distribution?

Response: For the *Math* data set, the largest standard deviation, 89.79, is only about one and a half times the smallest, 61.00. For the *Mileage* data set, the largest, 3.774, is more than three times the smallest, 1.188. Therefore, the *Math* data set is more reassuring in terms of the condition that population standard deviations are equal. As far as the rule of thumb goes, the largest is *not* more than twice the smallest for the *Math* standard deviations, but it *is* more than twice the smallest for the *Mileage* standard deviations.

Practice: *Try Exercise 11.38 on page 564.*

EXERCISES FOR SECTION 11.3

Inference for a Several-Sample Design with F: Analysis of Variance

Note: Asterisked numbers indicate exercises whose answers are provided in the Solutions to Selected Exercises section, on page 689.

*11.24 The Quantitative Environmental Learning Project reports that the second-biggest source of lead in municipal solid waste is from cathode ray tubes (CRTs), the major component of television screens and computer monitors. In a 1999 study by T. G. Townsend, a sample of discarded CRTs was tested for leachable lead concentration in milligrams per liter. The following table shows concentrations for CRTs manufactured by three companies.[11]

IBM	Memorex	Zenith
1.0	2.2	1.6
9.4	2.3	21.5
41.5	6.1	21.9
	9.1	54.5
	10.6	
	15.4	
	21.3	

   a. Does each of the columns represent a different variable? Explain.

   b. Report the number of groups I and the total sample size N.

   c. Use software to produce side-by-side boxplots of the three data sets.

   d. Which company's CRTs appear to have the highest concentration of lead?

   e. Which company's CRTs appear to have the lowest concentration of lead?

f. Which company has the least variability (spread) in lead concentrations?

g. Are the boxplots top-heavy (suggesting right-skewness) or bottom-heavy (suggesting left-skewness)?

h. Report the sample standard deviations.

i. Is the rule of thumb for use of ANOVA (largest sample standard deviation not more than twice the smallest) satisfied?

j. The F statistic can be found to be 1.26, which is not very large, because the distribution is centered near 1, with area 0.05 to the right of 4. Is the P-value small or not small?

k. If standard deviations are disparate, then a smaller P-value would be needed to claim statistical significance. Do the data suggest that mean lead concentrations differ significantly for CRTs produced by the three companies?

11.25 Exercise 11.24 compares lead concentrations in cathode ray tubes, depending on which company manufactured the tubes themselves. The same study also made a comparison, depending on which company manufactured the television screens and computer monitors. (Sometimes, the CRT manufacturer is different from the television or computer manufacturer.) The table below shows concentrations of lead for CRTs in televisions or computers manufactured by four companies.[12]

Toshiba	Samsung	Sharp	Zenith
3.2	60.8	1.5	1.6
54.1	15.4	4.4	21.5
2.2	1.0	35.2	21.9
10.6	6.9		
54.5			

a. Does each of the columns represent a different variable? Explain.

b. Report the number of groups I and the total sample size N.

c. Use software to produce side-by-side boxplots of the four data sets. Which company's screens and monitors appear to have the most lead?

d. Which company appears to have the least lead?

e. Which company has the most variability (spread) in lead concentrations?

f. Which company has the least variability in lead concentrations?

g. Are the boxplots top-heavy (suggesting right-skewness) or bottom-heavy (suggesting left-skewness)?

h. Report sample standard deviations for the four types of screen.

i. Tell whether or not the rule of thumb for use of ANOVA (largest standard deviation not more than twice the smallest) is satisfied.

j. The F statistic can be found to be 0.19, which is not large at all, since the distribution is centered near 1. Would the P-value be close to 0 or close to 1?

k. Do the data suggest that televisions and computers produced by the four companies have CRTs whose mean lead concentrations differ significantly?

*11.26 Exercise 11.18 on page 541 described how samples of fish were taken from the Spokane River and tested for lead content in milligrams per kilogram. The pooled two-sample t statistic can be found to be 2.35. In this chapter, we remarked that if just two groups are being compared, with equal sample sizes and standard deviations, then F is exactly the square of the two-sample t statistic. In this case, sample sizes and standard deviations are fairly close.

a. Calculate the square of the pooled two-sample t statistic.

b. Comment on how the square of t compares to the F statistic, 5.53.

*11.27 Tell whether each of these features characterizes a paired t, a two-sample t, or an F statistic, or none, or all three:

a. The numerator measures how far the observed data are from what is claimed in the null hypothesis.

b. The denominator contains information about how spread out the data values are.

c. The test statistic tends to be smaller for larger samples.

11.28 Math and Verbal SAT scores were examined for students in three types of introductory statistics course: one for social science majors, one for natural science majors, and one for business majors.

a. Mean Math SAT scores for the three groups were 589, 626, and 650; mean Verbal scores were 585, 601, and 574. If standard deviations and sample sizes were comparable, which *F* statistic should be larger: the one used to test for a difference in population mean Math scores or Verbal scores?

b. Standard deviations for the Math scores were 68, 69, and 69; for the Verbal

scores they were 73, 73, and 70. If differences among means for the three groups' math scores had been comparable to the differences among means for the three groups' verbal scores, which *F* statistic would be larger: the one used to test for a difference in population mean Math scores or Verbal scores?

*11.29 A state assessment test is a standards-based, criterion-referenced assessment used to measure a student's attainment of the academic standards while also determining the degree to which school programs enable students to attain proficiency of the standards. Every student in 5th, 8th, and 11th grades in the state is assessed in reading, math, and writing. Mean *scores* were compared for samples of schools at four different levels: elementary, elementary/middle, middle, and high school.

```
One-way ANOVA: MeanScore_E, MeanScore_EM, MeanScore_M, MeanScore_H
Analysis of Variance
Source      DF        SS        MS       F        P
Factor       3      9220      3073     XXXX     0.739
Error       80    585561      7320
Total       83    594780

                                   Individual 95% CIs For Mean
                                   Based on Pooled StDev
Level          N     Mean    StDev  -------+---------+---------+---------+
MeanScore_E 49     1228.3     82.4             (----*----)
MeanScore_EM 6     1263.5     40.3         (------------*------------)
MeanScore_M 17     1219.0     90.6      (-------*-------)
MeanScore_H 12     1223.2    104.7   (---------*---------)
                                   ------+---------+---------+---------+
Pooled StDev =     85.6          1200      1250      1300      1350
```

a. Which type of school had the highest sample mean?

b. Which type of school had the lowest sample mean?

c. In general, because a confidence interval for μ takes the form $\bar{x} \pm$ multiplier $\frac{s}{\sqrt{n}}$, smaller standard deviations tend to result in narrower intervals. Here, the combination elementary/middle schools had the smallest standard deviation, but their confidence interval is widest. Why?

d. What are the number of groups *I* and total sample size *N*?

e. Explain how the degrees of freedom for groups, 3, and error, 80, could have been calculated from the rest of the output.

f. Explain how the mean squares, 3,073 and 7,320, could have been calculated from the rest of the output.

g. The *F* statistic has been blanked out. Use information from the rest of the ANOVA table to report the value of *F*.

h. Based on the size of the *P*-value, would we consider the *F* statistic to be "large"?

i. If similar sample means and standard deviations had been obtained from hundreds of schools, instead of dozens, would the *F* statistic have been smaller, larger, or the same?

j. Judging from the confidence intervals, which of these means (if any) would be plausible for all four types of school: 1,200; 1,250; 1,300; 1,350?

11.30 The percentage of students classified as disadvantaged was compared for samples of schools at three different levels: elementary, middle, and high school. ANOVA was used to compare mean *percentages disadvantaged* for the three types of school.

```
Analysis of Variance
Source      DF        SS        MS        F         P
Factor       2      5986      2993      XXXX      0.000
Error       75     23604       315
Total       77     29590
                                      Individual 95% CIs For Mean
                                      Based on Pooled StDev
Level   N          Mean     StDev   ----------+---------+---------+------
%Disadv_e  49      70.98     18.25                        (---*---)
%Disadv_m  17      62.72     18.44                 (------*------)
%Disadv_h  12      46.39     14.09     (--------*-------)
                                      ----------+---------+---------+------
Pooled StDev  =    17.74                        48        60        72
```

a. Suppose students are classified as being economically disadvantaged based on a form that must be completed by parents regarding household income, and sent in to make students eligible for free or reduced school lunch. Explain how this could bring about a difference in reported percentages for the three types of school.

b. Disadvantaged students might tend to drop out before they have completed high school. Explain how this could bring about a difference in reported percentages for the three types of school.

c. Which type of school had the highest sample mean?

d. Which type of school had the lowest sample mean?

e. Are your answers to parts (c) and (d) consistent with your answers to parts (a) and (b)?

f. What are the number of groups I and total sample size N?

g. Explain how the degrees of freedom for groups (2) and error (75) could have been calculated from the rest of the output.

h. Explain how the mean squares, 2,993 and 315, could have been calculated from the rest of the output.

i. The F statistic has been blanked out. Use information from the rest of the ANOVA table to report the value of F.

j. Refer to the P-value in order to choose which *two* of these conclusions are correct:
   1. There is *no* evidence of a relationship between level of school and percentage of disadvantaged students.
   2. There *is* evidence of a relationship between level of school and percentage of disadvantaged students.
   3. Not all three mean percentages disadvantaged are the same for populations of schools at the various levels.
   4. All three mean percentages disadvantaged may be the same for populations of schools at the various levels.

k. Judging from the confidence intervals, which of these means (if any) would be plausible for all three types of school: 48, 60, 82?

*11.31 Exercise 11.96 will use software to explore whether or not a student's ears are pierced tells us something about the student's Math SAT score. What confounding variable plays a role in whether or not a student's ears are pierced, and also plays a role in Math SAT score?

*11.32 Exercise 11.100 will use software to explore whether or not a student's year in college tells us something about how long the student sleeps at night, based on data from 362 students classified as being in first, second, third, fourth, or "other" year. Find the values of the quantities needed to complete this ANOVA table obtained from the data.

Source	Degrees of Freedom	Sum of Squares	Mean Sum of Squares	F	P
Factor	DFG = ?	SSG = 22.29	MSG = ?	F = ?	P-value = 0.013
Error	DFE = ?	SSE = 620.82	MSE = ?		

a. DFG

b. DFE

c. MSG

d. MSE

e. *F*

11.33 Exercise 11.103 will use software to explore if a student's favorite color tells us something about the student's height, based on data from 362 students choosing from 8 colors.

    a. What confounding variable plays a role in a student's favorite color choice and also plays a role in height?

    b. Complete this ANOVA table obtained from the data.

Source	Degrees of Freedom	Sum of Squares	Mean Sum of Squares	F	P
Factor	DFG = ?	SSG = 543.6	MSG = ?	F = ?	P-value = 0.000
Error	DFE = ?	SSE = 5,635.2	MSE = ?		

*11.34 Suppose we obtained survey data to compare mean automobile accidents during the preceding year for individuals in various age groups: 16 to 25 years old, 26 to 65 years old, and over 65. Explain how bias in the reporting of variables' values could play a role in our results.

11.35 "Predictors and Consequences of Food Neophobia and Pickiness in Young Girls," published in *Journal of the American Dietetic Association* in June 2003, grouped girls into 4 classes according to how averse they were to trying new foods and how resistant they were to eating familiar foods. One response of interest was the amount of vegetable intake.

    a. According to the article, "ANOVA showed that there was a main effect of pickiness on vegetable consumption, $F_{3,186} = 4.43$, $P < 0.05$, with picky girls consuming fewer servings of vegetables."[13] Does this tell us that the area under the relevant *F* curve to the right of 4.43 is more than 0.05 or less than 0.05?

    b. Under what circumstances would the *F* statistic tend to be larger: if the sample means had differed more, if the standard deviations had been smaller, if the sample sizes had been larger, or all of these, or none of these?

    c. "A planned comparison ANOVA was performed to test the hypothesis that girls with high neophobia and high pickiness would report significantly lower vegetable intake than girls categorized as low on both neophobia and pickiness [. . .] Results supported this hypothesis $(F_{1,188} = 8.64, P < 0.01)$." According to the degrees of freedom, how many groups are being compared?

    d. Which test provides stronger evidence of an impact on vegetable intake, the one described in part (a) or the one described in part (c)? Explain.

    e. The article displayed vegetable intake for the four groups using side-by-side boxplots. If neophobia/pickiness had been assessed quantitatively, how would the relationship with vegetable intake be displayed?

*11.36 Psychometric scores for anxiety, depression, negative self, somatization, and hostility were combined into a single Global Severity Index (GSI). GSI was compared for 76 adolescents who were seen in the outpatient clinic for 7 different physical complaints (short stature, obesity, lack of weight gain, breast problems, genital problems, menstrual problems, and hirsutism).

   a. Report the explanatory variable and tell whether it is quantitative or categorical.

   b. Report the response variable and tell whether it is quantitative or categorical.

   c. The null hypothesis states that those variables are not related. Alternatively, it can be written in terms of population means. Write this null hypothesis about means using mathematical notation.

   d. Should the alternative state that not all population means are the same, or that all population means are different?

   e. How many degrees of freedom does the relevant F statistic have in the numerator and in the denominator?

   f. The F statistic is found to be 1.01. Keeping in mind that F distributions are centered near 1, is the P-value small enough to reject the null hypothesis and conclude that GSI is related to type of physical complaint?

   g. If psychometric scores differ significantly depending on the particular physical complaint, then clinicians could use that information to make referrals for psychiatric screening of clinic patients. Discuss the consequences of a Type II Error in this situation.

*11.37 ANOVA was used to compare samples of weekly "all-inclusive" hotel rates at four Mexican resorts: Cancun, Riviera Maya, Puerto Vallarta, and Los Cabos.

```
Analysis of Variance
Source     DF       SS        MS         F         P
Factor      3    352139    117380     XXXXXX    0.005
Error      21    422229     20106
Total      24    774369

                               Individual 95% CIs For Mean
                               Based on Pooled StDev
Level      N     Mean    StDev  ------+---------+---------+---------+
Cancun      8   1094.5   147.1    (------*------)
RivieraM    7   1227.9   165.7              (-------*------)
PuertoV     4   1108.5   125.1  (---------*---------)
LosCabos    6   1393.7   108.7                        (-------*-------)
                                      ------+---------+---------+---------+
Pooled StDev  =   141.8              1050      1200      1350      1500
```

   a. Which resort seems cheapest and which seems most expensive, as far as the sampled hotels are concerned?

   b. Does the alternative hypothesis state $\mu_1 \neq \mu_2 \neq \mu_3 \neq \mu_4$?

   c. State the alternative hypothesis correctly, using words.

   d. Do confidence intervals for the cheapest and most expensive resorts overlap?

   e. Do the data provide convincing evidence that mean weekly "all-inclusive" hotel rates are different at all four resorts? Explain.

   f. In fact, two-sample tests fail to show a significant difference between rates for three of the resorts, compared two at a time. Judging from the confidence intervals, which was the one resort whose rates were different enough from the other three to lead to our rejecting the null hypothesis in the F test?

*11.38 Exercise 11.29 showed output for a comparison of mean assessment test scores for schools at four different levels.

Level	N	Mean	StDev
MeanScore_E	49	1228.3	82.4
MeanScore_EM	6	1263.5	40.3
MeanScore_M	17	1219.0	90.6
MeanScore_H	12	1223.2	104.7

What aspect of the output casts doubt on the assumption, required for use of an *F* procedure, that the population standard deviations be equal?

11.39 The percentage of students taking state assessment tests was compared for samples of schools at 4 different levels: elementary, elementary/middle, middle, and high school.

```
Level        N    Mean    StDev
%Taking_e   49   98.10    2.58
%Taking_em   6   97.97    1.84
%Taking_m   17   94.68    5.93
%Taking_h   12   90.55    6.00
```

a. Use notation to write the null hypothesis.

b. Should the means 98.10 to 90.55 be identified as $\bar{x}_1$ to $\bar{x}_4$, or μ_1 to μ_4?

c. Should the standard deviations be identified as s_1 to s_4, or σ_1 to σ_4?

d. As far as the sample means are concerned, what relationship do you see between percentage taking the test and level of school?

e. Tell which level of school you would expect to have the lowest rate of truancy (failure to attend).

f. Which level should have the highest rate of truancy?

g. Explain how the different levels of truancy could have impacted percentages taking the tests.

h. Explain why the assumptions of ANOVA, which require equal population standard deviations, should not be made in this situation.

11.40 Student survey data were used to report means and standard deviations for number of credits taken by students of various years (1, 2, 3, 4, or other):

```
Level    N      Mean    StDev
1       179    15.682   1.591
2        81    15.346   2.175
3        49    15.959   1.541
4        38    15.105   2.798
other   13    12.846   4.598
```

a. First a test was carried out to see if there was a significant difference among mean credits taken by students in those five year levels, resulting in an *F* statistic of 6.90 and *P*-value 0.000. Is there evidence of a significant difference? If so, which group had the lowest mean number of credits taken?

b. Next the test was carried out, omitting the "other" students (several of whom studied only part-time), resulting in an *F* statistic of 2.03 and *P*-value 0.109. Is there evidence of a significant difference? If so, which group had the lowest mean number of credits taken?

CHAPTER 11 SUMMARY

We begin our review of inference for situations involving a categorical explanatory variable and a quantitative response

with a discussion by our four prototypical students.

Students Talk Stats

Reviewing Relationships between Categorical Explanatory and Quantitative Response Variables

*F*our statistics students are working on an extra-credit assignment. They need to identify the correct test, hypotheses, and conclusions for the following two studies, as described in Internet articles:

1. *"The return of the grapefruit diet?* Weight-loss diets that involve eating grapefruit or drinking grapefruit juice have been around for decades. But now there's clinical evidence that such a diet might work, at least for very overweight people. A 12-week study of 100 obese patients conducted at the Scripps Clinic in San Diego and sponsored by the Florida Department of Citrus found that people who ate half a grapefruit before each meal lost an average of 3.6 pounds and those who drank 8 ounces of grapefruit juice before meals lost an average of 3.3 pounds (though some lost more than 10 pounds). People who did neither lost an average of 1/2 pound. None of the study subjects altered his or her diet in any other way. Researchers speculate that some chemical property of grapefruit lowers insulin levels, reducing fat storage, says Ken Fujioka, M.D., medical director of the clinic's Nutrition and Metabolic Center."[14]

2. "Update on Migraine Headache: Treatment" [Researchers] assessed the efficacy of high-dose coenzyme Q10 (CoQ10) as prophylaxis against migraine headaches . . . The average number of days with migraine during the baseline period was 7.34, which was reduced significantly to 2.95 days after 3 months of therapy."[15]

Adam: *"For the first one, the null hypothesis is μ equals zero."*

Brittany: *"You better decide what test has to be done, first, and then say what the null hypothesis is. They're comparing weight losses, that's the quantitative response, and the explanatory variable is whether they ate half a grapefruit or drank grapefruit juice or did neither. Since there's three groups being compared, the researchers would have to do an ANOVA test. So the null hypothesis would say $\mu_1 = \mu_2 = \mu_3$ and the alternative would say not all the means are equal. They rejected the null and*

Students Talk Stats continued ➔

concluded that the three population mean weight losses wouldn't be the same. They'd be more for people on the grapefruit diet."

Carlos: *"I can't help but be suspicious about their results, since the study was paid for by citrus growers. They didn't make any effort to control for the placebo effect. Everybody's heard of grapefruit diets, and maybe people in the grapefruit treatment groups had a more optimistic attitude towards weight loss, and that's really why they lost more weight."*

Dominique: *"The other thing is that eating fruit or drinking juice right before meals could fill you up so you wouldn't eat as many foods with a lot of calories. I'd be more convinced that grapefruit makes mean weight losses differ if they had compared those people to people who ate some other kind of fruit or drank another juice before meals in the same amounts."*

Brittany's formulation of the null and alternative hypotheses is correct. Presumably, researchers produced a large enough F statistic to reject the null hypothesis of equal weight losses across the three treatment groups. But Carlos and Dominique raise legitimate concerns about the study's design. A small *P*-value in itself is not enough evidence to convince us that the explanatory variable really impacts the so-called response.

Now let's see what the students have to say about the migraine study.

Adam: *"Okay, then, the null hypothesis for the second problem is μ equals zero."*

Brittany: *"What's μ supposed to be? If we're comparing number of migraines for people who don't take CoQ10 and people who do, then the null hypothesis would be $\mu_1 - \mu_2 = 0$. And the alternative would be $\mu_1 - \mu_2 > 0$, because they're setting out to show that people on CoQ10 have fewer migraines."*

Carlos: *"But they're not comparing two groups. It's not a two-sample study, it's paired. They're comparing number of migraines for the same people, before and after three months of taking CoQ10. So the null hypothesis would be $\mu_d = 0$, and the alternative would be $\mu_d > 0$, if they're looking at before minus after. They must have used a paired t test, and gotten a small enough P-value to reject the null hypothesis."*

Dominique: *"I agree with Carlos that it's a paired design, but shouldn't they have looked at two samples? Because of the placebo effect they should have compared decrease in days with migraines for people who do and don't take CoQ10. Then the null and alternative hypotheses would have been like Brittany said, except μ_1 would be decrease in days with migraines for people taking CoQ10, and μ_2 would be decrease in days with migraines for people not taking it."*

Carlos has correctly identified the migraine study as one that involves paired data, and Dominique makes a good point: It is quite possible that the placebo effect would lead people to report fewer days with migraines after three months of treatment with *any* pill, even if it had no physiological benefit. Therefore, a combination two-sample/paired study, comparing improvements for treatment versus control groups, would have been more convincing. It is possible that the

Students Talk Stats continued →

An algebraically equivalent formulation of the two-sample hypotheses below, which might be helpful for students who are trying to decide which one-sided alternative is appropriate under the circumstances, is

$$H_0 : \mu_1 = \mu_2 \text{ versus } H_a : \begin{Bmatrix} \mu_1 > \mu_2 \\ \mu_1 < \mu_2 \\ \mu_1 \neq \mu_2 \end{Bmatrix}$$

> *Students Talk Stats continued*
>
> study actually did include a control group, and that this detail got "lost in the translation" when a reporter summarized the results. Tracking down the original journal article would be the best way to check what design was actually used. In this case, based on the preliminary study described above that did *NOT* use a placebo group, a randomized controlled double-blind study was subsequently carried out to confirm the effectiveness of CoQ10.

Outline of Hypothesis Test

When testing for a relationship between a categorical explanatory variable and quantitative response variable, the general steps in performing a test of hypotheses apply:

0. State null and alternative hypotheses.

1. Check that we have unbiased sample(s) from larger population(s) and large enough sample size(s).

2. Find the standardized test statistic; think about whether it seems "large."

3. Find the *P*-value; determine if it is "small."

4. State conclusions by choosing between the null and alternative hypotheses.

The specifics of the test depend on whether the data arise from a paired, two-sample, or several-sample design.

Stating Hypotheses for Paired, Two-Sample, and Several-Sample Designs

In such situations, we always test the null hypothesis of *no* relationship against the alternative that the two variables *are* related. To formulate the hypotheses more specifically in terms of the parameters of interest, we must think about which parameters are relevant for the three possible designs discussed.

■ **Paired design:** We focus on the single sample of differences between the pairs of observations for each individual, and do inference about the population mean of differences, μ_d, based on the sample mean of differences, $\bar{x}_d$. We write

$$H_0 : \mu_d = 0 \text{ versus } H_a : \begin{Bmatrix} \mu_d > 0 \\ \mu_d < 0 \\ \mu_d \neq 0 \end{Bmatrix}$$

■ **Two-sample design:** We do inference about the difference between population means $\mu_1 - \mu_2$, based on the difference between sample means $\bar{x}_1 - \bar{x}_2$. Our data consist of two independent sets of observations. The hypotheses are formulated in terms of the parameters μ_1 and μ_2.

$$H_0 : \mu_1 - \mu_2 = 0 \text{ versus } H_a : \begin{Bmatrix} \mu_1 - \mu_2 > 0 \\ \mu_1 - \mu_2 < 0 \\ \mu_1 - \mu_2 \neq 0 \end{Bmatrix}$$

■ **Several-sample design:** Our data consist of several independent sets of observations. In this case, we write

$$H_0 : \mu_1 = \mu_2 = \cdots = \mu_I \text{ versus}$$
$$H_a : \text{not all the } \mu_i \text{ are equal}$$

Conditions

No matter which of the three designs is used, the standardized test statistic follows the exact corresponding distribution—*t*, two-sample *t*, or *F*—only if the sample mean(s) can be said to follow a normal distribution.

The general guidelines are that the samples must appear fairly normal if the sample sizes are small. However, two-sample *t* procedures, and even more so the *F* procedures, are fairly robust against non-normality.

The Standardized Test Statistic

Depending on which design (paired, two-sample, or several-sample) applies, the relevant test statistic is t, two-sample t, or F.

- **Paired design:** Measure the relative distance of the mean of sampled differences from zero, which is what the mean of population differences would be if the null hypothesis were true. We have the paired t statistic

$$t = \frac{\bar{x}_d - 0}{s_d / \sqrt{n}}$$

If the null hypothesis of no difference overall between pairs is true, then this statistic follows a t distribution (symmetric about 0, standard deviation somewhat greater than 1, and bell-shaped) with $n - 1$ degrees of freedom, where n is the sample size.

- **Two-sample design:** Measure the relative distance of the difference between sample means from zero, which is what the difference between population means would be if the null hypothesis were true. We have the two-sample t statistic

$$t = \frac{(\bar{x}_1 - \bar{x}_2) - 0}{\sqrt{\dfrac{s_1^2}{n_1} + \dfrac{s_2^2}{n_2}}}$$

If the null hypothesis of equal population means is true, then this statistic follows a two-sample t distribution (symmetric about 0, standard deviation somewhat greater than 1, and bell-shaped) with degrees of freedom based on both sample sizes.

A special case of the two-sample procedure is when population standard deviations are assumed to be equal. In this case, the test statistic is computed a bit differently, and referred to as the **pooled** two-sample t. Unlike the usual two-sample t, this statistic truly follows a t distribution. Because the assumption of equal population standard deviations is rarely easy to justify, we do better to carry out ordinary rather than pooled procedures.

- **Several-sample design:** Measure the relative distance among sample means from the overall sample mean with the F statistic

$$F = \frac{[n_1(\bar{x}_1 - \bar{x})^2 + n_2(\bar{x}_2 - \bar{x})^2 + \cdots + n_I(\bar{x}_I - \bar{x})^2]/(I - 1)}{[(n_1 - 1)s_1^2 + (n_2 - 1)s_2^2 + \cdots + (n_I - 1)s_I^2]/(N - I)}$$

If the null hypothesis of equal population means is true, then this statistic follows an F distribution (strictly non-negative and centered near 1, all sorts of spreads possible depending on degrees of freedom, and always skewed right). Because F measures the ratio of mean variation among group means to mean variation within groups, the test procedure is referred to as Analysis of Variance, abbreviated ANOVA. Degrees of freedom in the numerator are $I - 1$, where I is the number of groups being compared. Degrees of freedom in the denominator are $N - I$, where N is the total sample size.

The above expression for an F statistic actually follows an F distribution only if the population standard deviations are equal. This assumption is thought to be reasonable if the largest sample standard deviation is no more than twice the smallest. If the largest is more than twice the smallest, then our F statistic should be larger than what we would otherwise require it to be, for it to be considered "large."

Because the F test to compare variances for two populations is not very robust, such tests are not included in this book. The ad hoc test that checks if one standard deviation is not more than twice the other is roughly the same as the formal F test. We stated this briefly in the context of a pooled two-sample t test because it served as a helpful stepping-stone to the analogous ad hoc test that compares several standard deviations before carrying out ANOVA.

Unlike z and t statistics, it is difficult to have a feel for whether or not an F statistic is large, except that any F less than 2 could almost never be considered "large."

Rejecting the null hypothesis when comparing several means results in a fairly general conclusion that not all the population means are equal. More detailed conclusions can be reached by using a technique that is not presented in this book, called "multiple comparisons."

P-*Value for Various Designs*

The *P*-value is, as always, the probability of the test statistic taking a value at least as extreme as the one observed, under the assumption that the null hypothesis is true.

- **Paired and two-sample designs:** The *P*-value may be a left-tail, right-tail, or two-tailed probability, depending on whether the alternative claims the parameter (μ_d or $\mu_1 - \mu_2$) to be less than, greater than, or different from zero.

- **Several-sample design:** The *P*-value must be a right-tail probability.

In any case, we use the same general criteria for deciding whether a *P*-value can be considered "small." Often 0.05 is used as a cut-off value, but there are many circumstances under which a smaller cut-off, such as 0.01, is appropriate.

Stating Conclusions

If the *P*-value is not especially small, then we continue to believe the null hypothesis may be true. In general, then, we conclude that there is not necessarily a relationship between the categorical explanatory and quantitative response variables.

- **Paired *t* test:** We are concluding specifically that the mean of all differences between pairs may be zero.

- **Two-sample *t* test:** We are concluding that the difference between population means may be

zero, which is the same as concluding that the two population means may be equal.

- **Several-sample test:** We are concluding that the several population means may all be equal.

If the *P*-value is small, by whatever criteria seem appropriate under the circumstances, then we reject the null hypothesis and conclude the alternative is true. In general, this means we believe there *is* a relationship between the categorical and quantitative variables of interest.

Confidence Intervals for Paired, Two-Sample, and Several-Sample Designs

The appropriate estimate and margin of error also depend on what type of study is involved.

- **Paired design:** The confidence interval for population mean of differences μ_d is

$$\overline{x}_d \pm \text{multiplier } \frac{s_d}{\sqrt{n}}$$

where $\overline{x}_d$ and s_d are the mean and standard deviation of the sample of differences. The multiplier is from the *t* distribution with $n - 1$ degrees of freedom.

- **Two-sample design:** The confidence interval for difference between population means $\mu_1 - \mu_2$ in a two-sample design is

$$\overline{x}_1 - \overline{x}_2 \pm \text{multiplier } \sqrt{\frac{s_1^2}{n_1} + \frac{s_2^2}{n_2}}$$

where $\overline{x}_1$ and s_1, $\overline{x}_2$ and s_2 are the means and standard deviations of the first and second samples. The two-sample *t* multiplier is similar to an ordinary *t* multiplier with appropriate degrees of freedom, which are based (in a rather complicated way) on the sample sizes.

- **Several-sample design:** Confidence intervals in ANOVA are best obtained via software. When scrutinizing several confidence intervals at once, we make a note of which ones do and do not overlap.

Because all of these procedures require the sample means to be normally distributed, the confidence intervals should not be taken at face value if samples are small and skewed.

Note: Asterisked numbers indicate exercises whose answers are provided in the Solutions to Selected Exercises section, on page 689.

Additional exercises appeared after each section: inference for paired design (Section 11.1) on page 525, inference for two-sample design (Section 11.2) on page 538, and inference for several-sample design (Section 11.3) on page 559.

Warming Up: RELATIONSHIPS BETWEEN CATEGORICAL AND QUANTITATIVE VARIABLES

11.41 "Sources of Individual Shy-Bold Variations in Antipredator Behaviour of Male Iberian Rock Lizards," published online in *Animal Behavior* in 2005, considered a variety of traits and measurements for lizards noosed in the mountains of central Spain, as well as their behavior under controlled low-risk and high-risk situations.[16] Tell whether each of these variables is explanatory or response, and whether it is quantitative or categorical.

a. Whether the lizard was subjected to a "low-risk" treatment (the experimenter walked slowly alongside the terrarium) or a "high-risk" treatment (the experimented approached the terrarium rapidly and tapped the lizard's tail with a brush)

b. The number of blue spots a lizard had on its sides (a possible indicator of vulnerability to predators)

c. Length of time that a lizard retreated after a simulated attack

d. A lizard's behavior rating from 0 (very shy) to 12 (very bold), based on how long it retreated under various attack conditions

11.42 "Sources of Individual Shy-Bold Variations in Antipredator Behaviour of Male Iberian Rock Lizards," published online in *Animal Behavior* in 2005, considered a variety of traits and measurements for lizards noosed in the mountains of central Spain, as well as their behavior under controlled low-risk and high-risk situations.[17] Tell whether each of the following focuses on data production, displaying and summarizing data, probability, or statistical inference.

a. "Lizards were more active in the low-risk than in the high-risk treatment

($\overline{X} \pm SE = 4.9 \pm 0.3$ times versus 3.4 ± 0.4 times)."

b. If lizards' activity did not depend on whether they were subjected to low-risk or high-risk treatment, the probability of observing a difference as extreme as 4.9 ± 0.3 versus 3.4 ± 0.4 is less than 0.0001.

c. "In contrast, leaning out of the refuge was not significantly different between treatments."

d. "The same person performed all predatory attacks while another immobile and hidden person recorded the lizard's behavior with binoculars from a vantage point."

11.43 Tell whether each of the following is a paired, two-sample, or several-sample design, and whether each would involve *t* or *F* as the standardized statistic.

a. Gather data to see if Verbal SAT scores differ significantly depending on whether a student's first language learned is English, another language, or English and another language both spoken since birth.

b. Gather data to see if disabled students' Math SAT scores are significantly lower than their Verbal scores.

c. Gather data to see if disabled students' Math SAT scores are significantly lower than those of nondisabled students.

*11.44 For each of the following identify the appropriate null hypothesis as $H_0: \mu_d = 0$ or $H_0: \mu_1 = \mu_2$ or $H_0: \mu_1 = \mu_2 = \mu_3$.

a. Gather data to see if Math SAT scores are higher for citizens of other countries than they are for U.S. citizens.

b. Gather data to see if total SAT scores differ for students who answer yes, no, or don't know to a question about whether they plan to apply for financial aid.

c. Gather data to see if Math SAT scores for citizens of other countries are higher than their Verbal scores.

11.45 For each of the following, identify the appropriate alternative hypothesis.

a. The first column of data consists of males' Math SAT scores, and the second column consists of females' Math SAT scores. We take the mean for the first column minus the mean for the second column, and carry out a two-sample test to see if males tend to do better than females in Math. Choose from $H_a: \mu_1 = \mu_2$, $H_a: \mu_1 < \mu_2$, $H_a: \mu_1 > \mu_2$, $H_a: \mu_1 \neq \mu_2$.

b. The first column of data consists of total SAT scores for students tested under standard conditions, and the second column consists of total SAT scores for students tested under nonstandard conditions. We take the mean for the first column minus the mean for the second column, and carry out a two-sample test to see if there is a significant difference between the two groups. Choose from $H_a: \mu_1 = \mu_2$, $H_a: \mu_1 < \mu_2$, $H_a: \mu_1 > \mu_2$, $H_a: \mu_1 \neq \mu_2$.

c. The first column of data consists of females' Math SAT scores, and the second column is their Verbal SAT scores. We take the first column minus the second column, and carry out a paired test to see if females tend to do better in Verbal than in Math. Choose from $H_a: \mu_d = 0$, $H_a: \mu_d < 0$, $H_a: \mu_d > 0$, $H_a: \mu_d \neq 0$.

11.46 An article entitled "Hurricane Love Songs" reports that Hurricane Charley's winds in August 2004 "apparently didn't faze fish in the midst of spawning. University of South Florida oceanographers, who regularly listen to the 'love songs' fish sing while spawning, said they expected Charley's winds and the increased water flow from its rain might silence the chorus. But when they reviewed tapes made from their hydrophones when Charley hit Charlotte Harbor, they found the fish just sang louder."[18] The oceanographers could have begun by setting up a null hypothesis that the spawning songs were equally loud before and during the hurricane, against the alternative that they were less loud during the hurricane. In a case like this where the data actually contradict the one-sided alternative hypothesis, what can you say about the size of the P-value?

11.47 "ID Bands May Harm Penguins," reported in *BioEd Online* in May 2004, explains: "Many bird species are monitored using metal bands around their legs. Researchers use information on individuals to deduce the birds' breeding and migration patterns. But penguins' legs are the wrong shape for bands, so the devices have to be attached to their flippers instead. This is a significant hindrance to the birds, say Michel Gauthier-Clerc of the Station Biologique de la Tour du Valat in Arles, France, and his colleagues. They suspect that aluminum or stainless-steel bands may hinder the penguins as they glide through the water."[19] Four students must decide what statistical test would be carried out to test the theory that banded penguins swim slower than unbanded penguins. Which student is correct?

Adam: You compare two groups of penguins so it's two-sided. It was probably paired because that's usually a better design.

Brittany: Comparing two groups makes it a two-*sample* design, not two-*sided*. But the alternative should be two-sided anyway, because that's more conservative.

Carlos: Comparing two groups makes it a two-sample design, but they should test a one-sided alternative because they suspect that the banded penguins swim slower.

Dominique: I think it's a paired test with a one-sided alternative.

Exploring the Big Picture: INFERENCE FOR PAIRED DESIGN

11.48 Illiteracy rates for adult men and women in a sample of 19 countries were recorded, and then for each country the *difference,* rate for men minus rate for women, was recorded. Results are displayed in a histogram.

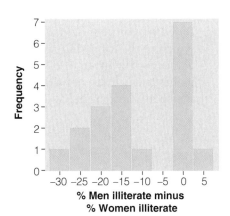

% Men illiterate minus
% Women illiterate

a. Does the histogram indicate that illiteracy rates in the sampled countries tended to be higher for men or for women?

b. Based on the histogram's appearance, and considering that the sample size is moderately large, would you expect a confidence interval for the mean of differences to contain zero?

c. Based on your answers to parts (a) and (b), would you expect to reject the null hypothesis against the alternative that the mean of all differences is negative?

11.49 "Superior Performance of Blind Compared with Sighted Individuals on Bimanual Estimations of Object Size," published in *Psychological Science* in 2005, reports that researchers suspected the ability to correctly estimate the size of an object using your hands with your eyes closed is related to whether you are blind or sighted. Blind and sighted individuals (24 of each) were blindfolded, then asked to indicate with their hands the dominant dimension of various familiar objects, like a package of spaghetti or a block of cheese. The *t* statistic for comparing actual to estimated sizes was 1.01 in the case of blind subjects and 8.52 in the case of sighted subjects.[20]

a. One of the *P*-values was reported to be less than 0.001 and the other was 0.32. Which was the *P*-value for the blind individuals?

b. Were estimates significantly different from actual sizes for the blind subjects, or the sighted subjects, or both, or neither?

Using Software [see Technology Guide]: PAIRED STUDIES

11.50 The Quantitative Environmental Learning Project presents data on widths and lengths of the native butter clam.[21] Here is a small random sample of dimensions for four of these clams that we will use to test whether, in general, the clams are longer than they are wide:

Width	Length
3.1	4.1
4.2	5.5
4.8	6.6
5.6	7.0

a. Use software to carry out a paired *t* test to see if the mean of differences, width minus length, is negative for the larger

population of clams from which the sample was taken: First report the *t* statistic.

b. Next report the *P*-value.

c. Is there evidence that the population mean is negative?

d. To see how choice of test procedure can play a role in conclusions, carry out a two-sample *t* test to see if the difference between population means is negative. (This is *not* the appropriate procedure because the samples of widths and lengths are not independent, but paired together.) Report the *t* statistic for this test.

e. Report the *P*-value.

f. Would the two-sample test provide evidence that the population mean is negative?

11.51 "Weighty Matter Pits Passengers Against Airlines," discussed in Exercise 10.59 on page 511, gives typical airline seat widths for first class seats on a sample of 5 airlines, and coach seats on the same airlines.[22]

Airline	First Class	Coach
USAirways	19.75	17.50
United	20.50	17.50
AmericaWest	20.80	17.35
Northwest	20.25	18.00
AirTran	22.00	18.00

a. Explain why a paired rather than a two-sample procedure should be used.

b. Which one of these would *not* be a good display of the sampled differences: stemplot, side-by-side boxplots, or histogram?

c. Use software to report a 95% confidence interval for the mean of the seat width differences, first class minus coach.

d. Based on your confidence interval, tell which of the following are plausible values for the mean of differences (in inches), which are not plausible, and which are borderline: 1, 2, 3, 4, 5

Exploring the Big Picture: INFERENCE FOR PAIRED OR TWO-SAMPLE DESIGN

11.52 An online article reported in June 2003 on a study carried out to test a new cavity preventive called CaviStat. Deterioration of teeth is measured with DMFS, the number of decayed, missing, and filled surfaces: "726 Venezuelan children [. . .] were divided into two groups and 321 test and 331 control subjects completed the study. The test group received the CaviStat[TM] dentifrice and the controls used a commercially available fluoride paste. [. . .] at one year, the control DMFS rose to 8.00 ± 4.18 whereas the test group DMFS decreased to 5.50 ± 4.15."[23]

a. Should the numbers 8.00 and 5.50 be denoted $\bar{x}_1$ and $\bar{x}_2$ or μ_1 and μ_2?

b. Explain why the numbers 4.18 and 4.15 must be reporting standard deviations s_i, not standard errors ($s_i/\sqrt{n}$) or margins of error ($2s_i/\sqrt{n}$).

c. Explain why confidence intervals can be set up based on probabilities from the z distribution.

d. Report a 95% confidence interval for control mean DMFS.

e. Report a 95% confidence interval for test (CaviStat) mean DMFS.

f. Explain why it is important to note that the two confidence intervals do not overlap.

g. Is 7 a plausible value for the DMFS of an *individual* in the CaviStat group, or in the control group, or both, or neither? Explain.

h. Is 7 a plausible value for the *mean* DMFS of all users of commercially available fluoride paste, or all users of CaviStat, or both, or neither? Explain.

i. Was this a paired, two-sample, or several-sample design?

j. To display DMFS for the two groups, would you use a pie chart, histogram, side-by-side boxplots, or scatterplot?

11.53 Suppose a pilot study of only 5 subjects had been carried out in order to test if users of a new toothpaste had significantly fewer cavities than what is typical for the population.

a. Which type of error is more likely to occur: concluding that the new toothpaste is better when it really isn't, or failing to conclude that the new toothpaste is better when it really is?

b. Tell whether the error you chose in part (a) is Type I or Type II.

11.54 "Early Television Exposure and Subsequent Attentional Problems in Children," published in *Pediatrics* in April 2004, investigated television-watching habits of 1,278 children aged 1 and 1,345 children aged 3 in the early 1990s. "Our main outcome was the hyperactivity subscale of the Behavioral Problems Index determined on all participants at age 7. Children who were ≥ 1.2 standard deviations above the mean were classified as having attentional problems. Our main predictor was hours of television watched daily at ages 1 and 3 years. [. . .] Children watched an average of 2.2 hours (SD: 2.91) of television per day at age 1 and 3.6 hours (SD: 2.94) per day at age 3."[24]

a. Tell what the main explanatory variable is, and whether it is quantitative or categorical.

b. Tell what the main response variable is, and whether it is quantitative or categorical.

c. One of these is the percentage of children who were classified as having attentional problems (those whose values were 1.2 or more standard deviations above the mean). Use what you know from the 68-95-99.7 Rule to tell which one it is: top 1.2%, top 2.1%, top 12%, or top 21%.

d. Explain why confidence intervals can be set up based on probabilities from the z distribution.

e. Report a 95% confidence interval for mean daily television hours watched by all children at age 1.

f. Explain why a 95% confidence interval for mean daily television hours watched by all children at age 3 would have a different center but roughly the same width.

g. The study found that "A 1-SD increase in the number of hours of television watched at age 1 is associated with a 28% increase in the probability of having attentional problems at age 7." Tell which one of these is *not* a correct interpretation, and why:

1. Children who had attentional problems at age 7 tended to have watched more TV at age 1.

2. Watching more TV at age 1 caused attentional problems at age 7.

3. Children who watched more TV at age 1 were more likely to have attentional problems at age 7.

4. Children who watched less TV at age 1 were less likely to have attentional problems at age 7.

11.55 "Early Television Exposure and Subsequent Attentional Problems in Children," published in *Pediatrics* in April 2004, investigated television-watching habits and subsequent rate of hyperactivity for a large group of children.

a. Was this an experiment or an observational study? How do you know?

b. The study found that "A 1-SD increase in the number of hours of television watched at age 1 is associated with a 28% increase in the probability of having attentional problems at age 7."[25] Can you describe another possible explanation for this result, besides the obvious cause-and-effect that the researchers had in mind?

c. The results summarized in part (b) suggest that television watching was handled as a quantitative variable, and behavior as categorical. Which of these plays the role of explanatory variable?

d. Suppose that television really does *not* cause hyperactivity, and the results observed were only due to confounding variables. If this were the case, and researchers had made claims of causation, would they have been committing a Type I or a Type II Error?

11.56 Researchers suspected that the ability to correctly estimate the size of an object using your hands with your eyes closed is related to whether you are blind or sighted. A group of statistics students is working on a problem in which they are to state the appropriate alternative hypothesis in terms of parameters. Which student states it correctly?

Adam: The alternative says there's a relationship between size estimate and whether you're blind or not.

Brittany: In terms of parameters, the alternative says the mean estimate for all blind people is different from the mean estimate for all sighted people.

Carlos: I think it was a paired study design, so the alternative would say that the mean of differences, blind estimate minus sighted estimate, does not equal zero.

Dominique: It can't be paired because some people are blind and a separate sample of people are sighted. The alternative says that the mean estimate for the sample of blind people is different from the mean for the sample of sighted people.

11.57 Tell whether each of these features characterizes a paired *t* confidence interval, a two-sample *t* confidence interval, or both, or neither:

a. If the interval contains zero, this suggests the null hypothesis of no difference is true.

    b. The interval is wider when the data have little spread.

    c. The interval is narrower when the sample size is large.

*11.58 *Math* and *Verbal* SAT scores for a sample of 100 students were used to perform inference about the population mean difference, Math minus Verbal.

```
95% CI for mean difference: (-25.2, 38.8)
T-Test of mean difference = 0 (vs not = 0): T-Value = 0.42 P-Value = 0.673
```

    a. Was this a paired or two-sample procedure?

    b. Is the *t* statistic relatively large, not large, or borderline?

    c. Does the *P*-value suggest that Math and Verbal SAT scores differed significantly?

    d. Explain how the confidence interval results are consistent with your answer to part (c).

    e. Is the confidence interval centered at μ_d, $\bar{x}_d$, or $\mu_1 - \mu_2$?

    f. Find the midpoint of the confidence interval in order to determine the sample mean of differences.

    g. Did the sampled students tend to score higher on Math or Verbal SATs?

11.59 *Math* and *Verbal* SAT scores for a sample of 100 *disabled* students were used to perform inference about the population mean difference, Math minus Verbal.

```
95% CI for mean difference: (-55.6, 5.4)
T-Test of mean difference = 0 (vs not = 0): T-Value = -1.63 P-Value = 0.105
```

    a. Was this a paired or two-sample procedure?

    b. Is the *t* statistic quite large, not large at all, borderline but on the small side, or borderline but on the large side?

    c. Does the *P*-value suggest that Math and Verbal SAT scores differed significantly?

    d. Explain how the confidence interval results are consistent with your answer to part (c).

    e. Which of these is the interval supposed to contain with 95% confidence: μ_d, $\bar{x}_d$, $\mu_1 - \mu_2$, or $\bar{x}_1 - \bar{x}_2$?

    f. Find the midpoint of the confidence interval to determine the sample mean of differences.

    g. Did the sampled students tend to score higher on Math or Verbal SATs?

11.60 *Math* SAT scores for a sample of 100 *disabled* students were compared to those of a sample of 100 *nondisabled* students (taking mean for the former minus mean for the latter), with output shown below.

```
95% CI for difference: (-109.5, -46.6)
T-Test of difference = 0 (vs not =): T-Value = -4.90 P-Value = 0.000 DF = 197
```

    a. Was this a paired or two-sample procedure?

    b. Does the confidence interval suggest that it is plausible for the difference between population means to be zero?

    c. Explain how the size of the *P*-value is consistent with your answer to part (b).

    d. Which of these is the interval supposed to contain with 95% confidence: μ_d, $\bar{x}_d$, $\mu_1 - \mu_2$, or $\bar{x}_1 - \bar{x}_2$?

    e. Find the midpoint of the confidence interval to determine the difference between sample means.

    f. Which group tended to score higher on the Math SATs?

11.61 *Verbal* SAT scores for a sample of 100 *disabled* students were compared to those of a sample of 100 *nondisabled* students (taking mean for the former minus mean for the latter), with output shown below.

```
95% CI for difference: (-79.0, -13.3)
T-Test of difference = 0 (vs not =): T-Value = -2.77 P-Value = 0.006 DF = 197
```

a. Was this a paired or two-sample procedure?

b. Does the confidence interval suggest it is plausible for the difference between population means to be zero?

c. Explain how the size of the P-value is consistent with your answer to part (b).

d. Is the confidence interval centered at μ_d, $\bar{x}_d$, $\mu_1 - \mu_2$, or $\bar{x}_1 - \bar{x}_2$?

e. Find the midpoint of the confidence interval in order to determine the difference between sample means.

f. Which group tended to score higher on the Verbal SATs?

11.62   Exercise 11.60 compares mean Math SAT scores for disabled versus nondisabled students, and Exercise 11.61 made the comparison of mean Verbal scores. Considering the confidence intervals and t statistics, is the difference between disabled and nondisabled students more dramatic for Math scores, or Verbal scores, or about the same?

Exploring the Big Picture: INFERENCE FOR TWO-SAMPLE DESIGN

11.63   Members of a statistics department recorded hours spent consulting on various projects in a particular semester, some for faculty clients and others for graduate student clients:

Faculty client	148	8	15	30	24	1							
Student client	20	5	50	18	48	3	30	15	10	20	2	1	5

Tell what would be the most noticeable feature if the data sets were graphed, and explain why it would not be appropriate to carry out a two-sample t test to see if on average, in the long run, more time is spent on projects for faculty than on those for graduate students.

11.64   The American Academy of Physician Assistants website reported on results of its 1999 census survey of all practicing PAs in the United States. Mean income was $58,000 for those who had been practicing for less than one year, and $76,000 for those who had practiced for more than 18 years. Standard deviation overall was $17,000.

a. What notation should be used for the numbers 58,000 and 76,000: $\bar{x}_1$ and $\bar{x}_2$ or μ_1 and μ_2?

b. What notation should be used for the number 17,000?

c. Explain why a formal inference procedure is not necessary to conclude that those who practiced for more than 18 years averaged more than those who had practiced for less than one year.

*11.65   "Cancer Survivors Found Happy As Others" describes a study by a pediatric cancer specialist at the City of Hope National Medical Center in California. "They questioned 90 children who had been successfully treated for cancer at least a year earlier [. . .] and a control group of 481 children who had never had cancer. The questions focused on physical issues, including pain and activity restrictions; [. . .] Scores ranged from 1 to 5, with 5 being most positive."[26]

a. Explain why this is a two-sample study, not paired.

b. If researchers were concerned that child cancer survivors would not be as happy as children who had never had cancer, then what would the alternative hypothesis state about the overall mean happiness rating μ_1 for cancer survivors compared to the mean μ_2 for the control group?

c. The survivors' sample mean score was $\bar{x}_1 = 4.15$, compared to the control mean $\bar{x}_2 = 4.05$. Explain why a formal test is not necessary for us to decide that the null hypothesis $\mu_1 = \mu_2$ will not be rejected against the alternative.

11.66   A comparison was made between number of cigarettes smoked in a day by a sample of females and a sample of males.

Sex	N	Mean	StDev	SE Mean
female	33	6.94	7.47	1.3
male	19	4.21	5.57	1.3

a. To start, we can write $n_1 = 33$. Use correct notation to identify the numbers 19, 6.94, 4.21, 7.47, and 5.57.

b. How is it possible that the standard errors are equal, even though the standard deviation was higher for the females?

c. Side-by-side boxplots are constructed to compare data for males and females. This focuses on which process (data production, displaying and summarizing data, probability, or statistical inference)?

d. Average number of cigarettes smoked per day may be the same for all male and female students. This focuses on which process?

e. Instead of asking, "On average, how many cigarettes do you smoke each day?" students were asked, "How many cigarettes did you smoke yesterday?" This focuses on which process?

f. If mean number of cigarettes smoked per day were identical for all males and females, it wouldn't be too unlikely to see sample means as different as 6.94 and 4.21. This focuses on which process?

11.67 "Meeting Mr. Farmer versus Meeting a Farmer: Specific Effects of Aging on Learning Proper Names," published in *Psychology and Aging* in September 2004, describes an experiment where young and older adults were tested on ability to remember the correct name and occupation to match a set of pictures of faces. The number of passes through the set of sixteen faces needed by the 16 younger adults to retain all the names and occupations had mean 8.38, standard deviation 2.63, and so a 95% confidence interval for population mean is (7.72, 9.04). "Pilot testing indicated that older adults had considerable difficulty learning 16 names and occupations and that they found the experiment distressing. Therefore, each older participant was presented only 12 stimuli."[27] The number of passes through a set of twelve faces needed by the 16 older adults to retain them all had mean 10.75, standard deviation 2.72, and so a 95% confidence interval for population mean is (10.07, 11.43).

a. Sketch a line showing possible mean scores (from about 7 to about 12) and use the reported confidence intervals to indicate the range of plausible means for all younger adults and the range of plausible means for all older adults.

b. What is it about the two intervals that suggests it is *not* plausible for the two population means to be equal?

c. If the sample sizes had been larger, would it be more likely or less likely for the intervals to overlap?

d. If the standard deviations had been larger, would it be more likely or less likely for the intervals to overlap?

e. If the sample means (8.38 and 10.75) had been farther apart, would it be more likely or less likely for the intervals to overlap?

Are a farmer and a baker more memorable than Mr. Farmer and Mr. Baker?

11.68 A study published in the *British Medical Journal* (BMJ) in January 2001 tracked a large sample of individuals born in 1946, noting their birthweights and scores on cognitive tests at ages 8, 11, 15, 26, and 43.

a. A 95% confidence interval for difference in mean cognitive scores at age 8 for the low-birthweight group compared with the middle-birthweight group (low minus middle) was (−0.42, −0.11). Explain why this provides evidence that cognitive ability at age 8 is adversely affected by having been a low-birthweight baby.

b. A 95% confidence interval for difference in mean verbal memory scores at age 43 for the low-birthweight group compared with the middle-birthweight group (low minus middle) was $(-0.29, +0.09)$. Explain why this does not provide evidence that verbal memory at age 43 is adversely affected by having been a low-birthweight baby.

  c. Tell which of these, if any, is a possible confounding variable that should be taken into account when examining the relationship between birthweight and cognitive scores: gender, or parents' socio-economic level, or both of these, or neither of these?

11.69   "Do People Value Racial Diversity? Evidence from Nielsen Ratings," published online by the *Berkeley Electronic Press* in 2005, tested the hypothesis that *younger* male viewers of Monday Night Football prefer to watch games with at least one black quarterback. Data on viewership for games between 1997 and 2001 were purchased from Nielsen Media Research, and averaged separately for 58 games featuring two white quarterbacks versus 24 games with at least one black quarterback. Among younger male viewers, mean and standard deviation (in thousands) for games featuring two white quarterbacks were 2,870 and 65.8; for games featuring at least one black quarterback they were 2,968 and 97.7.[28]

  a. Find the difference between sample means, viewership for games featuring two white quarterbacks minus viewership for games featuring at least one black quarterback.

  b. Does the sign of the difference between sample means support the researchers' initial suspicion?

  c. The standard error for the difference between sample means is
$$\sqrt{\frac{65.8^2}{58} + \frac{97.7^2}{24}} = 21.73.$$
Find the standardized difference between sample means, which is a two-sample t statistic, but behaves roughly like a z statistic because the samples are reasonably large.

  d. Keeping in mind that z statistics less than 1 in absolute value are common; closer to 1 than 2 are not unusual; around 2 are borderline; greater than 3 extremely improbable, tell whether the P-value would be not small at all, small, or borderline.

  e. If there were no preference in general among younger male viewers for games featuring at least one black quarterback, is the difference between sample mean viewerships likely to have occurred by chance?

  f. What do you conclude about the researchers' hypothesis?

  g. Among *middle-aged* male viewers, mean viewership was 3,870 thousand for games featuring two white quarterbacks, and 3,849 thousand for games featuring at least one black quarterback. Explain why a formal test is not necessary in order to conclude that the data fail to provide evidence in favor of the researchers' alternative hypothesis (that in general middle-aged male viewers prefer to watch games featuring at least one black quarterback).

Using Software [see Technology Guide]: TWO-SAMPLE STUDIES

11.70   Litter sizes are noted for a sample of female skunks, along with information regarding whether the skunks were born in the wild (W) or in captivity (C):

7(W)	7(W)	7(W)	6(W)	8(W)	5(C)	5(C)	5(W)	6(C)	5(C)	5(C)	6(C)	5(C)	7(W)	4(W)	5(C)

  a. Use software to produce a 95% confidence interval for the difference between population mean litter sizes for skunks born in the wild minus those born in captivity.

  b. Carry out a test; report the P-value.

  c. Do you conclude the means differ in general? If so, which type of skunk tends to have larger litters, those born in the wild or those born in captivity?

  d. If an interval were to be constructed at a higher level of confidence, would it be wider or narrower?

11.71   A car buyer wanted to compare prices of 3-year-old BMW and Mercedes Benz automobiles, and found these prices (in thousands of dollars) listed in the classified ads:

BMW	32	35	29	33	35	42	34	35	47	53
	27	54	27	27	34	32	28	51	28	
Mercedes	26	47	32	39						

a. Use software to produce sample means and standard deviations of prices.

b. Are the standard deviations similar enough that we can assume they arise from populations that share the same standard deviation?

c. Use software to carry out a pooled two-sample t test (assuming equal population variances); report the test statistic t and the P-value.

d. Use software to carry out an ANOVA (F) test, which requires the assumption of equal population variances; report the test statistic F and the P-value.

e. If sample sizes and standard deviations are equal, the F statistic is in fact the square of the two-sample t statistic. Find the square of your t statistic from part (c), and comment on whether or not it is about the same as the F statistic.

f. Comment on whether or not the P-values are similar for the pooled two-sample test compared to the ANOVA (F) test.

g. Comment on whether or not the P-values would be similar if the two-sample test had been carried out with a one-sided instead of two-sided alternative.

11.72   The *New York Times* reported that "from 2001 to 2003, World Health Organization surveys measured the prevalence of serious mental disorders in the populations of various countries."[29] A comparison was made between eight developed and seven less-developed countries.

Developed Countries	%	Less-Developed Countries	%
United States	7.7	Colombia	5.2
France	2.7	Ukraine	4.8
Belgium	2.4	Lebanon	4.6
Netherlands	2.3	Mexico	3.7
Japan	1.5	China (Shanghai)	1.1
Germany	1.2	China (Beijing)	0.9
Italy	1.0	Nigeria	0.4
Spain	1.0		

a. Give at least one reason why we may suspect rate of mental illness to be higher in undeveloped countries, and give at least one reason why we may suspect it to be higher in developed countries.

b. Given that either of the circumstances in part (a) could be expected, formulate appropriate null and alternative hypotheses.

c. Use software to produce side-by-side boxplots of the two data sets, and tell which country is responsible for the outlier.

d. Carry out a two-sample t test, reporting the t statistic and the P-value.

e. Delete the outlier and carry out the test again, reporting the t statistic and the P-value.

f. To what extent did the outlier affect the size of t, the size of the P-value, and the test's conclusion?

g. The article mentions that "embarrassment about disclosing mental illness varies from country to country"; in some countries, like Nigeria, women are reluctant to admit being depressed. What, if anything, can we conclude about comparative rates of mental illness, based on the size of the P-value?

11.73 Daily kilograms of horse cobs and pellets (in kilograms) are noted for a sample of 11 Indian rhinoceri, along with information on gender (M or F):[30]

| 3.9(M) | 3.1(F) | 7.5(M) | 5.7(F) | 9.5(M) | 7.9(F) | 5.3(F) | 3.2(M) | 2.7(F) | 2.7(F) | 2.7(F) |

    a. Use software to produce a confidence interval for the difference between population mean kilograms consumed for males minus females.

    b. Carry out the appropriate hypothesis test if we suspect males tend to eat more in general; report the *P*-value.

    c. Can we conclude that male rhinos eat more in general than females eat?

    d. Suppose amounts of cobs and pellets provided will be tailored to the two sexes in the future if a significant difference is found in the mean amounts consumed. Should this change be implemented?

Exploring the Big Picture: INFERENCE FOR SEVERAL-SAMPLE DESIGN

11.74 The Quantitative Environmental Learning Project reported current velocities measured on a number of transects across the Columbia River in Washington State, at three different depths: 5%, 55%, and 95%.[31] Mean velocities at the three depths have been compared using ANOVA.

```
Analysis of Variance
Source      DF        SS       MS       F        P
Factor       2     108.8     54.4     0.97    XXXXXXXXX
Error      210   11743.9     55.9
Total      212   11852.7
                                 Individual 95% CIs For Mean
                                 Based on Pooled StDev
Level       N     Mean    StDev   --+---------+---------+---------+----
depth  5% 71     4.714    7.392                (----------*-----------)
depth 55% 71     4.206    7.451             (-----------*-----------)
depth 95% 71     3.009    7.590   (-----------*-----------)
                                 --+---------+---------+---------+----
Pooled  StDev = 7.478             1.5       3.0       4.5       6.0
```

    a. In this context, is depth a quantitative or categorical variable?

    b. Which depth had samples that averaged the lowest velocity?

    c. Which depth averaged the highest velocity?

    d. Based on the sample standard deviations, is it reasonable to assume that population standard deviations are equal?

    e. The *P*-value has been crossed off from the output. Keeping in mind that *F* distributions are centered near 1, do the data provide convincing evidence that overall mean velocities differ at the various depths? Explain.

    f. Judging from the confidence intervals, which of these mean velocities (if any) would be plausible for all three depth levels: 1.5, 3.0, 4.5, 6.0?

11.75 *Percent of words stuttered* was recorded for 9 subjects whose disability had been classified as mild, moderate, or severe.

Mild	Moderate	Severe
11.5	6.4	12.0
10.3	11.0	25.0
7.3	12.0	
7.3		

a. Present the data as a column of quantitative responses (in increasing order) and a column of categorical explanatory values.

b. Recall that group degrees of freedom (in the numerator) are $I - 1$, where I is the number of groups. Error degrees of freedom (in the denominator) are $N - I$, where N is the total number of observations. If ANOVA were to be used to make a comparison, how many degrees of freedom would the F statistic have in the numerator and how many in the denominator?

c. A potential problem with the use of ANOVA for comparing the three groups is that the standard deviation for one of the groups is much larger than the other two. Tell which group it is, just by looking at how different the values are within each of the three groups.

11.76 *Mean duration of stuttering*, in seconds, was recorded for 9 subjects whose disability had been classified as mild, moderate, or severe.

Mean Duration	Classification
0.75	Mild
4.49	Severe
1.18	Moderate
0.93	Moderate
0.84	Mild
0.83	Moderate
0.90	Severe
0.52	Mild
1.73	Mild

a. Present the data as separate columns of quantitative responses for each of the various explanatory values.

b. If ANOVA is to be used to make a comparison, how many degrees of freedom will the F statistic have in the numerator and in the denominator?

*11.77 "Sources of Individual Shy-Bold Variations in Antipredator Behaviour of Male Iberian Rock Lizards," published online in *Animal Behavior* in 2005, considered behavior of lizards under controlled low-risk and high-risk situations.

a. Lizards were subjected to "low-risk" treatment (the experimenter walked slowly alongside the terrarium) and to "high-risk" treatment (the experimenter approached the terrarium rapidly and tapped the lizard's tail with a brush). A comparison was made of mean *activity* scores using repeated measures ANOVA, and the test statistic, which under the null hypothesis of no difference in activity between low- and high-risk treatments, follows an F distribution with 1 degree of freedom in the numerator and 33 in the denominator, was found to be 48.25.[32] Use the fact that the area under this curve to the right of 4 is approximately 0.05 to decide whether the P-value is quite large (close to 1), somewhat large, borderline, somewhat small, or quite small (close to 0).

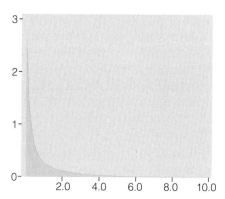

F distribution (1 df in numerator, 33 df in denominator)

b. Based on the size of the P-value, do the researchers have evidence that being subjected to low- or high-risk treatment has an effect on the lizards' rate of activity?

c. A comparison was also made of mean *frequency of lizards leaning out of their refuge* when subjected to low versus high risk treatments. The F statistic, which again has degrees of freedom 1 and 33, was found to be 0.03. Use the display of this F curve (shown in part [a]) to decide whether the P-value is quite large (close to 1), somewhat large, borderline, somewhat small, or quite small (close to 0).

d. Based on the size of the P-value, do the researchers have evidence that being subjected to low- or high-risk treatment has an effect on the lizards' frequency of leaning out of their refuge?

11.78 "An Exploration of Sexual Coercion at First Sexual Intercourse," published online at integrativepsychology.org, compared *age* at first intercourse for those whose first sexual intercourse experience was consensual, or a result of verbal coercion, or a result of force. Mean and standard deviation of ages were reported to be 13.92 and 1.96 for the consensual group, 13.66 and 1.92 for the verbal coercion group, and 12.51 and 2.18 for the forced group. The article reports that which of the three circumstances applied was significantly related to age at first intercourse: $F(2, 1,753) = 7.03$, $p < 0.001$.[33] Recall that we use I to denote number of groups and N to denote total sample size. We identify F with given degrees of freedom in the numerator $(I - 1)$ and denominator $(N - I)$, respectively, with the notation $F(I - 1, N - I)$.

a. What was apparently the total sample size N?

b. One of the sample mean ages seems quite different from the other two; tell which group this is, and whether age at first sexual intercourse seems noticeably younger or noticeably older than for the other two groups.

c. The null hypothesis states that mean age is the same for all three groups; is this referring to sample mean ages or population mean ages?

d. The researchers also tested for a significant difference among mean *number of partners* for the three groups. (Sample means were 2.34 for consensual, 2.54 for verbal coercion, 2.70 for forced.) This graph displays the F distribution for 2 degrees of freedom in the numerator and 1,753 in the denominator. The area to the right of 3.0 is exactly 0.05. If the F statistic was calculated to be 3.36, is the P-value much less than 0.05, a bit less than 0.05, a bit more than 0.05, or much more than 0.05?

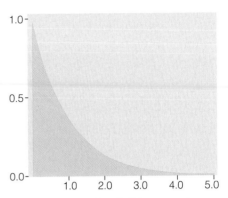

F distribution (2 df in numerator, 1,753 df in denominator)

e. The article also mentions that there was no statistically significant difference found for *frequency* of sexual intercourse among the three groups. Was this F statistic greater than 3 or less than 3?

11.79 Tell whether each of the following focuses on data production, displaying and summarizing data, probability, or statistical inference.

a. Great care is taken to ensure anonymity when surveying adolescents about their sexual experience, so that they will provide honest responses.

b. On average, *age* at first sexual experience was more than 1 year younger for respondents who had been forced.

c. If mean *frequency* of intercourse were the same for populations of adolescents in the three groups (first sexual experience consensual, a result of verbal coercion, or forced), it would not be unlikely to observe sample means such as those that were obtained in the survey.

d. In general, circumstances of the first intercourse experience play a role in *age* at first intercourse, but not in *frequency* of subsequent intercourse.

Using Software [see Technology Guide]: SEVERAL-SAMPLE STUDIES

11.80 Off-campus students at a certain university usually opt for housing in one of three areas: Oakland (a somewhat run-down area in the direct neighborhood of the campus), Shadyside (an upscale area a couple of miles northeast), and Squirrel Hill (a residential area a couple of miles southeast). Here are rents charged for one-bedroom apartments advertised for these areas in the classified section of the local newspaper:

Oakland	Shadyside	Squirrel Hill
475	790 600	625
550	597 550	545
450	702 720	595
350	739 650	550
485	750 625	650
430	865 665	550
650	750 675	425
350	750 550	400
495	525 550	779
425	675 780	690
475	795 765	
350	675 725	
	575 425	
	750	

a. Suppose mean rents really are equal overall in the three areas, but the data suggest otherwise. Based on the data, a student may refuse to consider apartments in the area with the highest sample mean. Would the student be committing a Type I or a Type II Error?

b. Suppose mean rents really differ in the three areas, but the data suggest otherwise. Based on the data, a student may not take location into account when thinking about affordability. Would the student be rejecting a true null hypothesis, or failing to reject a false null hypothesis?

c. Use software to test for a significant difference among mean rents; first report the sample means.

d. Next report the F statistic.

e. What is the P-value?

f. State your conclusions. If the null hypothesis is rejected, tell which area seems to be cheapest and which seems most expensive.

11.81 Lengths (in minutes) of movies showing during a week in 2004 were recorded to see if there is a significance difference in lengths for movies rated PG, PG-13, or R.

PG	PG-13	R
100	130	134
99	143	173
106	102	113
115	169	108
90	103	98
140	120	118
90	105	102
	120	123
	106	

a. Use software to compare mean lengths of movies with the different ratings; first report the F statistic.

b. What is the P-value?

c. Choose which one of the following conclusions is correct:

1. Mean lengths of sampled movies are the same for all three ratings.

2. Mean lengths of all movies are the same for all three ratings.

3. Mean lengths of all movies may be the same for all three ratings.

4. Mean lengths of all movies are different for all three ratings.

5. Mean lengths of all movies are different for at least two of the three ratings.

*11.82 Samples of three types of fish (rainbow trout, largescale sucker, and mountain whitefish) taken from the Spokane River were tested for *lead* content in milligrams per kilogram.[34]

Rainbow	Sucker	Whitefish
0.73	4.34	0.65
1.14	1.98	0.56
0.60	3.12	
1.59	1.80	

a. Use software to report means and standard deviations of lead content for the three types of fish, noting which type has the highest sample mean and which has the highest sample standard deviation.

b. Explain why an F procedure would not be appropriate for this data set.

11.83 Samples of three types of fish taken from the Spokane River were tested for *zinc* content in milligrams per kilogram.[35]

Rainbow	Sucker	Whitefish
45.3	150.0	35.4
50.8	106.0	28.4
40.2	90.8	
64.0	58.8	

a. Use software to produce side-by-side boxplots of zinc contents for the three types of fish, noting which type has the highest sample mean and which has the highest sample standard deviation.

b. For which of these reasons is ANOVA with F not an appropriate procedure for this data set: because the means are too different, because the standard deviations are too different, or because the shapes are too skewed?

Using Software [see Technology Guide]: PAIRED, TWO-SAMPLE, AND SEVERAL-SAMPLE STUDIES

11.84 An article on spatial organization of the honey badger in the southern Kalahari, published in the *Journal of Zoology* in 2005, reported home range sizes in square kilometers for four females and four males (not their mates) in the dry season and then for the same badgers in the wet season.[36]

Females (Dry Season)	Males (Dry Season)	Females (Wet Season)	Males (Wet Season)
76	555	88	615
104	699	89	426
83	214	184	335
123	425	139	624

a. If a comparison is to be made between home range sizes for females versus males, would a paired or two-sample procedure be used?

b. If a comparison is to be made between home range sizes for females versus males, should we do inference about the mean of differences or difference between means?

c. If a comparison is to be made between home range sizes in the dry versus the wet season, would a paired or a two-sample procedure be used?

d. If a comparison is to be made between home range sizes in the dry versus the wet season, should we do inference about the mean of differences or the difference between means?

e. Judging from the numbers in the table, which difference is more dramatic—the one between males and females or the one between dry and wet season?

f. Use software to test if, for all female honey badgers, it is plausible that the mean of differences between home range sizes, wet minus dry season, equals zero; first report the t statistic.

g. Report the P-value for the test in part (f).

h. State your conclusion.

i. For female badgers, report a 95% confidence interval for the mean of all differences in home range sizes, wet minus dry season.

j. Use software to test if, for all males, it is plausible that the mean of differences between home range sizes, wet minus dry season, equals zero; first report the t statistic.

k. Report the P-value for the test in part (j).

l. State your conclusion.

m. For male badgers, report a 95% confidence interval for the mean of all differences in home range sizes, wet minus dry season.

n. Use software to test if the mean home range size in the dry season for all female honey badgers could equal that for all males: first report the t statistic.

o. Report the P-value for the test in part (n).

p. State your conclusion.

q. For the dry season, report a 95% confidence interval for the difference in mean home range sizes, females minus males.

r. What would the P-value in part (o) be if we suspected in advance that home range size in the dry season is greater for males than for females?

s. Use software to test if the mean home range size in the wet season for all female honey badgers could equal that for all males; first report the t statistic.

t. Report the P-value for the test in part (s).

u. State your conclusion.

v. For the wet season, report a 95% confidence interval for the difference in mean home range sizes, females minus males.

w. What would the P-value in part (t) be if we suspected in advance that home range size in the wet season is greater for males than for females?

x. Which of these apparently has a significant effect on honey badgers' home range size: type of season (wet or dry), gender, both, or neither?

y. Consider the four hypothesis tests and the four confidence intervals produced in this exercise. What can we say about the confidence intervals when the data led us to reject the null hypothesis?

z. The researchers actually had data from about twice as many badgers, with results similar to those shown in the previous table. With a bigger sample size, would the P-values for your tests be larger or smaller?

*11.85 Researchers at the Max Planck Institute for Evolutionary Anthropology in Germany experimented on goats' ability to follow certain social cues, with results published in the online journal *Animal Behavior* in January 2005. "We tested goats' ability to use gaze and other communicative cues given by a human in a so-called object choice situation. An experimenter hid food out of sight of the subject under one of two cups. After baiting the cup the experimenter indicated the location of the food to the subject by using different cues [touching, pointing, gazing, or none for control]."[37] This table shows scores for 13 adult and 10 juvenile goats when given the various cues, where the maximum possible score each time was 18.

Adults Touch	Adults Point	Adults Gaze	Adults Control	Juveniles Touch	Juveniles Point	Juveniles Gaze	Juveniles Control
10	8	8	11	15	11	9	8
18	14	8	9	18	17	11	8
17	12	12	6	17	11	10	7
14	10	9	9	18	14	10	10
18	11	6	8	17	13	11	4
12	9	10	8	14	11	11	7
14	9	7	10	10	11	9	9
13	10	14	10	11	10	10	12
11	13	9	9	12	14	13	8
18	17	10	9	14	9	9	8
11	12	8	11				
11	7	8	11				
16	10	8	10				

a. For the *adult* goats, find the sample mean scores for gaze and control. Explain why a formal test is not necessary to draw this conclusion: The adult goats did not perform significantly better when cued with a gaze than they did with no cue (control).

b. Use software to carry out a paired test to see if the *juvenile* goats performed significantly better when cued with a gaze than they did with no cue. Report the mean of differences (gaze minus control), the standardized mean of differences (*t*), and the *P*-value, and state your conclusions.

c. If the mean of differences in part (b) had been negative, what would this tell us about performance when cued with a gaze compared to no cue at all, for the sample of juvenile goats?

d. Another way of determining whether or not juvenile goats respond to cues of gazing is to compare their mean gaze score to 9, which should be the overall mean if gazing does not help the goats in the 18 cup-selection tasks. Carry out a test to see if their mean score was significantly higher than 9; are our conclusions consistent with those of part (b)?

11.86 For this exercise, refer to the explanation and data for Exercise 11.85 about goats' response to social cues.

   a. Use software to carry out a two-sample test for a significant difference between scores of *adults and juveniles* when cued with gazing. First report the sample mean scores and tell which is higher.

   b. Report the *P*-value.

   c. Using $\alpha = 0.05$ as your cut-off for a small *P*-value, state whether or not the data provide convincing evidence of a difference.

   d. Suppose that researchers already had reason to believe that juveniles perform better than adults when cued with gazing. What would the *P*-value be in this case?

   e. Use $\alpha = 0.05$ as your cut-off for a small *P*-value, and state whether or not the data provide convincing evidence that juveniles' mean is higher.

   f. Suppose that researchers already had reason to believe that adults perform better than juveniles when cued with gazing. Do the data provide evidence that this is the case? Explain.

11.87 For this exercise, refer to the explanation and data for Exercise 11.85 about goats' response to social cues.

   a. If researchers want to construct a confidence interval to see how much better juvenile goats perform when cued with touching compared to pointing, is this a paired or two-sample design?

   b. Use software to produce the interval described in part (a).

   c. Does the interval that you reported in part (b) clearly contain zero, or just barely, or not quite, or not at all?

   d. Use your answer to part (c) to tell whether you expect the null hypothesis of no difference between touching and pointing to be rejected, or not rejected, or if results may be borderline.

   e. If researchers want to construct a confidence interval to see how much better juvenile goats perform compared to adults when cued with touching, is this a paired or two-sample design?

   f. Use software to produce the interval described in part (e).

   g. Does the interval you reported in part (f) contain zero clearly, just barely, not quite, or not at all?

   h. Use your answer to part (g) to tell whether or not you expect the null hypothesis of no difference between juveniles and adults to be rejected, or if results may be borderline.

11.88 A several-sample ANOVA procedure, studied in this chapter, is an extension of the two-sample procedure, in that a comparison is made of several independent samples. Repeated measures, not covered in this book, is an extension of the paired procedure, in that a comparison is made of several observations made on each of a group of individuals.

   a. If researchers want to compare goats' performances when cued with touch versus point versus gaze versus control, would they use several-sample ANOVA or repeated measures? Explain.

   b. Use software to produce side-by-side boxplots of the goats' scores (combining adults and juveniles) and comment on which type of cue seems to help goats the most.

   c. Which type of cue seems to help goats the least?

*11.89 In a particular race, the best times (in seconds) for swimming the 100 freestyle were 44.51, 45.91, 46.18, 46.62, and 46.89; the best times for the 100 backstroke were 50.02, 50.22, 50.34, 51.36, 52.85. Assuming these to be representative samples of all of the top times for swimming the two events, use software to produce a 95% confidence interval for the difference between mean times for the two events (freestyle minus backstroke); report whether the interval contains zero, or only positive numbers, or only negative numbers, and tell what this suggests.

11.90 Times (in seconds) for the 100 freestyle and 100 backstroke were recorded for three top swimmers on a university swim team: 46.18 and 50.02; 46.62 and 50.22; 46.89 and 52.85.

   a. Assuming these to be representative samples of all top swimmers' times for the two events, use software to produce a 95% confidence interval for the mean of the time differences, freestyle minus backstroke, for the two events.

   b. Report whether or not the interval contains zero, or only positive numbers, or only negative numbers.

   c. What does your answer to part (b) suggest?

*11.91 It is claimed that college-bound seniors tend to do a bit better on Math than on Verbal SATs. We would like to see if this is true for the larger population of students at a university, based on a sample of several hundred college students who took part in a survey.

   a. Does the claim that college-bound seniors do better on Math than on Verbal SATs constitute the null hypothesis or the alternative?

   b. Use software to access the student survey data, and perform the appropriate test. Report the mean of sampled differences, the standardized mean, and the P-value.

   c. Do the data support the above-mentioned claim?

   d. Use software to obtain a 95% confidence interval for the mean of differences, Math minus Verbal.

   e. Which of these are plausible values for the mean of differences, Math minus Verbal: −20, −10, 0, 10, or 20?

   f. Explain why we should not generalize about the difference between Math and Verbal scores to all universities, based on a sample of students from a particular university.

   g. This exercise considered a quantitative variable, score, compared for two kinds of test (Math or Verbal). What types of variables would be involved if we were interested in the relationship between Math and Verbal scores, so that we could predict a student's Math score, given his or her Verbal score?

11.92 Are students' mothers younger than their fathers in general, and if so, by how much?

   a. Use software to test if the mean of differences, mother's age minus father's age, is negative for the larger population of students; first report the mean of sampled differences.

   b. Report the standardized sample mean.

   c. Report the P-value.

   d. Do the data support the claim that overall mothers are younger?

   e. Use software to obtain a 95% confidence interval for the mean of differences, mother's age minus father's age.

   f. Tell whether each of these is a plausible value for the mean of all differences (in years): −3, −2, −1, 0, 1, 2, 3.

   g. This exercise considered a quantitative variable, age, compared for two genders of parent (mother or father). What types of variables would be involved if we were interested in the relationship between mothers' and fathers' ages, so that we could predict a student's mother's age, given his or her father's age?

11.93 Students were surveyed as to how many minutes they had exercised the day before. They were also asked whether or not they smoked.

   a. If one group exercised more, would you expect it to be the smokers or the nonsmokers?

   b. Use software to access the student survey data, and report the mean minutes exercised for smokers and for nonsmokers. Which sample mean is higher?

   c. Use software to carry out a (one-sided) test of the hypothesis that mean amount of exercise is the same for populations of smoking and nonsmoking students; report the *P*-value.

   d. State whether or not the hypothesis of equality should be rejected.

11.94 Students were surveyed as to how many minutes they had talked on the phone the day before. They were also asked whether or not they carried a cell phone.

   a. If one group talked on the phone more, would you expect it to be those who did or did not carry a cell phone?

   b. Use software to access the student survey data, and report the mean minutes on the phone for those who did and did not carry a cell phone. Which sample mean is higher?

   c. Use software to find the *P*-value for the two-sided test.

   d. What would be the *P*-value for the one-sided test?

   e. Can we conclude that overall students who carry cell phones tend to spend more time on the phone?

   f. Can we conclude that carrying a cell phone causes someone to talk on the phone more? Explain.

11.95 Do females on average do better than males on Verbal SAT tests? If so, how much better? Use software to access the student survey data and carry out a two-sample *t* procedure:

   a. Report the *P*-value.

   b. Using $\alpha = 0.05$ as your cutoff for a small *P*-value, tell whether your answer to part (a) clearly suggests that females do significantly better, or just barely suggests it, or not quite, or not at all.

   c. Report a 95% confidence interval for the difference in population mean scores, female minus male.

   d. State whether the interval you reported in part (c) clearly contains zero, or just barely, or not quite, or if it clearly contains strictly negative or strictly positive values.

*11.96 Does whether or not a student's ears are pierced tell us something about the student's Math SAT score?

   a. Use software to access the student survey data, and carry out a two-sample *t* test for a difference between population mean

Math SAT scores for students who do and do not have pierced ears. Report the *P*-value and state whether the difference is significant.

   b. Which students averaged higher Math SAT scores: those with or without pierced ears?

   c. What confounding variable plays a role in whether or not a student's ears are pierced, and also plays a role in Math SAT score?

   d. How could you control for the confounding variable when looking at the relationship between pierced ears and Math SAT score?

*11.97 Use software to access the student survey data and report a 95% confidence interval for how much taller college males are than females, on average. Is it plausible that on average males are half a foot taller than females?

11.98 Use software to access students' gender and weight values in the student survey data file.

   a. Report a 95% confidence interval for how much heavier college males are than females, on average.

   b. Is it plausible that on average males weigh 50 pounds more than females?

11.99 Is there a difference in mean hours slept by on-campus and off-campus students?

   a. Give at least one reason why on-campus students may get more sleep.

   b. Give at least one reason why on-campus students may get less sleep.

   c. Use software to access the student survey data, and report the mean hours of sleep for on-campus and off-campus students.

   d. Which sample mean is higher?

   e. By how many minutes is one sample mean higher than the other?

   f. Use software to carry out the appropriate test; report the *P*-value.

   g. The *P*-value is fairly small; does this mean we have a good deal of evidence that mean hours of sleep differ for on- and off-campus students, or does it mean we have evidence that mean hours of sleep differ a good deal for on- and off-campus students?

   h. Explain how age could be a possible confounding variable, and how it could be dealt with.

11.100 Is there a difference in mean hours slept for students in various years at college?

  a. Give at least one reason why students in earlier years may get more sleep.

  b. Give at least one reason why students in later years may get more sleep.

  c. Use software to access the student survey data, and report the mean hours of sleep for sampled students in each of the five year levels.

  d. Which sample mean is highest?

  e. Which sample mean is lowest?

  f. Use software to carry out the appropriate test; report the P-value.

  g. Two of these express the correct conclusions to draw, given the size of the P-value; which two are they?

    1. There is compelling evidence of a relationship between students' year at school and how much sleep they get, for populations of students in the various years.

    2. There is no compelling evidence of relationship between students' year at school and how much sleep they get, for populations of students in the various years.

    3. Mean amount of sleep may be equal for populations of students in the various years.

    4. Mean amount of sleep is not equal for populations of students in any of the various years.

    5. Mean amount of sleep is not equal for populations of students in at least two of the various years.

11.101 Suppose someone claims that students in higher years at school tend to earn more money, because they are older and have more work experience.

  a. Use software to access the student survey data, and find the sample means and standard deviations for earnings of 1st, 2nd, 3rd, 4th, and Other year students.

  b. Explain why it seems unlikely that population standard deviations are equal, as is required for use of ANOVA procedures to compare population means.

11.102 Is there a difference among ages of students who are vegetarians, non-vegetarians, or sometimes-vegetarians?

  a. Use software to access the student survey data; report the P-value.

  b. Is the age difference significant?

11.103 Does a person's favorite color tell us something about how tall the person should be?

  a. Use software to access the student survey data, and carry out an ANOVA to test for a difference among population mean heights for students preferring various colors; report the P-value.

  b. State whether the difference is significant.

  c. Which color was preferred by the tallest students and which by the shortest students?

  d. What confounding variable plays a role in what color a student prefers, and also plays a role in how tall the student is?

  e. How could you control for the confounding variable when looking at the relationship between height and color preference?

Discovering Research: CATEGORICAL AND QUANTITATIVE VARIABLES

11.104 Find a newspaper article or Internet report about a study that compares mean values of some quantitative variable for two or more populations, based on information from a sample (or samples). Explain whether there is reason to suspect bias because the sample is not representative of the larger population of interest.

Reporting on Research: CATEGORICAL AND QUANTITATIVE VARIABLES

11.105 Use results of Exercises 11.75 to 11.77 and relevant findings from the Internet to make a report on stuttering that relies on statistical information.

Inference for Relationships between Two Categorical Variables

Is the wearing of corrective lenses (contacts, glasses, or neither) related to gender for all students?

Contacts over glasses:
Girls more than guys?

This question typifies situations in which we are interested in the relationship between two categorical variables, not simply for a sample but for an entire population. In Section 5.2, we explored the relationship between gender and lenswear for a sample of 446 students. Now our goal is to go beyond making statements about gender and lenswear for the *sampled* students, and use that information to draw conclusions about the relationship between those variables in the larger *population* of students.

In Chapter 11, we discussed two different formulations of null and alternative hypotheses: more generally, in terms of variables, or more specifically, in terms of parameters. For example, in a two-sample problem about age and gender of students, the null hypothesis could either claim that age and gender (variables) are not related for the population of students, or it could claim that mean ages (parameters) are equal for populations of male and female students.

In this chapter, we are faced with a similar choice of formulations. Either the null hypothesis could claim that the variables gender and lenswear are not related, or it could claim that population proportions (or percentages) in the various lenswear categories are equal for males and females.

In the case of just two possibilities for each of the two categorical variables (data summarized in a 2-by-2 two-way table), expressing a one-sided alternative is a straightforward matter. In such situations, we will see how to use a z test to decide if population proportions in the response category of interest could be equal, or if there is evidence that one is less than, greater than, or different from the other.

Just as we saw in the case of comparing means in a several-sample design, contradicting the null hypothesis can become rather complicated when our categorical variables have more than two possible values. In such situations, the above-mentioned z test is no longer adequate, and we need the more general **chi-square** test.

The Big Picture:

A CLOSER LOOK

Just as the *F* test could be seen as a broader formulation of the two-sample *t* that compares just two means, the chi-square test is a broader formulation of the two-sample *z* that compares just two proportions. The Greek letter "chi" (pronounced like the word *sky* without the *s*) corresponds to our letter *x*, and a chi-square random variable can be written as X^2.

Besides writing the chi-square *distribution* as X^2, some books denote the chi-square *statistic* as X^2. To avoid confusion, we will simply write the words "chi-square distribution" or "chi-square statistic" or "chi-square random variable" in this book.

An illustration of the two possible approaches for the null hypothesis is featured in the *Teaching the Big Picture* **(TBP)** *Supplement* on page 952.

12.1 Comparing Proportions with a z Test

Is this first section, we will consider the simplest situation, where both categorical variables, explanatory and response, have just two possible values and a z test can be used. The data in such situations consist of two sample sizes n_1 and n_2 and two sample *counts* X_1 and X_2 in the response category of interest. To summarize responses for the two explanatory groups, we look at the sample *proportions* $\hat{p}_1 = X_1/n_1$ and $\hat{p}_2 = X_2/n_2$.

Our goal is to perform inference about the difference between population proportions, $p_1 - p_2$, based on the difference between sample proportions, $\hat{p}_1 - \hat{p}_2$. The hypotheses are formulated as

$$H_0 : p_1 - p_2 = 0 \text{ versus } H_a : \begin{cases} p_1 - p_2 > 0 \\ p_1 - p_2 < 0 \\ p_1 - p_2 \neq 0 \end{cases}$$

Note that the null hypothesis suggests "nothing is going on": In the larger populations, proportions in the response of interest are the same for the two groups compared.

To discover what $\hat{p}_1 - \hat{p}_2$ tells us about $p_1 - p_2$, we must establish what is known about the distribution of $\hat{p}_1 - \hat{p}_2$ as a random variable: What are its center, spread, and shape?

- The **mean** of $\hat{p}_1 - \hat{p}_2$ is $p_1 - p_2$, as long as our sampling and study designs are sound.

- The **standard error** of $\hat{p}_1 - \hat{p}_2$ is the rather complicated expression $\sqrt{\hat{p}(1 - \hat{p})\left(\dfrac{1}{n_1} + \dfrac{1}{n_2}\right)}$, where $\hat{p}$ is the pooled sample proportion. Under the assumption that the null hypothesis is true, both population proportions p_1 and p_2 equal some common value p. Because p is unknown, we estimate it with

$$\hat{p} = \frac{X_1 + X_2}{n_1 + n_2},$$

the sum of counts in the response of interest divided by the sum of sample sizes.

Instead of dwelling on the computation of the standard error, we should focus on the fact that it estimates the spread of $\hat{p}_1 - \hat{p}_2$, the same way that $\dfrac{s}{\sqrt{n}}$ estimates the spread of $\bar{x}$ when we perform inference about a single mean.

- The **shape** of the distribution of $\hat{p}_1 - \hat{p}_2$ is approximately normal as long as sample counts are large enough so that the individual sample proportions $\hat{p}_1$ and $\hat{p}_2$ follow approximately normal distributions.

As usual, our test statistic measures how extreme the sample results are, going under the assumption that the null hypothesis is true.

To get a feel for how the test statistic works, it is helpful to think of its three basic components.

Instead of formulating H_0 and H_a about p_1–p_2, students might prefer the equivalent formulations

$H_0 : p_1 = p_2$ versus

$H_a : \begin{cases} p_1 > p_2 \\ p_1 < p_2 \\ p_1 \neq p_2 \end{cases}$

- The appearance of $\hat{p}_1 - \hat{p}_2$ in the numerator of the standardized difference (z) means that our test statistic tends to be large in absolute value whenever the observed sample proportions are quite different. If they are different enough, then z will be large enough to result in a P-value small enough to reject the null hypothesis of equal population proportions.

Standardized Test Statistic and P-Value in Test Comparing Two Proportions

To test the null hypothesis $H_0: p_1 = p_2$ based on sample proportions $\hat{p}_1$ and $\hat{p}_2$ taken from samples of sizes n_1 and n_2, we calculate

$$z = \frac{(\hat{p}_1 - \hat{p}_2) - 0}{\sqrt{\hat{p}(1 - \hat{p})\left(\dfrac{1}{n_1} + \dfrac{1}{n_2}\right)}}$$

and find the *P*-value as the probability of a value this extreme in a standard normal (z) distribution. Results are approximately correct as long as there would be at least five in each category combination, under the assumption that the null hypothesis is true.

- Because of the way the pooled standard error is calculated, pooled sample proportions closer to the extremes 0 or 1 tend to make the standard error smaller and the test statistic larger.
- Sample sizes play an important role. As usual, they are divided in the denominator, so that larger sample sizes tend to make the test statistic large, helping to provide statistical evidence of a difference in the populations.

Before taking steps to perform inference about the larger population, it's always a good idea to think first about what the sample summaries are telling us.

EXAMPLE 12.1 COMPARING SAMPLE PROPORTIONS

Background: In Section 5.2 we discussed a report entitled "Wrinkle Fighter Could Help Reduce Excessive Sweating," where half of 322 patients were injected under the arm with Botox, the other half with salt water as a placebo. "A month later, 75% of the Botox users reported a significant decrease in sweating, compared with a quarter of the placebo patients . . ."[1] Treating Botox or placebo as the explanatory variable, recorded in rows, and sweating decreased or not as the response, recorded in columns, we constructed a two-way table for the data.

	Sweating decreased	Sweating not decreased	Total	Percent decreased
Botox	121	40	161	75%
Placebo	40	121	161	25%
Total	161	161	322	

Our sample sizes are 161 and 161, and the individual sample proportions are 0.75 and 0.25.

Question: What do the sample proportions suggest about the role of Botox injections in sweating?

Response: The difference in sample proportions certainly seems substantial. We could say, for instance, that the proportion with decreased sweating was three times as high in the Botox group compared to the placebo group.

Practice: *Try Exercise 12.2(a) on page 595.*

The Big Picture:

LOOKING AHEAD

We will go into more detail about our sample size requirement when we discuss chi-square tests in Section 12.2.

Illustrations of how the *P*-value is affected by the difference between sample proportions and by the sample sizes are featured in the **TBP** *Supplement* on pages 952 and 953.

On page 953 of the **TBP** *Supplement* is a two-way table illustrating the approach taken in this section: focusing on the difference between two proportions.

Now we go beyond the sample summaries to see what the data suggest about a larger population of Botox users.

*The*Big
Picture:
LOOKING BACK

In Chapter 10, if a two-sample *t* test showed a difference between sample means to be significant, we often proceeded to set up an interval estimate for the difference between population means. Similarly, if we have evidence of a difference between population proportions, we may want to quantify that difference with an interval estimate. This will be done in Example 12.4. As always, our interval takes this form: estimate ± margin of error.

EXAMPLE 12.2 INFERENCE TO COMPARE TWO PROPORTIONS BY HAND

Background: The Botox experiment described in Example 12.1 resulted in sample proportions 0.75 and 0.25 with decreased sweating, respectively, from samples of 161 subjects given Botox and 161 given placebo injections. The pooled sample proportion is $(121 + 40)/(161 + 161) = 0.50$.

Question: How could a test for significant effects of Botox be carried out by hand?

Response: The null hypothesis claims equal population proportions with decreased sweating: $H_0: p_1 = p_2$. The alternative should be one-sided because we suspect there would be a higher proportion in general with decreased sweating among those given Botox: $H_a: p_1 > p_2$. The difference between sample proportions is $0.75 - 0.25$, and we can standardize this difference, taking sample sizes and spread into account, using a z statistic.

$$z = \frac{(0.75 - 0.25) - 0}{\sqrt{0.50(1 - 0.50)(\frac{1}{161} + \frac{1}{161})}} = 9.0$$

We know that z as large as 9 is extremely unlikely, so our P-value must be very small. We reject the null hypothesis and conclude that, as long as the experiment was not flawed, Botox can decrease sweating in the larger population, not just the sample.

Practice: *Try Exercise 12.4 on page 597.*

Instead of carrying out the test by hand, it can be done easily with software.

EXAMPLE 12.3 TEST COMPARING TWO PROPORTIONS USING SOFTWARE

Background: Software was used to carry out a test of whether the proportion with reduced sweating was significantly higher for patients given Botox as opposed to a placebo.

```
Test and CI for Two Proportions
Sample      X      N  Sample p
1          121    161  0.751553
2           40    161  0.248447
Estimate for p(1) - p(2): 0.503106
95% lower bound for p(1) - p(2): 0.423887
Test for p(1) - p(2) = 0 (vs > 0): Z = 9.03 P-Value = 0.000
```

Question: What does the output tell us?

Response: The last line shows us that the test was one-sided, which is appropriate under the circumstances. The difference between sample proportions is 0.50 and the standardized difference is $z = 9.03$. Since z is so large, the P-value is zero to three decimal places. We conclude that the proportion with reduced sweating is significantly higher for subjects receiving Botox as opposed to salt water injections.

Practice: *Try Exercise 12.5 on page 597.*

Now that we have evidence of a significant difference between proportions with reduced sweating in the Botox experiment, we may want to report the extent to which Botox should have an effect on the general population of users.

EXAMPLE 12.4 CONFIDENCE INTERVAL COMPARING TWO PROPORTIONS USING SOFTWARE

Background: We saw the difference between *sample* proportions in our Botox example to be $0.75 - 0.25 = 0.50$. In order to estimate the difference between proportions with reduced sweating in larger *populations* of people, a confidence interval is appropriate. Software was used to request a 95% confidence interval for $p_1 - p_2$:

```
95% CI for p(1) - p(2): (0.408711, 0.597500)
Test for p(1) - p(2) = 0 (vs not = 0): Z = 9.03 P-Value = 0.000
```

Question: What does the output tell us?

Response: The confidence interval for $p_1 - p_2$ is approximately (0.41, 0.60). In general, the proportion of people with reduced sweating should be from 0.41 to 0.60 more when injected with Botox as opposed to with a placebo. Notice that the very small *P*-value is consistent with an interval that doesn't come close to containing zero.

Practice: *Try Exercise 12.8 on page 597.*

EXERCISES FOR SECTION 12.1

Comparing Proportions with a z Test

Note: Asterisked numbers indicate exercises whose answers are provided in the Solutions to Selected Exercises section, on page 689.

12.1 "Chopsticks May Cause Arthritis" reported in 2003 on a study of more than 2,500 residents in Beijing that "found that osteoarthritis was more common in the hands used to operate chopsticks—and in the fingers specifically stressed by chopstick use."[2]

a. Which one of these focuses on data production?
1. Sample proportions are actually fairly close.
2. The *P*-value is less than 0.05.
3. Because the hand that uses chopsticks would also be the hand used to perform many other tasks, researchers were careful to make a comparison involving the fingers particularly stressed by chopstick use.
4. For all users of chopsticks, there is a slightly elevated risk of hand osteoarthritis.

b. Which one of the statements in part (a) focuses on displaying and summarizing data?

c. Which one of the statements in part (a) focuses on probability?

d. Which one of the statements in part (a) focuses on statistical inference?

e. The article mentions that "the effect is not big" and that "the increase in risk associated with chopstick use is small." Keeping in mind that the sample size is quite large, can we infer that the *P*-value is not especially small, or that the sample proportions are not especially different, or both of these, or neither of these?

*12.2 The U.S. government collects hate crime data each year, classifying such criminal offenses according to motivation (race, religion, sexual orientation, etc.) and also according to race of the offender. The first bar graph compares proportions of crimes concerned with the victim's *religion* committed by blacks versus whites; the second one compares proportions concerned with the victim's *sexual orientation* committed by blacks versus whites.

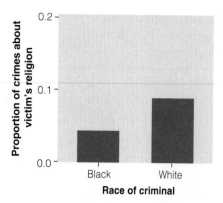

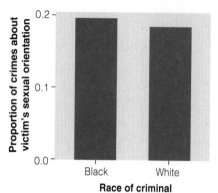

a. Which crime motivation appears to be related to the race of the criminal: religion or sexual orientation?

b. One of the z statistics is 0.84 and the other is 4.9. Which one of these is the statistic for the difference in proportions of crimes concerned with the victim's sexual orientation (second graph)?

c. One of the P-values is 0.406 and the other is 0.000. Which one of these is the P-value for the difference in proportions of crimes concerned with the victim's sexual orientation (second graph)?

12.3 "Study: Asking Teens About Suicide Doesn't Lead Them to Take Their Lives" responded to a concern by many parents and schools that surveying teens about suicidal thoughts may have harmful repercussions by planting such ideas in their heads. The study "involved 2,342 students at six suburban New York high schools who answered two mental health questionnaires two days apart. Half the students—the experimental group—also received about 20 suicide-related questions on both surveys. The questions included whether they had considered suicide and whether they thought it would be better if they were dead. The other half got suicide-related questions only on the second survey."[3] Roughly 4 percent

in both groups said they had had suicidal ideas since the first survey.

a. Describe the explanatory and response variables.

b. Which of these is known to equal 0.04? (There may be more than one.) $n_1, n_2, X_1, X_2, \hat{p}_1, \hat{p}_2, p_1, p_2$

c. Because the percentage with suicidal ideas was roughly the same for students in both groups, would the z statistic be close to zero, close to 2, or much larger than 2?

d. Would the P-value for a one-sided test be close to zero or close to 0.5?

e. The article mentions that each year 1,600 youngsters aged 15 to 19 succeed in committing suicide; since there are over 20 million in this age group, the proportion committing suicide is less than 1 in 10,000. Explain why it would be impractical to carry out a study where the response of interest is actually *committing* suicide—as opposed to *thinking* about suicide—after taking a survey.

f. The article also states that "the groups' scores on emotional-distress measures were similar before and after the first survey." Would a comparison be made using paired t, two-sample t, F, chi-square, or regression?

g. Which one of these focuses on data production?
   1. The sample proportions were found to be almost identical.
   2. If population proportions were equal, it would not be at all unlikely for sample proportions to be as different as those observed.
   3. We conclude that, in general, asking teenagers about suicide doesn't lead them to have suicidal thoughts.
   4. Within each of the selected classes, students were randomly assigned to receive suicide-related questions on both surveys or only on the second survey.

h. Which one of the statements in part (g) focuses on displaying and summarizing data?

i. Which one of the statements in part (g) focuses on probability?

j. Which one of the statements in part (g) focuses on statistical inference?

*12.4   In a survey conducted in 2003, the counts carrying cell phones were 233 of 282 females (sample proportion 0.83), and 116 of 162 males (sample proportion 0.72). The pooled sample proportion was $(233 + 116)/(282 + 162) = 0.79$. Carry out a one-sided *z* test by hand to see if the proportion carrying cell phones was significantly higher for females.

*12.5   For samples of male and female students taken in 2003, a *z* test was carried out to compare proportions who were carrying cell phones.

```
Sex                     X       N  Sample p
female               233     282  0.826241
male                 116     162  0.716049
Estimate for p(female) - p(male): 0.110192
95% CI for p(female) - p(male): (0.0278691, 0.192514)
Test for p(female) - p(male) = 0 (vs not = 0): Z = 2.62 P-Value = 0.009
```

a. Is the *z* statistic large, not large, or borderline?

b. Is the *P*-value small, not small, or borderline?

c. Do we conclude there was a significant difference between proportions carrying cell phones for males versus females?

12.6   In a survey conducted in 2003, the counts who smoked were 48 of 282 females (sample proportion 0.17), and 37 of 164 males (sample proportion 0.23). The pooled sample proportion was $(48 + 37)/(282 + 164) = 0.19$. Carry out a two-sided *z* test by hand to see if the difference in proportions who smoked between males and females was significant:

a. First calculate *z*, the standardized difference between sample proportions.

b. What can we say about the size of the *P*-value?

c. Was the difference significant?

12.7   For samples of male and female students, a *z* test was carried out to compare proportions who were smokers.

```
Sex                     X       N  Sample p
female                48     282  0.170213
male                  37     164  0.225610
Estimate for p(female) - p(male): -0.0553970
95% CI for p(female) - p(male): (-0.132962, 0.0221680)
Test for p(female) - p(male) = 0 (vs not = 0): Z = -1.40 P-Value = 0.162
```

a. Is the *z* statistic large, not large, or borderline?

b. Is the *P*-value small, not small, or borderline?

c. Do we conclude there was a significant difference between proportions smoking for males versus females?

d. Explain how the interval is consistent with the results of the *z* test.

*12.8   "Large Doses of Vitamin E Could Be Risky," reported online in the *Washington Post* in March 2005, warns that large doses of vitamin E "do not protect against heart attacks and cancer and might actually raise the risk of heart failure in people with diabetes or clogged arteries. [. . .] Research released last week on nearly 40,000 healthy women showed no heart benefits from vitamin E pills."[4] The article also tells of an American Medical Association study of 7,030 patients with diabetes or clogged arteries, randomly assigned to take a placebo or about 400 milligrams of vitamin E every day for several years: "Heart failure was diagnosed in 641 vitamin E patients, compared with 578 patients in the placebo group."

A 95% confidence interval and test for difference in population proportions have been obtained with software:

```
Estimate for p(1) - p(2): 0.0179232
95% CI for p(1) - p(2): (0.000228181, 0.0356182)
Test for p(1) - p(2) = 0 (vs not = 0): Z = 1.99 P-Value = 0.047
```

Explain how the interval is consistent with the results of the *z* test.

The **Big** *Picture:*
LOOKING BACK

Recall that our two-sample *t* statistic in Chapter 11 was based on a difference of means, whereas the *F* statistic was based on *squared* differences of means. Algebraically, for equal standard deviations and sample sizes, when only two groups are compared, *F* is exactly *t²*.

Similarly, our two-sample *z* statistic is based on a difference of proportions, whereas the χ^2 statistic is based on *squared* differences of observed from expected counts. In the simplest case, $\chi^2 = z^2$.

12.2 Comparing Counts with a Chi-Square Test

In this chapter, we present two approaches to performing inference about the relationship between two categorical variables. We began by making a comparison of *proportions*, such as the proportions with reduced sweating for those who were given Botox versus a placebo. The null hypothesis, which states that proportions are equal in the larger population, implicitly states that the variables in question are not related.

Another way to look for evidence that two categorical variables—like Botox and sweating—are related is to make a comparison not of two *proportions*, but of two *tables of counts*. The procedure, called a **chi-square test**, requires us first to calculate what table counts would be *expected* if Botox had no effect on sweating—that is, if the proportion with reduced sweating was exactly the same for those receiving Botox and for those receiving a placebo. Because the row and column totals all happen to be the same (161), the expected counts would all equal 80.5. The next step will be to compare that table of counts to the table of counts actually *observed* in our sample.

Chi-square procedure: Compare counts observed to counts expected if null hypothesis were true

Observed	Sweating decreased	Not decreased	Total
Botox	121	40	161
Placebo	40	121	161
Total	161	161	322

Expected	Sweating decreased	Not decreased	Total
Botox	80.5	80.5	161
Placebo	80.5	80.5	161
Total	161	161	322

Relating Chi-Square to z

The null hypothesis in a chi-square test states that the two categorical variables of interest are *not* related; the alternative states that they *are* related. Our test statistic, called the chi-square statistic and written χ^2, will measure how far the observed counts are from those expected under the null hypothesis of no relationship by taking the sum of standardized squared differences between observed and expected counts. If the null hypothesis is true, this statistic in the long run follows a very predictable pattern, known as the chi-square distribution. We will discuss the chi-square statistic and distribution in more detail after establishing how to find the expected counts for any two-way table. First, we see how inference based on counts is linked to inference based on proportions via the relationship between chi-square and *z*.

If only two explanatory groups are being compared, and the response allows for just two categories, χ^2 turns out to be identical to z^2.

EXAMPLE 12.5 RELATING Z^2 TO χ^2

Background: Our *z* statistic for the two-proportion test about Botox was 9.03. Output below shows the χ^2 statistic for the same data to be 81.50.

```
Chi-Sq = 20.376 + 20.376
        + 20.376 + 20.376 = 81.503
DF = 1, P-Value = 0.000
```

Question: How are *z* and χ^2 related?

Response: $z^2 = 9.03^2 = 81.5$; the chi-square statistic is the square of the *z* statistic.

Practice: *Try Exercise 12.10 on page 608.*

Just as the F procedure was a generalization of the two-sample t for comparing means, the χ^2 procedure is a generalization of the two-sample z for comparing proportions. As was the case for calculating t as opposed to F statistics, the mechanics of the computations for z as opposed to χ^2 seem quite different. Fortunately, though, the formula for our χ^2 statistic is quite intuitive, perhaps because it tends to be easy for us to think in terms of counts in a two-way table.

The Table of Expected Counts

To carry out a chi-square test for a relationship between two categorical variables, our strategy will be to compare the counts *observed* in the various category combinations to the counts *expected* if there were no relationship at all between the two variables.

Actually, we do not "expect" the variables' values to necessarily occur in this particular idealized configuration. Rather, we are thinking of these expected values as what the counts should *average* out to in the long run in repeated random samples, if the variables were not related. The context will be to address our opening question about whether gender and lenswear are related.

Before performing inference to draw conclusions about the relationship between gender and lenswear in the general population, we should first consider the relationship for the sample of students. We learned in Chapter 5 that the best summary of a relationship between two categorical variables is to compare proportions in the responses of interest for the various explanatory groups.

We saw in Example 5.10 on page 153 that the percentage wearing contacts was considerably higher for females (43% versus 26%). The percentage wearing glasses was considerably higher for males (23% versus 11%). The percentage needing no corrective lenses was somewhat higher for the males (52% versus 46%).

Our task now is to go beyond the sample data and decide whether those observed differences are extreme enough to convince us of a relationship between gender and lenswear in the larger *population* from which those students were sampled. To accomplish this task, we will shift our focus from proportions to counts.

The Big Picture:
LOOKING BACK

On page 278 in Part III, we mentioned that the mean of a random variable is sometimes referred to as its "expected value."

EXAMPLE 12.6 A TABLE OF EXPECTED COUNTS

Background: Data were gathered on counts in a sample of males and females wearing contacts, glasses, or no corrective lenses.

	Contacts	Glasses	None	Total
Female	121	32	129	282
Male	42	37	85	164
Total	163	69	214	446

Question: If there were no relationship between gender and lenswear, what counts would we expect to see in a two-way table, in which a group of 282 females and 164 males have altogether 163 wearing contacts, 69 wearing glasses, and 214 wearing neither?

Response: Altogether, 163 of 446 students wore contacts. If gender and lenswear were completely independent, then within the table we would expect to see this same proportion of both females and males wearing contacts. Thus, we would expect to see 163/446 of the 282 females wearing contacts: the expected count for this category combination would be

$$\frac{163 \times 282}{446} = 103$$

Continued

If time permits, we can prepare students for Example 12.6 by working through Example TBP 12.1 on page 953 of the *TBP Supplement*, which has them intuit the nature of the relationship between gender and lenswear. In addition, Example TBP 12.2 looks at the relevant sample proportions in more detail. We show how the expected counts tie in with the concept of independence in probability, and Example TBP 12.3 on page 955 confirms that the resulting table has equal conditional proportions.

The Big Picture:
A Closer Look

Although observed counts must be whole numbers, expected counts represent averages that are not necessarily integers. For ease of computation, we rounded our expected counts in Example 12.6 to the nearest whole number. When performing a chi-square procedure by hand, more decimal places are called for if, in the end, the size of the chi-square statistic is borderline.

Likewise, we would expect to see 163/446 of the 164 males wearing contacts: The expected count for this category combination would be

$$\frac{163 \times 164}{446} = 60$$

[Alternatively, since the total wearing contacts must be 163, we could subtract the expected count of females, 103, to conclude that the remaining 60 should be males with contacts.]

Similar reasoning for the other category combinations produces this table of expected counts:

Expected	Contacts	Glasses	None	Total
Female	(163 x 282)/446 = 103	(69 x 282)/446 = 44	(214 x 282)/446 = 135	282
Male	(163 x 164)/446 = 60	(69 x 164)/446 = 25	(214 x 164)/446 = 79	164
Total	163	69	214	446

Examination of the table above showing computation of expected counts reveals a pattern: Each expected count is simply the corresponding column total, multiplied by the row total, divided by the table total.

$$\text{expected count} = \frac{\text{column total} \times \text{row total}}{\text{table total}}$$

Practice: *Try Exercise 12.12(d) on page 608.*

Comparing Observed to Expected Counts

Now that we know what is expected under the null hypothesis of no relationship between gender and lenswear, our next step is to compare how far what we *observed* is from what would be *expected* under the null hypothesis. Referring to each category combination as a cell, we will look at the standardized squared differences, or *components* of chi-square, one cell at a time.

Definition The **components** of chi-square are the standardized squared differences between observed and expected counts:

$$\text{component} = \frac{(\text{observed} - \text{expected})^2}{\text{expected}}$$

If the numbers of possible values are r for the row variable and c for the column variable, then there are $r \times c$ components.

Our test for a relationship will be based on the chi-square statistic, which combines these standardized squared differences into one number. First, however, it is instructive to consider the components individually.

EXAMPLE 12.7 THE COMPONENTS OF CHI-SQUARE

Background: A chi-square procedure is being carried out to test for a relationship between gender and lenswear by comparing counts observed with those expected under the null hypothesis of no relationship.

Chi-square procedure: Compare counts observed to counts expected if null hypothesis were true									
Observed	Contacts	Glasses	None	Total	Expected	Contacts	Glasses	None	Total
Female	121	32	129	282	Female	103	44	135	282
Male	42	37	85	164	Male	60	25	79	164
Total	161	69	214	446	Total	163	69	214	446

Question: What are the individual components, and what do they suggest?

Response: Altogether, there are 2(3) = 6 pairs of counts to compare. Our six components are

$$\frac{(121 - 103)^2}{103} = 3.1 \quad \frac{(32 - 44)^2}{44} = 3.3 \quad \frac{(129 - 135)^2}{135} = 0.3$$

$$\frac{(42 - 60)^2}{60} = 5.4 \quad \frac{(37 - 25)^2}{25} = 5.8 \quad \frac{(85 - 79)^2}{79} = 0.5$$

Because 5.4 and 5.8 are the largest of these, we can say that the greatest differences occur because the observed number of males wearing contacts (42) is less than the number we'd expect (60) if there were no relationship, and the observed number of males wearing glasses (37) is more than the expected count (25). Because 0.3 and 0.5 are close to zero, we can say that the observed counts of females and males needing no lenses are relatively close to the counts we would expect if there were no relationship between gender and lenswear.

Practice: *Try Exercise 12.12(f–h) on page 608.*

The components of chi-square are combined into one statistic, called chi-square and written χ^2, which measures overall how far what we observed is from what would be the case if there were no relationship at all between the two variables of interest.

Definition   The **chi-square statistic** is the sum of the individual components, each of which calculates the standardized squared difference between observed and expected counts.

$$\text{chi-square} = \text{sum of } \frac{(\text{observed} - \text{expected})^2}{\text{expected}}$$

If the numbers of possible values are r for the row variable and c for the column variable, then the chi-square statistic has $r \times c$ terms.

EXAMPLE 12.8 CALCULATING THE CHI-SQUARE STATISTIC

Background: In the preceding example, we calculated the individual components of chi-square in the test for a relationship between gender and lenswear: 3.1, 3.3, 0.3, 5.4, 5.8, and 0.5.

Question: What is the value of the chi-square statistic?

Continued

Response: We simply sum the six individual components:

$$\chi^2 = 3.1 + 3.3 + 0.3 + 5.4 + 5.8 + 0.5 = 18.4$$

Practice: *Try Exercise 12.12(i) on page 608.*

In any test of hypotheses, once we have produced a test statistic, we need to determine whether or not it is large enough to constitute evidence of a statistically significant difference between what is observed and what is claimed in the null hypothesis. In tests where the test statistic followed a standard normal z distribution, it was fairly easy to get a feel for what would be a "large" z statistic: generally, anything that exceeded 2. Likewise, 2 would be a large value of a t statistic, unless the sample size is small, in which case the t distribution is such that 3 could usually be considered large. In Section 11.3, we encountered F statistics, whose relative size was difficult to gauge off-hand, because such a wide variety of F distributions are possible. We are now facing a similar difficulty with χ^2 statistics because there are many chi-square distributions possible, with very different spreads depending on the size of our two-way table.

We will return to our gender/lenswear example after a discussion of these distributions, at which point we will be ready to state whether or not 18.4 is "large" enough, in these circumstances, to constitute evidence of a relationship that goes beyond the sample to a larger population of students.

The Chi-Square Distribution

Because individual binomial counts in the long run follow a perfectly predictable pattern (normal) for large enough sample sizes, the sum of observed minus expected counts, squared and divided by expected counts, also follows a perfectly predictable pattern for large enough samples taken from a population with no relationship between the row and column variables. This pattern is known as the *chi-square distribution*. The degrees of freedom tell us which particular chi-square distribution applies.

Definition   The **chi-square degrees of freedom** equal $(r - 1) \times (c - 1)$, where r is the number of possible values for the row variable (usually explanatory) and c is the number of possible values for the column variable (usually response).

EXAMPLE 12.9 CALCULATING THE CHI-SQUARE DEGREES OF FREEDOM

Background: We would like to test for a relationship between gender (two possible values) and lenswear (three possible values).

Question: What are the chi-square degrees of freedom in this situation?

Response: Because gender allows for 2 possibilities and lenswear for 3, the degrees of freedom are $(2 - 1) \times (3 - 1) = 2$.

Practice: *Try Exercise 12.12(j) on page 608.*

Because the minimum number of possibilities for any categorical variable is 2, the smallest possible degrees of freedom for a chi-square random variable is $(2 - 1) \times (2 - 1) = 1$. Because 2-by-2 two-way tables are quite common, it is worth remembering that the chi-square distribution for 1 degree of freedom is such that the value that cuts off a right-tail probability of exactly 5% is 3.84.

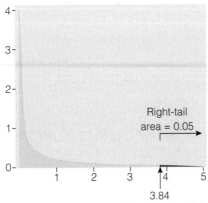

Chi-square with 1 df (for 2-by-2 table)

On the right side:

The Big Picture:
LOOKING BACK

On page 598, we observed that for a 2-by-2 table, χ^2 equals z^2. Thus, the square of the z value that corresponds to a tail probability of 0.05 is $1.96^2 = 3.84$, the same as the chi-square value that corresponds to a tail probability of 0.05 when df = 1.

In other words, for one degree of freedom (data in a 2-by-2 table), if chi-square is greater than 3.84 the *P*-value is less than 0.05.

The curve above gives us a glimpse of one particular chi-square distribution, that for 1 degree of freedom. There are all sorts of chi-square distributions, depending on the numbers of possible values for the two categorical variables involved, which determine the degrees of freedom. Still, these various distributions do have several features in common.

- **Non-negative:** First of all, since the squares in the numerators are at least zero and the expected counts in the denominators must be positive, the sum of components is non-negative. The minimum possible sum, zero, would occur only if the observed counts exactly match the counts expected under the null hypothesis of no relationship. In this case, response proportions would be identical for the various explanatory groups.

- **Mean of χ^2:** The chi-square distribution is always centered at the number of degrees of freedom, so for a 2-by-2 table (1 degree of freedom), it has a mean of 1.

- **Spread:** The distribution has more spread for larger degrees of freedom. For a 2-by-2 table (df = 1), chi-square values typically range from 0 to 4 or 5. For a 3-by-3 table (df = 4), values typically range from 0 to 10 or 11. Whereas a value of 3.84 could be considered unusual for chi-square with 1 degree of freedom, as in our Botox example, a value of 3.84 is not large at all for chi-square with 4 degrees of freedom, whose graph is shown below.

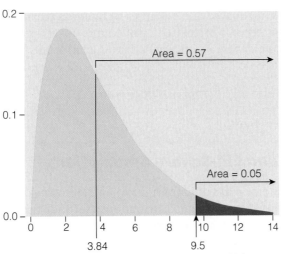

Chi-square with 4 df (for 3-by-3 table)

- **Shape:** All chi-square distributions are right-skewed. This comes about because the squaring process amplifies larger differences between observed and expected counts.

The Chi-Square Test

Now we know enough about the long-run behavior of chi-square statistics to complete our solution of the gender/lenswear example.

EXAMPLE 12.10 DRAWING CONCLUSIONS IN A CHI-SQUARE TEST

Background: In testing for a relationship between gender and lenswear, we found the chi-square statistic to be 18.4, and the degrees of freedom are $(2 - 1) \times (3 - 1) = 2$. The chi-square distribution that applies in this situation is shown here:

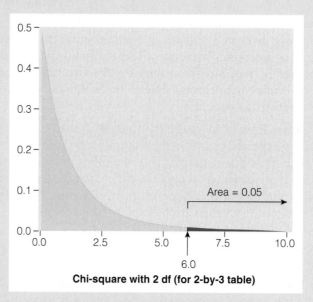

Chi-square with 2 df (for 2-by-3 table)

Question: Is there evidence that the wearing of corrective lenses (contacts, glasses, or neither) is related to gender for all students?

Response: The graph shows that for 2 degrees of freedom, chi-square values greater than 6 could be considered "large." Thus, it is almost impossible for chi-square with 2 degrees of freedom to take a value as high as 18.4, if the statistic is calculated from counts observed in a sample taken from a larger population where the variables gender and lenswear are not related. We conclude that gender and lenswear *are* related.

Practice: *Try Exercise 12.12(k) on page 608.*

Sample Size and Chi-Square Assumptions

As always, sample size plays an important role in inference conclusions: first, due to assumptions based on normal distributions; second, because larger samples tend to produce more evidence of a trend. As far as the assumption of normality of the underlying distributions of counts is concerned, we have the following guidelines.

Example 12.4 on page 955 of the *TBP Supplement* takes a different approach to the gender-lenswear problem by showing there to be no statistically significant relationship between gender and wearing corrective lenses in general, when *type* of lenses (contacts or glasses) is not specified.

The Big Picture: LOOKING BACK

Recall from Section 11.3 that rejecting the null hypothesis in an *F* test resulted in a fairly general conclusion that *not all the population means are equal*. In a comparison of several means, this conclusion allows for the possibility that some of the means are the same, just not all. Similarly, when we reject the null hypothesis in a χ^2 test in a table larger than 2-by-2, we reach the fairly general conclusion that the variables are somehow related. It is still possible that population proportions in certain response categories are equal for the explanatory groups, and not all of the proportions differ.

Guidelines for Use of a Chi-Square Procedure

If the null hypothesis of no relationship between the row and column variables is true, we can assume the chi-square statistic for a 2-by-2 table to follow a chi-square distribution with 1 degree of freedom as long as all of the expected counts are at least 5. A similar but less strict requirement holds for larger tables.

In the next example, we explore the impact of sample size on our chi-square test results. Note that the roles of explanatory and response variables in this situation are not as definite as in the lenswear examples, where gender was the obvious choice for explanatory variable.

The Big Picture:
LOOKING BACK

Our rule of thumb for a single sample proportion to follow a normal distribution, presented on page 306 in Part III, was for np and $n(1 - p)$ both to be at least 10. Our requirement for chi-square is similar, but we can allow for smaller expected counts because chi-square combines several normal distributions.

EXAMPLE 12.11 WHEN SAMPLES ARE TOO SMALL FOR CHI-SQUARE

Background: An article entitled "Why Booze and Smokes Go Together" describes a study in which "subjects were served a 'placebo' drink (fruit juice disguised with a whiff of pure alcohol to fool the drinker)." Researchers found that "the cigarette that followed just didn't satisfy as well. Neither did it provide subjects the same satisfying glow if they got a real drink but smoked a non-nicotine cigarette instead of their usual brand. Those findings . . . underscore that it's the nicotine itself, rather than the motions of smoking, that interacts with alcohol to light up the pleasure centers of the brain."[5]

Alcohol and tobacco:
a compelling combination?

Fisher's Exact Test, which is typically not covered in introductory statistics courses, provides a way of testing for a relationship between two categorical variables when samples are not large enough to satisfy our requirements for a chi-square test.

It is known that alcoholics tend to smoke (at a rate of 80% to 90%, as opposed to about 23% for the general population). Alternatively, we can say that smokers are more likely to be alcoholics than are nonsmokers. The above study confirms that there are chemical and physiological reasons for the connection, rather than the relationship merely coming about via some confounding variable such as socio-economic status or lifestyle tendencies.

Given that the rate of alcoholism in the United States is 4%, a random sample of 100 U.S. adults could result in the following hypothetical (but realistic) two-way table of counts.

	Alcoholic	Not Alcoholic	Total
Smoker	3	20	23
Nonsmoker	1	76	77
Total	4	96	100

Continued

The Big *Picture:*
LOOKING BACK

The problem with Example 12.11 is really the same kind of difficulty that we encountered in situations such as Exercise 9.12 on page 408, where we wanted to construct a 95% confidence interval for a population proportion based on a very small sample. The Central Limit Theorem allows us to assume counts or proportions or means to follow a normal distribution only if the sample size is large enough to offset non-normality in the underlying population.

Pages 956 to 959 of the **TBP** *Supplement* present the chi-square goodness of fit test for a *single* categorical variables with more than two possible values.

A chi-square test may be performed on the columns Alcoholic and Not Alcoholic, each of which contains just two counts: the first for smokers and the second for nonsmokers.

```
Chi-Square Test: Alcoholic, NotAlcoholic
Expected counts are printed below observed counts
       Alcoholic   NotAlcoholic   Total
   1        3           20          23
            0.92        22.08
   2        1           76          77
            3.08        73.92
Total       4           96         100
Chi-Sq =  4.703  +  0.196 +
          1.405  +  0.059 = 6.362

DF = 1
* WARNING * 1 cells with expected counts less than 1.0
          * Chi-Square approximation probably invalid
2 cells with expected counts less than 5.0
```

Question: Does the test provide evidence of a relationship in general between smoking and alcoholism?

Response: Before concluding from the size of the chi-square statistic, 6.362, that we have convincing evidence of a relationship between smoking and alcoholism, we should heed the warning included in the output. Two of our expected counts are less than 5, with one of them (0.92) even less than 1. Neither the pattern of behavior of individual counts of alcoholics smoking, nor the pattern for alcoholics not smoking, would follow a normal curve when only a handful of alcoholics are involved. Under the circumstances, we should refrain from pursuing the chi-square test.

Practice: *Try Exercise 12.12(m) on page 608.*

In the next example, we picture similar data coming from a larger sample size. Again, the proportions are consistent with what researchers have found to be true about smoking and alcoholism.

EXAMPLE 12.12 HOW LARGER SAMPLE SIZES AFFECT THE CHI-SQUARE STATISTIC

Background: Now let's imagine that a sample of *1,000* adults in the United States results in this two-way table of counts, with 10 times as many individuals in each of the category combinations compared to what we saw in Example 12.11.

	Alcoholic	Not Alcoholic	Total
Smoker	30	200	230
Nonsmoker	10	760	770
Total	40	960	1,000

A chi-square test is carried out using software.

```
Chi-Square Test: Alcoholic, NotAlcoholic
Expected counts are printed below observed counts
     Alcoholic NotAlcoholic Total
   1       30        200       230
            9.20     220.80
   2       10        760       770
           30.80     739.20
Total      40        960      1000
Chi-Sq = 47.026 +  1.959 +
         14.047 +  0.585 = 63.618
DF = 1, P-Value = 0.000
```

Questions:

1. How does the chi-square statistic compare to the one on page 606, which was based on a sample one-tenth the size?

2. Does the test provide evidence of a relationship in general between smoking and alcoholism?

3. How would our summary of the situation differ, depending on whether we take smoking or alcoholism as the explanatory variable?

Responses:

1. Now the sample is large enough so that expected counts in all category combinations are at least 5 (the smallest is 9.2). Multiplying the counts across the board by 10 results in a chi-square statistic (63.618) that is exactly 10 times the original chi-square statistic (6.362).

2. There is still just 1 degree of freedom, so we are still considering how extreme our chi-square statistic is relative to a distribution where anything over 3.84 could be called "large." Now the data easily produce sound statistical evidence of a relationship between smoking and alcoholism.

3. We could summarize by stating that smokers are about 10 times as likely to be alcoholics (30/230 = 13% versus 10/770 = 1.3%) or by stating that alcoholics are more than three times as likely to be smokers (30/40 = 75% versus 200/960 = 21%).

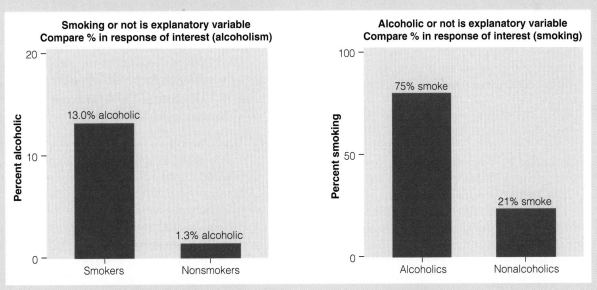

In the first of these two formulations, we are thinking of smoking or not as the explanatory variable. In the second, we are thinking of alcoholism or not as the explanatory variable. Which of these better reflects reality is perhaps no easier to decide than the answer to the question, "Which came first, the chicken or the egg?"

Practice: *Try Exercise 12.17 on page 612.*

By virtue of the mechanics of the calculation of the chi-square statistic, increasing the sample size directly impacts the size of χ^2, accordingly resulting in a smaller *P*-value and more evidence against the null hypothesis.

EXERCISES FOR SECTION 12.2

Comparing Counts with a Chi-Square Test

Note: Asterisked numbers indicate exercises whose answers are provided in the Solutions to Selected Exercises section, on page 689.

12.9 "Improving The Readability and Processability of a Pediatric Informed Consent Document," published in *Archives of Pediatric and Adolescent Medicine* in 2005, describes a study in which existing parental consent forms were modified to conform with federal guidelines that take into account that many Americans have poor literacy skills. Parents of children scheduled for minor elective surgical procedures were randomly (and evenly) assigned to receive information about a clinical study via the standard or the modified form. The proportion who described the form as "very clear" was 0.64 for the standard form, 0.77 for the modified form. The proportion who described the form as "easy to read" was 0.65 for the standard form, 0.86 for the modified form.[6] Sketch bar graphs, first for comparing proportions describing the form as *"very clear"* for standard versus modified forms, then for comparing proportions describing the form as *"easy to read"* for standard versus modified forms, and tell which of the two shows a more dramatic difference between standard and modified.

*12.10 Refer to Exercise 12.9, which reports proportions describing a consent form as *"very clear"* to be 0.64 for the standard form and 0.77 for the modified form, and proportions describing the form as *"easy to read"* to be 0.65 for the standard form and 0.86 for the modified form. Note that the difference was noticeably more dramatic in one of the two comparisons. Using additional information on sample sizes, various tests were performed, resulting in test statistics −4.27, −2.55, 6.492, and 18.226. Match one of each of those numbers to each of the following:

a. *z* statistic comparing responses of "very clear"

b. chi-square statistic comparing responses of "very clear"

c. *z* statistic comparing responses of "easy to read"

d. chi-square statistic comparing responses of "easy to read"

12.11 Refer to Exercises 12.9 and 12.10 on clarity and readability of consent forms: The proportion who described the form as "very clear" was 0.64 for the standard form, 0.77 for the modified form. The proportion who described the form as "easy to read" was 0.65 for the standard form, 0.86 for the modified form. Note that the difference was noticeably more dramatic in one of the two comparisons. Using additional information on sample sizes, various tests were performed, resulting in *P*-values 0.000, 0.000, 0.005, 0.01. Match one of each of those *P*-values to each of the following:

a. one-sided *P*-value for the *z* test comparing responses of "very clear"

b. *P*-value for the chi-square test comparing responses of "very clear"

c. one-sided *P*-value for the *z* test comparing responses of "easy to read"

d. *P*-value for the chi-square test comparing responses of "easy to read"

*12.12 "Influence of Patients' Requests for Direct-To-Consumer Advertised Antidepressants," published in the *Journal of the American Medical Association* in 2005, describes a study where actors playing the roles of patients visited a sample of physicians for help. The "patients" had been trained to sometimes request a brand-name antidepressant (Paxil), and other times to make a general request for an antidepressant, and yet other times to make no request.[7]

a. For which of the three groups would you expect to see the highest proportion receiving a prescription for Paxil from the physician?

b. The first table below shows counts observed to have received a prescription for Paxil or not. Calculate the sample proportions receiving Paxil for the three groups.

Observed	Received Paxil	No Paxil	Total
Paxil request	14	37	51
General request	1	49	50
No request	2	46	48
Total	17	132	149

Expected	Received Paxil	No Paxil	Total
Paxil request	5.82	45.18	51
General request	5.70	44.30	50
No request	5.48	42.52	48
Total	17	132	149

c. Which of the proportions, if any, seem very different from the others?

d. The second table shows expected counts in the various category combinations. Verify that each expected count equals column total times row total divided by table total.

e. Verify that the proportions receiving Paxil in the table of expected counts are the same for the three groups (Paxil, general, and no request).

f. For which group do the expected counts differ the most from the observed counts?

g. Output shows the χ^2 statistic as a sum of six components. Verify that each of these is the squared difference between observed and expected count, divided by expected count.

```
Chi-Sq = 11.503 + 1.481 +
          3.880 +  0.500 +
          2.207 +  0.284 = 19.855
     DF = 2, P-Value = 0.000
```

h. There are six category combinations considered, from "patients" requesting Paxil and receiving Paxil, to those making no request and not receiving Paxil. Use the size of the components to report which category combination has the observed count most different from what we would expect if prescriptions ordered by the physician were not at all related to what a patient requests.

i. Verify that the chi-square statistic is the sum of the individual components in part (g).

j. Explain why the degrees of freedom are shown to equal 2.

k. In an example on page 604, we showed that the area under the chi-square curve with 2 degrees of freedom to the right of 6.0 is 0.05. Can our chi-square statistic 19.855 be considered large, not large, or borderline?

l. What does your answer to part (k) suggest about the relationship between requesting medications and receiving prescriptions for them?

m. Suppose the first row (51 patients who made a request for Paxil) were omitted from the first table, for the purpose of checking for a significant difference between proportions obtaining a prescription for Paxil for those who made a general request compared to those who made no request. Explain why a chi-square procedure would not be appropriate.

12.13 The response of interest in Exercise 12.12 was whether or not the "patients" received Paxil. This exercise considers whether or not they received a prescription for *any* antidepressant.

a. For which of the three groups would you expect to see the lowest proportion receiving a prescription for any antidepressant from the physician?

b. The first table below shows counts observed to have received a prescription for an antidepressant medication or not. Calculate the sample proportions receiving medication for the three groups.

Observed	Received Med	No Med	Total
Paxil request	27	24	51
General request	38	12	50
No request	15	33	48
Total	80	69	149

Expected	Received Med	No Med	Total
Paxil request	27.38	23.62	51
General request	26.85	23.15	50
No request	25.77	22.23	48
Total	80	69	149

c. Do the proportions seem similar to one another or different?

d. The second table shows expected counts in the various category combinations. Verify that each expected count equals column total times row total divided by table total.

e. Verify that the proportions receiving medication in the table of expected counts are the same for the three groups (Paxil, general, and no request).

f. For which groups do the expected counts differ the most from the observed counts?

g. Output shows the χ^2 statistic as a sum of six components. Verify that each of these is the squared difference between observed and expected count, divided by expected count.

```
Chi-Sq = 0.005 + 0.006 +
         4.635 + 5.373 +
         4.502 + 5.220 = 19.742
         DF = 2, P-Value = 0.000
```

h. There are six category combinations considered, from "patients" requesting Paxil and receiving a prescription for an antidepressant medication, to those making no request and not receiving a prescription. For which category combinations are the observed counts almost identical to what we would expect if prescriptions ordered by the physician were not at all related to what a patient requests?

i. Explain why the degrees of freedom are shown to equal 2.

j. In an example on page 604, we showed that the area under the chi-square curve with 2 degrees of freedom to the right of 6.0 is 0.05. Can our chi-square statistic 19.742 be considered large, not large, or borderline?

k. What does the size of the chi-square statistic suggest about the relationship between requesting medications and receiving prescriptions for them?

12.14 "Mouth Piercings May Cause Gums to Recede" reported in 2005 that "researchers at Ohio State University looked at 58 young adults with an average age between 21 and 22. Half had pierced lips and the other half did not, although both groups were otherwise alike in age and gender. Among the subjects with a pierced lip, 41.4 percent had receding gums, although only 6.9 percent of those without a pierced lip suffered from this periodontal condition."[8]

a. Set up a two-way table of observed counts, based on information provided in the article, and construct a table of expected counts.

b. Calculate the chi-square statistic.

c. Comment on whether or not the data should convince us of a relationship between pierced lips and receding gums.

d. In your table of expected counts, find the expected proportions with receding gums for those who have pierced lips and for those who do not. Explain why these expected proportions are equal.

e. What two possible confounding variables were taken into account in the design of the study?

f. Which of these additional variables may also have played a role in whether or not a young adult had pierced lips and whether or not he or she had receding gums: smoking, or attentiveness to hygiene, or both, or neither? Explain.

g. Which one of the following focuses on data production?
1. Experts conclude that for all students, those with pierced lips are more likely to suffer from receding gums than those who don't have pierced lips.
2. In order to make a comparison, researchers attempted to look at two samples of students who were similar in important ways.
3. The observed counts are quite different from the expected counts.
4. A difference as large as the one observed is very unlikely to have come about by chance.

h. Which one of the statements in part (g) focuses on displaying and summarizing data?

i. Which one of the statements in part (g) focuses on probability?

j. Which one of the statements in part (g) focuses on statistical inference?

k. The article mentions that "in the pierced-lip group, recession of the gumline was, on average, twice as deep as it was among those with no pierced lip." Tell whether the variables of interest here are quantitative or categorical, and identify each as being explanatory or response.

l. The article also mentions that "the longer a subject had had a pierced lip, the more likely it was that he or she suffered from gum recession." Tell whether the variables of interest here are quantitative or categorical, and identify each as being explanatory or response.

m. Suppose we wanted to use the sample proportion of students without a pierced lip who had receding gums to set up a confidence interval for the population proportion. Explain why an interval based on a z multiplier may not be very accurate.

12.15 "Painkillers' Safety Doubts" warns that "smokers in Norway who took such drugs [as Advil, Motrin and Aleve] for at least six months had twice the risk of dying of a heart attack, stroke or other heart-related problem."[9] The article concedes that "the study was relatively small—908 people."

a. Is the size of the sample a drawback because not enough people would fall into certain explanatory categories, or because not enough people would fall into certain response categories? Explain.

b. Would 908 typically be considered too small a sample size to produce statistically significant results about the relationship between two categorical variables? Explain.

c. The alternative hypothesis in this situation could be formulated in terms of variables or parameters. Which *two* of the following are correct formulations of the alternative hypothesis?
1. There is a relationship between those drugs and heart-related problems.
2. There is no relationship between those drugs and heart-related problems.
3. The proportions with heart-related problems for populations of people who do and do not take those drugs are not equal.
4. The proportions with heart-related problems for populations of people who do and do not take those drugs are equal.

12.16 "Male Preference for Female Foot Colour in the Socially Monogamous Blue-Footed Booby," published online in *Animal Behaviour* in November 2004, explains that the authors "manipulated the foot colour of paired females to test whether this trait influences male courting behaviour."[10] Specifically, modified foot color of experimental females resembled that of birds in low nutritional state, which would presumably make them less attractive. Based on the information provided in the article, here are data for experimental and control females, indicating whether they received extrapair courtship (C) by male birds or not (N).

| Control: | C | N | C | N | N | C | N | N | N | N | C | | | |
| Experimental: | N | N | C | N | N | N | N | N | N | N | N | N | N | N |

a. What variable should be represented in the rows of a two-way table for this data set?

b. Tabulate the results in a two-way table.

c. Calculate the proportions receiving courtship for each group, and display them with a bar graph that has two bars, one for control and one for experimental birds.

d. About how many times as likely was it for a control bird to receive courtship? (Respond with the nearest whole number.)

e. Explain why a chi-square test for a relationship between foot color and receipt of courtship is not appropriate for this data set.

f. The researchers also compared the *amount* of courtship received by females in the experimental and control groups. Would this be analyzed with a paired t, two-sample t, ANOVA (F), chi-square, or regression?

Do bluer-footed boobies have more beaus?

Gerald & Buff Corsi/Getty Images

*12.17 "Obesity Among U.S. Immigrant Subgroups by Duration of Residence" reported in the *Journal of the American Medical Association* in December 2004 that "of 32,374 respondents, 14% were immigrants. The prevalence of obesity was 16% among immigrants and 22% among US-born individuals."[11]

a. Would proportions 0.16 and 0.22 be denoted p_1 and p_2 or $\hat{p}_1$ and $\hat{p}_2$?

b. The chi-square statistic for testing if the difference in proportions obese was significant equals 84.161, and the *P*-value is 0.000. Would the *P*-value still have been small if the same percentages had been obtained from a sample of 3,237 respondents instead of 32,374?

c. Researchers also compared BMI (weight in kilograms divided by height in meters squared) for immigrants who had been in the United States for less than 1 year, 10 to 15 years, or at least 15 years. Would this be accomplished with paired *t*, two-sample *t*, ANOVA (*F*), chi-square, or regression?

12.18 "Instead of Reading This, Maybe You Should Take a Nap" reported in the *New York Times* that the United States ranked fairly high (eleventh) in an ACNielsen survey of countries around the world, in terms of what percentage of adults go to bed after midnight (34%); the highest percentage (75%) was found in Portugal, and the next highest (69%) in Taiwan.[12]

a. The article does not mention sample sizes. Assume that 100 adults were surveyed in Portugal and 100 in Taiwan. Construct a table of observed counts going to bed after midnight or not, along with a table of counts expected if overall proportions were the same in the two countries (rounding to the nearest tenth).

b. Calculate the chi-square statistic.

c. State whether your chi-square statistic is large, not large, or borderline.

d. State whether the *P*-value is small, not small, or borderline.

e. Tell whether or not there is a significant difference in proportions going to bed after midnight in the two countries.

f. Recall that if all counts in a table are multiplied by the same number, the resulting chi-square statistic is also multiplied by that number. Would the conclusions that you reached in part (e) still hold if only 50 were sampled in each country instead of 100?

g. Would the conclusions you reached in part (e) still hold if 1,000 each were sampled in Portugal and Taiwan, instead of 100 in each country?

h. The top five countries in terms of percentage of "night owls" were Portugal, Taiwan, South Korea, Hong Kong, and Spain. Discuss the potential role played by climate, and propose two possible ways to test if climate affects the percentage of night owls in a country, one in which the explanatory variable is quantitative and one in which it is categorical.

CHAPTER 12   SUMMARY

When we are interested in the relationship between two categorical variables for a larger population, it's best to begin with a comparison of sample proportions in the response of interest for the various explanatory groups. For a 2-by-2 table, we have the option of comparing proportions with a z test. Otherwise, we use the more general chi-square test to compare observed and expected counts.

In the case of a 2-by-2 table, the chi-square statistic is equal to the square of the z statistic in a test for equality of population proportions.

The z Test

If each of the two variables allows for only two possible categories, testing for statistical evidence of a relationship in the larger population can be achieved by testing whether or not population proportions in the response of interest could be equal for the two explanatory groups. If population proportions are indeed equal, the standardized difference between sample proportions

$$z = \frac{(\hat{p}_1 - \hat{p}_2) - 0}{\sqrt{\hat{p}(1 - \hat{p})\left(\frac{1}{n_1} + \frac{1}{n_2}\right)}}$$

follows a standard normal (z) distribution. If the relative difference between sample proportions is large enough, then the P-value will be small and the null hypothesis will be rejected. The general conclusion would be that population proportions must differ, so the two variables are, in fact, related. It is also possible to carry out a z test with a one-sided alternative. The P-value would be a single-tailed probability, and the conclusion would be more specific—namely, that one particular population has a larger proportion in the category of interest than the other.

The Chi-Square Test

The more general case is when each of the categorical variables can take any number of possible values, not necessarily just two. In this case, we formulate the null hypothesis with a claim that the two variables are *not* related in the larger population from which the data arose. The alternative claims that they *are* related. A chi-square procedure tests the hypotheses by considering how different the observed counts are from expected counts—those that would arise, on average, in a sample for which the variables are completely independent of one another. Each expected count can be calculated by the following formula:

$$\text{expected count} = \frac{\text{column total} \times \text{row total}}{\text{table total}}$$

Comparisons are made, one entry of the table at a time, by calculating each component, or standardized squared difference between the count actually observed and the count expected if no relationship exists. Our test statistic combines all of these components by summing them up.

$$\text{chi-square} = \text{sum of } \frac{(\text{observed} - \text{expected})^2}{\text{expected}}$$

If the null hypothesis is true and the two variables are not related, this sum of components follows a **chi-square (χ^2) distribution** with degrees of freedom equal to $(r - 1) \times (c - 1)$ where r is the number of possible categories for the row variable and c is the number of possible categories for the column variable.

All chi-square random variables take values that cannot be negative, and their distributions always have *mean* equal to degrees of freedom and a *shape* that is right-skewed. *Spreads* are less for fewer degrees of freedom and greater for more degrees of freedom. For the chi-square distribution with 1 degree of freedom, a value of 3.84 can be considered large, as it cuts off a right-tail area of 0.05.

If the chi-square statistic can be considered large for the distribution with given degrees of freedom, then we have evidence that the counts observed differ significantly from what they would be on average if the null hypothesis were true. This evidence is summarized by the *P*-value, which tells the probability of chi-square taking a value at least as large as the one observed. A small *P*-value constitutes evidence against the null hypothesis, leading us to conclude that the variables are related for the larger population. Although the test is not especially difficult to carry out by hand, use of software is a much easier way to identify the chi-square statistic and *P*-value.

The sum of standardized squared differences known as chi-square can be assumed to follow a true chi-square distribution only if the distributions of observed counts are approximately normal. Our rule of thumb for a 2-by-2 table is that each expected count should be at least 5.

CHAPTER 12 EXERCISES

Note: Asterisked numbers indicate exercises whose answers are provided in the Solutions to Selected Exercises section, on page 689.

Additional exercises appeared after each section: comparing proportions with a z test (Section 12.1) on page 595 and chi-square tests (Section 12.2) on page 608.

Warming Up: RELATIONSHIPS BETWEEN TWO CATEGORICAL VARIABLES

12.19 "God and Evolution" reported that "a study of nearly 4,000 people in North Carolina, for example, found that frequent church-goers had a 46 percent lower risk of dying in a six-year period than those who attended less often. Another study involving nearly 126,000 participants suggested that a 20-year-old church-goer might live seven years longer than a similar person who does not attend religious services."[13]

    a. Which study considers the relationship between two categorical variables—the first or the second one mentioned?

    b. Tell what types of variables are involved in the other study, identifying each as being explanatory or response.

12.20 "Firm Believers More Likely to be Flabby, Purdue Study Finds" reported in March 1998: "Sociology professor Kenneth Ferraro found the correlation between being overweight and being religious was statistically significant regardless of a person's choice of faith."[14]

    a. Was weight (being overweight or not) apparently treated as a quantitative or categorical variable?

    b. Was religion (being religious or not) apparently treated as a quantitative or categorical variable?

    c. Would the relationship be explored with chi-square or with regression?

    d. Explain why "association" would be a better word to use in the circumstances than "correlation."

12.21 "Virginity Pledgers Still Take Sex Risks" explains that "virginity pledges emerged in the early 1990s based on the theory that young people would remain chaste if they had broader community support—or pressure—to remain abstinent." One virginity group called True Love Waits has youths sign a card stating: "Believing that true love waits, I make a commitment to God, myself, my family, those I date and my future mate to be sexually pure until the day I enter marriage." A study published in the *Journal of Adolescent Health* found that 20% of several thousand youths in a long-term study said they had taken a virginity pledge; some of these were termed "inconsistent pledgers," if their status or responses changed over time. "Almost 7% of the students who did not take a pledge were diagnosed with an STD (sexually transmitted disease), compared with 6.4% of the 'inconsistent pledgers' and 4.6% of the 'consistent pledgers.'"[15] The study's author, Peter Bearman, said these differences were not statistically significant, although spokesman Robert Rector from the conservative Heritage Institute said he interpreted the data to mean that young people committed to the abstinence pledge were less likely to become infected.

More exercises for this chapter are featured in the **TBP** Supplement on pages 962 through 965. End-of-chapter activities are described on page 959.

a. Who believed the differences among sample percentages could be attributed to chance in the sampling process, Bearman or Rector?

b. If Bearman is wrong, is he committing a Type I or Type II Error?

c. If Rector is wrong, is he committing a Type I or Type II Error?

d. Bill Smith, public policy vice president for the Sexuality Information and Education Council of the United States, said, "Not only do virginity pledges not work to keep our young people safe, they are causing harm by undermining condom use, contraception and medical treatment." Which chi-square test is Smith suggesting would have a small P-value: the one for a relationship between pledges and STDs or the one for a relationship between pledges and use of other preventive measures?

12.22 CBS reported on a study that explored the question of whether or not parents of dying children should talk to their children about death: "Using Sweden's comprehensive cancer and death records, the researchers found 368 children under 17 who had been diagnosed with cancer between 1992 and 1997 and who later died. They contacted the children's parents, and 80 percent of them filled out a long, anonymous questionnaire. Among the questions: "Did you talk about death with your child at any time?" Of the 429 parents who answered that, about one-third said they had done so, while two-thirds had not. None of the 147 who did so regretted talking about death. Among those who had not talked about death, 69 said they wished they had."[16] The P-value for testing if there is a relationship between talking about death or not and experiencing regrets later or not was 0.000. Based on the size of the P-value, students are to state whether or not parents of dying children should be encouraged to consider talking to their children about death. Whose answer makes the most sense, statistically?

Adam: You can't really draw any conclusions from this study, because only 80 percent of the parents filled out the questionnaire.

Brittany: I think 80 percent is a good enough response rate, but all of the families were from Sweden. I would only be convinced if they sampled from all countries.

Carlos: It would be hard enough to get all those records from one country. Anyway, going through the death of a child is probably similar for all parents, no matter where they're from. The small P-value convinces me that parents should be encouraged to talk about death with their kids, if they're dying.

Dominique: 429 is such a small number compared to all the parents in the world who go through the death of a child. It's not a good idea to generalize about what's true for the population when it's so much larger than the sample.

12.23 A pair of newspaper articles published side-by-side in 2005 presented two conflicting points of view. The first is "Random Student Drug Testing Works: It's About Public Health—Identifying Individuals Who Need Help and Treatment—Not Punishment," by the director of the White House Office of National Drug Control Policy.[17] The second is "Don't Believe The Hype: Random Drug Testing, a Humiliating Violation of Privacy, Has Not Been Proven to Deter Drug Use," by the director of the Safety First drug education project at the Drug Policy Alliance.[18]

a. Presumably both of the writers considered evidence from studies about the same two categorical variables. Briefly describe the variables, identifying which is explanatory and which is response.

b. What does the null hypothesis say about the relationship between those two variables?

c. Has the writer of the first article rejected that null hypothesis?

d. If that writer is wrong, has he committed a Type I or Type II Error?

e. Briefly describe the potential harmful consequences of committing this type of error in these particular circumstances.

f. Has the writer of the second article rejected the null hypothesis?

g. If that writer is wrong, has she committed a Type I or Type II Error?

h. Briefly describe the potential harmful consequences of committing this type of error in these particular circumstances.

Exploring the Big Picture: RELATIONSHIPS BETWEEN TWO CATEGORICAL VARIABLES

*12.24 "Men and the Frantic Life" reports on a study of 10,000 British workers done by the University College London, published in *Prevention* magazine. Men who are stressed at work are twice as likely to end up with diabetes than men who aren't. On the other hand, women's risk of diabetes was not related to being stressed at work.[19]

a. For which gender group was there a large chi-square statistic in testing for a relationship between stress and diabetes?

b. For each gender group, the null hypothesis could be formulated in terms of variables or parameters. Which *two* of the following are correct formulations of the null hypothesis?

1. There is a relationship between stress and diabetes.

2. There is no relationship between stress and diabetes.

3. The proportions developing diabetes for populations of people who are stressed or not stressed at work are equal.

4. The proportions developing diabetes for populations of people who are stressed or not stressed at work are not equal.

12.25 "Prostate Survival Studied," reporting on a study published in 2005 in the *Journal of the American Medical Association,* explains that "men with nonaggressive prostate cancer who were treated with hormones or took no action at all are unlikely to die of the disease even 20 years later, new research shows."[20] The study recommends that men with low-grade, localized cancers should avoid the surgery or radiation that can cause impotence and incontinence.

a. Apparently, a chi-square test was carried out to test for a relationship between treatment (hormones/nothing versus surgery/radiation) and outcome (long-term survival). Was the chi-square statistic for this test large or not large?

b. Was the *P*-value for the test described in part (a) small or not small?

c. Apparently, another chi-square test has been carried out to test for a relationship between treatment and side-effects such as impotence and incontinence. Was the chi-square statistic for this test large or not large?

d. Was the *P*-value for the test described in part (c) small or not small?

12.26 "Drug War Turned Toward Marijuana in '90s" reported in 2005 that "the focus of the drug war in the United States shifted significantly in the past decade from hard drugs to marijuana," specifying that the proportion of all drug arrests attributed to marijuana rose from 0.28 in 1992 to 0.45 in 2002. However, "the most widely quoted household survey on the topic has shown relatively little change in the overall rate of marijuana use over the same time period, experts say."[21]

a. In this situation, do 0.28 and 0.45 refer to $\hat{p}_1$ and $\hat{p}_2$ or p_1 and p_2?

b. Apparently, researchers tested for a relationship between year (1992 or 2002) and nature of the drug arrest (due to marijuana or hard drugs). Was their test statistic large or not large?

c. Was the *P*-value for the test described in part (b) small or not small?

d. Apparently, another test was carried out to test for a relationship between year (1992 or 2002) and whether or not a respondent used marijuana. Was the test statistic for this test large or not large?

e. Was the *P*-value for the test described in part (d) small or not small?

12.27 "Mental Illness Risk Rises After Death of a Child" tells of a Danish study that analyzed medical records of over a million parents. About 17,000 of the parents had lost a child under 18, and several hundred were hospitalized for psychiatric problems for the first time in the 5 years afterwards. Bereaved parents in the first year after the child's death were found to be about six times as likely as their nongrieving peers to be hospitalized for a mood disorder, like depression.[22]

a. If $\hat{p}_1$ denotes the proportion of bereaved parents hospitalized for mood disorders like depression, and $\hat{p}_2$ denotes the proportion of nongrieving parents hospitalized, which of the following is the appropriate alternative hypothesis: $p_1 > p_2$, or $p_1 < p_2$, or $\hat{p}_1 > \hat{p}_2$, or $\hat{p}_1 < \hat{p}_2$?

b. If we wanted to set up a confidence interval for the difference between population proportions, would the interval be centered at $p_1 - p_2$ or $\hat{p}_1 - \hat{p}_2$?

*12.28 For a sample of male and female students in a 2003 survey, the bar graph on top was constructed to compare proportions who were carrying cell phones; the bar graph on the bottom was constructed to compare proportions who were nonsmokers.

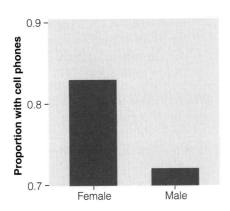

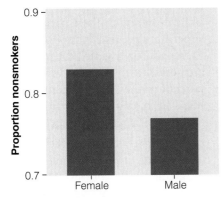

a. For which comparison is there a more pronounced difference between males and females: the one for proportions carrying cell phones or the one for proportions of nonsmokers?

b. Which chi-square statistic will be larger: the one for a relationship between gender and carrying cell phones, or the one for a relationship between gender and being a nonsmoker or not?

c. Which P-value will be smaller: the one for testing if there is a relationship between gender and carrying cell phones, or the one for testing if there is a relationship between gender and being a nonsmoker or not?

12.29 For a sample of male and female students, the bar graph on top was constructed to compare proportions who were vegetarians; the bar graph on the bottom was constructed to compare proportions who were business majors.

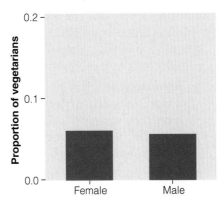

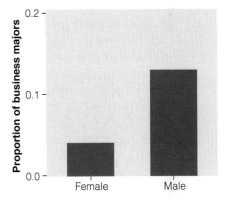

a. For which comparison is there a more pronounced difference between males and females: the one for proportions who are vegetarians or the one for proportions who are business majors?

b. Which chi-square statistic will be larger: the one for a relationship between gender and being a vegetarian or not, or the one for a relationship between gender and being a business major or not?

c. Which P-value will be smaller: the one for testing if there is a relationship between gender and being a vegetarian or not, or the one for testing if there is a relationship between gender and being a business major or not?

*12.30 Exercise 12.8 on page 597 discussed the article "Large Doses of Vitamin E Could Be Risky," which warns that large doses of vitamin E "do not protect against heart attacks and cancer and might actually raise the risk of heart failure in people with diabetes or clogged arteries. [. . .] Research released last week on nearly 40,000 healthy women showed no heart benefits from vitamin E pills."[23] The article also tells of an American Medical Association study of 7,030 patients with diabetes or clogged arteries, randomly assigned to take a placebo or about 400 milligrams of vitamin E every day for several years: "Heart failure was diagnosed in 641 vitamin E patients, compared with 578 patients in the placebo group."

a. Assuming the 7,030 patients were evenly divided between vitamin E and placebo, report the sample proportions with heart failure in the two groups, rounding to the nearest thousandth.

b. Do the numbers 641 and 578 refer to n_1 and n_2, X_1 and X_2, $\hat{p}_1$ and $\hat{p}_2$, or p_1 and p_2?

c. The chi-square statistic was found to be 3.929. Keeping in mind that for 1 degree of freedom (just two possible values for each variable), the probability of chi-square being greater than 3.84 is 0.05, tell whether the P-value is much larger than 0.05, a bit larger than 0.05, a bit smaller than 0.05, or much smaller than 0.05.

d. Is the conclusion that "large doses of vitamin E might raise the risk of heart failure in people with diabetes or clogged arteries" consistent with the size of the P-value?

e. The article mentions a large-scale study which showed no heart benefits from vitamin E pills. Can we infer that the chi-square statistic for the study was larger than 3.84, smaller than 3.84, or very close to 3.84?

f. A spokesperson for the makers of vitamin E supplements said the study is "not the final word on vitamin E." These companies would like people to believe that an error has been made when the study concluded vitamin E had no heart benefits. Would this have been a Type I or Type II Error?

g. Makers of vitamin E supplements would also like people to believe that an error has been made when the other study concluded that it might raise the risk of heart failure in certain people. Would this

have been a Type I Error (rejecting a true null hypothesis) or Type II Error (failing to reject a false null hypothesis)?

*12.31 "Pfizer Bares Belated Celebrex Study" reported in 2004 that "Pfizer Inc. revealed it completed a study four years ago that links its painkiller Celebrex to a 'statistically significant' increase in heart problems."[24]

a. Describe the two categorical variables of interest in Pfizer's study, identifying each as being explanatory or response.

b. Can we assume that Pfizer obtained a P-value that was more than 0.05 or less than 0.05?

c. Each of the variables you described in part (a) would have just two possible values, so the chi-square test would be based on a 2-by-2 two-way table. Was the chi-square statistic greater than 3.84 or less than 3.84?

12.32 "Ugly Kids Get Less Attention from Parents," reported in the University of Alberta's online medical news site, states that a researcher "has shown that parents are more likely to give better care and pay closer attention to good-looking children compared to unattractive ones."[25] A team of researchers observed over 400 2- to 5-year-old children with their parents in supermarkets, and independently graded each child on a scale of 1 to 10 on attractiveness. "Findings showed that 1.2 percent of the least attractive children were buckled in, compared with 13.3 percent of the most attractive youngsters."

a. The article does not mention how many children fall in the least and most attractive categories. Assume 1 in 100 least attractive children and 13 in 100 most attractive children were buckled in. Altogether, 14 children were buckled in, so how many would we expect to see buckled in for each group of 100 children if attractiveness was not a factor?

b. Complete tables of observed and expected counts.

c. Find the chi-square statistic for testing if the difference in proportions is significant.

d. Compare your chi-square statistic to 3.84 in order to decide if the difference is significant.

e. Before concluding that parents' attentiveness is influenced by their children's attractiveness, consider the possibility that causation occurs in the opposite direction, namely, that children's attractiveness is influenced by their parents' attentiveness. Explain how this could account for the differences observed.

f. The article does not mention how attractiveness was assessed. Would you be more convinced of the claim presented in the article's title if attractiveness were evaluated on the basis of symmetry of facial features or if it were evaluated on the basis of grooming?

g. If researchers conclude that, in general, ugly children get less attention from parents, which process is the focus: data production, displaying and summarizing data, probability, or statistical inference?

h. If attractiveness made no difference, it would be very unlikely to observe only 1 in 100 least attractive children, compared to 13 in 100 most attractive children, buckled in. Which of the four processes is the focus here?

i. In a bar graph, the bar for proportion buckled in is much taller for the attractive children. Which of the four processes is the focus here?

j. Because this was an observational study, researchers must make every effort to take into account possible confounding variables when they design their study. Which of the four processes is the focus here?

12.33 "Outcome of Surgery For Crooked Nose: An Objective Method of Evaluation," published in *Aesthetic Plastic Surgery* in 2004, explains that "Correction of a crooked nose poses one of the greatest challenges in septorhinoplasty."[26] A comparison was made of results for 13 surgeries on "C-shaped" noses (bent partway down) and 14 on "I-shaped" noses (angled out from the top). For the C-shaped noses, 1 repair was termed Excellent, 6 Good, 5 Acceptable, and 1 Unsuccessful; for the I-shaped noses, 2 repairs were Excellent, 9 Good, and 3 Acceptable.

a. Are sample sizes (13 and 14) large enough to expect at least 5 in each of the the 8 category combinations (type of nose and quality of repair)?

b. The article's authors combined excellent with good, and acceptable with unsuccessful, resulting in just two categories for quality of repair. Complete the tables for observed and expected counts (to the nearest hundredth) in the various category combinations:

Observed	Excellent/ Good	Acceptable/ Unsuccessful	Total
C-shaped			
I-shaped			
Total			

Expected	Excellent/ Good	Acceptable/ Unsuccessful
C-shaped		
I-shaped		

c. Notice that although the expected counts are not all at least 5, they do come quite close, so the chi-square procedure should give reasonably accurate results. Calculate the chi-square statistic.

d. Keeping in mind that for 2-by-2 tables the area to the right of 3.84 under the chi-square curve is 0.05, tell whether the P-value is small, not small, or borderline.

e. Is there a significant difference in repair quality for C-shaped versus I-shaped noses?

f. The researchers also looked at each nose's preoperative angle and postoperative angle. Was this a paired t, two-sample t, or F procedure?

g. In addition, the researchers compared improvements from preoperative to postoperative angle for the C-shaped noses versus the I-shaped noses. Was this a paired t, two-sample t, or F procedure?

12.34 "Family Lead Poisoning Associated With Occupational Exposure," published in *Clinical Pediatrics* in 2004, explains that "invisible toxins may be carried home to household members by inadequately protected workers on their clothes, shoes, or bodies, called 'take-home exposure.'"[27] Take-home lead exposures in California were studied, with information recorded on ages of household members and peak blood lead levels (BLL), in micrograms per deciliter:

	Infant	Toddler	School-Age	Total
BLL < 20	6	19	6	31
BLL ≥ 20	4	32	4	40
Total	10	51	10	71

a. Tell what are the explanatory and response variables, and how many possible values each has.

b. Is the explanatory variable displayed along rows or columns?

c. Tell why the chi-square statistic has 2 degrees of freedom.

d. The chi-square statistic is approximately 3. Refer to this sketch of the chi-square distribution with 2 degrees of freedom tell whether the *P*-value is small, not small, or borderline.

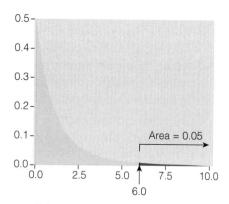

Chi-square with 2 df (for 2-by-3 table)

e. Which one of the following conclusions is correct?

1. There is no relationship between child's age group and blood lead levels being above or below 20.

2. The data do not provide convincing evidence of a relationship between child's age group and blood lead levels being above or below 20.

3. The data prove that there is a relationship between child's age group and blood lead levels being above or below 20.

4. The data provide convincing evidence of a relationship between child's age group and blood lead levels being above or below 20.

f. Suppose we wanted to use the sample proportion of infants with blood lead levels of at least 20 (4 out of 10) to set up a confidence interval for the population proportion. Explain why an interval based on a *z* multiplier may not be very accurate.

g. Briefly describe a way to assess values of age and blood lead levels so that the explanatory variable is categorical and the response is quantitative.

h. Describe a way to assess the variables so the explanatory variable is quantitative and the response is categorical.

i. Describe a way to assess the variables so both the explanatory and the response variables are quantitative.

12.35 An article published in the *New England Journal of Medicine* in 2005 describes a double-blind, randomized, placebo-controlled trial designed to test whether the antibiotic gatifloxacin could reduce the rate of cardiovascular events such as heart attacks. Approximately 4,000 patients were enrolled in the study, and we will assume that 2,000 each received gatifloxacin and placebo. The proportions with cardiovascular events after two years were 0.237 for the gatifloxacin group and 0.251 for the placebo group.[28]

a. Which group seemed to do better, as far as the sample was concerned: those who took gatifloxacin or those who took a placebo?

b. If we calculate 0.237(2,000) and 0.251(2,000), are we finding X_1 and X_2, or $\hat{p}_1$ and $\hat{p}_2$, or p_1 and p_2, or n_1 and n_2?

c. Complete all the information in the tables of observed counts, on the top, and expected counts, on the bottom:

Observed	Event	No Event	Total
Gatifloxacin			2,000
Placebo			2,000
Total	976		4,000

Observed	Event	No Event	Total
Gatifloxacin	488		2,000
Placebo			2,000
Total	976		4,000

d. The chi-square statistic, which is the combined standardized squared difference of observed minus expected counts, can be calculated to be 1.06. Use the fact that the area to the right of 3.84 under the chi-square distribution for a 2-by-2 table is 0.05 to decide if the *P*-value is not small at all, small, or borderline.

e. Which *two* of these are correct interpretations of the results?

1. There is evidence of a relationship between heart attacks or not and taking gatifloxacin or not.

2. The data prove that there is no relationship between heart attacks or not and taking gatifloxacin or not.

3. The data fail to provide evidence of a relationship between heart attacks or not and taking gatifloxacin or not.

4. The proportions having heart attacks for populations of people taking gatifloxacin or placebo are equal.

5. The proportions having heart attacks for populations of people taking gatifloxacin or placebo may be equal.

6. There is evidence that the proportions having heart attacks for populations of people taking gatifloxacin or placebo are different.

12.36 Refer to Exercise 12.35. Sample proportions taking gatifloxacin and placebo who experienced heart attacks were recorded by researchers.

a. A 95% confidence interval for population proportion of gatifloxacin-takers suffering heart attacks is (0.22, 0.26) and a 95% confidence interval for population proportion of placebo-takers suffering heart attacks is (0.23, 0.27). Do the intervals overlap?

b. Does your answer to part (a) suggest that gatifloxacin makes a difference?

c. A 95% confidence interval for difference between population proportions suffering heart attacks, gatifloxacin minus placebo, is (−0.04, +0.01). Does the interval contain zero?

d. Does your answer to part (c) suggest that gatifloxacin makes a difference?

12.37 Refer to Exercise 12.18 on page 612 about proportions of Portuguese and Taiwanese

who go to bed after midnight. Suppose 750 out of 1,000 Portuguese and 690 out of 1,000 Taiwanese are found to go to bed after midnight.

a. Use the fact that the standard error of sample proportion for Portuguese is $\sqrt{0.75(0.25)/1,000} = 0.01$ to set up a 95% confidence interval for the population proportion of "night owls" among the Portuguese.

b. Use the fact that the standard error of sample proportion for Taiwanese is $\sqrt{0.69(0.31)/1,000} = 0.01$ to set up a 95% confidence interval for the population proportion of "night owls" among the Taiwanese.

c. Report whether or not your confidence intervals overlap.

d. What does your answer to part (c) suggest in terms of whether or not population proportions could easily be the same in the two countries?

e. Use the fact that the difference between sample proportions is $0.75 − 0.69 = 0.06$ and that the standard error for difference between proportions is approximately 0.02 to set up a 95% confidence interval for the difference between population proportions.

f. Report whether or not your confidence interval contains zero.

g. What does your answer to part (f) suggest in terms of whether or not population proportions could easily be the same in the two countries?

h. If the results had arisen from sample sizes much smaller than 1,000, would we necessarily reach the same conclusions?

i. If the results had arisen from sample sizes much larger than 1,000, would we necessarily reach the same conclusions?

12.38 In "An Informal Look at Use of Bakery Department Tongs and Tissues," a researcher named Trinkaus reported: "Of 108 people observed extracting for purchase rolls or pastries from displayed bulk stock in food supermarket bakery departments, about 90% used their hands for item selection and withdrawal rather than the store provided tongs. In stores where tissues were provided instead of tongs, approximately 60% of the 133 people who were observed used their hands."[29]

a. The overall proportion using their hands was $\hat{p} = 0.73$. Explain why this is not the exact average of 0.90 and 0.60 (which is 0.75).

b. The P-value for the test of a relationship between use of hands and having tissues or tongs provided is 0.000. Is the chi-square statistic much less than 3.84, a bit less than 3.84, a bit more than 3.84, or much more than 3.84?

c. Explain how the study's results may be biased if observations were made in the morning for stores with tongs and in the evening for stores with tissues.

d. Explain how the study's results may be biased if stores with tongs tended to be located in areas with a large student population.

12.39 An article in *Nature* reports on a study of the relationship between kinship and aggression in wasps. In a controlled experiment, the proportion of 31 brother embryos attacked by soldier wasp larvae was 0.52, whereas the proportion of 31 unrelated male embryos attacked was 0.77.[30]

a. What are the explanatory and response variables?

b. Construct a table of (whole number) observed counts in the four possible category combinations, using rows for the explanatory variable and columns for the response.

c. Construct a table of counts expected if there were no relationship between kinship and aggression.

d. Compute the chi-square statistic, rounding to the nearest hundredth.

e. Is the P-value greater than 0.05 or less than 0.05?

f. Does the experiment provide evidence of a relationship between kinship and aggression?

12.40 An Internet report from January 2005 is titled, "Study: Anti-Seizure Drug Reduces Drinking in Bipolar Alcoholics." A chi-square test was carried out based on results mentioned in the report, which explains that takers of the drug (Valproate) and placebo were questioned after 6 months to see if they had engaged in heavy drinking (five or more drinks daily for men, four or more daily for women).[31]

	Heavy Drinking	No Heavy Drinking	Total
Valproate	14	18	32
Placebo	15	7	22
Total	29	25	54

a. Did the sample of Valproate-takers have a lower percentage engaging in heavy drinking?

b. The P-value was found to be 0.077. Was the chi-square statistic much less than 3.84, somewhat less than 3.84, somewhat greater than 3.84, or much greater than 3.84?

c. In order to produce more convincing evidence of the drug's benefits, what would be the most obvious change to make if a second study could be carried out?

d. What would the P-value have been if a one-sided z test had been carried out to see if population proportion engaging in heavy drinking is less for Valproate-takers than for placebo-takers?

e. The chi-square statistic was 3.13. What would the z statistic have been if a z test had been carried out instead of a chi-square test?

***12.41** A study at Duke University's Medical Center compared occurrences of post-operative nausea for women randomly assigned to receive drugs, acupuncture, or a placebo.[32] Output is shown on the left for the test carried out to see if proportions with nausea differed significantly for women in the *three* groups. Then results are combined for women receiving acupuncture or a placebo, with results shown on the right for comparing just *two* groups.

```
Expected counts are printed below observed counts
        NoNausea Nausea Total  |            NoNausea Nausea    Total
Drug      16       9      25   |Drug           16       9        25
          15.33    9.67        |               15.33    9.67
Acu       20       6      26   |Acu/Placebo    30      20        50
          15.95   10.05        |               30.67   19.33
Placebo   10      14      24   |Total          46      29        75
          14.72    9.28        |
Total     46      29      75   |
                              |
Chi-Sq = 0.029 + 0.046 +      |   Chi-Sq = 0.029 + 0.046 +
         1.030 + 1.634 +      |            0.014 + 0.023 = 0.112
         1.513 + 2.401 = 6.654|   DF = 1, P-Value = 0.737
         DF = 2, P-Value = 0.036|
```

a. Explain how the chi-square test results are affected by combining counts in the acupuncture and placebo groups.

b. Which results make the most sense to report—those on the left or those on the right?

c. For which table are counts large enough so that a chi-square procedure is appropriate: the one on the left, the one on the right, both, or neither?

*12.42 "Diversification Bias: Explaining The Discrepancy in Variety Seeking Between Combined and Separated Choices" by Daniel Read and George Loewenstein of Carnegie Mellon University, explained, "If you have just eaten an orange it might well make an immediate second orange less appealing, but it will probably have little effect on the pleasure of an orange eaten tomorrow."[33] The authors explored subjects' choices of snacks (such as candy bars, cookies, or chips) under a variety of conditions, including one circumstance in which they were to choose one from a variety of snacks *sequentially,* once each week for 3 weeks. In another circumstance, they were to *simultaneously* choose three from the various snacks. The table on the left shows some of the counts of subjects' choices, according to whether they were given sequential or simultaneous choices, and whether they opted for all three of one kind of snack, or two kinds, or all three different kinds.

a. Note that for any two-way table, the number of degrees of freedom corresponds to the number of cell counts that must be known in order to use the total counts to complete the rest of the table. How many degrees of freedom are involved here?

b. Fill in the remaining cell counts.

c. Compare the observed and expected counts: When people were given a *sequential* choice (once a week), did they pick just one kind of snack more often or less often than they would if conditions (sequential or simultaneous) made no difference?

d. When people were given a *simultaneous* choice (all at once), did they pick just one kind of snack more often or less often than they would if conditions (sequential or simultaneous) made no difference?

e. The chi-square statistic and *P*-value are shown here in computer output. Does type of choice (sequential or

Observed	One Kind	Two Kinds	Three Kinds	Total
Sequential choice	19	19		41
Simultaneous choice				56
Total	29	40	28	97

Expected	One Kind	Two Kinds	Three Kinds	Total
Sequential choice	12.26	16.91	11.84	41
Simultaneous choice	16.74	23.09	16.16	56
Total	29	40	28	97

simultaneous) have a significant impact on the degree to which people vary their selections?

```
Chi-Sq = 3.709  + 0.259 + 6.596 +
         2.715  + 0.190 + 4.829 = 18.297
DF = 2,  P-Value = 0.000
```

f. Based on this research, for which type of product should a marketer attempt to offer some appearance of variety: one that people tend to buy in bulk or one that people buy piecemeal?

12.43 "Diversification Bias: Explaining The Discrepancy in Variety Seeking Between Combined and Separated Choices" by Daniel Read and George Loewenstein of Carnegie Mellon University, described an experiment designed to test if trick-or-treaters' choice of two same or different candy bars depended on whether the candy bars were offered simultaneously at one house or sequentially at two houses. All 13 of 13 children offered to "choose whichever two candy bars you like"[34] from stacks of Three Musketeers and Milky Ways at one house chose two kinds (one of each). Only 12 of 25 children offered to choose a single candy bar from Three Musketeers and Milky Ways sequentially at two neighboring houses chose two kinds.

a. Use this information to set up two-way tables of observed and expected counts (rounded to the nearest hundredth).

b. Calculate the chi-square statistic.

c. Assess the P-value as being small or not.

d. State whether type of choice (simultaneous or sequential) had a significant impact on the children's decision to take two different kinds or both the same kind of candy bar.

Trick-or-treat selections provide a clue to market behavior.

Using Software [see Technology Guide]: TWO CATEGORICAL VARIABLES

*12.44 A study published in April 2000 in the *British Medical Journal* reported on a Scottish survey about high school students carrying weapons and engaging in illegal drug use.[35]

	Weapon	No Weapon	Total
Drugs	389	496	885
No drugs	248	1,978	2,226
Total	637	2,474	3,111

a. Use software to carry out a z test to check for evidence that, in general, drug users are more likely than non-users to carry weapons. Report the sample proportions to be compared, the z statistic, and the P-value. State your conclusion in terms of relevant population proportions.

b. Use software to carry out a z test to check for evidence that, in general, those who carry weapons are more likely than those who don't carry weapons to use drugs. Report the sample proportions to be compared, the z statistic, and the P-value. State your conclusion in terms of relevant population proportions.

c. Use software to carry out a chi-square test to produce evidence of a relationship between using drugs and carrying weapons. Report the chi-square statistic and the *P*-value. State your conclusion in terms of a relationship between relevant variables.

d. In which case is the square of the *z* statistic approximately equal to the value of the chi-square statistic: when drug use is taken to be the explanatory variable, when carrying of weapons is taken to be the explanatory variable, or both of these, or neither of these?

12.45 "Painless Heart Attacks More Lethal" reported in 2004 that "people who experience little or no chest pain during a heart attack are more likely to die from the attack."[36] International researchers studied data from 20,000 patients; "Of the 1,763 cardiac patients who did not experience chest pain, 13% died in the hospital, compared with 4.3% of those who experienced chest pain."

a. First, use the information provided to report counts observed for patients who did or did not experience chest pain, and those who did or did not die, rounding each to the nearest whole number.

b. Use software to carry out a chi-square test, including a table of expected counts and the individual terms of the chi-square statistic, and tell which one of the following does *not* contribute significantly to the evidence that pain and survival are related:

1. So many patients who did not have chest pain died.

2. So few patients who did not have chest pain survived.

3. So few patients who had chest pain died.

4. So many patients who had chest pain survived.

c. Which heart attack patients would tend to receive more appropriate treatment in the hospital: those who experience chest pain, or those who experience other symptoms such as shortness of breath, excessive sweating, or nausea and vomiting?

12.46 Refer to Exercise 12.45 on the relationship between chest pain and dying from a heart attack.

a. Based on the data provided, use software to report a 95% confidence interval for the population proportion of all those who do *not* experience chest pain to die of a heart attack.

b. Report a 95% confidence interval for the population proportion of all those who *do* experience chest pain to die of a heart attack.

c. Tell whether or not the intervals in parts (a) and (b) overlap.

d. Does your answer to part (c) suggest that the population proportions could be the same for both groups?

e. Explain why the interval for those experiencing pain is so much narrower than the interval for those who do not experience pain.

f. Use software to produce a 95% confidence interval for the difference in population proportions who die of a heart attack for those who do not minus those who do experience pain.

g. Tell whether or not the interval in part (f) contains zero, or if it contains only positive or only negative differences.

h. What does your answer to part (g) suggest about the population proportions for the two groups?

12.47 "Misperceptions, the Media and the Iraq War," published by the Program on International Policy Attitudes in October 2003, explored the relationship between Americans' primary news source and their susceptibility to misperceptions about the war in Iraq.[37] Specifically, besides reporting their primary source of news, a representative sample was asked if Iraq-al Qaeda links had been found, if weapons of mass destruction had been found, and if world public opinion favored the war. This table shows counts consistent with the reported frequency of each of the primary news sources, and how many of those respondents harbored at least one major misperception about the war.

	Misperception	No Misperception	Total
Print	118	132	250
Fox	152	38	190
CNN	94	76	170
NBC	83	67	150
ABC	73	47	120
CBS	64	26	90
PBS/NPR	7	23	30

  a. How many degrees of freedom apply?

  b. Use software to carry out a chi-square test; report the chi-square statistic.

  c. Report the *P*-value to confirm that having misperceptions was related to where respondents obtained their news.

  d. Which two sources corresponded to the highest percentages of people with misperceptions?

  e. Which two sources corresponded to the lowest percentages?

  f. Which four sources corresponded to the largest terms in the calculated chi-square statistic?

12.48 Does whether or not a person has ears pierced tell us something about whether the person wears contacts, glasses, or neither?

  a. Use software to access the student survey data, and carry out a chi-square test for a relationship between the two variables; report the chi-square statistic.

  b. Report the *P*-value, which provides evidence that the variables *are* related.

  c. Which sampled group has a higher proportion wearing glasses: those who do or those who do not have ears pierced?

  d. Explain why gender is a possible confounding variable in the relationship between pierced ears and eyewear.

  e. Use software to separate data on ears pierced and eyewear for males and females. Report the *P*-value for females.

  f. State whether or not there is evidence that for females, having ears pierced or not is related to eyewear.

  g. Report the *P*-value for males.

  h. State whether or not there is evidence that for males, having ears pierced or not is related to eyewear.

*12.49 Does a student's gender tell us something about how likely he or she was to eat breakfast? Does gender tell us something about how likely a student was to carry a cell phone in 2003?

  a. Use software to access the student survey data, and carry out a chi-square test for a relationship between gender and eating breakfast or not. Report the chi-square statistic and the *P*-value. Who was more likely to eat breakfast—males or females?

  b. Next, test for a relationship between gender and carrying a cell phone or not. Report the chi-square statistic and the *P*-value. Who was more likely to carry a cell phone—males or females?

  c. Based on your answers to parts (a) and (b), who was more likely to eat breakfast—students who did or did not carry a cell phone? Use software to report proportions eating breakfast for students who did and did not carry a cell phone. Next report the *P*-value, and state whether or not the relationship is significant.

12.50 Does whether or not a student smokes tell us something about how likely he or she is to live on campus?

  a. Explain why students who smoke may be more likely to live off campus than students who don't smoke.

  b. Use software to access the student survey data, and carry out a chi-square test for a relationship between smoking and living on campus or not. Report the chi-square statistic and the *P*-value.

  c. State whether or not there is statistical evidence of a relationship.

  d. Is the sample proportion living off campus higher for the smokers?

  e. Suppose a claim is made that students who live on campus are less likely to eventually die of cancer. Tell whether or not you are willing to believe this claim, and why.

12.51 Is there evidence of a relationship between gender and whether a student is a vegetarian, non-vegetarian, or sometimes-vegetarian?

  a. Use software to access the student survey data, and carry out a chi-square test for a relationship between the two variables; report the chi-square statistic and the *P*-value.

  b. State whether or not there is statistical evidence of a relationship.

12.52 There is strong evidence of a relationship between gender and color preference. Use software to access the student survey data and carry out a chi-square test for a relationship; refer to the observed and expected counts, along with the size of the terms of the chi-square statistic, in order to answer the following:

a. Explain why there are 7 degrees of freedom in the chi-square test.

b. Which two colors in particular contribute to making the chi-square statistic large because these colors are preferred significantly more often by males than by females?

c. Which two colors in particular contribute to making the chi-square statistic large because these colors are preferred significantly more often by females than by males?

12.53 Is there evidence of a relationship between gender and whether a student is left-handed, right-handed, or ambidextrous?

a. Use software to access the student survey data, and carry out a chi-square test for a relationship between the two variables; report the chi-square statistic and the P-value.

b. Is there statistical evidence of a relationship?

12.54 "Stuck for Life: Will Today's Hottest Names Stay That Way?" reported in 2005 that vowel endings commonly denote female names.[38] Obtain a roster of first names of students in your statistics class, with each student classified as male or female. Classify each name as ending with a vowel or not. Check if the proportion ending with a vowel is higher for females than for males, then carry out a chi-square test to see if there is statistical evidence of a difference.

Discovering Research: TWO CATEGORICAL VARIABLES

12.55 Find a newspaper article or Internet report about a study that compares proportions or percentages for two or more populations, based on information from samples. (In other words, the study is about a general relationship between two categorical variables.) Explain whether there is reason to suspect bias because of samples not being representative of the larger population of interest.

Reporting on Research: TWO CATEGORICAL VARIABLES

12.56 Use results of Exercises 12.15, 12.30, and 12.31, along with relevant findings from the Internet, to make a report on side effects of drugs or supplements that relies on statistical information.

CHAPTER 13

Inference for Relationships between Two Quantitative Variables

Are ages of all students' mothers and fathers related—that is, in the general population of students, does father's age tell us something about mother's age?

© iStockphoto.com/Escaflowne

How good is this guess: Mom's candles equal 14.5 plus 0.666 times dad's candles?

Q→Q   This question typifies situations in which we are interested in the relationship between two quantitative variables, not simply for a sample but for an entire population.

In Section 5.3, we learned to display the relationship between two quantitative variables with a scatterplot and summarize it by reporting the form, direction, and strength. If the form appeared linear, then we made a much more specific summary by describing the relationship with the equation of a straight line, called the least squares regression line. We also used the correlation *r* to specify the direction and strength of the relationship. All of this was done for the *sample* of explanatory and response pairs only. We did not attempt to draw conclusions about how the explanatory and response variables were related in the entire *population* from which the sample was taken.

Now that we are familiar with the principles of statistical inference, our goal in this chapter is to use sample explanatory and response values to draw conclusions about how the variables are related for the population. It should go without saying that such conclusions will be meaningful only if the sample is truly representative of the larger population. As usual, all results are based on probability distributions, which tell us what we can expect from *random* behavior.

The first step in this inference process is an important one: Examine the scatterplot to decide if the form of the relationship really does appear linear.

If linearity seems to be a reasonable assumption, then we can use inference to draw conclusions about what the line should be like for the entire population, and also about how much spread there is around the line. The unknown *slope* of the line that best fits the entire population of points will turn out to be critical in drawing conclusions about a relationship between the two quantitative variables of interest.

13.1 Inference for Regression: Focus on the Slope of the Regression Line

In general, whether we are performing inference in the form of confidence intervals or hypothesis tests, the spread of a distribution plays a crucial role. In particular, when we perform inference for a relationship between two quantitative variables, the amount of spread around the regression line for our sample of points plays an important role in the extent to which we can draw conclusions about the unknown slope of the line that best fits the larger population.

We saw in Section 5.3 that the single statistic used to measure the spread of sample points about the regression line was s, the typical residual size, calculated as

$$s = \sqrt{\frac{(y_1 - \hat{y}_1)^2 + \cdots + (y_n - \hat{y}_n)^2}{n - 2}}$$

where the y_i are observed responses (in the scatterplot) and $\hat{y}_i$ are predicted responses (on the line). These residuals are seen in a scatterplot as vertical distances of observed points from the fitted regression line, because they measure errors in predicting responses $\hat{y}_i$ from given explanatory values. If points are tightly clustered around a line, s will be relatively small; if they are loosely scattered, it will be large. Furthermore, if s is small, we can better pinpoint what should be true about the unknown slope of the line that best summarizes the relationship for the larger population.

> **The Big Picture: A Closer Look**
>
> If a scatterplot's points seem to cluster around a curve rather than a straight line, then other options must be explored. In more advanced treatments of relationships between two quantitative variables, methods are presented for transforming variables so that the resulting relationship is linear. In this book, we will proceed no further if the relationship is nonlinear.

EXAMPLE 13.1 THE ROLE OF S IN INFERENCE ABOUT THE SLOPE

Background: The following plots display s as the typical residual size in two regression problems, both based on data from a sample of nine schools. For the regression on the left, we are using the average Verbal SAT score of all students in each school to predict the average Math SAT score. For the regression on the right, we are using the percentage of teachers with advanced degrees at each school to predict the average Math SAT score of its students.

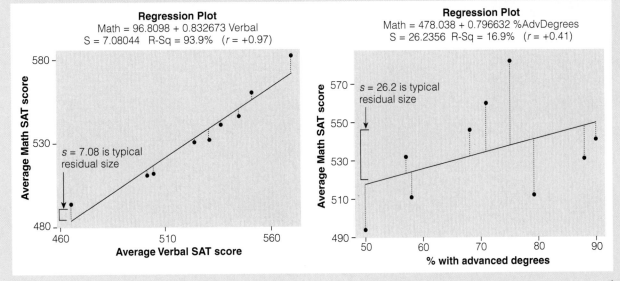

Continued

Question: For which relationship will we be better able to pinpoint the slope of the line that relates the two variables in the larger population of schools?

Response: The relationship between average Math and Verbal SATs is strong: The squared correlation R-Sq = 93.9% is close to 100%, and the points are tightly clustered around a line. The value of s, which measures the typical size of prediction error, is only about 7. In contrast, the relationship between average Math SAT and percentage of teachers with advanced degrees is weak, and the typical size of prediction error s is about 26. Clearly, we're in a better position to pinpoint the slope of the line for the larger population in the regression on the left, for Math and Verbal SATs.

Practice: *Try Exercise 13.1 on page 645.*

Conventional notation in regression can, unfortunately, be misleading. We can alert students to the fact that the letter *s* does *not* represent slope; nor does the letter *r* represent typical residual size.

Example TBP 13.1 on page 966 of the *Teaching the Big Picture* **(TBP)** *Supplement* guides students to first use their intuition to anticipate what sort of relationship would be expected for the ages of students' mothers and fathers.

The Big Picture:
A CLOSER LOOK

The typical size of sample prediction error is denoted capital S in the output.

The graphs in Example 13.1 should be kept in mind throughout this section whenever reference is made to typical residual size s, which may also be characterized as the spread about the regression line. Because we are now considering not just one but two quantitative variables, x and y, we denote their individual sample standard deviations as s_x and s_y. If there were absolutely no relationship between x and y, the regression line would be perfectly horizontal, and typical residual size s would equal s_y. As long as there is a relationship between the two variables, s should be less than s_y because information provided by the explanatory value x lets us be more precise in estimating y.

Setting the Stage: Summarizing a Relationship for Sampled Points

We consider now our opening question about the relationship between mother's age and father's age. These two variables are on equal footing in the sense that there is no obvious assignment of roles for explanatory and response variables. Arbitrarily, we phrased the question, "Does father's age tell us something about mother's age?" taking father's age as the explanatory variable. Before attempting to answer this question about the parents of the larger population of students, we should first determine what is true for the ages of parents of the sampled students.

EXAMPLE 13.2 WHAT DOES THE EXPLANATORY VARIABLE TELL US ABOUT THE RESPONSE VARIABLE FOR THE SAMPLE?

Background: Mother's age was regressed on father's age for a sample of several hundred students.

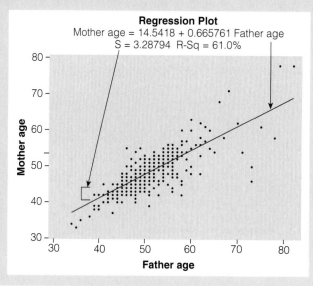

```
The regression equation is
MotherAge = 14.5418 + 0.665761 FatherAge
S = 3.28794        R-Sq = 61.0 %        R-Sq(adj) = 60.9 %
431 cases used 15 cases contain missing values
Predictor        Coef      SE Coef          T          P
Constant         14.542      1.317      11.05      0.000
FatherAge        0.66576     0.02571     25.89      0.000
Pearson correlation of FatherAge and MotherAge = 0.781
P-Value = 0.000
```

Question: What do the values of the slope (b_1), the intercept (b_0), and the typical residual size (s) tell us?

Response: The slope $b_1 = 0.665761$ tells us that as far as the sampled students are concerned, we predict one mother to be 0.666 years older than another if the father is 1 year older. The intercept $b_0 = 14.5418$ has little practical value because it doesn't make sense to predict the age of a student's mother when his or her father is zero years old. Technically, it is telling us that the line that best fits parents' age pairs for the sample of students crosses the y axis at about 14.5 years. The typical residual size $s = 3.28794$ tells us the typical error size when we use the regression line to predict mother's age for the sample of fathers' ages.

Practice: Try Exercise 13.2(d,f,h) on page 646.

Now that we have summarized the relationship between parents' ages for our *sample*, we are ready to go beyond the sample and think about the relationship for the larger *population* of students.

Distinguishing between Sample and Population Relationships

When we introduced the process of performing statistical inference about a single parameter (such as the population mean) based on a statistic (such as the sample mean), we acknowledged that although sample mean might be our best estimate for population mean, it is almost surely "off" by some amount. Similarly, although the least squares regression line is our best guess for the line that describes the relationship for the entire population, it is also probably "off" to some extent. In contrast to inference about a single parameter like the unknown population mean, when we perform inference about a relationship between two quantitative variables, there are actually three unknown parameters: slope, intercept, and spread. As always, proper notation is needed to distinguish these from the corresponding sample statistics.

Notation for Slope, Intercept, and Typical Residual Size for the Population Regression Line

The line that best fits the linear relationship between explanatory and response values for the population from which sample points were obtained has slope denoted β_1, intercept denoted β_0, and typical residual size denoted σ.

The *Big Picture:*

LOOKING AHEAD

You may have noticed that a *P*-value is always reported along with the correlation *r*, and that *t* statistics and *P*-values are included with the regression output. We will pay more attention to these once we have established a meaningful hypothesis test procedure in the regression context.

Students may perhaps wonder why *Mother age doesn't increase by a full year for every increase of one year in Father age:* As a student's father gets older, doesn't his or her mother have to age at exactly the same rate? It is important to recognize that ages are not being recorded as a time series, year by year for only one mother and father. Rather, we are thinking about an entire population of age pairs from which—at one point in time—we extract a sample of 431 *independent* age pairs. If one of these fathers is older than another by one year, then that mother may be older than the first mother, too, but not necessarily. On average, we expect her to be older than the first mother by about 0.666 years.

In the past, we have used σ to denote the standard deviation for a population of values of a single quantitative variable. When we consider the relationship between two quantitative variables x and y, we denote their individual standard deviations σ_x and σ_y, so there is no ambiguity when we denote the spread about the regression line as σ.

EXAMPLE 13.3 NOTATION FOR THE SLOPE, INTERCEPT, AND TYPICAL RESIDUAL SIZE IN A POPULATION RELATIONSHIP

Background: When George W. Bush ran against John Kerry in the 2004 presidential election, reporters speculated about each candidate's IQ, based on his SAT score.

Questions: How do we denote the standard deviation of all IQ scores and the standard deviation of all SAT scores? How do we denote the slope and intercept of the regression line that best fits the population of IQ and SAT scores? How do we denote the spread about this line?

Responses: Because reporters wanted to predict IQ based on SAT score, SAT score is the explanatory variable x and IQ the response y. Standard deviations are denoted σ_x for SAT score and σ_y for IQ. For the line that relates SAT score to IQ in general, the slope is denoted β_1 and the intercept is β_0. The spread is denoted σ.

How well can we estimate candidates' IQs based on their SATs?

Practice: Try Exercise 13.2(e,g,i,j) on page 646.

> *The Big Picture:*
> **A CLOSER LOOK**
>
> George Bush's SAT score was higher than John Kerry's by a few points, so the midpoint of his IQ interval estimate would be higher. However, because the relationship between SAT and IQ is far from perfect, the spread s is substantial and their intervals would overlap quite a bit. Thus, either candidate could easily have had the higher IQ.

In the next example, we contrast slope, intercept, and residual size for the sample and for the population.

EXAMPLE 13.4 SLOPE, INTERCEPT, AND SPREAD FOR A SAMPLE OR FOR THE POPULATION

Background: Mother's age was regressed on father's age for a sample of 446 students, resulting in a regression line with slope $b_1 = 0.666$, intercept $b_0 = 14.542$, and typical residual size $s = 3.288$.

Question: What can we say about the slope, intercept, and residual size for the line that best fits ages of mothers versus fathers for the entire population from which the sample of students was taken?

Response:

■ First of all, we only know the slope $b_1 = 0.666$ of the line that best fits our *sample*. The line that best fits the entire *population* may have more or less slope. We use β_1 to denote the unknown slope of the population regression line. The next graph shows that other slopes are plausible candidates for β_1.

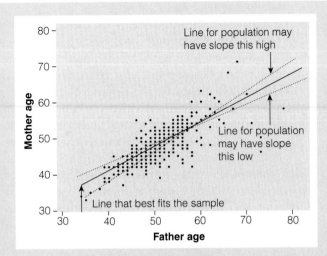

■ Next, we only know the intercept $b_0 = 14.542$ of the least squares line fitted from the *sample*. The line that best fits the entire *population* has an unknown intercept β_0. There is a whole range of plausible values for β_0, resulting in lines that may be lower or higher than the line constructed from our sample.

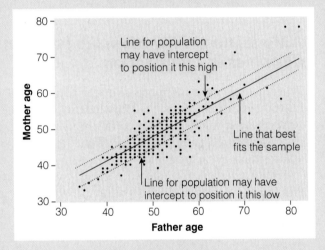

■ Thirdly, the typical size of the $n = 431$ residuals for our sample (from which 15 students with missing data have been excluded) is reported in the regression output to be $s = 3.288$. The spread σ about the population regression line for *all* age pairs is unknown. The population may exhibit less spread than what is seen in our sample, or more.

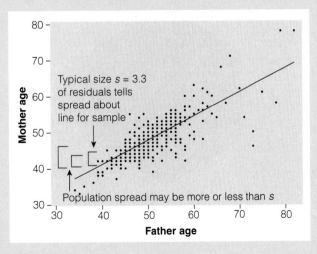

Practice: *Try Exercise 13.2(k) on page 646.*

When inference methods were first introduced in Chapter 9, we learned about three basic forms of inference: point estimates, confidence intervals, and hypothesis tests. For practical purposes, it is usually enough to use b_0 as a point estimate for the unknown intercept β_0 of the population regression line, and s as a point estimate for the unknown spread σ about the population regression line. Because of the special role played by the slope in the relationship between two quantitative variables, we will not merely use b_1 as a point estimate for the unknown slope β_1 for the population. Rather, we will go beyond the point estimate to carry out a hypothesis test about β_1 and to estimate it with a confidence interval.

Because the relationship between two quantitative variables is a fairly complex situation, various forms of inference can be carried out depending on what kinds of questions we want to answer. Arguably the most important of all the regression inference procedures is a hypothesis test to see if the slope of the regression line for the larger population could be zero. If we do not have convincing evidence that the slope is non-zero, then there is no convincing evidence that the so-called explanatory and response variables are truly related, and so other forms of inference are beside the point. Therefore, as we consider how the interplay between two quantitative variables in the population relates to their interplay in a sample, we will pay particular attention to the behavior of sample slope b_1 as a random variable, to see what it can tell us about the slope β_1 in the population.

A Model for the Relationship between Two Quantitative Variables in a Population

When we perform inference about a relationship in the larger population, we make "educated guesses," acknowledging that the exact truth remains unknown. Nevertheless, we begin with certain underlying assumptions about the relationship in the population. As always, the data should be checked to verify that these assumptions are reasonable.

Before performing inference about the population proportion in Chapter 9 and the population mean in Chapter 10, we took a great deal of care in Chapter 8 to think about the behavior of sample proportion relative to population proportion, and sample mean relative to population mean. Similar considerations will be helpful now, so that we can grasp the workings of the process of inference for regression. We can imagine a large population of explanatory and response values—ages of all students' fathers and mothers—from which a random sample is taken.

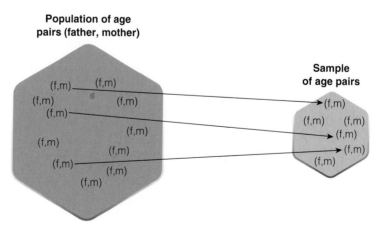

Intuitively, it makes sense that if the ages are related linearly in the population, they should also be related more or less linearly in the sample. If a certain slope β_1 holds for the population, then the slope b_1 in the sample should be in the same ballpark. Similarly, if a certain intercept β_0 holds for the population, then the intercept b_0 for the sample should be somewhere in that vicinity. Also, if responses for the entire population are spread about the line with some standard deviation σ, then the sample standard deviation s should be similar.

The behavior of statistics like sample slope b_1 in random samples taken from the larger population of explanatory/response pairs is perfectly predictable as long as the population relationship meets certain requirements. As we stated at the beginning of this chapter, the relationship must be linear. In addition, responses should vary normally about the population regression line with a constant standard deviation σ. The following graph is an oversimplification of the situation, in that it shows only 20 normally distributed Mother ages for each Father's age, instead of an infinite number. Likewise, the idealized model assumes Father ages to follow a (continuous) normal distribution, instead of just taking whole even-numbered age values as shown. Otherwise, it is a fair representation of how we imagine the population relationship between ages: It is positive and linear, with constant spread σ of points about the regression line following a normal pattern.

Population relationship expressed as $\mu_y = \beta_0 + \beta_1 x$

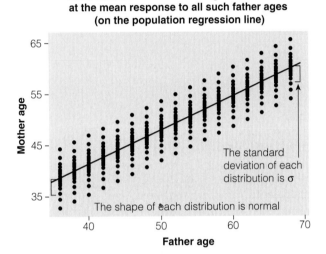

Each distribution of mother ages is centered at the mean response to all such father ages (on the population regression line)

Notice that a new symbol, μ_y, has been used to model the relationship in the larger population. Because statistics concerns itself with drawing conclusions about populations, based on samples, we must always be sure to distinguish between parameters (describing populations) and statistics (describing samples). In the case of a regression line, we have already used the notation $\hat{y}$ to refer to the response predicted for the sample: $\hat{y} = b_0 + b_1 x$, where b_0 and b_1 are calculated from the sample data. The corresponding parameter is $\mu_y = \beta_0 + \beta_1 x$, the unknown population mean response to a given explanatory value x.

Independence of the observations from one another is an additional condition for our inference procedure methods to yield accurate results, and the sampling process should always be considered in case there may be a violation of this condition.

EXAMPLE 13.5 REGRESSION INFERENCE REQUIRES INDEPENDENCE

Background: Suppose we look at the relationship between male students' heights and weights.

Question: Would methods developed in this chapter apply if our data consisted of height and weight measurements for the same student recorded each month over several years' time?

Continued

Response: No; the data must consist of height/weight pairs obtained randomly and independently from a population of male students.

Practice: *Try Exercise 13.6 on page 648.*

Whether we perform inference in the form of hypothesis tests or interval estimates, we must first check if we are justified in making the needed assumptions discussed above.

Guidelines for Regression Inference

Inference for regression should be carried out only if the following conditions are met:

- the scatterplot appears linear
- the sample size is large enough to offset any non-normality in the response values
- the spread of responses is fairly constant over the range of explanatory values
- the explanatory/response pairs are randomly selected and independent of one another

The Distribution of Sample Slope b₁

As always, we report the long-run behavior of a sample statistic by describing its distribution, specifically by telling its center, spread, and shape. If the above-mentioned requirements are met, then we can assert the following about the center, spread, and shape of the distribution of sample slope b_1:

- **Center:** The slope b_1 of the least squares line for repeated random samples of explanatory/response pairs has a mean equal to the unknown slope β_1 of the least squares line for the population.
- **Spread:** The standard deviation of sample slope b_1 is

$$\sigma_{b_1} = \frac{\sigma}{\sqrt{(x_1 - \overline{x})^2 + \cdots + (x_n - \overline{x})^2}}$$

Note that the quantity $\sqrt{(x_1 - \overline{x})^2 + \cdots + (x_n - \overline{x})^2}$, which appears in the denominator, involves *combined* squared distances of explanatory values from their mean. This quantity will be larger for larger sample sizes, so b_1 has less spread for larger samples. Again, our intuition tells us that we should be better able to pinpoint the unknown population slope β_1 if we obtain a sample slope from a larger sample.

which we estimate with the standard error of b_1,

$$SE_{b_1} = \frac{s}{\sqrt{(x_1 - \overline{x})^2 + \cdots + (x_n - \overline{x})^2}}$$

where s, the estimate for spread σ about the population regression line, measures typical residual size.

Although the above formula need not be used for calculations as long as software is available, it is worth examining SE_{b_1} to see how the residuals contribute to the spread of the distribution of sample slope. The appearance of s in the numerator of SE_{b_1} should make perfect intuitive sense: If the residuals as a group are small, then there is very little spread about the line, and we should be able to pinpoint its slope fairly precisely. Conversely, if the residuals are large, then there is much spread about the line and there is a much wider range of plausible slopes. This reinforces the conclusions we reached in Example 13.1 on page 629.

- **Shape:** Finally, b_1 itself has a normal shape if the residuals are normal, or if the sample size is large enough to offset non-normality of the residuals.

The graph below depicts what we have established about the distribution of sample slope b_1 for large enough sample sizes: It is centered at the population slope β_1, has approximate standard deviation SE_{b_1}, and follows a normal distribution.

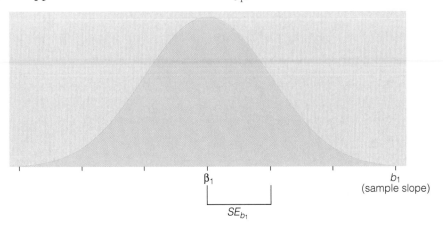

The **Big Picture:**
A CLOSER LOOK

To make the idea of the distribution of sample slope b_1 more concrete, you can picture taking repeated random samples from the population of mothers' and fathers' ages, as depicted on page 635. The relationship between mothers' and fathers' ages for different samples can have different slopes b_1 that are more or less close to the slope β_1 for the population of age pairs. SE_{b_1} estimates the extent to which these sampled slopes vary about β_1.

The Distribution of Standardized Sample Slope t

Recall that in Chapter 10, when we standardized the sample mean using the sample standard deviation s instead of the unknown population standard deviation σ, the resulting random variable $\frac{\bar{x} - \mu}{s/\sqrt{n}}$ followed a t distribution instead of z. In this section, we standardize the sample slope b_1 using SE_{b_1}, calculated from s because σ is unknown. The resulting standardized slope

$$t = \frac{b_1 - \beta_1}{SE_{b_1}}$$

follows a t distribution, and its degrees of freedom are $n - 2$.

> *Definition*   The **regression degrees of freedom** for performing inference about a quantitative response based on a single quantitative explanatory variable are $n - 2$, where the data consist of n pairs of explanatory and response values.

EXAMPLE 13.6 REGRESSION DEGREES OF FREEDOM

Background: Mean Math SAT score was regressed on percentage of teachers with advanced degrees for a sample of 9 schools.

Question: How many degrees of freedom apply?

Response: The regression degrees of freedom are $n - 2 = 9 - 2 = 7$.

Practice: *Try Exercise 13.8(b) on page 648.*

Remember that the t distribution is quite similar to that of z, especially for larger samples. The distribution of standardized sample slope is displayed at the top of page 638: It is centered at zero as is any t distribution. Its standard deviation is subject to the degrees of freedom, which are determined by the sample size (in particular, the standard deviation is close to 1 if the sample size is large enough to make t roughly the same as z). Like any t distribution, it is bell-shaped with heavier tails than z.

For a single variable x, $n - 1$ of the deviations of sampled values from their mean $\bar{x}$ vary freely; the nth is determined by those $n - 1$ values because they all must sum to zero. For the relationship between two variables x and y, $n - 2$ of the deviations of sampled points from the regression line vary freely. This is why we divide by $n - 2$ when we calculate s, and why our regression degrees of freedom are $n - 2$.

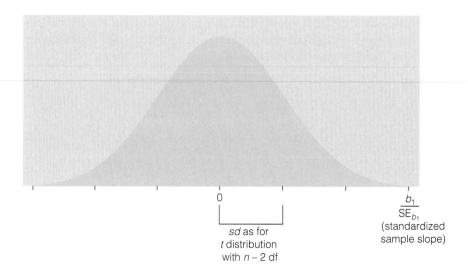

Now that we know more about the behavior of b_1 relative to β_1, and can put its size in perspective by standardizing, we will make use of the critical role played by β_1 in the relationship between explanatory and response variables, so as to set up a test for evidence of a relationship in the larger population.

Hypothesis Test about the Population Slope with t: A Clue about the Relationship

Knowing enough about the distribution of sample slope relative to population slope will help us find the answer to our earlier question about the relationship between parents' ages. Thus, we are ready to begin the process of statistical inference to draw conclusions about the relationship between two quantitative variables in a larger population, based on sample data about those variables.

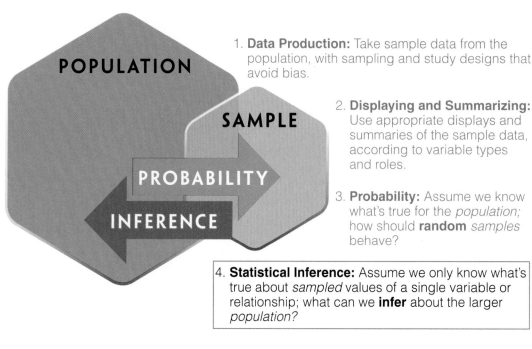

1. **Data Production:** Take sample data from the population, with sampling and study designs that avoid bias.

2. **Displaying and Summarizing:** Use appropriate displays and summaries of the sample data, according to variable types and roles.

3. **Probability:** Assume we know what's true for the *population;* how should **random** *samples* behave?

4. **Statistical Inference:** Assume we only know what's true about *sampled* values of a single variable or relationship; what can we **infer** about the larger *population?*

As we saw in our other chapters on inference for relationships, the most important inference procedure is designed to determine whether or not those variables are related in the larger population from which our sample originated. Thus, a hypothesis test typically takes precedence over a confidence interval.

As with our other hypothesis test procedures about the relationship between two variables, there are two formulations of the null and alternative hypotheses: one about the variables and their relationship; the other about a key parameter. As always, the null hypothesis H_0 claims that the variables are *not* related and the alternative H_a claims that they *are* related. When there are two quantitative variables of interest, H_0 states that the slope β_1 of the least squares line for the population is zero. This is equivalent to claiming that the mean population response does not depend on the so-called explanatory variable x: for $\beta_1 = 0$, we have

$$\mu_y = \beta_0 + \beta_1 x = \beta_0 + 0(x) = \beta_0$$

The alternative may be one-sided or two-sided. The two-sided alternative, $\beta_1 \neq 0$, is equivalent to the statement that the variables *are* related in the population. The one-sided alternatives $\beta_1 > 0$ or $\beta_1 < 0$ are more specific in that they express a claim not only that the variables are related, but also with regard to the direction of the purported relationship. To determine which formulation is appropriate, the wording and background of a problem must be carefully considered.

We have already established that the distribution of sample slope b_1, if certain conditions are met, is normal with a mean of β_1 and an approximate standard deviation of SE_{b_1}. Under the null hypothesis that $\beta_1 = 0$, the standardized test statistic

$$t = \frac{b_1 - 0}{SE_{b_1}}$$

follows a t distribution with $n - 2$ degrees of freedom. If the sample slope b_1 is relatively close to zero (taking sample size and spread into account), then the standardized test statistic t is not especially large. Consequently, the P-value is not small, and there is no compelling evidence of a non-zero population slope β_1. Thus, if the slope b_1 is too shallow, we cannot produce evidence that the two quantitative variables are related in the larger population.

Conversely, if the sample slope b_1 is relatively far from zero, then t is large in absolute value, the P-value is small, and we have statistical evidence that the population slope β_1 is *not* zero. In other words, a steep sample slope results in a small P-value and a conclusion that the variables *are* related.

Example TBP 13.2 on page 966 of the *TBP Supplement* explores the regression hypotheses in three different contexts.

Sample slope b_1 close to zero

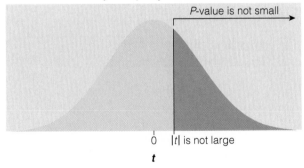

Sample slope b_1 far from zero

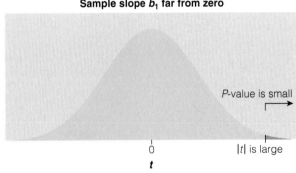

EXAMPLE 13.7 A HYPOTHESIS TEST ABOUT THE SLOPE OF THE REGRESSION LINE FOR A POPULATION

Background: Let's revisit the output for the regression of mother's age on father's age, which includes t statistics and P-values.

```
Predictor          Coef     SE Coef        T        P
Constant         14.542       1.317    11.05    0.000
FatherAge       0.66576     0.02571    25.89    0.000
Pearson correlation of FatherAge and MotherAge = 0.781
```

Continued

Question: What do our opposing hypotheses claim, and which one do the data suggest is true?

Response: The null hypothesis states that the slope β_1 of the line that relates mother's age to father's age in the population is zero. Equivalently, it states that mother's age and father's age are not related in the larger population. Common sense would suggest a positive relationship between the two variables, so our alternative hypothesis would be that $\beta_1 > 0$.

Since our inference procedure hinges on the slope of the regression line, we focus on the *second* row of the regression table, which starts with the slope $b_1 = 0.66576$ of the line that best fits the sampled points. Next comes its standard error, $SE_{b_1} = 0.02571$, which estimates how much slopes from a sample tend to vary about the unknown slope for the population.

The standardized sample slope is

$$t = \frac{b_1 - 0}{SE_{b_1}} = \frac{0.66576 - 0}{0.02571} = 25.89.$$

The *P*-value, 0.000, corresponds to a two-sided alternative. The *P*-value for our one-sided alternative is half the size, still 0.000. At any rate, it is small enough to reject the null hypothesis and conclude the alternative: $\beta_1 > 0$. Thus, we have strong statistical evidence of a positive relationship between parents' ages, not just in our sample, but also in the larger population of students.

Practice: *Try Exercise 13.8(d,e) on page 648.*

Motivated by the example above, we summarize the process of testing for a relationship between two quantitative variables, by testing the null hypothesis that the slope of the regression line for the population of explanatory and response values is zero.

> ## Hypothesis Test for a Relationship between Two Quantitative Variables
>
> 0. We formulate $H_0 : \beta_1 = 0$ versus $H_a : \beta_1 \neq 0$ about the slope β_1 of the population least squares regression line. Equivalently, H_0 claims the two variables are not related, and H_a claims that they are related. More specific one-sided alternatives can be formulated as $H_a : \beta_1 < 0$ or $H_a : \beta_1 > 0$.
>
> 1. The test should be carried out only if the guidelines on page 636 are followed.
>
> 2. Software should be used to produce the standardized sample slope $t = \frac{b_1 - 0}{SE_{b_1}}$, which follows a t distribution with $n - 2$ degrees of freedom.
>
> 3. The *P*-value to accompany the t test statistic is the probability of a t random variable being as extreme as the one observed, assuming H_0 is true. It is reported alongside the standardized slope t as part of the regression output.
>
> 4. If the *P*-value is small, we reject the null hypothesis and conclude that the variables are related in the larger population. Otherwise, we continue to believe that the null hypothesis may be true.

In Example 13.7, not only did we have strong evidence of a relationship (by virtue of the *P*-value being close to zero), but we also could assert that the relationship was fairly strong (by virtue of the correlation *r* being 0.78, which is fairly close to one). It is nevertheless possible to produce weak evidence of a strong relationship, or strong evidence of a weak relationship. These possibilities will be explored in the following examples. We will also consider an example where there is no statistical evidence of a relationship in the larger population. Note that sample size does not affect the strength of a relationship, but it can play an important role in the strength of our evidence that a relationship exists in the larger population.

EXAMPLE 13.8 WEAK EVIDENCE OF A STRONG RELATIONSHIP

Background: While most voters in a presidential election vote for the Democratic or Republican candidate, other parties do account for a small percentage of the popular vote in each state. This table looks at the relationship between percentages voting Democratic and Republican in the year 2000 for just a few states.

State	Democratic	Republican
Alabama	48.4	47.9
California	53.4	41.7
Ohio	46.4	50.0
Minnesota	47.9	45.5

The points in the scatterplot below do appear to cluster around some straight line, rather than a curve. The line has a negative slope because when the percentage voting Republican is low, the percentage voting Democratic is high, and vice versa. Part of the regression output is also shown.

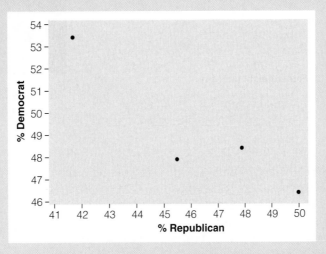

```
Pearson correlation of Democratic and Republican = −0.922
P-Value = 0.078
```

Question: What can we say about the relationship between the percentage voting Democratic and the percentage voting Republican for the population of 50 states?

Response: The fact that $r = -0.922$ is close to -1 suggests a strong negative relationship. On the other hand, the *P*-value (0.078) may not necessarily be considered small enough to provide statistical evidence of a relationship. Due to the small sample size (only 4), we do not have especially strong evidence of a relationship in the larger population of states, even though for the sample the relationship is apparently quite strong. In other words, we have *weak evidence of a strong relationship* between the percentage voting Republican and the percentage voting Democratic. A larger sample of states would have certainly supplied very strong evidence of such a relationship.

Practice: *Try Exercise 13.10 on page 649.*

In Example 13.8, we saw that although a linear relationship between two quantitative variables may be quite strong, with too small a sample we may only produce weak evidence of that relationship. In the next example, we see that with a large sample we may produce very strong evidence of a rather weak relationship in the population.

EXAMPLE 13.9 STRONG EVIDENCE OF A WEAK RELATIONSHIP

Background: In Section 5.3, we contrasted the rather strong relationship between mother's age and father's age with the relatively weak relationship between mother's height and father's height. A scatterplot for the latter is shown, followed by regression output.

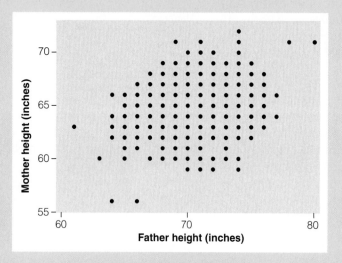

Is height a factor in couples' compatibility?

```
Pearson correlation of MomHT and DadHT = 0.225
The regression equation is
MomHT = 50.4 + 0.200 DadHT
431 cases used 15 cases contain missing values
Predictor          Coef      SE Coef          T        P
Constant         50.431        2.936      17.18    0.000
DadHT           0.20019       0.04178       4.79    0.000
S = 2.551       R-Sq = 5.1%        R-Sq(adj) = 4.9%
```

Question: What can we say about the relationship between mother's height and father's height for the population of students?

Response: Based on the appearance of the scatterplot and the value of r, there is apparently a slight tendency for relatively short fathers to be paired with relatively short mothers, and for relatively tall fathers to be paired with relatively tall mothers. Because height is such a minor factor when it comes to couples' compatibility, the relationship is naturally quite weak.

On the other hand, a test of whether the slope of the regression line could be zero for the general population of parents' heights produced a very large t statistic (4.79) and a very small P-value (0.000).

In this case, by virtue of a large sample (431 height pairs), we are able to produce very strong evidence of a relationship in the general population of parents' heights, but the relationship itself is rather weak.

Practice: *Try Exercise 13.12 on page 649.*

When we are testing the hypothesis that the mean of a single quantitative variable equals a certain proposed value, the sample mean almost always differs from that proposed value, even if the value is the correct one. Similarly, the sample correlation almost always differs from zero, even if the correlation for the population relationship really is zero. Before we take the value of the correlation r in the regression output too seriously, we should always pay attention to the P-value for testing whether or not there is statistical evidence of a relationship in the population.

Students Talk Stats

No Evidence of a Relationship

A website called "ratemyprofessors.com" reports students' ratings of their professors at universities around the country. These ratings are unofficial in that they are not monitored by the universities themselves. Besides listing average rating of the professors' teaching on a scale of 1 to 5, where 1 is the worst and 5 is the best, there is also a rating of how easy their courses are, where 1 is the hardest and 5 is the easiest.

Four students are discussing the relationship between the rating of professors and the rating of how easy their courses are, given the scatterplot and regression output for a random sample of 23 professors (all at the same university).

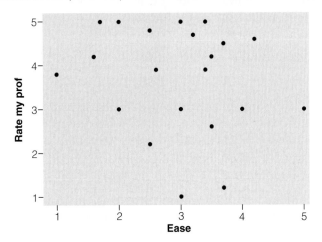

```
Pearson correlation of RateMyProf and Ease = −0.239
P-Value = 0.273
```

Adam: *"I knew r would be negative. I always give higher ratings to the professors if their courses are easy."*

Brittany: *"But the scale is going the other way, so a negative correlation means higher ratings of the professors tend to go with harder course ratings. I guess the best professors demand more of their students."*

Carlos: *"Brittany's right, but the relationship is really weak. You can tell from looking at the scatterplot, and because r is much closer to zero than to negative one."*

Dominique: *"But the P-value is 0.273, which isn't small at all, so there's no evidence that the relationship would hold in the larger population of professors' ratings. Overall, the ratings from students like Adam are probably cancelled out by ratings from students who appreciate good teaching, even if the course may be harder."*

Practice: *Try Exercise 13.13(b) on page 649.*

Pages 967–969 of the **TBP** *Supplement* go into more depth about constructing a confidence interval for the unknown slope of the regression line that best fits the relationship in a population.

Dominique takes the right approach, considering not just the correlation but also the *P*-value. It suggests that the overall ratings of teaching and ease could easily be unrelated, and we just happened to see a slightly negative relationship in our sample.

Confidence Interval for the Slope of the Population Regression Line

A 95% confidence interval for β_1 is constructed in the usual way, as

$$\text{estimate} \pm \text{margin of error.}$$

The estimate is of course b_1, and the margin of error is a multiple of the standard error SE_{b_1}, where the multiplier is the value of the relevant t distribution that corresponds to a symmetric area of 95%. We have already established that sample slope b_1 follows the t distribution with $n - 2$ degrees of freedom.

95% Confidence Interval for Slope β_1

If β_1 is the unknown slope of the regression line that relates x and y values in the population of interest, a 95% confidence interval for β_1 is

$$b_1 \pm \text{multiplier}(\text{SE}_{b_1})$$

where the multiplier comes from the t distribution with $n - 2$ degrees of freedom. Here b_1 is the slope of the line that best fits the sample of n points, and its estimated standard deviation is SE_{b_1}.

If n is large, the interval is approximately

$$b_1 \pm 2(\text{SE}_{b_1}).$$

This interval is appropriate only if the guidelines on page 636 are met.

EXAMPLE 13.10 EXAMINING A CONFIDENCE INTERVAL FOR THE SLOPE OF THE REGRESSION LINE

Background: Example 13.1 on page 629 looked at two regression problems, both based on data from a sample of 9 schools. For the regression on the left, we used the average Verbal SAT score of all students in each school to predict the average Math SAT score. For the regression on the right, we used the percentage of teachers with advanced degrees at each school to predict the average Math SAT score

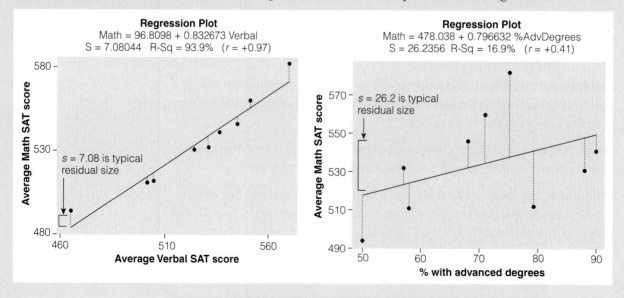

Regression Plot
Math = 96.8098 + 0.832673 Verbal
S = 7.08044 R-Sq = 93.9% (*r* = +0.97)

s = 7.08 is typical residual size

Regression Plot
Math = 478.038 + 0.796632 %AdvDegrees
S = 26.2356 R-Sq = 16.9% (*r* = +0.41)

s = 26.2 is typical residual size

of its students. Regression output is shown below, first for the regression on average Verbal scores, then for the regression on percentage with advanced degrees. The t multiplier for 95% confidence and 7 degrees of freedom, according to software or tables, is 2.365.

Predictor	Coef	SE Coef	T	P
Constant	96.81	42.04	2.30	0.055
Verbal	0.83	0.08	10.42	0.000

Predictor	Coef	SE Coef	T	P
Constant	478.04	47.99	9.96	0.000
%AdvDegr	0.80	0.67	1.19	0.272

Questions: Using 0.83 as b_1 and 0.08 as SE_{b_1}, what is a 95% confidence interval for the slope of the line relating average Math and *Verbal SAT* scores for the larger population of schools?

Using 0.80 as b_1 and 0.67 as SE_{b_1}, what is a 95% confidence interval for the slope of the line relating average Math and *percentage of teachers with advanced degrees* for the larger population of schools?

Are the confidence intervals consistent with the reported P-values?

Responses: The first interval, for the slope of the line relating all schools' average Math SAT score to their average Verbal SAT score, is $0.83 \pm 2.365(0.08) = (0.64, 1.02)$.

The second interval, relating all schools' average Math SAT score to their percentage of teachers with advanced degrees, is $0.80 \pm 2.365(0.67) = (-0.78, 2.38)$.

The first interval does *not* contain zero, which is consistent with the P-value 0.000 that is small enough to reject the hypothesis that $\beta_1 = 0$. The second interval *does* contain zero, which is consistent with the P-value 0.272 that is not small enough to reject the hypothesis that $\beta_1 = 0$.

Practice: *Try Exercise 13.15(b) on page 650.*

As we anticipated in Example 13.1 on page 629, we are better able to pinpoint the slope of the line for the larger population in the regression on the left, for Math and Verbal SATs. For this relationship, we have a narrow confidence interval for β_1 and a small P-value, thanks to the small amount of spread about the regression line, $s = 7.08$.

EXERCISES FOR SECTION 13.1

Inference for Regression: Focus on the Slope of the Regression Line

Note: Asterisked numbers indicate exercises whose answers are provided in the Solutions to Selected Exercises section, on page 689.

*13.1 A report on Southwest Airlines in 2004 looked at number of daily departures from various airports, along with number of gates at those airports and the year in which the airline was established at that particular airport.

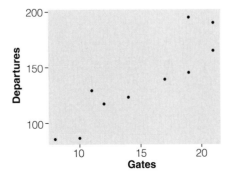
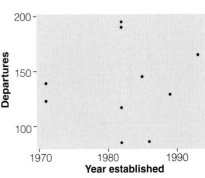

For which regression are we in a better position to pinpoint the slope of the regression line that relates the variables in general: for departures versus gates (on the left) or for departures versus year established (on the right)?

*13.2 "GOP Warns Democrats They'll Face Probes, Too," describes Republicans' reactions to accusations in 2005 that House Majority Leader Tom DeLay unethically accepted travel money from lobbyists. The article published a list of 39 trips between January 2000 and March 2005 financed by private interests for a state's members of Congress, including the length of travel (in days) and the dollar amount paid.[1] Output is shown for regression of dollar amount paid on trip length.

```
The regression equation is
Dollars = - 683 + 1176 Days
Predictor          Coef      SE Coef          T          P
Constant         -682.7        981.8      -0.70      0.491
Days             1175.9        164.2       7.16      0.000
S = 3401        R-Sq = 58.1%      R-Sq(adj) = 57.0%
Pearson correlation of Days and Dollars = 0.762
```

a. Explain why it would be natural for the relationship between days and dollars to be positive.

b. Is the opposite assignment of roles (dollars paid is explanatory and trip length is response) equally reasonable?

c. What amount do you predict would be paid for a 1-day trip?

d. What is the typical size of a prediction error for the sample?

e. How do we denote the typical size of a prediction error for the population: b_0, b_1, s, $\hat{y}$, β_0, β_1, σ, μ_y, or r?

f. How how much more money tended to be paid for each additional day traveled by the sample of congressional representatives?

g. Which of these is the correct notation for your answer to part (f): b_0, b_1, s, $\hat{y}$, β_0, β_1, σ, μ_y, or r?

h. How do we interpret the line's intercept?

i. How do we denote the intercept of the line that best fits the sample?

j. How do we denote the intercept of the corresponding line for the population?

k. Assume the data to be a representative sample taken from the population of all representatives' trip lengths and dollar amounts paid. Which of these may be different for the population as opposed to the sample: slope of the regression line, intercept of the regression line, spread around the regression line, all of these, or none of these?

l. Does the correlation suggest that the relationship is very weak, moderately weak, moderate, moderately strong, or very strong?

13.3 Refer to Exercise 13.2 on the relationship between trip length and amount paid for travel by a state's congressional representatives in the years 2000 to 2005.

a. Which one of the following conditions for the regression model is not necessarily met, based on the appearance of the histograms?

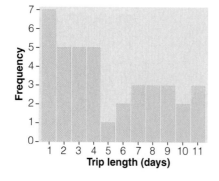
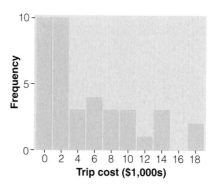

1. Scatterplot should appear linear.
2. Sample size should be large enough to offset non-normality in responses.
3. Spread of responses should appear fairly constant over the range of explanatory values.
4. Explanatory/response values should constitute a random sample of independent pairs.

b. Which one of the four conditions listed in part (a) is not necessarily met, based on the fact that there is less scatter for shorter trips and more for longer trips?

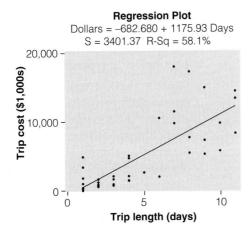

Regression Plot
Dollars = –682.680 + 1175.93 Days
S = 3401.37 R-Sq = 58.1%

13.4 The Quantitative Environmental Learning Project presented data on height and circumference of a sample of Douglas fir trees.[2] Notice that heights level off after circumferences exceed about 4 meters.

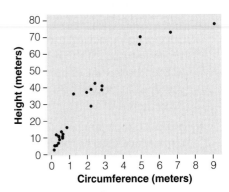

Which one of the following conditions for a regression model is not met:

a. Scatterplot should appear linear.

b. Sample size should be large enough to offset non-normality in responses.

c. Spread of responses should appear fairly constant over the range of explanatory values.

d. Explanatory/response values should constitute a random sample of independent pairs.

13.5 The Quantitative Environmental Learning Project reported widths and lengths (in centimeters) of a sample of 88 Puget Sound butter clams.[3] Output is shown for the regression of length on width.

```
Pearson correlation of Width and Length = 0.989
The regression equation is
Length = 0.257 + 1.22 Width
Predictor          Coef       SE Coef              T          P
Constant        0.25689      0.09293           2.76      0.007
Width           1.22013      0.01940          62.89      XXXXX
S = 0.3253       R-Sq = 97.9%      R-Sq(adj) = 97.8%
```

a. Explain why it would be natural for the relationship between length and width to be positive.

b. Is the opposite assignment of roles (length is explanatory and width is response) also reasonable?

c. If one clam is a centimeter wider than another clam, how much longer do you predict it to be?

d. Which of these is the correct notation for the number 0.257 seen in the regression equation?: $b_0, b_1, s, \hat{y}, \beta_0, \beta_1, \sigma, \mu_y$, or r?

e. What length do you predict for a clam that is 2 centimeters wide?

f. What is the typical size of a prediction error for the sample?

g. How do we denote typical vertical distance of clam length from the regression line for the population of all butter clams: $b_0, b_1, s, \hat{y}, \beta_0, \beta_1, \sigma, \mu_y$, or r?

h. Assume the data to be a representative sample taken from the population of all Puget Sound butter clams, with b_0, b_1, and s as reported in the output. Which of these do we know exactly for the population: β_0, β_1, σ, or all of these, or none of these?

   i. Does the correlation suggest that the relationship is very weak, moderately weak, moderate, moderately strong, or very strong?

   j. Does the reported value of the correlation tell the strength of the relationship in the sample or in the population?

   k. How many degrees of freedom hold for performing inference about the slope of the regression line for the larger population of butter clams?

   l. Suppose that the relationship between length and width of Puget Sound butter clams was *not* representative of the relationship for the larger population of all butter clams. Which of these (either, both, or neither) would be the case: the distribution of sample slope b_1 would still be centered at population slope β_1, or the distribution of standardized sample slope "t" would still be centered at zero?

   m. Suppose we wanted to use the same data set (butter clam widths and lengths) to set up a confidence interval to estimate how much longer than wide butter clams tend to be. Would the appropriate procedure be paired t, two-sample t, several-sample F, chi-square, or regression?

   n. The P-value has been X-ed out; use the size of the t statistic to get an idea of the size of the P-value, and conclude one of the following: $\beta_1 = 0$, $\beta_1 \neq 0$, $b_1 = 0$, or $b_1 \neq 0$.

*13.6 Consider the relationship between length and width of Puget Sound butter clams discussed in Exercise 13.5. Which one of the following conditions for a regression model is certainly not met if researchers repeatedly recorded the width and length of the same butter clam over the course of its lifetime (up to 20 years)?

   a. Scatterplot should appear linear.

   b. Sample size should be large enough to offset non-normality in responses.

   c. Spread of responses should appear fairly constant over the range of explanatory values.

   d. Explanatory/response values should constitute a random sample of independent pairs.

13.7 Consider the relationship between length and width of Puget Sound butter clams discussed in Exercise 13.5. Which one of the four conditions in Exercise 13.6 is more or less guaranteed to be met, based on what we know about the natural behavior of physical characteristics of living things?

*13.8 Exercise 13.2 on page 646 considers 39 trips between January 2000 and March 2005 financed by private interests for a state's members of Congress, including the length of travel (in days) and the dollar amount paid.

   a. Does the reported value of the correlation (0.762) tell the strength of the relationship in the sample or in the population?

   b. How many degrees of freedom hold for performing inference about the slope of the regression line for the larger population of representatives' trips?

   c. Suppose that for some reason, the relationship between travel length and amount paid for representatives in this particular state were not representative of the relationship for the larger population of representatives. Which of these (either, both, or neither) would be the case: The distribution of sample slope b_1 would not be centered at population slope β_1, or the distribution of standardized sample slope "t" would not be centered at zero?

   d. Which P-value—the first one (0.491) or the second one (0.000)—is relevant to test the null hypothesis that slope β_1 of the population regression line equals zero?

   e. Which *two* of these can be concluded from the size of the P-value?

     1. The slope of the regression line for the population may be zero.

     2. There is evidence that the slope of the regression line for the population is not zero.

     3. Length of travel and amount paid are not necessarily related for the larger population of representatives.

     4. There is evidence that length of travel and amount paid are related for the larger population of representatives.

*13.9 Which alternative hypothesis would make the most sense in performing inference about the relationship between representatives' trip lengths and amounts paid: $H_a: \beta_1 \neq 0$ or $H_a: \beta_1 < 0$ or $H_a: \beta_1 > 0$?

*13.10 Output in Exercise 13.5 on page 647 shows there to be a strong correlation ($r = +0.989$) between length and width, based on a large sample of Puget Sound butter clams. If only a handful of clams had been sampled, would we be likely to obtain weak evidence of a weak relationship, weak evidence of a strong relationship, strong evidence of a weak relationship, or strong evidence of a strong relationship?

13.11 A survey of several hundred students at the same university asked students to report the number of credits they were taking and their SAT scores. The fitted line plot on the left regresses Math SAT on credits for all the students in the sample; the one in the middle is for the regression using full-time students only (12 or more credits); the one on the right is for part-time students only (less than 12 credits). The correlation and P-value are, respectively, $r = +0.12$, P-value = 0.017 for all students together; $r = +0.07$, P-value = 0.19 for full-time students only; $r = +0.17$, P-value = 0.745 for part-time students only.

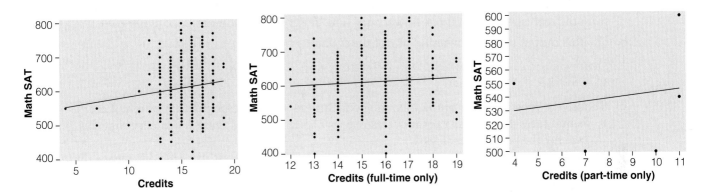

Write a paragraph or two discussing the relationship (if any) between number of credits and Math SAT score for the population of students from which the sample originated. Be sure to mention strength of relationship, strength of evidence, and possible confounding of variables.

*13.12 The scatterplot on the left in Exercise 13.11 shows the relationship between Math SAT score and number of credits taken for several hundred students at a university. The correlation was found to be $r = +0.12$ and the P-value was 0.017. Do these suggest that we have weak evidence of a strong relationship or strong evidence of a weak relationship?

*13.13 The 2005 International Business Owners Survey, conducted by Grant Thornton International, reported on percentage of businesses in a sample of 8 countries that exported to and imported from China.

Exports	54	21	25	29	14	14	11	37
Imports	29	29	19	17	12	9	6	5

a. How many degrees of freedom hold for performing inference about the slope of the regression line for the larger population of countries?

b. Use this output to choose the most accurate of the following conclusions.

```
Pearson correlation of Exports and Imports = 0.479
P-Value = 0.230
```

   1. Percentage importing increases as percentage exporting increases for the sample, and there is evidence that this is the case for the population as well.
   2. Percentage importing increases as percentage exporting increases for the sample, but there is no convincing evidence that this is the case for the population as well.
   3. Percentage importing does not increase as percentage exporting increases for the sample, but there is evidence of some relationship in the population.
   4. Percentage importing does not increase as percentage exporting increases for the sample, nor is there evidence of a relationship in the population.

c. Based on the size of the P-value, which one of these is the most plausible value for the t statistic: 1, 2, or 3?

d. What would the *P*-value have been if we had used a one-sided alternative, suspecting in advance that the slope is positive?

e. If the survey had just looked at individual companies (rather than percentages of companies in various countries importing to and exporting from China), asking whether or not each company imported from China, and whether or not it exported to China, what procedure would we use to test for a relationship between importing and exporting: paired *t*, two-sample *t*, several-sample *F*, or chi-square?

13.14 "Real Estate Rent, Vacancy Rates Don't Always Tell The Story" reported in a local paper in January 2005 that "At first glance, office space in the city's market seems to violate the law of supply and demand, which says that the greater the supply of something relative to demand, the lower its price should be."[4]

a. If the so-called law of supply and demand were to hold, what kind of correlation should we expect from the regression of rental rate on vacancy rate: closer to -1, closer to 0, or closer to $+1$?

b. Use this output to decide whether or not the *P*-value is small.

```
Pearson correlation of VacancyRate and RentalRate = 0.107
T =+0.36
```

c. Choose the most accurate of the following conclusions about the population of rental areas.
   1. Rental rates decrease as vacancy rates rise for the sample, and there is evidence that this is the case for the population as well.
   2. Rental rates do decrease as vacancy rates rise for the sample, but there is no evidence that this is the case for the population.
   3. Rental rates do not decrease as vacancy rates rise for the sample, but there is evidence of some relationship in the population.
   4. Rental rates do not decrease as vacancy rates rise for the sample, nor is there evidence of a relationship in the population.

d. Comment briefly on whether or not the article's title is appropriate, based on your answer to part (c).

e. Would the *P*-value have been small if we had carried out the test with a one-sided alternative $\beta_1 < 0$? Explain.

f. Refer to this scatterplot of the data. A regression of rental rate (in dollars per square foot) on vacancy rate reports two unusual observations: one that has a great deal of influence on the line but a residual that is not particularly large, and another with a large residual but no undue influence on the line. Which one of these corresponds to the area with vacancy rate 0.52 and rental rate $21.85 per square foot: the former (large influence) or the latter (large residual)?

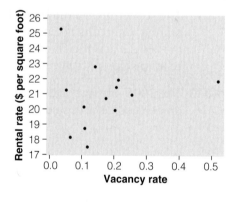

*13.15 Suppose height is regressed on age for a sample of children.

a. What kind of relationship, if any, do we expect to see between the two variables for the sample and for the population from which the sample was obtained?

b. Which of these confidence intervals for slope β_1 would convince us that the relationship is positive for the larger population of children: (2.0, 2.5), $(-1.0, 4.0)$, or $(-2.5, -2.0)$?

c. Which one of these would help to convince us that, in general, height increases with age: b_0 small, b_1 small, b_0 large, or b_1 large?

d. Suppose we performed the regression on just a few children. Would we be more likely to obtain weak evidence of a strong relationship or strong evidence of a weak relationship?

13.16 The regression of length on width for a large sample of butter clams, introduced in Exercise 13.5 on page 647, has $b_1 = 1.22$ and $SE_{b_1} = 0.02$. We are 95% confident that for every additional centimeter in width, a butter clam is longer by _____ to _____ centimeters. (Fill in the blanks to produce a 95% confidence interval for the slope of the regression line that best fits the population of butter clams.)

13.2 Interval Estimates for an Individual or Mean Response

In Section 13.1, we learned two important regression inference procedures: testing for statistical evidence of a relationship between the two quantitative variables of interest, and estimating the slope of the line that relates those variables in the larger population. For practical purposes, two other types of estimation are quite common. One is a *prediction interval* that should contain the *individual* response to a given explanatory value. The other is a *confidence interval* that should contain the *mean* of all responses to a given explanatory value.

Our first example in this section considers the distinction between a prediction interval and a confidence interval.

EXAMPLE 13.11 DECIDING WHICH IS APPROPRIATE: A PREDICTION INTERVAL OR A CONFIDENCE INTERVAL

Background: Reassessments of property values in a certain county in 2002 were extremely controversial, and some owners believed the assessment of their property was too high, resulting in unfairly high taxes. Suppose a homeowner was told that his land (which is 4,000 square feet in size) was reassessed at $40,000, and he wants to contest this as being unreasonably high. A sample of 29 land values in his neighborhood has a mean size of 5,619 square feet, and the mean assessed value is $34,624. A regression of value on size yields a correlation of $r = +0.927$. The regression equation is $\hat{y} = 1,551 + 5.885x$, and the typical residual size is $s = 6,682$, where the units are dollars. In addition to a scatterplot, interval estimates have been requested for an explanatory value of 4,000 square feet.

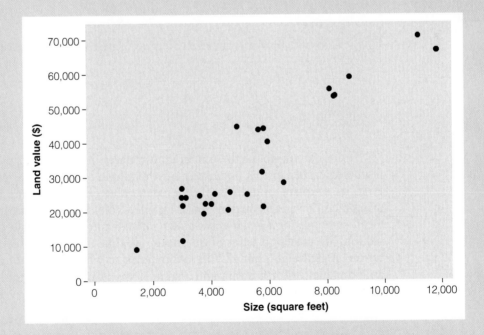

```
Predicted Values for New Observations
New Obs     Fit     SE Fit        95.0% CI              95.0% PI
1          25094       1446    (   22127,    28060)  (   11066,    39121)
```

Continued

Questions: What do the summaries suggest about the assessed value, based on the land size? Which interval estimate is relevant, and what does it suggest?

Responses: The correlation between size and value is strong and positive. The regression line predicts 4,000 square feet of land to be valued at $1,551 + 5.885(4,000) = 25,091$ dollars, considerably less than $40,000. The value of $s = \$6,682$ tells us the typical deviation from the regression line's prediction. Because the homeowner is concerned only about one particular assessment (his own), the prediction interval (11,066, 39,121) is relevant. It does suggest that $40,000 is an unusually high assessment, based on the size of his property.

Practice: *Try Exercise 13.18(b) on page 658.*

The Big Picture:
A CLOSER LOOK

Notice that the prediction interval (from about $11,000 to $39,000) in Example 13.11 extends roughly 2s on either side of the predicted value, about $25,000, since s is approximately $7,000.

To simplify matters, we begin by considering what could be called the "best-case scenario": The sample size is large, and an interval estimate is desired for an explanatory value that is close to the mean $\bar{x}$. Under these conditions, the 95% prediction interval extends roughly $2s$ on either side of the predicted response, whereas the confidence interval has $2\frac{s}{\sqrt{n}}$ as its approximate margin of error.

Approximate Prediction and Confidence Intervals in Regression

For a large sample size n and a value x that is close to the mean $\bar{x}$, an approximate 95% **prediction interval** for an *individual* response is

$$\text{PI} \approx \hat{y} \pm 2s$$

and an approximate 95% **confidence interval** for the *mean* response is

$$\text{CI} \approx \hat{y} \pm 2\frac{s}{\sqrt{n}}$$

where $\hat{y} = b_0 + b_1 x$ is the predicted response to the given x value and

$$s = \sqrt{\frac{(y_1 - \hat{y}_1)^2 + \cdots + (y_n - \hat{y}_n)^2}{n - 2}}$$

is the typical residual size in the sample.

To help think about these interval estimates in the context of other intervals discussed earlier in this book, our next example includes a variety of estimates. First, we estimate an individual or a mean value of a single quantitative variable, using methods established in earlier chapters. Next, we estimate an individual or mean response *for a given explanatory value*—a new skill that is the focus of this section. We present a series of questions, all alike in that they seek estimates concerning male weight, but all different in terms of whether an estimate is sought for an individual or for a mean, and also in terms of whether or not height information is provided.

EXAMPLE 13.12 ORDINARY INTERVAL ESTIMATES AND REGRESSION INTERVAL ESTIMATES

Background: A sample of 162 male weights have a mean of $\bar{y} = 170.8$ pounds and a standard deviation of $s_y = 33.1$ pounds. The shape of the distribution is close to normal. A regression on their corresponding height values (which average about 71 inches) shows strong evidence (*P*-value = 0.000) of a moderate relationship (*r* = +0.45). The relationship appears linear in the scatterplot, the least squares regression line is $\hat{y} = -188 + 5.08x$, and the typical spread about the line is $s = 29.6$ pounds.

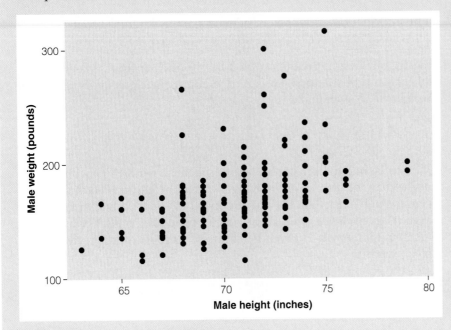

Questions: How do we estimate

1. the weight of an individual male?

2. the mean weight of all males?

3. the weight of an individual 71-inch-tall male?

4. the mean weight of all 71-inch-tall males?

Responses:

1. Using the methods discussed in Chapter 4, we can estimate where most weight values should be by using the 68-95-99.7 Rule, which is based on a normal distribution. About 95% of the time, we predict an individual weight to fall in the interval

$$\bar{y} \pm 2s_y = 170.8 \pm 2(33.1) = (104.6, 237.0)$$

2. Using the methods of Chapter 10, in which we learned to perform inference about the mean of a single quantitative variable, we can set up a 95% confidence interval for the *mean* weight of all male college students:

$$\bar{y} \pm 2\frac{s_y}{\sqrt{n}} = 170.8 \pm 2\frac{33.1}{\sqrt{162}} = (165.6, 176.0)$$

Because of dividing by the square root of the sample size, this confidence interval is much narrower than the interval that predicts an individual weight: It is much easier to pinpoint a mean as opposed to an individual value.

Continued

3. On average, we predict a 71-inch-tall male to weigh $\hat{y} = -188 + 5.08(71) = 172.7$ pounds. Since $s = 29.6$, an approximate 95% prediction interval for the weight of an individual 71-inch-tall male is

$$\text{PI} \approx \hat{y} \pm 2s = 172.7 \pm 2(29.6) = (113.5, 231.9)$$

The information about height helps make this interval about 14 pounds narrower than the one we produced in #1.

4. Again, our weight prediction for a height of 71 inches is $\hat{y} = 172.7$ pounds. An approximate 95% confidence interval for the *mean* weight of all such males is

$$\text{CI} \approx \hat{y} \pm 2\frac{s}{\sqrt{n}} = 172.7 \pm 2\frac{29.6}{\sqrt{162}} = (168.0, 177.4)$$

We can be much more precise about the mean for all 71-inch-tall males than we can for an individual of that height, and so this interval is much narrower than the one produced in #3. It's a bit narrower than the confidence interval for a mean produced in #2, because including information about height helps us to be more precise about mean weight.

Practice: *Try Exercise 13.20 on page 659.*

The interval estimate formulas on page 652 are a useful starting point to give us a feel for the regression prediction and confidence intervals, but they don't work very well for small sample sizes n or for values x that are far from the mean $\bar{x}$. Because the more accurate formulas for prediction and confidence intervals in regression are quite "messy," the most practical approach is to use software.

Before considering specific interval estimates, we think about the more general implications of making predictions about weight for a taller height.

EXAMPLE 13.13 HOW THE POINT ESTIMATE FOR A RESPONSE DIFFERS FOR A DIFFERENT EXPLANATORY VALUE

Background: A regression of a sample of males' weights on their heights produces the least squares regression line $\hat{y} = -188 + 5.08x$. On page 653 in Example 13.12, we estimated individual and mean weights when the height value is 71 inches.

Question: What would be the most noticeable change, if instead we produced interval estimates for a height of 76 inches?

Response: The slope 5.08 of the regression line tells us that if one male student is 1 inch taller than another, we estimate his weight to be about 5 pounds more. If the given height is 5 inches more—76 instead of 71— then we predict weight to be about 25 pounds more. Both the prediction interval and the confidence interval will be centered at a weight that is about 25 pounds heavier.

Practice: *Try Exercise 13.21(b) on page 659.*

Now we will scrutinize the interval estimates for weight when height is 76 inches, comparing them to those produced for a height of 71 inches. We will also confirm that the formulas on page 652 don't necessarily yield accurate approximations, due to the fact that 76 is far from the mean height of 71 inches.

EXAMPLE 13.14 INTERVAL ESTIMATES FOR AN UNUSUALLY LARGE EXPLANATORY VALUE

Background: In Example 13.12 on page 652 we constructed by hand an approximate confidence interval for the mean weight and a prediction interval for the individual weight when a male's height is 71 inches. Here are the intervals produced with software.

```
Predicted Values for New Observations
New Obs      Fit      SE Fit        95.0% CI              95.0% PI
1          172.83      2.35    ( 168.20,  177.47) ( 114.20,  231.47)
Values of Predictors for New Observations
New Obs   HT_male
1           71.0
```

We compare these to the interval estimates for a height of 76 inches.

```
Predicted Values for New Observations
New Obs      Fit      SE Fit        95.0% CI              95.0% PI
1          198.21      4.88    ( 188.58,  207.84) ( 138.97,  257.45)
Values of Predictors for New Observations
New Obs   HT_male
1           76.0
```

Questions: How do the centers of the intervals compare? How well do the intervals match the formulas PI $\approx \hat{y} \pm 2s$ and CI $\approx \hat{y} \pm 2\frac{s}{\sqrt{n}}$?

Responses: The CI and PI for $x = 76$ are centered at 198.21, whereas those for $x = 71$ are centered at 172.83. As we anticipated in Example 13.13, the intervals for 76 inches are centered at a weight that is about 25 pounds more.

For a height of 71 inches, which is close to average, the approximate intervals constructed by hand on page 654 in Example 13.12, CI = (168.0, 177.4) and PI = (113.5, 231.9), are quite close to the intervals produced with software.

For a height of 76 inches, we estimate $\hat{y}$ by hand to be $\hat{y} = -188 + 5.08(76) = 198.1$ pounds. Our approximate PI and CI would be

$$\text{PI} \approx 198.1 \pm 2(29.6) = (138.9, 257.3)$$

$$\text{CI} \approx 198.1 \pm 2\frac{29.6}{\sqrt{162}} = (193.4, 202.8)$$

The PI is close to the true interval (138.97, 257.45) produced with software. In contrast, the CI is *not* very close to the true interval (188.58, 207.84): It is too narrow, suggesting we know more about the mean response than we actually do.

Practice: *Try Exercise 13.21(c–e) on page 659.*

The Big Picture:

LOOKING AHEAD

An illustration of prediction interval and confidence interval bands on page 657 makes it clear that the confidence interval widens for values of *x* far from their mean.

Example TBP 13.4 on page 969 of the *TBP Supplement* demonstrates that both the confidence interval and the prediction interval tend to be narrower for stronger relationships.

Refer to page 970 of the *TBP Supplement* for the actual formulas for the prediction and confidence intervals in regression. A discussion by four students on page 971 presents an application of regression interval estimates using software, followed by a comparison with the corresponding intervals calculated by hand.

We can summarize the interval estimates found in Examples 13.12 and 13.14 with the display below.

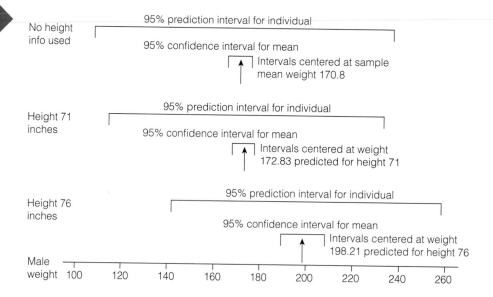

Note that this display shows us what to expect with no height information, and for two particular height values—71 and 76 inches. A scatterplot display, to be presented shortly, will show confidence and prediction interval "bands," displaying what can be expected over the entire range of possible height values.

Especially in the case of prediction intervals, if there is a substantial relationship between two quantitative variables, we can produce a narrower interval if we include information in the form of a given explanatory value. Confidence intervals for means will be considerably narrower than prediction intervals for individuals. Sample size plays an important role in the width of the confidence interval, with larger samples producing narrower intervals. Naturally enough, if the relationship is positive, then for higher values of the explanatory variable, both the confidence and the prediction intervals are centered at a higher response.

We have seen that when there is only a single quantitative variable y of interest (and its shape is close to normal), about 95% of individuals fall within $2s_y$ of their mean $\bar{y}$. A 95% confidence interval for population mean is within $2\frac{s_y}{\sqrt{n}}$ of the sample mean. Thus, it is division by the square root of sample size that makes our interval estimate for the mean so much narrower than an interval estimate for an individual.

The exact formulas for margin of error in regression prediction and confidence intervals are much messier than those for a single quantitative variable, but the predominant distinction between them is still that the confidence interval estimate for a mean response includes division by square root of sample size, producing narrower intervals for larger sample sizes.

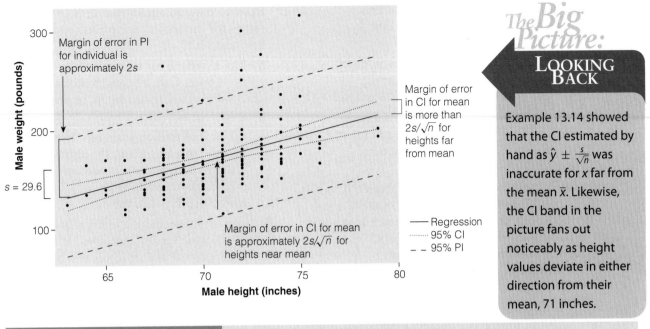

LOOKING BACK

Example 13.14 showed that the CI estimated by hand as $\hat{y} \pm \frac{s}{\sqrt{n}}$ was inaccurate for x far from the mean $\bar{x}$. Likewise, the CI band in the picture fans out noticeably as height values deviate in either direction from their mean, 71 inches.

EXERCISES FOR SECTION 13.2

Interval Estimates for an Individual or Mean Response

Note: Asterisked numbers indicate exercises whose answers are provided in the Solutions to Selected Exercises section, on page 689.

13.17 Researchers from the Department of Oceanography at Texas A&M University gathered data on ages (in millions of years) of fish fossils gathered at two sites and at various depths (in meters below sea floor, mbsf).

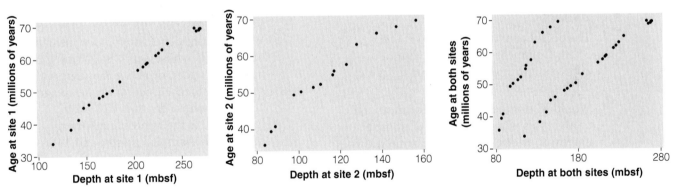

a. We may think of the age of a fossil as determining how deep it will be, or we may think of the depth of a fossil as providing information about its age. Based on the way the scatterplots have been constructed, which has been taken to be the explanatory variable, age or depth?

b. We may also consider the third variable, site. Tell whether it is explanatory or response, and whether it is categorical or quantitative.

c. Based on the appearance of the scatterplots, does the relationship between age and depth appear stronger at the first or the second site?

d. The scatterplot on the right shows the relationship between ages and depths for both sites combined. Does the appearance suggest it is better to study the sites separately or combined? Explain.

e. If we do inference about age based on depth of fossils, should we consider the population to be all fish fossils at any site or all fish fossils at the site from which the sample was obtained?

*13.18 Refer to data on ages and depths of fish fossils for the *first site* presented in the preceding exercise.

    a. The t statistic for regressing age on depth is +42.80. Can we conclude that the P-value is small, not small, or borderline?

    b. Which interval should contain the mean age of all fossils whose depth is 200 mbsf: a confidence interval or a prediction interval?

    c. When depth equals 200 mbsf, predicted age is 55.3 million years old. Use the fact that spread s about the regression line is 1.2 to construct an approximate 95% prediction interval for age of an *individual* fossil whose depth is 200 mbsf.

    d. The actual prediction interval is (52.8, 57.9). Comment on whether your approximate interval from part (c) came fairly close to this.

    e. When depth equals 200 mbsf, predicted age is 55.3 million years old. Use the fact that spread s about the regression line is 1.2 and sample size is 25 to construct an approximate 95% confidence interval for *mean* age of all fossils whose depth is 200 mbsf.

    f. The actual confidence interval is (54.9, 55.8). Comment on whether your approximate interval from part (e) came fairly close to this.

    g. Would a confidence interval for mean age of all fossils whose depth is 100 mbsf be narrower, wider, or about the same width as the confidence interval for mean age of all fossils whose depth is 200 mbsf? [Note: 200 is the approximate mean depth of the sampled fossils, and 100 is relatively far below this mean.]

    h. If we have no information about a fossil's depth, we would have to guess its age to be somewhere in the interval mean plus or minus 2 standard deviations in age: $55.5 \pm 2(10.5) = (34.5, 76.5)$. Explain why this interval is so much wider than the prediction interval you constructed in part (c).

13.19 Refer to data on ages and depths of fish fossils for the *second site* presented in Exercise 13.17.

    a. The t statistic for regressing age on depth is +16.02. Can we conclude that the P-value is small, not small, or borderline?

    b. When depth equals 120 mbsf, predicted age is 56.4 million years old. Use the fact that the spread s about the regression line is 2.3 to construct an approximate 95% prediction interval for age of a fossil whose depth is 120 mbsf.

    c. The actual prediction interval is (51.2, 61.6), which is somewhat wider than your interval in part (b). Is this because of how far 120 is from the mean depth, or because sample size (14) is relatively small?

    d. When depth equals 120 mbsf, predicted age is 56.4 million years old. Use the fact that the spread s about the regression line is 2.3 and sample size is 14 to construct an approximate 95% confidence interval for mean age of all fossils whose depth is 120 mbsf.

    e. The actual confidence interval is (55.0, 57.8). Is this wider or narrower than your approximate interval from part (d)?

    f. Would a confidence interval for mean age of all fossils whose depth is 140 mbsf be narrower, wider, or about the same width as the confidence interval for mean age of all fossils whose depth is 120 mbsf? [Note: 120 is the approximate mean depth of the sampled fossils, and 140 is relatively far above this mean.]

    g. If we have no information about fossils' depth, we would have to guess mean age of all fossils to be somewhere in the interval mean plus or minus 2 standard deviations in age, divided by square root of sample size: $53.9 \pm 2(10.5)/\sqrt{14} = (48.3, 59.5)$. Explain why this interval is so much wider than the confidence interval you constructed in part (d).

*13.20 Exercise 13.2 on page 646 looked at the relationship between trip length and amount paid for travel by a state's congressional representatives in the years 2000 to 2005. This output was produced by requesting interval estimates for 5 days and for 10 days, respectively.

Variable	N	Mean	Median	TrMean	StDev	SE Mean
Days	39	4.974	4.000	4.857	3.360	0.538
Dollars	39	5167	2622	4743	5184	830

Predicted Values for New Observations

Days	Fit	SE Fit	95.0% CI		95.0% PI	
5.00	5197	545	(4093,	6301)	(-1783,	12177)
10.0	11077	989	(9073,	13080)	(3899,	18254)

Identify each of the intervals in parts (a) through (f) by choosing one of the following for each:

1. Estimated amount paid (only roughly accurate) for an *individual* trip by a representative in the larger population, without information about trip length.
2. Estimated *mean* amount for all trips taken by the larger population of representatives, without information about trip length.
3. Estimated amount paid for an *individual 5-day* trip by a representative in the larger population.
4. Estimated *mean* amount for all *5-day* trips taken by the larger population of representatives.
5. Estimated amount paid for an *individual 10-day* trip by a representative in the larger population.
6. Estimated *mean* amount for all *10-day* trips taken by the larger population of representatives.

a. (9,073, 13,080)
b. (−1,783, 12,177)
c. (3,899, 18,254)
d. (4,093, 6,301)
e. $5,167 \pm 2(5,184)$
f. $5,167 \pm 2(5,184)/\sqrt{39}$

*13.21 Refer to Exercise 13.20 and the regression equation $\hat{y} = -683 + 1,176x$ for the relationship between trip length x in days and amount y paid for travel by a state's congressional representatives in the years 2000 to 2005.

a. Which interval should be narrower: the interval estimate of amount paid for an *individual* 5-day trip by a representative in the larger population, or the interval estimate of *mean* amount for all 5-day trips taken by the larger population of representatives?

b. How much higher should the center of the interval estimates be for the amount paid for a 10-day trip compared to the amount for a 5-day trip?

c. Note that the mean trip length was approximately 5 days. Which confidence interval should be narrower: interval estimate of mean amount paid for all 5-day trips, or interval estimate of mean amount paid for all 10-day trips?

d. Using the predicted amount for 10 days, $\hat{y} = -683 + 1,176(10) = 11,077$, the spread $s = 3,401$, and the sample size $n = 39$, find the interval $\hat{y} \pm 2\frac{s}{\sqrt{n}}$.

e. Explain why the interval you constructed in part (d) is not very accurate as a 95% confidence interval for the mean amount paid for a 10-day trip.

13.22 Exercise 13.5 on page 647 looked at the relationship between length and width of Puget Sound butter clams. The following output was obtained upon request of interval estimates for length, based on widths of 2 and 3 centimeters, respectively.

```
Variable          N      Mean     Median     TrMean        StDev   SE Mean
Width            88     4.444      4.200      4.450        1.798     0.192
Length           88     5.680      5.450      5.688        2.217     0.236

Width   Fit    SE Fit         95.0% CI             95.0% PI
2.00  2.6972   0.0587   ( 2.5804,  2.8139)   ( 2.0401,  3.3542)
3.00  3.9173   0.0446   ( 3.8287,  4.0059)   ( 3.2646,  4.5699)
```

Identify each of the intervals in (a) through (f) as one of the following:
1. Estimated length of an *individual* butter clam.
2. Estimated *mean* length of all butter clams.
3. Estimated *mean* length of all *3-cm-wide* butter clams in the larger population.
4. Estimated length of an *individual 3-cm-wide* butter clam in the larger population.
5. Estimated *mean* length of all *2-cm-wide* butter clams in the larger population.
6. Estimated length of an *individual 2-cm-wide* butter clam in the larger population.
   a. (2.5804, 2.8139)
   b. (3.8287, 4.0059)
   c. (2.0401, 3.3542)
   d. (3.2646, 4.5699)
   e. $5.680 \pm 2(2.217)$
   f. $5.680 \pm 2(2.217)/\sqrt{88}$

13.23 Refer to Exercise 13.22 on the relationship between length and width of Puget Sound butter clams.

a. Which interval should be narrower: interval estimate for mean length of all 3-cm-wide butter clams, or interval estimate for length of an individual 3-cm-wide butter clam?

b. Which interval should be centered at a higher length value: interval estimate of length of a 2-cm-wide butter clam, or interval estimate of length of a 3-cm-wide butter clam?

c. Note that the mean clam width was roughly 4 cm. Which confidence interval should be narrower: interval estimate for mean length of all 2-cm-wide clams, or interval estimate for mean length of all 3-cm-wide clams?

13.24 In September 2007, a museum curator examined "the square-toed, goatskin boots that Abraham Lincoln had on that night at Ford's Theater"[5] when he was assassinated. Lincoln's blood-stained clothes were being moved to a storage center while the theater museum was being renovated. His shoes would be a modern-day size 14, and his height was 6-foot-4. To determine if his foot size was unusually large for his height, we have regressed shoe size on height for a large sample of adult males and requested interval estimates for a height of 76 inches.

```
The regression equation is
Shoe = − 19.2 + 0.422 HT
444 cases used 2 cases contain missing values
Predictor          Coef      SE Coef           T        P
Constant       -19.1552       0.8253       -23.21    0.000
HT              0.42228       0.01231        34.30    0.000
S = 1.020       R-Sq = 72.7%      R-Sq(adj) = 72.6%

New Obs     Fit      SE Fit         95.0% CI               95.0% PI
1       12.9379     0.1217   ( 12.6987, 13.1772)   ( 10.9184, 14.9575)
Values of Predictors for New Observations
New Obs         HT
1              76.0
```

a. Use the output to determine if Lincoln's shoe size (14) could be considered unusually large for his height.

b. Verify that the prediction interval is approximately $\hat{y} \pm 2s$.

c. The confidence interval is noticeably wider than $\hat{y} \pm 2\dfrac{s}{\sqrt{n}}$. Is this because the sample size is too small, or because the explanatory value is too far from the mean?

*13.25 Exercise 13.1 on page 645 showed scatterplots based on a report about an airline's number of daily departures from various airports, along with the number of gates at those airports and the year in which the airline was established at that particular airport.

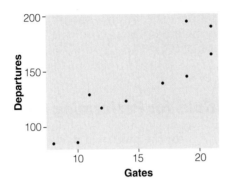
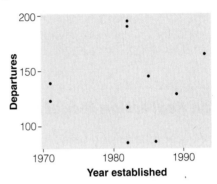

For which regression will our confidence interval and prediction interval estimates be narrower: for departures versus gates (on the left) or for departures versus year established (on the right)?

13.26 For a large sample of women, the relationship between their heights and the heights of their husbands has $r = 0.2$. The relationship between their heights and the heights of their daughters has $r = 0.5$. Which will be narrower: the prediction interval for the height of a woman whose husband is 71 inches tall (the average) or the prediction interval for the height of a woman whose daughter is 65 inches tall (the average)?

CHAPTER 13 SUMMARY

The purpose of this chapter is to establish what conclusions we can draw about the relationship between two quantitative variables in a larger population, based on the relationship observed in a sample. A scatterplot of the data should first be examined, to check if the relationship appears linear. If it does not, then a transformation (not presented in this book) would be necessary before applying the methods developed in this chapter. Our hypothesis test for a relationship can be formulated in terms of the slope β_1 of the line that best fits the population of explanatory and response pairs. We can also set up a confidence interval for β_1. In addition, we can produce interval estimates for an individual or mean response to a given explanatory value.

Population Regression Model and Conditions for Performing Inference

- When the linear relationship between two quantitative variables in a population is of interest, then the **population relationship** is expressed with the equation

$$\mu_y = \beta_0 + \beta_1 x.$$

  Responses for any explanatory value x are assumed to vary normally about the mean response μ_y with some standard deviation σ that is the same for all explanatory values.

- Inference about the unknown population relationship is performed based on the relationship between sampled explanatory and response values, summarized with the least squares regression line

$$\hat{y} = b_0 + b_1 x$$

  and the typical residual size s. The sample summaries b_0, b_1, and s are used as estimates

for the unknown parameters β_0, β_1, and σ. These summaries are reported in standard regression output and are rarely calculated by hand (formulas were presented in Section 5.3).

- Because inference procedures are based on several underlying assumptions, it is important not to proceed unless the corresponding conditions are met:

  1. Scatterplot should appear linear, not curved.
  2. Sample size should be large enough to offset non-normality in response values.
  3. Fairly constant spread of responses over the range of explanatory values should be evident.
  4. Explanatory/response values should constitute a random sample of pairs that are independent from one another.

Hypothesis Test about Slope

- Depending on the problem at hand, various forms of inference for regression may be relevant. First and foremost, we carry out a test of the null hypothesis that the slope β_1 of the population regression line is zero. This hypothesis must be rejected if we are to be convinced that there is in fact a relationship in the larger population from which the sample arose. The t statistic and P-value for a test of $H_0: \beta_1 = 0$ are reported in standard regression output. If sample slope b_1 is steep enough, the

t statistic will be large enough and the P-value will be small enough to reject H_0 and conclude that the population slope β_1 is not zero. As always, the P-value for a one-sided alternative can be found by taking half of the two-sided P-value. This is appropriate if there was an initial suspicion that the slope is specifically positive, or specifically negative.

- The steps of our hypothesis test reflect the *four basic processes* in the usual ways, after the preliminary step of formulating null and alternative hypotheses. First, the principles of good *data production* should be considered before we attempt to draw conclusions about the population based on the sample. If there is no reason to suspect bias arising from the study design, we *display and summarize* the relationship: Use software to produce a scatterplot and report the slope b_1 of the line that best fits the sample, along with its standardized value

$$t = \frac{b_1 - 0}{SE_{b_1}}$$

The *probability* that will let us decide between the null and alternative hypotheses is the *P*-value of the test. Stating our conclusion in terms of one of these hypotheses is the step that actually involves *statistical inference*.

- **Correlation** r plays an important role in any regression procedure. It tells the direction and strength of the relationship seen in sampled explanatory and response values. If the relationship is strong and r is close to 1 in absolute value, it is easier to produce evidence of a relationship in the larger population. Nevertheless, because of the role played by sample size, it is possible to obtain weak evidence of a strong relationship (small sample producing a *P*-value that is not especially small but $|r|$ is close to 1) or strong evidence of a weak relationship (large sample producing a *P*-value that is very small but r is close to 0). We may also have weak evidence of a weak relationship (a *P*-value that is not especially small and r is closer to 0 than to 1).

Confidence Interval for Slope

If $H_0 : \beta_1 = 0$ has been rejected, then we may be interested in a confidence interval for the unknown population slope β_1. An approximate 95% interval for β_1 is

$$b_1 \pm \text{multiplier}(SE_{b_1})$$

where SE_{b_1}, also reported in regression output, estimates the spread of the distribution of sample slope b_1 coming from a population relationship with slope β_1. Because SE_{b_1} is calculated from typical sample residual size s, the above interval tends to be wide for relationships that show loose scattering of points, and narrow for relationships that show tight clustering. The multiplier in the above interval is the value of the t distribution for $n - 2$ degrees of freedom associated with 95% confidence. This multiplier is approximately the same as the z multiplier 2 for large samples, and is somewhat more than 2 for small samples, but generally does not exceed 3.

Prediction and Confidence Interval Estimates for Responses

Besides test and confidence interval for slope β_1 of the regression line, two other interval estimates are frequently relevant. We may be interested in a prediction interval PI for an individual response to a given explanatory value x or a confidence interval CI for the mean of all responses to a given explanatory value x. Both intervals are centered at the predicted response $\hat{y} = b_0 + b_1 x$, but the confidence interval for mean response is narrower. When sample size is large and x is not far from $\bar{x}$, the 95% prediction interval for an individual response is approximately $\hat{y} \pm 2s$ and the 95% confidence interval for mean response is approximately $\hat{y} \pm 2\frac{s}{\sqrt{n}}$.

The rough estimates presented above should serve merely as a reference point; in practice, the precise prediction interval and confidence interval should be found using software.

CHAPTER 13   EXERCISES

Note: Asterisked numbers indicate exercises whose answers are provided in the Solutions to Selected Exercises section, on page 689.

Additional exercises appeared after each section: inference about slope (Section 13.1) on page 645 and interval estimates (Section 13.2) on page 657.

Warming Up: RELATIONSHIPS BETWEEN TWO QUANTITATIVE VARIABLES

13.27 In a study of the relationship between weight and lifespan, tell whether each of the following focuses on data production, displaying and summarizing data, probability, or statistical inference:

a. Researchers find the slope of the line that relates pounds overweight to years lived for people included in the study.

b. Researchers decide whether to treat weight as quantitative (pounds overweight) or categorical (obese or not).

c. If weight and lifespan were not related, it would be almost impossible to find a slope as steep as the one observed in the sample.

d. Researchers conclude that the more pounds a person is overweight, the shorter his or her life will be.

13.28 "Bigger Waistlines, Shorter Lifespans" is the title of a 2005 newspaper article.

a. Based on the title, tell what type of variables (quantitative or categorical) the explanatory and response variables seem to be.

b. How would the data be displayed?

c. The article reports that "obesity now shortens the average lifespan by about four months."[6] Tell what type of variables (quantitative or categorical) the explanatory and response variables seem to be, based on this quote.

d. Based on the quote in part (c), how would the data be displayed?

*13.29 The U.S. government published information on the number of hate crimes involving vandalism and the number of hate crimes against persons for each of the 50 states in a given year. Explain why it is not appropriate to use the data to perform inference about the relationship between hate crimes involving vandalism and hate crimes against persons in the larger population.

13.30 Data were collected on gross receipts and average ticket price for the top 25 rock concerts of the year. Explain why it is not appropriate to use the data to perform inference about the relationship between gross receipts and average ticket price for all rock concerts that year.

13.31 Researchers looked at how body core temperature changed over time for mice that had been exposed to hydrogen sulfide. Tell whether each of the following focuses on data production, displaying and summarizing data, probability, or statistical inference.

a. A scatterplot was used to see how core body temperature changed over time.

b. Researchers concluded that a certain rate of temperature decrease should hold for the population of mice.

c. Caution must be used in applying inference for regression methods, if temperature is recorded over time for the same mouse, because these measurements would not constitute an independent random sample.

d. It would be virtually impossible to see this pronounced a trend, if temperature in general did not change due to exposure to hydrogen sulfide.

More exercises for this chapter are featured in the **TBP** Supplement on pages 975 through 977. End-of-chapter activities are described on page 973.

Exploring the Big Picture: RELATIONSHIPS BETWEEN TWO QUANTITATIVE VARIABLES

13.32 "H_2S Induces a Suspended Animation-Like State In Mice," published in *Science* in March 2005, explains that exposure to hydrogen sulfide can produce states of suspended animation-like hibernation or torpor in mammals that normally maintain their core body temperature despite changes in environmental temperature.[7]

a. As time of exposure to hydrogen sulfide increased from 0 to 6 hours, temperature dropped quite steadily from about 38 to 14 degrees Celsius. Report the approximate slope of the regression line of temperature on time.

b. When the hydrogen sulfide was removed, temperatures of the mice rose steadily back to 38 degrees by the end of 3 hours. Report the approximate slope of this regression line.

c. Another part of the experiment looked at how temperature decrease related to concentration of hydrogen sulfide; the correlation was found to be -0.975. Would typical residual size s for this regression be closer to 0 or to 9 (the approximate standard deviation of the response temperature values)?

13.33 As of 2005, the United States had no guidelines on suggested caffeine intake for children and teenagers, but Canada did. On average, the recommended daily intake can be modeled by the equation $\mu_y = -24 + 1.3x$, where we think of μ_y as being the average maximum amount of caffeine in milligrams that is safely consumed per day by a child or teenager who weighs x pounds.

a. If one teenager weighs 10 pounds more than another, on average how many more milligrams of caffeine can he or she safely consume per day?

b. How should the slope for this model be denoted: b_1 or β_1?

*13.34 Children's height as a function of their age has been researched so extensively that we can consider known results to describe the relationship for all children in the United States. For instance, between the ages of 5 and 10, population mean height in inches satisfies $\mu_y = 30.75 + 2.25x$, where x is age in years. Spread about the line is 2 inches.

a. Notice that the slope of the regression line for the population is $\beta_1 = 2.25$. If we were to take repeated random samples of 25 children between the ages of 5 and 10 and regress their heights on their ages, then the slopes b_1 would vary from sample to sample. At what slope value would their distribution be centered?

b. If we were to take repeated random samples of children between the ages of 5 and 10 and regress their heights on their ages, then the slopes b_1 would vary from sample to sample. In which case would the distribution of sample slopes have less spread: when sampling 25 children or 250 children?

c. What notation is used for the spread about the line (2 inches): s or σ?

d. On average, how much taller do you predict a 9-year-old to be compared to a 6-year-old?

13.35 Children's height as a function of their age has been researched so extensively that we can consider known results to describe the relationship for all children in the United States. For instance, between the ages of 13 and 15, population mean height for teenage males (in inches) satisfies $\mu_y = 22 + 3x$, where x is age in years. Spread about the line is 3.1 inches.

a. Notice that the slope of the regression line for the population is $\beta_1 = 3$. If we were to take repeated random samples of 25 males between the ages of 13 and 15 and regress their heights on their ages, then the slopes b_1 would vary from sample to sample. At what slope value would their distribution be centered?

b. If we were to take repeated random samples of males between the ages of 13 and 15 and regress their heights on their ages, then the slopes b_1 would vary from sample to sample. In which case would the distribution of sample slopes have less spread: when sampling 10 males or 25 males?

c. What notation is used for the spread about the line (3.1 inches): s or σ?

d. On average, how much shorter do you predict a 13-year-old to be compared to a 15-year-old?

e. The linear regression model does a good job of summarizing the relationship between height and age for males in a particular age range, such as between 13 and 15 years old. Which *two* conditions would not be met if we attempted to perform inference about the height/age relationship based on a random sample of 250 males all the way from newborn to 25 years old?

   1. Scatterplot should appear linear.
   2. Sample size should be large enough to offset non-normality in responses.
   3. Spread of responses should appear fairly constant over the range of explanatory values.
   4. Explanatory/response values should constitute a random sample of independent pairs.

*13.36 Suppose we gather information from a random sample of men with regard to height, foot length, and salary. Note that the first two variables follow a normal distribution quite closely, but the distribution of salary would naturally exhibit a great deal of right-skewness, due to relatively few men earning unusually high salaries. Tell which one of these distributions would *not* follow a normal curve:

   a. Distribution of sample slope b_1 for regression of foot length on height for small random samples

   b. Distribution of sample slope b_1 for regression of foot length on height for large random samples

   c. Distribution of sample slope b_1 for regression of salary on height for small random samples

   d. Distribution of sample slope b_1 for regression of salary on height for large random samples

13.37 Suppose we gather information from a random sample of high school seniors with regard to IQ, SAT score, and daily hours of TV watched. Note that the first two variables follow a normal distribution quite closely, but the distribution of TV hours

would exhibit a great deal of right-skewness, due to a few students watching excessively long hours of TV. Tell which one of these distributions would *not* follow a t distribution:

   a. Distribution of standardized sample slope $(b_1 - \beta_1)/SE_{b_1}$ for regression of TV on IQ for small random samples

   b. Distribution of standardized sample slope $(b_1 - \beta_1)/SE_{b_1}$ for regression of TV on IQ for large random samples

   c. Distribution of standardized sample slope $(b_1 - \beta_1)/SE_{b_1}$ for regression of SAT on IQ for small random samples

   d. Distribution of standardized sample slope $(b_1 - \beta_1)/SE_{b_1}$ for regression of SAT on IQ for large random samples

13.38 Suppose we regressed daily hours of TV watched on IQ for a large sample of students.

   a. Which of these confidence intervals for β_1 would convince us that the relationship is negative for the larger population of students: $(-0.15, 0.40)$, $(-0.15, -0.05)$, or $(0.05, 0.15)$?

   b. Which one of these would help to convince us that IQ and TV watching are related: $|b_0|$ small, $|b_1|$ small, $|b_0|$ large, or $|b_1|$ large?

13.39 "The Social Services Safety Net Is Fraying" reported in March 2005 on the growing problem of waiting lists for mental retardation services in a certain state.[8] The data consist of numbers of emergency cases and critical cases in a given month over a series of many months:

Month	Emergency	Critical
February 2005	2,195	8,270
January 2005	2,182	8,131
December 2004	2,180	8,008
. . .	. . .	. . .

Students are to report which one of the conditions for a regression model is clearly not met; who has the best answer?

Adam: The problem is that the sample pairs aren't independent. If there are a lot of cases on the waiting list for one month, then the next month would also have a lot of cases, because it would include leftovers from the month before.

Brittany: I don't know about the rest of the scatterplot, but those three points don't fall on a straight line, so the data aren't linear like they're supposed to be.

Carlos: The sample size might not be large enough. That could be the problem because maybe the number of cases doesn't follow a normal distribution.

Dominique: We don't have enough data values to see what the spread looks like but I think the spreads might not be uniform from one end of the line to the other.

13.40 *The Black Death 1346–1353: The Complete History* by Ole Benedictow was featured in the *New England Journal of Medicine*'s March 2005 book review. The reviewer criticized the book's claim that the Black Death was the bubonic form of a rodent disease (*Y. pestis*) spread by fleas. Because the spread of *Y. pestis* depends on homebound rats, it is known to travel at a rate of only about 8 miles per *year*, whereas the Black Death "almost equalled that speed per *day*."[9] For each of the two diseases, the speed of spreading corresponds to the slope of the line that relates distance to time, which is not exactly known but could be approximated by experts with interval estimates.

  a. According to the critic of the theory that the Black Death and *Y. pestis* are one and the same, would confidence intervals for those two slopes overlap or not?

  b. This problem involves three variables: distance covered, time, and type of disease. Tell whether each is quantitative or categorical, and whether it plays the role of explanatory or response variable.

*13.41 "City Assessments Found Out of Line" reported that "a private study of 2,500 property sales in 2004 shows the prices to be widely different from the assessed values for the properties developed by the county. The comparison [...] found many properties were substantially underassessed or overassessed."[10] Suppose sale price is regressed on assessed price.

  a. Based on what the article is suggesting, would the value of r be closer to -1, closer to 0, or closer to $+1$?

  b. Would the value of s be relatively large (close to the standard deviation of sale prices) or relatively small (close to zero)?

  c. If a 95% confidence interval for the population slope β_1 contained zero, what would we conclude?

*13.42 "Environmental Mercury, Autism Linked by New Research" reported in *Environmental News Service* in March 2005 that Texas researchers had found a possible link between autism and mercury in the air and water. "The study compared mercury totals reported for 2001 in the 254 Texas counties to the rate of autism and special education services in nearly 1,200 Texas school districts. The districts, which range from urban to small metro to rural, enroll 4 million Texas children. 'The main finding is that for every 1,000 pounds of environmentally released mercury, we saw a 17 percent increase in autism rates,' said lead author Raymond Palmer, Ph.D., associate professor in the Health Science Center's department of family and community medicine."[11]

  a. Were the individuals studied best described as Texas counties, Texas school districts, or Texas children?

  b. Describe the two quantitative variables of interest, and tell which is explanatory and which is response.

  c. Is the slope of the regression line 1,000/0.17 or 0.17/1,000?

  d. Should researchers denote the slope for their findings as b_0, b_1, β_0, or β_1?

  e. Since the study produced evidence of a relationship, can we conclude that a 95% confidence interval for β_1 contains zero?

  f. Considering that the sample size was quite large, was the *P*-value probably much greater than 0.05, approximately 0.05, or much less than 0.05?

  g. Which one of these possible confounding variables would have been most important for the researchers to take into account: setting as urban, small metro, or rural; gender; time of year; age of children?

13.43 "Sources of Individual Shy-Bold Variations in Antipredator Behaviour of Male Iberian Rock Lizards" explored the relationship between lizards' physical characteristics (such as body size and immune response) in a small sample of lizards, and their behavior when subjected to some sort of risk. Behavior was measured in terms of how shy a lizard was found to be, with a maximum of 2 for shyest and minimum of −2 for boldest. The article reports that shy individuals tended to have larger body sizes, but immune system was not important.

a. Which of these is the correlation for shyness and body size (the other being correlation for shyness and immune response): 0.03, 0.38?

b. Which of these is the *P*-value for shyness and body size (the other being *P*-value for shyness and immune response): 0.026, 0.86?

c. Explain why inference results for this study should be based on probability results from a *t* distribution, not *z*.

13.44 A study looked at illiteracy rates of men and women in a sample of 19 countries.

```
The regression equation is
%WomenIlliterate = 4.49 + 1.32 %MenIlliterate
Predictor          Coef      SE Coef          T          P
Constant          4.493        2.483       1.81      0.088
%MenIlli        1.31848      0.09013      14.63      0.000
S = 7.910        R-Sq = 92.6%
```

a. Which of these suggests that lower illiteracy rates for men tend to be accompanied by lower rates for women, and similarly with higher rates for men and women: the fact that the intercept 4.49 is positive, or the fact that the slope 1.32 is positive?

b. Which of these suggests that illiteracy rates tend to be higher for women than for men: the fact that the intercept 4.49 is positive, or the fact that the slope 1.32 is positive?

c. Report the number in the output that tells us the relationship is strong.

d. Report the number in the output that tells us there is strong evidence of a relationship between illiteracy rates of men and women in the larger population of countries from which our sample originated.

e. Report the number in the output that tells typical spread of women's illiteracy rates about the regression line for those 19 countries.

13.45 "Sleep Disturbances in the Vietnam Generation: Findings from a Nationally Representative Sample of Male Vietnam Veterans," published in the *American Journal of Psychiatry* in July 1998, looked at difficulty in sleep onset, nightmares, and sleep maintenance difficulty in male Vietnam War veterans. Among the predictors studied was the degree of combat exposure.

a. To measure difficulty in sleep onset, researchers took the mean of responses to two questions that offered a 1- to 5-point response scale: "I fall asleep easily at night" (with 5 meaning this is never the case) and "I am afraid to go to sleep at night" (with 5 meaning this is always the case). According to the article, "The Pearson correlation coefficient for these two items is 0.41 ($p < 0.0001$, N = 1,167)."[12] Is there strong evidence of a moderate relationship between responses, or moderate evidence of a strong relationship?

b. To measure nightmares, researchers took the mean of responses to the items "I

have nightmares of experiences in the military that really happened" and "My dreams at night are so real that I waken in a cold sweat and force myself to stay awake." For these items, "($r = 0.60$, $p < 0.0001$, N = 1,167)." Compared to the relationship between the two sleep onset questions described in part (a), is there evidence of a stronger relationship, or stronger evidence of a relationship, for the two nightmare questions?

c. As far as relationship between explanatory and response variables is concerned, the article states: "Of interest, combat exposure was strongly correlated with frequency of nightmares, moderately correlated with sleep onset insomnia, and weakly correlated with disrupted sleep maintenance." One of the correlations was reported to be 0.14, another 0.46, and another 0.63. Which was the correlation for the relationship between degree of combat exposure and frequency of nightmares?

d. Explain why inference results for this study can refer to probabilities from a standard normal (z) distribution.

e. The study also looked at the relationship between whether someone was a combat veteran, non-combat veteran, or civilian, and whether or not he had sleep difficulties (where possible response options included "sometimes" and "very frequently"). Does this involve two quantitative variables, two categorical variables, or one of each?

13.46 The Quantitative Environmental Learning Project posted data on heat input (in trillions of BTUs) and carbon dioxide output (in tons) for a sample of electrical power plants in California in 1997. "By comparing heat input to CO_2 output, one can get a measure of the 'pollution efficiency' of each plant."[13] The relationship is displayed in a scatterplot, and software is used to regress CO_2 output on heat input.

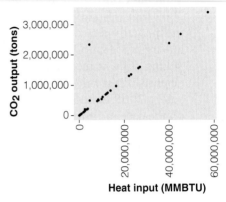

```
The regression equation is
CO2 output (tons) = 50306 + 0.0584 heat input (MMBTU)
Predictor        Coef      SE Coef           T         P
Constant        50306        45989        1.09     0.279
heat inp     0.058432     0.003188       18.33     0.000
S = 285,780      R-Sq = 86.6%      R-Sq(adj) = 86.3%
```

a. Both the appearance of the scatterplot and the positive value of the slope tell us that the correlation must be positive. Convert R-Sq to a decimal and take its positive square root to find the value of the correlation r to three decimal places (the nearest thousandth).

b. Report the typical size of a prediction error when the regression equation is used to predict CO_2 output from heat input.

c. The scatterplot shows there to be one outlier that conforms so poorly with the rest of the data that we may suspect it to have been falsely recorded. This output shows results of regression with the outlier omitted.

```
The regression equation is
CO2 output (tons) = 5633 + 0.0593 heat input (MMBTU)
Predictor        Coef      SE Coef           T         P
Constant         5633         5224        1.08     0.286
heat inp    0.0592588    0.0003592      165.00     0.000
S = 32,171       R-Sq = 99.8%      R-Sq(adj) = 99.8%
```

Now find the value of r and report the typical size of a prediction error.

d. Examine the intercept and slope of both equations, and choose one of the following to describe how the outlier most affected the line:

1. The outlier shifted the line down much lower.

2. The outlier shifted the line up much higher.

3. The outlier made the slope much shallower.

4. The outlier made the slope much steeper.

e. Which is true about interval estimates: Confidence interval for mean response is about one-tenth as wide when the outlier is omitted; or prediction interval for individual response is about one-tenth as wide when the outlier is omitted; or both of these; or neither of these? [Hint: CI is roughly $\hat{y} \pm 2s/\sqrt{n}$ and PI is roughly $\hat{y} \pm 2s$.]

13.47 "Inmate's Rising I.Q. Score Could Mean His Death," published in the *New York Times* in 2004, described the situation of death row inmate Daryl Atkins, who killed a man in Virginia in 1996 after forcing him to withdraw money from an ATM. The U.S. Supreme Court ruled in *Atkins v. Virginia* in 2003 that it is unconstitutional to execute the mentally retarded, for which the cutoff in Virginia is an IQ score of 70. In 1998, Atkins' IQ was recorded to be 59, but a defense expert retested it in 2004 to be 74, and in 2005 to be 76. A clinical psychologist on the case said that the more recent scores should be discounted because they were the result of "a forced march towards increased mental stimulation" provided by the case itself: "Oddly enough, because of his constant contact with the many lawyers that worked on his case, Mr. Atkins received more intellectual stimulation in prison than he did during his late adolescence and early adulthood. That included practicing his reading and writing skills, learning about abstract legal concepts and communicating with professionals." The article explains that there are other reasons why Atkin's IQ score may have risen: "I.Q. points are rarely completely stable and can drift, though within a relatively narrow range, typically by 5 points up or down. Psychologists recognize that practice drives scores higher. And I.Q.'s tend to rise over time, by about three points a decade."[14]

a. The article suggests that if you set up a prediction interval for a second IQ score in roughly the same time period, it would be centered at the first IQ score but there would be some variation. Does the number 5 describe the margin of error or the width of the prediction interval?

b. Based on the fact that Atkins scored 74 in 2004, is it plausible that another IQ test around the same time would yield a score less than 70?

c. Is it less plausible that another IQ test would yield a score less than 70, based on the fact that he also scored 76 in 2005?

d. Is the change from 59 in 1998 to 74 in 2004 and 76 in 2005 better explained by increased intellectual stimulation during that period or by the fact that IQ's tend to rise by about three points a decade?

*13.48 Exercise 13.1 on page 645 looked at the number of daily departures from various airports, along with the number of gates at those airports and the year in which the airline was established at that particular airport. Arrange in order each pair of possibilities presented in parts (a) through (g): first the one corresponding to the regression of departures on *gates* (plot on the top), then the one for regression of departures on *year established* (plot on the bottom).

a. correlations *r*: 0.08, 0.90

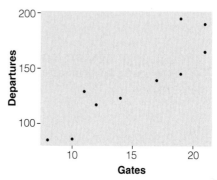

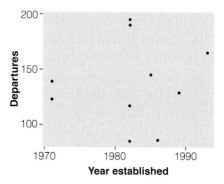

b. regression lines: $\hat{y} = -784 + 0.47x$, $\hat{y} = 29.2 + 7.12x$

c. spreads *s* about line: 17.55, 40.15

d. 95% confidence intervals for β_1: (4.32, 9.92), (−3.96, +4.89)

e. *P*-values to test if $\beta_1 = 0$: 0.000, 0.815

f. *t* statistics to test if $\beta_1 = 0$: 0.24, 5.85

g. 95% prediction intervals for daily departures when explanatory variable is equal to its mean: (40.3, 234.5), (94.96, 179.84)

13.49 On July 10, 2004, Andre Tolme became the first person to golf across Mongolia. He divided the country into 18 holes and set about completing the course, which was over 2 million yards long. Details, provided on the www.golfmongolia.com website, included information on how many shots Tolme needed to complete each hole, the par for each hole, and how many miles long it was. [By performing inference for regression, we are considering the relationships between the variables *shots versus par* or *shots versus miles* in general, taking these 18 holes to be a sample from a larger population of holes under similar circumstances.] Arrange in order each pair of possibilities presented in parts (a) through (g): first the one corresponding to the regression of number of shots on *par* (plot on the left), then the one for regression of shots on number of *miles* (plot on the right).

a. correlations r: 0.97, 0.55

b. regression lines: $\hat{y} = 134 + 0.822x$, $\hat{y} = -31.3 + 10.3x$

c. spreads s about line: 51.2, 180.9

d. 95% confidence intervals for β_1: (9.0, 11.6), (0.17, 1.48)

e. P-values to test if $\beta_1 = 0$: 0.000, 0.018

f. t statistics to test if $\beta_1 = 0$: 16.46, 2.63

g. 95% prediction intervals for number of shots when explanatory variable is equal to its mean: (282.1, 1,070.1), (564.7, 787.6)

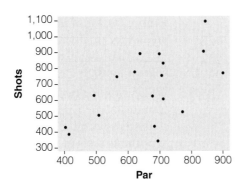

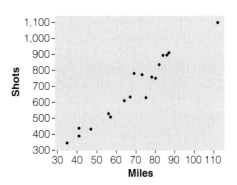

Using Software [see Technology Guide]: TWO QUANTITATIVE VARIABLES

*13.50 The Quantitative Environmental Learning Project reports on a study of river velocity versus depth: The data "were acquired at a station below Grand Coulee Dam at a distance of 13 feet from the edge of the river. The depth of the Columbia River at this spot was about 12 feet at the time of measurement. Velocities were measured at various heights in the water column."[15] Depths are recorded in feet and velocities in feet per second:

Depth	0.7	2.0	2.6	3.3	4.6	5.9	7.3	8.6	9.9	10.6
Velocity	1.55	1.11	1.42	1.39	1.39	1.14	0.91	0.59	0.59	0.41

a. Use software to produce a scatterplot of the data, and choose the correct word in each pair to complete this quotation from the report: "These data show a regular (1) *increase/decrease* of velocity with increasing depth of the river, as might be expected. The data are fairly (2) *linear/curved*, with a (3) *low/high* correlation coefficient."

b. If depth were recorded in meters instead of feet, which would be different: the value of r, the equation of the regression line, both of these, or neither of these?

c. How many degrees of freedom are appropriate for the t statistic used to test if the population slope β_1 of the regression line is zero?

d. Report the t statistic and the P-value for this test, and state a conclusion about whether or not depth and velocity are related in general.

e. Tell whether each of the following focuses on data production, displaying and summarizing data, probability, or statistical inference:

1. Finding slope b_1 and standardized slope t for the data

2. Finding the P-value

3. Deciding whether or not depth and velocity are related in general

4. Arriving at a method to obtain water depths and velocities

13.51 Samples of four rainbow trout and four largescale suckers taken from the Spokane River were tested for lead and zinc content in milligrams per kilogram.[16]

Rainbow Lead	Rainbow Zinc	Sucker Lead	Sucker Zinc
0.73	45.3	4.34	150.0
1.14	50.8	1.98	106.0
0.60	40.2	3.12	90.8
1.59	64.0	1.80	58.8

a. Use software to regress zinc on lead content for *rainbow trout;* first report the P-value.

b. State whether or not there is statistical evidence of a relationship for trout. If there is evidence of a relationship, state whether it appears to be positive or negative; strong, moderate, or weak.

c. Use software to regress zinc on lead content for *largescale suckers;* first report the P-value.

d. State whether or not there is statistical evidence of a relationship for suckers. If there is evidence of a relationship, state whether it appears to be positive or negative; strong, moderate, or weak.

e. Is it better to regress lead on zinc, or zinc on lead, or are they equally good?

f. If we did regress lead on zinc, instead of zinc on lead, would this affect the equation of the regression line, or the value of r, or both of these, or neither of these?

g. For *rainbow trout,* use the sample slope b_1 and standard error SE_{b_1} of the slope, and the fact that the t multiplier for 95% confidence and 2 degrees of freedom is 4.3, to construct an approximate 95% confidence interval for the population slope β_1, and fill in the blanks: If one rainbow trout has 1 more mg/kg of lead than another, we predict its zinc content to be higher by _____ to _____ mg/kg. (Round to the nearest tenth.)

h. For *largescale suckers,* use the sample slope b_1 and standard error SE_{b_1} of the slope, and the fact that the t multiplier for 95% confidence and 2 degrees of freedom is 4.3, to construct an approximate 95% confidence interval for the population slope β_1, and fill in the blanks: If one largescale sucker has 1 more mg/kg of lead than another, we predict its zinc content to be higher by _____ to _____ mg/kg. (Round to the nearest tenth.)

i. Which of your two confidence intervals contains zero? Explain how this is consistent with the results of your hypothesis tests in parts (b) and (d).

j. Suppose we wanted to use the data to set up a confidence interval to estimate the difference in mean lead contents for rainbow trout minus largescale suckers. Would the appropriate procedure be paired t, two-sample t, several-sample F, chi-square, or regression?

k. Suppose we wanted to use the data to set up a confidence interval to estimate the mean difference in lead and zinc contents for rainbow trout. Would the appropriate procedure be paired t, two-sample t, several-sample F, chi-square, or regression?

13.52 A large sample of students was surveyed at a particular university. Among other things, they were asked to report their weight and their age.

a. Explain why we can expect the relationship between weight and age to be positive.

b. Which makes the most sense to play the role of explanatory variable: weight or age; or are both equally good? Explain.

c. Suppose (just temporarily) that weight and age were not related, but that there were substantially more females than males who have unusually high age values. Would this lead to a negative or positive relationship between age and weight, if regression of weight on age were performed for males and females together?

d. Use software to separate out the weights and ages of males from females. Regress weight on age for each gender group and report the value of the correlation r and the P-value for males and for females.

e. Both gender groups contain high outliers for age and weight. Explain why the distribution of standardized sample slope should still be fairly close to a standard normal (z) distribution.

f. Do your regression results suggest that, in general, older students weigh more? Explain.

g. For males, use the sample slope b_1 and the standard error SE_{b_1} of the slope to construct an approximate 95% confidence interval for population slope β_1, and fill in the blanks: If one male is a year older than another, we predict him to be heavier by _____ to _____ pounds (round to the nearest tenth).

h. For females, use the sample slope b_1 and standard error SE_{b_1} of the slope to construct an approximate 95% confidence interval for population slope β_1, and fill in the blanks: If one female is a year older than another, we predict her to be heavier by _____ to _____ pounds (round to the nearest tenth).

i. Give at least one reason why one of your interval estimates for slope is wider than the other.

13.53 "Differentiation of Terminal Latewood Tracheids in Silver Fir Trees During Autumn," published online in the *Annals of Botany* in March 2005, describes research into the nature of the relationship between the trees' annual ring widths and the number of incompletely differentiated xylem cells per radial row.[17] The latter serve as an indication of how long it takes until the tree becomes dormant for the winter.

Ring Width	0.3	0.5	1.3	1.6	2.0	2.2	2.4	4.0	4.3	4.7
Inc. Diff. Cells	0.0	0.0	0.2	0.4	0.4	2.2	1.0	7.0	5.6	5.7

a. Use software to regress number of incompletely differentiated cells on annual ring width. Report the regression equation and tell whether the relationship is positive or negative for the sample of 10 trees.

b. Report the correlation and the P-value.

c. Choose the best summary from the following:

 1. There is weak evidence of a weak relationship in the population.

 2. There is weak evidence of a strong relationship in the population.

 3. There is strong evidence of a weak relationship in the population.

 4. There is strong evidence of a strong relationship in the population.

d. If a tree has very wide annual rings, what do you expect in terms of how late in the fall it becomes dormant?

*13.54 Researchers at the Max Planck Institute for Evolutionary Anthropology in Germany experimented on goats' ability to follow certain social cues, with results published in the online journal *Animal Behavior* in January 2005. "We tested goats' ability to use gaze and other communicative cues [touching, pointing] given by a human in a so-called object choice situation. An experimenter hid food out of sight of the subject under one of two cups. After baiting the cup the experimenter indicated the location of the food to the subject by using different cues."[18] This table shows scores for 13 goats when given the various cues, where the maximum possible score each time was 18, and the typical score for random guessing would be 9.

Touch	Point	Gaze
10	8	8
18	14	8
17	12	12
14	10	9
18	11	6
12	9	10
14	9	7
13	10	14
11	13	9
18	17	10
11	12	8
11	7	8
16	10	8

a. Use software to produce fitted line plots for regressing touch scores on point scores and touch scores on gaze scores. Which of the two plots shows tighter cluster about the regression line?

b. Report the value of s (typical prediction error size) for regression of touch score on *point* score.

c. Use software to produce a 95% prediction interval for touch score when a goat's point score equals 11 (the approximate mean point score value).

d. In some circumstances, the prediction interval's margin of error is close to $2s$, so the interval width is approximately $4s$. Explain why in this situation the interval is substantially wider than $4s$.

e. Report the value of s (typical prediction error size) for regression of touch score on *gaze* score.

f. Use software to produce a 95% prediction interval for touch score when a goat's gaze score equals 9 (the approximate mean gaze score value).

g. Report the width of your prediction interval in part (f) and verify that it is wider than $4s$.

h. Report correlations for the regression of touch score on point score and for the regression of touch score on gaze score; is the absolute value of the correlation closer to 1 for the larger or for the

smaller value of typical prediction size s? Explain why this is the case in terms of how tightly clustered or loosely scattered the scatterplot points are.

i. Both sample sizes are the same, but one of the P-values for testing for a relationship between touch score and the explanatory variable (point score or gaze score) is much smaller. Does it correspond to the regression with the absolute value of the correlation r closer to 0 or to 1?

j. If you wanted to predict touch score for another goat, would it be more helpful to know the goat's point score or gaze score?

13.55 The Quantitative Environmental Learning Project looked at "Characteristics of Selected Streams Along The West Side of The Sacramento Valley," including annual rainfall (in inches), drainage area (in square miles), and annual runoff (in inches per unit area).[19]

Creek	Rainfall	Drainage Area	Runoff
Middle Fork	40	244.0	14.1
Red Bank	24	93.5	6.4
Elder	30	136.0	9.6
Thomas	45	194.0	21.2
Grindstone	47	156.0	16.8
Stone Corral	21	38.2	2.2
Bear	27	100.0	6.0

a. Use software to produce fitted line plots for regressing runoff on rainfall and runoff on drainage; which of the two plots shows more scatter about the regression line?

b. Report the value of s (typical prediction error size) for regression of runoff on *rainfall*.

c. Use software to produce a 95% prediction interval for runoff when rainfall equals 30 (the approximate mean rainfall value).

d. In some circumstances, the prediction interval's margin of error is close to $2s$, so the interval width is approximately $4s$. Explain why in this situation the interval is substantially wider than $4s$.

e. Report the value of s (typical prediction error size) for regression of runoff on *drainage*.

f. Use software to produce a 95% prediction interval for runoff when drainage equals 140 (the approximate mean drainage value).

g. Report the width of your prediction interval in part (f) and verify that it is wider than $4s$.

h. Report correlations for the regression of runoff on rainfall and for the regression of runoff on drainage.

i. Is the correlation higher for the larger or for the smaller value of typical prediction size s? Explain why this is the case in terms of how tightly clustered or loosely scattered the scatterplot points are.

j. Both sample sizes are the same, but one of the P-values for testing for a relationship between runoff and the explanatory variable (rainfall or drainage) is much smaller. Does it correspond to the regression with the higher or lower value of correlation r?

k. If you wanted to predict annual runoff for another creek, would it be more helpful to know the annual rainfall or the drainage area at that location?

13.56 A large sample of students was surveyed at a particular university. Among other things, they were asked to report their age and how much money they had earned in the previous year, in thousands of dollars.

a. Use software to access the student survey data and produce a scatterplot of earnings versus age. Which of these best expresses the circumstances for this particular data set?

1. The responses are non-normal and the sample size is small.

2. The responses are non-normal and the sample size is large.

3. The responses are normal and the sample size is small.

4. The responses are normal and the sample size is large.

b. Find the correlation r and the P-value, and choose the best word in both cases to summarize the results: There is (1) *weak/borderline/strong* evidence of a (2) *weak/moderate/strong* relationship in the population.

c. Produce the regression equation and complete this rough summary of the relationship: Take a student's age and subtract _____ to find an estimate for how many thousands of dollars we predict to be earned.

d. According to the regression output, predictions of earnings based on age tend to be off by about how many dollars?

e. In general, which is narrower: a confidence interval for the mean response or a prediction interval for an individual response?

f. Considering that the students' mean age was about 20 years, which would be narrower: interval estimates when age equals 20 or when age equals 30?

g. Use software to produce a confidence interval for mean earnings and prediction interval for individual earnings when age equals 20, and also for when age equals 30. Indicate which is the narrowest of the four intervals and which is the widest.

h. A value of 3.5 thousand dollars is *not* plausible for which one of the following: mean earnings of all 20-year-old students in the population, mean earnings of all 30-year-old students in the population, earnings of an individual 20-year-old in the population, or earnings of an individual 30-year-old student in the population?

13.57 A large sample of students was surveyed at a particular university. Among other things, they were asked to report their weight, and how many minutes of television they had watched the day before.

a. Give at least two reasons why we can expect the relationship between weight and TV time to be positive.

b. If weight is taken to be the explanatory variable, what would this be suggesting in particular about weight and TV time?

c. If TV time is taken to be the explanatory variable, what would this be suggesting in particular about weight and TV time?

d. Explain why gender should be taken into account as a possible confounding variable.

e. Use software to separate out the weights and TV times of males from females. Regress weight on TV time for each gender group, and report the value of the correlation r and the P-value for males and for females, testing against the *one-sided alternative* $\beta_1 > 0$.

f. Although the correlations are practically identical, one of the P-values is considerably smaller than the other. What is the simplest explanation for how this came about?

g. Do your regression results suggest that, in general, watching more TV causes students to gain weight? Explain.

h. Do your regression results suggest that, in general, students who watch more TV tend to weigh more? Explain.

13.58 A survey was taken of a large sample of students at a particular university. Among other things, they were asked to report how many credits they were taking, and how many hours they had slept the night before.

a. If there is indeed a relationship between number of credits taken and hours slept, should we expect it to be positive or negative? Explain.

b. Use software to access the student survey data. Regress hours slept on credits; report the correlation r and the P-value.

c. Tell whether or not there is evidence of a relationship between credits and hours slept in the larger population of students. If there is, tell whether the relationship is positive or negative.

d. Either with software or by looking at the scatterplot, explain what all the influential observations have in common.

Discovering Research: TWO QUANTITATIVE VARIABLES

13.59 Find a newspaper article or Internet report about a study that looks at the relationship between two quantitative variables for a larger population, based on the relationship observed in a sample. Tell whether the relationship is positive or negative. Explain whether there is reason to suspect bias because of samples not being representative of the larger population of interest.

Reporting on Research: TWO QUANTITATIVE VARIABLES

13.60 Use results of Exercise 13.42 and relevant findings from the Internet to make a report on mercury and autism that relies on statistical information.

How Statistics Problems Fit into the Big Picture

© Jon Feingersh/Blend Images/CORBIS

B y now, all the pieces of the puzzle have fallen into place: We have progressed through all four stages in the process of performing statistics—data production, displaying and summarizing data, probability, and statistical inference. We have seen that within each stage, one of five situations typically applies—one categorical variable, one quantitative variable, one each categorical and quantitative, two categorical variables, or two quantitative variables. How can an understanding of these key aspects of the "big picture" help us to proceed when we are confronted with a real statistics problem in any context?

14.1 The Big Picture in Problem Solving

The very first step we take should be to consider the methods of data production. It is important to check if the values of a single variable, or for the relationship between variables, have been assessed in such a way as to accurately measure what is true for the sample. If so, then the appropriate display and summary tools can be applied, depending on which of the five variable-type situations is involved.

Also, before using information from the sample to perform statistical inference and draw conclusions about the larger population, the method of data production should again be considered. Now, our concern is whether or not we can assert that the sample is representative of the larger population in terms of the variables of interest. If this is the case, then the appropriate inference tools can be applied, again depending on which variable-type situation is involved.

The following table outlines the appropriate display/summary and inference tools for each of the five variable-type situations. Details can be found in Chapters 4 and 5 for displays and summaries, and in Chapters 9 through 13 for statistical inference.

Tools for Handling Various Situations	Displaying & Summarizing	Statistical Inference
1 categorical variable	Section 4.1 Display with pie chart or bar graph. Summarize with counts or (usually preferable) proportions or percentages in category of interest.	Chapter 9 Set up confidence interval for unknown population proportion, or test hypothesis that it equals a proposed value. Under the right conditions, standardized sample proportion follows standard normal (z) distribution.
1 quantitative variable	Section 4.2 Display with stemplot, histogram, boxplot, or (especially when normal) smooth curve. Summarize with five-number summary or (more often) mean and standard deviation.	Chapter 10 Set up confidence interval for unknown population mean, or test hypothesis that it equals a proposed value. Under the right conditions, standardized sample mean follows z distribution or t if sample is small and population standard deviation is unknown.
1 categorical & 1 quantitative variable	Section 5.1 **Paired design:** Display differences with histogram and summarize with mean and standard deviation. **Two- or several-sample design:** Display with side-by-side boxplots. Summarize by comparing five-number summaries or (more often) means and standard deviations.	Chapter 11 **Pairs:** Set up confidence interval for unknown population mean of differences, test hypothesis that it equals zero, using z or t procedure. **Two-sample:** Set up confidence interval for unknown difference between population means, or test hypothesis that it equals zero, using z or t procedure. **Several-sample:** Test hypothesis that population means are equal, using F procedure (analysis of variance, called ANOVA).
2 categorical variables	Section 5.2 Display with bar graph (graph explanatory variable horizontally). Summarize by comparing proportions or percentages in response categories of interest.	Chapter 12 If each variable has just two possibilities, set up confidence interval for difference between population proportions in category of interest, and use z test to see if they could be equal. In general, test if row and column variables are related using chi-square procedure.
2 quantitative variables	Section 5.3 Display with scatterplot. If linear, summarize with correlation and equation of regression line.	Chapter 13 Set up confidence interval for unknown slope of population regression line, or PI for individual response or CI for mean response to a given explanatory value. Test hypothesis that population slope of regression line is zero (equivalent to claim that the variables are not related) using t procedure.

Suppose four students are working on the practice final exam questions presented at the beginning of this book pages 1 and 2, using the table of tools shown above to determine a solution strategy for each.

Students Talk Stats

Choosing the Appropriate Statistical Tools: Question 1

Brittany: *"The question says, 'Suppose systolic blood pressures for 7 patients eating dark chocolate daily for two weeks dropped an average of 5 points, whereas those for a control group of 6 patients eating white chocolate remained unchanged. If the standardized difference between blood pressure decreases was 2.1, do we have convincing evidence that dark chocolate is beneficial?*

"There's a categorical explanatory variable for whether they ate dark chocolate or white, and blood pressure is the quantitative response. It's a two-sample design because it's two separate groups of patients. It's an inference question because we

Students Talk Stats continued ➔

Students Talk Stats continued

need to find out if the difference between dropping 5 points and 0 points is dramatic enough to convince someone that dark chocolate can lower blood pressure in general. So we need to refer to Chapter 11, but I'm not sure if it's going to be z or t."

Adam: *"It has to be two-sample t because the sample sizes—7 and 6—are small, and you can't expect them to know population standard deviations. So the standardized difference must have been calculated from sample standard deviations. A two-sample t statistic of 2.1 for just a few degrees of freedom isn't necessarily small enough to convince someone of a difference in the larger populations. I'd call the results borderline. Maybe if they tried again with more patients they'd be able to get more evidence that dark chocolate helps. I'd like to be in a study where all I had to do was eat chocolate for two weeks, and get paid for it!"*

Although the issue of data production is not raised explicitly in the question about chocolate, it is always worth considering. First, we would want some assurance that assignment to dark or white chocolate was randomized. Also, blood pressures must be measured without bias. As far as displays and summaries are concerned, a side-by-side boxplot—discussed in Section 5.1—would be appropriate; sample means are the relevant summary, specified in the problem statement.

Students Talk Stats

Choosing the Appropriate Statistical Tools: Question 2

Carlos: *"The next question says, 'According to a 2007 report, 47% of 1,623 U.S. Internet users surveyed by the Pew Internet & American Life Project had searched for information about themselves online. Give a 95% confidence interval for the percentage of all U.S. Internet users who searched online for information about themselves.'*

"This problem just has one categorical variable: whether or not Internet users have searched for information about themselves online. We look back at Chapter 9 and set up a 95% confidence interval for the population proportion just by plugging into the formula."

Adam: *"If they'd surveyed me, I would have told them I Google myself all the time. Sometimes I find out stuff about myself I didn't even know. Anyway, their sample size was large enough, so we're OK with normality. Otherwise the interval could be wrong."*

Adam is right to verify that the sample size warrants constructing an interval based on the standard normal distribution. For the interval to be truly accurate, the question should be posed in a straightforward way to elicit honest responses. Also, we would like some justification for assuming those 1,623 survey respondents to be fairly representative of all Internet users. Neither of these data production issues is particularly worrisome, because the Pew organization is reputable. Although a display is generally not needed for values of a single categorical variable like this, if desired a pie chart or bar graph could be used, as discussed in Section 4.1. The summary—sample percentage—has been reported in the problem statement.

Choosing the Appropriate Statistical Tools: Question 3

Dominique: *"The next question says, 'Researchers found that 9 out of 15 stroke patients receiving bat saliva had an excellent recovery, compared with 4 out of 17 who were untreated. Does this provide evidence that bat saliva is effective in treating stroke patients?*

"Now there's two categorical variables—whether a patient gets bat saliva or not, and whether or not there's excellent recovery. The table shows we need to refer to Chapter 12 and use chi-square. It should be pretty straightforward to find the expected counts and the chi-square statistic and see if it's large or not."

Adam: *"Since each of the variables just has two possibilities, you could also use a z test to see if the population proportion with an excellent recovery is higher for patients getting bat saliva. Then the P-value would be half of what it is for the more general chi-square test. If it was me, I'd want to see a pretty small P-value before I'd consider drinking bat spit."*

Whether a z or a chi-square test is used, we would want to know that having an "excellent recovery" was assessed for the patients without bias, and that they were randomly assigned to receive bat saliva or a placebo. The data could be displayed with a bar graph, and results (9/15 versus 4/17) could be converted to decimals as a way of summarizing and comparing responses for the two groups. These display and summary techniques were presented in Section 5.2.

These three practice final exam questions all required the students to perform statistical inference, which actually involves all four statistical processes together. Other problems, such as those in the upcoming chapter exercises, may focus on just one of these processes. These exercises will let you practice orienting yourself when confronted with a variety of statistical problems, so that you can identify the appropriate tools to use in any context.

First, we present a few examples.

EXAMPLE 14.1 DATA PRODUCTION FOR ONE CATEGORICAL VARIABLE

Background: The Census wants to record whether or not a citizen speaks another language besides English at home. If the form simply asks, "Do you speak another language besides English at home?" will the true proportion be measured accurately?

Question: Which of the five variable situations, and which of the four processes, are we interested in here?

Response: This involves a single categorical variable (whether or not the citizen speaks another language besides English at home). The process of interest is data production. Specifically, we must be concerned that some speakers of another language might not read English well enough to respond accurately to the question.

EXAMPLE 14.2 SUMMARIZING TWO CATEGORICAL VARIABLES

Background: The *New York Times* reported on grade inflation, based on a survey of 276,000 incoming freshmen at more than 400 colleges and universities, conducted by the Higher Education Research Institute at UCLA in 2003. "Almost half reported an A average in high school, up from 18 percent in 1968."[1]

Question: Which of the five variable situations, and which of the four processes, are we interested in?

Response: Here the explanatory variable is year, and it is categorical because just two year values (1968 and 2003) are being compared. The response is grade, also categorical because the study looked at whether or not a freshman had an A average in high school. The process is summarizing, because they report what was observed for the surveyed freshmen without making generalizations to all freshmen. Methods were presented in Section 5.2.

EXAMPLE 14.3 PROBABILITY ABOUT A CATEGORICAL EXPLANATORY AND A QUANTITATIVE RESPONSE VARIABLE

Background: Children's fitness was assessed by finding the distance, in meters, that they can run in 6 minutes. Researchers found the mean fitness scores of sampled children who did and did not watch TV daily were close enough to have come about by chance, if overall mean fitnesses were actually the same for all children who do and don't watch TV daily.

Question: Which of the five variable situations, and which of the four processes, are we interested in?

Response: This focuses on a categorical explanatory variable (daily TV watched or not) and a quantitative response (fitness score). The process is probability: Apparently, the probability of the observed difference coming about when sampling from two groups with equal mean fitness scores is not especially low. Methods for finding probabilities based on a normal approximation were established in Part III. (This probability calculation would pave the way for a statistical inference conclusion: Because the probability is not small, we would conclude that the study has *not* produced evidence to convince us that watching TV affects children's fitness score.)

Many real-life research studies feature situations that go beyond those outlined in the table on page 678. For instance, two-way ANOVA problems involve quantitative responses to two categorical explanatory variables. Multiple regression problems involve more than two quantitative variables. In addition, we have mentioned that methods based on normally distributed sample means are not always appropriate, in which case nonparametric methods should be considered. Two-way ANOVA, multiple regression, and nonparametrics are covered in the CD that accompanies this text. Furthermore, relationships between two quantitative variables may be nonlinear, requiring us to explore whether a transformation should be used.

Still, a vast number of statistical problems encountered in the real world can easily be handled with the methods presented in this book. Having mastered these techniques, you are now in a position to assess statistical claims encountered in the media, or in other college courses, or on the job. You are also equipped to analyze data yourself, and even to produce data in a thoughtful, effective way. From now on, you can use this newly acquired expertise to better understand and explain the complicated world that we live in, a skill that brings great rewards, both personal and professional.

Throughout this book we have focused at different times on each of the five variable-type situations within each of the four basic processes. These exercises let you practice pinpointing which situation and process apply.

CHAPTER 14   EXERCISES

Note: Asterisked numbers indicate exercises whose answers are provided in the Solutions to Selected Exercises section, on page 689.

For each of the following, identify type of variable or variables involved, and which of the four processes (data production, displaying and summarizing, probability, or statistical inference) applies. If the process is displaying and summarizing or statistical inference, tell what chapter or section presents the relevant tools.

14.1 "Boozy Bees May Offer Clues About Pickled People" describes a study in which some bees were given alcohol, while others were given plain sugar water. Researchers gave the bees a number rating of their industriousness.[2] The study's results would be undermined if the researchers knew whether or not a bee had been given alcohol when it was time to rate the bee's industriousness.

14.2 A study of wolf spiders found that, if overall proportions of male wolf spiders cannibalized were the same before and after mating, the probability of a difference between sample proportions as extreme as the one observed would be 0.572.[3]

Sexual cannibalism in spiders: hit or miss?

14.3 The Los Angeles *Daily News* reported the results of a study of several thousand babies born in California in the year 2000. Researchers found that babies born to mothers in the most polluted areas consistently weighed less—about 1 ounce less—than babies born to mothers who lived in clean-air cities.

14.4 Before the presidential election of 2004, the Gallup polling organization, in taking samples of "likely voters," made sure that the sample was comprised of 40% Republicans, 33% Democrats, and 28% Independents, even though the percentages voting in 2000 were 35% Republicans, 39% Democrats, and 26% Independents. Did this play a role in Gallup's reporting of which candidate had the majority of votes?

*14.5 If female damselfish have no general preference for larger males, the chance of at least 21 in 31 choosing the larger of two males is 0.035.

*14.6 In "Compliance With The Item Limit of The Food Supermarket Express Checkout Lane: An Informal Look," researcher J. Trinkaus reported, "75 15-min observations of customers' behavior at a food supermarket showed that only about 15% of shoppers observed the item limit of the express lane."[4]

*14.7 Based on a sample of Iberian rock lizards in experimental conditions, it was concluded that, in general, the amount of active behavior is higher for lizards in low-risk situations than for those in high-risk situations.

*14.8 Researchers asked parents of children who had died of cancer: "Did you talk about death with your child at any time?" None of the 147 who did so regretted talking about death, but 69 of the 282 who had not talked about death said they wished they had.[5] The difference is pronounced enough that we can conclude for all parents of dying children, they would be less likely to experience regrets if they talked about death with their children.

*14.9 Adult weekend lift ticket price was regressed on vertical drop of slope (in feet) for a sample of ski resorts in the Middle Atlantic states. An additional 3 cents were charged for every additional foot in vertical drop.

14.10 "What's in a Name? Studies Find That Afrocentric Names Often Incur a Bias" tells about two economists who wanted to research racial discrimination in hiring practices. They created fictitious resumes, and for every pair of similar-quality resumes sent in response to a help-wanted ad, one was randomly assigned a white-sounding name (such as Emily Walsh or Greg Baker) and the other a black-sounding name (such as Lakisha Washington or Jamal Jones). The resumes with white-sounding names received call-backs 10% of the time, whereas those with black-sounding names received call-backs only 7.5% of the time.[6] Because the difference is too large to be attributed to chance, we conclude that some employers do discriminate on the basis of race of applicants.

14.11 "Ugly Kids Get Less Attention from Parents," reported in the University of Alberta's online medical news site, states that a researcher "has shown that parents are more likely to give better care and pay closer attention to good-looking children compared to unattractive ones."[7] A team of researchers observed over 400 2- to 5-year-old children with their parents in supermarkets, and independently assessed the children's attractiveness. "Findings showed that 1.2 percent of the least attractive children were buckled in, compared with 13.3 percent of the most attractive youngsters." Because this was an observational study, we cannot rule out the possibility of causation in the opposite direction: Perhaps children's attractiveness is influenced by their parents' attentiveness.

*14.12 "Mouth Piercings May Cause Gums to Recede" reported in 2005 that "researchers at Ohio State University looked at 58 young adults with an average age between 21 and 22. Half had pierced lips and the other half did not, although both groups were otherwise alike in age and gender. Among the subjects with a pierced lip, 41.4% had receding gums, although only 6.9% of those without a pierced lip suffered from this periodontal condition."[8] Such a big difference is not at all likely to have occurred by chance if piercing had no effect on gums.

14.13 "Exercise Beats Calcium at Boosting Girl's Bones" reported on a study published in the *Journal of Pediatrics* in 2004, which found that "girls with better muscle development also had stronger bones."[9] Muscle development was measured in terms of the girls' lean body mass, and the study's author explained that for their sample of girls, "a 1 kilogram increase in lean mass was associated with a $2\frac{1}{2}\%$ increase in their bone strength."

*14.14 The American Time Use Survey of 2003 stated that the average American consumes 31 pounds of cheese in a year. A reporter speculated that Americans' love of cheese may play a role in the fact that they're getting heavier. If an observational study showed that the more cheese you eat, the more you weigh, can it be concluded that cheese in particular makes you gain weight? Could the theory be tested with an experiment instead of with an observational study?

14.15 A student wrote in to "Ask Marilyn" in *Parade* magazine about whether or not she should resist the urge to go back and change her answers in multiple-choice tests. Marilyn replied that in studies, about 50% of changes went from wrong to right; 25% went from right to wrong; and 25% went from wrong to wrong.

14.16 *Men's Health* magazine used data on body mass index, back-surgery rates, usage of gyms, etc. to grade the quality of men's "abs" (abdominal muscles). The average rating for men in Columbus was quite low, closer to the minimum 0 than to the maximum 4.

*14.17 In 2004, a 42-year-old man underwent surgery to reduce his weight of 1,072 pounds. If all male weights are normal with mean 190 pounds and standard deviation 30 pounds, how unlikely is it for a man to weigh this much?

*14.18 A recent study for Planned Parenthood found that children who watched the most sex-saturated television were twice as likely to engage in sexual activity within the next year as those who reported a low level of television watching. Before concluding that sex on TV increases the likelihood of sexual activity, we should consider the possibility that it was their heightened interest in sex that caused them to choose that type of programming. Unfortunately, it is difficult to rule out such confounding variables in an observational study.

*14.19 After the fatal crash of a small plane in North Carolina in January 2002, the FAA became concerned about excess weight on planes. Subsequently, passengers on small planes were asked how much they weighed, in order to ensure that the limit was not exceeded. The director of flight standards at the FAA stated that the airlines would need to take into account the fact that people usually under-report their weight to a certain extent.

14.20 The American Association of Retired People (AARP) conducted a survey, in which it discovered that, on average, those polled wanted to live to the age of 91. Does it matter whether the AARP surveyed Americans of all ages or just retired people?

*14.21 In the American Nurses Association online "Health and Safety Survey of 2001," participants were asked, "In the past year, have you been physically assaulted at work?"; 807 of 4,722 nurses answered yes.[10] Assuming the sample was representative, we can conclude that between 16% and 18% of *all* nurses had been assaulted that year.

14.22 The American Nurses Association found the proportion of *surveyed* nurses to have over 25 years of experience was $1,189/4,507 = 0.26$. Considering this was an online survey, 0.26 may be an underestimate, because older, more experienced nurses would be less likely to complete the survey.

14.23 If lizards' activity did not depend on whether they were subjected to low-risk or high-risk treatment, the probability of observing a difference as extreme as 4.9 ± 0.3 times emerging from the nest versus 3.4 ± 0.4 times is less than 0.0001.

14.24 In "The Height Gap," Burkhard Bilger of the *New Yorker* reports that tall men get married sooner, get promoted quicker, and earn higher wages. According to one recent study, for every additional inch in height a worker earns an additional $800 a year, give or take about $200.

14.25 The proportion of teenagers having suicidal thoughts was close enough for groups who had and had not been given a survey about suicide that we can conclude surveying teens about suicide doesn't make them have suicidal thoughts any more than they would otherwise.

14.26 In a study on Antarctic birds' use of scent to find their mates, 17 out of 20 birds selected the bag that had previously held their mate over another otherwise identical bag. If birds chose bags at random, the chance of doing this well would be only 0.0002.

*14.27 Workers were surveyed about neatness, as well as other background information. 11% of people making more than $75,000 annually described themselves as "neat freaks," but 66% of those earning less than $35,000 claimed that description.

14.28 A study looked at courtship behavior of damselfish, and found that in a sample of 31 females offered a choice between a small and a large male, 21 chose the large male.

*14.29 A survey asked people to say who was the most famous athlete of all time (top choice was Michael Jordan). Does it matter what time of year the survey was conducted?

14.30 "Drop In Temperatures Could Lower Ticket Prices, Too" was a sports page article that pointed out that "cold weather might reduce the cost of tickets for [Steelers] fans who are trying to scalp their way into Heinz Field for the AFC playoff game against the New York Jets Saturday [January 15, 2005]."[7] Some ticket brokers, however, believed that "the cold weather in the forecast isn't diminishing demand."[11] How could data be gathered to determine if prices tend to go down as the weather gets colder?

14.31 A statistical analysis was performed on stories published in *The New Yorker*, focusing on many variables, including main story topics. The percentages of topics for stories published between 1995 and 2001 were listed as follows: sex 47%, children 26%, travel 25%, drugs 5%, money 10%, religion 9%, illness 12%. Did the researcher allow for the possibility that a story had more than one main topic?

14.32 When reporting pounds lost by patients in a weight-loss study, researchers averaged in losses of patients who had dropped out by assuming those losses to equal zero.

14.33 Based on a survey of thousands of 12th graders in 2004 that asked, "How intelligent do you think you are compared to others your age?" we conclude that the population mean is higher than 4, which is the average of the response options (from 1 to 7).

14.34 A newspaper report on "regifting" claimed that most Americans engage in the practice of passing on unwanted gifts to others, since 323, or 64%, of 504 respondents admitted to regifting. A footnote to the description of the survey methodology mentions that 776 people responded to the survey, and only 504 qualified in the survey based on a screener question that was posed to filter out respondents who reported that they never received undesired holiday gifts. Should eBay (which conducted the survey as a promotional stunt to encourage selling unwanted gifts online) have screened out all the people who said they never received undesired holiday gifts? Does it make a difference in the reported percentage?

14.35 "Office Workers Give Away Passwords For a Chocolate Bar!" is Infosecurity Europe 2004's April 20 headline; the report goes on to describe how 71% of 172 office workers willingly revealed their computer password to a surveyor posted outside a London subway station at rush hour. However, no check was made to verify that the passwords provided in exchange for chocolate bars were authentic.

*14.36 A Harvard researcher produced evidence that, in general, the number of witchcraft trials in various years between 1520 and 1770 increased when temperature decreased, possibly because villagers tended to target "witches" as scapegoats when bad weather produced food shortages.

Blame the weather on witches?

*14.37 www.fairtest.org reported means and standard deviations of SAT scores for students in various income classes to show how much better higher-income students did than lower-income students.

14.38 Psychology researchers from the University of California, San Diego, set about finding an answer to the question, "Do dogs resemble their owners?" In their study, student judges were presented with a photo of a dog owner and photos of two dogs; one dog was the actual pet, the other was an imposter. If more than half of the judges correctly paired a given dog with his or her owner, this was considered a "match."[12] Although a majority of purebred dogs were correctly matched—16 out of 25—it is not so improbable for the judges to do this well by mere random guessing.

14.39 Based on a large study that took into account confounding variables such as household income, physical activity, smoking, etc., researchers concluded that, in general, the more children you have, the more you weigh.

14.40 A newspaper reported on an AARP Singles Survey of men and women ages 40 to 69 conducted in June 2003, where 3,501 singles were asked, "What for you is the desirable or preferred age of a dating partner?"[13] Of the women surveyed, 35% preferred an age younger than themselves; of the men surveyed, 80% preferred an age younger than themselves.

14.41 A study by the European School Survey Project on Alcohol and Other Drugs (ESPAD) found that 277 in a sample of 543 15- to 16-year-olds in the Faroe Islands had consumed five or more alcoholic beverages in a row at least once in the past month, compared to 1,207 in a sample of 8,940 15- to 16-year-olds in Poland. To best put the data in perspective, researchers should report proportions rather than counts.

14.42 In a sample of students from prominent Northeastern private schools, close to 10% received special accommodations for SATs. This is significantly higher than the percentage for all students nationwide (which is less than 2%), suggesting that, in general, private school students receive special accommodations more often than what is typical.

*14.43 A new weight-loss drug was tested by comparing pounds lost by patients randomly assigned to take the drug or a placebo. Both groups were given a diet and consultations with a dietician, in order to make their circumstances as similar as possible.

*14.44 Systolic blood pressures for 7 patients eating dark chocolate daily for two weeks dropped an average of 5 points, whereas those of a control group of 6 patients eating white chocolate remained unchanged. The difference was large enough that it is unlikely to have occurred by chance.

14.45 An article entitled "Piano Lessons Boost Math Scores" states that "second-grade students who took piano lessons for 4 months scored significantly higher on math than children who did not."[14] In order to decide how convincing the results are, we need to know if students (or parents) chose to take piano lessons or if they were randomly assigned.

*14.46 Researchers used mean and standard deviation of the amount of time it took a large sample of Americans to get to and from work in order to estimate the mean travel time for all Americans to be within a certain range.

14.47 A newspaper article entitled "Study Forced Orphans to Stutter" tells about a 1939 study carried out on 22 orphans in Iowa. One group of 11 was given positive speech therapy, and they were unaffected. The other 11 were induced to stutter by constant badgering on the part of their speech therapist: Out of those 11, 8 became chronic stutterers. Due to the unethical nature of the treatment, was there some way to gather the information via an observational study rather than an experiment?

14.48 "Remains Found of Downsized Human Species" reports that "once upon a time, on a tropical island midway between Asia and Australia, there lived a race of little people whose adults stood just 3.5 feet high."[15] The adult female skeleton discovered in 2003 was small enough to warrant identification as a new human species, called *Homo floresiensis* after the island of Flores where it was discovered. The skeleton's height can be put in perspective by considering that pygmies' heights have approximate mean 54 inches and standard deviation 2 inches. Would 3.5 feet (42 inches) be improbably low by these standards?

14.49 Mean number of chicks born to banded penguins in a study was so much less than the mean observed for unbanded penguins that we have convincing evidence that banded birds in general produce fewer offspring.

14.50 If there were no linear relationship between men's and women's illiteracy rates for all countries in the world, the chance of such a strong positive slope relating men's and women's illiteracy rates in a sample of 19 countries would be close to zero.

Solutions to Selected Exercises

Chapter 1

1.1 categorical

1.2 **a.** two quantitative variables **b.** one categorical and one quantitative variable **c.** one categorical and one quantitative variable **d.** two categorical variables

1.3 **a.** quantitative **b.** mean

1.4 **a.** The individuals are people around the world; the variable is whether they approve or disapprove of the Iraq war, and it is categorical. **b.** The individuals are countries; the variable is what percentage of a country's people disapprove of the Iraq war, and it is quantitative. **c.** The individuals are countries; the variable is whether the country as a whole approves or disapproves of the Iraq war, and it is categorical.

1.5 performing statistical inference

1.6 **a.** The individuals are adults, the variable is marital status, and it is categorical. **b.** The individuals are states, the variable is divorce rate, and it is quantitative. **c.** population

1.7 displaying and summarizing data

1.8 categorical

1.9 categorical

1.10 **a.** categorical (able to cope without cell phone or not) **b.** with a percentage

1.11 **a.** quantitative **b.** mean

1.12 **a.** location of first sexual encounter **b.** categorical **c.** with a percentage

1.13 performing statistical inference

1.14 population

1.15 Apparently the numbers arose from Census data, referring to entire populations, not samples.

1.16 **a.** sample **b.** Would you like to live to be at least 100? **c.** How old would you like to live to be?

1.17 **a.** (2) For each individual (appliance), a number value is recorded (percentage owning that appliance), and so there is one quantitative variable involved. **b.** (3) There is a categorical explanatory variable (which year—1987 or 2001) and a quantitative response variable (what percentage of households owned the appliance in that year). **c.** (2) There is one quantitative variable (how many television sets are owned).

1.18 **a.** appliances **b.** what percent of homes had the appliance **c.** quantitative

1.19 **a.** which year (1987 or 2001) **b.** categorical **c.** what percentage of homes had the appliance **d.** quantitative **e.** 2001

1.20 **a.** quantitative **b.** mean

1.21 **a.** $Q \to C$ **b.** $C \to C$ **c.** $Q \to Q$ **d.** $C \to Q$

1.22 data production

1.23 **a.** data production **b.** displaying and summarizing **c.** probability **d.** statistical inference

1.24 quantitative

1.25 displaying and summarizing data

1.26 **a.** gender **b.** categorical **c.** type of graffiti **d.** categorical **e.** proportions

1.27 response

1.28 explanatory

1.29 Carlos

1.30 probability

1.31 Responses will vary.

1.32 Responses will vary.

Chapter 2

2.1 **a.** Level of pain is the quantitative response. **b.** Marijuana or conventional treatment is the categorical explanatory variable. **c.** statistical inference

2.2 **a.** Deciding which customers to poll is concerned with sampling; deciding what to ask them is concerned with study design. **b.** Satisfaction would be categorical if customers were simply asked whether or not they were satisfied. It would be quantitative if they were asked to rate their level of satisfaction on a numerical scale. There are many other possibilities in either case.

2.3 **a.** Deciding which people should be polled focuses on sampling. **b.** Deciding how to assess people's physical activity focuses on study design. **c.** Physical activity could be categorical if they were asked whether or not they had engaged in physical activity beyond a certain level the day before, but there are many other possibilities. **d.** Physical activity could be quantitative if they were asked to report for how long they had engaged in physical activity in the past day, week, or month, but there are many other possibilities.

2.4   **a.** quantitative   **b.** mean   **c.** gender

2.5   **a.** nonrepresentative sample   **b.** higher

2.6   **a.** sampling frame different from population
b. volunteer sample   **c.** haphazard sample
d. nonresponse bias   **e.** convenience sample

2.7   haphazard sample

2.8   convenience sample

2.9   both

2.10   multi-stage sampling

2.11   Brittany's answer is best: take a stratified
(according to gender) sample.

2.12   e-mail, because a disproportionately high number
of respondents would use the Internet to get
sports information

2.13   Sample size doesn't matter because results are
biased anyway, due to the fact that respondents to
an e-mail survey are not representative of the
general population in terms of how often they use
the Internet to get sports information.

2.14   **a.** using a self-selected sample   **b.** It doesn't
make a difference because larger samples are not
helpful if the sample is not representative.

2.15   **a.** all introductory statistics students at that
university   **b.** all college-aged females

2.16   **a.** all humans   **b.** all male students at that
university

2.17   The top 20 are not a representative sample of all
the nation's universities, so we should not use
information from the study to draw more general
conclusions.

2.18   because all the countries in South America do not
represent any larger group

2.19   systematic sampling

2.20   **a.** categorical   **b.** proportion   **c.** younger
d. overestimate

2.21   self-selected

2.22   **a.** convenience sample   **b.** Marijuana cannot be
administered to a random sample of people.

2.23   cluster sample

2.24   random sample

2.25   the one who surveys four individuals

2.26   by stratifying first according to gender

2.27   **a.** at the sampling stage   **b.** sampling frame not
matching population

2.28   Sampling at random is the best way to take a
proper, scientific sample. The intended word was
probably "haphazard."

2.29   Responses will vary.

2.30   Responses will vary.

Chapter 3

3.1   **a.** The original design was an observational study.
b. The resident used anecdotal evidence.

3.2   several observational studies

3.3   anecdotal evidence

3.4   **a.** The NIH study was conducted by a well-
known and well-established governmental body,
and certainly would have considered a large
number and broad range of "get-tough" camps
before drawing its conclusions.   **b.** The book
would include very personal and detailed accounts
of the author's experiences.

3.5   If the study concludes they do nothing to prevent
criminal behavior, then these programs may be
reduced or eliminated, depriving some troubled
youths of the opportunity to benefit from them.

3.6   If the study concludes they are beneficial, then
parents or guardians would continue to rely on such
programs to benefit their children, when they should
be seeking some other more effective remedy.

3.7   observational study

3.8   the researchers

3.9   **a.** Obviously, it is harmful to victims who suffer
heart attacks as a result of being tasered. On the
other hand, if the deaths were coincidental, then
blaming them on Tasers could lead to police being
deprived of something that they consider helpful.
b. Using a very small sample poses more risk of
concluding Tasers in general are safe when in fact
some are not.

3.10   **a.** anecdotal evidence   **b.** sample survey
c. observational study

3.11   The question about whether the respondent feels
the national firearms registry program should be
abandoned needs to include a response option for
people who aren't sure or have no opinion.

3.12   nonsmokers

3.13   asking how many will be at Thanksgiving dinner

3.14   **a.** closed   **b.** The scale of 1 to 5 has a single
middle option (3) for people who want to give a
neutral response.

3.15   **a.** excellent, very good, good, fair, poor
b. excellent, very good, good, fair, or poor
c. both

3.16   Surveyers wanted respondents to be in favor.

3.17   For all four questions it is clear what particular
answer the surveyors want to elicit.

3.18   data production

3.19   ordered as above

3.20   Reverse order is arguably better, so that respondents
have a more concrete basis for their answer about
relative financial situation. There may be viable
theories for why the original order is better.

3.21   **a.** Researchers want to avoid bias that may result
if there is a tendency to agree with whatever
opinion was presented first (or whatever opinion
was presented second).   **b.** Researchers could see
if the proportions in favor of the registry program
are roughly the same, whether this opinion was
stated first or second.   **c.** 1,000 respondents
d. Make it less complicated.

3.22   **a.** good   **b.** overestimate   **c.** proportions

3.23 a. closed   **b.** 200

3.24 It's more important to assure respondents of their anonymity when asking how they rate their instructor's preparedness; otherwise, they may fear repercussions on their grade for the class.

3.25 the first

3.26 People tend to feel more anonymous when responding by computer, and would be less fearful of detection by their employers.

3.27 via computer lab facilities (provides more of a sense of anonymity)

3.28 hard-to-define concept

3.29 a. response variable imprecise   **b.** explanatory variable imprecise

3.30 a. observational study   **b.** confounding variables (those who are predisposed to be mentally—and physically—sharp would also tend to be more active walkers)   **c.** Study different age groups separately.   **d.** walking, (1)   **e.** mental impairment, (1)   **f.** proportions

3.31 a. gender   **b.** smoking (or second-hand smoke)

3.32 paired

3.33 a. paired   **b.** Statistical inference is not relevant because the top 20 universities are not a random sample of any larger population about which we could draw conclusions.

3.34 a. Teens could have been asked to recall how often they watched pro wrestling and how often they had started a date fight over the past several weeks or months. Faulty memories would be a major drawback to this design.   **b.** Teens could be asked to keep journals to record what TV shows they watch over the next several weeks or months, and also record their behavior on dates. The drawback to this design is that the teens might not behave naturally if the journals make them self-conscious about their TV viewing and/or date behavior. **c.** Teens with violent tendencies may be the ones who are more inclined to watch pro wrestling on TV; causation might be occurring in the opposite direction from what the headline suggests.

3.35 a. The study was retrospective because participants were asked to recall physical activity during the previous month.   **b.** Physical activity is treated as categorical, whether the respondents were inactive or not.   **c.** The explanatory variable is whether a participant lived in a small town or a large urban area, treated as categorical.

3.36 a. A study of whether acupuncture can relieve stress is more susceptible to the placebo effect because the idea of treatment might relax patients. In contrast, the idea of treatment could not really influence hair growth.   **b.** In the Rogaine study, it would be easier to make subjects blind by giving them a similar cream without the active ingredient. In contrast, it would be difficult to simulate the administration of acupuncture needles.

3.37 They compared weal sizes to avoid the experimenter effect: Reporting pain would be very subjective, and the experimenters were not blind.

3.38 lack of realism

3.39 the study that asks participants to have tissue removed from their upper arm

3.40 a. A random sample wouldn't necessarily consent to being given a puncture wound.   **b.** Writing about how they spent their free time was the control, as similar as possible to the treatment (writing about an upsetting experience) except for the aspect being tested—what they wrote about. **c.** The response variable was wound size after 2 weeks, apparently quantitative.   **d.** means **e.** lack of realism   **f.** They could first separate subjects by sex, then randomly assign one or the other treatment to the males, and similarly to the females.   **g.** paired

3.41 a. lack of realism   **b.** placebo effect   **c.** not important because temperature and melatonin are very objective measurements

3.42 small sample because otherwise it would be too expensive

3.43 observational studies because they aren't as expensive

3.44 The experiment to test if taking a blood pressure medication reduces the risk of heart attacks could easily include a control group taking a placebo pill instead of the blood pressure medication, and both groups of subjects would be blind to treatment.

3.45 a. If it were an observational study, math scores could have been higher because children whose parents enroll them in piano lessons would tend to have higher levels of academic achievement. (Type of family to actively seek piano lessons or not would be the confounding variable.) **b.** two-sample   **c.** paired   **d.** If the two-sample design was used, it is possible that students randomly assigned to take piano lessons were already better at math; if twins were used, their math skills are more likely to be comparable at the start of the experiment.   **e.** not so important because assessing math scores is a fairly objective process, whereby results would tend not to be affected by researchers' bias

3.46 The study to see if people can lower their cholesterol by eating oatmeal every day for a month uses a before-and-after design.

3.47 Male subjects could be randomly divided into two groups, both given unmarked tubes of cream; some contain Rogaine and others a similar preparation that does not include the active ingredient. Hair coverage is measured for both groups before and after the treatment period.

3.48 a. an experiment   **b.** second group **c.** randomly assigning participants to one of the three groups   **d.** lack of realism

3.49 a. observational study   **b.** people's behaviors affected by their awareness of participating in a prospective study

3.50 a. an experiment   **b.** treatments that are unethical to impose

3.51 a. Insects which the pesticide was designed to combat could thrive and be an annoyance or worse; the pesticide's manufacturer would also suffer financially. **b.** The manufacturer would be more in favor of avoiding this type of mistake.

3.52 a. Humans and their environment could suffer damage from the pesticide's chemicals. **b.** Environmentalists would be more in favor of avoiding this type of mistake.

3.53 age of the child

3.54 the experiment because results are produced for such a small sample

3.55 a. asking veterinarians **b.** calling homeowners

3.56 a. The article's title suggests that eating dinner with the family is the explanatory variable, and being adjusted or not is the response. **b.** "Well-adjusted teens eat dinner with the family," or something along these lines. **c.** quantitative (summarized with an average)

3.57 a. displaying and summarizing data **b.** statistical inference **c.** data production

3.58 a. closed question about a categorical variable **b.** open question about a quantitative variable **c.** anecdotal evidence

3.59 a. sensitive questions **b.** quantitative

3.60 a. closed **b.** open

3.61 a. open **b.** closed

3.62 All sorts of lyrics are possible. They should be assessed as to whether the question asked is correctly identified to be open or closed.

3.63 It is not possible to impose on people a "treatment" that requires them to be born in the fall or in the spring.

3.64 confounding variables

3.65 a. observational study **b.** confounding variables

3.66 a. two-sample **b.** experiment **c.** better study design

3.67 a. experiment **b.** The control group was bees that were given sugar water. **c.** It is unethical to administer alcohol to humans, especially in doses high enough to kill them. **d.** Assessment of sociability could be fairly subjective, so it is important for the researcher to be unaware of how much alcohol (if any) the bee consumed. **e.** Assessment of survival can be completely objective, so it is not important for the researcher to be unaware of how much alcohol (if any) the bee consumed. **f.** proportion

3.68 a. This was an experiment because a treatment (oatmeal) was imposed by researchers. **b.** oatmeal intake **c.** categorical **d.** whether or not cholesterol is lowered **e.** categorical **f.** The treatment group was 100 people in Lafayette, Colorado who volunteered to eat a good-sized bowl of oatmeal for 30 days. **g.** There was no randomized assignment to treatment or control because there was no control group. **h.** The participants, being conscious of the attempt to lower their cholesterol by eating oatmeal, may have

consciously or subconsciously made other changes in their eating habits that reduced their cholesterol. **i.** Hawthorne effect **j.** No, because larger samples are not helpful in flawed study designs. **k.** A better design would have been a randomized controlled double-blind experiment. Randomly divide subjects into two groups. One group is given oatmeal in some form (such as a bar or an unmarked cereal containing oats) to eat daily. The other group is given a food that is as similar as possible except it contains something other than oats. The subjects should not be told whether or not they've been given oatmeal. The measurement of cholesterol is objective enough that having researchers blind is a non-issue.

3.69 gender

3.70 the study that asks participants to use pesticides for 2 years

3.71 the study where the response of interest is how sociable a bee's behavior is

3.72 the study where response is people's feelings of self-esteem, because it is more subjective

3.73 the study that tests children's absorption of pesticides

3.74 the study that tests whether writing has an effect on healing when tissue has been removed from the upper arm under anesthesia

3.75 Dominique is correct: The study teaches us to be wary of retrospective observational studies because people's memories of past events or circumstances can be faulty.

3.76 Responses will vary.

3.77 Responses will vary.

3.78 Responses will vary.

3.79 Responses will vary.

Chapter 4

4.1 suicide, because $(1/12{,}091 > 1/15{,}440)$

4.2

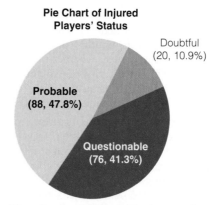

Pie Chart of Injured Players' Status

a. The slice for "doubtful" takes up about 11% of the pie, the one for "questionable" takes up 41% of the pie, and the one for "probable" takes up 48%. **b.** The bar for "doubtful" is of height 20, the bar for "questionable" is of height 76, and the bar for "probable" is of height 88 (see next page).

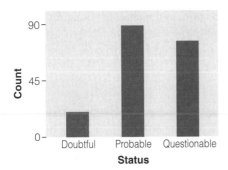

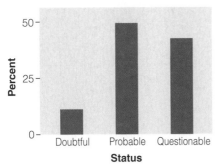

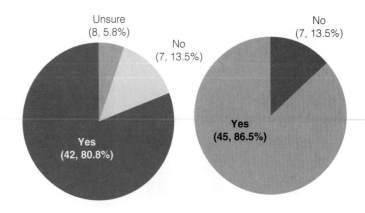

c. The bar for "doubtful" (see second bar graph) is of height 11%, the bar for "questionable" is of height 41% and the bar for "probable" is of height 48%   **d.** To include all players, we would need to know the count of uninjured players or the total count of players.

4.3 **a.** observational study   **b.** 25% and 67% are statistics; 12% and 83% are parameters   **c.** $\hat{p}$ **d.** pie chart on the right   **e.** higher   **f.** making a claim that racial profiling does not exist when it actually does   **g.** probability   **h.** 2   **i.** more convincing

4.4 **a.** favorite color, living situation, smoked or not, ate breakfast or not   **b.** favorite color   **c.** smoked less than a pack versus a pack or more (alternatively, smoked up to a pack versus more than a pack)   **d.** statistics   **e.** In this case, 15% might be an underestimate, if some students don't want to admit to being smokers. In any case, we can't say for sure that the population in general behaves the same as the sample.

4.5 **a.** vegetarian or not, ears pierced or not, year at school   **b.** year at school   **c.** part-time or full-time   **d.** statistics

4.6 **a.** compare heights of bars for blacks in population versus blacks stopped by traffic police   **b.** both about the same   **c.** No, because race doesn't follow a natural progression in amounts.

4.7 **a.** 25/48 = 52% preschool and 23/48 = 48% elementary school   **b.** preschool is the majority   **c.** mode   **d.** $\hat{p}$ **e.** First block into the two age groups, then do a random assignment to treatment (additional sugar) or control within each age group.

4.8 **a.** 42/52 = 81%   **b.** 7/52 = 13%   **c.** 3/52 = 6%   **d.** The pie chart (below, left) has three slices, of areas 81%, 13%, 6%.

e. Yes, 81% comes within 10% of 84%.
f. Now the pie chart (above, right) has only two slices, of areas 87% and 13%. It shows a considerably higher percentage answering "yes."

4.9 **a.** observational study   **b.** gender (categorical) and profession (general, neurologist, or headache specialist) also categorical   **c.** neurologists   **d.** The risk of migraines is 58% for female neurologists, 34% for male neurologists.   **e.** A majority of female neurologists have at least one migraine in a given year, whereas a minority of male neurologists have at least one migraine in a year.   **f.** bias in assessment   **g.** explanation for why neurologists may actually be different

4.10 **a.** 40%   **b.** parameter   **c.** See chart below (top): The slice for California takes up 35.4% of the pie, the one for New York takes up 24.3% of the pie, and the one for "other" takes up 40.3%.

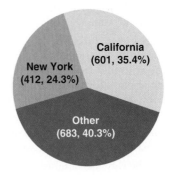

d. See graph below: The bar for California is of height 601, the bar for New York is of height 412, and the bar for "other" is of height 683.

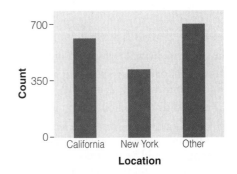

e. See graph below: The bar for California is of height 35.4%, the bar for New York is of height 24.3%, and the bar for "other" is of height 40.3%.

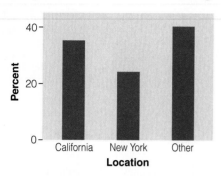

f. The bars could be ordered alphabetically, or shortest to tallest, or tallest to shortest.

g. Statistical inference would not be appropriate because the data are already for *all* cable and network series where the setting was known; there is no larger population to generalize to.

4.11 when considering whether a child suffers from strep throat

4.12 a. 0.51   **b.** 0.64   **c.** common   **d.** more convincing

4.13 a. 79%   **b.** 21%   **c.** higher now

4.14 a. 90/104 = 86.5% smoked less than a pack, 14/104 = 13.5% smoked a pack or more
b. The percentage of smoking students who smoke a pack or more a day would be higher because the denominator is smaller than that for the percentage of all students.

4.15 12/445 = 2.7% were part-time and 433/445 = 97.3% were full-time

4.16 Percentages in 1st, 2nd, 3rd, 4th, and Other are 8%, 58%, 23%, 8%, and 3%, respectively. They are not at all evenly divided; the majority are 2nd year, then about a fourth are 3rd year, 8% each in 1st and 4th, and only 3% are "Other."

4.17 No: the Middle Atlantic region is not very mountainous, so the vertical drop of its slopes could be biased toward smaller values.

4.18 because of the way the variable's values are assessed

4.19   0 00124677
      1 01125778
      2 9
      3 2
      4
      5 06

4.20 One of the 2 stems is missing.

4.21 The shape is skewed right, with high outliers.

4.22 Intervals that appear to be of equal width have different widths (4, 4, 2, and 4).

4.23 a. From 33 to 69 million years   **b.** left-skewed

4.24 The distribution of femur bone lengths for all *Tyrannosaurus rex* specimens that died in adulthood should be most normal (including other species could result in skewness in either

direction, and including young dinosaurs could result in low outliers).

4.25 a. used upright pianos in the classified ads
b.   0 14
      0 566
      1 122
      1 6
      2 123
c. The histogram is shown below.

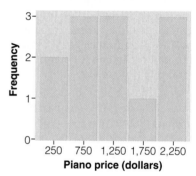

d. The histogram is shown below.

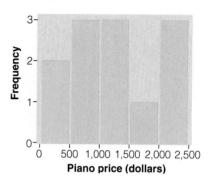

e. Only the scale of the vertical axis would change: Instead of a maximum frequency of 3, it would show a maximum percent of 3/12, or 25%. The shape would be the same.

4.26 a. fish fossils   **b.** 270 − 110 = 160 mbsf
c. 210 mbsf   **d.** left-skewed   **e.** less than
f. The sample would not have been random, but rather a convenience and/or systematic sampling of fossils at various depths.

4.27 a.

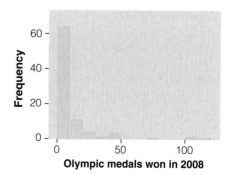

b. 1, 2, 4, 10, 110   **c.** 10 (the third quartile)

4.28 a. 1,150 dollars
b. 100, 575, 1,150, 1,850, 2,300; IQR = 1,275

c. 1.5(1,850 − 575) = 1,912.5; there are no values below 575 − 1,912.5 or above 1,850 + 1,912.5, so there are no outliers

d.

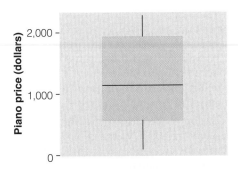

e. fairly symmetric

f. Prices can't be negative, so the value −600 should be omitted or converted to +600. Because it is conceivable that a special antique piano would be worth a lot of money, the value 3,100 should be retained.

4.29 a. The mean is approximately the same as the median because the shape is roughly symmetric.
b. ((12 × 1,175) + 8,000)/13 = 1,700 dollars
c. statistical inference **d.** $1,100 **e.** standard deviation 739 dollars **f.** 1175 − 0.65(739) = 695 dollars **g.** 24 pianos

4.30 a. The boxplot fails to show what seems to be a high outlier in the histogram. **b.** because of the high outlier **c.** 627 (the mean), 317.4 (the standard deviation)

4.31 a. 177 is the mean for crimes against persons. **b.** 78 is the standard deviation for crimes involving vandalism. **c.** 100 **d.** 25
e.

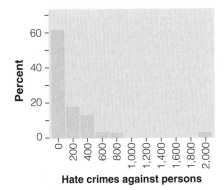

Hate crimes against persons

f. actual measurements of hate crimes reported for entire population

4.32 a.

```
 7  3
 8
 9  0034789
10  002556678
11  3555
12  03
13  00
14  0
15  02
16
17  3
```

b. 73, 98.5, 106, 121.5, 173 **c.** 121.5 + 1.5(121.5 − 98.5) = 156, so 173 is technically (and visually) a high outlier; 98.5 − 1.5(121.5 − 98.5) = 64, so 73 is not a low outlier.
d.

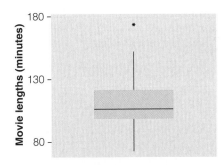

bottom whisker starts at 73, bottom of box at 98.5, line through box at 106, top of box at 121.5, top whisker to 152, 173 marked "*"
e. median, because right-skewness and the high outlier would inflate the mean **f.** statistic $\bar{x}$
g. 59 movies

4.33 The shape would be skewed right because the average is only 2.5 minutes but the maximum is 5 hours.

4.34 a. (31 + 33 + 36 + 37 + 43 + 54)/6 = 39 kilometers **b.** No, because these moons are not a random sample taken from any population. **c.** because of the high outlier (54)

4.35 a. females **b.** 32.25 **c.** 30.5 **d.** males **e.** Standard deviation for males is
$\sqrt{((33 − 32.25)^2 + (32 − 32.25)^2 + (32 − 32.25)^2 + (32 − 32.25)^2)/(4 − 1)} = 0.5$ **f.** years

4.36 a. 5 **b.** It is skewed left. **c.** 4.9 (somewhat less than the median) **d.** 1.2 (because 0.012 and 0.12 are too small, 12.0 is too large) **e.** both 4 **f.** because of the way the variable's values are assessed

4.37 a. 2.7 (greater than median because of right skewness, but 4.0 and 4.7 would be too large) **b.** 1.7

4.38 a. There is one very high outlier (148). **b.** only one **c.** No; most of the values are quite a bit closer to the mean.

4.39 a few months (in which case 4 years would be several standard deviations above the mean of 2 years)

4.40 a. (1,072 − 190)/30 = 29.4 **b.** parameter μ

4.41 a. 7/18 = 39%   **b.** 4/6 = 67%   **c.** $1,364,556
d. $756,897   **e.** The six directors whose salaries
are reported are likely to be among the highest
paid of the 18 American directors, and so their
mean salary would be an overestimate.

4.42 201; 47

4.43 a. 55.5   **b.** 10.5

4.44 a. Shape is somewhat skewed right but otherwise
bell-shaped.

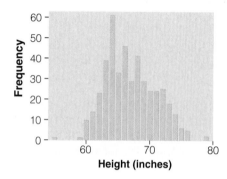
Height (inches)

b. No; there are more females (281 females,
163 males; or 63% versus 37%)
c. shape is close to normal

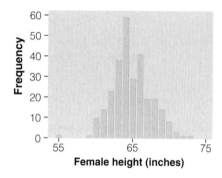
Female height (inches)

d. Shape is normal

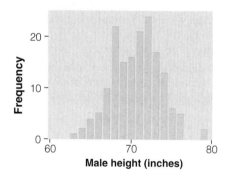
Male height (inches)

e. better to study them separately

4.45 a. 86, 125, 140, 160, 315.   **b.** The maximum,
315, is a high outlier because it is greater than
160 + 1.5(160 − 125).   **c.** 86, 117, 130, 140,
250.   **d.** The maximum, 250, is a high outlier
because it is greater than 140 + 1.5(140 − 117).
e. 115, 150, 165, 185, 315.   **f.** The maximum,
315, is a high outlier because it is greater than
185 + 1.5(185 − 150).   **g.** A males
h. B combined   **i.** C females

4.46 a. 1% + 2% + 4% = 7%   **b.** 1% + 2% +
4% + 34% = 41%   **c.** 34% + 24% + 28% +
7% = 93%   **d.** 24% + 28% + 7% = 59%

4.47 20% to 25%

4.48 a. (1,500.0 − 627.0)/317.4 = +2.75   **b.** no (the
maximum is 1,500.0)   **c.** negative   **d.** 627 +
0.86(317.4) = 900 feet   **e.** parameter, μ
f. statistic, $\bar{x}$ **g.** All the values would be
bunched close to the mean (627), hardly
extending below 620 or above 640.

4.49 a. 14/20 = 70% were within 1 standard
deviation of the mean, in the interval (8, 22)
b. 20/20 = 100% were within 2 standard
deviations away from the mean, in the interval
(1, 29)   **c.** squared years   **d.** The shape of the
distribution for age at death of humans would be
very left-skewed, with only relatively few dying
young.   **e.** statistical inference   **f.** 14 years

4.50 a. (Alternatively, the histogram could be
constructed to show endpoints rather than
midpoints of intervals.)

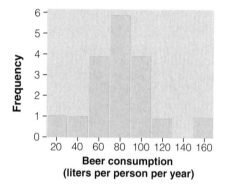
Beer consumption
(liters per person per year)

b. The rule should work well because the shape is
close to normal (symmetric and bell-shaped).
c. The interval (50, 110) extends 1 standard
deviation on either side of the mean.   **d.** 14/18 =
78% of values fall in this interval.   **e.** The
interval (20, 140) extends 2 standard deviations
on either side of the mean.   **f.** 17/18 = 94% of
values fall in this interval.   **g.** The interval (−10,
170) extends 3 standard deviations on either side
of the mean.   **h.** 18/18 = 100% of values fall in
this interval.   **i.** The z-score for Ireland is (155 −
80)/30 = +2.5; its value falls 2.5 standard
deviations above the mean.   **j.** 80 + 0.3(30) =
89; Australia   **k.** negative.

4.51 a. 19   **b.** z = (62.5 − 57.66)/13.58 = +0.36
c. fairly typical   **d.** z = (80.6 − 57.66)/13.58 =
+1.69   **e.** pretty high   **f.** The z-score might be
low because there were fewer people owning and
watching television in 1960.

4.52 mean 188 grams, standard deviation 48 grams

4.53 mean 12 kilograms, standard deviation 2
kilograms

4.54 a. Histogram is centered at 32; from left to right
mark circumferences of 17, 22, 27, 32, 37, 42, 47
to indicate circumferences within 1, 2, and 3
standard deviations of the mean.

68-95-99.7 Rule for Women's Waists

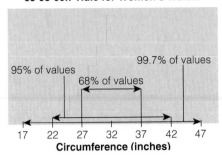

Circumference (inches)

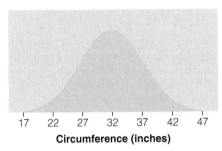

Circumference (inches)

b. The curve is a smoothed-out version of the histogram in part (a).   **c.** 2.5%   **d.** 27
e. Women in their twenties have more skewness because there is a bigger difference between their mean and median.   **f.** Both groups have right skewness because the mean is greater than the median.

4.55 a. μ **b.** $\bar{x}$ **c.** 10,000 women   **d.** $(32 - 32)/5 = 0$; intuitively, if a value exactly equals the mean, it is zero standard deviations away from the mean.
e. top 2.5%   **f.** unusually large
g. $32 + 2.4(5) = 44$ inches   **h.** $32 - 1.2(5) = 26$ inches

4.56 a. Curve is centered at 26; from left to right mark weight (pounds) of 17, 20, 23, 26, 29, 32, 35 to indicate weight (pounds) within 1, 2, and 3 standard deviations of the mean.

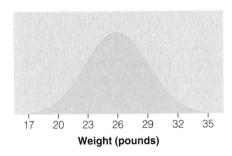

Weight (pounds)

b. $(20 - 26)/3 = -2$ **c.** $26 - 1.67(3) = 21$ pounds   **d.** 2.5%   **e.** pretty light   **f.** fairly typical

4.57 Without knowing that the shape is normal, we can't sketch the curve.

4.58 75% (z is negative so it must be below the mean)

4.59 16%

4.60 97.5%

4.61 a. Curve is centered at 15; from left to right mark numbers -3, 3, 9, 15, 21, 27, 33 to indicate

numbers of cigarettes smoked within 1, 2, and 3 standard deviations of the mean.

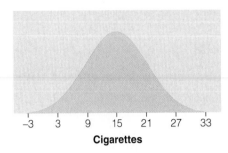

Cigarettes

b. The lower end of the curve is not perfectly consistent with reality because people don't smoke negative numbers of cigarettes.
c. $(20 - 15)/6 = +0.83$ **d.** not unusual
e. $(40 - 15)/6 = +4.17$ **f.** unusually high

4.62 a. approximately normal   **b.** skewed left/low outliers   **c.** skewed right/high outliers
d. skewed right/high outliers   **e.** skewed right/high outliers   **f.** approximately normal
g. skewed right/high outliers   **h.** skewed right/high outliers

4.63 a. skewed right/high outliers   **b.** skewed right/high outliers   **c.** approximately normal
d. skewed right/high outliers   **e.** skewed right/high outliers   **f.** approximately normal
g. skewed right/high outliers   **h.** skewed left/low outliers

4.64 a. $(42 - 64.5)/2.5 = -9$ **b.** $(42 - 54)/2 = -6$, so 6 standard deviations below average   **c.** σ

4.65 a. mean 1,569 kg, standard deviation 1,562 kg
b. $0/20 = 0\%$ less than 1 standard deviation below the mean   **c.** $2/20 = 10\%$ are more than 2 standard deviations above the mean   **d.** The data set does not conform well to the 68-95-99.7 Rule because of the high outliers.

4.66 a. mean 231, standard deviation 326
b. $18/23 = 78\%$ **c.** $0/23 = 0\%$ less than 1 standard deviation below the mean
d. $2/23 = 9\%$ **e.** The data set does not conform well to the 68-95-99.7 Rule because of the high outliers.

4.67 a. mean 112.0, standard deviation 21.4   **b.** $z = (73 - 112)/21.4 = -1.82$ **c.** $z = (173 - 112)/21.4 = +2.85$

4.68 0.3821

4.69 a. $z = -2.33$; weight is $188 - 2.33(48) = 76.2$
b. $z = -1.28$; weight is $188 - 1.28(48) = 126.6$
c. $z = +0.84$; weight is $188 + 0.84(48) = 228.3$
d. $z = +2.05$; weight is $188 + 2.05(48) = 286.4$

4.70 a. $z = -1.64$ or -1.65; weight is $12 - (1.64)2 = 8.72$ (or 8.7) kilograms   **b.** $z = -0.67$; weight is $12 - 0.67(2) = 10.66$ kilograms   **c.** $z = 0$; weight is 12 kilograms   **d.** $z = +1.88$; weight is $12 + 1.88(2) = 15.76$ kilograms [4.70 part f]

4.71 a. 0.1151   **b.** $1 - 0.1151 = 0.8849$

4.72 a. 0.0475   **b.** $z = (19 - 26)/3 = -2.33$; proportion is 0.0099.   **c.** $1 - 0.0099 = 0.9901$

d. $z = (28 - 26)/3 = +0.67$; proportion is $1 - 0.2514 = 0.7486$

4.73 0.3821

4.74 0.1587

4.75 0.0228

4.76 a. $z = (20 - 15)/6 = +0.83$; proportion is 0.2033.   **b.** $z = (40 - 15)/6 = +4.17$; proportion is smaller than 0.0013.

4.77 In an experiment, the researchers impose values of the explanatory variable to see the impact on the response. Thus, there should be two variables involved in an experiment, not just one.

4.78 College is more optional than high school, and apparently more females opt to attend college. The percentages in high school would be roughly 50/50, as in the general population.

4.79 Adam has a point: As students get older there would gradually be more of them with pierced ears. Brittany is also correct: There are more females in college, and females tend to have pierced ears more than do males.

4.80 whether they ate breakfast or not could differ the most between high school and college

4.81 a. statistic, $\hat{p}$ **b.** No, because we don't know how many shoppers were observed in each of these 15-minute periods.   **c.** convenience   **d.** inference

4.82 a. 1.13 million divided by 0.276 is about 4.09 million.   **b.** p

4.83 a. bias due to inaccurately assessing a variable's values   **b.** Because 0.05 is a sample proportion, we denote it $\hat{p}$.   **c.** The unknown population proportion is denoted p.

4.84 a. data production   **b.** 50%   **c.** a parameter   **d.** $17/20 = 85\%$ is a lot higher than 50%   **e.** all Antarctic prions

4.85 a. 37% males and 63% females   **b.** Yes, because if this is a representative sample, it clearly shows more females at the university than males.

4.86 a. blue   **b.** 43%   **c.** yellow   **d.** 4%   **e.** yes because the percentages are quite close

4.87 Responses will vary.

4.88 Responses will vary.

4.89 a. left-skewed   **b.** more symmetric

4.90 No, Hawking would *not* advocate treating intelligence as a categorical variable.

4.91 a. $288.4 + 2(129.4) = \$547,200$ (approximately)   **b.** $(547.2 - 643.8)/82.9 = -1.17$ **c.** Salaries may tend to differ according to region of the United States, and some areas may have more schools with a higher profile than other areas.   **d.** The mean salary of top college presidents summarizes that group only and, of course, would overestimate salaries of any other group of college presidents.

4.92 a. $150,000/150,000,000 = 0.001 = 0.1\%$ **b.** Curve is centered at 100; from left to right mark scores of 55, 70, 85, 100, 115, 130, 145 to

indicate scores within 1, 2, and 3 standard deviations of the mean.

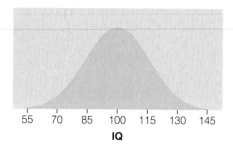

c. approximately 3 standard deviations below the mean (percentage less than 3 standard deviations below the mean is $(100\% - 99.7\%)/2 = 0.15\%$)   **d.** The harmful consequences of wrongly institutionalizing a person are numerous and obvious.   **e.** Failing to institutionalize people who are unable to function in society may make their lives more difficult. If they happen to be dangerous, there is a risk of harm to others. In either case, however, an IQ test is not the ideal way to determine whether or not people should be institutionalized.

4.93 a.

```
3  9
4
4  77
5  0011
5  6
6  012
```

b. The median is 51 days, or a little over 7 weeks.

4.94 a. $(40 - 32.4)/2.4 = +3.17$ **b.** $(40 - 115.3)/37.6 = -2.00$ **c.** 40 grams is more likely to be at the "fading ball of fluff" stage because its z-score is less extreme for this stage.

4.95 a. $(840 - 864)/100 = -0.24$ **b.** $(840 - 818)/91 = +0.24$ **c.** If a male mallard weighs 840 grams, he is just as likely to be at the "feathered-flightless" stage as at the "flying" stage: He is a bit light for the former and a bit heavy for the latter, but the z-scores have the same magnitude.

4.96 a. $(59 - 27)/6 = +5.33$; her age is 5.33 standard deviations above average   **b.** The distribution cannot be normal because it cannot be symmetric: There will be some unusually old mothers like this one, but the youngest mothers must be about 12, and their z-scores could not exceed about -2.5.   **c.** lower

4.97 Dominique has the best answer: Age of a mother at the time of delivery would have a few values that are surprisingly low.

4.98 a. mean 11.0, standard deviation 19.1   **b.** mean 8.8, standard deviation 12.5   **c.** standard deviation

4.99 The rents average to \$457, and they tend to differ from this average by about \$88.

4.100 **a.** $z = (40 - 32.4)/2.4 = 3.17$; proportion is less than 0.0013. **b.** $z = (40 - 115.3)/37.6 = -2.00$; proportion is 0.0228

4.101 **a.** $z = (840 - 864)/100 = -0.24$; proportion is 0.4052. **b.** $z = (840 - 818)/91 = +0.24$; proportion is 0.4052.

4.102 Responses will vary.

4.103 Responses will vary

Chapter 5

5.1 **a.** Testosterone levels are quantitative responses. **b.** Type of film is categorical explanatory with three possibilities. **c.** Gender is categorical explanatory with two possibilities.

5.2 **a.** two columns of quantitative responses, one for each of two categorical groups.
b.

Age	Sex
26	f
27	f
32	m
32	m
32	m
33	m
34	f
35	f

5.3 **a.** a column for values of quantitative responses and a column for values of a categorical explanatory variable
b.

Private	State	State-Related
273	2,050	604
329	2,195	4,296
340	2,338	5,369
353	2,566	7,047
365	4,627	
380		
409		
434		
761		
893		

c. number enrolled

5.4 **a.** private: mean 25.4, standard deviation 11.4 **b.** state: mean 34.6, standard deviation 3.1 **c.** state-related: mean 35.5, standard deviation 21.5 **d.** because the one outlier (66%) pulls up the value of the mean in this group; the other three values only have mean 25.3 **e.** state, because the standard deviation is smallest **f.** because the data sets are so small **g.** displaying and summarizing data

5.5 median

5.6

```
Private                State                  State-Related
1 | 1 2                1 |                    1 | 9
2 | 0 1 2 2 4          2 |                    2 | 2
3 |                    3 | 0 3 6 6 8          3 | 5
4 | 0 1 1              4 |                    4 |
5 |                    5 |                    5 |
6 |                    6 |                    6 | 6
```

5.7 **a.** two-sample **b.** Ordinary elementary schools have a lower center than elementary/middle combined. **c.** yes **d.** Ordinary elementary schools have more variable scores than elementary/middle combined schools. **e.** 40 **f.** no **g.** more convinced

5.8 **a.** several-sample **b.** Centers are comparable. **c.** no **d.** Spreads are comparable. **e.** no

5.9 **a.** $(1,300 - 1,228)/82 = +0.88$ **b.** $(1,300 - 1,219)/91 = +0.89$ **c.** $(1,300 - 1223)/105 = +0.73$ **d.** The z-scores for 1,300 are similar because the three school types have similar means and similar standard deviations.

5.10 gender

5.11 **a.** more **b.** higher **c.** People who consume a lot of soft drinks could weigh more and have higher blood pressures because of being overweight. **d.** separated **e.** observational study

5.12 **a.** High school students would cut class the most, and so they would have the lowest percentage participating. Elementary students would rarely cut class, and so they would have the highest percentage participating. **b.** no; elementary **c.** 91% **d.** elementary **e.** high school **f.** no

5.13 **a.** paired **b.** up by about 2 (mean of the difference is about +2) **c.** 3 (standard deviation of the difference) **d.** unusually large increase in deaths due to animals

5.14 **a.** observational study **b.** −0.61 **c.** Wal-mart **d.** more convincing **e.** statistical inference **f.** the store with more expensive prices **g.** smaller

5.15 **a.** females about 500 grams **b.** males about 600 grams **c.** positive **d.** negative **e.** ducks of all ages **f.** 35-week-old ducks only **g.** when the distributions' values are concentrated close to the means **h.** 40 ducks each **i.** 90

5.16 **a.** (4) **b.** (1) **c.** (1) **d.** mistake of concluding the drug *is* effective when it actually is not **e.** data production **f.** displaying and summarizing data **g.** statistical inference

5.17 **a.** relationship **b.** two single variables

5.18 two single categorical variables individually

5.19 **a.** relationship between earnings (explanatory) and neatness (response) **b.** earn less

5.20 **a.** the right-most column focuses on sending troops early or late **b.** the bottom row focuses on pulling troops early or late **c.** 8/36 = 0.22 **d.** 3/15 = 0.20 **e.** 5/21 = 0.24 **f.** whether troops were sent early or late **g.** (4)

5.21 **a.**

	Breakfast	No Breakfast	Total
Male	1	4	5
Female	8	5	13
Total	9	9	18

b. 20% **c.** 62%
d.

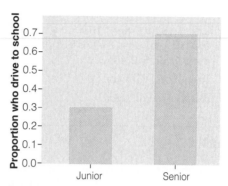

e. The sample is too small to give us an accurate picture of what is true for all male and female college students.

5.22 **a.** seniors
b.

	Drive	Don't	Total
Junior	3	7	10
Senior	7	3	10
Total	10	10	20

c. 30% **d.** 70%
e.

f. 50%
g.

	Drive	Don't	Total
Junior	5	5	10
Senior	5	5	10
Total	10	10	20

5.23 **a.** putting on a "slightly uncomfortable" necktie for 3 minutes **b.** none **c.** explanatory variable is whether or not they already had glaucoma, response is whether they had a significant rise in intraocular pressure
d.

	Pressure Increase	No Pressure Increase	Total
Glaucoma	12	8	20
No Glaucoma	14	6	20
Total	26	14	40

e. already having glaucoma or not

5.24 **a.** 14/32 = 44% **b.** 15/22 = 68% **c.** quantitative **d.** If valproate really is effective but researchers fail to prove this, then alcoholics would not be encouraged to take advantage of this drug, which could help them control their drinking.

5.25 It would be difficult (and expensive) to get a large sample of bipolar alcoholics and maintain them on drugs or placebo for 6 months.

5.26 white 679/3,712 = 0.18, black 210/1,082 = 0.19; slightly higher for blacks

5.27 **a.** parameters p_1 and p_2 (describe entire population, not sample) **b.** white $327/3,712 = 0.09$, black $46/1,082 = 0.04$ **c.** sexual orientation **d.** whites
e.

	Sexual Orientation	Religion	Other	Total
White Offender	679	327	2,706	3,712
Black Offender	210	46	826	1,082
Total	889	373	3,532	4,794

5.28 Dominique's answer is best: The relative difference is more dramatic for divorce rates than for abortion rates.

5.29 **a.**

	Pressure Increase	No Pressure Increase	Total
Glaucoma	13	7	20
No Glaucoma	13	7	20
Total	26	14	40

b. one **c.** no **d.** no

5.30 **a.** whether it was a brother or unrelated male embryo, and whether or not it was attacked
b.

	Attacked	Not Attacked	Total
Brother	16	15	31
Unrelated Male	24	7	31
Total	40	22	62

c. 20 and 20 **d.** Such a difference has more impact if it comes from larger as opposed to smaller samples.

5.31 **a.** Whether or not they talked about death with their children is the explanatory variable; whether or not they experienced regrets was the response.
b.

	Regrets	No Regrets	Total
Talked About Death	0	147	147
Didn't Talk About Death	69	213	282
Total	69	360	429

c. 24 **d.** 45 **e.** (2) **f.** data production **g.** statistical inference

5.32 **a.** Of students without pierced ears, $17/36 = 47\%$ prefer pink; of students with pierced ears, $28/39 = 72\%$ prefer pink. Thus, students with pierced ears tend to prefer pink. **b.** Gender: Females tend to have pierced ears and are more likely than males to prefer pink. **c.** For females, proportions preferring pink are $9/12 = 75\%$ for those without

pierced ears and $27/36 = 75\%$ for those with. For males, proportions preferring pink are $8/24 = 33\%$ for those without pierced ears and $1/3 = 33\%$ for those with. Neither female students nor male students with pierced ears tend to prefer pink.
d. the one in part (c)

5.33 two single quantitative variables

5.34 two single quantitative variables

5.35 relationship between two quantitative variables

5.36 **a.** linear **b.** If relatively high scores produce a high mean, then we expect a relatively high percentage of students to pass. **c.** Yes, the scatterplots show points sloping up in a positive direction. **d.** about -25% **e.** It doesn't make much sense to include a school whose mean is so low that the regression line predicts a negative percentage. **f.** displaying and summarizing

5.37 **a.** 2000 **b.** 1996; various percentages voting for a third-party candidate in each state would weaken the relationship between percentages voting Republican and Democratic.

5.38 **a.** top **b.** middle **c.** bottom **d.** We might expect there to be a negative relationship between percentage passing the test and percentage who are disadvantaged. In general, disadvantaged children would have fewer opportunities for academic progress, and so schools with more disadvantaged children would have fewer children passing the test.

5.39 **a.** We expect a correlation of zero. **b.** The scatterplot does appear to have zero correlation because it shows a random scattering of points with no pattern.

5.40 **a.** (3) is perfectly positive **b.** (2) is perfectly negative

5.41 (2) and (3) because they are perfect

5.42 **a.** $+0.30$ (weak positive) **b.** $+0.95$ (strong positive)

5.43 **a.** observational study **b.** sample **c.** positive **d.** slope b_1 **e.** statistic **f.** statistical inference

5.44 **a.** negative **b.** positive **c.** Sleep is quantitative, summarized with average. **d.** Weight is categorical, summarized with proportions overweight or obese.

5.45 The correlation would be unaffected.

5.46 **a.**

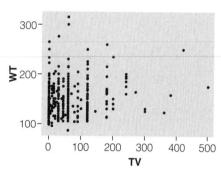

b. $r = 0.18$ **c.** weak and positive   **d.** males: $r = 0.15$; females: $r = 0.15$ **e.** yes   **f.** 167; estimated weight of males who watched no TV   **g.** $0.06(60) = 3.6$ pounds

5.47 stay the same

5.48 **a.**

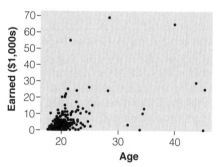

b. Both variables have high outliers.   **c.** $r = 0.49$ **d.** As students get older and gain more job experience, they tend to earn more money; also, some older students might be working full-time.

5.49 closer to 1

5.50 **a.** 1,250   **b.** 80   **c.** 40%   **d.** 20%   **e.** No, because the line would be too high.   **f.** No, because the line would be too high for below-average means and too low for above-average means.

5.51 slope $= 0.2$

5.52 We can sketch a line passing through the point of averages, $(\bar{x}, \bar{y}) = (4.4, 5.7)$. Its slope should be

$$b_1 = r\frac{s_y}{s_x} = 0.99\left(\frac{2.2}{1.8}\right) = 1.21$$

5.53 **a.** weak and negative   **b.** -0.36 **c.** #2   **d.** because this is the point of averages $(\bar{x}, \bar{y})$ [each is the average of the numbers 1 to 32]   **e.** $\frac{s_y}{s_x} = 1$, since $s_y = s_x$ (both are the standard deviation of the numbers 1 to 32)   **f.** equally good   **g.** equation of regression line

5.54 **a.** $Earned = -18.5526 + 1.0969\,(Age)$ **b.** 1 thousand   **c.** It's nonsensical to discuss earnings of students who are zero years old.

5.55 **a.** $r = -\sqrt{0.858} = -0.926.$ **b.** R-Sq $= 85.8\%$

5.56 **a.** $s = 4.9$, or about 5   **c.** parameter β_1

5.57 **a.** 600   **b.** 300   **c.** \$40   **d.** \$15   **e.** (3)   **f.** $20.5809 + 0.0281748(1,025) = 49.46$ **g.** inexpensive   **h.** $-\$9.46$ **i.** fairly typical   **j.** never   **k.** stay the same

5.58 s and s_y should be about the same because regression on explanatory values doesn't really give us any insight into response values.

5.59 **a.** neither   **b.** about the same size

5.60 **a.** implied that watching a lot of TV could make you heavier   **b.** equation of regression line

5.61 **a.** $+0.33$ because the relationship is weak and positive   **b.** Philadelphia   **c.** increase quite a bit   **d.** $1.76 + 0.2(9) = 3.56$ million   **e.** $1.7 - 3.56 = -1.86$ million   **f.** $s = 4.2$

5.62 **a.** The more pollutants are reduced, the more it costs the companies.   **b.** no effect   **c.** different   **d.** displaying and summarizing data   **e.** Motiva Enterprises   **f.** surprisingly low   **g.** steeper

5.63 **a.** b_1 **b.** β_1

5.64 Chance: two sets of five random x and y values could just happen to cluster around some line of negative or positive slope.

5.65 none; they are all curved

5.66 **a.** unadopted   **b.** adoptions   **c.** unadopted   **d.** Decreasing number of terminated ties might prevent some children from bonding with new parents, or may oblige some children to remain in "emotionally destructive" relationships with birth parents. Increasing the number of adoptions would be nice, but presumably all the obvious ways to accomplish this are already being attempted.

5.67 **a.**

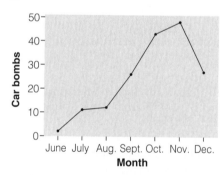

b. The most recent trend would predict a decrease from December's count of 27, whereas a regression line would predict an increase because the slope of the line would be positive.   **c.** 5.5

5.68 **a.** weather is explanatory and witchcraft trials is response   **b.** negative

5.69 **a.** age   **b.** response   **c.** response   **d.** explanatory

5.70 **a.** Celine Dion   **b.** a concert tour that made a lot of money in spite of low ticket prices   **c.** Prince   **d.** increase   **e.** Elton John   **f.** \$300,000   **g.** influential observation   **h.** \$350,000   **i.** \$16 million   **j.** \$16 million   **k.** both about the same   **l.** Average ticket price and shows would be explanatory, gross would be response.

5.71 **a.** both   **b.** $\bar{x}_1$ and $\bar{x}_2$

5.72 gender

5.73 b

5.74 **a.** 8.575 **b.** response, quantitative **c.** explanatory, categorical

5.75 **a.** In a lab, measure mean calorie expenditure for a certain time period for two groups randomly assigned to type on manual typewriters or computer keyboards. Convert to pounds gained or lost. Lack of realism is a major weakness. **b.** Compare mean weight of typists in the days of manual typewriters to mean weight of typists now using computers. A wide variety of outside variables could be responsible for increased weight.

5.76 **a.** two-sample **b.** paired **c.** Being more successful (including financially) might make it more likely for a man to find a wife.

5.77 Because the scale is different, making them look like centers are about the same, when actually the boxplot for fathers' heights is higher.

5.78 The distributions would have right-skewness and high outliers, so medians would be better summaries than means: Carlos's answer is best.

5.79 **a.** Obviously, graphic violence witnessed on television can have a much different effect on a child than whimsical violence in a nursery rhyme, which is generally read by a parent in a nurturing setting. **b.** depriving the child of quality time with the parent, and exposing the child to (potentially harmful) television **c.** The child may develop nightmares or presumably, according to the article, bad behavior. **d.** This is a matter of personal preference.

5.80 **a.** 2.5 **b.** lower **c.** better to report medians because the high outlier for the U.S. inflates the value of the mean for developed countries **d.** because population sizes vary **e.** 2.2 **f.** slightly higher **g.** bias in the assessment of a variable's values

5.81 **a.** first **b.** either **c.** second **d.** first **e.** symmetric **f.** $\bar{x}_1$ **g.** s_2 **h.** data production

5.82 **a.** two columns of quantitative responses **b.** 30, 47.5, 62, 81, 89 **c.** 22, 38, 47.5, 56, 70 **d.**

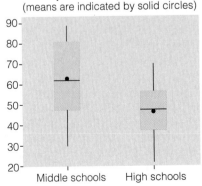

Boxplots of % Disadvantaged
(means are indicated by solid circles)

e. no; middle schools higher **f.** High school students and/or their parents may not be as conscientious about taking care of forms to make them eligible for free lunch. **g.** If economically disadvantaged students are more likely to have

dropped out by some time in high school, then the percentage of disadvantaged students would be lower in high schools than in middle schools. **h.** no; middle schools more variable **i.** fairly symmetric **j.** yes

5.83 **a.** yes, by about 10 pounds **b.** no **c.** sort of; it seems to apply only to females, and it may be more like 10 pounds, not 15 **d.** males **e.** female freshmen **f.** skewed right/high outliers **g.** Record weights of freshmen, record their weights a year later when they are sophomores, then consider the sample of weight differences.

5.84 **a.**

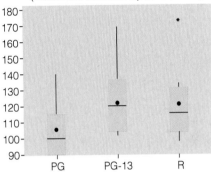

Boxplots of Movie Lengths
(means are indicated by solid circles)

b. Movies with one of the ratings tend to be shorter but lengths are comparable for movies with the other two ratings.

c.

Rating	N	Mean	StDev
PG	7	105.71	17.48
PG-13	9	122.00	22.44
R	8	121.13	23.93

d. We'd be more convinced if samples were larger. **e.** 20 **f.** s_1, s_2, s_3

5.85 **a.**

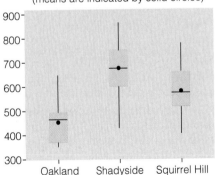

Boxplots of Rents for
One-Bedroom Apartments
(means are indicated by solid circles)

b.

Area	N	Mean	StDev
Oakland	12	457.1	87.9
Shadyside	27	674.7	102.2
Squirrel Hill	10	580.9	114.6

c. Oakland; 1; 2 **d.** 1 **e.** none of the three areas

5.86 **a.** mean 36 thousand, standard deviation 9 thousand   **b.** mean 36 thousand, standard deviation 9 thousand
c. BMW because the sample size is much larger (19 as opposed to 4)   **d.** $\bar{x}_2$ **e.** s_2 **f.** μ_1 **g.** σ_1

5.87 **a.**

Variable Earned	Year	N	Mean	Median	StDev
	1	35	3.229	1.000	5.375
	2	257	3.300	2.000	6.748
	3	102	3.843	3.000	4.240
	4	37	6.41	4.00	9.71
	other	14	6.71	4.50	6.28

b. yes **c.** yes

d.

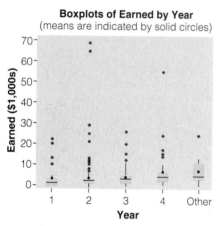

Boxplots of Earned by Year
(means are indicated by solid circles)

e. medians **f.** 2nd and 4th; yes

5.88 **a.** nonsmokers **b.** smokers 28.9, nonsmokers 43.2 **c.** nonsmokers **d.** major **e.** No, smoking does not necessarily cause a person to exercise less. Less health-conscious people may tend to smoke, and they may also tend toward exercising less.

5.89 **a.** on-campus 7.22; off-campus 7.01 **b.** on-campus **c.** minor **d.** statistical inference

5.90 **a.** bus 21.23, car 23.50, walk 20.29 **b.** walkers **c.** those who drive a car **d.** bus 20.29, car 21.05, walk 20.08 **e.** walkers **f.** those who drive a car **g.** using the sample mean age of 110 walkers to estimate the mean age of all students who commute by walking

5.91 Responses will vary.

5.92 Responses will vary.

5.93 What year (2002 or 2004) is the explanatory variable, and health (healthy or not) is the response.

5.94 **a.** (2) **b.** No; the youths would have difficulty remembering and estimating the amount of alcohol consumed. **c.** data production

5.95 **a.** observational study **b.** statistics **c.** $\hat{p}_1$ and $\hat{p}_2$ **d.** yes **e.** less convincing

5.96 **a.** Watching sex-saturated TV or not is the explanatory variable, engaging in sexual activity within the next year or not is the response. **b.** observational study **c.** Teens who were about to engage in sexual activity (because of heightened interest in sex) were more likely to watch sex-saturated television. This is certainly plausible. **d.** The study's results cannot provide evidence of

cause-and-effect the way an experiment might have (randomly expose some teens to sex-saturated television and others not, see if there is a difference in subsequent sexual activity). **e.** displaying and summarizing

5.97 **a.** observational study **b.** type of beer and whether the bear consumed it (for each can) **c.** Busch 1/2 = 50%; Rainier 35/35 = 100% **d.** Busch 1/35 = 3%; Rainier 35/35 = 100% **e.** the one in part (d) **f.** the one in part (d)

5.98 **a.** Percentages carrying weapons were 389/885 = 44% for drug-users and 248/2,226 = 11% for non-users. **b.** about 4 times as likely **c.** Percentages using illegal drugs were 389/637 = 61% for those who carried weapons, 496/2,474 = 20% for those who didn't carry weapons. **d.** about 3 times as likely

5.99 **a.** Course is categorical because the numbers refer to groups, not values with an arithmetic meaning. **b.** 200: 72%, 1000: 59%, 1100: 33% **c.** 200 has the highest percentage, 1100 has the lowest. **d.** There is a good possibility that males and females would have a tendency to major in different subject areas.

5.100 **a.** black **b.** pink, purple **c.** males: black 14%, blue 56%, green 16%, orange 3%, pink 1%, purple 2%, red 6%, yellow 2%; females: black 4%, blue 36%, green 13%, orange 3%, pink 13%, purple 18%, red 9%, yellow 4% **d.** green, orange, red, yellow

5.101 **a.** social science 74%, natural science 59%, business 42% **b.** gender **c.** Construct separate tables for each of the values of the possible confounding variable.

5.102 Responses will vary.

5.103 Responses will vary.

5.104 Correlation is appropriate for (b) because it involves two quantitative variables. It is not appropriate for (a) because the response is categorical; not appropriate for (c) because the explanatory variable is categorical; not appropriate for (d) because both explanatory and response variables are categorical.

5.105 Correlation is appropriate for (d) because it involves two quantitative variables. It is not appropriate for (a) because both explanatory and response variables are categorical; not appropriate for (b) because the explanatory variable is categorical; not appropriate for (c) because the response is categorical.

5.106 relationship between two quantitative variables

5.107 **a.** moderate   **b.** 114 to 134   **c.** 112 to 132
d. The predictions are far from perfect, and so the actual difference could easily go anywhere from Bush's IQ being 22 points higher to 18 points lower.   **e.** mean IQ of all those whose SAT score was 1206   **f.** β_0 and β_1

5.108 **a.** intercept   **b.** lower

5.109 **a.** temperature   **b.** negative   **c.** slope   **d.** data production

5.110 Ticket prices for each home game in a season could be checked in classified ads and on eBay. This should be done within a few days of the game, when weather forecasts are known. The forecasted temperature should also be recorded. Prices throughout the season should be regressed on temperature, to see if there is a positive relationship (lower prices for colder games, higher prices for warmer games).

5.111 **a.** 100 B.C.   **b.** 200 B.C.   **c.** 600
d. underestimate

5.112 Adam is correct: if $r = 0$, s is about the same size as s_y, 32 pounds.

5.113 **a.** both   **b.** regress earnings on weight separately for males and females

5.114 side-by-side boxplots

5.115 **a.**

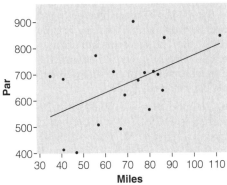

Regression Plot
Par = 416.168 + 3.55670 Miles
S = 125.521 R-Sq = 25.0% (r = +0.50)

moderate
b. 125.5
c.

Regression Plot
Shots = −31.2935 + 10.3187 Miles
S = 51.1519 R-Sq = 94.4%

strong
d. 51.2   **e.** shots and miles   **f.** The one for predicting shots from miles is smaller by 74.3 shots.

g.

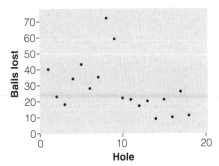

(3)
h. (2)
i.

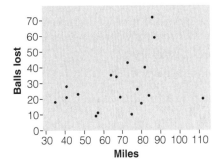

(2)   **j.** (3)   **k.** 12,170/509 = 24
l. 2,322,000/12,170 = 191

5.116 **a.** entire population   **b.** scatterplot shown with regression line in part (c)
c.

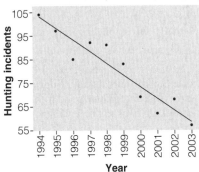

Regression Plot
HuntingIncidents = 9988.52 − 4.95758 Year
S = 5.56722 R-Sq = 89.1% (r = −0.94)

d. $r = -0.94$ **e.** The relationship is strong and negative.   **f.** 5, because the slope is approximately $b = -5$ **g.** 54   **h.** 6   **i.** the number of active hunters for each year

5.117 **a.** attendance ($r = 0.74$, compared to $r = 0.99$ for ticket price and $r = 0.97$ for gross)
b. average ticket price $6.35, gross $4,165 million, attendance 661 million   **c.** higher
d. higher **e.** higher   **f.** gross   **g.** decrease, because regressing average price on year overstated the strength of the relationship by eliminating much of the scatter

5.118 a.

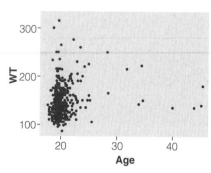

b. $r = +0.15$; weak and positive   **c.** positive
d. males: $r = +0.23$; females: $r = +0.15$ **e.** males
f. 1   **g.** 170 pounds   **h.** less than 33 pounds

5.119 a. $r = 0$; non-existent   **b.** It is possible that later in the semester, as workloads increase, students taking more credits would get less sleep.

5.120 Responses will vary.

5.121 Responses will vary.

Chapter 6

6.1 **a.** subjective assessment   **b.** equally likely outcomes   **c.** long-run set of observed outcomes

6.2 **a.** long-run set of observed outcomes
b. subjective assessment   **c.** equally likely outcomes

6.3 **a.** 0.686   **b.** long-run set of observed outcomes

6.4 **a.** 0.25   **b.** equally likely outcomes

6.5 $100\% - (47\% + 20\% + 6\% + 5\%) = 22\%$

6.6 $1 - 0.95 = 0.05$

6.7 **a.** $1 - (0.2 + 0.2 + 0.2) = 0.4$ **b.** $1,676,200/1,690,000 = 0.99$

6.8 **a.** dependent   **b.** approximately independent

6.9 **a.** independent   **b.** dependent

6.10 **a.** $0.14 + 0.04 = 0.18$ **b.** $0.14(0.14) = 0.196$
c. because those events would be dependent; people in the same household could tend to be similar in terms of making trips to the emergency room

6.11 **a.** $0.8(0.2) + 0.2(0.8) + 0.8(0.8) = 0.96$
b. $1 - (0.2)(0.2) = 0.96$

6.12 The probability of one or the other equals the sum, 0.100, minus the overlap, which is unknown but surely greater than zero because there must be some who both flew kites and danced.

6.13 **a.** statistic $\hat{p}$ **b.** Having three or more sex partners was more common because its probability was 0.23, whereas the probability of two sex partners was $1 - (0.06 + 0.53 + 0.23) = 0.18$.   **c.** The probability that both people from the same household had one sex partner cannot be found because there would be dependence. (Both of them living in the same household makes it more likely for them to be a couple.)   **d.** The probability that both of them had one sex partner is $0.53 \times 0.53 = 0.2809$.

6.14 a. 335   **b.** $335/1,030 = 0.325$ **c.** $335 + 170 + 306 = 811$ **d.** $811/1,030 = 0.787$ **e.** $P(Y) = $

$505/1,030 = 0.490$ **f.** No, they do not seem fairly representative of the general population of drivers in terms of age because the young seem to be overrepresented.   **g.** $P(S) = 641/1,030 = 0.622$ **h.** $0.787 = 0.490 + 0.622 - 0.325$
i. $P(S$ given $Y) = 335/505 = 0.66$ **j.** Young drivers were more likely to swear than drivers in general, but the difference was just a few percentage points.   **k.** likely to be dependent (not independent) and to overlap quite a bit

6.15 a. Any answer is correct here because it is a matter of opinion. Most answers would probably include sports cars, trucks, and utility vehicles.
b. $P(G$ given $E) = 79/360 = 0.22$, $P(G$ given $F) = 65/235 = 0.28$, $P(G$ given $L) = 16/61 = 0.26$, $P(G$ given $S) = 58/153 = 0.38$, $P(G$ given $T) = 42/119 = 0.35$, $P(G$ given $U) = 32/111 = 0.29$, $P(G$ given $V) = 8/47 = 0.17$ **c.** Highest probabilities were for sports cars and trucks.
d. $P(V) = 47/1,086 = 0.043$, $P(G) = 300/1,086 = 8/47$, $P(V$ and $G) = 8/1,086 = 0.007$ **e.** $P(V$ and $G) = 0.007 \neq P(V) \times P(G) = 0.043 \times 0.276 = 0.012$ because V and G are not independent.   **f.** $P(V$ and $G) = 8/1,086 = P(V) \times P(G$ given $V) = 47/1,086 \times 8/47$ because this is the general multiplication rule at work.
g. Most would suspect the probability of making insulting gestures *given* that someone drives a sports car to be higher; $P(G) = 0.28$, and $P(G$ given $S) = 0.38$.   **h.** $P(E$ or F or L or $V) = (360 + 235 + 61 + 47)/1,086 = 0.65$ **i.** $P(G$ given E or F or L or $V) = (79 + 65 + 16 + 8)/(360 + 235 + 61 + 47) = 0.24$.   **j.** The probability in (j) *is* lower than the overall probability of making insulting gestures, 0.28.   **k.** The surveyors did not allow for overlapping of categories because the numbers driving each type of car sum to the overall total of people surveyed, 1,086.

6.16 a. $P(C$ and $B) = 0.60(0.34) = 0.204$ **b.** $P($not C and $B) = 0.40(0.74) = 0.296$ **c.** closer to $P(B$ given $C) = 0.34$ **d.** $P(B) = 0.204 + 0.296 = 0.50$ **e.** $P(C$ given $B) = P(C$ and $B)/P(B) = 0.204/0.50 = 0.408$ **f.** $P(C) = 0.60$ and $P(C$ given $B) = 0.408$ are quite different because supporting stricter gun control laws and voting for Bush were highly dependent: A voter was much less likely to be in favor of stricter gun control laws if he or she voted for Bush.

6.17 a. $P(G$ and $B) = 0.04(0.25) = 0.01$ **b.** $P($not G and $B) = 0.96(0.50) = 0.48$ **c.** closer to 0.50   **d.** $P(B) = 0.01 + 0.48 = 0.49$ **e.** $P(G$ given $B) = P(G$ and $B)/P(B) = 0.01/0.49 = 0.02$

6.18 a. $P(R$ given $T) = 7/60 = 0.12$ **b.** $P(R$ given $TU) = 25/66 = 0.38$ **c.** These probabilities seem very different.   **d.** $\hat{p}_1$ and $\hat{p}_2$ **e.** 15   **f.** 17

Expected	Clots Removed	Not Removed
Just TPA	15	45
TPA & Ultrasound	17	49

g. 45 **h.** 49 **i.** These counts seem very different from the counts that were actually observed (each is 8 fewer or 8 more than the observed count). **j.** The researchers do seem justified in their claim that ultrasound enhances the standard clot-removal effectiveness of TPA. **k.** The potential harmful consequences of erroneously concluding that ultrasound is not helpful would be failing to treat clots with ultrasound and thereby lessening chances of their removal.

6.19 a. $P(C$ given $L) = 38/40 = 0.95$ and $P(C$ given $LN) = 90/93 = 0.97$ **b.** They are slightly different. **c.** $\hat{p}_1$ and $\hat{p}_2$

d.

Expected	Cured	Not Cured
Just Lotion	38.5	1.5
Lotion & Nit Removal	89.5	3.5

e. These counts are only slightly different from the counts that were actually observed. **f.** yes **g.** The most obvious consequence would be that the consumer takes a lot of (needless) trouble with nit removal in addition to using the lotion.

6.20 a. Probability of execution was $23/2,346 = 0.01$ in 1990 and $71/3,556 = 0.02$ in 2002. **b.** The rate doubled. **c.** parameters p_1 and p_2

6.21 a. Africa: $803/6,085 = 0.132$, projected to increase to 0.197 **b.** Europe: $730/6,085 = 0.120$, projected to decrease to 0.072

6.22 a. may overlap **b.** may not overlap **c.** may overlap **d.** may not overlap

6.23 a. may overlap **b.** may overlap **c.** may not overlap **d.** may not overlap **e.** may overlap

6.24 greater because they would remember those assaults when reporting on-the-job injuries

6.25 displaying and summarizing

6.26 data production

6.27 a. statistical inference **b.** underestimate

6.28 $1 - (3,915/4,722) = 0.17$

6.29 a. single variable **b.** $(105,397,000 - 50,992,000 - 50,455,000)/105,397,000 = 0.04$

6.30 $0.16 + 0.16 = 0.32$

6.31 $0.0015 + 0.0015 = 0.0030$

6.32 a. $0.17 + 0.21 + 0.26 + 0.16 = 0.80$ **b.** $0.33 + 0.07 = 0.40$ **c.** $0.80 \times 0.40 = 0.32$ **d.** $0.03 \times 0.11 = 0.0033$ **e.** $0.05 \times 0.35 = 0.0175$ **f.** It does not seem likely that a randomly chosen man and woman will be compatible in terms of age preferences, because the probabilities in (c), (d), and (e) sum to about 0.34, which is less than 0.50.

6.33 a. columns **b.** The probability of getting an A was much higher in 2003 than it was in 1970; the probability of lower grades was much higher in 1970 than in 2003. **c.** In 2003 there were students who were not accounted for in the four

grade categories because the proportions sum to 0.955, which is less than 1.

6.34 a. Some topics must overlap because the percentages sum to more than 100%. **b.** Minimum would be 0%, if there were no overlap. **c.** Maximum possible probability that she feared either "being gossiped about" or "being called names" (or both) is $0.24 + 0.18 - 0 = 0.42$ (when there is no overlap to subtract). **d.** Maximum would be 0.18, if all girls who responded "being called names" also responded "being gossiped about." **e.** Minimum possible probability that she feared either "being gossiped about" or "being called names" (or both) is $0.24 + 0.18 - 0.18 = 0.24$ (if all those who feared being called names also feared being gossiped about). **f.** No, they are probably dependent because some of the fears are more similar than others.

6.35 a. Some topics must overlap because the percentages sum to more than 100%. **b.** Minimum would be 0%, if there were no overlap. **c.** Maximum possible probability that the story is about sex or drugs (or both) is $0.47 + 0.05 - 0.00 = 0.52$ (when there is no overlap to subtract). **d.** Maximum would be 5%, if all stories about drugs were also about sex. **e.** Minimum possible probability that the story is about sex or drugs (or both) is $0.47 + 0.05 - 0.05 = 0.47$ (if all of the stories about drugs are also about sex). **f.** displaying and summarizing **g.** statistical inference **h.** data production

6.36 a. observational study **b.** $P(G) = 13/55 = 0.24$, $P(\text{not } S) = 32/55 = 0.58$, $P(G \text{ or not } S) = 45/55 = 0.82$ **c.** yes, $P(G \text{ or not } S) = P(G) + P(\text{not } S)$ because $45/55 = 13/55 + 32/55$ **d.** $P(G) = 13/55$, $P(S) = 23/55$, $P(G \text{ or } S) = 23/55$ **e.** no, $P(G \text{ or } S) \neq P(G) + P(S)$, because $23/55 \neq 13/55 + 23/55$ **f.** The probability of one event *or* the other did equal the sum of probabilities in the first case because the two events—being gray and being a nonsmoker—did not overlap. They were not equal in the second case because the events—being gray and being a smoker—did overlap.

6.37 a. observational study **b.** $P(G) = 117/275 = 0.43$, $P(A) = 196/275 = 0.71$. **c.** 104 **d.** $104/275 = 0.38$ **e.** $P(G)P(A) = 0.43(0.71) = 0.31$ does not equal $P(G \text{ and } A) = 0.38$ **f.** Because the events in (e) are not equal, this shows alcoholism/drug addiction and gray hair are dependent events.

6.38 a. independent **b.** non-overlapping

6.39 0.02 is $P(A$ given $W)$ and 1.00 is $P(W$ given $A)$

6.40 a. categorical **b.** $341/1,609 = 0.21$ **c.** $246/1,313 = 0.19$ **d.** From 1990 to 2000, the probability of being married for women who had abortions decreased slightly.

6.41 $0.27 \times 0.85 = 0.23$

6.42 $0.174 \times 0.368 = 0.064$

6.43 **a.** age   **b.** The probability of death by suicide is the highest for those aged 15–24 and 25–34 (both have probability 0.12).   **c.** The probability of death by suicide is the lowest for those aged 5–14 (probability 0.03) and aged 45–54 (probability 0.04).   **d.** parameters   **e.** p_1 to p_5

6.44 **a.** columns   **b.** If we let U denote the event of being uninsured, C the event of being college-aged (18–24), and O the event of being other than college-aged, then $P(U$ given $C) = 8.1/27.4 = 0.30$ and $P(U$ given $O) = 35.5/258.5 = 0.14$ **c.** Yes, the claim is justified.

6.45 **a.** $791,597/1,746,231 = 0.45$ **b.** parameter   **c.** $29,078/58,230 = 0.50$ **d.** more likely   **e.** English (only $149,331/405,227 = 0.37$ were male)

6.46 **a.** no, because the conditional probabilities differ (0.65, 0.56, 0.68, 0.40)   **b.** $0.65 \times 0.43 + 0.56 \times 0.43 + 0.68 \times 0.07 + 0.40 \times 0.07 = 0.60$ **c.** $0.65 \times 0.43/0.60 = 0.47$

6.47 **a.** $0.44 \times 0.38 + 0.56 \times 0.43 = 0.41$ **b.** gender

6.48 **a.** $0.43 \times 0.39 + 0.57 \times 0.49 = 0.45$ **b.** type of student

6.49 **a.** $P(Preg) = 0.5$, $P(\text{not } Preg) = 0.5$, $P(Pos$ given $Preg) = 0.75$, $P(Pos$ given not $Preg) = 0.25$, $P(Pos) = P(Preg) \times P(Pos$ given $Preg) + P(\text{not } Preg) \times P(Pos$ given not $Preg) = 0.5(0.75) + 0.5(0.25) = 0.5$, $P(Preg$ given Pos$) = P(Preg$ and $Pos)/P(Pos) = 0.5(0.75)/0.5 = 0.75$.   **b.** $P(Pos) = P(Preg) \times P(Pos$ given $Preg) + P(\text{not } Preg) \times P(Pos$ given not $Preg) = 0.8(0.75) + 0.2(0.25) = 0.65$, $P(Preg$ given Pos$) = P(Preg$ and $Pos)/P(Pos) = 0.8(0.75)/0.65 = 0.92$.   **c.** $P(Pos) = P(Preg) \times P(Pos$ given $Preg) + P(\text{not } Preg) \times P(Pos$ given not $Preg) = 0.2(0.75) + 0.8(0.25) = 0.35$, $P(Preg$ given Pos$) = P(Preg$ and $Pos)/P(Pos) = 0.2(0.75)/0.35 = 0.43$.   **d.** As the probability of having the condition in question decreases, so does the probability of having the condition, given that one tests positive for the condition.

6.50 **a.**

	Positive	Negative	Total
Gonorrhea	128	4	132
No Gonorrhea	1,997	97,871	99,868
Total	2,125	97,875	100,000

b. Of the 2,125 people who test positive, 128 actually have the disease: If someone tests positive, the probability of having the disease is $\frac{128}{2,125} = 0.06$.   **c.** higher

6.51 **a.** If exactly half of the transplants had been kidneys, the overall probability of surviving for at least a year would be $(0.98 + 0.88)/2 = 0.93$ **b.** $0.59 \times 0.98 + 0.41 \times 0.88 = 0.94$ **c.** $0.06 \times 26,000 = 1,560$ **d.** population   **e.** p_1 and p_2

6.52 The trend in probability of being liberal from 1970 to 2003 played a stronger role in attitude toward capital punishment because that probability decreased considerably, from 0.59 to 0.33, whereas the probability of being in favor of legalizing marijuana dropped slightly, from 0.41 to 0.39.

6.53 **a.**

Expected	Liberal	Not Liberal
Year 1970	$(60 \times 100)/200 = 30$	$(140 \times 100)/200 = 70$
Year 2003	$(60 \times 100)/200 = 30$	$(140 \times 100)/200 = 70$

b. 6   **c.** 6,000

6.54 **a.**

Expected	Against Death	For Death
Year 1970	$(92 \times 100)/200 = 46$	$(108 \times 100)/200 = 54$
Year 2003	$(92 \times 100)/200 = 46$	$(108 \times 100)/200 = 54$

b. 13   **c.** Yes, because they differ by 13.

6.55 **a.** $0.361 \times 0.316 = 0.114$ **b.** higher

6.56 Carlos is correct: The conditional probability of being a homicide victim is highest for black males $(6,780/17,245,000 = 0.000393)$ and lowest for white females $(3,074/116,705,000 = 0.000026)$.

6.57 **a.** War served in could allow for overlapping categories but age could not.   **b.** $P(G$ given $U) = 3,119/3,119 = 1$ and $P(U$ given $G) = 3,119/(3,119 + 307 + 223 + 101 + 28 + 6) = 0.82$ **c.** 55-59   **d.** World War II   **e.** decreased

6.58 **a.** $0.69 \times 0.15 = 0.1035$ **b.** Those two events should be dependent because Mexico is closer to Texas than to other states; Texas is closer to Mexico than to other countries.   **c.** higher

6.59 **a.** $0.32 \times 0.02 = 0.0064$ **b.** higher

6.60 race and marital status of citizens

6.61 Responses will vary.

6.62 Responses will vary.

Chapter 7

7.1 **a.** 0, 1, 2, 3, 4, 5, 6, 7
b.

X	0	1	2	3	4	5	6	7
Probability	0.20	0.05	0.05	0.05	0.05	0.50	0.05	0.05

7.2 **a.** 1, 2, 3, 4
b.

X	1	2	3	4
Probability	0.25	0.25	0.25	0.25

c. less than 2.5   **d.** 1

7.3 **a.** $1 - (0.02 + 0.04 + 0.34 + 0.24 + 0.28 + 0.07) = 0.01$

b.

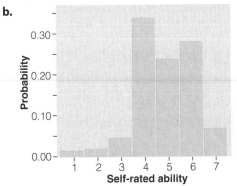

c. left-skewed   **d.** 5, 1

7.4 **a.** 5   **b.** because the distribution is skewed, not symmetric

7.5 **a.**

Outcome	X	Probability
NNN	0	0.75 x 0.75 x 0.75 = 0.421875
NND	1	0.75 x 0.75 x 0.25 = 0.140625
NDN	1	0.75 x 0.25 x 0.75 = 0.140625
DNN	1	0.25 x 0.75 x 0.75 = 0.140625
NDD	2	0.75 x 0.25 x 0.25 = 0.046875
DND	2	0.25 x 0.75 x 0.25 = 0.046875
DDN	2	0.25 x 0.25 x 0.75 = 0.046875
DDD	3	0.25 x 0.25 x 0.25 = 0.015625

X	Probability
0	0.421875
1	3(0.140625) = 0.421875
2	3(0.046875) = 0.140625
3	0.015625

b. skewed right   **c.** 1; 1

7.6 **a.**

Outcome	X	Probability
NN	0	0.75 x 0.75 = 0.5625
ND	1	0.75 x 0.25 = 0.1875
DN	1	0.25 x 0.75 = 0.1875
DD	2	0.25 x 0.25 = 0.0625

b.

X	Probability
0	0.5625
1	2(0.1875) = 0.3750
2	0.0625

c. $0(0.5625) + 1(0.3750) + 2(0.0625) = 0.5$
d. distances $-0.5, 0.5, 1.5$; squared distances $0.25, 0.25, 2.25$; weighted squared distances $0.25(0.5625) + 0.25(0.3750) + 2.25(0.0625) = 0.375$, square root 0.61.   **e.** 0.5 (mean), 0.61 (standard deviation)

7.7 **a.** A mean could be calculated for the second question only, because it involves a quantitative variable.   **b.** the principle of long-run observed outcomes

7.8 **a.** $0.01 + 0.02 + 0.04 = 0.07$.   **b.** Non-overlapping "Or" Rule   **c.** The problem arises because of the way the values of X are assessed (self-ratings are biased higher than true ability).   **d.** because ratings of friends are not independent (they would probably tend to be similar)   **e.** $0.01(0.01) = 0.0001$
f. $0.34 + 0.34 - 0.34(0.34) = 0.56$
g. $0.07/(0.24 + 0.28 + 0.07) = 0.12$

7.9 Weight 0 with $\frac{9}{16}$, 1 with $\frac{6}{16}$, and 2 with $\frac{1}{16}$: $0(\frac{9}{16}) + 1(\frac{6}{16}) + 2(\frac{1}{16}) = \frac{8}{16} = 0.5$

7.10 **a.** histogram for bulls below left.

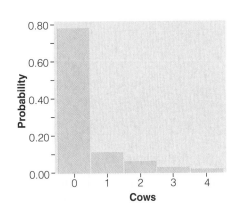

b. The histogram for cows is shown above right; both histograms are skewed right, but the histogram for bulls has a second peak at 2.   **c.** bullocks, since 0.28 is greater than 0.06   **d.** 0.66 + 0.04 + 0.28 = 0.98
e. 0.78 + 0.11 + 0.06 = 0.95   **f.** No; the Independent "And" Rule does not apply because the probability of owning no cows could be affected by whether or not bullocks are owned—B and C are likely to be *dependent*.
g. $\mu_B = 0(0.66) + 1(0.04) + 2(0.28) + 3(0.02) = 0.66$ **h.** $\mu_C = 0(0.78) + 1(0.11) + 2(0.06) + 3(0.03) + 4(0.02) = 0.40$ **i.** $(66(0) + 4(1) + 28(2) + 2(3))/100 = 0.66$, which equals the mean   **j.** 0, because a family never owns 0.40 cow

7.11 $(78(0) + 11(1) + 6(2) + 3(3) + 2(4)/100) = 0.40$

7.12 a. 0.5 is the average of the numbers 0 and 1
b. $\sqrt{0.5^2(0.5) + 0.5^2(0.5)} = 0.5$ **c.** 0.5 makes sense as the typical distance of the numbers 0 and 1 from their mean 0.5

7.13 a. $\sigma_B = \sqrt{(0 - 0.66)^2(0.66) + (1 - 0.66)^2(0.04) + (2 - 0.66)^2(0.28) + (3 - 0.66)^2(0.02)} = 0.95$
b. $\mu_{B + C} = 0.66 + 0.40 = 1.06$.   **c.** The formula can be used only if the random variables are independent, but as discussed above, B and C are likely to be dependent.

7.14 $\sigma_C = \sqrt{(0 - 0.4)^2(0.78) + (1 - 0.4)^2(0.11) + (2 - 0.4)^2(0.06) + (3 - 0.4)^2(0.03) + (4 - 0.4)^2(0.02)} = 0.88$

7.15 a. We cannot use the 68-95-99.7 Rule to find probabilities because the distribution is not normal.   **b.** $\mu = 1(0.01) + 2(0.02) + 3(0.04) + 4(0.34) + 5(0.24) + 6(0.28) + 7(0.07) = 4.9$
c. The typical distance of values from their mean couldn't be 0.012 or 0.12 (the histogram would have too little spread) or 12.0 (the histogram would have too much spread). Alternatively, we consider that the values range from 1 to 7.
d. $4.9 + 2(1.2) = 7.3$ **e.** $P(X > 7.3) = 0$
f. The probability of being more than 2 standard deviations above the mean equals 0, not $(1 - 0.95)/2 = 0.025$ as it would be if the 68-95-99.7 Rule held. The distribution is skewed left, not normal, and not at all smooth because only seven values are possible.   **g.** When $X = 1$, $Y = \frac{50}{3}(1) - \frac{50}{3} = 0$. When $X = 7$, $Y = \frac{50}{3}(7) - \frac{50}{3} = 100$.   **h.** $\mu_{-50/3 + (50/3)X} = -50/3 + (50/3)(4.9) = 65$ **i.** $\sigma_{-50/3 + (50/3)X} = (50/3)(1.2) = 20$

7.16 a. long-run observed outcomes   **b.** $1 - (0.13 + 0.27 + 0.25 + 0.10 + 0.07 + 0.05 + 0.03) = 0.10$ **c.** $0.25 + 0.10 + 0.07 + 0.05 + 0.03 = 0.50$ **d.** Non-overlapping "Or" Rule   **e.** higher numbers   **f.** lower numbers   **g.** The probability of going out every night is higher if a student's best friend goes out every night.   **h.** $0.03(0.03) = 0.0009$ **i.** $0.25 + 0.25 - 0.25(0.25) = 0.4375$
j. $0.27/(0.10 + 0.13 + 0.27) = 0.54$

7.17 a.

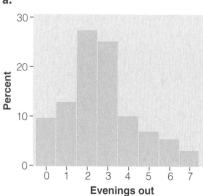

b. 2.5 (halfway between 2 and 3)   **c.** The histogram is skewed right, not normal, and far

from smooth because only eight values are possible.   **d.** greater than   **e.** $\mu = 0(0.10) + 1(0.13) + 2(0.27) + 3(0.25) + 4(0.10) + 5(0.07) + 6(0.05) + 7(0.03) = 2.68$, which rounds to 2.7.   **f.** The typical distance of values from their mean couldn't be 0.017 or 0.17 (the histogram would have too little spread) or 17.0 (the histogram would have too much spread).
g. $2.7 - 2(1.7) = -0.7$ **h.** $P(X < -0.7) = 0$
i. $P(X < -0.7) = 0$ not $(1 - 0.95)/2 = 0.025$ as it would be if the 68-95-99.7 Rule held. The probability conforms poorly to the rule because of the non-normal shape.
j. $\mu_Y = \mu_{X1} + \mu_{X2} + \ldots + \mu_{X52} = 52(2.7) = 140.4$ **k.** It would be difficult for students to remember and count or even just estimate all their evenings out for a whole year.   **l.** σ_Y would be less than 52(1.7) because the standard deviation of the sum is less than the sum of the standard deviations.

7.18 mean $\frac{9}{5}(30) + 32 = 86$, standard deviation $\frac{9}{5}(5) = 9$

7.19 mean $0.20(40) + 50 = 58$, standard deviation $0.20(10) = 2$

7.20 a. $0.66 + 0.66 = 1.32$ **b.** No, because standard deviations are not additive.

7.21 a. $0.4 + 0.4 = 0.8$ **b.** $\sqrt{0.88^2 + 0.88^2} = 1.24$

7.22 a. mean $4.7 + 4.7 = 9.4$, standard deviation $\sqrt{1.0^2 + 1.0^2} = 1.4$ **b.** The mean of the total days worked by both of them in a week can be computed as in part (a) but not standard deviation because days worked by co-workers would not be independent (they could tend to be similar, or to offset one another).

7.23 a. mean $42.6 + 42.6 = 85.2$, standard deviation $\sqrt{12.9^2 + 12.9^2} = 18.2$ **b.** The mean of the total hours worked by both of them in a week can be computed as in part (a) but not standard deviation because hours worked by co-workers would not be independent (they could tend to be similar, or to offset one another).

7.24 a. The number of children is fixed, so there is a fixed sample size $n = 3$. There is the same probability of sickle-cell disease each time, $p = 0.25$. The births are independent of each other, and for each child there are just two possibilities—disease or not.   **b.** $n = 3$ and $p = 0.25$.

7.25 a. not binomial because there are more than two possible values   **b.** not binomial because sample size n is not fixed   **c.** X is binomial.   **d.** not binomial because sampling without replacement from a relatively small population results in dependence of selections

7.26 a. not binomial because sampling without replacement from a relatively small population results in dependence of selections   **b.** X is binomial.   **c.** not binomial because there are more than two possible values   **d.** not binomial because sample size n is not fixed

7.27 a. when we sample 5 from 100 people   **b.** 25   **c.** 0.25

7.28 Depending on socio-economic level of students at a particular high school, there could be fewer or more single-child families. A private high school could tend to have students from smaller, wealthier families. If the sample is biased, then the distribution of sample proportion would not be centered at population proportion 0.05.

7.29 a. If $X = 3$ and $n = 100$, $\hat{p} = 3/100 = 0.03$.
   b. If $\hat{p} = 0.01$ and $n = 200$, $X = 0.01(200) = 2$
   c. Mean is $np = 50(0.02) = 1$ and standard deviation is
$\sqrt{np(1 - p)} = \sqrt{50(0.02)(0.98)} = 1.0$,
approximately.   **d.** On average, we expect to get about 1 married student in our sample, and the number who are married will tend to differ from this mean by about 1.   **e.** Mean is $p = 0.02$ and standard deviation is
$\sqrt{p(1 - p)/n} = \sqrt{0.02(0.98)/50} = 0.02$,
approximately.   **f.** Mean is $np = 500(0.02) = 10$ and standard deviation is
$\sqrt{np(1 - p)} = \sqrt{500(0.02)(0.98)} = 3.1$,
approximately.   **g.** Mean is $p = 0.02$ and standard deviation is
$\sqrt{p(1 - p)/n} = \sqrt{0.02(0.98)/500} = 0.01$,
approximately.   **h.** On average, we expect the proportion of married students in our sample to be about 0.02, and the proportion who are married will tend to differ from this by about 0.01.   **i.** Sample proportions are closer to 0.02 for the larger samples (500).

7.30 The mean is 0.02 but we cannot report the standard deviation because there is too much dependence; since 100 is not more than 10 times 40, the rule of thumb for approximate independence is not satisfied.

7.31 a. mean 0.001, standard deviation
$\sqrt{\frac{0.001(1 - 0.001)}{5,000}} = 0.0004$ **b.** Shape is not approximately normal because $5,000(0.001) = 5$ is not at least 10.

7.32 a.

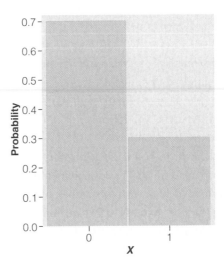

b. 2   **c.** The one on the bottom is more normal.

7.33 a.

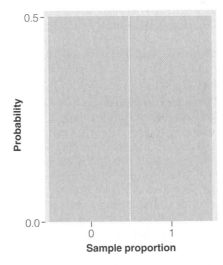

b. 5   **c.** The first one is more normal.

7.34 a. Centers would both be 0.25.   **b.** There would be less spread for samples of 40.   **c.** Shape would be closer to normal for samples of 40.

7.35 a. more normal for the larger sample size, 500   **b.** The distribution of X is approximately normal for samples of 500 but not 50: $500(0.02)$ and $500(0.98)$ are both at least 10, but $50(0.02)$ is less than 10.   **c.** The distribution of $\hat{p}$ is also very right-skewed because it has the same shape as X.

7.36 a. mean 0.25   **b.** standard deviation
$\sqrt{\frac{0.25(1 - 0.25)}{40}} = 0.07$ **c.** shape close to normal because $40(0.25) = 10$ and $40(1 - 0.25) = 30$ are both at least 10

7.37 a. categorical   **b.** $X = \hat{p}(n) = 0.06(150) = 9$ **c.** $\hat{p} = X/n = 8/200 = 0.04$ **d.** Mean is $np = 50(0.05) = 2.5$ and standard deviation is

$\sqrt{np(1-p)} = \sqrt{50(0.05)(0.95)} = 1.5$, approximately.   **e.** Mean is $p = 0.05$ and standard deviation is $\sqrt{p(1-p)/n} = \sqrt{0.05(0.95)/50} = 0.03$, approximately.   **f.** Mean is $np = 400(0.05) = 20$ and standard deviation is $\sqrt{np(1-p)} = \sqrt{400(0.05)(0.95)} = 4.4$, approximately.   **g.** Mean is $p = 0.05$ and standard deviation is $\sqrt{p(1-p)/n} = \sqrt{0.05(0.95)/400} = 0.01$, approximately.   **h.** The distribution of X is approximately normal for samples of 400 but not 50: 400(0.05) and 400(0.95) are both at least 10, but 50(0.05) is less than 10.   **i.** The distribution of X is also very right-skewed because it has the same shape as $\hat{p}$.

7.38 a. (2) Sample proportion of women in random samples of 100 is most normal (balanced population, large sample size) and (3) sample proportion of blacks in random samples of 10 is least normal (unbalanced population, small sample size).   **b.** (4) Smallest standard deviation is 0.03, for $p = 0.10$ and $n = 100$ (sample proportion of blacks in samples of 100); (1) largest standard deviation is 0.16, for $p = 0.50$ and $n = 10$ (sample proportion of women in samples of 10).

7.39 a. (1) Sample proportion speaking Chinese in random samples of 20 is least normal (more unbalanced population, small sample size).   **b.** (4) Sample proportion speaking Spanish in random samples of 200 is most normal (less unbalanced population, large sample size)   **c.** (2) Smallest standard deviation is 0.007, for $p = 0.01$ and $n = 200$ (sample proportion speaking Chinese in samples of 200)   **d.** (3) Largest standard deviation is 0.07, for $p = 0.11$ and $n = 20$ (sample proportion speaking Spanish in samples of 20).

7.40 the same

7.41 the same

7.42 X is discrete and it has an infinite number of possible values: 1, 3, 5, etc.

7.43 a. continuous quantitative   **b.** categorical   **c.** discrete quantitative   **d.** continuous quantitative   **e.** continuous quantitative   **f.** continuous quantitative   **g.** discrete quantitative

7.44 a. discrete quantitative   **b.** continuous quantitative   **c.** categorical   **d.** discrete quantitative   **e.** continuous quantitative   **f.** categorical   **g.** continuous quantitative

7.45 a. No, $P(X \geq 2)$ and $P(X > 2)$ aren't necessarily equal because X is discrete.   **b.** Yes, $P(X \geq 2)$ and $P(X > 2)$ should be equal because X, the mean of all values, is continuous.   **c.** Yes, because X is continuous.   **d.** Yes, because the random variable is continuous.

7.46 a. Yes, because X is continuous.   **b.** No, because X is discrete.   **c.** No, because X is discrete.

7.47

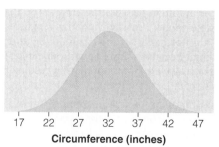

Circumference (inches)

7.48 a. 0.997, because these values are 3 standard deviations on either side of the mean.   **b.** $(1 - 0.68)/2 = 0.16$, since 127 is one standard deviation above the mean.   **c.** 112 and 132 (within 2 standard deviations of the mean)   **d.** 112 (2 standard deviations below the mean)

7.49 a. 0.025   **b.** This is somewhat unusual (on the large side).   **c.** between 0.0015 and 0.025 because 20 is between 17 and 22   **d.** this is very unusual (extremely small)   **e.** 12 inches below the mean, where there are 5 inches in a standard deviation: $(-12)/5 = -2.4$, so it is 2.4 standard deviations below the mean   **f.** $z = (20 - 32)/5 = -2.4$
g. $x = 32 + 0.8(5) = 36$

7.50 a. 0.95, because these are within 2 standard deviations of the mean   **b.** $(1 - 0.68)/2 = 0.16$ because 20 is 1 standard deviation below the mean   **c.** 10 and 40 (within 3 standard deviations of the mean)   **d.** 30 (more than 1 standard deviation above the mean)

7.51 a. $z = (117 - 100)/15 = +1.13$; unexceptional
b. $z = (144 - 100)/15 = +2.93$; exceptional
c. $z = (132 - 100)/15 = +2.13$; borderline
d. $z = (129 - 100)/15 = +1.93$; borderline

7.52 a. $z = (600 - 835)/111 = -2.12$; borderline
b. $z = (354 - 835)/111 = -4.33$; exceptional
c. $z = (742 - 835)/111 = -0.84$; unexceptional
d. $z = (623 - 835)/111 = -1.91$; borderline

7.53 a. less than 0.025   **b.** more than 0.025   **c.** more than 0.025   **d.** less than 0.025   **e.** more than 0.025   **f.** more than 0.025

7.54 a. 0   **b.** 1   **c.** 0   **d.** 1

7.55 a. 1   **b.** 0   **c.** 0   **d.** 1

7.56 a. more than 0.025   **b.** less than 0.025   **c.** more than 0.025   **d.** less than 0.025   **e.** more than 0.025   **f.** more than 0.025

7.57 a. between -1 and -2 because 0.10 is between 0.16 and 0.025   **b.** greater than $+3$ because 0.001 is less than 0.0015

7.58 a. between -1 and 0 because 0.4 is between 0.16 and 0.5   **b.** between $+2$ and $+3$ because 0.02 is between 0.025 and 0.0015

7.59 a. $z = (106 - 122)/5 = -3.2$; probability of this short less than 0.0015   **b.** $z = (125 - 122)/5 = +0.6$; probability of this tall between 0.5 and 0.16   **c.** $z = (116 - 122)/5 = -1.2$; probability of this short between 0.16 and 0.025

7.60 a. $z = (31.7 - 25)/5 = +1.34$; probability of this heavy between 0.16 and 0.025   **b.** $z = (47 - 25)/5 = +4.4$; probability of this heavy less than 0.0015   **c.** $z = (24 - 25)/5 = -0.20$; probability of this light between 0.16 and 0.50

7.61 a. Because 0.02 is between 0.025 and 0.0015, the z-score is between $+2$ and $+3$, so the height is between $122 + 2(5) = 132$ and $122 + 3(5) = 137$ centimeters.   **b.** Because 0.20 is between 0.16 and 0.5, the z-score is between -1 and 0, so the height is between $122 - (5) = 117$ and $122 - 0(5) = 122$ centimeters.

7.62 a. Because 0.002 is between 0.0015 and 0.025, the z-score is between -3 and -2 and so the weight is between $25 - 3(5) = 10$ and $25 - 2(5) = 15$ pounds.   **b.** Because 0.12 is between 0.025 and 0.16, the z-score is between $+2$ and $+1$ and the weight is between $25 + 2(5) = 35$ and $25 + 1(5) = 30$ pounds.

7.63 a. $z = -1.8$, probability between 0.025 and 0.05   **b.** $z = +2.9$, probability between 0.005 and 0   **c.** $z = +2.22$, probability between 0.025 and 0.01   **d.** $z = -2.41$, probability between 0.005 and 0.01

7.64 a. $z = +1.80$, probability between 0.05 and 0.025   **b.** $z = -2.22$, probability between 0.01 and 0.025   **c.** $z = -2.82$, probability between 0 and 0.005   **d.** $z = +3.30$, probability between 0.005 and 0

7.65 a. $z = (106 - 122)/5 = -3.2$; very short   **b.** $z = (125 - 122)/5 = +0.6$; somewhat tall   **c.** $z = (116 - 122)/5 = -1.2$; somewhat short

7.66 a. $z = (31.7 - 25)/5 = +1.34$; somewhat heavy   **b.** $z = (47 - 25)/5 = +4.4$; very heavy   **c.** $z = (24 - 25)/5 = -0.20$; somewhat light

7.67 a. less than 0.01   **b.** more than 0.01   **c.** less than 0.01   **d.** more than 0.01

7.68 a. less than 0.05   **b.** more than 0.05   **c.** less than 0.05   **d.** more than 0.05

7.69 a. $z = -2.576$, $x = 2.45 - 2.576(0.17) = 2.01$ **b.** $z = +1.645$, $x = 2.45 + 1.645(0.17) = 2.73$ **c.** $z = -1.960$, $x = 2.06 - 1.960(0.17) = 1.73$ **d.** $z = +2.326$, $x = 2.06 + 2.326(0.17) = 2.46$

7.70 a. $z = -1.960$, $x = 22.00 - 1.960(1.88) = 18.32$ **b.** $z = +2.576$, $x = 22.00 + 2.576(1.88) = 26.84$ **c.** $z = +2.326$, $x = 22.30 + 2.326(1.88) = 26.67$ **d.** $z = -1.645$, $x = 22.30 - 1.645(1.88) = 19.21$

7.71 a. histogram (because it is a quantitative variable)   **b.** mean   **c.** pie chart (because it is a categorical variable)   **d.** $\hat{p}$

7.72 a. pie chart   **b.** p because it describes the entire population of assaults   **c.** not necessarily, because sample proportion $\hat{p}$ varies   **d.** closer to 0.20 because larger samples behave more like the population   **e.** 23 is a count.   **f.** 0.15 is a proportion.   **g.** observational study

7.73 a. bar graph   **b.** p because it describes the entire population   **c.** not necessarily, because sample proportion $\hat{p}$ varies   **d.** farther from 0.90 because smaller samples can vary more   **e.** 0.87 is the only plausible value (it is between 0 and 1, and reasonably close to 90%).   **f.** 170 is the only plausible value (it is greater than 1, and reasonably close to 90% of 200).   **g.** observational study

7.74 probability

7.75 statistical inference

7.76 data production

7.77 a. overestimates   **b.** underestimates   **c.** overestimates   **d.** not obvious

7.78 a. underestimate   **b.** not obvious   **c.** overestimate   **d.** not obvious

7.79 a. scatterplot   **b.** histogram   **c.** bar graph   **d.** side-by-side boxplots

7.80 a. side-by-side boxplots   **b.** histogram   **c.** scatterplot   **d.** single pie chart

7.81 a. Median of M is 0 and median of F is 1.
b.

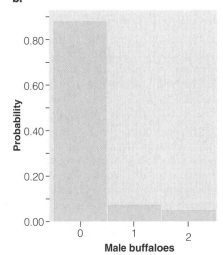

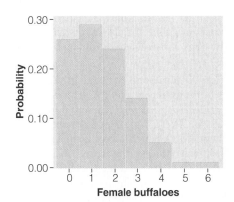

Both histograms are skewed right but the one for males has much more extreme right-skewness than that for females, because such a high

proportion have zero male buffaloes.   **c.** $P(M \geq 1)$ = $1 - P(M = 0) = 1 - 0.88 = 0.12$ or $P(M \geq 1)$ = $0.07 + 0.05 = 0.12$ **d.** $P(F \geq 1) = 1 - P(F = 0) = 1 - 0.26 = 0.74$ or $P(F \geq 1) = 0.29 + 0.24 + 0.14 + 0.05 + 0.01 + 0.01 = 0.74$ **e.** No, the Independent "And" Rule should not be applied because ownership of male and female buffaloes is likely to be dependent.   **f.** $P(M \geq 1$ and $F \geq 1) = P(M \geq 1) \times P(F \geq 1$ given $M \geq 1)$ = $0.12 \times 1 = 0.12$ **g.** $\mu_M = 0(0.88) + 1(0.07) + 2(0.05) = 0.17$ **h.** $\mu_F = 0(0.26) + 1(0.29) + 2(0.24) + 3(0.14) + 4(0.05) + 5(0.01) + 6(0.01)$ = 1.5 **i.** $\mu_{M + F} = \mu_M + \mu_F = 0.17 + 1.5 = 1.67$.   **j.** F has a larger standard deviation because its values are more spread, whereas those for M are very concentrated at zero.   **k.** The formula cannot be used because M and F are not independent.

7.82 a. $\mu_W = 0(0.15) + 1(0.61) + 2(0.21) + 3(0.03)$ = 1.12 and $\mu_M = 0(0.30) + 1(0.54) + 2(0.13) + 3(0.02) + 4(0.01) = 0.90$ **b.** The average for women is a bit more than that for men.
c. $\mu_{W + M} = \mu_W + \mu_M = 1.12 + 0.90 = 2.02$
d. No, W and M should be *dependent* because, presumably, the more women who collect firewood, the fewer men, and vice versa.
e. Yes, so $P(M = 0$ given $W = 0) = 0$. (At least one man has to collect in households where no women collect.)   **f.** probability

7.83 Brittany's answer is best: Other villages could easily have different situations in terms of how many cattle are owned, and in terms of who gathers firewood, because of varying economic and social norms.

7.84 a. $X_1 + X_2$ represents the thickness of bread for a sandwich constructed from two individual slices, and $2X_1$ represents the thickness of bread for a sandwich constructed by folding a single slice.
b. There is more of a tendency for extremely thin or thick sandwiches when a sandwich is constructed by folding over a single slice.
c. Mean of $2X_1$ is $2(0.5) = 1.0$ and mean of $X_1 + X_2$ is $0.5 + 0.5 = 1.0$; they are equal.
d. Standard deviation of $2X_1$ is $2(0.01) = 0.02$ and the standard deviation of $X_1 + X_2$ is $\sqrt{0.01^2 + 0.01^2} = 0.014$. Standard deviation of $2X_1$ is larger because there is more of a tendency for extremely thin or thick sandwiches when a sandwich is constructed by folding over a single slice.

7.85 a. $X_1 + X_2$ represents the student's score if she takes both midterms, and $2X_1$ represents her score if she takes just one midterm and doubles the score.   **b.** There is more of a tendency for unusually low or high scores if she takes just one midterm and doubles the score.   **c.** The mean of $2X_1$ is $2(80) = 160$ and the mean of $X_1 + X_2$ is $80 + 80 = 160$ **d.** The means are equal.
e. The standard deviation of $2X_1$ is $2(5) = 10$ and the standard deviation of $X_1 + X_2$ is $\sqrt{5^2 + 5^2} = 7.1$.   **f.** Standard deviation of $2X_1$ is larger because there is more of a tendency for

unusually low or high scores if she takes just one midterm and doubles the score.   **g.** No, there would be a substantial amount of dependence between one student's scores on both exams.

7.86 a. $800(1/365) = 2.19$
b. $\sqrt{800(1/365)(364/365)} = 1.48$
c. The z-score for 1 is $(1 - 2.19)/1.48 = -0.80$.
d. z is not unusually low so neither is 1, in this situation.   **e.** The sample size is not large enough to guarantee an approximate normal distribution because $np = 800(1/365) = 2.19$ is much less than 10.   **f.** between $2.19 - 2(1.48)$ and $2.19 + 2(1.48)$; in the interval $(-0.77, +5.15)$ **g.** Since 5 is about 2 standard deviations above the mean, the 68-95-99.7 Rule would estimate the probability to be $(1 - 0.95)/2 = 0.025$, which is fairly close to 0.02.   **h.** There is a substantial difference between 0 and 0.025.

7.87 a. categorical (under 23 or not)

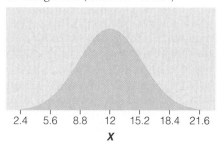

b.

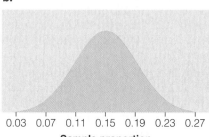

Sample proportion

c. Yes, because most of the area under the curve is to the left of 20.

d.

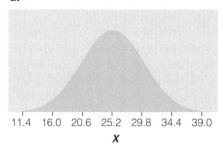

e. No, because there is almost no area under the curve to the left of 0.05.

7.88 a.

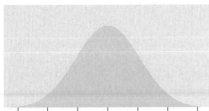

0.15 0.20 0.25 0.30 0.35 0.40 0.45
Sample proportion

b. No, because almost none of the area under the curve is to the right of 40. **c.**

d. Yes, because most of the area under the curve is to the right of 0.2.

7.89 a. mean $25(0.5) = 12.5$, standard deviation $\sqrt{25(0.5)(0.5)} = 2.5$ **b.** $z = (11 - 12.5)/2.5 = -0.60$ **c.** a bit low

d. mean 0.5, standard deviation $\sqrt{0.5(0.5)/25} = 0.1$ **e.** $z = (0.44 - 0.50)/0.1 = -0.60$ **f.** 0.6

7.90 a. mean $36(0.32) = 11.5$, standard deviation $\sqrt{36(0.32)(1 - 0.32)} = 2.8$ **b.** $z = (20 - 11.5)/2.8 = +3.04$ **c.** surprisingly high **d.** Yes; it is unlikely to see as many as 20 in a sample of 36 falling into the category of interest when the population proportion in that category is 0.32. **e.** mean 0.32, standard deviation $\sqrt{0.32(0.68)/36} = 0.08$

f. $z = (0.56 - 0.32)/0.08 = +3.00$
g. 3 **h.** underestimate **i.** because of a non-representative sample **j.** underestimate
k. because of the way the variable's values were assessed **l.** "How many days in the past month have you cut classes for the day?"

7.91 a. between 0.84 and 0.975 **b.** between 0.975 and 0.9985 **c.** between 0.16 and 0.50
d. between 0.975 and 0.9985 **e.** between 0.84 and 0.975 **f.** between 0 and 0.0015

7.92 a. between 0.975 and 0.9985 **b.** between 0.0015 and 0.025 **c.** between 0.9985 and 1
d. between 0.50 and 0.84 **e.** between 0.025 and 0.16 **f.** between 0.84 and 0.975

7.93 Responses will vary.

7.94 Responses will vary.

Chapter 8

8.1 a. population proportion p, a parameter
b. population mean μ, a parameter

8.2 a. sample mean $\bar{x}$, a statistic **b.** population proportion p, a parameter

8.3 a. population proportion **b.** both population proportion and sample size **c.** both population proportion and sample size

8.4 a. population proportion **b.** both population proportion and sample size **c.** both population proportion and sample size

8.5 a. both distributions centered at 0.66 **b.** less spread for samples of 50 students **c.** shape more normal for samples of 50 students

8.6 a. cannot use normal approximation because sample is too small **b.** sample proportion not centered at 0.66 because sample is biased; pre-meds may tend to have a different graduation rate **c.** can use methods presented

8.7 a. standard deviation $\sqrt{\frac{0.66(1 - 0.66)}{90}} = 0.05$, sample proportion $64/90 = 0.71$, standardized sample proportion $z = (0.71 - 0.66)/0.05 = +1$, probability approximately 0.16

8.8 a. both distributions centered at 0.61 **b.** less spread for samples of 20 athletes **c.** shape more normal for samples of 20 athletes

8.9 a. cannot use normal approximation because sample is too small **b.** can use methods presented **c.** sample proportion not centered at 0.61 because sample is biased

8.10 a. $\sqrt{\frac{0.61(1 - 0.61)}{29}} = 0.09$ **b.** $10/29 = 0.34$
c. $z = (0.34 - 0.61)/0.09 = -3$ **d.** 0.0015

8.11 a. $z = (0.93 - 0.88)/0.02 = +2.5$ **b.** between 0.025 and 0.0015 **c.** between 0.01 and 0.005
d. very unlikely **e.** (2) **f.** not improbable

8.12 a. $z = (0.18 - 0.16)/0.007 = +2.86$
b. between 0.025 and 0.0015 **c.** less than 0.005
d. extremely unlikely **e.** greater than 0.18

8.13 a. mean 0.80, standard deviation $\sqrt{0.80(1 - 0.80)/64} = 0.05$ **b.** The shape is approximately normal because $64(0.8)$ and $64(0.2)$ are both at least 10
c.

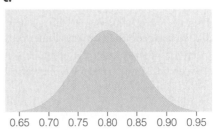

0.65 0.70 0.75 0.80 0.85 0.90 0.95
**Sample proportion believing in God
for samples of size 64**

d. No, because $48/64 = 0.75$ is just 1 standard deviation below the mean **e.** 0.80 is a parameter
f. p **g.** 0.75 is a statistic **h.** $\hat{p}$

8.14 Dominique's answer is best: at least 2% of sampled teenagers must have attended religious services in spite of not believing in God; it would be more than 2% if there were teenagers in the sample who did believe in God but it did not attend religious services.

8.15 a. population mean μ **b.** 20 **c.** 20

8.16 a. population mean μ **b.** 100 **c.** 100

8.17 a. population mean   **b.** population standard deviation and sample size   **c.** population shape and sample size

8.18 a. population mean   **b.** population standard deviation and sample size   **c.** population shape and sample size

8.19 a. Both distributions are centered at 10.5.   **b.** There should be less spread for the means of 16 selections.   **c.** Shape is more normal for 16 than for 9.

8.20 a. Both distributions are centered at 5.5.   **b.** There should be less spread for the means of 25 selections.   **c.** Shape is more normal for 25 than for 4.

8.21 a. to the right of 69   **b.** at 69   **c.** at 69   **d.** to the left of 69

8.22 a. at 144   **b.** to the left of 144   **c.** to the right of 144

8.23 a. $2.8/\sqrt{16} = 0.7$ **b.** $2.8/\sqrt{49} = 0.4$

8.24 a. $33/\sqrt{9} = 11$ **b.** $33/\sqrt{121} = 3$

8.25 a. extremely right-skewed   **b.** somewhat right-skewed   **c.** approximately normal

8.26 a. close to normal   **b.** close to normal   **c.** close to normal

8.27 a. more than 0.5   **b.** less than 0.16   **c.** more than 0.025

8.28 $z = (50 - 42.6)/3.0 = +2.47$, which is between $+2.326$ and $+2.576$, so the probability is between 0.01 and 0.005.

8.29 a. population mean μ **b.** 40 positive, 30 positive, 25 negative, 20 negative   **c.** 40 most extreme (farthest from 26)   **d.** 25 least extreme (closest to 26)

8.30 a. less than 0.0015   **b.** less than 0.5   **c.** less than 0.025

8.31 a. $z = (30 - 26.0)/2.0 = +2$ **b.** z is just over $+1.96$, so the probability is just under 0.025.

8.32 a. $z = (212 - 217)/(126/\sqrt{3{,}115}) = -2.21$ **b.** between 0.025 and 0.0015   **c.** between 0.01 and 0.025   **d.** very unlikely   **e.** (2)   **f.** $z = (212 - 217)/(126/\sqrt{9}) = -0.12$ close to zero, so the sample mean is fairly close to 217.

8.33 a. $z = (228 - 234)/(85/\sqrt{3{,}154}) = -3.96$ **b.** less than 0.0015   **c.** less than 0.005   **d.** extremely unlikely   **e.** (2)   **f.** $z = (228 - 234)/(85/\sqrt{25}) = -0.35$ **g.** z is close to zero, so the sample mean is fairly close to 234.

8.34 a. yes (numerator larger in absolute value for math than reading)   **b.** yes (denominator smaller for math than reading)   **c.** yes (denominator smaller for math than reading)

8.35 a. two categorical variables   **b.** one each, quantitative and categorical   **c.** one quantitative variable   **d.** one categorical variable

8.36 (c)

8.37 a. two-sample   **b.** paired   **c.** several-sample

8.38 a. one categorical   **b.** two categorical   **c.** two quantitative   **d.** one quantitative

8.39 (a)

8.40 The sample is too large relative to population size (should be no more than one-tenth population size, and it is half) and so samples without replacement have too much dependence.

8.41 The sample size (100) is more than one-tenth the population size (750).

8.42 a. $\hat{p}$ **b.** $\bar{x}$ **c.** n

8.43 a. probability   **b.** statistical inference   **c.** displaying and summarizing   **d.** data production

8.44 a. displaying and summarizing data   **b.** data production   **c.** statistical inference   **d.** probability

8.45 a. approximately normal   **b.** left-skewed/low outliers   **c.** right-skewed/high outliers   **d.** right-skewed/high outliers

8.46 a. right-skewed/high outliers   **b.** right-skewed/high outliers   **c.** approximately normal   **d.** left-skewed/low outliers

8.47 4, 3, 2, 1, respectively

8.48 not unlikely, fairly unlikely, very unlikely, extremely unlikely, respectively

8.49 40,000 because 40,000(1/4,000) = 10

8.50 3,650 because 3,650(1/365) = 10

8.51 a. 0.40   **b.** $\sqrt{0.40(1 - 0.40)/100} = 0.05$ **c.** positive   **d.** 0.10   **e.** $\sqrt{0.10(1 - 0.10)/100} = 0.03$ **f.** negative   **g.** 1. $z = (0.25 - 0.40)/0.05 = -3$, unusually low   2. $z = (0.25 - 0.10)/0.03 = +5$, unusually high   3. $z = (0.46 - 0.40)/0.05 = +1.2$, not unusual   4. $z = (0.16 - 0.10)/0.03 = +2$, unusually high

8.52 a. $\sqrt{0.34(1 - 0.34)/45} = 0.07$ **b.** $z = (0.29 - 0.34)/0.07 = -0.71$ **c.** somewhat low but not unusual   **d.** $\sqrt{0.23(1 - 0.23)/45} = 0.06$ **e.** $z = (0.29 - 0.23)/0.06 = +1.0$ **f.** somewhat high but not unusual   **g.** Yes, because the z-scores would be -7.1 for Europe (surprisingly low) and $+10$ for the United States (surprisingly high).   **h.** bar graph

8.53 a. categorical; consider the numbers of bedrooms in new single-family houses completed in 2003 and summarize with mean   **b.** close to symmetric

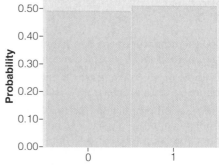

Sample proportion with exactly 3 bedrooms in samples of size 1

c. 0.51   **d.** $\sqrt{0.51(1-0.51)/6} = 0.20$
e. symmetric but not normal because the sample size is relatively small: $np = 6(0.51) = 3.06$ is less than 10   **f.** 0.51   **g.** $\sqrt{0.51(1-0.51)/24} = 0.10$
h. approximately normal because the sample size is relatively large: $np = 24(0.51) = 12.24$ and $n(1-p) = 24(0.49) = 11.76$ are both at least 10

8.54 0.40 negative (less than 0.51), 0.53 positive (greater than 0.51), 0.90 positive (greater than 0.51)

8.55 0.90 most extreme (farthest from 0.51), 0.53 least extreme (closest to 0.51)

8.56 a. $\hat{p} = 12/30 = 0.40$, $z = (0.40 - 0.51)/0.09 = -1.22$, not unusual   **b.** $\hat{p} = 16/30 = 0.53$, $z = (0.53 - 0.51)/0.09 = +0.22$, not unusual
c. $\hat{p} = 27/30 = 0.90$, $z = (0.90 - 0.51)/0.09 = +4.33$, unusually many

8.57 a. 0.51 plus or minus 2(0.09): between 0.33 and 0.69   **b.** No, because 0.70 is outside the range of sample proportions we would see 95% of the time.   **c.** 0.32

8.58 a. categorical   **b.** fairly symmetric but not normal

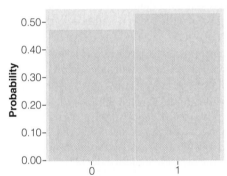

Sample proportion with 2 or
more stories in samples of size 1

c. 0.53   **d.** $\sqrt{0.53(1-0.53)/4} = 0.25$
e. symmetric but not normal because the sample size is relatively small: $np = 4(0.53) = 2.12$ is less than 10   **f.** 0.53   **g.** $\sqrt{0.53(1-0.53)/50} = 0.07$
h. approximately normal, since the sample size is relatively large: $np = 50(0.53) = 26.5$ and $n(1-p) = 50(0.47) = 23.5$ are both at least 10

8.59 a. negative (less than 0.53)   **b.** positive (more than 0.53)   **c.** negative (less than 0.53)

8.60 a. 0.20 most extreme (farthest from 0.53)
b. 0.50 least extreme (closest to 0.53)

8.61 a. $\hat{p} = 14/70 = 0.20$, $z = (0.20 - 0.53)/0.06 = -5.5$, unusually few   **b.** $\hat{p} = 49/70 = 0.70$, $z = (0.70 - 0.53)/0.06 = +2.83$, unusually many
c. $\hat{p} = 35/70 = 0.50$, $z = (0.50 - 0.53)/0.06 = -0.5$, not unusual

8.62 a. 0.53 plus or minus 0.06: between 0.47 and 0.59   **b.** Yes, since 0.49 is inside the range of sample proportions we would see 68% of the time.   **c.** 0.05

8.63 a. mean 0.05, standard deviation $\sqrt{0.05(1-0.05)/400} = 0.01$ **b.** The shape is approximately normal because 400(0.05) and 400(0.95) are both at least 10
c.

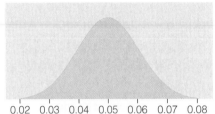

0.02 0.03 0.04 0.05 0.06 0.07 0.08
**Sample proportion who are gay in
samples of size 400**

d. Yes, because 160/400 = 0.40 would be an almost impossibly high sample proportion if sampling at random from a population with proportion 0.05 who are gay: $z = (0.40 - 0.05)/0.01 = +35$.   **e.** Yes, the high proportion could be explained by parents throwing them out of the home.

8.64 a. mean 0.44, standard deviation $\sqrt{\frac{0.44(1-0.44)}{66}} = 0.06$, shape approximately normal because 66(0.44) and 66(1 - 0.44) are both at least 10.   **b.** A sample proportion of 0.42 is not at all unusual because it is just a third of a standard deviation below the mean.

8.65 a. Proportion living on campus is 222/445 = 0.499, or 0.50 rounded to two decimal places.

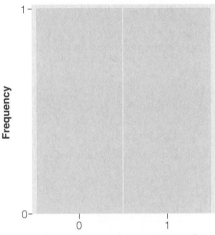

**Sample proportion on campus in
samples of size 1**

b. mean 0.5, standard deviation $\sqrt{0.5(1-0.5)/10} = 0.16$. Shape is symmetric and somewhat normal because although the sample size is small, the underlying distribution is nicely balanced.   **c.** mean 0.47, standard deviation 0.13

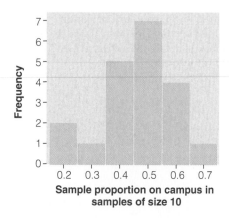

Sample proportion on campus in samples of size 10

d. The mean and standard deviation conform fairly well, and the shape is fairly normal.

8.66 a. Proportion living on campus is 222/445 = 0.499, or 0.50 rounded to two decimal places. **b.** mean 0.5, standard deviation $\sqrt{0.5(1 - 0.5)/40} = 0.08$. **c.** The shape should be approximately normal because the population distribution is balanced and the sample size is fairly large. **d.** mean 0.51, standard deviation 0.07

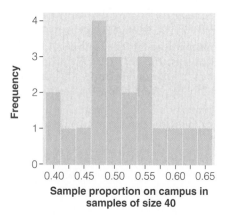

Sample proportion on campus in samples of size 40

e. Center and spread are quite close because 0.51 is close to 0.5 and 0.07 is close to 0.08. The shape is reasonably normal.

8.67 a. Proportion ambidextrous is 13/446 = 0.03.
b.

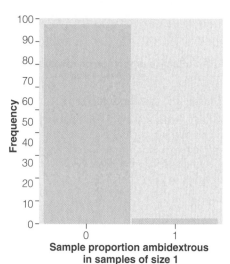

Sample proportion ambidextrous in samples of size 1

c. mean 0.03, standard deviation $\sqrt{0.03(1 - 0.03)/10} = 0.05$ **d.** Shape is skewed right because the population is very right-skewed and the sample is small. **e.** mean 0.02, standard deviation 0.04

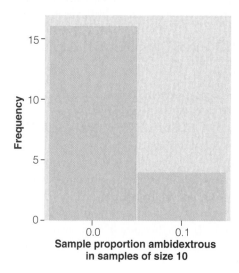

Sample proportion ambidextrous in samples of size 10

f. Mean is fairly close (0.02 is close to 0.03) and so is standard deviation (0.04 is close to 0.05); shape is right-skewed, but less so than the population.

8.68 a. proportion ambidextrous is 13/446 = 0.03 **b.** mean 0.03, standard deviation $\sqrt{0.03(1 - 0.03)/40} = 0.03$ **c.** The shape would still be skewed because the Rule of Thumb is not satisfied ($np = 0.03(40) = 1.2$) but less so than for samples of size 10 because larger samples do a better job of offsetting non-normality. **d.** mean 0.03, standard deviation 0.02

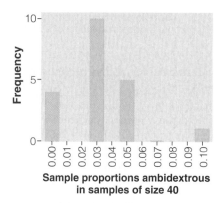

Sample proportions ambidextrous in samples of size 40

e. Center is about the same (0.03), spread is close (since 0.02 is close to 0.03), and shape is right-skewed.

8.69 Responses will vary.

8.70 a. somewhat left-skewed **b.** somewhat left-skewed **c.** close to normal

8.71 a. population mean μ **b.** 40 negative, 50 positive, 38 negative, 37 negative **c.** 50 most extreme (farthest from 42.6) and 40 least extreme (closest to 42.6)

8.72 a. 0, 1, 2, 3, 4, 5, 6, 7 **b.** 5 **c.** left-skewed **d.** 200 (larger sample because it has less spread)

e. (1) extremely improbable (2) very improbable (3) not improbable   **f.** compare means

8.73 a. 0, 1, 2, 3, 4, 5, 6, 7   **b.** 0 and 5   **c.** No, it would be somewhat left-skewed except for a peak at 0.   **d.** 100 (smaller sample because it has more spread)   **e.** extremely improbable   **f.** very improbable   **g.** not improbable   **h.** a histogram   **i.** side-by-side boxplots

8.74 a. Central Limit Theorem
b. $z = (2,820 - 2,860)/(440/\sqrt{572}) = -2.17$
c. unusually low   **d.** yes   **e.** Income, age, and location are a few possible confounding variables, but there are other possibilities.

8.75 a. mean 93, standard deviation $15/\sqrt{144} = 1.25$
b. mean 93, standard deviation $15/\sqrt{36} = 2.5$
c. sample mean MQ greater than 93
d. $z = (96.5 - 93)/1.25 = +2.8$, which is high enough to suggest that these children are not representative in terms of MQ: theirs tend to be higher than usual.   **e.** $(85.7 - 93)/2.5 = -2.92$, which is low enough to suggest that these children are not representative in terms of MQ: theirs tend to be lower than usual.

8.76 a. $15/\sqrt{25} = 3$ **b.** 93 plus or minus 2(3): the interval is (87, 99).   **c.** 0.32

8.77 a. mean 835, standard deviation 6.5
b. mean 835, standard deviation 18.0
c. sample mean fitness less than 835
d. $z = (834.1 - 835)/6.5 = -0.14$ **e.** z is not unusual, so these children do appear to be representative of the larger group.
f. $z = (838 - 835)/18.0 = +0.17$ **g.** z is not unusual, so these children do appear to be representative of the larger group.

8.78 a. $111/\sqrt{9} = 37$ **b.** 835 plus or minus 2(37): the interval is (761, 909)   **c.** 0.05

8.79 a. left-skewed   **b.** 0.18   **c.** mean 7.6 and standard deviation 0.19
d. $z = (9 - 7.6)/0.19 = 7.37$ **e.** virtually impossible   **f.** Sample mean rating would still be skewed for a small sample size (10).

8.80 a.

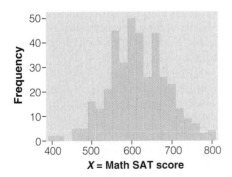

X = Math SAT score

b. mean 610, standard deviation $72/\sqrt{10} = 22.8$
c. Shape should be close to normal because the population is normal.   **d.** mean 607.0, standard deviation 24.0

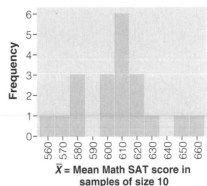

$\overline{X}$ = Mean Math SAT score in samples of size 10

e. Center 607 is close to 610, spread 24.0 is close to 22.8, and shape is approximately normal.

8.81 a. Mean is 610, standard deviation is $72/\sqrt{40} = 11.4$, shape should be close to normal because the population is normal.

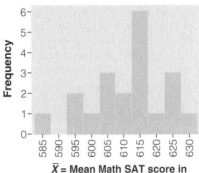

$\overline{X}$ = Mean Math SAT score in samples of size 40

b. mean 610.5, standard deviation 11.5
c. Means and standard deviations are very close; shape is bell-shaped but has a low outlier.
d. If we continued to take repeated random samples, some sample means would be on the high side to balance out those that are on the low side.

8.82 a.

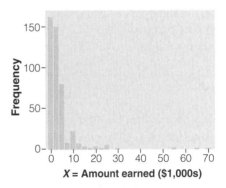

X = Amount earned ($1,000s)

b. mean 3.776, standard deviation $6.503/\sqrt{10} = 2.06$ **c.** Shape is right-skewed because the population is right-skewed and the sample is small.   **d.** mean 3.29, standard deviation 1.06

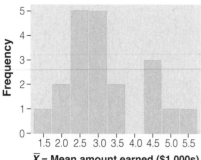

X̄ = Mean amount earned ($1,000s) in samples of size 10

e. Mean and standard deviation of the sample means are both somewhat less than the theoretical mean and standard deviation; shape is right-skewed as expected.

8.83 a. mean 3.776, standard deviation $6.503/\sqrt{40} = 1.03$ **b.** Shape is somewhat right-skewed because the population is very right-skewed, even though the sample size is moderate; there should less skewness than for samples of size 10 because larger samples do a better job of offsetting non-normality. **c.** mean 3.476, standard deviation 0.727

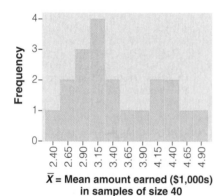

X̄ = Mean amount earned ($1,000s) in samples of size 40

d. Mean and standard deviation of the sample means are both a bit less than the theoretical mean and standard deviation; shape is right-skewed as expected.

8.84 Responses will vary.

Chapter 9

9.1 grade point average, for example

9.2 a. paired **b.** that 25 of the men had a dramatic decrease in blood pressure **c.** X **d.** $\hat{p}$ **e.** It is possible that blood pressure decreases when position is changed in either direction; this should be ruled out by determining if it only decreases when the men flip from face up to face down.

9.3 a. predicting a seizure and it does not occur **b.** overestimate, because people might want to boast about their dogs' abilities **c.** No, because the onset of an epileptic seizure could not really be simulated.

9.4 a. 0.53 **b.** It doesn't make sense to set up a 95% confidence interval for the proportion of all

Topeka voters who opposed the repeal because the data actually already represent all voters from that election. **c.** p

9.5 a. The survey from 1999 allowed for overlapping categories because they total to more than 100%. The survey from 2004 apparently did not because readers specified the *main* reason for choosing the last book they had read. **b.** 0.66 **c.** The difference can be attributed to the questions: For 66% the cover was one of several reasons for choosing a book; for 7% the cover was the predominant reason. **d.** (1) This interval has a 95% probability of containing the proportion of all people for whom a book's cover was *the* deciding factor in choosing the last book they read.

9.6 Those who come forward may be more likely, or less likely, to be male than abuse victims in general.

9.7 population proportion, 0.10

9.8 a. $0.60 \pm 2(0.035) = (0.53, 0.67)$ **b.** They should check if their sample was representative of all recent U.S. college graduates.

9.9 a. $\sqrt{0.10(1 - 0.10)/708} = 0.01$ **b.** 68, 640 **c.** $0.10 \pm 2(0.01) = (0.08, 0.12)$ **d.** only values greater than 0.05 **e.** Yes, because the range of plausible values is strictly higher than 0.05. **f.** Yes, because the population size would be much more than 10 times 708.

9.10 a. 0.90 **b.** $0.90(100) = 90$ **c.** $0.10(100) = 10$

9.11 $0.20 \pm 2\sqrt{0.20(1 - 0.20)/504} = 0.20 \pm 0.04 = (0.16, 0.24)$ or $0.20 \pm 1.96\sqrt{0.20(1 - 0.20)/504} = 0.20 \pm 0.03 = (0.17, 0.23)$

9.12 No: The multiplier 2 based on a normal distribution is incorrect because the number outside of the category of interest is too small (one was not right-handed).

9.13 Because the disease is contagious, it may not have infected other teams to the same degree. Also, a normal approximation is inappropriate because the sample size is too small (only five in the category of interest).

9.14 Using actual binomial probabilities would be preferable; because there are only two non-successes, a normal approximation would not be appropriate.

9.15 Using actual binomial probabilities would be preferable; because there are only two non-successes, a normal approximation would not be appropriate.

9.16 By reporting the data in this way, they are treating Rembrandt's vision as a quantitative variable (number of degrees).

9.17 a. the first survey, because all the interval's values are greater than 0.5 **b.** narrower **c.** $n = 1/0.04^2 = 625$

9.18 a. A 90% confidence interval would be narrower because the multiplier is 1.645 instead of 2. **b.** The point estimate for population proportion is halfway between 0.67 and 0.91: (0.67 +

0.91)/2 = 0.79. **c.** The margin of error is the distance from 0.79 to 0.67 or to 0.91, which is 0.12. **d.** The approximate standard deviation is half the margin of error, or 0.06. **e.** (3) We are 95% sure that population proportion falls in this interval. **f.** Yes, because the population (several thousand) is at least 10 times the sample size (75).

9.19 a. $1/\sqrt{16,000} = 0.008$ **b.** Yes, because $0.52 - 0.008$ is still greater than 0.5.
  c. $1/\sqrt{8,000} = 0.011$
  d. $1/\sqrt{.13(16,000)} = 0.022$ **e.** 0.53 is within 1 margin of error (0.022) of 0.52, and so it is a plausible value and the rate for the population of Hispanics may not have dropped at all. **f.** larger samples

9.20 a. more for subgroups because of dividing by a smaller sample size **b.** Those without a college degree have a smaller margin of error because there are more of them.

9.21 (d)

9.22 a. 3.5%, 6% **b.** There was apparently a larger sample size for "normal" parents because that interval is narrower.

9.23 a. The point estimate is halfway between 0.30 and 0.36, which is 0.33. **b.** The margin of error is the distance from 0.33 to 0.30, which is 0.03. **c.** The approximate standard deviation is half the margin of error, or 0.015. **d.** A 99% confidence interval would be wider because the multiplier is 2.576 instead of 2. Intuitively, an interval at a higher level of confidence must be wider because it has a better chance of containing the unknown population proportion. **e.** (4) We are 95% confident that population proportion falls in this interval. **f.** The interval is accurate only for that year; politics wouldn't be discussed as much in other years. **g.** The interval is accurate only for

November; politics wouldn't be discussed as much in other months.

9.24 a. No, we would expect those 100 children to be more likely to have imaginary companions because the subject apparently interested them.
  b. $0.65 \pm 2\sqrt{0.65(1 - 0.65)/100} = 0.65 \pm 0.10 = (0.55, 0.75)$ **c.** from 0.55 (20,000,000) = 11,000,000 to 0.75(20,000,000) = 15,000,000

9.25 a. $0.20 \pm 1.645\sqrt{0.20(1 - 0.20)/504} = 0.20 \pm 0.03 = (0.17, 0.23)$
  b. $0.20 \pm 2.326\sqrt{0.20(1 - 0.20)/504} = 0.20 \pm 0.04 = (0.16, 0.24)$ **c.** The 98% interval has a higher probability of containing the true population proportion. **d.** The 90% interval is narrower.

9.26 a. 0.045 is for administrators (largest margin of error for smallest sample) **b.** 0.011 is for teachers (middle margin of error for middle-sized sample) **c.** 0.003 is for students (smallest margin of error for largest sample)

9.27 a. 0.33 would be an overestimate if people received a visual cue to help them understand. **b.** 0.33 would be an overestimate if the sample included disproportionately many internationals.

9.28 We don't know the sample size.

9.29 Actual binomial probabilities should be used because there were too few in one of the categories to justify use of a normal approximation.

9.30 Neither, because in both situations there were only two in one of the categories.

9.31 The data come from nearly all the players (the population itself), so it is not appropriate to generalize to a larger population. Adam's answer is correct.

9.32 a. Confidence interval is (0.19, 0.25) (rounded).

```
Sample   X     N   Sample p        95.0% CI          Z-Value  P-Value
  1     150   680  0.220588  (0.189423, 0.251753)    −14.57    0.000
```

b. The interval would be centered to the left of it because the proportion would be much smaller if youths who were not headache patients were included. **c.** The interval would be centered to the left of it because the sample proportion would be smaller.

9.33 a. 1/8 = 0.125 **b.** Sample proportions are black 0.08, blue 0.43, green 0.14, orange 0.03, pink 0.08, purple 0.12, red 0.08, yellow 0.04.
  c. Black, orange, pink, purple, red, and yellow all have proportions lower than 0.125.
  d. Confidence intervals are black (0.05, 0.10), blue (0.39, 0.49), green (0.11, 0.18), orange (0.01, 0.04), pink (0.06, 0.11), purple (0.09, 0.15), red (0.05, 0.10), yellow (0.02, 0.05).
  e. The intervals for green and purple contain 0.125; the interval for blue is strictly above and the intervals for the rest are strictly below.

9.34 a. 0.05 **b.** This table includes answers to part (b).

No.	$\hat{p}$	CI	z	P-Value
1	0.02	(0.004,0.027)	−3.32	1.000
2	0.03	(0.014,0.045)	−2.02	0.978
3	0.04	(0.026,0.064)	−0.50	0.691
4	0.04	(0.019,0.054)	−1.36	0.914
5	0.04	(0.026,0.064)	−0.50	0.691

6	0.04	(0.026,0.064)	−0.50	0.691
7	0.08	(0.052,0.101)	2.54	0.006
8	0.04	(0.020,0.056)	−1.15	0.875
9	0.02	(0.010,0.039)	−2.46	0.993
10	0.02	(0.009,0.036)	−2.67	0.996
11	0.05	(0.027,0.067)	−0.28	0.611
12	0.06	(0.037,0.080)	0.80	0.211
13	0.11	(0.085,0.144)	6.24	0.000
14	0.05	(0.031,0.072)	0.15	0.440
15	0.05	(0.029,0.069)	−0.07	0.526
16	0.04	(0.022,0.059)	−0.93	0.825
17	0.15	(0.115,0.181)	9.49	0.000
18	0.05	(0.027,0.067)	−0.28	0.611
19	0.04	(0.019,0.053)	−0.50	0.691
20	0.03	(0.015,0.048)	−1.80	0.964

c. Sample proportion is higher than 0.05 for 7, 12, 13, and 17.   **d.** Confidence intervals are shown in the table.   **e.** The interval contains 0.05 for numbers 3, 4, 5, 6, 8, 11, 12, 14, 15, 16, 18, and 19. It is strictly above for 7, 13, and 17; strictly below for 1, 2, 9, 10, and 20.   **f.** wider

9.35 $100(0.95) = 95$

9.36 a. One point of view is that population proportion equals 0.05 and the other is that it is higher than 0.05.   **b.** One would hope that researchers were careful to obtain a representative sample of children and to perform the strep test carefully.   **c.** No: Certainly there would be more than 10 times 708 children in the city.   **d.** No: The sample size is large enough because we would expect $0.05(708) = 35$ with and $0.95(708) = 673$ without; both numbers are greater than 10.
e. $\hat{p} = 68/708 = 0.10$, $z = (0.10 - 0.05)/$
$0.01 = +5$ **f.** less than 0.0015 because +5 is greater than +3   **g.** (1) If researchers suspected that resistance rates were going to be higher in a particular city, the data would be more convincing than if they had just gone "fishing" for unusual values.

9.37 a. greater-than   **b.** $H_0 : p = 0.5$ vs. $H_a : p > 0.5$

9.38 a. shaded area shown in first graph below

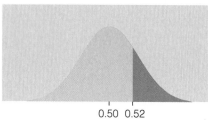

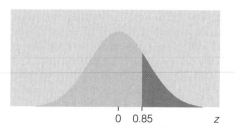

b. shaded area shown in graph above   **c.** shaded area shown in graph below

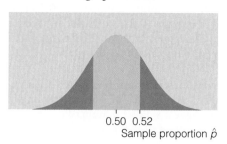

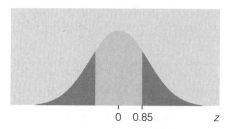

d. shaded area shown in graph above
e. No, because neither of the P-values is small.
f. Yes, because the null hypothesis that $p = 0.5$ is not rejected.

9.39 a. shaded area shown in graph below

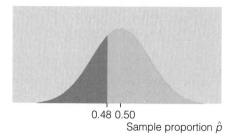

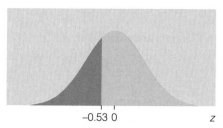

b. shaded area shown in graph above
c. shaded area shown in first graph at top of next page

0.48 0.50
Sample proportion $\hat{p}$

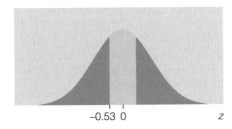

−0.53 0 z

d. shaded area shown in graph above
e. No, because neither of the P-values is small.
f. Yes, because the null hypothesis that $p = 0.5$ is not rejected.

9.40 a. $2,858/5,776 = 0.495$ **b.** $\hat{p}$ **c.** Yes, because it is less than 0.5.   **d.** greater than 0.16 because -0.79 is to the right of -1 **e.** z

9.41 a. $z = 0$ because $\hat{p}$ and p_0 are both 0.5.   **b.** The entire half of the normal curve to the right of 0.5 is shaded; the P-value is 0.5.   **c.** The entire half of the z curve to the right of 0 is shaded.
d. The entire area under the curve is shaded.
e. The entire area under the curve is shaded; the P-value is 1.0.   **f.** No, because the P-value is not small at all in either case.

9.42 a. $z = 0$, because $\hat{p}$ and p_0 are both 0.88.
b. The entire half of the normal curve to the left of 0.88 is shaded.   **c.** The entire half of the z curve to the left of 0 is shaded; the P-value is 0.5.
d. The entire area under the curve is shaded; the P-value is 1.0.   **e.** The entire area under the curve is shaded.   **f.** No, because the P-value is not small at all.

9.43 a. $700/1309 = 0.535$ **b.** $\hat{p}$ **c.** No, because 0.535 is greater than 0.5.   **d.** between $2(0.005)$ and $2(0.01)$ because 2.52 is between 2.326 and 2.576.   **e.** (2) There is convincing evidence that the proportion of all black cancer patients dying before Thanksgiving differs from 0.5.

9.44 a. $\hat{p} = 3547/6968 = 0.509$ **b.** No, because 0.509 is greater than 0.5.   **c.** between $2(0.025)$ and $2(0.16)$ because 1.51 is between 1 and 2
d. (1) There is no convincing evidence that the proportion of all elderly cancer patients dying before their birthday differs from 0.5.   **e.** p_0

9.45 a. 0.05   **b.** $0.05(100) = 5$ **c.** $0.05(20) = 1$
d. 1   **e.** (1) There is no convincing evidence that cancer patients die any more or less often before a special day as opposed to after.

9.46 a. z is more extreme for the House because the sample size is larger.   **b.** The P-value for the House is smaller because z is more extreme.

c. $0.040/2 = 0.020$ **d.** one-sided only, because 0.02 is less than 0.025 but 0.04 is not   **e.** 0.13

9.47 a. 0.11 (it is the smallest)   **b.** 0.20 (it is the largest)   **c.** 0.20 (it is the farthest from 0.15)
d. 0.14 (it is the closest to 0.15)

9.48 a. 0.05 (it is the farthest from 0.10)   **b.** 0.11 (it is the closest to 0.10)   **c.** 0.13 (it is the largest)
d. 0.05 (it is the smallest)

9.49 We have very strong evidence that this county's proportion of Caesarians does not conform to the national rate of 0.26.

9.50 not very small

9.51 a. $(70 + 86)/2 = 78$ **b.** $78/637 = 0.122$
c. $\sqrt{0.122(1 - 0.122)/637} = 0.013$
d. $107/637 = 0.168$ **e.** $z = (0.168 - 0.122)/0.013 = +3.54$ **f.** Yes, by the 68-95-99.7 Rule, it is less than 0.0015.   **g.** Yes, even if the null hypothesis is true, occasionally by chance the data will be unusual enough to reject it.

9.52 a. Type I (rejecting null hypothesis that the draws are random, even though it is true)   **b.** Type II (failing to reject null hypothesis that the draws are random, even though it is false)   **c.** Type I, because they would invest time, money, and effort into improving the lottery when it's actually fine.

9.53 a. Type I   **b.** Type II   **c.** Type II   **d.** If a Type I Error is committed, then dieters mistakenly believe they can lose weight by eating dairy products. This could prevent them from using another, more effective diet. If a Type II Error is committed, then dieters wouldn't be encouraged to try eating dairy products. This could prevent them from taking advantage of this effective method of losing weight.

9.54 a. The probability of a Type I Error (incorrectly "detecting" an innocent person to be a spy) is 0.16.   **b.** The consequences of these errors are basically the same as those in Example 9.28: Type I means convicting an innocent person.   **c.** The probability of a Type II Error (incorrectly failing to detect an actual spy) is $1 - 0.80 = 0.20$.
d. The consequence of a Type II Error would be letting an actual spy go free.

9.55 a. False-positive tests mean that the medications, etc. make it look like people use illegal drugs when they actually don't.   **b.** Type I

9.56 a. 0.05 is usually the default cutoff level α.
b. 0.01 should be used so that an athlete is not unfairly barred from participation in his sport.
c. 0.10 should be used because no immediate negative consequences would result from a positive test.

9.57 a. 0.01   **b.** 0.10

9.58 Type I

9.59 a. 11.04 is the z statistic for the test making a comparison to all *Americans* aged 18 to 44, because 0.955 is further from 0.855 than it is from 0.942.   **b.** Yes, the P-value is approximately zero, ecause the z-statistic is so high.

9.60 **a.** Yes, because the P-value is 0.000.
b. disproportionately high because the alternative uses a ">" sign **c.** different from because the alternative says "not =" **d.** because the sample proportion is actually considerably higher than 0.67, not lower

9.61 **a.** testing for a difference from proportion of all military personnel who were black, because 0.109 is further from 0.186 than it is from 0.13
b. testing for a difference from proportion of all military personnel who were black, because z is larger and the P-value is smaller

9.62 **a.** The null hypothesis says just half of dogs can be successfully matched; the alternative says more than half can be successfully matched. $H_0 : p = 0.5$ vs. $H_a : p > 0.5$. **b.** none, because none of the P-values is especially small **c.** both types together, because the counts in each category (23 and 22) are largest **d.** mixed breeds, because the counts in each category (7 and 13) are smallest
e. because only seven were observed in the category of interest, but with $p_0 = 0.5$, 10 each would be expected in and out of the category of interest

9.63 Yes, because the P-value is approximately zero.

9.64 Responses will vary.

9.65 **a.** The interval wouldn't come close to containing 0.13. **b.** $H_0 : p = 0.06$ and $H_0 : p = 0.14$ **c.** p_0 **d.** $z = 0$ if $\hat{p} = p_0$ **e.** P-value would be 1, twice the probability of z being greater than the absolute value of 0.

9.66 **d.** The data provide evidence that Group A strep in the city is more resistant to macrolides than it is in the United States in general.

9.67 **b.** The data fail to prove that women are more likely to die in the week after Christmas than in the week before.

9.68

```
Test of p = 0.5 vs p > 0.5
Sample      X      N   Sample p   95.0% Lower Bound   Z-Value   P-Value
1        1228   1706   0.719812          0.701928       18.16     0.000
```

a. $H_0 : p = 0.5$ vs. $H_a : p > 0.5$ **b.** $\hat{p} = 0.72$ (rounded) **c.** $z = 18.16$ **d.** P-value is 0.000 **e.** Yes, because the P-value is very small.

9.69

```
Test of p = 0.5 vs p not = 0.5
Sample   X    N   Sample p          95.0% CI          Z-Value   P-Value
1       18   31   0.580645   (0.406940, 0.754351)       0.90     0.369
```

a. $H_0 : p = 0.5$ vs. $H_a : p \neq 0.5$ **b.** 0.58 (rounded) **c.** $z = 0.90$ **d.** P-value is 0.369. **e.** The sample proportion could have come about by chance. **f.** Yes, because the P-value still wouldn't be small: half of 0.369 is 0.1845. **g.** (0.41, 0.75) (rounded) **h.** yes

9.70 **a.** $1/8 = 0.125$ **b.** Sample proportions are black 0.08, blue 0.43, green 0.14, orange 0.03, pink 0.08, purple 0.12, red 0.08, yellow 0.04.
c. Only blue and green have proportions higher than 0.125. **d.** Confidence intervals are black (0.05, 0.10), blue (0.39, 0.49), green (0.11, 0.18), orange (0.01, 0.04), pink (0.06, 0.11), purple (0.09, 0.15), red (0.05, 0.10), yellow (0.02, 0.05)
e. The intervals for green and purple contain 0.125; the interval for blue is strictly above and the intervals for the rest are strictly below.
f. narrower **g.** z scores are black −2.96, blue 19.65, green 1.18, orange −6.12, pink −2.68, purple −0.39, red −2.99, yellow −5.69.
h. P-values are black 0.999, blue 0.000, green 0.119, orange 1.000, pink 0.996, purple 0.653, red 0.999, yellow 1.000. **i.** We conclude the population proportion to be higher than 0.125 only for blue.

9.71 **a.** 0.05 **b.** Proportions for all 20 numbers are shown in the table below. **c.** The proportions are less than 0.05 for the numbers 1, 2, 3, 4, 5, 6, 8, 9, 10, 16, 19, and 20.

No.	$\hat{p}$	CI	z	P-Value
1	0.02	(0.004,0.027)	−3.32	0.000
2	0.03	(0.014,0.045)	−2.02	0.022
3	0.04	(0.026,0.064)	−0.50	0.309
4	0.04	(0.019,0.054)	−1.36	0.086
5	0.04	(0.026,0.064)	−0.50	0.309
6	0.04	(0.026,0.064)	−0.50	0.309
7	0.08	(0.052,0.101)	2.54	0.994
8	0.04	(0.020,0.056)	−1.15	0.125
9	0.02	(0.010,0.039)	−2.46	0.007
10	0.02	(0.009,0.036)	−2.67	0.004
11	0.05	(0.027,0.067)	−0.28	0.389
12	0.06	(0.037,0.080)	0.80	0.789

13	0.11	(0.085,0.144)	6.24	1.000
14	0.05	(0.031,0.072)	0.15	0.560
15	0.05	(0.029,0.069)	−0.07	0.474
16	0.04	(0.022,0.059)	−0.93	0.175
17	0.15	(0.115,0.181)	9.49	1.000
18	0.05	(0.027,0.067)	−0.28	0.389
19	0.04	(0.019,0.053)	−0.50	0.309
20	0.03	(0.015,0.048)	−1.80	0.036

d. Confidence intervals are shown in the table above.   **e.** The confidence intervals contain 0.05 for the numbers 3, 4, 5, 6, 8, 11, 12, 14, 15, 16, 18, 19. They are strictly above for the numbers 7, 13, 17. They are strictly below for the numbers 1, 2, 9, 10, 20. [Note that exact confidence intervals based on a binomial distribution will be slightly different, and the interval for the proportion choosing number 20 would just barely contain 0.05.]   **f.** z-scores are shown in the table above.   **g.** P-values are shown in the table above.   **h.** We conclude that overall students pick 1, 2, 9, 10, and 20 less than if they were choosing at random.

9.72 $z = +7.78$ goes "off the charts," so tables would not be helpful; we could say the P-value is approximately zero.

9.73 P-value is 0.2148.

9.74 P-value is $1 − 0.0059 = 0.9941$.

9.75 P-value is $2(0.0655) = 0.1310$.

9.76 P-value is 0.0154.

9.77 P-value is 0.1977.

9.78 P-value is 0.2981.

9.79 a. two quantitative   **b.** scatterplot   **c.** one each categorical and quantitative   **d.** histogram   **e.** side-by-side boxplots

9.80 experimenter effect

9.81 a. Compare people who do and do not engage in heavy physical exercise.   **b.** Compare players on fields that are and are not treated with fertilizers and herbicides—perhaps from various countries.

9.82 a. $14/40 = 0.35$
b. $\sqrt{0.35(1 − 0.35)/40} = 0.075$
c. yes (14 and 26)   **d.** $0.35 \pm 2(0.075) = (0.20, 0.50)$ **e.** both   **f.** (3)

9.83 a. $\hat{p} = 87/120 = 0.725$ **b.** Standard deviation is $\sqrt{0.725(1 − 0.725)/120} = 0.041$.   **c.** 95% confidence interval is $0.725 \pm 2(0.041) = (0.643, 0.807)$
d. $\hat{p} = 10/120 = 0.083$ **e.** Standard deviation is $\sqrt{0.083(1 − 0.083)/120} = 0.025$.

f. $0.08 \pm 2(0.025) = (0.03, 0.13)$ **g.** narrower
h. $\hat{p} = 10/87 = 0.115$ **i.** Standard deviation is $\sqrt{0.115(1 − 0.115)/87} = 0.034$.   **j.** $0.115 \pm 2(0.034) = (0.047, 0.183)$

9.84 a. Yes, 0.81 is the point estimate.   **b.** Sample size is needed to construct a confidence interval.   **c.** $n = 1/0.02^2 = 2,500$ **d.** Besides sample size, if conclusions are to be drawn in the form of a hypothesis test, a hypothetical population proportion p_0 must be proposed (possibly with a suspicion as to whether p is less than or greater than p_0).

9.85 a. Because we suspect a higher proportion to survive with the new protocol   **b.** Because there were only $123 − 118 = 5$ outside the category of interest; there should be at least 10 inside and outside the category of interest to justify use of the normal approximation.   **c.** Yes, because the P-value is 0.000.   **d.** No; the test shows that 0.80 is not a plausible value of population proportion.

9.86 a. The null hypothesis would say the proportion of all artists with misaligned eyes equals the population proportion with misaligned eyes (0.05); the alternative would say it is greater. $H_0 : p = 0.05$ vs. $H_a : p > 0.05$.   **b.** Yes, because 0.28 is greater than 0.05.   **c.** We verify that the general population size is much larger than 530 in order to assert that sample count is approximately binomial.   **d.** No, we would only expect $0.05(53) = 2.65$ with misaligned eyes.   **e.** The first set of output should be reported because it shows the actual binomial probability. Because the expected count in the category of interest is less than 10, the normal approximation should not be used.   **f.** (4) The data provide evidence that misaligned eyes are more common in artists.   **g.** The alternative hypothesis $H_a : p < 0.05$ can be ruled out just by looking at sample proportion because sample proportion is greater than 0.05.

9.87 Type I

9.88 a. Type I   **b.** avoiding beneficial treatment for breast cancer

9.89 a. The alternative claims that the proportion wearing braces who suffer such injuries is less than the overall proportion suffering such injuries. $H_a : p < p_0$.   **b.** Because sample proportion is actually greater than proposed population proportion p_0.   **c.** Several correct answers are possible, including the fact that athletes who wear braces tend to be more susceptible to injuries, and the fact that athletes who wear braces might take more risks because they feel protected.

9.90 a. Yes, because the confidence interval is completely above 0.5.   **b.** No, because the confidence interval contains values both below and above 0.5.   **c.** four men, because their sample proportion is much farther from 0.5   **d.** for men, because their z statistic is much larger

9.91 **a.** because the sample size (40) is not large enough for such an unbalanced distribution: $np = 40(0.03) = 1.2$ is not at least 10. **b.** 0.05 **c.** one **d.** none **e.** No, this will not always be the case; sometimes one or two will fail to capture population proportion p.

9.92 **a.** because z is for standardizing with a normal approximation **b.** 0.05 **c.** 19, 1 **d.** one; 0.031 **e.** No; sometimes none of the P-values will be small enough, other times perhaps two or even three of the P-values will be small enough. **f.** also one (0.031)

9.93 **a.** because a minority of the sample missed for that reason
b.

```
Sample   X   N   Sample p        95.0% CI
1       15  34   0.441176   (0.274278, 0.608075)
```

c. wider

9.94 **a.** (0.04, 0.08) **b.** no **c.** $z = +3.53$, P-value is 0.000; reject $H_0 : p = 0.03$ and conclude population proportion who never eat meat does not equal 0.03. **d.** 0.03 is not contained in the interval, and we reject the claim that $p = 0.03$. **e.** 0.000/2 = 0.000

9.95 **a.** (0.61, 0.70) **b.** no **c.** $z = 6.44$ **d.** P-value is 0.000; reject $H_0 : p = 0.50$ and conclude population proportion with pierced ears is not 0.50. **e.** 0.50 is not contained in the interval and we reject $H_0 : p = 0.50$. **f.** higher **g.** higher **h.** smaller

9.96 $z = +5$ goes "off the charts," so tables would not be helpful; we could say the P-value is approximately zero.

9.97 **a.** 0.4404 **b.** 0.0808 **c.** $1 - 0.0901 = 0.9099$

9.98 0.0197

9.99 **a.** $z = +7.27$ **b.** P-value is approximately zero. **c.** $z = +1.08$ **d.** P-value is 0.1401.

9.100 Responses will vary.

9.101 Instructors should evaluate students' discussion of article or report on Type I or II Error.

9.102 Responses will vary.

Chapter 10

10.1 **a.** 6.5 **b.** No, because the sample would not be representative of all Iberian rock lizards.

10.2 **a.** 1.9 **b.** sample size and standard deviation **c.** 0.005(1.9) = 0.0095

10.3 We know σ, so the standardized statistic is z.

10.4 **a.** μ and σ **b.** $504 \pm 2\frac{110}{\sqrt{121}} = (484, 524)$
c. We already know the population mean to be 504. **d.** Narrowest is (4). **e.** Widest is (1).

10.5 **a.** μ and σ **b.** yes **c.** We would not use the information to find a 95% confidence interval for mean income of all practicing PAs because we already are told what that mean is.

d. $68,000 \pm 2\frac{17,000}{\sqrt{100}} = (64,600, 71,400)$
e. Narrowest is (1). **f.** Widest is (4).

10.6 $2(20/\sqrt{16}) = 10$

10.7 $2(5/\sqrt{25}) = 2$

10.8 **a.** t procedure **b.** z procedure **c.** (11.08, 12.15) **d.** sample mean 11.614, P-value 0.000 **e.** Selections were apparently not truly random because the P-value is very small. **f.** Yes, because the P-value would have been half the size of 0.000. **g.** No, because sample mean is actually greater than 10.5. **h.** Because the sample mean was significantly greater than 10.5, people apparently perceive larger numbers to be more random. **i.** larger **j.** smaller

10.9 **a.** $9.04 **b.** because the sample size ($n = 82$) is fairly large **c.** $9.04 \pm 2(1.28/\sqrt{82}) = (8.76, 9.32)$ dollars **d.** Yes: $9.00 is well-contained in the confidence interval. **e.** narrower **f.** narrower **g.** $H_a : \mu \neq 9.00$

10.10 **a.** 4.55 **b.** (4.4722 + 4.6278)/2 = 4.55 **c.** because the confidence interval is built around the sample mean **d.** $4.55 \pm 2(0.0392) = (4.4716, 4.6284)$ is approximately the same as the reported interval **e.** (1) **f.** $(4.55 - 4.50)/0.0392 = 1.276$ **g.** 1.276 is not large for a z- or a t-statistic and so 4.50 is a plausible μ_0.

10.11 **a.** $H_0 : \mu = 22.6$ versus $H_a : \mu > 22.6$ **b.** because 5 is the population standard deviation **c.** $z = \frac{25.3 - 22.6}{5/\sqrt{6}} = +1.32$ **d.** not small because z is closer to 1 than to 2 **e.** no **f.** 2(1.32) = 2.64 would be significant.

10.12 **a.** $z = \frac{17.6 - 22.6}{5/\sqrt{7}} = -2.65$ **b.** There is evidence that mean cognitive ability score for those seven students was significantly lower than for the population of students in the course because z is unusually large negative. **c.** No; more likely, students with lower cognitive ability study more because they need to.

10.13 **a.** The P-value is quite small (0.007), so we reject the null hypothesis and conclude that $\mu > 7.151$ for the 20th century. **b.** Greater longevity in the latter century is a possible explanation for longer tenures. **c.** 2(0.007) = 0.014

10.14 because the standard deviation (1.362) is clearly more than 1

10.15 the one on the right (more spread)

10.16 **a.** $90.4 \pm 1.86(9.7/\sqrt{9}) = 90.4 \pm 6.0 = (84.4, 96.4)$ words per minute **b.** 1.645 **c.** narrower **d.** narrower **e.** wider

10.17 **a.** $52.6 \pm 3.36(3.2/\sqrt{9}) = 52.6 \pm 3.6 = (49.0, 56.2)$ **b.** narrower **c.** wider **d.** wider **e.** narrower

10.18 **a.** $H_0 : \mu = 1.0$ versus $H_a : \mu > 1.0$ **b.** $t = \frac{1.4 - 1.0}{1.35/\sqrt{10}} = +0.94$ **c.** The standardized sample mean is identified as t because it is calculated using s and not σ (and the sample size is small).   **d.** right-tailed   **e.** not small at all   **f.** The data do not provide evidence that mean number of calves sired by all male beluga whales in captivity exceeds 1.0.

10.19 a. $H_0: \mu = 6$ versus $H_a: \mu < 6$
b. $t = \frac{5.813 - 6.00}{1.109/\sqrt{16}} = -0.67$ **c.** The standardized sample mean is called t because the sample size is small and the sample mean was standardized with s, not σ.   **d.** left-tailed   **e.** not small at all   **f.** The data do not provide evidence that mean litter size for all captive female striped skunks is less than 6.   **g.** The sample standard deviation is zero because the three values 7, 7, and 7 have no spread.   **h.** We cannot find a standardized sample mean because it requires dividing by standard deviation, and we can't divide by zero.

10.20 The shape of the distribution of ages is close enough to normal but that of weights is not, because of right skewness and high outliers, and the fact that the sample size is rather small.

10.21 a. A z procedure is appropriate for both distributions because the sample size is so large; it doesn't matter if shape is non-normal.   **b.** If only 30 students had been sampled, a t procedure would be appropriate for evenings out but not for skipped days, because the former is only slightly skewed but the latter is very skewed.

10.22 a. $H_0: \mu = 44$ versus $H_a: \mu < 44$ **b.** to justify calling the standardized statistic "t" (otherwise, because of the small sample size, the distribution would not be symmetric and bell-shaped)   **c.** less than 44 because t is negative   **d.** 0.002 is small   **e.** The average price of Merlot wines is less than the company's wine prices in general.   **f.** $2(0.002) = 0.004$

10.23 a. B   **b.** B   **c.** B

10.24 a. B   **b.** B   **c.** B

10.25 a. 95%   **b.** 0.95(20) = 19   **c.** 19   **d.** No: 19 out of 20 is just what we'd expect in the long run.

10.26 a. 0.05   **b.** 19; 1   **c.** one (0.020)   **d.** It will not always be the case that exactly one P-value is small enough; sometimes none will be small enough, sometimes maybe two.   **e.** The interval will not contain 610.44.   **f.** because about half of the scores are below the mean and the other half above

10.27 a. $\bar{x}$ is approximately normal because the sample is large (192).   **b.** Standardized sample mean follows an approximate z distribution because for a large sample, s is close to σ.
c. $57 \pm 2(16/\sqrt{192}) = 57 \pm 2.3 = (54.7, 59.3)$
d. t **e.** 40 is not a plausible value for population mean because it is below the interval, not inside.
f. $\frac{57 - 40}{16/\sqrt{192}} = 14.72$ **g.** 40 is not a plausible value for population mean because then standardized sample mean would be too large to be believable.
h. $H_a: \mu \neq 40$ **i.** Yes, because 40 is not contained in the confidence interval.

10.28 a. because the sample is large (2,737)
b. Standardized sample mean follows an approximate z distribution because for a large sample, s is close to σ
c. $28.0 \pm 2(3.9/\sqrt{2,737}) = 28.0 \pm 0.15 =$ (27.85, 28.15)   **d.** 27.9 is plausible; 28.0 is plausible; 28.1 is plausible; 28.2 is not plausible, 30.0 is not plausible.   **e.** $\frac{28 - 30}{3.9/\sqrt{2,737}} = -26.8$
f. 30 is not a plausible value for population mean because then standardized sample mean would be too large (negative) to be believable.
g. $H_a: \mu \neq 30$ **h.** Yes, because 30 is not contained in the confidence interval.

10.29 a. $\frac{42.66 - 40}{12.46/\sqrt{25,000}} = +33.75$ **b.** The standardized sample mean is extremely large for a z statistic, so the probability of a sample mean this high if the population mean was only 40 is extremely small. We conclude the population mean is more than 40.

10.30 a. We have strong evidence that all male workers average more than 40 hours a week.   **b.** No, because according to the test 40 is not a plausible value for population mean.

10.31 a. $\frac{36.90 - 40}{11.93/\sqrt{25,000}} = -41.09$ **b.** z is extremely large negative, so the probability of a sample mean this low if the population mean was 40 is extremely small. We conclude the population mean is less than 40.

10.32 a. We have strong evidence that all female workers average less than 40 hours a week.
b. No, because according to the test 40 is not a plausible value for population mean.

10.33 a.

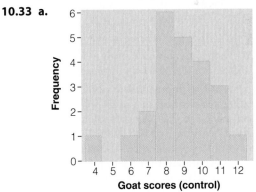

b. $H_0: \mu = 9$ versus $H_a: \mu > 9$ **c.** A formal test is not necessary to establish that the goats did not perform significantly better than chance because their sample mean (8.8) was worse than chance.
d. No. We can say that we have no compelling evidence that goats in general perform better than chance with the given social cues.
e. $8.8 \pm 2(1.8/\sqrt{23}) = 8.8 \pm 0.75 =$ (8.05, 9.55)

10.34 a. negative   **b.** positive   **c.** positive   **d.** negative

10.35 a. The standardized sample mean for touching would be higher because the mean is farther from 9.   **b.** If the standard deviations differed, the standardized value with higher sample mean wouldn't necessarily be higher.   **c.** If the sample sizes differed, the standardized value with higher sample mean wouldn't necessarily be higher.   **d.** The P-value for touching would be smaller because the standardized value is larger.   **e.** Both: z for pointing is unusually high, and according to part (a), z for touching would be even higher.

10.36 a. data production   **b.** probability
c. displaying and summarizing   **d.** statistical inference

10.37 a. negative   **b.** positive   **c.** positive
d. negative   **e.** negative   **f.** negative
g. positive

10.38 a. positive   **b.** positive   **c.** negative

10.39 $H_a: \mu < 1$

10.40 They should not be used because the sample represents only Mali, not sea otters in general. Gestation lengths for an individual otter may be shorter or longer than for other otters.

10.41 a. simply as a number of years   **b.** whether or not age is under 80 years

10.42 a. data production   **b.** displaying and summarizing   **c.** probability   **d.** statistical inference

10.43 a. 0.1822(100) = 18.22 dollars.   **b.** Because negative numbers are not possible, most of the spread occurs to the right of the mean, so it is skewed right.   **c.** The distribution is skewed, so normal probabilities for individuals would be incorrect.   **d.** Sample mean will be approximately normal because of the large sample size;
$0.1822 \pm 2(0.1899/\sqrt{264}) = 0.1822 \pm$
$0.0234 = (0.1588, 0.2056)$ **e.** No, because 0.5 is above the interval, not inside.   **f.** No, because 0.25 is above the interval, not inside.

10.44 a. It would be impractical to observe people's pirating behavior or to simulate offers with an experiment.   **b.** No, people may not be able to guess at how they would behave in real-life circumstances.   **c.** People's estimates could be rather inaccurate if they try to pin the percentage down precisely.   **d.** proportions, because the variable has categorical groups, not quantitative values

10.45 a. because the sample size is large (100)
b. $105.70 \pm 2(0.48) = (104.74, 106.66)$
c. 4.8, because 0.48 is 4.8 divided by the square root of 100.

10.46 a. both   **b.** The P-value for the women would be smaller because their test statistic is larger in absolute value.   **c.** because their sample mean is greater than 40   **d.** because their sample mean is less than 40

10.47 a. $H_0: \mu = 28.4$ versus $H_a: \mu \neq 28.4$;
$z = \frac{30.3 - 28.4}{19.7/\sqrt{1,278}} = +3.45$ **b.** P-value is close to zero because z is improbably large.   **c.** Reject H_0 and conclude that the mean for nonprofits differs

significantly from the population mean, 28.4 months.   **d.** $H_0: \mu = 28.4$ versus $H_a: \mu \neq 28.4$; $z = \frac{28.6 - 28.4}{19.7/\sqrt{17,209}} = +1.33$
e. P-value is not small because z is closer to 1 than to 2.   **f.** Do not reject H_0; conclude that the mean for independent assignees does not differ significantly from the population mean, 28.4 months.   **g.** smaller
h. smaller   **i.** 78% is too large a sample; for selections to be roughly independent, it shouldn't be more than 10%.   **j.** right-skewed   **k.** less than 28.4, because the mean is pulled above the median by the right-skewness and/or high outliers

10.48 (d)

10.49 a. $\frac{3 - 6}{2.6/\sqrt{140}} = -13.65$ can be called z because the sample size is large.   **b.** The difference is way too large to have come about by chance. A z value this extreme is nearly impossible.

10.50 a. The stemplot is roughly normal:

```
4  589
5  0000222
5  56778
6  00003
6  55
```

b. $(52.63 + 57.73)/2 = 55.18$ **c.** $5.10/2 = 2.55$
d. $2.55/2 = 1.275$ **e.** too long, because 60 is above the confidence interval

10.51 a. because there are 12 out of 14 in the category of interest, so only 2 outside the category of interest   **b.** no   **c.** yes   **d.** No, because $2(0.045) = 0.09$ is greater than 0.05.

10.52 a. because σ is known   **b.** σ (8.236) is larger than s (4.94).   **c.** t **d.** P-value based on t procedure

10.53 Dominique is correct. We failed to produce evidence that U.S. cardinals are significantly younger.

10.54 a. A formal test is not necessary because the sample performed at exactly chance (9.0).
b. Standardized sample mean would be zero because its numerator is $9.0 - 9$.   **c.** A 95% confidence interval for population mean score is guaranteed to contain 9 because it will be centered at 9 (sample mean).   **d.** $Q_3 + 1.5(Q_3 - Q_1) = 10 + 1.5(10 - 8) = 10 + 3 = 13$; 14 is a high outlier   **e.** In the long run with multiple testing, by chance a P-value will be "unusually small," even if the null hypothesis is true.

10.55
```
21  000000000
22  0
23
24
25
26  0
```

Standardized sample mean is neither z nor t because sample mean $\bar{x}$ is definitely not normal, due to a small sample size and a very high outlier.

10.56 The sample provides an overestimate because these were areas with highest earnings.

10.57 a. $20.7 \pm 2.78(0.4/\sqrt{5}) = 20.7 \pm 0.5 = (20.2, 21.2)$ **b.** $46.0 \pm 2.78(0.9/\sqrt{5}) = 46.0 \pm 1.1 = (44.9, 47.1)$ **c.** No; the population would be all times for the *best* swimmers in the event at that level (for comparable teams). **d.** Because the interval in part (b) contains numbers that are all more than twice the interval in part (a), it does not seem plausible that top swimmers on average can swim the 100 freestyle in twice the time it takes to swim the 50 freestyle.

10.58 a. $0.37 \pm 2.74(0.27/\sqrt{33}) = 0.37 \pm 0.13 = (0.24, 0.50)$ **b.** $0.37 \pm 2.576(0.27/\sqrt{33}) = 0.37 \pm 0.12 = (0.25, 0.49)$ **c.** slightly different **d.** a slight difference

10.59 a. implausible **b.** borderline **c.** plausible **d.** implausible **e.** data values themselves, to see if Southwest's seat size 17 is a low outlier

10.60 a.

```
4  05
5  257
6  225
7  057
8
9  7
```

b. (55.07, 71.09) (narrower)
c. $t = \frac{63 - 50}{15/\sqrt{12}} = 3.00$ **d.** Yes, because the probability of t being at least as high as 3.00 is less than 0.01. **e.** $H_a: \mu > 50$ **f.** paired

10.61 a.

```
1  05
2  05
3  0055
4  5
5  0
6
7  0
```

b. (16.86, 49.50) (wider) **c.** $\frac{33 - 25}{17/\sqrt{11}} = 1.56$
d. No, because the probability of t being at least as high as 1.56 is greater than 0.05. **e.** two quantitative variables

10.62 a. $t = \frac{19.6 - 15.2}{8.1/\sqrt{9}} = +1.63$ **b.** The standardized score should be written t and not z because the sample size is small, and sample standard deviation s is used, not σ. **c.** We would need to know σ. **d.** Because 1.63 is less than 1.86, the P-value is greater than 0.05, which is not small. **e.** Because 14.0 is actually less than 15.2; the P-value would be greater than 0.50.

10.63 a. Sample mean is far from μ_0. **b.** Values are concentrated around a sample mean that is different from μ_0. **c.** Sample size is large.

10.64 If a Type I Error is committed, a true null hypothesis is rejected, and people put their faith in a diet that is not really effective. If a Type II Error is committed, a false null hypothesis is not rejected, and people are deprived of the opportunity of learning about a diet that might work for them.

10.65 a. very compelling evidence that average weight after one year is less than what it was originally **b.** Zone **c.** Weight Watchers **d.** A smaller standard deviation would mean results are more predictable and less varied.

10.66 a. $\mu > 0$ **b.** $\mu < 0$ **c.** $\mu \neq 0$ **d.** 0.004

10.67 a. No, it is biased toward more weight loss because it is based only on the subjects who did not drop out. **b.** 0

10.68 No, because it is not plausible that the average weight loss is zero.

10.69 a. because no σ was given so s was used **b.** 95% **c.** 19 **d.** 18 **e.** No, this will not always be the case; sometimes 19 or 20 will contain it, or perhaps 17.

10.70 a. 0.05 **b.** 19 **c.** 1 **d.** 2 (both 0.004), **e.** This will not always be the case; sometimes 0 or 1 or maybe 3 will be small enough to reject H_0. **f.** It will not contain 3.776.

10.71 a. 0.0089 **b.** (3)

10.72 a. 0.0408 **b.** (2)

10.73 a. Age at first conception would also be right-skewed for human males because most would occur between the ages of 20 and 30, a few within a few years below 20, but some as much as 20 or 30 years more than 30.
b.

Variable	N	Mean	StDev	SE Mean	95.0% CI
BelugaAge	7	13.00	2.71	1.02	(10.49, 15.51)

c. $H_a: \mu < 12$

10.74 a.

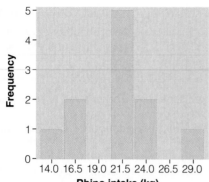

b. roughly normal   **c.** Yes, because even though the sample is small, the shape is close to normal.

d.
Variable	N	Mean	StDev	SE Mean	95.0% CI
RhinoIntake	11	20.75	4.29	1.29	(17.87, 23.64)

e. $H_a: \mu < 20$

10.75 a. A display would show an extremely high outlier (148).

b.
Variable	N	Mean	StDev	SE Mean	95.0% CI
ConsultingHours	21	23.10	32.09	7.00	(8.49, 37.70)

c. Center is 23.10, width is $37.70 - 8.49 = 29.21$

d.
Variable	N	Mean	StDev	SE Mean	95.0% CI
ConsultingHours	20	16.85	14.88	3.33	(9.88, 23.82)

e. Center is 16.85, width is $23.82 - 9.88 = 13.94$ **f.** The high outlier increased both the center and the width of the confidence interval, but the width was more dramatically affected because it was more than doubled, whereas the center just increased to 23.10 from 16.85, less than half again as much.

10.76 a. The histogram is roughly symmetric but not close to normal.

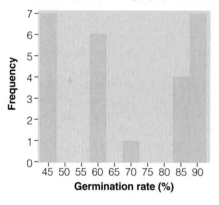

b. yes

c.
Variable	N	Mean	StDev	SE Mean	95.0% CI
Germination%	25	68.44	19.74	3.95	(60.29, 76.59)

10.77 a. The *P*-value is 0.857.   **b.** There is no compelling evidence that the mean mills for all the state's counties is lower than that for Allegheny County.

10.78 a. Test of mu = 580 vs mu not = 580

Variable	N	Mean	StDev	SE Mean
Verbal	391	591.84	73.24	3.70

Variable	95.0% CI		T	P
Verbal	(584.56,	599.12)	3.20	0.002

P-value is 0.002.   **b.** Yes, because the *P*-value is smaller than 0.05.

c. `Test of mu = 580 vs mu not = 580`
`The assumed sigma = 115`

Variable	N	Mean	StDev	SE Mean
Verbal	391	591.84	73.24	5.82

Variable	95.0% CI	Z	P
Verbal	(580.44, 603.24)	2.04	0.042

The test statistic is +2.04 and the *P*-value is 0.042. **d.** smaller **e.** larger **e.** (580.44, 603.24)

10.79 a. Both are quite possibly sources of bias.
   b. `Variable        95.0% CI`
   `   Math    ( 603.25,  617.62)`

10.80 a. *P*-value = 0.000; no **b.** *P*-value = 0.000; no **c.** *P*-value = 0.278; yes **d.** *P*-value = 0.685; yes

10.81 a. Sample mean is 15.2517. **b.** *P*-value is 0.009. **c.** (2)

10.82 a. (51.89, 65.01) **b.** 134 minutes a day is not plausible for students' population mean; they apparently watch much less. **c.** $H_0 : \mu = 134$ versus $H_a : \mu \neq 134$

10.83 a. (36.36, 44.54) **b.** 31 minutes a day is not plausible for students' population mean; they apparently exercise more. **c.** $H_0 : \mu = 31$ versus $H_a : \mu \neq 31$

10.84 a. (33.82, 42.01) **b.** 14.4 minutes a day is not plausible for students' population mean; they apparently talk on the phone much more. **c.** $H_0 : \mu = 14.4$ versus $H_a : \mu \neq 14.4$

10.85 a. (4.865, 7.866) **b.** because the range of plausible values is far below 30.3 **c.** because the range of plausible values is far below 19.1 **d.** People may not want to admit to a survey-taker, or even to themselves, that they smoke as much as they do. **e.** Due to increased awareness of the dangers of smoking, higher taxes, etc., the rate of smoking has decreased over time. **f.** College students could be part of a socio-economic bracket that tends not to smoke as much as the general population.

10.86 Responses will vary.

10.87 Responses will vary.

Chapter 11

11.1 a. hypothesis test to determine that conditions of stress do affect speech rates of stutterers in general

11.2 a. two-sample **b.** There is no relationship between age (adult or juvenile) and bucket-selection performance; or, population mean bucket-selection performance scores are the same for adults and juveniles. Symbolically, the latter can be written as $H_0 : \mu_1 = \mu_2$

11.3 a. paired **b.** There is no relationship between type of cue (touching or pointing) and bucket-selection performance; or, population mean of differences, performance scores for touching minus pointing, is zero. Symbolically, the latter can be written as $H_0 : \mu_d = 0$.

11.4 a. paired **b.** by reporting the standard deviation of the differences between normal and stressed speech rates **c.** histogram of differences **d.** inference about μ_d based on $\bar{x}_d$

11.5 a. two-sample **b.** by reporting means and standard deviations of speech rates under stress of stutterers and non-stutterers, respectively **c.** side-by-side boxplots **d.** inference about $\mu_1 - \mu_2$ based on $\bar{x}_1 - \bar{x}_2$ **e.** a hypothesis test to determine if stutterers in general are different from non-stutterers in terms of their speech rates

11.6 a. paired **b.** (2) **c.** No, a histogram should be used to display the single sample of differences.

d. $\mu_d = 0$ **e.** $\frac{16.69 - 0}{14.81 / \sqrt{16}} = 4.51$

f. yes **g.** $16.69 \pm 2.131 \frac{14.81}{\sqrt{16}} = (8.79, 24.58)$

h. Students might do better when they're older, or they might do better second time around because of having thought about the questions during the interim period. **i.** A better design would be to compare improvements for students who participated in the program with those of another group of similar students who did not participate. **j.** because it is roughly normal

11.7 a. paired **b.** because the standard deviation of the *difference* is most relevant in a paired design **c.** coliform

d.

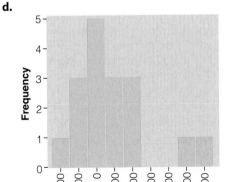

Differences (coliform minus *E. coli*)

Histogram suggests there are a few unusually large differences.   **e.** $t = 1.66$ **f.** P-value (for two-sided test) would be more than 0.05 because $z = 1.65$ would result in a 2-sided P-value of 0.10 and the tail area would be larger for t.   **g.** One type of bacteria is not necessarily more common overall.   **h.** $81.9 \pm 2.12\frac{203.3}{\sqrt{17}} = (-22.6, 186.4)$

i. The interval contains zero.   **j.** two quantitative

11.8   **a.** very large in absolute value and negative because the zinc contents are much larger than the lead contents   **b.** very small   **c.** $t = -10.01$ **d.** P-value = 0.002 (very small)   **e.** both correct

11.9   In each case, we see if the t statistic exceeds 2.   **a.** yes   **b.** yes   **c.** no   **d.** yes   **e.** no

11.10   **a.** yes   **b.** yes   **c.** no   **d.** yes   **e.** no

11.11   In each case, we see if the t statistic exceeds 2. If it does, we reject the null hypothesis and may be committing a Type I Error. If it does not, we do not reject, and may be committing a Type II Error.   **a.** Type I   **b.** Type I   **c.** Type II   **d.** Type I   **e.** Type II

11.12   **a.** In the long run, about 1 out of every 20 tests will reject a null hypothesis at the 0.05 level, even if the null hypothesis is true.   **b.** Type I

11.13   **a.** $25.3 - 17.57 = +7.73$ **b.** Those who didn't study did better.   **c.** $+7.73/3.33 = +2.32$ **d.** No, because the P-value is not less than $\alpha = 0.05$.   **e.** Yes, because the P-value is less than $\alpha = 0.05$.   **f.** larger   **g.** Brighter students may exaggerate how little they need to study, by way of bragging, and struggling students may exaggerate how much time they study, by way of complaining. Students could simply be asked to report hours studied in the previous week, or during any typical week, or they may be given journals for one or more weeks to record study hours. Either design has disadvantages: Retrospective is subject to students' faulty memories, and prospective may influence students' behaviors. Anonymity is important because students may over-report hours studied if they think their professors will have access to the information.

11.14   **a.** t statistic would be larger for the difference between ulna lengths because those sample means are farther apart.   **b.** t statistic would be larger for the difference between ulna lengths because that standard deviation is smaller.   **c.** 4.0 is for femurs and 7.3 is for ulnas.   **d.** both, because both t statistics are unusually large   **e.** larger

11.15   **a.** $10(3.5 - 2.7)/0.4 = 20$ **b.** $10(0.214 - 0.211)/0.053 = 0.57$ **c.** 0.57 is the one for spleens, because that t statistic is not very large.

11.16   **a.** No, because there is virtually no overlap.   **b.** Neither; 65 is too low for the volleyball players, too high for the gymnasts.

11.17   **a.** much larger   **b.** mild 0.96, moderate 0.98   **c.** $(0.96 - 0.98)/0.29 = -0.07$ **d.** One-sided, because we would want to demonstrate that

duration on average is longer for those with a moderate disability than for those with a mild disability.   **e.** not small at all   **f.** no convincing evidence   **g.** larger   **h.** smaller   **i.** larger   **j.** Type II

11.18 $(0.16 - 0.09) \pm 2\sqrt{\dfrac{0.11^2}{22} + \dfrac{0.06^2}{20}} =$

$0.07 \pm 0.05 = (0.02, 0.12)$

11.19   **a.** $3.2 - 2.6 = 0.6$ **b.** $0.6(60) = 36$ minutes   **c.** large sample sizes   **d.** very strong evidence that population means are different   **e.** only positive numbers   **f.** two categorical variables

11.20   **a.** Both, because the P-values, 0.021 and 0.024, are both fairly small.   **b.** Yes, because 0.11 is not more than twice 0.06.   **c.** yes   **d.** 0.012

11.21   No: The larger standard deviation is about three times the size of the smaller one.

11.22   **a.** $2.2 - 3.6 = -1.4$ **b.** $\bar{x}_1 - \bar{x}_2$ **c.** $-1.4 \pm 2(0.1) = (-1.6, -1.2)$ **d.** Yes, 3-year-olds watch more, and it's at least one hour more on average because the interval contains only negative numbers that exceed 1 in absolute value.   **e.** $-1.4 \pm 2.1(1.0) = (-3.5, +0.7)$ **f.** contains zero   **g.** This would suggest that the average for both groups could be the same.

11.23   **a.** $\mu_1 - \mu_2 < 0$

b. $t = \dfrac{(70.0 - 75.0) - 0}{\sqrt{\dfrac{12.4^2}{25} + \dfrac{13.0^2}{11}}} = -1.08$

c. not small at all, because t is not unusually large   **d.** Yes, because the null hypothesis of no curse is not rejected.   **e.** It will contain zero because it is plausible that the difference between means is zero.

11.24   **a.** No; the categorical explanatory variable is which company and the quantitative response variable is lead concentration. There is a column of responses for each categorical group.   **b.** $I = 3, N = 3 + 7 + 4 = 14$ **c.**

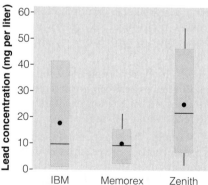

d. Zenith   **e.** Memorex   **f.** Memorex   **g.** top-heavy   **h.** 21.36, 6.98, 21.91   **i.** The sample standard deviations do not satisfy the rule because 21.91 is more than twice 6.98.   **j.** not small   **k.** no

11.25 a. No; the categorical explanatory variable is which company and the quantitative response variable is lead concentration. There is a column of responses for each categorical group.
b. $I = 4, N = 5 + 4 + 3 + 3 = 15$ **c.** Toshiba

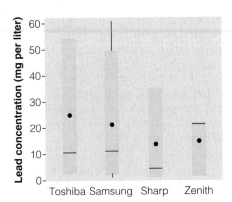

d. Sharp   **e.** Samsung   **f.** Zenith   **g.** top-heavy
h. 27.02, 27.17, 18.68, 11.61   **i.** No; 27.17 is more than 2(11.61).   **j.** close to 1   **k.** no

11.26 a. $t^2 = 2.35^2 = 5.52$ **b.** It is very close to $F = 5.53$.

11.27 a. all three   **b.** all three   **c.** none

11.28 a. Math, because those scores are more different.
b. Math, because those standard deviations are smaller.

11.29 a. elementary/middle schools   **b.** middle schools
c. because their sample size (6) was smallest
d. $I = 4$ and $N = 49 + 6 + 17 + 12 = 84$
e. $I - 1 = 4 - 1 = 3$ are the group degrees of freedom and $N - I = (49 + 6 + 17 + 12) - 4 = 84 - 4 = 80$ are the error degrees of freedom
f. MSG = SSG/DFG = 9,220/3 = 3,073, MSE = SSE/DFE = 585,561/80 = 7,320   **g.** $F = 3,073/7,320 = 0.42$ **h.** no   **i.** larger   **j.** 1,250

11.30 a. Parents of younger children could take a more proactive role in making sure the forms for free or reduced lunch are completed and sent in, so elementary schools could have the highest percent reported to be disadvantaged and high schools the lowest.   **b.** If disadvantaged students drop out, there would be a higher percentage disadvantaged in elementary school and a lower percentage in high school.   **c.** elementary   **d.** high school
e. Elementary highest and high school lowest are consistent with comments in parts (a) and (b).
f. $I = 3$ and $N = 49 + 17 + 12 = 78$ **g.** $I - 1 = 3 - 1 = 2$ are the group degrees of freedom and $N - I = (49 + 17 + 12) - 3 = 78 - 3 = 75$ are the error degrees of freedom   **h.** MSG = SSG/DFG = 5,986/2 = 2,993, MSE = SSE/DFE = 23,604/75 = 315   **i.** $F = 2,993/315 = 9.50$
j. (2) and (3)   **k.** None of the three is contained in all three intervals.

11.31 gender

11.32 The table has been completed with the particular values required.

Source	Degrees of Freedom	Sum of Squares	Mean Sum of Squares	F	P
Factor	DFG = 4	SSG = 22.29	MSG = 5.57	F = 3.20	P-value = 0.013
Error	DFE = 357	SSE = 620.82	MSE = 1.74		

a. 4   **b.** 357   **c.** 5.57   **d.** 1.74   **e.** 3.20

11.33 a. gender **b.**

Source	Degrees of Freedom	Sum of Squares	Mean Sum of Squares	F	P
Factor	DFG = 7	SSG = 543.6	MSG = 77.66	F = 4.88	P-value = 0.000
Error	DFE = 354	SSE = 5,635.2	MSE = 15.92		

11.34 Individuals in certain age groups could be more or less likely to admit to having been involved in automobile accidents than those in other age groups.

11.35 a. less than 0.05   **b.** all of these   **c.** 2, because $I - 1 = 1$ **d.** (c) because the P-value is smaller
e. scatterplot

11.36 a. Physical complaint is categorical.   **b.** GSI score is quantitative.   **c.** $\mu_1 = \mu_2 = \mu_3 = \mu_4 = \mu_5 = \mu_6 = \mu_7$ **d.** Not all population means are the same.   **e.** numerator $I - 1 = 7 - 1 = 6$,

denominator $N - I = 76 - 7 = 69$ **f.** no   **g.** If a Type II Error is made, then no attempt is made to refer the adolescents for psychiatric screening on the basis of their physical complaint; perhaps such screening would have benefitted the adolescents.

11.37 a. Cancun cheapest and Los Cabos most expensive   **b.** no   **c.** Not all the population means are equal.   **d.** no   **e.** No, they provide evidence that not all four are the same.
f. Los Cabos

11.38 The largest sample standard deviation (104.7) is more than twice the smallest (40.3).

11.39 **a.** $H_0: \mu_1 = \mu_2 = \mu_3 = \mu_4$ **b.** $\bar{x}_1$ to $\bar{x}_4$ **c.** s_1 to s_4 **d.** As level increases, percentage decreases. **e.** elementary **f.** high school **g.** More elementary students would be at school to take the test; fewer high school students would be at school to take the test. **h.** The largest standard deviation (6.00) is more than twice (even more than three times) the smallest standard deviation, 1.84.

11.40 **a.** Yes; lowest mean was for "other" students. **b.** no

11.41 **a.** explanatory, categorical **b.** explanatory, quantitative **c.** response, quantitative **d.** response, quantitative

11.42 **a.** displaying and summarizing **b.** probability **c.** statistical inference **d.** data production

11.43 **a.** several sample; F **b.** paired; t **c.** two-sample; t

11.44 **a.** $H_0: \mu_1 = \mu_2$ **b.** $H_0: \mu_1 = \mu_2 = \mu_3$ **c.** $H_0: \mu_d = 0$

11.45 **a.** $H_a: \mu_1 > \mu_2$ **b.** $H_a: \mu_1 \neq \mu_2$ **c.** $H_a: \mu_d < 0$

11.46 The P-value would be large (greater than 0.5).

11.47 Carlos

11.48 **a.** women **b.** no **c.** yes

11.49 **a.** 0.32 was the P-value for the blind individuals because their t statistic was not very large. **b.** only for sighted subjects

11.50 **a.** $t = -8.32$ **b.** P-value is 0.004 **c.** yes **d.** t would be -1.64. **e.** P-value would be 0.161. **f.** no

11.51 **a.** because two widths are recorded for each sampled airline **b.** side-by-side boxplots **c.** (1.959, 4.021) **d.** 1 not plausible, 2 borderline, 3 plausible, 4 borderline, 5 not plausible

11.52 **a.** $\bar{x}_1$ and $\bar{x}_2$ **b.** The numbers 4.18 and 4.15 are too large to be standard errors or margins of error, because the large sample sizes would make those quite small. **c.** because the samples are very large **d.** $8.00 \pm 2(4.18/\sqrt{321}) = (7.53, 8.47)$ **e.** $5.50 \pm 2(4.15/\sqrt{331}) = (5.04, 5.96)$ **f.** The fact that the two confidence intervals do not overlap indicates that population mean DMFS differs for control and CaviStat. **g.** 7 is a plausible value for an individual in either group, because its z score is $(7 - 8)/4.18 = -0.24$ for a control individual, $(7 - 5.5)/4.15 = +0.36$ for a CaviStat individual, neither of which is at all extreme. **h.** 7 is not a plausible value for either mean; it is way below the confidence interval for mean in the control group, and way above the confidence interval for mean in the CaviStat group. **i.** two-sample **j.** side-by-side boxplots

11.53 **a.** failing to conclude that the new toothpaste is better when it really is **b.** Type II

11.54 **a.** Explanatory variable is hours of television watched daily (quantitative). **b.** Response variable is having attentional problems or not (categorical). **c.** top 12% because $z = 1.2$ is between 1 and 2, so percentage should be between 16% and 2.5% **d.** because the samples are very large **e.** $2.2 \pm 2(2.91/\sqrt{1,278}) = 2.2 \pm 0.16 = (2.04, 2.36)$ **f.** For age 3, center would be at 3.6 instead of 2.2, but spreads are similar because standard deviations and sample sizes are very close. **g.** (2) Watching more TV at age 1 *caused* attentional problems at age 7 is not a correct interpretation because possible confounding variables prevent us from drawing a conclusion of causation.

11.55 **a.** observational study, because researchers did not impose a television treatment on small children **b.** Possibly children who are prone to attentional problems are more likely to show appreciation for the kind of stimulation that television provides, leading their parents to expose them to more television. **c.** television watching (the quantitative variable) **d.** Type I

11.56 Brittany is correct: The mean estimate for all blind individuals does not equal mean estimate for all sighted individuals ($\mu_1 \neq \mu_2$).

11.57 **a.** both **b.** neither **c.** both

11.58 **a.** paired **b.** not large **c.** no **d.** The confidence interval contains zero, so we would not reject the null hypothesis claiming the population mean of differences to be zero. **e.** $\bar{x}_d$ **f.** width of interval is $38.8 - (-25.2) = 64$; halfway between endpoints is $-25.2 + 32 = 6.8$ **g.** Math

11.59 **a.** paired **b.** borderline but on the small side **c.** no **d.** The confidence interval contains zero, so we would not reject the null hypothesis claiming the population mean of differences to be zero. **e.** μ_d **f.** The midpoint is $-55.6 + 30.5 = -25.1$ **g.** Verbal

11.60 **a.** two-sample **b.** no **c.** The P-value is small so it is not plausible that the difference between population means is zero. **d.** $\mu_1 - \mu_2$ **e.** $(-109.5 + (-46.6))/2 = -78.05$ **f.** nondisabled

11.61 **a.** two-sample **b.** no **c.** The P-value is small so it is not plausible that the difference between population means is zero. **d.** $\bar{x}_1 - \bar{x}_2$ **e.** $(-79.0 + (-13.3))/2 = -46.1$ **f.** nondisabled

11.62 more dramatic for Math scores (confidence interval is farther from zero, and t statistic is more extreme)

11.63 There is an extremely high outlier (148) for the faculty clients and so, due to the small sample sizes, $\bar{x}_1$ cannot be expected to follow a normal distribution, and the standardized difference between $\bar{x}_1$ and $\bar{x}_2$ does not follow a two-sample t distribution.

11.64 a. μ_1 and μ_2 **b.** σ **c.** because we already know that the one population mean is higher than the other

11.65 a. One group of children has had cancer, another independent group has not. **b.** $\mu_1 < \mu_2$ **c.** because $\bar{x}_1 > \bar{x}_2$

11.66 a. $19 = n_2$, $6.94 = \bar{x}_1$, $4.21 = \bar{x}_2$, $7.47 = s_1$, $5.57 = s_2$ **b.** because the females' sample size is larger **c.** displaying and summarizing **d.** statistical inference **e.** data production **f.** probability

11.67 a.

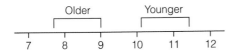

b. They don't overlap. **c.** less likely **d.** more likely **e.** less likely

11.68 a. because the difference in means is apparently negative, indicating that on average cognitive scores are lower for all those with a lower birthweight **b.** because the difference in means may be zero **c.** both

11.69 a. $2{,}870 - 2{,}968 = -98$ **b.** Yes, the fact that the difference is negative shows the mean was higher when there was a black quarterback. **c.** $-98/21.73 = -4.51$ **d.** small **e.** no **f.** Conclude there is overall a preference for games with a black quarterback, among young male viewers. **g.** A formal test is not necessary because the sample mean was actually less for games with black quarterbacks.

11.70 a. $(0.150, 2.350)$ **b.** The P-value is 0.031. **c.** Skunks born in the wild tend to have larger litters. **d.** wider

11.71 a. For BMW and Mercedes the means are 35.95 and 36.00; standard deviations are 9.03 and 9.06. **b.** yes **c.** $t = -0.01$, P-value $= 0.992$ **d.** $F = 0.00$, P-value $= 0.992$ **e.** $(-0.01)^2 = 0.00$; yes, it is the same to two decimal places. **f.** The P-values are identical. **g.** No; the one-sided P-value would be half of 0.992.

11.72 a. It could be higher in less-developed countries because of poverty, it could be higher in developed countries because of higher likelihood of detection/diagnosis. **b.** $H_0 : \mu_1 = \mu_2$ versus $H_a : \mu_1 \neq \mu_2$ **c.** U.S. is responsible for the outlier.

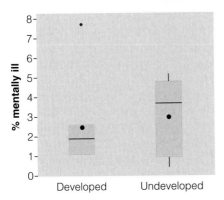

d. $t = -0.43$, P-value $= 0.671$ **e.** $t = -1.48$, P-value $= 0.183$ **f.** The outlier had a great effect on t and the P-value, but the test is still not significant either with or without it. **g.** Rates may be the same but it is a difficult variable to measure accurately.

11.73 a. Confidence interval is $(-2.94, 6.39)$. **b.** One-sided P-value is 0.181. **c.** no **d.** no

11.74 a. categorical **b.** 95% **c.** 5% **d.** yes **e.** No, because the P-value, which is the area to the right of 0.97, would be about 0.5, which is not small at all. **f.** 4.5

11.75 a.

Percentage	Classification
6.4	Moderate
7.3	Mild
7.3	Mild
10.3	Mild
11.0	Moderate
11.5	Mild
12.0	Moderate
12.0	Severe
25.0	Severe

b. $I - 1 = 3 - 1 = 2$ in the numerator, $N - I = 9 - 3 = 6$ in the denominator. **c.** Severe, because the numbers 12 and 25 are so different.

11.76 a.

Mild	Moderate	Severe
0.52	0.83	0.90
0.75	0.93	4.49
0.84	1.18	
1.73		

b. $I - 1 = 3 - 1 = 2$ in the numerator, $N - I = 9 - 3 = 6$ in the denominator.

11.77 a. quite small **b.** yes **c.** quite large **d.** no

11.78 a. Since $I - 1 = 2$, $I = 3$; since $N - I = 1{,}753$, $N = 1{,}753 + 3 = 1{,}756$ **b.** For the forced group, age is noticeably younger. **c.** population mean ages **d.** a bit less than 0.05 **e.** less than 3

11.79 a. data production **b.** displaying and summarizing **c.** probability **d.** statistical inference

11.80 a. Type I **b.** failing to reject a false null hypothesis **c.** The sample means are 457.1 (Oakland), 674.7 (Shadyside), and 580.9 (Squirrel Hill). **d.** 19.35 **e.** 0.000. **f.** Reject the null hypothesis, conclude population means differ; Oakland seems cheapest and Shadyside most expensive.

11.81 a. $F = 1.33$ **b.** P-value is 0.285   **c.** (3)

11.82 a. Means and standard deviations are Rainbow 1.015 and 0.446, Sucker 2.810 (highest mean) and 1.176 (highest sd), Whitefish 0.6050 and 0.0636   **b.** The sample standard deviations are too different.

11.83 a. Suckers have highest sample mean and highest sample standard deviation.

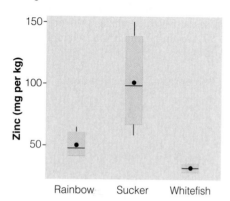

b. because the standard deviations are too different

11.84 a. two-sample   **b.** difference between means   **c.** paired   **d.** mean of differences   **e.** the one between males and females   **f.** $t = -1.13$ **g.** P-value = 0.339   **h.** Conclude the population mean of differences may be zero.   **i.** (−108.5, + 51.5)   **j.** $t = -0.26$ **k.** P-value = 0.813   **l.** Conclude the population mean of differences may be zero.   **m.** (−357, +304)   **n.** $t = -3.64$ **o.** P-value = 0.036   **p.** Conclude the difference between population means is not zero.   **q.** (−706, −47)   **r.** 0.018   **s.** $t = -4.99$ **t.** P-value = 0.015   **u.** Conclude the difference between population means is not zero.   **v.** (−614, −136)   **w.** 0.0075   **x.** gender   **y.** They do not contain zero.   **z.** smaller

11.85 a. Gaze 9.00 and control 9.31. A test is not necessary because the sample actually performed worse when cued with a gaze.   **b.** Mean of differences is 2.20, $t = 2.58$, P-value = 0.015 (one-sided). The juveniles did significantly better with gaze than no cue (control).   **c.** If the mean of differences in part (b) had been negative, there would have been no evidence of performing better when cued with a gaze.   **d.** Testing $H_0: \mu = 9$ versus $H_a: \mu > 9$ has $t = 3.28$, P-value = 0.005. The null hypothesis is rejected and we conclude that, in general, juvenile goats respond to gazing, which is consistent with our conclusion in part (b).

11.86 a. Sample means are 9.00 for adults and 10.30 for juveniles (higher).   **b.** P-value (two-sided) = 0.082   **c.** The data do not provide convincing evidence of a difference.   **d.** The one-sided P-value is 0.041.   **e.** The data do provide convincing evidence that juveniles score higher on average.   **f.** No, because the adults' sample mean is actually lower.

11.87 a. paired   **b.** (−0.01, +5.01)   **c.** It just barely contains zero.   **d.** Results are borderline: The null hypothesis may or may not be rejected, depending on whether the alternative is one-sided or two-sided, and on the level α used.   **e.** two-sample   **f.** (−2.08, +3.13)   **g.** It clearly contains zero.   **h.** We do not expect the null hypothesis of no difference between juveniles and adults to be rejected.

11.88 a. Repeated measures, because several observations are made for each goat.   **b.**

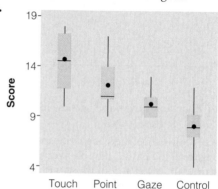

Touch seems to help the most.   **c.** Control was the least helpful (and gaze the next least).

11.89 The two-sample confidence interval (−6.522, −3.350) contains only negative numbers, suggesting times are shorter for freestyle overall on average.

11.90 a. The paired confidence interval is (−7.693, −1.240).   **b.** The interval contains only negative numbers.   **c.** This suggests swimmers swim faster in freestyle.

11.91 a. alternative   **b.** Mean of sampled differences is 14.75, standardized mean is $t = 3.46$, P-value is 0.001.   **c.** yes   **d.** (6.36, 23.13)   **e.** 10, 20   **f.** because certain universities would attract students with varying relative strengths or weaknesses in math   **g.** two quantitative

11.92 a. −2.321   **b.** −13.57   **c.** 0.000   **d.** yes   **e.** (−2.657, −1.985)   **f.** −2 is the only plausible value (just barely).   **g.** two quantitative

11.93 a. nonsmokers   **b.** 28.9 for smokers, 38.7 for nonsmokers (higher)   **c.** P-value is 0.06 for the one-sided test   **d.** Results are borderline.

11.94 a. those who did carry a cell phone   **b.** did: 34.5 (higher); did not: 22.8   **c.** 0.017   **d.** 0.009   **e.** yes   **f.** No, maybe it's people who talk on the phone a lot who choose to carry cell phones.

11.95 a. P-value is 0.06   **b.** not quite   **c.** (−3.18, 29.74)   **d.** The interval contains zero (but just barely).

11.96 a. P-value is 0.002 so the difference is significant.   **b.** those without pierced ears   **c.** gender   **d.** First separate males and females, then do two two-sample tests.

11.97 (−6.671, −5.431). Yes, because 6 inches is contained in the interval.

11.98 a. (35.09, 47.87)   **b.** No, because 50 pounds is not contained in the interval.

11.99 a. On-campus students may get more sleep than off-campus students because they don't have to get up earlier to commute.   **b.** On-campus students may get less sleep than off-campus students because of late-night noise in the dormitories.   **c.** on-campus 7.16, off-campus 6.80   **d.** On-campus is higher.   **e.** by 0.36 hours, or 21.6 minutes   **f.** P-value is 0.016   **g.** We have a good deal of evidence that mean hours of sleep differ for on- and off-campus students.   **h.** On-campus students tend to be younger; perhaps younger students sleep longer. To take age into account, separate students by age (or year at school) first, before studying the relationship between housing situation and hours slept.

11.100 a. Students in earlier years may get more sleep because they have fewer commitments and perhaps easier classes.   **b.** Students in later years may get more sleep because they budget their time better.   **c.** Means for 1, 2, 3, 4, Other, respectively, are 7.232, 6.791, 7.092, 6.545, 6.731.   **d.** 1st   **e.** 4th   **f.** 0.0013   **g.** (1) and (5)

11.101 a.

Level	Mean	StDev
1	2.282	3.444
2	3.951	5.747
3	3.673	3.217
4	8.553	11.913
other	19.692	21.379

b. because the largest (21.379) is way more than twice the smallest (3.217)

11.102 a. P-value is 0.712   **b.** no

11.103 a. P-value is 0.000.   **b.** Yes, results are significant.   **c.** Black was preferred by the tallest students and pink by the shortest students.   **d.** gender   **e.** First separate males and females, then do ANOVA.

11.104 Responses will vary.

11.105 Responses will vary.

Chapter 12

12.1 a. (3)   **b.** (1)   **c.** (2)   **d.** (4)   **e.** We can infer that the sample proportions are not very different (with such a large sample, the P-value may still be small).

12.2 a. religion   **b.** 0.84   **c.** 0.406

12.3 a. Explanatory variable is receiving questions about suicide on the first survey or not, response is having suicidal thoughts or not.   **b.** $\hat{p}_1$ and $\hat{p}_2$ **c.** close to zero   **d.** close to 0.5   **e.** The study would need to include tens of thousands of students so that we could expect at least five to commit suicide and base calculations on normal approximations.   **f.** paired t **g.** (4)   **h.** (1)   **i.** (2)   **j.** (3)

12.4 $H_0: p_1 = p_2$ versus $H_a: p_1 > p_2$;
$$z = \frac{(0.83 - 0.72) - 0}{\sqrt{0.79(1 - 0.79)\left(\dfrac{1}{282} + \dfrac{1}{162}\right)}} = 2.74;$$
because z is greater than 2.576, the P-value is less than 0.005 and we conclude the difference is significant.

12.5 a. large   **b.** small   **c.** yes

12.6 a. $z = \dfrac{(0.17 - 0.23) - 0}{\sqrt{0.19(1 - 0.19)\left(\dfrac{1}{282} + \dfrac{1}{164}\right)}} = -1.56$

b. Because z is less than 1.645 in absolute value, the two-sided P-value is greater than 0.10.   **c.** We conclude the difference was not significant.

12.7 a. not large   **b.** not small   **c.** no   **d.** The interval clearly contains zero, consistent with a P-value that is not small at all, showing that zero is a plausible value for the difference between population proportions.

12.8 The interval comes very close to containing zero, and the P-value is also somewhat borderline, just under 0.05.

12.9

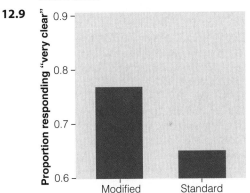

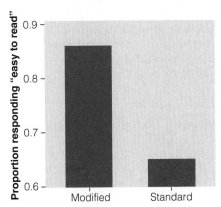

Responses for "easy to read" show a more dramatic difference.

12.10 a. −2.55   **b.** 6.492   **c.** −4.27   **d.** 18.226

12.11 a. 0.005   **b.** 0.01   **c.** 0.000   **d.** 0.000

12.12 a. for those requesting Paxil   **b.** Paxil request: 14/51 = 0.27; general request: 1/50 = 0.02; no request: 2/48 = 0.04   **c.** The proportion seems very different for those requesting Paxil.

d. $5.82 = 17(51)/149$; $5.70 = 17(50)/149$; $5.48 = 17(48)/149$; $45.18 = 132(51)/149$; $44.30 = 132(50)/149$; $42.52 = 132(48)/149$ **e.** $5.82/51 = 5.70/50 = 5.48/48 = 0.114$ **f.** for those requesting Paxil **g.** $11.503 = (14 - 5.82)^2/5.82$; $1.481 = (37 - 45.18)^2/45.18$; $3.880 = (1 - 5.70)^2/5.70$; $0.500 = (49 - 44.30)^2/44.30$; $2.207 = (2 - 5.48)^2/5.48$; $0.284 = (46 - 42.52)^2/42.52$. **h.** "patients" requesting Paxil and receiving Paxil **i.** $19.855 = 11.503 + 1.481 + 3.880 + 0.500 + 2.207 + 0.284$ **j.** There are $r = 3$ possibilities for the row variable and $c = 2$ possibilities for the column variable; the degrees of freedom are $(r - 1)(c - 1) = 2(1) = 2$ **k.** large, because it is considerably greater than 6.0 **l.** The size of chi-square suggests that, in general, there is a relationship between a patient's requests for medications and what, if anything, the doctor prescribes. **m.** because the expected counts would be too small (between 1 and 2)

12.13 a. for those making no request **b.** Paxil request: $27/51 = 0.53$; general request: $38/50 = 0.76$; no request: $15/48 = 0.31$ **c.** All three seem quite different from one another. **d.** $27.38 = 80(51)/149$; $23.62 = 69(51)/149$; $26.85 = 80(50)/149$; $23.15 = 69(50)/149$; $25.77 = 80(48)/149$; $22.23 = 69(48)/149$ **e.** $27.38/51 = 26.85/50 = 25.77/48 = 0.537$ **f.** general request and no request **g.** $0.005 = (27 - 27.38)^2/27.38$; $0.006 = (24 - 23.62)^2/23.62$; $4.635 = (38 - 26.85)^2/26.85$; $5.373 = (12 - 23.15)^2/23.15$; $4.502 = (15 - 25.77)^2/25.77$; $5.220 = (33 - 22.23)^2/22.23$ **h.** "patients" requesting Paxil and receiving a prescription for an anti-depressant medication and "patients" requesting Paxil and not receiving a prescription for an anti-depressant medication **i.** There are $r = 3$ possibilities for the row variable and $c = 2$ possibilities for the column variable; the degrees of freedom are $(r - 1)(c - 1) = 2(1) = 2$. **j.** large, because it is considerably greater than 6.0 **k.** It suggests that, in general, there is a relationship between a patient's requests for medications and whether or not the physician prescribes a medication.

12.14 a.

Observed	Receding	NotReceding	Total
Pierced	12	17	29
Not pierced	2	27	29
Total	14	44	58

Expected	Receding	NotReceding
Pierced	7	22
Not pierced	7	22

b. chi-square $= 3.57 + 3.57 + 1.14 + 1.14 = 9.42$ **c.** The data should convince us of a relationship because chi-square is larger than 3.84, so the P-value is smaller than 0.05. **d.** $7/29 = 0.24$ and $7/29 = 0.24$ are equal because the table is constructed to show counts that would be seen if proportions with receding gums were exactly equal in the two groups. **e.** age, gender **f.** both: Perhaps those who smoke are more likely to get their lips pierced and smoking may cause receding gums. Perhaps students less attentive to hygiene are more likely to get their lips pierced, and also more susceptible to receding gums. **g.** (2) **h.** (3) **i.** (4) **j.** (1) **k.** Lips pierced or not is the categorical explanatory variable; depth of gumline recession is the quantitative response. **l.** Length of time lips were pierced is the quantitative explanatory variable and suffering from gum recession is the categorical response. **m.** because the number observed (2) is too small (less than 5)

12.15 a. because not enough people would fall into certain response categories; only a small proportion would die of a heart attack **b.** No, it would only be too small if the proportion in the category of interest is too close to 0 or 1. **c.** (1) and (3)

12.16 a. whether a bird was in the experimental or control group for foot color
b.

	Courtship	No Courtship	Total
Control	4	7	11
Experimental	1	14	15
Total	5	21	26

c. sample proportions $4/11 = 0.36$ versus $1/15 = 0.07$; bar graph shown here:

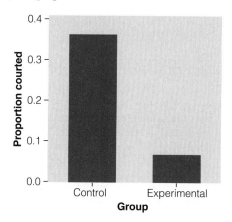

d. about 5 times as likely **e.** Expected counts are too small (some less than 5). **f.** two-sample t

12.17 a. $\hat{p}_1$ and $\hat{p}_2$ **b.** Yes, because chi-square would be 8.4161. **c.** ANOVA

12.18 a.

Observed	After	Before	Total
Portugal	75	25	100
Taiwan	69	31	100
Total	144	56	200

Expected	After	Before
Portugal	72	28
Taiwan	72	28

b. chi-square = 0.893   **c.** not large   **d.** not small   **e.** There is not a significant difference in proportions going to bed after midnight in the two countries.   **f.** Yes, because then chi-square would be even smaller and the P-value would be even larger.   **g.** No, because then chi-square would be 8.93 and the P-value would be smaller than 0.05.   **h.** People in warmer countries may tend to go to bed later when it cools down. Average temperature could be recorded for each country (quantitative variable) or climate zones could be recorded for each country (categorical).

12.19 a. the first   **b.** explanatory variable categorical (churchgoer or not) and response quantitative (length of life)

12.20 a. categorical   **b.** categorical   **c.** chi-square   **d.** because correlation is for two quantitative variables, not two categorical variables

12.21 a. Bearman   **b.** Type II   **c.** Type I   **d.** relationship between pledges and use of other preventive measures

12.22 Carlos's answer makes sense: Based on the small P-value, parents of dying children should be encouraged to consider talking to their children about death because a significantly smaller proportion of parents who talked about death experienced regrets later. The response rate was good and there's no reason to think that parents in other countries would be very different with respect to this issue. As for Dominique's objection, the P-value has taken sample size (429) into account.

12.23 a. Explanatory variable is being subjected to random drug testing or not, response is drug use deterred or not.   **b.** Null hypothesis says no relationship exists.   **c.** yes   **d.** Type I   **e.** Consequences of unnecessary random drug testing would be money needlessly spent and violation of students' privacy.   **f.** no   **g.** Type II   **h.** Consequences would be failure to supply a helpful deterrent to drug use.

12.24 a. men   **b.** (2) and (3)

12.25 a. not large   **b.** not small   **c.** large   **d.** small

12.26 a. p_1 and p_2 **b.** large   **c.** small   **d.** not large   **e.** not small

12.27 a. $p_1 > p_2$ **b.** $\hat{p}_1 - \hat{p}_2$

12.28 a. cell phones   **b.** gender and carrying cell phones   **c.** gender and carrying cell phones

12.29 a. business majors   **b.** gender and being a business major or not   **c.** gender and being a business major or not

12.30 a. 0.182, 0.164   **b.** X_1 and X_2 **c.** a bit smaller than 0.05   **d.** Yes, because the P-value is on the small side.   **e.** smaller than 3.84   **f.** Type II   **g.** Type I

12.31 a. Taking Celebrex or not is explanatory and having heart problems or not is response.   **b.** less than 0.05   **c.** greater than 3.84

12.32 a. 7 in each
b.

Observed	Buckled	Not Buckled	Total
Least attractive	1	99	100
Most attractive	13	87	100
Total	14	186	200

Expected	Buckled	Not Buckled
Least attractive	7	93
Most attractive	7	93

c. chi-square = 5.14 + 5.14 + 0.39 + 0.39 = 11.06   **d.** The difference is significant because 11.06 is greater than 3.84.   **e.** Perhaps attentive parents pay more attention to their children's appearance, thereby making them more attractive. These would also be the parents who are attentive enough to buckle their children into the cart.   **f.** Evaluation on the basis of symmetry of facial features would be more convincing.   **g.** statistical inference   **h.** probability   **i.** displaying and summarizing data   **j.** data production

12.33 a. no
b.

Observed	Excellent/ Good	Acceptable/ Unsuccessful	Total
C-shaped	7	6	13
I-shaped	11	3	14
Total	18	9	27

Expected	Excellent/ Good	Acceptable/ Unsuccessful
C-shaped	8.67	4.33
I-shaped	9.33	4.67

c. chi-square = 0.32 + 0.64 + 0.30 + 0.60 = 1.86   **d.** not small   **e.** no   **f.** paired t **g.** two-sample t

12.34 a. Age group is explanatory with three possibilities and blood lead level is response with two possibilities. **b.** columns **c.** $(3 - 1)(2 - 1) = 2$ **d.** not small **e.** (2) **f.** because there are too few in the response of interest **g.** age as infant, toddler, or school-age, and blood lead level as a number **h.** age as a number and blood lead level either less than or at least 20 **i.** age as a number and blood lead level as a number

12.35 a. those who took gatifloxacin **b.** X_1 and X_2 **c.**

Observed	Event	No Event	Total
Gatifloxacin	474	1,526	2,000
Placebo	502	1,498	2,000
Total	976	3,024	4,000

Expected	Event	No Event	Total
Gatifloxacin	488	1,512	2,000
Placebo	488	1,512	2,000
Total	976	3,024	4,000

d. not small at all **e.** (3) and (5)

12.36 a. They do overlap. **b.** No, it suggests gatifloxacin may not make a difference. **c.** It does contain zero. **d.** No, it suggests gatifloxacin may not make a difference.

12.37 a. $0.75 \pm 2(0.01) = (0.73, 0.77)$ **b.** $0.69 \pm 2(0.01) = (0.67, 0.71)$ **c.** The intervals do not overlap. **d.** This suggests that population proportions are not the same in the two countries. **e.** $0.06 \pm 2(0.02) = (0.02, 0.10)$ **f.** The interval does not contain zero. **g.** This suggests that population proportions are not the same in the two countries. **h.** no **i.** yes

12.38 a. because the sample sizes are different (0.73 is closer to the proportion for the larger sample size) **b.** much more than 3.84 **c.** Maybe people tend to use their hands more in the morning. **d.** Maybe students tend to use their hands more than do nonstudents.

12.39 a. Explanatory variable is brother or unrelated; response is attacked or not. **b.** Observed counts are shown in the first table.

Observed	Attacked	Not Attacked	Total
Brother	16	15	31
Unrelated	24	7	31
Total	40	22	62

Expected	Attacked	Not Attacked
Brother	20	11
Unrelated	20	11

c. Expected counts shown in the second table. **d.** chi-square = $0.80 + 1.46 + 0.80 + 1.46 = 4.52$ **e.** less than 0.05 **f.** yes

12.40 a. yes **b.** somewhat less than 3.84 **c.** use a larger sample size **d.** $0.077/2 = 0.0385$ **e.** $\sqrt{3.13} = 1.77$

12.41 a. When the three individual groups are compared the chi-square statistic is fairly large, the P-value is fairly small, and there is evidence at the 0.05 level of a relationship between treatment and nausea. In contrast, when the acupuncture and placebo groups are combined, the chi-square statistic is not large, the P-value is not small, and there is no evidence of a relationship. **b.** Report those on the left, because apparently acupuncture versus placebo makes a difference, and these groups should not be combined **c.** Both, because all counts are at least 5.

12.42 a. 2 (given the two counts of 19, there is enough information to fill in the rest of the table) **b.**

Observed	One Kind	Two Kinds	Three Kinds	Total
Sequential choice	19	19	3	41
Simultaneous choice	10	21	25	56
Total	29	40	28	97

c. more often **d.** less often **e.** yes **f.** one that people tend to buy in bulk

12.43 a. Observed counts are shown on the top and expected counts on the bottom.

Observed	One Kind	Two Kinds	Total
Simultaneous	13	12	25
Sequential	0	13	13
Total	13	25	38

Expected	One Kind	Two Kinds
Simultaneous	8.55	16.45
Sequential	4.45	8.55

b. Chi-square is $2.313 + 1.203 + 4.447 + 2.313 = 10.275$. **c.** P-value is very small because 10.275 is much greater than 3.84. **d.** We conclude that type of choice did have a significant impact on the children's decisions.

12.44 a. sample proportions $389/885 = 0.44$, $248/2,226 = 0.11$, $z = 20.46$, P-value = 0.000, conclude drug users are more likely to carry weapons than non-users **b.** sample proportions $389/637 = 0.61$, $496/2,474 = 0.20$, $z = 20.46$, P-value = 0.000, conclude those who carry weapons are more likely to use drugs   **c.** chi-square = 418.737, *P*-value = 0.000, conclude taking drugs or not and carrying weapons or not are related   **d.** both

12.45 a. No chest pain: 229 died and 1,534 survived; chest pain: 784 died and 17,453 survived.
b. (4)

```
          Died Survived    Total
NoPain     229     1534     1763
         89.30  1673.70
Pain       784    17453    18237
        923.70 17313.30
Total     1013    18987    20000
Chi-Sq =218.568 + 11.661 + 21.129 + 1.127
       = 252.486
DF = 1, P-Value = 0.000
```

c. those who experience chest pain

12.46 a. no chest pain: (0.115, 0.146)   **b.** chest pain: (0.040, 0.046)   **c.** The intervals do not overlap. **d.** It suggests the population proportions are not the same for both groups.   **e.** because the sample size is so much larger; also, because a sample proportion closer to 0 than to 0.5 results in a smaller standard deviation   **f.** (0.071, 0.103) **g.** The interval contains only positive differences. **h.** It suggests the population proportion is higher for those who had no chest pain.

12.47 a. (7 − 1)(2 − 1) = 6   **b.** chi-square = 72.278 **c.** *P*-value = 0.000, which confirms a relationship **d.** Fox and CBS highest   **e.** PBS/NPR and Print lowest   **f.** Fox, CBS, PBS/NPR, Print

12.48 a. chi-square = 15.161   **b.** *P*-value = 0.001 **c.** those who do not   **d.** males tend not to have their ears pierced, and they tend to wear glasses **e.** females' *P*-value = 0.370   **f.** no evidence of a relationship   **g.** males' *P*-value = 0.133   **h.** no evidence of a relationship

12.49 a. chi-square = 10.161, *P*-value = 0.001; females were more likely to eat breakfast   **b.** chi-square = 7.428, *P*-value = 0.006, females were more likely to carry a cell phone   **c.** Those who did carry a cell phone were more likely to eat breakfast: 0.56 of those who carried a cell phone ate breakfast; 0.54 of those who didn't carry a cell phone ate breakfast; the *P*-value is 0.741 so the relationship is not significant.

12.50 a. There would be rules against smoking in the dorms.   **b.** chi-square = 19.704, *P*-value = 0.000   **c.** There is evidence of a relationship. **d.** Yes: 0.71 of smokers live off campus, 0.45 of nonsmokers live off campus.   **e.** Yes, because smoking would be a confounding variable to make us see a relationship between living off campus and dying of cancer.

12.51 a. chi-square = 3.156, *P*-value = 0.206   **b.** no evidence of a relationship

12.52 a. (2 − 1)(8 − 1) = 7   **b.** black and blue **c.** pink and purple

12.53 a. chi-square = 3.574, *P*-value = 0.167   **b.** no evidence of a relationship

12.54 Responses will vary.

12.55 Responses will vary.

12.56 Responses will vary.

Chapter 13

13.1 for departures versus gates, on the left (there is less scatter and *s* will be smaller)

13.2 a. because longer trips cost more money   **b.** No, it is doubtful that representatives would base the length of their trip on how much money is paid. **c.** −683 + (1,176)(1) = 493 dollars   **d.** $3,401 **e.** σ **f.** 1,176 dollars   **g.** b_1 **h.** The intercept −683 should be interpreted theoretically as the *y*-value where the line crosses the *y*-axis; in actuality there would be no trips of length zero. **i.** b_0 **j.** β_0 **k.** all of these   **l.** moderately strong

13.3 a. (2)   **b.** (3)

13.4 Condition (a) is not met (scatterplot is not linear).

13.5 a. The wider a clam is, the longer it should be. **b.** yes   **c.** 1.22 centimeters   **d.** b_0 **e.** 0.257 + 1.22(2) = 2.697 centimeters   **f.** 0.3253 centimeters   **g.** σ **h.** none of these   **i.** very strong   **j.** in the sample   **k.** 88 − 2 = 86 **l.** neither   **m.** paired *t*   **n.** *t* is extremely large so *P*-value is extremely small; conclude $\beta_1 \neq 0$.

13.6 (d)

13.7 (b)

13.8 a. in the sample   **b.** 39 − 2 = 37   **c.** both **d.** 0.000   **e.** (2) and (4)

13.9 $H_a : \beta_1 > 0$ because we expect the relationship to be positive.

13.10 weak evidence of a strong relationship

13.11 There is fairly strong evidence of a weak relationship between number of credits and Math SAT score for all students, but this relationship is apparently due to the confounding variable type of student: Full-time students take more credits than part-time students, and their Math SAT scores tend to be higher. When full-time and part-time students are separated, there is no evidence of a relationship between number of credits and Math SAT score for either group.

13.12 strong evidence of a weak relationship

13.13 a. 8 − 2 = 6   **b.** (2) because *r* is of moderate size but the *P*-value is not small at all   **c.** 1 **d.** 0.23/2 = 0.115   **e.** chi-square

13.14 a. closer to −1   **b.** *P*-value is not small because *t* is not large.   **c.** (4) because *r* is positive and the *P*-value is not small   **d.** The title is appropriate, because vacancy rate does not seem to affect price in general for this market.   **e.** No; the *P*-value would have been greater than 0.5 because the sample slope is actually positive.   **f.** former (large influence)

13.15 a. Because children grow taller as they get older, we expect a positive relationship: correlation r greater than zero. Age tells us quite a lot—but not everything—about how tall a child will be, so we expect r to be somewhere between 0.5 and 1.0. This should be true for the larger population of children, not just the sample.   **b.** (2.0, 2.5)   **c.** b_1 large   **d.** weak evidence of a strong relationship

13.16 $1.22 - 2(0.02) = 1.18$, $1.22 + 2(0.02) = 1.26$

13.17 a. depth   **b.** explanatory, categorical   **c.** first   **d.** separately, because the regression lines are very distinct   **e.** all fish fossils at the site from which the sample was obtained

13.18 a. small   **b.** confidence interval   **c.** $55.3 \pm 2(1.2) = (52.9, 57.7)$ **d.** Yes, it came quite close.   **e.** $55.3 \pm 2(1.2)/\sqrt{25} = (54.82, 55.78)$ **f.** Yes, it came quite close.   **g.** wider   **h.** because depth tells us a lot about age; without information about depth, it is difficult to pin down the age

13.19 a. small   **b.** $56.4 \pm 2(2.3) = (51.8, 61.0)$ **c.** because sample size is relatively small (120 is in fact quite close to the mean)   **d.** $56.4 \pm 2(2.3)/\sqrt{14} = (55.2, 57.6)$ **e.** wider   **f.** wider   **g.** because depth tells us a lot about age; without information about depth, it is difficult to pin down mean age

13.20 a. (6)   **b.** (3)   **c.** (5)   **d.** (4)   **e.** (1)   **f.** (2)

13.21 a. interval estimate of mean amount for all 5-day trips taken by the larger population of representatives   **b.** $2(1,176) = 2,352$ dollars because 10 days is 2 times as long as 5 days   **c.** interval estimate of mean amount paid for all 5-day trips   **d.** (9,988, 12,166)   **e.** The interval is not very accurate because 10 is too far from the mean trip length, 5 days.

13.22 a. (5)   **b.** (3)   **c.** (6)   **d.** (4)   **e.** (1)   **f.** (2)

13.23 a. interval estimate for mean length of all 3-cm-wide butter clams   **b.** interval estimate of length of a 3-cm-wide butter clam   **c.** interval estimate of mean length of all 3-cm-wide clams

13.24 a. It is not unusual because 14 is contained in the prediction interval.
b. $\hat{y} = -19.2 + 0.422(76) = 12.872$, $s = 1.020$, $\hat{y} \pm 2s = 12.872 \pm 2(1.020) = (10.832, 14.912)$ which is close to (10.9184, 14.9575) [or closer if we use the calculated fit, 12.9379, as $\hat{y}$]
c. because the explanatory value is too far from the mean

13.25 for departures versus gates (on the left)

13.26 the prediction interval for the height of a woman whose daughter is 65 inches tall, because that relationship is stronger

13.27 a. displaying and summarizing   **b.** data production   **c.** probability   **d.** statistical inference

13.28 a. both quantitative (size of waistline is explanatory, length of life is response)   **b.** scatterplot   **c.** Being obese or not is the categorical explanatory variable; length of life is the quantitative response.   **d.** side-by-side boxplots

13.29 A government report about all 50 states tells us everything about the population; there is no larger group to generalize to.

13.30 The relationship for *top 25* concerts is not necessarily representative of the relationship for all concerts.

13.31 a. displaying and summarizing   **b.** statistical inference   **c.** data production   **d.** probability

13.32 a. Slope is $(14 - 38)/(6 - 0) = -4$.   **b.** Slope is $(38 - 14)/(3 - 0) = +8$ or $(38 - 14)/(9 - 6) = +8$ **c.** closer to 0 because there is very little spread about the line

13.33 a. $10(1.3) = 13$ **b.** β_1

13.34 a. Distribution of b_1 should be centered at $\beta_1 = 2.25$.   **b.** 250 children   **c.** σ **d.** $3(2.25) = 6.75$ inches

13.35 a. Distribution of b_1 should be centered at $\beta_1 = 3$.   **b.** 25 males   **c.** σ **d.** $2(3) = 6$ inches   **e.** (1) (scatterplot will not appear linear because slope is changing) and (3) spread of responses varies (for example, σ for the age range discussed in the preceding exercise was 2; in this exercise it is 3.1)

13.36 (c) [small sample with non-normal responses]

13.37 (a) [b_1 is not normal for small sample and non-normal responses, so standardized b_1 is not t]

13.38 a. $(-0.15, -0.05)$ **b.** $|b_1|$ large

13.39 Adam is correct; responses are not an independent random sample due to the way they are collected from one month to the next.

13.40 a. They would not overlap because the critic believes the speed of spread of the Black Death was significantly faster than the speed of spread of *Y. pestis*.   **b.** distance covered: quantitative response; time: quantitative explanatory; type of disease: categorical explanatory

13.41 a. closer to 0   **b.** relatively large because predictions of sale price based on assessed price are not very accurate   **c.** Conclude there is no evidence of a relationship between sale price and assessed price for the larger population of properties.

13.42 a. Texas school districts (for each district, record rate of autism and how much mercury is released in the county where that district is located)   **b.** Explanatory variable (quantitative) is pounds of environmentally released mercury in 2001; response variable (also quantitative) is rate of autism.   **c.** 0.17/1,000   **d.** b_1 **e.** No, the interval would not contain zero.   **f.** much less than 0.05   **g.** Setting as urban, small metro, or rural could play a role in mercury pollution, and also in autism rates via a variety of socio-economic factors.

13.43 a. 0.38   **b.** 0.026   **c.** because the sample size is small

13.44 a. the fact that the slope 1.32 is positive **b.** the fact that the intercept $+4.49$ is positive **c.** R-Sq = 92.6% **d.** P-value = 0.000 **e.** $S = 7.910$

13.45 a. strong evidence of a moderate relationship between responses **b.** evidence of a stronger relationship **c.** 0.63 (the highest) **d.** because the sample size is very large **e.** two categorical variables

13.46 a. $r = +\sqrt{0.866} = +0.931$
b. $S = 285{,}780$ tons
c. $r = +\sqrt{0.998} = +0.999$, $s = 32{,}171$ tons
d. (2) **e.** both

13.47 a. margin of error **b.** Yes, typically it could range from 69 to 79 (within 5 points of 74). **c.** Yes, typically it could range from 71 to 81. **d.** The increase is better explained by increased intellectual stimulation; 3 points a decade isn't enough to explain this great an increase.

13.48 a. 0.90 (closer to 1), 0.08 **b.** $\hat{y} = 29.2 + 7.12x$ (steeper slope), $\hat{y} = -784 + 0.47x$ **c.** 17.55 (less prediction error), 40.15 **d.** (4.32, 9.92) (interval contains only positive slopes), $(-3.96, +4.89)$ **e.** 0.000 (small P-value), 0.815 **f.** 5.85 (large t), 0.24 **g.** (94.96, 179.84) (narrower interval), (40.3, 234.5)

13.49 a. 0.55, 0.97 (closer to 1) **b.** $\hat{y} = 134 + 0.822x$, $\hat{y} = -31.3 + 10.3x$ (steeper slope), **c.** 180.9, 51.2 (less spread) **d.** (0.17, 1.48) (centered at 0.822), (9.0, 11.6) (centered at 10.3) **e.** 0.018, 0.000 (smaller) **f.** 2.63, 16.46 (larger) **g.** (282.1, 1070.1), (564.7, 787.6) (narrower)

13.50 a.

![Scatterplot of Velocity (feet per second) versus Depth (feet)](velocity-depth-plot)

(1) decrease (2) linear (3) high **b.** the equation of the regression line **c.** $10 - 2 = 8$ **d.** $t = -6.80$, P-value is 0.000; there is strong evidence of a relationship in general between depth and velocity. **e.** **1.** displaying and summarizing **2.** probability **3.** statistical inference **4.** data production

13.51 a. P-value is 0.013. **b.** There is statistical evidence of a relationship and the relationship is positive and strong because $r = +0.99$. **c.** P-value is 0.176. **d.** There is no statistical evidence of a relationship. **e.** equally good **f.** just the equation of the regression line **g.** $22.605 \pm 4.3(2.63) = 11.3$ to 33.9 **h.** $26.6 \pm 4.3(12.89) = -28.8$ to $+82.0$ **i.** The interval for rainbow trout does not contain zero, which is

consistent with our conclusion in part (b). The interval for suckers contains zero, which is consistent with our conclusion in part (d). **j.** two-sample t **k.** paired t

13.52 a. People tend to gain weight as they get older. **b.** Age should be explanatory: Being older may cause you to weigh more, but weighing more cannot cause you to be older. **c.** negative **d.** males: $r = +0.23$, P-value is 0.003; females: $r = +0.15$, P-value is 0.010 **e.** because sample sizes are both large **f.** Yes, slightly, because the P-values are small and the correlations are positive (but closer to 0 than to 1). **g.** $3.864 \pm 2(1.298) = (1.3, 6.5)$; 1.3 to 6.5 **h.** $0.9710 \pm 2(0.3732) = (0.2, 1.7)$; 0.2 to 1.7 **i.** The interval for males is wider because their sample size is smaller and their standard error s is larger.

13.53 a. Inc. Diff. Cells $= -1.59 + 1.65$ RingWidth; positive **b.** correlation $r = +0.923$, P-value is 0.000 **c.** (4) **d.** If a tree has very wide annual rings we expect it to become dormant relatively late.

13.54 a. touch on point

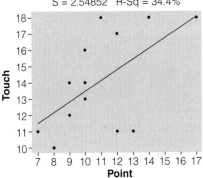

Regression Plot
Touch $= 6.90442 + 0.656637$ Point
$S = 2.54852$ R-Sq $= 34.4\%$

Regression Plot
Touch $= 14.4103 - 0.0370370$ Gaze
$S = 3.14569$ R-Sq $= 0.1\%$

b. $s = 2.549$ **c.** (8.306, 19.949) **d.** because the sample size is small **e.** $s = 3.146$ **f.** (6.892, 21.262) **g.** $21.262 - 6.892 = 14.37$ is wider than $4(3.146) = 12.584$ **h.** touch on point $r = +0.59$, touch on gaze $r = 0.03$; r is closer to 1 for the smaller s because the points are more tightly clustered **i.** Smaller P-value corresponds to r closer to 1. **j.** point score

13.55 a.

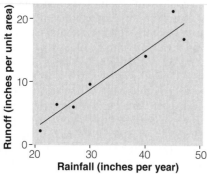

Regression Plot
Runoff = –9.77576 + 0.618506 Rainfall
S = 2.05776   R-Sq = 92.2%

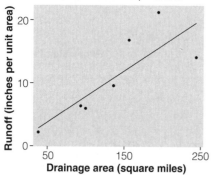

Regression Plot
Runoff = –0.252198 + 0.0811744 Drainage Area
S = 4.18909   R-Sq = 67.8%

Plot for regression of runoff on drainage shows more scatter. **b.** $s = 2.058$ **c.** (3.080, 14.479) **d.** because the sample size (7) is small **e.** $s = 4.189$ **f.** (−0.40, 22.63) **g.** width 22.63 + 0.40 = 23.03 is wider than 4(4.189) = 16.756 **h.** $r = +0.96$ for the regression on rainfall and $r = +0.82$ for the regression on drainage **i.** higher correlation for smaller s because the points are more tightly clustered **j.** higher value of r **k.** annual rainfall

13.56 a. (2)

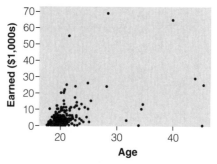

b. $r = +0.49$, P-value is 0.000; (1), (2)
c. *Earned* $= -18.6 + 1.1$ *Age*; 18.6 **d.** \$5,682
e. a confidence interval for the mean response
f. interval estimates when age equals 20 **g.** For age 20, $CI = (2.852, 3.920)$ (narrowest), $PI = (-7.794, 14.566)$; for age 30, $CI = (12.523, 16.188)$, $PI = (3.039, 25.672)$ (widest) **h.** mean

earnings of all thirty-year-old students in the population

13.57 a. Watching TV might prevent students from being active and burning calories; it might encourage snacking; finally, being overweight may make watching TV preferable to active pastimes like sports. **b.** This would suggest that being heavy causes a student to watch more TV than a lighter student. **c.** This would suggest that watching more TV causes a student to be heavier than a student who doesn't watch as much TV. **d.** Perhaps one gender group watches more TV than the other; because females tend to be lighter, this could lead us to see a positive or negative relationship. **e.** males: $r = +0.15$, P-value is 0.028; females: $r = +0.15$, P-value is 0.0055 **f.** P-value is smaller for females because their sample size is larger. **g.** No, we can't conclude TV *causes* weight gain because there may be confounding variables, or causation in the opposite direction as explained in part (b). **h.** Yes, slightly, because both correlations are positive and both P-values are small.

13.58 a. negative, because students with more credits would have more work to do and less time to sleep **b.** $r = -0.03$, P-value is 0.631 **c.** no evidence of a relationship between credits and hours slept in the larger population of students **d.** All of the influential observations have unusually low numbers of credits; they are all part-time students.

13.59 Responses will vary.

13.60 Responses will vary.

Chapter 14

14.14 two quantitative variables; data production

14.15 one categorical variable; displaying and summarizing (Section 4.1)

14.16 one quantitative variable; displaying and summarizing (Sections 4.2–4.4)

14.17 one quantitative variable; probability

14.18 two categorical variables; data production

14.19 one quantitative variable; data production

14.20 one quantitative variable; data production

14.21 one categorical variable; statistical inference (Chapter 9)

14.22 one categorical variable; data production

14.23 categorical explanatory and quantitative response variables; probability

14.24 two quantitative variables; statistical inference (Chapter 13)

14.25 two categorical variables; statistical inference (Chapter 12)

14.26 one categorical variable; probability

14.27 two categorical variables; displaying and summarizing (Section 5.2)

14.28 one categorical variable; displaying and summarizing (Section 4.1)

14.29 one categorical variable; data production

14.30 two quantitative variables; data production

14.31 one categorical variable; data production

14.32 one quantitative variable; displaying and summarizing (Sections 4.2–4.4) or data production

14.33 one quantitative variable; statistical inference (Chapter 10)

14.34 one categorical variable; data production

14.35 one categorical variable; data production

14.36 two quantitative variables; statistical inference (Chapter 13)

14.37 categorical explanatory and quantitative response variables; displaying and summarizing (Section 5.1)

14.38 one categorical variable; probability

14.39 two quantitative variables; statistical inference (Chapter 13)

14.40 two categorical variables; displaying and summarizing (Section 5.2)

14.41 two categorical variables; displaying and summarizing (Section 5.2)

14.42 one categorical variable; statistical inference (Chapter 9)

14.43 categorical explanatory and quantitative response variables; data production

14.44 categorical explanatory and quantitative response variables; probability

14.45 categorical explanatory and quantitative response variables; data production

14.46 one quantitative variable; statistical inference (Chapter 10)

14.47 two categorical variables; data production

14.48 one quantitative variable; probability

14.49 categorical explanatory and quantitative response variables; statistical inference (Chapter 11)

14.50 two quantitative variables; probability

Teaching the Big Picture

TBP Chapter 1

Introduction: Variables and Processes in Statistics

1.1 Details

Explanatory and response variables were defined on page 7. Students should be aware that in other contexts, the response is referred to as the *dependent variable*, and the explanatory is the *independent variable*. In this book, we avoid using these expressions to describe the roles of variables, reserving the term "independent" to refer to two events that are not related in a probabilistic sense, to be discussed in Part III.

If students need additional guidance in identifying the four processes, an easy way to determine if a statement is focusing on the process of Probability is to see if the word "probability" occurs, or "chance" or "likelihood"; the latter two are the only synonyms we tend to encounter for the word "probability". Displaying and Summarizing differs from Statistical Inference in that inference makes a claim about the larger population, often employing expressions like "in general" or "for all". Data Production is concerned with the initial steps of taking a sample and deciding on a study design.

1.2 Activities

Activities Involving Student Data

Many of the activities in our teaching supplement utilize data about the students themselves. For the sake of efficiency, it is preferable for students to complete a survey early on, reporting their values for the following variables: gender, major decided or not, year at school (1, 2, 3, 4, or other), live on campus or not, smoke or not, ear(s) pierced or not, corrective lenses worn (contacts, glasses, or neither), handedness (right, left, or both), ate breakfast that morning or not, height, shoe size, number of minutes spent talking on the phone the day before, number of minutes spent watching TV the day before, number of minutes spent exercising the day before, number of minutes spent on the computer the day before, number of hours slept the night before (to the nearest half hour), age in years (to the nearest tenth), age of mother, age of father, number of siblings, number of credits taken, how much money (to the nearest thousand dollars) they earned the preceding calendar year.

[Note: A computer survey automatically converts information about a student's birthday to his or her age in years, to the nearest tenth. Students may be asked to come up with an easy way to make a similar conversion when the data are gathered by hand.]

When the data must be accessed, starting with the activity for Chapter 3, the instructor should make results available on a spreadsheet to be accessed online. If this is not feasible, then students should access data from the book's existing data file

```
http://www.pitt.edu/~nancyp/bigpicture/surveydata.txt
```

about several hundred students surveyed previously. This data file should be used for the activities starting with Chapter 7 when normal random variables are discussed.

As a last resort, values for the variables of interest can be reported out loud by students in the computer lab and entered on the spot; however, this method tends to be both time-consuming and error-prone. Also, it cannot be used in activities for Chapters 8 through 13, which require students to take samples from a population of several hundred values.

Activity: Identifying Variable Types and Roles

Using the Computer

Students search online news websites and other Internet resources to locate reports of statistical studies involving each of the five variable situations (one quantitative, one categorical, one of each, two categorical, and two quantitative). For the class as a group, the goal is to find one of each type of situation. When a student finds a study involving a variable situation not yet found, he or she reports to the class, describing the study so they can decide if they agree that the study does, in fact, involve the types of variables as claimed. [By quoting a key phrase of the report, the student may help classmates locate the article with a search engine such as Google so they can examine it for themselves.] The instructor keeps track of the studies found by students and what types of variables they involve, until all five situations are represented.

In the Classroom

(Before conducting this activity, the instructor should accumulate at least a week's worth of newspapers and/or magazines.) Students search through newspapers and magazines in an effort to locate reports of statistical studies involving each of the five variable situations (one quantitative, one categorical, one of each, two categorical, and two quantitative). For the class as a group, the goal is to find one of each type of situation. When a student finds a study involving a variable situation not yet found, he or she reports to the class, describing the study so they can decide if they agree that the study does, in fact, involve the types of variables as claimed. The instructor keeps track of the studies found by students and what types of variables they involve, until all five situations are represented.

Alternatively, the instructor may make a handout of study descriptions, such as those in the Supplemental Part I Review Exercises beginning on page 763, and the students screen these for the five variable situations.

1.3 Guide to Exercise Topics

Variable types: 1.1*, 1.2*, 1.3(a), 1.4, 1.6*(a,b), 1.8*, 1.9, 1.11*(a), 1.12(a,b), 1.16(b,c), 1.18, 1.19(a-d), 1.20(a), 1.24, 1.26(a-d)

Handling data: 1.3(b), 1.6*(c), 1.10*, 1.11*(b), 1.12(c), 1.14*, 1.15, 1.20(b), 1.26(e)

Roles of variables: 1.17*, 1.19(c), 1.21, 1.26(c), 1.27, 1.28, 1.29
Four processes of statistics: 1.5, 1.7, 1.13, 1.22, 1.23*, 1.25, 1.30

1.4 Supplemental Exercises

1.1 The *New York Times* study of homes reported average house size in 2001 to be 2,428 square feet, compared with an average of 2,150 square feet in 1987.

   a. For each of the homes studied, values of two variables have been recorded—what are they?

   b. Tell whether each of the two variables is quantitative or categorical.

   c. Tell which plays the role of explanatory variable and which is the response.

   d. Does the study compare means or percentages?

1.2 Suppose a study of homes over the years recorded the year from 1987 to the present, as well as the size of the house in square feet, to see if average house size increased steadily over time.

   a. There are two variables mentioned here—what are they?

   b. Tell whether each of the two variables is quantitative or categorical.

   c. Which plays the role of explanatory variable and which is the response?

1.3 Makers of a blood pressure medication studied a group of heart disease patients whose blood pressures were considered normal at the outset. They found there was less likelihood of suffering heart attacks for those who had their blood pressure lowered further by taking additional medication compared to those whose blood pressure was allowed to remain at the original normal level.

   a. There are two variables involved here—what are they?

   b. Tell whether each of the two variables is quantitative or categorical.

   c. Tell which plays the role of explanatory variable and which is the response.

   d. Would researchers use means or proportions to make a comparison between those who did and did not take additional medication?

1.4 Researchers believe that alcohol consumption during pregnancy can affect a baby's birth weight. Describe a possible study corresponding to each of the following:

   a. Explanatory variable is categorical and response variable is categorical.

   b. Explanatory variable is categorical and response variable is quantitative.

   c. Explanatory variable is quantitative and response variable is categorical.

   d. Explanatory variable is quantitative and response variable is quantitative.

1.5 Solutions to Supplemental Exercises

1.1 **a.** which year (1987 or 2001) and the size of the house **b.** Year is categorical and size of the house is quantitative. **c.** Year is explanatory and size of house is response. **d.** means

1.2 **a.** year and house size **b.** Both are quantitative. **c.** Year is explanatory and size of house is response.

1.3 **a.** whether blood pressure was lowered, and whether patients suffered heart attacks **b.** Both are categorical. **c.** Whether blood pressure was lowered further with medication is explanatory and whether the patients suffered heart attacks is the response. **d.** proportions

1.4 **a.** Determine whether or not a mother drank a certain amount of alcohol during pregnancy, and whether the baby was normal birth weight or below. **b.** Determine whether or not a mother drank a certain amount of alcohol during pregnancy, and record the baby's birth weight. **c.** Record the amount of alcohol consumed during pregnancy, and whether the baby was normal birth weight or below. **d.** Record the amount of alcohol consumed during pregnancy, and record the baby's birth weight.

TBP Chapter 2

Sampling: *Which* Individuals Are Studied

2.1 Details and Examples

To supplement our discussion of random number selection at the beginning of Chapter 2 (page 18), the following activity can be carried out in class and the results examined for bias in the selection process: Each student picks a whole number at "random" from 1 to 20. Although each student might believe that he or she has made an unbiased selection, certain numbers in particular, and certain types of numbers, give more of an impression of being "random," and these are more heavily favored in the long run. If the selections were truly random, then each of the 20 numbers should be selected equally often in the long run, 5% of the time. The count of students who selected each number should be examined to see if certain numbers are preferred, and others avoided. Also, for truly random selections, the average of all the numbers picked should be roughly 10.5, which is the average of the numbers from 1 to 20. Students' selected numbers should be averaged and checked to see if there is systematic favoring of lower or higher numbers. Results from the student survey that accompanies this book (available on disk or a website) can also be checked.

Probability Sampling Plans

Some fairly straightforward sampling designs were discussed beginning on page 20 in Chapter 2. Real-life sampling tends to be rather more complicated than the examples and exercises in this book, which are designed to expose students to the basic principles. Moreover, sampling techniques must evolve constantly to keep pace with changes in society.

Probability sampling plans often end up by contacting the selected individuals via telephone. Because using a phone book would reduce the sampling frame to people with listed numbers, telephone surveys began many years ago to use random digit dialing. Now pollsters are faced with a new difficulty, as more and more people are abandoning traditional land-line phone service. People also screen and block calls routinely, making it difficult for surveyors to reach them. According to Larry Jacobs, director of the 2004 Elections Project at the University of Minnesota, response rates dropped from 40% a couple of decades ago to just about 25%. Some polling firms are experimenting with use of e-mail and the Internet to replace the traditional telephone polling system.

From Sample to Population: To What Extent Can We Generalize?

In Example 2.4 on page 22, we considered the question of what population is represented by a given sample. In theory, the various processes of statistics are carried out in this order:

1. Researchers wonder what is true about particular variables or relationships in a specified population—for instance, what is the relationship between

The Big Picture: A Closer Look

Notice that in our "random" number activity, we can focus on whether or not a particular number was selected, so that the underlying variable is categorical. Alternatively, we can focus on the size of the numbers selected, making our variable of interest quantitative.

smoking and cancer for all human beings? Or, does gender play a role in the extent to which American teenagers in general suffer from depression?

2. A *representative* sample is taken from the entire population of interest, and those variables or relationships are evaluated for the sample. Thus, researchers would take a representative sample of human beings and study the relationship between smoking and cancer in that sample. Or, they would obtain a representative sample of American teenagers and compare frequency or levels of depression for males and females.

In practice, there may be some deviations from this ideal. First of all, it often happens that data have already been collected before a researcher has thought about what he or she wants to learn, and about what population. Researchers may in fact take advantage of *available data* that someone else has produced. Based on the available data, they would like to draw some broader conclusions.

Secondly, even though a researcher may have in mind a specified population, he or she might be obliged to study a nonrandom sample, such as a convenience sample or volunteers. Experiments almost always work with volunteers because otherwise it would be difficult to get people to allow researchers to "take over" the values of whatever variables they are interested in. Still, the researchers would like to use those results to draw more general conclusions.

2.2 Activities

Activity: Potential Bias in Nonrandom Samples

Using the Computer

Without the aid of any tools for random selection, each student does his or her best at selecting three states at random from the following list, circling the three that are chosen. Discuss why "haphazard" does a better job than "random" to describe this type of sampling. [To avoid influencing students' selections, it is recommended that students are given a sheet with only state names listed exactly as shown (in three columns), so they do not have the opportunity to read ahead to the questions that follow.

Alabama	Louisiana	Ohio
Alaska	Maine	Oklahoma
Arizona	Maryland	Oregon
Arkansas	Massachusetts	Pennsylvania
California	Michigan	Rhode Island
Colorado	Minnesota	South Carolina
Connecticut	Mississippi	South Dakota
Delaware	Missouri	Tennessee
Florida	Montana	Texas
Georgia	Nebraska	Utah
Hawaii	Nevada	Vermont
Idaho	New Hampshire	Virginia
Illinois	New Jersey	Washington
Indiana	New Mexico	West Virginia
Iowa	New York	Wisconsin
Kansas	North Carolina	Wyoming
Kentucky	North Dakota	Washington, D.C.

1. Have the students as a group use software to generate 100 random selections of three numbers from the numbers 1 to 51. For example, if there are 20 students in the class, each student makes 5 random selections of three numbers from 1 to 51.

2. Determine what proportion of students chose exactly one state from each column in their original (haphazard) selection. Then determine what proportion of computer-aided (random) selections have the equivalent of one state from each column—that is, one of the three numbers between 1 and 17, one of the three numbers between 18 and 34, and one between 35 and 51. (The proportion should be fairly close to 0.24.) Is the proportion of haphazard selections with one state from each column close to the proportion of random selections that result in one from each column? If not, discuss how bias, and people's ideas of how random samples should look, may have entered into the haphazard selections.

3. Now determine what proportion of students (haphazardly) chose all three states from one column. Then determine what proportion of computer-aided (random) selections have all three numbers between 1 and 17, or all three between 18 and 34, or all three between 35 and 51. (The proportion should be fairly close to 0.10.) Is the proportion of haphazard selections with all three states in one column close to the proportion of random selections that result in all three in one column? If not, discuss how bias, and people's ideas of how random samples should look, may have entered into the haphazard selections.

   Note to instructors: Students typically are biased toward selections that are spread out as opposed to clumped together. Most likely their haphazard selections result in considerably more than 0.24 with one state from each column, and considerably less than 0.10 with all three states in one column. This provides evidence that their selections were not truly random.

Using a Random Digits Table

First students make their haphazard selection of three states as in the computer activity described above.

1. Have the students as a group use a random digits table to generate 100 random selections of three numbers from the numbers 1 to 51. For example, if there are 20 students in the class, each student makes 5 random selections of three numbers from 1 to 51.

2. Determine what proportion of students chose exactly one state from each column in their original (haphazard) selection. Then determine what proportion of random selections (with the table) have the equivalent of one state from each column—that is, one of the three numbers between 1 and 17, one of the three numbers between 18 and 34, and one between 35 and 51. (The proportion should be fairly close to 0.24.) Is the proportion of haphazard selections with one state from each column close to the proportion of random selections that result in one from each column? If not, discuss how bias, and people's ideas of how random samples should look, may have entered into the haphazard selections.

3. Now determine what proportion of students (haphazardly) chose all three states from one column. Then determine what proportion of random selections (with the table) have all three numbers between 1 and 17, or all three between 18 and 34, or all three between 35 and 51. (The proportion should be fairly close to 0.10.) Is the proportion of haphazard selections with all three states in one column close to the proportion of random selections that result in all three in one column? If not, discuss how bias, and people's ideas of how random samples should look, may have entered into the haphazard selections.

Note that methods of combinatorics would be needed to solve for the actual probabilities. Specifically, the probability of choosing exactly 1 state in each of 3 columns is

$$\frac{\binom{17}{1}\binom{17}{1}\binom{17}{1}}{\binom{51}{3}} = 0.2359$$

and the probability of choosing all 3 states in any one of the 3 columns is

$$\frac{3\binom{17}{3}}{\binom{51}{3}} = 0.0980$$

2.3 Guide to Exercise Topics

Sampling bias: 2.6*, 2.9, 2.12, 2.14(a), 2.20, 2.24, 2.27

Probability sampling plans: 2.7, 2.8, 2.10*, 2.11, 2.19, 2.21, 2.22, 2.23, 2.25, 2.26, 2.28

Role of sample size: 2.13*, 2.14(b)

Generalizing from a sample to a population: 2.15*, 2.16, 2.17*, 2.18

2.4 Supplemental Exercises

2.1 A poll was taken to determine what percentage of employers are loyal to their workers. The percentage could be reported as either 77% or 41%, depending on whether results are reported only for respondents who are workers, or only for respondents who are employers. Which percentage do you think corresponds to responses from employers?

2.2 Suppose the committee for cultural activities at a college wants to know how satisfied all the college's students are with the quality of on-campus concert programming, so they conduct a survey.

   a. Describe at least one way in which the results could be biased due to a nonrepresentative sample.

   b. Describe at least one way in which the results could be biased due to a poor design for assessing the sample.

2.3 In January 2003, newsPolls.org posted results of a survey where one of the questions was, "What is your favorite season of the year? Is it Spring, Summer, Fall or Winter?"

   a. Is the variable of interest quantitative or categorical?

   b. Would the results be summarized with means or proportions?

   c. For this particular question, it is most important to obtain a sample that is representative in terms of which one of these: gender, region of the United States, or political party?

   d. If the survey was conducted online and had a disproportionate number of young respondents, specify whether the sample proportion who prefer winter would be an overestimate or an underestimate for the proportion preferring winter in the general population.

2.4 Suppose a utility company wants to assess overall customer satisfaction.

   a. If the company wants a representative sample, should it draw a sample from its list of customers or sample from customers who telephone the company with concerns?

b. If the company contacts every fiftieth customer on its list, is this a random sample, a volunteer sample, a convenience sample, or a systematic sample?

c. If the company mails a questionnaire to a random sample of customers on its list, which of these is most likely to be a problem: sampling frame not matching population, nonresponse, or having a sample that is entirely self-selected?

d. In which case would the company have a better idea about customer satisfaction—if 20% or if 40% respond to questionnaires; or doesn't it make a difference?

2.5   Suppose a utility company wants to assess overall customer satisfaction. Tell whether each of the following focuses on data production, displaying and summarizing data, probability, or statistical inference.

a. The company decides to ask its customers to rate their satisfaction on a scale of 1 to 10, instead of just asking if they are satisfied or not.

b. The company decides that, based on the results of the sample, average satisfaction rating of all customers should be somewhere between 7.5 and 8.5.

c. The company finds mean satisfaction rating for the sample of customers.

2.6   A poll taken by AP-Ipsos in May 2004 asked respondents to report their height and weight. Based on those numbers, 49% of the respondents qualify as overweight.

a. In fact, there is good reason to expect that 49% is not entirely accurate; is it probably an underestimate or an overestimate of the percentage of all Americans who are overweight?

b. Is the reported percentage who are overweight biased because the sample was not representative of all Americans, or because individuals did not necessarily provide honest answers?

2.7   The May 2004 poll mentioned in the previous exercise found that 56% of respondents attempt to restrict fat in their diets. An August 2004 poll by Mark Clements Research, Inc. reported that 40% of Americans are eating low-fat foods. What is the best explanation for the pronounced difference in percentages—56% versus 40%: a change in attitudes between May and August, a difference in the wording of the questions, or different sampling techniques?

2.5   Solutions to Supplemental Exercises

2.1   77%

2.2   Many responses are possible besides these:
a. If they survey students who are attending one of the concerts, then they would be nonrepresentative, and tend to have a higher degree of satisfaction than students who do not attend.   **b.** The survey might be worded in such a way as to suggest that if the concerts are not appreciated, they will be reduced, in which case students might be careful to express a higher level of satisfaction than they actually feel. If, on the other hand, students suspect that dissatisfaction could lead to the booking of better musicians, they may exaggerate their complaints.

2.3   **a.** categorical   **b.** proportions   **c.** region of the United States   **d.** overestimate

2.4   **a.** from its list of customers   **b.** systematic sample   **c.** nonresponse   **d.** 40%

2.5   **a.** data production   **b.** statistical inference   **c.** displaying and summarizing data

2.6   **a.** underestimate   **b.** because individuals did not necessarily provide honest answers

2.7   a difference in the wording of the questions

TBP Chapter 3

Design: *How* Individuals Are Studied

3.1 Details and Examples

Role of Sample Size: Bigger Is Better If Design Is Sound

Example 2.3 on page 22 demonstrated that larger samples are better, but only if the sampling plan avoids bias. Similarly, larger samples cannot improve study designs that are flawed. As long as the sample is random and the study is well designed, then studying more individuals is better because it gives us more information. The precise impact of sample size on a study's results will become clear later in the book, when we study sampling distributions and statistical inference.

EXAMPLE TBP 3.1 SAMPLE SIZE AND STUDY DESIGN

Background: Suppose researchers want to examine the effectiveness of SAT prep courses. One possibility is to conduct an *observational study*: They will compare score improvements for a group of students who had enrolled in such a course with those of a group of students who had not. (The students have taken the SATs a first time, and after either attending a prep course or not, they will take the SATs a second time.) Another possibility is to carry out a *randomized controlled experiment*: Randomly assign some students to be enrolled in such a class, and others not; then compare score improvements.

Questions: If the observational study is conducted, which will give us a better idea of the prep course's effectiveness for the general population of students: if they look at 10 students altogether, 100 students altogether, or doesn't it matter? Which is better if the experiment is carried out?

Responses: Because the observational study design is flawed by a confounding variable (the type of student who enrolls for such a course is likely to be the type of student to do better anyway), it doesn't help to use a larger sample size.

In the case of the experiment, because the study design is fairly sound, the larger sample is better.

Practice: *Try Exercise TBP 3.2(d) on page 761.*

Bias through Ordering of Survey Questions

In our discussion of deliberate bias, we mentioned on page 40 that surveyors may at times design a question for the purpose of influencing responses to later questions.

EXAMPLE TBP 3.2 PLANTING IDEAS WITH SURVEY QUESTIONS

Background: In the year 2002, there was much controversy over the fact that the Augusta National Golf Club, which hosts the Masters Golf Tournament each year, does not accept women as members. Defenders of the club created a survey that included the following statements, to which respondents were supposed to tell if they agreed or disagreed:

1. "The First Amendment of the U.S. Constitution applies to everyone regardless of gender, race, religion, age, profession, or point of view."

2. "The First Amendment protects the right of individuals to create a private organization consisting of a specific group of people based on age, gender, race, ethnicity, or interest."

3. "The First Amendment protects the right of organizations like the Boy Scouts, the Girls Scouts, and the National Association for the Advancement of Colored People to exist."

4. "Individuals have a right to join a private group, club, or organization that consists of people who share the same interests and personal backgrounds as they do if they so desire."

5. "Private organizations that are not funded by the government should be allowed to decide who becomes a member and who does not become a member on their own, without being forced to take input from other outside people or organizations."

Question: What was the purpose of the first four statements?

Response: The first and second statements steer people to favor the opinion that specialized groups may form private clubs. The third statement reminds people of organizations that are formed by minorities, setting the stage for them to agree with the fourth statement, which supports people's rights to join any private club. This in turn leads into the fifth statement, which focuses on a private organization's right to decide on its membership. As a group, the questions attempt to relentlessly steer a respondent toward ultimately agreeing with the club's right to exclude women.

Practice: *Try Exercise 3.19 on page 45.*

The Big Picture:
A Closer Look

Prospective observational studies, defined on page 32, include **longitudinal** studies, where individuals' changes or developments are recorded as they occur, often over several years' time.

Confounding Variables in an Observational Study

Notice that in our Response in Example 3.16 on page 47, we did not say that controlling for gender would allow us to make a *definite* claim of causation, we just said that we would be "closer" to establishing a causal connection. This lack of a definite conclusion is due to the fact that other confounding variables may also be involved. Students may be able to come up with some of these possible confounding variables themselves.

EXAMPLE **TBP 3.3** MORE THAN ONE POSSIBLE CONFOUNDING VARIABLE

Background: Gender is a possible confounding variable in the relationship between sugar intake and hyperactivity.

Questions: What are other possible confounding variables in this relationship? How easily could they be controlled for?

Responses:

- Parenting style is one possibility: Perhaps children of permissive parents are free to consume more sweets, and they also may tend toward hyperactive behavior. This possible confounding variable, because of its subjective nature, would be more difficult to separate out than something objective like gender.

- Similarly, socio-economic level could possibly be tied in with sugar intake and hyperactive behavior. Researchers have developed a variety of methods to group individuals according to this potential confounding variable.

- Another possible confounding variable would be caffeine commonly consumed in foods like chocolate or in some carbonated beverages that also have high sugar content. Yet another would be the artificial colors and flavors contained in many kinds of candy. These could be handled by identifying and then separating out the various sources of sugar in each child's diet.

Practice: *Try Exercise 3.69 on page 68.*

Do All Experiments Include a Control Group?

On page 52, we define the control group in an experiment. A common misconception is for students to believe that an experiment *must* include a control group of individuals receiving no treatment per se. There may be situations where a complete lack of treatment is not an option, or where including a control group is ethically questionable, or where researchers explore the effects of a treatment without making a comparison.

EXAMPLE **TBP 3.4** NO CONTROL GROUP BECAUSE ALL SUBJECTS SHOULD BE TREATED

Background: Suppose doctors want to experiment whether Prograf or Cyclosporin is more effective as an immunosuppressant for transplant patients.

Question: Why would they not include a control group of patients who receive neither treatment?

Response: It would be unethical to include a control group of patients not receiving any immunosuppressants, because this could lead to rejection of the transplanted organ.

Practice: *Try Exercise TBP 3.7 on page 758.*

EXAMPLE TBP 3.5 NO CONTROL GROUP BECAUSE SIMULATED TREATMENT IS RISKY

Background: Recently, in an attempt to combat the effects of Parkinson's disease, experiments have been conducted wherein the treatment is a highly invasive surgery that inserts stem cells into the brain.

Question: What are the ethical concerns in including a control group?

Response: The only way to have a legitimate control group in this case is to randomly assign half of the subjects to undergo the entire surgery except for the actual treatment component (inserting stem cells into the brain). It can be considered unethical to subject someone to this risk for the sake of experimentation, when as a member of the control group the subject would receive no known benefits to offset the risk.

Practice: *Try Exercise TBP 3.8 on page 759.*

There may even be an experiment designed with only a single treatment.

EXAMPLE TBP 3.6 NO CONTROL GROUP IN POORLY DESIGNED EXPERIMENT

Background: Makers of a new hair product asked a sample of individuals to treat their hair with that product over a period of several weeks, then assess how manageable their hair had become.

Question: Was this an experiment?

Response: This design is clearly flawed because of the absence of a comparison group, but it is still an experiment because use of the product has been imposed by its manufacturers, rather than chosen naturally by the individuals. A flawed experiment is nevertheless an experiment.

Practice: *Try Exercise 3.68(g) on page 67.*

Modifications to a Completely Randomized Design

The idea of blocking in experiments was mentioned briefly on page 57. This example provides more detail about blocked and paired designs.

EXAMPLE TBP 3.7 EXPERIMENT WITH BLOCKED OR PAIRED DESIGN

Background: A study was conducted to test the theory that because people using stronger sunscreens don't feel the effects of sunburn as quickly, they spend more time outside and increase their risk of skin cancer.

An observational study would not be appropriate to test this theory because people who choose different sunscreens may also differ in terms of how long they are inclined to spend in the sun. In fact, a randomized controlled blind experiment was carried out: "In a study of 87 French and Swiss college students, researchers gave half of them sunscreen with a protection factor of 10 and the other half with a factor of 30. The students, who weren't told which lotion they received, went on summer vacations and recorded the amount of time they spent in the sun. Users of the stronger sunscreen spent 25% more time in the sun, mostly sunbathing, the study found . . . students in the study often waited until their skin turned red before rushing to the shade. Those unknowingly using the stronger sunscreen waited longer and had greater exposure to cancer-causing ultraviolet radiation . . ."[1]

Questions: How could the design have incorporated blocking, if the researchers had felt that location could play an important role in the relationship between type of sunscreen and time spent in the sun? How could the blocking be extended so that the design was paired?

Responses: The researchers could have blocked first by vacation region—Europe, Caribbean, etc.—and then randomly assigned one of the two types of sunscreen. In the extreme, they could have carried out a study of pairs of students who are vacationing together: Within each pair, randomly assign one to receive each of the two types of sunscreen.

Practice: *Try Exercise 3.40(f) on page 60.*

Note that the relationship between two variables is being explored: type of sunscreen (categorical explanatory variable) and time spent in the sun (quantitative response variable).

In the context of paired designs, we mentioned before-and-after studies on page 58. Here is an example of such a study.

EXAMPLE TBP 3.8 BEFORE-AND-AFTER EXPERIMENTS

Background: Suppose the manufacturer of a hair-loss drug would like to produce evidence of its effectiveness.

Question: How could the drug's manufacturer carry out an experiment to produce evidence of its effectiveness using a before-and-after design?

Response: The drug manufacturer could compare hair coverage before and after treatment for a group of male subjects. The categorical explanatory variable would be taking the drug or not, and the response, hair coverage, may be measured quantitatively. Ultimately, researchers would focus on the difference in hair coverage, before minus after (or vice-versa), to assess if the drug is effective.

Practice: *Try Exercise 3.46 on page 61.*

We mentioned on page 58 that it is very common for drug studies to combine two-sample and paired designs. Here is an example of such a study.

EXAMPLE TBP 3.9 COMBINING PAIRED AND TWO-SAMPLE DESIGNS

Background: Studies in the 1990s on the effectiveness of a medicinal compound called sildenafil citrate for heart problems accidentally came upon an interesting side-effect: It improved erectile function in men. Many clinical trials followed in the late 1990s, as the drug was being screened for marketing under the name of Viagra. One type of design used was to randomly assign some men to Viagra, others to a placebo. Erectile function was assessed for each man before and after the period of treatment. These studies produced overwhelming evidence of considerably more improvement for those men who took Viagra.

Question: What aspect of the described design is paired, and what aspect is two-sample?

Response: Comparing function before and after uses pairs of values; comparing improvements for Viagra versus placebo uses two samples.

Practice: *Try Exercise 3.47 on page 61.*

3.2 Activities

Activity: Identifying Study Design

Using the Computer

Students search online news websites and other Internet resources to locate reports of statistical studies involving each of these designs: a prospective observational study, a retrospective observational study, a single-blind experiment, a double-blind experiment, a paired study, a two-sample study, and a several-sample study. (For the latter three, students should identify the study as being an experiment or an observational study.) For the class as a group, the goal is to find studies representing all of the above-mentioned designs. When a student finds a study using a design not yet found, he or she reports to the class, describing the study so they can decide if they agree that the type of design has been correctly identified. [By quoting a key phrase of the report, the student may help classmates locate the article with a search engine such as Google so they can examine it for themselves.] The instructor keeps track of the studies found by students and what designs they use, until all seven types of design mentioned above are represented.

In the Classroom

Students search a collection of newspapers, journals, and magazines to locate reports of statistical studies involving each of the above-mentioned designs.

Alternatively, the instructor may make a handout of study descriptions, such as those in the Supplemental Part I Review Exercises beginning on page 763, and the students screen these for the various study designs.

Activity: Formulating a Survey Question

In the Classroom

At the beginning of the lecture devoted to sample surveys, the instructor can explain that in 2005, a popular movie sparked speculation: how common is it for a

40-year-old male to be a virgin? Students can be asked to imagine that a representative sample of 40-year-old males is available, and the students, task is to design a survey question to find out what proportion are virgins. They should jot down their question, and reconsider it at the end of the lecture.

After they have learned about various issues in survey question design (open vs. closed questions, what response options to provide for closed questions, how to elicit honest responses to sensitive questions, and whether the concept of interest is well-defined) students should discuss whether or not they are satisfied with the phrasing of their question, and—if not—how they would rephrase it.

Note that "The Basics; Pure Speculation: The Aging Virgin," published in the *New York Times* in 2005, discusses the difficulties of determining the true proportion of 40-year-olds who are virgins. It does mention a University of Chicago study that reported 1.2 percent of men saying they were virgins when they turned 40.

3.3 Guide to Exercise Topics

Various designs: 3.1*, 3.2, 3.3, 3.4, 3.7*, 3.8*, 3.10, 3.48(a), 3.49(a), 3.50(a), 3.58(c), 3.63, 3.65(a), 3.66(b), 3.67(a), 3.68*(a)

Errors: 3.5, 3.6, 3.9*, 3.51, 3.52, 3.54

Sample surveys: 3.11*, 3.12, 3.13, 3.14*, 3.15, 3.16*, 3.17, 3.19*, 3.20, 3.21*(a,b,d), 3.22, 3.23(a), 3.24*, 3.25*, 3.26, 3.27*, 3.28*, 3.29, 3.58(a,b), 3.59, 3.60*, 3.61, 3.62

Observational studies: 3.30*, 3.31, 3.32*, 3.33, 3.34*, 3.35, 3.49(b), 3.53, 3.64, 3.65(b), 3.69, 3.75

Experiments: 3.36*, 3.37*, 3.38*, 3.39*, 3.40*, 3.41, 3.42, 3.43, 3.44, 3.45*, 3.46*, 3.47*, 3.48(b–d), 3.50(b), 3.66(c), 3.67(b–f), 3.68*(b–h), 3.70, 3.71*, 3.72, 3.73*, 3.74

3.4 Supplemental Exercises

3.1 In August 2003, newsPolls.org posted results of a survey in which one of the questions was: "Who is the most famous athlete, either active or retired, in America today?"

   a. Is the variable of interest quantitative or categorical?

   b. Would the results be summarized with a mean or with proportions?

   c. If the survey were conducted in the winter, what sort of bias might occur—preference of football players or preference of baseball players?

3.2 A market research firm reported recently that more than two-thirds of all Americans eat yogurt.

   a. Is this result likely to be based on a multistage sample, a haphazard sample, or a convenience sample?

   b. Is the variable of interest quantitative or categorical?

   c. In using survey results to draw conclusions about the eating habits of all Americans, is the firm concerned with the process of data production, displaying and summarizing data, or statistical inference?

   d. For which sample size would you have more faith in the firm's report of what proportion of all Americans eat yogurt: 30 or 3,000; or doesn't it make a difference?

3.3 An article entitled "1 In 10 Students Subject to Abuse" reported findings by the American Association of University Women delivered to Congress as part of the requirement of the No Child Left Behind Law. The article mentions that "some educators took issue with the way the report combines sexual abuse with other behaviors, such as inappropriate jokes, in one broad category of sexual misconduct."[2] Based on the educators' concerns, do we have reason to suspect that the reported proportion of 1 in 10 is higher than what the educators feel is accurate, or lower?

3.4 An article entitled "Male Marital Outlook Tied to Upbringing" found that "men with negative attitudes [about marriage] were far more likely than the rest to have been raised by a divorced parent in a non-churchgoing family."[3]

   a. Does the article's title make upbringing the explanatory variable, the response, or is there no clear suggestion of causation?

   b. One of the following, more than the others, should prevent us from concluding that being raised by a divorced parent in a non-churchgoing family necessarily causes men to have a negative attitude about marriage; which is it: confounding variables, faulty memory in a retrospective study, or failure to respond honestly to sensitive questions?

   c. The article goes on to state that married men are "less likely to hang out in bars, to abuse alcohol or drugs." Does this suggest that less use of alcohol and drugs explains marriage or is a response to marriage; or is there no suggestion of causation?

3.5 "Afternoon Light Helps Babies Sleep" tells of a study that "compared babies who slept well with problem sleepers and found that the good sleepers had been exposed to twice as much light between noon and 4 p.m. The study's author [. . .] said that the worst period for crying for babies, beginning around six weeks, was also the time when the body appeared to be establishing circadian rhythms, by regulating the output of the melatonin, a brain chemical that reacts to light."[4] However, the author "conceded that the findings might just

reflect greater 'energy or enthusiasm for outdoor activities' among mothers whose sleep was being interrupted less."

   a. Was this an experiment or an observational study?

   b. The title suggests which variables to be playing the roles of explanatory and response variables?

   c. The author's closing comment acknowledges the possibility of causation in the reverse direction. Explain what roles the variables would be playing in this case.

3.6 Suppose an instructor would like to know how much time his students spend on homework exercises each week throughout the semester.

   a. Describe the design of a retrospective observational study that the instructor could carry out. What is the main drawback of this design?

   b. Describe the design of a prospective observational study that the instructor could carry out. What is the main drawback of this design?

   c. Tell which design is better overall, and why: the retrospective or the prospective study?

3.7 In a large group of postmenopausal women at high risk for developing breast cancer, half were randomly assigned to take tamoxifen, and the rest were assigned to take a new drug called raloxifene. Explain why the researchers did not include a control group of women receiving neither drug.

3.8 Starting in the 1970s, Dr. Peter Janetta at the University of Pittsburgh developed a revolutionary but effective type of brain surgery to cure trigeminal neuralgia, whose sufferers are subject to acute facial pain. Explain why inclusion of a control group could have been problematic if the effectiveness of his methods were to be tested via an experiment.

3.5 Solutions to Supplemental Exercises

3.1 **a.** categorical **b.** proportions **c.** preference of football players

3.2 **a.** multistage sample **b.** categorical **c.** statistical inference **d.** 3,000

3.3 higher

3.4 **a.** no clear suggestion of causation ("tied to" is noncommittal) **b.** confounding variables **c.** suggests less use of alcohol and drugs is a response to marriage

3.5 **a.** observational study **b.** Afternoon light is explanatory variable, babies' sleep is response. **c.** If babies' sleep (explanatory variable) is good, then mothers have the energy or enthusiasm to take them out for exposure to afternoon light (response variable).

3.6 **a.** Ask the students at the end of the semester how much time they spent on homework

assignments. The main drawback of this design is students' faulty memories. **b.** Ask students at the beginning of the semester to keep an ongoing log of how many hours they spend on homework. The main drawback of this design is that their homework hours may be influenced by their consciousness of keeping track of them. **c.** The prospective design is better, because the influence on homework hours would not be too dramatic, and would probably be beneficial anyway.

3.7 It would be unethical to include a control group receiving neither drug because the women are known to be at high risk for developing breast cancer, and need to be given some treatment.

3.8 It may be considered to be unethical to subject someone to brain surgery but not administer any treatment that is considered beneficial.

3.6 Review of Introduction and Part I

In Chapters 1 through 3, we discussed the five possible variable situations ($C, Q, C \rightarrow Q, C \rightarrow C, Q \rightarrow Q$) and the four processes in statistics (data production, displaying and summarizing, probability, and statistical inference).

The first phase of data production—sampling—must be carried out carefully to ensure that the sam-

ple represents the larger population without bias. The second phase, study design, must be planned carefully to ensure that the variable or variables of interest are assessed without bias for the sampled individuals.

3.7 Supplemental Part I Review Exercises

A statistical study can be examined in the context of each of the four processes—data production, displaying and summarizing, probability, and statistical inference. To highlight the fact that for any given situation we can focus on any of these four processes, the review exercises for Parts II (page 810), III (page 883), and IV (page 979) feature the same settings as these 15 exercises. For now, the focus is on data production.

3.9 A drug for female sexual dysfunction called Intrinsa was tested in 2004, both for efficacy and for possible dangerous side-effects before being considered for approval by the Food and Drug Administration. A report of clinical trials states: "Fifty-two percent of those [women] given the drug said they experienced a 'meaningful benefit' in their

sex-lives—but so did 31 percent of those who were given the placebo."[5]

   a. Tell what variables are involved here, which is explanatory and which is response, and whether they are quantitative or categorical. If a variable is categorical, how many possible values can it take?

   b. Was this an experiment or an observational study?

   c. Are the results in the quotation focusing on efficacy or on dangerous side-effects?

3.10 Researchers at the University of Montreal reported that "blind people are better than sighted controls at judging the direction of pitch change between sounds [. . .] but only if they became blind at an early age. The younger the onset of blindness, the better is the performance."[6]

   a. Identify the three variables involved and tell whether each is categorical or quantitative, and whether each is playing the role of explanatory or response variable.

   b. Was this an experiment or an observational study or a sample survey?

3.11 In 1999, Harvard Medical School researchers produced evidence that when television was introduced to the island of Fiji in the mid-1990s, teenage girls began to suffer from eating disorders because of body image issues resulting from seeing thin actresses on their favorite shows.

   a. Was this an experiment, an observational study, or a sample survey?

   b. Which one of these should be considered most seriously before concluding that the eating disorders in Fiji were caused by the introduction of television: if the sample of girls was representative; the possibility of confounding variables; the placebo effect; the experimenter effect?

3.12 According to a Pew report, by the year 2007, one in every 100 Americans was in prison.

   a. Was the information most likely obtained from a representative sample of Americans, a nonrepresentative sample of Americans, or the population of Americans?

   b. If we want to see if the difference between proportion of Hispanics in the general population and proportion of Hispanics imprisoned could easily have come about by chance, are we mainly concerned with data production, displaying and summarizing data, probability, or statistical inference?

3.13 The *Harvard Gazette Archives* reported: "Cognition unaffected by pot use; but other studies suggest marijuana smokers are not a happy lot."[7] A study recruited heavy users, former users, and non-users, who took a variety of cognition tests 0, 1, 7, and 28 days after quitting the drug. Another study said that "most heavy users admitted that the drug has a negative impact on all aspects of their lives from job performance

and physical health to mental well-being and satisfactory socializing."

   a. Was the first study an experiment, an observational study, or a sample survey?

   b. What are the two explanatory variables of interest in the first study?

   c. Was the response variable in the first study most likely quantitative or categorical?

   d. Was the second study an experiment, an observational study, or a sample survey?

   e. As far as the second study is concerned, a researcher admitted that causality could occur in either direction. Explain how marijuana use could play the role of response variable in this context.

3.14 "Acupuncture Helps Ease Arthritis Pain" describes a National Institutes of Health study where participants "were randomly assigned to receive one of three treatments: acupuncture, sham acupuncture—a procedure designed to prevent patients from being able to detect if needles are actually inserted at treatment points—or participation in a control group that followed the Arthritis Foundation's self-help course for managing their condition . . . Overall, those who received acupuncture had a 40 percent decrease in pain and 40 percent improvement in function."[8]

   a. Tell what variables are involved here, and whether they are quantitative or categorical. If categorical, tell how many possible values a variable can take.

   b. The article only reported the improvement in patients who received genuine acupuncture. Can we assume that there was no improvement in the other patients?

3.15 According to a newspaper report, "the bigger your brood, the likelier it is to show on your waistline. And that's not just for women, who may retain some of the pounds they gain during pregnancy. Fathers tend to gain weight, too, increasing their risk of obesity with the number of offspring, suggesting that eating habits are to blame."[9] Researchers found the relationship between family size and body size held, regardless of household income, physical activity, smoking, and other factors.

   a. Was this an experiment, an observational study, or a sample survey?

b. Besides family size and weight, researchers apparently recorded values for at least four other variables for each individual studied; tell what those variables are.

c. When researchers decided what possible confounding variables should be considered when they would interview participants in their study, were they mainly concerned with data production, displaying and summarizing data, probability, or statistical inference?

3.16 A study conducted by AAA looked at other driving distractions besides cell phones. It was reported that drivers are engaged in many such distracting behaviors: 62% acknowledged fiddling with the radio dial while driving in the previous 6 months; 57% reported eating, 44% tried to pick something up from the floor or between the seats, 32% wrote something down, 32% stretched to reach the glove compartment, and 23% cleaned the inside of their windshield.

a. Does this information involve single categorical variables or the relationship between categorical variables?

b. It was also reported that men were more than twice as likely as women to have steered the car with their thighs or driven with no hands. Does this information involve single categorical variables or the relationship between categorical variables?

c. Was this an experiment or an observational study or a sample survey?

3.17 A report on sexual health by the Alan Guttmacher Institute says that "men of all ages tend to overstate their sexual activity when surveyed, while women understate theirs."[10]

a. Not counting age, there are actually three variables whose values researchers needed to know here; tell what they are and whether they are quantitative or categorical.

b. When the Institute had to come up with a way of measuring actual as opposed to claimed sexual activity, was it mainly concerned with data production, displaying and summarizing data, probability, or statistical inference?

3.18 Every week in football season, data are recorded for the types of injuries suffered by the players on the NFL list of injured players. During a particular week, the most common—knee injury—was suffered by 49 of the 234 players, whereas the least common—a blister on the foot—was suffered by only 1 player.

a. Suppose we also wanted to include information on the position of each of the injured players—quarterback, running back, etc. What would be the explanatory variable: injury or position?

b. When deciding whether to report counts or proportions, are we mainly concerned with data production, displaying and summarizing data, probability, or statistical inference?

3.19 The *Los Angeles Daily News* reported the results of a study of thousands of babies born in California in the year 2000. Researchers found that babies born to mothers in the most polluted areas consistently weighed less—about 1 ounce less—than babies born to mothers who lived in clean-air cities.

a. Tell what variables are involved here, and whether they are quantitative or categorical. Which is explanatory and which is response?

b. When deciding which areas to include in their study, were researchers mainly concerned with data production, displaying and summarizing data, probability, or statistical inference?

3.20 "Soft Drink Link to Diabetes Found" reports that "as consumption of sugar-sweetened drinks increased, women put on more pounds and increased their likelihood to develop diabetes."[11]

a. Tell what variables are involved, whether they are quantitative or categorical, and what role each plays (explanatory or response).

b. If researchers want to issue a warning, based on these results, that any woman who consumes too many sugar-sweetened drinks may be putting herself at risk for diabetes, are they mainly concerned with data production, displaying and summarizing data, probability, or statistical inference?

3.21 Columnist Maureen Dowd of the *New York Times* discussed two studies published in 2004 on what men are looking for in a woman. The first study "suggests that men going for long-term relationships would rather marry women in subordinate jobs than women who are supervisors."[12] The second study "found that a high IQ hampers a woman's chance to get married, while it is a plus for men. The prospect for marriage increased by 35% for guys for each 16-point increase in IQ; for women, there is a 40% drop for each 16-point rise."

   a. The first study features one variable; tell what it is, and if it is quantitative or categorical.

   b. The second study features two variables in addition to the explanatory variable gender. Tell what they are, whether each is quantitative or categorical, and whether each is explanatory or response.

3.22 According to the *New York Times*, economics professor David Zimmerman at Williams College studied the impact of college roommates on political leanings and on grades. He "looked at the political views of 3,500 students who had shared rooms as freshmen, noting their leanings when they started college and again 3 years after graduation. Generally, roommates kept the same political persuasion—except those freshmen whose roommates were on the far left of the political spectrum. No matter what their politics at enrollment, they were more likely than similar students to be *conservative* as adults. [. . .] In separate research, Zimmerman and Gordon C. Winston, another Williams economics professor, uncovered more unsettling evidence of peer influence: Freshmen rooming with the weakest students experienced a slight drop in grades. The researchers divided 5,000 one-time roommates at four colleges into three groups: those who scored in the top 15% of the SAT verbal scores admitted to the college, those in the bottom 15%, and everyone in between. On average, grades of the typical students who roomed with low scorers were pulled down by a tenth of a grade point by graduation. No other impact was noticed."

   a. Which would be an easier study design for the researchers to implement in order to compare political leanings from freshman year to 3 years after graduation: retrospective or prospective?

   b. What would be the main drawback of a retrospective design?

3.23 A wine merchant advertised prices of its California Cabernet wines, per bottle. The minimum price was $10 and the maximum was $130. The mean price was $41. Which one of the five variable situations applies: C, Q, $C \rightarrow Q$, $C \rightarrow C$, or $Q \rightarrow Q$?

3.8 Solutions to Supplemental Part I Review Exercises

3.9 a. Taking the drug or a placebo is the categorical explanatory variable, and experiencing a 'meaningful benefit' in their sex lives is the categorical response variable. Both can take just two possible values. **b.** experiment **c.** efficacy

3.10 a. Being blind or sighted is a categorical explanatory variable; age at onset of blindness is a quantitative explanatory variable; ability to detect direction of pitch change is a quantitative response variable. **b.** observational study

3.11 a. observational study **b.** the possibility of confounding variables

3.12 a. population of Americans **b.** probability

3.13 a. experiment **b.** degree of marijuana use and amount of time since quitting **c.** quantitative **d.** sample survey **e.** People who have problems with their jobs, health, mental well-being, or social life might be more likely to use marijuana than people who are doing well in these aspects of their lives.

3.14 a. Which treatment is the categorical explanatory variable; it can take three possible values. Amount of pain and ability to function are two quantitative response variables. **b.** No, they probably improved, too, due to the placebo effect.

3.15 a. observational study **b.** gender (mother or father), household income, physical activity, and smoking **c.** data production

3.16 a. single categorical variables **b.** relationship between categorical variables **c.** sample survey

3.17 a. gender (categorical), claimed amount of sexual activity (quantitative), actual amount of sexual activity (quantitative) **b.** data production

3.18 a. position   **b.** displaying and summarizing data

3.19 a. Whether the baby was born in a most polluted area or a clean-air city is the categorical explanatory variable, and birth weight is the quantitative response.   **b.** data production

3.20 a. Amount of soft drinks consumed is a quantitative explanatory variable; weight (or weight increase) is a quantitative response, and whether or not they developed diabetes is a categorical response.   **b.** statistical inference

3.21 a. whether the men prefer women in subordinate jobs or those who are supervisors   **b.** IQ is a quantitative explanatory variable, and whether women (or men) of that IQ are married is a quantitative response variable.

3.22 a. retrospective   **b.** faulty memories

3.23 Q

TBP Chapter 4

Displaying and Summarizing Data for a Single Variable

4.1 Details and Examples

Raw Categorical Data: Starting from Scratch

In Example 4.1, which was about breakfast, and in most of the examples students see in textbooks—as well as in real-life applications with categorical variables—the data have been processed for the reader, with results summarized as counts or proportions. At times, however, there are situations in which we need to start from scratch, working with a data set in its original form as responses at the individual level. If time permits, a class can discuss and agree on a survey design to produce data about the students' own drinking habits, keeping in mind the importance of anonymity. Alternatively, they can start with the results from the author's class, as tabulated in this example.

EXAMPLE TBP 4.1 FINDING A PROPORTION FROM RAW DATA

Background: Each year over 1,000 college students die in alcohol-related deaths, often in cases that involve binge drinking. Harvard School of Public Health reported in 2004 that 44% of college students are binge drinkers. In an informal anonymous survey conducted in a statistics class shortly after the Harvard report was released, students were asked:

> "In the past two weeks, have you had:
> (males) more than five alcoholic drinks on one occasion?
> (females) more than four alcoholic drinks on one occasion?"

[This is how experts classify a student to be a binge drinker or not.] Their responses are listed in this table.

yes	no	yes	no	no	yes
no	yes	yes	no	yes	no
yes	yes	no	no	yes	yes
yes	no	yes	yes	no	no
yes	no	yes	yes	yes	yes
no	no	yes	no	yes	no
no	yes	no	no	yes	no
no	no	no	no	yes	yes
yes	no	no	no	no	no
no	no	no	no	no	no
no	yes	yes	no	no	yes

Questions: How can we summarize these results? Do they seem consistent with the Harvard School of Public Health report?

Responses: Altogether, there are 66 responses, of which 28 are "yes" and 38 are "no." The percentage answering "yes" is 28/66 = 42%, which is actually quite close to 44%, Harvard's reported percentage.

The percentage reported by the Harvard School of Public Health was itself based on a sample survey, and in that respect would be considered a statistic. In the context of this example, where the ad hoc classroom survey is being checked for conformity, we might consider Harvard's proportion (0.44) to be a parameter p, and our classroom summary (0.42) to be a statistic $\hat{p}$.

Practice: *Try Exercise 4.7(a) on page 80.*

Pie Charts and Bar Graphs

After learning about bar graphs in Example 4.5 on page 76, students may wonder which of our two displays for categorical data is "better." We can ask them to consider the subtle difference in the visual information provided by pie charts versus bar graphs. When we look at a pie chart, we tend to focus on how each category percentage (area of a pie slice) compares to the entire 100% of individuals studied (area of entire pie). When we look at a bar graph, we tend to focus on how each category percentage (height of a bar) compares to that of other categories (heights of other bars).

EXAMPLE TBP 4.2 OPTING FOR PIE CHART OR BAR GRAPH

Background: A report on foreign student enrollment tells the numbers of students coming from each of 15 countries of origin.

Questions: What display should be used if a reporter wants to stress that more than an eighth of all foreign students come from India? What if a reporter wants to stress that most students come from India, China, Korea, Japan, and Taiwan, in that order?

Responses: In the first case, a pie chart would be most helpful; in the second case, the reporter should use a bar graph.

Practice: *Try Exercise 4.6(b) on page 80.*

By opting for dog breeds in order of decreasing numbers registered in Example 4.5 on page 76, we produced a graph that listed bars left to right from most to least common. We can mention to students that this was a rather arbitrary choice over many other options, such as listing the breeds alphabetically, or from least to most common, etc. The horizontal axis in this case is for purely categorical values, not quantitative, and there is no single required ordering as there would be for numbers (which are always listed left to right from lowest to highest). However, if a quantitative variable has been converted to categorical by forming groups in certain ranges, then the accompanying bar graph should list bars in their natural numerical progression, with ranges of smaller values to the left and ranges of larger values to the right.

EXAMPLE TBP 4.3 BARS IN INCREASING ORDER

Background: "Light Drinking in Pregnancy Has Long-Term Effects on Kids" tells of a study where pregnant women were classified as light drinkers (less than 1.5 drinks per week), moderate drinkers (1.5 drinks per week to less than one drink per day), and heavy drinkers (one or more drinks per day). Of course, some women consumed no alcohol, and they were classified as nondrinkers.

Question: If the drinking habits of the women studied were to be depicted in a bar graph, is there a "best" way of ordering the bars?

Response: In this case, because the variable (drinking habits) deals with amounts, its values should be shown in increasing order left to right: the left-most bar would be for the nondrinkers, followed by bars for light, moderate, and heavy drinkers, in that order.

Practice: *Try Exercise 4.6(c) on page 80.*

Details about Center, Spread, and Shape

In addition to studying Example 4.21 on page 100, which shows the role played by left- or right-skewness in the relationship between the mean and the median, students can also consider examples like this one, where the mean provides a misleading summary.

EXAMPLE TBP 4.4 WHEN THE MEDIAN IS PREFERABLE TO THE MEAN

Background: For the purpose of informing potential students about their job prospects after graduation, universities gather data about starting salaries of former students with various majors. The mean starting salary of geography majors from the University of North Carolina was remarkably high compared to the means from other schools. This was a result of just one high outlier by the name of Michael Jordan. Averaging in his unusually high salary as a star pro basketball player inflated the value of the mean. The median would not have been affected.

Question: Which measure of center should be used?

Response: In this case (and, in general, with any data for monetary variables) the median should be used as a measure of center, because high outliers tend to distort the value of the mean.

Practice: *Try Exercise 4.34(a,c) on page 105.*

After the formula for standard deviation has been presented on page 101, the following example can be used for instructors who want their students to be able to calculate standard deviations by hand.

EXAMPLE **TBP 4.5** CALCULATING THE STANDARD DEVIATION BY HAND

Background: Number of credits taken by 14 nontraditional students were introduced in Example 4.11.

4 7 11 11 11 13 13 14 14 15 17 17 17 18

Question: How would the standard deviation be calculated by hand?

Response: We find the square root of the average squared deviation from the mean as follows:

1. Find the mean by averaging all the values (shown in the first column).

2. Find the deviations from the mean, shown in the second column.

3. Find the squared deviations from the mean, shown in the third column.

4. Average the squared deviations, dividing their sum by the number of observations minus one. This gives us the variance s^2.

5. Take the square root of the variance to find the standard deviation, 4.

Value	Deviation from Mean	Squared Deviation
4	$4 - 13 = -9$	$-9^2 = 81$
7	$7 - 13 = -6$	$-6^2 = 36$
11	$11 - 13 = -2$	$-2^2 = 4$
11	$11 - 13 = -2$	$-2^2 = 4$
11	$11 - 13 = -2$	$-2^2 = 4$
13	$13 - 13 = 0$	$0^2 = 0$
13	$13 - 13 = 0$	$0^2 = 0$
14	$14 - 13 = +1$	$+1^2 = 1$
14	$14 - 13 = +1$	$+1^2 = 1$
15	$15 - 13 = +2$	$+2^2 = 4$
17	$17 - 13 = +4$	$+4^2 = 16$
17	$17 - 13 = +4$	$+4^2 = 16$
17	$17 - 13 = +4$	$+4^2 = 16$
18	$18 - 13 = +5$	$+5^2 = 25$
$\bar{x} = 13$		Sum = 208
		"Average" $= s^2 = \frac{208}{14-1} = 16$
		$s = \sqrt{s^2} = \sqrt{16} = 4$

Practice: *Try Exercise 4.35(e) on page 106.*

The following example can be discussed with students after Example 4.22 on page 101 to help give them a feel for standard deviations in the context of discussing shape, center, and spread.

EXAMPLE TBP 4.6 GETTING A FEEL FOR SHAPE, CENTER, AND SPREAD

Background: Consider the distribution of ages for three groups: a random sample of high school students, a random sample of high school seniors, and a random sample of college students (which includes some nontraditional students).

Question: What results can we expect in terms of shape, center (mean), and spread (standard deviation) for each of the three samples?

Response:

■ *High school students:*

1. The shape of the distribution of their ages should be fairly symmetric but there may be a few unusually old seniors who had to repeat one or more years, resulting in a bit of right-skewness or a few high outliers. (Unusually young freshmen, although not impossible, would be quite rare.)

2. The mean would be somewhere around 16.

3. The standard deviation, or typical distance of all ages from this mean, would probably be about 1 year.

■ *High school seniors:*

1. The shape of the distribution of their ages would also have some right-skewness or high outliers, again because of students who had to repeat a year.

2. The mean would be around 17 or 18 (depending on what time of year they are surveyed).

3. The standard deviation would be a few months, because typically ages would differ from the mean by just a few months. Obviously, the ages of high school seniors would have much less spread than the ages of all high school students together, from freshmen to seniors.

■ *College students:*

1. The shape of the distribution of their ages would have more right-skewness and high outliers than the distribution for high school students: Most students graduate from high school in 4 years because of its mandatory nature, but it is quite common for students to take some time off before or during their time at college. Moreover, it has been found that, in fact, a majority of college students take more than 4 years to graduate. Therefore, although most college students are between 18 and 22, there would still be quite a few who are older. A histogram of the distribution could show quite a long right tail.

2. The mean would be somewhat inflated by the presence of some unusually old students, and so it would be somewhat higher than 20.

3. The standard deviation could be 2 or 3, because quite a few students' ages would be more than just 1 year away from 20 or so.

Students may get a better feel for the role played by the spread of a distribution if they compare histograms that have the same mean but very different standard deviations. A graph with an unrealistically small or large standard deviation can be sketched with the same scale as the original (correct) histogram, to illustrate how different they are. This example supplements Example 4.23 on page 102.

EXAMPLE TBP 4.7 PICTURING STANDARD DEVIATION

Background: Household size in the United States has a mean of approximately 2.5 people and a standard deviation of approximately 1.4 people.

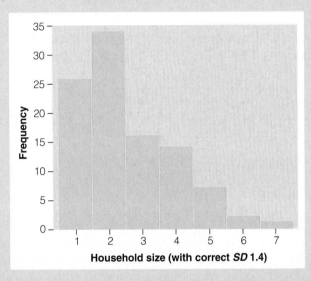

Questions: How would the histogram appear if the standard deviation were only 0.14 instead of 1.4? How would it appear if the standard deviation were 14.0?

Responses: If the standard deviation were only 0.14, household sizes would be bunched very closely around 2.5, hardly extending down to 2 or up to 3 people. The situation would look like the histogram on the left. If the standard deviation were 14.0, household sizes would vary below 2.5 all the way down to negative numbers, and above into sizes indicating dozens of people in the same household. A histogram would appear as the one on the right. Clearly, neither of these could be consistent with reality.

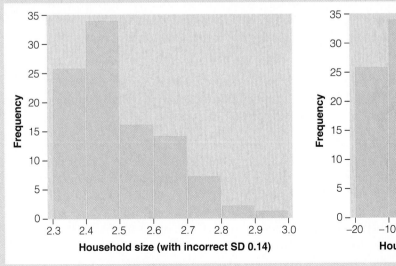

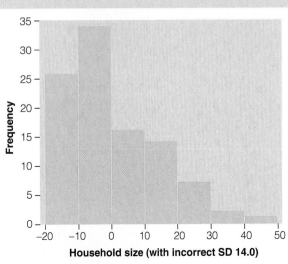

In Part III, which discusses probability, we will present a theory for the behavior of sample means and sample proportions. Under the right circumstances, their distributions will have a normal shape, even if the population of values does not. This result will enable us to apply rules for the behavior of normal distributions so that we can draw conclusions about population mean or proportion, based on sample mean or proportion. In order to draw formal conclusions, we will rely heavily on the theory that we will gradually develop. For now, students can use their intuition to make some educated guesses at whether or not a proposed value for the population mean is plausible. This pair of examples serves to preview typical inference questions, and demonstrate that intuition is the best way to start, but more is certainly needed to draw informed conclusions. They can be discussed after Example 4.28 on page 114, which distinguishes between the sample mean and the population mean.

EXAMPLE TBP 4.8 A PROPOSED POPULATION MEAN THAT IS PLAUSIBLE FOR A GIVEN SAMPLE MEAN

Background: A sample of 162 male college students had a mean weight of $\bar{x} = 171$ pounds.

Question: Are you willing to believe the claim (on one of many Internet sites devoted to such statistics) that mean weight of all adult males is $\mu = 170$ pounds?

Response: It should seem plausible that the population mean is 170, and our random sample produced a mean slightly higher by chance. However, in order to make a truly informed decision about the unknown population mean weight, additional information is needed—such as the relevant standard deviation, and whether or not the normal distribution applies. In Part IV of this book, on statistical inference, we learn to solve this type of problem.

EXAMPLE TBP 4.9 A PROPOSED POPULATION MEAN THAT IS IMPLAUSIBLE FOR A GIVEN SAMPLE MEAN

Background: A random sample of 19 female students at a university reported their weights for a survey. The reported mean was $\bar{x} = 129$ pounds.

Question: Does this sample mean seem consistent with the National Center for Health Statistics' report that mean weight of all young adult American females is $\mu = 142$ pounds?

Response: The difference between sample mean 129 pounds and reported population mean 142 pounds seems very large. In Part IV of this book, we revisit this example and, with the help of additional information on the spread of the distribution of weights, we will conclude that 129 and 142 are "significantly different": Either those students were not representative of the larger population studied by the NCHS, or perhaps they were tending to under-report their weights (a common phenomenon).

The Role of Sample Size: Why Some Means Tell Us More Than Others

Once we have distinguished between sample and population means in Example 4.28 on page 114, we can look ahead to inference by intuiting that a sample mean is better at pinning down the unknown value of the population mean if it arises from a larger sample.

EXAMPLE TBP 4.10 MEANS FROM DIFFERENT SAMPLE SIZES

Background: Suppose we want to convince someone that the mean running time of all new movies this year is less than 2 hours (120 minutes).

Question: Which of these would provide more convincing evidence that the mean running time of all movies is less than 120 minutes: if a random sample of 3 movies had a mean of only 112 minutes, or if a random sample of 30 movies had a mean of only 112 minutes?

Response: Even if the mean time of all movies was not less than 120 minutes, it's easy to imagine that if we sample only 3 movies, we may happen to get a sample mean as low as 112. On the other hand, it seems less likely to sample 30 movies and get a sample mean as low as 112, if the overall mean is not less than 120. Therefore, a mean of 112 minutes in a sample of 30 movies should provide more convincing evidence that the overall mean is less than 120 minutes.

Practice: *Try Exercise 4.55(c) on page 121.*

Details about the Normal Distribution

After the 68-95-99.7 Rule has been introduced on page 111, teachers may show students examples like this one, where the Empirical Rule is confirmed quite nicely. In contrast, data sets that are far from bell-shaped, like that in Exercise TBP 4.22 on page 785, can be shown to conform poorly to the rule.

EXAMPLE TBP 4.11 ASSESSING THE ACCURACY OF THE 68-95-99.7 RULE

Background: Recall our list of 19 female weights:

110 110 112 120 120 120 125 125 130 130 132 133 134 135 135 135 145 148 159

The stemplot looked fairly bell-shaped:

```
11 | 0  0  2
12 | 0  0  0  5  5
13 | 0  0  2  3  4  5  5  5
14 | 5  8
15 | 9
```

and we found the mean to be $\bar{x} = 129$ and standard deviation $s = 13$ (rounding to the nearest whole number).

Continued

Question: What does the 68-95-99.7 Rule tell us to expect for the distribution of weights, and how closely do the weights conform to the rule?

Response: According to the rule, approximately

- 68% of the weights should fall within 1 standard deviation of the mean: in the interval $(129 - 13, 129 + 13) = (116, 142)$;
- 95% of the weights should fall within 2 standard deviations of the mean: in the interval $(129 - 2(13), 129 + 2(13)) = (103, 155)$;
- 99.7% of the weights should fall within 3 standard deviations of the mean: in the interval $(129 - 3(13), 129 + 3(13)) = (90, 168)$.

In fact, the rule works quite well for this data set. The diagram below shows that 68% of the weights actually do fall within 1 standard deviation of the mean; 95% within 2 standard deviations, and 100% (which is, of course, quite close to 99.7%) fall within 3 standard deviations of the mean.

19/19 = 100% within 3 sds of mean (between 90 and 168)

18/19 = 95% within 2 sds of mean (between 103 and 155)

13/19 = 68% within 1 sd of mean (between 116 and 142)

110 110 112 120 120 120 125 125 130 130 132 133 134 135 135 135 145 148 159

Instructors who want their students to use normal tables can go beyond what's mentioned on page 119. The first normal table at the end of the book gives areas under the standard normal (z) curve to the left of z values $-3.0, -2.9, \cdots, -0.1$ and to the right of z values $+0.1, +0.2, \cdots, +3.0$. These are shown alongside a sketch of the normal curve, and it may be helpful to think of them as providing details to supplement the 68-95-99.7 Rule, which really only gives us the "tip of the iceberg." Whereas the rule can tell us that the proportion of normal values greater than 2 standard deviations above the mean is $(1 - 0.95)/2 = 0.025$, the table tells us that the proportion of normal values greater than 1.9 standard deviations above the mean is 0.0287, and the proportion greater than 2.1 standard deviations above the mean is 0.0179.

The second normal table gives areas under the z curve to the left of z values $-3.09, -3.08, \cdots, -0.01, 0.00$ and to the right of $+0.01, +0.02, \cdots, +3.00$. This table reveals even more of the "iceberg," providing details for z values to two decimal places instead of just one. For example, the first table tells us that the area to the left of $z = -2.10$ is 0.0179, whereas the second table tells us that the area to the left of $z = -2.11$ is 0.0174, the area to the left of $z = -2.12$ is 0.0170, and so on.

Because the normal curve is not flat, these proportions do not progress at a constant rate; nevertheless, we could say that the area to the left of -2.115 is approximately halfway between 0.0174 and 0.0170, or 0.0172. This estimation technique, called *interpolation*, was commonly practiced before software became available.

Here are some examples that utilize information from the standard normal table.

Example TBP 4.12 USING THE TABLE WHEN A Z-SCORE IS GIVEN

Background: In Example 4.30 on page 116, we used the 68-95-99.7 Rule to get a feel for the performances of two students whose z-scores on an exam were -0.4 and $+1.5$, respectively.

Question: What does the normal table tell us about the relative performances of these students?

Response: The normal table shows us that the proportion scoring less than $z = -0.4$ is 0.3446: about a third of all the students did worse than this score. The proportion scoring better than $z = +1.5$ is 0.0668: This student's score is at roughly the top 7% of the class.

Practice: *Try Exercise 4.71 on page 124.*

EXAMPLE TBP 4.13 USING THE TABLE WHEN AN ORIGINAL VALUE IS GIVEN

Background: Male foot lengths (in inches) have mean 11 and standard deviation 1.5.

Question: What does the normal table tell us about the relative size of a male's foot that is 7 inches long?

Response: First we find $z = \frac{7 - 11}{1.5} = -2.67$. Then we look in the normal table to find that the proportion below $z = -2.67$ is 0.0038. Less than half a percent of all males have feet that short.

Practice: *Try Exercise 4.100 on page 131.*

Because -2.67 is between -3 and -2, the 68-95-99.7 Rule would tell us that the proportion of foot lengths less than this is somewhere between $(1 - 0.997)/2 = 0.0015$ and $(1 - 0.95)/2 = 0.025$. The table gives more accuracy, but with the rule you can estimate proportions or percentages in your head.

Besides using the table to find the proportion of normal values in a certain interval, we can also use it to solve problems in the other direction. That is, given a certain proportion above or below, we can report the corresponding z value.

EXAMPLE TBP 4.14 USING THE TABLE WHEN A PROPORTION IS GIVEN

Background: Male foot lengths, in inches, have a mean of 11 and a standard deviation of 1.5.

Question: What is the cutoff length for the longest 4% of males' feet?

Response: First we look for the proportion 0.04 inside the table. The closest we can find is 0.0401. Because this corresponds to a z value of $+1.75$, we know that the longest 4% are more than 1.75 standard deviations above the mean—that is, longer than $11 + 1.75(1.5) = 13.625$ inches.

Practice: *Try Exercise 4.69 on page 124.*

There are a variety of ways normal tables can present information. Instead of showing probabilities of exceeding a certain z value in either direction, some show *cumulative* proportions or percentages. That is, they only report the proportion *below* a certain *z* value, whether *z* is positive or negative. The third normal table shows these cumulative probabilities.

A few textbooks show proportions *within* a certain distance of $z = 0$. Also, some textbooks only present proportions for *positive z* values, assuming that students can solve problems with negative *z* values by invoking the symmetry of the normal curve.

4.2 Activities

Activity: Displaying and Summarizing Data

Find (and distribute) a newspaper or journal article or Internet report about a study that involves a single quantitative variable *whose values are specified*. Discuss how the data were produced—was it an experiment or an observational study? Discuss if results are being reported for a sample or for an entire population. Discuss if there is reason to suspect bias that arises if the sample is not representative, or bias in the design for assessing the variable's values. Display the data with a stemplot, histogram, and/or boxplot and discuss the center, spread, and shape of the distribution as evidenced in the display.

Activity: Displaying and Summarizing Data; Assessing Conformity with the 68-95-99.7 Rule

Find (and distribute) a newspaper or journal article or Internet report about a study that involves a single quantitative variable *whose values are specified*. Discuss how the data were produced—was it an experiment or an observational study? Discuss if the variable is summarized with mean, median, or neither. Use software to find the mean and standard deviation of the data set. Display the data and discuss the shape of the distribution. Report how well or badly the data set conforms to the 68-95-99.7 Rule. Discuss if results are being reported for a sample or for an entire population. Is there reason to suspect bias that arises if the sample is not representative, or bias in the design for assessing the variable's values?

Activity: z-scores for Normal and Non-normal Data

1. Assume all female heights (in inches) to have mean 65 and standard deviation 2.5. Each female in the class uses a calculator to find her *z*-score for height and reports it to the class. Together the class constructs a histogram to display all the *z*-scores and comments on its shape, noting whether there are both large negative and large positive *z*-scores. Determine what percentage of *z*-scores are less than 1, 2, and 3 in absolute value to see how well females' heights in the class conform to the 68-95-99.7 Rule. Discuss whether results would differ for a larger class.

2. Assume all male heights (in inches) to have mean 70 and standard deviation 3. The class examines *z*-scores for male heights as done for females in part (1).

3. Students report data on the number of minutes spent watching TV the day before (or doing school work, or on the computer, or on the phone), and the leader uses a calculator to find the mean and standard deviation. Students calculate and report their individual *z*-scores, then the class constructs a histogram for the data, comments on its shape, and notes whether there are both large negative and large positive *z*-scores. Deter-

mine what percentage of *z*-scores are less than 1, 2, and 3 in absolute value to check conformity with the 68-95-99.7 Rule. Discuss whether results would differ for a larger class.

4. Depending on how much time is available, students examine their *z*-scores for other variables such as number of hours slept the night before (to the nearest half hour), age in years (to the nearest tenth), number of siblings, credits taken, etc.

4.3 Guide to Exercise Topics

Single categorical variables: 4.1, 4.2, 4.3*, 4.4*, 4.5, 4.6*, 4.7*, 4.8, 4.9, 4.10, 4.11, 4.12, 4.13, 4.14*, 4.15, 4.16, 4.81, 4.82, 4.84, 4.85, 4.86

Single quantitative variables and the shape of a distribution: 4.19*, 4.20*, 4.21*, 4.22, 4.23, 4.24, 4.26*, 4.27(a), 4.32(a), 4.50(a), 4.62*, 4.63, 4.89, 4.97

Center and spread of a distribution: 4.26*, 4.27, 4.28*, 4.29*, 4.30*, 4.31, 4.32, 4.33, 4.34*, 4.35, 4.37, 4.38*, 4.39, 4.40, 4.41, 4.42*, 4.43, 4.44*, 4.45, 4.98, 4.99

Normal distributions: 4.46*, 4.47, 4.48*, 4.49, 4.50, 4.51, 4.52*, 4.53, 4.54*, 4.55*, 4.56, 4.57, 4.58, 4.59*, 4.60, 4.61, 4.62*, 4.63, 4.64, 4.65*, 4.66, 4.67, 4.91, 4.92, 4.93, 4.94*, 4.95, 4.96

Using the normal table: 4.68, 4.69*, 4.70, 4.71*, 4.72, 4.73, 4.74*, 4.75, 4.76, 4.100*, 4.101

4.4 Supplemental Exercises

4.1 In 2004, Congress approved a $6 million budget for the promotion of international tourism in the United States with a marketing campaign that is based on pop culture. The U.S. Department of Commerce's Office of Travel and Tourism Industries studied the origins and destinations of international tourists to the United States in 2003:

- 12.66 million from Canada, 9.67 million from Mexico, 18.03 million from overseas
- 23.3% to Florida, 23.3% to New York state, 22.1% to California, 10.8% to Hawaii, 7.6% to Nevada
- 22.1% to New York City, 11.8% to Los Angeles, 11.5% to Miami, 9.8% to Orlando, 9.4% to San Francisco

a. Origins are reported in counts; convert them to percents.

b. What percentage of tourists visited other parts of New York state besides New York City?

c. What percentage of tourists visited other parts of Florida besides Miami and Orlando?

d. Does this pie chart depict the information for destinations that are states or cities?

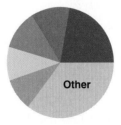

4.2 National Football League coaches are supposed to classify injured players as being "doubtful" if their chance of playing in the next game is 25%, "questionable" if the chance is 50%, and "probable" if the chance is 75%.

a. Are the percentages 25%, 50%, and 75% statistics or parameters?

b. Of 20 players listed as "doubtful" on a Friday in November 2004, just 1 played in the next game. Does the percentage conform well to the 25% chance that presumably applies to these players?

c. Of 76 players listed as "questionable," 37 played in the next game. Does the percentage conform well to the 50% chance that presumably applies to these players?

d. Of 88 players listed as "probable," 83 played in the next game. Does the percentage conform well to the 75% chance that presumably applies to these players?

e. Which one classification is apparently used more often than it should be by the NFL coaches—doubtful, questionable, or probable? Explain.

4.3 National Football League coaches classify their injured players as "doubtful," "questionable," or "probable," depending on their likelihood of playing in the next game.

a. 5% of players listed as "doubtful" on a particular Friday were able to play in Sunday's game. Would this be fairly helpful in persuading someone that for all the weeks that year, a minority of players listed as "doubtful" were able to play?

b. 49% of players listed as "questionable" on a particular Friday were able to play in Sunday's game. Would this be fairly helpful in persuading someone that for all the weeks that year, a minority of players listed as "questionable" were able to play?

c. What do we call the process whereby results from a single week are used to make a general statement about all weeks?

4.4 In 2004, the U.S. Census Bureau reported that 27% of adults age 25 and older have a college degree. It also compared percentages with at least a high school education in the 50 states: The highest was New Hampshire, with 92.1% having a high school diploma, followed closely by Minnesota and Wyoming. West Virginia, with 78.7%, was next to the bottom.

a. Keeping in mind that the information comes from the U.S. Census Bureau, should we treat the above percentages as statistics or parameters?

b. Is the above information treating college education as a quantitative or a categorical variable? Who or what are the individuals studied?

c. Is the above information treating high school education as a quantitative or a categorical variable? Who or what are the individuals studied?

d. Make a general statement about high school and college education in the United States, using the words "minority" and "majority."

e. Why is the information about high school education in the various states reported as percents rather than counts?

f. Why would a pie chart be impractical if we wanted to convey what percentage of the U.S. population resides in each of the 50 states?

4.5 A *New York Times* article from June 1, 2004, entitled "New York Fiction, by the Numbers" tells about an undergraduate engineering student at Princeton who performed a statistical analysis of stories published in *The New Yorker* under two different editors. She focused on many variables, such as writer's gender, characters' religion, and main story topics. The percentages of topics for stories published between 1995 and 2001 were listed as follows:

Sex	Children	Travel	Drugs	Money	Religion	Illness
47%	26%	25%	5%	10%	9%	12%

Find what the percentages add up to, and explain why it is more than 100%.

4.6 "Contraception Shots Work in Male Monkeys" tells about an injection that results in levels of certain antibodies that are high enough to prevent conception. "In the experiments, designed in the United States and carried out in India, seven of the nine males tested developed high antibody levels. Five of the seven recovered fertility once the immunization stopped."[1]

a. What percentage of the monkeys studied were apparently rendered infertile on a more permanent basis?

b. Obviously, the most important aspect of the contraception shots that must be tested is whether or not they are effective in preventing conception. Manufacturers would not want to make the mistake of claiming the shots to be effective when they are not; nor would they want to make the mistake of concluding the shots to be ineffective when they actually work. Which of these mistakes would be more harmful in general?

c. Another important aspect of the contraception shots that must be tested is whether or not they produce unwanted side effects, such as permanent infertility. Manufacturers would not want to make the mistake of concluding that the shots cause permanent infertility when in fact they actually don't; nor would they want to make the mistake of concluding that the shots do not cause permanent infertility when they actually do. Which of these mistakes would be more harmful in general?

d. Which type of error are we more at risk to make due to the sample size being so small: concluding there *are* side effects when in fact there are *not,* or concluding there are *not* side effects when in fact there *are*?

4.7 A 4-year study in a private school in a certain city led to the newspaper report "Study Finds Sea of Strep; Some Kids Just Carriers." According to the report, "six out of every 10 students tested positive for strep at least once during a school year" but "a bit more than half of those who tested positive had no symptoms."[2]

a. The study included 125 children. Approximately what number tested positive for strep at least once during a school year?

b. Was the number of children who tested positive but had no symptoms closer to 10, 20, 30, 40, or 50?

c. Why should we hesitate to conclude that six out of every 10 students in all schools in that city would test positive for strep at least once during a school year?

d. The article explains that researchers swabbed the students' throats every 2 weeks of the school year for 4 years. Explain the difficulties that would be involved in studying a sample of children that is more representative of all the city's school children.

4.8 This display shows costs for adult weekend ski lift tickets in various resorts in the Middle Atlantic states for the winter of 2004.

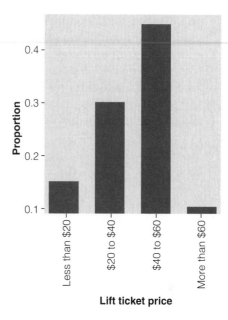

Explain why this graph should be called a bar graph, *not* a histogram.

4.9 Data have been gathered on the amount for which 5,000 New Orleans slaves were sold during the first half of the 19th century.

a. Explain why a histogram or boxplot would be a better display tool than a stemplot.

b. If we want a display that calls attention to amounts that are high outliers, should we use a histogram or a boxplot?

c. If we want a display that gives a clear picture of the shape of the distribution, should we use a histogram or a boxplot?

d. When deciding whether to use a histogram or boxplot, are we mainly concerned with data production, displaying and summarizing data, probability, or statistical inference?

4.10 Data have been gathered on ages of eight Olympic beach volleyball players.

a. Explain why a histogram or stemplot would be a better display tool than a boxplot.

b. If we want a display that lets us see specific age values, should we use a histogram or a stemplot?

c. When deciding whether to use a histogram or stemplot, are we mainly concerned with data production, displaying and summarizing data, probability, or statistical inference?

4.11 Here are stemplots for estimated weights (in thousands of kilograms) for 20 dinosaur specimens, ranging from 30 to 5,654 kilograms, and for body mass index (BMI) of 13 of our nation's presidents, from 17.0 for James Madison to 42.3 for William Howard Taft. [BMI is a way of measuring body fat, taking weight and height into account.]

```
Dinosaurs          Presidents
 0  00124677       1  79
 1  01125778       2  12334
 2  9              2  5688
 3  2              3  0
 4                 3
 5  06             4  2
```

a. What is the most obvious similarity between the two stemplots?

b. In order to understand weights of dinosaurs, which additional information would be helpful—species of dinosaur, age at death, or both of these?

c. In 1998 the National Heart Institute redefined the limit for being considered overweight as having a BMI of 25 or over. By this criterion, what percentage of those 13 presidents would be considered overweight?

d. The article "Tell the Truth: Does This Index Make Me Look Fat?" states that almost half of all American presidents have been overweight by this standard. Is the sample of 13 BMI values consistent with the article's summary?

e. The official limit for being considered not just overweight, but obese, is having a BMI of 35 or over. How many of these presidents would be considered obese by this criterion?

4.12 Researchers Robert W. Fogel and Stanley L. Engerman investigated over 20,000 slave hires in various southern states between the years 1785 and 1865, with number of hires peaking around the year 1860. Generally the hiring period lasted a year. This histogram displays the hiring prices listed in transaction documents.

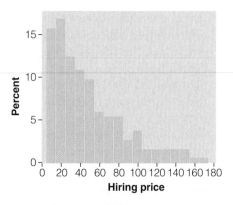

a. Half of the hiring prices were how many dollars or less—35, 65, or 95?

b. If the mean hiring price was $44, assuming this was for one year's time, what was the mean hiring price per day?

4.13 Here are data for the elevation (in meters) of 18 volcanoes around the world:

Volcano	Elevation	Volcano	Elevation
Etna	3,340	Mt. Fuji	3,776
Hekla	1,491	Mt. Rainier	4,392
Kilauea	4,000	Mt. Shasta	4,322
Krakatoa	813	Mt. St. Helens	2,550
Mauna Loa	4,170	Novarupta	841
Mauna Kea	4,205	Surtsey	174
Mt. Baker	3,285	Tanbora	2,850
Mt. Erebus	3,794	Teide	3,717
Mt. Hood	3,429	Vesuvius	1,281

a. Display the data with a stemplot, first truncating the tens and ones digits, then using thousands for stems and hundreds for leaves.

b. Display the data with a stemplot constructed as above but with stems split in two.

c. Report the five-number summary values.

d. Use the 1.5 × IQR Rule to determine which values, if any, should be considered outliers.

e. Would the distribution best be described as left-skewed, having low outliers, symmetric, right-skewed, or having high outliers?

f. Explain why the mean (2,913) is so much less than the median (3,384.5).

g. Sketch a boxplot of the data.

4.14   Another form of display tool is the dotplot, which records each quantitative data value as a dot over a horizontal axis. Which would give you a better picture of the shape of the distribution of volcano elevations: a stemplot as constructed in Exercise TBP 4.13, or the dotplot shown below?

4.15   Here is a data set for salaries (in thousands of dollars) of our nation's 42 presidents, starting with George Washington in 1789 and ending with Barack Obama in 2008.

25	25	25	25	25	25	25	25	25	25	25	25	25	25
25	25	25	38	50	50	50	50	50	50	75	75	75	75
75	75	88	100	100	100	200	200	200	200	200	200	400	400

   a. Report the five-number summary values.

   b. Use the $1.5 \times IQR$ Rule to determine which values, if any, should be considered outliers.

   c. Sketch a boxplot of the data.

   d. Explain why the mean (85.7) is so much higher than the median (50).

   e. The mean is 85.7 and the standard deviation is about 91. Explain why it is not possible for a president's salary to have a z-score less than -1.

   f. Should we think of these summaries as statistics (describing a sample) or parameters (describing a population)?

   g. For a better understanding of the data, which one of these additional variables would be most useful to consider: president's age when in office, year that president was elected, or number of popular votes received?

   h. The standard deviation of salaries is 91 thousand dollars. Suppose all the salaries were adjusted for inflation—for example, George Washington's salary of 25 thousand (which, by the way, he refused) would be comparable to roughly 238 thousand dollars in the year 2008. Would the standard deviation of the adjusted data set still be 91?

   i. If we take inflation into account, which president received more pay: Richard Nixon, who became president in 1969 with a salary of $200,000, or Bill Clinton, who became president in 1993 with a salary of $200,000?

4.16   "Pace Affects Pedometer Accuracy" tells of a 2004 *Consumer Reports* review of a dozen pedometers: "only three out of the 12 were accurate within 5% when used at 2.5 mph" and "some were off by as much as 2 miles when they reached 5 miles (either registering 3 miles or up to 7)."

   a. One approach taken by *Consumer Reports* was to consider each pedometer in terms of a categorical variable. Tell what that variable is, and how it is summarized.

   b. Another approach taken by *Consumer Reports* was to consider each pedometer in terms of a quantitative variable. Is there more concern about the mean of that variable, or about its standard deviation? Explain.

4.17   A newspaper reported on the fact that incoming freshmen at the local university were better qualified than before: "The average SAT score for all freshmen entering in fall 2004 was 1231, up from 1213 last year. Forty-six percent of the students were in the top 10 percent of their high school classes, compared with 43 percent last year."[3]

   a. One approach to show that students in 2004 were better qualified was to cite changes in a categorical variable. Tell what that variable is, and how it is summarized.

   b. Another approach to show that students in 2004 were better qualified was to cite changes in a quantitative variable. Tell what that variable is, and how it is summarized.

4.18 Exercise TBP 4.12 on page 782 considered data on slave *hires*; the same researchers also investigated a sample of 5,000 slave *sales* in New Orleans between the years 1804 and 1862. This histogram displays the amounts on the notarized bills of sale stored in the New Orleans Notarial Archival Office.

a. Two measures of center are found to be $650 and $700. Use the shape of the histogram to report which one of these is the mean.

b. Half of the selling prices were how many dollars or less?

c. Exercise TBP 4.12 reported that the mean *hiring* price (typically for the period of one year) of slaves was $44. Why is the mean selling price more than 10 times greater than the mean hiring price?

4.19 "Bad News for Women Here" reports that a certain city is a fairly unhealthy place for women: "Smoking was the biggest pitfall. Women here on average smoked 121 cigarettes a month, compared with a national average of 93."[4]

a. In this instance, smoking is handled as a quantitative variable, summarized with an average (mean). How is it usually handled and summarized?

b. The average number of cigarettes reported takes *all* women, not just smokers, into account. Suppose a sample of 100 women from that city averages 121 cigarettes in a month, and that sample includes 25 smokers and 75 non-smokers. [Roughly 25% of American adults smoke.] How many cigarettes per month do the smokers average?

c. If we assume there are 30 days in a month, how many cigarettes a day do the smoking women average?

d. Suppose a sample of 100 women in the nation average 93 cigarettes a month, and this sample also includes 25 smokers and 75 nonsmokers. How many cigarettes a day do the smoking women average?

4.20 This output was produced to summarize contributions made on a day in early December to a newspaper's "Goodfellows Toy Fund," which buys toys for underprivileged children.

Variable	N	Mean	Median	TrMean	StDev	SE Mean
Contribution	111	59.2	25.0	40.3	111.6	10.6
Variable	Minimum	Maximum	Q1	Q3		
Contribution	20.0	1000.0	25.0	50.0		

a. How many contributions were made that day?

b. Use two of the numbers shown in order to find what the total contributions were that day.

c. Would a display of the data show the distribution to be skewed left/having low outliers, or roughly symmetric, or skewed right/having high outliers?

d. Half of the contributions were no more than how many dollars?

e. The top 25% of the contributions were more than how many dollars?

f. How would the fact that the first quartile and the median are equal (both 25) affect the appearance of a boxplot of the data?

g. If a reporter wants to give readers the impression that typical donations are larger, will he/she report the mean or the median contribution?

4.21 Part (e) of Exercise TBP 4.20 asked you to find the value for which 25% of charitable toy fund contributions were higher. Besides showing values for the quartiles, the output also shows the mean to be $59.2 and standard deviation $111.60.

a. Use the normal table or a computer to find the *z* value corresponding to the top 25% of a normal distribution.

b. If the distribution of contributions were normal, for what value would 25% be higher?

c. Is your answer to part (b) reasonably close to the actual value for the top 25%?

4.22 This table, posted on the Internet by nationmaster.com in 2004, shows the number of McDonald's restaurants in 39 countries.

Country	Number of McDonald's
United States	12,804
Japan	3,598
Canada	1,154
United Kingdom	1,115
Germany	1,091
France	857
Australia	701
Taiwan	338
China	326
Italy	290
Spain	276
South Korea	243
Philippines	235
Sweden	227
Netherlands	205
Mexico	205
Poland	181
Hong Kong	177
New Zealand	149
Austria	148
Malaysia	139
Turkey	133
Singapore	121
Switzerland	119
Denmark	99

Country	Number of McDonald's
Finland	93
Portugal	91
Thailand	88
Hungary	76
Indonesia	75
Belgium	64
Ireland	62
Czech Republic	60
Norway	55
Greece	48
Slovakia	10
Luxembourg	6
Iceland	3
Brunei	1

a. Half of the countries have a number of McDonald's restaurants less than or equal to what value?

b. The mean number of McDonald's is 658. Find what percentage of countries have a number of McDonald's restaurants less than or equal to this number.

c. Explain why the median is a better report of what is "typical" for this data set than the mean.

d. The standard deviation for number of McDonald's is 2,089. Find the *z*-score for the smallest number in the data set; find the *z*-score for the largest number in the data set.

e. Find what percentage of the 39 values are within just 1 standard deviation of their mean.

f. Explain why the 68-95-99.7 Rule does not work well for this data set.

g. The United States is an extreme high outlier. Should it be removed from the data set? Explain.

4.23 "Conflict of Interest Discovered in New Cholesterol Guidelines" expresses concern that "most of the heart disease experts who urged more people to take cholesterol-lowering drugs this week have made money from the companies selling those medications [. . .] The new guidelines . . .

were written by nine of the country's top cholesterol experts. At least six have received consulting or speaking fees, research money, or other support from makers of the most widely used anti-cholesterol drugs. The new guidelines would add about 7 million more Americans to the 36 million already encouraged to take the pills to lower their cholesterol . . ."[5] The guidelines, updated in 2004, recommend that people with high risk of heart attack get their level of LDL (bad) cholesterol "below 100, instead of the current goal of below 130."

a. Some sources report LDL cholesterol levels to have mean 160, standard deviation 30, and a shape that is normal. Use the 68-95-99.7 Rule to sketch a curve for this distribution, marking off the levels that are within 1, 2, and 3 standard deviations of the mean.

b. What percentage of the levels would be low enough by the previous standards, which recommended LDL cholesterol levels below 130?

c. What percentage of the levels would be low enough by the new standards, which recommend LDL cholesterol levels below 100?

d. Discuss the harmful consequences of setting a level that is not as low as it should be for determining which patients at risk for heart attacks should take preventive medication.

e. Discuss the harmful consequences of setting a level that is lower than it needs to be for determining which patients at risk for heart attacks should take preventive medication.

4.24 Illiteracy rates for adult men and women in a sample of 19 countries were recorded:

| Men: | 1.0 | 4.1 | 7.5 | 32.7 | 45.9 | 1.1 | 17.0 | 23.8 | 0.2 | 0.3 | 3.0 | 76.2 | 19.6 | 1.0 | 0.3 | 26.4 | 1.1 | 18.6 | 7.2 |
| Women: | 2.1 | 4.4 | 25.6 | 55.5 | 76.5 | 1.9 | 31.1 | 46.6 | 0.2 | 0.5 | 2.2 | 91.5 | 16.9 | 2.7 | 0.6 | 39.6 | 2.3 | 39.4 | 15.4 |

a. There are actually two variables of interest here. Tell what they are, whether they are quantitative or categorical, and which is explanatory and which is response.

b. Report the mean and median illiteracy rates for the men, and tell which does a better job of reporting what is typical.

c. Report the mean and median illiteracy rates for the women, and tell which does a better job of reporting what is typical.

d. Explain how the relative sizes of mean and median indicate that the distribution for women has more right skewness or high outliers than that for the men.

e. Obtain boxplots for both data sets. Only one of the data sets can be characterized as having a high outlier. Is it the data set for men or women?

4.25 Some physical characteristics, like shoe size, naturally follow a normal shape for specific age and gender groups. Use software to access the student survey data and complete the following tasks.

a. Find the mean and standard deviation for shoe sizes of all surveyed students.

b. Separate the data by gender and find the mean and standard deviation for shoe sizes of surveyed females.

c. Find the mean and standard deviation for shoe sizes of surveyed males.

d. Is the combined mean halfway between the mean for females and males, or closer to that for females, or closer to that for males? Explain how this result is affected by the relative numbers of females and males surveyed.

e. Is the combined standard deviation less than the individual standard deviations, in between them, or more than the individual standard deviations?

f. Report medians for all surveyed students, for females only, and for males only. For which group is the mean noticeably higher than the median?

4.5 Solutions to Supplemental Exercises

4.1 **a.** Canada 31%, Mexico 24%, overseas 45%
b. 1.2% **c.** 2.0% **d.** cities

4.2 **a.** parameters **b.** 1/20 = 5% does not conform
well because it is not close to 25%. **c.** 37/76 =
49% does conform well because it is close to
50%. **d.** 83/88 = 94% does not conform well
because it is not close to 75%. **e.** "Probable"
(94% is much higher than 75%)

4.3 **a.** Yes, because 5% is so much less than 50%.
b. No, because 49% is not much less than 50%.
c. statistical inference

4.4 **a.** parameters **b.** categorical, with individuals
being adults in the U.S. age 25 and over
c. quantitative, with individuals being states
d. A majority of U.S. adults age 25 and over
have a high school education, and a minority
have a college degree. **e.** Percents are used,
rather than counts, because states have very
different population sizes. **f.** because there are
too many (50) different values

4.5 134%, more than 100% because some stories
dealt with more than one of those topics

4.6 **a.** 2 out of 9, or 22% **b.** Claiming the shots to
be effective when they are not is more harmful.
c. Concluding that the shots do not cause
permanent infertility when they actually do
would be more harmful. **d.** concluding there
are not side effects when in fact there are

4.7 **a.** 60% of 125 is 75. **b.** A bit more than half of
75 is about 40. **c.** This was not a representative
sample, and because strep is a contagious disease,
certain schools could have disproportionately
high numbers of students with strep throats.
d. It would be much more expensive and time-
consuming to swab the throats of students in a
sample of schools throughout the city every
two weeks.

4.8 This graph is not a histogram because the
variable of interest (lift ticket costs) is treated as
categorical groups.

4.9 **a.** A stemplot would be impractical for such a
large data set. **b.** boxplot **c.** histogram
d. displaying and summarizing data

4.10 **a.** The data set is too small for a boxplot.
b. A stemplot lets us see specific age values.
c. displaying and summarizing data

4.11 **a.** The most obvious similarity between the two
stemplots is the presence of right-skewness/high
outliers. **b.** Both species of dinosaur and age at
death should help explain weight.
c. 6/13 = 0.46 **d.** Yes, because 0.46 is almost
half. **e.** just one (Taft at 42)

4.12 **a.** 35 **b.** 44/365 = 0.12 (12 cents)

4.13 **a.** 0 188
         1 24
         2 58
         3 234777
         4 01233

b. 0 1
        0 88
        1 24
        1
        2
        2 58
        3 234
        3 777
        4 01233

c. 174 1,491 3,384.5 4,000 4,392 **d.** 1,491 −
1.5(4,000 − 1,491) = −2,272.5 (no low outliers);
4,000 + 1.5(4,000 − 1,491) = 7,763.5 (no high
outliers) **e.** left-skewed **f.** The mean is so
much less than the median because of the left-
skewness.

g.

4.14 The stemplot gives more detail of shape because
the dotplot doesn't make peaks obvious.

4.15 **a.** 25, 25, 50, 100, 400 **b.** $IQR = 75$; $1.5 \times
IQR = 112.5$; $Q1 − 1.5 \times IQR = −87.5$ so of
course there are no low outliers. $Q3 + 1.5 \times
IQR = 100 + 112.5 = 212.5$ so the two salaries
of 400 thousand are designated as outliers.

c.

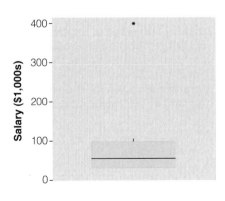

d. The mean is much higher than the median because the distribution is very right-skewed, with high outliers.   **e.** 1 standard deviation below the mean is already a negative number ($85.7 - 1(91) = -5.3$); negative salaries are not possible.   **f.** These are parameters, summarizing salaries of all presidents.   **g.** Because of inflation, we should take into account year that the president was elected.   **h.** No; adjusting for inflation would reduce the spread.   **i.** Nixon

4.16   **a.** Whether or not the pedometer was accurate within 5% when used at 2.5 mph is the categorical variable, summarized with the proportion 3/12.   **b.** There is more concern about the standard deviation of the variable that tells what distance was registered when the pedometer was worn for 5 miles.

4.17   **a.** The categorical variable is whether or not the students were in the top 10 percent of their high school classes, summarized with percents (from 43% in 2003 to 46% in 2004).   **b.** The quantitative variable is SAT score, summarized with mean (average went from 1213 to 1231).

4.18   **a.** $700 (it is greater than the median because of right-skewness)   **b.** $650 (the median)   **c.** because an owner would count on many years' labor from a slave

4.19   **a.** Smoking is usually handled as a categorical variable (smoker or not), summarized with a proportion.   **b.** $(121 \times 100)/25 = 484$ **c.** $484/30 = 16.1$ **d.** $(93 \times 100)/25 = 372$ per month; $372/30 = 12.4$ per day

4.20   **a.** 111   **b.** $111(59.2) = 6{,}571$ **c.** skewed right/having high outliers   **d.** 25 (the median)   **e.** 50 (the third quartile Q_3)   **f.** You wouldn't see a line through the box.   **g.** mean because it is higher

4.21   **a.** $+0.67$ **b.** 133.97   **c.** No; 133.97 is far from the third quartile, 50.

4.22   **a.** Half are less than or equal to the median, 148.   **b.** $32/39 = 82\%$ are less than or equal to 658.   **c.** The median's value is not distorted by the extremely high values at the top of the list; the mean is inflated by these values, and only a small percentage (18%) are this high or higher.   **d.** The z-score for the smallest number is $(1 - 658)/2{,}089 = -0.3$; the z-score for the largest number is $(12{,}804 - 658)/2{,}089 = +5.81$.   **e.** $37/39 = 95\%$ of the values are within 1 standard deviation of the mean.   **f.** The 68-95-99.7 Rule does not apply because the data set is far from normal.   **g.** No, the United States should not be removed; it is, in a way, the most important value in the data set, in terms of seeing how many McDonald's there are in the world.

4.23   **a.** Curve is centered at 160; from left to right mark levels of 70, 100, 130, 160, 190, 220, 250 to indicate levels within 1, 2, and 3 standard deviations of the mean.

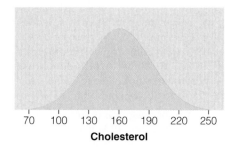

Cholesterol

b. Percentage below 130 is 16%.   **c.** Percentage below 100 is 2.5%.   **d.** If the level is not as low as it should be, people at high risk are not taking steps to prevent heart attacks.   **e.** If the level is lower than it needs to be, people are taking medication that they do not necessarily need.

4.24   **a.** Gender is explanatory and categorical; illiteracy rate is response and quantitative.   **b.** mean 18.8, median 17; median probably better because mean seems inflated   **c.** mean 29.3, median 25.6; median probably better because mean seems inflated   **d.** The distribution for women apparently has more right-skewness or high outliers than that for the men because its mean is relatively high compared to the median.   **e.** the one for the men

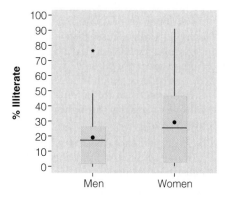

4.25   **a.** mean 9.1056, standard deviation 1.9484   **b.** mean 8.0053, standard deviation 1.2105   **c.** mean 11.009, standard deviation 1.452   **d.** closer to that for females because there are more females   **e.** more than the individual standard deviations   **f.** All students' median is 9; females' median is 8; males' median is 11; mean is noticeably higher for all students.

TBP Chapter 5
Displaying and Summarizing Relationships

5.1 Details and Examples

One Categorical and One Quantitative Variable

Display Alternatives

Other displays besides side-by-side boxplots, introduced on page 136, are sometimes used for relationships between a categorical explanatory and quantitative response variable. If there are only two groups being compared, a "back-to-back stemplot" may be constructed, with both sets of values sharing the same list of stems. Leaves for one group precede the stems right to left, and leaves for the other group follow the stems left to right. This is a useful tool for displaying distributions by hand only when the data sets are small.

An alternative for data from a two-sample design is to superimpose histograms for the two groups, using the same horizontal scale. This technique can give a good picture for comparison and is available in some software packages. It would be quite tedious to produce by hand.

When Gender and Age Arise from a Two-Sample Design

The following example serves as a contrast to the example featured in Students Talk Stats on page 139, in which the relationship between *parents'* genders and ages was identified as coming from a paired design.

EXAMPLE TBP 5.1 REVIEWING TWO-SAMPLE DISPLAYS AND SUMMARIES

Background: Survey data include information on students' ages and genders.

Question: What displays and summaries would be appropriate if we wanted to compare the ages of male and female students?

Response: Side-by-side boxplots could be used for display. Because ages have right-skewness and high outliers, we could compare five-number summaries.

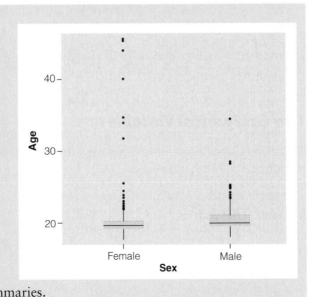

Continued

The ages of males and females seem comparable—perhaps the males are a bit older, looking at the vertical positions of the two boxes. On the other hand, the females have several high outliers that are noticeably higher than those for the males, indicating that our sample included several women in their forties.

Two-Sample Output

Because of the pivotal role played by spreads of distributions in situations like Example 5.5 on page 141, it is important to get into the habit of scrutinizing not just means but also standard deviations of quantitative data. This will be the focus of our next example.

EXAMPLE TBP 5.2 HOW STANDARD DEVIATIONS TELL SPREADS

Background: These summaries correspond to the boxplots on the left and right, respectively, in Example 5.5 on page 141.

```
Side-by-side boxplots on left (large amounts of spread)
Variable            N         Mean        StDev
Gum                29         83.62       12.30
NoGum              27         78.81       14.21

Side-by-side boxplots on right (small amounts of spread)
Variable            N         Mean        StDev
Gum                29         83.62       3.005
NoGum              27         78.81       3.793
```

Question: How do the means and standard deviations compare for the boxplot on the left versus the one on the right?

Response: Pairwise, means are the same ($\bar{x}_1 = 83.62$ versus $\bar{x}_2 = 78.81$) in both sets of output. However, standard deviations differ dramatically: $s_1 = 12.30$ and $s_2 = 14.21$ for the data represented in the boxplot on the left, $s_1 = 3.005$ and $s_2 = 3.793$ for the data represented in the boxplot on the right.

Practice: *Try Exercise 5.15(g) on page 148.*

Two Categorical Variables

This example goes into more detail regarding the table of observed counts featured in Example 5.14 on page 157.

EXAMPLE TBP 5.3 COMPARING PERCENTAGES IN A TWO-WAY TABLE

Background: Polls conducted in the United States in 2002 by Princeton Data Source, and in Canada by Environics, asked whether people agreed with the statement, "It is necessary to believe in God to be moral."

[Only about 2% did not respond, and they are included with those who answered 'No.']

	It is necessary to believe in God to be moral...		
	Yes	No (or no answer)	Total
U.S.	870	630	1,500
Canada	150	350	500
Total	1,020	980	2,000

We consider nationality to be the explanatory variable, and whether or not people agree that it is necessary to believe in God to be moral is the response.

Questions: Which country had a higher *count* answering no (or no answer)? Which country had a higher *percentage* answering no (or no answer)? What can we say about the relative percentages answering yes?

Responses: The *count* of Americans answering No or no answer (630) is almost twice as high as the *count* of Canadians answering No or no answer (350). Nevertheless, the *percentage* of Americans with this response is only 630/1500 = 42%, as opposed to 350/500 = 70% for the Canadians.

If we compare percentages answering Yes, we see they are 870/1,500 = 58% for the United States, and 150/500 = 30% for Canada, so the rate of agreement with the statement was almost twice as high in the United States as it was in Canada. As far as a comparative summary of the data is concerned, the percentages give us a good idea of how nationality played a role in whether or not someone agreed that it was necessary to believe in God to be moral.

Practice: *Try Exercise 5.26 on page 162.*

Two Quantitative Variables

Nonlinear Scatterplot

Recall that for a *single* quantitative variable, we establish whether the shape of the distribution is normal, in which case we may draw more specific conclusions about the variable's behavior. Similarly, when the relationship between *two* quantitative variables is of interest, determining the form to be *linear* will enable us to proceed with a very well-developed theory, where we summarize the relationship with the equation of a straight line.

Many relationships between two quantitative variables naturally fall into a curved, rather than a linear, pattern. Attempting to fit such relationships with a straight line is like trying to fit a "square peg in a round hole," as the saying goes. Typically, such relationships can be handled by transforming one or both of the variables using logarithms, square roots, or other operations. These methods are not presented in this book, but it is important for students to be aware that they exist, and that many data sets should not be handled immediately by least squares regression. Students are warned about the possibility of a curved relationship on page 166.

Example TBP 5.4 CURVED RELATIONSHIP

Background: Paleontologists explored the relationship between age and size of *Tyrannosaurus rex*, based on specimens of dinosaurs that had died at various ages.

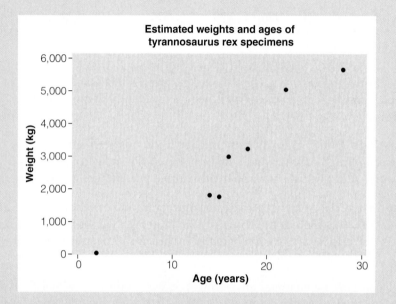

Question: Would a straight line provide a good summary of the relationship between dinosaurs' ages and sizes?

Response: Just as humans' growth over many years fits a curve rather than a straight line, the weights of these dinosaurs do appear to level off by a certain age, after 20 years or so. In order to produce an equation that predicts dinosaur weight from age, some transformation would first need to be performed.

Practice: *Try Exercise 5.65 on page 200.*

Calculating r by Hand

On page 170, we defined the correlation to be the "average" product of standardized x and y values:

$$r = \frac{1}{n-1}\left[\left(\frac{x_1 - \bar{x}}{s_x}\right)\left(\frac{y_1 - \bar{y}}{s_y}\right) + \cdots + \left(\frac{x_n - \bar{x}}{s_x}\right)\left(\frac{y_n - \bar{y}}{s_y}\right)\right]$$

Here, $\bar{x}$ and s_x, $\bar{y}$ and s_y are the mean and standard deviation of x and y, respectively. Note that, just as was done for standard deviation, the "average" is found by summing the values and dividing by sample size *minus one*.

Rather than devoting time and energy to performing tedious calculations to compute r, it is best to leave the arithmetic to the calculator or computer software, and concentrate instead on getting a feel for how r assesses the direction and strength of a linear relationship between two quantitative variables.

Nevertheless, it is worthwhile to take a look at the formula for r, not just as a tool for calculations by hand, but also because it gives us insight into how r manages to reflect a relationship's direction and strength.

In case software is not available, the following steps may be taken to solve for r:

1. Find the means and standard deviations of the x and y variables. [These calculations were demonstrated in Section 4.3 on center and spread of a quantitative distribution.]

2. Standardize the x and y values to (value − mean)/standard deviation, using the mean and standard deviation of x and of y, respectively. That is, we find each $\frac{x_i - \bar{x}}{s_x}$ and $\frac{y_i - \bar{y}}{s_y}$.

3. Find the product of each pair of standardized values.

4. Take the "average" by summing all products and dividing by sample size minus one. This is r.

Recall the scatterplot for the relationship between 17 male students' heights and weights, which was positive and somewhere between the relationships between parents' heights ($r = 0.224$) and parents' ages ($r = 0.781$) in terms of strength. In fact, the correlation is calculated below as $r = 0.646$, indicating a positive relationship that is moderate in strength. [Notice that the standardized heights are found by taking each height value and subtracting the mean 69.765 inches and dividing by the standard deviation 2.137 inches. The standardized weights are found by taking each weight value and subtracting the mean 170.59 pounds and dividing by the standard deviation 28.87 pounds.]

Height x	Weight y	Standardized Height	Standardized Weight	Product
65	140	−2.22976	−1.05958	2.36260
68	130	−0.82592	−1.40596	1.16121
68	181	−0.82592	0.36058	−0.29781
68	150	−0.82592	−0.71320	0.58905
69	180	−0.35798	0.32594	−0.11668
69	172	−0.35798	0.04884	−0.01748
69	125	−0.35798	−1.57915	0.56530
69	185	−0.35798	0.49913	−0.17868
69	150	−0.35798	−0.71320	0.25531
70	168	0.10997	−0.08971	−0.00987
70	180	0.10997	0.32594	0.03584
71	175	0.57791	0.15275	0.08828
71	214	0.57791	1.50364	0.86897
71	145	0.57791	−0.88639	−0.51225
72	195	1.04586	0.84551	0.88429
73	175	1.51380	0.15275	0.23124
74	235	1.98175	2.23104	4.42136
$\bar{x} = 69.765$	$\bar{y} = 170.59$			Sum = 10.33
$s_x = 2.137$	$s_y = 28.87$			$r = \frac{10.33}{17 - 1} = 0.646$

Notice that what contribute most to the size of r in the male height versus weight example are pairs such as (65, 140), where both x and y are considerably below average, resulting in a pair of substantially negative standardized values whose product

(2.36260) is substantially positive; also pairs such as (74, 235), where both x and y are considerably above average, resulting in a pair of substantially positive standardized values whose product (4.42136) is substantially positive. Averaging such products together results in a fairly large positive r, closer to $+1$.

For strong negative relationships, when x is far below its average, y tends to be far above its average, and the product is a large negative number. Likewise, when x is far above its average, y tends to be far below its average, and the product is again a large negative number. Averaging these together results in a relatively large negative r, close to -1.

Finally, for very weak relationships, when x is below its average, there's no telling what y will be—sometimes below and sometimes above average. These products are sometimes positive and sometimes negative. Likewise, when x is above its average, y is sometimes below and sometimes above average, resulting again in products that are sometimes positive and sometimes negative. Averaging these positive and negative products together results in a value of r that is closer to zero.

Correlation Based on Averages

We mentioned on page 176 that the correlation based on averages tends to overstate the strength of a relationship. Here is an example to illustrate this phenomenon.

EXAMPLE TBP 5.5 CORRELATION BASED ON AVERAGES OVERSTATES STRENGTH

Background: Instead of looking at the relationship between height and weight of a group of males, we could look at the relationship between height and *average* weight for each possible height value.

Ht	65	68		69				70		71			72	73	74
Wt	140	130	150 181	125	150 172	180 185		168	180	145	175 214		195	175	235
AvWt	140	153.7		162.4				174.0		178.0			195	175	235

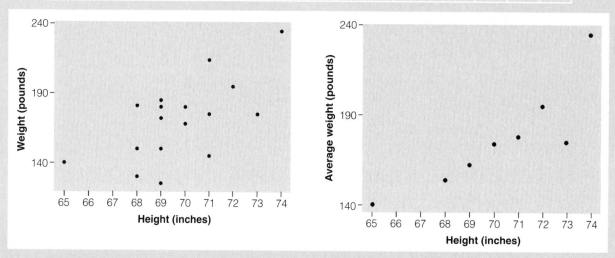

Questions: Which relationship appears to be stronger? What do the correlations ($r = +0.65$ for weight versus height, shown on the left, and $r = +0.87$ for average weight versus height, shown on the right) tell us?

Responses: The relationship between height and average weight, shown on the right, appears stronger. This is confirmed by the fact that its correlation is closer to 1. By combining all weights for each height value into one average weight value, we have reduced the amount of scatter in the plot.

Practice: *Try Exercise 5.49 on page 196.*

Details about Slope and Intercept

The slope and intercept of the regression line are defined on page 180. It is common to express the equation of the least squares line as $\hat{y} = b_0 + b_1 x$, where $\hat{y}$ denotes the *predicted* response for a given explanatory value x, as opposed to the actual *observed* value y. Calculation of the slope b_1 and intercept b_0 of the least squares line by hand is extremely tedious because it involves the calculation of r, which is in itself very labor-intensive, even for a small data set. To begin the task, you would calculate means and standard deviations of each of the two variables, and then the correlation r. Thus, you need to know $\bar{x}$, s_x, $\bar{y}$, s_y, and r.

The slope b_1 of the least squares line is calculated as $b_1 = r\frac{s_y}{s_x}$. This formula is worth thinking about because it expresses the fact that for the least squares line, an increase of 1 standard deviation in the horizontal x direction is accompanied by a change of r standard deviations in the vertical y direction (which amounts to an increase if r is positive, a decrease if r is negative). This provides us with a new perspective on the way r accounts for direction and strength. The fact that the slope is $r\frac{s_y}{s_x}$ (where s_y and s_x are, by definition, always positive) confirms that if r is positive, the slope is positive and if r is negative, the slope is negative. If r is close to -1 or $+1$, y is very responsive to x in that it will change by almost a whole standard deviation if x changes by a standard deviation. If r is close to 0, y is hardly impacted by x in that it will change by only a small fraction of a standard deviation when x changes by a whole standard deviation.

The intercept of the least squares line is calculated as $b_0 = \bar{y} - b_1\bar{x}$. This formula is also instructive: According to the least squares line equation, when x takes its mean value $\bar{x}$, the predicted response is $\hat{y} = b_0 + b_1\bar{x}$. Substituting $b_0 = \bar{y} - b_1\bar{x}$ we have $\hat{y} = (\bar{y} - b_1\bar{x}) + b_1\bar{x} = \bar{y}$. In other words, when x takes its mean value $\bar{x}$, the line predicts y to take its mean value $\bar{y}$.

The slope of the regression line, denoted b_1, provides us with valuable information because it tells us by how much the response variable increases or decreases for every unit change in the explanatory variable. For Example 5.28 on page 178, the fact that the slope b_1 is -1287.64 tells us that for every additional year in age, we predict a used Grand Am to cost about $1,287.64 less. Of course, this prediction is not perfect because the points don't line up exactly along the line with that slope.

The intercept of the regression line, denoted b_0, tells us what response the line predicts when the explanatory value is zero. If zero is outside the range of plausible explanatory values, then the intercept can only be interpreted in a technical way—for instance, the intercept for regression of weight on height is not very meaningful because it makes no sense to predict the weight of a person who is zero inches tall. In the case of Example 5.28, although it is possible for a Grand Am to be zero years old (when it is brand new), we should refrain from using this regression line to predict its price because the line only applies to *used* Grand Ams. There is bound to be a jump in price when we make the transition from a used car—even if it's just a few days old—to a brand-new car. This ties in with the concept of *extrapolation*.

EXAMPLE TBP 5.6 INTERPRETING SLOPE AND INTERCEPT

Background: At the beginning of this chapter we posed the question "Are ages of sampled students' mothers and fathers related?" and by now have reported the correlation in this situation to be $r = +0.781$, suggesting that there is a fairly strong positive relationship. Because the scatterplot

Continued

appeared linear, it makes sense to summarize the relationship with the equation of a straight line, which can be found using software.

```
The regression equation is
MotherAge = 14.5 + 0.666 FatherAge
```

Question: What do the slope and intercept of the line tell us?

Response: The fact that the slope is 0.666 tells us that if one father is a year old than another, we predict the first mother to be about 0.666 years (or about 8 months) older than the second one. The intercept does not have a very meaningful interpretation because a father would not be zero years old. Nevertheless, it tells us that if we extended the line to the y-axis, it would cross at the point where mother's age is equal to 14.5.

Practice: *Try Exercise 5.51 on page 196.*

The line in this example was constructed based on ages ranging from the thirties to the eighties, and so we should refrain from predicting mother's age based on a father's age outside this range.

Details about s and s_y

Example 5.32 on page 183 compared s (the value of the typical residual size) and s_y (the typical distance of responses from their mean).

If we only have information about a single quantitative variable, then the best prediction we can make for a value of that variable is the mean value. For example, if all we know is that the mean of 17 male students' weights is 175, then when asked to guess a male student's weight without seeing him, 175 is the best we can do. The standard deviation of those 17 weights, $s = 29$, tells us about how far off our guess will tend to be from the student's actual weight: about 29 pounds.

If, on the other hand, we have regressed weights on heights and produced the equation weight $= -438 + 8.72 \times$ height, and we are asked to guess a male student's weight, then we would do well to find out his height. When the regression equation is used to predict weight, based on height, then the typical residual size, $s = 23$, tells us about how far off our guess will tend to be: only about 23 pounds. To avoid confusing ordinary standard deviations with this residual, we would denote the ordinary standard deviation of weights as $s_y = 29$.

5.2 Activities

Activity: One Categorical and One Quantitative Variable

Using the Computer

Students discuss whether values for each of these variables—age, shoe size, minutes spent talking on the phone the day before, minutes spent exercising the day before, amount of money earned the year before—would tend to be higher for females, higher for males, or about the same for both gender groups. Students access data about the variables mentioned, create side-by-side boxplots of males' and females' values for each variable, and discuss whether they were apparently correct in predicting if values for one gender group would be higher. They also discuss whether spreads for each pair of boxplots appear to be comparable. Other variables' values for males versus females can be explored if time permits.

In the Classroom

Together, the students choose one of the variables that they agree should show a difference for males and females. Instead of accessing the data online, students in each gender group one at a time report their values for the chosen variable, then the class together creates back-to-back stemplots (or side-by-side boxplots) of males' and females' values, and discusses whether they were apparently correct in predicting values for one gender group to be higher. They also discuss whether spreads appear to be comparable for males and females. If there is time, students choose a variable that they believe should *not* differ much for the two gender groups, and explore those values as described above.

Activity: Two Categorical Variables

Using the Computer

Students discuss whether they expect any pairs of the following variables to be related—gender, major decided or not, whether or not they smoke, whether they live on campus or not, whether or not they earned at least $1,000 the year before, whether they ate breakfast the morning of the survey, whether or not ears are pierced. Students access data about the variables of interest. For pairs of variables that are suspected to be related, students should come to agreement on which is explanatory and which is response, then predict which explanatory group will have a higher proportion in a particular response category of interest. For example, do they expect the proportion living on campus to be higher or lower or about the same for students who smoke compared to those who don't smoke? Next, software is used to construct tables of counts, and proportions in response categories, after which students discuss to what extent their predictions were correct. If time permits, a bar graph should be produced and examined. Another topic for further discussion is whether or not students would expect to see similar relationships for a larger population of students, not just a sample of class members.

In the Classroom

Together, the students agree on two variables that they suspect *will* be related. First they should come to agreement on which is explanatory and which is response, then predict which explanatory group will have a higher proportion in a particular response category of interest. For example, do they expect the proportion living on campus to be higher or lower for students who smoke compared to those who don't smoke? Next, a two-way table of counts is constructed by getting a show of hands for students who are in each category combination. Then proportions in response categories are found and compared; students discuss to what extent their prediction of a relationship seems correct. If time permits, a bar graph can be produced and examined. Another topic for further discussion is whether or not students would expect to see similar relationships for a larger population of students, not just the sample of class members.

If there is time, students next choose a pair of variables that they suspect are *not* related, and analyze them together as described above. In the end, they should discuss to what extent their prediction of no relationship seems correct, and what they think they would see in a larger population of students.

Activity: Two Quantitative Variables

Using the Computer

Students discuss whether pairwise they expect any of these variables—student's age (to the nearest tenth of a year), age of mother, age of father, number of siblings, amount of money earned the year before, minutes spent watching TV the day before, minutes spent on the phone the day before, minutes spent on the computer the day before, number of credits taken, hours slept the night before (to the nearest half hour)—to be related. Students access data about the variables of interest. For pairs of variables that are suspected to be related, students should come to agreement on which is explanatory and which is response, then predict whether the relationship will be positive or negative. Next, software is used to construct a scatterplot and compute the correlation r, after which students discuss to what extent their predictions were correct. Another topic for further discussion is whether or not students would expect to see similar relationships for a larger population of students, not just a sample of class members.

In the Classroom

Students choose two variables that they suspect *will* be related, come to agreement on which is explanatory and which is response, then predict whether the relationship will be positive or negative. One by one they report their pair of values so that the class together can construct a scatterplot. The instructor uses a calculator to compute the correlation r, after which students discuss to what extent their predictions were correct. Another topic for further discussion is whether or not students would expect to see similar relationships for a larger population of students, not just a sample of class members.

If there is time, students next choose a pair of variables that they suspect are *not* related, and analyze them together as described above. In the end, they should discuss to what extent their prediction of no relationship seems correct, and what they think they would see in a larger population of students.

5.3 Guide to Exercise Topics

Previewing displays and summaries for one categorical and one quantitative variable: 5.71*(b), 5.73, 5.74, 5.75, 5.76, 5.78, 5.81(f,g), 5.84*(f), 5.86(d)

Two-sample designs: 5.2*, 5.7*, 5.77, 5.80, 5.81, 5.82, 5.86, 5.88*, 5.89

Several-sample designs: 5.3, 5.4, 5.5*, 5.6, 5.8*, 5.9, 5.10*, 5.12, 5.83(a–f); Using Software: 5.84*, 5.85, 5.87, 5.90(a–f)

Paired designs: 5.13*, 5.14(a–c), 5.76, 5.83(g)

The role of spreads: 5.15, 5.16

The role of sample size: 5.7(g), 5.14(d–g), 5.15*(h), 5.16(a,b), 5.84*(d), 5.86(c), 5.90(g)

Previewing relationships between two categorical variables: 5.17*, 5.18, 5.19, 5.93

Summarizing and displaying two categorical variables: 5.19, 5.20*, 5.21*, 5.22(a–f), 5.23*(a–d), 5.26*, 5.27, 5.28, 5.94, 5.97, 5.98

The role of sample size: 5.23*(i), 5.24, 5.25*, 5.30(d), 5.95(e)

Expected counts in a table: 5.22(g), 5.23*, 5.29*, 5.30, 5.31

Confounding variables: 5.23*(e), 5.32*, 5.96; Using Software: 5.101

Previewing relationships between two quantitative variables: 5.33*, 5.34, 5.35, 5.104*, 5.105, 5.106

Displaying and summarizing two quantitative variables: 5.36*(a–c), 5.37*, 5.38*, 5.57(e), 5.59(a)

Correlation: 5.39*, 5.40*, 5.53(a–c), 5.107(a)

A closer look at correlation: 5.45*, 5.47*, 5.49, 5.57(k), 5.107(e), 5.117(g)

The least squares regression line: 5.36*(d–f), 5.43, 5.50*, 5.51, 5.52*, 5.54*, 5.57(f–i), 5.70(h), 5.108, 5.109; Using Software: 5.54*

A closer look at least squares regression: 5.36*(d,e), 5.39*, 5.41, 5.50*, 5.51, 5.52, 5.53(d–g), 5.54*, 5.55*, 5.57(f–j), 5.59(b), 5.60*, 5.61*, 5.62*, 5.70(a–k), 5.107(b–d), 5.112; Using Software: 5.48, 5.115, 5.116(b–i), 5.117, 5.119

Relationships for samples versus populations: 5.43(b), 5.56*, 5.63*, 5.107(f), 5.116(a)

The role of sample size: 5.64*

Time series: 5.65, 5.66*, 5.67, 5.68, 5.111

Additional variables: 5.46*, 5.69*, 5.70(l), 5.113, 5.118

Errors in studies' conclusions: 5.79

5.4 Supplemental Exercises

CATEGORICAL AND QUANTITATIVE VARIABLES

5.1 Researchers suspect that exposure to the common industrial chemical benzene may reduce the number of disease-fighting white blood cells. Which one of these designs for producing data involves a categorical explanatory variable and a quantitative response?

a. Measure the number of white blood cells for workers who are exposed to more than 1 ppm (part per million) of benzene, and for workers who are exposed to less than 1 ppm.

b. Measure workers' number of white blood cells, and measure the amount of benzene they are exposed to in their work environment.

c. Measure the amount of benzene workers are exposed to, and classify them as having normal or reduced numbers of white blood cells.

5.2 An article entitled "Bored Teens Pick Up Bad Habits in Summer" reported in 2004: "The National Survey on Drug Use and Health found that June and July were the most popular time for teens to try marijuana, with about 6,300 new users a day during those months. That compares with about 4,700 new users a day during other times of the year."[1]

a. If we round to 30 days per month, how many new users were there altogether in June and July?

b. If we round to 30 days per month, how many new users were there altogether during the other 10 months?

c. What is the average number of new users a day in general, without distinguishing between which time of year it is?

d. Can we assume the numbers 6,300 and 4,700 are estimates, or were they actually measured for the entire population?

5.3 Students were surveyed as to how much cash they were carrying, to the nearest dollar. They were also asked to report their gender and their year at school. A comparison was made, first for mean amount of cash carried by females versus males, then for mean amount of cash carried by students in various years 1 through 4.

Gender	N	Mean	StDev
female	280	24.0	39.6
male	159	34.2	58.4

Year	N	Mean	StDev
1	35	26.57	33.67
2	254	26.02	44.18
3	101	29.60	59.66
4	36	30.68	38.50

a. Which variable seems to play more of a role in amount of cash carried: gender or age?

b. Report the z-score for a female carrying $100 in cash.

c. Report the z-score for a male carrying $100 in cash.

d. Report the z-score for a first-year student carrying $100 in cash.

e. Report the z-score for a fourth-year student carrying $100 in cash.

f. Based on your z-scores, for which type of student is it most uncommon to be carrying at least $100: a female, a male, a first-year student, or a fourth-year student?

5.4 "For Younger Latinos, a Shift to Smaller Families" reports in the *New York Times* that the national fertility rate for Latinas dropped to 2.7 children per woman in 2002 from 2.9 children per woman in the early 1990s.

a. Do the numbers 2.7 and 2.9 represent means, medians, or proportions?

b. Which of these would be the best guess for standard deviation of number of children per Latina woman in 2002: 0.05, 1.5, 4.5, or 5.5?

c. If the data arose from a census, would the standard deviation be written s or σ?

d. Which of these would be the best guess for shape of the distribution of number of children: symmetric, skewed left, or skewed right?

e. If the data arose from a census, would the numbers 2.7 and 2.9 be statistics or parameters?

5.5   The mean Math SAT score for students whose family income was less than $10,000 a year is approximately 440, with a standard deviation of 100. The mean Math SAT score for students whose family income was more than $100,000 a year is approximately 570, with a standard deviation of 100.

a. If a student in the under-$10,000 income bracket scored 500 on the Math SAT test, what is his z-score relative to others in this income bracket?

b. If a student in the over-$100,000 income bracket scored 500 on the Math SAT test, what is his z-score relative to others in this income bracket?

5.6   Students completed a survey where they reported their gender and age, as well as mother's age and father's age.

a. Which do you think should be closer: mean ages of male and female college students, or mean ages of students' mothers and fathers?

b. Who would you expect to be older on average—students' mothers or students' fathers?

c. If we compare ages of male and female students, is this a paired or a two-sample design?

d. If we consider age differences between students' mothers and fathers, is this a paired or a two-sample design?

e. Which should have a higher standard deviation: ages of students or ages of students' parents?

5.7   In the course of the 1990s, was there a reduction in opportunities for low-income students to study at the nation's best schools? This data set shows the percentages of students with Pell Grants (for low-income students) at the top 20 national universities, in the academic years 1992–93 and 2001–02.

University	% 1992–93	% 2001–02	Change
Harvard	4.6	6.8	+2.2
Princeton	6.8	7.4	+0.6
Yale	9.9	10.1	+0.2
M.I.T.	16.3	12.4	−3.9
C.I.T.	17.1	15.3	−1.8
Duke	8.5	10.1	+1.6
Stanford	12.6	11.7	−0.9
U. Penn	11.6	9.8	−1.8
Dartmouth	10.9	10.9	0
Washington	8.6	8.0	−0.6
Columbia	16.8	14.9	−1.9
Northwestern	10.8	9.5	−1.3
Chicago	18.4	12.4	−6.0
Cornell	14.0	16.3	+2.3
Johns Hopkins	7.9	9.6	+1.7
Rice	13.1	12.5	−0.6
Brown	9.4	9.7	+0.3
Emory	17.1	12.2	−4.9
Notre Dame	9.4	8.0	−1.4
Vanderbilt	11.1	10.0	−1.1

a. For the data to support a claim that recently, fewer low-income students are being given opportunities to study at the best schools, would the mean change be positive or negative?

b. Calculate the mean change.

c. Based on the mean, characterize the situation as one of the following: overall a large decrease in percentages, overall a slight decrease in percentages, overall a slight increase in percentages, or overall a large increase in percentages.

d. By looking at a histogram of the data, we can say that most of the percentages went up or down by about 1%, but in a few schools the percentage of students with Pell grants went down by several percent. Is the histogram skewed left, symmetric, or skewed right?

e. Was the study design paired, two-sample, or several-sample?

5.8 Suppose someone claims that students with decided majors tend to earn more money, because of their "decisive" personalities.

a. Use software to access the student survey data, and find the mean earnings for students with decided majors and for students with undecided majors.

b. The mean is higher for students with decided majors, but this is not necessarily due to their personalities. Tell which one of these is the most likely suspect for a confounding variable: age (older students tend to have decided on a major, and they also tend to earn more); or smoking (smokers tend to have decided on a major, and they also tend to earn more); or weight (heavier students tend to have decided on a major, and they also tend to earn more).

5.9 Students were surveyed as to how many minutes they had talked on the phone the day before. They were also asked whether or not they carried a cell phone.

a. If one group talked on the phone more, would you expect it to be those who did or did not carry a cell phone?

b. Use software to access the student survey data, and report the mean minutes on the phone for those who did and did not carry a cell phone.

c. Whose sample mean was higher?

d. Does the difference appear to be major or minor?

e. Can we conclude that carrying a cell phone causes someone to talk on the phone more? Explain.

USING THE NORMAL TABLE [SEE END OF BOOK] OR SOFTWARE: CATEGORICAL AND QUANTITATIVE VARIABLES

5.10 Exercise TBP 5.4 reports mean number of children for Latino women to be 2.7 in 2002. The standard deviation was 1.5. If a normal variable has mean 2.7 and standard deviation 1.5, find the proportion of values less than zero, and explain why this is a poor estimate for the proportion of values of this particular variable that are negative.

5.11 According to Exercise TBP 5.5, the mean Math SAT score for students whose family income was less than $10,000 a year is approximately 440, with a standard deviation of 100. The mean Math SAT score for students whose family income was more than $100,000 a year is approximately 570, with a standard deviation of 100.

a. Suppose a student in the under-$10,000 income bracket scored 500 on the Math SAT test. If the distribution were normal, what percentile is this student's score, relative to others in the same income bracket?

b. Suppose a student in the over-$100,000 income bracket scored 500 on the Math SAT test. If the distribution were normal, what percentile is this student's score, relative to others in the same income bracket?

5.12 Lengths (in micrometers) of the first type of grain shown in Exercise 5.81 on page 209 have mean 22, standard deviation 4.5. Lengths of the second type of grain have mean 30, standard deviation 3.5. We assume each distribution to be approximately normal.

a. For the first type of grain, the longest 20% are longer than how many micrometers?

b. For the second type of grain, the shortest 10% are shorter than how many micrometers?

5.13 Subjects taking a placebo in the weight loss study described in Exercise 5.16 on page 149 lost an average of 5 pounds. Assume the distribution to be approximately normal.

a. If the standard deviation for pounds lost were 10, what would be the proportion of placebo-takers who *gained* weight?

b. If the standard deviation for pounds lost were 4, what would be the proportion of placebo-takers who *gained* weight?

5.14 Scores on a state assessment test were averaged for all the schools in a particular district, which were classified according to level (see Exercise 5.9 on page 146). Assume distribution of school means to be approximately normal.

a. Mean scores for elementary schools had mean 1,228, standard deviation 82. What proportion of elementary schools have a mean score greater than 1,300?

b. Mean scores for middle schools had mean 1,219, standard deviation 91. What proportion of middle schools have a mean score greater than 1,300?

c. Mean scores for high schools had mean 1,223, standard deviation 105. What proportion of high schools have a mean score greater than 1,300?

5.15 Percentages taking state assessment tests for various high schools were roughly normally distributed with mean 91%, standard deviation 6% (see Exercise 5.12 on page 147). The top 10%, in terms of participation, had approximately what percentage of students taking the tests?

5.16 Weights (in pounds) of a large group of freshman females were shown in Exercise 5.83 on page 210 to have mean 122 and standard deviation 12; weights of freshman males had mean 175 and standard deviation 40. Assume both distributions to be approximately normal. Suppose a freshman in this group weighs 140; find the proportion of females weighing this much, and the proportion of males weighing this little, then tell your best guess for whether the student is female or male.

TWO CATEGORICAL VARIABLES

5.17 The *New York Times* reported on grade inflation, based on a survey of 276,000 incoming freshmen at more than 400 colleges and universities, conducted by the Higher Education Research Institute at UCLA in 2003. "Almost half reported an A average in high school, up from 18 percent in 1968."[2]

a. If we were displaying this information with a bar graph, what variable should be shown on the horizontal axis?

b. Is it plausible that only about 18% of all incoming freshmen in 2003 had A averages in high school, but there just happened to be almost 50% with A averages in the sample?

c. In 1968, about 22% of students had C or below. One of these is the correct percentage with C or below for those surveyed in 2003—which is it: 5%, 50%, or 55%?

d. As reported here, the two variables of interest are treated as categorical. Describe how both variables could be treated as quantitative.

e. When researchers must decide whether to ask students, "What was your grade point average in high school?" or "Did you have an A average in high school?" are they mainly concerned with data production, displaying and summarizing data, probability, or statistical inference?

5.18 "Combo of Two Blood Pressure Drugs Tied to Higher Deaths in Women" reports that in a study, "women who combined diuretics with calcium channel blockers—among the most frequently prescribed drugs for high blood pressure—had nearly twice as many fatal heart attacks and other cardiovascular deaths as women on diuretics plus beta blockers or ACE inhibitors. Still, the number of heart-related deaths was relatively small: 31 out of 1,223 women taking the calcium channel blocker combination versus 18 out of 1,380 on the beta blocker combination and 17 out of 1,413 on the ACE inhibitor duo."[3]

a. Tell what variables are involved here, whether they are explanatory or response, and whether they are quantitative or categorical. If categorical, tell how many possible values a variable can take.

b. Calculate the proportions of heart-related fatalities (to three decimal places) for the three groups and verify that the first is about twice as high as either of the other two.

c. Would the results be more worrisome or less worrisome if the numbers were 31 out of 122, 18 out of 138, and 17 out of 141?

d. A critic of the study noted that it "was based only on observations and was not a randomized trial—the gold standard of medical research—in which participants are randomly assigned treatment." In other words, it is possible that the observed differences were due to a confounding variable. Which one of these is the most likely culprit: gender, seriousness of illness when drugs were prescribed, whether the women complied with the doses, or region of the United States?

e. In drawing a conclusion about whether or not the combination of diuretics with calcium channel blockers can lead to fatal heart attacks, two erroneous conclusions are possible. Describe the type of error that would have the most unfortunate consequences for women with high blood pressure.

5.19 In a small community with population a little under 10,000, number and causes of deaths were recorded for 1990 and for 2000. In each of those years, the number of deaths was about 140 and the most common causes of death were heart disease and cancer. This chart shows the proportion of deaths due to each of those causes in each of those years.

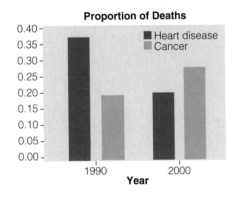

a. What are the explanatory and response variables?

b. Was the proportion of deaths due to other causes in 2000 about 0.2, 0.3, 0.4, or 0.5?

c. Which of these best characterizes the difference between 1990 and 2000: a noticeable decrease in the proportion of heart disease deaths, a noticeable increase in the proportion of cancer deaths, or both, or neither?

5.20 "TV Combat Fatigue on the Rise" describes results of a survey carried out by the Pew Research Center during the third and fourth weeks of March 2003, when the Iraq War had just begun. Respondents were asked, "In general, would you rate the job the press has done in covering the war in Iraq excellent, good, only fair, or poor?"[4] This table shows favorable responses (excellent or good) and unfavorable responses (only fair or poor) for those two weeks.

	Favorable	Unfavorable	Total
March 20–22	760	143	903
March 23–24	474	118	592
Total	1,234	261	1,495

a. Find the proportion of the 1,495 respondents who were surveyed March 20–22, and the proportion surveyed March 23–24.

b. Find the proportions with favorable responses during each of the two time periods.

c. Discuss whether or not the data support the title, *TV combat fatigue on the rise.*

5.21 "Survey Finds Church-Goers Growing Bolder" explains that "Church-going Americans have grown increasingly intolerant in the past 4 years of politicians making compromises on such hot issues as abortion and gay rights,"[5] based on surveys carried out in 2000 and again in 2004. Respondents were asked, "Should elected officials set their convictions aside to get results in government?" Results were approximately as shown in this table.

	Yes	No	Total
Year 2000	1,260	240	1,500
Year 2004	740	260	1,000
Total	2,000	500	2,500

a. What is the explanatory variable?

b. Report the percentages agreeing that politicians should set convictions aside, for 2000 and for 2004.

c. Tell whether the percentage increased or decreased over those 4 years, and by how much.

5.22 A survey was taken of students at a large university in the fall of 2003; among other things, students were asked to report whether or not they smoked, and whether they were non-vegetarian, a sometimes-vegetarian, or vegetarian.

a. First, we'll treat smoking as the explanatory variable. Suppose a professor anticipates that smokers tend not to be health-conscious and that very health-conscious students tend to be vegetarians. Would the professor expect to see a higher or lower percentage of vegetarians (and sometimes-vegetarians) among the smokers, compared to the nonsmokers?

b. Use software to access the student survey data. Combine percentages for vegetarians and sometimes-vegetarians, and report these separately for the smokers and for the nonsmokers. Which group has a higher percentage of vegetarians—the smokers or the nonsmokers?

c. Next, we'll treat vegetarianism as the explanatory variable. If the professor anticipates that students' degree of health-consciousness could play a role in their values for both variables, would she expect to see a higher or lower percentage of smokers among the vegetarians (or sometimes-vegetarians), compared to the non-vegetarians?

d. The combined percentage smoking for vegetarians and sometimes-vegetarians is 25%, and the percentage smoking for

non-vegetarians is 18%. Is this consistent with what we would anticipate if health-consciousness plays a significant role in these two variables' values?

e. Often, the variable whose values occur first chronologically is taken to be the explanatory variable. Explain why, according to this criterion, there is no clear choice of roles for explanatory and response in this situation.

f. In fact, the differences in the percentages that you reported in part (b) could easily have come about by chance if we were sampling at random from a larger population where smoking and vegetarianism were not related. Can we conclude that these variables are related for the larger population?

TWO QUANTITATIVE VARIABLES

5.23 Data are shown for three students' years of birth x and ages y. Each of these has been standardized by subtracting the mean and dividing by the standard deviation.

x = Birth Year	y = Age	Standardized Year	Standardized Age	(b)Product
1988	22	−1	+1	(i)?
1990	20	0	0	(ii)?
1992	18	+1	−1	(iii)?
$\bar{x}$ = 1990	$\bar{y}$ = 20			(c)r = "Average" product = ?
s_x = 2	s_y = 2			

a. Sketch a scatterplot of the original x and y values, and describe the relationship.

b. Calculate the products (i), (ii), and (iii) of standardized years and ages.

c. Find the "average" product r by summing the products and dividing by sample size minus 1.

d. Explain why the correlation r is consistent with the appearance of your scatterplot.

e. Would r be the same for a larger sample of students?

5.24 Data are shown for five students' ages x and heights y. Each of these has been standardized by subtracting the mean and dividing by the standard deviation.

x = Age	y = Height	Standardized Age	Standardized Height	(b)Product
18	62	−1	−1	(i)?
18	70	−1	+1	(ii)?
20	66	0	0	(iii)?
22	62	+1	−1	(iv)?
22	70	+1	+1	(v)?
$\bar{x}$ = 20	$\bar{y}$ = 66			(c)r = "Average" product = ?
s_x = 2	s_y = 4			

a. Sketch a scatterplot of the original x and y values, and describe the relationship.

b. Calculate the products (i), (ii), (iii), (iv), and (v) of standardized ages and heights.

c. Find the "average" product r by summing the products and dividing by sample size minus 1.

d. Explain why the correlation r is consistent with the appearance of your scatterplot.

e. Would r be the same for a larger sample of students?

f. Would r be the same for a sample of younger students?

g. If heights were recorded in centimeters, tell whether each of these would be different or the same: (i) the value of mean height; (ii) the value of standard deviation of heights; (iii) standardized heights; (iv) correlation r.

5.25 Data are shown for three students' heights x in inches and heights y in centimeters. Each of these has been standardized by subtracting the mean and dividing by the standard deviation.

x = Height (in)	y = Height (cm)	Standardized Height (in)	Standardized Height (cm)	(b)Product
62	155	−1	−1	(i)?
66	165	0	0	(ii)?
70	175	+1	+1	(iii)?
$\bar{x} = 66$	$\bar{y} = 165$			(c)r = "Average" product = ?
$s_x = 4$	$s_y = 10$			

a. Sketch a scatterplot of the original x and y values, and describe the relationship.

b. Calculate the products (i), (ii), and (iii) of standardized heights in inches and centimeters.

c. Find the "average" product r by summing the products and dividing by sample size minus 1.

d. Explain why the correlation r is consistent with the appearance of your scatterplot.

e. Would r be the same for a larger sample of students?

5.26 Using data published by the Bureau of Labor Statistics, unemployment rate was regressed on year, from 1985 to 2004.

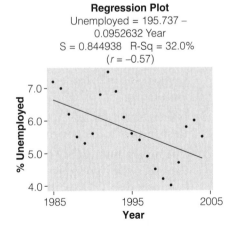

Regression Plot
Unemployed = 195.737 − 0.0952632 Year
S = 0.844938   R-Sq = 32.0%
(r = −0.57)

a. Use the regression equation to predict unemployment rate for 1980.

b. Use the regression equation to predict unemployment rate for 1970.

c. Due to extrapolation, which prediction is in more danger of yielding inaccurate results: the one for 1980 or the one for 1970?

d. The actual unemployment rate was 7.1 in 1980 and 4.9 in 1970. Which prediction was worse: the one for 1980 or the one for 1970, or were they about equally good or bad?

e. Do the scatterplot points appear to be randomly scattered around the regression line, or does their scatter seem to follow a pattern?

f. If a time series plot were drawn for the scatterplot points shown, how many peaks would we see in the unemployment rate from 1985 to 2004?

g. Which does a better job of summarizing the relationship: the regression line or the time series plot?

5.27 This time series shows number of new smoke-free restaurants opened in a certain city over the course of several years.

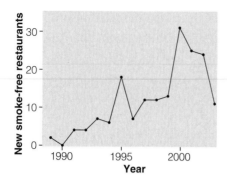

a. In what two particular years were there substantial increases in the number of new smoke-free restaurants opened?

b. So far, the pattern has been a gradual increase, followed by a steep increase, then a drop to a value that is still higher than the starting point. Can we expect this pattern to increase for about 5 more years, 10 more years, 15 more years, or possibly not at all? Explain.

5.28 This time series plot shows numbers of births of black and white babies in a small community over two recent decades.

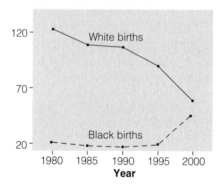

a. There are three variables of interest here. Tell what they are, whether each is quantitative or categorical, and which role each plays (explanatory or response).

b. For each racial group, report whether it is showing a general growth or decline in births.

5.29 Researchers put forth a variety of theories as to why the percentage of low-birth-weight babies is higher for blacks than for whites. This time series plot shows percentage of low-birth-weight babies born to women in a small community over two recent decades.

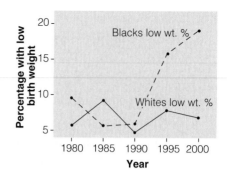

a. Comment on the general trends in percentages of low-birth-weight babies for black and white mothers in this community.

b. In general, the percentage of low-birth-weight babies is said to be more than twice as high for blacks as for whites. Are the percentages in this community consistent with what is true for the general population?

c. Smoking is known to be responsible for low-birth-weight babies. Explain how to produce data to explore whether or not smoking could explain the higher percentage of low-birth-weight babies for black women over the past decade or two.

5.30 It is commonly believed that cigarette smoking can stunt your growth; height of surveyed female smokers was regressed on number of cigarettes smoked to see if these variables provided evidence of a relationship.

```
The regression equation is
HT_female = 64.3 + 0.0766
Cigs_female
```

a. Why was height regressed on cigarettes smoked for females separately from males?

b. If there is a relationship, is there reason to suspect it to be positive or negative?

c. The minimum number of cigarettes in the data set used to produce the regression equation was 1. Does the equation make a reasonable prediction for the height of a female who smoked 0 cigarettes?

d. How would the correlation r change if heights were recorded in centimeters instead of inches: increase, decrease, or no change?

e. Does the regression equation support the notion that cigarette smoking can stunt your growth? Explain briefly.

f. Instead of using regression (with two quantitative variables) to look for evidence that cigarette smoking can stunt your growth, we could compare heights of smoking females and nonsmoking females. In this case, what display could be used?

5.31 "Life Expectancy Up Again" reports that "Life expectancy in the United States in 1900, at birth, was 47.3 years. By the 1929 stock market crash, it had climbed to 57.1. At the end of World War II [1945], it was 65.9. When Ronald Reagan became president in 1980, it had risen to 73.7. During the more than two decades since, as disease detection and treatment have improved, life expectancy has climbed [in 2002] another 3.7 years."[6]

a. By hand or with software, produce a scatterplot of the data; does the relationship appear linear or curved?

b. Use software to perform a regression of life expectancy on year, based on the numbers provided, and report the regression equation.

c. According to the regression output, what is the typical size of the prediction error (in years) for these 5 points?

d. An expert on longevity predicts that life expectancy will level off once it has increased by another 8 years or so. Use the fact that the slope of the regression line is about 0.3 to estimate about how many years it will be until life expectancy levels off, according to this expert.

e. Another demographer believes people will live well beyond 100 during this century. If the rate of increase seen in your regression line continues to the year 2100, what is the predicted life expectancy for that year?

5.32 A survey was taken of students at a large university in the fall of 2003; among other things, students were asked to report their Math and Verbal SAT scores.

a. Use software to access the student survey data. Produce the five-number summary, mean, and standard deviation for the individual variables, Math and Verbal SAT.

b. Given the individual summaries for Math and Verbal scores, is there only one scatterplot that is possible?

c. Produce a scatterplot of the data, taking Verbal SAT as the explanatory variable, and describe the relationship as extremely weak, fairly weak, fairly strong, or extremely strong.

d. The scatterplot shows one of the variables to have a couple of very noticeable low outliers; are they unusually low Math or Verbal scores?

e. Carry out a regression of Math on Verbal scores. Use the regression line to predict the Math SAT score of a student whose Verbal SAT was equal to the mean (part of your answer to part [a]), and verify that the predicted Math SAT is also the mean.

f. Without any information about a student's Verbal SAT score, we would have to predict Math SAT to equal its mean, and our prediction error's typical size would be s_y, which is about 72. If we use regression on Verbal SAT to predict Math SAT, what is the typical size of our prediction error?

g. Would it have been better, worse, or equally good to take Math SAT as the explanatory variable?

h. If Math SAT were taken as the explanatory variable instead of Verbal SAT, which of these would change: the equation of the regression line, the value of the correlation, or both, or neither?

5.5 Solutions to Supplemental Exercises

5.1 (a)

5.2 a. 378,000 **b.** 1,410,000 **c.** 4,899
 d. estimates

5.3 a. gender **b.** $(100 - 24)/39.6 = +1.92$
 c. $(100 - 34.2)/58.4 = +1.13$ **d.** $(100 -$

$26.57)/33.67 = +2.18$ **e.** $(100 - 30.68)/38.50 = +1.80$ **f.** a first-year student

5.4 a. means **b.** 1.5 **c.** σ **d.** skewed right
 e. parameters

5.5 **a.** $(500 - 440)/100 = +0.6$ **b.** $(500 - 570)/100 = -0.7$

5.6 **a.** mean ages of male and female college students   **b.** students' fathers   **c.** two-sample design   **d.** paired   **e.** ages of students' parents

5.7 **a.** negative   **b.** -0.87 **c.** overall a slight decrease in percentages   **d.** skewed left   **e.** paired

5.8 **a.** decided 4.29 thousand dollars, undecided 3.20 thousand dollars   **b.** age (older students tend to have decided on a major, and they also tend to earn more)

5.9 **a.** those who did carry a cell phone   **b.** cell phone 42.6, no cell phone 21.1   **c.** cell phone carriers   **d.** major   **e.** No; maybe people who like to use the phone a lot are the ones who make it a point to carry a cell phone.

5.10 $z = (0 - 2.7)/1.5 = -1.8$; probability is 0.0359. This is a poor estimate because the distribution is right-skewed, not normal; the actual probability of having a negative number of children must be zero.

5.11 **a.** $z = (500 - 440)/100 = +0.6$; probability of z this *high* is 0.2743, so the student is in the 73rd percentile.   **b.** $z = (500 - 570)/100 = -0.7$; probability of z this *low* is 0.2420, so the student is in the 24th percentile.

5.12 **a.** The longest 20% have $z = +0.84$, so the length is $22 + 0.84(4.5) = 25.78$.   **b.** The shortest 10% have $z = -1.28$, so the length is $30 - 1.28(3.5) = 25.52$.

5.13 **a.** To gain weight, pounds lost would have to be less than zero: $z = (0 - 5)/10 = -0.5$; the probability of being less than this is 0.3085.   **b.** $z = (0 - 5)/4 = -1.25$; the probability of being less than this is 0.1056.

5.14 **a.** $z = (1,300 - 1,228)/82 = +0.88$; probability is 0.1894.   **b.** $z = (1,300 - 1,219)/91 = +0.89$; probability is 0.1867.   **c.** $z = (1,300 - 1,223)/105 = +0.73$; probability is 0.2327.

5.15 The top 10% have $z = +1.28$; percentage is $91 + 1.28(6) = 98.68$.

5.16 A 140-pound female has $z = (140 - 122)/12 = +1.5$; probability of being this high is 0.0668. A 140-pound male has $z = (140 - 175)/40 = -0.875$; probability of being this low is between 0.1922 and 0.1894, or about 0.19. Best guess is that the student is a male, because it isn't as improbably low for a male as it is improbably high for a female.

5.17 **a.** year   **b.** No, because the sample is so huge.   **c.** 5%   **d.** number-valued year between 1968 and 2003, and grade point average (from 0 to 4.0)   **e.** data production

5.18 **a.** Which drug combination is the categorical explanatory variable with three possibilities (diuretics plus calcium channel blockers, or diuretics plus beta blockers, or diuretics plus ACE inhibitors), and whether the women died from a heart-related cause is the categorical response variable with two possibilities.   **b.** 0.025, 0.013, 0.012   **c.** more worrisome   **d.** seriousness of illness when drugs were prescribed   **e.** Erroneously concluding that the combination of diuretics with calcium channel blockers does not lead to fatal heart attacks when, in fact, it does would have the most unfortunate consequences for women with high blood pressure who take the drugs.

5.19 **a.** Year is explanatory and cause of death is response.   **b.** 0.5   **c.** both

5.20 **a.** $903/1,495 = 0.60$ surveyed March 20–22; $592/1,495 = 0.40$ surveyed March 23–24   **b.** March 20–22: $760/903 = 0.84$ favorable; March 23–24: $464/592 = 0.80$ favorable   **c.** The title does seem appropriate because over just a few days' time, people's rating of press coverage of the war went down by 4 percentage points. Although the difference is small, the sample size is large, suggesting that it may reflect a real change in public opinion.

5.21 **a.** year (2000 or 2004)   **b.** $1,260/1,500 = 84\%$ in 2000, and $740/1,000 = 74\%$ in 2004   **c.** decreased by 10%

5.22 **a.** lower   **b.** smokers: 18% vegetarian and sometimes-vegetarian, nonsmokers: 13% vegetarian and sometimes-vegetarian; smokers' percentage is higher   **c.** lower   **d.** no   **e.** Sometimes the choice to smoke comes first and sometimes the choice to become a vegetarian comes first.   **f.** no

5.23 **a.** It is a perfect negative relationship.

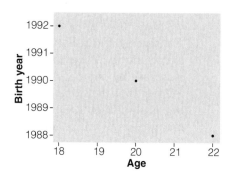

b. (i) -1 (ii) 0 (iii) -1 **c.** $\frac{-1 + 0 - 1}{3 - 1} = -1$ **d.** $r = -1$ is consistent with a perfect negative relationship.   **e.** yes

5.24 **a.** There is no relationship.

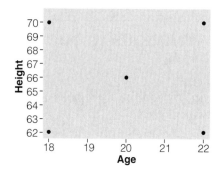

b. (i) $+1$ (ii) -1 (iii) 0 (iv) -1 (v) $+1$
c. $\frac{1 - 1 + 0 - 1 + 1}{5 - 1} = 0$ **d.** $r = 0$ is consistent
with no relationship.   **e.** not necessarily
f. r could be positive and substantial for younger
students, whose height is still increasing with age.
g. (i) different (ii) different (iii) same (iv) same

5.25 a. It is a perfect positive relationship.

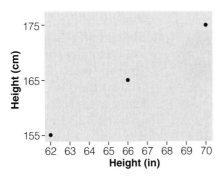

b. (i) $+1$ (ii) 0 (iii) $+1$ **c.** $\frac{1 + 0 + 1}{3 - 1} = 1$
d. $r = +1$ is consistent with a perfect positive
relationship.   **e.** yes

5.26 a. 7.1   **b.** 8.1   **c.** 1970   **d.** The prediction for
1970 was worse.   **e.** Their scatter seems to
follow a pattern.   **f.** 3   **g.** time series plot

5.27 a. 1995, 2000   **b.** possibly not at all; at some
point the market cannot sustain any more smoke-
free restaurants because most restaurants will
already be smoke-free

5.28 a. Year is a quantitative explanatory variable; race
is a categorical explanatory variable; number of
births is a quantitative response variable.
b. growth for blacks, decline for whites

5.29 a. The trend increases dramatically for blacks,
and remains relatively stable for whites.   **b.** yes
c. Smoking rates should be compared for black
and white women to see if the rate is increasing
more for black women.

5.30 a. in case gender is a confounding variable
b. negative   **c.** yes   **d.** no change   **e.** No,
because the slope is positive.   **f.** side-by-side
boxplots

5.31 a. The scatterplot (shown in regression answer to
part [b]) is linear.   **b.** Life expectancy $=$
$-517.417 + 0.298123(\text{Year})$

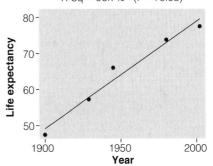

Regression Plot
Life expectancy $= -517.417 +$
0.298123 Year
$S = 2.58746$
R-Sq $= 96.7\%$ ($r = +0.98$)

c. 2.6 years   **d.** $8/0.3 = 26.7$ **e.** $-517.417 +$
$0.298123(2,100) = 108.6$

5.32 a.

Variable	N	N*	Mean	Median	TrMean	StDev
Math	390	56	610.44	610.00	610.23	72.14
Verbal	391	55	591.84	590.00	591.60	73.24

Variable	SE Mean	Minimum	Maximum	Q1	Q3
Math	3.65	400.00	800.00	560.00	660.00
Verbal	3.70	300.00	800.00	540.00	640.00

b. no (any relationship is possible, from strong negative to strong positive)   **c.** fairly weak

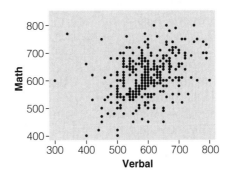

d. Verbal   **e.** Mean Verbal is 591.84; predict Math $= 385.548 + 0.379703(591.84) = 610$, which is the mean.
f. $S = 67$ can be found in regression output.   **g.** equally good   **h.** equation of regression line

5.6 Review of Part II

In Chapters 4 and 5, we covered displays and summaries for the five possible variable situations:

1. **One categorical variable:** Display with a pie chart or bar graph. Summarize by reporting count or (usually preferable) proportion or percentage in a given category.

2. **One quantitative variable:** Display with a stemplot, boxplot, histogram, or (especially if the shape is normal) with a smooth curve. Summarize by reporting center, spread, and shape, with some mention of outliers. The five-number summary is sometimes used because of its resistance to outliers and the fact that it corresponds to the boxplot display. In general, however, we use mean to tell center and standard deviation to tell spread.

3. **Categorical explanatory and quantitative response variable:** The most common display is side-by-side boxplots, one for each value of the categorical explanatory variable. These lead to a visual comparison of medians, ranges, and interquartile ranges, but the most common way to compare centers is with means, and spreads with standard deviations.

4. **Relationship between two categorical variables:** Display with a bar graph, with explanatory values along the horizontal axis and counts, proportions, or percentages in the response(s) of interest graphed vertically. Summarize by comparing counts, proportions, or percentages in the response(s) of interest for the various categorical groups.

5. **Relationship between two quantitative variables:** Display with a scatterplot; if linear, include the regression line. If linear, summarize by reporting the correlation r to tell the direction and strength of the relationship, and the equation of the regression line. Typical residual size s may also be reported.

5.7 Supplemental Part II Review Exercises

A statistical study can be examined in the context of each of the four processes—data production, displaying and summarizing, probability, and statistical inference. To highlight the fact that for any given situation we may focus on any of these four processes, the review exercises for Parts I (page 763), III (page 883), and IV (page 979) feature the same settings as these 15 exercises. For now, the focus is on displaying and summarizing.

5.33 A drug for female sexual dysfunction, Intrinsa, was tested in 2004, both for efficacy and for possible dangerous side effects before being considered for approval by the Food and Drug Administration. A report of clinical trials states: "Fifty-two percent of those [women] given the drug said they experienced a 'meaningful benefit' in their sex lives—but so did 31% of those who were given the placebo."[7]

a. How would the study's results be displayed: a single pie chart, a bar graph, a histogram, side-by-side boxplots, or a scatterplot?

b. Suppose 200 women were included in the study, with half each taking the drug and a placebo. Construct a table of counts in the four possible category combinations, using rows for the explanatory variable and columns for the response.

5.34 Researchers at the University of Montreal reported that "blind people are better than sighted controls at judging the direction of pitch change between sounds [. . .] but only if they became blind at an early age. The younger the onset of blindness, the better is the performance."[8]

a. How could researchers summarize how much better blind people are than sighted people at judging the direction of pitch change between sounds, measured by percent correct on a sound test: by comparing means, by comparing proportions, or by reporting the correlation and regression line?

b. How could researchers summarize how ability to judge the direction of pitch change between sounds, measured by percent correct on a sound test, relates to age of onset of blindness: by comparing means, by comparing proportions, or by reporting the correlation and regression line?

5.35 In 1999, Harvard Medical School researchers produced evidence that when television was introduced to the island of Fiji in the mid-1990s, teenage girls began to suffer from eating disorders because of body image issues resulting from seeing thin actresses on their favorite shows.

a. Suppose the data recorded percentage of teenage girls suffering from eating disorders for each of the years between 1990 and 2000. How would the data be displayed?

b. Suppose the data recorded whether or not teenage girls in a sample were anorexic, in 1995 and again 3 years later, after television viewing was well-established. How would the data be displayed?

c. Suppose the data recorded weights of a sample of teenage girls, in 1995 and again 3 years later, after television viewing was well-established. How would the data be displayed?

5.36 According to a Pew report, by the year 2007, one in every 100 Americans was in prison.

a. If we want to display how the prison population has increased steadily in recent years, would we use a pie chart, stemplot, side-by-side boxplots, or time series plot?

b. If we want to display the make-up of the prison population, according to racial/ethnic groups, would we use a pie chart, histogram, side-by-side boxplots, or scatterplot?

c. If we want to show that blacks are more likely to be imprisoned than whites, do

we compare means, compare percentages, or report correlation?

5.37 The *Harvard Gazette Archives* reported: "Cognition unaffected by pot use; but other studies suggest marijuana smokers are not a happy lot."[9] A study recruited heavy users, former users, and non-users, who took a variety of cognition tests 0, 1, 7, and 28 days after quitting the drug. Another study said that "most heavy users admitted that the drug has a negative impact on all aspects of their lives from job performance and physical health to mental well-being and satisfactory socializing."

a. How could we display cognition test scores for heavy users versus former users versus non-users?

b. How would we summarize the results of the study referenced in the second quotation?

5.38 "Acupuncture Helps Ease Arthritis Pain" describes a National Institutes of Health study where participants "were randomly assigned to receive one of three treatments: acupuncture, sham acupuncture—a procedure designed to prevent patients from being able to detect if needles are actually inserted at treatment points—or participation in a control group that followed the Arthritis Foundation's self-help course for managing their condition . . . Overall, those who received acupuncture had a 40% decrease in pain and 40% improvement in function."[10]

a. Is 40% summarizing the values of a categorical variable or the amount of change in a quantitative variable?

b. How could we display amount of pain still suffered by participants undergoing the three different treatments for pain reduction?

5.39 According to a newspaper report, "the bigger your brood, the likelier it is to show on your waistline. And that's not just for women, who may retain some of the pounds they gain during pregnancy. Fathers tend to gain weight, too, increasing their risk of obesity with the number of offspring, suggesting that eating habits are to blame."[11] Researchers found the relationship between family size and body size held, regardless of household income, physical activity, smoking, and other factors.

a. Explain why this study, which explored the relationship between the number of offspring and whether or not an individual was obese, does not conform to any of the five situations C, Q, C → Q, C → C, or Q → Q.

b. If researchers considered how many pounds an individual was overweight, instead of considering whether or not an individual was obese, then how could they summarize the relationship with number of offspring: with a mean, a proportion, or a slope?

5.40 A study conducted by AAA looked at other driving distractions besides cell phones. It was reported that drivers are engaged in many such distracting behaviors: 62% acknowledged fiddling with the radio dial while driving in the previous 6 months; 57% reported eating, 44% tried to pick something up from the floor or between the seats, 32% wrote something down, 32% stretched to reach the glove compartment, and 23% cleaned the inside of their windshield.

a. Explain why a pie chart would be inadequate to display the data.

b. What additional information would be needed in order to report the count of drivers in each of the categories mentioned?

5.41 A report on sexual health by the Alan Guttmacher Institute says that "men of all ages tend to overstate their sexual activity when surveyed, while women understate theirs."[12]

a. Suppose that, for each individual studied, researchers were able to record the actual number of sexual encounters in the preceding week, as well as the claimed number. Would results best be displayed with a bar graph, a histogram, or side-by-side boxplots?

b. Apparently, the mean of differences for number of sexual encounters, actual minus claimed, was positive for one gender group and negative for the other. For which group was it positive—men or women?

5.42 Every week in football season, data are recorded for the types of injuries suffered by the players on the NFL list of injured players. During a particular week, the most common—knee injury—was suffered by 49 of the 234 players, while the least common—such as a blister on the foot—was suffered by only one player.

a. What would be the best display for the data, if we want to make it clear that about one-fifth of all the injuries were knee injuries?

b. What would be the best display for the data, if we want to show how the prevalence of knee injuries compared to that of various other injuries?

5.43 The Los Angeles Daily News reported the results of a study of thousands of babies born in California in the year 2000. Researchers found that babies born to mothers in the most polluted areas consistently weighed less—about 1 ounce less—than babies born to mothers who lived in clean-air cities.

a. How could the data be displayed: with a pie chart, a bar graph, a histogram, side-by-side boxplots, or a scatterplot?

b. Is 1 ounce referring to a difference between proportions, a difference between means, or a slope?

5.44 "Soft Drink Link to Diabetes Found" reports that "as consumption of sugar-sweetened drinks increased, women put on more pounds and increased their likelihood to develop diabetes."[13]

a. How could the data for sugar-sweetened drinks and weight be displayed: with a pie chart, a bar graph, a histogram, side-by-side boxplots, or a scatterplot?

b. How could the data for sugar-sweetened drinks and weight best be summarized: with means, standard deviations, proportions, or a correlation?

5.45 Columnist Maureen Dowd of the New York Times discussed two studies published in 2004 on what men are looking for in a woman. The first study "suggests that men going for long-term relationships would rather marry women in subordinate jobs than women who are supervisors."[14] The second study "found that a high IQ hampers a woman's chance to get married, while it is a plus for men. The prospect for marriage increased by 35% for guys for each 16-point increase in IQ; for women, there is a 40% drop for each 16-point rise."

a. Would the results of the first study be summarized with proportions, means, or a slope?

b. Are the numbers 35% and 40% for the second study referring to a quantitative or a categorical variable?

5.46 According to the *New York Times*, economics professor David Zimmerman at Williams College studied the impact of college roommates on political leanings and on grades. He "looked at the political views of 3,500 students who had shared rooms as freshmen, noting their leanings when they started college and again three years after graduation. Generally, roommates kept the same political persuasion—except those freshmen whose roommates were on the far left of the political spectrum. No matter what their politics at enrollment, they were more likely than similar students to be *conservative* as adults. [. . .] In separate research, Zimmerman and Gordon C. Winston, another Williams economics professor, uncovered more unsettling evidence of peer influence: Freshmen rooming with the weakest students experienced a slight drop in grades. The

researchers divided 5,000 onetime roommates at four colleges into three groups: Those who scored in the top 15% of the SAT verbal scores admitted to the college, those in the bottom 15%, and everyone in between. On average, grades of the typical students who roomed with low scorers were pulled down by a 10th of a grade point by graduation. No other impact was noticed."[15]

a. Keeping in mind the types of variables involved, how would the relationship between political persuasion at the start of college and political persuasion three years after graduation be displayed?

b. Keeping in mind how the researchers treated the variables involved, how would the relationship between roommates' SAT and students' grades be displayed?

5.47 A wine merchant advertised prices of its California Cabernet wines, per bottle. The minimum price was $10, and the maximum was $130. The mean price was $41. Explain how you know that the shape of the histogram for prices is skewed right and/or has high outliers.

5.8 Solutions to Supplemental Part II Review Exercises

5.33 a. a bar graph
b.

	Benefit	No Benefit	Total
Drug	52	48	100
Placebo	31	69	100
Total	83	117	200

5.34 a. by comparing means   **b.** by reporting the correlation and regression line

5.35 a. time series plot (or scatterplot or bar graph with years in order as explanatory variable)
b. bar graph   **c.** side-by-side boxplots

5.36 a. time series plot   **b.** pie chart   **c.** compare percentages

5.37 a. side-by-side boxplots   **b.** percentage or proportion

5.38 a. amount of change in a quantitative variable
b. side-by-side boxplots

5.39 a. The situation is $Q \rightarrow C$.   **b.** slope

5.40 a. A pie chart would be inadequate because the categories overlap.   **b.** sample size

5.41 a. histogram   **b.** women

5.42 a. pie chart   **b.** bar graph

5.43 a. side-by-side boxplots   **b.** a difference between means

5.44 a. scatterplot   **b.** correlation

5.45 a. proportions   **b.** categorical

5.46 a. bar graph   **b.** side-by-side boxplot

5.47 The minimum is only $31 below the mean, whereas the maximum is $89 above the mean. Clearly the maximum is a high outlier or one of several values on a long right tail, indicating right skewness.

TBP Chapter 6

Finding Probabilities

6.1 Details and Examples

Non-overlapping "Or" Rule

The Non-overlapping "Or" Rule was presented on page 232. An extremely useful application of this rule will arise in Part IV, when we seek the probability that a normal variable could take a value as extreme as the one observed, under the assumption that it has a given mean and standard deviation. Such an application is seen in the following example.

EXAMPLE TBP 6.1 APPLYING THE NON-OVERLAPPING "OR" RULE TO THE NORMAL CURVE

Background: Assume adult male foot lengths (in inches) have a mean of 11 and a standard deviation of 1.5. If we randomly sample 100 adult male foot lengths, the probability of the sample mean being less than 10.7 is 0.025, and the probability of being greater than 11.3 is also 0.025.

Question: What is the probability of sample mean foot length being less than 10.7 or more than 11.3?

Response: The events are non-overlapping, so we simply take $0.025 + 0.025 = 0.05$.

Practice: *Try Exercise 6.30 on page 258.*

Two Solution Methods for Problems about Occurring "at Least Once"

After completing Example 6.14 on page 235, students can handle problems like the following two examples that require them to apply several of the basic probability rules.

EXAMPLE TBP 6.2 USING THE "OR" RULE FOR THE PROBABILITY OF OCCURRING AT LEAST ONCE

Background: The probability of a single coin toss resulting in heads is 0.5.

Question: What is the probability of getting at least one head in two tosses?

Response: As the sketch below indicates, two tosses of a coin may result in 4 possible outcomes, each of which has probability $1/2 \times 1/2 = 1/4$. In 3 of the 4 outcomes, we see at least one head. The outcomes are non-overlapping, and so by the Non-overlapping "Or" Rule, the probability of at least one head in two tosses is $1/4 + 1/4 + 1/4 = 3/4$.

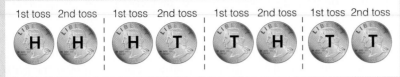

| 1st toss | 2nd toss | 1st toss | 2nd toss | 1st toss | 2nd toss | 1st toss | 2nd toss |
| H | H | H | T | T | H | T | T |

Practice: *Try Exercise 6.11(a) on page 237.*

The solution to Example TBP 6.2 was manageable because there aren't too many possible outcomes to consider in just two tosses of a coin. In contrast, the next example features 10 coin tosses, where the number of possibilities is dauntingly large. Fortunately, we can simplify matters greatly by immediate application of the "Not" Rule.

EXAMPLE TBP 6.3 USING THE "NOT" RULE FOR THE PROBABILITY OF OCCURRING AT LEAST ONCE

Background: The probability of a single coin toss resulting in heads is 0.5.

Question: What is the probability of getting at least one head in 10 tosses?

Response: Solving this by the "brute force" method would require a prohibitive amount of work, specifying all the possible outcomes that have at least one head, from TTTHTTTTTT to HHHHHHHHHH—there are over 1,000 of them!—next using the Independent "And" Rule to calculate each probability, then using the Non-overlapping "Or" Rule to add them all up. A much simpler alternative is provided by the "Not" Rule, which tells us that $P(A) = 1 - P(\text{not } A)$ for any event A. In this case, the event of interest is $A =$ "getting at least one head." The negation of this event, not $A =$ "not getting at least one head," is in fact the same as the event "getting all tails."

$$P(A) = 1 - P(\text{not } A) = 1 - P(TTTTTTTTTT) =$$

$$1 - \frac{1}{2} \times \frac{1}{2} \times \cdots \times \frac{1}{2} = 1 - \left(\frac{1}{2}\right)^{10} = 1 - 0.001 = 0.999.$$

Notice that the Independent "And" Rule let us find the probability of all 10 tails—10 independent events—by successively multiplying their probabilities.

Practice: *Try Exercise 6.11(b) on page 237.*

"Or" and "And" Probabilities in a Table

Example 6.15 on page 238 illustrated "or" and "and" probabilities in a two-way table. Alternatively, we may shade the females in the table with horizontal lines, and the A students with vertical lines. Those who are female *or* got an A are the

	A	Not A	Total
Female			
Male			
Total			

ones with any shading at all. Those who are female *and* got an A are the ones with the mesh of both horizontal and vertical shading.

General "Or" Rule

In Example 6.17 on page 240, we illustrated the General "Or" Rule as the sum of the probabilities of two events, minus the probability of their overlap. Alternatively, we can fill in the missing information in the two-way table, and solve for the probability of being female *or* getting an A, by applying the Non-overlapping "Or" Rule for the individual categorical variables. For example, if the probability of being female and getting an A is 0.15, and altogether the probability of being female is 0.60, then the probability of being female and *not* getting an A must be 0.45. Similarly, the probability of *not* being female and getting an A must be 0.25 − 0.10 = 0.15. Then we can add to find the probability of the shaded region to be $P(Female$ or $A) = 0.15 + 0.45 + 0.10 = 0.70$.

	A	Not A	Total
Female	0.15	0.45	0.60
Male	0.10	0.30	0.40
Total	0.25	0.75	1.00

	A	Not A	Total
	P (Female or A)		
Female	= 0.15 + 0.45 + 0.10		
Male	= 0.70		
Total			

Although our solution as sketched in the table is entirely correct, it is somewhat unsatisfactory because it does not make clear how the answer (0.70) relates to the information provided: $P(Female) = 0.60$, $P(A) = 0.25$, $P(Female$ and $A) = 0.15$. The solution method in Example 6.17 in the textbook works directly with those probabilities.

General "And" Rule

In Example 6.19 on page 241, we solve for the probability of getting two quarters when sampling two coins without replacement from two quarters and two nickels. The sketch below shows how to get the same answer by thinking about equally likely outcomes. The specific quarters and nickels are denoted as $Q1$, $Q2$, $N1$, and $N2$. Altogether there are 12 ways to pick two coins in a row, and 2 of those 12 ways result in getting a quarter both times. Therefore, the probability of getting a quarter both times is 2/12 = 1/6.

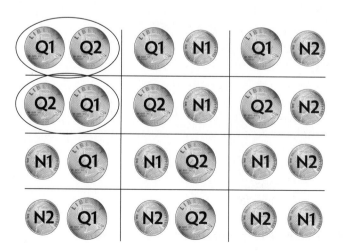

This solution is perfectly correct, but it would be nice to express our answer in terms of the individual probabilities involved, to bring us closer to establishing a general rule. Example 6.19 on page 241 solves the problem by working with the probabilities given in the problem statement.

Rule of Conditional Probability

The definition of conditional probability presented on page 241 makes a lot of sense when we look at a two-way table of counts, such as in our gender/ear piercings example.

P(E given M) = 20/200 = 0.10

	Ears Pierced	Ears Not Pierced	Total
Female	270	30	300
Male	20	180	200
Total	290	210	500

We found the probability of ears pierced, given a student was male, to be $P(E$ given $M) = 20/200 = 0.10$. By dividing each of the counts 20 and 200 by the total number of possible outcomes 500, we can convert our answer so that it is in terms of probabilities, instead of counts.

$$P(E \text{ given } M) = \frac{20}{200} = \frac{20/500}{200/500} = \frac{P(E \text{ and } M)}{P(M)}$$

This is exactly consistent with our definition of conditional probability as stated in the rule $P(B \text{ given } A) = \dfrac{P(A \text{ and } B)}{P(A)}$ on page 246, with E substituted for B and M for A.

Displaying Probabilities

When taking a mathematical approach to probability, it is common to depict unions and intersections of events with a Venn diagram. Typically, there is no attempt made to represent probabilities by areas: Events A and B are represented by circles of equal area, even if one is more probable than the other. The fact that a Venn diagram displays the events A (as opposed to not A) and B (as opposed to not B) on equal footing is a disadvantage from a statistical standpoint, because statistical applications tend to think in terms of one variable being explanatory and the other response.

A tree diagram, such as the one featured in the game show activity at the end of this chapter's supplementary material, does take the perspective that one variable (for the first branch-off) is explanatory and the other (for the second branch-off) is response. Just as we make an effort to put the explanatory variable in the rows of our two-way table, we consider the explanatory variable first when sketching a tree diagram. Like the Venn diagram, a tree diagram fails to illustrate probability sizes graphically: It simply labels each branch with a number corresponding to its probability, using conditional probabilities for the second layer of branch-offs.

Because neither Venn diagrams nor tree diagrams actually represent probabilities by area, we can think of them as "displaying" information to the same extent that a two-way table does. Like tree diagrams, two-way tables let us approach the information with an explanatory variable in mind, if we adhere to the convention of putting the explanatory variable in rows. Their advantage over tree diagrams, which only represent probabilities, is that they can just as easily show counts (as is the case with Venn diagrams, as well).

In this book we concentrate on the use of two-way tables to help students visualize probabilities. Besides making the roles of explanatory and response variables evident, they allow students to see the natural progression from frequencies to relative frequencies, through a simple division of counts by population size. The depiction of "or" and "and" probabilities is also evident, as demonstrated in Example 6.15 on page 238. Moreover, the use of two-way tables in the context of probability is reinforced by their use in displaying and summarizing relationships between two categorical variables, which students have already seen in Chapter 5. In turn, exposure to two-way tables in the probability context paves the way for inference for two categorical variables in later material on chi-square procedures. Thus, two-way tables help students see how applications of the more general probability rules fit the C → C situation, a familiar aspect of the "big picture."

Bar graphs can be used to display conditional probabilities in the same way that they display conditional proportions. Their drawback is that they do not illustrate the difference in sizes of probabilities of being in the various explanatory categories. Thus, a bar graph showing the probability of pierced ears to be 10% for the males and 90% for the females would look the same, whether the ratio of females to males is 3 to 2 or 1 to 1.

Unfortunately, what is arguably the best depiction of probabilities for two variables—a mosaic display—is also the rarest seen. These graphs were proposed by Hartigan & Kleiner in 1981 and further developed by Michael Friendly beginning in 1991. Here is a mosaic illustrating the proportions in three lenswear (response) categories for two gender (explanatory) groups. These sample proportions could just as well be representing probabilities for a larger population. The mosaic display reflects the two-way table's assignment of the explanatory variable to rows and the response to columns. It divides the area vertically in proportion to the likelihood of occurring in the explanatory categories, and horizontally in proportion to the likelihood of occurring in the response categories. Thus, we can grasp explanatory probabilities by comparing heights, response probabilities by comparing widths, and overall probabilities by comparing areas. Counts can be substituted for probabilities if we want to begin with the raw numbers.

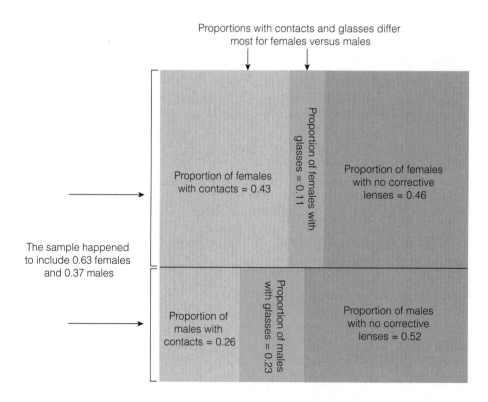

Proportions with contacts and glasses differ most for females versus males

The sample happened to include 0.63 females and 0.37 males

Proportion of females with contacts = 0.43

Proportion of females with glasses = 0.11

Proportion of females with no corrective lenses = 0.46

Proportion of males with contacts = 0.26

Proportion of males with glasses = 0.23

Proportion of males with no corrective lenses = 0.52

Contrasting Non-overlapping Events and Independent Events

We discussed the notion of non-overlapping events on page 232. We defined independent events on page 233. One of the most frequently asked questions by students when they learn probability rules is "What's the difference between non-overlapping (same as disjoint or mutually exclusive) and independent events?" Let's formulate an answer to this question by considering once again our two-way table for students' gender and grade (A or not).

EXAMPLE TBP 6.4 NON-OVERLAPPING EVENTS MUST BE DEPENDENT

Background: We know that the events "Female" and "Male" are non-overlapping.

Question: Are the events "Female" and "Male" also independent?

Response: We recall that for two independent events, knowing whether or not one occurs does not give us any information about the probability of the other occurring. If we know that a student is female, this certainly gives us information about the probability that the student is male! For two non-overlapping events, if one occurs the probability of the other occurring must be zero: The events are highly *dependent*. If there are only two outcomes possible, as is the case for many categorical variables studied, then if one does not occur, the probability of the other occurring must be one.

Practice: *Try Exercise 6.38(b) on page 261.*

EXAMPLE TBP 6.5 INDEPENDENT EVENTS MUST OVERLAP

Background: It has been found that for a certain population of students, the events "Female" and "A" (getting an A in their statistics class) are independent.

	A	Not A	Total
Female	0.15	0.45	0.60
Male	0.10	0.30	0.40
Total	0.25	0.75	1.00

Question: Do the events "Female" and "A" overlap?

Response: They do overlap, and the amount of overlap, corresponding to $P(F \text{ and } A)$, is precisely enough so that it equals the product $P(F) \times P(A)$. In a previous example, we found the amount of overlap to be $0.60 \times 0.25 = 0.15$.

Practice: *Try Exercise 6.38(a) on page 261.*

In conclusion, non-overlapping events are by nature dependent, not independent. Independent events overlap, and the exact amount of overlap can be determined by multiplying their individual probabilities.

Contrasting Conditional Probabilities

Conditional probabilities are widely considered to be among the most misunderstood concepts in statistics. They are also among the most important, for various reasons. First of all, recall our approach to describing the relationship between two categorical variables, as stated at the end of Section 5.2: "Summarize with conditional percentages in the response categories of interest, given each explanatory category. Compare percentages to determine if they differ; if so, consider the extent to which they differ." If we think of each individual as a randomly chosen member of the group represented in the two-way table, then conditional probabilities are the same thing as conditional percentages, and they are our standard tool for summarizing relationships between two categorical variables.

A more subtle use of conditional probabilities enters into the decisions we will make in Part IV, when we want to draw conclusions about a population parameter. We will base our decision on the "P-value," which is actually a conditional probability. It tells the conditional probability of a random sample producing data such as we have observed, *given* that the parameter takes a claimed value, or *given* that there is no relationship between two variables being considered. Thus, a conditional probability is the key to what conclusions we draw, no matter which of the five basic situations applies.

Thinking about the difference between $P(B$ given $A)$ and $P(A$ given $B)$ will help us gain insight into the meaning of conditional probabilities.

EXAMPLE TBP 6.6 CONTRASTING P(B GIVEN A) AND P(A GIVEN B)

Background: Recall our lie detector example, in which the probability of "detecting" someone to be a spy, given that he or she actually *is* a spy, is 80%; the probability of "detecting" someone to be a spy, given that he or she *is not* a spy, is 16%. We assume that 10 of every 10,000 employees actually are spies. Based on this information, it is possible to fill in all the cells of a two-way table representing the two variables (being a spy or not, and being "detected" or not) for 10,000 employees:

Question: Are $P(D$ given $S)$ and $P(S$ given $D)$ the same?

Response: The probability of detection, given that someone is a spy, is in fact provided as part of the problem statement: 8 of 10 actual spies are detected to be spies, as shown in our two-way table: $P(D$ given $S) = 8/10 = 0.80$. In contrast, $P(S$ given $D)$ is found to be $8/1{,}606 = 0.005$.

$P(D$ given $S) = 8/10 = 0.80$			
	D	Not D	Total
S	8	2	10
Not S	1,598	8,392	9,990
Total	1,606	8,394	10,000

$P(S$ given $D) = 8/1606 = 0.005$			
	D	Not D	Total
S	8	2	10
Not S	1,598	8,392	9,990
Total	1,606	8,394	10,000

Practice: *Try Exercise 6.39 on page 261.*

In Section 5.2 on displaying and summarizing relationships between two categorical variables, we pointed out that these account for a vast number of situations studied by researchers, who often treat naturally quantitative variables as categorical by grouping values. It is essential to know what conditional probabilities—or percentages—to compare in such situations, because clearly it matters which is the given event, corresponding to a value of the explanatory variable.

The convention, which is generally employed in this book, is to use the rows of a two-way table for the explanatory variable, in which case conditional probabilities are found as in the two-way table on the left in the preceding example. However, it is not uncommon to have real-life data presented in a two-way table that uses columns for the explanatory variable, as in the table shown on the right. For practical applications, it is good to be in the habit of thinking about what should be the explanatory variable before seeking a conditional probability or percentage.

A discussion among the four students helps to contrast $P(B$ given $A)$ and $P(A$ given $B)$.

Students Talk Stats

When Conditional Probabilities Are Equal

*F*our statistics students are working together on their probability homework. One problem

	A	Not A	Total
Female	0.15	0.45	0.60
Male	0.10	0.30	0.40
Total	0.25	0.75	1.00

features the two-way table below for the variables gender (*F* or not *F* for female or male) and getting an A or not, and asks if the conditional probabilities $P(A$ given $F)$ and $P(F$ given $A)$ are equal.

Adam: *"First you check for independence. Since probability of A times probability of F equals probability of A and F, they're independent. So that means the conditional probabilities are the same."*

Brittany: *"You're right that 0.25 times 0.60 equals 0.15, but being independent doesn't mean those two conditional probabilities are the same."*

Carlos: *"Being independent means probability of A given F is just probability of A, which is 0.25. And probability of F given A is just probability of F, which is 0.60. Those conditional probabilities aren't equal, because 0.25 doesn't equal 0.60."*

Dominique: *"So if A and F are independent, the only way for P(A given F) and P(F given A) to be equal is if A and F have the same probabilities. I wish the probability of getting an A in this course was 0.60."*

6.2 Activities

Activity: Randomness and the Game of Rock, Paper, Scissors

In the Classroom

The instructor or students can do some background investigation concerning the human brain's inability to mimic random selections, and the need for tools like random digits tables or computer-generated randomizations. (The former can be demonstrated by examining the bias that occurs when people are asked to randomly pick a number from 1 to 20). Next, there can follow a discussion of what would be the optimal strategy in the game of rock, paper, scissors (RPS). As far as offense is concerned, a player seeks to perceive patterns in his or her opponent's throws, and to react accordingly. As far as defense is concerned, if a player has no idea what the opponent will throw next, the best approach would be to make his or her own throw unpredictable. Thus, he or she would need to choose randomly from rock, paper, and scissors. Information about RPS tournaments abounds on the Internet, and there is mention of some players who undertake to memorize the digits of pi to internalize a random number generator within their brains. Others favor aptly named gambits like "avalanche," "bureaucrat," or "paper dolls."

Keeping these strategies in mind, students can compete in their own RPS tournament in the classroom. Because competitors must be paired off successively in one-on-one matches, the optimal class size is a power of 2. A qualifying round can be held to achieve this. For example, if the class size N is more than 16 but fewer than 32, have $2(N - 16)$ students (randomly selected, of course!) compete in the qualifying round. For this and all subsequent rounds, best out of nine throws is a manageable number as long as the class isn't much larger than 30 students.

The qualifying round eliminates $N - 16$ players, resulting in $N - (N - 16) =$ 16 players. Pair them off randomly for the next round, then pair off the winners of each, and so on, until the final one-on-one match. Afterwards, the players—and especially the winner—can be "interviewed" about the strategies they employed, and asked if randomness could be said to enter in.

Activity: Applying the Rules of Probability

Using the Computer

First, students (preferably as a group) identify all of the following: the probability that a randomly chosen number from 1 to 10 is . . .

 a. even

 b. less than 4

 c. greater than 4

 d. even or less than 4

 e. less than 4 or greater than 4

 f. even and less than 4

 g. even and greater than 4

 h. even, given that it is less than 4

 i. even, given that it is greater than 4

Also, keeping in mind the "or" rule for non-overlapping or overlapping events, and the "and" rule for independent or dependent events, as well as the rule for conditional probabilities, they should discuss whether

 1. the probability in (d) equals the sum of probabilities (a) and (b)?

 2. the probability in (e) equals the sum of probabilities (b) and (c)?

 3. the probability in (f) equals the product of probabilities (a) and (b)?

 4. the probability in (g) equals the product of probabilities (a) and (c)?

 5. the probability in (a) equals the probability in (h)?

 6. the probability in (a) equals the probability in (i)?

Next, each student uses software to take a random sample (with replacement) of 10 numbers from 1 to 10, and finds the proportion of numbers that are even. Discuss to what extent these short-run proportions match the actual probability. Find the long-run proportion of even numbers by summing counts of even numbers randomly selected, then dividing by 10 times the number of students. Discuss to what extent this long-run proportion matches the actual probability. If time permits, students can compare short-run and long-run proportions for events (b) through (i).

Activity: Applying the Rules of Probability to Birthdays

In the Classroom

This activity gives students practice using the Non-overlapping "Or" Rule, the Independent "And" Rule, and the "Not" Rule. It is more effective for larger groups (say, at least 50 students). However, it can be modified for a smaller group by considering not only the birthdays of the students present, but also those of their parents. For example, for a class of 20 students we ask what is the probability that at least two in a group of 60 people have the same birthday. In the end, check for matches among birthdays of students *and* their parents.

Students should begin by thinking about this question: What is the chance that at least two people in a class of 50 share the same birthday? At their seats they write down a guess; then the instructor sketches a quick histogram of their guesses, with ranges of 0 to 0.1, 0.1 to 0.2, all the way up to 0.9 to 1.0. Their guesses will vary considerably, showing that intuition is not very helpful in this case.

Here is an easier example to discuss before tackling the previous, more difficult one: What is the chance that at least two people in a group of 3 share the same birthday? (Assume all days to be equally likely, and disregard leapyear.) If we call the students A, B, and C, then at least two can share the same birthday in any of these ways: AB or AC or BC or ABC. (If there are students whose names begin with A, B, and C, use their names to make the possibilities more concrete.) These four possibilities are non-overlapping, and so by the Non-overlapping "Or" Rule, the probability of any one *or* the other happening is the sum of the four probabilities. Look first at the probability of A and B having the same birthday, and C different. Whatever A's birthday is, the probability of B having the same birthday is $\frac{1}{365}$, and the probability of C's birthday being different is $\frac{364}{365}$. So, by the Independent "And" Rule, the probability of B being the same *and* C being different is $\frac{1}{365} \times \frac{364}{365}$. Similarly, the probabilities of A and C or B and C being the same are each $\frac{1}{365} \times \frac{364}{365}$. The probability that A and B and C are all the same is $\frac{1}{365} \times \frac{1}{365}$. Altogether, the probability is $\frac{1}{365} \times \frac{364}{365} + \frac{1}{365} \times \frac{364}{365} + \frac{1}{365} \times \frac{364}{365} + \frac{1}{365} \times \frac{1}{365} = 0.0082$.

Next, consider this problem: What is the probability of at least two out of 10 people sharing the same birthday? If we call the people A, B, C, D, E, F, G, H, I, J, at least two can share the same birthday in more than 1,000 ways! AB AC AD ... AJ BC BD ... ABC ... ABCDEFGHIJ. Imagine how much more complicated it would be for the original problem, with 50 students instead of 10!

The solutions are much easier if we employ an alternate strategy, taking advantage of the "Not" Rule, which tells us the probability of something happening must equal 1 minus the probability of *not* happening. (This is because the probabilities of all possibilities together must sum to 1.) First we'll apply this strategy to re-do the easiest problem, the chance of at least 2 out of 3 sharing a birthday.

The probability of at least 2 out of 3 sharing the same birthday must equal 1 minus the probability of all 3 having different birthdays. The probability of all 3 different is the probability of B different from A $[\frac{364}{365}]$ times the probability of C different from both $[\frac{363}{365}]$. Thus, the probability of at least 2 the same is $1 - \frac{364}{365} \times \frac{363}{365} = 0.0082$ (the same answer we got originally).

Now, we will use this strategy on the probability of at least two out of 50 sharing a birthday = 1 minus probability of all 50 birthdays being different

$$= 1 - \frac{364}{365} \times \frac{363}{365} \times \frac{362}{365} \cdots \times \frac{316}{365} = 1 - \frac{364 \times 363 \times \cdots \times 316}{365^{49}} = 0.97$$

It is almost certain that at least two people in a class of 50 share the same birthday! The fact that students' intuitive guesses for the probability of this event tend to be much lower than 0.97 demonstrates that intuition is often an inadequate substitute for systematic application of the laws of probability. (Note: The probability is approximately 0.5 that two students in a class of 23 have the same birthday; in a class of 80, the probability of at least two birthdays the same is 0.999915.)

The instructor can finish the activity by going through the months one at a time and asking students born that month to tell the date, in order to discover if there are at least two with the same birthday.

Activity: Solving for Game Show Probabilities with a Tree Diagram

The instructor should be prepared with three envelopes, preferably of three different colors, and labeled A, B, C. One of the envelopes hides a prize—for example, a dollar bill. The instructor plays the role of game show host, and chooses a volunteer student to play the role of contestant. The instructor explains that a prize is hidden in one of the three envelopes A, B, or C. After the student picks one of the three, the instructor offers the student a "golden opportunity": The instructor reveals one of the remaining two envelopes, showing no prize. The instructor gives the student a chance to switch to the envelope he or she did not select originally. After the student makes the decision to "keep" or "switch," ask the rest of the class if this was a wise choice: Is the probability of winning the prize higher with the "keep" strategy, or the "switch" strategy, or perhaps the same for both? Students will almost surely differ in their opinions, confirming that this is a probability problem for which our ordinary intuition tends not to be adequate. At the board the instructor can show the class how to construct probability trees to calculate the probability of winning using each strategy.

If the "keep" strategy is used...

Prize	Pick	Prob	Result

Probability of winning = 1/9 + 1/9 + 1/9 = 1/3

If the "switch" strategy is used...

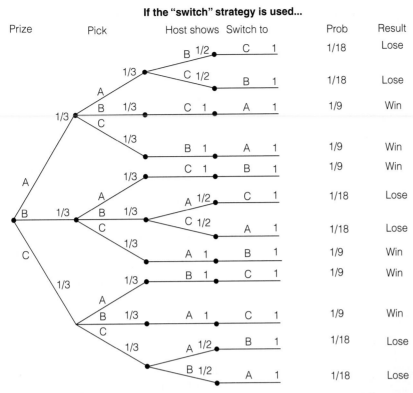

Probability of winning = 1/9 + 1/9 + 1/9 + 1/9 = 2/3

Thus, the probability of winning is only 1/3 if the student keeps the originally selected envelope, but increases to 2/3 if the student switches to the envelope not selected (and not shown by the instructor). Discuss the importance of thinking of these probabilities as long-run chances: If the instructor were to offer the student the chance to play this game every class, in the long run the student would win about twice as often if the "switch" strategy is used. On a one-time-only basis, it is of course possible to win with the "keep" strategy or to lose with the "switch" strategy.

6.3   Guide to Exercise Topics

The meaning of probability: 6.1*, 6.2, 6.3*(b), 6.4(b), 6.61

Basic probability rules: 6.3*(a), 6.4(a), 6.5*, 6.6*, 6.7, 6.8*, 6.9, 6.10*, 6.11*, 6.12, 6.13, 6.22, 6.23, 6.28, 6.29, 6.30*, 6.31, 6.32

General probability rules: 6.14*, 6.15, 6.16*, 6.17, 6.18*, 6.19, 6.33, 6.34*, 6.35, 6.36, 6.37, 6.38*, 6.39*, 6.40, 6.41, 6.42, 6.43, 6.44, 6.45, 6.46, 6.47*, 6.48, 6.49*, 6.50, 6.51, 6.52, 6.53, 6.54, 6.55*, 6.56, 6.57, 6.58, 6.59

Four processes: 6.25, 6.26, 627

6.4   Supplemental Exercises

6.1   Of the 688 U.S. prisoners under sentence of death in 1980, 268 were never married, 229 were married, and 217 were widowed or divorced. Of the 3,557 U.S. prisoners under sentence of death in 2002, 1,746 were never married, 709 were married, and 1,102 were widowed or divorced.

a. Tell what the variables of interest are, and whether each is explanatory or response.

b. For U.S. prisoners under sentence of death, did the probability of being never married substantially decrease, or increase, or stay about the same from 1980 to 2002?

c. For U.S. prisoners under sentence of death, did the probability of being married substantially decrease, or increase, or stay about the same from 1980 to 2002?

d. For U.S. prisoners under sentence of death, did the probability of being widowed or divorced substantially decrease, or increase, or stay about the same from 1980 to 2002?

6.2   In the American Nurses Association online Health and Safety Survey of 2001, nurses were asked, "Over the past 12 months, how many times have you been injured on the job, including needlestick injuries?"[1]

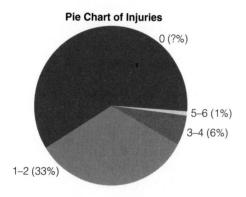

Pie Chart of Injuries

0 (?%)

5–6 (1%)

3–4 (6%)

1–2 (33%)

a. What is the probability that one of these nurses had *not* been injured in the past 12 months?

b. The question about how many times the nurses have been injured on the job was followed by the question, "Of these injuries, how many did you report?" The ANA website posts the percentage answering zero, but explains that some of the nurses who had *not* been injured also answered the question, resulting in a disproportionately high percentage. Of 4,826 nurses, 386 were not injured and did not respond to the question; 2,487 were not injured and responded that they reported zero injuries; 831 had been injured and responded that they reported zero injuries, and 1,122 had been injured and did report the injuries. The website calculated the percentage to be (2,487 + 831)/(2,487 + 831 + 1,122) = 75%. Find the more appropriate percentage that tells the probability of not reporting an injury, *given* that a nurse *had* been injured.

6.3   This table shows the probabilities of American adults having attended each specified art activity at least once in the year 2002.

Jazz	Classical	Opera	Musical	Play	Ballet	Art Museum	Historic Park	Craft Fair
0.11	0.12	0.03	0.17	0.12	0.04	0.27	0.32	0.33

a. Does this problem involve a single variable or a relationship?

b. How do we know that some American adults attended more than one of those art activities?

c. What is the maximum probability of an American adult attending either a jazz or classical concert in 2002?

d. What is the minimum probability of an American adult attending either a jazz or classical concert in 2002?

e. Explain why the actual probability of attending either a jazz or classical concert is almost surely part-way between the minimum and maximum.

6.4   This table shows the probabilities of an adult in the United States in 2003 being in various racial and marital status category combinations. Notice that these are ordinary, not conditional, probabilities, and so they sum to one.

	Never Married	Married	Widowed	Divorced
White	0.182	0.502	0.055	0.084
Black	0.045	0.048	0.008	0.014
Other	0.018	0.037	0.003	0.004

a. Find the probability of *not* being married.

b. Find the probability of being widowed or divorced.

c. Find $P(W)$, $P(B)$, and $P(O)$, where W, B, and O represent the events of being white, black, or other, respectively.

d. Find the conditional probability of being divorced, given that a U.S. adult was white; that is, find $P(D$ given $W)$, where D represents the event of being divorced. Find the overall probability of being divorced, and verify that the two are equal.

e. Are being white and being divorced independent or dependent events?

f. As an alternative check for independence, find $P(W) \times P(D)$ and tell whether or not it equals $P(W$ and $D)$.

g. Find the conditional probability of being never married, given that a U.S. adult was black; that is, find $P(N$ given $B)$, where N represents the event of being never married. Find the overall probability of being never married, and verify that the two are different.

h. Are being black and being never married independent or dependent events?

i. As an alternative check for independence, find $P(B) \times P(N)$ and tell whether or not it equals $P(B$ and $N)$.

j. Explain why it makes sense to take race as the explanatory variable and marital status as the response, instead of the other way around.

6.5 Births in the United States in 2002 are classified according to the mother's smoking status and race, and according to whether the baby's birth weight is low or normal.

	Low Birth Weight	Normal	Total
Smoker	0.02	0.18	0.20
Nonsmoker	0.06	0.74	0.80
Total	0.08	0.92	1.00

	Low Birth Weight	Normal	Total
Black	0.03	0.18	0.21
White	0.05	0.74	0.79
Total	0.08	0.92	1.00

a. There are three variables involved here; tell what they are, and whether each plays the role of explanatory or response variable.

b. Find the probabilities of a baby having low birth weight, for smokers and nonsmokers; in other words, find $P(L$ given $S)$ and $P(L$ given $N)$ where L is the event of the baby having low birth weight, S is the event of the mother being a smoker, and N is the event of the mother being a nonsmoker.

c. The probability of having a low birth weight baby is higher for smoking mothers; is it at least twice as high as it is for nonsmokers?

d. Find the probabilities of a baby having low birth weight, for blacks and whites; in other words, find $P(L$ given $B)$ and $P(L$ given $W)$ where L is the event of the baby having low birth weight, B is the event of the mother being black, and W is the event of the mother being white.

e. The probability of having a low birth weight baby is higher for black mothers; is it at least twice as high as it is for whites?

f. Which factor seems to play more of a role in low birth weights: smoking or race?

g. The above probabilities are based on all but four states (California, Indiana, New York, and South Dakota) which did not require reporting of tobacco use during pregnancy. Are there any obvious reasons why the relationship between smoking and birth weight should be different in those four states?

6.6 Of the 167,334 U.S. patents issued in 2002, the probability of being for durable goods was 0.76 and the probability of being for nondurable goods was 0.17. Given that a patent was for durable goods, the probability of being for an electronic product was 0.40. Given that a patent was for nondurable goods, the probability of being for a chemical product was 0.74. Altogether, what was the probability of a patent being for an electronic or chemical product?

6.7   The *Statistical Abstract of the United States* reports rates for people of various gender and racial groups who made visits to healthcare facilities in 2002.

a. The probability of at least one visit to a healthcare facility was $P(H$ given $M) = 0.787$ for males and $P(H$ given $F) = 0.881$ for females. The probability of at least one visit to a healthcare facility was $P(H$ given $B) = 0.836$ for blacks and $P(H$ given $W) = 0.841$ for whites. Is making healthcare visits more dependent on gender or on race?

b. Assume $P(M) = P(F) = 0.5$—that is, assume equal proportions of males and females—and use the information for males and females to find $P(H)$, the overall probability of at least one visit to a healthcare facility.

6.8   Let's suppose 100 students surveyed in 1970 and another 100 in 2003 said whether or not they were in favor of legalizing marijuana, with counts corresponding to the probabilities reported in Exercise 6.52 on page 264.

Counts Observed

	Make legal	Keep illegal	Total
Year 1970	41	59	100
Year 2003	39	61	100
Total	80	120	200

Counts Expected If Year and Opinion About Marijuana Were Independent

	Make legal	Keep illegal	Total
Year 1970			100
Year 2003			100
Total	80	120	200

a. Use the formula

$$\text{expected count} = \frac{\text{row total} \times \text{column total}}{\text{table total}}$$

to fill in the table of counts that would be expected if year and opinion about legalizing marijuana were independent.

b. Each of the counts in your table differs from the observed counts by how many?

c. If attitudes about marijuana really didn't change from 1970 to 2003, would it be surprising to see counts as reported in the observed table, instead of as in the expected table (where probability of being in favor of legalization is exactly the same in 1970 as in 2003)?

6.5   Solutions to Supplemental Exercises

6.1   a. Year is explanatory and marital status is response.   **b.** substantially increased, from 268/688 = 0.39 to 1,746/3,557 = 0.49   **c.** substantially decreased, from 229/688 = 0.33 to 709/3,557 = 0.20   **d.** stayed about the same, from 217/688 = 0.32 to 1,102/3,557 = 0.31

6.2   a. 60%   **b.** 831/(831 + 1,122) = 43%

6.3   a. single variable   **b.** The sum of probabilities exceeds 1.   **c.** 0.11 + 0.12 = 0.23 (if there was no overlap at all)   **d.** 0.12 (if all who attended jazz also attended classical)   **e.** Almost surely, some of those who attended jazz did attend classical concerts and others didn't.

6.4   a. 1 − (0.502 + 0.048 + 0.037) = 0.413   **b.** 0.055 + 0.008 + 0.003 + 0.084 + 0.014 + 0.004 = 0.168   **c.** $P(W)$ = 0.182 + 0.502 + 0.055 + 0.084 = 0.823, $P(B)$ = 0.045 + 0.048 + 0.008 + 0.014 = 0.115, and $P(O)$ = 0.018 + 0.037 + 0.003 + 0.004 = 0.062   **d.** $P(D$ given $W)$ = 0.084/0.823 = 0.102; $P(D)$ = 0.084 + 0.014 + 0.004 = 0.102   **e.** independent because $P(D$ given $W) = P(D)$ **f.** $P(W) \times P(D)$ = 0.823 × 0.102 = 0.084 = $P(W$ and $D)$.   **g.** $P(N$ given $B)$ = 0.045/0.115 = 0.391 and $P(N)$ = 0.182 + 0.045 + 0.018 = 0.245, and so the two are different.   **h.** dependent because $P(N$ given $B) \neq P(N)$ **i.** $P(B) \times P(N)$ = 0.115 × 0.245 = 0.028, which does not equal $P(B$ and $N)$ = 0.045.   **j.** Race can, to some extent, play a role in a person's marital status, but marital status cannot affect race.

6.5   a. Smoking or not is explanatory, race is explanatory, birth weight is response.   **b.** $P(L$ given $S)$ = 0.02/0.20 = 0.10 and $P(L$ given $N)$ = 0.06/0.80 = 0.08   **c.** Probability of low birth weight babies is not at least twice as high for smokers as it is for nonsmokers because 0.10 is less than twice 0.08.   **d.** $P(L$ given $B)$ = 0.03/0.21 = 0.14 and $P(L$ given W = 0.05/) = 0.05/0.79 = 0.06   **e.** The probability of having a low birth weight baby is at least twice as high for blacks as it is for whites because 0.14 is more than twice 0.06.   **f.** race   **g.** no

6.6 $0.76 \times 0.40 + 0.17 \times 0.74 = 0.43$

6.7 **a.** Making healthcare visits is more dependent on gender because $P(H$ given $M)$ and $P(H$ given $F)$ are more different from each other than are $P(H$ given $B)$ and $P(H$ given $W)$. **b.** $P(H) = P(H$ given $M)P(M) + P(H$ given $F)P(F) = 0.5 \times 0.787 + 0.5 \times 0.881 = 0.834$

6.8 **a.**

Expected	Make Legal	Keep Illegal
Year 1970	$80 \times 100/200 = 40$	$120 \times 100/200 = 60$
Year 2003	$80 \times 100/200 = 40$	$120 \times 100/200 = 60$

b. 1 **c.** No, because they only differ by 1.

TBP Chapter 7

Random Variables

7.1 Details and Examples

Discrete Random Variables

The Mean of a Random Variable

We mentioned on page 278 that we sometimes call the mean of a random variable its "expected value." This expression is somewhat misleading because we wouldn't necessarily expect the random variable to take this value, and for many discrete random variables, the mean itself is not a possible value.

EXAMPLE TBP 7.1 MEAN NOT NECESSARILY A POSSIBLE VALUE OF A RANDOM VARIABLE

Background: Recall the distribution of household size:

X	1	2	3	4	5	6	7
P(X = x)	0.26	0.34	0.16	0.14	0.07	0.02	0.01

Question: What is the mean of the distribution, and what is the probability that the random variable for household size actually equals its mean value?

Response: According to the formula, we have

$$\mu = (1 \times 0.26) + (2 \times 0.34) + \cdots + (7 \times 0.01) = 2.5$$

(where we have rounded to the nearest tenth).

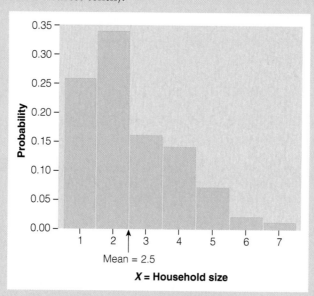

The variable never takes the mean value itself because households cannot consist of 2.5 people.

Practice: *Try Exercise 7.10(i,j) on page 287.*

Illustrating Rules for Means and Standard Deviations

To supplement the material beginning on page 280, a series of examples (*TBP 7.2* through 7.5) will look at combinations of random variables where the underlying situation is the roll of a die. We begin with this very simple random variable.

EXAMPLE TBP 7.2 MEAN AND STANDARD DEVIATION OF SINGLE DICE ROLL

Background: This table shows the probability distribution for number X rolled on a single die.

X = Number rolled	1	2	3	4	5
$P(X = x)$	1/6	1/6	1/6	1/6	1/6

Question: What are the mean and standard deviation of X, and how can we interpret them in the context of a probability histogram for X?

Response: The mean of X is

$$\mu = (1 \times 1/6) + (2 \times 1/6) + (3 \times 1/6) + (4 \times 1/6) + (5 \times 1/6) + (6 \times 1/6) = 21/6 = 3.5$$

The standard deviation is

$$\sigma = \sqrt{(1 - 3.5)^2\left(\frac{1}{6}\right) + (2 - 3.5)^2\left(\frac{1}{6}\right) + \cdots + (6 - 3.5)^2\left(\frac{1}{6}\right)}$$

$$= \sqrt{\left(6.25 \times \frac{1}{6}\right) + \left(2.25 \times \frac{1}{6}\right) + \left(0.25 \times \frac{1}{6}\right) + \left(0.25 \times \frac{1}{6}\right) + \left(2.25 \times \frac{1}{6}\right) + \left(6.25 \times \frac{1}{6}\right)}$$

$$= \sqrt{(6.25 + 2.25 + 0.25 + 0.25 + 2.25 + 6.25) \times \frac{1}{6}} = \sqrt{2.92} = 1.7$$

The mean number rolled with a single die is 3.5. Sometimes the roll is quite close to 3.5 (such as when a 3 or a 4 is rolled) and sometimes it is rather far from 3.5 (such as when a 1 or a 6 is rolled). Since the standard deviation is 1.7, this tells us that the typical distance of the numbers 1, 2, 3, 4, 5, 6 from their mean 3.5 is 1.7.

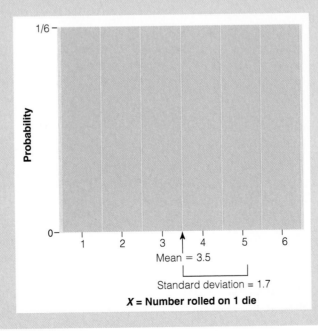

X = **Number rolled on 1 die**

The random variables of most interest to us—sample proportion and sample mean—are based on simpler random variables whose sum must be divided by sample size, which is the same thing as multiplying by $\frac{1}{n}$. Thus, we need to consider what happens to mean and standard deviation when a random variable is multiplied by a constant.

Example TBP 7.3 WHEN RANDOM VARIABLES ARE MULTIPLIED BY A CONSTANT

Background: This table shows the probability distribution for D, double the number rolled on a single die.

D = Double the number rolled	2	4	6	8	10	12
$P(D = d)$	1/6	1/6	1/6	1/6	1/6	1/6

Question: What are the mean and standard deviation of D, and how can we interpret them in the context of a probability histogram for D?

Response: The values 2, 4, 6, 8, 10, 12 are easily averaged together to find the mean $\mu_D = 7$. The standard deviation is

$$\sigma = \sqrt{(2 - 7)^2\left(\frac{1}{6}\right) + (4 - 7)^2\left(\frac{1}{6}\right) + \cdots + (12 - 7)^2\left(\frac{1}{6}\right)}$$

$$= \sqrt{\left(25 \times \frac{1}{6}\right) + \left(9 \times \frac{1}{6}\right) + \left(1 \times \frac{1}{6}\right) + \left(1 \times \frac{1}{6}\right) + \left(9 \times \frac{1}{6}\right) + \left(25 \times \frac{1}{6}\right)}$$

$$= \sqrt{(25 + 9 + 1 + 1 + 9 + 25) \times \frac{1}{6}} = \sqrt{11.7} = 3.4$$

The typical distance of those numbers from their mean, 7, is the standard deviation, 3.4.

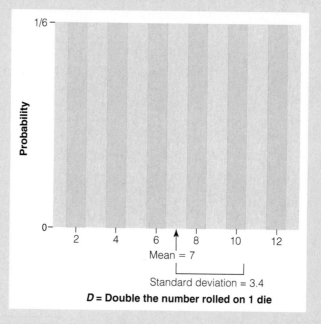

D = Double the number rolled on 1 die

We see that if the roll of a die is multiplied by 2, its mean (3.5) is multiplied by 2 to get 7; its standard deviation (1.7) is also multiplied by 2 to get 3.4.

Sample mean and sample proportion as random variables are formed by *summing* simpler random variables, then dividing by sample size. Thus, we also need to consider what happens to mean and standard deviation when we take a sum of random variables.

EXAMPLE TBP 7.4 WHEN RANDOM VARIABLES ARE ADDED TOGETHER

Background: We are interested in the random variable T, the total rolled with two dice. There are 36 possible outcomes altogether when two dice are rolled, shown in this interim table, along with their probabilities and the associated values t of the total rolled T.

Outcomes	T	Prob
(1, 1)	2	1/36
(1, 2)	3	1/36
(2, 1)	3	1/36
(1, 3)	4	1/36
(2, 2)	4	1/36
(3, 1)	4	1/36
⋮	⋮	⋮
(6, 6)	12	1/36

Next we use the Non-overlapping "Or" Rule to combine multiple probabilities of the same value of T, in order to produce the probability distribution of T.

T = Total on 2 dice	2	3	4	5	6	7	8	9	10	11	12
$P(T = t)$	1/36	2/36	3/36	4/36	5/36	6/36	5/36	4/36	3/36	2/36	1/36

Question: What are the mean and standard deviation of T, and how can we interpret them in the context of a probability histogram for T?

Response: The mean is the weighted average of the totals 2 through 12. A glance at the probability histogram for T (sketched below) shows a symmetric distribution centered at 7, so 7 must be the mean. The standard deviation is

$$\sigma = \sqrt{(2 - 7)^2\left(\frac{1}{36}\right) + (3 - 7)^2\left(\frac{2}{36}\right) + (4 - 7)^2\left(\frac{3}{36}\right) + \cdots + (12 - 7)^2\left(\frac{1}{36}\right)}$$

$$= \sqrt{\left(25 \times \frac{1}{36}\right) + \left(16 \times \frac{2}{36}\right) + \left(9 \times \frac{3}{36}\right) + \cdots + \left(25 \times \frac{1}{36}\right)}$$

$$= \sqrt{(25 + 16(2) + 9(3) + \cdots + 25) \times \frac{1}{36}} = \sqrt{5.89} = 2.4$$

The typical distance of those numbers from their mean, 7, is the standard deviation, 2.4.

We see that if two random variables for the roll of a die are added together, the mean of their sum (7) equals the sum of their means (3.5 plus 3.5). However, the standard deviation of their sum (2.4) does *not* equal the sum of their standard deviations (1.7 plus 1.7).

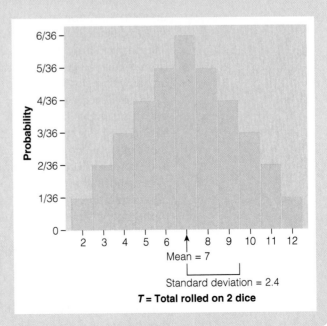

T = Total rolled on 2 dice

EXAMPLE TBP 7.5 DOUBLING A RANDOM VARIABLE'S VALUES DIFFERS FROM ADDING TWO IDENTICAL RANDOM VARIABLES

Background: In the past three examples, we have explored the distributions of a single dice roll X, double the roll of a die D, and the total rolled with two dice T.

Question: How do the shapes, centers, and spreads of the distributions of the random variables X, D, and T compare?

Response:

- **Shape:** Because all six possible rolls of a single die are equally likely, the histogram for X has a flat (and symmetric) shape that is called *uniform*. The six possible values of double the number rolled must also be equally likely, and so the histogram for D is also uniform. In contrast, the possible totals of two dice are not equally likely. There are many ways to get a total of 7 (namely, the pairs (1,6), (2,5), (3,4), (4,3), (5,2), (6,1)), and progressively fewer ways to get totals toward the extremes of 2 and 12. There is only one way for T to equal 2 and one way to equal 12. The result is a probability histogram with a symmetric triangular shape: It is highest in the middle (7), and falls away evenly on either side of 7.

- **Center:** The mean roll for one die is 3.5; the mean of double the number rolled for one die is twice that, $2(3.5) = 7$. The mean total roll for two dice is the sum of the two means, $3.5 + 3.5 = 7$.

- **Spread:** The standard deviation for the roll of one die is 1.7. The standard deviation of double the number rolled is twice 1.7, or 3.4. The standard deviation for the *total* of two dice is *not* twice 1.7, it is only 2.4!

The fact that the distribution of T (total rolled with two dice), has less spread than the distribution of D (doubling a single roll) is the manifestation of a natural phenomenon that lies at the heart of sampling theory and statistical inference. By "sampling" two dice, instead of taking twice the value of one die, we are dealing with a random variable that has a tendency to take values closer to its mean. If such a tendency is already conspicuous when we sample two dice instead of one, just imagine how pronounced it becomes when a random variable's values arise from taking much larger samples. This phenomenon will be the focus of Chapter 8, on Sampling Distributions.

The preceding examples showed us a specific case of behavior that is typical for means and standard deviations of random variables. This behavior is formalized in the rules for means and standard deviations of random variables that take the form $aX + b$ or $X_1 + X_2$. The rules enable us to derive formulas for the mean and standard deviation of counts or proportions, which will be useful if we want to get a normal approximation for the probability of a count or proportion falling in a certain interval. First, we'll put these approximation methods in context by outlining the various ways to solve binomial probability problems.

Various Approaches to Probability for Binomial Random Variables

We stated on page 295 that our preferred approach to solving probability problems for binomial random variables is to first reformulate (make it a statement about proportions instead of counts), then use a normal approximation. To keep things in perspective, it is helpful to consider that other approaches are sometimes taken.

- Use the "binomial formula" $P(X = k) = \binom{n}{k}p^k(1 - p)^{n-k}$ for $k = 0, \ldots,$ n. This formula isn't very useful for hand calculations useful unless we are finding probabilities for very small samples.

- Use binomial tables. This method spares us some tedious calculations, but once again the applications typically involve smaller samples.

- Use a calculator or computer software. In Part IV, we will discuss the use of computer software to perform inference about categorical data, focusing on *proportions* and bypassing the step in between that focuses on binomial *counts*.

- Use a normal approximation to find probabilities about the sample count X in the category of interest, such as $P(X \leq ?)$. This is closer to what we have in mind because it works well for large sample sizes. However, we generally prefer to draw conclusions in terms of proportions, rather than counts, because they provide a summary in relative terms, taking sample size into account.

Binomial Random Variables: Center, Spread, and Shape

Deriving Formulas for Mean and Standard Deviation of Counts and Proportions

Deriving formulas for mean and standard deviation of sample proportion is a rather "mathematical" undertaking, but all the groundwork has already been laid, and knowing the origins of these formulas may help make them seem less mysterious when they are invoked repeatedly throughout the rest of the book. In the end, students should focus on the results that tell us center, spread, and shape of the distribution of sample proportion. These results are deceptively brief, as you may confirm by looking at the summary on page 307. But a very rich and far-reaching theory is condensed into these conclusions, on which we will rely heavily in Part IV.

We have already seen an example where the random variable for number of tails in two coin flips can be thought of as the sum of two individual random variables for count of tails in a single coin flip. In this example, the sample size n happened to be 2 and the probability p of being in the category of interest (tails) happened to be 0.5. But the same kind of reasoning works for any sample size n and any underlying probability p.

Below is the very simple probability distribution for the count X_1 falling in the category of interest for the 1st individual in a sample. Obviously, if only 1 individual is selected, then the only possible counts in the category of interest are 0 and 1. The probability of being in that category is called p, so the probability of X_1 taking the value 1 is p. By the Sum-to-One Rule, the probability of X_1 taking the value 0 must be $1 - p$.

X_1 = no. in category of interest for 1st individual	0	1
$P(X_1 = x_1)$	$1 - p$	p

The same distribution applies to each of the n individuals in a random sample. As long as the sample is not more than one-tenth of the population size, sampling without replacement will have little effect on the probability p of each individual falling in the category of interest. You should picture n such distributions altogether, ending with this one:

X_n = no. in category of interest for nth individual	0	1
$P(X_n = x_n)$	$1 - p$	p

For each individual, the formula for calculating mean number in the category of interest can be applied. Multiplying each possible value by its probability and adding them together, we have

$$\mu_{X_1} = 0(1 - p) + 1(p) = p$$

and similarly for each of the n individuals, ending with this one:

$$\mu_{X_n} = 0(1 - p) + 1(p) = p$$

Next, we construct the binomial random variable X for count in the category of interest for the entire sample of n individuals by summing the n individual random variables X_1 through X_n:

$$X = X_1 + \cdots + X_n$$

Mathematicians refer to each of the individual random variables X_i, whose possible values are only 0 and 1, as "Bernoulli," and say that a binomial random variable is the sum of independent Bernoulli random variables.

Now we can apply our rule that tells us the mean of the sum of random variables equals the sum of the means. Each mean is p and there are n of them:

$$\mu_X = \mu_{X_1 + \cdots + X_n} = \mu_{X_1} + \cdots + \mu_{X_n} = p + \cdots + p = np$$

This interim result is useful if you want to solve for probabilities in terms of counts, rather than proportions. It tells us that when a random sample of size n is taken from a population with proportion p in the category of interest, then the mean number of sampled individuals falling in that category is np.

The spread of a binomial distribution is not so intuitive, but we will verify that the formula "makes sense," and yields the same results as what we found doing problems "the long way."

Just as we did for means, to get a formula for binomial standard deviation we begin with the very simple probability distributions for the count X_1 falling in the category of interest for the 1st individual in a sample, etc., up to the count X_n falling in the category of interest for the nth individual.

X_1 = no. in category of interest for 1st individual	0	1
$P(X_1 = x_1)$	$1 - p$	p

X_n = no. in category of interest for nth individual	0	1
$P(X_n = x_n)$	$1 - p$	p

For each individual, the formula for calculating standard deviation can be applied. Each time we subtract the mean p from each of the values 0 and 1, square the difference, weight each of the two differences with its respective probability $1 - p$ or p, sum these up, and take the square root.

$$\sigma_{X_1} = \sqrt{(0 - p)^2(1 - p) + (1 - p)^2(p)} =$$
$$\sqrt{p^2(1 - p) + (1 - p)^2 p} = \sqrt{p(1 - p)}$$

and similarly for each of the n individuals, ending with this one:

$$\sigma_{X_n} = \sqrt{p(1 - p)}$$

Again, we think of the binomial random variable X for count in the category of interest for the entire sample of n individuals as the sum of n individual random variables X_1 through X_n:

$$X = X_1 + \cdots + X_n$$

Then we apply our rule that tells us the standard deviation of the sum of random variables is the square root of the sum of squared standard deviations. This is the point at which we see the need for the requirement of independent selections (or population at least 10 times sample size, so the selections in sampling without replacement are approximately independent). Our rule for finding the standard deviation of a sum of random variables *applies only* when those variables are *independent*. Each standard deviation is $\sqrt{p(1-p)}$, so each squared standard deviation is just $p(1-p)$. Altogether there are n of them:

$$\sigma_X = \sqrt{\sigma_{X_1}^2 + \cdots + \sigma_{X_n}^2} = \sqrt{p(1-p) + \cdots + p(1-p)} = \sqrt{np(1-p)}$$

To find the mean of the random variable for *proportion*, not count, we note that the sample proportion $\hat{p}$ in the category of interest is just the sample count X in that category, divided by sample size n:

$$\hat{p} = X/n$$

Then we make use of the rule for means of random variables that are formed when we multiply another random variable by a constant.

$$\mu_{\hat{p}} = \mu_{X/n} = \frac{1}{n}\mu_X = \frac{1}{n}(np) = p$$

Once we have derived a rule for the standard deviation of count X, it is easy to find the standard deviation of $\hat{p}$. Since $\hat{p} = \frac{1}{n}(X)$, we simply apply the rule for standard deviations of random variables that are formed when we multiply another random variable by a constant:

$$\sigma_{\hat{p}} = \sigma_{X/n} = \frac{1}{n}\sigma_X = \frac{1}{n}\sqrt{np(1-p)} = \sqrt{\frac{p(1-p)}{n}}$$

Results about Normality Needed in Addition to Results about Mean and Standard Deviation

In the discussion among four students on page 297 it was established that the count of left-handed people in a sample of size 100 has a mean of 10 and a standard deviation of 3. This suggests that it wouldn't be unusual to get as few as 7 or as many as 13 left-handed people in a sample of 100. But it would be unusual for the sample count of left-handed people to be more than 2 standard deviations away from the mean, so we wouldn't expect to get fewer than 4 or more than 16 left-handed people in a sample of 100. However, if we want to draw precise conclusions about the probability of sample count falling in a certain interval, as we did informally just now, then it is not enough to know the mean and standard deviation. In addition, we must have a result that tells us about the *shape* of the distribution of counts. If the distribution of counts is very skewed, then it may be routine to fall a certain number of standard deviations above the mean, and virtually impossible to fall that number of standard deviations below the mean.

Similarly, the sample proportion left-handed in samples of size 100 has a mean of 0.10 and a standard deviation of 0.03. In a sample of 100 people, it wouldn't seem unusual to get a sample proportion of left-handed people as low as 0.07 or as high as 0.13. But it would seem unusual to get a sample proportion as much as 2 standard deviations away from the mean, so we wouldn't expect to see a sample proportion lower than 0.04 or higher than 0.16 in our sample of 100 people. This is an informal application of the 68-95-99.7 Rule, which really requires additional justification—namely, some support for our implicit assumption that the distribution's shape is approximately normal.

Checking for Approximate Normality of Sample Proportion

To supplement Example 7.31 on page 306, we check how well various examples discussed in Section 7.2 conform to the rule of thumb for approximate normality.

EXAMPLE TBP 7.6 CHECKING RULE OF THUMB FOR APPROXIMATE NORMALITY

Background: Example 7.28 on page 299 considered the distribution of sample proportions of tails in various numbers of coin flips; underlying population proportion of tails is $p = 0.5$. Example 7.30 on page 303 considered the distribution of sample proportions of left-handed or right-handed people for various sample sizes; underlying population proportions are $p = 0.1$ and $p = 0.9$, respectively.

Question: Is the rule of thumb for approximate normality of the distribution of sample proportion satisfied in each of the following?

1. $n = 4$ and $p = 0.5$

2. $n = 16$ and $p = 0.5$

3. $n = 20$ and $p = 0.5$

4. $n = 16$ and $p = 0.1$

5. $n = 16$ and $p = 0.9$

6. $n = 100$ and $p = 0.1$

7. $n = 100$ and $p = 0.9$

Response:

1. The rule is not satisfied at all for $n = 4$ and $p = 0.5$ because $np = 4(0.5) = 2$, which is much less than 10.

2. The rule isn't quite satisfied for $n = 16$ and $p = 0.5$ because $np = 16(0.5) = 8$, which is just under 10.

3. The rule is just barely satisfied for $n = 20$ and $p = 0.5$ because $np = 20(0.5) = 10$ and $n(1 - p) = 20(1 - 0.5) = 10$. Thus, if $p = 0.5$, as for the coin flips, any sample size of 20 or more would be considered "large enough."

4. The rule is not satisfied at all for $n = 16$ and $p = 0.1$ because $np = 16(0.1) = 1.6$, which is much less than 10.

5. Nor is the rule satisfied for $n = 16$ and $p = 0.9$; although $np = 16(0.9) = 14.4$ is more than 10, the skewness in the other direction gives $n(1 - p) = 16(1 - 0.9) = 16(0.1) = 1.6$, which is way too small.

6. The rule is just barely satisfied for $n = 100$ and $p = 0.1$ because $np = 100(0.1) = 10$ and $n(1 - p) = 100(1 - 0.1) = 100(0.9) = 90$.

7. Likewise, the rule is just barely satisfied for $n = 100$ and $p = 0.9$ because $np = 100(0.9) = 90$ and $n(1 - p) = 100(1 - 0.9) = 100(0.1) = 10$. If $p = 0.1$ or $p = 0.9$, any sample size of 100 or more is "large enough."

Binomial Random Variables: Permutations and Combinations

Although the majority of inference applications work with large enough sample sizes that a normal approximation is justified, some instructors like to expose their students to combinatorics and the binomial formula. The next several pages provide detailed material for such instructors, and the **TBP** Exercises for this chapter include plenty of problems for practice and for assignments.

In Section 7.2, we introduced a binomial random variable as one that counts the number of values in a certain category when sampling at random from a population of categorical values, where just two values are possible. We identified the fixed sample size as n, and specified the probability of falling in the category of interest as p.

Many—but certainly not all—situations with binomial random variables in elementary statistics applications involve large enough sample sizes that a normal curve fits the distribution fairly closely. This phenomenon was explored in Examples 7.28, 7.29, and 7.30 starting on page 299. Thus, for a large enough sample size, we can use a normal approximation to find a binomial probability.

There are still many contexts where a *small* sample is taken and we want to know the probability that a certain number of sampled individuals fall in a particular category. We will concentrate now on situations in which the sample size is too small to use a normal approximation. Still, the population must be large enough relative to sample size so that selections are more or less independent—otherwise the random variable for count in the category of interest would *not* follow a binomial distribution. A series of examples will be presented to demonstrate that in order to find binomial probabilities, we need to know how to count selections called *combinations*, which in turn require the counting of *permutations*.

Binomial Probability Distributions

To get a feel for the general pattern of binomial probabilities, it helps to consider entire probability distributions.

EXAMPLE TBP 7.7 A BINOMIAL PROBABILITY DISTRIBUTION

Background: Suppose both parents have brown eyes with a recessive blue gene. According to the laws of genetics, each time they have a child, the probability of the child having blue eyes is 0.25.

Questions: If this couple intends to have 3 children, what is the probability distribution for number X having blue eyes out of those 3 children? What patterns are evident in how each probability relates to the values of X, n, and p?

Responses: To determine probabilities, we begin with a list of all possible outcomes, labeling a child with blue eyes as B and not-blue eyes as N, along with the accompanying count X of children with blue eyes. The Independent "And" Rule helps us find the probability of each sequence. For instance, the probability of the first child with blue eyes *and* the second with blue eyes *and* the third with not-blue eyes is $0.25 \times 0.25 \times 0.75$.

Continued

Outcome	X	Probability
NNN	0	0.75 × 0.75 × 0.75
NNB	1	0.75 × 0.75 × 0.25
NBN	1	0.75 × 0.25 × 0.75
BNN	1	0.25 × 0.75 × 0.75
NBB	2	0.75 × 0.25 × 0.25
BNB	2	0.25 × 0.75 × 0.25
BBN	2	0.25 × 0.25 × 0.75
BBB	3	0.25 × 0.25 × 0.25

The Non-overlapping "Or" Rule allows us to combine probabilities for NNB, NBN, and BNN (the three different ways for X to equal 1), and to combine probabilities for NBB, BNB, and BBN (the three different ways for X to equal 2). Thus, our interim table leads to the following probability distribution table:

X	Probability
0	$1(0.25)^0(0.75)^3 = 0.421875$
1	$3(0.25)^1(0.75)^2 = 0.421875$
2	$3(0.25)^2(0.75)^1 = 0.140625$
3	$1(0.25)^3(0.75)^0 = 0.015625$

For each value of X, the probability of blue eyes ($p = 0.25$) is raised to the power equalling the count of children x with blue eyes, and the probability of not-blue eyes ($1 - p = 0.75$) is raised to the power equalling the count of children $n - x$ with not-blue eyes (where $n = 3$ is our sample size). There is no immediately obvious explanation for why the coefficients are, respectively, 1, 3, 3, and 1.

The relationship between the coefficients and the values of X, n, and p requires more thought; we will do another example before outlining the pattern.

In this and other examples, it is extremely important that the "selection" of individuals be independent. In the case of a couple having children, whether or not each child ends up with blue eyes is independent of whether other children have blue eyes; the process is equivalent to sampling *with* replacement. In contrast, suppose that parents picked their 3 children at random from a cabbage patch containing 8 children, 2 of whom had blue eyes. Certainly at the outset, the probability of obtaining a child with blue eyes is $p = 2/8 = 0.25$, but this is a sampling-*without*-replacement scenario, and the probability will change after the first child has been selected. For instance, the probability of obtaining all 3 children with blue eyes would be $2/8 \times 1/7 \times 0/6 = 0$, which is different from the sampling-with-replacement probability $0.25^3 = 0.015625$ established in our example above.

Our next example involves choosing an American household at random. Technically, we are sampling without replacement, but because the population of all households is so vast, removing 4 households, one at a time, for our sample has virtually no effect on any of the probabilities. Just as we have required for the selection of large samples so far in Chapter 7, we continue to require now for the selection of small samples that the population be at least 10 times the sample size. That way, sampling without replacement has relatively low impact, and the Independent "And" Rule still yields fairly accurate probabilities.

EXAMPLE TBP 7.8 BINOMIAL DISTRIBUTION FOR SAMPLE OF SIZE 4

Background: The probability of an American household owning a cat is 0.3.

Questions: If 4 households are selected at random, what is the probability distribution for count of households in those 4 that own a cat? What patterns are evident in how each probability relates to the values of X, n, and p?

Responses: Now our sample size is $n = 4$ and the probability of falling in the category of interest (owning a cat) is $p = 0.3$. We first produce an interim table listing all possible sequences of households C with and N without a cat, along with the number X with cats and the accompanying probability (calculated via the Independent "And" Rule):

Outcome	X	Probability	Outcome	X	Probability
NNNN	0	$0.3^0 0.7^4$	CNNC	2	$0.3^2 0.7^2$
NNNC	1	$0.3^1 0.7^3$	CNCN	2	$0.3^2 0.7^2$
NNCN	1	$0.3^1 0.7^3$	CCNN	2	$0.3^2 0.7^2$
NCNN	1	$0.3^1 0.7^3$	NCCC	3	$0.3^3 0.7^1$
CNNN	1	$0.3^1 0.7^3$	CNCC	3	$0.3^3 0.7^1$
NNCC	2	$0.3^2 0.7^2$	CCNC	3	$0.3^3 0.7^1$
NCNC	2	$0.3^2 0.7^2$	CCCN	3	$0.3^3 0.7^1$
NCCN	2	$0.3^2 0.7^2$	CCCC	4	$0.3^4 0.7^0$

Again, we combine like values of X via the Non-overlapping "Or" Rule to produce the probability distribution table:

X	Probability
0	$1(0.3)^0(0.7)^4 = 0.2401$
1	$4(0.3)^1(0.7)^3 = 0.4116$
2	$6(0.3)^2(0.7)^2 = 0.2646$
3	$4(0.3)^3(0.7)^1 = 0.0756$
4	$1(0.3)^4(0.7)^0 = 0.0081$

And again, the probability (0.3) of falling in the category of interest (owning a cat) for each household is raised to the power equalling the count x of households in that category, and the probability of not owning a cat (0.7) is raised to the power equalling the count $n - x$ of households without cats.

Finally, we would like an explanation for how the coefficients 1, 4, 6, 4, 1 arise. For instance, why is 6 the coefficient of $(0.3)^2(0.7)^2$? Again, there is no obvious answer to this question.

The rather deceptively simple question of how binomial coefficients arise requires some degree of understanding within the realm of a branch of mathematics called *combinatorics*, which deals with counting the number of possibilities in various types of situations.

To explain the origin of binomial coefficients, we need to be able to count combinations. To count combinations, we need to be able to count permutations. To count permutations, it helps to be familiar with factorial notation.

Factorials

Factorials are products of whole numbers in descending order down to 1. The factorial notation, written as an exclamation point, saves us from writing a long list of numbers, and also helps us concentrate on the numbers that are most important in a problem. As an example, we will say "one factorial equals one" and write "$1! = 1$." Our general rule will be that $0! = 1$ and $n! = n \times (n - 1) \times (n - 2) \times \ldots \times 1$ for any whole number n that is one or more. Here is a list of factorial values for the first few numbers:

$$0! = 1$$
$$1! = 1$$
$$2! = 2 \times 1 = 2$$
$$3! = 3 \times 2 \times 1 = 6$$
$$4! = 4 \times 3 \times 2 \times 1 = 24$$
$$5! = 5 \times 4 \times 3 \times 2 \times 1 = 120$$

and so on.

This notation will be quite helpful in spelling out rules for counting possibilities in various types of situations, starting with *ordered* arrangements of objects.

Permutations

> *Definition*   A **permutation** is an arrangement of objects where the order matters.

EXAMPLE TBP 7.9 COUNTING PERMUTATIONS OF 3 LETTERS

Background: Our "objects" consist of the letters A, B, and C.

Question: In how many different ways can we arrange the letters A, B, and C? In other words, how many permutations are there of the letters A, B, and C?

Response: There are 3 possibilities for the first letter in our arrangement. For each of these, there are 2 possibilities for the second letter, because one letter has already been used. For each of these two-letter arrangements, there is only 1 remaining possibility for the third letter. Altogether there are $3 \times 2 \times 1 = 3! = 6$ possibilities. We can list the possibilities as follows:

$$ABC \quad BAC \quad CAB$$
$$ACB \quad BCA \quad CBA$$

Practice: *Try Exercise TBP 7.1 on page 858.*

This simple example leads to the following general rule:

> There are $n!$ ways to arrange n different objects. In other words, the number of permutations of n different objects is $n!$.

The preceding example required us to arrange *all* of the objects in a group. For our purposes, we need to be able to count arrangements of a *subset* of objects.

Permutations of Objects Taken from a Larger Group

EXAMPLE TBP 7.10 COUNTING PERMUTATIONS OF 5 FROM 26 LETTERS

Background: Now our "objects" consist of all 26 letters of the alphabet, but we only consider ordered arrangements of 5.

Question: How many permutations are there consisting of 5 different letters taken from the entire alphabet?

Response: Because there 26 alphabet letters altogether, there are 26 ways to pick the first letter in our ordered arrangement. For each of these 26 possibilities for a first letter, there are 25 ways to pick a different second letter. For each of these two-letter arrangements, there are 24 ways to pick a third letter different from the first two. For each of these three-letter arrangements, there are 23 ways to pick a different fourth letter, and for each of these four-letter arrangements, there are 22 ways to pick a different fifth letter. Altogether there are

$$\overbrace{26 \times 25 \times 24 \times 23 \times 22}^{\text{5 factors}}$$

ways to pick five different alphabet letters.

Practice: *Try Exercise TBP 7.2(a) on page 858.*

Whenever we seek to establish a general rule, based on an example problem, it helps to discover how the problem's solution relates to the background information provided. In the case of permuting subsets of objects, this can be accomplished by expressing our solution in terms of factorials.

EXAMPLE TBP 7.11 COUNTING PERMUTATIONS OF SUBSETS OF OBJECTS WITH FACTORIALS

Background: In the preceding example, we found that the number of permutations of 5 letters taken from 26 is $26 \times 25 \times 24 \times 23 \times 22$.

Questions: How can we write $26 \times 25 \times 24 \times 23 \times 22$ using factorials? How can we write it as an expression involving only the numbers 5 and 26 appearing in the problem statement?

Continued

Responses: To complete the factorial, we multiply by $21 \times 20 \times \ldots \times 2 \times 1$. Dividing by $21 \times 20 \times \ldots \times 2 \times 1$ gets us back to the original number. Thus, we can write

$$26 \times 25 \times 24 \times 23 \times 22 =$$

$$\frac{26 \times 25 \times 24 \times 23 \times 22 \times 21 \times 20 \times \ldots \times 2 \times 1}{21 \times 20 \times \ldots \times 2 \times 1} = \frac{26!}{21!}$$

Another way to write this is

$$\frac{26!}{21!} = \frac{26!}{(26 - 5)!}$$

which lets us express the number of permutations using only the original numbers 26 and 5: The number of permutations of 5 objects taken from 26 different objects is $\frac{26!}{(26 - 5)!}$.

Practice: *Try Exercise TBP 7.2(b) on page 858.*

Now we can count the number of permutations of a subset of objects taken from a larger group using an expression that involves the size of the subset and the size of the larger group.

The number of permutations of r objects taken from n different objects is

$$\overbrace{n \times (n - 1) \times \ldots \times (n - r + 1)}^{r \text{ factors}} = \frac{n!}{(n - r)!}$$

The binomial coefficients that we originally sought are really counting *unordered* selections, or *combinations*. When we say that order does not matter in a combination, we mean that red, white, blue is the same color combination as red, blue, white; the same as white, red, blue; the same as white, blue, red; the same as blue, red, white; the same as blue, white, red. These represent just one "combination," not six, of three colors.

Combinations

Definition A **combination** is a selection from a group of distinct objects where order does not matter.

We will motivate our rule to count combinations by looking first at an example.

EXAMPLE TBP 7.12 COUNTING COMBINATIONS OF 3 FROM 5 LETTERS

Background: We are interested in a subset of 3 from 5 letters where order does not matter.

Question: How many combinations of three letters can we make from the letters A, B, C, D, and E?

$$\overbrace{}^{\text{3 factors}}$$

Response: First, we know there are $5 \times 4 \times 3 = 60$ *permutations*, or *ordered arrangements* of three letters taken from five different letters:

Permutations									
ABC	ABD	ABE	ACD	ACE	ADE	BCD	BCE	BDE	CDE
ACB	ADB	AEB	ADC	AEC	AED	BDC	BEC	BED	CED
BAC	BAD	BAE	CAD	CAE	DAE	CBD	CBE	DBE	DCE
BCA	BDA	BEA	CDA	CEA	DEA	CDB	CEB	DEB	DEC
CAB	DAB	EAB	DAC	EAC	EAD	DBC	EBC	EBD	ECD
CBA	DBA	EBA	DCA	ECA	EDA	DCB	ECB	EDB	EDC

But there are fewer *combinations,* or arrangements where order does not matter. In fact, the number of permutations of three letters is six times the number of combinations. This is because each combination of three letters is rearranged $3! = 6$ times when we count permutations. For example, the combination ABC, which takes up the first column above, includes the six permutations ABC, ACB, BAC, BCA, CAB, and CBA. To count combinations, we just divide the number of permutations by $3!$, and find altogether

$$\dfrac{\overbrace{5 \times 4 \times 3}^{\text{3 factors}}}{\underbrace{3 \times 2 \times 1}_{3!}} = \dfrac{5 \times 4}{2 \times 1} = 10$$

combinations of three letters taken from five letters.

Combinations									
ABC	ABD	ABE	ACD	ACE	ADE	BCD	BCE	BDE	CDE

Looking at our list of permutations above, we could count the number of combinations by counting the number of columns—there are 10 of them.

Practice: *Try Exercise TBP 7.3(a) on page 858.*

Notation for Combinations

Because counting combinations is essential in the expression for binomial coefficients, the following shorthand notation is used: For any non-negative whole numbers n and r (with r no greater than n), we write

$$\binom{n}{r} = \dfrac{\overbrace{n \times (n-1) \times \ldots \times (n - r + 1)}^{r \text{ factors}}}{\underbrace{r \times (r-1) \times \ldots \times 2 \times 1}_{r!}}$$

called "n choose r" because this counts the number of ways to *choose* r objects from n different objects.

Notice that, because the numerator is the same as $\frac{n!}{(n-r)!}$, we can also write $\binom{n}{r} = \frac{n!}{r!(n-r)!}$.

> The number of combinations of r objects taken from a group of n different objects is $\binom{n}{r} = \frac{n!}{r!(n-r)!}$.

EXAMPLE TBP 7.13 APPLYING THE FORMULA TO COUNT COMBINATIONS

Background: We are interested in the number of combinations of 5 letters taken from 26.

Question: According to the formula above, how many possible combinations are there of 5 alphabet letters?

Response: The number of combinations of 5 objects taken from a group of 26 different objects is $\binom{26}{5} = \frac{26!}{5!(26-5)!} = \frac{(26)(25)(24)(23)(22)}{(5)(4)(3)(2)(1)} = 65{,}780$.

Practice: *Try Exercise TBP 7.3(b) on page 858.*

Note that there is only one way to choose zero objects from any number of objects: $\binom{n}{0} = 1$ for any positive whole number n. Also, the number of ways to choose one object from a group of objects is the same as the number of objects: $\binom{n}{1} = n$. Finally, there is only one way to choose all of the objects from a group: $\binom{n}{n} = 1$.

Some useful shortcuts can be made when counting combinations; one of these is demonstrated by using the solution to a problem about taking combinations of 3 from 5 in order to find the solution to a problem about taking 2 from 5.

EXAMPLE TBP 7.14 INTUITING A SHORTCUT FOR COUNTING COMBINATIONS

Background: We are interested in combinations of 2 letters taken from 5 different alphabet letters.

Question: How many possible combinations are there of 2 from 5?

Response: We could start "from scratch" and take $\binom{5}{2} = \frac{5!}{2!3!} = 10$. Alternatively, we note that the number of combinations of 2 chosen from 5 is actually the same as the number of combinations of 3 that are left *unchosen*, or $\binom{5}{3} = 10$ as we found in Example **TBP 7.12**.

For n different objects and a whole number r between 0 and n.

$$\binom{n}{r} = \binom{n}{n-r}.$$

EXAMPLE TBP 7.15 APPLYING THE SHORTCUT FOR COUNTING COMBINATIONS

Background: In a previous example, we found the number of combinations of 5 letters taken from 26 to be 65,780.

Question: How many combinations of 21 letters can be taken from 26?

Response: Applying the above formula, we have

$$\binom{26}{21} = \binom{26}{26-21} = \binom{26}{5} = 65{,}780.$$

Practice: *Try Exercise TBP 7.3(c) on page 858.*

Calculating Binomial Coefficients

Let's return to Example **TBP 7.8**, where we wondered why the coefficient of $0.3^2 0.7^2$ was 6 when solving for the probability that 2 in a random sample of 4 households owned a cat.

In fact, referring to the list of possibilities CCNN, CNCN, CNNC, NCCN, NCNC, NNCC we see that $6 = \binom{4}{2} = \frac{4 \times 3}{2 \times 1}$ is the number of *combinations* of 2 C's (and the rest N's) from 4 letters: 1st and 2nd, 1st and 3rd, 1st and 4th, 2nd and 3rd, 2nd and 4th, 3rd and 4th. Similarly, $\binom{4}{1} = 4$ is the coefficient of $0.3^1 \times 0.7^3$, the number of ways to choose 1 C and the rest N's from 4 letters. Combining this result with the patterns already established in binomial probabilities, we can now present a formula for finding the probability that a binomial random variable takes any one of its possible values.

In general, the probability of getting x in a random sample of size n falling in the category of interest where each has probability p of falling in that category is

$$P(X = x) = \binom{n}{x} p^x (1 - p)^{n-x}$$

EXAMPLE TBP 7.16 APPLYING THE BINOMIAL FORMULA

Background: In World Series baseball, the first team to win four games is the champion. Clearly, the fewest games possibly played would be four, and the most would be seven. In 2003, a sports columnist observed that

Continued

24 of the last 50 World Series—that is, 0.48—lasted the full seven games. For the purpose of this example, we'll assume the two teams were always evenly matched (the probability of a given team winning each game is 0.5).

Question: What is the probability of a World Series lasting seven games?

Response: We calculate the binomial probability of exactly 3 wins for a team in 6 games played, when each time the probability of a win is 0.5:

$$P(X = 3) = \binom{6}{3}0.5^3(1 - 0.5)^{6-3} = 0.3125$$

Practice: *Try Exercise TBP 7.13 on page 859.*

Because unevenly matched teams would make it even *less* likely to last the full seven games, our solution to this example suggests that there may be psychological forces at work, with a tendency for the team that is behind to make a comeback.

The above formula is often cumbersome, especially to find probabilities over intervals, which requires solving for several probabilities and summing them. The traditional alternative was to use binomial tables; the current method of choice is to use a calculator or computer, specifying the sample size n, probability p of falling in the category of interest each time, and the particular count x in the category of interest for which we want to find a probability. Software commonly reports the *cumulative* probability for x, which is the probability $P(X \le x)$ of *up to* x falling in the category of interest. For instance, the probability of up to 2 children with blue eyes in our first example can be found as

```
Cumulative Distribution Function
Binomial with n = 3 and p = 0.250000
       x      P( X <= x )
     2.00        0.9844
```

By hand, we would take

$$1(0.25)^0(0.75)^3 + 3(0.25)^1(0.75)^2 + 3(0.25)^2(0.75)^1 =$$
$$0.421875 + 0.421875 + 0.140625 = 0.984375$$

Similarly, to find the probability of no more than 1 household with cats in a random sample of 4 households, we get

```
Cumulative Distribution Function
Binomial with n = 4 and p = 0.300000
       x      P( X <= x )
     1.00        0.6517
```

Definition   The **cumulative probability** $P(X \le x)$ is the probability of a random variable X taking a value up to and including a specified x.

If we use software to find a probability that is not the exact cumulative probability—that is, a binomial probability over some other interval besides $P(X \le c)$—then appropriate adjustments need to made.

EXAMPLE TBP 7.17 ADJUSTING CUMULATIVE PROBABILITY FOR BINOMIAL RANDOM VARIABLE

Background: An ad agency seeks comments on a commercial that aired during TV coverage of the Super Bowl. The proportion of all U.S. adults watching was 0.4. The agency takes a random sample of 5 adults.

Question: What is the probability that *at least three* were watching?

Response: We can find the probability of interest either by applying the formula or by employing software.

1. (solution with formula) The sample number X watching the Super Bowl is binomial with $n = 5$, probability of being in the category of interest (having watched the Super Bowl) is $p = 0.4$.

$$P(X \geq 3) = P(X = 3) + P(X = 4) + P(X = 5)$$

$$= \binom{5}{3}0.4^3 0.6^2 + \binom{5}{4}0.4^4 0.6^1 + \binom{5}{5}0.4^5 0.6^0$$

$$= 0.2304 + 0.0768 + 0.01024 = 0.31744$$

2. (solution with software) In general, software gives us a cumulative probability of the form $P(X \leq c)$ and we are seeking a probability of the form $P(X \geq c)$. According to the "Not" Rule, $P(X \geq 3) = 1 - P(X \leq 2)$. For $n = 5$, $p = 0.4$, we find

```
Cumulative Distribution Function
Binomial with n = 5 and p = 0.400000
       x      P( X <= x )
    2.00        0.6826
```

$P(X \leq 2) = 0.6826$ and so $P(X \geq 3) = 1 - 0.6826 = 0.3174$.

Practice: *Try Exercise TBP 7.18 on page 859.*

Summary of Binomial Probabilities

Whereas a *permutation* is an ordered arrangement of individuals, a *combination* is a selection where ordering is not taken into account. There are $n!$ permutations of n different objects, $\frac{n!}{(n - r)!}$ permutations of r objects taken from n different objects, and $\binom{n}{r} = \frac{n!}{r!(n - r)!}$ combinations of r objects taken from a group of n different objects. The exact binomial probability of getting x in the category of interest can be found by using the formula

$$P(X = x) = \binom{n}{x}p^x(1 - p)^{n-x}$$

where n is the sample size and p is the probability each time of falling in that category. This formula is useful for small sample sizes n.

Alternatively, either a computer or calculator can be used to find binomial probabilities. Care should be taken to distinguish between the *cumulative* probability $P(X \leq x)$ and the individual probability $P(X = x)$.

Continuous Random Variables and the Normal Distribution

Discrete versus Continuous Random Variables

This example supplements our discussion of the distinction between discrete and continuous random variables on page 315.

EXAMPLE TBP 7.18 WHEN PROBABILITIES FOR ORDINARY AND STRICT INEQUALITIES ARE THE SAME

Background: A commuter could wonder about the probability that his commute time on a given day is less than half an hour, or he may wonder if his commute time is no more than half an hour.

Question: Are the two probabilities different or the same?

Response: Commute time is a continuous random variable, so the two probabilities $P(X < 0.5)$ and $P(X \leq 0.5)$ are the same.

Practice: *Try Exercise 7.45 on page 331.*

Integrals provide us with a way to solve for areas under density curves by mathematically smoothing out the process of summing up areas of rectangles. Whereas for a discrete random variable X we have

$$P(a \leq X \leq b) = P(X = a) + \cdots + P(X = b) = \sum_{x=a}^{x=b} P(X = x)$$

with $P(X = x)$ the probability distribution of X, the analogous formula for continuous X is

$$P(a \leq X \leq b) = \int_{x=a}^{x=b} f(x)dx$$

where $f(x)$ is the height of the density curve for the probability distribution of X. Like most introductory statistics textbooks, this book does not require an understanding of calculus or integrals.

Standardized and Unstandardized Normal Values

These two examples provide more detailed review of the process of standardizing or unstandardizing values of normal random variables, mentioned on page 325.

EXAMPLE TBP 7.19 THE STANDARDIZED VALUE OF A NORMAL RANDOM VARIABLE

Background: Typical nightly hours slept by college students are normal with a mean of 7 and a standard deviation of 1.5.

Question: How many standard deviations below or above the mean time is 9 hours?

Response: Since the mean is 7 hours, 9 hours is *2 hours* above the mean. Since a standard deviation is 1.5 hours, this would be 2/1.5 = 1.33 *standard deviations* above the mean. Combining these two steps, we can write

$$(9 \text{ hours} - 7 \text{ hours})/(1.5 \text{ hours per standard deviation})$$

$$= \frac{9-7}{1.5} \text{ standard deviations} = +1.33 \text{ standard deviations}$$

On the left, we see how far a time of 9 hours is above the mean 7, and the graph on the right shows this distance in standard deviations.

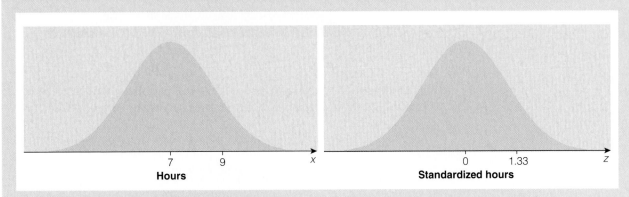

Practice: *Try Exercise 7.49(e) on page 331.*

   In the language of statistics, we have just found the "*z*-score" for a sleep time of 9 hours to be $z = +1.33$. Or, to put it another way, we have "standardized" the value of 9. Next, we review how to "unstandardize" a *z*-score.

EXAMPLE TBP 7.20 STANDARDIZING AND UNSTANDARDIZING VALUES OF NORMAL RANDOM VARIABLES

Background: Typical nightly hours slept by college students are normal with a mean of 7 and a standard deviation of 1.5.

Questions:

1. What is the standardized value for a time of 4.5 hours?

2. If a student's standardized time slept is +2.5, how many hours is this?

Responses:

1. $z = (4.5 - 7)/1.5 = -1.67$. This time is 1.67 standard deviations below average.

2. If $z = +2.5$, then time slept is 2.5 standard deviations above average: $7 + 2.5(1.5) = 10.75$ hours.

Practice: *Try Exercise 7.49(f,g) on page 331.*

Using the 68-95-99.7 Rule to Estimate Probabilities

These sketches illustrate the probabilities estimated in parts 1 and 2 of Example 7.39 on page 321.

   1. According to the sketch, $P(Z < +2.8)$ will be close to the area under the entire curve, which is 1. (Tables or software give a precise answer of 0.9974.)

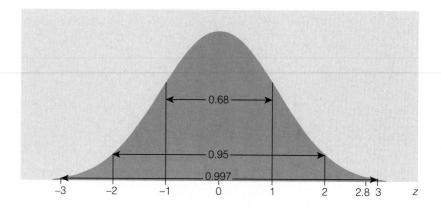

2. According to the sketch, $P(Z < -1.47)$ will be somewhere between 0.025 and 0.16. (Tables or software give a precise answer of 0.0708.)

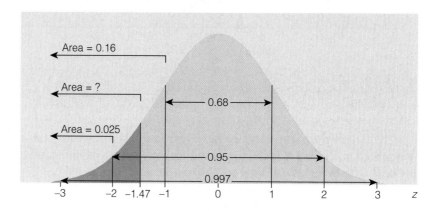

Here is a sketch for the response to the second part of Example 7.41 on page 323 that asked, "The probability is 0.15 that a standardized normal variable takes a value above what value of z?"

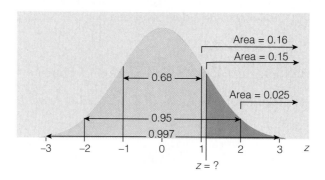

Here is a sketch of the quartiles of the z curve, to accompany the second part of Example 7.42 on page 324.

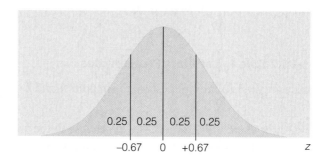

Example 7.43 on page 325 asked, "The probability is 0.04 that a randomly chosen student will sleep less than how many hours?" After solving the problem, we mentioned that the question could have been rephrased to ask, "What sleep time is in the 4th percentile?" Here is an example that helps students to think about percentiles.

EXAMPLE TBP 7.21 THINKING IN TERMS OF PERCENTILES

Background: The height X (in inches) of a randomly chosen woman is a normal random variable with mean 65, standard deviation 2.5.

Question: What is the approximate height of a woman who is at the 58th percentile?

Response: According to the sketch, the value of z with area 0.58 to the left must be somewhere between 0 and 1 (closer to 0 than to 1). Her height is somewhere between 65 and 67.5 inches (closer to 65). (Tables or software give a precise answer of $z = 0.20$, which unstandardizes to $x = 65 + 0.20(2.5) = 65.5$ inches.)

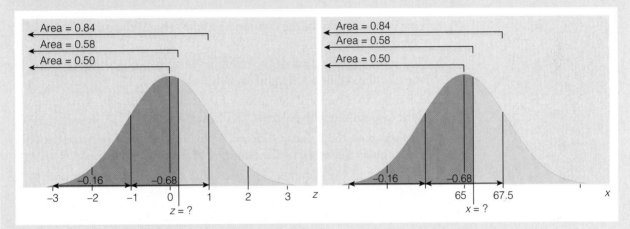

Practice: *Try Exercise 7.61(b) on page 333.*

Using the 90-95-98-99 Rule to Estimate Probabilities

We note that the information about the tails of the normal curve on page 327 lets us conclude the probability is 0.10, 0.05, 0.02, 0.01 (respectively) that a normal random variable takes a value as many as 1.645, 1.960, 2.326, 2.576 (respectively) standard deviations away from the mean *in either direction*. This last statement actually makes use of the "Or" Rule for non-overlapping events. We can write

$$P(|Z| \geq 1.645) = P(Z \leq -1.645 \text{ or } Z \geq +1.645) =$$

$$P(Z \geq -1.645) + P(Z \geq +1.645) = 0.05 + 0.05 = 0.10$$

This result will turn out to be useful for finding P-values for two-tailed hypothesis tests.

7.2 Activities

Activity: Random Variables and Rules for Means and Variances

Using the Computer

Discuss whether these pairs of variables should be dependent or independent for college students: height and shoe size; height and age. Then students access survey data (preferably the large data file that accompanies this book; otherwise data for their own class can be used). *http://www.pitt.edu/~nancyp/bigpicture/surveydata.txt* Students add to the existing columns Height, Shoesize, and Age by creating additional columns for height with a 1-inch heel "HeightPlus1," height in centimeters "2.5TimesHeight," sum of height and shoesize "HeightPlusShoe," and sum of height and age "HeightPlusAge."

Now find means and standard deviations of Height, Shoesize, Age, HeightPlus1, 2.5TimesHeight, HeightPlusShoesize, HeightPlusAge. Verify the following, and explain:

1. One plus the mean of the column "Height" equals the mean of the column "HeightPlusOne."

2. The standard deviation of the column "Height" equals the standard deviation of the column "HeightPlusOne."

3. 2.5 times the standard deviation of the column "Height" equals the standard deviation of the column "2.5TimesHeight."

4. The mean of the column "Height" plus the mean of the column "Shoesize" equals the mean of the column "HeightPlusShoesize."

5. The mean of the column "Height" plus the mean of the column "Age" equals the mean of the column "HeightPlusAge."

Calculate variances of Height, Shoesize, Age, HeightPlusShoesize, and HeightPlusAge by squaring standard deviations. Explain why the variance of the column "Height" plus the variance of the column "Shoesize" does *not* equal the variance of the column "HeightPlusShoesize." Verify that they are in fact quite different.

Explain why the variance of the column "Height" plus the variance of the column "Age" *approximately* equals the variance of the column "HeightPlusAge." Verify that they are, in fact, quite close.

In Chapter 7, we will establish a formula for standard deviation of sample mean $\overline{X} = (X_1 + X_2 + \cdots + X_n)/n$ by claiming that

$$Variance[(X_1 + X_2 + \cdots + X_n)/n] =$$

$$(Variance[X_1] + Variance[X_2] + \cdots + Variance[X_n])/n$$

Discuss why this cannot be claimed if the sampled values X_1 to X_n are *dependent*.

In the Classroom

Discuss whether these variables should be dependent or independent: the number X on the first roll of a die and the number Y on the second roll of the die.

Each student rolls a die twice. Together, the class creates columns X and Y for the values of their first and second rolls. Students create additional columns X + 1 for the values of the first roll plus one, 2X for doubling the values of the first roll, and X + Y for the total of each pair. Either the class together or just the instructor finds means and standard deviations of X, Y, X + 1, 2X, and X + Y.

Verify the following, and explain:

1. One plus the mean of the column "X" equals the mean of the column "$X + 1$."

2. The standard deviation of the column "X" equals the standard deviation of the column "$X + 1$."

3. 2 times the standard deviation of the column "X" equals the standard deviation of the column "$2X$."

4. The mean of the column "X" plus the mean of the column "Y" equals the mean of the column "$X + Y$."

5. The standard deviation of the column "X" plus the standard deviation of the column "Y" does not equal the standard deviation of the column "$X + Y$."

Calculate variances of X, Y, and $X + Y$. Explain why these *are* (approximately) equal, and verify: The variance of the column "X" plus the variance of the column "Y" approximately equals the variance of the column "$X + Y$."

Discuss whether these variables should be dependent or independent: The number X on the first roll of a die and the total $X + Y$ of the first and second rolls.

Create a new column $X + (X + Y)$ by summing the first roll X with the total of two rolls $X + Y$. Explain why these should be *not* be equal, and verify that they are different: The variance of the column "X" plus the variance of the column "$X + Y$" does not equal the variance of the column "$X + (X + Y)$."

In Chapter 8, we will establish a formula for standard deviation of sample mean $\overline{X} = (X_1 + X_2 + \cdots + X_n)/n$ by claiming that

$$Variance[(X_1 + X_2 + \cdots + X_n)/n] =$$

$$(Variance[X_1] + Variance[X_2] + \cdots + Variance[X_n])/n$$

Discuss why this cannot be claimed if the sampled values X_1 to X_n are *dependent*.

Activity: Binomial Random Variables and the Behavior of Sample Proportion

Using the Computer

Discuss and predict center (mean), spread (standard deviation) and shape of the distribution of proportion of heads in (a) 1 coin flip (b) 4 coin flips (c) 20 coin flips. (Use values of n and p, and formulas for mean and standard deviation of sample proportion $\hat{p}$.)

Each student creates a column "Coin flip" with just two values, H and T.

a. Each student uses software to randomly sample 1 coin flip value and reports aloud the proportion of heads as being 0 or 1. The instructor constructs a histogram of the class's sample proportions so shape can be discussed; software is used to calculate the mean and standard deviation of the class's sample proportions, and these are compared to the exact mean and standard deviation discussed in (a) above.

b. Each student uses software to randomly sample (*with* replacement) 4 coin flip values and reports aloud the proportion of heads as being 0, 0.25, 0.5, 0.75, or 1. The instructor constructs a histogram of the class's sample proportions so shape can be discussed; software is used to calculate the mean and standard deviation of the class's sample proportions, and these are compared to the exact mean and standard deviation discussed in (b) above. (Optional: Why is sampling with replacement appropriate for simulating coin flips?)

c. Each student uses software to randomly sample (*with* replacement) 20 coin flip values and reports aloud the proportion of heads as being

0, 0.05, 0.10, etc. up to 1. The instructor constructs a histogram of the class's sample proportions so shape can be discussed; software is used to calculate the mean and standard deviation of the class's sample proportions, and these are compared to the exact mean and standard deviation discussed in (c) above.

Which of the three histograms has a shape closest to normal? Would the activity's results be any different if the class size were much larger?

In the Classroom

Each student needs a coin to flip; alternatively, each student can roll a die and count even numbers as heads and odds as tails.

Discuss and predict center (mean), spread (standard deviation) and shape of the distribution of proportion of heads in (a) 1 coin flip (b) 4 coin flips (c) 20 coin flips. (Use values of n and p, and formulas for mean and standard deviation of sample proportion $\hat{p}$.)

a. Each student flips a coin 1 time and reports aloud the proportion of heads as being 0 or 1. The instructor constructs a histogram of the class's sample proportions so shape can be discussed; mean and standard deviation of the class's sample proportions are found (either by everyone in the class or by the instructor) with a calculator, and these are compared to the exact mean and standard deviation discussed in (a) above.

b. Each student flips a coin 4 times and reports aloud the proportion of heads as being 0, 0.25, 0.5, 0.75, or 1. The instructor constructs a histogram of the class's sample proportions so shape can be discussed; mean and standard deviation of the class's sample proportions are found, and these are compared to the exact mean and standard deviation discussed in (b) above.

c. Each student flips a coin 20 times and reports aloud the proportion of heads as being 0, 0.05, 0.10, etc. up to 1. The instructor constructs a histogram of the class's sample proportions so shape can be discussed; mean and standard deviation of the class's sample proportions are found, and these are compared to the exact mean and standard deviation discussed in (c) above.

Which of the three histograms has a shape closest to normal? Would the activity's results be any different if the class size were much larger? Discuss. Students may also discuss to what extent their histograms would differ if they recorded counts instead of proportions.

Activity: Normal Random Variables

Using the Computer

This activity helps to reinforce the 68-95-99.7 Rule as well as more specific information about the tails of the normal curve (the 90-95-98-99 Rule).

First, students review the proportion of standard normal values between -1 and $+1$; between -2 and $+2$; between -3 and $+3$.

Next, each student accesses data from the book's existing data file about several hundred students surveyed previously; specifically, they will work with the column of 391 Verbal SAT scores, whose distribution is quite close to normal, with mean 591.84 and standard deviation 73.24. To standardize these values, create a column VerbalZ from the original column Verbal by subtracting the mean 591.84 and dividing by the standard deviation 73.24. Sort this column from lowest to highest. Produce histograms of the original and standardized scores to verify that centers, spreads, and shapes appear as they should. Then students report to the instructor how many of the 391 z-scores are less than -3, less than -2, less than -1, greater than $+1$, greater than $+2$, and greater than $+3$. Using this information, they calculate together the proportion of standardized values between -1 and $+1$; between -2 and $+2$; between -3 and $+3$. Looking at these proportions, the class should discuss how well the z-scores conform to the 68-95-99.7 Rule.

Now discuss the fact that for standard normal values z, 1% exceed 2.576 in absolute value, 2% exceed 2.326 in absolute value, and 10% exceed 1.645 in absolute value. Students report to the instructor how many of the 391 z-scores are less than -2.576, less than -2.326, less than -1.645, greater than $+1.645$, greater than $+2.326$, and greater than $+2.576$. Using this information, they calculate together the proportion of standardized values exceeding 2.576, 2.326, and 1.645 in absolute value, and discuss how well the z-scores conform to a perfectly normal distribution.

In the Classroom

This activity makes use of the fact that the sum of 12 randomly chosen (with replacement) digits from 0 to 9 follows an approximately normal distribution with mean 54 and standard deviation 10.

Each student is assigned several sets of 12 random digits listed below, so that altogether all 100 sets of digits are used. (For example, if there are 20 students in the class, each is assigned 5 sets of digits.) Each student calculates the sum x of 12 digits in his or her assigned sets, and standardizes each sum x to z by subtracting the mean 54 and dividing by the standard deviation 10. For example, the sum of the first set is $x = 0 + 3 + 3 + 7 + 9 + 1 + 0 + 3 + 9 + 7 + 2 + 5 = 49$ and its standardized value is $z = (49 - 54)/10 = -0.5$.

1	033791039725	26	865000191950	51	112613209178	76	851147167752
2	524985161402	27	753663073694	52	092205731239	77	786101721703
3	222556463562	28	478158061081	53	190766022391	78	613249924822
4	933265639738	29	149766142777	54	252564625394	79	518121858176
5	770073116216	30	517492373451	55	456092135276	80	475865175155
6	322410845199	31	584862307358	56	295532587426	81	264645553342
7	419424015724	32	168754806934	57	558621777394	82	035359813094
8	791129611829	33	225264557638	58	980833340028	83	510360028361
9	927991431116	34	704998019750	59	716204759114	84	326213906024
10	886249205541	35	254712792887	60	523134595469	85	555444204204
11	101149666986	36	131294819430	61	592638856271	86	929340330716
12	820005513872	37	782913872937	62	942496087301	87	031470037466
13	873689245058	38	891948263218	63	267870185647	88	610162783853
14	284086415262	39	630662091167	64	624827786470	89	923081014671
15	229469795710	40	827869396711	65	786268681435	90	058672468109
16	475522389148	41	794196697658	66	070430319963	91	023864415548
17	187699838924	42	050407125414	67	590602978758	92	120663412928
18	204144121560	43	578235603673	68	982062524443	93	415060605242
19	195220791596	44	482401391600	69	057507765780	94	068912043284
20	513811288935	45	872877062806	70	978865098488	95	846705818784
21	717404612211	46	117536782328	71	690988927386	96	567237741558
22	099944155955	47	317547052249	72	609148986486	97	820018106832
23	916002025292	48	626455505213	73	461982550517	98	958233693743
24	370217689643	49	736480004732	74	193587141135	99	041398668400
25	628934608210	50	837957114053	75	687801494943	100	390600050627

Then students report to the instructor how many of the 100 z-scores are less than -3, less than -2, less than -1, greater than $+1$, greater than $+2$, and greater than $+3$. Using this information, they calculate together the proportion of standardized values between -1 and $+1$; between -2 and $+2$; between -3 and $+3$. Looking at these proportions, the class should discuss how well the z-scores conform to the 68-95-99.7 Rule.

Now discuss the fact that for a population of standard normal values z, 1% exceed 2.576 in absolute value, 2% exceed 2.326 in absolute value, and 10% exceed 1.645 in absolute value. Students report to the instructor how many of the 100 z-scores are less than -2.576, less than -2.326, less than -1.645, greater than $+1.645$, greater than $+2.326$, and greater than $+2.576$. Using this information, they calculate together the proportion of standardized values exceeding 2.576, 2.326, and 1.645 in absolute value, and discuss how well the z-scores conform to a perfectly normal distribution.

7.3 Guide to Exercise Topics

Discrete random variables: 7.1*, 7.2, 7.3*, 7.4*, 7.5*, 7.6, 7.7*, 7.8*, 7.9*, 7.10*, 7.11, 7.12*, 7.13*, 7.14, 7.15*, 7.16, 7.17, 7.18*, 7.19, 7.20*, 7.21, 7.22*, 7.23, 7.81, 7.82, 7.83, 7.84*, 7.85

Binomial random variables: 7.24*, 7.25*, 7.26, 7.27*, 7.28*, 7.29*, 7.30*, 7.31, 7.32*, 7.33, 7.34*, 7.35*, 7.36*, 7.37, 7.38*, 7.39, 7.40*, 7.41, 7.86, 7.87*, 7.88, 7.89*, 7.90

Continuous random variables in general: 7.42*, 7.43*, 7.44, 7.45*, 7.46

Normal random variables: 7.47*, 7.48*, 7.49*, 7.50, 7.51*, 7.52, 7.53*, 7.54*, 7.55, 7.56, 7.57*, 7.58, 7.59*, 7.60, 7.61*, 7.62, 7.63*, 7.64, 7.65*, 7.66, 7.67*, 7.68, 7.69*, 7.70, 7.91*, 7.92

7.4 Supplemental Exercises

PERMUTATIONS, COMBINATIONS, AND BINOMIAL FORMULA

7.1 In how many ways can seven people stand in line to have their picture taken?

7.2 A photographer wants to line up (in order) three people out of a group of seven to have their picture taken.

    a. Find how many ways this can be done by multiplying the numbers of possibilities for the first, second, and third person in the arrangement.

    b. Find how many ways this can be done by using a formula involving factorials.

7.3 We are interested in the number of combinations of three taken from a group of seven people.

    a. Find how many ways this can be done by dividing the number of permutations of 3

from 7 by the number of permutations of 3 objects.

    b. Find how many ways this can be done by using the formula for $\binom{n}{r}$.

    c. Use your answer to part (a) or (b) to report the number of combinations of 4 taken from a group of 7 people.

7.4 Suppose a wedding party—bride, groom, parents, ushers, maids of honor—has 20 people altogether. How many ways are there to photograph all possible combinations of 4 people taken from those 20 (where order does not matter)?

7.5 How many combinations of 16 people taken from 20 are possible?

7.6 A single octave of white keys on a keyboard contains 8 notes. How many "melodies" of

3 notes in a row are possible if notes may be repeated?

7.7 From an octave containing 8 notes, how many melodies of 3 notes are possible if notes may not be repeated?

7.8 From an octave containing 8 notes, how many "chords" of 3 (different) simultaneous notes are possible?

7.9 Fill in the binomial coefficients (a) through (c) for the binomial probability distribution when a random sample of size 2 is taken and for each individual the probability of falling in the category of interest is p.

X	Probability
0	(a) ? $(p)^0(1 - p)^2$
1	(b) ? $(p)^1(1 - p)^1$
2	(c) ? $(p)^2(1 - p)^0$

7.10 Use information from the table completed in the preceding exercise to find the probability that 1 in a random sample of 2 individuals falls in the category of interest, when altogether 40% of the population fall in that category.

7.11 Fill in the binomial coefficients (a) through (f) for the binomial probability distribution when a random sample of size 5 is taken and for each individual the probability of falling in the category of interest is p.

X	Probability
0	(a) ? $(p)^0(1 - p)^5$
1	(b) ? $(p)^1(1 - p)^4$
2	(c) ? $(p)^2(1 - p)^3$
3	(d) ? $(p)^3(1 - p)^2$
4	(e) ? $(p)^4(1 - p)^1$
5	(f) ? $(p)^5(1 - p)^0$

7.12 Use information from the table completed in the preceding exercise to find the probability that 3 in a random sample of 5 individuals fall in the category of interest, when altogether 50% of the population fall in that category.

7.13 The proportion p of all assaults on law enforcement officers that are made with weapons (as opposed to fists, etc.) is 0.2.

Suppose we look at a random sample of 6 assaults; use the formula $P(X = x) = \binom{n}{x} p^x (1 - p)^{n-x}$ to find the probability that exactly 1 of those assaults is made with a weapon.

7.14 In the United States, 90% of all drug seizures are of marijuana. Use the formula $P(X = x) = \binom{n}{x} p^x (1 - p)^{n-x}$ and the Non-Overlapping "Or" Rule to find the probability that no more than 2 in a random sample of 5 drug seizures are of marijuana.

7.15 The proportion of all U.S. bankruptcies in 2005 that were due to medical bills was 0.5. Use the binomial formula to find the probability that in a random sample of 4 bankruptcies, fewer than 2 were due to medical bills.

7.16 In the state of Connecticut, the proportion of blacks is about 0.1.

  a. Find the probability that in a random sample of 10 Connecticut residents, fewer than 3 are black.

  b. Use your answer to part (a) to find the probability that in a random sample of 10 Connecticut residents, at least 3 are white.

USING SOFTWARE: BINOMIAL PROBABILITIES

7.17 The proportion p of all assaults on law enforcement officers that are made with weapons (as opposed to fists, etc.) is 0.2. Suppose we look at a random sample of 6 assaults; use software to find the probability that exactly 1 of those assaults is made with a weapon.

7.18 In the United States, 90% of all drug seizures are of marijuana. Use software to find the probability that no more than 2 in a random sample of 5 drug seizures are of marijuana.

7.19 The proportion of all U.S. bankruptcies in 2005 that were due to medical bills was 0.5. Use software to find the probability that in a random sample of 4 bankruptcies, fewer than 2 were due to medical bills.

7.20 In the state of Connecticut, the proportion of blacks is about 0.1.

a. Find the probability that in a random sample of 10 Connecticut residents, fewer than 3 are black.

b. Use your answer to part (a) to find the probability that in a random sample of 10 Connecticut residents, at least 3 are black.

NORMAL PROBABILITIES FOR DIFFERENCES BETWEEN RANDOM VARIABLES

7.21 Math SAT scores in 2002 had mean 534 for males and 500 for females. Standard deviations for each gender group were approximately 100.

a. Let M be the Math SAT score of a randomly chosen male and F the Math SAT score of a randomly chosen female. Find μ_{M-F}, the mean of the difference in their Math SAT scores.

b. Find σ_{M-F}, the standard deviation of the difference in Math SAT scores for a randomly chosen male and female.

c. Math SAT scores for males and for females both have approximately normal distributions, so the distribution of the difference in scores $M - F$ is also approximately normal. Use the 68-95-99.7 Rule to sketch a normal curve for the distribution of the difference, whose mean you found in part (a) and standard deviation you found in part (b).

d. Draw a vertical line in your sketch roughly above the point where the difference is zero; if $M - F$ is less than zero, whose score is higher—the male's or the female's?

e. It is true that on average for the entire population, males have higher Math SAT scores than females. Is it also true that if an individual male and female were selected at random, the male's math SAT score is almost sure to be higher than that of the female? Explain.

f. In part (e), we assume SAT scores are known for all males and females in the population, and we want to draw conclusions about an individual randomly sampled male score and female score. Is this the process of data production, displaying and summarizing, probability, or statistical inference?

7.22 Children's fitness is assessed by finding the distance X, in meters, that they can run in 6 minutes. Overall, this distance varies fairly normally, with mean 835 and standard deviation 111.

a. Explain why distances run by the same student on two separate occasions should not be considered as two independent observations of the random variable X.

b. Would the standard deviation for distances run by the same student on multiple occasions be more or less than 111?

c. Let X_1 be the distance run in 6 minutes by one randomly chosen child, and X_2 the distance run by another randomly chosen child. Find $\mu_{X_1-X_2}$, the mean of the difference in the distances run.

d. Find $\sigma_{X_1-X_2}$, the standard deviation of the difference in distances run.

e. Because distances X are normal, differences $X_1 - X_2$ are also normal. Use the 68-95-99.7 Rule to sketch a normal curve for the distribution of the difference, whose mean you found in part (c) and standard deviation you found in part (d).

f. Use your sketch to estimate the probability that one student out-distances the other by more than 314 meters. Remember that this can happen if the first distance is at least 314 meters greater *or* if it is at least 314 meters less.

7.23 Male shoulder heights are normal with mean 56.65, standard deviation 2.46, in inches. Male crotch heights are normal with mean 33.05, standard deviation 1.85.

a. Suppose a man is picked at random, and we let S denote his shoulder height and C his crotch height. Find the mean of the distance $S - C$ from crotch to shoulder height.

b. If shoulder and crotch height were independent, what would be the standard deviation of the distance $S - C$ from crotch to shoulder height?

c. The actual standard deviation of the distance $S - C$ from crotch to shoulder height is 2.16 inches. Explain why the difference exhibits less spread than it would if a man's shoulder and crotch heights were independent.

7.24 Female shoulder heights are normal with mean 52.50, standard deviation 2.49, in inches. Female knee heights are normal with mean 18.95, standard deviation 1.06.

   a. Suppose a woman is picked at random, and we let S denote her shoulder height and K her knee height. Find the mean of the distance $S - K$ from knee to shoulder height.

   b. If shoulder and knee height were independent, what would be the standard deviation of the distance $S - K$ from knee to shoulder height?

   c. The actual standard deviation of the distance $S - K$ from knee to shoulder height is 1.78 inches. Explain why the difference exhibits less spread than it would if a woman's shoulder and knee heights were independent.

USING THE NORMAL TABLE: NORMAL RANDOM VARIABLES [SEE END OF BOOK]

7.25 In Exercise 7.57 we estimated z-scores using the 68-95-99.7 Rule. Now use tables to find the precise z-score corresponding to the given probabilities:

   a. The probability is 0.10 that a z-score is below what value?

   b. The probability is 0.001 that a z-score is above what value?

7.26 In Exercise 7.58 we estimated z-scores using the 68-95-99.7 Rule. Now use tables to find the precise z-score corresponding to the given probabilities:

   a. The probability is 0.4 that a z-score is below what value?

   b. The probability is 0.02 that a z-score is above what value?

7.27 In Exercise 7.61, we estimated heights of first-grade girls, given probabilities. Now use tables to find the precise heights, based on a distribution with a mean of 122 centimeters and a standard deviation of 5 centimeters:

   a. The probability is 0.02 that a girl at the start of first grade is taller than what height?

   b. The probability is 0.20 that a girl at the start of first grade is shorter than what height?

7.28 In Exercise 7.62, we estimated weights of first-grade boys, given probabilities. Now use tables to find the precise weights, based on a distribution with a mean of 25 kilograms and a standard deviation of 5 kilograms:

   a. The probability is 0.002 that a boy at the start of first grade is less than what weight?

   b. The probability is 0.12 that a boy at the start of first grade is more than what weight?

7.29 Exercise 7.29 reported that the proportion of all high school seniors who are married is 0.02. For a random sample of 500 seniors, find the mean and standard deviation (to the nearest thousandth) of sample proportion married, and find the probability that sample proportion is *less* than 0.03.

7.30 Exercise 7.37 reported that the proportion of all high school seniors with no siblings is 0.05. For a random sample of 400 seniors, find the mean and standard deviation (to the nearest thousandth) of sample proportion with no siblings, and find the probability that sample proportion is *more* than 0.04.

7.31 For samples of 80 Grand Canyon group hiking leaders, the *count* who were college-aged has mean 12 and standard deviation 3.2, whereas the *proportion* has mean 0.15 and standard deviation 0.04. Both distributions are approximately normal.

   a. Find the probability that fewer than 20 of the 80 group leaders are college-aged.

   b. Find the probability that the sample proportion of group leaders who are college-aged is less than 0.05.

7.32 Exercise 7.88 reported that for samples of 84 Grand Canyon hikers, the *count* preferring less-developed areas has mean 25.2 and standard deviation 4.6, whereas the *proportion* has mean 0.3 and standard deviation 0.05. Both distributions are approximately normal.

   a. Find the probability that at least 40 in a sample of 84 hikers prefer less-developed areas.

   b. Find the probability that the proportion preferring less-developed areas is at least 0.2.

7.33   In Exercise 7.89, for a sample of 25 U.S. bankruptcies, the proportion due to medical bills has mean 0.5 and standard deviation 0.1. Find the probability that sample proportion is less than 0.44.

7.34   According to Exercise 7.38, the proportion of females in the state of Connecticut is about 0.50. Find the mean and standard deviation of sample proportion for samples of size 80, and find the probability that no more than 31 in a sample of 80 potential jury members (presumably chosen at random) are female.

7.35   According to Exercise 7.39, the proportion of people in the United States speaking Spanish is about 0.11. Find the mean and standard deviation of sample proportion for samples of size 108, and find the probability that for a presumably representative sample of 108 people in the U.S. responding to an Internet survey, the proportion of Spanish speakers is more than 0.18.

7.36   In Exercise 7.53, the 68-95-99.7 Rule was used to report whether probabilities were more or less than 0.025. Use normal tables to report those probabilities more precisely.

7.37   In Exercise 7.56, the 68-95-99.7 Rule was used to report whether probabilities were more or less than 0.025. Use normal tables to report those probabilities more precisely.

7.38   According to Exercise 7.65, heights in centimeters of girls at the start of first grade are approximately normal with mean 122, standard deviation 5. For each of the following heights, find the z-score and the probability of being that short (or shorter) if it's negative, that tall (or taller) if it's positive.

    a. 106 centimeters

    b. 125 centimeters

    c. 116 centimeters

7.39   According to Exercise 7.66, weights in kilograms of boys at the start of first grade are approximately normal with mean 25, standard deviation 5. For each of the following weights, find the z-score and the probability of being that light (or lighter) if it's negative, that heavy (or heavier) if it's positive.

    a. 31.7 kilograms

    b. 47 kilograms

    c. 24 kilograms

7.40   In Exercise 7.91, the 68-95-99.7 Rule was used to estimate probabilities of children's gross motor quotient being less than a certain value, given that MQ scores are normal with mean 100 and standard deviation 15. Use tables to find these probabilities more precisely.

7.41   In Exercise 7.92, the 68-95-99.7 Rule was used to estimate probabilities of distance run by children in 6 minutes being greater than a certain value, given that distances are normal with mean 835 and standard deviation 111. Use tables to find these probabilities more precisely.

7.42   In Exercise 7.67, information about the tails of the normal curve was used to report whether probabilities regarding MQ scores were more or less than 0.01. Use normal tables to report these probabilities more precisely.

7.43   In Exercise 7.68, information about the tails of the normal curve was used to report whether probabilities regarding fitness scores were more or less than 0.05. Use normal tables to report these probabilities more precisely.

7.44   According to Exercise 7.63, chest sizes are approximately normal, with mean and standard deviation (in inches) 37.35 and 2.64 for males, 35.15 and 2.64 for females. Find the z-score for each of the given chest sizes; if it is negative, find the probability of a chest size that low or lower; if positive, find the probability of being that high or higher.

7.45   According to Exercise 7.64, waist sizes are approximately normal, with mean and standard deviation (in inches) 32.35 and 3.31 for males, 28.15 and 2.89 for females. Find the z-score for each of the given waist sizes; if it is negative, find the probability of a waist size that low or lower; if positive, find the probability of being that high or higher.

7.5 Solutions to Supplemental Exercises

7.1 $7! = 7 \times 6 \times 5 \times 4 \times 3 \times 2 \times 1 = 5{,}040$

7.2 **a.** $7 \times 6 \times 5 = 210$
  b. $\frac{7!}{(7-3)!} = 7 \times 6 \times 5 = 210$

7.3 **a.** The number of permutations of 3 from 7 is $7 \times 6 \times 5 = 210$ and the number of permutations of each of those 3 is $3 \times 2 \times 1 = 6$. Dividing 210 by 6, we get 35.
  b. $\binom{7}{3} = \frac{7!}{3!4!} = \frac{7 \times 6 \times 5}{3 \times 2 \times 1} = 35$ **c.** The number of combinations of 4 from 7 is the same as the number of combinations of 3 from 7, or 35.

7.4 $\binom{20}{4} = \frac{20!}{4!16!} = \frac{20 \times 19 \times 18 \times 17}{4 \times 3 \times 2 \times 1} = 4{,}845$

7.5 $\binom{20}{16} = \binom{20}{20-16} = \binom{20}{4} = 4{,}845$

7.6 $8 \times 8 \times 8 = 512$

7.7 $8 \times 7 \times 6 = 336$

7.8 $\binom{8}{3} = \frac{8 \times 7 \times 6}{3 \times 2 \times 1} = 56$

7.9 **a.** $\binom{2}{0} = 1$ **b.** $\binom{2}{1} = 2$ **c.** $\binom{2}{2} = 1$

7.10 $2(0.4)^1(0.6)^1 = 0.48$

7.11 **a.** $\binom{5}{0} = 1$ **b.** $\binom{5}{1} = 5$ **c.** $\binom{5}{2} = 10$
  d. $\binom{5}{3} = 10$ **e.** $\binom{5}{4} = 5$ **f.** $\binom{5}{5} = 1$

7.12 $10(0.5)^3(0.5)^2 = 0.3125$

7.13 $P(X = 1) = \binom{6}{1}0.2^1(1 - 0.2)^{6-1} = 0.393216$

7.14 $\binom{5}{0}0.9^0 0.1^5 + \binom{5}{1}0.9^1 0.1^4 + \binom{5}{2}0.9^2 0.1^3 =$ $0.00001 + 0.00045 + 0.00810 = 0.00856$

7.15 $\binom{4}{0}0.5^0 0.5^4 + \binom{4}{1}0.5^1 0.5^3 = 0.0625 +$ $0.2500 = 0.3125$

7.16 **a.** $\binom{10}{0}0.1^0 0.9^{10} + \binom{10}{1}0.1^1 0.9^9 +$ $\binom{10}{2}0.1^2 0.9^8 = 0.3487 + 0.3874 + 0.1937 =$ 0.9298 **b.** same as (a) (0.9298)

7.17 0.3932 (typical output shown here)
```
Probability Density Function
Binomial with n = 6 and p = 0.200000
        x       P( X = x )
      1.00      0.3932
```

7.18 0.0086 (typical ouput shown here)
```
Cumulative Distribution Function
Binomial with n = 5 and p = 0.900000
        x       P( X <= x )
      2.00      0.0086
```

7.19 0.3125 (typical ouput shown here)
```
Cumulative Distribution Function
Binomial with n = 4 and p = 0.500000
        x       P( X <= x )
      1.00      0.3125
```

7.20 **a.** 0.00860.9298 (typical ouput shown here) Cumulative Distribution Function
```
Binomial with n = 10 and p = 0.100000
        x       P( X <= x )
      2.00      0.9298
```
  b. $1 - 0.9298 = 0.0702$

7.21 a. $\mu_{M-F} = \mu_M - \mu_F = 534 - 500 = 34$
b. $\sigma_{M+F} = \sqrt{\sigma_M^2 + \sigma_F^2} = \sqrt{100^2 + 100^2} = \sqrt{20,000} = 141$ **c.**

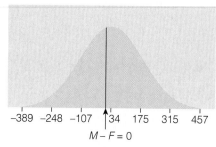

Difference (M – F)

d. Zero line is shown in the sketch above. If $M - F$ is less than zero then the female's score is higher. **e.** No, there is a substantial probability (roughly .4) that the female's score is higher. **f.** probability

7.22 a. Distances run by the same student on two separate occasions are not independent observations. If he or she runs a short distance on one occasion, the distance on another occasion is also likely to be short (and similarly if he or she runs a long distance). **b.** less
c. $\mu_{X_1-X_2} = 835 - 835 = 0$

d. $\sigma_{X_1-X_2} = \sqrt{111^2 + 111^2} = 157$ **e.**

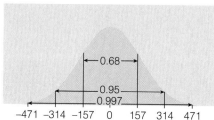

Difference in distances run in 6 minutes (in meters)

f. $0.025 + 0.025 = 0.05$
g. $P(|X_1 - X_2| > 314) = 0.025 + 0.025 = 0.05$

7.23 a. $56.65 - 33.05 = 23.60$
b. $\sqrt{2.46^2 + 1.85^2} = 3.08$ **c.** The difference is not as unpredictable, because a small value of S wouldn't often occur with a large value of C, and vice versa.

7.24 a. mean $52.50 - 18.95 = 33.55$
b. $\sqrt{2.49^2 + 1.06^2} = 2.71$ **c.** The difference is not as unpredictable, because a small value of S wouldn't often occur with a large value of K, and vice versa.

7.25 a. -1.28 **b.** $+3.08$ or $+3.09$

7.26 a. -0.25 **b.** $+2.05$

7.27 a. The top 0.02 has $z = +2.05$ so $x = 122 + 2.05(5) = 132.25$ centimeters. **b.** The bottom 0.20 has $z = -0.84$ so $x = 122 - 0.84(5) = 117.8$ centimeters.

7.28 a. The bottom 0.002 has $z = -2.88$ so $x = 25 - 2.88(5) = 10.6$ kilograms. **b.** The top 0.12 has $z = +1.17$ or $+1.18$ so $x = 25 + 1.17(5) = 30.85$ or $x = 25 + 1.18(5) = 30.9$

7.29 Mean is 0.02, standard deviation is $\sqrt{0.02(1 - 0.02)/500} = 0.006$, $z = (0.03 - 0.02)/0.006 = +1.67$. Probability of z greater than $+1.67$ is 0.0475, so probability of z less than $+1.67$ is $1 - 0.0475 = 0.9525$.

7.30 Mean is 0.05, standard deviation is $\sqrt{0.05(1 - 0.05)/400} = 0.011$, $z = (0.04 - 0.05)/0.011 = -0.91$. Probability of z less than -0.91 is 0.1814 so probability of z more than -0.91 is $1 - 0.1814 = 0.8186$.

7.31 a. $z = (20 - 12)/3.2 = 2.5$; probability of z greater than 2.5 is 0.0062, so probability of z less than 2.5 is $1 - 0.0062 = 0.9938$. **b.** $z = (0.05 - 0.15)/0.04 = -2.5$; probability of z less than -2.5 is 0.0062.

7.32 a. $z = (40 - 25.2)/4.6 = 3.22$; probability of z at least 3.22 is less than 0.0013. **b.** $z = (0.2 - 0.3)/0.05 = -2$; probability of z at least -2.0 is $1 - 0.0228 = 0.9772$.

7.33 $z = (0.44 - 0.5)/0.1 = -0.6$; probability of z less than -0.6 is 0.2743.

7.34 Mean is 0.5, standard deviation is $\sqrt{0.5(1 - 0.5)/80} = 0.056$, sample proportion is $31/80 = 0.388$, $z = (0.388 - 0.5)/0.056 = -2$; probability of z less than or equal to -2 is 0.0228.

7.35 Mean is 0.11, standard deviation is $\sqrt{0.11(1 - 0.11)/108} = 0.03$, $z = (0.18 - 0.11)/0.03 = 2.33$; probability of z greater than 2.33 is 0.0099.

7.36 a. less than 0.0013, or approximately zero
b. 0.0668 **c.** $1 - 0.0668 = 0.9332$
d. 0.0179 **e.** 0.0446 **f.** $1 - 0.2420 = 0.7580$

7.37 a. 0.0668 **b.** 0.0062 **c.** more than $1 - 0.0013$, or approximately 1 **d.** less than 0.0013, or approximately zero **e.** 0.3821 **f.** $1 - 0.0968 = 0.9032$

7.38 a. $z = (106 - 122)/5 = -3.2$; probability is less than 0.0013 **b.** $z = (125 - 122)/5 = 0.6$; probability is 0.2743 **c.** $z = (116 - 122)/5 = -1.2$; probability is 0.1151

7.39 a. $z = (31.7 - 25)/5 = 1.34$; probability is 0.0901 **b.** $z = (47 - 25)/5 = 4.4$; probability is less than 0.0013, or approximately zero **c.** $z = (24 - 25)/5 = -0.2$; probability is 0.4207

7.40 a. $z = (117 - 100)/15 = 1.13$; probability is $1 - 0.1292 = 0.8708$ **b.** $z = (132 - 100)/15 = 2.13$; probability is $1 - 0.0166 = 0.9834$ **c.** $z = (89 - 100)/15 = -0.73$; probability is 0.2327 **d.** $z = (144 - 100)/15 = 2.93$; probability is $1 - 0.0017 = 0.9983$ **e.** $z = (129 - 100)/15 = 1.93$; probability is $1 - 0.0268 = 0.9732$ **f.** $z = (51 - 100)/15 = -3.27$; probability is less than 0.0013, or approximately zero

7.41 **a.** $z = (600 - 835)/111 = -2.12$; probability is $1 - 0.0170 = 0.9830$ **b.** $z = (1092 - 835)/111 = 2.32$; probability is 0.0102 **c.** $z = (354 - 835)/111 = -4.33$; probability is greater than $1 - 0.0013$, or approximately 1 **d.** $z = (742 - 835)/111 = -0.84$; probability is $1 - 0.2005 = 0.7995$ **e.** $z = (960 - 835)/111 = 1.13$; probability is 0.1292 **f.** $z = (623 - 835)/111 = -1.91$; probability is $1 - 0.0281 = 0.9719$

7.42 **a.** 0.0082 **b.** 0.0287 **c.** less than 0.0013, or approximately zero **d.** 0.3446

7.43 **a.** 0.0287 **b.** 0.0808 **c.** 0.0446 **d.** 0.0548

7.44 **a.** $z = (32.60 - 37.35)/2.64 = -1.80$; probability of this low is 0.0359 **b.** $z = (45.00 - 37.35)/2.64 = 2.90$; probability of this high is 0.0019 **c.** $z = (41.00 - 35.15)/2.64 = 2.22$; probability of this high is 0.0132 **d.** $z = (28.00 - 35.15)/2.64 = -2.71$; probability of this low is 0.0034

7.45 **a.** $z = (38.30 - 32.35)/3.31 = 1.80$; probability of this high is 0.0359 **b.** $z = (25.00 - 32.35)/3.31 = -2.22$; probability of this low is 0.0132 **c.** $z = (20.00 - 28.15)/2.89 = -2.82$; probability of this low is 0.0024 **d.** $z = (37.70 - 28.15)/2.89 = 3.30$; probability of this high is less than $1 - 0.0013$, or approximately zero

TBP Chapter 8
Sampling Distributions

8.1 Details and Examples

Sample Proportion and Population Proportion

To supplement Example 8.2 on page 347, we can illustrate various random selections of students, with various sample proportions as shown in the figures below, for repeated random samples of size 10.

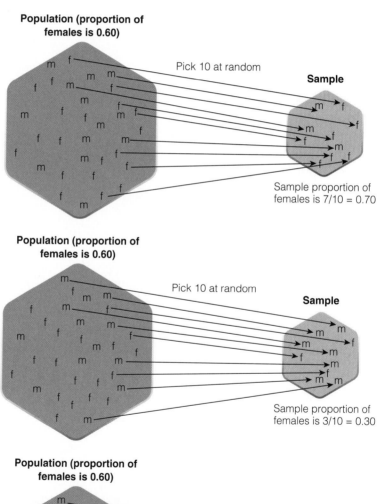

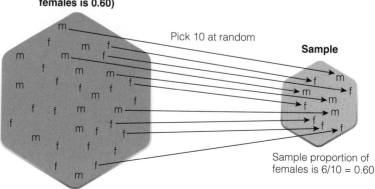

These are just three of many possibilities that can occur in random selections.

The parameter in Example 8.1 on page 346, for the proportion of times a number picked at random from 1 to 20 should equal seven, is obvious and exact because of the principle of equally likely outcomes. We often work with parameters that are less precise.

EXAMPLE TBP 8.1 PARAMETER BASED ON LONG-RUN OBSERVATIONS OR SUBJECTIVE OPINION

Background: A university spokesman claims that one-third of its commuting students commute by car. In a sample of 232 commuters, 72 commute by car.

Questions: What are the parameter and accompanying statistic in this situation? Under what principle has the parameter been determined?

Responses: The parameter is population proportion p commuting by car, said to be one third (or about 0.33). The accompanying statistic is the sample proportion $\hat{p}$ commuting by car, observed to be $72/232 = 0.31$. The parameter was apparently determined by some combination of the principle of long-run observed outcomes (commuting habits observed by the spokesman) and subjective opinion (his educated guess). Even if this proportion is not guaranteed to be accurate, we treat it as a parameter because it is purported to describe the entire population of interest, not a sample taken from that population.

Practice: *Try Exercise TBP 8.5(a) on page 877.*

Anticipating Both Forms of Inference

When we perform inference in the form of confidence intervals in Part IV, we will use conclusions like those in Example 8.4 on page 350 to make statements like, "If we sample at random from a population with unknown proportion p of females, we can be 95% confident that p is within 2 standard deviations of the sample proportion $\hat{p}$."

The other form of inference, hypothesis tests, uses what we know about the normal distribution to make decisions based on whether or not a value is what we'd consider to be unusual.

EXAMPLE TBP 8.2 TYPICAL VALUES OF SAMPLE PROPORTION BASED ON 68-95-99.7 RULE

Background: If students each pick a whole number at random from 1 to 20, then the overall proportion picking each of the numbers should be $1/20 = 0.05$. Suppose 400 students are asked to pick a number at random from 1 to 20.

Questions:

1. What are the mean and standard deviation of sample proportion picking the number seven?

Continued

2. What can we say about the shape of the distribution of sample proportion picking the number seven?

3. What does the 68-95-99.7 Rule show us about the distribution of sample proportion picking the number seven?

4. The probability is approximately 95% that the sample proportion picking the number seven would be within what distance of the population proportion?

5. If students truly picked numbers at random, would it be unusual for the sample proportion picking the number seven in a sample of 400 students to be as high as 0.075?

Responses:

1. As long as students do not influence one another, the selections are independent. This situation actually involves sampling with replacement because the supply of numbers is in no way depleted as students think of their chosen numbers. The sample size n is 400, and the proportion p in the category of interest (being the number seven) is 0.05. According to our formulas, mean is $p = 0.05$ and standard deviation is $\sqrt{\frac{p(1-p)}{n}} = \sqrt{\frac{0.05(1-0.05)}{400}} = 0.01$.

2. Our conditions for approximate normality are met: $np = 400(0.05) = 20 \geq 10$ and $n(1-p) = 400(0.95) = 380 \geq 10$. Therefore, the shape of the distribution of sample proportion picking the number seven is approximately normal.

3. The 68-95-99.7 Rule yields the following sketch for the distribution of sample proportion picking the number seven:

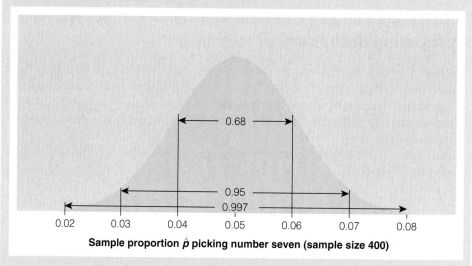

Sample proportion $\hat{p}$ picking number seven (sample size 400)

4. According to the sketch, the probability is 0.95 that the sample proportion picking seven would be within 2 standard deviations of population proportion—that is, within 0.02 of 0.05, or from 0.03 to 0.07.

5. If 400 students truly picked numbers at random, it would be unusual for the sample proportion picking the number seven to be as high as 0.075 because it falls outside the range of what we'd see 95% of the time.

Practice: *Try Exercise 8.57(a,b) on page 376.*

Checking Sample Size

Example 8.6 on page 351 demonstrated that the distribution of sample proportion has more spread for smaller samples. The other important aspect of sample size to keep in mind is that it must be large enough to justify approximating the distribution of sample proportion with a normal curve.

EXAMPLE TBP 8.3 WHEN THE DISTRIBUTION OF SAMPLE PROPORTION DOES NOT FOLLOW A NORMAL CURVE

Background: A coin is tossed 10 times.

Question: What is the probability that the proportion of tails is less than or equal to 0.4?

Response: We should not attempt to solve this problem using a normal approximation, because the sample size $n = 10$ is too small. The population proportion of tails is $p = 0.5$, and we see that $np = 10(0.5) = 5$ is smaller than 10. The probability histogram, although symmetric, would not conform well to a smooth normal curve because it only has 11 bars (for possible values 0 through 10). Instead of using a normal approximation, the correct solution method would be to find the binomial probability of count X of tails being less than or equal to 4, using tables, or software, or the binomial formula. According to the latter, the probability we seek is

$$P(\hat{p} \le 0.4) = P(X \le 4) = P(X = 0) + \cdots + P(X = 4)$$

$$= \binom{10}{0}0.5^0 0.5^{10-0} + \cdots + \binom{10}{4}0.5^4 0.5^{10-4} = 0.3770$$

Note that a normal approximation would result in a probability of 0.2643, which is off by about 30%.

Practice: _Try Exercise TBP 8.5(e) on page 819._

A Sample Proportion That Provides No Evidence of Bias

Researchers use statistics to produce evidence that "something is going on," such as the systematic tendency to under-represent Hispanics in prime-time television programs, as illustrated in Example 8.7 on page 352. In many cases, the data fail to show evidence of anything unusual.

EXAMPLE TBP 8.4 A SAMPLE PROPORTION THAT CONFORMS TO THE POPULATION PROPORTION

Background: A university program offers courses to high school students for college credit. Assuming high school students are evenly divided between males and females, the proportion of females would be 0.5.

Continued

Therefore, in samples of 267 students, sample proportion of females would have mean 0.5 and standard deviation $\sqrt{\frac{0.5(1-0.5)}{267}} = 0.03$. The shape should be normal because $267(0.5) = 133.5$ is more than 10.

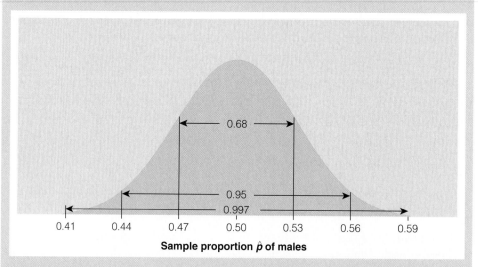

Sample proportion $\hat{p}$ of males

Suspecting that females might be in the majority in this college-in-high school program, an administrator looked at a sample of 267 students from several thousand who were enrolled, and found that 139 were female.

Question: What does the sketch of the distribution of sample proportion suggest about the administrator's suspicions that females would be in a majority overall?

Response: As a proportion, 139 out of 267 equals 0.52. Our sample proportion is a bit high compared to 0.5, but the sketch shows that it is not at all unusual. There seems to be no basis for the administrator's suspicion that females overall are in a majority.

Practice: *Try Exercise 8.64 on page 377.*

Sample Mean and Population Mean

To supplement Example 8.9 on page 357, we can illustrate various rolls of two dice, with various sample means as shown in the figures below.

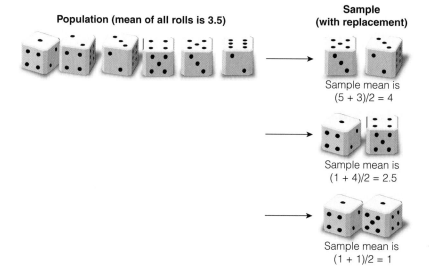

Population (mean of all rolls is 3.5)

Sample (with replacement)

Sample mean is (5 + 3)/2 = 4

Sample mean is (1 + 4)/2 = 2.5

Sample mean is (1 + 1)/2 = 1

These are just three of many possibilities that can occur in rolls of two dice.

In Section 8.1, we treated the number picked at random from 7 to 20 as a categorical variable: either the number was seven or it was not. In the next example, we treat the number picked at random as a quantitative variable. Like Example 8.8 on page 356, we want to identify the parameter of interest and the accompanying statistic.

EXAMPLE TBP 8.5 RANDOM NUMBER SELECTION AS A QUANTITATIVE VARIABLE

Background: A sample of 400 students picked a number "at random" from 1 to 20, and the mean of their selections was 11.6. The numbers 1 to 20 have a mean of 10.5.

Question: What are the parameter and the accompanying statistic in this situation?

Response: The parameter is the population mean number, $\mu = 10.5$. The accompanying statistic is the sample mean number picked, $\bar{x} = 11.6$.

Practice: *Try Exercise 8.53(a) on page 375.*

8.2 Activities

Activity: Distributions of Sample Proportion Living on Campus and Ambidextrous

Using the Computer

The first activity for this chapter helps students understand the sampling distribution of sample proportion, including the roles played by sample size and underlying population proportion. It is similar to Exercises 8.65, 8.66, 8.67, and 8.68 in the textbook but provides a more active look at the behavior of sample proportion.

First predict the center (mean), spread (standard deviation), and shape of the distribution of sample proportion for random samples of:

1. Size $n = 10$ from a population of students with proportion $p = 0.5$ living on campus
2. Size $n = 40$ from a population of students with proportion $p = 0.5$ living on campus
3. Size $n = 10$ from a population with proportion of ambidextrous people $p = 0.03$
4. Size $n = 40$ from a population with proportion of ambidextrous people $p = 0.03$

Next, each student accesses data from the book's existing data file about several hundred students surveyed previously; specifically, they will work with the column "Live," in which 0.5 of the students live on campus, and the column "Handed," in which 0.03 of the students are ambidextrous (both left- and right-handed).

Each student randomly samples 10 rows from Live and stores them in LiveSmallSample, 40 rows from Live and stores them in LiveLargeSample, 10 rows from

Handed and stores them in HandedSmallSample, and 40 rows from Handed stored in HandedLargeSample. Then each student sorts or tallies the columns to report his or her:

1. Proportion living on campus in samples of size 10
2. Proportion living on campus in samples of size 40
3. Proportion ambidextrous in samples of size 10
4. Proportion ambidextrous in samples of size 40

and the instructor keeps track of all of their sample proportions to construct histograms and calculate means and standard deviations of sample proportions for situations (1) through (4). Together the students discuss to what extent center, spread, and shape of the distribution of sample proportion are impacted by sample size and by whether p is such that the underlying distribution is fairly symmetric or fairly skewed.

Activity: Distribution of Sample Proportion of Blue M&M's

In the Classroom

This activity goes hand-in-hand with Example 8.2 on page 347. Materials needed are several bags of mini M&M's (about one bag for every 10 students), a bowl, a teaspoon, a tablespoon, and students' own calculators for finding sample proportions; also, one sheet of paper for recording sample proportions of blue M&M's in teaspoons and another for tablespoons.

In practice, just one random sample is taken from a population of categorical values and the statistic $\hat{p}$, sample proportion, is found—one time only. In theory, we may consider values of $\hat{p}$ for repeated samples, in order to get an idea of how sample proportion as a *variable* behaves. For samples taken at random, sample proportion is a *random variable*. The purpose of this activity is to show students how such a random variable behaves by exploring its *sampling distribution*: the distribution of values taken by the statistic in all possible samples of the same size from the same population. Results will be only approximately correct because instead of looking at an infinite number of samples, the number of samples is just the number of students in the class. Also, sample sizes will vary a bit because teaspoons and tablespoons are not entirely precise.

Each student randomly samples (without replacement) a level teaspoon of M&M's from the bowl and passes it on to the next student. Each divides the number of blues sampled by the total number sampled and records this sample proportion on a sheet of paper that follows the bowl of M&M's (more slowly) around the room. When all students have sampled a teaspoon, the bowl circulates again, this time with a tablespoon. A second sheet is used to record sample proportions for tablespoons. [For larger classes of more than 40 students, have half sample teaspoons and half sample tablespoons so there is enough time to complete the activity.] Meanwhile, the instructor discusses the sampling distribution more or less as follows:

Based on the author's experience as of 2009, the (population) proportion of blue M&M's in the bags of minis is one-sixth, or $p = 0.17$. We'll assume that a teaspoon consists of about 25 M&M's and a tablespoon about 75. What kind of values would sample proportion $\hat{p}$ of blue M&M's take for repeated samples of:

1. Size $n = 25$ (about a teaspoon) from a population of M&M's with proportion $p = 0.17$ that are blue.
2. Size $n = 75$ (about a tablespoon) from a population of M&M's with proportion $p = 0.17$ that are blue.

Discuss with students that if numerous samples or repetitions of the same size are taken,

1. **Center**—The mean of the distribution of sample proportion $\hat{p}$ will be the true proportion p from the population. [Thus, $\hat{p}$ is an unbiased estimator for p.]

2. **Spread**—Standard deviation of sample proportion is

$$\sqrt{\frac{p(1-p)}{n}}$$

Thus, the spread decreases as sample size increases.

3. **Shape**—The frequency curve made from proportions from the various samples will be approximately normal [Central Limit Theorem].

Applying these rules to the M&M selections, we can predict that:

1. For a teaspoon (sample size 25),
   a. The histogram of sample proportion values will be centered around population proportion, 0.17.
   b. The standard deviation of $\hat{p}$ should be approximately
   $$\sqrt{\frac{0.17 \times (1 - 0.17)}{25}} = 0.075$$
   c. The histogram should be sort of normal, but the sample size may be too small to guarantee a true symmetric bell-shape.

2. For a tablespoon (sample size 75),
   a. The histogram should also be centered at 0.17.
   b. The standard deviation should be approximately
   $$\sqrt{\frac{0.17 \times (1 - 0.17)}{75}} = 0.043$$
   c. The histogram should be closer to normal.

Because 0.17(75) is well over 10, the Empirical Rule allows us to set up probability intervals for the sample proportion of blues in tablespoons. (The rule may not work very well for teaspoons, because 0.17(25) is only about 4.)
For samples of size 75, approximately:

- 68% of sample proportions should be within 1×0.043 of 0.17, that is, in [0.127, 0.213].
- 95% of sample proportions should be within 2×0.043 of 0.17, that is, in [0.084, 0.256].
- 99.7% of sample proportions should be within 3×0.043 of 0.17, that is, in [0.041, 0.299].

At this point, students should check how well their own sample proportions as a group conformed to the 68-95-99.7 Rule.

Activity: Distribution of Sample Mean SAT Score or Earnings

Using the Computer

This activity helps students understand the sampling distribution of sample mean, including the roles played by sample size and center, spread, and shape of the underlying population. It is similar to Exercises 8.80, 8.81, 8.82, and 8.83 in the textbook but provides a more active look at the behavior of sample mean.

First predict the center (mean), spread (standard deviation), and shape of the distribution of sample mean for random samples of:

1. Size $n = 10$ from a fairly normal population with mean 610, standard deviation 72

2. Size $n = 40$ from a fairly normal population with mean 610, standard deviation 72

3. Size $n = 10$ from a skewed population with mean 3.776, standard deviation 6.503

4. Size $n = 40$ from a skewed population with mean 3.776, standard deviation 6.503

Next, each student accesses data from the book's existing data file about several hundred students surveyed previously; specifically, they will work with the column of Math SAT Scores "Math," which is fairly normal with mean 610 and standard deviation 72, and the column of earnings (in thousands of dollars) "Earned," which is quite right-skewed with mean 3.776 and standard deviation 6.503. Produce histograms of the two distributions and verify the centers, spreads, and shapes to be as described above.

Each student randomly samples 10 rows from Math and stores them in Math-SmallSample, 40 rows from Math and stores them in MathLargeSample, 10 rows from Earned and stores them in EarnedSmallSample, and 40 rows from Earned stored in EarnedLargeSample. Then each student summarizes the columns of samples to report his or her:

1. Mean of a sample of 10 values from a fairly normal population whose mean is 610, standard deviation is 72

2. Mean of a sample of 40 values from a fairly normal population whose mean is 610, standard deviation is 72

3. Mean of a sample of 10 values from a skewed population whose mean is 3.776, standard deviation is 6.503

4. Mean of a sample of 40 values from a skewed population whose mean is 3.776, standard deviation is 6.503

and the instructor keeps track of all of their sample means to construct histograms and calculate means and standard deviations of sample means for situations (1) through (4). Together the students discuss to what extent center, spread, and shape of the distribution of sample mean are impacted by sample size and by whether the underlying distribution is fairly normal or skewed.

Activity: Distribution of Sample Mean Dice Roll

In the Classroom

This activity goes hand-in-hand with Example 8.9 on page 357. Materials needed are many ordinary (six-sided) dice: either one per student or eight for each row of students; students' own calculators for finding sample means; also, sheets of paper for recording sample mean rolls of 2 dice and for sample mean rolls of 8 dice.

In practice, just one random sample is taken from a population of quantitative values and the statistic $\bar{x}$, sample mean, is found—one time only. In theory, we may consider values of $\overline{X}$ for repeated samples, to get an idea of how sample mean as a *variable* behaves. For samples taken at random, sample mean is a random variable. The purpose of this activity is to show students how such a random variable behaves by exploring its sampling distribution: the distribution of values taken by the statistic in all possible samples of the same size from the same population. Results will be only approximately correct because, instead of looking at an infinite number of samples, the number of samples is just the number of students in the class.

Each student rolls a die twice (or rolls 2 dice and passes them on to the next student). Each averages the two numbers and records this sample mean on a sheet of paper that circulates around the room. When all students have found the mean of 2 rolls, they next find the mean of 8 rolls with the aid of a calculator. (A second sheet is used to record sample mean of 8 rolls.) Meanwhile, the instructor discusses the sampling distribution more or less as follows:

We know that the mean of all possible rolls of a die is $\mu = (1 + 2 + 3 + 4 + 5 + 6)/6 = 3.5$ and the standard deviation is

$$\sigma = \sqrt{\frac{1}{6}(1 - 3.5)^2 + \frac{1}{6}(2 - 3.5)^2 + \frac{1}{6}(3 - 3.5)^2 + \frac{1}{6}(4 - 3.5)^2 + \frac{1}{6}(5 - 3.5)^2 + \frac{1}{6}(6 - 3.5)^2} = 1.7$$

What kind of values would sample mean roll $\overline{X}$ take for repeated samples of:

1. $n = 2$?
2. $n = 8$?

Discuss with students that if numerous samples or repetitions of the same size n are taken from a population of quantitative values for a random variable X having mean μ and finite standard deviation σ, then the following hold for the sampling distribution of sample mean $\overline{X}$:

1. The mean of the distribution of $\overline{X}$ is μ [$\overline{X}$ is an unbiased estimator of μ].
2. The standard deviation of $\overline{X}$ is $\frac{\sigma}{\sqrt{n}}$, where σ is population standard deviation.

Thus, we can tell precisely how much the spread decreases as sample size increases: Increasing from 2 to 8 dice means the spread of $\overline{X}$ decreases from $\frac{1.7}{\sqrt{2}} = 1.2$ to $\frac{1.7}{\sqrt{8}} = 0.6$.

3. For large sample size n, the sampling distribution of $\overline{X}$ is approximately normal [Central Limit Theorem]. How large is large enough? It depends on the shape of the population distribution. More observations are required if the shape of the population distribution is far from normal.

Applying these rules to the dice experiment, we can predict that:

1. For 2 dice,
   a. The histogram of sample mean values will be centered around population mean, 3.5.
   b. The standard deviation of $\overline{X}$ should be approximately $\frac{1.7}{\sqrt{2}} = 1.2$.
   c. The most likely mean roll is 3.5 (resulting from (1,6), (2,5), (3,4), (4,3), (5,2), or (6,1)). Lower or higher mean rolls are progressively less likely, with 1 (two 1s are rolled) and 6 (two 6s are rolled) being least likely. Thus, the shape should be somewhat triangular: highest in the middle at 3.5, descending on either side.

2. For 8 dice,
   a. The histogram should also be centered at 3.5.
   b. The standard deviation should be approximately $\frac{1.7}{\sqrt{8}} = 0.6$.
   c. The histogram should be closer to normal.

Because the underlying distribution is perfectly symmetric, the Empirical Rule should provide fairly accurate probability intervals for the sample mean roll of 8 dice. (The rule may not work very well for only 2 dice.)

For samples of size 8, approximately

- 68% of sample means should be within 1×0.6 of 3.5, that is, in [2.9, 4.1].
- 95% of sample means should be within 2×0.6 of 3.5, that is, in [2.3, 4.7].
- 99.7% of sample means should be within 3×0.6 of 3.5, that is, in [1.7, 5.3].

At this point, the class should check how well their own sample means as a group conformed to the 68-95-99.7 Rule.

8.3 Guide to Exercise Topics

Previewing sample proportions and sample means: 8.35*, 8.36*, 8.37*, 8.38, 8.39, 8.40*, 8.41, 8.42, 8.43, 8.44, 8.45*, 8.46, 8.47*, 8.48

Distribution of sample proportion: 8.1*, 8.2, 8.3*, 8.4, 8.5*, 8.6*, 8.7*, 8.8, 8.9, 8.10, 8.11*, 8.12, 8.13*, 8.14, 8.49*, 8.50, 8.51*, 8.52, 8.53*, 8.54*, 8.55*, 8.56*, 8.57*, 8.58, 8.59, 8.60, 8.61, 8.62, 8.63, 8.64, 8.69; Using Software: 8.65*, 8.66, 8.67, 8.68

Distribution of sample mean: 8.15*, 8.16, 8.17*, 8.18, 8.19*, 8.20, 8.21*, 8.22, 8.23*, 8.24, 8.25*, 8.26, 8.27*, 8.28*, 8.29, 8.30, 8.31, 8.32*, 8.33, 8.34, 8.70, 8.71*, 8.72*, 8.73, 8.74, 8.75*, 8.76*, 8.77, 8.78, 8.79; Using Software: 8.80, 8.81*, 8.82, 8.83

8.4 Supplemental Exercises

Warming Up

8.1 Researchers want to explore the question of the effect of charter school education on students' performances on math tests. Tell whether each of these possible designs features one quantitative, one categorical, one each quantitative and categorical, two categorical, or two quantitative variables:

a. Compare math scores for a sample of charter school students to math scores for a sample of non-charter school students.

b. For a large sample of students, determine whether they go to regular or charter school, and whether their math scores are below proficiency.

c. For a sample of students who attend charter schools, find the proportion whose math scores are below proficiency, and compare it to the known national proportion below proficiency for all students.

d. Find the mean math score for a sample of charter school students, and compare it to the known national average for all students.

8.2 Tell whether each of the following uses a paired, a two-sample, or a several-sample design:

a. Fourth-grade math scores are compared for 2003, 2004, 2005, and 2006.

b. Reading scores for charter school students are compared to reading scores of noncharter school students.

c. For a sample of students, the difference between their reading and math scores is examined.

8.3 MQ scores are used to assess children's gross motor development. Tell whether each of the following focuses on data production, displaying and summarizing data, probability, or statistical inference:

a. Researchers want to show the difference between MQ scores of sampled children who did and did not participate in sports.

b. Researchers want to see if children who participate in sports tend to have higher MQ scores, and must decide whether to survey the children about participation in any sports, or just formal club or team sports.

c. Researchers consider whether the mean MQ for a sample of children who participate in sports is unusually high, assuming they sampled from a group whose mean MQ is the same as it is for all children in general.

d. Based on MQ scores of a sample of children who participate in sports, researchers want to decide if the mean MQ of all children who participate in sports is higher than it is for children in general.

8.4 Children's fitness is assessed by finding the distance, in meters, that they can run in 6 minutes. Tell whether each of the following focuses on data production, displaying and summarizing data, probability, or statistical inference:

a. Researchers want to see if children who watch TV daily tend to have lower fitness scores; they must obtain permission from the children's parents to have them run for 6 minutes during gym class.

b. Researchers consider whether the mean fitness score for a sample of children who watch TV on a daily basis is unusually low, assuming they sampled from a group whose mean fitness is the same as it is for all children in general.

c. Based on fitness scores of a sample of children who watch TV daily, researchers want to decide if the mean fitness of all children who watch TV daily is lower than it is for children in general.

d. Researchers want to show the difference between fitness scores of sampled children who did and did not watch TV on a daily basis.

8.5 In a comprehensive study of twelfth graders across the country in 2002, the proportion who claimed never to have tried marijuana was 0.88.

a. In this problem, 0.88 is presented as a parameter, the population proportion. Is its value based on the principle of equally likely outcomes or on the principle of long-run observed outcomes?

b. The underlying distribution (sample proportion who never tried marijuana for samples of size 1) has just two possible values, 0 and 1. Sketch its probability histogram, and describe it as left-skewed, right-skewed, or symmetric.

c. If we took repeated random samples of 16 students from this population and recorded the proportion claiming never to have tried marijuana in each sample, what should be the mean of all these sample proportions?

d. What should be the standard deviation (to the nearest hundredth) of all sample proportions for samples of size 16?

e. Tell whether the shape of the distribution of sample proportions for samples of size 16 would be left-skewed, right-skewed, symmetric but not normal, or approximately normal. (Justify your answer.)

f. If we took repeated random samples of 121 students from this population and recorded the proportion claiming never to have tried marijuana in each sample, what should be the mean of all these sample proportions?

g. What should be the standard deviation (to the nearest hundredth) of all sample proportions for samples of size 121?

h. Tell whether the shape of the distribution of sample proportions for samples of size 121 would be left-skewed, right-skewed, fairly symmetric but not normal, or approximately normal. (Justify your answer.)

i. In general, when does distribution of sample proportion have a smaller standard deviation: for larger or for smaller sample sizes?

j. In general, when does distribution of sample proportion have a more normal shape: for larger or for smaller sample sizes?

8.6 In a comprehensive survey of teenagers across the country in 2002, the proportion who did not attend religious services was 0.16.

a. The underlying distribution (sample proportion for samples of size 1) has just two possible values, 0 and 1. Sketch its probability histogram, and describe it as left-skewed, right-skewed, or symmetric.

b. If we took repeated random samples of 36 students from this population and recorded the proportion not attending religious services in each sample, what should be the mean of all these sample proportions?

c. What should be the standard deviation (to the nearest hundredth) of all sample proportions for samples of size 36?

d. Tell whether the shape of the distribution of sample proportions for samples of size 36 would be left-skewed, right-skewed, symmetric but not normal, or approximately normal. (Justify your answer.)

e. If we took repeated random samples of 324 students from this population and recorded the proportion never attending religious services in each sample, what should be the mean of all these sample proportions?

f. What should be the standard deviation (to the nearest hundredth) of all sample proportions for samples of size 324?

g. Tell whether the shape of the distribution of sample proportions for samples of size 324 would be left-skewed, right-skewed, fairly symmetric but not normal, or approximately normal. (Justify your answer.)

h. In general, when does distribution of sample proportion have a larger standard deviation: for larger or for smaller sample sizes?

i. In general, when does distribution of sample proportion have a less normal shape: for larger or for smaller sample sizes?

USING THE NORMAL TABLE: PROPORTIONS [SEE END OF BOOK]

8.7 In part (g) of Exercise 8.51, z-scores were found for various sample proportions of students who sought counseling, given that population proportion was 0.40 at expensive private institutions and 0.10 at larger, public institutions. Report the z-scores for the sample proportions listed in part (g), and find the probability of sample proportion being that high or that low.

8.8 Parts (b) and (e) of Exercise 8.52 asked for z-scores if sample proportions smoking were 0.29 in Europe and in the United States, respectively. Report those z-scores, then find the probability of sample proportion being that low in Europe, and the probability of sample proportion being that high in the United States.

8.9 Exercise 8.56 reported that the distribution of sample proportion of new houses in the United States with exactly three bedrooms in samples of size 30 had mean 0.51, standard deviation 0.09, and a shape that is approximately normal. Report the sample proportion and the z-score for each of the given sample counts, and find the probability of a sample proportion this far or farther from 0.51 *in either direction*.

8.10 Exercise 8.61 reported that the distribution of sample proportion of new houses in the United States with at least two stories in samples of size 70 had mean 0.53, standard deviation 0.06, and a shape that is approximately normal. Report the sample proportion and the z-score for each of the given sample counts, and find the probability of a sample proportion this far or farther from 0.53 *in either direction*.

8.11 Exercise 8.11 reported that for U.S. twelfth graders in 2002, the proportion who claimed never to have tried marijuana was 0.88. The distribution of sample proportion claiming never to have tried marijuana for samples of size 250 has mean 0.88, standard deviation 0.02, and a shape that is approximately normal, due to the large sample size. Find the z-score if sample proportion was found to be 0.93, and find the probability of being this high or higher.

8.12 Exercise 8.12 reported that for U.S. twelfth graders in 2002, the proportion who did not attend religious services was 0.16. The distribution of sample proportion who do not attend religious services for samples of size 3,000 has mean 0.16, standard deviation 0.007, and a shape that is approximately normal, due to the large sample size. Find the z-score if the sample proportion was found to be 0.18, and find the probability of being this high or higher.

8.13 Exercise 8.63 reported that 0.05 of all U.S. teenagers are gay or lesbian, and asked for the mean and standard deviation of sample proportion for samples of size 400. Find the z-score if 160 in a sample of 400 teenagers are found to be gay or lesbian, and explain why normal tables would not be used to find the probability of a proportion this high.

8.14 According to the 1990 U.S. Census, travel time X to work had a mean of about 22 minutes. The standard deviation was about 20 minutes.

a. Does the random variable $2X$ represent total travel time to work for two randomly selected workers, total travel time to and from work for one randomly selected worker, or double the travel time to work for one randomly selected worker?

b. Does the random variable $X_1 + X_2$, where X_1 and X_2 are independent, represent total travel time to work for two randomly selected workers, total travel time to and from work for one randomly selected worker, or double the travel time to work for one randomly selected worker?

c. Use the formulas $\mu_{aX} = a\mu_X$ and $\mu_{X_1 + X_2} = \mu_{X_1} + \mu_{X_2}$ to find the mean of $\frac{1}{2}(X_1 + X_2)$, sample mean travel time to work for a random sample of $n = 2$ workers, and verify that it equals the mean of X.

d. Use the formulas $\sigma_{aX} = a\sigma_X$ and $\sigma_{X_1 + X_2} = \sqrt{\sigma_{X_1}^2 + \sigma_{X_2}^2}$ to find the standard deviation of $\frac{1}{2}(X_1 + X_2)$, sample mean travel time for a random sample of $n = 2$ workers.

e. The rule for sample means states that the standard deviation of sample mean is population standard deviation divided by square root of sample size. Calculate this for a population standard deviation equal to 20, and a sample size of 2, and verify that your answer is the same as your answer to part (d).

f. Explain why a normal approximation cannot be used to find the probability that sample mean travel time takes a value over a certain interval, for samples of size 2.

8.15 Length X in centimeters of a newborn baby has mean 50 and standard deviation 5.

a. If $X_1 + X_2$ represents the combined lengths of newborn twins, are X_1 and X_2 dependent or independent? Explain.

b. Use the formulas $\mu_{aX} = a\mu_X$ and $\mu_{X_1 + X_2} = \mu_{X_1} + \mu_{X_2}$ to find the mean of $\frac{1}{2}(X_1 + X_2)$, sample mean weight of $n = 2$ randomly chosen newborns, and verify that it equals the mean of X.

c. Use the formulas $\sigma_{aX} = a\sigma_X$ and $\sigma_{X_1 + X_2} = \sqrt{\sigma_{X_1}^2 + \sigma_{X_2}^2}$ to find the standard deviation of $\frac{1}{2}(X_1 + X_2)$, sample mean weight of $n = 2$ randomly chosen newborns.

d. The rule for sample means states that the standard deviation of sample mean is population standard deviation divided by square root of sample size. Calculate this for a population standard deviation equal to 5, and a sample size of 2, and verify that your answer is the same as your answer to part (c).

e. Can a normal approximation be used to find the probability that sample mean length takes a value over a certain interval, for samples of size 2? Explain.

8.16 Ages of first-time students at the University of Washington in the fall of 1999 had mean 19.80 and standard deviation 0.32.

a. Explain why the shape of the distribution of ages of incoming students would be more uniform (flat) than normal (bell-shaped), with right-skewness and high outliers rather than left-skewness and low outliers.

b. The shape of the distribution of sample mean age for samples of size 16 should be roughly normal; what are its mean and standard deviation (to the nearest hundredth)?

c. Use the 68-95-99.7 Rule to sketch the distribution of sample mean age for samples of size 16.

d. Use your sketch to characterize the probability of a sample mean age as high as 19.9 years in a sample of size 16—is it not improbable, somewhat improbable, very improbable, or extremely improbable?

e. The shape of the distribution of sample mean age for samples of size 64 should be close to normal; what are its mean and standard deviation?

f. Use the 68-95-99.7 Rule to sketch the distribution of sample mean age for samples of size 64.

g. Use your sketch to characterize the probability of a sample mean age as high as 19.9 years in a sample of size 64—is it not improbable, somewhat improbable, very improbable, or virtually impossible?

8.17 High school GPA of first-time students at the University of Washington in the fall of 1999 had mean 3.63 and standard deviation 0.32.

a. Explain why the shape of the distribution of high school GPA's may have more left-skewness and low outliers than right-skewness and high outliers.

b. The shape of the distribution of sample mean GPA for samples of size 4 should be roughly normal; what are its mean and standard deviation?

c. Use the 68-95-99.7 Rule to sketch the distribution of sample mean GPA for samples of size 4.

d. According to your sketch, is the probability of a sample mean GPA higher than 4.0 in a sample of size 4 not improbable, somewhat improbable, very improbable, or extremely improbable?

e. Is your sketch consistent with a system of grades where GPA cannot exceed 4.0? Explain.

f. The shape of the distribution of sample mean GPA for samples of size 256 should be close to normal; what are its mean and standard deviation?

g. Use the 68-95-99.7 Rule to sketch the distribution of sample mean GPA for samples of size 256.

h. Describe what happens to the spread of the distribution of sample mean in general as sample size increases.

USING THE NORMAL TABLE: MEANS [SEE END OF BOOK]

8.18 Exercise 8.28 stated that the distribution of hours worked per week by husbands in the United States in the early 1990s had mean 42.6 and standard deviation 12.9. For samples of size 18, the shape of sample mean hours would be very close to normal, with mean 42.6 and standard deviation $12.9/\sqrt{18} = 3.0$. Use tables to find the probability that sample mean hours worked . . .

a. exceeds 40

b. exceeds 50

c. falls below 38

d. falls below 37

8.19 Exercise 8.31 stated that the distribution of hours worked per week by wives in the United States in the early 1990s had mean 26.0 and standard deviation 17.2. For samples of size 74, the shape of sample mean hours would be close to normal, with mean 26.0 and standard deviation $17.2/\sqrt{74} = 2.0$. Use tables to find the probability that sample mean hours worked. . .

a. exceeds 40

b. exceeds 30

c. falls below 25

d. falls below 20

8.20 Exercise 8.72 stated that the number of days per week worked by U.S. husbands in the early 1990s had mean 5.2 and standard deviation 0.7. Use tables to find the probability of each of the following:

a. Sample mean days worked by a random sample of 200 husbands is less than 5.0.

b. Sample mean days worked by a random sample of 50 husbands is less than 5.0.

8.21 Exercise 8.73 stated that the number of days per week worked by U.S. wives in the early 1990s had mean 4.7 and standard deviation 1.0. Use tables to find the probability of each of the following:

a. Sample mean days worked by a random sample of 400 wives is at least 5.0.

b. Sample mean days worked by a random sample of 100 wives is at least 5.0.

8.22 According to Exercise 8.100, ages of first-time students at the University of Washington in the fall of 1999 had mean 19.80 and standard deviation 0.32. Find the probability of sample mean age as high as 19.9 years . . .

a. in a sample of size 16

b. in a sample of size 64

8.23 According to Exercise 8.74, birth weights of babies in Guatemala were found to have mean 2,860 grams and standard deviation 440 grams. The mean weight of 572 babies of mothers who cooked on open wood fires was 2,820 grams. Find the probability of a sample mean weight this low (or lower), if the sample had been random.

8.24 According to Exercise 8.75, children's overall motor quotient (MQ) is normal with mean 93 and standard deviation 15.

a. A sample of 144 children who participated in both club sports and regular sports had a mean MQ of 96.5. Find the probability of a sample mean MQ this high (or higher) if the sample had been random.

b. A sample of 36 obese children had a mean MQ of 85.7. Find the probability of a sample mean MQ this low (or lower) if the sample had been random.

8.25 According to Exercise 8.77, the distance (in meters) children can run in 6 minutes varies normally, with mean 835 and standard deviation 111.

a. A sample of 289 children who watched TV daily ran a mean distance of 834.1 meters. Find the probability of a sample mean this low (or lower) if the sample had been random.

b. A sample of 38 underweight children ran a mean distance of 838 meters. Find the probability of a sample mean this high (or higher) if the sample had been random.

8.26 According to Exercise 8.32, fourth-grade reading scores in 2003 had mean 217 and standard deviation 126. Find the probability that in a sample of 3,115 fourth graders, the mean reading score was 212 or lower.

8.27 According to Exercise 8.33, fourth-grade math scores in 2003 had mean 234 and standard deviation 85. Find the probability that in a sample of 3,154 fourth graders, the mean math score was 228 or lower.

8.5 Solutions to Supplemental Exercises

8.1 **a.** one each quantitative and categorical **b.** two categorical **c.** one categorical **d.** one quantitative

8.2 **a.** several-sample **b.** two-sample **c.** paired

8.3 **a.** displaying and summarizing **b.** data production **c.** probability **d.** statistical inference

8.4 **a.** data production **b.** probability **c.** statistical inference **d.** displaying and summarizing

8.5 **a.** principle of long-run observed outcomes **b.** The distribution is left-skewed.

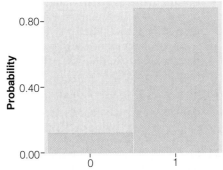

Sample proportion who never tried marijuana in samples of size 1

c. 0.88 **d.** $\sqrt{0.88(0.12)/16} = 0.08$ **e.** still left-skewed because the sample size is relatively small: $n(1 - p) = 16(0.12) = 1.92$ is less than 10
f. 0.88 **g.** $\sqrt{0.88(0.12)/121} = 0.03$
h. approximately normal because the sample size is relatively large: $np = 121(0.88) = 106.48$ and $n(1 - p) = 121(0.12) = 14.52$ are both at least 10
i. larger **j.** larger

8.6 **a.** The distribution is right-skewed.

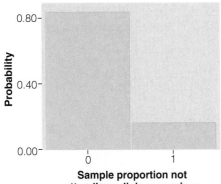

Sample proportion not attending religious services for samples of size 1

b. 0.16 **c.** $\sqrt{0.16(0.84)/36} = 0.06$ **d.** still right-skewed because the sample size is relatively small: $np = 36(0.16) = 5.76$ is less than 10
e. 0.16 **f.** $\sqrt{0.16(0.84)/324} = 0.02$
g. approximately normal because the sample size is relatively large: $np = 324(0.16) = 51.84$ and $n(1 - p) = 324(0.84) = 272.16$ are both at least 10 **h.** smaller **i.** smaller

8.7 **a.** $z = -3$; probability of that low is 0.0013
b. $z = +5$; probability of that high is less than 0.0013, or approximately zero **c.** $z = +1.2$; probability of that high is 0.1151 **d.** $z = +2$; probability of that high is 0.0228

8.8 For Europe $z = -0.71$; probability of that low is 0.2389; for U.S. $z = +1.0$; probability of that high is 0.1587.

8.9 **a.** $\hat{p} = 0.40$, $z = -1.22$, probability is $2(0.1112) = 0.2224$ **b.** $\hat{p} = 0.53$, $z = +0.22$, probability is $2(0.4129) = 0.8258$ **c.** $\hat{p} = 0.90$, $z = +4.33$, probability is less than $2(0.0013)$, or approximately zero

8.10 **a.** $\hat{p} = 0.20$, $z = -5.5$, probability is less than $2(0.0013)$, or approximately zero **b.** $\hat{p} = 0.70$, $z = +2.83$, probability is $2(0.0023) = 0.0046$ **c.** $\hat{p} = 0.50$, $z = -0.50$, probability is $2(0.3085) = 0.6170$

8.11 $z = +2.50$; probability of this high or higher is 0.0062

8.12 $z = +2.86$; probability of this high or higher is 0.0021

8.13 $z = +35$; normal tables would not be used because 35 is way "off the chart" (most z values are between -3 and $+3$)

8.14 **a.** double the travel time to work for one randomly selected worker **b.** total travel time to work for two randomly selected workers (times to and from for the same worker would be dependent) **c.** mean of $\frac{1}{2}(X_1 + X_2)$ is $\frac{1}{2}(22 + 22) = 22$, which is the same as the mean of X **d.** standard deviation of $\frac{1}{2}(X_1 + X_2)$ is $\frac{1}{2}\sqrt{20^2 + 20^2} = 14.14$
e. $20/\sqrt{2} = 14.14$, the same as part (d)
f. The population distribution may be skewed, and two is too small a sample size to expect sample mean to have an approximately normal shape.

8.15 a. dependent, because sizes of twins tend to be similar   **b.** mean of $\frac{1}{2}(X_1 + X_2)$ is $\frac{1}{2}(50 + 50) = 50$, which is the same as the mean of X **c.** standard deviation of $\frac{1}{2}(X_1 + X_2)$ is $\frac{1}{2}\sqrt{5^2 + 5^2} = 3.54$ **d.** $5/\sqrt{2} = 3.54$, the same as part (c)   **e.** Yes, because lengths themselves would follow a normal distribution.

8.16 a. The shape would be flatter than normal because ages should be fairly evenly spread within a half year or so of 19.8; the right-skewness and high outliers would come from a few relatively old first-time students.   **b.** mean 19.8, standard deviation $0.32/\sqrt{16} = 0.08$

c.

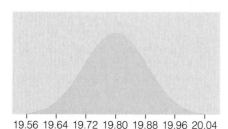

19.56 19.64 19.72 19.80 19.88 19.96 20.04
Sample mean age for samples of size 16

d. not improbable   **e.** mean 19.8, standard deviation $0.32/\sqrt{64} = 0.04$

f.

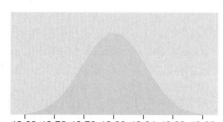

19.68 19.72 19.76 19.80 19.84 19.88 19.92
Sample mean age for samples of size 64

g. very improbable

8.17 a. The shape may have more left-skewness and low outliers because a few students would have an unusually low GPA; many students would have a high GPA, close to 4.0, and it can't get any higher than 4.0.   **b.** mean 3.63, standard deviation $0.32/\sqrt{4} = 0.16$

c.

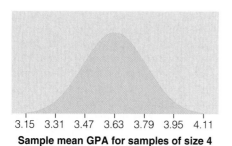

3.15 3.31 3.47 3.63 3.79 3.95 4.11
Sample mean GPA for samples of size 4

d. very improbable   **e.** No; the sketch makes it look like sample mean GPA greater than 4.0 is possible.   **f.** mean 3.63, standard deviation $0.32/\sqrt{256} = 0.02$

g.

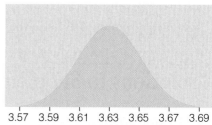

3.57 3.59 3.61 3.63 3.65 3.67 3.69
Sample mean GPA for samples of size 256

h. As sample size increases, spread decreases.

8.18 a. $z = (40 - 42.6)/3.0 = -0.87$; probability of z greater than -0.87 is $1 - 0.1922 = 0.8078$ **b.** $z = (50 - 42.6)/3.0 = +2.47$; probability of z greater than 2.47 is 0.0068   **c.** $z = (38 - 42.6)/3.0 = -1.53$; probability of z less than -1.53 is 0.0630   **d.** $z = (37 - 42.6)/3.0 = -1.87$; probability of z less than -1.87 is 0.0307

8.19 a. $z = (40 - 26.0)/2.0 = +7$; probability of z greater than 7 is approximately zero   **b.** $z = (30 - 26.0)/2.0 = +2$; probability of z greater than 2 is 0.0228   **c.** $z = (25 - 26.0)/2.0 = -0.5$; probability of z less than -0.5 is 0.3085   **d.** $z = (20 - 26.0)/2.0 = -3$; probability of z less than -3 is 0.0013

8.20 a. $z = \frac{5 - 5.2}{0.7/\sqrt{200}} = -4.04$; probability is less than 0.0013, or approximately zero   **b.** $z = \frac{5 - 5.2}{0.7/\sqrt{50}} = -2.02$; probability is 0.0217

8.21 a. $z = \frac{5 - 4.7}{1.0/\sqrt{400}} = +6$; probability is less than 0.0013, or approximately zero   **b.** $z = \frac{5 - 4.7}{1.0/\sqrt{100}} = +3$; probability is 0.0013

8.22 a. $z = \frac{19.9 - 19.8}{0.32/\sqrt{16}} = +1.25$; probability is 0.1056   **b.** $z = \frac{19.9 - 19.8}{0.32/\sqrt{64}} = +2.50$; probability is 0.0062

8.23 $z = -2.17$; probability is 0.0150

8.24 a. $z = +2.8$; probability is 0.0026   **b.** $z = -2.92$; probability is 0.0018

8.25 a. $z = -0.14$; probability is 0.4443   **b.** $z = +0.17$; probability is 0.4325

8.26 $z = -2.21$; probability is 0.0136

8.27 $z = -3.96$; probability is approximately zero

8.6 Review of Part III

There are three ways to determine an individual probability: equally likely outcomes, long-run relative frequency, or subjective opinion. Various rules tell us how probabilities behave, such as the probability of one event *or* another occurring, or the probability of one event *and* another occurring.

Random variables are quantitative variables whose values are subject to the laws of probability. These values are specified via the random variable's probability distribution. The probability distribution is displayed with a histogram and summarized by reporting its mean, standard deviation, and shape.

Sample proportion and sample mean are random variables of particular interest in statistics. Based on information about the population from which the samples were taken, we can identify the mean and standard deviation of the distribution of sample proportion or sample mean. Under the right circumstances, we can assert the shape to be normal and assess probabilities based on a normal distribution.

8.7 Supplemental Part III Review Exercises

A statistical study can be examined in the context of each of the four processes—data production, displaying and summarizing, probability, and statistical inference. To highlight the fact that for any given situation we may focus on any of these four processes, the review exercises for Parts I (page 763), II (page 810), and IV (page 979) feature the same settings as these 15 exercises. For now, the focus is on probability.

8.28 A drug for female sexual dysfunction called Intrinsa was tested in 2004, both for efficacy and for possible dangerous side effects before being considered for approval by the Food and Drug Administration. A report of clinical trials states: "Fifty-two percent of those [women] given the drug said they experienced a 'meaningful benefit' in their sex lives—but so did 31% of those who were given the placebo."[1]

   a. Suppose 200 women were included in the study, with half each taking the drug and a placebo. Construct a table of counts in the four possible category combinations, using rows for the explanatory variable and columns for the response.

   b. Construct a table of counts that would be expected if the probabilities of experiencing benefits were identical for both groups of women.

8.29 Researchers at the University of Montreal reported that "blind people are better than sighted controls at judging the direction of pitch change between sounds [. . .] but only if they became blind at an early age. The younger the onset of blindness, the better is the performance."[2]

   a. Suppose researchers consider sample mean performance on the sound test for blind study participants as a random variable. To decide whether or not the random variable's distribution is approximately normal, which of these should be checked: the sample size, the shape of the distribution of performances, both of these, or neither of these?

   b. In which case would we be more convinced that being blind or sighted plays a role in the ability to judge the direction of pitch changes: if the difference in performances between blind and sighted subjects could easily occur by chance, or if the difference is too large to be explained by chance?

8.30 In 1999, Harvard Medical School researchers produced evidence that when television was introduced to the island of Fiji in the mid-1990s, teenage girls began to suffer from eating disorders because of body image issues resulting from seeing thin actresses on their favorite shows. Assume that the proportion of girls suffering from eating disorders in the years before television is known to be p, and the proportion for a sample of size n taken after the introduction of television is found to be $\hat{p}$.

   a. What is the mean of the distribution of $\hat{p}$, if we are sampling from a population whose proportion with eating disorders is still p?

   b. What is the standard deviation of the distribution of $\hat{p}$?

c. What should we check before claiming that the shape of the distribution of $\hat{p}$ is approximately normal?

8.31 According to a Pew report, by the year 2007, one in every 100 Americans was in prison.

  a. If two Americans were chosen at random, what would be the probability that one or the other was in prison?

  b. Suppose we took a random sample of 400 Americans in 2007. What are the mean and standard deviation for the *count* in prison?

  c. Suppose we took a random sample of 400 Americans in 2007. What are the mean and standard deviation for the *proportion* in prison?

  d. Is the shape of the distribution of proportion in prison for random samples of size 400 skewed left, approximately normal, or skewed right?

8.32 The *Harvard Gazette Archives* reported: "Cognition unaffected by pot use; but other studies suggest marijuana smokers are not a happy lot."[3] A study recruited heavy users, former users, and non-users, who took a variety of cognition tests 0, 1, 7, and 28 days after quitting the drug. Another study said that "most heavy users admitted that the drug has a negative impact on all aspects of their lives from job performance and physical health to mental well-being and satisfactory socializing."

  a. For which group might we expect cognition test score and number of days (0, 1, 7, or 28) to be dependent: heavy users, former users, or non-users?

  b. If we let H denote the event of being happy, and M the event of being a marijuana smoker, which of these probabilities should be the largest, according to the second study: $P(H$ given $M)$, $P(H$ given not $M)$, $P(H$ and $M)$, or $P(H$ and not $M)$?

8.33 "Acupuncture Helps Ease Arthritis Pain" describes a National Institutes of Health study where participants "were randomly assigned to receive one of three treatments: acupuncture, sham acupuncture—a procedure designed to prevent patients from being able to detect if needles are actually inserted at treatment points—or participation in a control group that

followed the Arthritis Foundation's self-help course for managing their condition. . . Overall, those who received acupuncture had a 40 percent decrease in pain and 40 percent improvement in function."[4]

  a. The probability of a randomly chosen patient being in the acupuncture group is one-third. Is this based on the principle of equally likely outcomes, long-run observed outcomes, or a subjective assessment?

  b. Are the events of being in the acupuncture group and being in the sham acupuncture group non-overlapping, independent, both, or neither?

8.34 According to a newspaper report, "the bigger your brood, the likelier it is to show on your waistline. And that's not just for women, who may retain some of the pounds they gain during pregnancy. Fathers tend to gain weight, too, increasing their risk of obesity with the number of offspring, suggesting that eating habits are to blame."[5] Researchers found the relationship between family size and body size held, regardless of household income, physical activity, smoking and other factors.

  a. Are the study's findings based on the principle of equally likely outcomes, long-run observed outcomes, or a subjective assessment?

  b. According to the reported findings, which of these conditional probabilities would we expect to be higher: the probability of being overweight given that an individual has two children, or the probability of being overweight given that an individual has three children?

8.35 A study conducted by AAA looked at other driving distractions besides cell phones. It was reported that drivers are engaged in many such distracting behaviors: 62% acknowledged fiddling with the radio dial while driving in the previous six months; 57% reported eating, 44% tried to pick something up from the floor or between the seats, 32% wrote something down, 32% stretched to reach the glove compartment, and 23% cleaned the inside of their windshield.

  a. What additional information would be needed in order to find the probability of fiddling with the radio dial or eating?

b. It was also reported that men were more than twice as likely as women to have steered the car with their thighs or driven with no hands. Are the events of steering without hands and being male overlapping, dependent, both, or neither?

8.36 A report on sexual health by the Alan Guttmacher Institute says that "men of all ages tend to overstate their sexual activity when surveyed, while women understate theirs."[6]

   a. One approach to the data would be to consider the sign of the difference, actual number minus claimed number of sexual encounters over a certain time period. If we use the letter P to denote the event that the number is positive, M to denote the event that an individual is male and F the event that an individual is female, which should be higher: $P(P$ given $M)$ or $P(P$ given $F)$?

   b. Suppose the population mean amount of actual sexual activity in a week for men is μ, and researchers consider the sample mean amount of claimed sexual activity in a week, $\overline{X}$, for a random sample of men. Is the distribution of $\overline{X}$ centered at μ?

8.37 Every week in football season, data are recorded for the types of injuries suffered by the players on the NFL list of injured players. During a particular week, the most common—knee injury—was suffered by 49 of the 234 players, while the least common—such as a blister on the foot—was suffered by only one player.

   a. The probability of a knee injury during the given week is approximately 0.2. If two players are chosen at random from those 234, what is the probability that both suffer knee injuries?

   b. Suppose we added the probabilities of suffering from the various injuries listed. Under which circumstance would the sum equal one: If the NFL listed only one injury per player, or if the NFL listed more than one injury for some of the players?

8.38 The *Los Angeles Daily News* reported the results of a study of thousands of babies born in California in the year 2000. Researchers found that babies born to mothers in the most polluted areas consistently weighed less—about 1 ounce less—than babies born to mothers who lived in clean-air cities.

   a. Suppose $\overline{X}_1$ is the sample mean weight of babies born in the most polluted areas and $\overline{X}_2$ is the sample mean weight of babies born in clean-air cities. According to the study, which distribution is centered at higher values, $\overline{X}_1$ or $\overline{X}_2$?

   b. Why can we assume $\overline{X}_1$ and $\overline{X}_2$ to be approximately normally distributed?

8.39 "Soft Drink Link to Diabetes Found" reports that "as consumption of sugar-sweetened drinks increased, women put on more pounds and increased their likelihood to develop diabetes."[7]

   a. If we use the letter D to denote the event that a woman develops diabetes and O to denote the event of being overweight, does the study suggest that D and O are non-overlapping, dependent, both, or neither?

   b. Considering that the probability of being overweight is much higher than the probability of suffering from diabetes, which of these would you expect to be higher: $P(D$ given $O)$ or $P(O$ given $D)$?

8.40 Columnist Maureen Dowd of the *New York Times* discussed two studies published in 2004 on what men are looking for in a woman. The first study "suggests that men going for long-term relationships would rather marry women in subordinate jobs than women who are supervisors."[8] The second study "found that a high IQ hampers a woman's chance to get married, while it is a plus for men. The prospect for marriage increased by 35 percent for guys for each 16-point increase in IQ; for women, there is a 40 percent drop for each 16-point rise."

   a. Suppose a study is conducted in which eligible men are given a description of a woman (including her type of job), and are asked to identify the probability that they would consider marrying the woman. Would the reported probability be based on the principle of equally likely outcomes, long-run observed outcomes, or a subjective assessment?

   b. Let M denote the event that an individual is married, and X denote the individual's IQ. According to the second study, which of these should be higher: $P(M$ given $X = 130)$ for men or $P(M$ given $X = 130)$ for women?

8.41 According to the *New York Times*, economics professor David Zimmerman at Williams

College studied the impact of college roommates on political leanings and on grades. He "looked at the political views of 3,500 students who had shared rooms as freshmen, noting their leanings when they started college and again three years after graduation. Generally, roommates kept the same political persuasion—except those freshmen whose roommates were on the far left of the political spectrum. No matter what their politics at enrollment, they were more likely than similar students to be *conservative* as adults. [. . .] In separate research, Zimmerman and Gordon C. Winston, another Williams economics professor, uncovered more unsettling evidence of peer influence: Freshmen rooming with the weakest students experienced a slight drop in grades. The researchers divided 5,000 onetime roommates at four colleges into three groups: Those who scored in the top 15 percent of the SAT verbal scores admitted to the college, those in the bottom 15 percent, and everyone in between. On average, grades of the typical students who roomed with low scorers were pulled down by a 10th of a grade point by graduation. No other impact was noticed."[9]

a. Suppose a political pollster used a cluster sampling method to survey college students, taking random samples of apartments and dorms, and recording the opinions of all individuals in each dwelling. Would we expect the responses for two individuals in the same dwelling to be dependent or independent?

b. Let C denote the event of having conservative opinions three years after graduation, L the event of having left-wing opinions three years after graduation, RC the event of having had a conservative roommate in freshman year, and RL the event of having had a left-wing roommate in freshman year. Which of these was apparently the case: $P(C$ given $RC) > P(L$ given $RC)$ or $P(C$ given $RL) > P(L$ given $RL)$ or both or neither?

8.42 A wine merchant advertised prices of its California Cabernet wines, per bottle. The minimum price was $10, and the maximum was $130. The mean price was $41. Is the distribution of sample mean price approximately normal for small samples, large samples, or samples of any size?

8.8 Solutions to Supplemental Part III Review Exercises

8.28 a.

	Benefit	No Benefit	Total
Drug	52	48	100
Placebo	31	69	100
Total	83	117	200

b.

	Benefit	No Benefit	Total
Drug	41.5	58.5	100
Placebo	41.5	58.5	100
Total	83	117	200

8.29 a. both   **b.** if the difference is too large to be explained by chance

8.30 a. p **b.** $\sqrt{\frac{p(1-p)}{n}}$ **c.** if np and $n(1-p)$ are both at least 10

8.31 a. $0.01 + 0.01 - 0.01(0.01) = 0.0199$
b. mean $400(0.01) = 4$, standard deviation $\sqrt{400(0.01)(1-0.01)} = 1.99$ **c.** mean 0.01,

standard deviation $\sqrt{\frac{0.01(1-0.01)}{400}} = 0.005$
d. skewed right

8.32 a. heavy users   **b.** $P(H$ given not $M)$

8.33 a. equally likely outcomes   **b.** non-overlapping

8.34 a. long-run observed outcomes   **b.** the probability of being overweight given that an individual has three children

8.35 a. the probability of fiddling with the radio dial *and* eating   **b.** both

8.36 a. $P(P$ given $F)$ **b.** No, $\overline{X}$ would be centered to the right of μ because of men's tendency to overstate the variable's value.

8.37 a. $0.2(0.2) = 0.04$ **b.** if the NFL listed only one injury per player

8.38 a. $\overline{X}_2$ **b.** because the samples are large and because the distribution of weights themselves tends to be normal

8.39 a. dependent   **b.** $P(O$ given $D)$

8.40 a. subjective assessment   **b.** $P(M$ given $X = 130)$ for men

8.41 a. dependent   **b.** both

8.42 large samples (because the distribution must be right-skewed)

TBP Chapter 9

Inference for a Single Categorical Variable

Preview: Notation for Statistics and Random Variables

In the Overview of Statistical Inference on page 386, we contrast the behavior of statistics relative to known parameters with inference for an unknown parameter, based on a sample statistic. When we discuss the long-run behavior of a standardized statistic, such as standardized sample proportion, then we are thinking of the statistic's values as values of a *random variable*. Under the right circumstances, this random variable follows a known distribution, such as the standard normal distribution. To distinguish a standard normal *distribution* from a standard normal *value*, we use a boldface **z** to denote the random variable, and an ordinary z to denote a particular value called the z statistic. For consistency's sake, the original random variable, denoted X in Part III, will now be denoted **x**. Depending on which situation applies, the relevant standardized distribution may be the familiar standard normal **z**, or the pattern may turn out to be one of several new distributions to be introduced in the coming chapters: t, two-sample t, F, or X^2. Although the letter z can be used to denote a standardized value of any quantitative variable, even if the shape does not happen to be normal, in this part of the book identifying a variable or value as "z" suggests that it is standard *normal,* as opposed to some other standardized distribution.

Preview: Illustrations of Inference in Five Situations

These graphs may help give students a visual sense of how the two forms of inference will be carried out in each of the five variable situations.

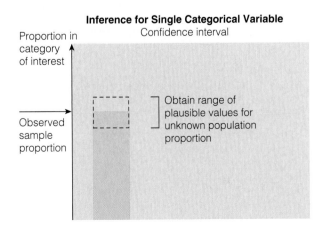

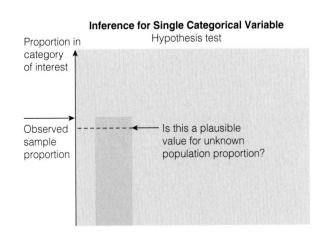

Inference for Single Quantitative Variable
Confidence interval

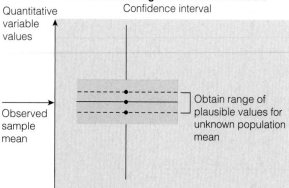

Quantitative variable values

Observed sample mean

Obtain range of plausible values for unknown population mean

Inference for Single Quantitative Variable
Hypothesis test

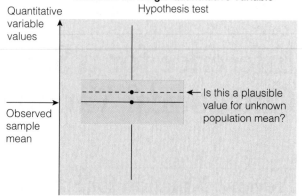

Quantitative variable values

Observed sample mean

← Is this a plausible value for unknown population mean?

Inference for Categorical Explanatory and Quantitative Response Variable
Confidence interval

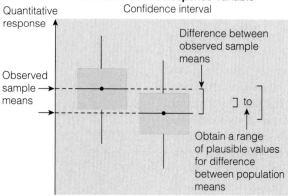

Quantitative response

Difference between observed sample means

Observed sample means

] to

Obtain a range of plausible values for difference between population means

1st categorical explanatory value   2nd categorical explanatory value

Inference for Categorical Explanatory and Quantitative Response Variable
Hypothesis test

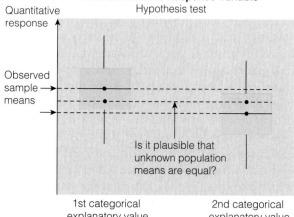

Quantitative response

Observed sample means

Is it plausible that unknown population means are equal?

1st categorical explanatory value   2nd categorical explanatory value

Inference for Two Categorical Variables
Confidence interval

Proportion in response category of interest

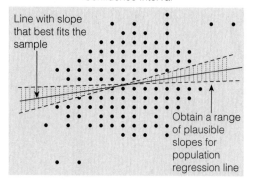

Difference between observed sample proportions

Observed sample proportions

] to

Obtain a range of plausible values for difference between population proportions

1st categorical explanatory value   2nd categorical explanatory value

Inference for Two Categorical Variables
Hypothesis test

Proportion in response category of interest

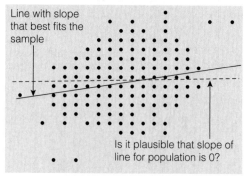

Is it plausible that unknown population proportions are equal?

Observed sample proportions

1st categorical explanatory value   2nd categorical explanatory value

Inference for Two Quantitative Variables
Confidence Interval

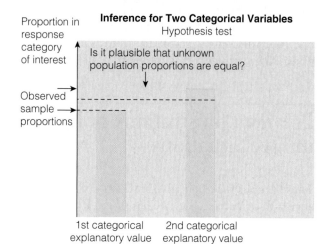

Line with slope that best fits the sample

Obtain a range of plausible slopes for population regression line

Inference for Two Quantitative Variables
Hypothesis Test

Line with slope that best fits the sample

Is it plausible that slope of line for population is 0?

9.1 Details and Examples

Explaining the Shift from Probability to Confidence

Although our results on page 348 about the center, spread, and shape of the distribution of sample proportion for a known population proportion are perfectly correct, they have limited practical use. In reality, we rarely know what is true about an entire population. All we know for sure is what we see in the sample; based on this information, we want to make an educated guess at what is true for the population.

To keep things simple at first for students as we make the transition from probability to inference, we invoke the "95" part of the 68-95-99.7 Rule, and apply it to our random number selection example. It asserts that 95% of the time in the long run, sample proportion will fall within 2 standard deviations of population proportion 0.05—that is, within 2(0.01) = 0.02 of 0.05. This is a typical probability statement, in that it tells us about the behavior of the random variable sample proportion, relative to known population proportion. From a grammatical perspective, we could say that *sample proportion was the subject of our sentence*. What we need to do at this point is turn our statement around and make it an inference statement instead: Tell what should be true about unknown population proportion, based on the sample proportion we observed. In other words, we want to *make population proportion the subject of our sentence*.

Confidence Intervals

For students who need additional reminders about the importance of checking that methods based on a normal approximation are justified, here is an example demonstrating that our methods fail if there are not enough individuals *in* the category of interest. Exercise 9.12 on page 401 involves a case where there are not enough individuals *outside* the category of interest. Both the example and the exercise can be presented along with Example 9.7 on page 396, in which both conditions $X \geq 10$ and $n - X \geq 10$ are met and a normal approximation is appropriate.

EXAMPLE TBP 9.1 SAMPLE SIZE FAILING THE REQUIREMENT FOR A NORMAL APPROXIMATION

Background: In a sample of 16 students, 1 was left-handed (sample proportion 0.0625).

Question: Can we construct a 95% confidence interval for the proportion of all students who are left-handed?

Response: We should not proceed with setting up the confidence interval, because the multiplier 2 applies only for a normal distribution, and sample proportion for such a small sample taken from such an unbalanced population has a skewed distribution. We encountered such a distribution on page 304 of Chapter 7, in our discussion of the shape of the distribution of counts or proportions.

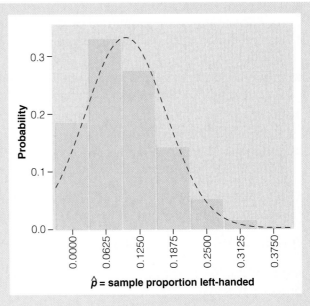

In Chapter 7, we had direct knowledge of the shape of the sampling distribution because we knew that the population proportion p was 0.1. Now our knowledge that the shape of the sampling distribution is skewed comes indirectly from the sample: The observed count in the category of interest is too small because only 1 of the 16 students was left-handed, and 1 is less than 10.

After students have been shown how to construct a confidence interval, as in Example 9.9 on page 398, we can point out that the method incorporates skills from the *four basic processes* that are presented in this book:

- Principles of *data production*, developed in Part I, let us check if the sample was collected in such a way that sample proportion provides an unbiased estimate for population proportion. We also consider if the sample size is large enough to ensure that a multiplier from the normal distribution is legitimate, and if the population is at least 10 times the sample size, so that our formula for the standard error is approximately correct.
- Methods of *summarizing data* from Part II are implemented in calculating sample proportion and its standard error.
- *Probability* theory from Part III lets us state that sample proportion has a certain probability of falling within some distance of population proportion.
- Finally, *statistical inference,* the focus of Part IV, lets us state that we are confident at a certain level that population proportion is contained within some distance of sample proportion.

After students have mastered the methods for constructing a confidence interval by the end of Section 8.1, instructors may want to expose them to an example like this one, so that they understand the level of confidence as a long-run probability of the interval's success in capturing the unknown parameter.

EXAMPLE TBP 9.2 CONFIDENCE INTERVAL AND LONG-RUN BEHAVIOR

Background: Imagine that someone did not know that the proportion of all coin flips resulting in heads is 0.5, and he wanted to use 20 flips of a coin to set up a confidence interval for the "unknown" population proportion of heads. We consider what would happen in the long run if 20 coin flips were repeatedly used to set up 95% confidence intervals.

- The coin is flipped 20 times, and the proportion of heads is found to be $9/20 = 0.45$. A 95% confidence interval for proportion of all flips that result in heads is calculated as $(0.23, 0.67)$. This interval does contain the population proportion of all flips that result in heads, which we know to be 0.5.
- In another 20 flips, the proportion of heads is found to be $8/20 = 0.40$ and the 95% confidence interval is $(0.19, 0.61)$. Again, the interval succeeds in capturing the population proportion 0.5.
- In yet another 20 flips, the sample proportion is $12/20 = 0.60$ and the 95% confidence interval is $(0.39, 0.81)$. It does contain 0.5.
- In the next 20 flips, the sample proportion is $15/20 = 0.75$ and the 95% confidence interval is $(0.56, 0.94)$. This interval does *not* contain 0.5.

We can picture many repetitions of 20 coin flips, for each of which a sample proportion of heads is found and a confidence interval for population proportion of heads is constructed.

Question: What can we say about the long-run performance of those confidence intervals?

Response: In the long run, 95% of those confidence intervals should contain the true population proportion, 0.50.

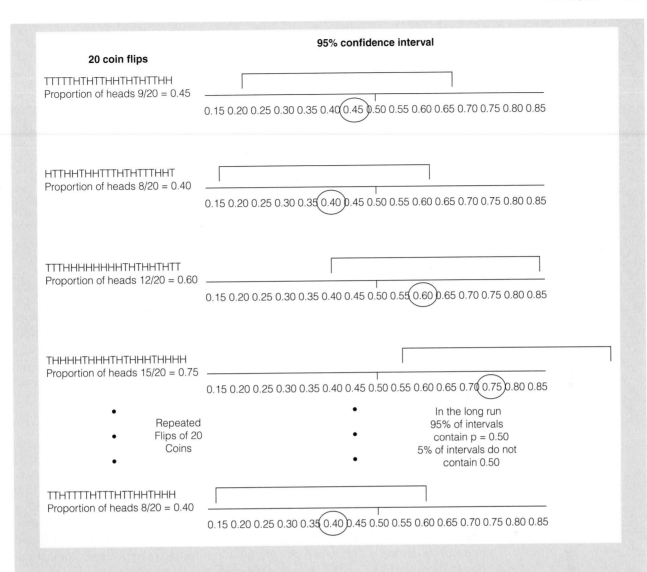

Thus, if someone used a single set of 20 flips of a coin to produce a 95% confidence interval for the proportion of all flips that are heads, chances are the interval will indeed contain that proportion, which we know to be 0.5. But there is a 5% chance that the interval will not contain 0.5.

Practice: *Try Exercise TBP 9.15 on page 907.*

   Notice that the requirement of a large enough sample size for a normal approximation isn't quite met in this example, but the counts of successes and failures are close enough to 10 that the confidence intervals should be fairly accurate. As for the issue of sample size relative to population size, this is not a concern here because flipping a coin is essentially sampling *with* replacement: We could flip over and over without depleting the supply of heads and tails. The population in this situation is a rather abstract entity—namely, all flips of a coin.
   We can modify the illustration of many 95% confidence intervals to show how wider intervals, at a higher confidence level, have a higher probability of containing the population proportion, as discussed in Example 9.12 on page 401. If we look at a set of 99% confidence intervals based on sample proportions 0.45, 0.40, 0.60, and 0.75, we see that each is a bit wider than the corresponding 95% interval because we use the multiplier 2.576 instead of 1.96. The fourth of these intervals, constructed around 0.75, goes from (0.56, 0.94) for 95% confidence to (0.50, 1.00) for 99% confidence. In the long run, more of the 99% confidence intervals will manage to contain $p = 0.50$ because they are wider.

Wilson Estimate

For more accuracy in a confidence interval for an unknown population proportion, it is possible to work with the *Wilson estimate* for sample proportion, which replaces $\hat{p} = \frac{X}{n}$ with $\widetilde{p} = \frac{X+2}{n+4}$. This adjustment moves the sample proportion slightly away from the extremes, 0 and 1, by adding two successes and two failures to the actual counts. $\widetilde{p}$ is approximately normal with a mean of p and a standard error of

$$SE_{\widetilde{p}} = \sqrt{\frac{\widetilde{p}(1 - \widetilde{p})}{n + 4}}$$

as long as the sample size is at least 5. Notice that $\widetilde{p}$ is substituted for p in the above formula for standard error because p is unknown. The modified 95% confidence interval takes the form $\widetilde{p} \pm 1.96 \sqrt{\frac{\widetilde{p}(1 - \widetilde{p})}{n + 4}}$.

Hypothesis Tests

In this book, we have chosen to formulate our null hypothesis as a simple equality $H_0: p = p_0$. This approach is quite common, but it is not the only possible way to go. In fact, many treatments of hypothesis tests would have written our null and alternative hypotheses in Example 9.17 on page 417 as follows, replacing the "=" sign in H_0 with "≤" or "≥" for the one-sided tests:

a. $H_0: p \leq 0.05$ versus $H_a: p > 0.05$

b. $H_0: p \geq 0.50$ versus $H_a: p < 0.50$

c. $H_0: p = 0.30$ versus $H_a: p \neq 0.30$

As far as matching the problem statement is concerned, students will find that sometimes the simple equality is a closer translation of the wording, and at other times an inequality (not strict) better expresses the premise of the null hypothesis. There is one aspect of the formulation of H_0 with an inequality that makes it preferable—namely, that it makes the null and alternative hypotheses logical opposites because together they cover all possible values of p.

On the other hand, the solution strategy for deciding between null and alternative hypotheses is to assume the null hypothesis to be true, and then see how unlikely it would be to get a sample proportion at least as extreme as the one we observed. This will require us to work with a sampling distribution that is centered directly at p_0. Our original formulation $H_0: p = p_0$ is consistent with this solution strategy, and that is why we opt in this book to express H_0 with an equality. Results are always identical, no matter which formulation of H_0 is used. Either way, the alternative hypothesis H_a *must* be expressed as a strict inequality, using $<$ or $>$ or $\neq$.

In case students are curious about how researchers determine the appropriate cutoff level for a small P-value, here are some examples of why both past and future considerations should be taken into account. These are designed to supplement the brief discussion after Example 9.23 on page 429.

EXAMPLE TBP 9.3 FUTURE CONSIDERATIONS WARRANTING VARIOUS CUTOFFS FOR P-VALUE

Background: Suppose a bookstore chain is thinking of opening up a new store in a certain metropolitan area. Because the proportion of all Americans with a college degree is 0.26, the chain's operators have decided to open the new store if there is evidence that the proportion of college graduates in that area is higher than the national rate. They take a random sample of residents, find the sample proportion of college graduates in their sample, and obtain a z statistic and P-value.

Questions: What would be the most appropriate cutoff level for the P-value—0.10 or 0.05 or 0.01—under each of the following circumstances?

1. No other information is provided.

2. The chain is enjoying considerable profits and its operators are eager to pursue new ventures.

3. The chain is experiencing financial difficulties and could not afford to cope with losses from an unsuccessful store in an area with not enough college graduates as potential patrons.

Responses:

1. Use the conventionally accepted level of 0.05.

2. Use 0.10, which can more easily lead to rejecting the null hypothesis and deciding to open the new store.

3. Use the smallest level 0.01, so that the new store will be opened only if there is very convincing evidence that the proportion of college graduates in the area is higher than the national rate.

Practice: *Try Exercise 9.56 on page 445.*

EXAMPLE TBP 9.4 WHEN FUTURE CONSIDERATIONS WARRANT A HIGH CUTOFF FOR P-VALUE

Background: The proportion of contents of a certain medication consisting of the active ingredient is supposed to be 2%. In the interest of quality control, manufacturers want to take a sample of doses and test if they conform to this standard.

Question: What would be the most appropriate cutoff level for the P-Value—0.10 or 0.05 or 0.01?

Response: The null hypothesis would state $H_0: p = 0.02$ and the alternative would be $H_a: p \neq 0.02$. In this case, the null hypothesis of conformity should be rejected if there are any doubts at all. If we employed a very small cutoff level, such as 0.01, then there would be a tendency for the manufacturer not to react unless the observed proportion was very different from the 0.02 that is supposed to be in effect. This is not to be recommended because problems could arise if users of the medication are not getting the proper amount of that ingredient. The right approach would be to set a fairly high cutoff level, such as 0.10 or even more. That way, the manufacturer would tend to respond even to less extreme deviations from the target level, and take the necessary measures to improve the production process.

The preceding two examples showed that *future* considerations should be taken into account when deciding on a cutoff level, whereby *P*-values below that level will cause us to reject the null hypothesis. In the next examples, we see that *past* considerations should also be taken into account.

EXAMPLE TBP 9.5 WHEN PAST CONSIDERATIONS WARRANT
A LOW CUTOFF FOR P-VALUE

Background: It is taken to be common knowledge that the proportion of coin flips resulting in heads is 0.5. Suppose a statistician theorizes that the proportion of heads is actually less than 0.5, because of the raised image on the head of the coin making that side a bit heavier and more likely to hit the landing surface first.

Question: What would be the most appropriate cutoff level for the *P*-value—0.10 or 0.05 or 0.01?

Response: This is a situation where the null hypothesis is what we'd call "tried and true," and it would take very convincing evidence to shatter our faith in the long-held belief that half of all coin flips results in heads. The cutoff level should be set at 0.01 or even smaller.

EXAMPLE TBP 9.6 WHEN PAST CONSIDERATIONS WARRANT
A HIGH CUTOFF FOR P-VALUE

Background: The administrator of a statistics tutoring center has a somewhat vague impression that about one-fourth of the students utilizing the center are business majors. She administers a questionnaire to a sample of students who visit the tutoring center and uses the sample proportion identifying themselves as business majors in order to test her hypothesis.

Question: What would be the most appropriate cutoff level for the *P*-value—0.10 or 0.05 or 0.01?

Response: Now the null hypothesis, that population proportion of business majors among students using the tutoring center is 0.25, was by no means "written in stone," and so a fairly high cutoff probability, such as 0.05 or 0.10, would be fine.

Students are often baffled by the idea of statistical significance, and it helps to explain it to them in a variety of ways, to increase the likelihood that at least one of these explanations will make the concept clear to them. Additional discussion may be appropriate after statistical significance is defined on page 431. If data are statistically significant, then what we observed is relatively far from what is proposed in the null hypothesis. For the given sample size and standard deviation, if $\hat{p}$ is far enough from p_0 to result in a standardized proportion z that is far from zero, producing a small *P*-value, then the difference between $\hat{p}$ and p_0 cannot easily be explained away by chance. A difference that is statistically significant is one for which the unpredictability of random selections does not provide an adequate explanation. Instead, it suggests that "something is going on," in contrast to the null hypothesis' claim that "nothing is going on."

In practice, only one test is carried out, with one sample. But because the *P*-value is really telling us about probabilities in the long run, we consider in this example what could happen in repeated tests of the hypothesis $H_0: p = 0.5$. It parallels Example **TBP 9.2** on page 890, which explored the long-run behavior of confidence intervals.

EXAMPLE TBP 9.7 HYPOTHESIS TEST CONCLUSIONS IN THE LONG RUN

Background: Imagine that someone did not know that half of all coin flips result in heads, and she wanted to use 20 flips of a coin to test the null hypothesis that population proportion of heads equals 0.5. We consider what would happen in the long run if 20 coin flips were repeatedly used to test this hypothesis against the two-sided alternative. The cutoff for "small" P-values will be taken to be 0.05.

- The coin is flipped 20 times, and the proportion of heads is found to be $9/20 = 0.45$. The z statistic is calculated to be -0.45 and the P-value is 0.655. Because the P-value is not smaller than 0.05, we do not reject $H_0: p = 0.5$.

- In another 20 flips, the proportion of heads is found to be $8/20 = 0.40$; $z = -0.89$ and P-value is 0.371. Again, we do not reject H_0.

- In yet another 20 flips, the sample proportion is $12/20 = 0.60$; $z = +0.89$ and P-value is 0.371. Once again, we do not reject H_0.

- In the next 20 flips, the sample proportion is $15/20 = 0.75$. This time $z = +2.24$ and the P-value is 0.025. Now we reject $H_0: p = 0.5$ and conclude (erroneously) that the proportion of all coin flips resulting in heads is *not* 0.5.

We can picture many repetitions of 20 coin flips, for each of which a sample proportion of heads is found, along with its standardized value z and the P-value, to decide between the null and alternative hypotheses.

Question: What can we say about the long-run results of those hypothesis tests?

Response: In the long run, 5% of the P-values will be small enough (less than 0.05) to reject the null hypothesis that $p = 0.5$. Thus, 5% or 0.05 is the probability of committing a Type I Error.

20 coin flips	Test $H_0: P = 50$ vs. $H_a: P$ not equal 0.50 (reject if P-value < 0.50)
TTTTTHTHTTHHTHTHTTHH Proportion of heads 9/20 = 0.45	$z = 0.45$, P-value = 0.655 → do not reject H_0
HTTHHTHHTTTHTHTTTHHT Proportion of heads 8/20 = 0.40	$z = -0.89$, P-value = 0.371 → do not reject H_0
TTTHHHHHHHHHTHTHHTHTT Proportion of heads 12/20 = 0.60	$z = +0.89$, P-value = 0.371 → do not reject H_0
THHHHTHHHHTHTHHHTHHHH Proportion of heads 15/20 = 0.75	$z = +2.24$, P-value = 0.025 → do not reject H_0
• • Repeated Flips of 20 Coins •	• In the long run • 95% of the tests do not reject H_0 5% of tests reject H_0 •
TTHTTTTHTTTHTTHHTHHH Proportion of heads 8/20 = 0.40	$z = -0.89$, P-value = 0.371 → do not reject H_0

Continued

Recall that we presented the same thought-experiment of repeated flips of 20 coins in an example designed to help us correctly interpret the meaning of confidence intervals. In that case, the rule of thumb for large enough sample size wasn't quite met because *observed* counts of heads or tails were less than 10. In the case of hypothesis tests, where a value p_0 of population proportion is proposed, we check that counts in and out of the category of interest *expected* under the assumption that $p = p_0$ are at least 10. Now the criteria *are* met, because $np_0 = 20(0.5) = 10$ and $n(1 - p_0) = 20(1 - 0.5) = 10$. (If the null hypothesis is true, we expect to get 10 heads and 10 tails in 20 flips.) Just as we discussed for the example about confidence intervals, there is no problem with sample size being too large relative to population size. Flipping a coin is sampling *with* replacement, in the sense that we can flip all the heads or tails we want and the "supply" of either is in no way depleted.

Practice: *Try Exercise TBP 9.16 on page 907.*

When discussing Type I and II Errors, some instructors like to show their students a table like this one, outlining the *probabilities* of the four possible combinations involving what is true and what the test concludes. This table can supplement the one on page 433 of the textbook, which simply identified conclusions as being correct or in error.

	Do Not Reject H_0	Reject H_0
H_0 true	Prob. $1 - \alpha$	Prob. of Type I Error is α
H_0 false	Prob. of Type II Error is β	Prob. $1 - \beta$ = power

In a z test about the population proportion p, the probability of a Type II Error—incorrectly failing to reject the null hypothesis when the alternative is true—can be calculated only if we are told specifically the actual value of the population proportion. Thus, we need to know the true *alternative* proportion that contradicts the null hypothesized proportion. What we do *not* need in order to calculate the probability of Type II Error is the value of an observed proportion $\hat{p}$. Our probability is about the test itself, not about the results.

Here are two supplementary examples about errors in medical testing.

EXAMPLE TBP 9.8 SENSITIVITY AND SPECIFICITY IN MEDICAL TESTS

Background: A medical test is used to detect HIV. If HIV is actually present in the bloodstream, the test results are positive with probability 0.997 (called the **sensitivity** of the test), and negative with probability 0.003. If HIV is not present, the test is positive with probability 0.015, negative with probability 0.985 (called the **specificity** of the test).

Question: What constitute Type I and Type II Errors in this context, and what are their probabilities?

Response: The null hypothesis would be that a person does not have HIV. If HIV is present (the null hypothesis is false), the test may turn up negative and fail to reject the null hypothesis with probability 0.003; this is the probability of a Type II Error. If HIV is not present (the null hypothesis is true), the test may turn up positive and incorrectly reject the null hypothesis with probability 0.015. This is the probability of a Type I Error.

The four possible combinations of actuality (no HIV or HIV) and the test's decision (negative or positive) are shown in the table below.

⇓ Actuality	Decision	
	Negative (don't reject H_0)	Positive (reject H_0)
No HIV (H_0 true)	*Correct* Prob = **specificity** = 0.985	*Incorrect* (false positive) **Type I Error** (Prob = 0.015)
HIV (H_a true)	*Incorrect* (false negative) **Type II Error** (Prob = 0.003)	*Correct* Prob = **sensitivity** = 0.997

EXAMPLE TBP 9.9 ERRORS IN TEST FOR GONORRHEA

Background: A medical test is used to detect gonorrhea, a common sexually transmitted disease. If the case of an actual gonorrhea infection, the test results are positive with probability 0.983 (called the *sensitivity* of the test), and negative with probability 0.017. If gonorrhea is not present, the test is positive with probability 0.022, negative with probability 0.978 (called the *specificity* of the test).

Question: What constitutes Type I and Type II Errors in this context, and what are their probabilities?

Response: The null hypothesis would be that a person does not have gonorrhea. If gonorrhea is present (the null hypothesis is false), the test may turn up negative and fail to reject the null hypothesis with probability 0.017; this is the probability of a Type II Error. If gonorrhea is not present (the null hypothesis is true), the test may turn up positive and incorrectly reject the null hypothesis with probability 0.022. This is the probability of a Type I Error. The four possible combinations of actuality (no gonorrhea or gonorrhea) and the test's decision (negative or positive) are shown in the table below.

⇓ Actuality	Decision	
	Negative (don't reject H_0)	Positive (reject H_0)
No gonorrhea (H_0 true)	*Correct* Prob = **specificity** = 0.978	*Incorrect* (false positive) **Type I Error** (Prob = 0.022)
Gonorrhea (H_a true)	*Incorrect* (false negative) **Type II Error** (Prob = 0.017)	*Correct* Prob = **sensitivity** = 0.983

Both of these are examples of higher probabilities for Type I Error than for Type II Error in a medical context, as discussed in Example 9.27 on page 434.

The probability (0.015) of incorrectly telling a healthy person that he or she is HIV positive is higher than the probability (0.003) of incorrectly telling someone that he or she does not have HIV. Likewise, the probability (0.022) of incorrectly telling a healthy person that he or she does have gonorrhea is higher than the probability (0.017) of incorrectly telling an infected person that he or she does not have gonorrhea.

The graph on page 898 illustrates how lessening the probability of one type of error leads to an increase in the probability of the other type of error.

In the context of medical tests, the decision of whether a patient tests positive or negative can be based on a sample, such as a blood sample. The amount of the deciding factor—such as number of "unusual" cells—is measured, and if it goes beyond a certain level, the test is deemed positive. In reality, whereas healthy patients tend to have lower levels and diseased patients higher levels, there is a "gray area" where the two overlap.

One extreme would be if the cutoff for testing positive is set at the minimum in the overlap, in which case only Type I Errors would be committed. At the other extreme, if the cutoff for testing positive is set at the maximum in the overlap, only Type II Errors would be committed. The medical community may decide to set the cutoff at a compromise point that makes the probability of a Type II Error somewhat less than the probability of a Type I Error. This would be done because the consequences of failing to diagnose a diseased person tend to be more worrisome than those for when a healthy person incorrectly tests positive. In the latter situation, more discerning follow-up tests may be carried out and, it is hoped, reach the correct decision.

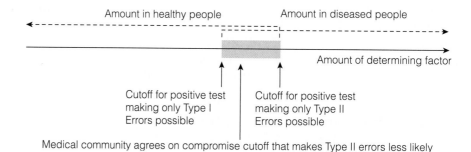

We can also impress on students that two types of error are possible in many decisions made in people's everyday lives.

EXAMPLE TBP 9.10 CONSEQUENCES OF TWO TYPES OF ERROR

Background: In a survey of teenagers, the proportion reported to be virgins was 0.62. For those reported to be virgins, the proportion of mothers who said their teenage child was a virgin was 0.97. For those who had had sex, the proportion of mothers who said their teenage child was a virgin was 0.50.

Question: What would be the consequences of mothers committing either type of error?

Response: We identified the probability of a Type I Error (incorrectly believing a teenager to have had sex when he or she did not) as 0.03. The consequences of this type of error could be subtle strains on the parent-child relationship. The probability of a Type II Error (incorrectly believing a teenager to be a virgin when he or she is not) is 0.50. The consequences of this type of error would include failure to take steps to guide the child toward safe sex practices. There could also be general communication problems.

Carlos' comment in Students Talk Stats on page 438 serves as another reminder of the imperfect nature of hypothesis testing. He is absolutely correct that a sample proportion of 0.48 cannot *prove* that population proportion is 0.50. Rather, a sample proportion of 0.48 in this situation tells us that 0.50 is within a range of plausible values for population proportion. There are infinitely many other plausible values besides 0.50. The following example explores this phenomenon.

EXAMPLE TBP 9.11 SAMPLE DATA CAN SUPPORT MORE THAN ONE NULL HYPOTHESIS

Background: If a sample of size 230 produces 111 individuals in the category of interest (sample proportion approximately 0.48), as in the example above, then software can be used to test various null and alternative hypotheses.

Questions: What would be concluded in each of the following tests?

1. $H_0: p = 0.51$ versus $H_a: p < 0.51$

2. $H_0: p = 0.52$ versus $H_a: p < 0.52$

3. $H_0: p = 0.53$ versus $H_a: p < 0.53$

4. $H_0: p = 0.54$ versus $H_a: p < 0.54$

Responses:

1. Test $H_0: p = 0.51$ versus $H_a: p < 0.51$ results in $z = -0.83$, P-value = 0.203; we do not reject H_0, because the P-value is not less than 0.05.

2. Test $H_0: p = 0.52$ versus $H_a: p < 0.52$ results in $z = -1.14$, P-value = 0.128; we do not reject H_0, because the P-value is not less than 0.05.

3. Test $H_0: p = 0.53$ versus $H_a: p < 0.53$ results in $z = -1.44$, P-value = 0.075; we do not reject H_0, because the P-value is not less than 0.05.

4. Test $H_0: p = 0.54$ versus $H_a: p < 0.54$ results in $z = -1.75$, P-value = 0.040; we *do* reject H_0, because the P-value is less than 0.05.

Practice: *Try Exercise 9.47 on page 444.*

In this example, not only is 0.50 a plausible value for the population proportion, but 0.51, 0.52, and 0.53 are also plausible. In contrast, $H_0: p = 0.54$ is rejected, because 0.54 is not low enough to be included in a range of plausible values for unknown population proportion, when sample proportion is found to be 0.48. Ordinarily, of course, a research context leads us to test only one proposed value of p, not several as we have done here to make a point.

Students can discuss the way conclusions are stated in a legal context, where the null hypothesis claims the defendant is innocent and the alternative claims he is guilty. A trial weighs the evidence, and in the end the conclusions are *guilty* (reject the null hypothesis) or *not guilty* (do not reject the null hypothesis). Note that a jury's verdict is **not** a decision of guilty or *innocent*! If the trial has failed to prove the defendant is guilty, it has not proven the defendant to be innocent, but under our legal system, a person is presumed innocent until proven guilty. Similarly, because our null hypothesis in general represents the status quo or traditionally accepted position, it is also "presumed innocent until proven guilty": We will continue to believe it is plausible, unless there is convincing evidence to the contrary.

Once the discussion of hypothesis tests for a categorical variable that allows for just two possible values has been completed on page 438, we can remind students that we occasionally need to carry out a test when the categorical variable allows for more than two possibilities. Our treatment of single categorical variables in Chapter 9 is still based on the binomial model introduced in Section 7.2 of Chapter 7, which permits only two possible categorical values. If a categorical variable permits more than two possibilities, we can reduce the possibilities to two by singling out one particular categorical value of interest and considering whether or not the variable takes that value. In Example 9.14 on page 403, the categorical variable "transportation" originally took four possible values (car, bus, bike, or walking), but we reduced the possible values to two (walking or not walking).

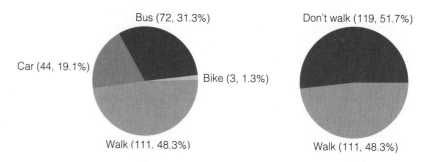

To handle situations involving a single categorical variable with more than two possibilities, a *chi-square goodness of fit* test is used. This method will be presented in Chapter 12 because it is very similar to methods developed in that chapter for doing inference about the relationship between two categorical variables.

9.2 Activities

Activity: Confidence Intervals and Tests for Proportions

Using the Computer

This set of activities helps students understand the meaning of confidence levels and of significance levels in setting up intervals for, and tests about, unknown population proportion.

Each student accesses data from the book's existing data file about several hundred students surveyed previously. Specifically, they will work with the column "Pierced," in which 0.6525 of the students have pierced ear(s). Each student randomly samples 40 values from that column, puts them in a column PiercedSample, and constructs a 95% confidence interval for "unknown" population proportion with pierced ears based on the sampled values. This is done several times by each student so that altogether the class has constructed 100 95% confidence intervals. (For example, if there are 20 students in the class, each should construct five confidence intervals.) Then the presenter checks to see what count, then percentage, of 95% confidence intervals contain the population proportion with pierced ears, 0.6525. If there is time, students also construct several 90% and 99% confidence intervals to see what percentage contain 0.6525 in each case. In the context of this activity, students should discuss the meaning of a 95% (or other) confidence interval.

Now each student uses the columns of sampled values to carry out several tests of $H_0: p = 0.6525$ against the two-sided alternative $H_a: p \neq 0.6525$. Altogether, the class as a group should carry out 100 tests. Then the presenter checks to see what count, then percentage, of the students' tests have a P-value less than 0.05. If there is time, the presenter can also check to see the count and percentage of tests with a P-value less than 0.10 and less than 0.01.

In the context of this activity, students should discuss the meaning of rejecting a null hypothesis with a *P*-value less than 0.05 (or other level).

Finally, discuss the relationship between confidence intervals and hypothesis test results.

Activity: Confidence Intervals and Tests for Proportions with M&M's

In the Classroom

This activity helps students understand the meaning of confidence levels and of significance levels in setting up intervals for, and tests about, "unknown" population proportion.

Materials needed: several bags of mini baking M&M's (about one bag for every 10 students), a bowl, a tablespoon, and students' own calculators for finding sample proportion.

Each student randomly samples (without replacement) a tablespoon of M&M's from the bowl and passes it on to the next student. Each divides the number of blues sampled by the total number sampled to find the sample proportion of blue M&M's, then sets up 68%, 95%, and 99.7% confidence intervals for population proportion of blue M&M's *p* based on sample proportion $\hat{p}$.

Meanwhile, the class discuss confidence intervals for proportions as follows: An approximate

- 68% confidence interval for *p* is $\hat{p} \pm 1(\sqrt{\frac{\hat{p}(1 - \hat{p})}{n}})$
- 95% confidence interval for *p* is $\hat{p} \pm 2 (\sqrt{\frac{\hat{p}(1 - \hat{p})}{n}})$
- 99.7% confidence interval for *p* is $\hat{p} \pm 3 (\sqrt{\frac{\hat{p}(1 - \hat{p})}{n}})$

For example, if 75 M&M's are sampled, then we would substitute 75 for *n* and sample proportion of blues for $\hat{p}$. Suppose a student samples 75 M&M's and find the sample proportion of blue M&M's to be $\hat{p} = \frac{10}{75} = 0.13$. Then the accompanying 68% confidence interval for population proportion *p* of blues $0.13 \pm \sqrt{\frac{0.13(0.87)}{75}} = 0.13 \pm 0.04 = (0.09, 0.17)$. This interval just barely contains *p*, which we happen to know is 0.17. [There are six different colors of baking M&M's, and apparently there are equal proportions of each.] Someone else's 68% confidence interval might fail to contain *p*. In the long run, the probability of successfully capturing 0.17 is 68%—about two-thirds of the class should succeed. Similarly, the probability of successfully capturing 0.17 with a 95% confidence interval is 95% almost all of the class members are expected to succeed.

Now the instructor checks to see what count, then percentage, of 68%, 95%, and 99.7% confidence intervals contain the population proportion which we happen to know is 0.17.

Next, each student uses his or her sample proportion of blue M&M's to calculate standardized sample proportion $z = \dfrac{\hat{p} - 0.17}{\sqrt{\frac{0.17(1 - 0.17)}{n}}}$ and carry out a test of

$H_0 : p = 0.17$ against the two-sided alternative $H_a : p \neq 0.17$.

Then the instructor checks to see what count, then percentage, of the students' tests have a *P*-value less than 0.05. The instructor may also want to check to see the count and percentage of tests with a *P*-value less than 0.10 and less than 0.01.

In the context of these activities, students should discuss the meaning of a 95% (or other) confidence interval and the meaning of rejecting a null hypothesis with a *P*-value less than 0.05 (or other level).

In the Classroom

Find (and distribute) an article or report that includes mention of a margin of error or a *P*-value concerning a population proportion when there is a single categorical variable of interest. If sample proportion and sample size are mentioned, construct the interval or carry out the test yourself to verify the reported results. Discuss sampling and study design. Discuss the implications of the study's conclusions.

9.3 Guide to Exercise Topics

Point estimates: 9.4*(a), 9.5*(b), 9.6*, 9.18(b), 9.84(a)

Confidence intervals for proportions: 9.4*, 9.5*, 9.7*, 9.8*, 9.9*, 9.10, 9.11, 9.13, 9.14*, 9.15, 9.17, 9.18*, 9.19*, 9.20, 9.21* 9.22, 9.23, 9.24, 9.25, 9.26, 9.27, 9.28, 9.29*, 9.30, 9.31, 9.32, 9.33, 9.34, 9.35*, 9.70(a–e), 9.82, 9.83, 9.84(b,c), 9.91, 9.93(b,c), 9.94(a),(b), 9.95(a,b), 9.100

Hypothesis tests for proportions: 9.36*, 9.37*, 9.38*, 9.39, 9.40*, 9.41*, 9.42, 9.43, 9.44, 9.45, 9.46*, 9.47*, 9.48, 9.49*, 9.50*, 9.51, 9.52*, 9.53, 9.54, 9.55, 9.56*, 9.57, 9.58, 9.59*, 9.60, 9.61, 9.62, 9.63, 9.64, 9.65*, 9.66*, 9.67*, 9.68, 9.69, 9.70(g–i), 9.71(f–h), 9.85, 9.86, 9.87, 9.88, 9.89, 9.90, 9.92, 9.93(a), 9.94(c–e), 9.95(c–h), 9.101

Using tables: 9.72, 9.73*, 9.74, 9.75, 9.76*, 9.77*, 9.78, 9.96*, 9.97, 9.98*, 9.99

9.4 Supplemental Exercises

9.1 Researchers reported their findings on the disease amyotrophic lateral sclerosis (ALS). Identify which of these variable situations applies for each of the following.

a. "The longer an athlete played, the greater his risk of contracting ALS." C, Q, $C \to Q$, $Q \to C$, $C \to C$, or $Q \to Q$?

b. "The mean age at which the athletes developed the disease was 51, 10 years younger than the general population." C, Q, $C \to Q$, $Q \to C$, $C \to C$, or $Q \to Q$?

c. The proportion having the disease was higher for Italian soccer players compared with the general population. C, Q, $C \to Q$, $Q \to C$, $C \to C$, or $Q \to Q$?

9.2 Researchers reported their findings on the disease amyotrophic lateral sclerosis (ALS). For which one of the following would the methods of this chapter apply?

a. "The longer an athlete played, the greater his risk of contracting ALS."

b. "The mean age at which the athletes developed the disease was 51, 10 years younger than the general population."

c. The proportion having the disease was higher for Italian soccer players compared with the general population.

9.3 A study of wolf spiders by Persons and Uetz was published in the online journal *Animal Behavior* in November 2004.

a. The study looked at the proportion of females attempting cannibalism. Were the researchers focusing here on one categorical, one quantitative, one each categorical and quantitative, two categorical, or two quantitative variables?

b. The study found that "there was no significant difference in the proportion of males cannibalized before versus after mating."[1] Were the researchers focusing here on one categorical, one quantitative, one each categorical and quantitative, two categorical, or two quantitative variables?

c. The study mentioned that the researchers were able to record all mating events because "copulation duration is exceptionally long in this species (mean ± $SD = 223.44 \pm 31.60$ min; $N = 84$)." Were the researchers focusing here on one categorical, one quantitative, one each categorical and quantitative, two categorical, or two quantitative variables?

d. The article explains that male wolf spiders have "tufts of bristles on their first pair of legs, which are waved up and down during courtship." For background information, the researchers looked at the relationship between body length and tuft size. Were the researchers focusing here on one categorical, one quantitative, one each categorical and quantitative, two categorical, or two quantitative variables?

e. The researchers wanted to establish if larger males were less likely to be cannibalized by females. Here the focus is on one quantitative (size) and one categorical (cannibalization) variable. Does size play the role of explanatory or response variable?

f. For each of the females who mated twice, the researchers compared tuft size for the first mate with that of the second mate, and found that tufts of second mates were significantly larger than those of first mates. Was this a paired, two-sample, or several sample design?

9.4 A study of wolf spiders by Persons and Uetz was published in the online journal *Animal Behavior* in November 2004. Tell whether each of the following focuses on data production, displaying and summarizing data, probability, or statistical inference.

a. "Cannibalism was slightly lower among virgin females (17% combined premating and postmating cannibalism) than among previously mated females (24% combined)."

b. If overall proportions of male wolf spiders cannibalized were the same before and after mating, the probability of a difference between sample proportions as extreme as the one observed would be 0.572.

c. "Overall, our results support the conclusion that larger male body size and larger tuft size are potentially subject to selection from both sexual cannibalism and female mate choice . . ."

d. "In keeping with the Guidelines for the Treatment of Animals in Research

(Section 4c), the container size, with associated litter, allowed sufficient space and hiding places for either sex to avoid the other."

9.5 Patricia Garfield, a researcher of dreams who was trained in clinical psychology, conducted a web survey of 500 dreamers during the late 1990s, with results reported in the article "From Falling to Failing, It's the Same Old Stories." "Topping her list of negative dreams were being chased (80 percent reported these dreams); falling or drowning (64 percent); being lost or trapped (58 percent); being naked or inappropriately dressed (52 percent); and being accidentally injured, ill or dying (48 percent)."[2]

a. Assuming Garfield's sample is representative, which of these could we construct based on this information:
   1. A confidence interval for the proportion of all dreams that are about being chased.
   2. A confidence interval for the proportion of all negative dreams that are about being chased.
   3. A confidence interval for the proportion of all people who dream about being chased.

b. The article elaborates: "only 25 percent of people responding to her survey reported being attacked or chased by animals. The main culprit, she says, is a dark stranger, often dressed in black, which was found in 40 percent of attack/chase dreams." Are 25% and 40% referring to the same sample? Explain.

c. Suppose 25% of 500 dreamers report being chased by animals, and the standard deviation of sample proportion is 0.02. What is a 95% confidence interval for the proportion of all dreamers who are chased by animals in their dreams?

9.6 A 2005 report on the 109th Congress included information on gender of the 434 members of the House and 100 members of the Senate. Two tests (the first for the House and the second for the Senate) were carried out using software, based on the fact that 68 House members and 14 Senate members were women. The null hypothesis would claim equal proportions of men and women.

```
Test and CI for One Proportion
Test of p = 0.5 vs p < 0.5
Sample      X      N  Sample p  95.0% Upper Bound  Z-Value  P-Value
1          68    434  0.156682            0.185382   -14.30    0.000

Test of p = 0.5 vs p < 0.5
Sample      X      N  Sample p  95.0% Upper Bound  Z-Value  P-Value
1          14    100  0.140000            0.197074    -7.20    0.000
```

a. About 16% of the House and 14% of the Senate members were women. Explain why standardized proportion (z) of women is more extreme for the House than for the Senate.

b. *P*-values for both tests are reported as 0.000. Which *P*-value is actually smaller: the one for the House or the one for the Senate? Explain.

c. In both tests, the null hypothesis would be rejected, and we would conclude that women are under-represented in both the House and the Senate. Would we also reject the null hypothesis if two-sided tests had been carried out instead of one-sided? Explain.

d. According to the test output above, what is the assumed proportion of all adult Americans who are women?

e. What notation should be used for the assumed proportion of all adult Americans who are women: p, p_0, or $\hat{p}$?

f. What notation should be used for the number 0.140000 reported in the output for the second test?

g. If the first test had been carried out against the opposite one-sided alternative, $H_a: p > 0.5$, would the *P*-value be 0, 0.5, or 1? Explain.

9.7 "Survey Reveals Majority of College Students Breaking Even or Flat Broke While in School" is the headline of an Internet report posted by Ebay. "The Survey.com study was conducted in December 2004 with 500 college students between the ages of 19 and 25 as participants."[3] Besides reporting on the percentage of students who broke even or were broke, the article also includes information on students shopping for textbooks online, helping friends or classmates sell books online, or using the Internet to compare textbook prices. To test whether all students in a given category are in a majority (greater than 0.5), the correct standard deviation is $\sqrt{0.5(1 - 0.5)/500} = 0.02$

a. The sample proportion who used the Internet to compare textbook prices was 0.65. How many standard deviations above 0.50 is this?

b. The sample proportion who used the Internet to help a friend or classmate sell textbooks online was 0.53. How many standard deviations above 0.50 is this?

c. Explain why the survey's results *would* let us claim that a majority of all students used the Internet to compare textbook prices, but we could *not* claim that a majority of all students used the Internet to help a friend or classmate sell textbooks online.

d. The article reports that "more than 50 percent have shopped on Half.com for their textbooks," without specifying the exact sample proportion. Keep in mind that the standard deviation of the sample proportion (taking the population proportion to be 0.5) is 0.02. What sample percentage would begin to convince us that the population percentage is more than 0.50, if we agree that sample proportions more than 2 standard deviations above the mean are high enough to be considered improbable?

9.8 Exercise TBP 9.7 tested if a majority of students have used the Internet to help a friend or classmate sell textbooks online, based on a proportion of 0.53 who had done so in a sample of 500 students. Use the fact that standard deviation of sample proportion under the null hypothesis would be 0.02 to find the z statistic, then use tables to find the *P*-value.

9.9 An article entitled "Courtship in the Monogamous Convict Cichlid; What Are Individuals Saying to Rejected and Selected

Mates?," written by Nick Santangelo and published online in the journal *Animal Behavior* in November 2004, considered female damselfish' choice of mates. Of 31 females, 21 chose the larger of two potential male mates.

a. Explain why the conditions for use of a normal approximation to set up a confidence interval are just barely satisfied.

b. Find the sample proportion choosing the larger male, rounding to the nearest thousandth.

c. The approximate standard deviation of sample proportion is 0.084. Report a 95% confidence interval for the proportion of all female damselfish who would choose the larger of two males.

d. Based on your confidence interval, which one of these conclusions is most appropriate?
   1. The data show without a doubt that the population proportion of female damselfish choosing a larger male mate is greater than 0.5.
   2. The data provide no evidence that the population proportion of female damselfish choosing a larger male mate is greater than 0.5.
   3. The data may barely indicate that the population proportion of female damselfish choosing a larger male mate is greater than 0.5.

9.10 An article entitled "Courtship in the Monogamous Convict Cichlid; What Are Individuals Saying to Rejected and Selected Mates?," written by Nick Santangelo and published online in the journal *Animal Behavior* in November 2004, considered female damselfish' choice of mates. Of 31 females, 21 chose the larger of two potential male mates.

a. Explain why the conditions for use of a normal approximation to test the hypothesis $H_0: p = 0.5$ are satisfied.

b. If we suspect females prefer larger males, should we use a one-sided or two-sided alternative?

c. Find the sample proportion choosing the larger male, rounding to the nearest hundredth.

d. Assuming the null hypothesis to be true, the standard deviation of sample

proportion is 0.09. Find the standardized sample proportion z.

e. In our discussions of normal distributions in Part III, we stated that standardized values z considerably greater than 2 in absolute value are generally considered *exceptional*. Values close to 2 in absolute value may be called *borderline*. Otherwise, a value may be considered *unexceptional*. Using these criteria, which one of the following conclusions is most appropriate?
   1. The data show without a doubt that the population proportion of female damselfish choosing a larger male mate is greater than 0.5.
   2. The data provide no evidence that the population proportion of female damselfish choosing a larger male mate is greater than 0.5.
   3. The data may barely indicate that the population proportion of female damselfish choosing a larger male mate is greater than 0.5.

f. Whereas the normally approximated probability of a sample proportion as high as 21/31 is about 0.025, the actual binomial probability is 0.035. Does this provide more evidence or less evidence against the null hypothesis than was obtained with the normal approximation?

g. The actual (binomial test) P-value for testing $H_0: p = 0.5$ against the one-sided alternative $H_a: p > 0.5$ is 0.035. What would the P-value be if we'd had no initial suspicion that larger males would be preferred over smaller males?

9.11 An article entitled "Courtship in the Monogamous Convict Cichlid; What Are Individuals Saying to Rejected and Selected Mates?," written by Nick Santangelo and published online in the journal *Animal Behavior* in November 2004, considered courtship behavior of male and female damselfish. Tell whether each of the following focuses on data production, displaying and summarizing data, probability, or statistical inference.

a. "Fish were fed by dropping eight pellets of trout crumbles in each experimental compartment every day. This eliminated any bias in resource quality between potential mates."

b. "The null hypothesis for male courtship was rejected because courtship rates of selected and rejected males differed significantly."

c. "21 chose the large male, 10 chose the small male."

d. If in general female damselfish have no preference for larger males, the chance of at least 21 in 31 choosing the larger male is 0.035.

9.12 A December 2005 *New York Times* article reports: "In 1990, 44 talented teenagers came from around the world to the Juilliard School yearning for a career in classical music. Ten years after graduation, nearly half of those who could be traced had dropped out of performing."[4] Specifically, 14 of the 36 who could be traced had dropped out of performing.

a. To the nearest hundredth, find the sample proportion (of those who could be traced) who had dropped out of performing.

b. Show that the approximate standard deviation of sample proportion is 0.08.

c. If we decided to focus on the proportion who *were* performing, instead of the proportion who were *not* performing, what would the sample proportion and its approximate standard deviation be?

d. Assuming those 36 are a representative sample from a larger population of classical music students, report a 95% confidence interval for the population proportion who would have dropped out of performing by 10 years after graduation.

e. Of the 44 incoming students from 1990, only 36 could be traced. As far as the other 8 are concerned, is there reason to believe that they are similar to those 36 in terms of performing? If not, is there reason to believe that more of them or fewer of them had dropped out of performing? Explain.

9.13 A December 2005 *New York Times* article reported on the careers, 10 years after graduation, of classical music students who began studying at the Juilliard School in 1990. Quite a few had dropped out of performing, and 10 out of the 36 students who could be traced were working in a profession that did not involve music at all.

a. State the null and alternative hypotheses if we want to test if fewer than half of all such students would be working in a non-musical profession ten years after graduation.

b. To the nearest hundredth, find the sample proportion who were working in a non-musical profession, and verify that it is less than one half.

c. Show that, assuming population proportion to be 0.5, the standard deviation of sample proportion is 0.083.

d. Explain why the requirements for a normal approximation are satisfied.

e. Find z, the standardized sample proportion.

f. Use your z-score and a sketch of the tails of the normal curve to tell whether the probability of a sample proportion equal to 10/36 or lower—when the population has proportion 0.5 in nonmusical professions—is greater than 0.05, between 0.05 and 0.025, between 0.025 and 0.01, between 0.01 and 0.005, or less than 0.005.

g. Do we conclude that the proportion of all such students ending up in a nonmusical profession ten years after graduation may be half, or is it clearly less than half?

h. Of the 44 incoming students from 1990, only 36 could be traced. Suppose that of the remaining 8, all 8 were working in a nonmusical profession. If this were the case, report the sample proportion in nonmusical professions, and standardized sample proportion z, using the fact that the standard deviation for samples of size 44 is 0.075.

i. If 18 out of 44 students ended up in nonmusical professions, can we conclude that the population proportion is less than half?

9.14 A *New York Times* online article from March 2005 begins, "Why soccer would be a risk for amyotrophic lateral sclerosis [ALS., or Lou Gehrig's disease] is a mystery. But a new study has found that Italian professional soccer players get the disease at a rate nearly six times as great as the general population."[5] The article goes on to describe results of a study carried out in Turin: "The study's subjects included all native Italian male professional soccer players who were on a team roster from 1970 to 2002 and who had played in at least one official match. The total came to more than 7,000 men. Eighteen cases of ALS were identified."

a. Assuming that the proportion of ALS cases in the study was six times as large as the proportion of cases in the general population, how many cases would we expect to see in a sample of size 7,000?

b. Explain why the conditions for carrying out a hypothesis test with a normal approximation in this case are not satisfied.

c. Show that the approximate standard deviation for sample proportion, based on a sample proportion of $18/7{,}000 =$

0.0026, is 0.0006, to the nearest ten-thousandth.

d. Because 18 and $7{,}000 - 18$ are both greater than 10, the conditions for setting up a confidence interval are satisfied. Assuming those Italian soccer players are a representative sample of all soccer players, report a 98% confidence interval for the proportion of all soccer players with ALS.

e. The rate of ALS in the general population is apparently about $3/7{,}000 = 0.0004$. Considering your confidence interval in part (d), is 0.0004 a plausible value for the rate of ALS among all soccer players?

9.15 In a population of several hundred students, the proportion who live on campus is 0.5. Repeated random samples of size 40 were taken, and for each sample a 95% confidence interval was constructed for the population proportion living on campus. This was done 20 times, for a total of 20 confidence intervals.

Variable	X	N	Sample p	95.0% CI	Z-Value	P-Value
Livelargesample	20	40	0.500000	(0.345051, 0.654949)	0.00	1.000
Livelargesample	23	40	0.575000	(0.421804, 0.728196)	0.95	0.343
Livelargesample	17	40	0.425000	(0.271804, 0.578196)	-0.95	0.343
Livelargesample	26	40	0.650000	(0.502188, 0.797812)	1.90	0.058
Livelargesample	16	40	0.400000	(0.248182, 0.551818)	-1.26	0.206
Livelargesample	18	40	0.450000	(0.295828, 0.604172)	-0.63	0.527
Livelargesample	19	40	0.475000	(0.320245, 0.629755)	-0.32	0.752
Livelargesample	21	40	0.525000	(0.370245, 0.679755)	0.32	0.752
Livelargesample	22	40	0.550000	(0.395828, 0.704172)	0.63	0.527
Livelargesample	19	40	0.475000	(0.320245, 0.629755)	-0.32	0.752
Livelargesample	16	40	0.400000	(0.248182, 0.551818)	-1.26	0.206
Livelargesample	20	40	0.500000	(0.345051, 0.654949)	0.00	1.000
Livelargesample	20	39	0.512821	(0.355949, 0.669692)	0.16	0.873
Livelargesample	25	40	0.625000	(0.474972, 0.775028)	1.58	0.114
Livelargesample	19	40	0.475000	(0.320245, 0.629755)	-0.32	0.752
Livelargesample	20	40	0.500000	(0.345051, 0.654949)	0.00	1.000
Livelargesample	22	40	0.550000	(0.395828, 0.704172)	0.63	0.527
Livelargesample	19	40	0.475000	(0.320245, 0.629755)	-0.32	0.752
Livelargesample	22	40	0.550000	(0.395828, 0.704172)	0.63	0.527
Livelargesample	24	40	0.600000	(0.448182, 0.751818)	1.26	0.206

a. In general, what is the probability that a 95% confidence interval contains the true value of the parameter?

b. If 20 intervals are produced, each with 95% confidence, in the long run about how many will succeed in capturing the true value of the parameter?

c. How many of the 20 intervals above contain the population proportion, 0.5? Will this be exactly the case in every set of 20 confidence intervals? Explain.

9.16 In a population of several hundred students, the proportion who live on campus is 0.5. Repeated random samples of size 40 were taken, and for each sample a hypothesis test was carried out, testing if the population proportion living on campus equals 0.5. This was done 20 times, for a total of 20 tests. The preceding exercise shows the standardized sample proportion on campus, z, and the accompanying P-value for each test.

a. In general, what is the probability that a test of a null hypothesis that is actually true rejects it, using 0.05 as the cutoff level α for what is considered to be a small P-value?

b. If 20 tests of a true null hypothesis are carried out at the 0.05 level, in the long run about how many will (correctly) fail to reject it? How many will (incorrectly) reject it?

c. How many of the 20 P-values above are small enough to reject $H_0: p = 0.5$ at the $\alpha = 0.05$ level? Will this be exactly the case in every set of 20 tests? Explain.

d. How many of the 20 P-values above are small enough to reject $H_0: p = 0.5$ at the $\alpha = 0.10$ level?

e. Explain why roughly half of the z statistics are negative.

9.17 The proportion of all births in the United States that were Caesarian deliveries in 2002 was 0.26. One particular county found that 35,600 of its 143,000 births were Caesarian that year.

a. Use software to test if the proportion of Caesarian deliveries in that county differs significantly from the population proportion of Caesarians: State H_0 and H_a mathematically, report the sample proportion $\hat{p}$, the standardized sample proportion z, and the P-value.

b. Does the proportion of Caesarians in that county differ significantly from 0.26?

c. If both sample size and sample count of Caesarians were divided by 100 (356 of 1,430 births are Caesarian), then the sample proportion would not change. Would standardized sample proportion z change? If so, what would its new value be?

d. If 356 of 1,430 births are Caesarian, does this differ significantly from 0.26? Explain.

e. Which confidence interval would be narrower: one based on proportion of Caesarians in 143,000 births, or one based on proportion of Caesarians in 1,430 births; or would they be the same?

f. Based on your answers to parts (b) and (d), which confidence interval would contain 0.26: one based on 35,600 in 143,000 births, or one based on 356 in 1,430 births, or both, or neither? Explain.

g. Suppose that there are 1,000 counties in the United States for which the proportion of Caesarian births is 0.26. If a large number of births are sampled in each county and the sample proportion of Caesarians is used each time to produce a 99% confidence interval for the population proportion of Caesarians, about how many of the 1,000 counties will have intervals that do *not* contain 0.26?

h. Suppose that there are 1,000 counties in the United States for which the proportion of Caesarian births is 0.26. If a large number of births are sampled in each county and the sample proportion of Caesarians is used each time to test the null hypothesis that the population proportion equals 0.26 against the two-sided alternative, about how many of the 1,000 tests will reject the null hypothesis using 0.01 as the cutoff probability α?

9.18 A student survey was completed by 446 students in introductory statistics courses at a large university in the fall of 2003. Students reported their sex as male or female.

a. Use software to access the survey data and produce a 95% confidence interval for the proportion of all students who are male, assuming the surveyed students were a representative sample.

b. According to the U.S. Statistical Abstract, the proportion of college students who are male (as of 2002) is 0.44. Does your interval contain 0.44?

c. Test whether the proportion of males in the larger population from which surveyed students were sampled could equal 0.44. Draw your conclusions, using 0.05 as the cutoff for a small P-value.

d. Explain how your answers to parts (b) and (c) are consistent with one another.

9.19 A student survey was completed by 446 students in introductory statistics courses at a large university in the fall of 2003. Students reported whether or not they smoked.

a. Use software to access the survey data and produce a 95% confidence interval for the proportion of all students who smoke, assuming the surveyed students were a representative sample.

b. The proportion of adult Americans who smoke is reported to be 0.25. Does your interval contain 0.25?

c. Test whether the proportion of smokers in the larger population from which surveyed students were sampled could equal 0.25. Draw your conclusions, using 0.05 as the cutoff for a small *P*-value.

d. Explain how your answers to parts (b) and (c) are consistent with one another.

e. Report the *P*-value if you had tested against the one-sided alternative that proportion of all such students who smoke was *less than* 0.25.

9.20 A student survey was completed by 446 students in introductory statistics courses at a large university in the fall of 2003. Students reported whether or not their major was decided.

a. Use software to access the survey data and produce a 95% confidence interval for the proportion of all students whose major is decided, assuming the surveyed students were a representative sample.

b. Does your interval contain 0.50?

c. Test whether the proportion of decided majors in the larger population from which surveyed students were sampled could equal 0.50. Draw your conclusions, using 0.05 as the cutoff for small *P*-values.

d. Explain how your answers to parts (b) and (c) are consistent with one another.

e. Would sample proportion be higher or lower if only fourth-year students were surveyed?

f. Would standardized sample proportion *z* be higher or lower if only fourth-year students were surveyed?

g. Would the *P*-value be larger or smaller if only fourth-year students were surveyed?

9.21 Exercise 9.112 tested if a majority of female cichlids prefer a larger male mate, based on a sample proportion of 21/31 with this preference. Report the standardized sample proportion *z* and the *P*-value for this test.

9.22 Exercise 9.115 tested if fewer than half of all classical music students end up with a career in the music profession, based on a sample proportion of 10/36. Use the fact that standard deviation of sample proportion under the null hypothesis would be 0.083 to find the *z* statistic to carry out the test, then use tables or software to find the *P*-value.

9.23 Exercise 9.117 reported 20 confidence intervals for population proportion of students living on campus, and the output included 20 *z* values. Use tables or software to report the 20 corresponding *P*-values (to 4 decimal places) for a two-sided alternative.

9.5 Solutions to Supplemental Exercises

9.1 **a.** $Q \rightarrow C$ **b.** Q **c.** C

9.2 (c) (one categorical variable)

9.3 **a.** one categorical **b.** two categorical **c.** one quantitative **d.** two quantitative **e.** explanatory **f.** paired

9.4 **a.** displaying and summarizing data **b.** probability **c.** statistical inference **d.** data production

9.5 **a.** (3) a confidence interval for the proportion of all people who dream about being chased. **b.** No; 25% refers to sampled people and 40% refers to sampled attack/chase dreams. **c.** $0.25 \pm 2(0.02) = (0.21, 0.29)$

9.6 **a.** *z* is more extreme for the House because the sample size is larger. **b.** The *P*-value for the House is smaller because *z* is more extreme. **c.** Yes, because twice 0.000 is still 0.000 (or at most 0.001). **d.** 0.5 **e.** p_0 **f.** $\hat{p}$ **g.** $P(Z > -14.30) = 1$

9.7 **a.** $0.15/0.02 = 7.5$ **b.** $0.03/0.02 = 1.5$ **c.** Because the *P*-value for the first is approximately zero, whereas the *P*-value for the second is not especially small (greater than 0.05 because *z* is less than 1.645). **d.** 0.54 because it is 2 standard deviations above 0.50

9.8 $z = 1.5$; *P*-value is 0.0668

9.9 **a.** There are exactly 10 who did not choose the larger male. **b.** $21/31 = 0.677$ **c.** $0.677 \pm 2(0.084) = (0.509, 0.845)$ **d.** (3) The data may barely indicate that the population proportion of female damselfish choosing a larger male mate is greater than 0.5.

9.10 **a.** 31(0.5) and 31(1 − 0.5) are both at least 10. **b.** one-sided **c.** $\hat{p} = 21/31 = 0.68$ **d.** $z = (0.68 - 0.5)/0.09 = +2$ **e.** (3) The data may barely indicate that the population proportion of female damselfish choosing a larger male mate is greater than 0.5. **f.** less evidence **g.** $2(0.035) = 0.070$

9.11 a. data production   **b.** statistical inference   **c.** displaying and summarizing data   **d.** probability the chance of at least 21 in 31 choosing the larger male is 0.035.

9.12 a. $14/36 = 0.39$ **b.** $\sqrt{0.39(1 - 0.39)/36} = 0.08$ **c.** sample proportion $1 - 0.39 = 0.61$, same standard deviation 0.08   **d.** $0.39 \pm 2(0.08) = (0.23, 0.55)$ **e.** No, probably more of them had dropped out. (If they were still performing, they would have been easier to locate.)

9.13 a. $H_0 : p = 0.5$ versus $H_a : p < 0.5$ **b.** $\hat{p} = 10/36 = 0.28$ is less than 0.5   **c.** $\sqrt{0.5(1 - 0.5)/36} = 0.083$ **d.** Under the null hypothesis, we expect 18 in and 18 out of the music business.   **e.** $z = (0.28 - 0.5)/0.083 = -2.65$ **f.** less than 0.005 because z is less than

-2.576 **g.** clearly less than half   **h.** $\hat{p} = 10/44 = 0.23$, $z = (0.23 - 0.5)/0.075 = -3.6$ **i.** Yes

9.14 a. One-sixth of 18 is three.   **b.** 3 is not at least 10.   **c.** $\sqrt{0.0026(1 - 0.0026)/7,000} = 0.0006$ **d.** $0.0026 \pm 2.326(0.0006) = 0.0026 \pm 0.0014 = (0.0012, 0.0040)$ **e.** No, because it is not contained in the interval.

9.15 a. 95%   **b.** $0.95(20) = 19$ **c.** 20 contain 0.5, but this will not always be the case; sometimes only about 18 or 19 will contain 0.5.

9.16 a. 0.05   **b.** 19, 1   **c.** None, but this will not always be the case; sometimes one or two will reject.   **d.** one (0.058)   **e.** because about half of the sample proportions will be below 0.5 and the other half above

9.17 a.

```
Test of p = 0.26 vs p not = 0.26
Sample      X       N  Sample p           95.0% CI          Z-Value    P-Value
1       35600 143000  0.248951   (0.246710, 0.251192)      -9.53      0.000
H₀:p = 0.26 vs. Hₐ:p ≠ 0.26, p̂ = 0.25 (rounded), z = -9.53, P-value is 0.000
```

b. yes   **c.** Yes, z would be one-tenth its value, or minus -0.953.   **d.** No, because the P-value would be greater than $2(0.16) = 0.32$, since $|z| < 1$ (applying the 68-95-99.7 Rule).   **e.** Confidence interval based on proportion of Caesarians in 143,000 births would be narrower.   **f.** Confidence interval based on 356 in 1,430 births would contain 0.26, because for this sample we would not reject $H_0 : p = 0.26$.   **g.** $0.01(1000) = 10$ **h.** $0.01(1000) = 10$

9.18 a. (0.32, 0.41)   **b.** no   **c.** $z = -3.08$, P-value is 0.002; reject $H_0 : p = 0.44$ and conclude the population proportion of males from which the sample was obtained does not equal 0.44.   **d.** 0.44 is not contained in the interval, and we reject the claim that $P = 0.44$.

9.19 a. (0.15, 0.23)   **b.** no   **c.** $z = -2.90$, P-value is 0.004; reject $H_0 : p = 0.25$ and conclude population proportion of smokers from which the sample was obtained does not equal 0.25.   **d.** 0.25 is not contained in the interval, and we reject the claim that $P = 0.25$.   **e.** $0.004/2 = 0.002$

9.20 a. (0.49, 0.58)   **b.** yes   **c.** $z = +1.52$, P-value is 0.129; do not reject $H_0 : P = 0.50$ and conclude population proportion whose major is decided may be 0.50.   **d.** 0.50 is contained in the interval and we do not reject $H_0 : P = 0.50$ **e.** higher   **f.** higher   **g.** smaller

9.21 $z = +1.97$, P-value is 0.0244

9.22 $z = 2.68$; P-value is 0.0037

9.23 1.000, 0.3422, 0.3422, 0.0574, 0.2076, 0.5286, 0.7490, 0.7490, 0.5286, 0.7490, 0.2076, 1.000, 0.8728, 0.1142, 0.7490, 1.000, 0.5286, 0.7490, 0.5286, 0.2076.

TBP Chapter 10

Inference for a Single Quantitative Variable

10.1 Details and Examples

Means versus Proportions: Similarities and Differences in Inference Procedures

To simultaneously review principles established in Chapter 9 and preview principles to be covered in Chapter 10, we can outline for students the similarities and differences in performing inference for means as opposed to proportions.

Similarities to Inference for Proportions

- Our three forms of inference about unknown population mean will be point estimates, confidence intervals, and hypothesis tests.
- Our sample statistic (in this case, sample mean) as a single point estimate will be shown to be an unbiased estimator for population parameter (population mean).
- Our confidence interval will be of the form

  estimate $\pm$ margin of error

  = sample statistic $\pm$ multiplier $\times$ standard deviation of sample statistic

  where estimate is our sample statistic (sample mean) and margin of error is a multiple of the standard deviation of the sampling distribution of our sample statistic. The sample statistic should be unbiased, the sample size should be large enough so that we are justified in using a multiplier from, say, a z distribution, and the population should be at least 10 times the sample size so that our expression for standard deviation of sample statistic is correct.
  - The multiplier in the margin of error depends on the level of confidence, among other things. In general, higher levels of confidence are associated with wider intervals.
  - The most important aspect of the standard deviation of the sampling distribution is the way it impacts the width of the confidence interval: If the distribution itself has a lot of spread, the interval will be wider; if its values are fairly concentrated, the interval will be narrower. Because the expression for standard deviation of the sampling distribution features sample size in the denominator, margin of error is larger for small samples, smaller for large samples.
  - The correct interpretation of the confidence interval is that we are confident (at a specific level) that the unknown population parameter is contained in that interval. Alternatively, we can say the specific probability of producing an interval that succeeds in capturing the unknown population parameter.

■ Inference in the form of a hypothesis test is designed to decide whether or not to believe the claim that the population parameter (in this case, population mean) equals a proposed value. The decision is based on the value of the sample statistic (sample mean).

■ There are three forms of alternative hypothesis, expressed with either a ">", "<", or "≠" sign.

■ Once the null and alternative hypotheses are stated, a four-step strategy is used to come to a decision; the strategy involves assuming that the null hypothesis is true, and then finding the probability of an outcome as extreme as what was observed:

0. State null and alternative hypotheses.

1. Methods require that the sample must be representative of the population (ideally, the sample is random). When sampling without replacement, sample size should not be more than one-tenth of population size. The sample size must be large enough that a normal approximation works well.

2. Produce the relevant statistic (in this case, sample mean), standardize to the test statistic, and get a feel for whether or not it is "large."

3. Find the P-value (probability of a test statistic at least as extreme as the one observed, assuming the null hypothesis to be true) and assess whether or not it is "small."

4. Draw conclusions: If the P-value is small, reject the null hypothesis and conclude the population parameter (sample mean) is less/greater/different than the proposed value. If it is not small, do not reject the null hypothesis; conclude that it may be true.

■ Care should be taken in setting up the alternative as either one-sided or two-sided. The P-value for a two-sided alternative is twice that for a one-sided alternative.

■ In order to choose an appropriate cutoff level a for how small a P-value must be to reject the null hypothesis, both past and future considerations should be taken into account. The most commonly used cutoff level is $\alpha = 0.05$.

■ The most obvious circumstance that leads to rejection of the null hypothesis is when the sample statistic is very far from the proposed value of the parameter (in this case, if sample mean is far from hypothesized population mean). But sample size also plays a role: Larger samples make it easier to reject the null hypothesis. Furthermore, spread of the distribution of the sample statistic enters in: The difference between what is observed and what is hypothesized is more pronounced if the standard deviation (either known σ or its estimate s) is small.

■ Two types of error can be made when carrying out a test of hypotheses: rejecting the null hypothesis when it is in fact true, or failing to reject it when it is false.

■ If a cutoff level α for what P-values will be considered small has been selected, then in fact α tells the probability of rejecting a true null hypothesis (Type I Error).

■ Confidence intervals are related to hypothesis tests in a specific way.

Differences from Inference for Proportions

When working with categorical variables, the standard deviation of sample proportion was calculated, or estimated, using a formula involving hypothesized population proportion, or observed sample proportion, plus sample size n. Now that we are working with quantitative variables, we have no way of knowing or estimating standard deviation unless it is given in the problem statement, or calculated from the data.

Also, when the variable is categorical, the population proportion p tells us how balanced or unbalanced the underlying shape is, and we can spell out a neat rule of thumb for what constitutes a large enough sample size n relative to that shape. In contrast, when the variable of interest is quantitative, the only information we generally have about the shape of the population distribution comes from looking at a graph of the sample data. Thus, displaying the data is an important part of our inference procedure. For certain variables, such as physical characteristics, we may be justified in assuming the population shape to be normal.

The examples presented in this chapter will involve just a single quantitative variable. When we perform inference, we have in mind a larger population of individuals, and for each individual that variable takes some number value. The diagram below represents various number values with a "#." The mean of all those values in the population is unknown, and in order to gain information about it, a random sample is taken. By looking at the sample mean, we can draw conclusions about the unknown population mean.

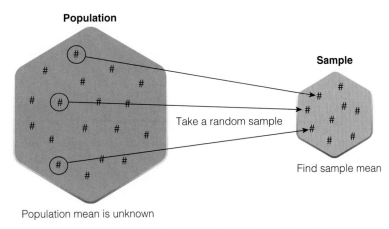

Probability versus Confidence for Means

These graphs illustrate the margin of error found in Example 10.6.

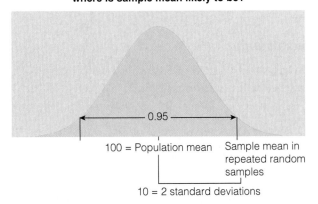

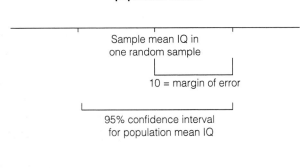

Assessing Normality of Sample Data

Normal probability plots can be explained to the more advanced students after the Guidelines for Approximate Normality of the Sample Mean have been presented on page 466.

The probability that a standard normal variable takes a value below -3 is 0.0015, the probability of taking a value below -2 is 0.025, below -1 is 0.16, below 0 is 0.5, below $+1$ is 0.84, below $+2$ is 0.975, and below $+3$ is 0.9985. If we plot the probabilities 0.0015, 0.025, 0.16, 0.5, 0.84, 0.975, 0.9985 against the values $-3, -2, -1, 0, 1, 2, 3$, then the result is a curve that starts flat, rises steeper, then flattens again. It is possible to re-scale the vertical axis to make the plot linear. The z-values and probabilities mentioned above are just the "tip of the iceberg": If we plot any set of standard normal values along the x-axis, and re-scaled probabilities on the y-axis, the result should be a straight line. For that matter, they need not be standard normal: If they are unstandardized, there's just a different scale on the horizontal axis.

If, on the other hand, the data do not conform well to a normal distribution, the graph of re-scaled normal probabilities versus data values will deviate noticeably from a straight line. Statistical software packages include a test for normality like the one described above, and we start with a visual test: A plot that appears linear suggests that the data set is normal. There are also a variety of test statistics and accompanying P-values.

Margin of Error in a Confidence Interval for a Mean

These graphs supplement the discussion about the margin of error for female weights by the four students on page 469. The graph on the left illustrates the standard deviation of the underlying population and the one on the right shows standard deviation of sample mean, which is multiplied by 2 to produce the margin of error. The confidence interval extends one margin of error on either side of the sample mean.

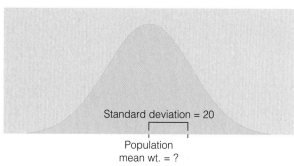

Standard deviation = 20

Population mean wt. = ?

Sample mean wt. in repeated random samples

Standard deviation = 4.59

129.37 = observed sample mean wt.

Margin of error = 2(4.59)

95% confidence interval for unknown population mean wt.

Details about Confidence Intervals with z

After the basic z confidence interval is constructed in Example 10.8 on page 470, further aspects of the interval can be explored if time permits.

EXAMPLE TBP 10.1 WHEN THE SAMPLE MEAN IS NON-NORMAL

Background: Assume standard deviation for number of credits taken by all college students is 2.

Question: Can we construct a 95% confidence interval for mean number of credits taken by all nontraditional students, based on this sample of credits taken by 14 nontraditional students?

| 4 | 7 | 11 | 11 | 12 | 13 | 13 | 14 | 14 | 17 | 17 | 17 | 17 | 18 |

Response: First, we examine a histogram of the data.

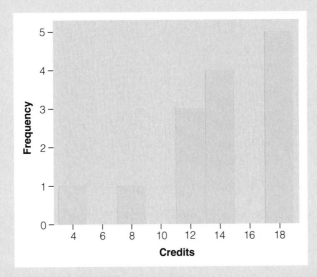

The distribution looks skewed to the left, which is to be expected because there are bound to be part-time students in the group, who take unusually few credits. The sample size, only 14, is too small for the Central Limit Theorem to guarantee an approximately normal distribution of sample mean. A larger sample would be needed to do inference about this variable.

Practice: *Try Exercise TBP 10.8(b,c) on page 929.*

Later on in Chapter 10, we carry out a formal test of hypothesis about a proposed value for unknown population mean. Meanwhile, we can informally assess the plausibility of a proposed mean by checking whether or not it is contained in our confidence interval.

EXAMPLE TBP 10.2 THE CONFIDENCE INTERVAL AS A RANGE OF PLAUSIBLE VALUES

Background: Assume standard deviation for shoe sizes of all male college students is 1.5 and we have a random sample of 9 shoe sizes:

| 11.5 | 12.0 | 11.0 | 15.0 | 11.5 | 10.0 | 9.0 | 10.0 | 11.0 |

Continued

A histogram of the data has a gap, but knowing that measurements like shoe size do follow a normal curve, we can attribute the gap to the fact that so few students were sampled.

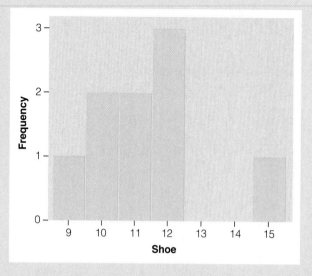

A 95% confidence interval for mean shoe size of all male college students is found using software:

```
The assumed sigma = 1.5
Variable           N      Mean    StDev    SE Mean         95.0% CI
Shoe               9    11.222    1.698     0.500    ( 10.242, 12.202)
```

Question: Does it seem plausible that the mean of all shoe sizes of male college students is 11.0?

Response: Because 11.0 is well within the confidence interval, it does seem like a plausible value for population mean.

Practice: *Try Exercise 10.9(a–d) on page 478.*

In Example **TBP** 10.2, we identified a proposed value of population mean as being plausible because it was well-contained in our confidence interval. Conversely, a proposed value is considered implausible if it is clearly outside the confidence interval.

EXAMPLE TBP 10.3 USING A CONFIDENCE INTERVAL TO IDENTIFY AN IMPLAUSIBLE VALUE FOR THE POPULATION MEAN

Background: Number of police employed per 10,000 residents is recorded for a sample of 21 mid-sized cities. The mean is found to be 23.42 and the standard deviation is assumed to be 10 (where units are police per 10,000 residents). A histogram of the data, shown on page 917, has a bit of right-skewness, but with a sample of size 21 we can assume the sample mean to follow a reasonably normal distribution.

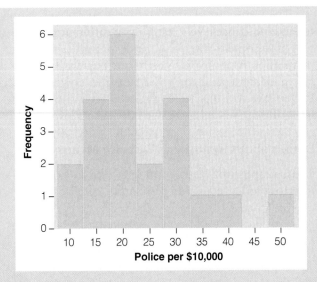

A 95% confidence interval has been produced with software.

```
One-Sample Z: police
The assumed sigma = 10
Variable          N      Mean   StDev   SE Mean        95.0% CI
police           21     23.42    9.96      2.18    (  19.14, 27.70)
```

Question: Based on the output shown, is 30 a plausible value for the mean number of police per ten thousand residents in all mid-sized cities?

Response: The 95% confidence interval does not contain 30. Therefore, 30 would not be considered a plausible value for the population mean number of police per ten thousand residents.

Practice: *Try Exercise 10.27(c–e) on page 500.*

Example 10.10 on page 472 demonstrated how the width of a confidence interval varied for levels 90% to 99%. The level used can make a big difference for "borderline" values.

EXAMPLE TBP 10.4 PROPOSED VALUE PLAUSIBLE OR IMPLAUSIBLE DEPENDING ON LEVEL OF CONFIDENCE.

Background: A 90% confidence interval for population mean female weight has been found to be (121.82, 136.92) and a 99% confidence interval is (117.55, 141.19).

Questions: Is 120 a plausible value for population mean weight? Is 140 plausible?

Responses: If we work with the 90% confidence interval, then neither 120 nor 140 is contained in the interval, and we dismiss these as being implausible. If on the other hand we work with the 99% confidence interval, both 120 and 140 are contained in the interval, and either of these seems like a plausible value for population mean.

Practice: *Try Exercise 10.5(e,f) on page 477.*

The same sort of ambiguity that arises in Example **TBP** 10.4, because of different confidence levels resulting in different interval widths, also arises in the context of the other form of inference, hypothesis testing. Just as we saw in tests about population proportion, whether or not we reject the null hypothesis about population mean depends on what cutoff level we have decided to use for our *P*-value. If we want to translate confidence interval results to hypothesis test results, the level of confidence ties in with the cutoff level used.

Details about Hypothesis Tests for Means with *z*

These graphs, for instructors who like to explain *P*-values with pictures in addition to words, accompany Example 10.12 on page 476.

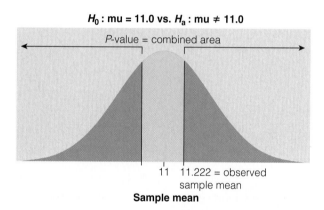

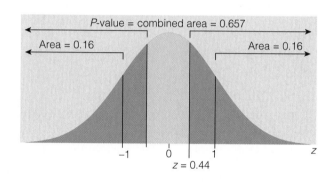

Details about Confidence Intervals for Means with *t*

The confidence intervals based on *z* or *t* in Example 10.14 on page 483 were quite different because the sample size (9) was so small. Example 10.5 illustrates that by the time sample size is increased to 19, the difference between a *z* or *t* interval is not so pronounced.

EXAMPLE TBP 10.5 COMPARING CONFIDENCE INTERVALS FOR POPULATION MEAN WITH T VERSUS Z FOR LARGER N

Background: We have a random sample of weights of 19 female college students:

110	110	112	120	120	120	125	125	130	130	132	133	134	135	135	135	145	148	159

Question: What is the difference between 95% confidence intervals for population mean weight using a *t* multiplier (with no assumptions about σ) versus a *z* multiplier (assuming population standard deviation equals 12.82)?

Response: First we look at the *t* confidence interval:

```
One-Sample T: Weight
Variable          N     Mean    StDev   SE Mean          95.0% CI
Weight           19   129.37    12.82      2.94   (  123.19, 135.55)
```

Next, we consider what the interval would have been if we had somehow known 12.82 to be population standard deviation:

```
One-Sample Z: Weight
The assumed sigma = 12.82
Variable          N     Mean   StDev   SE Mean         95.0% CI
Weight           19   129.37   12.82      2.94   ( 123.60, 135.13)
```

The difference between *t* and *z* intervals is very slight (widths 12.36 and 11.53, respectively).

Practice: *Try Exercise TBP 10.12 on page 929.*

Because the *t* distribution looks so much like the *z* distribution for larger samples, we can substitute *z* multipliers when constructing a confidence interval by hand based on sample mean and sample standard deviation from a large sample. When using software, *t* is required if σ is unknown.

EXAMPLE TBP 10.6 CONFIDENCE INTERVAL FOR A MEAN WHEN σ IS UNKNOWN BUT N IS LARGE

Background: We have data for number of problem teeth (decayed, filled, or missing) in a sample of 331 Venezuelan children. The mean is 8.0 and the standard deviation is 4.0.

Questions: If we want to construct by hand a 95% confidence interval for population mean of problem teeth, should we use a *z* or a *t* multiplier? If we want to construct the interval with software, should we use a *z* or *t* procedure?

Responses: By hand, we could use the *z* multiplier 2, because for such a large sample the *t* multiplier will be virtually identical. With software, we would request a *t* procedure because population standard deviation is unknown.

Practice: *Try Exercise 10.27(b–d) on page 500.*

Example 10.15 on page 485 showed that higher levels of confidence produced wider intervals. Conversely, lower levels of confidence produce narrower intervals.

EXAMPLE TBP 10.7 NARROWER INTERVAL AT LOWER LEVEL OF CONFIDENCE

Background: A sample of 20 masses of dinosaur specimens (in kilograms) has mean 1,569 and standard deviation 1,562. According to our table, the multiplier for a sample of size 20 (with *df* = 20 − 1 = 19) and 90% confidence is 1.73.

	Confidence Level			
	90%	95%	98%	99%
z (infinite *n*)	1.645	1.960 or 2	2.326	2.576
t: df = 19 (*n* = 20)	1.73	2.09	2.54	2.86
t: df = 11 (*n* = 12)	1.80	2.20	2.72	3.11
t: df = 3 (*n* = 4)	2.35	3.18	4.54	5.84

Question: What is a 90% confidence interval for mean mass of all such dinosaurs, and how does it compare to a 95% confidence interval?

Continued

Response: Our 90% confidence interval constructed by hand is

$$\bar{x} \pm \text{multiplier} \frac{s}{\sqrt{n}}$$

$$= 1{,}569 \pm 1.73\left(\frac{1{,}562}{\sqrt{20}}\right) = 1{,}569 \pm 604 = (965,\, 2{,}173)$$

We get the same interval using software:

Variable	N	Mean	StDev	SE Mean	90.0% CI
DinoMass	20	1569	1562	349	(965, 2173)

The interval is narrower than the 95% interval, which uses multiplier 2.10 instead of 1.73:

Variable	N	Mean	StDev	SE Mean	95.0% CI
DinoMass	20	1569	1562	349	(837, 2300)

We can pinpoint the unknown population mean more precisely if we sacrifice some confidence that our interval is correct.

Practice: *Try Exercise 10.60(b) on page 512.*

To supplement the formula on page 483 for a confidence interval based on the t distribution, it is instructive to consider how this interval compares to the one based on a z distribution.

■ For larger sample sizes n, s is close to σ and the t multiplier is close to the z multiplier (approximately 2 for 95% confidence). By hand, we can substitute z multipliers when n is large. With software, we always specify a t procedure if σ is unknown.

■ For smaller sample sizes, the t distribution has considerably more spread than the standard normal z distribution, and the multiplier is larger, although seldom more that 3.

■ Multipliers for t confidence intervals at other levels of confidence follow similar patterns to those for z intervals at other levels of confidence, in that t multipliers are less for lower confidence levels, and more for higher confidence levels. Thus, the usual trade-off occurs: we may obtain a narrower interval at a lower confidence level or a wider interval at a higher confidence level.

■ The most important difference between a z confidence interval (σ known) and a t confidence interval (σ unknown) is that the t interval is wider.

Details about Hypothesis Tests for Means with *t*

To stress the difference between tests about means using t or z. we can revisit Example 10.12 on page 476, for which we originally assumed a known value of population standard deviation. This time we make no such assumption.

EXAMPLE TBP 10.8 TEST (WITH SOFTWARE) ABOUT A MEAN WHEN THE POPULATION STANDARD DEVIATION IS UNKNOWN

Background: We have a random sample of 9 shoe sizes of college males:

11.5	12.0	11.0	15.0	11.5	10.0	9.0	10.0	11.0

Question: Is 11.0 a plausible value for mean shoe size of all male college students, or do the data provide evidence that population mean differs from 11.0?

Response: Now we simply enter the data values and request a *t* test about a mean, specifying the proposed population mean 11.0.

```
One-Sample T: Shoe
Test of mu = 11 vs mu not = 11
Variable           N       Mean    StDev    SE Mean
Shoe               9     11.222    1.698      0.566
Variable               95.0% CI            T        P
Shoe            (  9.917,   12.527)     0.39    0.705
```

0. The null and alternative hypotheses are confirmed in the output:
   $H_0: \mu = 11.0$ versus $H_a: \mu \neq 11.0$,

1. All three conditions are fulfilled, as discussed in the context of a *z* test: sample apparently representative, sample mean normally distributed, and sample not too large relative to population size.

2. The relevant statistic is sample mean shoe size 11.222, and standardized test statistic is shown to be *t* = 0.39. The fact that *t* is quite close to zero suggests that sample mean $\bar{x} = 11.222$ is relatively close to hypothesized population mean $\mu_0 = 11.0$.

3. The *P*-value is calculated as a two-tailed probability on the *t* curve for 8 degrees of freedom, the probability of sample mean as different (in either direction) from 11.0 as 11.222 is. This is the same thing as *t* being greater than 0.39 in absolute value, or twice the probability of *t* being greater than +0.39. The probability is shown in the output to be quite large, 0.705.

4. The *P*-value is not small at all, so we have no evidence whatsoever to reject the null hypothesis in favor of the alternative. Because we do not reject the null hypothesis, we should acknowledge 11 as a plausible value for population mean shoe size, based on the data provided.

Practice: *Try Exercise 10.73 on page 515.*

Example 10.17 on page 487 demonstrated that we should not carry out a *t* test if the sample is small and the data appear non-normal. In the following supplemental example, because the variable of interest—SAT score—is known to be normal, we can assume the standardized statistic to follow a *t* distribution, even though the sample is very small.

EXAMPLE TBP 10.9 VERY SMALL SAMPLES PERMISSIBLE FOR T TEST ON NORMAL DATA

Background: Reports of SAT scores often state that the national average in Math is about 500. We want to use a sample of 4 scores from a random sample of students taking introductory statistics at a large university to see if they represent a population whose scores have a mean that is higher than 500. The sample scores were 580, 760, 640, and 570.

Continued

Questions: Do the data provide evidence that population mean is greater than 500? Do hand calculations, along with this sketch of the *t* curve for 3 degrees of freedom, confirm our conclusion?

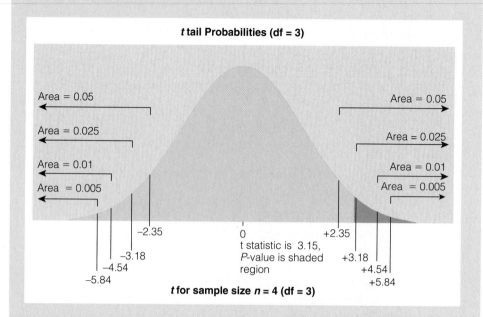

Responses: Carrying out the test with software, we enter the 4 SAT scores, state the test mean to be 500, and opt for a greater-than alternative. According to the output, the *t* statistic is 3.15.

```
One-Sample T: MathSAT
Test of mu = 500 vs mu > 500
Variable            N         Mean       StDev       SE Mean
MathSAT             4         637.5       87.3        43.7
Variable       95.0% Lower Bound            T            P
MathSAT                      534.7        3.15         0.026
```

The *P*-value is shown to be 0.026, which is small enough to cast doubt on the claim that the mean Math SAT score of the population of students from which our sample originated is only 500. Because these students went on to college after taking the SAT in high school, and because they are in a rather math-oriented course, their overall average Math SAT apparently exceeds the national mean of 500.

To carry out the test by hand, we would need to find the mean and standard deviation of those 4 values, then standardize to $t = 3.15$. In general, if the sample size is fairly large, then a large *t* is roughly what a large *z* would be, namely greater than about 2. If the sample size is small, then there is usually reason to call *t* large if its size exceeds 3. In this case, because the sample is very small and *t* is just over 3, we can't just "eyeball" the *t* statistic to draw our conclusion. Referring to the sketch provided, we see that $t = 3.15$ is just under 3.18, which corresponds to a right-tail area of 0.025, so the *P*-value must be just over 0.025. This is perfectly consistent with the value 0.026 provided by software, and the same conclusion would be reached.

Practice: *Try Exercise 10.73 on page 515.*

t Tables

Teachers may opt to supplement the material in Section 10.2 by explaining the use of *t* tables to perform inference about an unknown population mean when the sample size is small and, as is usually the case, the population standard deviation σ is unknown.

The use of *t* tables can be bypassed in this book's treatment of inference about a mean when population standard deviation is unknown, because it is assumed that if *t* procedures were actually being carried out in practice, software would be used. However, the use of tables has become a tradition in the teaching of statistics, so we present here a brief guide to finding multipliers for *t* confidence intervals or ranges for *P*-values in *t* tests. The table itself can be found at the end of the book.

Because there is only one standard normal (*z*) distribution, on a single page we were able to present probabilities for over 600 *z* values, ranging from -3.09 to $+3.09$ in increments of 0.01. Because there are so many *t* distributions—one for each possible degrees of freedom—space does not permit such detailed tables of probabilities. For practical purposes, knowing the *t* values for 90%, 95%, 98%, and 99% confidence should suffice for setting up confidence intervals, and these same values are enough to determine if the *P*-value in a one-sided test is greater than 0.05, between 0.05 and 0.025, between 0.025 and 0.01, between 0.01 and 0.005, or less than 0.005. For a two-sided test the endpoints of those intervals are doubled. Thus, only eight *t* values are shown in the table for each of the featured degrees of freedom. In fact, because the *t* distribution is symmetric about zero, four of those eight are redundant.

For comparison, the table begins with the *z* values corresponding to the above-mentioned confidence levels and tail probabilities: ± 1.645, ± 1.96, ± 2.326, and ± 2.576. For large degrees of freedom (resulting from large sample sizes) *s* should be quite close to σ and the *t* distribution is virtually identical to the *z* distribution. For smaller degrees of freedom, *s* provides less information about the actual standard deviation, and so the *t* distribution has more spread than *z*. At the bottom of the page, the *t* distribution for just 1 degree of freedom is shown; clearly it is more spread out than the *z* curve at the top, and its tails are much "heavier."

EXAMPLE TBP 10.10 USING T TABLE FOR CONFIDENCE INTERVAL

Background: A sample of 11 college presidents' salaries during the year 2002–2003, in thousands of dollars, had mean 288.4 and standard deviation deviation 129.4.

Questions: According to the *t* table provided at the end of the book, what is the multiplier for a 99% confidence interval for mean salary of all college presidents? What is the interval?

Responses: We refer to the *t* table for $11 - 1 = 10$ degrees of freedom and 99% confidence: The multiplier is 3.169 and our interval is

$$288.4 \pm 3.169\left(\frac{129.4}{\sqrt{11}}\right) = (164.8, 412.0)$$

The interval is quite wide because the level of confidence is high, the standard deviation is large, and the sample size is small.

Practice: *Try Exercise TBP 10.32 on page 931.*

The same table can be used to carry out a t hypothesis test; we simply refer to tail probabilities, instead of inside probabilities, in order to get a range for our P-value.

EXAMPLE TBP 10.11 USING T TABLE FOR HYPOTHESIS TEST

Background: A sample of 4 Math SAT scores has mean 637.5, standard deviation 87.3, and so the standardized sample mean is $t = \frac{637.5 - 500}{87.3/\sqrt{4}} = 3.15$. If we want to test, as before, against the one-sided alternative $H_a: \mu > 500$, the P-value is the probability of $t \geq 3.15$ when t has $4 - 1 = 3$ degrees of freedom.

Questions: How does our t statistic compare to relevant values in the t table? What is a range for the P-value? What do we conclude?

Responses: We refer to the t table for $4 - 1 = 3$ degrees of freedom. Since 3.15 is between the "critical values" 2.353 and 3.182 for 3 df, the P-value is between 0.05 and 0.025. When we carried out this example with software, the P-value was shown to be 0.026: It is just over 0.025, because 3.15 is just under 3.182. As before, we have some evidence to conclude that the population mean exceeds 500.

Practice: *Try Exercise 10.33 on page 931.*

If the alternative in the preceding example had been two-sided, then the P-value would have been the probability of $|t| \geq 3.15$. This two-tailed probability would lie between $2(0.05) = 0.10$ and $2(0.025) = 0.05$.

10.2 Activities

Activity: Confidence Intervals and Tests about Mean Hours Slept

Using the Computer

This activity helps students understand the meaning of confidence levels and of significance levels in setting up intervals for, and tests about, unknown population mean.

Each student accesses data from the book's existing data file about several hundred students surveyed previously. Specifically, they will work with the column "Sleep" of hours slept the night before students were surveyed, whose mean is 7.1 (hours). Each student randomly samples 40 values from that column, puts them in a column Sleep Sample and constructs a 95% confidence interval for "unknown" population mean hours slept based on the sampled values. This is done several times by each student so that altogether the class has constructed 100 95% confidence intervals. Then the instructor checks to see what count, then percentage, of 95% confidence intervals contain the population mean 7.1. If there is time, students also construct several 90% and 99% confidence intervals to see what percentage contain the mean (7.1) in each case.

Next, each student uses the columns of sampled sleep times to carry out several tests of $H_0: \mu = 7.1$ against the two-sided alternative $H_a: \mu \neq 7.1$. Altogether, the class as a group should carry out 100 tests. Then the instructor checks to see what count, then percentage, of the students' tests have a P-value less than 0.05. If there is time, the instructor can also check to see the count and percentage of tests with a P-value less than 0.10 and less than 0.01.

In the context of these activities, students should discuss the meaning of a 95% (or other) confidence interval and the meaning of rejecting a null hypothesis with a P-value less than 0.05 (or other level).

Activity: Confidence Intervals and Tests about Mean Dice Roll

In the Classroom

Materials needed: many ordinary (six-sided) dice: either one per student or eight for each row of students; students' own calculators for finding sample means.

Each student rolls a die 8 times (or rolls 8 dice and passes them on to the next student). Each averages the 8 numbers with the aid of a calculator, records this sample mean $\bar{x}$, and uses it to construct 68%, 95%, and 99.7% confidence intervals for "unknown" population mean μ. This should be done using known standard deviation $\sigma = 1.7$ (as well as sample size $n = 8$).

Meanwhile, the instructor reviews the following: An approximate

- 68% confidence interval for μ is $\bar{x} \pm 1(\frac{\sigma}{\sqrt{n}})$
- 95% confidence interval for μ is $\bar{x} \pm 2(\frac{\sigma}{\sqrt{n}})$
- 99.7% confidence interval for μ is $\bar{x} \pm 3(\frac{\sigma}{\sqrt{n}})$

For example, suppose 8 dice are rolled. Because σ for the population of rolls 1,2,3,4,5,6 is 1.7, an approximate

- 68% confidence interval for μ is $\bar{x} \pm 1(\frac{1.7}{\sqrt{8}}) = \bar{x} \pm 0.6$
- 95% confidence interval for μ is $\bar{x} \pm 2(\frac{1.7}{\sqrt{8}}) = \bar{x} \pm 1.2$
- 99.7% confidence interval for μ is $\bar{x} \pm 3(\frac{1.7}{\sqrt{8}}) = \bar{x} \pm 1.8$

Suppose a student rolls 8 dice and gets a sum of 23, so $\bar{x} = \frac{23}{8} = 2.875$. Then a

- 68% confidence interval for μ is $2.875 \pm 0.6 = (2.275, 3.475)$
- 95% confidence interval for μ is $2.875 \pm 1.2 = (1.675, 4.075)$
- 99.7% confidence interval for μ is $2.875 \pm 1.8 = (1.075, 4.675)$

The 68% confidence interval either captures the population mean μ or it does not. We happen to know that μ in this case is 3.5, so the interval (2.275, 3.475) did *not* capture it. Somebody else's 68% confidence interval might well contain 3.5. In the long run, 68% of such intervals should succeed in capturing μ. If 20 people each roll 8 dice and set up a 68% confidence interval for μ based on each sample mean $\bar{x}$, then about 14 of them should succeed in capturing μ—that is, roughly 14 of those intervals will contain 3.5. Similarly, about 95%—roughly 19—of their 95% confidence intervals should contain 3.5, and it's practically guaranteed that all of their 99.7% confidence intervals will contain 3.5.

Now the instructor checks to see what count, then percentage, of 68%, 95%, and 99.7% confidence intervals contain the true population mean, which we happen to know is 3.5.

Next, each student uses his or her sample mean roll of 8 dice to carry out a test of $H_0: \mu = 3.5$ against the two-sided alternative $H_a: \mu \neq 3.5$ based on the test statistic $z = \frac{\bar{x} - 3.5}{1.7/\sqrt{8}} = 0.6(\bar{x} - 3.5)$. Then the instructor checks to see what count, then percentage, of the students' tests have a z statistic greater than 1.96 in absolute value, and therefore a *P*-value less than 0.05. If there is time, the instructor can also check to see the count and percentage of tests with $|z| > 1.645$ (*P*-value less than 0.10) and with $|z| > 2.576$ (*P*-value less than 0.01).

In the context of these activities, students should discuss the meaning of a 95% (or other) confidence interval and the meaning of rejecting a null hypothesis with a *P*-value less than 0.05 (or other level).

Activity: Power to Detect a False Null Hypothesis about Math SAT Scores

Using the computer

Consider our several hundred surveyed students to be a population whose Math SAT scores have $\mu = 610.44$, $\sigma = 72.14$.

1. Sample 100 with replacement and test $H_0: \mu = 590$ versus $H_a: \mu > 590$ at the $a = 0.05$ level. Notice that the alternative is in fact correct. What is the probability of correctly rejecting H_0?

   In general, we reject H_0 in favor of $H_a: \mu > \mu_0$ at the 0.05 level when our standardized statistic $z = \frac{\bar{x} - \mu_0}{\sigma/\sqrt{n}}$ is greater than 1.645. In this case, we reject when

   $$\frac{\bar{x} - 590}{72.14/\sqrt{100}} > 1.645 \rightarrow \bar{x} > 590 + \frac{1.645(72.14)}{\sqrt{100}} = 601.87$$

   What is the probability of getting a sample mean greater than 601.87, given $\mu = 610.44$ and $\sigma = 72.14$? Find

   $$P(\bar{X} > 601.87 \text{ given } \mu = 610.44) = P\left(Z > \frac{601.87 - 610.44}{72.14/\sqrt{100}}\right) =$$
   $$P(Z > -1.19) = 0.883$$

   There is an 88% chance, in this case, that our hypothesis test will correctly favor the claim that $\mu > 590$: This is the power of the test.

   Have each student access the survey data and randomly sample 100 *with* replacement from all the Math SAT scores, store them in column "sample1", and carry out a *z* test as outlined above. Determine what percentage get a *P*-value small enough to reject—that is, less than 0.05.

2. What if $n = 10$ instead of $n = 100$? Should we have more or less power with a smaller sample size? Discuss, calculate, carry out the activity based on samples of size 10, stored in column "sample2."

3. What if we test $H_0: \mu = 605$ versus $H_a: \mu > 605$ instead of $H_0: \mu = 590$ versus $H_a: \mu > 590$? Should we have more or less power now? Discuss, calculate, carry out the activity using "sample1" but specifying the new alternative.

4. What if we increase α from 0.05 to 0.10? Should we have more or less power now? In this case, the critical *z* changes from 1.645 to 1.28. Discuss, calculate, review the *P*-values from the first test to see how many are less than 0.10 instead of less than 0.05.

To summarize, discuss whether power increases with smaller or larger sample sizes. Does it increase with alternatives that are farther from or closer to the true μ? Does it increase with a smaller or a larger cutoff level α?

10.3 Guide to Exercise Topics

Previewing inference for means: 10.34, 10.35, 10.36, 10.37*, 10.38, 10.39, 10.40

Inference for means with z: 10.1*, 10.3*, 10.4*(a–c), 10.5(a–c), 10.21(a); Confidence Intervals: 10.2, 10.4*(d,e), 10.5(c–f), 10.6*, 10.7, 10.9*(a–f), 10.10, 10.27*(a–e), 10.28(a–d), 10.43, 10.45; Confidence Intervals Using Software: 10.8*(c), 10.78(f); Hypothesis Tests: 10.9*(g), 10.11*, 10.12, 10.13*, 10.27*(f–i), 10.28(e–h), 10.29, 10.31, 10.46, 10.47, 10.48, 10.49, 10.51, 10.52, 10.53; Hypothesis Tests Using Software: 10.8*(c–h), 10.78(c)

Inference for means with t: 10.14*, 10.15, 10.20, 10.21(b), 10.55; Confidence Intervals: 10.16*, 10.17, 10.33(e), 10.50, 10.54(c), 10.57, 10.58, 10.59, 10.60*(b), 10.61(b); Confidence Intervals Using Software: 10.73*(a–b), 10.74(a–d), 10.75, 10.76, 10.79, 10.82*(a–b), 10.83(a–b), 10.84(a–b), 10.85(a–c); Hypothesis Tests: 10.18, 10.19, 10.60*(c–e), 10.61(c,d), 10.62, 10.63, 10.73*(c), 10.74(e), 10.82*(c), 10.83(c), 10.84(c); Hypothesis Tests Using Software: 10.8*(d–j), 10.77, 10.78(a,b), 10.80, 10.81

A closer look at inference for means: 10.22*, 10.23*, 10.24, 10.25, 10.26*, 10.27*(i), 10.28(h), 10.30*, 10.32, 10.33, 10.46, 10.54(e), 10.64, 10.65, 10.66, 10.67, 10.68, 10.69, 10.70, 10.71*, 10.72

10.4 Supplemental Exercises

10.1 "Family Lead Poisoning Associated with Occupational Exposure," published in *Clinical Pediatrics* in November/December 2004, states that take-home lead exposure is suspected if there is a household member and working adult in the home with blood lead levels greater than or equal to 10 mg/dL, and an identified workplace source of lead. Tell whether each of the following involves one categorical variable, one quantitative, one of each, two categorical, or two quantitative.

a. Test if blood lead levels are higher, the longer workers have been exposed to lead.

b. Test if blood lead levels of employees at a particular plant are higher on average than what is known to be normal for an American.

c. Test if having elevated blood lead levels is related to type of workplace (radiator repair, metal casting, ceramics manufacture, furniture refinishing, or battery repair).

d. Test if the level of lead in the blood differs for workers in various types of workplace.

e. Test if the percentage of families with a household member and working adult

having blood lead levels greater than or equal to 10 mg/dL is higher for employees at a particular plant than what it is known to be for workers in general.

10.2 Suppose a hypothesis test is carried out using a sample of employees at a particular workplace to see if their blood lead levels are significantly higher than what is normal.

a. For the sake of employees' health, which type of error would be more harmful—Type I or Type II? Explain.

b. Would the type of error you chose in part (a) be more likely to occur with a smaller sample or with a larger sample?

10.3 Suppose a hypothesis test is carried out using a sample of employees at a particular workplace to see if their blood lead levels are significantly higher than what is normal. Tell whether each of the following focuses on data production, displaying and summarizing, probability, or statistical inference:

a. Researchers decide to record a precise blood lead level for each employee in the sample, treating it as a quantitative variable.

b. Researchers find the sample mean blood lead level.

c. Researchers find the probability of a sample mean as high as the one observed, assuming the employees were a random sample taken from the entire U.S. population whose mean blood lead level is presumed to be known.

d. Researchers conclude that the population of employees at that workplace have a higher mean blood lead level than that of the U.S. population.

10.4 Researchers suspected that students who study more tend to have lower grades, because needing to study a lot reflects the fact that these are students for whom it is a struggle to learn what is required. For each of the following possible designs, tell whether the explanatory variable is quantitative or categorical, and whether the response is quantitative or categorical. Assume that the goal is to predict grade performance, based on how much a student studies.

a. Classify study time as 0, 0 to 2, 2 to 4, 4 to 6, 6 to 9, or more than 9 hours per week; record course performance as top 20%, bottom 20%, or middle 60%.

b. Record study time in hours per week; record course performance as top 20%, bottom 20%, or middle 60%.

c. Classify study time as 0, 0 to 2, 2 to 4, 4 to 6, 6 to 9, or more than 9 hours per week; record course performance as percentage, from 0 to 100.

d. Record study time in hours per week; record course performance as percentage, from 0 to 100.

10.5 A random sample of students produced the following 95% confidence interval for population mean Math SAT score: (559, 607).

a. Report the width of the interval, the margin of error, and the standard error.

b. Tell which one of these is the correct interpretation of the interval (559, 607):
   1. The probability is 0.95 that the sample mean falls in this interval.
   2. The probability is 0.95 that the population mean falls in this interval.
   3. We are 95% confident that the sample mean falls in this interval.
   4. We are 95% confident that the population mean falls in this interval.

   5. 95% of all Math SAT scores fall in this interval.
   6. 95% of sampled Math SAT scores fell in this interval.

c. Note that 610 is *not* contained in the interval. If we tested against $H_a : \mu \neq 610$ at the 5% level, would we reject $H_0 : \mu = 610$?

d. A 99% confidence interval for population mean is (551, 615). If we tested against $H_a : \mu \neq 610$ at the 1% level, would we reject $H_0 : \mu = 610$?

10.6 A report, "What Determines Environmental Performance at Paper Mills?," published online by the *Berkeley Electronic Press* in 2003, examined data on 68 paper mills during the 1980s.

a. Sulfur dioxide emissions, in tons per year (to the nearest 100 tons) were found to have mean 3,200 and standard deviation 3,700. Report a 95% confidence interval for mean yearly emissions for all such paper mills during the time period from which the data were obtained.

b. What is the correct interpretation of the interval you constructed in part (a)?
   1. 95% of all emission levels fall in this interval.
   2. 95% of sampled emission levels fell in this interval.
   3. The probability is 0.95 that the population mean falls in this interval.
   4. The probability is 0.95 that the sample mean falls in this interval.
   5. We are 95% confident that the population mean falls in this interval.
   6. We are 95% confident that the sample mean falls in this interval.

c. Pollution abatement capital (value of the plant's pollution reduction equipment, in thousands of dollars) was found to have mean $7,900 and standard deviation $7,800. Report a 95% confidence interval for mean pollution abatement capital for all such paper mills during the time period from which the data were obtained.

d. The authors report that "emissions are significantly lower in plants with a larger air pollution abatement capital stock: a 10% increase in abatement capital stock appears to reduce emissions by 6.9%."[1] Was this a paired, two-sample, or regression study?

10.7   Heights (in inches) of college-aged males are reported to have mean 70, standard deviation 3. A test is carried out, based on heights of a large sample of male students in introductory statistics classes, with results as shown.

```
One-Sample Z: HT_male
Test of mu = 70 vs mu > 70
The assumed sigma = 3
Variable              N        Mean     StDev    SE Mean
HT_male             163      70.626     2.940      0.235
Variable        95.0% Lower Bound        Z         P
HT_male                     70.239     2.66     0.004
```

   a. Explain how the results could be used to argue that those students represented a biased sample in terms of their actual heights.

   b. Explain how the results could be used to argue that there was bias in the students' reporting of their heights.

10.8   Based on what you can guess about the shape of certain distributions, tell whether or not we can assume sample mean to be approximately normal in each of the following situations where we would like to perform inference using z or t. Give a brief explanation for each.

   a. Sample mean height for a sample of 6 male college students.

   b. Sample mean earnings for a sample of 12 female college students.

   c. Sample mean commute time for a sample of 90 college students.

   d. Sample mean wing length for a sample of 3 flies.

10.9   Based on what you can guess about the shape of certain distributions, tell whether or not we can assume sample mean to be approximately normal in each of the following situations where we would like to perform inference using z or t. Give a brief explanation for each.

   a. Sample mean time spent watching television per day, for a sample of 50 toddlers.

   b. Sample mean tongue lengths, for a sample of 5 college students.

   c. Sample mean cups of coffee consumed per day, for a sample of 75 college students.

   d. Sample mean distance of a college campus from parents' homes, for a sample of 14 students.

USING TABLES: INFERENCE FOR MEANS [SEE END OF BOOK]

10.10   If we use a hypothesis test to solve Exercise 10.9(b), our standardized statistic is $\frac{9.04 - 10}{1.28/\sqrt{82}} = -6.79$ and the z distribution can be used because the sample size is large. What does the z table at the end of the book suggest about the probability that z takes a value at least as extreme as -6.79?

10.11   Use the z table to find a more precise answer to Exercise 11.54(c)—that is, the probability that a normal variable takes a value more than 1.2 standard deviations above its mean.

10.12   Exercise 10.27(c) asks for an approximate 95% confidence interval, based on a sample of size 192. What would the multiplier be if the t table with 100 degrees of freedom were used, instead of using the z multiplier 1.96, which we sometimes round to 2?

10.13   Exercise 10.28(c) asks for an approximate 95% confidence interval, based on a sample of size 2,737. What would the multiplier be if the t table with 1,000 degrees of freedom were used, instead of using the z multiplier 1.96, which we sometimes round to 2?

10.14   Exercise 10.50(d) states that the t multiplier for a sample of size 22 is roughly 2. Use the t table to get a more precise value for this multiplier. Degrees of freedom are $22 - 1 = 21$, so refer to the closest smaller df in the table—namely, 20.

10.15 Exercise 10.16(a) states that the t multiplier for 95% confidence and 8 degrees of freedom is 2.31. Use the t table to report this multiplier to three decimal places instead of two.

10.16 Exercise 10.17(a) states that the t multiplier for 99% confidence and 8 degrees of freedom is 3.36. Use the t table to report this multiplier to three decimal places instead of two.

10.17 Exercise 10.33(d) states that the t multiplier for 22 degrees of freedom is roughly 2. According to the t table, the multiplier for 20 degrees of freedom (and 95% confidence) is 2.086. Would the multiplier for 22 degrees of freedom be slightly more or slightly less than 2.086?

10.18 Exercise 10.35 states that the standardized statistic for a sample of size 23 follows an approximate z distribution. The value of this statistic was found to be +5.4, which is statistically significant for z. For what degrees of freedom would the sample size be so small that a test statistic of +5.4 no longer produces a right-tail probability less than 0.05? (Refer to the t table.)

10.19 In Exercise 10.47(b), a z test statistic can be found to equal +1.33. Use the z table to find the probability of z taking a value at least as extreme (in either direction) as +1.33.

10.20 In Exercise 10.11, a population of students taking a test of cognitive ability had scores with mean 22.6, standard deviation 5; a sample of 6 students who studied zero hours per week had mean 25.3, standard deviation 7.7.

    a. If we standardize using population standard deviation, the test statistic is $z = \frac{25.3 - 22.6}{5/\sqrt{6}} = +1.32$. Use the z table to find the probability of a z-score this high.

    b. If population standard deviation were unknown, and we standardized with sample standard deviation, the test statistic would be $t = \frac{25.3 - 22.6}{7.7/\sqrt{6}} = +0.86$. Use the t table with appropriate degrees of freedom to give a range for the probability that a t score is this high.

10.21 In Exercise 10.12, a population of students taking a test of cognitive ability had scores with mean 22.6, standard deviation 5; a sample of 7 students who studied 9 or more hours per week had mean 17.6, standard deviation 2.8.

    a. If we standardize using population standard deviation, the test statistic is $z = \frac{17.6 - 22.6}{5/\sqrt{7}} = -2.65$. Use the z table to find the probability of a z-score this low.

    b. If population standard deviation were unknown, and we standardized with sample standard deviation, the test statistic would be $t = \frac{17.6 - 22.6}{2.8/\sqrt{7}} = -4.72$. Use the t table with appropriate degrees of freedom to give a range for the probability that a t score is this low.

10.22 Exercise 10.91(a) mentioned recording course performance as top 20%, bottom 20%, or middle 60%. Use the z table to report how many standard deviations away from the mean a score would have to be to cut off the top or bottom 20%.

10.23 Exercise 10.57 mentions that the t multiplier for 95% confidence and 4 degrees of freedom is 2.78. Use the t table to report this multiplier to an additional decimal place.

10.24 In Exercise 10.13, output shows the one-sided P-value for $z = 2.47$ to be 0.007. Use the z table to report this probability to an additional decimal place.

10.25 In Exercise 10.51, output shows the one-sided P-value for $z = 1.69$ to be 0.045. Use the z table to report this probability to an additional decimal place.

10.26 In Exercise 10.52, output shows one-sided P-values, first when standardizing with σ, then when standardizing with s from a sample of size 14.

    a. The one-sided P-value for $z = -0.78$ is shown to be 0.218. Use the z table to report this probability to an additional decimal place.

    b. The one-sided P-value for $t = -1.30$ is shown to be 0.108. Refer to the t table with 10 degrees of freedom to report a range for this probability.

10.27 Based on the t statistic (3.00) found in Exercise 10.60(b) for a sample of 12 deaf adults, use the t table with 10 degrees of freedom to give a range for the (one-sided) P-value.

10.28 Based on the *t* statistic (1.56) found in Exercise 10.61(b) for a sample of 11 deaf adults, use the *t* table with 10 degrees of freedom to give a range for the (one-sided) *P*-value.

10.29 Exercise 10.58(a) states 2.74 is the *t* multiplier for 32 degrees of freedom and 99% confidence.

   a. Use the *t* table to find the multiplier for 30 degrees of freedom and 99% confidence.

   b. In general, is the *t* multiplier smaller or larger for lower degrees of freedom?

   c. Use the *t* table to find the multiplier for 30 degrees of freedom and 90% confidence.

   d. In general, is the *t* multiplier smaller or larger for lower levels of confidence?

10.30 Exercise 10.59 displays a 95% *t* confidence interval for a sample of size 12. According to the *t* table, what is the approximate multiplier in this situation?

10.31 Based on the *t* statistic (0.94) found in Exercise 10.18(b) for a sample of 10 beluga whales, use the *t* table with 9 degrees of freedom to give a range for the (one-sided) *P*-value.

10.32 Exercise 10.73(b) asks you to use software to produce a 95% confidence interval for population mean age of beluga fathers at first conception, based on a sample of 7 whales. Use the *t* table to report the multiplier used.

10.33 In Exercise 10.65(a), the *t* statistic for 39 degrees of freedom was 2.77.

   a. Use the *t* table with 40 degrees of freedom to report a range for the probability of *t* being 2.77 or higher.

   b. The *P*-value was reported to be 0.009. Was this obtained from testing against a one-sided or a two-sided alternative?

10.5 Solutions to Supplemental Exercises

10.1 a. two quantitative b. one quantitative c. two categorical d. one categorical and one quantitative e. one categorical

10.2 a. Type II, because in this case it would be concluded that lead exposure is not a problem, when in fact it is and should be dealt with. b. smaller sample

10.3 a. data production b. displaying and summarizing c. probability d. statistical inference

10.4 a. both categorical b. explanatory quantitative, response categorical c. explanatory categorical, response quantitative d. both quantitative

10.5 a. $607 - 559 = 48$ is the width of the interval; the margin of error is half that, 24, and the standard error is half that, or 12. b. (4) We are 95% confident that population mean falls in this interval. c. yes d. No, because 610 is contained in the interval.

10.6 a. $3,200 \pm 2(3,700/\sqrt{68}) = 3,200 \pm 897 = (2,303, 4,097)$ tons b. (5) We are 95% confident that population mean falls in this interval. c. $7,900 \pm 2(7,800/\sqrt{68}) = 7,900 \pm 1,892 = (6,008, 9,792)$ thousand dollars d. regression

10.7 a. The null hypothesis is rejected against the alternative that population mean height is greater than 70 inches, suggesting that these students tend to be taller than what is true for the general population of college-aged males. b. The null hypothesis is rejected against the alternative that population mean height is greater than 70 inches, suggesting that these students may have over-reported their height values.

10.8 a. Yes, because even though the sample size is small, the population would be normal. b. No, because the population would be right-skewed and the sample size is small. c. Yes, because even though the population would be right-skewed, the sample size is large. d. Yes, because even though the sample size is small, the population would be normal.

10.9 a. Yes, because even though the population would be right-skewed, the sample size is large. b. Yes, because even though the sample size is small, the population would be normal. c. Yes, because the sample size is large, so the shape doesn't matter. d. No, because the population would be right-skewed and the sample size is small.

10.10 Because -6.79 is larger than 3 in absolute value, the probability of being at least this extreme (in either direction) is less than $2(0.0013) = 0.0026$.

10.11 0.1151

10.12 1.984

10.13 1.962

10.14 2.086

10.15 2.306

10.16 3.355

10.17 slightly less

10.18 For 1 degree of freedom, test statistic must be more than 5.4 (at least 6.314) to produce a right-tail probability less than 0.05.

10.19 2(0.0918) = 0.1836

10.20 a. 0.0934   **b.** greater than 0.05

10.21 a. 0.0040   **b.** less than 0.005

10.22 0.84

10.23 2.776

10.24 0.0068

10.25 0.0455

10.26 a. 0.2177   **b.** greater than 0.05

10.27 between 0.01 and 0.005

10.28 greater than 0.05

10.29 a. 2.75   **b.** larger   **c.** 1.697   **d.** smaller

10.30 2.228

10.31 greater than 0.05

10.32 2.447

10.33 a. less than 0.005   **b.** two-sided

TBP Chapter 11

Inference for Relationships between Categorical and Quantitative Variables

---

11.1 Details and Examples

Before beginning Section 11.1 on page 522, students may profit from a review of notation.

EXAMPLE TBP 11.1 NOTATION IN PAIRED OR TWO-SAMPLE OR SEVERAL-SAMPLE DESIGN

Background: We have data on the ages of students' mothers and fathers, on the ages of the students themselves, and on the students' year at school.

Question: How do we denote means and standard deviations of the following, both for the sample and for the population?

1. differences in ages of mothers and fathers

2. ages of male students and ages of female students

3. ages of first-year, second-year, third-year, and fourth-year students

Response:

1. The sample of differences has mean denoted $\bar{x}_d$ and standard deviation s_d. The population of differences has mean μ_d and standard deviation σ_d.

2. Ages of sampled male students have mean $\bar{x}_1$ and standard deviation s_1. Population mean and standard deviation can be written μ_1 and σ_1. For females, we can denote mean and standard deviation and s_2 for the sample, μ_2 and σ_2 for the population.

3. The sample means and standard deviations for ages of students in the 4 years can be written $\bar{x}_1$ through $\bar{x}_4$ and s_1 through s_4. For the populations we write μ_1 through μ_4 and σ_1 through σ_4.

Practice: *Try Exercise 11.4(d) on page 526.*

Inference for a Paired Design

Distinguishing between Paired and Two-Sample Designs

Because both involve a categorical explanatory variable that takes two possible values and a quantitative response, students often have difficulty distinguishing between paired and two-sample designs. It helps to think about many examples, and to keep in mind that in a paired study, two measurements of the quantitative variable are recorded for each "individual," where the individual may actually be a paired unit such as a married couple or twins. Also, a before-and-after study almost always uses a paired design. The following example can be discussed toward the beginning of Chapter 11, to remind students of the difference between the paired and two-sample designs.

EXAMPLE TBP 11.2 IDENTIFYING PAIRED DESIGN

Background: We have data on the ages of students' mothers and fathers and want to determine if there is a relationship between the variables "age of a parent" and "sex of a parent" (that is, if fathers or mothers tend to be older).

Question: Is this a paired or two-sample design?

Response: If we want to determine whether the sex of a parent gives us a clue about relative age, then we look at *pairs* of ages for students' fathers and mothers, not two independent samples. For each pair, we would look at the difference, say, DadAge minus MomAge. If the mean of the sampled differences is close to zero, then this would suggest that the null hypothesis is true, and sex of parent does not play a role in his or her age. If the mean of sampled differences is far from zero and positive, then this would suggest that overall fathers tend to be older. If it is far from zero and negative, we would have evidence that overall mothers tend to be older. The picture below illustrates that we are looking at a sample of age differences taken from a population of age differences. The sample mean age difference can help us conclude whether the population mean age difference could be zero, or whether there is evidence that it is greater or less than zero.

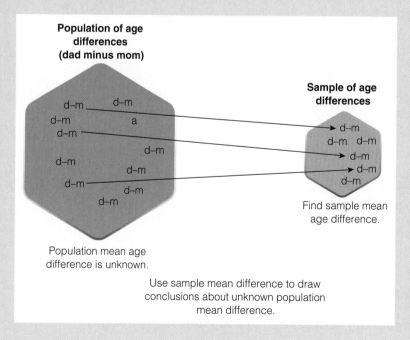

Practice: *Try Exercise 11.6(a) on page 526.*

Although the solution process for such problems is quite simple, understanding the roles of the variables involved requires some careful thinking. Even though the raw data values are usually provided in the form of two columns of numbers, these columns do *not* represent the two variables of interest. For the preceding example, the two variables of interest are not MomAge and DadAge, but ParentAge and ParentSex, as stated at the outset.

Notice that a different issue would be raised if we'd asked if there is a *relationship* between "age of father" and "age of mother," in which case those two quantitative variables would be handled with a regression procedure. Such an approach will be taken in a later chapter.

These illustrations accompany the first two paragraphs of Section 11.2 on page 528 to remind students of the important difference between a two-sample and a paired design.

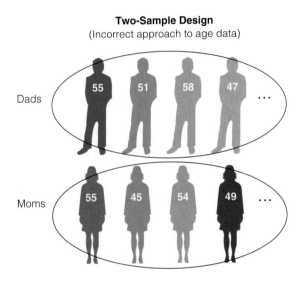

Two-Sample Design
(Incorrect approach to age data)

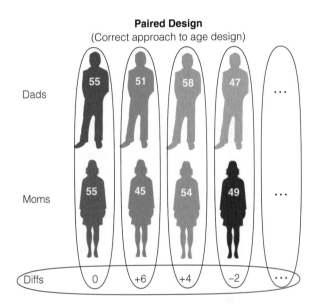

Paired Design
(Correct approach to age design)

EXAMPLE TBP 11.3 HOW USING THE WRONG PROCEDURE CAN AFFECT OUR CONCLUSIONS

Background: In Example TBP 11.4 on page 936, we will use a paired t procedure to test if cars' mileages are higher on the highway than in the city. Due to a P-value of 0.002, we will reject H_0, concluding that they *are* higher on the highway, in general.

Question: If the data were (incorrectly) handled with a two-sample procedure, as shown in the output below, would we reach the same conclusions?

```
Two-sample T for City vs Highway
          N     Mean      StDev     SE Mean
City      5     26.40     5.73       2.6
Highway   5     31.80     5.76       2.6
Difference = mu City - mu Highway
Estimate for difference:  -5.40
95% upper bound for difference: 1.48
T-Test of difference = 0 (vs <): T-Value = -1.49 P-Value = 0.090 DF = 7
```

Response: Now the P-value is not especially small. We could not conclude that driving on the highway results in higher mileages, on average.

Concentrating on the difference between mileages, city minus highway, wipes out the rather pronounced differences among mileages for various cars (from 20 to 34 and from 25 to 40) and lets us focus on the effect of where each car was driven. In general, a paired procedure tends to provide more evidence, if a difference exists.

To calculate the interval by hand, we need to know that the t multiplier for 95% confidence and $5 - 1 = 4$ degrees of freedom is 2.78. This can be verified with software, or by consulting the t table at the end of the book. The sample mean difference is -5.20, the sample standard deviation is 1.92, and the sample size is 5, so the interval is

$$-5.20 \pm 2.78(1.92/\sqrt{5}) = -5.20 \pm 2.39 = (-7.59, -2.81)$$

Because data in a paired design reduce to a single sample of differences, solution methods for such problems are identical to those that applied in Chapter 10 when we performed inference for a single quantitative variable. In fact, the paired t procedure may be considered superfluous because simple data manipulation could produce a single column of differences, on which an ordinary t procedure could be used to test if the mean of the population from which that column was sampled could equal zero.

It is important to remember that these methods require the distribution of sample mean differences to be approximately normal. In a supplemental chapter on nonparametrics, we present a method that can be used when this requirement is not met—that is, when the sample size is small and the sample of differences has skewness or outliers.

Here is an example to reinforce the guidelines on page 525 for use of a paired t procedure.

EXAMPLE TBP 11.4 CHECKING THE CONDITIONS FOR A PAIRED T PROCEDURE BEFORE PERFORMING INFERENCE

Background: We suspect that cars' mileages should be higher on the highway than in the city. We collect a data set of mileages for a random sample of 5 cars, each tested in the city and on the highway.

City	Highway	Mileage Diff
20	28	−8
34	40	−6
26	32	−6
30	34	−4
22	25	−3

Questions: Is it appropriate to perform inference about the population of mileages, city versus highway? If so, does a car's gas mileage (in miles per gallon) depend on whether it's driven in the city or on the highway? If it does, then to what extent?

Responses: We'll take the preliminary step of entering the data and formulating hypotheses on the computer, so that we can request the relevant display (histogram) for checking the guidelines for a paired t procedure.

0. Because we suspect highway miles to be higher, we formulate $H_0: \mu_d = 0$ versus $H_a: \mu_d < 0$ about the population mean difference, $\mu_d =$ city minus highway miles per gallon.

```
Paired T for City - Highway
              N        Mean      StDev     SE Mean
City          5        26.40     5.73      2.56
Highway       5        31.80     5.76      2.58
Difference    5        -5.400    1.949     0.872
95% upper bound for mean difference: -3.541
T-Test of mean difference = 0 (vs < 0): T-Value = -6.19 P-Value = 0.002
```

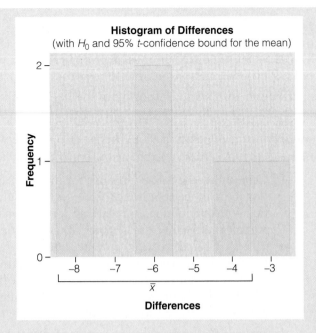

Histogram of Differences
(with H_0 and 95% t-confidence bound for the mean)

1. The histogram seems roughly normal, so we proceed with the test.

2. The sample mean of differences is -5.4, which standardizes to $t = -6.19$. Because the sample size is so small ($n = 5$), the t distribution has more spread than a z distribution. Nevertheless, a t that is larger than 3 in absolute value is extreme even when t just has a few degrees of freedom.

3. Our alternative hypothesis stated that $\mu_d < 0$, so the P-value is the probability of a t statistic being *less* than or equal to -6.19. According to the output, this probability is 0.002, which is very small by any standards.

4. Because the P-value is very small, we reject H_0 and conclude H_a is true: We conclude that the mean of all differences, city minus highway miles per gallon, would be negative for the entire population of cars from which our sample originated. In terms of the variables involved, we would say that whether a car is driven in the city or on the highway plays a role in its gas mileage, and mileages tend to be higher on the highway.

Because our test rejected the null hypothesis that mean of differences equals zero, a confidence interval can be examined in order to quantify how much less the mileages tend to be in the city as opposed to on the highway:

```
95% CI for mean difference: (-7.588, -2.812)
```

The confidence interval suggests that miles per gallon for city driving tend to be less than those for highway driving by about 2.8 to 7.6 miles per gallon.

Practice: *Try Exercise 11.6(j) on page 526.*

Inference for a Two-Sample Design

The two-sample t distribution is described briefly on page 528. To understand the behavior of this random variable, it helps to recall what we have learned about the distribution of a standard normal $z = \frac{\bar{x} - \mu}{\sigma/\sqrt{n}}$ and the similar, but not identical, random variable $t = \frac{\bar{x} - \mu}{s/\sqrt{n}}$ obtained when the sample standard deviation s is substituted for the population standard deviation σ. We will address one at a time the issues of center, spread, and shape of these random variables.

1. **Center:** Because sample mean $\bar{x}$ for random samples is centered at population mean μ, the appearance of $\bar{x} - \mu$ in the numerator of both z and t means that both distributions are centered at zero. Similarly, it can be established using rules for means from Chapter 7 that the *difference* between sample means $\bar{x}_1 - \bar{x}_2$ is centered at the *difference* between population means $\mu_1 - \mu_2$. If the categorical explanatory variable (being in category 1 or 2) has no effect on the quantitative response, then it should be true that $\mu_1 - \mu_2 = 0$. Therefore, the distribution of $\bar{x}_1 - \bar{x}_2$ should be centered at zero when the null hypothesis is true, and so should the two-sample t distribution.

2. **Spread:** We know that the standard deviation of $z = \frac{\bar{x} - \mu}{\sigma/\sqrt{n}}$ is 1 and the standard deviation of $t = \frac{\bar{x} - \mu}{s/\sqrt{n}}$ is more than 1, especially for small samples. The spread of the two-sample t distribution is not identical to the spread of the single-sample t, but it is also more than 1, to a greater or lesser extent depending on both sample sizes n_1 and n_2.

3. **Shape:** As far as shape is concerned, we must keep in mind that we are typically hoping the Central Limit Theorem will enable us to assume that sample means follow a normal distribution. Specifically, the distribution of $\frac{\bar{x} - \mu}{\sigma/\sqrt{n}}$ is really only normal if the sample mean $\bar{x}$ is normal, which will be the case if

   - the underlying distribution variable x itself is normal; or
   - the distribution of x is close to normal and the sample is small; or
   - the distribution of x is fairly symmetric (not necessarily normal) and the sample is of moderate size; or
   - the sample is very large

   In other words, if the population isn't normal, the sample needs to be large enough to offset its non-normality. Likewise, for $\frac{\bar{x} - \mu}{s/\sqrt{n}}$ to truly follow a t distribution (which is symmetric about zero and bell-shaped but somewhat different from the standard normal z), either x should be normal or the sample should be large enough relative to the shape of x.

This graph accompanies Example 11.6 on page 531, to give students a more concrete picture of the process of taking independent samples from populations of females and males, respectively.

Two-Sample Design

Population of female ages

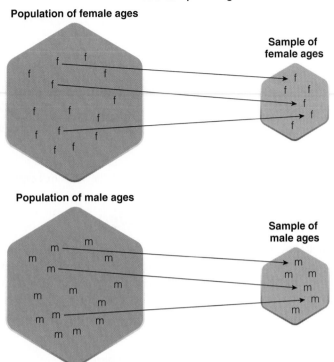

Sample of female ages

Population of male ages

Sample of male ages

This illustration shows how the size of the difference between sample means affects the size of the two-sample t statistic and the size of the P-value, as discussed in Example 11.7 on page 532.

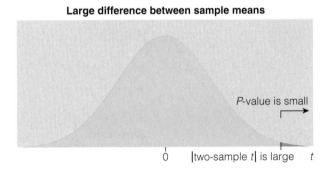

Large difference between sample means

P-value is small

0 |two-sample t| is large t

Small difference between sample means

P-value is not small

0 |two-sample t| is not large t

This illustration shows how the size of the sample standard deviations affects the size of the two-sample t statistic and the size of the P-value, as discussed in Example 11.8 on page 532.

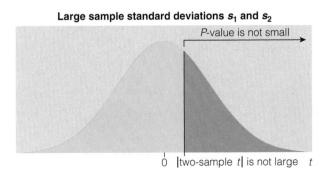

Large sample standard deviations s_1 and s_2

P-value is not small

0 |two-sample t| is not large t

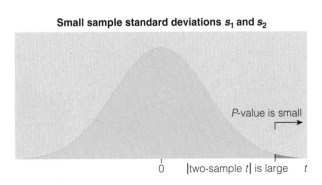

Small sample standard deviations s_1 and s_2

P-value is small

0 |two-sample t| is large t

This illustration shows how the sample sizes affect the size of the two-sample t statistic and the size of the P-value, as discussed in Example 11.9 on page 534.

Large sample sizes n_1 and n_2

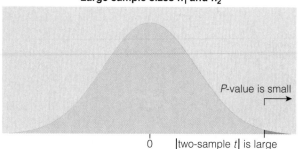

P-value is small

0 |two-sample *t*| is large

Small sample sizes n_1 and n_2

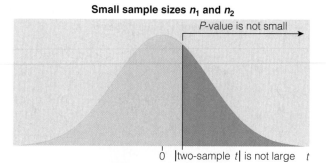

P-value is not small

0 |two-sample *t*| is not large   *t*

Downtown	Near Campus
495	500
380	475
650	650
1,100	450
725	525
860	710
425	575
	575

Here are the data to accompany the Students Talk Stats example on page 537.

Inference for a Several-Sample Design

Below is an illustration of the scenarios discussed on page 549. Whether the samples are large or small, either scenario comes about from a basic several-sample design, whereby samples are taken from several independent populations. In this context, the populations are the three racial/ethnic groups, from which we take random samples and record values for the variable of interest, salary.

Several-Sample Design

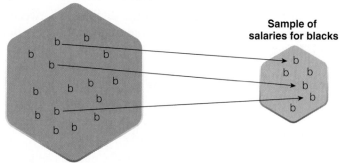

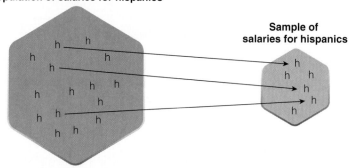

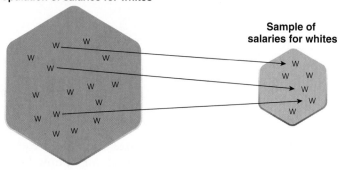

In contrast to the results for Math SAT scores in Example 11.20, on page 554, an *F* test for Verbal SAT scores, carried out in the next example, fails to show significant differences among students of various years.

EXAMPLE TBP 11.5 WHEN F TEST PRODUCES NO EVIDENCE OF A DIFFERENCE AMONG POPULATION MEANS

Background: Data have been gathered on students in introductory statistics courses at a particular university, including their year of study and their Verbal SAT scores. Software was used to carry out an analysis of variance, and then to produce side-by-side boxplots of sample scores for each of the five year possibilities (1st, 2nd, 3rd, 4th, and Other).

```
One-way ANOVA: Verbal versus Year
Analysis of Variance for Verbal
Source      DF        SS        MS        F        P
Year         4     23559      5890     1.10    0.357
Error      386   2068465      5359
Total      390   2092024

                                  Individual 95% CIs For Mean
                                  Based on Pooled StDev
Level      N      Mean     StDev ------+---------+---------+---------+
1         32    596.25     86.91                      (------*------)
2        234    592.76     65.87                         (-*--)
3         86    596.51     77.26                        (---*----)
4         29    579.83     79.47                  (-------*------)
other     10    551.00    124.32  (------------*------------)
                                  ------+---------+---------+---------+
Pooled StDev =     73.20               525       560       595       630
```

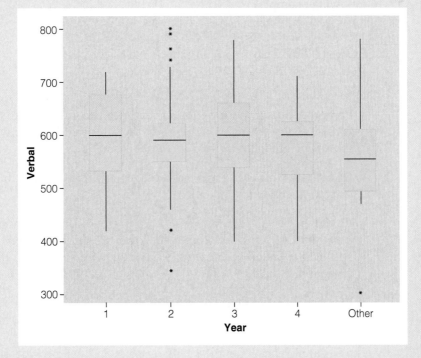

Question: Is there evidence that mean Verbal SAT scores are not all the same for students of various years?

Continued

Response: The side-by-side boxplots, already examined in Section 5.1, appear to be quite similar for students of various years, although that for "Other" students was somewhat lower than the rest. And yet, there must have been a few "Other" students with fairly high scores, because the upper whisker of their plot extends quite high, resulting in plenty of overlap with the first- through fourth-year plots.

According to the output, most of the sample mean Verbal scores were quite close to one another, and the most different mean (551.00 for "Other" students) would not carry as much weight because that group size was only 10. Whereas the sample standard deviations for Math scores ranged between 60 and 90, those for Verbal scores range between 65 and 125. Whatever differences we see among sample means are offset by a considerable amount of variation within each group of Verbal scores. In the end, the P-value (0.357) tells us that the F statistic, 1.10, is not large at all. The amount of variation that we observe among sample means of Verbal SAT scores could easily arise when sampling at random from five populations who share the same mean Verbal score. Looking at the boxplots and sample summaries, we could imagine a mean in the upper 500s as being plausible for all students in each of the five year groups.

Practice: *Try Exercise 11.77(c,d) on page 582.*

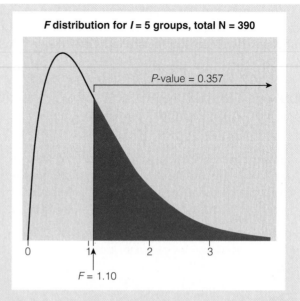

F distribution for $I = 5$ groups, total $N = 390$

P-value = 0.357

$F = 1.10$

Example 11.20 showed that bias can arise from non-representative samples. We should also be on the lookout for bias in the assessment process, as seen in the following example.

EXAMPLE TBP 11.6 HOW BIAS IN REPORTING VARIABLES' VALUES CAN AFFECT THE F TEST RESULTS

Background: Suppose we found that mean scores reported by college students for a test taken in high school differ significantly, with means *increasing* gradually as year increases from 1 to 4.

Question: How could this trend be explained by the fact that the scores were self-reported?

Response: If the scores were self-reported, we should consider the possibility that as students get older, they might forget their exact scores, and tend to round up more than down, a perfectly natural human tendency.

Practice: *Try Exercise 11.34 on page 563.*

To supplement Example 11.23 on page 557, we provide output for the two-sample test that shows no significant difference between two of the five sample means that were, as a group, found to differ significantly.

```
Two-sample T for Math_2 vs Math_3
             N      Mean     StDev    SE Mean
Math_2     233     613.9      61.0        4.0
Math_3      87     601.8      89.8        9.6
Difference = mu Math_2 - mu Math_3
Estimate for difference: 12.1
95% CI for difference: (-8.6, 32.7)
T-Test of difference = 0 (vs not =): T-Value = 1.16 P-Value = 0.249 DF = 116
```

Using mathematical notation for the parameters involved (population mean scores), the null hypothesis about means for the five year levels is written as

$$H_0 : \mu_1 = \mu_2 = \mu_3 = \mu_4 = \mu_5$$

Students must resist the temptation to simply replace all the $=$ signs with $\neq$ signs when writing H_a. This would be only one of many ways to disagree with H_0. If you were to write them all out, there would be 26 of them, such as

$$H_a : \mu_1 = \mu_2 \neq \mu_3 \neq \mu_4 \neq \mu_5 \text{ or}$$

$$H_a : \mu_1 \neq \mu_2 = \mu_3 \neq \mu_4 \neq \mu_5 \text{ or}$$

$$H_a : \mu_1 \neq \mu_2 \neq \mu_3 = \mu_4 \neq \mu_5 \text{ or}$$

$$\vdots$$

$$H_a : \mu_1 \neq \mu_2 \neq \mu_3 \neq \mu_4 \neq \mu_5$$

Clearly, it is much easier to express the ANOVA alternative hypothesis in plain English instead of mathematical notation, and write

$$H_a : \text{not all the population means are equal}$$

where "population means" can be replaced by "μ_i" if you like.

If the null hypothesis has been expressed in terms of the variables involved (stating that they are not related), instead of with respect to the relevant parameters (stating that population means are all equal), then the alternative hypothesis should also be framed in terms of the relationship.

Assumptions of ANOVA

The following discussion supplements the guidelines for use of an F procedure presented on page 558. Recall that in the two-sample case, we could carry out either an ordinary or a pooled t test for equal population means. Results of an ordinary test held whether or not population standard deviations were equal. Essential quantities in the pooled test, such as the degrees of freedom, the two-sample t statistic itself, and consequently the P-value, were all calculated under the assumption of equal population standard deviations.

Users of a two-sample t procedure can first decide whether or not this assumption is justified, and then opt for an ordinary or pooled procedure. One criterion for making this decision is based on sample standard deviations: If the largest is not more than twice the smallest, then presumably the sample standard deviations are close enough that one could conclude that the unknown population standard deviations may be equal. If the largest sample standard deviation is more than twice the smallest, then it is safer to use the non-pooled procedure.

In the several-sample case, we have no choice but to assume—or hope—that population standard deviations are equal, because all the calculations that make up the F procedure are based on this assumption. In other words, there is only a procedure analogous to the pooled two-sample t, and no corresponding extension of the ordinary two-sample t. The criterion for deciding whether we can safely assume population standard deviations to be equal is just like the one mentioned for the two-sample procedure: Check if the largest of the sample standard deviations is not more than twice the smallest. If it is less than twice the smallest, then presumably the assumption of equal population standard deviations is a reasonable one. And what if it isn't?

Fortunately, the F procedure is not completely inappropriate if the sample standard deviations are quite different, indicating a difference among population standard deviations as well. Rather, if this is the case, then we should insist on "larger" values of F than we would otherwise in order to conclude that population means are not all equal. In other words, we would need an even smaller P-value than usual in order to reject the null hypothesis.

As far as other assumptions are concerned, the F distribution (like z, t, and two-sample t) technically only applies when sample means are normally distributed. Again, we need not completely discount the test's results if the samples show skewness and/or outliers. The F procedure is fairly robust—that is, resistant to non-normality. Just as with the single- and two-sample procedures, we should check if sample sizes seem large enough to offset any non-normality that is apparent in displays of the data sets. It helps if sample sizes are not too disparate.

11.2 Activities

Activity: Distinguishing between Paired and Two-Sample Studies

Using the Computer

Access the student survey data and unstack heights, moms' heights, and dads' heights by the variable "sex of student." Is there a significant difference between mean height of female students and mean height of the mothers? Decide whether the test should be paired or two-sample, then carry it out and state conclusions. Next, carry out the wrong test and see if the same conclusions are reached. Likewise, test for a difference between mean heights of male students and fathers, then compare results to those for the incorrect procedure.

If there is a subtle difference, are we better equipped to detect it with a paired or with a two-sample test?

Activity: Roles of Differences between Means, Sizes of Standard Deviations, and Sample Sizes in the Two-Sample t Procedure

Using the Computer

The purpose of this activity is to explore the roles played by difference between sample means, by sample sizes, and by sample spreads in the size of the two-sample t statistic and subsequently the P-value in a test for equality between two population means.

In the first of three parts, we compare a sample of students' ages to a sample of ages that average just one year older, then compare to a sample that average three years older. This comparison lets us focus on the role played by the difference $\bar{x}_1 - \bar{x}_2$ when we seek evidence of a significant difference between population means $\mu_1 - \mu_2$.

Students access or create a sample data set Age consisting of values 18, 19, 21, 23, 23, 23, 23, 23, 25, 27, 28 whose mean is 23 and standard deviation is 3; create another data set AgePlusOne (whose mean is 24 and standard deviation is still 3) by adding 1 to each entry of Age, and create another data set AgePlusThree (whose mean is 26 and standard deviation is still 3) by adding 3 to each entry of Score.

1. Are the data in AgePlusOne significantly different from the data in Age? Carry out a two-sided two-sample t test, report the P-value, and decide.

2. Are the data in AgePlusThree significantly different from the data in Age? Carry out a two-sided two-sample t test, report the P-value, and decide.

3. Discuss the role played by the size of the difference between sample means $\bar{x}_1 - \bar{x}_2$ when testing for a difference between population means based on the two-sample t statistic

$$\frac{\bar{x}_1 - \bar{x}_2}{\sqrt{\dfrac{s_1^2}{n_1} + \dfrac{s_2^2}{n_2}}}$$

In the second of three parts, we compare a large sample of students' ages to another large sample of ages that average just one year older. This comparison lets us focus on the role played by sample sizes n_1 and n_2 when we seek evidence of a significant difference between population means $\mu_1 - \mu_2$.

Students access or create a data set AgeLargeSample consisting of 9 18's, 9 19's, 9 20's, 45 23's, 9 25's, 9 27's, and 9 28's; this data set has mean 23 and standard deviation 2.875. Create another data set AgePlusOneLargeSample (whose mean is 24 and standard deviation is also 2.875) by adding 1 to each entry of Age-LargeSample.

1. Are the data in AgePlusOneLargeSample significantly different from the data in AgeLargeSample? Carry out a two-sided two-sample t test, report the P-value, and decide.

2. Recall that in the first part of this activity, we compared two small data sets of ages, both of which had standard deviation 3, where the sample mean ages differed by just 1 year. We were not able to find a significant difference between those mean ages. In this part, we compare two large data sets of ages, both of which again have standard deviation 3 and whose sample means again differ by just 1 year. In this context, discuss the role played by sample sizes n_1 and n_2 when testing for a difference between population means based on the two-sample t statistic $\dfrac{\bar{x}_1 - \bar{x}_2}{\sqrt{\dfrac{s_1^2}{n_1} + \dfrac{s_2^2}{n_2}}}$.

In the third of three parts, we compare a small sample of students' ages with very little spread to another small sample with very little spread, whose average is just one year older. This comparison lets us focus on the role played by sample standard deviations s_1 and s_2 when we seek evidence of a significant difference between population means $\mu_1 - \mu_2$.

Students access or create a date set AgeLessSpread consisting of values 21, 22, 23, 23, 23, 23, 23, 23, 23, 24, 25, whose mean is 23 and standard deviation is just 1; create another data set AgeLessSpreadPlusOne (whose mean is 24 and standard deviation is still just 1) by adding 1 to each entry of AgeLessSpread.

1. Are the data in AgeLessSpreadPlusOne significantly different from the data in AgeLessSpread? Carry out a two-sided two-sample t test, report the P-value, and decide.

2. Recall that in the first part of this activity, we compared two data sets of ages, both of which had standard deviation 3, where the sample mean ages differed by just 1 year. We were not able to find a significant difference between those mean ages. In this part, we compare two data sets of ages whose sample means also differ by just 1 year, but now each has standard

deviation 1 instead of 3. In this context, discuss the role played by the size of the standard deviations s_1 and s_2 when testing for a difference between population means based on the two-sample t statistic $\dfrac{\bar{x}_1 - \bar{x}_2}{\sqrt{\dfrac{s_1^2}{n_1} + \dfrac{s_2^2}{n_2}}}$.

In the Classroom

The purpose of this activity is to explore the roles played by difference between sample means, by sample sizes, and by sample spreads in the size of the two-sample z statistic and subsequently the P-value in a test for equality between two population means. It makes use of the fact that the mean of all dice rolls is 3.5 and the standard deviation is 1.7. Also, the mean of the numbers 3 and 4 is 3.5, too, but the standard deviation is only 0.5.

In the first of three parts, we compare a sample of dice rolls to a sample of dice rolls that average just one more, then compare to a sample that average two more. This lets us focus on the role played by the difference $\bar{x}_1 - \bar{x}_2$ when we seek evidence of a significant difference between population means $\mu_1 - \mu_2$.

Students roll a die 9 times, record those values in a column X_1, and find the mean $\bar{x}_1$. They create another column X_2 by adding 1 to each entry of X_1 and note that its mean $\bar{x}_2$ is exactly one more than $\bar{x}_1$. They create yet another column X_3 by adding 2 to each entry of X_1 and note that its mean $\bar{x}_3$ is exactly two more than $\bar{x}_1$.

1. Are the data in X_2 significantly different from the data in X_1? Carry out a two-sided two-sample z test by finding

$$\frac{\bar{x}_1 - \bar{x}_2}{\sqrt{\dfrac{\sigma_1^2}{n_1} + \dfrac{\sigma_2^2}{n_2}}} = \frac{\bar{x}_1 - \bar{x}_2}{\sqrt{\dfrac{1.7^2}{9} + \dfrac{1.7^2}{9}}} = 1.25(\bar{x}_1 - \bar{x}_2)$$

Determine if the two-sample z statistic is larger than 2 in absolute value. If not, the P-value is not smaller than 0.05, and there is no significant difference between the data in the two columns.

2. Are the data in X_3 significantly different from the data in X_1? Carry out a two-sided two-sample z test by finding

$$\frac{\bar{x}_1 - \bar{x}_3}{\sqrt{\dfrac{\sigma_1^2}{n_1} + \dfrac{\sigma_2^2}{n_2}}} = \frac{\bar{x}_1 - \bar{x}_3}{\sqrt{\dfrac{1.7^2}{9} + \dfrac{1.7^2}{9}}} = 1.25(\bar{x}_1 - \bar{x}_3)$$

Determine if the two-sample z statistic is larger than 2 in absolute value. If so, the P-value is smaller than 0.05, and there is a significant difference between the data in the two columns.

3. Discuss the role played by the size of the difference between sample means when testing for a difference between population means based on the two-sample z statistic.

In the second of three parts, we compare a small sample of dice rolls to another small sample that average two more. This comparison lets us focus on the role played by sample sizes n_1 and n_2 when we seek evidence of a significant difference between population means $\mu_1 - \mu_2$.

Students roll a die 4 times, record those values in a column X_1, and find the mean $\bar{x}_1$. They create another column X_2 by adding 2 to each entry of X_1 and note that its mean $\bar{x}_2$ is exactly two more than $\bar{x}_1$.

1. Are the data in X_2 significantly different from the data in X_1? Carry out a two-sided two-sample z test by finding

$$\frac{\bar{x}_1 - \bar{x}_2}{\sqrt{\dfrac{\sigma_1^2}{n_1} + \dfrac{\sigma_2^2}{n_2}}} = \frac{\bar{x}_1 - \bar{x}_2}{\sqrt{\dfrac{1.7^2}{4} + \dfrac{1.7^2}{4}}} = 0.83(\bar{x}_1 - \bar{x}_2)$$

Determine if the two-sample z statistic is larger than 2 in absolute value. If not, the P-value is not smaller than 0.05, and there is no significant difference between the data in the two columns.

2. Recall that in the first part of this activity, we compared two larger data sets of numbers, both of which had standard deviation 1.7, where the sample means differed by 2. We probably *were* able to find a significant difference between those means. In this part, we compare two smaller data sets, both of which again have standard deviation 1.7 and whose sample means again differ by 2. In this context, discuss the role played by sample sizes n_1 and n_2 when testing for a difference between population means based on the two-sample z statistic $\dfrac{\bar{x}_1 - \bar{x}_2}{\sqrt{\dfrac{\sigma_1^2}{n_1} + \dfrac{\sigma_2^2}{n_2}}}$.

In the third of three parts, we compare a sample of dice rolls with very little spread to another sample with very little spread, whose average is just one more. This comparison lets us focus on the role played by standard deviations σ_1 and σ_2 when we seek evidence of a significant difference between population means $\mu_1 - \mu_2$.

Students create a column X_1 of 3s and 4s by rolling a die nine times and recording the value as 3 if it is 3 or less, 4 if it is 4 or more. Then they find the mean $\bar{x}_1$. They create another column X_2 by adding 1 to each entry of X_1 and note that its mean $\bar{x}_2$ is exactly one more than $\bar{x}_1$.

1. Are the data in X_2 significantly different from the data in X_1? Carry out a two-sided two-sample z test by finding

$$\frac{\bar{x}_1 - \bar{x}_2}{\sqrt{\dfrac{\sigma_1^2}{n_1} + \dfrac{\sigma_2^2}{n_2}}} = \frac{\bar{x}_1 - \bar{x}_2}{\sqrt{\dfrac{.5^2}{9} + \dfrac{.5^2}{9}}} = 4.24(\bar{x}_1 - \bar{x}_2)$$

Determine if the two-sample z statistic is larger than 2 in absolute value. If so, the P-value is smaller than 0.05, and there is a significant difference between the data in the two columns.

2. Recall that in the first part of this activity, we compared two columns of numbers, both of which had standard deviation 1.7, where the sample means differed by just one. We probably were not able to find a significant difference between those means. In this part, we compare two data sets whose sample means also differ by just 1 year, but now each has standard deviation 0.5 instead of 1.7. In this context, discuss the role played by the size of the standard deviations σ_1 and σ_2 when testing for a difference between population means based on the two-sample z statistic $\dfrac{\bar{x}_1 - \bar{x}_2}{\sqrt{\dfrac{\sigma_1^2}{n_1} + \dfrac{\sigma_2^2}{n_2}}}$.

Activity: How I and N Affect the F Distribution and the F Statistic

Using the Computer

First we consider how I and N impact the *distribution* of F.

Suppose the sample size is $N = 20$. These individuals might be divided into 2 groups of 10, or 4 groups of 5, or 5 groups of 4, or 10 groups of 2. Use software (for example, "Calc>Probability Distributions>F" in MINITAB) to find the inverse cumulative probability for the correct degrees of freedom in the numerator (DFG) and in the denominator (DFG) in each of the four above-mentioned situations ($I = 2, 4, 5,$ or 10), inputting 0.95 as the constant. This identifies the F value that yields 0.05 as the tail probability, and tells us how large our F statistic must be to let us reject at the 0.05 level.

In general, as far as the spread of the distribution of F is concerned, is it easier to reject the null hypothesis when our sample is divided into few groups or many groups?

Now suppose the sample size is $N = 40$. These individuals might be divided into 2 groups of 20, or 4 groups of 10, or 10 groups of 4, or 20 groups of 2. Use software to find the inverse cumulative probability for the correct degrees of freedom in the numerator (DFG) and in the denominator (DFG) in each of these situations, again inputting 0.95 as the constant.

As far as the spread of the distribution of F is concerned, is it easier to reject the null hypothesis when our sample is divided into few groups or many groups? (Do you see the same trend for $N = 40$ as you saw for $N = 20$?)

As far as the distribution of F is concerned, is it easier to reject the null hypothesis for a smaller total sample size N or a larger N?

Next we consider how I and N impact the size of the F *statistic*.

Our formula for F can be rearranged to show that SSG/SSE is being multiplied by $\frac{N-I}{I-1}$. For $N = 20$, does this quantity increase or decrease as I increases from 2 to 4 to 5 to 10? As far as the size of F is concerned, is it easier to reject the null hypothesis when our sample is divided into few groups or many groups?

For $N = 40$, does the quantity increase or decrease as I increases? (Do you see the same trend for $N = 40$ as you saw for $N = 20$?)

As N increases from 20 to 40, does $\frac{N-I}{I-1}$ increase or decrease? As far as the size of F is concerned, is it easier to reject the null hypothesis for a smaller total sample size N or a larger N?

In summary, can we say that our P-value tends to be smaller when the data are divided into few or many groups I? Can we say that our P-value tends to be smaller for smaller or larger total sample size N?

11.3 Guide to Exercise Topics

Previewing inference for relationships between a categorical and a quantitative variable: 11.1*, 11.2*, 11.3, 11.4*, 11.5, 11.41, 11.42, 11.43, 11.44*, 11.45

Inference for paired designs: 11.6*, 11.7, 11.8, 11.48, 11.49, 11.58*, 11.59; Using Software: 11.50, 11.51, 11.84(f–m), 11.85*(b,c), 11.87(a–d), 11.90*, 11.91*, 11.92

Inference for two-sample designs: 11.9*, 11.10, 11.11, 11.12, 11.13*, 11.14*, 11.15, 11.16, 11.17, 11.18*, 11.19*, 11.20*, 11.21, 11.22, 11.23, 11.52, 11.53, 11.54, 11.55, 11.56, 11.60, 11.61, 11.62, 11.63, 11.64, 11.65*, 11.66, 11.67, 11.68, 11.69; Using Software: 11.70, 11.71, 11.72, 11.73, 11.84(h–w), 11.86, 11.87(e–h), 11.89*, 11.93, 11.94, 11.95, 11.96*, 11.97*, 11.98, 11.99

Inference for a several-sample design: 11.26*, 11.27*, 11.28*, 11.29*, 11.30, 11.31*, 11.32*, 11.33, 11.34*, 11.35, 11.36*, 11.37*, 11.38*, 11.39, 11.40, 11.71, 11.74, 11.75, 11.76, 11.77*, 11.78, 11.79, 11.108(e); Using Software: 11.24*, 11.25, 11.80, 11.81, 11.82*, 11.83, 11.100, 11.101, 11.102, 11.103

11.4 Supplemental Exercises

11.1 Tell whether each of the following involves one categorical, one quantitative, one of each, two categorical, or two quantitative variables:

    a. Each individual in a study is classified as having a serious mental disorder or not.

    b. For each country in a sample, the percentage of people with a serious mental disorder is recorded.

    c. For each country in a sample, the percentage of people with a serious mental disorder is recorded, along with information as to whether the country is developed or less developed.

11.2 Tell whether each of the following involves one categorical, one quantitative, one of each, two categorical, or two quantitative variables:

    a. For one individual, a sample of spoken words is examined and each word is classified as having been stuttered or not.

    b. For each person in a group of speech therapy patients, the percentage of words stuttered on a spoken evaluation is recorded.

    c. Each person in a group of speech therapy patients has been classified as having a mild, moderate, or severe disability. An evaluation records the percentage of words stuttered for each person, and a comparison is made of scores among the three groups.

11.3 A study published in the *British Medical Journal* (BMJ) in January 2001 tracked a large sample of individuals born in 1946, noting their birth weights and scores on cognitive tests at ages 8, 11, 15, 26, and 43. Birth weights were classified as being less than 2.51 kg, between 2.51 and 3.00 kg, between 3.01 and 3.50 kg, between 3.51 and 4.00 kg, and 4.01 to 5.00 kg. Identify each of these variables as being categorical or quantitative, and as being explanatory or response.

    a. birth weight

    b. cognitive test score

    c. age

11.4 "Comparison of the Atkins, Ornish, Weight Watchers, and Zone Diets for Weight Loss and Heart Disease Reduction," published in the *Journal of the American Medical Association* in January 2005, reported on an experiment in which 40 subjects were randomly assigned to each of the 4 diets.

    a. For any given diet, subjects' initial weights were compared with weights after 12 months. Would this involve a paired or two-sample procedure?

    b. Weight losses were compared for subjects on the four diets. Would this involve a t or an F procedure?

    c. Weight loss after 12 months (assuming no change from baseline for participants who discontinued the study) was 2.1 kilograms for those on the Atkins diet, with standard deviation 4.8 kilograms. If weight loss followed an approximately normal distribution (so that the 68-95-99.7 Rule applies), can we conclude that almost all of the subjects actually lost weight? Explain with words or a sketch.

    d. *P*-values for testing whether or not on average weight is lost with each of the four diets were, respectively, 0.009, 0.002, 0.001, and 0.007. Due to the very small *P*-values, do we conclude there is evidence that a large amount of weight is lost on average with each of the diets, or do we conclude there is a large amount of evidence that on average some weight is lost with each of the diets?

    e. The *P*-value for comparing mean weight losses on the four diets was 0.40. Do you conclude that type of diet makes a difference overall?

    f. Considering your answer to part (e), is it possible that you made a Type I Error or a Type II Error?

    g. Researchers also looked at the relationship between weight decrease and waist size. Does this involve two quantitative variables, two categorical variables, or one of each?

    h. The article reports that "all diets reduced mean LDL cholesterol levels at 1 year, although this did not reach statistical significance in the case of the Atkins group . . ."[1] Can we conclude that the *P*-value for testing cholesterol reduction on the Atkins diet was more than 0.05 or less than 0.05?

USING TABLES: PAIRED AND TWO-SAMPLE STUDIES [SEE END OF BOOK]

11.5 In Exercise 11.49, a t statistic comparing estimates for size of an object made by 24 blind subjects with and without blindfolds was found to be 1.01. What can we say about the size of the P-value for a two-sided alternative, if we refer to the t table using 20 degrees of freedom?

11.6 Exercise 11.58 showed $t = 0.42$ for a paired test comparing 100 students' Math and Verbal SAT scores. Because the sample is large enough for z probabilities to be approximately correct, use the normal table to estimate the P-value for the two-sided test.

11.7 Exercise 11.59 showed $t = -1.63$ for a paired test comparing 100 disabled students' Math and Verbal SAT scores. Because the sample is large enough for z probabilities to be approximately correct, use the normal table to estimate the P-value for the two-sided test.

11.8 Exercise 11.61 compared Verbal SAT scores of 100 disabled students to those of a sample of 100 nondisabled students, producing a two-sample t statistic of -2.77. Because the sample is large enough for z probabilities to be approximately correct, use the normal table to estimate the P-value for the two-sided test.

11.9 Exercise 11.9 reported two-sample t statistics for tests comparing psychometric scores of male versus female adolescents, and explained that the samples were large enough for the two-sample t to behave roughly the same as a z distribution. Use the z table to report the (two-sided) P-value for each of the five t statistics.

  a. anxiety: $t = +2.89$

  b. depression: $t = +3.83$

  c. hostility: $t = +0.70$

  d. negative self: $t = +3.50$

  e. somatization (physical complaints caused by psychological problems): $t = +1.11$

11.10 Exercise 11.10 reported two-sample t statistics for tests comparing psychometric scores of early- versus mid-adolescents, and explained that the samples were large enough for the two-sample t to behave roughly the same as a z distribution. Use

tables to report the (two-sided) P-value for each of the five t statistics.

  a. anxiety: $t = 3.36$

  b. depression: $t = 3.56$

  c. hostility: $t = 1.25$

  d. negative self: $t = 2.85$

  e. somatization $t = 1.35$

11.11 Exercise 11.13 compared test scores for 6 students who studied zero hours per week and 7 students who studied at least nine hours per week; the two-sample t statistic was 2.32. The conservative approach using tables would refer to $6 - 1 = 5$ degrees of freedom. Report whether the P-value is less than $2(0.05) = 0.10$ for a two-sided test.

11.12 In Exercise 11.15, a two-sample t statistic for comparing physical characteristics of large samples of male and female mice was found to be 0.57. Use z tables to report the approximate P-value for a two-sided test.

11.13 In Exercise 11.17, the two-sample t statistic comparing duration of words stuttered for 4 patients with mild versus 3 with moderate speech disabilities was found to be $t = -0.07$. The conservative approach using tables would be to refer to $3 - 1 = 2$ degrees of freedom. Report the t value that corresponds to a left-tail area of 0.05. Do we have evidence of a small P-value?

11.14 Exercise 11.23 required the calculation of a two-sample t statistic comparing mean age at death for 25 westerners present at the opening of King Tut's tomb with mean age at death for 11 Westerners who were in Egypt but not exposed to the "mummy's curse." Report the two-sample t statistic and give a range for the P-value, using $11 - 1 = 10$ degrees of freedom and a one-sided alternative. What is the table value closest to your t statistic?

11.15 Exercise 11.108 reported one-sided P-values testing for significant weight loss for 40 subjects on each of four diets: 0.009, 0.002, 0.001, and 0.007. Degrees of freedom would be $40 - 1 = 39$, and the conservative approach would be to refer to 35 rather than 40 degrees of freedom in the t table. Since 0.009 is between 0.005 and 0.01, the first t statistic would have been approximately between 2.438 and 2.734. Give a range for the other three t statistics, based on the given P-values.

11.5 Solutions to Supplemental Exercises

11.1 **a.** one categorical   **b.** one quantitative   **c.** one categorical and one quantitative

11.2 **a.** one categorical   **b.** one quantitative   **c.** one categorical and one quantitative

11.3 **a.** categorical, explanatory   **b.** quantitative, response   **c.** categorical, explanatory

11.4 **a.** paired   **b.** F **c.** No, because 0 would be just $(0 - (-2.1))/4.8 = 0.44$ standard deviations above the mean; it is quite common for a normal variable to be this far above the mean or more.   **d.** Conclude there is a large amount of evidence that on average some weight is lost with each of the diets.   **e.** no   **f.** Type II   **g.** two quantitative variables   **h.** more than 0.05

11.5 Since 1.01 is less than 1.725, the two-sided P-value is greater than $2(0.05) = 0.10$.

11.6 P-value is approximately $2(.3372) = 0.6744$

11.7 P-value is approximately $2(.0516) = 0.1032$

11.8 P-value is approximately $2(.0028) = 0.0056$

11.9 **a.** $2(0.0019) = 0.0038$ **b.** less than $2(0.0013) = 0.0026$ **c.** $2(0.2420) = 0.4840$ **d.** less than $2(0.0013) = 0.0026$ **e.** $2(0.1335) = 0.2670$

11.10 **a.** P-value less than $2(0.0013) = 0.0026$ **b.** P-value less than $2(0.0013) = 0.0026$ **c.** P-value $2(0.1056) = 0.2112$ **d.** P-value $2(0.0022) = 0.0044$ **e.** P-value $2(0.0885) = 0.1770$

11.11 For 5 degrees of freedom, 2.32 is between 2.015 and 2.571, so the P-value is between $2(0.05) = 0.10$ and $2(0.025) = 0.05$; it is less than 0.10.

11.12 P-value is approximately $2(0.2843) = 0.5686$

11.13 For 2 df, $t = -2.92$ has left-tail area 0.05; the P-value is not small at all.

11.14 $t = -1.08$; P-value is greater than $2(0.05) = 0.10$ because t is not as extreme as -1.812, which is the closest table value.

11.15 For P-value 0.002, t must be greater than 2.724; for P-value 0.001, t must be greater than 2.724; for P-value 0.007, t must be between 2.438 and 2.724.

TBP Chapter 12

Inference for Relationships between Two Categorical Variables

12.1 Details and Examples

These tables accompany our discussion on page 591 about formulating hypotheses in terms of variables (gender and lenswear) or parameters (proportions of males and of females in various lenswear categories).

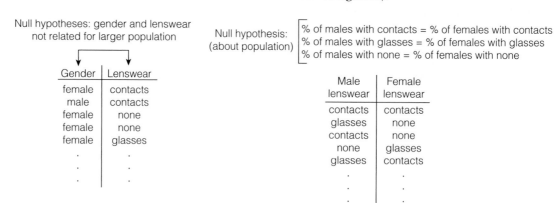

Null hypotheses: gender and lenswear not related for larger population

Gender	Lenswear
female	contacts
male	contacts
female	none
female	none
female	glasses
.	.
.	.

Null hypothesis: (about population)

% of males with contacts = % of females with contacts
% of males with glasses = % of females with glasses
% of males with none = % of females with none

Male lenswear	Female lenswear
contacts	contacts
glasses	none
contacts	none
none	glasses
glasses	contacts
.	.
.	.

Another issue to be considered is whether the data were sampled from a single population, after which each individual was classified according to values of both categorical variables of interest. In this case, the chi-square test is formulated as a test of *independence* of those two variables. If, instead, the individuals have been sampled from separate populations, the test is for *homogeneity* of those groups with respect to the response variable. Either way, the same chi-square procedure, to be presented in this chapter, can be used.

Comparing Proportions with a z Test

Here is a graphical depiction of the relationship between the size of the difference between sample proportions and the size of the *P*-value, as discussed on page 592.

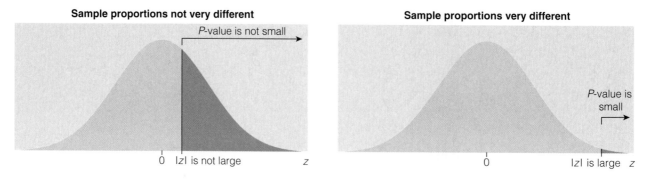

Sample proportions not very different — *P*-value is not small — 0 |z| is not large   z

Sample proportions very different — *P*-value is small — 0 |z| is large   z

These graphs show the impact of sample sizes on the size of the *P*-value.

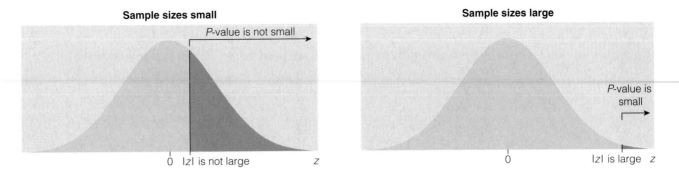

This two-way table can be presented when discussing the z procedure to compare two proportions on page 593, to be contrasted with chi-square, which compares two tables of counts.

z procedure: Compare difference between observed proportions (0.75 − 0.25 = 0.50) to difference expected if null hypothesis were true (0)

	Sweating decreased	Sweating not decreased	Total	Percent decreased
Botox	121	40	161	0.75
Placebo	40	121	161	0.25
Total	161	161	322	

Inference with Chi-Square

The following two examples supplement Example 12.6 on page 599 by preceding the calculation of expected counts with a discussion of what we might intuit in terms of a relationship between the variables gender and lenswear, as well as a thorough examination of the observed proportions.

EXAMPLE TBP 12.1 INTUITING RELATIONSHIP BETWEEN GENDER AND LENSWEAR

Background: We are interested in the variables lenswear (contacts, glasses, or none) and gender.

Question: Would you expect those variables to be related for populations of male and female college students?

Response: Before looking at data, and simply based on what we notice in our everyday lives, we may have reason to suspect that a relationship between the variables is possible. Specifically, females may opt for contacts instead of glasses for cosmetic purposes. As far as the need for *any* corrective lenses is concerned, it seems that if poor eyesight were more prevalent in one of the gender groups, it would by now be fairly common knowledge, like the fact that baldness is a predominantly male trait. Thus, we may anticipate that gender and lenswear are related, not because of poorer eyesight in one gender group, but because of differences in choice of corrective lenses.

Practice: *Try Exercise 12.12(a) on page 608.*

EXAMPLE TBP 12.2 COMPARING SAMPLE PROPORTIONS IN LENSWEAR CATEGORIES

Background: In Section 5.2, we used gender as the explanatory variable, and produced a table recording counts and also percentages in the various lenswear categories (responses) for females and males.

	contacts	glasses	none	All
female	121	32	129	282
	42.91%	11.35%	45.74%	100.00%
male	42	37	85	164
	25.61%	22.56%	51.83%	100.00%
All	163	69	214	446

Question: What do the data tell us about gender and lenswear for the sample of students?

Response: Certainly differences between males and females existed for the sample of students—such as 42.91% of the females wearing contacts as opposed to only 25.61% of the males, and only 11.35% of the females wearing glasses as opposed to 22.56% of the males. The difference between percentages wearing no corrective lenses—45.74% for the females versus 51.83% for the males—is not as pronounced.

Practice: *Try Exercise 12.12(b) on page 608.*

The calculation of expected counts, as in Example 12.6 on page 599, is worth further discussion, first of all because of its connection to our study of probability. Secondly, Example **TBP 12.3** reminds students that, by construction, we are producing a table where the explanatory groups have equal proportions in the response of interest.

The formula for expected counts is actually equivalent to the requirement that all event combinations be independent, so that the Independent "And" Rule of probability from Chapter 6 holds: $P(A \text{ and } B) = P(A) \times P(B)$. For example, for the events to be independent, probability of being female *and* wearing contacts

$$P(F \text{ and } C) = \frac{(163 \times 282)/446}{446}$$

must equal probability of being female *multiplied* by probability of wearing contacts

$$P(F)P(C) = \frac{282}{446} \times \frac{163}{446}$$

Our null hypothesis can be formulated in terms of variables (gender and lenswear are not related) or parameters (population proportions of males and of females in the various lenswear categories are equal). Likewise, the table of counts expected under the null hypothesis not only reflects what counts would be seen if the variables were not related, but also what counts would be seen if proportions were equal.

EXAMPLE TBP 12.3 RESPONSE PROPORTIONS EQUAL IN TABLE OF EXPECTED COUNTS

Background: In Example 12.6 on page 599, a table was produced showing what counts we would expect if gender and lenswear were not related.

Question: What are the proportions of males and females in each lenswear category occurring in our table of expected counts?

Response: The expected proportions wearing contacts are $103/282 = 0.365$ for females and $60/164 = 0.366$ for males; wearing glasses are $44/282 = 0.156$ females and 0.155 males; wearing neither are $135/282 = 0.479$ females and $79/164 = 0.482$ males. The proportions are virtually the same for males and females, and would be identical if expected counts had not been rounded to the nearest whole number.

Practice: *Try Exercise 12.12(e) on page 608.*

After drawing the conclusion in Example 12.10 on page 604 that gender and lenswear are related, we can pinpoint which category combinations are the main contributors to the conclusion of a statistically significant relationship by examining the individual components (terms) of the χ^2 statistic to see which ones make the statistic large. When we looked at these components in Example 12.7 on page 600, we noted that the largest, 5.4 and 5.8, arose because significantly fewer males were observed (42) to wear contacts than what was expected (60) if gender and lenswear were not related, and significantly more males were observed (37) to wear glasses than what was expected (25). There was also a substantial contribution from the terms 3.1 and 3.3, because of more females wearing contacts and fewer wearing glasses. In contrast, there was very little contribution from the terms 0.3 and 0.5: The observed counts wearing no lenses were quite close, for both females and males, to the counts expected if equal proportions wore no lenses in the two gender groups. Apparently, it is not the general need for corrective lenses that differs between the sexes, it is the choice of which type of lenses to wear, contacts or glasses. This is consistent with our initial conjecture, made earlier in the section before beginning the formal problem solution.

To make the above conclusion official, we can present the data differently, combining counts with contacts and glasses, to see if the wearing of any corrective lenses is related to gender.

EXAMPLE TBP 12.4 HOW THE CHI-SQUARE TEST CAN BE AFFECTED BY COMBINING CATEGORIES

Background: Data on gender and lenswear are presented in a two-way table, where counts for contact lenses and glasses have been combined.

	Corrective Lenses	None	Total
Female	153	129	282
Male	79	85	164
Total	232	214	446

Continued

This affects the percentages to be compared, as shown in the bar graphs below.

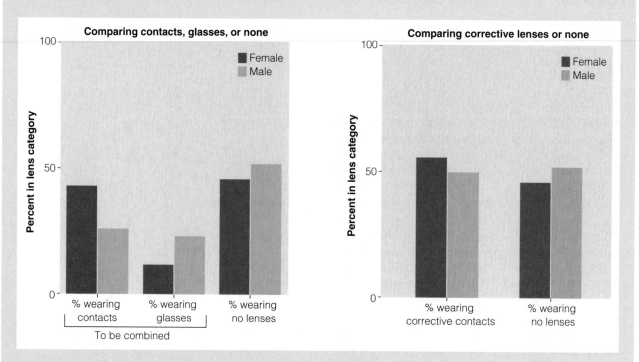

A chi-square test is carried out on the new set of counts, with results shown below.

```
Expected counts are printed below observed counts
      CorrectiveLenses  None       Total
Female      153          129       282
            146.69       135.31
 Male        79           85       164
             85.31        78.69
Total       232          214       446
Chi-Sq =  0.271 +  0.294 +
          0.467 +  0.506 = 1.538
DF = 1, P-Value = 0.215
```

Question: Do we reach the same conclusions as in the preceding example, which handled counts for contacts and glasses separately?

Response: The new chi-square statistic is just 1.538, not large at all for a chi-square distribution with 1 degree of freedom (no longer 2 degrees of freedom because we now have just a two-by-two table). This is confirmed by the fact that the *P*-value, 0.215, is not small at all. Now, we conclude there is no evidence of a relationship between gender and lenswear (need for any corrective lenses) in the larger population from which the students were sampled.

Practice: *Try Exercise 12.41 on page 622.*

This example should serve as a caution because it shows that when categorical data may take more than two possible values, the choice of which groups—if any—to combine can profoundly impact a test's conclusions.

Goodness of Fit Test for a Single Categorical Variable

Although inference for single categorical variables was already covered in Chapter 9, the special case of a variable with more than two possible category values is best mentioned in this chapter because of the need for a chi-square procedure. The circumstances that warrant a goodness-of-fit test are not nearly as common as those that warrant an ordinary chi-square test for a relationship. For this reason, many instructors do not include such tests in their curriculum.

In Chapter 9, we learned to use a z procedure to test whether or not a proposed value for a population proportion was plausible. For instance, we tested whether or not the proportion of all students eating breakfast could be 0.5, or whether or not the proportion of all people getting a seven when picking a number "at random" from 1 to 20 could be 1/20, or 0.05. Our methods were based on a binomial model, where the categorical variable of interest can have just two possible values.

It often arises that the categorical variable of interest has more than two possible values. For example, students may be polled as to which is their favorite meal—breakfast, lunch, or dinner—and we could use the data to answer the question of whether all three meals are equally favored (proportions one-third) in the larger population. Or the proportion of people selecting each of the 20 numbers from 1 to 20 could be examined to see, if overall, each could have a probability of 0.05 of being selected. In the next example, ethnicity data on television characters is examined to see if it fairly reflects proportions that hold for the U.S. population. In each of these situations, a chi-square "goodness of fit" test would be used to determine if the observed counts in the various categories fit closely enough to the proposed model for the general behavior of the categorical variable. Just as in our test about a relationship between two variables, we standardize with the statistic

$$\text{chi-square} = \text{sum of } \frac{(\text{observed} - \text{expected})^2}{\text{expected}}$$

When a chi-square goodness of fit test is conducted on values of a single categorical variable, the degrees of freedom equal the number of possible categories minus one.

EXAMPLE TBP 12.5 SAMPLE PROPORTIONS IN SEVERAL CATEGORIES FOR ONE VARIABLE

Background: A watchdog group called Children Now regularly examines the ethnicity of prime-time television characters to document under-representation of certain racial and ethnic groups. Examination of all the characters featured in the first two episodes of every entertainment show on the six networks that aired at the start of the fall season in 2002 showed proportions seen in the first column of numbers. In contrast, the proportions in the United States are shown in the next column. A bar graph displays these proportions.

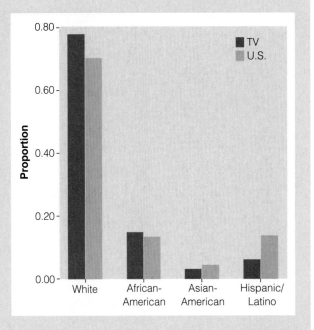

Race/Ethnicity	TV	U.S.
White	0.77	0.70
African-American	0.14	0.13
Asian-American	0.03	0.04
Hispanic/Latino	0.06	0.13

Continued

Question: How do the proportions observed for television characters compare to those for the general U.S. population?

Response: Some discrepancy is evident, in particular that whites (non-Hispanic) are more commonly seen on prime-time television, and Hispanics are under-represented.

Practice: *Try Exercise TBP 12.3(a,b) on page 962.*

If we took a random sample of "characters" from the general population of the United States, chances are their ethnicities would not conform perfectly to those shown in the table on the right, just because of the variability of random samples. To convince someone of inequity, inference is needed to demonstrate that the observed proportions are too different from what's true for the general population to have come about by chance.

EXAMPLE TBP 12.6 INFERENCE FOR SINGLE CATEGORICAL VARIABLE WITH SEVERAL CATEGORIES

Background: The number of characters examined in the preceding example was not reported, but let's assume it to have been 1,000, since 4 prime-time shows times 6 networks times at least 6 characters per show times 7 days a week would be at least 1,008.

When we looked for evidence of a relationship between two categorical variables, we compared the observed counts in each category combination with the counts expected if there were no relationship between the variables. Similarly, we will now compare the observed counts in each of the four racial/ethnic categories with what they would have been if they were perfectly representative of the make-up of the U.S. population.

Race/Ethnicity	Observed (TV)	Expected (U.S.)	$\dfrac{(Observed - Expected)^2}{Expected}$
White	770	700	7.00
African-American	140	130	0.77
Asian-American	30	40	2.50
Hispanic/Latino	60	130	37.69
			$\chi^2 = 47.96$

Since the degrees of freedom equal the number of possible categories minus one, and we are considering 4 racial/ethnic groups, we have 3 degrees of freedom. A sketch shows the behavior of this particular chi-square distribution.

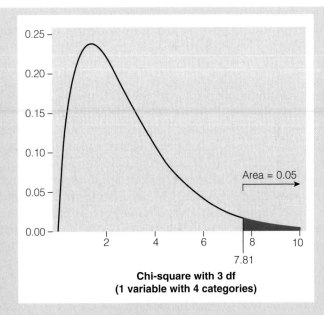

**Chi-square with 3 df
(1 variable with 4 categories)**

Question: Is there evidence of under-representation of some ethnic groups?

Response: Our conclusion of whether or not the television characters are a poor reflection of the actual population hinges on whether or not the chi-square statistic, 47.96, could be considered "large." For chi-square with 3 degrees of freedom, anything larger than 7.81 could be considered unusually large. Clearly, 47.96 is large enough to produce a P-value very close to zero, and we can reject the null hypothesis that the failure of characters' ethnicity to conform to that of the general population could have come about by chance. The fact that the largest component by far (37.69) is the one arising from a discrepancy in the Hispanic/Latino category indicates that this is the trouble spot. Apparently the networks are not airing shows with enough Hispanic characters to reflect the group's substantial share of our population.

Practice: *Try Exercise TBP 12.3(c–f) on page 962.*

The group Children Now feels it is important for children of all racial and ethnic groups to see characters like themselves on television. They also raise concerns about roles played by the characters, and compare percentages cast in the role of villain for various racial and ethnic groups.

12.2 Activities

Activity: Long-run Behavior of the Chi-Square Statistic

Using the Computer

The purpose of this activity is to examine behavior of the chi-square statistic and accompanying P-value in the long run for many tests of a true null hypothesis (that is, when two categorical variables are *not* related in the larger population).

Each student accesses data from the book's existing data file about several hundred students surveyed previously; specifically, they will work with the columns "Smoke" (whether the student smokes or not) and "Dec?" (major decided or not). As it happens, the two variables are completely independent for this large group of students: The proportion with a decided major is roughly 54%, both for smokers and nonsmokers. The chi-square statistic is approximately zero, and the *P*-value is approximately 1.

Each student takes a random sample of size 50 from the columns Smoke and Dec?, carries out a chi-square test, reports the value of the chi-square statistic and checks if the *P*-value is less than 0.05. This process should be repeated several times by each student so that as a group, the class has carried out 100 tests altogether. The instructor sketches a histogram of the chi-square statistics, and checks to see what proportion of the 100 tests have a *P*-value small enough (less than 0.05) to reject the (true) null hypothesis of no relationship between Smoke and Dec?. For those cases that rejected the null hypothesis, discuss whether each suggests smokers or nonsmokers are more likely to have decided on a major. Discuss what it means to reject the null hypothesis of no relationship at the 0.05 level.

In the Classroom

The purpose of this activity is to examine behavior of the chi-square statistic (and accompanying *P*-value) in the long run for many tests of a true null hypothesis (that is, when two categorical variables are *not* related in the larger population). Each student needs a calculator.

Suppose a population of job applicants consists of 50% each men and women, and no matter if the applicant is male or female, the chance of being qualified to be hired for a job in a large company is 10%. Thus, for the larger population, there is actually no relationship between gender and hiring.

The process of screening 100 job applicants can be simulated by taking a random sample of 100 digits and classifying them as follows: 0 corresponds to a male who is hired; 1 corresponds to a female who is hired; 2, 3, 4, 5 correspond to males who are not hired; 6, 7, 8, 9 correspond to females who are not hired. Each student takes a different set of 100 random digits from the table provided. (For classes of more than 25 students, other random digits tables can be used.) Each student fills out a table of observed counts like the one shown below by tallying the count of 0s, 1s, and numbers 2 through 5; the remaining count of numbers 6 through 9 can be found by subtracting the sum of other counts from 100. Then each student completes a table of expected counts and calculates the chi-square statistic. When all the students have finished, the instructor records their chi-square statistics and constructs a histogram to display them. Discuss the shape of the histogram and compare it to displays in the textbook showing the chi-square distribution for two-by-two tables.

Keeping in mind that for two-by-two tables, the *P*-value is less than 0.05 whenever chi-square is greater than 3.84, the class determines what percentage of their chi-square statistics are greater than 3.84, which is the percentage of *P*-values that are small enough to reject the null hypothesis of no relationship between gender and being hired by the company. For those cases that rejected the null hypothesis, discuss which type of error has been committed; discuss whether each suggests hiring practices that favor men or women. Discuss what it means to reject the null hypothesis of no relationship at the 0.05 level. [Note: Random digits sets #7 and #23 result in chi-square statistics that are greater than 3.84.]

Observed	Hired	Not Hired	Total
Male			
Female			
Total			

1	96096	92840	52519	78899	27039	17580	26875	09944	06974	46749
	55071	19471	18078	94511	46787	01623	92375	81014	31566	83506
2	85718	67598	88641	59194	98188	37349	22637	01611	52483	54868
	31654	12878	04674	55931	63102	85422	06966	21288	32329	61805
3	78911	24222	84117	01776	96593	25969	07396	32810	25817	53469
	24658	93522	48856	75202	74978	25023	90167	82304	88486	91752
4	51813	26099	05401	14877	74337	37024	13086	28646	30265	32235
	88723	40714	37650	07414	16172	00117	39790	23818	25212	56513
5	95113	73764	34201	62970	78494	71483	10925	68808	14589	67788
	48744	78026	00684	87684	81498	96138	72083	51802	47187	41394
6	17021	89767	89899	93622	64640	61577	22085	45211	86542	74229
	69332	29348	15094	02633	47199	48956	10556	88053	80600	90348
7	08890	90792	18647	30739	75012	59634	67748	62271	85035	85758
	07840	79350	44520	49984	99842	20633	70565	95674	41596	84836
8	10447	62342	50934	98579	95380	91600	02527	92099	09599	15385
	53385	99257	90076	53191	47936	37638	71779	74850	28347	84094
9	26880	09722	42643	09483	41456	23911	23289	19487	40416	46099
	65430	43221	30020	69010	98022	17067	71629	93730	14484	27266
10	01753	65202	75034	43340	68922	81113	41711	48873	05091	92216
	60703	99736	74500	04967	93278	36615	51169	03266	97652	71951
11	40037	03289	56387	75262	82092	14974	53444	68127	67591	62074
	90714	35317	34685	14750	32968	12741	92499	49509	10223	70346
12	06087	59808	81196	10098	14364	48182	14620	31729	01743	32908
	88097	74915	07346	43888	45615	73857	71830	88466	66428	13879
13	08123	21849	01980	53552	13040	08661	39498	60479	54639	07562
	57666	75252	47741	68435	07388	00509	24618	59973	40105	87228
14	63346	34036	91936	38910	58551	44716	37373	77263	72683	86254
	14030	71050	15985	71626	44748	54879	53104	13896	88449	64389
15	35272	93680	59466	57673	09324	03901	00369	90528	89444	54184
	50317	26638	81673	31792	13258	66646	08047	45627	52200	99799
16	48278	25046	61378	55919	30034	87434	76033	12086	78294	34774
	97856	39301	18118	05798	85243	74342	13347	84594	24432	35449
17	54045	57205	02630	46301	13773	65283	35036	83349	63720	49928
	27251	36542	80758	64552	08636	52149	05026	20774	90009	53183
18	36131	10510	36356	88512	92713	87649	83642	53545	52552	39323
	79323	62554	47790	75477	40056	38471	36082	79376	14076	58520
19	60483	16605	71260	50137	97323	90233	51991	48550	45921	41299
	22780	36291	08571	66506	59273	73954	95944	76293	10149	71851
20	49961	30805	48438	93348	40107	59022	44045	15491	46601	71037
	56461	11998	11701	62819	75495	77781	44897	18746	81498	21312
21	98612	50419	86764	48788	27283	88979	59157	24035	34701	86740
	62127	09812	06869	40387	34198	11217	56806	23655	28021	84879
22	90621	43489	72785	74519	43839	35963	72224	54069	33209	64948
	12792	82440	80066	58816	32124	02419	69506	29361	21182	81536
23	17400	47416	92191	16032	31208	62986	85789	15967	98763	20700
	58360	06007	71238	45608	38339	97618	99913	65338	97267	09760
24	71999	63617	46425	70256	63988	79593	20444	35473	82838	84194
	43015	72619	89435	60671	54544	11041	32073	15197	45634	18313
25	00514	04433	52235	78591	48706	64841	31506	71007	28759	24694
	75314	52525	14868	46802	96881	51607	16609	96325	24381	33841

12.3 Guide to Exercise Topics

Previewing inference for two categorical variables: 12.1, 12.19, 12.20, 12.21, 12.22, 12.23

Inference comparing two proportions: 12.2*, 12.3, 12.4*, 12.5*, 12.6*, 12.7, 12.8*, 12.9, 12.16(a–d), 12.27, 12.36, 12.37(a–g); Using Software: 12.44*(a,b), 12.46

Chi-square tests: Relating Chi-square to z: 12.10*, 12.11, 12.40(d),(e); Using Software: 12.44*(c,d); Table of Expected Counts: 12.12*(d–f), 12.13(d–f), 12.14(a,b), 12.32(a,b), 12.33(b), 12.35(a–c), 12.39(a–c); Chi-Square Distribution and Test: 12.12*, 12.13, 12.14, 12.17, 12.18, 12.24*, 12.25, 12.26, 12.28*, 12.29, 12.30*, 12.31*, 12.32, 12.33, 12.34, 12.35, 12.38, 12.39, 12.40(b), 12.41*, 12.42*, 12.43; Using Software: 12.45, 12.47, 12.48, 12.49*, 12.50, 12.51, 12.52, 12.53, 12.54, 12.55; Sample Size: 12.3(e), 12.15, 12.16(e), 12.17(b), 12.18(f,g), 12.37(h,i), 12.40(c)

12.4 Supplemental Exercises

12.1 Daniel Klein, a professor of economics at Santa Clara University, studied the political orientation of professors. He found that at Berkeley, Democrats outnumbered Republican faculty 9.9-to-1; at Stanford, Democrats outnumbered the Republicans 7.6-to-1. Among the humanities and social sciences, there were 16 Democrats for one Republican. His sample apparently included hundreds of professors. Discuss whether each of the following is a valid conclusion:

a. Democrats outnumber Republicans on all college campuses.

b. If Berkeley and Stanford are representative of all college campuses in terms of professors' political orientation, then the proportion of Democrats among all college professors is substantially higher than the proportion of Republicans.

c. Democrats are more interested in academic jobs so they can work for the public good and social justice.

d. Republicans are discriminated against when they apply for academic jobs.

12.2 A study by the European School Survey Project on Alcohol and Other Drugs (ESPAD) found that 277 in a sample of 543

15-to-16-year-olds in the Faroe Islands had consumed five or more alcoholic beverages in a row at least once in the past month, compared to 1,207 in a sample of 8,940 15-to-16-year-olds in Poland.

a. Report sample proportions who had consumed five or more alcoholic beverages in a row for the Faroe Islands and for Poland; are these denoted p_1 and p_2 or $\hat{p}_1$ and $\hat{p}_2$?

b. The chi-square statistic is 546. Is it extremely large because the sample proportions are so different, or because the sample sizes are quite large, or both of these, or neither of these?

c. What is the approximate P-value?

d. Express your conclusion two ways: first in terms of the variables excessive alcohol consumption and regions (Faroe Islands or Poland), then in terms of the parameters population proportion with excessive alcohol consumption in each of the two regions.

12.3 People in general, and those belonging to various demographic groups in particular, may have pronounced color preferences. Here are the counts preferring various colors in a sample of 446 university students.

Black	Blue	Green	Orange	Pink	Purple	Red	Yellow
35	193	64	13	37	53	35	16

a. If all these colors were liked by equal numbers of students, what proportion of students would prefer each color? What count would prefer each color?

b. Which two colors were preferred by disproportionately high numbers of sampled students, and which two by disproportionately low numbers?

c. Calculate the chi-square goodness-of-fit statistic.

d. How many degrees of freedom does the chi-square random variable have?

e. A chi-square random variable with degrees of freedom identified correctly in part (d) takes a value greater than 14 with probability 0.05. What can you say about the size of the P-value for this test?

f. Assuming these students are a representative sample, is there evidence that certain colors are preferred more than others in the general student population?

12.4 There may be a tendency at a certain university for students in some years of study to be more likely to take introductory statistics than students in other years. In a lab class of 20 undergraduate introductory statistics students, there were 2 first-year students, 13 second-year, 5 third-year, and 0 fourth-year.

a. If all years had equal numbers of students taking introductory statistics, what proportion, and what count, of students would be in each year?

b. Calculate the chi-square goodness-of-fit statistic.

c. How many degrees of freedom does the chi-square random variable have?

d. A chi-square random variable with degrees of freedom identified correctly in part (c) takes a value greater than 7.8 with probability 0.05. What can you say about the size of the P-value for this test?

e. Is there evidence that, in the general population of students, those in some years of study are more likely to take introductory statistics than those in other years?

12.5 An article entitled "Study Indicates Racial Disparity in Traffic Stops" reports on a study of 2,000 traffic stops by police in a certain city. "Overall, the study showed 25% of all stops during a six-month period involved black motorists, even though blacks account for 12% of the city's driving-age population. Whites were involved in 67% of the stops, but are 83% of the city's driving-age population."[1]

a. First, report the observed counts in the three possible race categories: black, white, and other.

b. Next, report the counts we would expect to see if those 2,000 motorists were exactly representative of the city's driving-age population.

c. Carry out a chi-square goodness-of-fit test: report the value of the chi-square statistic.

d. Refer to this sketch of the chi-square distribution with 2 degrees of freedom, and tell whether or not there is evidence that disproportionately many minorities are targeted by city police in traffic stops.

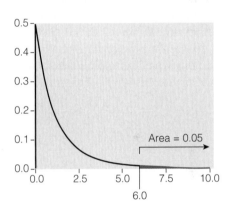

Chi-square with 2 df (2-by-3 table)

12.6 In 2005, public television stations were involved in a controversy over the airing of an episode of the children's program "Postcards from Buster," where an animated rabbit visited the home of a real child who had two (lesbian) mothers. One station reported receiving 28 calls and emails after the program was aired, 8 in support of the station and 11 against. We will assume that the remaining 9 calls were neutral.

a. If the population of viewers were evenly split into three categories—for, against, and neutral—what counts would we expect to see in each category for a sample of 28 viewers?

b. Carry out a chi-square goodness-of-fit test: Report the value of the chi-square statistic.

c. For 2 degrees of freedom, the probability of a chi-square statistic taking a value greater than 6 is 0.05. Does the study provide convincing evidence that viewers are unequally divided among the three categories, assuming that the viewers who contacted the station are representative of all viewers?

d. In fact, the proportion of viewers in one of the three categories is practically guaranteed to be *higher* in the general population than it was for the viewers who contacted the station: Which category is it?

12.7 "Selective Seed Abortion Affects the Performance of the Offspring in Bauhinia Ungulata" describes a study "in which ovules from either the stylar (treatments 1 and 2) or the basal (treatments 3 and 4) half of fruits were destroyed, to evaluate whether these patterns of selective seed abortion have an effect on the vigour of the offspring."[2] This table shows how many seeds did and did not germinate, when the first or second ovule in either the stylar or basal halves were destroyed with pin pricks, or when no ovules were destroyed (control).

	Germinated	Not Germinated	Total
Control	171	153	324
Treatment 1	66	130	196
Treatment 2	86	110	196
Treatment 3	96	100	196
Treatment 4	113	108	221

a. If germination is to be compared for all five conditions, state the null hypothesis in terms of the parameters population proportion germinated in each group.

b. Does the alternative state that all five population proportions differ, or that at least two of the five differ?

c. The highest sample proportion germinated is for the control group: 171/324 = 0.5278; calculate the other four proportions and report which treatment group has the lowest proportion germinated.

d. Use software to carry out a test; report the degrees of freedom, the value of the chi-square statistic, and the *P*-value.

e. What do you conclude about population proportions germinated under the various conditions?

f. Do you conclude that there is a relationship between what condition is imposed and whether or not the seed germinates?

g. Keeping in mind that treatments 1 and 2 involve destruction of a stylar ovule and treatments 3 and 4 involve destruction of a basal ovule, look at the sample proportions you found in part (c) and tell which type of ovule destruction seems to have more of an effect: stylar or basal?

h. Eliminate data for treatments 1 and 2 and repeat the chi-square test; report the degrees of freedom, the value of the chi-square statistic, and the *P*-value.

i. What do you conclude about population proportions germinated under the various conditions: control or treatment 3 or treatment 4?

j. The authors state that "Seed sets in fruits from treatments 1 and 2 showed a significantly lower (33–43%) percentage of germination; the germination of seeds from fruits in treatments 3 and 4 (49–51%) did not differ from control seeds." Is this supported by the conclusions you reached in part (e) and in part (i)? Explain.

12.8 "Combo of Two Blood Pressure Drugs Tied to Higher Deaths in Women" reports that in a study, "women who combined diuretics with calcium channel blockers—among the most frequently prescribed drugs for high blood pressure—had nearly twice as many fatal heart attacks and other cardiovascular deaths as women on diuretics plus beta blockers or ACE inhibitors. Still, the number of heart-related deaths was relatively small: 31 out of 1,223 women taking the calcium channel blocker combination versus 18 out of 1,380 on the beta blocker combination and 17 out of 1,413 on the ACE inhibitor duo."[3]

a. Note that the variables of interest are type of drugs taken and whether or not the women had a heart-related death. How many degrees of freedom does the chi-square statistic have?

b. Calculate the proportions of heart-related fatalities (to three decimal places) for the three groups and verify that the first is about twice as high as either of the other two.

c. Use software to test for a relationship between type of drug and suffering a heart-related death or not: Report the chi-square statistic and the P-value, and state whether or not the data provide statistical evidence of a relationship.

d. Examine the observed and expected counts, and the six terms of the chi-square statistic, and decide which one of these plays the most important role in the test's results:
   1. The number of women taking the calcium channel blocker combination who had a heart-related death was higher than what we'd expect if there were no relationship.
   2. The number of women not taking the calcium channel blocker combination who had a heart-related death was lower than what we'd expect if there were no relationship.

3. The number of women taking the beta blocker combination who had a heart-related death was lower than what we'd expect if there were no relationship.
4. The number of women taking the ACE inhibitor duo who had a heart-related death was lower than what we'd expect if there were no relationship.

e. A critic of the study noted that it "was based only on observations and was not a randomized trial—the gold standard of medical research—in which participants are randomly assigned treatment."[4] In other words, it is possible that the observed differences were due to a confounding variable, such as whether or not the woman's blood pressure problem was considered to be serious when the doctor decided which type of drug to prescribe. Explain how to design an observational study that takes this possible confounding variable into account.

12.5 Solutions to Supplemental Exercises

12.1 **a.** This is not a valid conclusion if we don't know the sampled campuses were representative of all campuses. **b.** This is a valid conclusion. **c.** This is just speculation, not a valid conclusion. **d.** This is also speculation.

12.2 **a.** $277/543 = 0.51$, $1207/8940 = 0.14$ denoted $\hat{p}_1$ and $\hat{p}_2$ **b.** both **c.** zero **d.** Alcohol consumption and region are related; population proportion differs for the two regions.

12.3 **a.** proportion 0.125, count 55.75 **b.** blue and green; orange and yellow **c.** 422.1 **d.** 7 **e.** The P-value is very small. **f.** yes

12.4 **a.** proportion 0.25, count 5 **b.** 19.6 **c.** 3 **d.** The P-value is very small. **e.** yes

12.5 **a.** $0.25(2,000) = 500$, $0.67(2,000) = 1,340$, $0.08(2,000) = 160$ **b.** $0.12(2,000) = 240$, $0.83(2,000) = 1,660$, $0.05(2,000) = 100$ **c.** $(500 - 240)^2/240 + (1,340 - 1,660)^2/1,660 + (160 - 100)^2/100 = 378.4$ **d.** Yes, there is evidence because the P-value is extremely small.

12.6 **a.** 9.33 in each **b.** $0.19 + 0.30 + 0.01 = 0.50$ **c.** no **d.** those who are neutral

12.7 **a.** $H_0: p_1 = p_2 = p_3 = p_4 = p_5$ **b.** At least two of the five differ. **c.** They are, respectively, 0.34 (lowest), 0.44, 0.49, 0.51. **d.** Degrees of freedom are $(5 - 1)(2 - 1) = 4$, chi-square $= 20.907$, P-value $= 0.000$. **e.** Population proportions differ. **f.** yes **g.** stylar **h.** Degrees of freedom are $(3-1)(2-1) = 2$, chi-square $= 0.708$, P-value $= 0.702$. **i.** They may be equal. **j.** Yes, because the difference was significant when the first two treatments were included: not significant when only the second two treatments were compared to control.

12.8 **a.** $(3 - 1)(2 - 1) = 2$ **b.** $31/1,223 = 0.025$, $18/1,380 = 0.013$, $17/1,413 = 0.012$; 0.025 is about twice 0.013 or 0.012. **c.** Chi-square $= 8.687$, P-value $= 0.013$; the data do provide evidence of a relationship. **d.** (1) **e.** Separate women first according to how serious their condition was judged to be by their doctors.

TBP Chapter 13

Inference for Relationships between Two Quantitative Variables

13.1 Details and Examples

Our opening example in Chapter 13 concerns the relationship between ages of students' mothers and fathers. Before using software in Example 13.2 on page 630 to specify the nature of the relationship, we can encourage students to think about what their common sense would suggest.

EXAMPLE TBP 13.1 INTUITING THE RELATIONSHIP FOR THE SAMPLE AND FOR THE POPULATION

Background: We are interested in the relationship between ages of students' mothers and their fathers.

Question: How would we expect these variables to be related for a sample of students and for the larger population of students?

Response: Because couples tend to have ages that are reasonably close to one another, we would expect the mother to be on the young side if the father is young, and on the old side if the father is old. There is reason to expect a rather steady increase in the variable MotherAge as values of the variable FatherAge increase. Therefore, we do expect the relationship to be positive and linear, not just for a sample of age pairs but also for the larger population.

Practice: *Try Exercise 13.2(a) on page 646.*

Regression Hypotheses

This example supplements our discussion on page 639 of the formulation of null and alternative hypotheses in regression.

EXAMPLE TBP 13.2 THE NULL AND ALTERNATIVE HYPOTHESES IN REGRESSION INFERENCE

Background: We are interested in several possible relationships between quantitative variables: mother's age and father's age for all students, percentages voting Democratic and Republican for all 50 states, and ratings of professor's teaching and how easy or difficult their courses are for a population of professors.

Questions: How would we formulate null and alternative hypotheses to answer the following?

1. Is there statistical evidence of a relationship between mother's age and father's age for all students?

2. Based on information from a sample of 4 states, can we conclude that for all states there is a negative relationship between percentage voting Democratic and percentage voting Republican?

3. A website called "ratemyprofessors.com" reports students' ratings of their professors at universities around the country. These are unofficial in that they are not monitored by the universities themselves. Besides listing average rating of the professors' teaching on a scale of 1 to 5, where 1 is the worst and 5 is the best, there is also a rating of how easy their courses are, where 1 is the hardest and 5 is the easiest. Is there a relationship between the rating of teaching and the rating of ease?

Responses:

1. We could pose the first question as $H_0 : \beta_1 = 0$ versus $H_a : \beta_1 \neq 0$ where β_1 is the slope of the line that relates ages of fathers and mothers for the entire population of students. Because common sense would tell us to expect a positive relationship, we may go so far as to formulate the alternative as one-sided: $H_0 : \beta_1 = 0$ versus $H_a : \beta_1 > 0$.

2. For the second question, we would write $H_0 : \beta_1 = 0$ versus $H_a : \beta_1 < 0$.

3. Offhand, we may suspect that students would favor easy teachers, in which case the relationship between professor's rating and course's level of easiness would be positive. On the other hand, teachers who are more conscientious might maintain higher standards, not just for their students but also for themselves. Thus, because the direction could really go either way, we should keep a more general two-sided alternative, writing $H_0 : \beta_1 = 0$ versus $H_a : \beta_1 \neq 0$.

Practice: *Try Exercise 13.9 on page 648.*

Confidence Interval for the Population Slope β_1

To supplement Example 13.10 on page 644, we can discuss a confidence interval for the slope of the regression line in our parent age example. Ages of students' fathers and mothers produced the following regression output.

```
Pearson correlation of FatherAge and MotherAge = 0.781
P-Value = 0.000

The regression equation is
MotherAge = 14.5 + 0.666 FatherAge
431 cases used 15 cases contain missing values
Predictor        Coef      SE Coef           T          P
Constant        14.542        1.317       11.05      0.000
FatherAge      0.66576      0.02571       25.89      0.000
S = 3.288        R-Sq = 61.0%      R-Sq(adj) = 60.9%
```

The fact that the correlation r is $+0.781$ tells us there is a fairly strong positive relationship between x and y data values. Based on the fact that $b_1 = 0.666$, our best guess for how MotherAge responds to FatherAge is to predict that if one student's father is 1 year older than a second student's father, his mother would be 0.666 years older than the second student's mother. By now, we know enough about behavior of samples to realize that there must be some margin of error attached to this slope. For every additional year of FatherAge in the population, does MotherAge tend to be an additional 0.666 years, give or take about 0.1 years? Or 0.666 years, give or take about 1 year? As usual, the size of the margin of error will supply important information. In the former case, having evidence that population slope is in the interval $(+0.566, +0.766)$ would convince us of a positive relationship, whereas in the latter case, where the range of plausible values $(-0.334, +1.666)$ for unknown population slope straddles zero, we could not claim to have statistical evidence of a relationship.

The confidence interval can be requested using software, or it can be constructed from the usual regression summaries if the correct multiplier from the t distribution is known.

EXAMPLE TBP 13.3 INTERVAL ESTIMATE FOR SLOPE OF REGRESSION LINE FOR POPULATION

Background: For a sample of students, mother's age was regressed on father's age:

Predictor	Coef	SE Coef	T	P
Constant	14.542	1.317	11.05	0.000
FatherAge	0.66576	0.02571	25.89	0.000

Question: If one father is a year older than another, what is an interval estimate for how much older (if at all) we expect the mother to be?

Response: The point estimate b_1 for the unknown slope β_1 of the line that relates the variables MotherAge and FatherAge in the larger population is shown not only in the regression equation, but also as the coefficient of FatherAge in the second row of the output table.

It is reported to 5 decimal places as 0.66576, and its standard error, 0.02571, appears in the next column. The output shows our sample size to be 431, and so there are 429 degrees of freedom. With such a large sample, the t multiplier is virtually identical to the z multiplier for 95% confidence, which is approximately 2. Our 95% confidence interval for β_1 is

$$0.666 \pm 2(0.02571) = 0.666 \pm 0.051 = (0.615, 0.717)$$

More specifically, for every additional year of FatherAge, we are 95% confident that the corresponding value of MotherAge is an additional 0.617 to 0.715 years.

Practice: *Try Exercise 13.15(b) on page 650.*

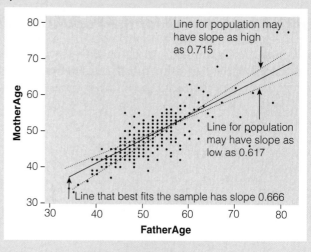

The fact that the confidence interval for the slope of the line relating mother's age to father's age for all students contains only positive numbers suggests evidence of a positive relationship between fathers' and mothers' ages in the population. This is consistent with the small P-value (0.000) obtained in the hypothesis test about the slope.

In practice, a confidence interval is most useful as a way of estimating the extent to which one variable responds to another, once we have established via a hypothesis test that our two quantitative variables are in fact related.

Our first step in learning to perform inference about proportions in Chapter 9 was to set up a confidence interval. By checking if the interval contained a proposed value of population proportion, we were able to make a rather informal decision as to whether that value was plausible, based on whether or not the value was contained in the interval. Later in the chapter we learned to carry out a formal test of hypotheses about unknown population proportion, expressing two opposing points of view and following four basic steps.

Similarly, we used the confidence interval in our example above to informally conclude that the value of β_1 is not zero. A more formal way to reach this conclusion is by carrying out a test of hypotheses.

Details of Confidence and Prediction Intervals

On page 656, we discussed various influences on our prediction intervals or confidence intervals for individual or mean responses in regression. If there were no relationship between the explanatory and response values, the prediction interval would be no different from the interval that extends two ordinary standard deviations (s_y) in y on either side of the mean response. If there is a strong relationship between explanatory and response values, the prediction interval is noticeably more precise than the interval obtained without taking the explanatory value into account.

EXAMPLE TBP 13.4 NARROWER INTERVALS IN A STRONGER RELATIONSHIP

Background: Example 13.1 on page 629 pointed out that we can better pinpoint the unknown slope of a relationship in the larger population if the relationship is strong, with little scatter about the regression line. For a sample of schools, we considered the regression of average Math SAT scores on average Verbal SAT scores, which was quite strong, with $r = 0.97$. In contrast, the regression of average Math SAT scores on the percentage of teachers with advanced degrees was moderate-to-weak, with $r = 0.41$. Now we have produced interval estimates for average Math score when average Verbal score takes its mean value, and when percentage with advanced degrees takes its mean value.

```
New Obs      Fit      SE Fit        95.0% CI              95.0% PI
1          533.96       2.36    ( 528.38,  539.55)   ( 516.30,  551.62)
New Obs      Fit      SE Fit        95.0% CI              95.0% PI
1          534.36       8.75    ( 513.67,  555.05)   ( 468.92,  599.80)
```

Question: How do the intervals compare?

Response: Both the confidence and the prediction intervals are much narrower for the first regression (average Math on average Verbal), with approximate widths 11 and 35, compared with widths 41 and 131 for the second regression (average Math on percentage with advanced degrees).

Practice: *Try Exercise 13.25 on page 661.*

Although it is strongly recommended to use software to produce prediction intervals and confidence intervals in regression, for the sake of completeness we include this material to supplement the discussion on page 656.

Because the t distribution applies, the multiplier for either the prediction interval or the confidence interval will be close to 2 for large samples, and not much higher than 3 for very small samples. The only difference between the confidence and prediction intervals arises from the standard error.

The formula for the standard error corresponding to a prediction interval for a given explanatory value x^* is rather daunting:

$$s\sqrt{1 + \frac{1}{n} + \frac{(x^* - \bar{x})^2}{(x_1 - \bar{x})^2 + \cdots + (x_n - \bar{x})^2}}$$

but we should note that as long as the sample size n is large, the term $\frac{1}{n}$ inside the square root will be negligible. Furthermore, if the sample is large, the denominator of the third term tends to be considerably larger than the numerator, and this term is also negligible. Therefore, for large samples, the standard error for a prediction error is roughly $s\sqrt{1} = s$. For very small samples, the term $\frac{1}{n}$ makes some contribution and the standard error is somewhat more than s: As usual, smaller samples have the effect of rendering our predictions less precise. Also, if x^* is quite far from the mean $\bar{x}$, then there will be some noticeable contribution from the third term. In the best-case scenario, where the sample is large and the given value x^* is close to the mean, the standard error for predicting an individual response to x^* is roughly equal to s, and the prediction interval is roughly equal to the estimated response plus or minus $2s$.

The formula for standard error corresponding to the confidence interval for mean response to a given explanatory value x^* is also quite involved:

$$s\sqrt{\frac{1}{n} + \frac{(x^* - \bar{x})^2}{(x_1 - \bar{x})^2 + \cdots + (x_n - \bar{x})^2}}$$

However, as long as x^* is pretty *close* to $\bar{x}$, the expression inside the square root is dominated by $\frac{1}{n}$, and the standard error is approximately $s\left(\sqrt{\frac{1}{n}}\right) = \frac{s}{\sqrt{n}}$. Just as when we set up a simple confidence interval for the mean of a quantitative variable, under ideal conditions we can estimate the spread of sample mean values with standard deviation divided by square root of sample size.

On the other hand, when predicting the mean response to an explanatory value that is *far* from the mean of all explanatory values, there is a substantial contribution from the numerator $(x^* - \bar{x})^2$ of the second term, and the standard error is considerably larger than $\frac{s}{\sqrt{n}}$.

To get a general feel for the two standard errors, it may help to note that they differ only in that $1 + \frac{1}{n}$ plus the messy term involving distances from $\bar{x}$ appears inside the square root sign for the prediction interval, as opposed to just $\frac{1}{n}$ plus the same last term for the confidence interval. Thus, under the ideal circumstances of a large sample size and an explanatory value close to the mean, the biggest contributor to the standard error for a prediction interval is $s(\sqrt{1}) = s$, whereas the biggest contributor for a confidence interval is $s\left(\sqrt{\frac{1}{n}}\right) = \frac{s}{\sqrt{n}}$.

Here are some general guidelines for understanding the prediction interval for an individual response and the confidence interval for a mean response in the regression setting.

Both 95% prediction interval (PI) and 95% confidence interval (CI) should be obtained in the regression setting by using software.

The **95% prediction interval** for an individual response to a given explanatory value x^* is

estimate $\pm$ margin of error $=$ estimate $\pm$ multiplier (standard error)

where

- the estimate is $\hat{y} = b_0 + b_1 x^*$, the predicted response to x^*
- the multiplier is from the t distribution with $n - 2$ degrees of freedom, corresponding to 95% confidence
- the standard error estimates spread of *individual* sample responses about unknown population mean response

For large samples, the multiplier is approximately 2 and the standard error is approximately s, where

$$s = \sqrt{\frac{(y_1 - \hat{y}_1)^2 + \cdots + (y_n - \hat{y}_n)^2}{n - 2}}$$

is the typical residual size in the sample.

The **95% confidence interval** for mean of all responses to a given explanatory value x^* is

estimate $\pm$ margin of error $=$ estimate $\pm$ multiplier (standard error)

where

- the estimate is $\hat{y} = b_0 + b_1 x^*$, the predicted response to x^*
- the multiplier is from the t distribution with $n - 2$ degrees of freedom, corresponding to 95% confidence
- the standard error estimates spread of sample *mean* response about unknown population mean response

For large samples, the multiplier is approximately 2. If the sample size is large *and* x^* is relatively close to $\bar{x}$, the standard error is approximately $\frac{s}{\sqrt{n}}$.

To review regression interval estimates at the end of Section 13.2, we consider the following situation, where four students discuss the relationship between professor evaluations posted on the website www.ratemyprofessors.com and the official university evaluations that are also available online at some schools.

Students Talk Stats

An Application of Regression Interval Estimates

*F*our students are thinking about signing up for a course by a professor with a RateMyProf rating of 4.0. The university ratings website lists ratings for two professors with that same last name: One is a 3.5 and the other is 5.0. The students would like to figure out which is more likely to correspond to the RateMyProf rating of 4.0. They begin by looking at summaries of the two variables for a random sample of 22 professors.

Students Talk Stats continued →

Students Talk Stats continued

Variable	N	N*	Mean	Median	TrMean	StDev
RateMyProf	22	0	3.765	4.000	3.838	1.199
UniversityRating	22	0	4.280	4.500	4.311	0.585

Variable	SE Mean	Minimum	Maximum	Q1	Q3
RateMyProf	0.250	1.000	5.000	3.000	4.800
UniversityRating	0.125	2.930	5.000	4.023	4.750

Adam: *"The mean for RateMyProf is 3.765 and for UniversityRating is 4.280, which is about half a point higher. So if this professor was rated 4.0 by RateMyProf, his UniversityRating should be 4.5. That doesn't match either 3.5 or 5.0, so maybe it's a third guy with the same last name."*

Brittany: *"Just because one mean is higher than the other, you don't know the individual values are related. And even if they are, the relationship isn't going to be perfect, so you can't make an exact prediction. You have to look at the scatterplot first and then do a regression and a prediction interval if it looks linear."*

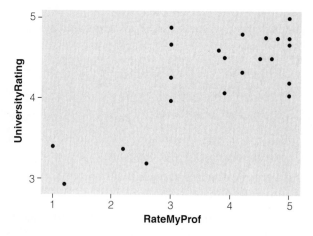

The scatterplot looks positive and linear, so you can regress UniversityRating on RateMyProf and request a prediction interval for UniversityRating when RateMyProf equals 4.

```
The regression equation is
UniversityRating = 2.95 + 0.353 RateMyProf
Predictor        Coef      SE Coef         T         P
Constant       2.9536       0.2830     10.44     0.000
RateMyPr      0.35315      0.07180      4.92     0.000
S = 0.4036      R-Sq = 54.7%     R-Sq(adj) = 52.5%
Predicted Values for New Observations
New Obs    Fit      SE Fit        95.0% CI            95.0% PI
1       4.3662      0.0878   ( 4.1830, 4.5494) ( 3.5047, 5.2277)
Values of Predictors for New Observations
New Obs RateMyPr
1          4.00
```

Carlos: *"There really does seem to be a relationship between the two types of rating, because the P-value is 0.000. And it must be fairly strong, because r is the square root of 0.547, which is more than 0.7. But neither 3.5 nor 5.0 falls in the 95% confidence interval, so maybe Adam's right and neither of the two ratings is the one we're looking for."*

Students Talk Stats continued →

Students Talk Stats continued

> **Dominique:** *"The confidence interval is telling you where the* mean *of all university ratings should be when the RateMyProf rating was 4. We want to know where* one *professor's rating is likely to be, so we look at the prediction interval. Since 5.0 is well within the interval from 3.5047 to 5.2277, and 3.5 is just outside, I think it's probably the professor with the UniversityRating of 5.0. We should sign up for his course."*

The above discussion by four students includes output with confidence and prediction interval estimates. Notice that we could have roughly approximated the 95% *prediction* interval by taking 2 standard deviations on either side of the estimated UniversityRating for when RateMyProf equals 4. The estimate itself is $2.95 + 0.353(4) = 4.362$ and because $s = 0.4036$, we take

$$4.362 \pm 2(0.4036) = (3.55, 5.17),$$

which is reasonably close to the prediction interval reported in the output, (3.5047, 5.2277).

The standard error for a *confidence* interval is roughly $\frac{s}{\sqrt{n}} = \frac{0.4036}{\sqrt{22}} = 0.0860$. If we take 2 standard errors on either side of the estimate 4.362, we get the interval

$$4.362 \pm 2(0.0860) = (4.19, 4.53),$$

which is fairly close to the confidence interval reported in the output, (4.1830, 4.5494). Note, however, that the interval may have been too narrow if we'd been making a prediction for a RateMyProf value like 2.0, which is quite far from the mean 3.765 of all RateMyProf values.

13.2　Activities

Activity: Distribution of Sample Slope

Using the Computer

This activity gives students a look at the long-run behavior of sample slope when sampling at random from a population relationship whose regression line has a certain known slope. It also shows students the role played by sample size in whether or not the null hypothesis of no relationship between two quantitative variables can be rejected.

Each student accesses data from the book's existing data file about several hundred students surveyed previously. Specifically, they will work with the columns Height and Shoe (shoe size). First, the relationship between these two variables should be displayed with a scatterplot and summarized with a regression equation. Note that the relationship is linear, moderately strong and positive ($r = +0.85$). The slope of the regression line for this population is $\beta_1 = +0.422$ when Shoe is regressed on Height.

Each student uses software to take a random sample of 4 paired values for Height and Shoe, stored in HeightSmallSample and ShoeSmallSample. Each student regresses ShoeSmallSample on HeightSmallSample and reports the slope b_1 and *P*-value. The instructor constructs a histogram of sample slopes b_1 for the class, and together the class discusses center, spread, and shape of the distribution of b_1. They also check to see how many *P*-values are small enough (less than 0.05) to reject the null hypothesis that $\beta_1 = 0$, thus concluding that the sample provides evidence of a (linear) relationship between Height and Shoesize in the larger population from which the sample was taken.

Next, each student takes a random sample of 10 paired values for Height and Shoe, stored in HeightLargeSample and ShoeLargeSample. Each student regresses ShoeLargeSample on HeightLargeSample and reports the slope b_1 and P-value. The instructor constructs a histogram of sample slopes b_1 for the class, and together the class discusses center, spread, and shape of the distribution of b_1 for the larger samples. They also check to see how many P-values are small enough (less than 0.05) to reject the null hypothesis that $\beta_1 = 0$, and discuss how sample size impacts the ability of a sample to produce evidence of a relationship in the larger population.

In the Classroom

This activity gives students a look at the long-run behavior of sample slope when sampling at random from a population relationship whose regression line has a certain known slope.

Each student reports his or her height to the nearest inch, and shoe size. These are written on the board along with a number to identify 1st, 2nd, 3rd, and so on to the nth student in the class. If time permits, a scatterplot is sketched on the board to show that the relationship appears linear, moderately strong, and positive. The instructor uses a calculator to solve for the slope β_1 of the line regressing shoe size on height for the entire class, which is taken to be the population. The regression line can be sketched onto the scatterplot.

Now each student uses a different line from the table of random digits presented in the activity for Chapter 7 to randomly select another student's height and shoe size from the n pairs listed on the board. (For example, if there are 35 students in the class, then usable labels consist of the pairs 01 through 35; the first student should use line 1 and will sample student #03; the second student should use line 2 and will sample student #16, since 52, 49, and 85 are not usable; the third student should use line 3 and will sample student #22, and so on.)

0	3	3	7	9	1	0	3	9	7	2	5
5	2	4	9	8	5	1	6	1	4	0	2
2	2	2	5	5	6	4	6	3	5	6	2

Together with his or her own height and shoe size, each student now has a sample of two height/shoe pairs, from which the sample slope can be calculated as b_1 = (Shoe2 minus Shoe1)/(Height2 minus Height 1). Discuss under what conditions the sample slope would turn out to be negative. Also discuss what happens to the slope if both students happen to have the same height.

The most extreme sample lines can be sketched onto the scatterplot to show the wide range of possible sample slopes that arise. Discuss how results would differ if samples of more than just two height/shoe pairs had been taken. The instructor constructs a histogram of sample slopes b_1 for the class and together the class discusses center, spread, and shape of the distribution of b_1, and how these relate to the known population slope β_1.

13.3 Guide to Exercise Topics

The role of s; summarizing relationships between two quantitative variables in the sample and in the population: 13.1*, 13.2*, 13.5*(a–j), 13.17, 13.27, 13.28, 13.29*, 13.30, 13.31, 13.32, 13.41*(a,b), 13.42*, 13.46(a–d)

The regression model and the distribution of b_1: 13.3, 13.4, 13.5(k–m), 13.6*, 13.7, 13.8*(a–c), 13.13*(a), 13.34*, 13.35, 13.36*, 13.37, 13.38, 13.39

Hypothesis tests and confidence intervals for the slope of the regression line: 13.5(l–n), 13.8*(d,e), 13.9*, 13.10*, 13.11, 13.12*, 13.13*, 13.14, 13.15*, 13.16, 13.40, 13.41*, 13.42*(e–g), 13.43, 13.44, 13.45, 13.59; Using Software: 13.50*, 13.51, 13.52, 13.53, 13.56, 13.57, 13.58

Prediction intervals for an individual response and confidence intervals for a mean response: 13.18*, 13.19, 13.20*, 13.21*, 13.22, 13.23, 13.24, 13.25*, 13.26, 13.46, 13.47, 13.48, 13.49*, 13.54*, 13.55, 13.56

13.4 Supplemental Exercises

13.1 "In Salary Arbitration, Old Math Matters Most," published in the *New York Times* in 2005, explained that for baseball players, "Salary arbitration hearings allow the club and the player to argue for one salary or another based largely on the player's statistics and how the statistics compare to those of similar players."[1] Below are batting averages and following year's salaries (in millions) for some players in 2004, along with number of home runs hit the previous season:

Player	Batting Average	Salary (in millions)	Home Runs
Lance Berkman	0.316	10.500	30
Carlos Lee	0.305	8.000	31
Mike Lowell	0.276	6.500	32
Aubrey Huff	0.297	4.917	29
Craig Wilson	0.264	3.000	29
Erubiel Durazo	0.259	2.100	21

a. Use software to produce a scatterplot of salary versus batting average, and verify that its appearance is linear.

b. Regress salary on batting average: Report the equation of the regression line, the value of the correlation, and the *P*-value.

c. Based on the small *P*-value, choose two appropriate conclusions from the following:
   1. There is evidence of a relationship between salary and batting average in the larger population of players.
   2. There is no evidence of a relationship between salary and batting average in the larger population of players.
   3. There is evidence that the slope of the regression line relating salary to batting average in the larger population of players is not zero.
   4. The slope of the regression line relating salary to batting average in the larger population of players could be zero.

d. Note that Durazo's salary is a bit lower than the rest, but it is his low value of the explanatory variable (only 21 home runs) that would make him especially unusual if salary were regressed on home runs. Would this tend to make Durazo's scatterplot point one with a large residual or one with a large amount of influence on the regression line?

e. Regress salary on homeruns: Report the equation of the regression line, the value of the correlation, and the *P*-value.

f. Explain why the regressions suggest that batting average should have more impact on salary than number of home runs does.

g. At the time the article was written, Cubs player Aramis Ramirez's salary was under negotiation to be either $8 million or $10.25 million. The regression line predicts someone with his batting average (0.318) to earn a salary of $9.705 million. Which of the two proposed salaries ($8 or $10.25 million) comes closer to this prediction?

h. Another player whose salary was under negotiation at the time was Shea Hillenbrand of the Blue Jays, whose batting average was 0.310 (but number of home runs was only 15). Use this output to decide whether either, both, or neither of his proposed salaries ($3.450 or $4.350 million) is reasonable, based on the regression on batting average. Explain your answer briefly.

```
BattingA    Fit     SE Fit       95.0% CI            95.0% PI
0.310      8.733    0.967   (  6.048,  11.418)  (  3.604,  13.862)
```

13.2 Refer to the preceding exercise on baseball players' salaries. The article also included information on pitchers' salaries (in millions) and ratio of games won to lost, which can be converted to proportion of games won.

Player	Proportion Won	Salary
Mark Buehrle	0.50	30.500
C. C. Sabathia	0.59	2.700
Roy Halladay	0.76	6.000
Brad Penny	0.58	3.725

a. Produce a scatterplot of the data and regress salary on proportion of games won to report the correlation r and the P-value.

b. The P-value is not small enough to convince us that salary and proportion of games won are related in the larger population of pitchers. Does this seem to be due to the fact that the sample values themselves show no increase in salary as proportion of games won increases, or because the sample size is too small?

c. Using $\alpha = 0.05$ as the cutoff, would the P-value have been small enough to reject $\beta_1 = 0$ if a one-sided test had been carried out?

d. Roy Oswalt of the Astros, whose games had 0.67 as the proportion of wins, was under negotiation to receive a salary of $7.8 or $6.0 million. Use this output to decide if either, both, or neither of these proposed salaries is reasonable:

```
New Obs     Fit    SE Fit       95.0% CI            95.0% PI
1          4.659   0.568   (  2.217,  7.101)  (  -0.092,  9.411)
```

13.3 The Quantitative Environmental Learning Project reported on environmentalists' concerns that chicken farms are a source of groundwater pollution: "In this study, monitoring wells were installed at five Florida broiler farms and monitored quarterly from March 1992 through January 1993."[2] Among collected data were nitrate and potassium concentrations, in milligrams per Liter:

Potassium	1.5	1.8	1.6	1.3	0.7	0.7	0.6	0.6	0.4	0.4	0.4	0.1
Nitrate	18	19	20	21	9.4	10	11	26	5.2	5.4	5.0	4.9

a. Use software to produce a scatterplot of nitrate versus potassium. Report the potassium and nitrate values for the conspicuous outlier in the plot.

b. Regress nitrate on potassium; report the regression equation, the correlation r, the P-value, and typical residual size s.

c. If you had regressed potassium on nitrate (instead of nitrate on potassium), which of these would be different: the value of r, or the equation of the regression line, or both, or neither?

d. Produce a 95% confidence interval for mean nitrate concentration for all water samples whose potassium concentration is 1 mg/L, and a 95% prediction interval for individual nitrate concentration when potassium is 1 mg/L.

e. Report the widths of your confidence and prediction intervals, to the nearest tenth (one decimal place).

f. Delete the outlier and again regress nitrate on potassium. Report the new regression equation, the correlation r, the P-value, and typical residual size s.

g. With the outlier deleted, produce 95% confidence and prediction intervals when potassium concentration is 1 mg/L.

h. Report the widths of your new confidence and prediction intervals, to the nearest tenth (one decimal place).

i. Comment on the role that outliers can play in regression inference procedures, in terms of how accurately we can estimate response or mean response to a given explanatory value.

j. Tell whether each of the following focuses on data production, displaying and summarizing data, probability, or statistical inference:

  1. Reporting an interval that has a 95% chance of containing mean nitrate concentration for all water samples whose potassium concentration is 1 mg/mL.

  2. Deciding which chicken farms are to be included in the study.

  3. Finding the intercept b_0 and slope b_1 of the line that best fits the data.

13.4 A large sample of students was surveyed at a particular university. Among other things, they were asked to report their Math and Verbal SAT scores.

a. An example in this chapter regressed *mean* Math SAT score on *mean* Verbal SAT score for a sample of nine schools. Would that regression tend to have more scatter or less scatter than a regression of Math SAT on Verbal SAT for *individual* students?

b. Use software to access the student survey data and regress Math on Verbal scores. Which observations tend to be more influential: those with extreme Math or extreme Verbal values?

c. Which observations tend to be outliers, in the sense of having large residuals: those with extreme Math or extreme Verbal values?

d. If we took Verbal scores to be the response instead of the explanatory variable, tell whether each of these would change: the equation of the regression line; the value of s; the value of r.

e. Report the correlation and the P-value, and use them to summarize the relationship (if any) between Math and Verbal SAT scores in the larger population of students from which the sample was obtained.

USING TABLES: TWO QUANTITATIVE VARIABLES [SEE END OF BOOK]

13.5 In Exercise 13.43, the P-value for a (two-sided) test of a relationship between shyness and physical attributes for a sample of 34 lizards was reported to be 0.026. Since regression degrees of freedom would be $34 - 2 = 32$, refer to the t table for 30 degrees of freedom to report an approximate range for the t statistic, keeping in mind that the single tail probability would be $0.026/2 = 0.013$.

13.6 Exercise 13.13 reported a regression P-value of 0.230 in testing for a relationship between percentage of businesses exporting to and importing from China in a sample of 8 countries. Since regression degrees of freedom would be $8 - 2 = 6$, refer to the t table for 6 degrees of freedom to report an approximate range for the t statistic, keeping in mind that the single tail probability would be $0.230/2 = 0.115$.

13.7 Exercise 13.14 found a t statistic of 0.36 in testing for a relationship between rental rates and vacancy rates for 13 areas in a city. Degrees of freedom are $13 - 2 = 11$; to be conservative we would refer to the t table using 10 degrees of freedom. What does the table tell us about the size of the (two-sided) P-value?

13.5 Solutions to Supplemental Exercises

13.1 a.

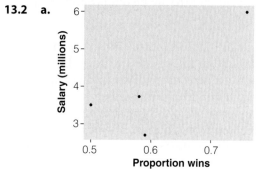

The form is linear.   **b.** Salary = −28.9 + 122 Batting Average, $r = +0.89$, P-value is 0.016.
c. (1) and (3)   **d.** one with a large amount of influence on the regression line   **e.** Salary = −9.31 + 0.529 Home Runs, $r − +0.66$, P-value is 0.154.   **f.** because the regression on batting average has a small P-value and a value of r closer to 1   **g.** $10.25 is closer.   **h.** $4.35 million is reasonable, in that it is contained in the 95% prediction interval for salary when batting average is 3.10; $3.45 million is not.

13.2 a.

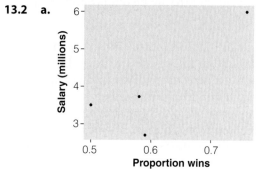

$r = +0.84$, P-value is 0.162   **b.** because sample size (4) is too small   **c.** No (P-value would be 0.081, still larger than 0.05)   **d.** either

13.3 a. potassium 0.6, nitrate 26

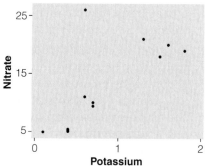

b. Nitrate = 4.90 + 9.52 Potassium, correlation $r = 0.71$, P-value 0.010, $s = 5.536$ **c.** the equation of the regression line   **d.** CI = (10.70, 18.13), PI = (1.53, 27.30)   **e.** 18.13 − 10.70 is about 7.4, 27.3 − 1.53 is about 25.8   **f.** Nitrate = 2.46 + 10.7 Potassium, correlation $r = 0.95$, P-value 0.000, $s = 2.189$ **g.** CI = (11.642, 14.718), PI = (7.995,18.366)   **h.** 14.718 − 11.642 is about 3.1, 18.366 − 7.995 is about 10.4   **i.** Confidence and prediction intervals were more than twice as wide with the single outlier included compared to with the outlier omitted: The outlier made it difficult to estimate response or mean response accurately.   **j.** (1) statistical inference (2) data production (3) displaying and summarizing

13.4 a. less scatter   **b.** Verbal   **c.** Math   **d.** The equation of the regression line would change; the value of s would change; the value of r would not.   **e.** $r = 0.384$, P-value is 0.000; there is strong evidence of a moderately weak relationship between Math and Verbal SAT scores in the larger population.

13.5 Since 0.013 is between 0.01 and 0.025, t should be approximately between 2.042 and 2.457 in absolute value.

13.6 Since 0.115 is greater than 0.05, t must be less than 1.943 in absolute value.

13.7 Since 0.36 is less than 1.812, the P-value is greater than 2(0.05) = 0.10.

13.6   Review of Part IV

In Chapters 9 through 13, we have covered inference procedures for the five possible variable situations:

1. **One categorical variable:** Set up a confidence interval or carry out a hypothesis test for the unknown population proportion p in the category of interest. These are based on a sample proportion $\hat{p}$ that standardizes to z, assuming the sample is large enough.

2. **One quantitative variable:** Set up a confidence interval or carry out a hypothesis test for the unknown population mean response μ. These are based on a sample mean that standardizes to z if σ is known or (by hand) if the sample is large. They are based on a standardized t statistic if σ is unknown. Whether z or t is used, the sample must be large enough to offset non-normality in the distribution of the quantitative variable's values.

3. **Categorical explanatory and quantitative response variable:** Depending on the study design, test for a relationship using paired t, two-sample t, or F (ANOVA). If there is evidence of a relationship, confidence intervals can be constructed to estimate the impact of the explanatory variable on the response.

4. **Relationship between two categorical variables:** If each of the two variables has just two possible values, a z test can be performed to determine if the proportion in the response of interest is significantly higher, lower, or different for one group compared to the other. If the difference is significant, a confidence interval can be constructed to estimate the extent of the difference for the larger populations. More generally, a chi-square procedure can be used to test for a relationship between the two variables.

5. **Relationship between two quantitative variables:** As long as the relationship appears linear, test if the slope β_1 of the regression line for the larger population could be zero, based on a sample slope b_1 standardized to a t statistic. If there is evidence of a relationship, a confidence interval can be constructed for the unknown population slope. It is also possible to set up an interval to predict an individual response to a given explanatory value, or a confidence interval for the mean response for a subgroup of individuals with a given explanatory value.

13.7   Supplemental Part IV Review Exercises

A statistical study can be examined in the context of each of the four processes—data production, displaying and summarizing, probability, and statistical inference. To highlight the fact that for any given situation we may focus on any of these four processes, the review exercises for Parts I (page 763), II (page 810), and III (page 883) feature the same settings as these 15 exercises. For now, the focus is on statistical inference.

13.8   Intrinsa, a drug for female sexual dysfunction, was tested in 2004, both for efficacy and for possible dangerous side effects before being considered for approval by the Food and Drug Administration. A report of clinical trials states: "Fifty-two percent of those [women] given the drug said they experienced a 'meaningful benefit' in their sex-lives—but so did 31 percent of those who were given the placebo."[1] Suppose 200 women were included in the study, with half each taking the drug and a placebo.

a. A test comparing proportions who experienced benefits for the two groups results in a test statistic $z = 3.0$. Report the approximate P-value for a one-sided test, and state whether or not the test provides evidence that the drug is beneficial in general.

b. A test for a relationship between taking the drug or not and experiencing benefits or not results in a chi-square statistic of 9.08. Tell whether or not the *P*-value is less than 0.05, and whether or not the test provides evidence of a relationship.

13.9   Researchers at the University of Montreal reported that "blind people are better than sighted controls at judging the direction of pitch change between sounds [. . .] but only if they became blind at an early age. The younger the onset of blindness, the better is the performance."[2]

 a. To test if blind people's scores in judging the direction of pitch change between sounds are significantly better than those of sighted people, which procedure would researchers perform: paired *t*, two-sample *t*, chi-square, or inference for regression?

 b. To test if the ability to judge the direction of pitch change between sounds (measured by percent correct on a sound test) relates to age of onset of blindness, which procedure would researchers perform: paired *t*, two-sample *t*, chi-square, or inference for regression?

13.10   In 1999, Harvard Medical School researchers produced evidence that when television was introduced to the island of Fiji in the mid-1990s, teenage girls began to suffer from eating disorders because of body image issues resulting from seeing thin actresses on their favorite shows.

 a. Suppose the data recorded percentage of teenage girls suffering from eating disorders for each of the years between 1990 and 2000. Which of the four conditions for carrying out inference for regression would be violated?

 b. Suppose the data recorded whether or not teenage girls in a sample were anorexic, in 1995 and again 3 years later, after television viewing was well-established. Would we carry out a test using two-sample *t*, chi-square, or regression?

 c. Suppose the data recorded weights of a sample of teenage girls, in 1995 and again 3 years later, after television viewing was well-established. Would we carry out a test using two-sample *t*, chi-square, or regression?

13.11   According to a Pew report, by the year 2007, one in every 100 Americans was in prison.

 a. Suppose that for a random sample of 1,600 women in 2007, the proportion in prison was 0.001. Explain why we should not use the data to construct a confidence interval for the proportion of all women who were in prison, using a multiplier from the *z* distribution.

 b. Suppose that for a random sample of 1,600 women in 2007, the proportion in prison was 0.001. Standardize this sample proportion to *z*, based on a hypothesized population proportion of 0.01, and report how unlikely it would be for *z* to be this low. Based on this probability (the *P*-value), decide whether or not the women were a representative sample of the general population, in terms of being in prison or not.

13.12   The *Harvard Gazette Archives* reported: "Cognition unaffected by pot use; but other studies suggest marijuana smokers are not a happy lot."[3] A study recruited heavy users, former users, and non-users, who took a variety of cognition tests 0, 1, 7, and 28 days after quitting the drug. Another study said that "most heavy users admitted that the drug has a negative impact on all aspects of their lives from job performance and physical health to mental well-being and satisfactory socializing."

 a. Was the *P*-value for the test of a relationship between pot use and cognition apparently small or not small?

 b. According to the second study's conclusion, would a test to see if the proportion claiming to be happy among marijuana users is significantly lower than the proportion among non-users produce a small *P*-value?

13.13   "Acupuncture Helps Ease Arthritis Pain" describes a National Institutes of Health study where participants "were randomly assigned to receive one of three treatments: acupuncture, sham acupuncture—a procedure designed to prevent patients from being able to detect if needles are actually inserted at treatment points—or participation in a control group that followed the Arthritis Foundation's self-help course for managing their condition . . .

Overall, those who received acupuncture had a 40 percent decrease in pain and 40 percent improvement in function."[4]

a. To compare improvements for the three groups, would researchers use a single-sample z, a paired t, a two-sample t, an F, or a chi-square statistic?

b. Does the title suggest that the test statistic was relatively large or not large?

13.14 According to a newspaper report, "the bigger your brood, the likelier it is to show on your waistline. And that's not just for women, who may retain some of the pounds they gain during pregnancy. Fathers tend to gain weight, too, increasing their risk of obesity with the number of offspring, suggesting that eating habits are to blame."[5] Researchers found the relationship between family size and body size held, regardless of household income, physical activity, smoking and other factors.

a. If researchers considered how many pounds an individual was overweight, instead of considering whether or not an individual was obese, then how could they test for a relationship with number of offspring: with a paired t, two-sample t, ANOVA, chi-square, or inference for regression procedure?

b. Would a confidence interval for the slope of the line relating pounds overweight to number of offspring contain zero?

13.15 A study conducted by AAA looked at other driving distractions besides cell phones. It was reported that men were more than twice as likely as women to have steered the car with their thighs or driven with no hands.

a. To produce evidence of a relationship in general between gender and driving with no hands, would researchers use a z test comparing two proportions or a chi-square test or either or neither?

b. Would the study's results on the relationship between gender and driving with no hands produce a smaller P-value if the sample size were 100 or 400?

13.16 A report on sexual health by the Alan Guttmacher Institute says that "men of all ages tend to overstate their sexual activity when surveyed, while women understate theirs."[6]

a. Suppose that, for each individual studied, researchers were able to record the actual number of sexual encounters in the preceding week, as well as the claimed number. Would they test for significance using a paired t, a two-sample t, or chi-square?

b. If the test statistic standardizes the mean of differences, actual minus claimed, what signs would this test statistic have for the men and for the women?

13.17 Every week in football season, data are recorded for the types of injuries suffered by the players on the NFL list of injured players. During a particular week, the most common—knee injury—was suffered by 49 of the 234 players, while the least common—such as a blister on the foot—was suffered by only one player.

a. Suppose we used the sample proportion with knee injuries that week as a point estimate for the proportion of players suffering knee injuries in general for any week of the year. Explain how this sample proportion could produce a biased estimate.

b. Explain why a binomial distribution would not be adequate to model the behavior of counts suffering from the various possible injuries.

13.18 The Los Angeles Daily News reported the results of a study of thousands of babies born in California in the year 2000. Researchers found that babies born to mothers in the most polluted areas consistently weighed less—about 1 ounce less—than babies born to mothers who lived in clean-air cities.

a. Is 1 ounce reporting a mean of differences or a difference between means?

b. Would researchers test for significance using a paired t or a two-sample t?

13.19 "Soft Drink Link to Diabetes Found" reports that "as consumption of sugar-sweetened drinks increased, women put on more pounds and increased their likelihood to develop diabetes."[7]

a. Would the relationship between sugar-sweetened drinks and weight be explored via a two-sample t, ANOVA, chi-square, or inference for regression?

b. Which would be centered at higher values: a confidence interval for the mean weight of all women who average one sweetened drink a day, or a confidence interval for the mean weight of all women who average three sweetened drinks a day?

13.20 Columnist Maureen Dowd of the *New York Times* discussed two studies published in 2004 on what men are looking for in a woman. The first study "suggests that men going for long-term relationships would rather marry women in subordinate jobs than women who are supervisors." The second study "found that a high IQ hampers a woman's chance to get married, while it is a plus for men. The prospect for marriage increased by 35 percent for guys for each 16-point increase in IQ; for women, there is a 40 percent drop for each 16-point rise."[8]

a. One way to gather additional evidence to support the first study's conclusion would be to compare the proportion married for women in subordinate jobs with the proportion married for women of a similar age who are supervisors. Suppose the z statistic in this comparison equalled 3. What would the chi-square statistic be if we tested for a relationship between type of job and marriage, based on the same data?

b. Explain why inference for regression would not be appropriate to test for a relationship between IQ score and whether or not an individual is married.

13.21 According to the *New York Times*, economics professor David Zimmerman at Williams College studied the impact of college roommates on political leanings and on grades. He "looked at the political views of 3,500 students who had shared rooms as freshmen, noting their leanings when they started college and again 3 years after graduation. Generally, roommates kept the same political persuasion—except those freshmen whose roommates were on the far left of the political spectrum. No matter what their politics at enrollment, they were more likely than similar students to be *conservative* as adults. [. . .] In separate research, Zimmerman and Gordon C. Winston, another Williams economics professor, uncovered more unsettling evidence of peer influence: Freshmen rooming with the weakest students experienced a slight drop in grades. The researchers divided 5,000 onetime roommates at four colleges into three groups: those who scored in the top 15% of the SAT verbal scores admitted to the college, those in the bottom 15%, and everyone in between. On average, grades of the typical students who roomed with low scorers were pulled down by a tenth of a grade point by graduation. No other impact was noticed."[9]

a. Would results in the first study be explored with paired t, two-sample t, ANOVA, chi-square, or inference for regression?

b. Would results in the second study be explored with paired t, two-sample t, ANOVA, chi-square, or inference for regression?

13.22 A wine merchant advertised prices of its California Cabernet wines, per bottle. The minimum price was $10, and the maximum was $130. The mean price was $41. What other information would be needed if we wanted to use a sample of 40 such wines to test if their mean price differs significantly from the mean price of all California Cabernet wines?

13.8 Solutions to Supplemental Part IV Review Exercises

13.8 **a.** *P*-value is less than 0.0015; there is evidence of a benefit. **b.** Yes, because chi-square is greater than 3.84.

13.9 **a.** two-sample t **b.** inference for regression

13.10 **a.** The explanatory/response pairs are randomly selected and independent of one another. **b.** chi-square **c.** two-sample t

13.11 **a.** Because $np = 1,600(0.001) = 1.6$ is clearly less than 10; the distribution of sample proportion is not approximately normal for samples of size 1,600 if the population proportion is estimated to be 0.001.
b. $z = (0.001 - 0.01)/\sqrt{0.01(1 - 0.01)/1,600} = -3.62$, so the probability of z this low is less than 0.0015, according to the 68-95-99.7 Rule. These

women were not representative of the general
population in terms of being in prison or not.

13.12 a. not small   **b.** yes

13.13 a. F **b.** large

13.14 a. inference for regression   **b.** no

13.15 a. either   **b.** 400

13.16 a. paired t **b.** negative for men, positive for
women

13.17 a. It could be biased toward lower or higher
values depending on whether it was early or late
in the season.   **b.** There are more than two
possible values for type of injury.

13.18 a. a difference between means   **b.** two-sample t

13.19 a. inference for regression   **b.** a confidence
interval for the mean weight of all women who
average three sweetened drinks a day

13.20 a. 9   **b.** because the response variable is
categorical, not quantitative

13.21 a. chi-square   **b.** ANOVA

13.22 a. standard deviation of prices

TBP Chapter 14

How Statistics Problems Fit into the Big Picture

14.1 Details and Examples

This table provides a brief example of each of the 20 possible combinations: five variable situations within four processes.

Situations in the "Big Picture"	Data Production	Displaying, Summarizing	Probability	Statistical Inference
1 categorical variable	Before surveying people about whether they had a permanent tattoo on their body, pollsters had to decide whether to offer response options yes/no or yes/no/unsure.	In a survey of drivers, 62% admitted fiddling with the radio dial while driving in the past 6 mos.; 57% reported eating, and 44% tried to pick something up from the floor. Can we use one piechart to display this information?	If 35% of all workers call in sick at least once a year when they're not really sick, what is the chance that more than half in a random sample of 50 workers take off work for a "phantom illness"?	Before a weekend in NFL football season, 49 of 234 injured players suffered from knee problems. Can we conclude that overall at least a fifth of all injuries are knee problems?
1 quantitative variable	Thousands of 12th graders were surveyed about how often they cut class in a month. Would the fact that the survey was conducted in class create any bias?	Some families with epileptic children said their dogs showed evidence of anticipating a seizure. Researchers want to report what is typical, based on a variety of anticipation times mentioned by the families.	Age of mothers at the time of delivery has mean 27 and standard deviation 6 years. If the distribution were normal, what would be the probability of a 59-year-old woman giving birth? (This happened in Dec. 2004.)	An AARP survey showed that on average, people wanted to live to the age of 91. Based on their survey date, we'd like to determine if on average people in general want to live to be at least 90.
1 categorical & 1 quantitative variable	Researcher's stated that men's actual amount of sexual activity tends to be less than claimed amount. It's easy enough to measure what's claimed, but how can researcher's find out the actual amount?	Grades of students who roomed with weak students (bottom 15% of SAT scores) averaged a tenth of a grade point lower than the ones with roommates who were stronger students. How do we graph the data?	Half of students taught dental anatomy over a 3-day period were assigned to chew gum during classes, while the other half didn't. Gum-chewers scored higher on the test. What is the chance of this happening if gum-chewing makes no difference?	Based on weights of 24 incoming female freshman (mean 122 lbs.) and 172 females sophomores (mean 132 lbs.) we want to see if there is evidence for or against the theory of the "Freshman Fifteen."
2 categorical variables	Anthropologists studied gender differences in public restroom graffiti, noting if it was in a men's or women's room, and if it was competitive/derogatory or advisory/sympathetic. What criteria are used for this classification?	10 out of 67 teenage boys interviewed in 1962 believed it was OK to have sex during high school. 34 years later, 29 of them "remembered" believing sex in high school was OK at the time. How much of a discrepancy is this?	A bear at a Washington lake resort finished 36 of 36 cans of Rainier beer found in coolers, but drank only 1 of 36 cans of Busch. Could this have happened by chance if the bear really had no preference for Rainier?	9 of 15 stroke patients treated with vampire bat saliva had an excellent recovery, compared with 4 of 17 untreated stroke patients. Should this convince us that bat saliva makes a difference?
2 quantitative variables	Computer simulations indicated that as temperatures increased with global warming, rice crops decreased. Researchers wanted to design a study to gather data on the relationship using actual rice crops in the Philippines.	Sociologists studied family size and IQ, and had to decide whether to report how IQ decreased as number of siblings increased, or how number of siblings decreased as IQ increased.	In a study of only 8 countries, the percentage of left-handed people increased with homicide rates. What is the chance of seeing such a relationship in the sample of countries, if being left-handed really isn't related to homicide in general?	Scientists measured age and ear length of a sample of people and concluded that in general, our ears grow about 0.01 inches in a year.

For a review that goes beyond the confines of individual chapter topics, this discussion by the four students can be used as a starting point for in-class discussion of a variety of important principles on summary and inference methods. It is based on the report in Exercise 14.38 which claimed dogs tend to resemble their owners. The study was also featured in Exercises 4.12 and 9.62.

Students Talk Stats

Summaries and Inference for Categorical Variables

Suppose four students are discussing a study that explored whether or not dogs tend to resemble their owners: "Forty-five dogs took part in the study—25 purebreds and 20 mutts. [. . .] Overall, there were just 23 matches. However, the judges had an easier time with the purebred dogs: 16 matches, versus 7 for the mixed breeds." A "match" was achieved if a judge correctly identified the dog's owner from two photographs. Thus, the success rate would average only 50% if a judge performed no better than random guessing.

Adam: *"Looks like they really were able to match up the purebreds with their owners: 16 matches instead of 7 shows they got more than twice as many right."*

Brittany: *"The counts aren't the best summaries because they had more purebreds to work with. You should compare percentages, and say that 16 out of 25 were matched for the purebreds, which is 64%, as opposed to 7 out of 20 for the mixed breeds, which is 35%. It's not twice as much but they still did much better with the purebreds."*

Carlos: *"I'm not impressed. To see if we're convinced that the difference in results for purebreds and mixed breeds is large enough to conclude that it goes beyond the sample, you find the chi-square statistic to be 3.74, and the P-value is 0.053. The difference is not quite statistically significant."*

Dominique: *"Do we really care about the difference between purebreds and mixed breeds? The main result is that they got altogether 23 matches out of 45 dogs, which is only 51%. A single-proportion test to see if overall correct matches would be in a majority would standardize the difference between 51% and 50%, which gives you a z statistic that isn't large at all, so the P-value isn't small at all. Even if you restrict yourself to the purebreds, the difference between 64% and 50% isn't statistically significant for such a small sample. I think the headlines' claim that "Purebred dogs resemble their owners" is misleading."*

Endnotes

Chapter 1

1. Kenneth R. Weiss, "New Test-Taking Skill: Working the System," *Los Angeles Times,* January 9, 2000.

2. "Racial Gaps in Education Cause Income Tiers," *The Michigan Daily,* March 21, 2003.

3. Bootle Cosgrove-Mather, "Are Feeding Tubes Over-Prescribed?" CBS News, July 2, 2003.

4. Trevor Butterworth, "The Duh Report: Smarties Stay Sober, Narcissists Crave Fame, Cell Phones Addictive," STATS, September 15, 2006.

5. "Stronger Sunscreens May Increase Exposure, Cancer Risk," Augusta Chronicle, August 4, 1999.

6. "Teens Most Likely to Have Sex at Home," *USA Today,* September 26, 2002.

7. "Living Longer," *The New York Times,* September 16, 2007.

8. "Where You Live Can Affect How Long You Live," NPR Morning Edition, September 11, 2006.

9. "Smoke Out/Teens Get the Message on the Hazards of Tobacco," Editorial, *Pittsburgh Post-Gazette,* July 8, 2004.

Chapter 2

1. Marylynn Uricchio, "Larry Flint," *Pittsburgh Post-Gazette,* October 15, 2001.

2. Scripps Survey Research Center at Ohio University, newspoll.org (accessed October 28, 2002).

3. "1 in 4 Credit Reports Has Serious Errors, Group Says," *USA Today,* June 17, 2004.

4. Scripps Survey Research Center at Ohio University, newspoll.org (accessed August 15, 2003).

5. Pricing Strategy Associates, http://www.pricingpsychology.com (accessed May 3, 2009). Copyright 2004–2007, Marlene Jensen.

6. Scripps Survey Research Center at Ohio University, newspoll.org (accessed May 18, 2003).

7. Linda Wilson Fuoco, "Dogs That Fail the 'Pinch Test,'" *Pittsburgh Post-Gazette,* December 8, 2004.

8. "Couch Potato Nation," *Pittsburgh Post-Gazette,* January 12, 1999.

9. "Written Word Helps Wounds Heal," BBC News, September 6, 2003.

10. Bob Herbert, "Countdown to Execution No. 300," *The New York Times,* March 10, 2003.

Chapter 3

1. Letter to the Editor, *Pittsburgh Post-Gazette,* March 13, 1997.

2. *Pittsburgh Post-Gazette,* November 13, 2004.

3. Rita Healy, "Where You Will Live the Longest," Health & Science, *Time,* September 12, 2006.

4. "'Get Tough' Programs for Youths Critized," *The Boston Globe,* October 16, 2004.

5. *Pittsburgh Post Gazette,* November 17, 2004.

6. Emily F. Oster, "Witchcraft, Weather and Economic Growth in Renaissance Europe," *Journal of Economic Perspectives,* Winter 2004, posted March 30, 2004.

7. "FDA: More Tests on Female Sexual Dysfunction Drug," *St. Augustine Record,* December 3, 2004.

8. Anabelle Garay, Associated Press, "As Orders Soar, Concerns Over Stun Guns Grow," November 30, 2004.

9. "Stress Found in Returning Soldiers," *Pittsburgh Post-Gazette,* July 1, 2004.

10. [personal experience of the author, Glacier National Park, approx 2000.]

11. Robert Frost, "Happiness Makes Up in Height for What It Lacks in Length," 1942. Albert Camus, unsourced.

12. Anita Srikameswaran, "Survey Find County Enjoys Good Health," *Pittsburgh Post-Gazette,* February 26, 2004.

13. Dennis Gilbert, "Hamilton College Youth and Guns Poll," Hamilton College, August 21, 2000.

14. "Data Found Lacking on Effects of Gun Control Efforts," *USA Today,* December 16, 2004.

15. Edison/Mitofsky, United States General Exit Poll, November 2, 2004.

16. Edison/Mitofsky, United States General Exit Poll, November 2, 2004.

17. "Majority Support for Gun Control; Majority Support Continuation of National Firearms Registry," Environics Research Group, February 21, 2003.

18. "Phantom Illness," *The Augusta Chronicle,* November 1, 2004.

19. "Moderate Walking Helps the Mind Stay Sharper," *Pittsburgh Post-Gazette,* September 22, 2004.

20. "Couch Potato Nation," *Pittsburgh Post-Gazette,* January 12, 1999.

21. "Study Forced Orphans to Stutter," *Seattle Times,* June 11, 2001.

22. Anahad O'Connor, "The Claim: Bee Stings Can Be Treated by Scraping Out Stingers," *The New York Times,* May 30, 2006.

23. David Biello, "Washing Hands Reduces Moral Taint," *Scientific American,* September 7, 2006.

24. Bob Herbert, "Countdown to Execution No. 300," *The New York Times,* March 10, 2003.

25. Sandra Blakeslee, "Study Offers Surprise on Working of Body's Clock," *The New York Times,* January 16, 1998.

26. "Piano Lessons Boost Math Scores," Personal MD, March 18, 1999.

27. "When Your Hair's a Real Mess, Your Self-Esteem is Much Less," *Pittsburgh Post-Gazette,* January 26, 2000.

28. Carey Hamilton, "How Healthy Is Our State for Kids? Study Will Tell," *The Salt Lake Tribune,* September 30, 2005.

29. Juliet Eilperin, "Study of Pesticides and Children Stirs Protests," *Washington Post,* October 30, 2004.

30. "Watching TV May Hurt Toddlers' Attention Spans," msnbc, April 5, 2004.

31. "Watching TV May Hurt Toddlers' Attention Spans," msnbc, April 5, 2004.

32. "Family Dinners Benefit Teens," Briefs, *Pittsburgh Post-Gazette,* August 26, 1997.

33. "Don't Count Out Prostitutes," *The Philadelphia Inquirer,* October 10, 2000.

34. "High Heels Can Drive You Literally Crazy," *The Citizen,* July 25, 2005.

35. "Breast Milk Benefit," *The Pittsburgh Post-Gazette,* September 9, 1998.

36. Fox Chase Pediatric, "Breast-Feeding Benefits Bolstered," January 23, 2001.

37. Quaker Oats Company, Quaker Oats Oatmeal Product Label, 1999.

38. "Normal Teenagers are Not Ticking Time Bombs," news-medical.net, September 10, 2004.

Chapter 4

1. Chris Conway, "The DNA 200," *The New York Times,* May 20, 2007.

2. David Carr, "New York Fiction, by the Numbers," *The New York Times,* June 1, 2004.

3. Marilyn vos Savant, "Ask Marilyn," by *Parade Magazine,* February 29, 2004.

4. "Lab Still Most Popular Dog," *Pittsburgh Post-Gazette,* February 18, 2004.

5. "Office Workers Give Away Passwords for a Chocolate Bar!," M2 Presswire, April, 2004, BNET (online).

6. "Study Indicates Racial Disparity in Traffic Stops," *The Pittsburgh Post-Gazette,* April 22, 2002.

7. Eric Nagoumey, "A Big Professional Headache," *The New York Times,* December 2, 2003.

8. "Study: TV Shows Tend to be Bi-coastal," *USA Today,* November 22, 2004.

9. Michael Roy and Nicholas Christenfeld, "Do Dogs Resemble Their Owners?" *Chance Magazine,* March 31, 2004.

10. Matthew Wald, "F.A.A. Reviews Rules on Passenger Weight After Crash," *The New York Times,* January 28, 2003.

11. "Colleges Still Unsure How to Use New SAT," *Pittsburgh Post-Gazette,* February 25, 2007.

12. Fogel, Robert W., and Stanley L. Engerman. New Orleans Slave Sale Sample, 1804–1862 [Computer file]. Compiled by Robert W. Fogel and Stanley L. Engerman, University of Rochester. ICPSR07423–v2. Ann Arbor, MI: Inter-university Consortium for Political and Social Researcher [product and distributor].

13. Johnston, Lloyd D., Jerald G. Bachman, Patrick M. O'Malley, and John E. Schulenberg. Monitoring the Future: A Continuing Study of American Youth (8th and 10th Grade Surveys), 2004 [Computer file]. Conducted by University of Michigan, Institute for Social Research, Survey Research Center. ICPSR04263-v1. Ann Arbor, MI: Inter-university Consortium for Political and Social Research.

14. Geoff Koch, "Study Confirms Dogs Can Sense Seizures," *The Dallas Morning News*, June 28, 2004.

15. Johnston, Lloyd D., Jerald G. Bachman, Patrick M. O'Malley, and John E. Schulenberg. Monitoring the Future: A Continuing Study of American Youth (8th and 10th Grade Surveys), 2004 [Computer file]. Conducted by University of Michigan, Institute for Social Research, Survey Research Center. ICPSR04263-v1. Ann Arbor, MI: Inter-university Consortium for Political and Social Research.

16. Anahad O'Connor, "In Michigan, a Milestone for a Mouse Methuselah," April 13, 2004.

17. Blair Tindall, "The Plight of the White-Tie Worker," *The New York Times*, Sunday, July 4, 2004.

18. "Food Statistics>Beer consumption (most recent) by country," reported online at http://www.nationmaster.com/graph/foo_bee_con-food-beer-consumption.

19. Nicholas Wade [for *New York Times*], "Remains Found of Downsized Human Species," *Pittsburgh Post-Gazette*, October 28, 2004.

20. J. Trinkaus, "Compliance with the Item Limit of the Food Supermarket Express Checkout Lane: An Informal Look," *Psychological Reports*, 73, no. 1 (August 1993): 105–6.

21. Mark Sherman [credited to Associated Press], "Caesarian Deliveries Hit U.S. Record," *The Seattle Times*, November 24, 2004.

22. "Antarctic Birds Use Scent to Find Their Mates," *USA Today*, October 29, 2004 [credited to Associated Press].

23. Wines, Michael, and Sharon Lafraniere,"Hollowed Generation: Plunge in Life Expectancy; Hut by Hut, AIDS Steals Life in a Southern Africa Town," *The New York Times*, November 28, 2004.

24. Deborah Solomon, "The Science of Second-Guessing," interview, *New York Times*, December 12, 2004.

25. Anthony Walton, "Review of 'The State Boys Rebellion' by Michael D'Antonio," *The New York Times*, June 27, 2004.

26. Gollop, J. B., and W. H. Marshall. "A Guide for Aging Duck Broods in the Field, Mississippi Flyway Council Technical Section," p. 14 Northern Prairie Wildlife Research Center Home Page, 1954.

Chapter 5

1. "Study: Chewing Gum and CDs May Help Students Master Dental Anatomy," Global Health Nexus, NYU College of Dentistry, Winter 2004.

2. Luther Carpenter, "Job Redistribution a la Francaise," *Dissent Magazine* (online).

3. Lyric Wallwork Winik, "Films and hormones," *Parade Magazine*, October 10, 2004.

4. "Link Between Caffeine Consumption and High Blood Pressure Found in Adolescents," *PsychCentral*, April 29, 2004.

5. "Oh, Deer!," *Pittsburgh Post-Gazette*, November 21, 2004.

6. Gina Kolata, "Dream Drug Too Good to Be True?," *The New York Times*, reported in *The Pittsburgh Post-Gazette*, December 5, 2004.

7. "Wrinkle Fighter Could Help Reduce Excessive Sweating" [attributed to The Associated Press], *Pittsburgh Post-Gazette,* February 8, 2004.

8. Clifford Krauss, "Canada's View on Social Issues is Opening Rifts with the U.S.," *The New York Times,* December 2, 2003.

9. Justin Bachman, "This & That: You Do What?!?," The *Pittsburgh Post-Gazette,* July 12, 2004.

10. Lyric Wallwork Winik, "Make a Mess—and Money," *Parade Magazine,* March 6, 2005.

11. Steven R. Weisman, "Chart: The Other Troops in Iraq," *The New York Times,* November 21, 2004.

12. "Tight Ties Could Damage Eyesight," BBC News (online), July 28, 2003.

13. "Study: Anti-Seizure Drug Reduces Drinking in Bipolar Alcoholics," *Bipolar Central* (online), January 6, 2005.

14. Eduardo Porter, "Values Gap: Where Playboy and 'Will and Grace' Reign," November 21, 2004.

15. Giron, D., D. Dunn, I. Hardy, and M. Strand, "Aggression by Polyembryonic Wasp Soldiers Correlates with Kinship but not Resource Competition," *Nature,* 430 (5 August 2004): 676–79.

16. Jaime Holguin, "How to Talk to Dying Children," CBS News (online), September 15, 2004 [attributed to Associated Press].

17. "Pounds and Penance," *The Guardian,* January 15, 2001.

18. Christopher Snowbeck, "Perspiration, Not Procreation," *Pittsburgh Post-Gazette,* July 7, 2002.

19. "Life by the Numbers: What Do Americans Like?" [attributed to Associated Press], *St. Petersburg Times* (online), December 8, 2004.

20. "Life by the Numbers: What Do Americans Like?" [attributed to Associated Press], *St. Petersburg Times* (online), (accessed December 8, 2004).

21. Dan Lewerenz, "Exercise Beats Calcium at Boosting Girls' Bones," *Pittsburgh Post-Gazette* [attributed to Associated Press], June 15, 2004.

22. Lee Bowman, "Too Few z's May Result in Too Many Pounds," Scripps Howard News Service, www.sitnews.us, December 7, 2004.

23. Hull, Joseph, and Greg Langkamp, "Puget Sound Butter Clams Length v. Width," Quantitative Environmental Learning Project (QELP).

24. Lawrence Walsh, "A Complete Guide to the Region's Slopes," *Pittsburgh Post-Gazette,* November 14, 2004.

25. Michael Janofsky, "E.P.A. Cuts Pollution Levels with Refinery Settlements," *The New York Times,* October 10, 2004.

26. Barbara White Stack, "Law to Increase Adoptions Results in More Orphans," *Pittsburgh Post-Gazette,* reported on seattlepi.com (accessed January 3, 2005).

27. Nick Wadhams, The Associated Press, "Cars Becoming Weapon of Choice," reported in *Pittsburgh Post-Gazette,* January 13, 2005.

28. Emily F. Oster, "Witchcraft, Weather and Economic Growth in Renaissance Europe," *Journal of Economic Perspectives,* Winter 2004, posted March 30, 2004.

29. Richard Bernstein, "Modern German Duty: The Obligation to Play," *The New York Times,* July 2, 2003.

30. Stacey Hirsh, "Sitting Is a Spreading Occupational Hazard," *The Baltimore Sun,* April 15, 2004.

31. Hal R. Varian, "Studies Find That for Men, It Pays to Be Married," *International Herald Tribune,* July 30, 2004.

32. Witte, Griff, and Nell Henderson, "Wealth Gap Widens for Blacks, Hispanics," *The Washington Post,* October 18, 2004.

33. "Busting the Nursery Rhymes," *Pittsburgh Post-Gazette,* November 30, 2004.

34. Donald G. McNeil Jr., "Large Study on Mental Illness Finds Global Prevalence," *The New York Times,* June 2, 2004.

35. Piperno, D., E. Weiss, I. Holst, and D. Nadel, "Processing of Wild Cereal Grains in the Upper Palaeolithic Revealed by Starch Grain Analysis," *Nature,* 430 (5 August 2004): 670–73.

36. C. Brown, "The Information Trail of the 'Freshman 15'—A Systematic Review of a Health Myth within the Research and Popular Literature," *Health Information Libraries Journal,* 25, no 1 (March 2008): 1–12.

37. John Heilprin, "Coral Reefs Less Healthy Now than 2 Years Ago," *Pittsburgh Post-Gazette,* December 7, 2004.

38. Hibell, B., B. Andersson, T. Bjarnason, A. Kokkevi, M. Morgan, and A. Narusk, "The European School Survey Project on Alcohol and Drugs (ESPAD)," 1995 Report.

39. Trinkaus, J., "An Informal Look at Use of Bakery Department Tongs and Tissues," *Perceptual and Motor Skills,* December 1998.

40. Mackenzie Carpenter, "Study Links Teen Sex, Suggestive TV Fare," *Pittsburgh Post-Gazette* [Reported in the *Cleveland Plain Dealer*], September 9, 2004.

41. "The Best & Worst of Everything: Our Annual Year-End Roundup," *Parade Magazine,* December 26, 2004.

42. McKeganey, N., J. Norrie, "Association Between Illegal Drugs and Weapon Carrying in Young People in Scotland: Schools' Survey," *British Medical Journal,* 320 (April 8, 2000): 982–84.

43. Eric Nagourney, "Prevention: Harder Water and Longer Lives," *The New York Times,* January 27, 2004.

44. Eric Nagourney, "Power of Smell—Flavonoids Counter Reactive Oxygen in Body. The Stronger an Onion Tastes, the More Likely It Is to Help Fight Cancer and Other Diseases, Scientists at Cornell Have Found," *The Telegraph of Calcutta, India,* November 1, 2004.

45. Genaro C. Armas [Associated Press], "Life by the Numbers," SouthCoastTODAY.com, May 19, 2009.

46. "African AIDS Patients More Diligent in Taking Medicine Than in U.S.," *Pittsburgh Post-Gazette,* September 3, 2003.

47. "Warming Reducing Rice Yields," *Pittsburgh Post-Gazette,* July 5, 2004.

48. "Drop in Temperatures Could Lower Ticket Prices, Too," *Pittsburgh Post-Gazette,* January 13, 2005.

49. James Brooke, "Golfing Mongolia: A 2.3-Million-Yard par 11,880," *The New York Times,* July 4, 2004.

50. Paula Reed Ward, "PA Hunting Season Claimed 3 Lives," *Pittsburgh Post-Gazette,* December 12, 2004.

Chapter 6

1. Brewer, P., and C. Wilcox, "Same-Sex Marriage and Civil Unions," *Public Opinion Quarterly,* 69, no. 4 (2005): 599–616.

2. John Houle, Cornerstone Communications Group, "Health & Safety Survey," American Nurses Association online, September 2001.

3. "Asides," *Pittsburgh Post-Gazette,* July 4, 2004.

4. McKeganey, N., J. Norrie, "Association Between Illegal Drugs and Weapon Carrying in Young People in Scotland: Schools' Survey," *British Medical Journal,* 320 (April 8, 2000): 982–84.

5. Byron Spice, "How Not to Catch a Spy: Use a Lie Detector," *Pittsburgh Post-Gazette,* October 9, 2002.

6. "Sweating the Details," *Pittsburgh Post-Gazette,* July 27, 2004.

7. "Ultrasound Improves Stroke Blood Clot Clearance," *Future Pundit* online news, November 18, 2004.

8. Dale Lawrence Pearlman, MD, "A Simple Treatment for Head Lice: Dry-On, Suffocation-Based Pediculicide," *Pediatrics Online Journal,* September 1, 2004.

9. John Houle, Cornerstone Communications Group, "Health & Safety Survey," American Nurses Association online, September 2001.

10. Xenia Montenegro, "Lifestyles, Dating and Romance: A Study of Midlife Singles," *AARP Knowledge Management,* September 2003.

11. "Taunts Cut Girls More than Sticks or Stones," *Pittsburgh Post-Gazette,* November 12, 2003.

12. David Carr, "New York Fiction, By the Numbers," *The New York Times,* June 1, 2004.

13. R. Trueb, "Association Between Smoking and Hair Loss: Another Opportunity for Health Education Against Smoking?," *Dermatology,* 206 (2003): 189–91.

14. "Fewer Drinks——Fewer Gray Hairs," *Pittsburgh Post-Gazette,* February 20, 2008.

15. "Home Pregnancy Tests Reviewed," *Bandolier Journal* (online), June 1999.

Chapter 7

1. Johnston, Lloyd D., Jerald G. Bachman, Patrick M. O'Malley, and John E. Schulenberg, Monitoring the Future: A Continuing Study of American Youth (8th- and 10th-Grade Surveys), 2004 [Computer file]. Conducted by University of Michigan, Institute for Social Research, Survey Research Center. ICPSR04263-v1. Ann Arbor, MI: Inter-university Consortium for Political and Social Research [producer and distributor], 2005–12–15. doi:10.3886/ICPSR04263.

2. Axinn, William G., Arland Thornton, Jennifer S. Barber, Susan A. Murphy, Dirgha Ghimire, Thomas Fricke, Stephen Matthews, Dharma Dangol, Lisa Pearce, Ann Biddlecom, Sundar Shrehtha, and Douglas Massey, Chitwan Valley [Nepal] Family Study: Changing Social Contexts and Family Formation [Computer file]. ICPSR04538-v3. Ann Arbor, MI: Inter-university Consortium for Political and Social Research [distributor], 2009–05–13. doi:10.3886/ICPSR04538.

3. Axinn, William G., Arland Thornton, Jennifer S. Barber, Susan A. Murphy, Dirgha Ghimire, Thomas Fricke, Stephen Matthews, Dharma Dangol, Lisa Pearce, Ann Biddlecom, Sundar Shrehtha, and Douglas Massey, Chitwan Valley [Nepal] Family Study: Changing Social Contexts and Family Formation [Computer file]. ICPSR04538-v3. Ann Arbor, MI: Inter-university Consortium for Political and Social Research [distributor], 2009–05–13. doi:10.3886/ICPSR04538.

4. Johnston, Lloyd D., Jerald G. Bachman, Patrick M. O'Malley, and John E. Schulenberg, Monitoring the Future: A Continuing Study of American Youth (8th- and 10th-Grade Surveys), 2004 [Computer file]. Conducted by University of Michigan, Institute for Social Research, Survey Research Center. ICPSR04263-v1. Ann Arbor, MI: Inter-university Consortium for Political and Social Research [producer and distributor], 2005-12-15. doi:10.3886/ICPSR04263.

5. Grand Canyon National Park Northern Arizona Tourism Study, April 2005.

6. Maggie Fox, "Half of Bankruptcy Due to Medical Bills—U.S. Study," Reuters, February 2, 2005.

7. Habler, H. J., W. Janig, M. Krummel, and O. A. Peters, "Reflex Patterns in Postganglionic Neurons Supplying Skin and Skeletal Muscle of the Rat Hindlimb," *Journal of Neurophysiology,* Vol 72, Issue 5 2222–2236.

8. "Tall Enough?," *Pittsburgh Post-Gazette,* November 4, 2003.

9. Axinn, William G., Arland Thornton, Jennifer S. Barber, Susan A. Murphy, Dirgha Ghimire, Thomas Fricke, Stephen Matthews, Dharma Dangol, Lisa Pearce, Ann Biddlecom, Sundar Shrehtha, and Douglas Massey, Chitwan Valley [Nepal] Family Study: Changing Social Contexts and Family Formation [Computer file]. ICPSR04538-v3. Ann Arbor, MI: Inter-university Consortium for Political and Social Research [distributor], 2009–05–13. doi:10.3886/ICPSR04538.

Chapter 8

1. Veronica Torrejon, "U.S. Teens share Parents' Religion, Survey Finds," *The Los Angeles Times,* February 26, 2005.

2. Veronica Torrejon, "U.S. Teens Share Parents' Religion, Survey Finds," *The Los Angeles Times,* February 26, 2005.

3. Skrbinsek, A., and A. Bath, "Attitudes of Rural and Urban Public Toward Wolves in Croatia," *Conservation and Management of Wolves in Croatia,* 2005.

4. "Criminal Pasts Cited for Many City School Bus Drivers," *Pittsburgh Post-Gazette,* November 19, 2003.

5. L.A. Johnson, "Passing Along (or Recycling) Unwanted Gifts Can Be Fraught with Peril," *Pittsburgh Post-Gazette,* December 25, 2004.

6. Boy, E. N. Bruce, and H. Delgado, "Birth Weight and Exposure to Kitchen Wood Smoke During Pregnancy in Rural Guatemala," *Environmental Health Perspectives,* no. 1 (January 2002): 109–14.

Chapter 9

1. "Does Anybody Really Know Quelle Heure Est-il?," *Pittsburgh Post-Gazette,* February 20, 2005.

2. "Criminal Pasts Cited for Many City School Bus Drivers," *Pittsburgh Post-Gazette,* November 19, 2003.

3. "The Comfort of a Familiar Scent," *Pittsburgh Post-Gazette,* June 1, 2005.

4. Robert Barr [Associated Press], "Princess Diana Remembered," reported on an ABC Action News website (accessed August 31, 2007).

5. Trockel, Mickey, Michael Barnes, and Dennis Egget, "Health Related Variables and Academic Performance among First-Year College Students: Implications for Sleep and Other Behaviors," *Journal of American College Health,* 49, no 3 (2000): 125–31.

6. Daniel J. DeNoon, "Sleep Face Down for Lower Blood Pressure," *WebMD Health News,* October 11, 2004.

7. Kirton, A., E. Wirrell, J. Zhang, and L. Hamiwka, "Seizure-Alerting and -Response Behaviors in Dogs Living with Epileptic Children," *Neurology,* 62 (2004): 2303–5.

8. John Hanna [Associated Press], "Topeka Voters Reject Ordinance Repeal, Anti-Discrimination Law Will Stand," reported online in *Common Ground Common Sense,* March 1, 2005.

9. "What Readers Think About Reading——a 1999 Survey," *The Bookseller,* November 19, 1999; reported online by the National Reading Campaign.

10. "A Friendly Word Is the Best Way of Turning a Book into a Bestseller," *Independent,* March 3, 2005; reported online by the National Reading Campaign.

11. Statement of Dr. Kathleen McChesney, Office of Media Relations, United States Conference of Catholic Bishops, February 18, 2005.

12. "13th Annual 'Attitudes in the American Workplace' Poll conducted by Harris Interactive for The Marlin Company Results," 2007.

13. "Antibiotic Resistance Puzzle," *Pittsburgh Post-Gazette,* February 18, 2004.

14. L.A. Johnson, "Passing Along (or Recycling) Unwanted Gifts Can Be Fraught with Peril," *Pittsburgh Post-Gazette,* December 25, 2004.

15. S. Kazakova et al., "A Clone of Methicillin-Resistant Staphylococcus Aureus Among Professional Football Players," *New England Journal of Medicine,* 352 (February 3, 2005): 468–75.

16. Livingstone, M. S., and B. R. Conway, "Was Rembrandt Stereoblind?" *New England Journal of Medicine,* 351 (September 16, 2004): 1264.

17. "Hospital Chiefs Wary of Mandate on Error Reports," *Pittsburgh Post-Gazette,* March 16, 2005.

18. Ben Feller [Associated Press], "Survey: Most Young Adults Value College; Nonetheless, Many Fall Short of Getting There or Graduating," February 8, 2005.

19. "65 Percent of Children Have Had an Imaginary Companion," *The Medical News,* December 6, 2004.

20. "First Amendment No Big Deal, Students Say," MSNBC (online) [Associated Press], January 31, 2005.

21. Maxim Kelly, "Rude Health: Sound Warning on Your Lungs," *The Sunday Business Post Online,* June 26, 2005.

22. "Contraception Shots Work in Male Monkeys," *Pittsburgh Post-Gazette,* November 12, 2004.

23. "Obesity Rampant in NFL, Study Says," *The Daughtry Times* [Associated Press], March 1, 2005.

24. "Kids Overdo Headache Meds," *Pittsburgh Post-Gazette,* June 15, 2004.

25. "Full Moon Exerts No Pull on Frequency of Epileptic Seizures," *Bio-Medicine* (online), May 25, 2004.

26. "Half of Moms Are Unaware of Children Having Sex," *Pittsburgh Post-Gazette,* September 5, 2002.

27. Sandra G. Boodman, "New Rules for Safer Surgery," *The Washington Post,* [reported in *Post-Gazette Now*], July 13, 2004.

28. "Antibiotic Resistance Puzzle," *Pittsburgh Post-Gazette,* February 18, 2004.

29. Young, Donn, and Erinn Hade, "Holidays, Birthdays, and Postponement of Cancer Death," *The Journal of the American Medical Association (JAMA),* 292, no. 24 (December 22/29, 2004).

30. "Study Proves Number Bias in UK Lottery," usamega.com [Archived lottery news website] (accessed December 11, 2004).

31. Daniel J. DeNoon, "Dairy Food No Magic Bullet for Weight Loss," Fox News (online), Friday, November 19, 2004.

32. Byron Spice, "How Not to Catch a Spy: Use a Lie Detector," *Pittsburgh Post-Gazette,* October 9, 2002.

33. "Amgen Will Stop Providing Parkinson's Drug," AP Online, February 13, 2005.

34. Roy, Michael, and Nicholas Christenfeld, "Do Dogs Resemble Their Owners?," *Chance Magazine,* March 31, 2004.

35. "Federal Intervention in Schiavo Case Prompts Broad Public Disapproval," ABC News (online), Monday, March 21, 2005.

36. "Antibiotic Resistance Puzzle," *Pittsburgh Post-Gazette,* February 18, 2004.

37. Jean Koppen, "Medical Uses of Marijuana: Opinions of U.S. Residents 45+," *AARP Policy & Research,* December 2004.

38. "2004 a Bad Year for the Grizzly Bear," *Pittsburgh Post-Gazette,* December 20, 2004.

39. Nick Santangelo, "Courtship in the Monogamous Convict Cichlid; What Are Individuals Saying to Rejected and Selected Mates?" *Animal Behaviour,* 68, no. 1, (January 2005): 143–49.

40. Nick Santangelo, "Courtship in the Monogamous Convict Cichlid; What Are Individuals Saying to Rejected and Selected Mates?" *Animal Behaviour,* 68, no. 1, (January 2005): 143–49.

41. Chio, A., G. Benzi, M. Dossenal, R. Mutani, and G. Mora, "Severely Increased Risk of Amyotrophic Lateral Sclerosis Among Italian Professional Football Players," *Brain,* January 5, 2005.

42. Persons, Matthew, and George Uetz, "Sexual Cannibalism and Mate Choice Decisions in Wolf Spiders: Influence of Male Size and Secondary Sexual Characters," *Animal Behavior,* 69, no. 1 (January 2005): 83–94.

43. "Poll: U.S. May Be Ready for Female President," Foxnews.com [Associated Press], February 23, 2005.

44. "New Transplant Protocol Improves Survival Rate," *Pittsburgh Post-Gazette,* December 13, 2004.

45. Livingstone, M. S., and B. R. Conway, "Was Rembrandt Stereoblind?" *New England Journal of Medicine,* 351 (September 16, 2004): 1264–65.

46. "Radiation Risk Overstated," *Pittsburgh Post-Gazette,* March 16, 2005.

47. Linda Lyons, Education and Youth Editor, "Oh, Boy: Americans Still Prefer Sons," *Gallup,* September 23, 2003.

48. Lacy, Naomi, Audrey Paulman, Matthew Reuter, and Bruce Lovejoy, "Why We Don't Come: Patient Perceptions on No-Shows," *Annals of Family Medicine,* 2, no. 6, (November/December 2004): 541–45.

Chapter 10

1. Lopez, P., D. Hawlena, V. Polo, and J. Martin, "Sources of Individual Shy-Bold Variations in Antipredator Behaviour of Male Iberian Rock Lizards," *Animal Behavior,* 69 (January 2005): 1–9.

2. Durham, Yvonne, Matthew Roelofs, and Stephen Standifird, "eBay's Buy-It-Now Function: Who, When, and How," *Topics in Economic Analysis & Policy,* 4, no. 1 (2004).

3. Kaminski, Juliane, Julia Riedel, Josep Call, and Michael Tomasello, "Domestic Goats, Capra Hircus, Follow Gaze Direction and Social Cues in an Object Choice Task," *Animal Behavior,* 69, no 1 (January 2005): 11–18.

4. Kahneman, Daniel, Alan Krueger, David Schkade, Norbert Schwarz, and Arthur Stone, "A Survey Method for Characterizing Daily Life Experience: The Day Reconstruction Method," *Science,* 306, no. 5702 (December 3, 2004): 1776–80.

5. Popp, David, Ted Juhl, and Daniel Johnson, "Time in Purgatory: Examining the Grant Lag for U.S. Patent Applications," *The Berkeley Electronic Press,* 4, no. 1 (2004).

6. Oster, Sharon, and Fiona Scott Morton, "Behavioral Biases Meet the Market: The Case of Magazine Subscription Prices," *The Berkeley Electronic Press,* 5, no. 1 (2005).

7. Da Silva, I., and S. Larson, "Predicting Reproduction in Captive Sea Otters," *Zoo Biology,* 24, no. 1, (2005): 73–81.

8. Håkan J. Holm, "Can Economic Theory Explain Piracy Behavior?" *Berkeley Electronic Press,* 3, no. 1 (2003).

9. Håkan J. Holm, "Can Economic Theory Explain Piracy Behavior?" *Berkeley Electronic Press,* 3, no. 1 (2003).

10. Harvey, N. C., J. D. Dankovchik, C. M. Kuehler, et al., "Egg Size, Fertility, Hatchability, and Chick Survivability in Captive California Condors (Gymnogyps californianus)," *Zoo Biology,* 23 (2004): 489–500.

11. Popp, David, Ted Juhl, and Daniel Johnson, "Time In Purgatory: Examining the Grant Lag for U.S. Patent Applications," *The Berkeley Electronic Press,* 4, no. 1 (2004).

12. Olivares, Orlando, "An Analysis of the Study-Time Grade Association," *Radical Pedagogy* (2002).

13. Zwolan, T. A., P. R. Kileny, and S. A. Telian, "Self-Report of Cochlear Implant Use and Satisfaction by Prelingually Deafened Adults," *Ear & Hearing,* 17, no. 3 (June 1996): 198–210.

14. Dansinger, Michael, Joi Augustin Gleason, John Griffith, Harry Selker, and Ernst Schaefer, "Comparison of the Atkins, Ornish, Weight Watchers, and Zone Diets for Weight Loss and Heart Disease Risk Reduction," *Journal of the American Medical Association (JAMA)* 293, no. 1 (2005): 43–53.

15. Caruso, Anthony, Wojtek Chodzko-Zajko, Debra Bidinger, and Ronald Sommers, "Adults Who Stutter: Responses to Cognitive Stress," *Journal of Speech and Hearing Research,* 37 (August 1994): 746–754.

16. Caruso, Anthony, Wojtek Chodzko-Zajko, Debra Bidinger, and Ronald Sommers, "Adults Who Stutter: Responses to Cognitive Stress," *Journal of Speech and Hearing Research,* 37 (August 1994): 746–754.

17. Robeck, T. R., S. L. Monfort, P. P. Calle, J. L. Dunn, E. Jensen, J. R. Boehm, S. Young, and S. T. Clark, "Reproduction, Growth and Development in Captive Beluga," *Zoo Biology,* 24, no. 1 (2005): 29–49.

18. Clauss, M., C. Polster, E. Kienzle, H. Wiesner, K. Baumgartner, F. von Houwald, W. Streich, and E. Dierenfeld, "Energy and Mineral Nutrition and Water Intake in the Captive Indian Rhinoceros," *Zoo Biology,* 24 (2005): 1–14.

Chapter 11

1. Caruso, Anthony, Wojtek Chodzko-Zajko, Debra Bidinger, and Ronald Sommers, "Adults Who Stutter: Responses to Cognitive Stress," *Journal of Speech and Hearing Research,* 37 (August 1994): 746–754.

2. Kaminski, Juliane, Julia Riedel, Josep Call, and Michael Tomasello, "Domestic Goats, Capra Hircus, Follow Gaze Direction and Social Cues in an Object Choice Task," *Animal Behavior,* 69, no. 1 (January 2005): 11–18.

3. Hull, Joseph and Greg Langkamp, "Lake Washington Bacteria Counts," Quantitative Environmental Learning Project (QELP).

4. Hull, Joseph and Greg Langkamp, "Lead v. Zinc Concentrations in Spokane River Fish," Quantitative Environmental Learning Project (QELP).

5. Faith Mehmet Kislal, "Psychiatric Symptoms of Adolescents with Physical Complaints Admitted to an Adolescence Unit," *Clinical Pediatrics,* 44, no. 2 (2005): 121–130.

6. Orlando J. Olivares, "An Analysis of the Study-Time Grade Association," *Radical Pedagogy* (2002).

7. Hull, Joseph and Greg Langkamp, "Lead Concentrations in Spokane River Dish," Quantitative Environmental Learning Project (QELP).

8. Barger et al, "Extended Work Shifts and the Risk of Motor Vehicle Crashes Among Interns," *The New England Journal of Medicine,* 352 (January 13, 2005): 125–133.

9. Christakis, D., F. Zimmerman, D. DiGiuseppe, and C. McCarty, "Early television exposure and subsequent attentional problems in children," *Pediatrics,* 113, no. 4 (April 2004).

10. "Science Lifts 'Mummy's Curse,'" BBC News World Edition, December 20, 2002.

11. Hull, Joseph and Greg Langkamp, "Leachable Lead Concentrations in CRTs" Quantitative Environmental Learning Project (QELP).

12. Hull, Joseph and Greg Langkamp, "Leachable Lead Concentrations in CRTs" Quantitative Environmental Learning Project (QELP).

13. Galloway, A., Y. Lee, and L. Birch, "Predictors and Consequences of Food Neophobia and Pickiness in Young Girls," *Journal of American Dietary Association,* 103, no. 6 (June 2003): 692–98.

14. Kelly DiNardo, "Ask the Nutritionist; The Return of the Grapefruit Diet?," *BNET Health Publications* (online), September 2004.

15. S. Silberstein, "Update on Migraine Headache: Treatment," posted on *Medscape Today,* 2002.

16. Lopez, P., D. Hawlena, V. Polo, and J. Martin, "Sources of Individual Shy-Bold Variations in Antipredator Behaviour of Male Iberian Rock Lizards," *Animal Behavior,* 69 (January 2005): 1–9.

17. Lopez, P., D. Hawlena, V. Polo, and J. Martin, "Sources of Individual Shy-Bold Variations in Antipredator Behaviour of Male Iberian Rock Lizards," *Animal Behavior,* 69 (January 2005): 1–9.

18. "Hurricane Love Songs," *Pittsburgh Post-Gazette,* November 15, 2004.

19. Michael Hopkin, "ID Bands May Harm Penguins," *BioEd Online,* May 19, 2004.

20. Smith, M., E. Franz, S. Joy, and K. Whitehead, "Superior Performance of Blind Compared with Sighted Individuals on Bimanual Estimations of Object Size," *Psychological Science,* 16, no. 1, January 2005.

21. Hull, Joseph and Greg Langkamp "Puget Sound Butter Clams Length v. Width," Quantitative Environmental Learning Project (QELP).

22. Dan Fitzpatrick, "Weighty Matter Pits Passengers Against Airlines," *Pittsburgh Post-Gazette,* March 13, 2005.

23. Machado, C., M. S. Wolfe, and I. Kleinberg, "2749 Initial Examination of a CaviStat(r)-Containing Dentifrice on Caries Development in Venezuelan Children," 81st General Session of the International Association for Dental Research (June 25–28, 2003).

24. Christakis, D., F. Zimmerman, D. DiGiuseppe, and C. McCarty, "Early Television Exposure and Subsequent Attentional Problems in Children," *Pediatrics* 113, no. 4 (April 2004)

25. Christakis, D., F. Zimmerman, D. DiGiuseppe, and C. McCarty, "Early Television Exposure and Subsequent Attentional Problems in Children," *Pediatrics* 113, no. 4 (April 2004).

26. "Child Cancer Survivors Found Happy as Others," *Pittsburgh Post-Gazette,* February 7, 2005.

27. L.E. James, "Meeting Mr. Farmer versus Meeting a Farmer: Specific Effects of Aging on Learning Proper Names, *Psychology and Aging,* 19, no. 3 (September 2004): 515–22.

28. Aldrich, E., P. Arcidiacono, and J. Vigdor, "Do People Value Racial Diversity?" *The Berkeley Electronic Press,* 5, no 1 (February 8, 2005).

29. Donald G. McNeil Jr., "Large Study on Mental Illness Finds Global Prevalence" *The New York Times,* June 2, 2004.

30. Clauss, M., C. Polster, E. Kienzle, H. Wiesner, K. Baumgartner, F. von Houwald, W. Streich, and E. Dierenfeld, "Energy and Mineral Nutrition and Water Intake in the Captive Indian Rhinoceros," *Zoo Biology,* 24, no. 1 (2005): 1–14.

31. Hull, Joseph, and Greg Langkamp, "Columbia River Velocities," Quantitative Environmental Learning Project (QELP).

32. Lopez, P., D. Hawlena, V. Polo, and J. Martin, "Sources of Individual Shy-Bold Variations in Antipredator Behaviour of Male Iberian Rock Lizards," *Animal Behavior,* 69 (January 2005): 1–9.

33. Jones, K., T. Smith, and S. Ketring, "An Exploration of Sexual Coercion at First Sexual Intercourse," *Journal of Integrative Psychology,* 5 (2004): 1–9.

34. Hull, Joseph, and Greg Langkamp, "Lead v. Zinc Concentrations in Spokane River Fish," Quantitative Environmental Learning Project (QELP).

35. Hull, Joseph, and Greg Langkamp, "Lead v. Zinc Concentrations in Spokane River Fish," Quantitative Environmental Learning Project (QELP).

36. Begg, C., K. Begg, J. Du Toit, and M. Mills, "Spatial Organization of the Honey Badger Mellivora Capensis in the Southern Kalahari: Home-Range Size and Movement Patterns," *Journal of Zoology* (May 5, 2004).

37. Kaminski, Juliane, Julia Riedel, Josep Call, and Michael Tomasello, "Domestic Goats, Capra Hircus, Follow Gaze Direction and Social Cues in an Object Choice Task," *Animal Behavior*, 69, no. 1 (January 2005): 11.

Chapter 12

1. "Wrinkle Fighter Could Help Reduce Excessive Sweating" [attributed to the Associated Press], *Pittsburgh Post-Gazette,* February 8, 2004.

2. "Chopsticks May Cause Arthritis," TVNZ online, October 25, 2003.

3. Lindsey Tanner [Associated Press], "Study: Asking Teens About Suicide Doesn't Lead Them to Take Their Lives," *Pittsburgh Post-Gazette,* April 6, 2005.

4. Lindsey Tanner [Associated Press], "Large Doses of Vitamin E Could Be Risky," *The Washington Post,* March 16, 2005.

5. "Why Booze and Smokes Go Together," *Pittsburgh Post-Gazette,* April 6, 2004.

6. Tait, A., T. Voepel-Lewis, Shobha Malviya, and S. Philipson, "Improving the Readability and Processability of a Pediatric Informed Consent Document," archives of *Pediatrics & Adolescent Medicine,* 159, no. 4 (April 2005).

7. Kravitz, R., R. Epstein, M. Feldman, C. Franz, R. Azari, M. Wilkes, L. Hinton, and P. Franks, "Influence of Patients' Requests for Direct-to-Consumer Advertised Antidepressants," *Journal of the American Medical Association [JAMA]* 293, no. 16 (April 27, 2005).

8. "Mouth Piercings May Cause Gums to Recede," *Pittsburgh Post-Gazette,* April 5, 2005.

9. "Painkillers' Safety Doubts," *Pittsburgh Post-Gazette,* April 19, 2005.

10. Torres, R., and A. Velando, "Male Preference for Female Foot Colour in the Socially Monogamous Blue-footed Booby," *Animal Behaviour,* 69, no. 1 (January 2005).

11. Goel, M., E. McCarthy, R. Phillips, and C. Wee, "Obesity Among U.S. Immigrant Subgroups by Duration of Residence," *Journal of the American Medical Association,* 292, no. 23 (December 15, 2004).

12. Hubert B. Herring, "Instead of Reading This, Maybe You Should Take a Nap," *The New York Times,* April 10, 2005.

13. Nicholas D. Kristof, "God and Evolution" (was "God and Evolution: An Inclination to Faith May Be in Our Genes"), *The New York Times,* February 12, 2005.

14. "Firm Believers More Likely to Be Flabby, Purdue Study Finds," *Purdue News,* March 1998.

15. Ceci Connolly, "Virginity Pledgers Still Take Sex Risks," *The Washington Post,* reported in the *Pittsburgh Post-Gazette,* March 19, 2005.

16. Jaime Holguin, "How to Talk to Dying Children," CBS News (online), September 15, 2004.

17. "Random Student Drug Testing Works," *Pittsburgh Post-Gazette,* May 4, 2005.

18. "Don't Believe the Hype," *Pittsburgh Post-Gazette,* May 4, 2005.

19. "Men and the Frantic Life," *Pittsburgh Post-Gazette,* May 4, 2005.

20. "Prostate Survival Studied," *Pittsburgh Post-Gazette,* May 4, 2005.

21. "Drug War Turned Toward Marijuana in '90s," *Pittsburgh Post-Gazette,* May 4, 2005.

22. Benedict Carey, "Mental Illness Risk Rises After Death of a Child," *The New York Times* [published in the *Pittsburgh Post-Gazette*], March 24, 2005.

23. Lindsey Tanner [Associated Press], "Large Doses of Vitamin E Could Be Risky," *The Washington Post,* March 16, 2005.

24. "Pfizer Bares Belated Celebrex Study," *Pittsburgh Post-Gazette,* February 1, 2005.

25. "Ugly Kids Get Less Attention from Parents," *The Medical News* (online), April 12, 2005.

26. Okur, E., I. Yildirim, B. Aydogan, and M. Akif Kilic, "Outcome of Surgery for Crooked Nose: An Objective Method of Evaluation," *Aesthetic Plastic Surgery,* 28, no. 4 (July–August 2004): 203–7.

27. Hipkins, K., B. Materna, S. Payne, and L. Kirsch, "Family Lead Poisoning Associated with Occupational Exposure," *Clinical Pediatrics,* 43, no. 9 (November–December 2004): 845–49.

28. Cannon, C., E. Braunwald, C. McCabe, J. Grayston, B. Muhlestein, R. Giugliano, R. Cairns, and A. Skene, "Antibiotic Treatment of Chlamydia Pneumoniae After Acute Coronary Syndrome," *New England Journal of Medicine,* 352 (April 21, 2005): 1646–54.

29. J. Trinkaus, "An Informal Look at Use of Bakery Department Tongs and Tissues," *Perceptual and Motor Skills,* December 1998.

30. Giron, D., D. Dunn, I. Hardy, and M. Strand, "Aggression by Polyembryonic Wasp Soldiers Correlates with Kinship but Not Resource Competition," *Nature,* 430 (August 5, 2004): 676–79.

31. "Study: Anti-Seizure Drug Reduces Drinking in Bipolar Alcoholics." *Bipolar Central* (online), January 4, 2005.

32. "Acupuncture Eases Postoperative Nausea," *HealthDayNews,* September 22, 2004.

33. Read, Daniel, and George Loewenstein, "Diversification Bias: Explaining the Discrepancy in Variety Seeking Between Combined and Separated Choices," *Journal of Experimental Psychology,* I, no. 1 (1995): 34–49.

34. Read, Daniel, and George Loewenstein, "Diversification Bias: Explaining the Discrepancy in Variety Seeking Between Combined and Separated Choices," *Journal of Experimental Psychology,* I, no. 1 (1995): 34–49.

35. McKeganey, N., and J. Norrie, "Association Between Illegal Drugs and Weapon Carrying in Young People in Scotland: Schools' Survey," *British Medical Journal,* 320 (April 8, 2000): 982–84.

36. William Hathaway, "Painless Heart Attacks More Lethal," *The Hartford Courant,* reported in the *Pittsburgh Post-Gazette,* August 17, 2004.

37. Steven Kull, "Misperceptions, the Media, and the Iraq War," *Program on International Policy Attitudes (PIPA),* October 2, 2003.

38. "Stuck for Life: Will Today's Hottest Names Stay That Way?" *Pittsburgh Post-Gazette,* May 10, 2005.

Chapter 13

1. "GOP Warns Democrats They'll Face Probes, Too," *Pittsburgh Post-Gazette,* April 29, 2005.

2. Hull, Joseph, and Greg Langkamp, "Biometrics of Douglas Fir," Quantitative Environmental Learning Project (QELP).

3. Hull, Joseph, and Greg Langkamp, "Puget Sound Butter Clams Length v. Width," Quantitative Environmental Learning Project (QELP).

4. "Real Estate Rent, Vacancy Rates Don't Always Tell the Story," *Pittsburgh Post-Gazette,* January 30, 2005.

5. Michael E. Ruane, "In Touch with Lincoln's Last Hours," *The Washington Post,* September 7, 2007.

6. "Bigger Waistlines, Shorter Lifespans," *Pittsburgh Post-Gazette,* March 17, 2005.

7. Blackstone, E., M. Morrison, and M. Roth, *Science,* 308, no. 5721 (April 22, 2005): 518.

8. Steve Twedt, "The Social Services Safety Net Is Fraying," *Pittsburgh Post-Gazette,* March 28, 2005.

9. Ole J. Benedictow, "The Black Death 1346–1353: The Complete History," *New England Journal of Medicine,* 352 (March 2005): 1054–55.

10. "City Assessments Found Out of Line," *Pittsburgh Post-Gazette,* February 25, 2005.

11. "Environmental Mercury, Autism Linked by New Research," *BNET (online) Environment News Service,* March 2005.

12. Leskin, G., S. Woodward, H. Young, and J. Sheikh, "Sleep Disturbances in the Vietnam Generation: Findings from a Nationally Representative Sample of Male Vietnam Veterans," *Journal of Psychiatric Research,* 36, no. 6 (November–December 2002): 449–452.

13. Hull, Joseph, and Greg Langkamp, "Electric Power Plant C0$_2$ Output versus Energy Input," Quantitative Environmental Learning Project (QELP).

14. Adam Liptak, "Inmate's Rising I.Q. Score Could Mean His Death," *The New York Times,* February 6, 2005.

15. Hull, Joseph, and Greg Langkamp, "Columbia River Velocity Versus Depths," Quantitative Environmental Learning Project (QELP).

16. Hull, Joseph, and Greg Langkamp, "Lead v. Zinc Concentrations in Spokane River Fish," Quantitative Environmental Learning Project (QELP).

17. Gricar, J., K. Cufer, P. Oven, and U. Schmitt, "Differentiation of Terminal Latewood Tracheids in Silver Fir Trees During Autumn," *Annals of Botany,* 95, no. 6 (May 2005).

18. Kaminski, Juliane, Julia Riedel, Josep Call, and Michael Tomasello, "Domestic Goats, Capra Hircus, Follow Gaze Direction and Social Cues in an Object Choice Task," *Animal Behavior,* 69, no 1 (January 2005): 11–18.

19. Hull, Joseph, and Greg Langkamp, "Characteristics of Selected Streams Along the West Side of the Sacramento Valley," Quantitative Environmental Learning Project (QELP).

Chapter 14

1. Abigail Sullivan Moore, "Blackboard: Grades; Gimme an A (I insist!)," *The New York Times,* April 25, 2004.

2. Bill Hendrick [Cox News Service], "Boozy Bees May Offer Clues About Pickled People," *Pittsburgh Post-Gazette,* November 15, 2004.

3. Persons, Matthew, and George Uetz, "Sexual Cannibalism and Mate Choice Decisions in Wolf Spiders: Influence of Male Size and Secondary Sexual Characters," *Animal Behavior,* 69, no. 1 (January 2005): 83–94.

4. J. Trinkaus, "Compliance with the Item Limit of the Food Supermarket Express Checkout Lane: An Informal Look," *Psychological Reports,* 73, no. 1, (August 1993): 105–6.

5. Jaime Holguin, "How to Talk to Dying Children," CBS News (online), September 15, 2004.

6. "What's In a Name? Studies Find That Afrocentric Names Often Incur a Bias," *Pittsburgh Post-Gazette,* November 25, 2003.

7. "Ugly Kids Get Less Attention from Parents," *The Medical News* (online), April 12, 2005.

8. "Mouth Piercings May Cause Gums to Recede," *Pittsburgh Post-Gazette,* April 5, 2005.

9. Dan Lewerenz, "Exercise Beats Calcium at Boosting Girls' Bones," *Pittsburgh Post-Gazette* [attributed to Associated Press], June 15, 2004.

10. John Houle, Cornerstone Communications Group, "Health & Safety Survey," American Nurses Association online, September 2001.

11. "Drop in Temperatures Could Lower Ticket Prices, Too," *Pittsburgh Post-Gazette,* January 13, 2005.

12. Roy, Michael, and Nicholas Christenfeld, "Do Dogs Resemble Their Owners?" *Chance Magazine,* March 31, 2004.

13. Xenia Montenegro, "Lifestyles, Dating and Romance: A Study of Midlife Singles," *AARP Knowledge Management,* September 2003.

14. Personal MD, "Piano Lessons Boost Math Scores." March 18, 1999.

15. Nicholas Wade [for *New York Times*], "Remains Found of Downsized Human Species," *Pittsburgh Post-Gazette,* October 28, 2004.

TBP Endnotes

TBP Chapter 3

1. "Stronger Sunscreens May Increase Exposure, Cancer Risk," *Augusta Chronicle,* August 4, 1999.

2. *Pittsburgh Post-Gazette,* July 1, 2004.

3. David Crary, Associated Press, *Pittsburgh Post-Gazette,* June 24, 2004.

4. *Pittsburgh Post-Gazette,* December 7, 2004.

5. Charles Homans, "FDA Calls for More Testing on Female Sexuality Drug," Knight Ridder, December 3, 2004.

6. Gougoux, F. et al., "Pitch Discrimination in the Early Blind," *Nature,* 430 (15 July 2004): 309.

7. William J. Cromie, "Cognition Unaffected by Pot Use," *Harvard Gazette* archives, October 18, 2001.

8. Virginia Linn, *Pittsburgh Post-Gazette,* December 21, 2004.

9. "Bigger Families, Bigger Waistlines," *Pittsburgh Post-Gazette,* March 30, 2004.

10. "Guys Need to Get a Clue about Sexuality," *Pittsburgh Post-Gazette,* March 12, 2002.

11. Kawanza L. Griffin, *Milwaukee Journal Sentinel,* August 25, 2004.

12. Maureen Dowd, "Men Just Want Mommy," *New York Times,* January 13, 2005.

13. Kate Stone Lombardi, "Roommates: It's Enough to Make You Conservative," *New York Times,* January 16, 2005.

TBP Chapter 4

1. Randolph E. Schmid, Associated Press, *Pittsburgh Post-Gazette,* November 12, 2004.

2. Byron Spice, *Pittsburgh Post-Gazette,* November 21, 2004.

3. "Pitt Students Gifted," *Pittsburgh Post-Gazette,* October 31, 2004.

4. *Pittsburgh Post-Gazette,* November 18, 2003.

5. Linda A. Johnson, Associated Press, *Pittsburgh Post-Gazette,* July 17, 2004.

TBP Chapter 5

1. Martha Irvine, Associated Press, *Pittsburgh Post-Gazette,* June 5, 2004.

2. Abigail Sullivan Moore, "Blackboard: Grades; Gimme an A (I Insist!)," *New York Times,* April 25, 2004.

3. Lindsey Tanner, Associated Press, *Pittsburgh Post-Gazette,* December 15, 2004.

4. Pew Research Center, March 28, 2003.

5. Michael Conlon, Reuters, January 23, 2005.

6. *Pittsburgh Post-Gazette,* March 21, 2004.

7. Charles Homans, "FDA Calls for More Testing on Female Sexuality Drug," Knight Ridder, December 3, 2004.

8. Gougoux, F. et al., "Pitch Discrimination in the Early Blind," *Nature,* 430 (15 July 2004): 309.

9. William J. Cromie, "Cognition Unaffected by Pot Use," *Harvard Gazette* archives, October 18, 2001.

10. Virginia Linn, *Pittsburgh Post-Gazette,* December 21, 2004.

11. "Bigger Families, Bigger Waistlines," *Pittsburgh Post-Gazette,* March 30, 2004.

12. "Guys Need to Get a Clue about Sexuality," *Pittsburgh Post-Gazette,* March 12, 2002.

13. Kawanza L. Griffin, *Milwaukee Journal Sentinel,* August 25, 2004.

14. Maureen Dowd, "Men Just Want Mommy," *New York Times,* January 13, 2005.

15. Kate Stone Lombardi, "Roommates: It's Enough to Make You Conservative," *New York Times,* January 16, 2005.

TBP Chapter 8

1. Charles Homans, "FDA Calls for More Testing on Female Sexuality Drug," Knight Ridder, December 3, 2004.

2. Gougoux, F. et al., "Pitch Discrimination in the Early Blind," *Nature,* 430 (15 July 2004): 309.

3. William J. Cromie, "Cognition Unaffected by Pot Use," *Harvard Gazette* archives, October 18, 2001.

4. Virginia Linn, *Pittsburgh Post-Gazette,* December 21, 2004.

5. "Bigger Families, Bigger Waistlines," *Pittsburgh Post-Gazette,* March 30, 2004.

6. "Guys Need to Get a Clue about Sexuality," *Pittsburgh Post-Gazette,* March 12, 2002.

7. Kawanza L. Griffin, *Milwaukee Journal Sentinel,* August 25, 2004.

8. Maureen Dowd, "Men Just Want Mommy," *New York Times,* January 13, 2005.

9. Kate Stone Lombardi, "Roommates: It's Enough to Make You Conservative," *New York Times,* January 16, 2005.

TBP Chapter 9

1. Persons, Matthew, and George Uetz, "Sexual Cannibalism and Mate Choice Decisions in Wolf Spiders: Influence of Male Size and Secondary Sexual Characters," *Animal Behavior,* 69, no. 1 (January 2005): 83–94.

2. *Pittsburgh Post-Gazette,* December 7, 2003.

TBP Chapter 11

1. Dansinger, Michael L., MD, et al, "Comparison of the Atkins, Ornish, Weight Watchers, and Zone Diets for Weight Loss and Heart Disease Risk Reduction," *Journal of the American Medical Association (JAMA)*, 293, no. 1 (2005): 43–53.

TBP Chapter 12

1. "Study Indicates Racial Disparity in Traffic Stops," *Pittsburgh Post-Gazette*, April 22, 2002.
2. Jorge I. Mena-Ali and Oscar J. Rocha, *Annals of Botany*, March 4, 2005.
3. Lindsey Tanner, Associated Press, *Pittsburgh Post-Gazette*, December 15, 2004.

TBP Chapter 13

1. Charles Homans, "FDA Calls for More Testing on Female Sexuality Drug," Knight Ridder, December 3, 2004.
2. Gougoux, F. et al., "Pitch Discrimination in the Early Blind," *Nature*, 430 (15 July 2004): 309.
3. William J. Cromie, "Cognition Unaffected by Pot Use," *Harvard Gazette* archives, October 18, 2001.
4. Virginia Linn, *Pittsburgh Post-Gazette*, December 21, 2004.
6. "Guys Need to Get a Clue about Sexuality," *Pittsburgh Post-Gazette*, March 12, 2002.
7. Kawanza L. Griffin, *Milwaukee Journal Sentinel*, August 25, 2004.
8. Maureen Dowd, "Men Just Want Mommy," *New York Times*, January 13, 2005.
9. Kate Stone Lombardi, "Roommates: It's Enough to Make You Conservative," *New York Times*, January 16, 2005.

Index

Standard Normal (*z*) Distribution

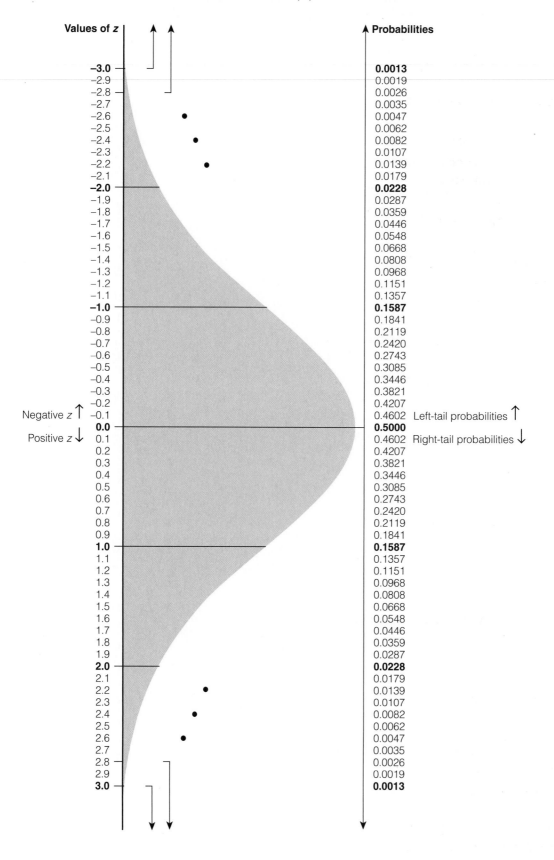

Standard Normal Values (to Hundredths) and Probabilities

z	⎵·⎵0	⎵·⎵1	⎵·⎵2	⎵·⎵3	⎵·⎵4	⎵·⎵5	⎵·⎵6	⎵·⎵7	⎵·⎵8	⎵·⎵9	
−3.0	0.0013	0.0013	0.0013	0.0012	0.0012	0.0011	0.0011	0.0011	0.0010	0.0010	
−2.9	0.0019	0.0018	0.0018	0.0017	0.0016	0.0016	0.0015	0.0015	0.0014	0.0014	
−2.8	0.0026	0.0025	0.0024	0.0023	0.0023	0.0022	0.0021	0.0021	0.0020	0.0019	
−2.7	0.0035	0.0034	0.0033	0.0032	0.0031	0.0030	0.0029	0.0028	0.0027	0.0026	
−2.6	0.0047	0.0045	0.0044	0.0043	0.0041	0.0040	0.0039	0.0038	0.0037	0.0036	
−2.5	0.0062	0.0060	0.0059	0.0057	0.0055	0.0054	0.0052	0.0051	0.0049	0.0048	
−2.4	0.0082	0.0080	0.0078	0.0075	0.0073	0.0071	0.0069	0.0068	0.0066	0.0064	
−2.3	0.0107	0.0104	0.0102	0.0099	0.0096	0.0094	0.0091	0.0089	0.0087	0.0084	
−2.2	0.0139	0.0136	0.0132	0.0129	0.0125	0.0122	0.0119	0.0116	0.0113	0.0110	
−2.1	0.0179	0.0174	0.0170	0.0166	0.0162	0.0158	0.0154	0.0150	0.0146	0.0143	
−2.0	0.0228	0.0222	0.0217	0.0212	0.0207	0.0202	0.0197	0.0192	0.0188	0.0183	
−1.9	0.0287	0.0281	0.0274	0.0268	0.0262	0.0256	0.0250	0.0244	0.0239	0.0233	
−1.8	0.0359	0.0351	0.0344	0.0336	0.0329	0.0322	0.0314	0.0307	0.0301	0.0294	
−1.7	0.0446	0.0436	0.0427	0.0418	0.0409	0.0401	0.0392	0.0384	0.0375	0.0367	
−1.6	0.0548	0.0537	0.0526	0.0516	0.0505	0.0495	0.0485	0.0475	0.0465	0.0455	
−1.5	0.0668	0.0655	0.0643	0.0630	0.0618	0.0606	0.0594	0.0582	0.0571	0.0559	
−1.4	0.0808	0.0793	0.0778	0.0764	0.0749	0.0735	0.0721	0.0708	0.0694	0.0681	
−1.3	0.0968	0.0951	0.0934	0.0918	0.0901	0.0885	0.0869	0.0853	0.0838	0.0823	
−1.2	0.1151	0.1131	0.1112	0.1093	0.1075	0.1056	0.1038	0.1020	0.1003	0.0985	
−1.1	0.1357	0.1335	0.1314	0.1292	0.1271	0.1251	0.1230	0.1210	0.1190	0.1170	
−1.0	0.1587	0.1562	0.1539	0.1515	0.1492	0.1469	0.1446	0.1423	0.1401	0.1379	
−0.9	0.1841	0.1814	0.1788	0.1762	0.1736	0.1711	0.1685	0.1660	0.1635	0.1611	
−0.8	0.2119	0.2090	0.2061	0.2033	0.2005	0.1977	0.1949	0.1922	0.1894	0.1867	
−0.7	0.2420	0.2389	0.2358	0.2327	0.2297	0.2266	0.2236	0.2206	0.2177	0.2148	
−0.6	0.2743	0.2709	0.2676	0.2643	0.2611	0.2578	0.2546	0.2514	0.2483	0.2451	
−0.5	0.3085	0.3050	0.3015	0.2981	0.2946	0.2912	0.2877	0.2843	0.2810	0.2776	
−0.4	0.3446	0.3409	0.3372	0.3336	0.3300	0.3264	0.3228	0.3192	0.3156	0.3121	
−0.3	0.3821	0.3783	0.3745	0.3707	0.3669	0.3632	0.3594	0.3557	0.3520	0.3483	
−0.2	0.4207	0.4168	0.4129	0.4090	0.4052	0.4013	0.3974	0.3936	0.3897	0.3859	Left-
−0.1	0.4602	0.4562	0.4522	0.4483	0.4443	0.4404	0.4364	0.4325	0.4286	0.4247	tail
0.0	0.5000	0.4960	0.4920	0.4880	0.4840	0.4801	0.4761	0.4721	0.4681	0.4641	probabilities ↑
0.1	0.4602	0.4562	0.4522	0.4483	0.4443	0.4404	0.4364	0.4325	0.4286	0.4247	Right-
0.2	0.4207	0.4168	0.4129	0.4090	0.4052	0.4013	0.3974	0.3936	0.3897	0.3859	tail
0.3	0.3821	0.3783	0.3745	0.3707	0.3669	0.3632	0.3594	0.3557	0.3520	0.3483	probabilities ↓
0.4	0.3446	0.3409	0.3372	0.3336	0.3300	0.3264	0.3228	0.3192	0.3156	0.3121	
0.5	0.3085	0.3050	0.3015	0.2981	0.2946	0.2912	0.2877	0.2843	0.2810	0.2776	
0.6	0.2743	0.2709	0.2676	0.2643	0.2611	0.2578	0.2546	0.2514	0.2483	0.2451	
0.7	0.2420	0.2389	0.2358	0.2327	0.2297	0.2266	0.2236	0.2206	0.2177	0.2148	
0.8	0.2119	0.2090	0.2061	0.2033	0.2005	0.1977	0.1949	0.1922	0.1894	0.1867	
0.9	0.1841	0.1814	0.1788	0.1762	0.1736	0.1711	0.1685	0.1660	0.1635	0.1611	
1.0	0.1587	0.1562	0.1539	0.1515	0.1492	0.1469	0.1446	0.1423	0.1401	0.1379	
1.1	0.1357	0.1335	0.1314	0.1292	0.1271	0.1251	0.1230	0.1210	0.1190	0.1170	
1.2	0.1151	0.1131	0.1112	0.1093	0.1075	0.1056	0.1038	0.1020	0.1003	0.0985	
1.3	0.0968	0.0951	0.0934	0.0918	0.0901	0.0885	0.0869	0.0853	0.0838	0.0823	
1.4	0.0808	0.0793	0.0778	0.0764	0.0749	0.0735	0.0721	0.0708	0.0694	0.0681	
1.5	0.0668	0.0655	0.0643	0.0630	0.0618	0.0606	0.0594	0.0582	0.0571	0.0559	
1.6	0.0548	0.0537	0.0526	0.0516	0.0505	0.0495	0.0485	0.0475	0.0465	0.0455	
1.7	0.0446	0.0436	0.0427	0.0418	0.0409	0.0401	0.0392	0.0384	0.0375	0.0367	
1.8	0.0359	0.0351	0.0344	0.0336	0.0329	0.0322	0.0314	0.0307	0.0301	0.0294	
1.9	0.0287	0.0281	0.0274	0.0268	0.0262	0.0256	0.0250	0.0244	0.0239	0.0233	
2.0	0.0228	0.0222	0.0217	0.0212	0.0207	0.0202	0.0197	0.0192	0.0188	0.0183	
2.1	0.0179	0.0174	0.0170	0.0166	0.0162	0.0158	0.0154	0.0150	0.0146	0.0143	
2.2	0.0139	0.0136	0.0132	0.0129	0.0125	0.0122	0.0119	0.0116	0.0113	0.0110	
2.3	0.0107	0.0104	0.0102	0.0099	0.0096	0.0094	0.0091	0.0089	0.0087	0.0084	
2.4	0.0082	0.0080	0.0078	0.0075	0.0073	0.0071	0.0069	0.0068	0.0066	0.0064	
2.5	0.0062	0.0060	0.0059	0.0057	0.0055	0.0054	0.0052	0.0051	0.0049	0.0048	
2.6	0.0047	0.0045	0.0044	0.0043	0.0041	0.0040	0.0039	0.0038	0.0037	0.0036	
2.7	0.0035	0.0034	0.0033	0.0032	0.0031	0.0030	0.0029	0.0028	0.0027	0.0026	
2.8	0.0026	0.0025	0.0024	0.0023	0.0023	0.0022	0.0021	0.0021	0.0020	0.0019	
2.9	0.0019	0.0018	0.0018	0.0017	0.0016	0.0016	0.0015	0.0015	0.0014	0.0014	
3.0	0.0013	0.0013	0.0013	0.0012	0.0012	0.0011	0.0011	0.0011	0.0010	0.0010	

Standard Normal Values and Cumulative Probabilities
(for z being less than the value shown in the margin)

z	.00	.01	.02	.03	.04	.05	.06	.07	.08	.09
−3.0	0.0013	0.0013	0.0013	0.0012	0.0012	0.0011	0.0011	0.0011	0.0010	0.0010
−2.9	0.0019	0.0018	0.0018	0.0017	0.0016	0.0016	0.0015	0.0015	0.0014	0.0014
−2.8	0.0026	0.0025	0.0024	0.0023	0.0023	0.0022	0.0021	0.0021	0.0020	0.0019
−2.7	0.0035	0.0034	0.0033	0.0032	0.0031	0.0030	0.0029	0.0028	0.0027	0.0026
−2.6	0.0047	0.0045	0.0044	0.0043	0.0041	0.0040	0.0039	0.0038	0.0037	0.0036
−2.5	0.0062	0.0060	0.0059	0.0057	0.0055	0.0054	0.0052	0.0051	0.0049	0.0048
−2.4	0.0082	0.0080	0.0078	0.0075	0.0073	0.0071	0.0069	0.0068	0.0066	0.0064
−2.3	0.0107	0.0104	0.0102	0.0099	0.0096	0.0094	0.0091	0.0089	0.0087	0.0084
−2.2	0.0139	0.0136	0.0132	0.0129	0.0125	0.0122	0.0119	0.0116	0.0113	0.0110
−2.1	0.0179	0.0174	0.0170	0.0166	0.0162	0.0158	0.0154	0.0150	0.0146	0.0143
−2.0	0.0228	0.0222	0.0217	0.0212	0.0207	0.0202	0.0197	0.0192	0.0188	0.0183
−1.9	0.0287	0.0281	0.0274	0.0268	0.0262	0.0256	0.0250	0.0244	0.0239	0.0233
−1.8	0.0359	0.0351	0.0344	0.0336	0.0329	0.0322	0.0314	0.0307	0.0301	0.0294
−1.7	0.0446	0.0436	0.0427	0.0418	0.0409	0.0401	0.0392	0.0384	0.0375	0.0367
−1.6	0.0548	0.0537	0.0526	0.0516	0.0505	0.0495	0.0485	0.0475	0.0465	0.0455
−1.5	0.0668	0.0655	0.0643	0.0630	0.0618	0.0606	0.0594	0.0582	0.0571	0.0559
−1.4	0.0808	0.0793	0.0778	0.0764	0.0749	0.0735	0.0721	0.0708	0.0694	0.0681
−1.3	0.0968	0.0951	0.0934	0.0918	0.0901	0.0885	0.0869	0.0853	0.0838	0.0823
−1.2	0.1151	0.1131	0.1112	0.1093	0.1075	0.1056	0.1038	0.1020	0.1003	0.0985
−1.1	0.1357	0.1335	0.1314	0.1292	0.1271	0.1251	0.1230	0.1210	0.1190	0.1170
−1.0	0.1587	0.1562	0.1539	0.1515	0.1492	0.1469	0.1446	0.1423	0.1401	0.1379
−0.9	0.1841	0.1814	0.1788	0.1762	0.1736	0.1711	0.1685	0.1660	0.1635	0.1611
−0.8	0.2119	0.2090	0.2061	0.2033	0.2005	0.1977	0.1949	0.1922	0.1894	0.1867
−0.7	0.2420	0.2389	0.2358	0.2327	0.2297	0.2266	0.2236	0.2206	0.2177	0.2148
−0.6	0.2743	0.2709	0.2676	0.2643	0.2611	0.2578	0.2546	0.2514	0.2483	0.2451
−0.5	0.3085	0.3050	0.3015	0.2981	0.2946	0.2912	0.2877	0.2843	0.2810	0.2776
−0.4	0.3446	0.3409	0.3372	0.3336	0.3300	0.3264	0.3228	0.3192	0.3156	0.3121
−0.3	0.3821	0.3783	0.3745	0.3707	0.3669	0.3632	0.3594	0.3557	0.3520	0.3483
−0.2	0.4207	0.4168	0.4129	0.4090	0.4052	0.4013	0.3974	0.3936	0.3897	0.3859
−0.1	0.4602	0.4562	0.4522	0.4483	0.4443	0.4404	0.4364	0.4325	0.4286	0.4247
0.0	0.5000	0.5040	0.5080	0.5120	0.5160	0.5199	0.5239	0.5279	0.5319	0.5359
0.1	0.5398	0.5438	0.5478	0.5417	0.5557	0.5596	0.5636	0.5675	0.5714	0.5753
0.2	0.5793	0.5832	0.5871	0.5910	0.5948	0.5987	0.6026	0.6064	0.6103	0.6141
0.3	0.6179	0.6217	0.6255	0.6293	0.6331	0.6368	0.6406	0.6443	0.6480	0.6517
0.4	0.6554	0.6591	0.6628	0.6664	0.6700	0.6736	0.6772	0.6808	0.6844	0.6879
0.5	0.6915	0.6950	0.6985	0.7019	0.7054	0.7088	0.7123	0.7157	0.7190	0.7224
0.6	0.7257	0.7291	0.7324	0.7357	0.7389	0.7422	0.7454	0.7486	0.7517	0.7549
0.7	0.7580	0.7611	0.7642	0.7673	0.7703	0.7734	0.7764	0.7794	0.7823	0.7852
0.8	0.7881	0.7910	0.7939	0.7967	0.7995	0.8023	0.8051	0.8078	0.8106	0.8133
0.9	0.8159	0.8186	0.8212	0.8238	0.8264	0.8289	0.8315	0.8340	0.8365	0.8389
1.0	0.8413	0.8438	0.8461	0.8485	0.8508	0.8531	0.8554	0.8577	0.8599	0.8621
1.1	0.8643	0.8665	0.8686	0.8708	0.8729	0.8749	0.8770	0.8790	0.8810	0.8830
1.2	0.8849	0.8869	0.8888	0.8907	0.8925	0.8944	0.8962	0.8980	0.8997	0.9015
1.3	0.9032	0.9049	0.9066	0.9082	0.9099	0.9115	0.9131	0.9147	0.9162	0.9177
1.4	0.9192	0.9207	0.9222	0.9236	0.9251	0.9265	0.9279	0.9292	0.9306	0.9319
1.5	0.9332	0.9345	0.9357	0.9370	0.9382	0.9394	0.9406	0.9418	0.9429	0.9441
1.6	0.9452	0.9463	0.9474	0.9484	0.9495	0.9505	0.9515	0.9525	0.9535	0.9545
1.7	0.9554	0.9564	0.9573	0.9582	0.9591	0.9599	0.9608	0.9616	0.9625	0.9633
1.8	0.9641	0.9649	0.9656	0.9664	0.9671	0.9678	0.9686	0.9693	0.9699	0.9706
1.9	0.9713	0.9719	0.9726	0.9732	0.9738	0.9744	0.9750	0.9756	0.9761	0.9767
2.0	0.9772	0.9778	0.9783	0.9788	0.9793	0.9798	0.9803	0.9808	0.9812	0.9817
2.1	0.9821	0.9826	0.9830	0.9834	0.9838	0.9842	0.9846	0.9850	0.9854	0.9857
2.2	0.9861	0.9864	0.9868	0.9871	0.9875	0.9878	0.9881	0.9884	0.9887	0.9890
2.3	0.9893	0.9896	0.9898	0.9901	0.9904	0.9906	0.9909	0.9911	0.9913	0.9916
2.4	0.9918	0.9920	0.9922	0.9925	0.9927	0.9929	0.9931	0.9932	0.9934	0.9936
2.5	0.9938	0.9940	0.9941	0.9943	0.9945	0.9946	0.9948	0.9949	0.9951	0.9952
2.6	0.9953	0.9955	0.9956	0.9957	0.9959	0.9960	0.9961	0.9962	0.9963	0.9964
2.7	0.9965	0.9966	0.9967	0.9968	0.9969	0.9970	0.9971	0.9972	0.9973	0.9974
2.8	0.9974	0.9975	0.9976	0.9977	0.9977	0.9978	0.9979	0.9979	0.9980	0.9981
2.9	0.9981	0.9982	0.9982	0.9983	0.9984	0.9984	0.9985	0.9985	0.9986	0.9986
3.0	0.9987	0.9987	0.9987	0.9988	0.9988	0.9989	0.9989	0.9989	0.9990	0.9990